THE NEW INTERNATIONAL COMMENTARY ON

THE NEW TESTAMENT

F. F. BRUCE, *General Editor*

THE GOSPEL ACCORDING TO JOHN

THE ENGLISH TEXT
WITH INTRODUCTION, EXPOSITION AND NOTES

by
LEON MORRIS

Principal, Ridley College,
Melbourne

WM. B. EERDMANS PUBLISHING CO.
GRAND RAPIDS, MICHIGAN

Fourth printing, November 1977

Acknowledgment is made to the following publishers for permission to quote from the publications indicated: Cambridge University Press, New York, 1953: *The Interpretation of the Fourth Gospel* by C. H. Dodd; Faber & Faber, London, 1947: *The Fourth Gospel* by Edwin C. Hoskyns and F. Noel Davey; Hodder & Stoughton, London, 1950: *Jesus the Revelation* by C. J. Wright; Macmillan, London, 1945, and St. Martin's Press, New York, 1945: *Readings in St. John's Gospel* by William Temple; Oxford University Press, New York, 1956: *St. John's Gospel* by R. H. Lightfoot; Saint Andrew Press, Edinburgh, 1956, and Westminster Press, Philadelphia, 1958: *The Gospel of John*, vols. 1 and 2, translated and interpreted by William Barclay; SCM Press, London, 1955: *The Fourth Gospel* by Robert H. Strachan; S.P.C.K., London, 1955: *Gospel according to St. John* by C. K. Barrett; T. & T. Clark, Edinburgh, 1928: *A Critical & Exegetical Commentary on the Gospel according to St. John* by J. H. Bernard.

THIS BOOK IS FOR CHARLIE

CONTENTS

EDITOR'S FOREWORD

In any series of New Testament commentaries the work on the Fourth Gospel must occupy a position of central importance. When Professor C. H. Dodd delivered his inaugural lecture in the Norris-Hulse Chair at Cambridge in 1936, on *The Present Task in New Testament Studies*, he suggested that the understanding of this Gospel, "one of the outstanding tasks of our time", might be the crucial test of our success or failure in solving the problem of the New Testament as a whole – that the Fourth Gospel, in fact, might prove to be the keystone of an arch which at present fails to hold together. Many scholars, pre-eminently Professor Dodd himself, have laboured at this task since then, but they have not moved appreciably nearer to unanimity. Not one but several "new looks" on the Fourth Gospel have been presented in recent years: if we have John Robinson's new look, we also have Ernst Käsemann's. We may look hopefully to fresh discoveries in Near Eastern religious history of the relevant period, and in some degree our hopefulness is rewarded (as in the comparative study of the Fourth Gospel and the literature of Qumran), but the heart of the problem of the Fourth Gospel lies within the document itself. One thing is certain: proponents of one interpretation act without warrant when (as they still do at times) they rule another interpretation out of court or dismiss it as being no longer tenable.

The choice of Dr. Leon Morris to contribute the commentary on this Gospel to the New International series was made by the late General Editor, Dr. Stonehouse. It was a wise choice. Dr. Morris has over the years given ample proof of his qualities as biblical theologian and exegete. To this series he contributed the volume on the Epistles to the Thessalonians in 1959. In the Editor's Foreword to that volume some account was given of Dr. Morris's career until then. At that time he was Vice-Principal of Ridley College, Melbourne. Soon afterwards he came to Cambridge as Warden of Tyndale House; he returned to Australia in 1964 to become Principal of Ridley College.

It will be evident at a glance that a commentary of this scale and character is the fruit of many years' study. From time to time in the course of these years Dr. Morris has given us by-products of his work in this field – monographs on *The Dead Sea Scrolls and St John's Gospel* (London, 1960) and *The New Testament and the Jewish Lectionaries* (London, 1964), and most recently a volume of *Studies in the Fourth Gospel* (Grand Rapids and Exeter, 1969). These *hors d'oeuvres* have whetted our appetite for the main course, and now at last we greet it. If one out of many praise-worthy features of the work may be mentioned, it is Dr. Morris's capacity for making up his own mind, after surveying the evidence and the opinions of others, and for telling us unambiguously where he thinks the truth of the matter lies. Here is wealth in which the student of Scripture will rejoice; the General Editor counts him-self happy to have had the opportunity of rejoicing in it before Dr. Morris's other readers, to whom he now commends it.

F. F. BRUCE

AUTHOR'S PREFACE

It is ten years and more since I accepted the invitation of the late Professor N.B. Stonehouse to write this volume. I cannot say that I have worked uninterruptedly on this commentary throughout that period. I have had a number of other commitments, and the stress of two moves, one from Australia to England and the other from England back to Australia, did not make for concentrated literary activity. Most of all the demands of the post of Principal of a College which is both a University College and a theological College have restricted the time available for writing. But through all these years this book has been constantly in my thoughts and I have worked at it whenever I could. As it goes forth I am conscious of its many shortcomings. But I am conscious also that I have had a great deal of assistance from many quarters.

I have tried to indicate my principal indebtednesses in the footnotes. I have learned a great deal from B. F. Westcott's great commentary. And I never forget that my enthusiasm for Johannine studies was kindled in the first instance by Archbishop Bernard's two volumes in the International Critical Commentary series. Of more recent works I have learned most from the commentaries of Sir Edwyn Hoskyns and Professor C. K. Barrett. A host of friends and several classes of students have stimulated and helped me. To all, though I cannot mention them by name, I express my profound gratitude.

Let me also express my appreciation of the courtesy and helpfulness shown me by Professor Stonehouse. I greatly appreciated his invitation to contribute this volume and his understanding when its appearance was delayed. I discussed a few points with him and this would have been a better commentary had I had opportunity of doing this more often. He was a fine Christian scholar and I gladly acknowledge my debt to him.

Finally I am grateful to the present editor of the series, Professor F. F. Bruce, for his understanding of my difficulties in completing this work, for the many valuable suggestions he has made for its improvement and for his steady encouragement.

LEON MORRIS

PRINCIPAL ABBREVIATIONS

AA	Matthew Black: *An Aramaic Approach to the Gospels and Acts* (Oxford, 1946)
Abbott	Edwin A. Abbott: *Johannine Grammar* (London, 1906)
ABR	*The Australian Biblical Review*
AG	W. F. Arndt and F. W. Gingrich: *A Greek-English Lexicon of the New Testament* (Chicago and Cambridge, 1957)
Amplified	*The Amplified New Testament* (Grand Rapids, 1958)
ANF	Ante-Nicene Fathers (American Reprint of the Edinburgh Edition, Grand Rapids, n.d.)
AO	C. F. Burney: *The Aramaic Origin of the Fourth Gospel* (Oxford, 1922)
ARV	*The American Revised Version* (or, *The American Standard Version*)
AS	G. Abbott-Smith: *A Manual Greek Lexicon of the New Testament* (Edinburgh, 1954)
Augustine	Nicene and Post-Nicene Fathers (American Reprint of the Edinburgh Edition, Grand Rapids, 1956), First Series, Volume VII, *Homilies on the Gospel of John, Homilies on the First Epistle of John, Soliloquies*
AV	*The Authorized Version*
BA	*The Biblical Archaeologist*
Bailey	R. F. Bailey: *Saint John's Gospel* (London, 1957)
Barclay	William Barclay: *The Gospel of John*, 2 vols. (Edinburgh, 1956)
Barrett	C. K. Barrett: *The Gospel according to St. John* (London, 1955)
BDF	F. Blass and A. Debrunner: *A Greek Grammar of the New Testament*, trans. R. W. Funk (Chicago and Cambridge, 1961)
Berkeley	*The Holy Bible, The Berkeley Version* (Grand Rapids, 1959)
Bernard	J. H. Bernard: *A Critical and Exegetical Commentary on the Gospel according to St. John*, The International Critical Commentary, 2 vols. (Edinburgh, 1928)
BJRL	*The Bulletin of the John Rylands Library*
BNT	*The Background of the New Testament and its Eschatology*, ed. W. D. Davies and D. Daube (Cambridge, 1956)
Brown	Raymond E. Brown: *The Gospel according to John (i-xii)*, The Anchor Bible (New York, 1966)
BS	A. Deissmann: *Bible Studies* (Edinburgh, 1901)
BT	*The Bible Translator*
Bultmann	Rudolf Bultmann: *Das Evangelium des Johannes* (Göttingen, 1956)
Calvin	John Calvin: *The Gospel according to St. John*, trans. T. H. L. Parker (Grand Rapids, vol. I, 1959, vol. II, 1961)
CBQ	*The Catholic Biblical Quarterly*

1

Chrysostom	Nicene and Post-Nicene Fathers (American Reprint of the Edinburgh edition, Grand Rapids, 1956), First Series, Volume XIV, *Homilies on the Gospel of St. John and Hebrews*
CQR	*The Church Quarterly Review*
Danby	H. Danby: *The Mishnah* (Oxford, 1933)
Dods	Marcus Dods: *The Gospel of St. John*, The Expositor's Greek Testament (London, 1897)
DSS	Millar Burrows: *The Dead Sea Scrolls* (London, 1956)
EB	*Encyclopaedia Biblica*, ed. T. K. Cheyne and J. S. Black (London, 1914)
ERE	*Encyclopaedia of Religion and Ethics*, ed. J. Hastings, 12 vols. (Edinburgh, 1908-21)
ExT	*The Expository Times*
FF	Ferrar Fenton: *The Holy Bible in Modern English* (London, 1922)
FG	Hugo Odeberg: *The Fourth Gospel* (Uppsala, 1929)
FGRCI	W. F. Howard: *The Fourth Gospel in Recent Criticism and Interpretation*, rev. C. K. Barrett (London, 1955)
Field	F. Field, *Notes on the Translation of the New Testament* (Cambridge, 1899)
Filson	F. V. Filson: *Saint John*, The Layman's Bible Commentaries (London, 1963)
Findlay	J. Alexander Findlay: *The Fourth Gospel* (London, 1956)
GNT	*The Greek New Testament being the Text Translated in the New English Bible 1961*, ed. R. V. G. Tasker (Oxford and Cambridge, 1964)
Godet	F. L. Godet: *Commentary on the Gospel of John*, 2 vols. (Grand Rapids, n.d.)
Goodspeed	Edgar J. Goodspeed: *The New Testament, An American Translation* (Chicago, 1923)
GT	*A Greek-English Lexicon of the New Testament*, being Grimm's Wilke's Clavis Novi Testamenti, trans. and rev. J. H. Thayer (Edinburgh, 1888)
Hamilton	William Hamilton: *John*, The Modern Reader's Guide to the Gospels (London, 1966)
HDB	*A Dictionary of the Bible*, ed. James Hastings, 5 vols. (Edinburgh, 1898)
HDCG	*A Dictionary of Christ and the Gospels*, ed. James Hastings, 2 vols. (Edinburgh, 1906)
Hendriksen	William Hendriksen: *Exposition of the Gospel according to John*, 2 vols. (Grand Rapids, 1953)
HHT	John Lightfoot: *Horae Hebraicae et Talmudicae* (London, 1823)
Hoskyns	Sir Edwyn Hoskyns: *The Fourth Gospel*, ed. F. N. Davey (London, 1947)

HTFG	C. H. Dodd: *Historical Tradition in the Fourth Gospel* (Cambridge, 1963)
HThR	*The Harvard Theological Review*
Hunter	A. M. Hunter: *The Gospel according to John*, The Cambridge Bible Commentary (Cambridge, 1965)
IB	*The Interpreter's Bible*, vol. 8, *The Gospel according to St. John*, Introduction and Exegesis by W. F. Howard, Exposition by A. J. Gossip (New York, 1952)
IBNTG	C. F. D. Moule: *An Idiom Book of New Testament Greek* (Cambridge, 1953)
IFG	C. H. Dodd: *The Interpretation of the Fourth Gospel* (Cambridge, 1953)
ISBE	*The International Standard Bible Encyclopaedia*, 5 vols. (Chicago, 1937)
JBL	*The Journal of Biblical Literature*
JThS	*The Journal of Theological Studies*
Kleist-Lilly	James A. Kleist and Joseph L. Lilly: *The New Testament* (Milwaukee, 1956)
Knox	Ronald Knox: *The Holy Bible, A Translation from the Latin Vulgate* (London, 1955)
LAE	A. Deissmann: *Light from the Ancient East* (London, 1927)
Lagrange	M. J. Lagrange: *Évangile selon Saint Jean* (Paris, 1936)
Lenski	R. C. H. Lenski: *The Interpretation of St. John's Gospel* (Columbus, Ohio, 1956)
Lightfoot	R. H. Lightfoot: St. John's Gospel (Oxford, 1956)
Loyd	Philip Loyd: *The Life according to S. John* (London and Oxford, 1936)
LS	*A Greek-English Lexicon*, compiled by H. G. Liddell and R. Scott, new ed., H. S. Jones and R. McKenzie, 2 vols. (Oxford, 1940)
LT	A. Edersheim: *The Life and Times of Jesus the Messiah*, 2 vols. (London, 1890)
Luther	*Luther's Works* (Concordia Publishing House, St. Louis)
Lüthi	Walter Lüthi: *St John's Gospel* (Edinburgh and London, 1960)
M, I	J. H. Moulton: *A Grammar of New Testament Greek*, vol. I, *Prolegomena* (Edinburgh, 1906)
M, II	*Ibid.*, vol. II, *Accidence and Word-Formation*, ed. W. F. Howard (Edinburgh, 1919)
M, III	*Ibid.*, vol. III, *Syntax*, by Nigel Turner (Edinburgh, 1963)
MacGregor	G. H. C. MacGregor: *The Gospel of John*, Moffatt New Testament Commentary (London, 1928)
Mantey	G. A. Turner and J. R. Mantey: *The Gospel according to John*, The Evangelical Commentary (Grand Rapids, n.d.)
McClymont	J. A. McClymont: *St. John*, The Century Bible (Edinburgh, 1901)

MiM	W. Milligan and W. F. Moulton: *Commentary on the Gospel of St. John* (Edinburgh, 1898)
ML	Millar Burrows: *More Light on the Dead Sea Scrolls* (London, 1958)
MNTC	The Moffatt New Testament Commentary
MM	J. H. Moulton and G. Milligan: *The Vocabulary of the Greek Testament* (London, 1914-29)
Moffatt	James Moffatt: *The New Testament, A New Translation* (London, n.d.)
Moods	E. de W. Burton: *Syntax of the Moods and Tenses in New Testament Greek* (Edinburgh, 1955)
Morgan	G. Campbell Morgan: *The Gospel according to John* (London and Edinburgh, 1951)
MS(S)	Manuscript(s)
MT	The Massoretic Text
Murray	J. O. F. Murray: *Jesus according to S. John* (London, 1936)
NBD	*The New Bible Dictionary*, ed. J. D. Douglas *et al.* (London, 1962)
NEB	*The New English Bible, New Testament* (Oxford and Cambridge, 1961)
NICNT	The New International Commentary on the New Testament
NPNF	The Nicene and Post-Nicene Fathers (American Reprint, Grand Rapids, 1956)
NTS	*New Testament Studies*
NTT	E. Stauffer: *New Testament Theology* (London, 1955)
ODCC	*The Oxford Dictionary of the Christian Church*, ed. F. L. Cross (London, 1958)
Phillips	J. B. Phillips: *The Gospels in Modern English* (London, 1957)
Pilcher	G. Venn Pilcher: *The Gospel according to St. John* (Sydney, n.d.)
Plummer	A. Plummer: *The Gospel according to S. John*, Cambridge Greek Testament (Cambridge, 1882)
Reynolds	H. R. Reynolds: *The Gospel of St. John*, The Pulpit Commentary, 2 vols. (London, 1888)
Richardson	Alan Richardson: *The Gospel according to Saint John*, The Torch Bible Commentaries (London, 1959)
Rieu	E. V. Rieu: *The Four Gospels* (Penguin Books, 1952)
RSV	*The Revised Standard Version*
RThR	*The Reformed Theological Review*
Ryle	John Charles Ryle: *Expository Thoughts on the Gospels, St. John*, 3 vols. (London, 1957)
SBk	H. L. Strack und P. Billerbeck: *Kommentar zum Neuen Testament aus Talmud und Midrasch*, 4 vols. (München, 1922-28)

4

Schonfield	H. J. Schonfield: *The Authentic New Testament* (London, 1956)
SDSS	T. H. Gaster: *The Scriptures of the Dead Sea Sect* (London, 1957)
SE, I	*Studia Evangelica*, vol. I, ed. K. Aland *et al.* (Berlin, 1959)
SE, II	*Ibid.*, vol. II, ed. F. L. Cross (Berlin, 1964)
SE, III	*Ibid.*, vol. III, ed. F. L. Cross (Berlin, 1964)
SFG	Leon Morris: *Studies in the Fourth Gospel* (Grand Rapids, 1969)
SJT	*The Scottish Journal of Theology*
SNT	*The Scrolls and the New Testament*, ed. K. Stendahl (London, 1958)
Strachan	R. H. Strachan: *The Fourth Gospel* (London, 1955)
Tasker	R. V. G. Tasker: *The Gospel according to St. John*, Tyndale Bible Commentaries (London and Grand Rapids, 1960)
TDNT	*Theological Dictionary of the New Testament*, being a translation by G. W. Bromiley of *TWNT*, vols I-VI (Grand Rapids, 1964-69)
Temple	William Temple: *Readings in St. John's Gospel* (London, 1947)
Tenney	Merrill C. Tenney: *John: The Gospel of Belief* (Grand Rapids, 1948)
Torrey	C. C. Torrey: *The Four Gospels, A New Translation* (London, n.d.)
Turner	G. A. Turner and J. R. Mantey: *The Gospel according to John*, The Evangelical Commentary (Grand Rapids, n.d.)
TWBB	*A Theological Word Book of the Bible*, ed. A. Richardson (London, 1950)
Twentieth Century	*The Twentieth Century New Testament* (London and New York, 1904)
TWNT	*Theologisches Wörterbuch zum Neuen Testament*, ed. G. Kittel and G. Friedrich (Stuttgart, 1933-)
v.l.	*varia lectio* (variant reading)
Westcott	Brooke Foss Westcott: *The Gospel according to St. John* (Grand Rapids, 1954)
Weymouth	R. F. Weymouth: *The New Testament in Modern Speech* (London, 1907)
Williams, C. B.	Charles B. Williams: *The New Testament, A Translation in the Language of the People* (Chicago, 1950)
Williams, C. K.	Charles Kingsley Williams: *The New Testament, A New Translation in Plain English* (London, 1952)
Wright	C. J. Wright: *Jesus the Revelation of God* (London, 1950)
Wuest	Kenneth S. Wuest: *The New Testament, An Expanded Translation* (London, 1961)
ZATW	*Zeitschrift für die Alttestamentliche Wissenschaft*
ZNTW	*Zeitschrift für die Neutestamentliche Wissenschaft*

Quotations from the Bible are normally from ARV, those from the Mishnah from the translation by H. Danby, from the Midrash and the Talmud from the Soncino translation, from Josephus and Philo from the Loeb translation, from the Apostolic Fathers from J. B. Lightfoot's translation, from the Pseudepigrapha from the edition of Charles. Statistics are often taken from R. Morgenthaler, *Statistik des Neutestamentlichen Wortschatzes* (Zürich, 1958)

INTRODUCTION

I like the comparison of John's Gospel to a pool in which a child may wade and an elephant can swim. It is both simple and profound. It is for the veriest beginner in the faith and for the mature Christian. Its appeal is immediate and neverfailing.

It is a simple Gospel. The humblest believer can read it and understand it and profit by it. Sir Edwyn Hoskyns put his finger on something important when he wrote: "The critic may range the gospel with Philo and the Alexandrian philosophers; but, and the question is important, did the poor and the ignorant, when they lay a-dying, ever ask their Rabbis to read to them out of the voluminous writings of Philo or of those like him?"[1] The poor and the ignorant have often found in this Gospel something that matters intensely both for life and for death.

But that is not the whole story. A little later Hoskyns writes of the critical commentator who applies himself to the close study of this book, "he will not be true to the book he is studying if, at the end, the gospel does not still remain strange, restless, and unfamiliar."[2] There are unplumbed depths in the limpid clarity of this writing. What at first appears plainly obvious is presently seen to pose problems. Most students would agree with Hoskyns that years of close study of this Gospel do not leave one with a feeling of having mastered it, but rather with the conviction that it is still "strange, restless, and unfamiliar".

An Introduction to this book could accordingly be a long and complicated affair. However, the book I am writing is primarily a commentary, and this introduction is not meant to be comprehensive. I propose to do little more than notice some of the important problems. There is a multitude of books on particular aspects of this Gospel for those who wish to pursue these questions

---

[1] P. 20.
[2] *Loc. cit.*

further.[3] But there are some aspects of the Gospel on which something must be said and we proceed to them.

I. Authorship[4]

Some have urged that the authorship of this Gospel matters little. We do not have the information to determine the point, they say, and in any case it is of no great importance. It is not who wrote the words that counts, but what is written. There is something in this. It is certainly the case that the important thing is to give heed to what is said, and further, that this is more urgent than indulging in scholarly arguments about authorship. It is also true that the Gospel as it stands is anonymous. Even the most conservative among us need not feel bound to espouse any particular view of authorship. But the subject is not unimportant, for all that. If we can feel that there are good grounds for thinking of an eyewitness, and specifically of John the Apostle, as being behind it our view of what it says will be one thing. But if we see it as written by a second-century Christian who had never set eyes on Jesus it will be quite another. While complete certainty may be unattainable, the question is one which we may discuss to our profit.

Continental scholars have for the most part long since abandoned the idea that this Gospel was written by the Apostle John, whereas in Britain scholarship has been much more hospitable to the idea. Most British scholars have thought either that John wrote the Gospel or that he was closely associated with it in some way, *e.g.* he may have been the witness behind it. In recent years there has been something of a shift of opinion in Britain. Most scholars there, other than conservative evangelicals, would not now hold that the author was the Apostle John. A good number would still maintain that his witness is behind the Gospel, but opinion is now much more akin to that on the continent. The position is much the same in America.

This impressive body of opinion must be given due weight. But we must also bear in mind that a good deal of it appears to be

---

[3] I have examined some of the more important problems in my *Studies in the Fourth Gospel* (Grand Rapids, 1969). For fuller statements about some of the matters referred to in this Introduction may I refer readers to that volume.

[4] For a fuller account see *SFG*, ch. 4.

due more to the prevailing climate of opinion of our day than to any new evidence. It is interesting to notice that Westcott, who held firmly to the Johannine authorship, was well aware of the three reasons that A. M. Hunter gives for rejecting it. Hunter points to the use of the Synoptists by the author of this Gospel, the difference in style between this and the other three Gospels, and the improbability that the Apostle John would have called himself, "the disciple whom Jesus loved". Hunter concludes: "For these and other reasons, scarcely a reputable scholar in this country nowadays is prepared to affirm that the Fourth Gospel was written by John the Apostle."[5] Westcott long ago took notice of these (and other) points.[6] But he held that other considerations outweighed them, and that the best solution to the problem on the basis of the evidence available is to see John the Apostle as the author. Westcott has not so much been confuted as bypassed. Nobody seems to have dealt adequately with his massive argument. But scholars today evaluate the evidence differently. They are not necessarily wrong in this but we should be clear that for the most part it is the same evidence. It is not the case that new discoveries have made the older view untenable. Lightfoot, indeed, reminds us that "This traditional ascription still receives support, and has never been shown to be impossible."[7]

The basic reason for holding that the author was John the Apostle is that this appears to be what the Gospel itself teaches. In the concluding chapter, after a reference to "the disciple whom Jesus loved", we read: "This is the disciple that beareth witness of these things, and wrote these things" (21 : 24). The following words "and we know that his witness is true" show that the statement comes from others than the author. But their commendation is quite early, for no manuscript of the Gospel is known which lacks it. We have, then, a statement, probably contemporary with the publication of the Gospel, that its author was the disciple

---

[5] *Introducing the New Testament* (London, 1945), p. 50.
[6] See the full examination of the evidence in the Introduction to his Commentary.
[7] P. 2.

9

whom Jesus loved. The Gospel itself seems to indicate that this man was John the Apostle.[8]

The other information we glean about the Beloved Disciple is as follows. At the Last Supper he "was at the table reclining in Jesus' bosom" and, when Jesus predicted the betrayal, at Peter's suggestion he "leaning back, as he was, on Jesus' breast saith unto him, Lord who is it?" (13 : 23, 25). This seems to betoken an intimacy with the Lord, and this is strengthened by the fact that as He hung on the cross Jesus commended His mother to this man's care (19 : 26f.). As he is the only follower of Jesus, apart from the women, who is said to have been at the cross he may well be the witness of the water and blood which came out of Jesus' side (19 : 34f.). On the resurrection morning he raced Peter to the empty tomb but did not go in (20 : 2–5).[9] When Peter came up and entered he followed this example "and he saw, and believed" (20 : 8). He it was who recognized Jesus on the shore of the lake after the miraculous catch of fish (21 : 7), and finally he was the subject of Jesus' words to Peter, "If I will that he tarry till I come, what is that to thee?" (21 : 20ff.). It is possible that he was the unnamed disciple of 1 : 35–40, and again the "other disciple" who was "known unto the high priest" and who brought Peter into the high priest's courtyard (18: 15f.). But in neither case is the evidence clear enough to enable us to be certain.

From the list of names given in 21 : 2 (Peter, Thomas, Nathanael, the sons of Zebedee and two others) it seems that the Beloved Disciple was one of the sons of Zebedee or else one of the unnamed disciples. If the latter, he must still have been one of the Twelve for he was present at the Last Supper and it seems that only the Twelve were present on that occasion (Matt. 26 : 20; Mark 14 :

---

[8] It is sometimes said that, since ch. 21 is a supplement, added later than chs. 1–20, the words refer only to the author of ch. 21. Granted that the final chapter is to be regarded as a supplement (and we must bear in mind that, while some scholars regard it as from the hand of another author than chs. 1–20, others do not), T. Zahn's point is still valid: "if it was necessary to assure the readers that chap. xxi. was written by the beloved disciple of Jesus, it was even more important to make clear to them who wrote chaps. i.–xx." (*Introduction to the New Testament*, III, Edinburgh, 1909, p. 237). If it was a different author we are justified in looking for some hint.

[9] The verb used in 20 : 2 is φιλέω, in the other passages ἀγαπάω.

17, 20; Luke 22 : 14, 30). This rules out suggestions like Lazarus[10] and John Mark.[11] The Beloved Disciple appears to have stood in close relationship to Peter (13 : 24; 20 : 2; 21 : 7). From the other Gospels we know that Peter, James and John formed a trio (and that they were singled out as specially close to Jesus). As James was martyred early (Acts 12 : 2), this leaves John.[12]

This may be supported by the curious fact that John is not mentioned by name anywhere in this Gospel. It is not easy to think of a reason why any early Christian, other than John himself, should have completely omitted all mention of such a prominent Apostle.[13] It is also the case that in this Gospel we do not read of "John the Baptist" as in the other Gospels but simply of "John". It is difficult to see why any informed early Christian

---

[10] Advocated, for example, by F. V. Filson (pp. 21–25); see also his contribution to *Current Issues in New Testament Interpretation*, ed. W. Klassen and G. F. Snyder (London, 1962), pp. 119–123. J. N. Sanders distinguishes between the disciple whom Jesus ἠγάπα (Lazarus) and him whom Jesus ἐφίλει (John the Elder, who is identical with John Mark). He sees the former as the witness behind this Gospel and the latter as responsible for its "publication" (*Studies in the Fourth Gospel*, ed. F. L. Cross, London, 1957, pp. 72–82).

[11] See, for example, Lewis Johnson, *ExT*, LXXVII, 1965–66, pp. 157f., and the comments on the idea by Donald Rogers, *ExT*, LXXVII, 1965–66, p. 214. So also J. Ernest Davey, *The Jesus of St. John* (London, 1958), pp. 23–29.

[12] Some follow more or less the procedure we have been following and look for the "witness" among people mentioned in the New Testament and see him as the Beloved Disciple, but then take a different line by suggesting that another was the actual author of the Gospel. Thus MacGregor approves of Swete's suggestion that the rich young ruler was the Beloved Disciple ("Jesus looking upon him loved him", Mark 10 : 21), but he sees John the Elder as the writer of the Gospel (pp. lxiii f.). While the ruler satisfies the criterion of being the recipient of Jesus' love there is no evidence that he ever became a disciple. Those who see John the Apostle as the Beloved Disciple and the "witness", and a follower of his, perhaps John the Elder, as the Evangelist, are more numerous. An ingenious view is that of Robert Eisler who saw Lazarus as the Beloved Disciple and John the son of the high priest Annas (mentioned in Acts 4 : 6) as the Evangelist, with the heretic Marcion as his amanuensis (*The Enigma of the Fourth Gospel*, London, 1928).

[13] MacGregor mentions approvingly the curious hypothesis of "the deliberate cancellation by the Redactor, in the interest of his theory that the Beloved Disciple is John, of all independent references to John by name" (p. xlix). There is, of course, not a shred of evidence for this, and the suggestion is noteworthy only as showing that, as the evidence stands, the case for identifying the Beloved Disciple with John is convincing.

11

(who must have known there were two Johns) should thus court confusion. But it would have been quite natural for John the Apostle to speak of his namesake simply as "John". This point is all the more significant in that in this Gospel people are consistently distinguished. Thus the Judas who asked the question at the Last Supper is expressly said to be not Judas Iscariot (14 : 22). Thomas is usually identified by the addition of his Greek name, Didymus (11 : 16; 20 : 24; 21 : 2), a name not used by the Synoptists. Judas Iscariot is the son of a certain Simon who is not mentioned outside this Gospel (6 : 71; 13 : 2, 26). So we might go on. In view of this care with other names some reason is needed for his speaking of the Baptist simply as John.

The biggest objection to this identification, in my opinion, is the contention that a man is not likely to refer to himself as "the disciple whom Jesus loved". I agree. It does not seem a natural way of describing oneself.[14] But then, it is countered, it is not a very natural way of describing anyone else either. There is force in this. Why should any Christian single out one disciple as specially beloved by Jesus? While it is possible it is not very natural. And this fact means that the objection we are considering has rather less weight than at first appears. So, while we recognize the fact that the objection is weighty, it does not seem weighty enough to cancel out the arguments adduced earlier.[15]

These arguments are reinforced by a variety of considerations which are urged to show that the author of the Gospel knew Palestine well. For example, he clearly knew of the connection

---

[14] Yet we should not overlook the point made long ago by W. Sanday. He reminds us that Jesus referred to Himself as "the Son of man" and thinks that His follower may have adopted "a similar method of oblique and allusive reference". Sanday thinks that "The beloved disciple had a special reason for not wishing to obtrude his own personality. He was conscious of a great privilege, of a privilege that would single him out for all time among the children of men. He could not resist the temptation to speak of this privilege. The impulse of affection responding to affection prompted him to claim it. But the consciousness that he was doing so, and the reaction of modesty led him at the same moment to suppress, what a vulgar egotism might have accentuated, the lower plane of his own individuality. The son of Zebedee (if it was he) desired to be merged and lost in 'the disciple whom Jesus loved' " (*The Criticism of the Fourth Gospel*, Oxford, 1905, pp. 79f.).

[15] *Cf.* A. M. Hunter: "after all the conjectures have been heard, the likeliest view is that which identifies the Beloved Disciple with the Apostle John" (*Interpreting the New Testament 1900–1950*, London, 1951, p. 86).

of Elijah with Jewish messianic expectations (1 : 21), the low view held of women (4 : 27), the importance attaching to the religious schools (7 : 15), the hostility between Jews and Samaritans (4 : 9), and the contempt the Pharisees had for ordinary people (7 : 49). He knew the importance of the Sabbath, and the fact that, while it was not lawful to carry a bed on it (5 : 10), the need to circumcise a child overrode it (7 : 22f.). His topography is remarkably accurate, and he includes mention of places like Cana, which are mentioned in no earlier writing known to us.[16] Much more of this kind of thing could be cited.

The style is that of a Jew. C. F. Burney[17] and C. C. Torrey[18] indeed both had the idea that the Gospel was originally written in Aramaic and that our present Gospel is a translation. Few subsequent scholars have accepted this view, but most agree that Aramaic thinking lies behind our Gospel, and often Aramaic expressions.[19]

This has received a strong reinforcement in recent times by the discovery of the Dead Sea Scrolls. These have demonstrated, by their many parallels to this Gospel both in ideas and expression, that John is essentially a Palestinian document. As A. M. Hunter says, "To put the matter in one sentence, the Scrolls have

---

[16]   See R. D. Potter, *SE*, I, pp. 329–337.

[17]   *The Aramaic Origin of the Fourth Gospel* (Oxford, 1922).

[18]   *Our Translated Gospels* (London, n.d.). He begins his Preface with this uncompromising statement: "The material of our Four Gospels is all Palestinian, and the language in which it was originally written is Aramaic, then the principal language of the land, with the exception of the first two chapters of Lk., which were composed in Hebrew." I should perhaps add that he thinks John 21 formed no part of the original, but that it was composed in Greek by the translator.

[19]   An exception is E. C. Colwell. He examines the case made out by Burney and Torrey and concludes:

"(I) The method employed by Burney and the other Aramaic scholars is unsound – for (1) they use no adequate control; (2) they are inaccurate and inconsistent; (3) they point to the cumulative force of a list of Aramaisms of the weakest sort. (II) Their results are not at all convincing: (1) they do not pick the same Aramaisms when they work independently; (2) they reject each other's mistranslations; (3) the vast majority (about 90 per cent) of their Aramaisms have been shown by this study to be paralleled in Greek; (4) what remains is the inevitable minimum of Semitisms in a gospel which inherited the earlier Christian traditions. There is here nothing to justify the claim that the author of the Fourth Gospel thought in Aramaic or wrote in Aramaic" (*The Greek of the Fourth Gospel*, Chicago, 1931, pp. 130f.).

established its essential Jewishness."[19a] This does not mean that
John's position is essentially that of the scrolls. There are fundamental differences, many of which stem from the fact that for
John the Messiah has come. This is the essential truth. He sees
all things in the light of Christ, whereas for the scrolls the coming
of Messiah (or Messiahs) is still future. But there are parallels
both of concepts and language which enable us to say that John
is at home against a Palestinian background. This is reinforced
by the parallels which may be adduced from the writings of the
Rabbis.[20]

We should also notice that there are touches which many have
felt indicate an eyewitness.[21] This is not universally agreed, but
then it is difficult to know what all would agree does indicate
the eyewitness. What to one is unmistakable evidence of first-
hand observation is to another no more than a touch introduced
to give an air of verisimilitude to the narrative. But it is difficult
to think that that is an adequate explanation of all the passages

[19a] *ExT*, LXXI, 1959–60, p. 166. Later he says, "The trend of recent
studies has been to make the Evangelist's links with Palestine much stronger
than many of us have allowed" (*op. cit.*, p. 222).

[20] See, for example, the many passages cited by SBk. Curiously W. G.
Kümmel says, "any kind of familiarity with the views of the rabbis nowhere
is evident in John" (*Introduction to the New Testament*, London, 1965, p. 155).
It is better to take the verdict of Israel Abrahams than this sweeping statement.
Abrahams speaks of "the Fourth Gospel's close acquaintance with Hebraic
traditions" (*Studies in Pharisaism and the Gospels*, First Series, Cambridge, 1917,
p. 135). S. Neill reports him as saying, "to us Jews the Fourth Gospel is the
most Jewish of the four" (*The Interpretation of the New Testament*, London, 1964,
p. 315). Neill immediately goes on, "If a learned Jew makes a remark of this
kind, it is impossible for a Christian to say that he does not know what he is
talking about." Again, Odeberg detects "already, at a superficial reading,
passages, sentences and words revealing a terminology all but identical with
the Rabbinic" (*FG*, p. 5). It seems clear that John has points of contact both
with official Judaism as represented by the Pharisees, and also with unorthodox
Judaism as depicted in the Qumran scrolls.

[21] For example, W. C. van Unnik says, "Many things in this Gospel are
suggestive of personal reminiscence (1 : 39f.; 4 : 6; 13 : 21 ff., especially in
chs. 18 to 21)" (*The New Testament, Its History and Message*, London, 1964,
p. 61). So also Barclay: "Many of these things are such apparently unimportant
details that they are inexplicable unless they are the memories of a man who
was there" (I, p. xx). B. P. W. Stather Hunt goes as far as to say, "no other
Gospel bears upon its face such undeniable proof that its author was an eyewitness of the scenes which he records" (*Some Johannine Problems*, London,
1958, p. 7).

adduced in this Gospel. Sometimes these concern the time of day at which a thing happened (1 : 39; 4 : 6, *etc.*), or perhaps they link it with one of the feasts (2 : 13, 23, *etc.*). Place names are brought in very naturally, and often for no apparent reason save that it was there that the incident happened (*e.g.* Cana in ch. 2). Many have seen the reminiscence of an eyewitness in the way the call of the disciples is described (1 : 35–51), or again the episode of the feet-washing (13 : 1–20). With this we should take information about persons not mentioned elsewhere such as Nicodemus, Lazarus and others. It is difficult to see a reason for introducing the name of Nicodemus into the narrative, for example, other than that this was in fact the inquirer's name. And why else should we be told that the name of the high priest's servant whose ear Peter cut off was Malchus (18 : 10)? Or that he was related to one of those who accused Peter of being a follower of Jesus (18 : 26)? To personal knowledge again we should surely ascribe the information that Annas was father-in-law to Caiaphas (18 : 13). All in all the information supplied by this Gospel gives good reason for us to hold that its author knew the facts at first hand and wrote of what he knew and had seen.

It is also the case that there are some claims to eyewitness testimony. The first is in 1 : 14, "we beheld his glory". Some see this as meaning, "we Christians", "believers generally". But in the first instance this is a very unnatural way to take the words, and in the second the word "see" appears to mean, "see with the outward eye".[22] It is much more likely that the words refer to what the writer and his friends have seen physically. A second appeal to witness appears in 19 : 35, "he that hath seen hath borne witness, and his witness is true: and he knoweth that he saith true, that ye also may believe." There is a problem as to whether the writer means that he himself has borne the witness or that someone else has done so. But there is good reason for

---

[22] The verb is $\theta\varepsilon\acute{\alpha}o\mu\alpha\iota$ of which AS says, "in NT apparently always in literal, physical sense of 'careful and deliberate vision which interprets . . . its object' ".

seeing eyewitness testimony behind the statement (see the note on the passage).[23]

With this we should consider the controversies referred to in the Gospel. These are not the kind of questions that Christians discussed among themselves in the second century (like episcopacy, Gnostic emanations, the date of keeping Easter, *etc.*), nor are they the standard disputes between Christians and Jews. There is an authentic note about them as of the kind of subject that was in dispute in first century Palestine. So we get discussions of the use and abuse of the Sabbath (ch. 5), about the Messiah and his credentials and whether he would rescue the Jews from the Romans (6 : 15; 11 : 47–50), about true and false Judaism. P. Borgen has made a close study of the sixth chapter and he points out that in subject matter and method this is authentic Palestinian.[24] From another angle Raymond E. Brown has discussed the concept of the *Logos* in this Gospel. He has shown that it is not a Hellenistic philosophical idea that has strayed into a Jewish work, but that the form and content given it by John shows it to be of Palestinian origin.[25]

The writer of this Gospel had a good knowledge of the apostolic band. He recalls words the Twelve spoke among themselves (4 : 33; 16 : 17; 20 : 25; 21 : 3,7). He shows knowledge of their thoughts on occasion (2 : 11, 17, 22; 4 : 27; 6 : 19, 60f.). He knows the places they frequented (11 : 54; 18 : 2). Sometimes he speaks of mistakes they made which were later corrected (2 : 21f.; 11 : 13; 12 : 16). If he were one of their number all this would fall into place.

From all this it is clear that the evidence in favour of the

---

[23] Sanday refers to "all those marks of an eye-witness which we shall see to be present in great number and strength. They point to a first-hand relation between the author and the facts which he records. If the Gospel is not the work of an eye-witness, then the writer has made a very sustained and extraordinary effort to give the impression that he was one" (*op. cit.*, p. 70).

[24] *Bread from Heaven* (Leiden, 1965). The book is sub-titled, "An Exegetical Study of the Concept of Manna in the Gospel of John and the Writings of Philo". He sees both Philo and John as interpreting Jewish traditions in the face of non-Jewish ideas.

[25] *The Gospel according to John (i–xii)* (New York, 1966), pp. 519–24. He concludes, "In sum, it seems that the Prologue's description of the Word is far closer to biblical and Jewish strains of thought than it is to anything purely Hellenistic" (*op. cit.*, p. 524). See also W. F. Howard, *FGRCI*, p. 11.

Johannine authorship is by no means negligible. Those who disagree generally concede that the evidence shows that the author was a Palestinian Jew, perhaps also that he had some unusual knowledge of what went on in the days of Jesus. But they would reject a good deal of the preceding, regarding it as no more than an attempt at verisimilitude. Thus whereas it has been contended that the writer knew what the apostles said on certain occasions it would be countered that he did not really know what they said. He knew only what they ought, in his opinion, to have said and he said that they said it. I think it may be fairly replied that it is difficult to do this kind of thing consistently without giving oneself away. The writer of this Gospel does it often, and what he writes rings true.

Another point to tell against the traditional view is the curious fact that most of the action takes place in Judea, whereas we would have expected John the son of Zebedee to be more interested in Galilee. This is certainly difficult, but the theological interest of this writer must be borne in mind. He certainly knew some interesting things about Jesus' ministry in Galilee, for he tells us of incidents like the wedding in Cana which are mentioned nowhere else. But he saw Jerusalem as the place where the Messiah must be accepted or rejected, so he put his emphasis on what took place there.

Some find it difficult to date the Gospel as early as John the Apostle on the grounds that it reflects Gnostic ideas. These ideas are also seen as evidence that the writer was probably not the Apostle for there is no reason for thinking that Jesus numbered a Jewish Gnostic among His followers. Everything here depends on the "Gnostic ideas" in John. In my opinion they are better spoken of as "pre-Gnostic". As far as I am aware no one has succeeded in showing that developed Gnosticism is anywhere present in John. E. F. Scott can say, "the approximations to Gnosticism in the Fourth Gospel are in many respects more apparent than real . . . John was led to conclusions which bear a superficial resemblance to those of the Gnostics, but on closer analysis are radically different."[26] On these grounds there is no objection

---

[26] *The Fourth Gospel* (Edinburgh, 1906), p. 100. He locates the writing of this Gospel in the "period of truce" before the conflict with Gnosticism (*op. cit.*, p. 103).

either to an early date, or to an Apostle as the author.[27]

The omissions of this Gospel are also to be noticed. Two of the more striking are those of the Transfiguration and the Agony in Gethsemane. Some go so far as to say that these omissions of incidents where John, along with Peter and James, had a special place of privilege, are sufficient to show that John did not write this Gospel. This is a strong argument. But perhaps both omissions are due to the fact that our author makes the essential point otherwise. He may have found it difficult to find a place for the Transfiguration (which concentrates the manifestation of Jesus' glory into one magnificent story) in the face of the fact that one of his major themes is that Jesus' glory was manifested continually in the path of lowly service, and that it was preeminently shown on the cross. Where is there a place for the Transfiguration in this scheme? The Agony is more difficult.[28] But it must be borne in mind that many have seen a counterpart in the scene in which Jesus says, "Now is my soul troubled; and what shall I say? Father, save me from this hour" (12 : 27). He may have felt that this is the essential thing. It is also possible that the writer, who clearly saw Jesus' lowliness as all-pervasive, did not wish to concentrate it into one narrative.[29] Any argument on omissions must further reckon with the fact that, on any showing, this writer has some extraordinary omissions. No really satisfactory explana-

---

[27] Some draw attention to the role of the Qumran writings in this connection. Thus A. Feuillet: "as Father Mollat justly points out, at the very heart of Judaism there was a whole school of thought, now brought to light by the Dead Sea Scrolls, which attributed great importance to knowledge and used a vocabulary which makes one think of Hellenism. If a Greek influence was brought to bear on St. John, perhaps it was only in this way, and therefore very indirectly. Further research will be able to clear up these delicate points" (A. Robert and A. Feuillet, *Introduction to the New Testament*, New York, 1965, p. 884). It seems to me that this may be ascribing too large a function to the Scrolls. If John was intended for an audience living in a centre of Greek culture it is not unnatural to hold that its author had direct experience of Greek thought. Nevertheless Feuillet does well to remind us that we should look carefully at what the Scrolls can tell us and not assume Hellenistic influence too readily.

[28] Strachan thinks this Gospel was written in part with people like the Stoics in mind. "Gethsemane, to the Stoic, would represent a moral breakdown." While retaining what is essential (12 : 27), John omits what would repel such readers (p. 58). This at least deserves consideration.

[29] See further *SFG*, pp. 184f.

tion has ever been produced, for example, for the surprising fact that, though his account of the events in the upper room is much the fullest of the four we have, he says nothing about the institution of the Holy Communion.[30] He must have known of this. It is important. Yet he omits it. We need not be too surprised then if he omits other incidents we regard as important.

The difference in style between this Gospel and the others is often urged with great confidence as proving that John did not write it. This, I think, does not follow. There is no reason for holding that all the apostolic band saw everything in the same way, or that they thought in the same way, or that they wrote in the same style. It is more convincing to put the objection in the form that if Jesus was as He is depicted in the Synoptic Gospels He could not be as John depicts Him. Therefore the author could not have known the real Jesus and thus he was not a member of the apostolic band. But this is to assume that the Synoptists have caught for us all that Jesus was. We are, however, familiar with the fact that a great man will show different facets to different people. It may fairly be disputed that the Jesus of St John is incompatible with the Jesus of the Synoptics.[31] He who gave rise to the Christian movement was certainly no ordinary man. Through the years Christianity has made its appeal to men who find themselves at home in the matter-of-fact atmosphere of the Synoptic Gospels. But it has also attracted those who find the Fourth Gospel more congenial, and, for that matter, to those who are attracted by the Christ who inspired the Pauline Epistles, or to the great High Priest they find in the Epistle to the Hebrews, or to the triumphant Lamb of the Apocalypse. We must face the fact that in history Jesus has proved a gigantic figure. It is not

---

[30] It is usually said, sometimes quite dogmatically, that the omission is due to a desire to keep information about this "holy mystery" from the uninitiated. *Cf.* J. Jeremias: "All difficulties disappear, however, when it is realized that the author of the Fourth Gospel consciously omitted the account of the Last Supper because he did not want to disclose the sacred formula to the heathen" (*The Eucharistic Words of Jesus*, Oxford, 1955, p. 73). But this immediately confronts us with the problem: If the "sacred formula" is to be kept from outsiders why do Matthew and Mark and Luke all include it in their Gospels?

[31] *Cf.* R. H. Lightfoot: "the Church has never been aware of any fundamental incompatibility between the portrait of the Lord in this gospel and that in the other three. This question has long ago been settled by the religious consciousness of Christendom" (p. 1).

at all impossible, accordingly, that He is the Sitter behind both Gospel portraits, that the Synoptists depict Him from one aspect, John from another. The fact that we are not able to put the two pictures together satisfactorily may mean no more than that we are not big enough to comprehend the whole Christ.

This point was made emphatically by W. F. Albright. He said: "One of the strangest assumptions of critical New Testament scholars and theologians is that the mind of Jesus was so limited that any apparent contrast between John and the Synoptics must be due to differences between early Christian theologians. Every great thinker and personality is going to be interpreted differently by different friends and hearers, who will select what seems most congenial or useful out of what they have seen and heard. From Socrates to the most recent men of eminence there are innumerable examples. The Christian might *a fortiori* suppose the same to be true of his Master."[32] Along the same lines C. L. Mitton can say: "It is not that the Johannine portrait is right and the Synoptics wrong, but rather that in each there may be preserved a true emphasis which the other fails to do full justice to. The Fourth Gospel may therefore have its own contribution to make, not only to those who wish to grasp the eternal significance of Jesus Christ, but also to those who wish to gain a clear insight into the historical personality of Jesus of Nazareth."[33]

Nevertheless the difference in style is held by many to be decisive. Kümmel, for example, says forthrightly, "the Gnostic language of the Johannine Jesus discourses makes impossible the composition of John by an eyewitness."[34] I do not think that he (or for that matter, anyone else) has shown that the language of the discourses is Gnostic. But plainly the style is sufficient of itself to rule out for Kümmel the possibility that the author was the Apostle or anyone else of his day. Everyone must think this point through for himself. To some the undoubted difference in style is decisive. To others it simply indicates the gigantic stature of Jesus.

As noted elsewhere in this Introduction, there is also the im-

---

[32] *BNT*, p. 171, n. 1.

[33] *ExT*, LXXI, 1959–60, p. 340.

[34] *Op. cit.*, p. 174. *Cf.* also D. Moody Smith Jr.: "If Jesus actually spoke as he speaks in the various strands of the Synoptic tradition, I find it impossible to believe that he also spoke as does the Johannine Christ" (*Interpretation*, XXI, 1967, p. 475).

portant point that Riesenfeld and others have in recent years developed an interesting way of reconciling the two portraits.[35] They point out that any teacher in antiquity had what we might call his public teaching, striking sayings which he caused his disciples to commit to memory, and as well teaching of a more informal kind. They suggest that behind the Synoptic Gospels there lies the public teaching of Jesus, whereas the Fourth Gospel gives us rather the informal teaching of Jesus among His friends, and His equally informal encounters with His enemies. This may or may not be the way of it. I simply point out that in the judgment of this eminent scholar and those who think with him the problem is not insuperable. They see the Jesus of the Synoptics and the Jesus of St John as quite compatible.

When we turn to the external evidence we are confronted by the fact that, while John the son of Zebedee is not named as the author of this Gospel in the earliest days, there is no other name in the tradition. The first person of whom we have record who definitely ascribes this Gospel to John appears to be Theophilus of Antioch (c. A.D. 180). Irenaeus also says it was written by John the Apostle, and his source appears to have been Polycarp, who knew John personally.[36] This is considerably later than we might have expected. Those who oppose apostolic authorship insist that it is impossible to trace the tradition much if anything behind this date. They suggest that there is a significant gap and that we must regard the tradition as of little value.

Yet we must not overlook the fact that there is little Christian literature before this period. Westcott can point out that Christian theological literature to all intents and purposes begins with Irenaeus, Clement of Alexandria, and Tertullian, all of whom

---

[35] See below, pp. 45ff.

[36] *Adv. Haer.*, II. xxii. 5; III. i. 1; III. iii. 4. Eusebius cites a letter of Irenaeus to Florinus in which he speaks of what he learned from Polycarp who had known John (*HE*, V. xx. 5f.). The importance of this should not be minimized. *Cf.* R. H. Malden: "A historical fact which appears in a contemporary or nearly contemporary letter may generally be accepted without demur, for the reason that the author is not trying to write history . . . When historical facts are referred to in letters, it shows that they were matters of common knowledge in the circle in which the writer and his correspondent moved" (cited by H. P. V. Nunn, *The Authorship of the Fourth Gospel*, Eton, 1952, pp. 37f.).

see John the Apostle as the author.[37] In considering the absence of earlier attestation we must bear in mind that this may be accounted for in part by the fact that heretics gave this Gospel a warm welcome, and this may have deterred the orthodox. A Gospel which differed so much from the Three might well have perplexed the simple faithful. They were hesitant about it. And their hesitation was increased when they found that certain heretics made a good deal of use of it.

There can be no doubt about the Gnostic use of John. It appears to have been the favorite Gospel among the Gnostics. The first commentary on it was written by the Gnostic Heracleon.[38] The Chenoboskion literature shows that John was widely used and highly esteemed by the Gnostics. The importance of this find for Johannine criticism does not seem always to have been realized. But these documents show conclusively that John's Gospel was accepted as authoritative in the circles from which they came in the first half of the second century. We are speaking now about the acceptance of the Gospel as authoritative, not of the explicit use of the Apostle John's name in connection with it.[39] Our Gospel was clearly important to the writer of the "Gospel of Truth" (probably Valentinus). This writing is dated by K. Grobel "150 if not earlier",[40] by G. Quispel "earlier than 150, say about

---

[37]   P. lix. H. P. V. Nunn reminds us that some of those who commended this Gospel in early days knew what persecution was. Irenaeus may have witnessed the persecution at Lyons and certainly succeeded the martyr Pothinus. Tertullian gave up a brilliant career to become a Christian, and he lived through the persecution of Severus. Origen's father was killed in this persecution and he himself nearly suffered the same fate. Nunn proceeds: "It is not usual for exceptionally well educated men living under these conditions to accept the capital documents on which their faith depends without enquiry or examination, when such are possible, as they undoubtedly were at that time. They were even less likely to compose a spurious Gospel and to find acceptance for it when they had seen men and women put to horrible deaths for believing statements which this Gospel was intended to commend" (*op. cit.*, p. 101).

[38]   Sanday brings out the importance of Heracleon: "To recognize a writing is one thing; to recognize it as sacred is another; to comment upon it as so sacred and authoritative that its contents can be interpreted allegorically is a third; and all this is so early as *c*. 170" (*op. cit.*, p. 240).

[39]   The Chenoboskion documents show only that the Gospel was held in high esteem. But Irenaeus adds the information that Ptolemaeus and his followers held this Gospel to have been written by "John, the disciple of the Lord" (*Adv. Haer.*, I. viii. 5; ANF, I, p. 328).

[40]   K. Grobel, *The Gospel of Truth* (London, 1960), p. 28.

140",[41] and by W. C. van Unnik "round about 140–45".[42] Its importance for our present purpose is put in a nutshell by Quispel: "the 'Gospel of Truth' has borrowed more than a little from the Gospel of St. John, *as from a writing which was already old and held in high repute*".[43] It seems equally clear that John was known to the writer of the "Gospel of Philip". R. McL. Wilson points out that "of the four Gospels, the author's preference is clearly for Matthew and John".[44] This work is dated by H.-Ch. Puech "in the 2nd century, or at latest in the beginning or the middle of the 3rd."[45] If the earlier date should prove correct this document is relevant to our study, and it may be worth noticing that Wilson finds "a number of indications which seem to point to the second century."[46]

The "Apocryphon of John", according to S. Giversen, shows "a thorough knowledge" of the New Testament,[47] and he specifically mentions John's Gospel.[48] This writing is dated by Puech "before 180", and he proceeds, "It is scarcely too much to assume that it was composed in the first half of the second century."[49] R. M. Grant dates it earlier, "at the beginning of the second century".[50]

We should not overlook the "Gospel of Thomas", dated by many in the vicinity of 140–150.[51] It is a sayings document, and much more akin to the Synoptic Gospels than to John, but most who have studied it appear to hold that there are Johannine

---

[41] *The Jung Codex, Three Studies*, by H. C. Puech, G. Quispel, W. C. van Unnik (London, 1955), p. 54.

[42] *Ibid.*, p. 104.

[43] *Op. cit.*, p. 49 (my italics).

[44] *The Gospel of Philip* (London, 1962), p. 7.

[45] E. Hennecke, *New Testament Apocrypha*, ed. W. Schneemelcher, I (London, 1963), p. 278.

[46] *Op. cit.*, p. 3.

[47] *Apocryphon Johannis* (Copenhagen, 1963), p. 152.

[48] *E. g., op. cit.*, pp. 140, 153, 155.

[49] *Op. cit.*, p. 330.

[50] Puech, *op. cit.*, p. 331.

[51] "Hitherto there has been a fair measure of agreement over the date A.D. 140–150" (B. Gärtner, *The Theology of the Gospel of Thomas*, London, 1961, p. 271).

reminiscences as well as Synoptic.[52] It adds its quota to the evidence that our Gospel was accepted at this period.[53]

All this adds up to a substantial body of evidence that John's Gospel was well known and regarded as authoritative in the first half of the second century. We cannot dismiss this as merely a heretical aberration, for Valentinus, most agree, wrote his "Gospel of Truth" at about the time of his exclusion from the church of Rome where he was so honored a member that he was seriously considered for the position of bishop. Clearly he must have acquired his essential attitude to this Gospel while a member of the Roman church in good standing. At the same time, once he and his followers came to be regarded as heretics the fact that they made such use of John may have made the orthodox suspicious of the book.

This evidence has not, of course, been known for very long. But now that it has come to light its importance for this aspect of Johannine studies should not be overlooked. These Gnostic writings give good grounds for holding that John was known and accepted in the early part of the second century. This is all the

---

[52] The official edition lists parallels to passages in all four Gospels. See *The Gospel according to Thomas*, by A. Guillaumont, H.-Ch. Puech, G. Quispel, W. Till and Yassah 'Abd Al Masih (London, 1959), pp. 59–62. *Cf.* H. E. W. Turner: "As compared with the Synoptic Gospels the Fourth Gospel recedes into the background, but there is much to be said in favour of the view of Kasser that if the compiler appears to quote the Synoptists by preference, his style is formed on the Johannine mould" (H. Montefiore and H. E. W. Turner, *Thomas and the Evangelists*, London, 1962, pp. 31f.).

[53] It is likely that this should be extended yet further. Thus the "Acts of John" undoubtedly presupposes the Gospel, and M. R. James dates it "not later than the middle of the second century" (*The Apocryphal New Testament*, Oxford, 1926, p. 288). But K. Schäferdiek thinks the evidence "suggests the 3rd century; there are certainly no compelling reasons for assuming an earlier date" (E. Hennecke, *New Testament Apocrypha*, ed. W. Schneemelcher, II, London, 1965, pp. 214f.). C. K. Barrett, however, who is not prone to seeing early evidence for John, accepts a date of 150–160, and regards it "of some importance that there were in Asia in the middle of the second century Christians (though heretical Christians) who found it at least credible that the apostle John had worked in their country" (p. 86). Thus the date is not certain, but opinion seems to incline to the mid-second century. Quite different, but very early is a piece of evidence cited by Bernard. He thinks that there is a reference to John 1 : 9 in the apocalypse known as "The Rest of the Words of Baruch", dated by Rendel Harris soon after A.D. 136 (p. lxxii).

more valuable in that some dispute the evidence of Ignatius and Justin Martyr.[54]

The fact that, with all these heretical associations, John still became universally accepted as canonical is surely significant. Why was it included in the canon? Not because of the pressure of opinion in the church, because it was quoted but little. The opponents of Johannine authorship make very effectively the point that this writing was not widely used. If it were known to have been written by an apostle we can understand its inclusion. But unless this was firmly believed it is difficult to see why the book should ever have been accepted in the church, in view of its sparse use by the orthodox and its popularity among the heretics.

It is true that after a time it began to dawn in on some of the faithful that, so far from giving aid and comfort to the Gnostics, this Gospel was the most effective refutation of their point of view. So they, too, began to use it extensively. But in view of the hesitation of very many[55] we can be sure that its credentials were subjected to very close scrutiny. That is what makes the fact that no other name than John has been suggested as its author so very significant. Some in the early church would surely have been ready to have this writing rejected and one obvious way of doing this would have been to discredit it by pointing to an heretical author. Even if a heretical origin could not be demonstrated it would

---

[54] Barrett examines the passages in which it has been said Ignatius depends on John and concludes: "There is nothing in these (or any other) passages to prove that Ignatius had read John" (p. 93). Similarly he says after a similar treatment of Justin Martyr: "These passages do not prove that Justin had read John; yet they are sufficient to give some plausibility to that hypothesis" (p. 94). These estimates, especially the latter, are far from being unchallenged. Thus Bernard thinks it "in accordance with all probabilities, that Ignatius had read this famous book . . . He uses several Johannine phrases after a fashion which is difficult to explain if they are no more than reflexions of current Christian teaching" (p. lxxi). As for Justin, Bernard thinks that he had not only read John but that "Justin's doctrinal system is dependent as a whole upon the Fourth Gospel" (p. lxxv). In view of such uncertainties it is good to have this solid evidence for the acceptance of this Gospel at such an early date.

[55] Yet this should not be exaggerated. *Cf.* T. E. Pollard: "There is no evidence that the Fourth Gospel was treated with suspicion anywhere other than in Rome, and then only by a small group, although we must allow the possibility that some writers like Justin Martyr, the contemporary and strong critic of Valentinus, hesitated to use it openly" (*ABR*, VII, 1959, p. 45).

have helped to have been able to draw attention to some non-apostolic Christian as the author. The fact that we have no evidence of any other name must be held to be significant.

It is also worth noting that according to a very probable reading of the evidence Marcion held the Apostle John to be the author of this Gospel. Tertullian speaks of this man as laboring "very hard to destroy the character of those Gospels which are published as genuine and under the name of apostles" by drawing attention to Paul's rebuking even of apostles in Gal. 2 : 13f.[56] It is difficult to see the drift of Marcion's argument unless he did in fact think that John wrote this Gospel. His point apparently was not that John did not write it, but that John did write it and was wrong![57] As Marcion seems to have come to Rome *c.* 140 this is quite early testimony.[58]

Another feature of the external evidence for authorship is that quite often in the early church others were associated with John in the writing of the Gospel. Clement of Alexandria, for example, says that John "was urged on by his disciples, and, divinely moved by the Spirit, composed a spiritual Gospel".[59] The Muratorian Canon says that "it was revealed to Andrew, one of the Apostles, that John should narrate all things in his own name as they remembered them."[60] This kind of statement leads many recent writers to think of a "school" of John, and others to hold that John did not actually write the Gospel, but that he was the "witness" behind it, the one whose recollections are embodied in this writing. This does not necessarily mean that he dictated the book, and some who hold the view think that John's reminiscences were carried on in oral tradition for quite some time before one of the Johannine "school" (who had probably not seen Jesus)

---

[56] *Contra Marc.*, IV. iii (ANF, III, p. 348).

[57] Lagrange thinks that the evidence of Marcion points to an accepted view that John was the author (pp. XLVIIf.).

[58] Some cite Celsus as bearing testimony to John. From Origen's *Contra Celsum* it is clear that that opponent of Christianity referred to the Fourth Gospel (*e.g.* I. 70). As Celsus appears to have been active during the third quarter of the second century this is early testimony to the fact that Christians regarded the book as authoritative. But Celsus, naturally enough, does not use the name "John", so we cannot cite him for authorship.

[59] Cited from Eusebius, *HE*, VI. xiv. 7 (Loeb trans.).

[60] Cited from H. Bettenson, *Documents of the Christian Church* (London, 1944), p. 40.

decided to write them down. This it is held would account for the persistence of the tradition which links the name of John with the Gospel and at the same time would fit in with that part of the evidence which leads so many recent scholars to find Johannine authorship totally unacceptable. It would probably be true to say that most scholarship finds some such solution to the problem.

Some find it helpful to think of a second John, usually referred to as "John the Elder". They suggest that he wrote the Gospel, but that confusion of names led to its ascription to his namesake the Apostle. The trouble is that, for all its popularity in some circles, there is little evidence for the existence of such a figure.[61] It amounts to Eusebius's interpretation of one sentence in Papias and a much later traveller's tale of two tombs in Ephesus each said to be John's. The sentence in Papias does not necessarily refer to two Johns at all, so that this evidence cannot be said to be impressive.[62]

The big weakness in all views of this type is what we might call "the disappearance of the hero". Those who hold such views affirm that the tradition embodied in this Gospel derives ultimately from the revered Apostle. He is the founder of the "school" (not necessarily in any formal sense). It is his reminiscences which are brought together in this volume. He is a great and honored figure. Why then should he be ignored so completely that his name is not so much as mentioned even once? This appears to be a major difficulty in the way of the acceptance of such a theory, but it is rarely faced. But unless some credible reason can be given for

---

[61] C. S. Petrie has made a careful examination of the evidence in his article, "The Authorship of 'The Gospel according to Matthew': a Reconsideration of the External Evidence" (*NTS*, 14, 1967–68, pp. 15–32). He speaks of John the Elder as "that elusive mythical figure that for so long has bedevilled students of the Fourth Gospel." He goes on: "We must see just how Eusebius brings him into the picture and why; and then, after wondering at the fuss he has been allowed to cause, consign him to oblivion" (*op. cit.*, p. 20).

[62] Sometimes the view is reinforced by the assertion that the Apostle John was martyred early. But the evidence for this is very shaky. See *SFG*, pp. 280ff. It is a curious fact that those who put forward this view do not usually take notice of the fact that, even if it be accepted at its face value, it does not say *when* John was martyred. At best it says that James and John were both killed by the Jews. It says nothing about time or place, or whether the two were martyred together. Yet this is obviously the critical point.

such an extraordinary procedure it is difficult to see how the theory can stand.

It has also to be reckoned with that on this view the actual author of the Gospel has not only allowed his hero to drop out of sight, but he has dropped some fairly broad hints that he himself was "the beloved disciple". The man who could do this has been termed "a psychological monstrosity".[63] It is, to say the least of it, a curious procedure. But this, too, does not seem to have been explained by those who put forward the theory.[64]

Some archaeological evidence should be mentioned. There is first the fact that in the catacombs the raising of Lazarus appears on some quite early murals. H. P. V. Nunn speaks of one such in the Capella Graeca in the catacomb of Priscilla, which, he says, is early second century. There is also a representation of the Eucharist with the baskets connected with the miracle of the loaves and fishes on the table. This is thought to show that John 6 is in mind. Nunn points out that the crypt of the Acilii Glabriones, "one of the most aristocratic families in Rome, some of the members of which were Christians in the first century", is close to this. He concludes: "This is quite sound archaeological evidence that long before the middle of the second century some of the most characteristic teaching of the Fourth Gospel was well known in Rome, so well known that the most noble members of the Roman Church used representations of it to express their most cherished hopes and to decorate their tombs."[65] This is important evidence, all the more so since no one argues that John was written in Rome.

---

[63] A. H. N. Green-Armytage, *John Who Saw* (London, 1952), p. 132.

[64] B. H. Streeter, for example, argued that John the Elder need not have come into contact with the Apostle very much (he thinks that he derived most of his facts from Mark or Luke): "We need only postulate for him a connection with the Apostle and an attitude to his memory comparable to that of Irenaeus towards Polycarp. A brief and, as it seemed in the halo of later recollection, a wonderful connection with the Apostle – perhaps also a few never-to-be-forgotten words of Christ derived from his lips – would make the attitude towards the Beloved Disciple expressed in the Gospel psychologically explicable" (*The Four Gospels*, London, 1930, p. 433). That is what it would not do. Plainly Streeter did not reflect on his analogy. Irenaeus clearly thought a great deal of Polycarp. But the point is that he said so. He mentioned the name and he spoke of things Polycarp said and did. But Streeter asks us to believe that the Elder John all but obliterated his hero. This is psychologically impossible.

[65] *The Son of Zebedee* (London, 1927), p. 86.

Allowing time for it to travel to that city and be accepted as authoritative there, we cannot date the Gospel very late.

Another piece of archaeological evidence is the inscription of Abercius. This man was bishop of Hieropolis in Phrygia. He composed an inscription to be used on his tomb, which says in part, "My name is Abercius, the disciple of the Holy[66] Shepherd, who feeds his flocks of sheep on the hills and plains and who has great eyes that look in every place. For he taught me the faithful letters of life...."[67] The difficulty here is twofold: knowing whether this implies knowledge of the Fourth Gospel, and the dating of the inscription. The reference to the Shepherd recalls John 10 and the "letters of life" remind us of "the words of eternal life" (John 6 : 68). On the whole it seems that Abercius knew and valued our Gospel. If his death is correctly dated by Nunn *c.* 150 this will be important early testimony. But others date it later, perhaps near A.D. 200,[68] when it would lose some of its force.

Stather Hunt is impressed by a very different consideration from any so far indicated, namely the difficulty of finding another author. He draws our attention to evidence that there is an eyewitness behind this Gospel, notably "the underlying intensity with which the Gospel is written". He goes on to point out that "there does not appear to be any known person of sufficient calibre to have written it except the son of Zebedee."[69] This will not carry the same conviction to all minds. But it is a relevant point nevertheless.

Plainly the evidence is not such as to enable us to say without a shadow of doubt "This is the solution". No theory so far put forward is without difficulties. It is a matter of choosing that which presents us with the fewest. Many recent scholars make telling criticisms of the view that John the Apostle was the author. But when we turn to their own views we find little to inspire. The suggested reconstructions are often difficult to follow, some-

---

[66] Or "Pure"; the word is ἁγνοῦ.
[67] Cited from H.P.V. (wrongly given on the title page as H.V.P.) Nunn, *Christian Inscriptions* (Eton, 1951), p. 30.
[68] E.g. *ODCC, s.v.* "Abercius".
[69] *Op. cit.*, p. 8.

29

times bordering on the bizarre.[70] There is certainly none which is free from serious objection. It is a matter then of accepting that solution which best accounts for the facts and which has the fewest difficulties in its way. It is for this reason that I accept the view that John the Apostle was the author of the Gospel. I agree that this view does not account for all the evidence. But then neither does any other view known to me. This one seems to account for the facts best.

II. Date

It is usually held by conservatives and radicals alike, that the Fourth Gospel is of comparatively late date. This view goes back to ancient times for Patristic writers often regarded this Gospel as the latest of the four. Most writers these days put it in the last decade of the first century, though some prefer a date in the early second century.[71] It cannot be late in the second century because a papyrus fragment of the first half of that century has been found in Egypt. Allowing for the time it would have taken for the Gospel to travel from the place of its composition to Egypt this means that the early second century is as late as we can reasonably place it. But most see very little reason for putting it much earlier. It is hard to see why there should be such a consensus, for there is very little real evidence for it.[72]

One of the points urged by those who favor a late date is the contention that the manner of referring to "the Jews" points to a time when they had become confirmed enemies of the church.

---

[70] R. A. Edwards gives as one reason for his accepting the Johannine authorship that "the alternative suggestions seemed far too complicated for them to be possible in a real world where living men met and talked" (*The Gospel according to St. John*, London, 1954, p. ix).

[71] Sometimes the position is oversimplified. M. S. Enslin, for example, could say: "every critic, whatever his views as to the author, agrees that the gospel cannot antedate the year 100" (*Christian Beginnings*, New York and London, 1938, p. 448). That was not true in 1938 and it is not true now.

[72] *Cf.* C. C. Torrey: "At the annual meeting of the Society of Biblical Literature and Exegesis in New York City, in December, 1934, I challenged my New Testament colleagues to designate even *one* passage, from any of the Four Gospels, giving clear evidence of a date later than 50 A.D., or of origin outside Palestine. The challenge was not met, nor will it be, for there is no such passage" (*op. cit.*, p.x). At least this incident shows that the evidence for a late date is not obvious.

This, it is said, is not natural, neither during the lifetime of Jesus, nor for many years afterwards. We require time for the development of opposition so that the followers of Jesus and "the Jews" stand as hostile groups. This, however, does not follow. After our Lord's crucifixion and after the kind of opposition the Jews consistently showed to the early Christian preachers this kind of language is natural. It does not require a prolonged period of development.

It is often said that John made use of some at least of the Synoptists. Most critics would hold that he used Mark at any rate, perhaps also Luke, though few would hold that he used Matthew. If this is in fact the case, then John will presumably be dated towards the end of the century. But the evidence seems slight.[73] After P. Gardner-Smith's examination it does not seem as though the case has been made out. A significant number of recent scholars insist that John is independent of the Synoptic Gospels. We cannot build on a hypothesis which is far from being universally accepted, and in some quarters is vigorously repudiated.

Some suggest that this Gospel gives evidence of lateness in its syncretism (combination of religious ideas from a variety of sources), and in the indications in the Gospel itself that its teaching has undergone a lengthy period of development. Concerning the first, the evidence of the Qumran scrolls shows that the point is not to be taken seriously. The scrolls show conclusively that many ideas previously regarded as Hellenistic circulated in Palestine before the time of Christ. There is nothing in John along these lines that demands a date later than the Scrolls. The second point is a matter of debate. It is put forward very seriously but the evidence for development is not apparent to all. Nor is the case helped when, as not infrequently happens, the contention of one critic is the refutation of another.

There is no reference in this Gospel to the destruction of Jerusalem. This, it is held, indicates that it was written either before that event or long enough after it for interest to have waned. Since few people think it was written before the destruction of Jerusalem this puts us somewhere near the end of the first century. However, it does not exclude the possibility that the Gospel was composed before the fall of Jerusalem.

---

[73] See below, pp. 49ff.

The highly developed theology of John is thought by many to indicate a late date. Time must be allowed for the development of this full theology. This argument, however, will not stand up to examination. There is nothing in the theology of John which demands a date later than the theology of the Epistle to the Romans. But that Epistle must have been written in the 50's, so that John need not be very late.[74]

We must be more respectful of a kindred argument, one which sees the development not so much in theology as in the evolution of tradition. R. H. Fuller puts it concisely, "Since the evangelist stands at the end of a process of tradition, Palestinian, Hellenistic, and Jewish-heterodox-Baptist, it is impossible to accept the traditonal (sic) . . . ascription of this gospel to John bar Zebedee."[75] This is more weighty than the previous argument, but it comes short of demonstration. It is plain from a variety of sources that Palestine in the early first century was a place where many ideas met. From the time of Antiochus Epiphanes Hellenism had been a keenly contested issue, and all the other strands Fuller notes were Palestinian in origin. It is difficult to see why their conjunction is regarded as necessarily later than John the son of Zebedee.

Sometimes use is made of individual expressions in John. Thus there are references to excommunication (9 : 22; 12 : 42; 16 : 2). It is laid down that the Christians were not excluded from the synagogues until the 80's. However this is far from certain. What we *know*, as opposed to surmise, about excommunication does not allow us to say this did not take place until the 80's. There is little definite information, but we can say that as far as our knowledge goes there is nothing in John on this subject which demands a late date.

Thus none of the contentions usually brought forward is beyond dispute. The late date is not demonstrated. In recent years a

---

[74] *Cf.* R. M. Grant: "The only grounds on which this point [*i.e.* that John is earlier or later than the Synoptics] can definitely be 'proved' lie in a general theory of the development of early Christian thought, and the chief support of this theory is provided by the Gospel itself. Since the argument is circular we shall do well to neglect it" (*A Historical Introduction to the New Testament*, London, 1963, p. 155).

[75] *A Critical Introduction to the New Testament* (London, 1966), p. 176.

number of critics have drawn attention to some considerations which favour an early date.

John's ignorance of the Synoptic Gospels may be important. As we have already noticed, some who argue for a later date suggest that this is indicated by John's dependence on some at any rate of the Synoptic Gospels. But as it is becoming increasingly clear that John did not use any of these Gospels an early date becomes more possible. The later we put John the more difficult it is to account for his failure to make use of the other Gospels.

A number of John's expressions seem to indicate an early date. Thus he speaks of the immediate followers of Jesus not as "apostles" but as "disciples" and further he normally uses the expression "His disciples" rather than "the disciples". In the days of His ministry Jesus' disciples would be distinguished from those of other teachers by some such expression. But when Christianity had begun to develop there was no question about whose disciples were being referred to and "*the* disciples" became the standard expression. It is interesting that John makes use of this early locution.

G. A. Turner and J. R. Mantey similarly find John's use of "the Jews" early. They point out that Judaism was much more powerful before the destruction of Jerusalem in A.D. 70 than afterwards. They point out further that in writings like 1 Thess. 2 : 15 f. Christianity is on the defensive, but that a century later when Justin Martyr wrote to Trypho the Jew the positions were reversed. The Fourth Gospel reflects the earlier and not the later situation. Considerations such as these "point to a possible if not probable date contemporary with the Pauline Epistles."[76]

A somewhat similar point is that in John 5 : 2 we read concerning the pool of Bethesda "there is" not "there was". It is, of course, possible for John to use the present tense referring to something that is past. But it is more natural for it to refer to something existent.

Many people have been impressed by the discoveries made at Qumran. The scrolls have many points of contact with the Fourth Gospel, more, in fact, than with any other book in the New Testament. But the monastery at Qumran seems to have been destroyed completely before A.D. 70. This means that any point

---

[76] P. 18.

33

of contact must be quite early. It does not prove an early date for the Gospel, but it is more consistent with an early date than a late one.

John's concern over the followers of John the Baptist has seemed to some an argument for an early date, for the church does not seem to have been greatly concerned about this problem in later days.[77]

Considerations of this kind have convinced a number of recent scholars that this Gospel is earlier than has customarily been thought. W. F. Albright, for example, maintains that, "All the concrete arguments for a late date for the Johannine literature have now been dissipated".[78] He prefers a date in "the late 70's or early 80's". Others think it may possibly be even earlier. C. C. Tarelli can say, "To suggest a date before A.D. 70 is perhaps too daring, and yet the Palestinian atmosphere which many scholars find in the Gospel is certainly the atmosphere of Palestine before that date".[79] B. P. W. Stather Hunt thinks it "natural to date our Gospel just before A.D. 70".[80]

The dating of the Gospel is thus not easy. There is nothing to indicate with any great precision what date is to be preferred. If we give full weight to the general atmosphere of the Gospel which, as Tarelli says, is that of Palestine before A.D. 70, and to early locutions like "his disciples" and "there is in Jerusalem" we would think of a date before A.D. 70. It seems to me that this is about as far as we can go in the present state of our knowledge.[81]

Before leaving this subject it may be well to point out that in recent times a number of scholars have argued for an early date for part at any rate of the tradition embodied in this Gospel and a late date for its actual composition. We have seen some of the thinking behind this in our discussion of authorship. The thought is that there was a Johannine "school", perhaps going back to

[77] *Cf.* R. M. Grant: "This outside evidence, scanty though it is, confirms our impression that the evangelist is dealing with the real problem presented by those who revered the Baptist more highly than Jesus. This feature of his gospel suggests that it was written at a relatively early date" (*op. cit.*, p. 153).

[78] *New Horizons in Biblical Research* (London, 1966), p. 46.

[79] *JThS*, XLVII, 1947, p. 209.

[80] *Op. cit.*, p. 113.

[81] A. M. Hunter comes somewhere near this when he says, "It might have been written about 80; but then again it might have been written a decade earlier" (*op. cit.*, p. 222). C. L. Mitton mentions this verdict approvingly (*op. cit.*, p. 340).

John the Apostle. This "school" passed on its traditions, some at any rate of which comprised very early accounts, possibly those of an eyewitness. The origins of this Gospel thus go back to early times. But the tradition is held to have been retained in oral tradition for a long time and finally reduced to writing at around the turn of the century.[82] This is a way of trying to get the best of both worlds. It gives a credible account of the early date of some of the material and at the same time of that part of the evidence which convinces many that the Gospel is late. Such views are not, in my opinion, as probable as that the date is pre-A.D. 70. But they certainly cannot be ruled out.

III. Purpose

A wide variety of purposes have been attributed to this Evangelist. It has commonly been held, for example, that he wrote to supplement the Synoptic Gospels.[83] This view means that he had these Gospels before him and that he was dissatisfied with some aspects, at any rate, of what they contained. Having further knowledge himself he decided to make it available to the Christian public. A difficulty is the widespread conviction at the present time that John is completely independent of the Synoptics. I do not see how any theory of dependence can be made to stand up. And if John did not know the Synoptics then clearly he did not write to supplement them.[84] The same objection may be be urged against a somewhat different theory, namely that John was written

---

[82] *Cf.* J. A. T. Robinson: "The decisive question is the status and origin of the Johannine tradition. Did this come out of the blue round about the year A.D. 100? Or is there a real continuity, not merely in the memory of one old man, but in the life of an on-going community, with the earliest days of Christianity? What, I think, fundamentally distinguishes the 'new look' on the fourth Gospel is that it answers that question in the affirmative" (*SE*, I, p. 350).

[83] This is as old as Clement of Alexandria, who thought that John was content with the "bodily facts" (τὰ σωματικά) in the Synoptists, but wrote as well "a spiritual Gospel" (πνευματικὸν εὐαγγέλιον) (Eusebius *HE*, VI. xiv. 7).

[84] A. Wikenhauser further points out that "if it was John's intention to supplement the Synoptics, he would certainly have shown clearly how his account was to be harmonized with theirs" (*New Testament Introduction*, New York, 1958, p. 301). The difficulties in harmonizing the accounts are, of course, notorious.

to supersede the Synoptic Gospels.[85] If they were not written at the time John wrote then obviously he was not trying to supersede them.

Others have felt that John had a polemic aim. Some have thought that he tried to combat Gnosticism.[86] Usually this is put in the form that he was confronting Docetism. However, Gnosticism as a movement comes before us in history only during the second century.[87] A number of scholars, it is true, are impressed with "pre-Gnostic" elements in early writings, notably the Qumran scrolls. But, when full allowance is made for these early appearances of individual concepts which were later important to the Gnostics, it still seems that Gnosticism is a second-century phenomenon. If any writing is out to combat it then it must be of that date. Thus if we hold to a fairly early date for this writing there is no question of a combat with Gnosticism.

It is, however, quite possible that one of John's aims was to combat false teaching of a docetic type. The Docetists were men who held that the Christ never really became incarnate. Everything was "seeming".[88] That the docetic heresy did not appear in the first century seems clear.[89] But certain elements which later were to be embodied in this heresy seem to have been quite early. In other words while John certainly did not have before him the fully-fledged docetic heresy, there seems nothing in the way of the view that he was confronted by false teachers of a docetic turn of mind. This is especially clear in I John, but it is also apparent in the Gospel. This would account for such things as his emphatic assertion that "the Word was made flesh" (1 : 14). Throughout his Gospel he is concerned to emphasize the genuine

---

[85] D. Guthrie cites H. Windisch, supported by W. Bauer, for this view (*New Testament Introduction, The Gospels and Acts*, London, 1965, p. 249 and n. 1).

[86] This view is as old as Irenaeus who saw the Gospel as written to oppose Cerinthus (*Adv. Haer.*, III. xi. 1).

[87] See the comments by R. M. Grant and J. Munck on p. 63 below.

[88] Gk $\delta o\varkappa\varepsilon\tilde{\iota}\nu$, "to seem", gives the name to the heresy.

[89] J. N. D. Kelly points out that the first to mention Docetists ($\delta o\varkappa\eta\tau\alpha\acute{\iota}$) is Serapion of Antioch (*fl.* 200). "But Docetism was not a simple heresy on its own; it was an attitude which infected a number of heresies, particularly Marcionism and Gnosticism" (*Early Christian Doctrines*, London, 1958, p. 141). The attitude appears to have been earlier than the emergence of fully developed Docetism.

humanity of Jesus and at the same time the fact that Jesus really came from God. But this does not mean that the principal purpose of this Gospel was to combat an early form of Docetism. The false teaching is opposed almost by the way.[90] The main thrust of this Gospel is certainly elsewhere.

Others have held that John is concerned to write a polemic against unbelieving Jews. The one strong point in favor of this is the way in which the term "the Jews" is used throughout the Gospel. Our Evangelist makes use of this expression far more often than does any of the others and he certainly cannot be said to be warmly disposed toward "the Jews".[91] However this is but one aspect of this Gospel, and it is far from being the most prominent. It cannot be said that a case has really been made out for regarding this as the principal aim.

Again some have maintained that John was writing to oppose the continuing followers of John the Baptist.[92] He certainly makes it clear that the Baptist's place was a subordinate one and it may well be that he had in mind some of that prophet's followers.[93] But again this is too subdued a note for us to think of it as the dominant purpose.

Others again think that John was concerned with opposing

---

[90] A curiosity of scholarship is the view of E. L. Titus that this Gospel teaches Docetism: "with the descent of the Spirit – the point of the Incarnation – that humanity ceased to operate, except in terms of the physical organism: he walked about, used the voice mechanism, *etc.*, but the mental and spiritual qualities were no longer those of a man. From the point of the Incarnation, the continuum of the human element remained only in the minds of the Jews" (*The Message of the Fourth Gospel*, New York, 1957, p. 33). If this is not Docetism it is Apollinarianism. Either way Titus makes our author a heretic.

[91] C. F. D. Moule points out that this Gospel "contains tough polemic against Jews". He thinks that here there "may be good traditions of the actual controversies of Christ's own life-time, preserved and re-set in such a way as to be entirely topical to the evangelist's own circumstances" (*The Birth of the New Testament*, London, 1962, pp. 94, 95).

[92] W. Baldensperger is usually cited as the outstanding example of a scholar who saw John this way. I do not think that any recent writer sees this as the dominant purpose of the Evangelist. Many see it as one of his subordinate aims (*e.g.* Strachan, pp. 109–112).

[93] For John's followers as a continuing movement see C. H. H. Scobie, *John the Baptist* (London, 1964), ch. XII.

Christian teachers who gave too much place to the sacraments[94] or too little place to the sacraments.[95] Here everything depends on how much it is held that John had the sacraments in view. It is, of course, the case that he never mentions either Christian Baptism or the Lord's Supper throughout the Gospel. It is quite possible to hold that he never refers, even obliquely, to either. On the other hand some have felt that particularly in chapters 3 and 6 he is concerned with these two sacraments. As precisely opposite conclusions have been drawn from this evidence the argument clearly rests on no certain basis. And to make this the main aim of the Gospel is certainly flying in the face of the evidence.

Some have felt that John's principal aim was to present to the world a kind of "Hellenized" Christianity.[96] He was interested in making an intellectually respectable form of Christianity available

---

[94] Thus in discussing John 6 Odeberg refers to the views of J. Kreyenbühl who, he says, "maintains that the section really speaks of the Eucharist, but not by way of advocating it but by way of a strong rejection of this sacrament, as being a *ritus*, an institution of the Church. The object of the Evangelist is, acc. to Kreyenbühl, to put against the Sacrament of the Church . . . his own spiritual understanding: the real flesh and blood of the Son of Man (= the Evangelist) are his teaching, his religion, his life in God and of God, and these only are potent of eternal Life" (*FG*, p. 237). Cf. also E. C. Colwell and E. L. Titus: "We would go so far as to say that the Fourth Gospel represents a reaction to an increasing suppression of spontaneous religious experience through the substitution of an *ex opere operato* sacramental ritual" (*The Gospel of the Spirit*, New York, 1953, p. 52).

[95] Cf. O. Cullmann: "Scholars have long ago observed and commentators fittingly commented upon the author's deep interest in the sacraments, in this or that passage. We mean to go further, however, and to show how the Gospel of John regards it as one of its chief concerns to set forth the connexion between the contemporary Christian worship and the historical life of Jesus" (*Early Christian Worship*, London, 1954, p. 37). K. and S. Lake think of this Gospel as written "by a Hellenistic Christian in order to support the sacramental theology which finds a centre in the divine Jesus" (*An Introduction to the New Testament*, London, 1938, p. 51; see also pp. 61f.).

[96] Cf. E. F. Scott: "In order that the religion might naturalise itself in the larger Gentile world to which, since the days of Paul, it had chiefly appealed, it required to find expression in the Hellenic modes of thought . . . The writer of the Fourth Gospel, not content with employing a Greek idea here and there, attempts an entire re-statement of the Christian message in terms of the current philosophy" (*op. cit.*, p. 6).

to as wide a public as possible.[97] They point to the use of terms like *Logos* and suggest that John was a Hellenist interested in commending Christianity to other Hellenists.

This view has had its popularity, but it cannot be said to square with the facts. For it is becoming increasingly evident these days that, however this Gospel is to be understood, it is a product of Jewish and not Hellenistic ways of thinking.[98] Some have held that it was originally composed in Aramaic. Most think that this is too extreme, but they point out that there are many Aramaisms in this writing and that there is evidence of Aramaic thinking behind it. It cannot be said that the view that the Gospel is a manifesto of Hellenistic Christianity has very much to commend it.

In any case due consideration ought to be given to the fact that John tells us in so many words why he wrote: "these are written, that ye may believe that Jesus is the Christ, the Son of God; and that believing ye may have life in his name" (20 : 31). There seems no reason for ignoring this express statement. John says plainly that he is out to show Jesus as the Christ, the Son of God. And he does this not in order to give to his readers some interesting new information but in order that he may bring them

---

[97] This seems to be the view of C. H. Dodd: "It seems therefore that we are to think of the work as addressed to a wide public consisting primarily of devout and thoughtful persons . . . in the varied and cosmopolitan society of a great Hellenistic city such as Ephesus under the Roman Empire" (*IFG*, p. 9).

[98] H. G. G. Herklots makes an important point as he concludes his discussion of John: "The Greek world wanted Jesus at its own price, as a spiritual influence only, and not as one who had taken on flesh and blood. It was only through being lifted up from the earth, in the bitter anguish of crucifixion, that He began the process in which history finds its meaning and consummation, of drawing all men to Himself" (*A Fresh Approach to the New Testament*, London, 1950, p. 121). This Gospel makes good use of terms intelligible in the Hellenistic world, but it is to impress ideas which are not Hellenistic.

to a place of faith and accordingly to new life in Christ's name.[99]

Not only does John tells us this in set terms, but close examination of his Gospel shows that this is, in fact, what he has done.[100] Again and again he brings before us evidence that Jesus is indeed the Christ. He does not make as extensive use of the term itself as we might possibly have expected. But the idea is often present, and the term is also found on occasion. Moreover, John constantly lets us see the challenge posed by the message of Jesus. Men divide in the presence of this message. Either they commit themselves to Christ in faith and so enter life or they refuse to commit themselves and remain in darkness and a condition of lostness. There seems no reason why John's statement should be rejected. This is what he said he would do and this it seems is what he has done.[101]

IV. History and Theology[102]

That the writer of the Fourth Gospel has a serious theological

---

[99] There is a textual problem as to whether the present or the aorist subjunctive of the verb πιστεύω should be read. On the whole it seems that the present is somewhat more probable. Some argue from this that the meaning is, "that you may continue to believe", so that John wrote primarily to Christians to strengthen their faith. Thus F. V. Filson thinks there is no doubt about John's purpose, and he cites this text. But a little later he says, "he aimed, not primarily to win new converts or to convince his opponents, but to state the role of Jesus Christ in such a way that his role as Son of God, as the Father's agent in creating and upholding the world, and as the Savior and Lord of the world, would be plain, and so the church would be saved from despising or disparaging the historical Jesus" (*A New Testament History*, London, 1965, pp. 374, 376f.). But this seems to be reading a good deal into the tense.

[100] C. H. Dodd points out that, quite apart from grammatical considerations, the Gospel shows that its author "is thinking in the first place, not so much of Christians who need a deeper theology, as of non-Christians who are concerned about eternal life and the way to it, and may be ready to follow the Christian way if this is presented to them in terms that are intelligibly related to their previous religious interests and experience" (*IFG*, p. 9).

[101] *Cf.* C. F. D. Moule: "This Gospel, unlike the others, answers the question, 'What must I do to be saved?' The others mainly confine themselves to the story of discipleship; the Fourth Gospel speaks in terms not only of following and imitation, but of belief and incorporation" (*The Birth of the New Testament*, London, 1962, p. 94). He immediately goes on, "What is less often noticed is that it also answers the question 'What must *I* do ...' – it is an extremely individualistic message ... St John sees Jesus as the source of life, to be connected with whom is, for each individual, life eternal." In a number of places Moule insists on the individualism of this Gospel.

[102] See further, *SFG*, ch. 2.

40

purpose is surely beyond doubt. As we saw in the preceding section he tells us in set terms that his purpose in writing is to show that Jesus is the Christ, God's Son, and by writing in this strain to persuade people to believe in Him and so to enter into life. The question at issue is not whether John is interested in conveying theological meaning. It is rather whether he has completely subordinated his historical sense to this aim, or whether he has a concern for facts as well as for theology.

It is worth noticing at the outset that interpretation does not necessarily mean distortion of the facts. Indeed the absence of interpretation may sometimes mean distortion. Thus one can say with truth "Nicholas Ridley was executed". But if this is all that one says a wrong impression may be conveyed. It means more to say, "Bishop Nicholas Ridley was burned at the stake" and still more to say, "Bishop Nicholas Ridley was martyred". The last statement carries a fuller meaning than the earlier two. It may, of course, be disputed. That is the penalty one pays for the fuller light conveyed by the interpretative statement. There is a parallel here with John's Gospel. It is undoubtedly an interpretative document. It selects its material omitting much that the other Gospels include, and including much that they do not. And if one does not agree with John's view of Jesus much may be disputed (as it is by many radical scholars). But if John is right, if the Word was indeed made flesh and dwelt among us, then this interpretative document is of the utmost importance for those who want the fullest light on the facts.

There are many writers who assure us that there is no question of taking the history in this Gospel seriously. To some it appears so obvious that John's one interest is theology that they pay no attention to the historical information John provides unless they have some corroboration from some outside source. Since so very little in this Gospel is in this way corroborated this means that they regard the Gospel as to all intents and purposes a work of theology.[103]

---

[103] *Cf.* Titus: "it is natural for the modern mind, unaccustomed to ways of antiquity, to view the material as history. This view has vitiated even the best of modern commentaries"; "If, at any point, his narrative conveys information on the subject, it is more by accident than by intent"; "the question of the historical accuracy of the medium of communication is quite beside the point" (*op. cit.*, pp. 13, 14, 21).

This attitude is becoming increasingly hard to sustain. Many recent writers have shown us that there is good reason for regarding this or that story in John as authentic. C. H. Dodd in his great work, *Historical Tradition and the Fourth Gospel*, has carried out a systematic examination as a result of which he concludes that behind this Gospel there lies a very ancient tradition, quite independent of that embodied in the Synoptic Gospels. It is difficult to go through such a sustained examination and still regard John as having little concern for history.

The fact is that John is concerned with historical information. Again and again he drops into his narrative pieces of topographical information, for example, or time notes. Thus theologically there seems no particular reason for telling us that such and such an incident happened in such and such a place, or that Jesus met such and such a person at such and such a time. I do not deny that some exegetes have been able to read edifying meanings into some of these notes. But I think it has never been proved that these notes are intended to be taken in this way. John apparently records this kind of information because he believes it to be accurate.

It is also the case that John is remarkably accurate in a number of areas in which he can be tested. One result of the finding of the Dead Sea Scrolls has been to convince a number of scholars that this Gospel contains reliable information.[104] There can be no doubt that there are very many points of contact between the Scrolls and this Gospel. But on the hypothesis that John is a late theologian there is not the slightest reason why there should be such agreement. It would mean that in the first instance he was writing at a considerable distance both in time and in place from the milieu in which the Scrolls were circulated. And it would also mean that his purpose was such that he would be impatient of archaeological research. The fact that John is in agreement with the Scrolls in many points makes it clear that there is reliable information here.

Elsewhere I have examined some of John's teaching about John

---

[104] A good example is W. H. Brownlee's verdict on what the Scrolls have shown us about the teaching of John the Baptist: "The most astonishing result of all is the validation of the Fourth Gospel as an authentic source concerning the Baptist" (*SNT*, p. 52).

the Baptist.[105] I have tried to show that, while John's purpose in dealing with the Baptist is clear (he depicts him always and only as a "witness" to Jesus Christ), yet he does not distort his facts. Recent research has shown that the information on the Baptist in this Gospel is remarkably accurate. Now if John can write accurately while he is setting forth the Baptist in one capacity only, ignoring all other aspects of his ministry, what reason have we for regarding him as unable to do the same thing elsewhere?

It must be stressed that this is a place where we must not be swayed by *a priori* presumptions. It is simply not good enough to say "John is a theologian; therefore we need take no notice of his historical notes", or to say "John is invariably accurate; anything he says must be taken as factual." I see no reason why John should not have written, as many scholars suggest he did, with a concern for theological truth only. After all, the parable is a well attested vehicle of theological teaching in the Synoptic Gospels and no one suggests that we must take everything in a parable as literally true. Similarly I see no reason for maintaining that John must necessarily tell a factual story. It seems to me quite clear that did he so choose John could write a theological narrative cast in the form of a series of historical anecdotes. We could ignore the anecdotes and concentrate on the theological meaning.

This would, of course, be subject to the heavy discount implied in the question, "What is the theological meaning of something that never happened?" This question should be taken more seriously than it is by many critics who regard this as John's method of writing. It is important to be clear that there is a difference between parables and real happenings considered as teaching media. In the parable we are saying, "God's truth appears to me like this." Then the factuality or otherwise of the story is of little consequence. The story is an illustration. Everyone understands it so. It does not matter whether it happened or not. But if we say, "God's truth is shown in this happening, God's grace is shown in that", the case is very different. Then if this did not happen we cannot say God's truth has in fact been revealed, His grace has in fact been shown. Our story may be edifying. It may tell a lot about our ideas. But we should be clear that it is our ideas that it reveals. It tells us nothing about God. The question

---

[105] See *SFG*, pp. 110ff.

THE GOSPEL ACCORDING TO JOHN

is whether John is telling us what he thinks about God, or whether he is telling us what God has done. We should never minimize the importance of the distinction between "God's truth is like –" and "God's truth is seen in –".

The question, then, is not whether the parabolic kind of writing is theoretically possible. The question is what John has in fact done. Here it seems that too many critics have been content to lay it down dogmatically that John has written in this or that fashion. What they have not done is to adduce evidence to prove the point. To lay it down that John has written theology not history can be countered by the simple device of saying John has written history but not theology. One dogmatic statement can be met by another. What is required here is evidence. And the evidence is that where he can be tested John is remarkably accurate. The inference is that he is accurate also in other places.

There is also the point that, as we noted earlier, there seems reason for holding that part of John's aim was to counter false teachers of a docetic type. These men held that there was no real incarnation. Jesus only "seemed" to eat and drink and move among men. As a counter to this kind of teaching John insists that Jesus was a real man. He insists on "the flesh" of the Son of man and in all makes it quite clear that Docetism is incompatible with Christianity. But if John was writing as the kind of critic we are thinking of maintains he writes, he would have given his whole case against the Docetists away. The Docetists would have been quite happy with an incarnation of this type. So long as they could be assured that the things that Jesus is alleged to have done he did not actually do, that the stories are no more than the vehicles of authentic teaching, they would have been content to accept them. It always seems surprising to me that critics will affirm so forthrightly at one and the same time that John was trying to oppose Docetists, and that his facts are not to be relied upon. Unless he knew that his facts were reliable, that they would stand up to challenge, he was highly vulnerable to any docetic attack and he must have known it.[106]

---

[106] *Cf.* B. W. Bacon: "In an age so eagerly bent on ascertaining the historic facts regarding Jesus' life, and the true sequence of events (Luke i. 1–4), it is insupposable that an author so strenuous to uphold the concrete reality of the church's historic tradition should not give real history so far as he was able. He could not afford to depreciate it in the face of Doketic myth and fancy

It is a further point to be considered that there is a great difference in style between John and the Synoptists. One must always regard with a healthy respect the objection which says, "If Jesus was as He is depicted in Matthew and Mark and Luke, He cannot have been as He is depicted in John. The two are incompatible." It certainly is the case that there are significant differences between these two portraits. The usual way of accounting for this difference is to say that in the Fourth Gospel we have the result of the prolonged meditation of the Beloved Disciple and that what he has produced is his view of what God has done in Christ rather than a factual account of what happened.

I have more respect for this argument than for any of the others. But I do not think it will carry the weight that many scholars place upon it. It is possible to account for it, at least in some measure, and Riesenfeld has drawn attention to the importance of considering the way in which Jewish Rabbis carried on their instruction of scholars.[107] We are almost incurably convinced that the use of notebooks is essential to the learning process. This, however, was not the case in the first century. Then it was often held that if a man had to look a thing up in a book he did not really know it. The true scholar was a person who had committed to memory the things he learned. Until a man had a teaching in his memory he was not considered really to have mastered it. The regular process of instruction, then, consisted in the teacher selecting certain items to be committed to memory and the student memorising them. There was a regular system of instruction among the Rabbis and an accepted body of oral teaching. This oral teaching was not the kind of thing that was expected to be altered in transmission. It would, of course, be nonsense to maintain that in practice it never was. From generation to generation of teachers

---

and contempt for a 'Christ in the flesh' " (*The Making of the New Testament*, London, n.d., p. 222). Bacon, it is true, thinks that John wrote late and that "real history was no longer attainable" (*op. cit.*, p. 223). But that is another matter. If John was early or had access to reliable tradition real history was attainable and on Bacon's showing he must have used it.

[107] See "The Gospel Tradition and its Beginnings" in *SE*, I, pp. 43–65. The point of view is argued more fully by B. Gerhardsson in *Memory and Manuscript* (Uppsala, 1961). This view has been vigorously criticized, as, for example, by C. F. Evans in *Theology*, LXI, 1958, pp. 355–62. J. J. Vincent summarizes, in *SE*, III, pp. 105–118. I have written at somewhat greater length on this in *SFG*, pp. 131ff.

and students there is not the slightest doubt that modifications were introduced. But the point is that nobody felt that tradition was free and open to the modification of anyone who came along.

We may perhaps bring out this point by drawing attention, as Riesenfeld does, to the idea which is often held as to how the early Christian church carried on its teaching. Let me give this in Riesenfeld's own words. He thinks that the picture often given is that "it was the custom in the primitive Church to preach freely and without restraint, and in this process sayings and narratives were created and invented. And then from this extensive body of material the evangelists or their predecessors made a well-considered selection."[108] Riesenfeld immediately continues, "But this romantic picture has no relation to reality. On the contrary, it is probable both that from Jesus' own days the material was far more strictly limited and also that it was handed down in a far more rigid and fixed form."

There is nothing unlikely about this. Riesenfeld gives the Jewish system in this way: "The ideal pupil was one who never lost one iota of the tradition. That variations in the material took place in the process of tradition for psychological reasons is obvious, and this circumstance enables us to investigate the development of the tradition from another angle. For, however great its receptive capacities, even an Oriental mind is not a tape-recorder."[109]

We must always be on our guard against reading back our methods of instruction and of retention into the circumstances of Jesus and His Apostles. They came out of a different culture and understood the learning process in an entirely different fashion. There can be little doubt but that memorization played an important part in the carrying on of the original Christian teaching. Broadly speaking we may say that it is Riesenfeld's contention that in the Synoptic Gospels we have by and large the public teaching of Jesus, i.e. the teaching which He caused His disciples to commit to memory. This does not mean, of course, that there would be no variation. The differences between the Synoptic Gospels show that there was in fact variation. But it does mean that this is a recognizably homogeneous whole. This was the kind

---

[108] *SE*, I, p. 61.
[109] *Op. cit.*, p. 55.

of thing which was carried on orally and was meant from the first to be carried on orally. Riesenfeld sees it this way: "In the Gospels we are shown very clearly that Jesus was a teacher, and especially in his relation to his disciples. This means more than his mere preaching in their presence. He gave them instruction and in this we are reminded, *mutatis mutandis*, of the method of the Jewish rabbi. And this implies that Jesus made his disciples, and above all the Twelve, learn, and furthermore that he made them learn by heart."[110] Riesenfeld sees evidence for this in the form in which Jesus' sayings are formulated in the Synoptic Gospels, in the preservation of some original Aramaic terms, *etc.*

But any teacher does more than engage in public discussion and instruction. There is also more informal teaching which takes place in private. Riesenfeld thinks that the Gospel according to St John takes its origin in this kind of thing: "here the starting point is to be found in the discourses and 'meditations' of Jesus in the circle of his disciples, such as certainly took place side by side with the instruction of the disciples proper, with its more rigid forms. Such a view is not incompatible with this line of tradition having also undergone a long and complex development."[111]

It is not necessary to endorse everything that Riesenfeld has said to be convinced that there is an interesting and suggestive possibility here. Nor is it necessary to argue that this must have been the way it was. All that I am contending is that Riesenfeld has shown us one possible way in which two views of Jesus' teaching as divergent as those in the Synoptic Gospels and in John could nevertheless originate from the one Teacher. It is quite possible that this is the explanation. It is quite possible that something else is the explanation. But in view of Riesenfeld's argument it does not seem possible any longer to maintain that the teaching of Jesus as given to us in the Synoptic Gospels is incompatible with that that we see in the Fourth Gospel.

From all this it appears that we ought not to think of John as a writer who is not at all interested in history. He is certainly a theologian, but he has a reverence for the facts. There is no real reason for thinking that he composed edifying stories which had

110 *Op. cit.*, p. 59.
111 *Op. cit.*, p. 63.

theological meaning but bore little relationship to what had actually happened.

Something like this is often widely assumed. Indeed it is almost a commonplace of modern Johannine criticism. Yet we should bear in mind that the process does not appear to be evident in the ancient world, at least among careful writers. A. W. Mosley has a most interesting article entitled, "Historical Reporting in the Ancient World",[112] in which he argues that many assumptions commonly made about the way in which the ancients wrote should be discarded. He is able to show that quite a number of writers of antiquity tell us how they understood their task. In the process they show a respect for how things actually happened. They did on occasion, it is true, compose speeches and put them in the mouths of historical characters. But they did this only where they had nothing else to go on. And when they did compose speeches they tried to make their characters say what they probably did say at the time. In other words historians did not regard themselves as having unlimited freedom. And Mosley makes this further point, which is of the utmost significance for our present enquiry, that, while they might compose speeches in this way, they did not compose accounts of events. This does not mean that we cannot find legendary accounts in antiquity. We can. But these are not found among careful and honest writers. They are found among the second-rate, or among those who are not avowedly attempting to give us accounts of what occurred. The accepted standards in the ancient world among Greeks, Romans, and Hebrews, were different from and higher than what a number of New Testament scholars have all too readily assumed.

The point of Mosley's article for our present enquiry is that there is no doubt but that John is a careful and honest writer. If he tells us that a certain thing happened we have no reason for thinking that this is simply a theological construction. The presumption must always be that John has a respect for the truth. To say otherwise is to depart from the standards, not of our own day only, but of the first century.

Hoskyns makes the important point that the very theological significance which John is trying to bring out demands that we take his history seriously. "His whole conscious intention", says

---

[112] *NTS*, 12, 1965–66, pp. 10–26.

Hoskyns, "is to force his readers back upon the life of Jesus in the flesh and upon His death in the flesh, as *the place of understanding*: he is therefore guilty of gross self-deception if he is inventing or distorting the visible likeness of Jesus to further his purpose."[113] This point is important. His theological purpose being what it is he cannot invent or distort history without making that purpose difficult or impossible of attainment.

It seems then that we should take with the utmost seriousness the account that John has given. It is true that it differs in important respects from what we see in the Synoptists. But then we must bear in mind that the Jesus whom all four Evangelists depict was a gigantic figure, greater by far than can be comprehended in any one Gospel.[114]

V. The Relationship of the Fourth Gospel to the Synoptics[115]

It has usually been accepted that John wrote after Matthew, Mark and Luke. And since he wrote later than the others, and since their writings were regarded very highly in the early church, it has seemed a natural corollary that John must have made use of those Gospels. When we add to this the fact that there are certain striking coincidences of language (for example in the story of the anointing of Jesus by the woman at Bethany, or in certain aspects of the ministry of John the Baptist), it has seemed proven beyond any reasonable doubt that John made use of the other Gospels. Sometimes it has been held indeed that he wrote in order to correct misapprehensions which might arise from what they said. Sometimes it has been held that, while he agreed with his predecessors, he felt that there were certain aspects of the ministry of Jesus which they had not dealt with or had not dealt

---

113 P. 117.

114 William Temple thinks that "A good photograph is vastly preferable to a bad portrait. But the great portrait painter may give a representation of a man which no photographer can emulate." He goes on to suggest that the Synoptists "may give us something more like the perfect photograph; St John gives us the more perfect portrait" (p. xvi). It might be more accurate to speak of the Synoptists as also giving us portraits (after all, different painters may paint differing, but worthwhile portraits of the same sitter). Each brings out some aspect of the original which the others miss. See further the comments by Albright and Mitton, p. 20 above.

115 This topic is treated at greater length in *SFG*, ch. 1.

with adequately. So he wrote to supplement them. Either way it is felt that he had some at any rate of the earlier Gospels before him and that he wrote with a knowledge of what was in them. In recent years not many have been found to espouse the view that John had all three synoptists before him. Usually it has been agreed that John made some use of Mark.[116] It has been held to be a little more uncertain that he made use of Luke but a good number of scholars feel that he did this.[117] But his use of Matthew has been held to be much more problematical. While some scholars, including some recent ones, have felt that he used Matthew,[118] most have felt that the points of contact are so few that probably he did not.

In recent years, however, all this has been called in question. Probably the greatest impetus to the new way of thinking was given by P. Gardner-Smith. He made a very close examination of the alleged case for dependence and concluded that it cannot be substantiated.[119] Since then others have followed in Gardner-Smith's steps and there is an increasing conviction in recent times that John is independent of the Synoptists.[120]

Perhaps the most cogent argument for seeing dependence in recent times is that of Barrett. Barrett is impressed basically by two things: the occurrence of a number of passages in Mark and John in the same order, and some striking verbal resemblances. His list of passages is as follows:[121]

  (a) The work and witness of the Baptist
  (b) Departure to Galilee

---

[116] See for example E. K. Lee, "St Mark and the Fourth Gospel", *NTS*, 3, 1956–57, pp. 50–58.

[117] See the evidence set out by J. M. Creed, *The Gospel according to St. Luke* (London, 1950), pp. 318–21.

[118] H. F. D. Sparks argues that John knew Matthew, *JThS*, n.s., III, 1952, pp. 58–61. See also the reply by P. Gardner-Smith, *JThS*, n.s., IV, 1953, pp. 31–35.

[119] *Saint John and the Synoptic Gospels* (Cambridge, 1938).

[120] Kümmel cites as supporters of John's independence of the Synoptists Michaelis, Manson, Menoud, J. A. T. Robinson, Sanders, Wilkens, Higgins. He lists others who hold that John knew none of the Synoptists though he did know the tradition they reproduce, namely Feine-Behm, Connick, Noack, Mendner, Feuillet, Klijn, Heard, F. C. Grant, Bultmann, Dodd, Hunter, Käsemann, Borgen, Haenchen, Grundmann. Buse and Temple think John knew one of Mark's sources (*op. cit.*, pp. 143f.).

[121] Pp. 34f.

(c)   Feeding the multitude
(d)   Walking on the lake
(e)   Peter's confession
(f)   Departure to Jerusalem
(g)   The entry ⎫
      The anointing ⎬ (transposed in John)
(h)   The Last Supper with predictions of betrayal and denial
(i)   The Arrest
(j)   The Passion and Resurrection.

Barrett clearly regards the occurrence of these in the same order in Mark and John as being very significant. He repeats the statement and he puts it in italics. Yet with all respect to a great scholar this is not a very impressive list. (a) must come first. Where else are we to put the work of the Baptist? (b) must follow (a) and (c) must follow (b). But the case for dependence is weakened when one takes notice of the fact that Mark puts (c) 211 verses after (b) and John 99 verses after it. The conjunction of (c) and (d) is more impressive. This is the kind of sequence which is necessary if Barrett's case is to be established.[122] If there were more of this kind of sequence we would agree that the order was important. The placing of (e) Peter's Confession after (d) Walking on the lake is a sequence of the same type, or would be could we be sure that Mark and John are describing the same event. I do not think they are. There are important differences between Mark's scene at Caesarea Philippi and John's sequel to the synagogue sermon at Capernaum.[123] And if these are not the same event then the item cannot be included in the list. (f) The departure to Jerusalem cannot come anywhere earlier in the list and the following items cannot come before it. It is not without its significance that Barrett brackets two items under (g) and they are in reverse order in the two Gospels. I do not see how (h), (i) and (j) can come in any other than the order given.

---

[122]   Gardner-Smith, however, suggests that "it may have been customary at quite an early period to relate the story of Christ's walking on the water immediately after the story of the feeding of the five thousand" (*op. cit.*, p. 89, n.). If this were so Barrett's point would have less force.

[123]   *Cf.* E. B. Redlich: "This is identification run riot, for the words of confession are too unlike to be referred to one event; besides, the locality is not the same" (*An Introduction to the Fourth Gospel*, London, 1939, p. 71).

From all this it is plain that the argument from the order of events is not really impressive. It is difficult to see how any other order could be adopted for most of the items Barrett singles out. There is no better case for verbal dependence. Presumably Barrett has not omitted any cogent evidence, but he gives us only twelve passages with verbal coincidences, most of which are single verses and the agreements are rarely very close. When we reflect that Mark contains 12,000 words this is not very convincing.[124]

The case for dependence on Luke and that for dependence on Matthew are, of course, even less cogent. There is no point in examining either in detail.[125]

It is true that there are some interesting coincidences of language in the Fourth Gospel and the other Gospels. One might adduce, as an example of the kind of thing which impresses, the use of the expression "valuable pistic nard" in both Mark and John with reference to the ointment used at the Anointing. This is an unusual expression. But, precisely because it is unusual, it is the kind of thing that might well stick in the mind and be preserved in more than one line of oral tradition.[126] What seems very clear to many who have examined the evidence closely is that the kind of thing which is common to John and the Synoptists is precisely the kind which one would anticipate finding in oral tradition. In fact if we think of the development of oral tradition in different parts of the church with a great respect for the incidents which are being narrated we have the kind of situation which would account for both the resemblances and the differences. In other words while there is some relationship between the tradition embodied in the Synoptists and that in John there is no valid reason, it would seem, for maintaining that the connection is written. It is much more likely to be oral.

---

124 *Cf.* Kümmel: "The number of texts for which a dependence of John upon the Synoptics can be defended with any reason is astonishingly small, and by closer inspection even for those texts the number of divergencies is far greater than that of the agreements" (*op. cit.*, p. 144; he thinks however that John probably had Mark and Luke in mind "and used them from memory", *op. cit.*, p. 145).
125 For a fuller treatment see *SFG*, pp. 15ff.
126 Thus Gardner-Smith draws attention to three verbal correspondences in the narratives of the Anointing and proceeds, "All these three are of a kind very easily remembered, striking in character, and therefore likely to become stereotyped in oral tradition" (*op. cit.*, p. 49).

VI. DISLOCATIONS

The Fourth Gospel does not read smoothly throughout. There are several places where it has seemed to a number of writers that the sequence of thought would be improved immensely if we rearranged the text.[127] The most plausible example is the reversal of the order of chs. 5 and 6. Chapter 5 deals with incidents in Jerusalem whereas the sixth begins, "After these things Jesus went away to the other side of the sea of Galilee". This would follow naturally enough from the end of ch. 4, where John has been talking about the healing of the nobleman's son in Galilee. Jesus is then in a position to cross the sea. The reference to crossing the sea with the point of departure in Jerusalem is not so immediately obvious. If this rearrangement be carried out there is also an improved sequence at the other end. As it reads, ch. 7 begins "And after these things Jesus walked in Galilee: for he would not walk in Judea, because the Jews sought to kill him". This does not follow very naturally upon ch. 6 which is located in Galilee, but it would follow very well on ch. 5 which is located in Jerusalem and which speaks of a conflict between Jesus and the Jews which might well have reached serious dimensions.

Another suggested rearrangement takes its origin from the words in the farewell discourse, "Arise, let us go hence" (14 : 31). This looks like a preparation for leaving the Upper Room, but there are three more chapters before Jesus and His friends leave for Gethsemane. It would obviously improve matters if the end of ch. 14 could be located somewhere near the end of the discourse. Accordingly a number of modern students suggest that ch. 14 should immediately precede ch. 17. Bernard sees other difficulties in the Farewell Discourse and he suggests a rearrangement to give the order 13 : 1–30; 15; 16; 13 : 31–38; 14; 17.[128]

And so one might go on. A number of suggested rearrangements have been made some of which do in fact give a smoother sequence. This is not true of every such rearrangement. In fact it might almost be laid down that every rearrangement suggested is attended by some disadvantages. For example, G. H. C. MacGregor and A. Q. Morton are among those who wish to rearrange the Fare-

---

[127] Howard summarizes the principal theories of textual dislocation, *FGRCI*, p. 303.
[128] P. xx.

well Discourse. But having given their rearrangement which puts ch. 14 after chs. 15, 16, they point out that, "If we adopt that suggested above, Thomas's question in XIV.5 seems unnatural after Jesus's words in XVI.5ff. Also, of the two allusions to the 'Comforter' in XIV.16f. and XV.26 the former reads like the first and indeed seems presupposed in the latter. There are moreover in ch. XIV many almost needless repetitions of the thought of ch. XV and XVI."[129]

Objections can be urged even against the most plausible of all the suggestions, namely the reversal of order of chs. 5 and 6. Thus Dodd stresses the need for the establishment of Jesus' position as the Divine Son (5 : 19–47) to precede His claims in ch. 6 and concludes: "We see therefore how important it is for our author's argument that the discourse in ch. v should precede the present discourse."[130] Some feel that the crisis at the end of ch. 6 (where many left Jesus and He challenged the Twelve, "Would ye also go away?" 6 : 67) comes too early if it precedes ch. 5. Others point out that a quick removal to Galilee would follow very naturally on the conflict mentioned in ch. 5. So, though many have been convinced, it cannot be said that the case has been made out beyond any shadow of doubt.

This seems to be more or less the position throughout. The rearrangements are normally suggested for subjective reasons. As the text stands it seems to some that the sequence is poor and that it would be improved by a rearrangement. But when the rearrangement is carried through, normally other disadvantages appear.

There is moreover the problem of accounting for the present disorder. If any suggested rearrangement is to be accepted we must have some convincing explanation of how the present text came into existence. For what seems so obvious to us must surely have been apparent to whoever it was put the text in the present order. It is, further, not easy to see how a manuscript could get into such disorder.

Sometimes a note of objectivity is brought into this. It is suggested that originally the manuscript was in separate sheets. A

---

[129] *The Structure of the Fourth Gospel* (Edinburgh and London, 1961), p. 70.
[130] *IFG*, p. 340.

calculation may be made, as, for example, by Bernard.[131] He suggests that each leaf of two pages contained about 750 letters, a figure he arrives at by postulating a page of thirty-four lines, each of eleven letters. He then finds that the various major displacements he sees in the Epistle represent a multiple of approximately this amount of space. But to get this he must insist on approximation. His sixth major section, for example, 12 : 36b–43, contains 598 letters, which is a not inconsiderable distance away from his average. In fact, most have thought that we must make so many allowances for this sort of thing that the apparent note of objectivity cannot be sustained.

A more serious objection is in seeing how the manuscript could come to be scattered in the way postulated. We do not know anything about the way manuscripts were commonly written in antiquity which encourages us to think a leaf would be written in this way and not form part of a roll or a book. If it were in a roll or codex it could not be detached. Bernard does not seem to have given consideration to the fact that in a roll sheets are fastened together in such a way that if these were written on back and front the passages on the two sides of one sheet would not be consecutive, while in a codex form two leaves (four pages) would form a unit, not one (two pages).[132]

Even if this improbability could be overcome we are faced with a further difficulty. We must postulate that modern critics without the separate pages before them are better able to discern the right sequence than the first or second-century editor who had the leaves actually in his hands. If he could not perform this feat it is difficult to think that we can. It must also be borne in mind that the theory asks us to think that each page where a displacement occurs conveniently coincided with the end of a sentence. Haphazard displacement is much more likely to find sentences broken, at least in some cases. All in all it cannot be

---

[131] Pp. xxviii ff.

[132] There is a further difficulty concerning the dating if the use of the codex form. Bernard's view will not stand, I think, if the roll form was used for the original writing of this Gospel. The codex form does not seem to have been widely used until the second century A. D. (F. G. Kenyon, *Our Bible and the Ancient Manuscripts*, London, 1939, pp. 12f.). It may be just early enough for the autograph of John, but it is a near thing. As Guthrie puts it, "there is no certain evidence to show whether codices were used quite as early as this" (*op. cit.*, p. 287).

said that the hypothesis of dislocations has been successfully made out.

One cannot help thinking that sufficient attention is not being given to the author's intention. We all too readily assume that he must have had more or less the same canons of consistency as we have. But if he was not interested in producing the kind of consistency which we take for granted he may well have had different standards as to what part of his writing should follow what other part. In other words it is always better to try and make sense of the manuscript as it stands than to try our hand at varying the order. And a number of modern writers, for example, C. K. Barrett,[133] C. H. Dodd,[134] and R. H. Lightfoot,[135] are convinced that we should take the present order of John rather than try to rearrange it. C. J. Wright goes further and suggests that in our rearrangements we may be missing something important, "In trying to make a book conform to standards of our own, we may fail to understand the author's type of mind."[136]

VII. Sources

A number of scholars have attempted to demonstrate the existence of sources used by this Evangelist.[137] Sometimes this is done in a fairly modest way. For example, it may be reasoned that 20 : 30f. is clearly the end point of an original Gospel. Therefore ch. 21 is an addition by some later hand. But it is possible to go on from there. If this later hand is responsible for ch. 21 perhaps

---

[133] "Neither displacement theories nor redaction theories are needed to explain the present state of the gospel" (p. 20).

[134] "Unfortunately, when once the gospel has been taken to pieces, its reassemblage is liable to be affected by individual preferences, preconceptions and even prejudices ... If ... it should appear that the structure of the gospel as we have it has been shaped in most of its details by the ideas which seem to dominate the author's thought, then it would appear not improbable that we have his work before us substantially in the form which he designed" (*IFG*, p. 240).

[135] "It is reasonable to hold that no attempt should be made to alter the order of the text as we have it" (p. 8).

[136] P. 29. He goes on: "Not only so, but by the multiplicity and diversity of our schemes of rearrangement we are in danger of making our conclusions a laughing-stock to those not yet bereft of a sense of humour."

[137] There is a useful summary of "Theories of Partition and Redaction" in Howard, *FGRCI*, pp. 297ff. See also D. Guthrie, *op. cit.*, pp. 275ff.

it is responsible for other parts of the Gospel also. In other words, the very presence of ch. 21 may be held to be evidence of the activity of a Redactor. This figure, acting as editor as he was, may then be held to be responsible for a number of verses, mainly of a connective character. The Redactor, it is then plausibly urged, has worked over the Gospel material putting it in its present shape.[138]

Another approach is to point out that there is some evidence that John made use of Mark and Luke, at any rate, possibly Matthew also. This, it is maintained, gives evidence of some use of sources. Since the Evangelist used these sources he may well have used others also. This argument, however, is not very convincing in the light of the improbability that John used any of the Synoptists. As we have looked at this possibility and rejected it there seems no point in pursuing this particular theory of sources.

Perhaps the most interesting of recent attempts to disentangle sources is that of Rudolf Bultmann. Bultmann thinks that the enumeration of the "signs" in 2 : 11 and 4 : 54 can scarcely have originated with the Evangelist, for the Evangelist says that Jesus did a large number of signs (2 : 23; 4 : 45). The "sign" at the end of ch. 4 is thus not Jesus' "second sign" as 4 : 54 says. Again Bultmann feels that 20 : 30, which speaks of Jesus as having done "many other signs . . . in the presence of the disciples", is not a very suitable conclusion for the Gospel. But he thinks it would be quite in place for a conclusion to a narrative of "signs". From these and other considerations Bultmann is lead to postulate the existence of a "signs" source. When the "signs" are separated out from the Gospel the most notable further feature is the discourses. Bultmann goes on accordingly to deduce that there was a "revelation" source, which he thinks was of Gnostic origin. A third source is to be discerned in the Passion and Resurrection narrative. In addition to all this Bultmann finds evidence of the activity of a Redactor.

Unfortunately for any idea of sources in this Gospel the precise

---

[138] R. H. Strachan in the earlier editions of his commentary worked on the theory of redaction, but abandoned it in the third edition, where he says: "All attempts . . . to discover the work of different hands in the Gospel, have reached hardly any agreement, and are open to the charge of oversubtlety" (p. 81).

delineation is very difficult. There seems little question but that the style of the Gospel is uniform.[139] If John did take sources he has so re-worked them and made them his own that in the judgment of many competent scholars it is now impossible to discern which were sources and which was John's own material. What B. H. Streeter said about a particular view has a much wider application: "if the sources have undergone anything like the amount of amplification, excision, rearrangement and adaptation which the theory postulates, then the critic's pretence that he can unravel the process is grotesque. As well hope to start with a string of sausages and reconstruct the pig."[140] It seems much safer to take the Gospel as it stands and assume it comes from the Evangelist. There is no need to deny that he made use of sources. He may well have done this. But he has so thoroughly made them his own that they cannot now be recovered.[141] Any criticism of this Gospel which rests on the detection of sources must be regarded as suspect.[142]

---

[139] Howard produces tables which show the incidence of certain stylistic characteristics. He says, "It would be absurd to claim that they amount to a demonstration. We may, however, point out that there is a remarkable distribution of these characteristics through all parts of the Gospel, narrative and discourse, Galilean and Judaean" (*FGRCI*, p. 107; the tables are found in Appendix B, pp. 276ff.).

[140] *Op. cit.*, p. 377.

[141] Even when an author does not impose his own stamp as thoroughly as does John the difficulty of detecting sources may be immense. If I may quote Streeter again, "In Mark we have extant one of the main sources of both Matthew and Luke. But if we had before us *only* Matthew, or *only* Luke, no critic on earth would have been able to reconstruct a source like Mark. Even where we have two copies of a lost document to help us, we are at times baffled; witness the fact that no one has yet made a convincing reconstruction of Q" (*op. cit.*, p. 378).

[142] W. G. Kümmel examines and rejects a number of different source theories with comments like: "these partition hypotheses have proved to be inadequately grounded in respect to methodology" (*op. cit.*, p. 141); "the tenability of such source theories has been fundamentally disputed with the help of vocabulary statistics" (*loc. cit.*): "The more far-reaching hypotheses of Wellhausen, Schwarz, and Hirsch, according to which John arose through extensive expansion of a 'Grundschrift,' can only be designated as arbitrary and undemonstrable" (*op. cit.*, p. 150). He rejects the theories of Eckhardt, Boismard, Broome, and MacGregor and Morton. He is more respectful to Bultmann but rejects his views, too (*op. cit.*, pp. 150ff.).

VIII. Place of Composition

It is, of course, not known where the Gospel was written, but there are three places urged with some show of probability. The first of these is the traditional site, namely Ephesus. This goes back to Irenaeus who says, "Afterwards, John, the disciple of the Lord, who also had leaned upon His breast, did himself publish a Gospel during his residence at Ephesus in Asia."[143] This is not proof, but it is a fairly early indication, and, as we noted earlier, Irenaeus had had personal contact with Polycarp who knew John personally. So the tradition is entitled to be heard. It is supported by the fact that Ephesus is not far from Phrygia, the centre of the Montanist movement, and the Montanists made early use of this Gospel. It is also the case that one of the minor features of this Gospel is an insistence on the minor role played by John the Baptist. We know that there were continuing disciples of the Baptist in the vicinity of Ephesus (Acts 19 : 1–7), and it may well be that this state of affairs continued until the writing of this Gospel.

The most popular alternative suggestion is that the Gospel comes from the general region of Antioch. It is pointed out that there are parallels to the "Odes of Solomon"[144] which are thought to belong to Syria. There are also some coincidences of language with the writings of Ignatius, who was bishop of Antioch. Those who see evidences of a Gnostic way of thinking in John also point out that the type of Gnosticism presupposed is one which has affinities with Judaism, and this is likely to have arisen in such a centre as Antioch on the borders of Judaism. The fact that the first orthodox commentary on John came from Antioch (written by Theophilus) may also be relevant.

The third suggestion is Alexandria[145] or somewhere else in Egypt. It is pointed out that the earliest manuscript of this Gospel was found in Egypt, which indicates early use of our Gospel in that

---

[143] *Adv. Haer.*, III. i. 1 (ANF, I, p. 414).

[144] Turner and Mantey however discount this. They say, "The Odes of Solomon were viewed by Harnack as affording an important source of ideas for the Fourth Gospel, but subsequent research has modified this judgment and virtually annulled it" (p. 7). Barrett thinks that "The major resemblances (such as they are) between the two works are due to this common drawing upon a non-Christian source of religious terminology" (p. 55).

[145] So K. and S. Lake, *op. cit.*, p. 53.

land. It is also the case that the teaching of John is held to have points of contact with the allegorical method thought to have been characteristic of Egypt. Perhaps more relevant is the fact that Egypt was a centre of early Gnosticism. The Gnostics made a good deal of use of John, and it may be that this was due in part to the fact that this Gospel was there in Egypt to be used.

None of these suggestions can be said to be convincing and in the end we are left without certain proof. Perhaps there is a little more to be said for Ephesus than for either of the others.

IX. Background

A good deal of attention has been given to the background presupposed by this Gospel. This is, of course, important for its interpretation, for we must know the kind of milieu in which the author moved if we are to be sure we understand his meaning. One reason why different scholars understand this Gospel differently is that they have different ideas of its background.

There can be no doubt but that the Old Testament played a large part in the author's thinking. He had obviously read it well and pondered it long. He quotes it a number of times. Sometimes his citations are from the Septuagint, while sometimes it would appear he makes his own translation from the Hebrew. But quite apart from specific quotation it is clear that he had absorbed the teaching of the Old Testament. In his treatment of the Good Shepherd (ch. 10) and of the true Vine (ch. 15) he has unmistakable allusions to the Old Testament without specific quotation. Again and again this is the case. It is clear that he knew his Bible very well indeed.

With this we must take Judaism. There can be little doubt that the teachings of the Rabbis lie behind part of the teaching of this Gospel, though we must be on our guard here because of the late date of the rabbinic sources. Experts in rabbinics agree, however, that, while the writings as we have them are later than New Testament times, they embody much ancient material. Some of it certainly goes back to the times of John, and even of Jesus. The parallels adduced in Strack-Billerbeck are sufficient to show that this is an area which must not be overlooked. But Judaism was not monolithic. The rabbinic writings give us what we may term normative Judaism, but there were other currents in first century Judaism. H. Odeberg has given a good deal of attention to Jewish mysticism, and has been able to show that there are many points of contact.[146] We should also notice here the importance of the Qumran scrolls. These give us a useful insight into another section of unorthodox Judaism and here again there are connections with John.[147] Others have seen acquaintance with Jewish apocalyptic thought.[148] It must be stressed that while the resemblances between the Fourth Gospel and each of these types of Judaism are real, so also are the differences. In fact this should be obvious from the very fact of the widespread nature of the resemblances. It is impossible that any writing should at one and the same time reflect accurately the essential positions of normative Judaism, mystical Judaism, and Qumran. But something of each is to be discerned in the background.

There is also a Hellenistic background. Some have seen this preeminently in the Prologue, with its reference to the *Logos*, a concept found among the Greek philosophers. In the note on this concept it is pointed out that John's is not the typical Greek use, but he may have had the Greek use in mind for all that. It is plain from his habit of explaining Jewish terms, even common ones like "Rabbi" (1 : 38; even Mark does not feel the necessity to explain this term, Mark 9 : 5, *etc.*) that he wrote for people who were not Jews. Now any group of cultured people in the first century would have had some acquaintance with Hellenistic thought. When we know that Judaism is not the whole story allowance must be made for a Greek background. Some scholars think that this is especially the case with the writings of Philo.[149] This man appears to have been influential in Hellenistic Judaism, and his writings may well have been known to the first readers of this Gospel. Many see some affinities with Philo in the Prologue.

Another possible background is discerned in the *Hermetica*, a group of writings of a philosophical and religious nature. These were attributed to Hermes Trismegistus. C. H. Dodd has made a thorough examination of these tractates[150] and he thinks that this kind of approach to life is presupposed at points in our Gospel.

---

[146] See *FG*, *passim*.
[147] See *SFG*, ch. 6.
[148] *E.g.* Barrett, p. 26.
[149] C. H. Dodd sees Philo as important (*IFG*, pp. 54–73). So also A. W. Argyle, *ExT*, LXIII, 1951–52, pp. 385f.
[150] *IFG*, pp. 10–53; *The Bible and the Greeks* (London, 1954), pp. 99–248.

This may well be the case, but Dodd's results must be used with caution. G. D. Kilpatrick has shown that some of the characteristic concepts of the *Hermetica* are totally absent from John, and that the vocabulary is different. He finds much more affinity with the Septuagint, which is an important conclusion.[151] The Hellenistic world knew other religions of salvation than that brought before us in the *Hermetica*, and John appears to some to have some acquaintance with the kind of thinking found in them. The mystery religions brought men the concept of life, and some of John's phraseology recalls it.

A number of students have suggested that Gnosticism is the proper background. Sometimes this is precisely located in Mandaism. Mandaeans are continuing Gnostics of a non-Christian type. All the other Gnosticism we know comes before us as a Christian heresy. The Mandaeans are often hailed as showing that Gnosticism was not of Christian origin. And some go further, maintaining that John takes shape only when seen against this background. But despite the confident statements of some who have examined this literature closely it is difficult to agree with them. The Mandaean documents as we know them are late. Even allowing for the fact that the sixteenth century manuscripts known to us go back to earlier originals it is difficult to date this literature early enough to be significant. Dodd thinks that, "The compilation of the Mandaean Canon, therefore, cannot be dated much, if at all, before A.D. 700."[152] Some of its ideas may, of course, be considerably older than the compilation of the canon, but these dates show that it is most unlikely that this kind of thinking had any real effect on John.

Bultmann is an outstanding example of a modern commentator who sees Gnosticism as the important part of the background to John. He holds that the Gnostic redeemer myth lies behind John's idea of a Christ who came forth from God and who returns to God. This can be made to sound convincing, for there can be no doubt that the thought that Christ came down from heaven

---

[151] See *Studies in the Fourth Gospel*, ed. F. L. Cross (London, 1957), pp. 36–44. He concludes that "we can discard the *Hermetica* along with the Mandaean texts and other evidences of Gnosticism. They constitute no significant part of the background of the Gospel, they do not provide the key to its interpretation" (*op. cit.*, p. 43).

[152] *IFG*, p. 115.

and that He returns there having accomplished His mission of salvation is of great importance to John. But the existence of this redeemer-myth in any pre-Christian form is far from having been proved.[153] So for all its popularity in some circles this idea must be discarded.[154] The Gnosticism we know is definitely second-century. There is no reason for thinking that it sprang full grown from nothing, and Gnosticism was certainly hospitable to ideas from a multitude of sources. We may well hold, accordingly, that some of the ideas that ultimately were to form an integral part of Gnosticism were in existence when John wrote. Indeed, I have earlier suggested that one of John's aims was to combat docetic ideas.[155] But this is not the same thing as seeing Gnosticism as a coherent system at the time John wrote,[156] nor of thinking even of its essential ideas as his background. For either of these the evidence is lacking.

It must be insisted that the background to John is the early Christian church. John's fundamental ideas are the basic Christian ideas. He presents an individual picture indeed, but it is a picture

---

[153] *Cf.* R. M. Grant: "The most obvious explanation of the origin of the Gnostic redeemer is that he was modelled after the Christian conception of Jesus. It seems significant that we know no redeemer before Jesus, while we encounter other redeemers (Simon Magus, Menander) immediately after his time" (*Gnosticism*, London, 1961, p. 18). Again Quispel, writing on the Gnostic documents of Chenoboskion, sees the possibility of giving "the death-sentence to Bultmann's hypothesis of a pre-Christian Gnostic Redeemer" (*op. cit.*, p. 38).

[154] J. Munck has an incisive criticism of Bultmann: "Bultmann believes he can prove that the Gospel of St. John presupposes this redeemer myth and can only be understood in the light of it. But no attempt has been made at a critical evaluation of the material cited, and the author does not distinguish between probable dependence, the use of the same *terminus technicus* in the same sense and in quite another sense, and the use of the same imagery in the same sense and in quite another, and therefore probably entirely irrelevant, sense. For these reasons the data so meritoriously assembled form only a kind of valuable raw material for defining concepts and have not the power of a proof, as Bultmann believed" (*Current Issues in New Testament Interpretation*, ed. W. Klassen and G. F. Snyder, London, 1962, pp. 227f.).

[155] See above, pp. 36f.

[156] Munck objects even to the term "proto-gnostic" (as implying "that the proto-gnostic forms a preliminary to Gnosticism"), and prefers "syncretistic" as "a term which does not definitely anticipate the specially gnostic but merely describes an observed phenomenon as a single expression of the religious mixture from which Gnosticism derives" (*op. cit.*, pp. 236f.).

of the same Christ, and of the same religion as other Christian writers. We have rejected the idea that John is dependent on the Synoptic Gospels, but the fact that the contention can be seriously put forward shows that the teaching in these Gospels must be taken as part of the Johannine background. So must the exposition of the faith that we see in the Pauline Epistles. Not all would agree with E. F. Scott when he says, "The evangelist is everywhere indebted to Paul".[157] But he does point us to something of importance. The Evangelist is not a Paulinist, but he knows the same Christ that Paul knows. John is an authentic Christian document and for its full meaning to be appreciated it must be seen in company with the other early Christian writings, the remaining books of the New Testament.

---

[157] *Op. cit.*, p. 46. James Moffatt puts "Paulinism" at the head of his list of "the main currents which flow through the gospel" apart from the Old Testament (*An Introduction to the Literature of the New Testament*, Edinburgh, 1927, p. 522).

ANALYSIS OF THE GOSPEL ACCORDING TO JOHN

I. THE PROLOGUE, 1 : 1–18
   1. The Word and God, 1 : 1, 2
   2. The Word and creation, 1 : 3–5
   3. The Word and John the Baptist, 1 : 6–8
   4. The Word incarnate, 1 : 9–14
   5. The Word's surpassing excellence, 1 : 15–18
II. THE BEGINNINGS OF JESUS' MINISTRY, 1 : 19–51
   1. The witness of John, 1 : 19–34
      (a) *John and the Pharisees*, 1 : 19–28
      (b) *John and Jesus*, 1 : 29–34
   2. The first disciples, 1 : 35–51
      (a) *Andrew and Peter*, 1 : 35–42
      (b) *Philip and Nathanael*, 1 : 43–51

III. THE SIGNS AND PUBLIC DISCOURSES OF THE CHRIST, 2 : 1 – 12 : 50
   1. First Sign – Water into wine, 2 : 1–11
      Interlude, 2 : 12
   2. Cleansing the temple, 2 : 13–17
   3. Destroying and raising the temple, 2 : 18–22
   4. Jesus and men, 2 : 23–25
   5. First Discourse – The new birth, 3 : 1–36
      (a) *The new birth*, 3 : 1–15
      (b) *Reflection*, 3 : 16–21
      (c) *Jesus and John the Baptist*, 3 : 22–36
         (i) A question about purifying, 3 : 22–26
         (ii) The reply of John the Baptist, 3 : 27–30
         (iii) Reflection, 3 : 31–36
   6. Second Discourse – The water of life, 4 : 1–42
      (a) *Jesus' departure for Galilee*, 4 : 1–3
      (b) *Living water*, 4 : 4–14
      (c) *The woman and her husbands*, 4 : 15–19
      (d) *True worship*, 4 : 20–26

(e) *The woman's witness,* 4 : 27–30
(f) *Christ's meat,* 4 : 31–38
(g) *Samaritan believers,* 4 : 39–42
    Interlude in Galilee, 4 : 43–45
7. Second Sign – Healing the nobleman's son, 4 : 46–54
8. Third Sign – The healing of the lame man, 5 : 1–18
  (a) *The healing,* 5 : 1–9a
  (b) *Dispute over the Sabbath,* 5 : 9b–18
9. Third Discourse - The Divine Son, 5 : 19–47
  (a) *The Father and the Son,* 5 : 19–24
  (b) *The Son and judgment,* 5 : 25–29
  (c) *Witness to the Son,* 5 : 30–47
10. Fourth Sign – Feeding the multitude, 6 : 1 –15
11. Fifth Sign – Walking on the water, 6 : 16–21
12. Fourth Discourse – The bread of life, 6 : 22–66
  (a) *The audience gathers,* 6 : 22–25
  (b) *Food that abides,* 6 : 26f.
  (c) *The words of God,* 6 : 28f.
  (d) *The bread of life,* 6 : 30–40
  (e) *Christ and the bread,* 6 : 41–51
  (f) *Eating the flesh and drinking the blood,* 6 : 52–59
  (g) *Words that are spirit and life,* 6 : 60–66
13. Peter's confession, 6 : 67–71
14. Fifth Discourse – The life-giving Spirit, 7 : 1–52
  (a) *Jesus' discussion with His brothers,* 7 : 1–9
  (b) *The reaction of the multitudes,* 7 : 10–13
  (c) *Righteous judgment,* 7 : 14–24
  (d) *Is this the Christ?* 7 : 25–31
  (e) *An attempt at arrest,* 7 : 32
  (f) *The return to the Father,* 7 : 33–36
  (g) *A prophecy of the Spirit,* 7 : 37–39
  (h) *Division,* 7 : 40–44
  (i) *The failure to arrest Jesus,* 7 : 45–52
15. Sixth Discourse – The Light of the world, 8 : 12–59
  (a) *The witness of the Father,* 8 : 12–20
  (b) *Dying in sins,* 8 : 21–24
  (c) *The Father and the Son,* 8 : 25–30
  (d) *Slaves of sin,* 8 : 31–47

2. The Disciples' questions, 13 : 31 – 14 : 31
   (a) *The new commandment,* 13 : 31–35
   (b) *A prophecy of the denial,* 13 : 36–38
   (c) *Christ, the Way,* 14 : 1–7
   (d) *The Father and the Son,* 14 : 8–14
   (e) *The coming of the Spirit,* 14 : 15–17
   (f) *The manifestation of Christ to the disciples,* 14 : 18–24
   (g) *"I go unto the Father",* 14 : 25–31
3. The true Vine, 15 : 1–16
4. Persecution, 15 : 17–25
   (a) *Suffering for Christ's sake,* 15 : 17–21
   (b) *Christ reveals men's sin,* 15 : 22–25
5. The work of the Holy Spirit, 15 : 26 – 16 : 15
   (a) *The witness of the Spirit,* 15 : 26f.
   (b) *A warning of coming persecutions,* 16 : 1–4
   (c) *The work of the Spirit,* 16 : 5–15
6. Some difficulties solved, 16 : 16–33
   (a) *The disciples' perplexity,* 16 : 16–18
   (b) *The disciples' joy,* 16 : 19–24
   (c) *The disciples' faith,* 16 : 25–30
   (d) *The disciples' peace,* 16 : 31–33
7. The High Priestly Prayer, 17 : 1–26
   (a) *Prayer for the glorification of the Son,* 17 : 1–5
   (b) *Prayer for the disciples,* 17 : 6–19
   (c) *Prayer for those who will in future believe,* 17 : 20–26

V. THE CRUCIFIXION, 18 : 1 – 19 : 42
   1. The arrest, 18 : 1–12
   2. The Jewish trial and the denials, 18 : 13–27
      (a) *Jesus brought before Annas,* 18 : 13f.
      (b) *Peter's first denial,* 18 : 15–18
      (c) *The examination before Annas,* 18 : 19–24
      (d) *Peter's second and third denials,* 18 : 25–27
   3. The Roman trial, 18 : 28 – 19 : 16
      (a) *Jesus delivered up to Pilate,* 18 : 28–32
      (b) *Jesus examined before Pilate,* 18 : 33–40
      (c) *Behold, the Man,* 19 : 1–6a
      (d) *Pilate's final decision,* 19 : 6b–16

ANALYSIS

4. Jesus put to death, 19 : 17–42
    (a) *Jesus crucified*, 19 : 17–22
    (b) *The division of Jesus' clothing*, 19 : 23–25a
    (c) *Jesus provides for Mary*, 19 : 25b–27
    (d) *The death of Jesus*, 19 : 28–30
    (e) *The piercing of Jesus' side*, 19 : 31–37
    (f) *The burial*, 19 : 38–42

VI. THE RESURRECTION, 20 : 1–29
  1. The empty tomb, 20 : 1–10
  2. The appearances, 20 : 11–29
    (a) *The appearance to Mary*, 20 : 11–18
    (b) *The appearance to the ten*, 20 : 19–23
    (c) *The appearance to Thomas*, 20 : 24–29

VII. THE PURPOSE OF THE GOSPEL, 20 : 30f.

VIII. THE EPILOGUE, 21 : 1–25
  1. The miraculous draught of fishes, 21 : 1–14
  2. Peter restored, 21 : 15–19
  3. The role of the Beloved Disciple, 21 : 20–23
  4. Authentication, 21 : 24f.

Appendix – The woman taken in adultery, 7 : 53 – 8 : 11

CHAPTER I

I. THE PROLOGUE, 1 : 1–18

The first eighteen verses of this Gospel form a Prologue to the whole.[1] Some have thought that this section was originally separate, perhaps being composed by someone other than the Evangelist.[2] They see it as having no real connection with the Gospel, but as being adapted more or less successfully to its present situation. It is more likely that it is original, for it accords so well with what follows. These verses bring before us some of the great thoughts that will be developed as the narrative unfolds; the excellency of Christ, who is the Word of God, the eternal strife between light and darkness, and the witness borne by the Baptist, that greatest of the sons of Israel. But the principal topic in these verses is the incarnation, together with its astounding sequel, the rejection of the Word by those who might have been expected to welcome Him.

Of particular interest and importance is the use of the term *Logos* or Word, which is applied to Christ in these verses, and in these verses alone in this Gospel (for that matter the term is rare elsewhere, Rev. 19 : 13 being the only other place where there can be no doubt about it, and there it is not "the Word" simply, but

---

[1] Morgan points out that we should not understand the term "Prologue" merely in the sense "Preface". "It is far more than a preface. In these eighteen verses we have an explanation of everything that follows from the nineteenth verse of chapter one, to the twenty-ninth verse of chapter twenty. All that follows is intended to prove the accuracy of the things declared in the first eighteen verses . . . it is a summation; everything is found in those first eighteen verses." Similarly Godet sees it as "the summary of the testimonies which Jesus bore to Himself in the course of His ministry . . . it is at once the most normal and the richest expression of the consciousness which Jesus had of His own person" (I, p. 291). R. H. Lightfoot is emphatic: "These verses give the key to the understanding of this gospel, and make clear how the evangelist wishes his readers to approach his presentation of the Lord's work and Person".

[2] R. E. Brown, for example, describes it as "An early Christian hymn, probably stemming from Johannine circles, which has been adapted to serve as an overture to the Gospel narrative of the career of the incarnate Word" (p. 1).

71

"the Word of God"). But, though the term is not used in this way elsewhere in John, the idea that Christ stands to the Father in the relationship that it denotes permeates the whole. As E. F. Scott says, "it pervades the Gospel and supplies the key by which its teaching must be interpreted."[3] The Gospel is a Gospel about the Word. The Prologue sounds the keynote.

Some have thought that it should be understood as poetry.[4] It is true that it is possible to arrange it to look like verse. Bernard, for example, has done this in Greek,[5] and Rieu in his English translation. It is also undoubtedly true that some of the attributes of poetry are to be found in it. But, as Barrett justly remarks, those who regard it as verse differ markedly in their verse arrangements,[6] and in what they regard as prose insertions. It is also the case that their methods, applied elsewhere, could make "poetry" of almost any part of the Gospel. It is better to regard the Prologue as elevated prose. It is written in a meditative strain (but then so is much of this Gospel). This lends a musing air to the passage. But it does not make it poetry.

The *Logos*, the Word, is the theme right through the Prologue. We can divide the passage into short sections for purposes of study, and every one of them will be concerned with one aspect or other of the Word's relationships.

1. THE WORD AND GOD, 1 : 1, 2

1 In the beginning was the Word, and the Word was with God, and the Word was God. 2 The same was in the beginning with God.

1 The opening words, "In the beginning", are probably a conscious reminiscence of the first words of the Bible. The first book of the Hebrew Bible was named "In the beginning" (from its opening words) so the expression would be widely known. John is

---

[3] *The Fourth Gospel* (Edinburgh, 1906), p. 146.

[4] Schonfield, for example, maintains that "The Prologue consists of a hymn interspersed with brief remarks. The hymn is antiphonal, the alternate lines being chanted as a response" (p. 451, n. 1). This is, of course, pure assertion. Schonfield may be right, but there is no evidence.

[5] See his Introduction, I, p. cxliv f.

[6] Brown cites eight different reconstructions, and adds his own (p. 22). But the only parts all agree belong to the original poem are vv. 1, 3–4, 10–11.

writing about a new beginning, a new creation, so he uses words which recall the first creation. He soon goes on to use other words which loom large in Genesis 1, such as "life" (v. 4), "light" (v. 4), and "darkness" (v. 5). Genesis 1 described God's first creation. John's theme is God's new creation. Like the first, the second is not carried out by some subordinate being. It is brought about through the agency of the *Logos*, the very Word of God. There is continuity with the old creation. The Word was "in the beginning". This means that He was before all else.[7] But it probably means more. The term rendered "beginning" can also denote "origin" in the sense of basic cause.[8] Temple is probably right in thinking that the phrase here combines two meanings, "in the beginning of history", and "at the root of the universe". John is fond of using expressions with more than one meaning. If it happened only occasionally we might regard it as coincidence and make a serious effort to decide between the two meanings. But it happens so often that it must be regarded as deliberate. It is John's way of bringing out the fuller meaning of whatever term he is using. So here it seems to me that he has both meanings in mind and wants us to see both meanings in his words. It is quite in his manner to begin his Gospel with an expression that is to be taken in two ways. Both are important. There never was a time when the Word was not. There never was a thing which did not depend on Him for its very existence. The verb "was" is most naturally understood of the eternal existence of the Word: "the Word continually was".[9] We should not press the tense unduly, but certainly the verb

---

[7] Knox renders, "At the beginning of time", but John's ἐν ἀρχῇ is at once more concise, more far-reaching, and more impressive. We might get something of its force by considering the slightly different ἀπ᾽ ἀρχῆς which is used in I John 1 : 1. This draws attention to what took place from the beginning on, whereas our present passage tells us that in the beginning "the Word was already there" (Barclay). Barth says finely, "this Word was not, like all other words, a created human word, merely relating to God, merely speaking from God and about God. As the Word it is spoken in the place where God is, namely, ἐν ἀρχῇ, *in principio* of all that is" (*Church Dogmatics*, I, 1, Edinburgh, 1955, p. 459).

[8] Thus AG gives the first meaning of the word as "beginning" and the second as "the first cause". Tertullian makes a good deal of the double meaning of the term ἀρχή in LXX of Gen. 1 : 1 in his argument against Hermogenes (XIX; ANF, III, p. 488).

[9] "Was" is ἦν not ἐγένετο, which is used in vv. 3, 6, 14 (see 8 : 58 for a good illustration of the difference between γίνομαι and εἰμί). It is relevant to notice

denotes neither a completed state, nor a coming into being. It is appropriate to eternal, unchanging being. John is affirming that the Word existed before creation, which makes it clear that the Word was not created. It is of the utmost importance to grasp this. Others, particularly among the Jews with their emphasis on the one God as the source of all things, had thought of the Word as of excellent dignity, but as subordinate, as a created being. It is fundamental to John that the Word is not to be included among created things. "In the beginning" (with all the fulness of meaning that these words can hold) the Word "was".

For "the Word" (*Logos*) see Additional Note A, pp. 115ff. The introduction of the term, as something familiar, in the very first line of the Gospel brings before us one of the difficulties that will remain with us throughout. It is not proven beyond doubt whether the term, as John uses it, is to be derived from Jewish or Greek or some other source.[10] Nor is it plain precisely what he meant by it. John does not tell us and we are left to work out for ourselves the precise allusion and its significance. Again and again we will find ourselves in this situation. I do not mean that John's thought is confused or that we cannot follow what he is saying. On the contrary, his thought is clear and his style lucid. But his combination of simplicity and profundity often leaves us wondering whether we have caught all his meaning.

This at any rate can be said: "the Word" points to the truth that it is of the very nature of God to reveal Himself. A man's word is the means whereby he reveals what he is thinking. "The

---

that exactly the same verb, ἦν, occurs in the next clause, where Knox brings out the continuous force by rendering, "God had the Word abiding with him". Westcott draws attention to the fact that, whereas the opening of Genesis takes us back to the beginning and that which starts from that point, "St. John lifts our thoughts *beyond* the beginning and dwells on that which 'was' when time, and with time finite being, began its course." Calvin thinks little of any argument derived from the tense of the verb and looks for "weightier reasons", *viz.*, "that the Evangelist sends us to the eternal sanctuary of God and teaches us that the Word was, as it were, hidden there before He revealed Himself in the outward workmanship of the world."

[10] *Cf.* R. P. Casey: the Prologue's "principal difficulty lies neither in its style nor in its terminology but in the fact that its author has his feet planted firmly in two worlds: that of the O.T. and that of Hellenistic philosophy and allows his gaze to wander easily from one to the other. At every important point he has not only two thoughts instead of one, but two sets of allusions in mind" (*JThS*, n.s., IX, 1958, p. 270).

Word of God is His thought (if we may put it so) uttered so that
men can understand it."[11] God is not to be thought of as aloof
and indifferent. He reveals Himself. But He reveals Himself as
He chooses.[12] He is sovereign in revelation as in all else. We must
guard against two misinterpretations. The one is that of thinking
of the revelation as static. It is more than the revelation of certain
truths about God. To know God is life eternal (17 : 3). The
knowledge of God that the Word brings is not merely information.
It is life. The Word is creative.[13] The other is that of thinking of
the Word as nothing more than an attribute or even an activity
of God. John thinks of the Word as coming to earth in the person
of Jesus of Nazareth (v. 14). At the same time He partakes of the
innermost being of God, for "the Word was God". It is probably
impossible for us to read the Prologue without thoughts of Jesus
of Nazareth. But it is worth bearing in mind that there is nothing
to link the two until we come to v. 14. Up till that point the first
readers of this Gospel would have thought of the Word in terms
of a supremely great Being or Principle. If we are to evaluate the
intended impact of these words we must bear this in mind.

"The Word was with God" is probably as good a translation
as we can manage for a difficult Greek expression.[14] If the prep-

---

[11] C. H. Dodd, *How to Read the Gospels* (London, 1944), p. 29. *Cf.* also
R. F. Bailey: "Self-revelation in active expression of His will and in rational
order is part of God's nature."

[12] Karl Heim points out that "The word distinguishes itself only from the
dark foil of silence. If there is no silence the speaker cannot make himself
understood at all. His words then are drowned in noise. Therefore there is
no understanding of the word of God in all those philosophies which do not
acknowledge the distinction between these two forms of God's presence, silence
and speech, which hold the opinion either that God is equally beyond reach
everywhere, or that He can be experienced everywhere in the same way and
is always equally near" (*Jesus the Lord*, Edinburgh and London, 1959, p. 154).

[13] *Cf.* Barrett: "the term Logos is seen to describe God in the process of
self-communication – not the communication of knowledge only, but in a self-
communication which inevitably includes the imparting of true knowledge.
The Logos is a Word of God which at the same time declares his nature and
calls into being a created life in which a divine power circulates" (p. 61).

[14] ὁ Λόγος ἦν πρὸς τὸν θεόν. Many commentators (*e.g.* Bernard, Boismard)
deny that πρός with the accusative differs from παρά with the dative. J. Rendel
Harris says bluntly that the construction used here is due to "the writer's or
the translator's Greek, or if we prefer it, want of Greek" (*The Origin of the*

osition is to be taken literally it means "the Word was towards God". John thinks of no opposition between the Word and the Father. The whole existence of the Word was oriented towards the Father. Probably we should understand from the preposition the two ideas of accompaniment and relationship. That the thought is of importance and is no casual expression is indicated by the fact that the statement is repeated in v. 2. It marks an advance on the previous statement (*cf.* also 1 John 1 : 2). There John established the personal existence of the Word. Now he goes on to the Word's personal character in relation to the Father. Not only did the Word exist "in the beginning", but He existed in the closest possible connection with the Father. The expression does differentiate between the two. Perhaps John is by implication refuting any idea that the Word is an emanation from God, quite distinct from the Godhead. The Word and God are not identical. But they are at one.

The high point is reached in the third affirmation: "the Word was God". Nothing higher could be said. All that may be said about God may fitly be said about the Word. This statement should not be watered down. Moffatt renders, "the Logos was divine" (similarly Goodspeed, Schonfield, *et al.*). While this English

---

Prologue to St John's Gospel, Cambridge, 1917, p. 5). But the Greek of this Gospel is not slipshod. Dods maintains that the preposition "implies not merely existence alongside of but personal intercourse. It means more than μετά or παρά, and is regularly employed in expressing the presence of one person with another." For its use with persons *cf.* Matt. 13 : 56; Mark 6 : 3. According to A. T. Robertson, "the literal idea comes out well, 'face to face with God' " (*A Grammar of the Greek New Testament in the light of Historical Research*, London, n.d., p. 623). He also says, "face-to-face converse" is in mind (*op. cit.*, p. 625). MacGregor thinks that the preposition "expresses *nearness* combined with the sense of *movement towards* God, and so indicates an active relationship. The Logos and God do not simply exist side by side, but are on terms of living intercourse, and such fellowship implies separate personality." It is hard to see less. B. F. C. Atkinson sees a sense of intimacy, and finds in the construction "the sense of home". He cites as examples of this use, "I will arise and go *home* to my father . . . And he arose and went *home* to his father" (Luke 15 : 18, 20). This passage he takes to mean, "The word was in God's home" (*The Theology of Prepositions*, London, n.d., p. 19). BDF sees the construction as signifying, "with, in the company of" (239(1)). MiM sees in it "not merely being beside, but maintaining communion and intercourse with", and cites Mark 6 : 3; 1 John 1 : 2; 2 : 1.

probably means much the same as does that of ARV the emphasis is different, and the modern translation is no improvement.[15] John is not merely saying that there is something divine about Jesus. He is affirming that He is God,[16] and doing so emphatically as we see from the word order in the Greek.

---

[15] The Greek is Θεὸς ἦν ὁ Λόγος. The adjective "divine" would be θεῖος. This word was available and it is found in the New Testament (e.g. Acts 17 : 29; II Pet. 1 : 3). But Godet thinks that the use of this term of the Logos would denote "a quasi-divinity, a condition intermediate between God and the creature". John is not affirming this, but full deity of the Logos. Abbott points out that it is more common to have an adjective than a noun in this position (1994a; he cites 6 : 60), which makes John's use of the noun all the more significant. The difficulty about the construction is the absence of the article with Θεός. Strachan says dogmatically, "the word theos has no article, thus giving it the significance of an adjective." But this is too simple. How else in Greek would one say, "the Word was God"? And, as Westcott says, an article would equate Θεός and Λόγος, and would be "pure Sabellianism". Had this been John's meaning he could not have said "the Word was with God".

The true explanation of the absence of the article appears to be given by E. C. Colwell, who has shown that in the New Testament definite nouns which precede the verb regularly lack the article (JBL, LII, 1933, pp. 12–21). On this verse he comments: "The absence of the article does not make the predicate indefinite or qualitative when it precedes the verb; it is indefinite in this position only when the context demands it. The context makes no such demand in the Gospel of John" (op. cit., p. 21). See further B. M. Metzger's comments on Colwell's view (ExT, LXIII, 1951–52, pp. 125f.), and the discussion by J. Gwyn Griffiths (ExT, LXII, 1950–51, pp. 314–6). Strachan's statement ignores the usage of the New Testament as do the translations of Moffatt, Goodspeed, Schonfield, etc. On Moffatt's reading N. Turner comments, "Once again dilution of the high Christology of a New Testament author is seen to be based on a fallacious appeal to unfounded grammatical principles" (Grammatical Insights into the New Testament, Edinburgh, 1965, p. 17). NEB renders, "what God was, the Word was", and J. A. T. Robinson makes a good deal of this rendering in his objection to the conventional understanding of the words (Honest to God, London, 1963, p. 71). E. D. Freed, however, in an article entitled "Honest to John" (ExT, LXXV, 1963–64, pp. 61ff.) maintains that Robinson's treatment of this and other Johannine passages can scarcely be accepted. He argues for the rendering, "the Word was God". This is the way RSV takes it (as also Knox, Weymouth, etc.).

[16] Cf. E. M. Sidebottom: "One cannot help feeling that the tendency to write 'the Word was divine' for θεὸς ἦν ὁ λόγος springs from a reticence to attribute the full Christian position to John. It will not do to say that the meaning is that the Word 'belongs to the same sphere of being as God'; Philo could have accepted some such formula as that . . . But Philo was a Jew. He could not have accepted what the Church taught about Christ" (The Christ of the Fourth Gospel, London, 1961, pp. 48f.).

If that is a staggering affirmation to us there is no reason for thinking that it was any less so to the Jewish author of this Gospel. To the Jews of the day monotheism was more than a belief commonly held. It was a conviction to be clung to and defended with a fierce tenacity. The Jews might be ground down under the heel of the Roman conquerors, but they could do more than hate their military superiors. They could despise them. The Romans were no more than ignorant idolaters, and, crass folly, believed in many gods! The Jews knew with an unshakable certainty that there was, there could be, only one God. When John says, "the Word was God", this must be understood in the light of Jewish pride in monotheism. Even though this writer regarded monotheism as a central tenet in his religion he yet could not withhold from the Word the designation "God".

He says "the Word was God", not, "God was the Word". The latter would have meant that God and the Word were the same. It would have pointed to an identity. But John is leaving open the possibility that there may be more to "God" than the "Word" (clearly he thought of the Father as God, and his later references indicate a similar status for the Spirit). But when he thinks of the Word he lays it down unequivocally that nothing less than God will do for our understanding of the Word.[17]

2 Nothing new is added in this verse, but two points are repeated from v. 1 and thereby given emphasis.[18] The Word was "in the beginning" and the Word was "with God". The eternity of the Word is not to be overlooked or minimized. The other point concerns the close relationship between the Father and the Word.

---

[17] D. M. Baillie finely brings out the importance of this: "when Justin, Irenaeus, Tertullian, Clement and Origen set themselves to grapple with the question as to whether the Logos was of the very being of God Himself from all eternity, the discussion was not on some remote point of ancient metaphysics. The question was: Is the redeeming purpose which we find in Jesus part of the very being and essence of God? Is that what God is? Is it His very nature to create, and to reveal Himself, and to redeem His creation? Is it therefore not some subordinate or intermediate being, but the Eternal God Himself, that reveals Himself to us and became incarnate in Jesus for our salvation?" (*God was in Christ*, London, 1955, p. 70).

[18] The use of the pronoun οὗτος also serves to add a measure of emphasis to the statement. John is very fond of using this pronoun in this way. The absence of a connecting particle is to be noted. Both Burney (*AO*, pp. 49ff.)

These two are not the same, but they belong together. The fact that One may be said to be "with" the Other clearly differentiates them. Yet though they are distinct, there is no disharmony. John's expression points us to the perfect unity in which they are joined.

2. THE WORD AND CREATION, 1 : 3-5

3 All things were made through him; and without him [1]was not anything made that hath been made. 4 In him was life; and the life was the light of men. 5 And the light shineth in the darkness; and the darkness [2]apprehended it not.

[1] Or, *was not anything made. That which hath been made was life in him; and the life* & *c.* [2] Or, *overcame.* See ch. 12.35 (Gr.).

It is no accident that John goes straight from his statement about the relation between the Word and God to the phenomenon of creation. As Cullmann puts it, "The self-communication of God occurs first of all in creation. That is why creation and salvation are very closely connected in the New Testament. Both of them have to do with God's self-communication."[19] The development of the theme of the *Logos* leads naturally to the revelation made in creation.

3 From the relationship of the Word to the Father John turns to His relationship to creation. He makes the assertion that all created things[20] were brought into being through Him. The verb "were made" does not in itself mean specifically "were created" so much as "came into being". But in this context the difference is not significant. John is saying that everything owes its existence

---

and Black (*AA*, pp. 38ff.) note this construction as specially frequent in this Gospel and find in it evidence for a Semitic background. Burney thinks it evidence that the Gospel was originally written in Aramaic. Black sees the construction as specially typical of the sayings of Jesus and he finds evidence of this in the sayings in the Synoptics. He concludes: "John may not be as a whole a translation of an Aramaic original, but, in the sayings and speeches of Jesus, as in the Synoptics, may contain translations of an Aramaic tradition, edited and rewritten by the author of the Gospel in Greek" (*AA*, p. 43). This is part of the evidence that we have reliable information in this Gospel.

[19] *The Christology of the New Testament* (London, 1959), p. 267.

[20] He says πάντα not τὰ πάντα nor ὁ κόσμος. This perhaps points to all things taken individually rather than to the universe considered as a totality.

to the Word.[21] He does not say that all was made "by" Him, but "through" Him. This way of putting it safeguards the truth that the Father is the source of all that is.[22] The relation of the first two Persons of the Trinity in the work of creation is of interest. There is a careful differentiation of the parts played by the Father and the Son in 1 Cor. 8 : 6. Creation was not the solitary act of either. Both were at work (and for that matter, still are; cf. 5 : 17, 19). The Father created, but He did it "through" the Word.

A feature of Johannine style is the enunciation of a proposition in positive form, and then immediately its repetition in the negative. We see this here. The second expression is emphatic, and we could render, "without him there was not even one thing made".[23] The whole of creation is included in one broad sweep. Nothing is outside the range of His activity. There is a change of tense. "Were made" (aorist) regards creation in its totality, as one act. But "hath been made" is perfect, and this conveys the thought of the continuing existence of created things. What we see around us did not come into existence apart from the Word, any more than what appeared in the first day of creation.

The emphatic assertion of the exclusive role of the Word in creation is probably to be understood against some contemporary ideas. There are those who think of John as written in part to oppose Gnosticism. I do not think that this can be demonstrated, for on our present information Gnosticism appeared later than any date that is feasible for the composition of this Gospel. But Gnosticism did not appear fully fashioned in a moment of time. It was an eclectic movement, gathering ideas from a variety of sources. It is not in the least unlikely that some were putting out at this time some such view of creation as was later gathered into the various Gnostic systems (though we have no complete evidence

---

[21] C. H. Dodd says, "the whole creation is a revelation of the thought or purpose of God" (loc. cit.). This, however, is not quite the thought. John is not here speaking of revelation at all. J. D. McCaughey in a private communication says, "What John is doing is making an affirmation of faith: πάντα δι' αὐτοῦ ἐγένετο. It is quite arbitrary to go on from there to assert that πάντα, the whole creation, is a revelation of God's thought and purpose. The Prologue asserts that *all things were made through the Word*; it does not assert that the Word can be recognized through all things."

[22] Yet it should be noted that in Rom. 11 : 36; Heb. 2 : 10 the preposition διά is used also of the Father.

[23] οὐδὲ ἕν, "not even one" is stronger than οὐδέν, "nothing".

for the point). This view saw matter as inherently evil. Therefore the good God could have had nothing to do with it. But it was held that there were various "emanations" of spirit beings from Him, until eventually there appeared one powerful enough to create and foolish enough not to see that this would be a mistake. John strongly repudiates all such ideas. The world is due to God Himself[24] acting through His Word.[25] The universe is not eternal, nor is it due to some foolish inferior being. This world is God's world.[26]

4 There is a punctuation problem here. Many scholars take the last words of the previous verse with the opening words of this one to give some such meaning as that of ARV mg., "That which hath been made was life in him", or, alternatively, "That which hath been made in him was life". In our earliest manuscripts there are, of course, few or no punctuation marks, so that either reading is possible. It is perhaps worth noting that the earliest manuscripts which do have punctuation seem usually to place the point before the disputed words, and thus put them in v. 4, not v. 3. So do most other ancient authorities, whether translations

---

[24] Temple sees in the thought of creation by the Word the expression of the conviction "that all things are in their measure an expression of that Will which sustains but also moulds and guides all things, so that the unity of the world, its principle of rational coherence, is the Divine Personality in self-expression" (*Nature, Man and God*, London, 1940, p. 302). But see n. 21 above.

[25] Luther makes this verse the occasion of a strong statement of the divinity of Christ. "If Christ is not true and natural God, born of the Father in eternity and Creator of all creatures, we are doomed . . . we must have a Savior who is true God and Lord over sin, death, devil, and hell. If we permit the devil to topple this stronghold for us, so that we disbelieve His divinity, then His suffering, death, and resurrection profit us nothing" (vol. 22, pp. 21f.).

[26] Some see a connection with the concluding psalm in the Qumran *Manual of Discipline*: "By his knowledge everything comes to pass; and everything that is he establishes by his purpose; and without him it is not done" (*DSS*, p. 388). But, though the last expression could be rendered, "without him it is not made", Burrows' translation is preferable. The psalmist is not thinking about creation but about providence. More apposite is 1 QS iii. 15, "From the God of knowledge is all that is and that is to be" (*DSS*, p. 374). Perhaps closer parallels are to be found in the Apocrypha, as "O God . . . who hast made all things by thy word" (Wis. 9 : 1, and *cf.* Sir. 42 : 15). Perhaps we should also note the *Odes of Solomon* 16 : 20, "the worlds were made by His word". This, however, may be of Christian rather than Jewish origin (see J. Rendel Harris, *The Odes and Psalms of Solomon*, Cambridge, 1911, pp. 112f.).

81

into other languages or quotations in the Fathers.[27] It was not until this way of understanding the text was used to support heretical views[28] that the Fathers tended to adopt the other view. Despite this it seems to me that the text is to be preferred to the margin, and that the point should go after the words in question so that they are read as part of v. 3. To take the text is to get a terse forceful statement in v. 4, while the retention of the disputed words in the previous verse is natural and adds to the emphasis that is there built up. But the margin gives us an exceedingly complicated expression in v. 4. I am not sure that those who adopt this view really face the difficulties. Barrett goes so far as to say that both ways of rendering the words with this verse division ("That which came into being – in it the Word was life", and "That which came into being – in the Word was its life") "are almost impossibly clumsy". Moreover the sense is not easy to accept. That the Word is the source of life is a typically Johannine idea. That everything that has been made is life is not, even if we add, "in him".

Following the usual verse division then, we move on from creation in general to the creation of life, the most significant element in creation. Life is one of John's characteristic concepts. He uses the term 36 times, whereas no other New Testament writing has it more than 17 times (this is Revelation; next comes Romans with 14 times and I John 13 times). Thus in this one writing there occur more than a quarter of all the New Testament references to life. "Life" in John characteristically refers to eternal life (see on 3 : 15), the gift of God through His Son. Here, however, the term must be taken in its broadest sense. It is only because there is life in the *Logos* that there is life in anything on earth at

---

[27] Westcott has a long note in which he cites the principal authorities, and accepts this division of the sentences (pp. 59–63). He takes the meaning to be, "Creation has not 'life in itself' (v. 26), but it had and has life in the Word" (p. 61). I doubt whether this is the meaning of δ $\gamma\acute{e}\gamma o\nu\epsilon\nu$ $\grave{e}\nu$ $a\grave{v}\tau\tilde{\phi}$ $\zeta\omega\grave{\eta}$ $\tilde{\eta}\nu$. Though an impressive list of modern commentators supports the verse division of ARV mg. (and for a long list of Fathers in support see M. E. Boismard, *St. John's Prologue*, London, 1957, p. 14), I do not find their reasons convincing. C. K. Barrett finds that P66 "inclines slightly" to the division I have supported, by reason of its punctuation marks (*ExT*, LXVIII, 1956–57, p. 175).

[28] The words were understood by some to signify that the Spirit was created by the Son.

all. Life does not exist in its own right. It is not even spoken of
as made "by" or "through" the Word, but as existing "in" Him.
There is probably a characteristic Johannine double meaning here.
The life of which John writes is in the first instance the kind of
life that we see throughout this earth. But this will call to mind
that spiritual life which is so much the more significant that John
can speak of it as "the life". Neither will be out of mind here.
This Gospel constantly associates life with the Word. He came
that men might have life and have it more abundantly (10 : 10).
He died that men might have everlasting life (3 : 16). He gave
His flesh for the life of the world (6 : 51). Only those who eat
His flesh and drink His blood have life (6 : 53f.), and similarly
only those who come to Him have life (5 : 40). When He gives
life men perish no more (10 : 28). He said that He had power
to lay down his life and to take it again (10 : 18), and He did
just that. As Lord of life He raised Lazarus from the dead (ch.
11). Twice He said that He was "the life" (11 : 25; 14 : 6), a
thought to which we are very close in the Prologue. The basic
source of all life is the Father who "hath life in himself" (5 : 26;
where see note). But the Father "gave . . . to the Son also to have
life in himself" (*ibid.*), and it is this latter point to which attention
is directed here.

What is the meaning of "the life was the light of men"?[29] GT
equates the light with "intelligence", and explains the verse in
this way: "because the life of men is self-conscious, and thus a
fountain of intelligence springs up".[30] But this is to take the words
in an unnatural way. There is no indication in the context that
intelligence is in mind, and in any case there seems no reason
for confining the words to any one aspect of man.[31] It is more
likely that we should think of Old Testament passages which refer
to God as the source of light and life. Thus we read, "For with
thee is the fountain of life: In thy light shall we see light" (Ps.

---

[29] John moves easily between the thoughts of life and light. See 3 : 16–19;
8 : 12; 12 : 46–50, *etc.*

[30] *Sub* ζωή.

[31] Marcus Dods thinks that the words mean "that the life which appears
in the variety, harmony, and progress of inanimate nature, and in the wonderfully manifold yet related forms of animate existence, appears in man as 'light,'
intellectual and moral light, reason and conscience."

36 : 9).[32] It is this kind of thing that the writer has in mind. But he is writing about the Word, so his meaning will be that the Word, Himself the life, is also "the light of men".[33] John is preparing the way for the thought which he will develop throughout his Gospel, that Jesus is *the* life-bringer and light-bearer.

Just as John links life with Christ, so does he link light. Christ is "the light of the world" (8 : 12; 9 : 5). He is come "a light into the world" (12 : 46). Indeed, the man who follows Him "shall not walk in the darkness, but shall have the light of life" (8 : 12). Men can be urged to believe in the light (12 : 36) just as they are urged to believe in Him. And just as He who is life gave life to dead Lazarus, so He who is the light of the world gave sight to the man born blind (ch. 9). In Gen. 1 : 3 the first thing God says is "Let there be light". Similarly in this chapter the Word is the source of light. All the light that men have, and that whether they walk in it or turn their backs on it, they owe to the Word.[34]

5 Over against light is darkness.[35] The antithesis is a natural one whether we are thinking of the physical world or the spiritual world. It is the function of light to shine precisely in the darkness, to oppose darkness, to dispel darkness. The opposition of light and darkness is a major theme of this Gospel, a feature it shares with

---

[32] For this thought in later Judaism *cf.* 1 Baruch 4 : 2f.,
"All they that hold it (the Torah) fast are appointed to life;
But such as leave it it shall die.
Turn thee, O Jacob, and take hold of it;
Walk towards her shining in the presence of the light thereof."

[33] McClymont stresses the definite article before "light" which, he thinks, "brings out its universality as it exists in the Word." Similarly Plummer, "the one true Light".

[34] The imagery of light was very widespread in the ancient world. Dodd cites evidence to show that such expressions as this verse "would be entirely in place in a Hermetic writing" (*IFG*, p. 18). John's words would have a widespread appeal. He is very interested in light, and he uses the term φῶς 23 times, almost a third of its New Testament occurrences (more than a third if we add the 6 occurrences in I John). The term is used next most frequently in Acts where it is found 10 times.

[35] John's word is σκοτία, which he uses 8 times, and again 6 times in I John. This total of 14 out of 17 New Testament occurrences make it almost exclusively a Johannine word. The other writers prefer σκότος which occurs only once in this Gospel and once in I John, but 30 times in the New Testament. There appears to be no difference in meaning.

the Qumran scrolls.[36] Not too much can be made of this since the antithesis is such a natural one, and very widespread in antiquity. Probabably most religions express it in greater or less measure. But in both John and Qumran it is a prominent theme.

Notice that John changes his tense. Up till now he has used the past exclusively. But the light, he says, "shineth". The light is continually in action. Even as John writes it is shining. The light of the world, the light of men, never ceases to shine. Discussions of whether John has in mind the pre-incarnate Christ or the in-carnate Christ seem quite beside the point. He is not dealing here with the incarnation, but with the fact that it is of the very essence of light that it shines.[37]

According to ARV the darkness "apprehended it not".[38] The Greek verb[39] is not easy to translate. It contains the idea of laying hold on something so as to make it one's own (*cf.* its translation as "attain" with reference to a prize, 1 Cor. 9 : 24). This can lead to meanings like "lay hold with the mind", and thus "comprehend" (AV) or "apprehend". That the verb can bear such a meaning is not in dispute. Whether it is relevant to the present context is another matter. Darkness is not usually conceived of as trying to understand light. To take this meaning is really to understand "darkness" as equivalent to certain men, or perhaps mankind at large. But in this Gospel darkness is not so much men as the evil

---

[36] So prominent is this theme in the Scrolls that a complete writing is given over to it, *The War of the Sons of Light with the Sons of Darkness*. And, of course, the idea is found in many other places in the Scrolls.

[37] φαίνει points to the essential action of light in itself (so Westcott), rather than to the effect of light in illuminating men, which latter we see in φωτίζει in v. 9.

[38] The negative οὐ (οὐκ) is unusually common in John, where it occurs more often than in any other book of the New Testament. John has it 286 times, whereas Matthew uses it 204 times, Mark 117 times and Luke 174 times. Similarly he uses οὐδείς 52 times (Matthew 19 times, Mark 26 times, Luke 33 times). This is not the case with μή, which John uses 117 times, whereas Matthew has it 129 times and Luke 142 times. He never employs μηδείς, though it is found in each of the other three Gospels. Again John's use of the emphatic οὐχί, namely 5 times, is well below that of Luke (17 times), or even of the much shorter 1 Corinthians (12 times). We are perhaps to connect John's preference for οὐ partly with the simplicity of his style, which favors the use of the objective negative, and partly with the subject matter. John has a good deal to say about the conflict between Jesus and His enemies, light and darkness, good and evil. This calls for some resounding negations.

[39] κατέλαβεν.

environment in which men find themselves.[40] The theme of the perpetual conflict between darkness and light is found throughout it. It is men's condemnation that they loved darkness rather than light (3 : 19). Jesus calls on men to follow Him so that they do not walk in darkness (8 : 12). They are to walk while they have the light, lest darkness "overtake" or "overcome" them (12 : 35, the same verb as here). He came "a light into the world" so that whoever believes on Him "may not abide in the darkness" (12 : 46). Jesus' whole mission was a conflict between the light and the darkness. The verb we are discussing has a rarer, but sufficiently attested meaning, "overcome". It is that that is required here. The light is shining in the darkness. And[41] the darkness was unable to overcome the light. The aorist tense of the verb "overcame" is unexpected. We would have anticipated a present to give a timeless truth: "The light shines in the darkness, and the darkness does not overcome it."[42] The most natural way of taking the aorist, however, is as referring to a single occasion. It may be that we are to understand it of creation, the subject of the present passage. There the light triumphed and not the darkness (and its attendant chaos). Some discern a reference to the fall of man (Gen. 3). Perhaps more likely is a reference to Calvary (so Murray). There the light and the darkness came into bitter and decisive conflict and the darkness could not prevail. Probably in his usual manner John is using an expression which should be taken as true on more than one level.[43]

---

[40] *Cf.* D. W. Baldensperger: "By the term *darkness* we must not understand unbelieving men, but the Satanic world, set against God. This is an allusion to an accepted theological tenet in Judaism: the struggle of the Messias (Logos) against Satan" (cited in Boismard, *op. cit.*, p. 21).

[41] καί is sometimes used, as here, in the sense, "and yet" (which is more properly expressed by καίτοι, a word found only 3 times in the New Testament). It joins two affirmative clauses, but the sense conveyed is adversative.

[42] The aorist could, of course, be a gnomic aorist with much this meaning. Or it could be constative, regarding a prolonged conflict as a completed whole. But a single action seems more probable.

[43] Morton Smith argues for the translation "master" as preserving some of the ambiguity of κατέλαβεν (*JBL*, 64, 1945, pp. 510f.). Temple makes the point that John is "most modern" in that "The evil which for him presents the problem is not only in men's hearts; it is in the whole ordered system of nature. That ordered system is infected; it 'lieth in the evil one' (*1 John* v, 19). St. John might have had all the modern problem of the callousness and cruelty of nature before his mind. Anyhow, his approach is the modern approach. He does not conceive of Nature as characterised by a Wordsworthian perfection, which is only spoilt by fallen mankind".

We have already noticed that the opposition of light and darkness is one of the great themes which John shares with the men of Qumran. Like John the men of the desert community saw the two as locked in mortal struggle. But we should not overlook the fact that for them there is no equivalent of John's past tense here. They looked and longed for the ultimate triumph of light. But they could not rest in a victory already won as John could.[44]

3. THE WORD AND JOHN THE BAPTIST, 1 : 6-8

6 There came a man, sent from God, whose name was John. 7 The same came for witness, that he might bear witness of the light, that all might believe through him. 8 He was not the light, but came that he might bear witness of the light.

It is curious at first sight that there should be this mention of John the Baptist in the Prologue. There is no difficulty about his appearing in the narrative sections, but it is certainly perplexing to find him in this brief introduction to the teaching of the Gospel. It may be that the answer is to be found in the prominence accorded the Baptist by some of his followers.[45] While the Gospels depict him as pointing men to Christ, and as regarding his whole mission as that of a forerunner, it seems that some of his followers

---

[44] *Cf.* F. F. Bruce: "the affinities in vocabulary should not make us overlook the new element in John's use of these terms. When he speaks of the true light, he is not thinking in abstractions; he is not primarily concerned with a body of teaching or a holy community; to him the true light is identical with Jesus Christ, the Word made flesh" (*Second Thoughts on the Dead Sea Scrolls*, London and Grand Rapids, 1956, p. 134).

[45] J. A. T. Robinson scouts the idea that the followers of the Baptist ever formed a distinct sect: "I cannot find a shred of reliable historical evidence for them at the time – that is for the mere existence of disciples of John after his death who were not in some way Christians, let alone for those who were actively anti-Christian" (*NTS*, 4, 1957–58, p. 278; on p. 279, n. 2 he traverses the evidence and finds it unconvincing, though he does not mention the passage from the Clementine Homilies cited in the following note). But quite apart from the evidence of the Clementines, there is the existence of the followers of John mentioned in Acts 18 : 25; 19 : 3. Granted that these were in some sense Christian their existence at all is inexplicable if there was no Baptist "sect". And if there was one, nothing in Robinson's treatment tells against the view that by the time of the Clementines they were hostile to Christians. But with his contention that in the New Testament period there was no such sect actively opposed to Christians we have no quarrel. That is exactly the position taken up by the Evangelists.

did not accept this assessment of their leader. From the beginning some wondered whether he were the Christ (Luke 3 : 15). And as time went by it seems that some of his followers preferred to keep themselves aloof from the Christian movement, regarding John as a more important figure than Jesus ("Just as a man, overcome at the sight of dawn, would not deign to look at the sun"[46]). Some had baptized in John's name as far afield as Ephesus (Acts 19 : 3),[47] and they may have gone farther. The great Apollos is first introduced as one "knowing only the baptism of John" (Acts 18 : 25). Our author does not enter directly into controversy with such people, but he insists more than any of the other Evangelists on the subordinate place of the Baptist. One of the aims of this Gospel plainly was to show how clearly and consistently John had pointed men to Jesus. Apparently the movement associated with the Baptist's name was particularly strong in the region where this Gospel was written. If, as seems probable, the author of the Gospel come from the group originally centred round John his interest in his former teacher would be natural. This interest would not be lessened by the fact that John's was the witness borne to Christ by the last of the prophets of the old covenant.

6 The word rendered "came" is that translated "made" three times in v. 3. While in this verse there is no particular emphasis on the act of creation (we may well accept the translation "came"), yet the use of this word must be held to point a contrast between Jesus and John. Jesus "was" in the beginning. John "came into existence". The contrast is continued when John is described as "a man", for Jesus has already been spoken of as "the Word". But though John's place was a subordinate one it was an important

---

[46] Calvin. J. B. Lightfoot speaks of a new attitude towards Christianity developed by the followers of John the Baptist: "His name is no longer the sign of imperfect appreciation, but the watchword of direct antagonism. John had been set up as a rival Messiah to Jesus" (*St Paul's Epistles to the Colossians and to Philemon*, London, 1876, p. 403). That there were some who came to regard John as the Messiah is attested by the *Clementine Recognitions* (1 : 54, 60). This aroused such hostility from the Christian side that John was even called a false prophet (such appears to be the meaning of *Clementine Homilies*, 2 : 17). Our Evangelist is more balanced. He recognizes both the greatness of John and the superiority of Christ.

[47] It is, of course, just possible that some were baptized in Palestine and later moved to Ephesus. But it is unlikely that the whole company would have done this.

one. While the Evangelist is concerned that John should not be accorded the place that belongs to Jesus he is also concerned that John's true greatness should be seen. John was "sent from God" (*cf.* 1 : 33; 3 : 28).[48] His mission was not of human, but of divine origin. This bold assertion at the very first mention of the Baptist is clear evidence that the Evangelist is not engaging on a campaign of denigration. He fully recognizes the greatness of the fore-runner.[49]

7 From the divine commission we come to the actual work of the Baptist. He came "for witness".[50] Witness is one of the key concepts of this Gospel,[51] and it is quite in accordance with this that right on the threshhold John the Baptist is characterized in terms of witness. This is emphasized, first by drawing attention to the man ("the same", not simply "he"), and then by the twofold reference to witness. John often emphasizes a concept by the simple device of repeating it. He speaks of John as a witness often and only. In the Synoptists John's preaching of repentance and his practice of baptism are noted. In this Gospel his one function is to bear witness to Jesus. We know him as "John the Baptist"

---

[48] ἀπεσταλμένος παρὰ Θεοῦ. The perfect indicates the permanent character of his mission. He continues in the character of a man sent. παρὰ Θεοῦ does not indicate the same close relationship as does πρὸς τὸν Θεόν in v. 1, but too much should not be made of this for Jesus can say that He came παρά the Father (17 : 8). This Gospel makes frequent use of the idea that the Father sent the Son into the world. There may, however, be significance in the fact that the verb is always in the active when it refers to Christ, never passive as here and 3 : 28. For the alleged distinction between ἀποστέλλω and πέμπω see on 3 : 17.

[49] For the greatness of John the Baptist see *SFG*, pp. 59f. The simple description of the man, "whose name was John", invites comment. It has traditionally been taken as pointing to John the Apostle as the author of the Gospel. Who else would introduce the Baptist without qualification as John? Support for this is found in the fact that the Evangelist is usually very careful with names that might be confused as we see from his treatment of Judas (6 : 71; 12 : 4; 13 : 2; 14 : 22; 18 : 2), Mary (11 : 2; 19 : 25), and Joseph (19 : 38). The Synoptists, of course, also sometimes refer to the Baptist simply as John (*e.g.* Matt. 11 : 2; Mark 2 : 18). But when full allowance is made for this, the use of "John" in the Fourth Gospel is sufficiently unusual for the point to have weight.

[50] εἰς μαρτυρίαν signifies "for witness", not "to be a witness". It is the activity rather than the man that receives the stress.

[51] The noun μαρτυρία is found 14 times in this Gospel (not in Matthew, 3 times in Mark, once in Luke), and the verb μαρτυρέω 33 times (once each in Matthew and Luke, not in Mark). In both cases John uses the word far more often than anyone else in the New Testament.

but in this Gospel the references to his baptism are incidental. It is perhaps significant that there is no mention of his baptizing Jesus. But there is repeated reference to his witness; *cf.* 1 : 7, 8, 15, 19, 32, 34; 3 : 26 (*cf.* 3 : 28); 5 : 33. For this Evangelist John's witness is what matters. He came for witness and nothing else that he did can be compared in importance to this.

In this Gospel there are seven who bear witness to Jesus. Each of the three Persons of the Trinity is involved, the Father (5 : 31f., 34, 37; 8 : 18), Christ Himself (8 : 14, 18; *cf.* 3 : 11, 32; 8 : 37), and the Spirit (15 : 26; *cf.* 16 : 14). A fourth and fifth are related thereto, namely the works of Jesus (5 : 36; 10 : 25; *cf.* 14 : 11; 15 : 24), and the sacred Scripture (5 : 39; *cf.* 5 : 45ff.). A sixth witness is John the Baptist, and in the seventh place we notice a variety of human witness consequent on the ministry of Jesus, the disciples (15 : 27; *cf.* 19 : 35; 21 : 24), the Samaritan woman (4 : 39), the multitude (12 : 17). This emphasis on testimony should not be overlooked. There is a legal air about it. Testimony is a serious matter and it is required to substantiate the truth of a matter. It is clear that our author wants us to take what he writes as reliable. He is insistent that there is good evidence for the things he sets down. Witness establishes the truth.

It does more. It commits a man. If I take my stand in the witness box and testify that such-and-such is the truth of the matter I am no longer neutral. I have committed myself. John lets us see that there are those like John the Baptist who have committed themselves by their witness to Christ. But he is also bold enough to think that God has committed Himself. He has borne witness in various ways. He has committed Himself before the world in all that the Son was and did. The men who have borne their witness have committed themselves, but the important thing is the witness of God.[52]

[52] Gabriel Marcel makes much of the commitment aspect of witness, as in *The Philosophy of Existence* (London, 1948), pp. 67–76. He says, for example, "To be a witness is to act as a guarantor. Every testimony is based on a commitment and to be incapable of committing oneself is to be incapable of bearing witness. This is indeed the reason for the preliminary oath which is administered in a law court. By taking the oath I bind myself, I give up the possibility of withdrawing myself, as it were, from what I have said" (*op. cit.*, p. 68). See also his, *The Mystery of Being*, II (London, 1951), ch. VIII. Similarly J. H. Oldham says, "Unless you commit yourself, unless you stake everything on the truth of what you say, you cannot be a witness" (*Life is Commitment*, London, 1953, p. 11).

John's work was to "bear witness of the light". This somewhat indefinite expression does not tell us what he said, nor how or when he said it. We might possibly understand "the light" to denote goodness in general were it not for the previous references to light (vv. 4f.), and for the subsequent avowal that John was not the light. All this makes it certain that by "the light" Christ is meant. The verb "bear witness" incidentally is in the aorist. The meaning is not that John continually witnessed (though that, too, was true), but that he accomplished a finished work. He bore his witness to the Word, and there was nothing more that he could do.

This bearing of witness was not an end in itself. Behind it was the purpose "that all might believe through him". Grammatically "him" might refer either to "the light" or to the subject, "he". The sense of the passage requires the latter. Men are said to believe "in" Christ, not "through" Him. For John, on the other hand, it was a great privilege to be the means of bringing men to the place of faith.[53] "Believe" is not in the continuous tense, and this is perhaps significant. John came to bring men to decide, to make the definitive act of faith.

8 The greatness of the Baptist had, as we have seen, caused some of his followers to entertain exaggerated ideas about him. They appear to have held him to be the Messiah. But the Evangelist vigorously repudiates this. *He*[54] "was not the light".[55] Just as he brings out the true greatness of John so does he make clear his limitations. He goes on to repeat the truth that John came to bear witness. That was the whole reason for his appearance. That was why he was "sent from God". Those who did not see this were misinterpreting his whole mission. There is nothing in the Greek

---

[53] There is a contrast between John's preaching to all that they might believe and the attitude of the men of Qumran. For them, "There must be no admonitions or contention with the men of the pit, for the counsel of the law must be concealed among the men of error" (*DSS*, p. 383).

[54] ἐκεῖνος is used to emphasize the subject. The pronoun is a favourite with John who uses it 70 times, more than any other New Testament writer (Matthew 54 times, Mark 23 times, Luke 33 times, Acts 22 times, Paul 21 times). He uses it significantly often of Christ (10 times), of the Father (6 times) and of the Holy Spirit (5 times). The pronoun is often a way of giving emphasis. Indeed, except when it is used in dialogue it is usually emphatic in this Gospel.

[55] John is ὁ λύχνος, "the lamp" (5 : 35), but he is not τὸ φῶς, "the light".

corresponding to "came". This lends a note of abruptness, even eagerness, to the verse. Taken with the strong adversative, "but",[56] it puts a little more emphasis on the words that follow.[57] The writer cannot get to the words about "witness" quickly enough. There was a singleness of purpose about the Baptist (and about the Evangelist's description of him).

4. THE WORD INCARNATE, 1 : 9-14

9 [1]There was the true light, even the light which lighteth [2]every man, coming into the world. 10 He was in the world, and the world was made through him, and the world knew him not. 11 He came unto [3]his own, and they that were his own received him not. 12 But as many as received him, to them gave he the right to become children of God, even to

---

[56] ἀλλ'. John is very fond of ἀλλά, which he uses 101 times. This is more than in any other book in the New Testament (next is I Corinthians with 72 occurrences).

[57] The ἵνα is usually taken as telic after an ellipsis of "he came" or the like. It has, however, been suggested that this is an example of imperatival ἵνα. For this construction see C. J. Cadoux, *JThS*, XLII, 1941, pp. 165ff.; H. G. Meecham *JThS*, XLIII, 1942, pp. 179f.; A. R. George, *JThS*, XLV, 1944, pp. 56ff.; C. F. D. Moule, *IBNTG*, pp. 144f.; M, I, pp. 178f., III, pp. 94f. (and the literature there cited). Such discussions make it clear that this construction is more widespread than is commonly assumed. But it is questionable whether John lends as much support as Cadoux, for example, claims. Thus if in the present passage ἵνα were imperatival we should translate, "let him bear witness", which is an impossible sense. Cadoux suggests, "he had to bear witness". But this is not an imperative. It sounds more like a construction based on δεῖ. Further, ἵνα occurs in other Johannine passages with no preceding principal verb (1 : 22; 9 : 3, 36; 13 : 18; 14 : 30f.; 15 : 24f.; 18 : 8f., 31f.; 19 : 24). In some of these the imperatival sense is quite impossible, and in none of them does it yield a better sense than the supposition of an ellipsis. Sometimes, as here, a verb may readily be supplied from the context. Sometimes no verb in the context is suitable (*e.g.* 13 : 18; 15 : 24f.). It may be that John uses the construction as a way of hinting at the divine purpose which he sees working out in each of the happenings where this construction occurs. The telic force in ἵνα would be favourable to such a significance. John incidentally is very fond of constructions with ἵνα. The word occurs in this Gospel 147 times, which is far and away the highest total in any New Testament book. Next is Mark with 65 times, while Matthew and Luke have it 41 times and 46 times respectively.

them that believe on his name: 13 who were ⁴born, not of
⁵blood, nor of the will of the flesh, nor of the will of man,
but of God. 14 And the Word became flesh, and ⁶dwelt
among us (and we beheld his glory, glory as of ⁷the only
begotten from the Father), full of grace and truth.

¹ Or, *the true light, which lighteth every man, was coming* ²Or, *every man as
he cometh* ³ Gr. *his own things.* ⁴ Or, *begotten* ⁵ Gr. *bloods.* ⁶ Gr. *tabernacled.*
⁷ Or, *an only begotten from a father* Comp. Heb. 11.17.

Attention is now fastened on the incarnation. Two points are
specially emphasized. The one is the astonishing fact that the
Word of God, true God as He is, yet took upon Him man's nature.
The other is the even more astonishing fact that when He did
so men would have nothing to do with Him. John is concerned
that we should miss neither the good news of the incarnation of
God, nor the tragedy of man's rejection of God.
9 The Greek of this verse is somewhat awkward, as the verb
"was" appears to have no subject. We could overcome this by
taking "the true light" as the subject, and reading the sentence
as in ARV mg., "The true light, which lighteth every man, was
coming...." The objection to this is that the two constituent parts
of the verb "was coming" would then be separated by a relative
clause, a difficult if not impossible construction.[58] It is better to
understand the subject from the preceding verses: "(That light)
was the true light...." But there is another problem, namely
whether we should take "coming into the world" with "man"[59]
or with "light". In the former case the meaning might be "every
man at the time of his birth". Or we could take the whole expression "every man that cometh into the world" to mean simply
"all men" (the Rabbis used the expression with just this meaning[60]).
But the sense of the whole passage is against such meanings. And

---

[58] There is a note on the construction in Abbott, 2277. John does often
separate participles from ἦν (*cf.* v. 28), and it may be that we should take
ἐρχόμενον with ἦν accordingly. But it will probably be in the sense, "That
was the true light ... coming. ..."
[59] No argument should be based on the occurrence of ἄνθρωπον, for John
uses the redundant ἄνθρωπος quite often (*cf.* 2 : 10; 3 : 1, 27 *etc.*).
[60] There is an interesting parallel to the present passage, namely, "Thou
givest light ... to all who enter into the world" (Lev. Rab. XXXI. 6; Soncino
edn., p. 401). Test. Lev. 14 : 4 speaks of the Law as given "to lighten every
man".

it is against Johannine custom. John does not normally speak of men at large as "coming into the world". This is a description he reserves for Christ. Moreover this verse stands at the head of a section dealing with the incarnation, where a statement about the incarnation rather than one about men in general seems required. I take the words to apply accordingly to "the light".[61] The awkwardness of the verse appears to arise from the fact that John is saying two things and he has run them together: "He was the true light", and further, He was "coming into the world". Fortunately our uncertainty about the construction does not extend to the sense. The Evangelist is speaking about the Word as "the true light", and leading on from that, about the illumination He gives to men. Other lights "were flickers of the truth; some were faint glimpses of reality; some were will o' the wisps which men followed, and which led men out into the dark and left them there" (Barclay). But Christ is the genuine light. He is the light that brings real illumination to men. There is nothing unreal or shadowy about the light which is Christ.[62]

His giving light "to every man"[63] is not closely defined. There

---

[61] The participle might be held to mean, "by coming into the world". This, however, does not seem to be the significance of the incarnation in John, so should be rejected. If the present tense, $\dot{\varepsilon}\varrho\chi\acute{o}\mu\varepsilon\nu o\nu$, be held to be continuous the meaning will be that the light continuously came in many ways (cf. Westcott: "He came in type and prophecy and judgement"), but especially in the incarnation. In 6 : 33, 50 we read similarly of a continuous coming of Christ ($\dot{o}$ $\varkappa\alpha\tau\alpha\beta\alpha\acute{\iota}\nu\omega\nu$), while in 6 : 51, 58, the reference to the single coming in the incarnation is plain ($\dot{o}$ $\varkappa\alpha\tau\alpha\beta\acute{a}\varsigma$).

[62] The word for "true" is $\dot{a}\lambda\eta\theta\iota\nu\acute{o}\varsigma$, which Bernard distinguishes from $\dot{a}\lambda\eta\theta\acute{\eta}\varsigma$ "as the genuine from the true" (though he admits that the distinction is not always easy). This leads to comments like that of Godet: "It designates the fact as the adequate realization of the idea. It contrasts, therefore, not the true with the false, but the normal appearance with the imperfect realization." Barrett thinks that in this Gospel $\dot{a}\lambda\eta\theta\acute{\eta}\varsigma$ is applied to opinions and statements and those who hold them, whereas $\dot{a}\lambda\eta\theta\iota\nu\acute{o}\varsigma$ means "real", "genuine", "authentic". G. D. Kilpatrick, however, has shown that John's use of $\dot{a}\lambda\eta\theta\iota\nu\acute{o}\varsigma$ is probably always attributive and of $\dot{a}\lambda\eta\theta\acute{\eta}\varsigma$ predicative (BT, 11, 1960, pp. 174f.; the doubt arises because of textual variants). Kilpatrick's position seems to be the right one. John's distinction between the two words in this case is purely grammatical, and we should not look for any essential difference in meaning. Both words cover various shades of meaning including "true" and "genuine". AG gives both meanings for both words.

[63] The use of the singular, $\pi\acute{a}\nu\tau\alpha$ $\ddot{a}\nu\theta\varrho\omega\pi o\nu$, rather than the plural, $\pi\acute{a}\nu\tau\alpha\varsigma$, may be meant to indicate every man individually rather than all men in the mass.

is a sense in which the Word gives light only to those who believe, for those who do not believe in Him are yet in darkness (3 : 19f.). But, as James tells us, "Every good gift and every perfect gift is from above" (Jas. 1 : 17). There is a general illumination of mankind. It is the common teaching of the New Testament writers that God has revealed something of Himself to all men (Rom. 1 : 20), sufficient at least for them to be blameworthy when they take the wrong way instead of the right way.[64] John attributes this general illumination to the activity of the Word. For "world" see Additional Note B, pp. 126ff.

10 John has a way of emphasizing a word by the simplest of all devices, repetition. He does this here. Three times he repeats the word "world" and each time it comes first in its clause. Clearly John wishes to fasten attention on it. He says three things. First, the light (or the Word) was "in the world". The verb conveys the thought of continuity. He did not simply pay a fleeting visit, but was there continuously. The second point is a reminder that the world owes its very existence to the Word. "The world was made through him" employs the same vocabulary and construction as the similar words in v. 3 (where see note). The third point deals with the rejection of the Word by the world, and this rejection is heightened by the way John leads up to it. The Word was in the world continuously, that world that He had made. And yet the world did not know Him.[65] Notice the subtle shift in meaning of the word "world". On the first two occasions it refers to the earth together with all that is in it, including man. But on this third occasion it signifies men at large, more partic-

---

[64] Calvin says that men "bear the distinction between right and wrong engraven in their conscience. Thus there is no man to whom some awareness of the eternal light does not penetrate." Strachan denies that the words mean that "in every man, irrespective of race or religion, there is some knowledge of God, however faint." He thinks the words have much the same sense as 3 : 21 and that John has in mind the effect of the message. Thus "the idea of Judgment is prominent".

[65] The pronoun αὐτόν is masculine and means "Him". But grammatically it refers to φῶς and should be neuter. It is possible that we are to understand the real subject as the Λόγος now regarded in His aspect of light. Or John may already be thinking of the incarnate Christ. Both, of course, could be true. Dodd notices the point and discusses some of its implications (*IFG*, pp. 268ff.).

ularly those men who came into contact with Jesus of Nazareth. See further Additional Note B, pp. 126ff.

"Knew[66] him not" we might render, "did not come to know him", "did not recognize him". More than intellectual knowledge is in mind. There is also the thought of failing to know intimately, to know and love as a friend, to be in right relation. The tense is aorist, which perhaps indicates a single action. The world missed its great opportunity. It did not come to know the Word when the Word was in its very midst. The world did not know Him. The world never does. The world's characteristic reaction is that of indifference.

11 With vivid touches John highlights the tragedy of the rejection.[67] We might translate the opening words, "he came home".[68] It is the exact expression used of the beloved disciple when, in response to Jesus' word from the cross, he took Mary "unto his own home" (19 : 27; cf. 16 : 32). When the Word came to this world He did not come as an alien. He came home. Moreover, He came to Israel. Had He come to some other nation it would have been bad enough, but Israel was peculiarly God's own people. The Word did not go where He could not have expected to be known. He came home, where the people ought to have known Him.

And it was the home folk, "they that were his own",[69] that "received him not". This designation brings the rejectors into special relation with the Rejected. They should have known better. We must see here a reference to the Jewish nation. They

---

[66] The verb is γινώσκω. Some suggest that this verb signifies knowledge acquired by effort and attention, whereas οἶδα would denote rather an intuitive knowledge. It is more than doubtful whether this distinction can be shown to hold in this Gospel. See further on 2 : 24.

[67] In a well known passage Augustine speaks of having read in the writings of the Platonists something equivalent to the teaching of the Prologue up to this point. "But I did not read in those books that *He came unto His own, and His own received Him not*" (*Confessions*, vii. 9). Here is the distinctively Christian note, that which sets the gospel apart from the writings of the philosophers.

[68] The Greek is εἰς τὰ ἴδια ἦλθεν. W. F. Howard accepts this meaning, but adds, "there is also warrant for translating it 'his own possession'" (*IB*). Luther distinguishes between the coming of Christ into the world mentioned earlier in the Prologue, and this coming which he calls "His real advent". He understands it to refer to His entering on His public ministry at His baptism (*op. cit.*, p. 77).

[69] οἱ ἴδιοι. Note the change from and the link with εἰς τὰ ἴδια.

had enjoyed many advantages, more particularly the revelation made known to them "by divers portions and in divers manners" (Heb. 1 : 1). This time John does not say that they did not know Him, but that they did not receive Him. The verb may be used of taking a person to oneself in intimate fellowship. It is used in this way of Joseph taking Mary as his wife (Matt. 1 : 20, 24), and of Christ taking believers to Himself in heaven (14 : 3). This was the kind of welcome that His own people ought to have given Him when He went home. But they "received him not". The aorist tense here, as in the previous verse points to the decisive act of rejection.[70] It fastens our attention on the crisis rather than the continuing result.

In passing we may notice that this is an excellent example of John's emphasis on the fact of the incarnation. He is not content with a series of "mythological" antagonisms, with setting "light" over against "darkness", and the rest. He writes in personal terms and in concrete terms.

12 John does not wish to leave the impression (which might be gained from v. 11) that nobody responded to the Word. The bulk of the people did not respond, but there were some who did. John now turns his attention to them. The unusual grammatical construction in the Greek is reproduced in ARV, where "as many as received him" does not fit smoothly into the sentence.[71] This has the effect of setting them over against the rejectors of the last two verses and of putting a certain emphasis on those who received the Lord. To them did the Word give "the right"

---

[70] Some, *e.g.* Plummer, distinguish between the meaning of παρέλαβεν here and ἔλαβον in the next verse. The former verb means "to take from the hand of another, accept what is *offered*", he says, whereas the latter "denotes the *spontaneous* acceptance of *individuals*, Jews or Gentiles." Christ was offered to the Jewish nation, but they did not avail themselves of the offer. Moffatt makes another distinction with his renderings, "welcome" in v. 11 and "accepted" in v. 12. But Moulton denies any distinction, taking this to be an example of "a classical idiom by which the preposition in a compound is omitted, without weakening the sense, when the verb is repeated" (M, I, p. 115). In view of John's penchant for using synonyms with no appreciable difference of meaning (see on 3 : 5, and *SFG*, pp. 293-319), it would not be wise to build much on a difference of meaning here.

[71] This is the first of twenty-seven examples cited by Burney of the use of the *casus pendens* followed by a pronoun, which he regards as evidence of a Semitic origin (*AO*, pp. 64f.). The construction is found in many languages,

or "the authority" to become God's children. There are three important words here. (i) "Gave". The end of the story is not the tragedy of rejection, but the *grace* of acceptance. There were men to whom He *gave* the gift that they should receive the Word and become children of God. (ii) "The right".[72] John does not speak of power, as in the sense of power over sin (though in fact they receive that, too). His thought is that of status.[73] They have received full authority to this exalted title. He does not say "to be" but "to become". Not only is there a status, but there is a change of status. Elsewhere it is spoken of as passing from death to life (5 : 24). (iii) "Children". John refers to them as "children" rather than as "sons" of God. The term he uses is one which draws attention to community of nature (*cf*. II Pet. 1 : 4, "that . . . ye may become partakers of the divine nature"), rather than one which would stress the rights and privileges of sonship.[74] While the New Testament sees God as the Father of all men, paradoxically it does not think of all men as sons of God. God's attitude to all men is that of a Father. All are His sons in the sense that He made them, and that He provides for them. But men are His sons in the full sense only as they respond to what He does for them in Christ. When they receive the Word they are born again (ch. 3) into the heavenly family. It is only in this way that they are really God's "children".

The "children" then are those who believe. In the opening part of the verse John has spoken of receiving Him, now as believing

---

including Greek, so that it is not its occurrence, but its frequency that is significant. Thus Burney found twenty-one examples only in the whole range of the Synoptic Gospels, so that John does use the construction significantly often. Black points out that after the Prologue most are in sayings of Jesus, and all are in direct speech (*AA*, p. 35; it may be asked whether this is in fact the case with 3 : 32). This points to Aramaic behind the sayings in this Gospel.

[72] ἐξουσίαν.

[73] "Authorization, an imparted title to a new status, rather than an inherent ability, is the root meaning of the word" (*IB*).

[74] The term John uses is τέκνα. He never uses υἱός of men's sonship to God, but keeps this term for Christ. He alone has full rights to what the term denotes. The nearest John gets to it is when he refers to men becoming υἱοί φωτός (12 : 36). By contrast, Paul speaks of men as both υἱοί and τέκνα. He uses the former term to refer to the rights Christ confers on those adopted into the heavenly family, rather than the community of nature they share.

on His name.[75] These are different ways of looking at the same spiritual change wherein a man ceases to rely on his own merits and achievements and puts his trust in Christ instead. Like the opening words of the verse, these are linked with the construction rather loosely. The effect is to give them a certain emphasis. That faith is the way is important. John does not wish his readers to miss it. Notice that they are to believe "on his name". The "name" meant much more to people of antiquity than it does to us. For us it is a mere appellative, a convenient label whereby we distinguish one person from another. We ask, "What's in a name?" and answer (with Shakespeare), "that which we call a rose by any other name would smell as sweet." The name for us is a matter of indifference. Not so in the ancient world. For men then it stood for the whole personality. When, for example, the Psalmist spoke of loving the name of God (Ps. 5 : 11), or when he prayed, "The name of the God of Jacob set thee up on high" (Ps. 20 : 1), he did not have in mind simply the uttering of the name. He was thinking of all that "God" means. The name in some way expressed the whole person.[76] To believe "on the name" of the Word, then, means to trust the person of the Word. It is to believe in Him as He is. It is to believe that God is the God we see revealed in the Word and to put our trust in that God. This is more than simple credence. It is not believing that what He says is true, but trusting Him as a person. It is believing "in" or "on" Him. The same Greek expression as is used here is found in the papyri in connection with accounts *etc.*, and it seems to be linked with

---

[75] The expression is τοῖς πιστεύουσιν εἰς τὸ ὄνομα αὐτοῦ. Notice that while John uses the verb πιστεύω 98 times (as against Matthew 11 times, Mark 14 times, Luke 9 times, Acts 37 times, Paul 54 times) he never uses the noun πίστις. This may, as some think, be due in part to the use made of the noun by heretical thinkers. But it is clear that he thought of faith as an activity, as something that men do. His favourite construction is to follow the verb with εἰς and the accusative (36 times). Of this W. Turner writes, "The sense must be that the believer throws himself upon his Lord in loving, self-abandoning faith and trust" (*ExT*, LXIV, 1952–53, p. 51). By contrast the simple dative means believing that what someone says is true. But in the last resort if one believes God one acts on that belief, so probably there is not much difference in ultimate meaning. See further Additional Note E, pp. 335ff.

[76] For the use of "the name" in antiquity see the note by S. New in *The Beginnings of Christianity*, ed. F. J. Foakes Jackson and K. Lake, V (London, 1933), pp. 121–40.

the idea of possession.[77] If the New Testament retains anything of this usage the expression will convey the additional thought that when we believe we yield ourselves up to be possessed by Him in whom we believe.

13 We move on to the way men enter the heavenly family. In place of the plural "who were born" (read by all Greek MSS and the great majority of versions and citations), which will refer to the believers mentioned in the previous verse, a few Latin authorities read "who was born", thus taking the words to refer to the Virgin Birth.[78] The attestation of the plural is so overwhelming that it should surely be accepted. Yet it is not at all unlikely that John of set purpose uses words which will conjure up associations of the Virgin Birth, as Temple and Hoskyns (to name no others) hold. He will thus remind his readers that their spiritual existence depends on what Christ has done for them.

The origin of the "children of God" is described three times negatively and once positively. They are "not of bloods". The plural is curious, as is the use of "blood" at all in this connection. But there was an idea in antiquity that birth took place as the result of the action of blood. Thus in the *Wisdom of Solomon* we read, "in the womb of a mother I was molded into flesh, within the period of ten months, compacted with blood, from the seed

---

[77] See MM *sub* ὄνομα (5). They think that the use of this expression in connection with baptism signifies "baptized into the possession of".

[78] The singular is read by the Old Latin MS *b*, and the verb though not the pronoun appears to be singular in syr[c]. There is patristic support, notably from Irenaeus (Latin translation) and Tertullian. The latter vigorously defends the singular (*de carn. Chr.*, 19), and regards the plural as an invention of the heretics. For Irenaeus see *Adv. Haer.* III. 16. 2. Justin can say, "His blood did not spring from the seed of man, but from the will of God" (*Dial. Try.*, 63), which may possibly imply this reading. In modern times the singular is accepted by Burney, Torrey, Boismard, and others (see the list in Boismard, *op. cit.*, p. 39, n. 1). There are good notes in Hoskyns, pp. 163–6, and Boismard, *op. cit.*, pp. 35–45. Torrey regards the usual text as giving us "an impossible saying". He thinks that the past tense of the verb rules out any possibility of the saying being a promise of the new birth, and goes on: "Only one being could be described in the phrases used here" (*Our Translated Gospels*, London, n.d., pp. 151–3). But we should not overlook MacGregor's caution, "the words in question would exclude the idea of human mother no less than of human father (*cf.* Heb. 7 : 3)". We should also bear in mind that John does not elsewhere speak of the virgin birth, whereas he does refer to regeneration (ch. 3; it is an important topic in 1 John, see 2 : 29; 3 : 9; 4 : 7; 5 : 1, 4, 18).

of a man and the pleasure of marriage" (Wis. 7 : 1f.). The plural here may point to the action of both parents, or it may refer to blood as made up of many drops.[79] "Nor of the will[80] of the flesh" points to sexual desire, though we should bear in mind that John does not use the term "flesh" in the evil sense which is common in Paul. For him it denotes man's bodily nature in its weakness rather than in its sinfulness. "The will of the flesh" is that desire that arises out of man's bodily constitution. "Nor of the will of man" may be meant to denote much the same thing. The word for "man" is not that used in v. 6, but one which often denotes "husband".[81] We could translate here, "of the will of a husband". Or the expression may be taken more generally, "nor of any human volition whatever". The piling up of these expressions is to be understood in the light of Jewish pride of race. The Jews held that because of the "Fathers", *i.e.* their great ancestors, God would be favourable to them. John emphatically repudiates any such idea. Nothing human, however great or excellent, can bring about the birth of which he speaks.

Over against this[82] John sets the way men are born into the heavenly family. The new birth is always sheer miracle. All human initiative is ruled out.[83] Men are born "of God". They can be born in no other way. John uses bold imagery here, for his word "are born" is the verb commonly used of the action of the male parent in begetting children (see further on 3 : 3).[84]

---

[79] Hoskyns thinks that the writer could not say that "the Christians were not born of blood (singular), because their birth does in fact depend upon a death which later he describes as involving the outpouring of blood (xix. 34)."

[80] John is rather fond of the word θέλημα which he uses 11 times (more than any other New Testament book). Here there is an implicit reference to the will of God, and such a reference, implicit or explicit, is found in every passage where the word occurs. The frequency with which John uses the term is indicative of his deep interest in the way God's will is wrought out.

[81] ἀνδρός.

[82] Note the strong adversative ἀλλ'.

[83] Lucetta Mowry sees a reference throughout this section to the Qumran idea of two groups of men, but with a different basis of division. Here "one recalls the Essene ceremonies when men were elevated or lowered in rank according to their ethical achievements during the past year. But John maintains that one must be transformed into the other order by a power outside the self. The divine spirit transforms men" (*BA*, XVII, Dec. 1954, p. 92).

[84] On the basis of patristic citations Boismard reconstructs the text of vv. 12, 13 to read,

14 Now comes the most concise statement of the incarnation. "The Word" (see on v. 1, and Additional Note A, pp. 115ff.) refers to Him who is nothing less than God. "Became" is in the aorist tense, and indicates action at a point of time. "Flesh" is a strong, almost a crude way of referring to human nature. John does not say, "the Word became man", nor "the Word took a body". He chooses that form of expression which puts what he wants to say most bluntly. It seems probable that he was confronted by opponents of a Docetic type, men who were ready to think of Jesus of Nazareth as the Christ of God, but who denied the reality of His humanity. They thought of Him as appearing only to move among men. Since God could not, on their premises, defile Himself by real contact with mankind, the whole life of Jesus must be appearance only. John deliberately chooses his strong term to leave no room for such fancies. He is clear on the deity of the Word. But he is just as clear on the genuineness of His humanity.[85]

Notice that this is the first time in the Gospel that John indicates that the Word and Jesus are to be taken as the same. Up till this point it would have been quite possible for the reader to have taken "the Word" to refer to some supreme cosmic principle or the like. But in one short, shattering expression John unveils the great idea at the heart of Christianity that the very Word of God took flesh for man's salvation.

The Word "dwelt among us". Properly the verb signifies "to

    "All those who received him,
      He gave them to become children of God,
      He whom *(sic)* neither of flesh nor of blood
      But of God was begotten" (*op. cit.*, p. 35).
The value of quotations in the Fathers is not to be denied, but I do not see that they justify us in rejecting the testimony of the MSS in this case.
[85] Laurence Housman brings out something of the wonder of it all:
    "Light looked down and beheld Darkness.
    'Thither will I go,' said Light.
    Peace looked down and beheld War.
    'Thither will I go,' said Peace.
    Love looked down and beheld Hatred.
    'Thither will I go,' said Love.
      So came Light and shone.
      So came Peace and gave rest.
      So came Love and brought life.
    And the Word was made flesh and dwelt among us."

pitch one's tent". It may thus denote a temporary visit (Moffatt, "tarried among us"). But this cannot be insisted upon, and any exegesis which deduces a limited incarnation from the fact that the Word "tabernacled" among men is in error. The word had come to be used in a conventional fashion of settling down permanently in a place (*e.g.* Rev. 12 : 12). But the word might, at least in Jewish ears, arouse other associations. The place of worship during the wanderings of Israel in the wilderness, the place where God had vouchsafed His presence was "the Tabernacle". The noun corresponds to the verb used here. That John means us to recall God's presence in the tabernacle in the wilderness seems clear from the immediate reference to "glory",[86] for glory was associated with the tabernacle. When, for example, it was first set up, "the glory of Jehovah filled the tabernacle. And Moses was not able to enter into the tent of meeting, because the cloud abode thereon, and the glory of Jehovah filled the tabernacle" (Exod. 40 : 34f.). It is possible that we should see other symbolism here also. There seems no doubt but that John saw Jesus as a new and greater Moses, and a number of students have seen evidence for this here.[87] It is possible that the Sinai theophany or other Old Testament incident may be in mind. But certainly the glory associated with

---

[86] There is a valuable note on glory in Strachan, pp. 103-6. Two notable comments are, "When the Evangelist says *We beheld his glory*, he is really saying that the final purpose of God is already achieved in the historical person Jesus", and, "The 'glorifying' of Jesus always means His dying" (p. 106). See also the articles by Paula von Mirtow in *Theology*, XLIX, 1946, pp. 336–40, 359–65. See also on δοξάζω on 7 : 39 below.

[87] Many see a reference to the Sinai theophany rather than to the setting of the tabernacle. The points of contact with Exod. 33 are especially numerous:

Exodus 33		John 1	
7	Now Moses used to take the tabernacle		
9	the pillar of cloud (the Shekinah) descended	14	the Word became flesh and tabernacled among us
10	all the people saw the pillar of cloud		we beheld his glory.
11	Jehovah spake unto Moses face to face	17	the law was given through Moses
20	thou canst not see my face	18	No man hath seen God at any time
23	thou shalt see my back; but my face shall not be seen		the only begotten Son . . . hath declared him.

All this strengthens the view that John wants us to see Jesus as the new and greater Moses.

the tabernacle will be part of John's meaning. The glory resulting from the immediate presence of the Lord is referred to quite often in Jewish writings. It came to be linked with the *Shekinah*, a word which means "dwelling" *i.e.* God's dwelling among His people. In the Targums this term was sometimes substituted for the divine name. There were various ways in which the Jews used the term, and it is likely that John has more than one of them in mind. As A. M. Ramsey says, "We are reminded both of the tabernacle in the wilderness, and of the prophetic imagery of Yahweh tabernacling in the midst of His people, and of the Shekinah which He causes to dwell among them... The place of His dwelling is the *flesh* of Jesus." He goes on to bring out the force of the present passage by saying, "*All* the ways of tabernacling of God in Israel had been transitory or incomplete: *all* are fulfilled and superseded by the Word-made-flesh and dwelling among us."[88] That is the great point. What had been hinted at and even realized in a dim, imperfect fashion earlier was perfectly fulfilled in the Word made flesh.

That John had in mind the *Shekinah* and the glory that was associated with it seems further indicated by the express statement that the glory was "glory as of the only begotten from the Father".[89] The verb "beheld" is invariably used in John (as, for that matter, in the whole New Testament) of seeing with the bodily eye. It is not used of visions.[90] John is speaking of that glory that was seen in the literal, physical Jesus of Nazareth. As He came in lowliness we have an example of the paradox that John uses so

---

[88] *The Glory of God and the Transfiguration of Christ* (London, 1949), pp. 59f. So also W. Nicholls, "By the play on *skene, eskenosen*, St. John implies that Christ as the Word made flesh was the true *Shekinah*, the true presence of God with men" (*Jacob's Ladder*, London, 1958, p. 19).

[89] Yet against this we should note Barrett's two points that *Shekinah* means not the glory of God, but the presence of God, and that σκηνόω and its compounds are not regularly used to render שכן.

[90] D. E. Holwerda emphasizes this: "The 'we' of 1 : 14 does not refer to the 'Apostolic Church' (Barrett, *Comm.*) or to believers in general, both pre- and post-resurrection (Bultmann, *Comm.*). The 'we' must be restricted to those who saw Jesus' σκηνοῦν. It is true, as Bultmann says, that not all who were eyewitnesses of Jesus saw His glory and that, therefore, θεάομαι refers to a seeing in faith. But this gives no cause for extending this seeing to all believers. Every believer sees Jesus in faith, but he does not see the earthly *(σκηνοῦν)* Jesus" *(The Holy Spirit and Eschatology in the Gospel of John*, Kampen, 1959, p. 3, n. 8).

forcefully later in the Gospel, that the true glory is to be seen, not in outward splendour, but in the lowliness with which the Son of God lived for men and suffered for them. John thinks, it is true, that the miracles showed the glory of Christ (2 : 11; 11 : 4, 40). But in a deeper sense it is the cross of shame that manifests the true glory (12 : 23f.; 13 : 31). The repetition of the word "glory" emphasizes its reality. John will not have us misled by appearances. The true glory was there, in the earthly life of the Word.[91] And it was seen.[92]

We should not read too much into "only begotten". To English ears this sounds like a metaphysical relationship, but the Greek term means no more than "only", "unique".[93] It is used, for example, of the widow of Nain's "only" son (Luke 7 : 12; cf. also Luke 9 : 38). It is used also of Jairus's "only" daughter (Luke 8 : 42). Perhaps even more instructive is the use of the term with reference to Isaac (Heb. 11 : 17), for Isaac was not Abraham's only son. But he was "unique". He was the only son given to Abraham by God's promise. Used here, though the word does not necessarily indicate a metaphysical relationship, it does at the least show that Jesus is God's Son in a unique way. No other is or can be the Son of God as He is. The unique character of the relationship between the Father[94] and the Son is one of the great

---

[91] C. J. Wright comments: "Whatever awakens us to the reality of the presence of God is a manifestation of the Divine glory. *Tintern Abbey* was this to Wordsworth. *The Thames* was this to Francis Thompson. The *'flower in the crannied wall'* was this to Tennyson." All this is doubtless true, but it is misleading to see in it a parallel to John's thought. For him Jesus was the unique embodiment of the glory of God. Because of His character as the Word we see in Him the divine glory, and we see it nowhere else. See further on 3 : 14.

[92] All this has implications for Christian service. As C. H. Dodd reminds us, "Because the Lord is King, and His claim upon all His creatures is absolute, the word of God is first of all a call or command. Christ as λόγος is God's call to us, His command laid upon us . . . Unless our worship includes this element of whole-hearted allegiance, it has not reckoned with the full gravity of the statement: 'the *Word* became flesh' " (*Studies in the Fourth Gospel*, ed. F. L. Cross, London, 1957, p. 21).

[93] It should not be overlooked that μονογενής is derived from γίνομαι not γεννάω (one ν, not two). Etymologically it is not connected with begetting. See further the note by D. Moody, *BT*, 10, 1959, pp. 145-7.

[94] John makes "Father" the characteristic word for God, as may be seen by the fact that he uses the term more than twice as often as anyone else and almost entirely of God. The figures for the Gospels are Matthew 64 times, Mark 18 times, Luke 56 times, John 137 times. Of John's total of 137 no less than 122 refer to God.

themes of this Gospel. What John here briefly indicates in one word he subsequently develops powerfully. From this point on, as R. H. Lightfoot notes, "St. John leaves behind him the use of the word Logos, in order henceforth, throughout the book, to use not only the historical name 'Jesus', but also the more personal terms of 'Father' and 'Son'."

There is a small problem of knowing with what we should connect the expression "full of grace and truth". ARV is probably correct in putting "and we beheld . . . the Father" in parentheses, and taking it with "the Word". But many of the early Fathers understood it to qualify "glory", and some commentators (*e.g.* MacGregor) take it that way still. Others again think it goes with "the only begotten".[95] The problem is one of Greek grammar, and not of meaning, for on any showing it is the incarnate Word who is full of grace and truth. "Grace" is one of the great Christian words, and it is a minor mystery that John uses it three times in the Prologue and not again throughout his Gospel. The word basically denotes "that which causes joy", and so "winsomeness". It comes to signify "good-will", "kindness", and the like, often with the notion that the favor shown is undeserved. In the Christian understanding of things grace is especially seen in that God has provided for man's spiritual need in sending His Son to be man's Saviour. From this we get the thought of the good gifts that God bestows on those who are saved, and finally that of the attitude of thankfulness that men ought to have to God for all His goodness to them. Nowhere do we see more clearly what the grace of God means than in the Word made flesh.

With this John links "truth". This is another important Johannine word. It is found twenty-five times in John, so that clearly it is a topic in which he is deeply interested. We usually understand truth simply as the opposite of falsehood, and John may use the term in much this way (*e.g.* 8 : 45). But for him the term is of wider meaning. Like "life" and "light", with which we were dealing earlier, truth is closely linked with Jesus. He could even say, "I am . . . the truth" (14 : 6). See Additional Note D (pp. 293ff.) for the richness of this Johannine concept. It is plain that for John

---

[95] If πλήρης is rightly regarded as masculine and nominative it must go with λόγος. But the word is often treated as indeclinable, in which case it could agree with either δόξαν or μονογενοῦς. John does not use the adjective elsewhere, so we are left to the general probabilities.

truth is many-sided and many-splendoured. When he speaks of the incarnate Word as full of grace and truth he is pointing us to the fact that truth and the complete reliability of God are bound up with one another.[96] Truth as he sees it is not basically something that can be known apart from God. The Word is the revelation of truth as well as of grace. Grace taken by itself may have given men an unbalanced picture. Not only is God the God of grace. He is that, but He is also the God who demands of men "truth in the inward parts" (Ps. 51 : 6). Men must "do" the truth (3 : 21).[97]

5. THE WORD'S SURPASSING EXCELLENCE, 1 : 15–18

15 John beareth witness of him, and crieth, saying, [1]This was he of whom I said, He that cometh after me is become before me: for he was [2]before me. 16 For of his fulness we all received, and [3]grace for grace. 17 For the law was given through Moses; grace and truth came through Jesus Christ. 18 No man hath seen God at any time; [4]the only begotten Son, who is in the bosom of the Father, he hath declared him.

[1] Some ancient authorities read *(this was he that said)*. [2] Gr. *first in regard of me.* [3] Or, *grace upon grace* [4] Many very ancient authorities read *God only begotten.*

The Prologue concludes with a little section underlining the uniqueness of Christ. First we are reminded of His superiority to the Baptist, then that He supplies all the need of His people. He is shown to surpass Moses by supplying grace and truth instead of the Law. The Prologue concludes with the point that He is the one revealer of the God whom no man has seen.

15 The use of the present tense indicates the continuance of the witness of John. The Evangelist still hears his voice.[98] The

---

[96] He is probably also pointing to the frequent conjunction of *hesedh* and *'emeth* in the Old Testament (*cf.*, *e.g.*, Exod. 34 : 6).

[97] The four concepts "mercy", "dwell", "grace" and "truth" which we meet here are found together also in Ps. 85 : 9f.

[98] The perfect κέκραγεν is used in the sense of the present, as Moulton has shown (M, I, p. 147; so also E. de W. Burton, *Moods*, p. 39). Abbott (2479) suggests that one reason for the use of this tense and not the aorist is that the latter tense is used several times of Christ's preaching (7 : 28, 37; 12 : 44). This may be so, but here the primary reason surely is that the Evangelist thinks of the Baptist's voice as still sounding.

report of John's words is not without its difficulties. We should have expected "This *is* he" (as in v. 30, and as Rieu actually renders here). The use of "was" may indicate that the Baptist had spoken of Jesus before and be pointing back to that occasion. More probably it is a way of referring to the continuing existence of the Word. Throughout the Prologue the present tense is never used of the Word, with but one exception, the "shineth" of v. 5.[99] The continuous imperfect is used of Him again and again (vv. 1, 2, 4, 9, 10), a way of speaking which puts some stress on His continuing existence.

In the second half of the verse there is a change in the sphere of reference of the prepositions from that of time to that of importance. "He that cometh after me" refers to the fact that John's ministry preceded that of Jesus in point of time.[100] "Is become before me" indicates that notwithstanding this Christ's ministry was first in point of importance. This was a noteworthy statement for in antiquity it was widely held that chronological priority meant superiority.[101] Men were humble about their own generation, and really thought that their fathers were wiser then they –

---

[99]   In v. 4 the present, $\dot{\epsilon}\sigma\tau\iota\nu$, is read by אD syr^c sa, some Old Latin MSS, and a few other authorities. Most editors and commentators, however, agree that this is a correction of $\ddot{\eta}\nu$, and not the true text. An exception is Boismard, who not only accepts the present, but alters the next verb to the present also (without any MS support) because "it is clear that the second verb 'to be' should be in the same tense as the first" (*op. cit.*, p. 13). But this is an argument that cuts both ways.

[100]   It is possible, however, to take the words differently. $\dot{o}\pi\dot{\iota}\sigma\omega$ in the New Testament is used much more often of place than of time. In particular $\ddot{\epsilon}\varrho\chi o\mu\alpha\iota\ \dot{o}\pi\dot{\iota}\sigma\omega\ \tau\iota\nu\dot{o}\varsigma$ is used of following someone, *i.e.* of becoming or being a disciple (*e.g.* Mark 8 : 34). The expression here could be taken to mean, "A follower of mine has taken precedence of me, for he (always) was before me, my superior."

[101]   Thus O. Cullmann draws attention to the Jewish apologetic that reasoned that Moses preceded the Greek philosophers and poets and was therefore superior to them (*The Early Church*, London, 1956, pp. 177–82). The Clementine literature by contrast developed the opposite idea that chronological priority means inferiority (Cain preceded Abel, Ishmael was born before Isaac, Esau came before Jacob, Aaron was prior to Moses, *Clementine Homilies*, 2 : 16). It goes on to assert that this gives the means of distinguishing the evil principle from the good, and thus John, who came before Jesus, is regarded as a false prophet. But this unusual approach highlights the more normal attitude.

incredible as this may sound to our generation! They really believed in "the good old days". But John indicates a reversal in the case of John and Jesus. Till Jesus came John occupied the centre of the stage. But He who was later in time "came to be before" His forerunner. We should probably think of a reversion to priority in time in the expression at the end of the verse.[102] Though Jesus appeared on the earthly scene *after* John the Baptist He was really *before* him. As v. 1 has made clear, He pre-existed from eternity. So He actually was before John. However the Greek is somewhat unusual, and literally means "first of me".[103] Some take "first" to mean not "first in time", "before", but "first in importance", which will give such a meaning as "he was my Chief".[104] This, however, seems an unnatural meaning for the expression. Most agree that it should be taken to refer to time: "He existed before me". But it is an unusual and emphatic expression.[105] As Westcott points out it denotes not merely relative priority but absolute priority. The Word was not only "former" but "first". The pre-existence of Jesus shows His superiority[106] (*cf.* Moffatt, "my successor has taken precedence of me, for he preceded me").

16 V. 15 shows that John thought of Jesus as far surpassing him. The point of the "for" which links that verse and this is perhaps that Christians in general can support this verdict, "for" they have experienced the good gifts that He gives.[107] "Fulness" will have

---

[102] John introduces the proposition with ὅτι, "for". He is unusually fond of this conjunction, and employs it altogether 271 times. No other book of the New Testament has it more than 173 times (Luke), so John's usage stands out. It is a mark of his style.

[103] πρῶτός μου.

[104] So Murray, and Abbott (1896–1900, 2665–66, 2799a).

[105] There is something of a parallel, however, in the ἐμὲ πρῶτον ὑμῶν μεμίσηκεν of 15 : 18.

[106] Wright says that here "The language of *time* is used to express the notion of *quality*, as in the utterance found at 8⁵⁸, 'Before Abraham was, I am.' "

[107] Some MSS read "And", but the attestation of "For" is superior and should be accepted. The view that John the Baptist is still the speaker in v. 16 does not seem to be correct (though it can claim the support of great names, *e.g.* Origen and Luther). The sense seems against it. Grace is explicitly associated with Christ in vv. 14, 17, in the latter of which it is explicitly contrasted with the preceding Judaism. If John be held to have uttered the words, "we all" will mean "all the prophets".

here the active meaning, "that which fills".[108] Christ is the source of all our blessings. There is a hint at the infinite extent of His resources, for "all" receive from Him.[109] We might have thought that the receiving of Christ's fulness would be described as continuous. But John uses the same verb and the same tense as he has used of the single act of receiving Christ in v. 12. He prefers to concentrate attention on our becoming participators in the fulness when we first received Christ.[110] "Grace for grace" is an unusual expression.[111] Literally it means "grace instead of grace". Clearly John intends to put some emphasis on the thought of grace. Probably also he means that as one piece of divine grace (so to speak) recedes it is replaced by another. God's grace to His

---

[108] J. B. Lightfoot has an important note on πλήρωμα (op. cit., pp. 257-73). He argues from the form (the -μα ending) that the word must be passive in meaning. J. Armitage Robinson shows, however, that usage does not support Lightfoot. Words of this type sometimes do have the active meaning (St Paul's Epistle to the Ephesians, London, 1907, pp. 255-59). MM remind us that in the papyri nouns in -μα and nouns in -σις were drawing closer in meaning at this period (sub voc.). See also the articles on "Pleroma" in HDB and "Fulness" in ISBE. This is the only place in the Johannine writings where the term is found.

[109] "The thought is of the inexhaustible resources of grace ('grace upon grace') which the people of Christ find in Him, and on which they may freely draw" (F. F. Bruce, NICNT on Col. 1 : 19, n. 122). Perhaps we should notice also that we may have here a foretaste of the later Gnostic view. The Gnostics held that the totality of spiritual beings emanated from the high good God, and they denoted the totality of such beings by the word πλήρωμα. If the idea is as early as New Testament times Paul will be hitting at it when he insists on the uniqueness of Christ by saying that it was the Father's good pleasure "that in him should all the fulness dwell" (Col. 1: 19), or again "in him dwelleth all the fulness of the Godhead bodily" (Col. 2 : 9). And John will then mean that what these curious speculations spread over a multitude of divine beings is in fact concentrated in Christ.

[110] R. E. Brown sees a possible reference to the Qumran doctrine of the coming of the Messiahs (SNT, p. 204). If this is so, John will mean that what the covenanters looked for in vain Jesus completely supplied.

[111] χάριν ἀντὶ χάριτος. The καί which links this to the preceding words means "and, what is more". It should not be taken to signify "namely", or "that is to say". Abbott thinks this use is probably absent from John altogether (2146a). There is an interesting parallel to the expression in Philo. He speaks of God as granting "graces", χάριτας, and ἑτέρας ἀντ' ἐκείνων καὶ τρίτας ἀντὶ τῶν δευτέρων, "and others in their stead, and third ones in place of the second" (de post. Cain, 145). John does not use the preposition ἀντί apart from this passage.

people is continuous and is never exhausted. Grace knows no interruption and no limit. In contrast with the Law it stresses the dynamic character of the Christian life. Law can be mastered. A man may acquire merit by conforming to it. He knows the precise requirements that are demanded of him. But grace is always an adventure. No man can say where grace will lead him. Grace means an ever deepening experience of the presence and the blessing of God.

17 "The law" strictly stands for the first five books of the Old Testament. These books were sacred Scripture *par excellence* to the Jews of that day (and for that matter, of this). But because they were so eminent the title came to be used simply to mean Scripture, *i.e.* the whole Old Testament. From that it could mean the whole of Judaism considered as a system based on Scripture. In this verse there is probably a mingling of the first and last meanings. The Jews thought of Moses as the author of the first five books of the Bible, but not of the whole of the Old Testament. Thus the second meaning is excluded. But John is not concentrating on five books of the Bible. He is contrasting the old with the new, Judaism with Christianity. All that Moses could produce was "law". He did not even originate that, for it was "given through" him. It came from God. Over against the idea of law is that of "grace and truth" (see on v. 14).[112] There is a good deal of Jewish thought which regards these two divine attributes as revealed through Moses (see SBk on v. 14). John may well be claiming accordingly that God's revelation of these attributes was wrongly ascribed to Moses. They were not revealed through him, but they came through Jesus. The association of truth with the gospel revelation in Jesus Christ is clear in this verse, for in its more usual sense truth certainly came by Moses. But John's concern is with the whole way of salvation by grace as it was revealed and established in the ministry of Christ. This was God's way, and His more excellent way at that. Since it "came" through Christ it

---

[112] "Grace" and "truth" both have the article here, though neither has it in v. 14. The meaning may be "the" grace and "the" truth already mentioned, or the well known, outstanding grace and truth. This verse affords a good example of John's habitual paratactic style. We should have expected the contrasting μέν and δέ. But John simply puts the two statements side by side.

points to His surpassing excellence. The verb is somewhat curious, and not what we would have expected.[113] It associates grace and truth more closely with Christ than the law with Moses, though the retention of the preposition "through" ensures that the divine origin is not overlooked. This is John's first use of the human name, Jesus (though the idea of the Word made flesh came earlier). He is fond of it, using it in all 237 times (Matthew uses it 150 times, Mark 81 times, and Luke 89 times). This is more than a quarter of the total New Testament occurrences of the word (905 times). But it is otherwise with the compound title Jesus Christ, found elsewhere in this Gospel only in 17 : 3 though *cf.* 20 : 31). John uses the term "Christ", however, more often than the other Evangelists (Matthew 17 times, Mark 7 times, Luke 12 times, John 19 times). This will accord with his aim of writing that men might believe that Jesus is the Christ (20 : 31). This title depicts Him as the Messiah of Israel (see further on v. 20). There is point in using the full name Jesus Christ with all solemnity in this passage where His superiority to Moses is being brought out. The contrast of the Christian way with the Jewish and the function of Moses as subordinate to and pointing forward to the Christ is a recurring theme in this Gospel (see 5 : 39, 46; 6 : 32; 8 : 32ff.; 9 : 28ff.). We have already seen that John depicts Jesus as a second Moses. T. F. Glasson has written a book to show that the contrast of Moses and Christ is one of John's major themes.[114]

18 At first sight this verse may seem to be very loosely connected with the preceding if in fact it is connected at all. But in reality it forms the climax to the entire Prologue, stressing as it does that Christ is in the closest possible relation to the Father. There is also the thought that, though Moses was highly esteemed by all Jews, yet in the system he inaugurated nobody could "see" God. By contrast, Jesus Christ has revealed Him.

---

[113] ἐγένετο (used in vv. 3, 6, 10, 12, 14, 15; the perfect in v. 4) signifies "became", "came into being". In some of its previous occurrences it refers to the Word's creative activities (3, 10, 12), and its use here may be meant to associate grace and truth with the work of Christ. As Christians understand it, grace is always "the grace of our Lord Jesus Christ", and they can speak of truth "as truth is in Jesus" (Eph. 4 : 21). There is point in linking them both to Christ's creative work.

[114] *Moses in the Fourth Gospel* (London, 1963).

The emphatic declaration, "No man[115] hath seen [116] God at any time" (notice that the word "God" is in an emphatic position) is in line with Exod. 33 : 20, where the Lord says, "man shall not see me and live" (*cf.* John 5 : 37; 6 : 46). Yet there are some passages like Exod. 24 : 9–11 which explicitly affirm that some men have seen God. What then does John mean? Surely that in His essential being God has never yet been seen of men. Men had had their visions of God, but these were all partial. The theophanies of the Old Testament did not and could not reveal God's essential being. But Christ has now made such a revelation. As Calvin puts it, "When he says that none has seen God, it is not to be understood of the outward seeing of the physical eye. He means generally that, since God dwells in inaccessible light, He cannot be known except in Christ, His lively image."

Instead of "the only begotten Son" (ARV) a number of very good manuscripts read "God only begotten" (ARV mg).[117] The second reading seems to have both better attestation and transcriptional probability on its side. It is objected that "only begotten God" is not a usual Johannine expression, and that the following mention of "Father" makes "Son" more natural. But these very reasons would incline scribes to alter "God" to "Son", all the more so since "only begotten God" is a startling expression. It is not easy to see what would cause anyone who had "Son" before him to alter this to "God". It seems that we should accept as the correct reading "only begotten God". But in any case the sense is scarcely affected. Christ is elsewhere called both "Son" and "God", so there is no point of doctrine involved. For "only begotten" see on v. 14. It is possible that we should punctuate with a comma after "begotten", thus giving us three titles of Christ: "Only-begotten, God, He who is in the bosom of the

---

[115] For John's frequent use of οὐδείς see on v. 5.

[116] John is fond of the verb ὁράω which he uses 31 times, far more than in any other book of the New Testament (next is Acts with 16 times). For the difficulty of discerning a difference of meaning in John's various words for seeing see on 2 : 23.

[117] *(ὁ) μονογενὴς Θεός* is read by P66 P75 ℵBC*L33 boh syrᵖ and a good deal of patristic evidence, including some heretics (Valentinians, Arius). ὁ μονογενὴς Υἱός is read by AC³KΘ fl f13 28 565 700 vg syrᶜ and much patristic evidence. On the basis of quotations in the Fathers Boismard reads simply μονογενής.

Father". This final expression[118] expresses the closeness of the Father and the Son. It also carries overtones of affection (*cf.* our "the wife of his bosom"). The copula "is" expresses a continuing union.[119] The only begotten is continually in the bosom[120] of the Father. When the Word became flesh His cosmic activities did not remain in abeyance until the time of the earthly life was ended. There are mysteries here that man cannot plumb, but we must surely hold that the incarnation meant the adding of something to what the Word was doing, rather than the cessation of most of His activities.[121] The verb "declared"[122] (here only in John) is used of setting forth a narrative (*cf.* Luke 24 : 35, where it is rendered "rehearsed"). It indicates that Jesus has now given a full account of the Father. This does not mean that there is nothing more to be learned of Him. The term is not precise enough for that. But it does point to the adequacy of the revelation made in Christ. We may have confidence that God is as Christ revealed Him. The word is used in the mystery religions and elsewhere as a technical term for the revelation of divine secrets. Often it is used of the gods themselves making a disclosure. Such associations fitted the word to be used of a full and authoritative revelation of the divine Being. Such a revelation could, of course, be made

---

[118] The expression is εἰς τὸν κόλπον, not ἐν τῷ κόλπῳ (13 : 23), "into the bosom", rather than "in the bosom". If the distinction can be pressed we have an expression analogous to πρὸς τὸν Θεόν of 1 : 1, with the thought of the orientation of the Son towards the Father. But, as often in Hellenistic Greek, εἰς may be simply equivalent to ἐν. Abbott, however, denies that John uses εἰς loosely (2706–13), as does I. de la Potterie (*Biblica*, XLIII, 1962, pp. 366–87). The latter sees the significance of the present passage as "'tourné vers le sein du Père', comme pour décrire le Fils, éternellement conscient de recevoir de ce sein toute sa vie, tout son être" (*op. cit.*, p. 385). But we must not overlook John's habit of using synonyms without significant difference of meaning (see on 3 : 5).

[119] In the Greek it is the participle ὁ ὤν.

[120] The word κόλπος is found in the New Testament only in Luke and John. John 3 : 13 is a parallel to the present passage if the appropriate words are rightly read there.

[121] Augustine has some fine sayings, *e.g.* "Man was added to Him, God not lost to Him"; "He emptied Himself not by losing what He was, but by taking to Him what He was not" (*Homilies on the Gospel of John*, VIII. 3; XVII. 16).

[122] ἐξηγήσατο. From this root we derive our word "exegesis". It is a suggestive thought that Christ is the "exegesis" of the Father.

only by One uniquely qualified in the manner made clear by the references to Him in the earlier part of the verse.[123]

ADDITIONAL NOTE A: THE LOGOS (THE WORD)

The term *Logos* was in frequent use among the Greeks.[124] The word might be thought of as remaining within a man, when it denoted his thought or reason. Or it might refer to the word going forth from the man, when it denoted the expression of his thought, *i.e.* his speech.[125] The *Logos*, as a philosophical term, depended on the former use. It denoted something like the world-soul, the soul of the universe. It was an all-pervading principle, the rational principle of the universe. It was a creative energy. All things in one sense came from it. In another, men derived their wisdom from it.[126] The concept is as old as Heraclitus (sixth century B.C.). This philosopher declared that the *Logos* "is always existent", and again that "all things happen through this *Logos*".[127] He thought of the ultimate reality sometimes as Fire, sometimes as God, sometimes as *Logos*. "In Heraclitus the three conceptions, *Logos*, Fire, and God, are fundamentally the same. Regarded as the *Logos*, God is the omnipresent Wisdom by which all things are steered".[128] Heraclitus found men conceiving the universe in

---

[123] This will be the point of the emphatic ἐκεῖνος (for this term see on v. 8) "*He* and no other".

[124] For that matter "the Word" was used in many religions (see F. W. Dillistone, *Christianity and Symbolism*, London, 1955, pp. 141–51). For its use among the Greeks *cf.* R. H. Pfeiffer, *History of New Testament Times* (New York, 1949), pp. 122–27; art. "Logos" by A. F. Walls in *Baker's Dictionary of Theology* (Grand Rapids, 1960).

[125] These are distinguished as λόγος ἐνδιάθετος and λόγος προφορικός. Sometimes we read also of the λόγος σπερματικός, the "seminal" or "generative" reason, the creative force in nature. This last term is often in the plural. Justin used it in the singular of Christ, saying concerning the philosophers, "each man spoke well in proportion to the share he had of the spermatic word" (*Second Apol.*, 13).

[126] Origen seems to understand λόγος in much this way: "all who are rational beings are partakers of the word, *i.e.*, of reason, and by this means bear certain seeds, implanted within them, of wisdom and justice, which is Christ" (*De Prin.*, I. iii. 6).

[127] James Adam, *The Religious Teachers of Greece* (Edinburgh, 1909), p. 217.

[128] Adam, *op. cit.*, p. 233. We must be on our guard against thinking that "God" meant the same to Heraclitus as it does to us. He could say, "God is day and night, winter and summer, war and peace, satiety and hunger. But he is changed, just as fire, when mingled with different kinds of incense, is named after the flavour of each" (Adam, *op. cit.*, p. 225).

physical terms. He introduced the idea of the *Logos* to account for the order he saw in the *kosmos*. It was the stabilizing, directing principle of the universe.[129]

Later thinkers for the most part failed to follow this thought up. For example, though Plato occasionally mentions the *Logos*, he is more concerned with his distinction between this material world and the real, heavenly world of "ideas". It was the Stoics who really developed the concept of the *Logos*. They abandoned Plato's heavenly archetypes in favor of the thought (more akin to Heraclitus) that the universe is pervaded by the *Logos*, the eternal Reason. The term *Logos* gave expression to their deep conviction of the rationality of the universe. They did not think of the *Logos* as personal, so they did not understand it as we would God. For them it was essentially a principle or force. But the important thing is that if it was a principle it was the supreme principle of the universe. It was the force that originated and permeated and directed all things.

When John used the term *Logos*, then, he used a term that would be widely recognized among the Greeks.[130] The average man would not know its precise significance to the philosophers (any more than his modern counterpart knows what the scientist understands by, say, "nuclear fission"). But he would know that it meant something very important. John could scarcely have used the Greek term without arousing in the minds of those who used the Greek language thoughts of something supremely great in the universe. But, though he would not have been unmindful of the associations aroused by the term, his essential thought does

---

[129] T. F. Glasson, following J. Burnet, questions whether Heraclitus really had a *Logos* doctrine (*JThS*, n.s., III, 1952, pp. 231–38). It may be doubted whether he has made his point, though clearly John owes nothing directly to Heraclitus.

[130] John also has affinities with strands of Greek thought which do not use the *Logos* concept. Thus Dodd is able to point out that there are parallels in the *Poimandres* to several things said about the *Logos* in John. He goes on, "we may say that the Johannine conception of Christ has in some measure combined the roles assigned in the *Poimandres* to four distinct beings" (*IFG*, p. 33). There is no question of literary dependence. But John has clearly used a form of expression which would strike many chords among his Greek readers.

not derive from the Greek background.[131] His Gospel shows little
trace of acquaintance with Greek philosophy and less of dependence upon it.[132] And the really important thing is that John in
his use of *Logos* is cutting clean across one of the fundamental
Greek ideas. The Greeks thought of the gods as detached from
the world, as regarding its struggles and heartaches and joys and
fears with serene divine lack of feeling. John's idea of the *Logos*
conveys exactly the opposite idea. John's *Logos* does not show us
a God who is serenely detached, but a God who is passionately
involved. The *Logos* speaks of God's coming where we are, taking
our nature upon Himself, entering the world's struggle, and out
of this agony winning men's salvation.[133]

More important for our understanding of this Gospel in general
and of its use of this term in particular is its Jewish background.
The opening words "In the beginning" compel a comparison
with Gen. 1 : 1, while "the Word" irresistibly turns our attention

---

[131] F. V. Filson shows that there is no complete parallel in Greek thought
to the Johannine concept (*The New Testament against its Environment*, London,
1950, pp. 89f.). He reminds us that "in the Christian account the Son or Logos
is linked with the historical Christ and not, as logic would lead us to expect,
with the Spirit. This most notable difference is striking, but it is often overlooked.
The fact shows that the Christian doctrine of the Spirit is not a borrowing
from Stoic sources, either directly or indirectly. It derives from a historical
career and its sequel, rather than from a Greek philosophy" (*op. cit.*, p. 90).
See also W. J. Phythian-Adams, *CQR*, CXXXIX, 1944–45, pp. 1ff. But if
John's idea of the *Logos* cannot be derived from Greek concepts the effects
of its Greek associations were important. A. C. Headlam says: "It enabled
Christianity to express itself in terms of Greek thought . . . It enabled a Christian
philosophy to be built up in harmony with current thought" (*Christian Theology*,
Oxford, 1934, p. 334). For the importance of the *Logos* concept to early Christian
theologians see G. L. Prestige, *God in Patristic Thought* (London, 1952), and
especially ch. VI.

[132] Yet it is surely going too far to say, as J. Burnet does, "the Johannine
doctrine of the λόγος has nothing to do with Herakleitos or with anything at
all in Greek philosophy" (*Early Greek Philosophy*, London, 1945, p. 133, n. 1).
It would be impossible to use a term so widely known in Greek philosophy
in a writing in the Greek language, probably published in a centre of Greek
culture, without being mindful of the associations the term would arouse.

[133] *Cf.* W. Barclay: "John spoke to a world which thought of the gods in
terms of passionless *apatheia* and serene *detachment*. He pointed at Jesus Christ
and said: 'Here is the mind of God; here is the expression of the thought of
God; here is the Logos.' And men were confronted with a God who cared so
passionately and who loved so sacrificially that His expression was Jesus Christ
and His emblem a cross" (*ExT*, LXX, 1958–59, p. 82).

to the repeated "and God said" of the opening chapter of the Bible. The Word is God's creative Word (v. 3). The atmosphere is unmistakably Hebraic.

A feature of Old Testament teaching that was receiving attention in the first century was its use of concepts like "the Word", "Wisdom" and the like. While nothing was said to compromise the basic monotheism of Judaism attention was increasingly directed to passages where such entities are given an almost independent existence. Thus throughout the Old Testament the Word of the Lord is thought of as an effective agent for the accomplishing of the divine will. "By the word of Jehovah were the heavens made" (Ps. 33 : 6). When God speaks He does something. His word is a divine action.[134] God's revelatory act is often described by saying that the word of the Lord "came" to the prophet. In keeping with this a prophet may ascribe a more or less independent existence to the Word, as when he reports God as saying, "so shall my word be that goeth forth out of my mouth: it shall not return unto me void, but it shall accomplish that which I please, and it shall prosper in the thing whereto I sent it" (Isa. 55 : 11). And in Psalm 29 "the voice" of the Lord is regarded in much the same way.

There are also semi-personalizations of Wisdom or the Law. Thus Wisdom can be spoken of very much like a divine person:

"Jehovah possessed me in the beginning of his way,
Before his works of old.

---

[134] "There can be little doubt that the Hebrew concept of *word as deed* plays a major role in understanding the meaning of the Logos. In Old Testament history and prophecy the *debar Yahweh* always meant Yahweh's *activity* in creation, revelation and redemption" (Richard Morgan, *Interpretation*, XI, 1957, pp. 159f.). Thorlief Boman puts a good deal of emphasis on the dynamic significance of *dabhar* (though he rejects the idea of the word as "a connecting link between Jahveh and his creation. It is of moment to the prophets and the other great personalities of the Old Testament to trace the creation directly back to Jahveh", *Hebrew Thought compared with Greek*, London, 1960, p. 64). He notices Faust's translation of John 1 : 1, "In the beginning was the deed", and comments, "Actually Goethe is on solid linguistic ground because he goes back to the Hebrew (Aramaic) original and translates its deepest meaning; for if *dabhar* forms a unity of word and deed, in our thinking the deed is the higher concept in the unity" (*op. cit.*, p. 66). The linguistics behind all this have been severely criticized, notably by James Barr in *The Semantics of Biblical Language* (Oxford, 1961). But, when full allowance has been made for his strictures the connection of *logos* with deed is noteworthy.

I was set up from everlasting, from the beginning,
Before the earth was . . .
When he established the heavens, I was there . . .
Then I was by him, as a master workman;
And I was daily his delight" (Prov. 8 : 22ff.).

The parallelism in Isa. 2 : 3 and Mic. 4 : 2 shows that "the Law"
and "the Word" mean very much the same thing. In such passages
"Wisdom" or "the Law" or "the Word" is in some sense divine,
yet not quite the same as God.[135]

There is another use of some importance, namely that in the
Targums. When Hebrew ceased to be a spoken language the
Scripture was still read in that language in the services of the
synagogue. As a concession to the weakness of the flesh there
arose the custom of giving a running translation. This was called
a Targum. At first the Targums were oral only, but in later times
they were written down. Those that have survived enable us to
see that they were rather free paraphrases rather than exact
translations. The Targumists tried to give the sense of the passage
being read, and not simply to translate mechanically. These
Targums were produced at a time when, from motives of reverence
and from a fear of breaking the third commandment, Jews had
ceased to pronounce the divine name. When they came to this
name in the original the readers and translators substituted some
other expression they thought more reverent, such as "the Holy
One" or "the Name". Sometimes they said "the Word (*Memra*)".[136]
For example, where our Bible says, "And Moses brought forth the
people out of the camp to meet God" (Exod. 19 : 17) the Targum
reads "to meet the Word of God". This kind of thing is quite

---

[135] See G. A. F. Knight, *A Biblical Approach to the Doctrine of the Trinity*
(Edinburgh, 1953), for a discussion of several Old Testament terms of this
kind. He thinks that "the Word of God" in the Old Testament is an *"alter
ego* of God" (*op. cit.*, p. 16).
[136] W. F. Albright refers to the manuscript Targum Neofiti 1 (a complete
Palestinian Targum) as "An important new Aramaic targum of the Pentateuch" which "has come to light in the Vatican library". It is "two or three
centuries older than any previously known targum". In it, Albright tells us,
"the 'Word' of God appears as a surrogate for the name of God, Yahweh"
(*New Horizons in Biblical Research*, London, 1966, p. 45). See M. McNamara,
The New Testament and the Palestinian Targum to the Pentateuch (Rome, 1966);
G. J. Cowling, "New Light on the New Testament? The significance of the
Palestinian Targum", *TSF Bulletin*, No. 51 (Summer 1968), pp. 6 ff.

common. Barclay says that in the Targum of Jonathan[137] alone the expression is used in this way about 320 times. It is often said that this Jewish use is not relevant, because it does not denote a being in any way distinct from God. It is just a reverent way of referring to God Himself.[138] But this is hardly the point. The point is that wherever people were familiar with the Targums they were familiar with "the Word" as a designation of the divine.[139] The Johannine use is not that of the Targums, but to those familiar with the Targums it must necessarily arouse these associations.

In the period between the two Testaments there was a marked extension of the usages we have been discussing. There are some striking statements about Wisdom.[140] Thus in the book *Ecclesiasticus* Wisdom is reported as saying, "I came forth from the mouth of the Most High, and covered the earth like a mist. I dwelt in high places, and my throne was in a pillar of cloud. Alone I have made the circuit of the vault of heaven and have walked in the depths of the abyss" (Sir. 24 : 3ff.). Clearly Wisdom stands in close relationship to God, though the writer is careful to speak of her as a created being: "From eternity, in the beginning, he created me" (Sir. 24 : 9). In the *Wisdom of Solomon* we find that Wisdom "glorifies her noble birth by living with God" (Wis. 8 : 3), and

---

[137] A Targum on the Former and Latter Prophets, *i.e.* the books in our Bible from Joshua to II Kings (excluding Ruth), and the prophetical books (excluding Daniel).

[138] SBk, II, pp. 302–33, makes it clear that *Memra* is used as another name for God. It is not an intermediary. Bultmann directs attention to the point that the Targums always use *Memra* with a genitive. It is "the *Memra* of the Lord" or the like, not simply "the *Memra*", as in John's use of "the Word". E. M. Sidebottom gives the force of it in these terms: "Memra then is not a mediating principle of any kind, and not the creative Word of the psalms . . . it is the Name of God himself, with perhaps the suggestion especially of God as self-revealing" (*op. cit.*, p. 39).

[139] M. McNamara sees the Targums as an important part of the background of John's *Logos* concept ("*Logos* of the Fourth Gospel and *Memra* of the Palestinian Targum (Ex 12⁴²)", *ExT*, LXXIX, 1967–68, pp. 115–7). He can go so far as to say, "Johannine tradition may yet well prove to be mainly influenced by liturgical Jewish tradition, particularly of the form found in the Targums" (*op. cit.*, p. 117). This may be going too far, but the influence of the Targums on John should certainly not be overlooked.

[140] Rendel Harris argues strongly that the *Logos* must be understood in terms of the Wisdom literature. Again and again he suggests that the Prologue is to be understood against this background: "the Prologue to the Gospel can be turned back from a Logos-Hymn to a Sophia-Hymn" (*op. cit.*, p. 39).

that she "is an initiate in the knowledge of God, and an associate in his works" (Wis. 8 : 4). The writer can pray, "O God of my fathers, and Lord of mercy, who hast made all things by thy word, and by thy wisdom hast formed man" (Wis. 9 : 1f., a passage which incidentally shows that the author put little difference between Wisdom and the Word). There is an even bolder personification of the Word: "For while gentle silence enveloped all things, and night in its swift course was now half gone, thy all-powerful word leaped from heaven, from the royal throne . . . a stern warrior . . . and touched heaven while standing on the earth" (Wis. 18 : 14ff.).[141] While it would be too much to say that these writers thought of Wisdom or the Word as having any distinct existence of their own, yet their bold imagery was certainly preparing the way for John's idea of the *Logos*.

It is difficult to know whether Philo should be thought of as a Jewish or Greek thinker. The great Alexandrian Jew really effected a synthesis of Greek philosophy and Old Testament thought. He spoke much about the Word,[142] and his various sayings do not readily harmonize. Sometimes he speaks of the *Logos* as a "second God", sometimes as the one God in action (is it too much to see in this his Greek philosophy and his Hebrew religion respectively?). If we might venture on a generalization, he saw the *Logos* as a philosophically respectable bridge between a transcendent God and this material universe.[143] He had no intention of abandoning the Old Testament. But he accepted the philosophical ideas of the day, and interpreted the Old Testament in terms of them.[144] Thus his view of the *Logos* is rather that of

---

[141] Similarly there was a development in the personification of the Law, the Torah. This had a great vogue among the Rabbis, as may be seen from the passages cited in SBk, II, pp. 353ff., where we see the *Torah* depicted as pre-existent, as eternally existent with God, as God's daughter, as active in creation, as the life of Israel and the light of Israel.

[142] W. F. Howard says that Philo used the term "no fewer than thirteen hundred times" (*Christianity according to St. John*, London, 1943, pp. 36f.).

[143] D. M. Baillie reminds us that "in the Philonic tradition the Logos, so far as hypostatized at all, was conceived as an intermediate being, between God and man" (*op. cit.*, p. 70, n. 1). This is very different from John's idea of a *Logos* who "became flesh", *i.e.* who was both God and man.

[144] *Cf.* Westcott: "He found a 'Logos' in the Greek Bible which he accepted as the record of revelation, and he applied to that what Greek writers had said of the 'Logos,' without thinking it necessary to inquire into the identity of the terms" (p. xxxvi).

current philosophy, somewhat modified, than the religious conception of the Old Testament.[145]

C. H. Dodd takes very seriously the idea that the Philonic understanding of the *Logos* is part of the background to the Johannine Prologue.[146] He thinks that Philo helps us to understand expressions very difficult to explain in terms of a merely Jewish background, for example, "the Word was God". His conclusion is that the opening words of the Prologue "are clearly intelligible only when we admit that $\lambda\acute{o}\gamma o\varsigma$, though it carries with it the associations of the Old Testament Word of the Lord, has also a meaning similar to that which it bears in Stoicism as modified by Philo, and parallel to the idea of Wisdom in other Jewish writers".[147] This, however, seems to assume that the whole of the Johannine concept of the Word must be explicable in terms of some part of its background, be it Jewish, Hellenistic, or what you will. This I would strongly contest. John's thought is his own. He uses a term which would be full of meaning to men whatever their background. But whatever their background they would not find John's thought identical with their own. His idea of the *Logos* is essentially new.

We may sum up this part of the discussion in the words of

---

[145] Against this A. W. Argyle argues that Philo thought of the *Logos* very much as he did of God ("The Logos of Philo: Personal or Impersonal?" in *ExT*, LXVI, 1954–55, pp. 13f.). On the question of the personality of the *Logos* in Philo, A. C. Headlam says, "if we ask what it was in itself, whether it was personal or impersonal, we get no satisfying answer. Philo never asked or answered the question. He remains always vague and poetical" (*op. cit.*, p. 331).

[146] See for example, the list of parallels he gathers (*IFG*, pp. 71f., 276f.). Another who stresses Philo is A. W. Argyle (*ExT*, LXIII, 1951–52, pp. 385f.). He questions whether "any fully satisfactory alternative interpretation" of the Fourth Gospel has been found to that which sees it in the light of Philo. He cites an impressive list of parallels and concludes: "Their cumulative force suggests that to deny any connexion between the Johannine Logos conception and that of Philo would be to throw away a valuable clue to the understanding of the mind and thought of the fourth evangelist."

[147] *IFG*, p. 280. He proceeds to apply this concept to the expression "the Word became flesh". It is curious that he selects this passage, for from the time of Augustine on, many have felt that this is a thought completely out of harmony with Philo. Argyle, for example, says bluntly, "Philo could not have said" it (*op. cit.*, p. 385). Indeed, Philo says explicitly of the life $\pi\varrho\grave{o}\varsigma\ \Theta\varepsilon\acute{o}v$ that it "has never come down to us, nor submitted to the constraints of the body" (*Quis rer. div. her.*, 45).

William Temple. The *Logos*, he says, "alike for Jew and Gentile represents the ruling fact of the universe, and represents that fact as the self-expression of God. The Jew will remember that 'by the Word of the Lord were the heavens made'; the Greek will think of the rational principle of which all natural laws are particular expressions. Both will agree that this Logos is the starting-point of all things."[148] John was using a term which, with various shades of meaning, was in common use everywhere. He could reckon on all men catching his essential meaning.[149]

This, then, is the background to John's thought. But it is not his thought itself.[150] He had a richer, deeper, fuller idea than that of any of his predecessors. For him the Word was not a principle, but a living Being and the source of life; not a personification, but a Person and that Person divine.[151] The Word was nothing less than God. John gave full expression to this, but it is important to see that this was but the culmination of a tendency inherent in

---

[148] P. 4.

[149] MacGregor dismisses as "a singularly futile dispute" the question of whether John's *Logos* concept owes more to Greek or Jewish sources. He says: "John must certainly have been indebted to both; if he was able adequately to present the Gospel to a heterogeneous Church, it was just because in the forefront of his Gospel so many converging streams of thought are gathered into one clear pool in which is reflected the face of Jesus Christ" (p. xxxv). Similarly, B. H. Streeter thinks that "The interpretative fusion of Greek philosophic mysticism with the conception of a Personal God reached by the Hebrew Prophets, modified by the religious experience of the Early Church, obtained its classical expression in the Prologue of the Fourth Gospel" (*The Four Gospels*, London, 1930, p. 374). In an article entitled "Ambiguity of Word Meaning in John's Gospel" (*Classical Weekly*, XXXVII, 1943–44, p. 77), F. W. Gingrich points out that it is characteristic of John to use words with two meanings. He thinks that λόγος is used here to convey both the Hebrew "word" and the Greek "reason".

[150] In discussions on John's use of the *Logos* not all have borne in mind the principle of which C. J. Wright reminds us: "the 'ancestry' of an 'idea' is not the idea itself" (p. 65).

[151] Godet thinks that the writer "wished to describe Jesus Christ as the *absolute revelation* of God to the world, to bring back all divine revelations to Him as their living centre, and to proclaim the matchless grandeur of His appearance in the midst of humanity" (I, p. 290). Cullmann maintains that "this title expresses very forcefully an important aspect of New Testament Christology – the unity in historical revelation of the incarnate and the pre-existent Jesus" (*The Christology of the New Testament*, London, 1959, p. 258). His whole discussion of the term is very valuable.

Christianity from the first.[152] The "word" stands for the whole Christian gospel in such passages as Mark 2 : 2 (where it applies to the preaching of Jesus) and Mark 8 : 32 (where it has special reference to the death of the Son of man).[153] Allan D. Galloway can regard *Logos* as referring to the work of Christ, rather than to His Person.[154] That is to say, it is a term which gathers up into itself the universal saving significance of Christ. He, the Word, is no tribal saviour, but the one hope of all mankind. The Word and the gospel are intimately connected. When Luke speaks of those who were "eyewitnesses and ministers of the word" (Luke 1 : 2) it is difficult to escape the impression that by "the word" he means more than teaching. He is thinking of the intimate relationship between Christ and the gospel, and is coming very close to calling Jesus "the Word". Again, he does not seem to put much difference between preaching the word (Acts 8 : 4) and preaching Jesus (Acts 11 : 20). A number of times Paul speaks of preaching Christ (1 Cor. 1 : 23; II Cor. 4 : 5; Gal. 3 : 1). In Col. 1 : 25ff. he explains "the word of God" as "the mystery", and this in turn as "Christ in you". Though the step of calling Christ "the Word" is not often taken (though *cf.* 1 John 1 : 1; Rev. 19 : 13) it is clear that the way had been prepared. There is a preparation also in the realm of ideas, for in passages like Phil. 2 : 5ff., Col. 1 : 15ff., though the terminology is different, Paul ascribes to Christ qualities and activities akin to those postulated of Wisdom in the Old Testament and elsewhere. The conclusion seems inescapable that, while John uses a term which was widely familiar, and which would convey a meaning to men of very diverse backgrounds, his thought

---

[152] "The compelling urge which led the Evangelist to pen, or make use of, the Logos Hymn, is not any of the external factors which from time to time have been proposed, but the dynamic fact of Christ Himself" (Vincent Taylor, *The Names of Jesus*, London, 1953, p. 164).

[153] On ἕνεκεν ἐμοῦ καὶ ἕνεκεν τοῦ εὐαγγελίου in Mark 10 : 29 Vincent Taylor comments, "together with the Synoptic variants, it is important as indicating an identification of Jesus Himself with the 'Gospel' and the 'Kingdom' in primitive Christian thought" *(in loc.)*.

[154] He says, "in the long run, it is primarily as an assertion of the cosmic significance of the *work* of Christ that we should see it" (*The Cosmic Christ*, London, 1951, p. 54). He compares the openings of the Second and Fourth Gospels and goes on: "Both Mark and John, while using very different language and symbolism, imply the same claim for the universal significance of the redeeming work of the Christ" (*op. cit.*, pp. 54f.).

is essentially Christian.[155] When he speaks of Jesus as the *Logos* he does but put the coping stone on an edifice that was being erected throughout the New Testament.[156]

After the Prologue John does not apply the specific term *Logos* to Jesus, but it should not be overlooked that he puts a good deal of stress on "the word(s)" of Jesus or of God.[157] He makes it clear that Jesus' words are God's words (3 : 34; 14 : 10, 24; 17 : 8, 14), which makes it very important to believe them (5 : 47). Indeed to abide in Jesus' "word" is the same as to be His disciple (8 : 31). Jesus' words bring life (5 : 24; 6 : 68; 8 : 51), and in fact are life (6 : 63). They bring cleansing (15 : 3) and power in prayer (15 : 7). The reverse side of the coin is that the refusal to heed Jesus' word or words brings judgment (12 : 47f.). Those who refuse to hear belong to the devil (8 : 47, *cf.* 44). It is important to "keep" Jesus' word (14 : 23; 15 : 20; 17 : 6). There is a good deal more. It is quite plain that the use of *Logos* on the threshold of this Gospel is not a casual expression. It is meaningful, and leads us into an

---

[155] Against this E. F. Scott thinks that "There can be little doubt that by thus importing the doctrine of the Logos into the Gospel record, John is not only compelled to do violence to historical fact, but empties the life of Christ of much of its real worth and grandeur, while seeming to enhance it. The moral attributes, trust, pity, forgiveness, infinite sympathy, are replaced by certain metaphysical attributes, which are supposed to belong more essentially to the divine nature" (*op. cit.*, p. 173). But it is more than doubtful whether John's use of the *Logos* is a device for replacing "moral attributes" by "metaphysical" ones. It is rather a question of the *Logos* adding something than of it replacing anything. If we are to think of a real incarnation, then there must be genuine deity as well as genuine humanity. John insists strongly on both. His use of the *Logos* concept is part of his way of drawing attention to the deity. Nowhere can it be justly held to minimize the humanity. Scott's idea that the doctrine of the *Logos* is "born of philosophical theory" (*op. cit.*, p. 175) perhaps accounts for his point of view. But, as we have seen, for John the idea is more religious than philosophical, more dependent on the Old Testament than on the Stoics, and more dependent on Christian experience and thought than either. The Prologue is the expression, not of a philosophical theory, but of a religious faith.

[156] With a different metaphor Hoskyns says: "The workshop in which the Word of God was forged to take its natural place among the great theological descriptions of Jesus and His Work is a Christian workshop: the tools are Christian tools" (p. 162). He develops the point convincingly (pp. 159–63). See also K. Harper, "Christ the Word" in *ExT*, LX, 1948–49, pp. 200–02.

[157] There does not appear to be much difference between his use of ῥήματα (always plural) and λόγος (nor between λόγος and λόγοι; see on 14 : 24).

important idea for the understanding of the Gospel.[158]

ADDITIONAL NOTE B: THE WORLD

The word κόσμος has an especially Johannine ring about it in the New Testament. Altogether it occurs 185 times, of which 78 occurrences are in John, 24 in the Johannine Epistles, and 3 in Revelation. Its occurrence in the Synoptic Gospels is not frequent (Matthew 8 times, Mark and Luke 3 times each). It occurs in the Pauline Epistles a total of 47 times. It is thus a word of some importance for John and to a lesser extent for Paul, but it is not much used by other New Testament writers.

Basically the word denotes an ornament, a use which we may still see in 1 Pet. 3 : 3 (and which has given us our word "cosmetic"). The universe with all its harmonious relationships is the outstanding ornament, and thus the term came to be used of the universe at large. It is probably this use that we see in John 1 : 10, "the world was made through him" (cf. 1 : 3, "All things were made through him"). It is likely that when Christ is referred to as "the light of the world" (8 : 12; 9 : 5), or of coming or being sent "into the world" (3 : 17; 11 : 27, etc.) it is the universe at large that is meant, though, of course, it cannot be ruled out as impossible that it is this world that is in mind. For men this earth is the most significant part of the universe so it is not surprising that the term came to be used of this world in which we live.[159] We see this in such a passage as "In the world ye have tribulation" (16 : 33).

From this it is a natural transition to seeing the world as the majority of men, or a large number of men, as when the Pharisees said despairingly, "lo, the world is gone after him" (12 : 19). But the majority of men have not usually been conspicuous for their zealous service of God. In the case of Christ, the world at large opposed Him, rejected Him, and finally crucified Him. So it is not surprising that "the world" is used of mankind in opposition

---

[158]   J. Ernest Davey maintains that the emphasis on the word(s) of God or of Christ is "One of the leading features in the Gospel" (*The Jesus of St John*, London, 1958, p. 83). He also says, "the main suitability of the word Logos to *John's* conception of Christ's significance lies in the central importance for him of the teaching or message of God which Christ mediated to men in His actual words and life on earth" (*op. cit.*, p. 88).

[159]   Interestingly, as H. Sasse notes, it was used among the Greeks also for heaven (*TDNT*, III, pp. 871f.). This use is not found in the New Testament.

to Christ. Sasse can speak of the world as "the sum of the divine creation which has been shattered by the fall, which stands under the judgment of God, and in which Jesus Christ appears as the Redeemer."[160] The world "is in some sense personified as the great opponent of the Redeemer in salvation history."[161]

It is this use of "the world" as hostile to Christ and all that He stands for which is the significantly new use the term acquires in the New Testament. It does not appear to have such a meaning in Greek writings at large. There it is rather something attractive, the order and the beauty of the universe. But for John and for Paul the shattering thing was that the men who inhabit this beautiful and ordered universe acted in an ugly and unreasonable way when they came face to face with Christ.[162] The world hates His followers, and He could say, "ye know that it hath hated me before it hated you" (15 : 18). Long before this He said to His brothers, "The world cannot hate you; but me it hateth" (7 : 7). In line with this there are several passages which speak of the evil one as "the prince of this world" or the like (12 : 31; 14 : 30; 16 : 11). The world rejoices when the disciples are lamenting (16 : 20). There is a blindness about the world. When the Word came into the world, the world He had made, "the world knew him not" (1 : 10). Nor does it know the Father (17 : 25). Nor can it receive nor does it know the Spirit (14 : 17).[163]

---

[160]   *Op. cit.*, p. 893. He is referring primarily to Pauline usage, but these words apply also to John.

[161]   *Op. cit.*, p. 894.

[162]   Bultmann sees the ugly thing in man's determination to live for himself: "The delusion that arises from the will to exist of and by one's self *perverts truth into a lie, perverts the creation into the 'world.'* For in their delusion men do not let their quest for life become a question about themselves so as to become aware of their creaturehood, but instead they give themselves the answer so as to have a security of their own. They take the temporary for the ultimate, the spurious for the genuine, death for life" (*Theology of the New Testament,* II, London, 1955, p. 27). The entire section, "The Perversion of the Creation into 'the World' " is important. Towards the end Bultmann says, "the world creates for itself a *security* of its own and operates within it as that which is *familiar and to be taken for granted.* It shrugs off the disturbance which is created for it by the appearing of Jesus with its incredulous question: 'How can this be?' (3 : 9), or with similar 'how's' (6 : 42; 7 : 15; 8 : 33; 12 : 34)" (*op. cit.,* p. 32).

[163]   Barclay says, "There is only one thing certain about *the kosmos, the world* – the *kosmos* is not what it was meant to be. Something has gone wrong. What is that something? It is sin" (II, pp. 21f.).

But John does not leave us with a picture of unremitting hostility between God and the world. It is true that the world is not interested in the things of God, but it is not true that God reciprocates. On the contrary God loves the world (3 : 16). Christ speaks to the world the things He has heard from God (8 : 26). The whole work of salvation which God accomplishes in Christ is directed to the world. Thus He takes away the sin of the world (1 : 29). He is the Saviour of the world (4 : 42). He gives life to the world (6 : 33). This is at cost for He gives His flesh for the life of the world (6 : 51). Christ came specifically to save the world, not to judge it (3 : 17; 12 : 47). His success is shown by the references to the overthrow of Satan, the prince of this world (12 : 31; 14 : 30; 15 : 11). The victory remains with Christ (16 : 33), but this does not alter the fact that the world basically opposed Him. This will perhaps account for the fact that the term "world" does not appear, either in John or elsewhere in the New Testament, for the eschatological sphere of blessing. For that some other term is used.

The term thus has many shades of meaning. This diversity must be kept in mind in studying this Gospel, because the boundaries between the classifications are not hard and fast. John moves freely from one to another, or even uses the term in ways which evoke more than one of its possible meanings.

II. THE BEGINNING OF JESUS' MINISTRY, 1 : 19-51

1. THE WITNESS OF JOHN, 1 : 19-34

(a) John and the Pharisees, 1 : 19-28

19 And this is the witness of John, when the Jews sent unto him from Jerusalem priests and Levites to ask him, Who art thou? 20 And he confessed, and denied not; and he confessed, I am not the Christ. 21 And they asked him, What then? Art thou Elijah? And he saith, I am not. Art thou the prophet? And he answered, No. 22 They said therefore unto him, Who art thou? that we may give an answer to them that sent us. What sayest thou of thyself? 23 He said, I am the voice of one crying in the wilderness, Make straight the way of the Lord, as [1] said Isaiah the prophet. 24 [2] And they had been sent from the Pharisees. 25 And they asked him, and said unto him, Why then baptizest thou, if thou art not the Christ, neither Elijah, neither the prophet? 26 John answered them, saying, I baptize [3] in water: in the midst of you standeth one whom ye know not, 27 even he that cometh after me, the latchet of whose shoe I am not worthy to unloose. 28 These things were done in [4] Bethany beyond the Jordan, where John was baptizing.

[1] Is. xl. 3. [2] Or, *And* certain *had been sent from among the Pharisees.* [3] Or, *with* [4] Many ancient authorities read *Bethabarah,* some *Betharabah.* Comp. Josh. 15.6, 61; 18.22.

The opening of the narrative proper might well be understood as the account of the happenings of one momentous week. John does not stress the point, but he does give notes of time which seem to indicate this. The first day is taken up with a deputation from Jerusalem which interrogates the Baptist. "On the morrow" we have John's public pointing out of Jesus (29-34). Day 3 tells of two disciples of the Baptist who followed Jesus (35-40). It seems probable that we should take v. 41 to refer to day 4 (see the notes on v. 39). It tells of Andrew's bringing of Peter to Jesus. Day 5 (43–51) is the day when Philip and Nathanael come to Him. There are no events recorded on day 6, but the marriage in Cana is two days after the previous incident (2 : 1–11). If we are correct in thus seeing the happenings of one momentous week set forth at the beginning of this Gospel we must go on to ask what significance is to be attached to this beginning. The parallel with the days of creation in Gen. 1 suggests itself, and is reinforced by the "In the beginning" which opens both chapters. Just as the opening words of this chapter recall Gen. 1, so is it with the framework. Jesus is to engage in a new creation. The framework unobtrusively suggests creative activity.

The first activity to be recorded is that of an official party of questioners who came to interrogate the Baptist. This gave him the opportunity of bearing his witness to the One who was to come after. Characteristically the writer says nothing of John's baptismal activities. He concentrates on his witness (see on v. 7).

19 We do not read in the other Gospels of these messengers who were sent to John from "the Jews". But it is plain enough that John's preaching attracted a good deal of attention. Matthew, for example, tells us that there went out to him "Jerusalem, and all Judaea, and all the region round about the Jordan" (Matt. 3 : 5). It is accordingly not only natural, but to be expected, that the authorities would make diligent inquiry about the new religious movement. They could not ignore a man with such a following. Jews in high places were very sensitive to movements which might culminate in disorders and lead to trouble with the Romans. The inquisitors came from Jerusalem[1] from "the Jews". This expression is rare in the Synoptic Gospels. Each of them refers a few times to "the King of the Jews" and scarcely uses the term otherwise. But in John it is used some seventy times. Sometimes the Evangelist employs it in a neutral sense (*e.g.* 2 : 6, "the Jews' manner of purifying"). He can even use it in a good sense (*e.g.* "salvation is from the Jews", 4 : 22). But much more often he uses it to denote

---

[1] This Evangelist always uses the Hellenized form of the name Ἱεροσόλυμα (preferred also by Matthew and Mark) rather than Ἱερουσαλήμ, the transliteration of the Hebrew, which is the form used in LXX. Luke uses both forms, but prefers the latter.

the Jewish nation as hostile to Jesus. It does not necessarily denote the whole nation. In fact characteristically it means the Jews of Judea, especially those in and around Jerusalem.[2] Now and then it is used in such a way as to exclude some of those who were certainly Jews by race. Thus the parents of the man born blind were certainly members of the Jewish nation, but they are said to fear "the Jews" (9 : 22). It is the aspect of hostility to Jesus that "the Jews" primarily signifies. It may mean the Jews of Galilee (6 : 41, 52), but more usually it points to those in and around Jerusalem. Not infrequently it refers to the leaders of the nation. We should probably deduce from this and from the composition of the delegation mentioned here that it came from the Sanhedrin.[3]

It is not certain whether we are to understand v. 24 to indicate that the whole delegation was Pharisaic. Probably this is not the meaning of that verse (see note). But it is plain that Pharisees were prominent in connection with the inquiry, and it is equally clear that the Pharisees were the real religious leaders of the nation. So it is not surprising that Pharisees should be linked with "the Jews". Consistently the nation which should have welcomed Jesus opposed Him. Consistently the religious leaders led the way in this opposition and rejection. As the Gospel unfolds this antagonism becomes clearer and clearer.

---

[2] In a very valuable note G. J. Cuming argues that in this Gospel " 'the Jews' . . . means Judaeans as opposed to Galileans". Especially does it apply to "the chief priests and the Pharisees, whom he depicts as our Lord's bitterest opponents. The indictment is not drawn against the whole Jewish nation but against its religious leaders. The choice of the word 'Judaeans' to describe them strongly suggests that the Evangelist was a Galilean" (*ExT*, LX, 1948–49, p. 292). This last point is not to be overlooked. Some maintain that the use of the term makes the author a foreigner, whereas it is sufficient explanation that he came from Galilee.

[3] The composition of the delegation brings together two terms neither of which is found again in this Gospel, and which are not linked elsewhere in the New Testament, namely, "priests and Levites". John is apparently stressing the part played by official Judaism. The words point to an official embassy. Support for this has been claimed by suggesting that the inquiry constituted a trial of "a false prophet", which was the prerogative of the Sanhedrin (Mishnah, *Sanh.* 1 : 5). But this seems far-fetched. The point is clear enough without this dubious argument.

The delegation is said to have consisted of "priests and Levites".[4] We might have expected some Sadducees[5] since the high-priestly families mostly came from this group, or some scribes. But for some reason John never mentions either group.[6] We should probably understand them to be included under the general term "the Jews". Among the lower priests some were sympathetic to the Pharisees,[7] and it is likely that some were sent on this errand. As the Baptist came of a priestly family (Luke 1 : 5ff.), the priests would be especially interested in his behaviour.[8] From all this it seems that the delegation was official and widely representative. It asked[9] a simple question, "Who art thou?" John was a puzzle. He did not conform. Officialdom wanted to know more about him.

20 No one in the delegation is reported to have said anything about Messiah. But John discerned the drift of the inquiry.

---

[4] For the Levites in New Testament times see E. Schürer, *A History of the Jewish People* (Edinburgh, 1885), II, i, pp. 264ff.; A. Edersheim, *The Temple* (London, n.d.), pp. 63ff. Their principal duties were to provide the Temple police and to supply music at the Temple services (for which latter there must always be at least twelve of them on the platform, *Arak.* 2 : 6). McClymont reminds us of the connection of the Levites with teaching (II Chron. 35 : 3; Neh. 8 : 7–9). If this continued in later times the Levites would have special reason for examining the new teacher. But the regulations scattered throughout the Mishnah stress two functions only, those of providing music (orchestral, *Sukk.* 5 : 4, *Kel.* 15 : 6, and especially vocal, *RH.* 4 : 4, *Tam.* 7 : 3, 4, *etc.*), and of acting as guards (*Midd.* 1 : 1, 2, 5, *etc.*).

[5] Some commentators (*e.g.* Wright) speak of Sadducees as being in this delegation. This is not unlikely, but there is no evidence.

[6] "Scribes" are mentioned in 8 : 3, but there is no reason for regarding this as part of the Gospel.

[7] Josephus is an example of a man who was both a priest and a Pharisee (*Vit.* 1 : 2).

[8] Barclay makes the point that Jewish orthodoxy frowned on John because he did not conform to the accepted ideas either of a priest or a preacher. He reminds us that the Church is always in danger of repeating the mistake.

[9] The verb is ἐρωτάω, which John uses 27 times (Matt. 4 times, Mark 3 times, Luke 15 times). The use of αἰτέω is not so distinctively Johannine. It is found in this Gospel 11 times (Matthew 14 times, Mark 9 times, Luke 11 times). This is probably mostly a matter of style, for in the New Testament the words do not appear to differ greatly in meaning. Properly, of course, ἐρωτάω means "ask a question", and it is thus appropriate in the present passage. See further on 11 : 22.

Messianic speculations were in the air,[10] and he framed his reply accordingly. The Evangelist might have written simply, "And he said". Instead we have a rather complicated expression: "And he confessed, and denied not; and he confessed. . . ." This piling up of one expression on top of another is perhaps intended to indicate the seriousness of the Baptist's reply. He vigorously repudiated any suggestion that he might be the Messiah.[11] The impression conveyed by the solemn way of introducing his reply to the question is strengthened by his use of the emphatic pronoun "I": "I am not the Christ" (as though to say, "It is not *I* who am the Christ!"). This emphatic pronoun is a marked feature of John's speech in this chapter. He uses it constantly, and each time he contrasts himself with Jesus and takes the lower place. He says: "*I* am the voice" (v. 23), "*I* baptize" (v. 26), "*I* am not worthy" (v. 27), "of whom *I* said" (v. 30), "*I* knew him not" (vv. 31, 33), "*I* came baptizing" (v. 31), and "*I* have seen" (v. 34). The series is noteworthy, and the effect is to make it quite clear that John claimed a subordinate position.[12]

In this verse the point is that, whatever John was, he was certainly not the Christ. There was a Christ, but it was not he. With us "Christ" has become little more than a personal name for Jesus. But properly it is a title, "the Christ", and it means

---

[10] J. B. Lightfoot points out that we learn more about contemporary Jewish views on the Messiah from John than we do from the Synoptics. The topic is discussed in Galilee (1 : 41, 45, 49, *etc.*), in Samaria (4 : 25, 29, 42), in Judea (5 : 39, 45f.; 7 : 26f., *etc.*). "Among friends, among foes, among neutrals alike, it is mooted and discussed. The person and character of Jesus are tried by this standard. He is accepted or he is rejected as he fulfils or contradicts the received ideal of the Messiah" (E. Abbot, A. P. Peabody and J. B. Lightfoot, *The Fourth Gospel*, London, 1892, p. 152). See also on v. 41.

[11] S. Mowinckel points out that the term "Messiah" has an eschatological character but also that "it has a political sense from the beginning" (*He that Cometh*, Oxford, 1959, p. 7). This must be borne in mind in estimating the sparse use of the term in the New Testament.

[12] The emphatic pronoun ἐγώ is unusually frequent throughout this Gospel. John uses it 465 times, while figures for the other Gospels are Matthew 210 times, Mark 104 times, Luke 215 times. It is plain that John is much more ready than the others to use this emphatic form. This is not the case with the plural ἡμεῖς (Matthew 49 times, Mark 24 times, Luke 69 times, John 48 times), nor with σύ (Matthew 207 times, Mark 89 times, Luke 224 times, John 151 times), nor with ὑμεῖς (Matthew 247 times, Mark 75 times, Luke 220 times, John 255 times).

"the anointed" (as does "Messiah").[13] In the Old Testament various people were anointed, but notably priests and kings (for the latter, *cf.* the phrase, "the Lord's anointed"). The rite was used to set men apart for special functions. When in due course the expectation grew up that one day God would send into the world an especially great Person, a mighty Deliverer, One who would represent Him in a very special sense, this coming great One was thought of not as "an anointed", but as "*the* anointed one", "*the* Messiah". Among those set apart by God for special functions He stood out. So the title was applied by believers to Jesus, and it remains to remind us of this public and official aspect of His ministry.[14]

21 It had been foretold by the prophet Malachi that before "the great and terrible day of Jehovah" God would send Elijah the prophet (Mal. 4 : 5). This was understood to mean that Elijah would precede the Messiah. Accordingly when John made it so clear that he was not the Christ his interrogators bethought them of this prophecy and inquired whether then[15] he was Elijah. His denial puzzles many, for Jesus explicitly asserted that John was "Elijah, that is to come" (Matt. 11 : 14). This is one of the passages which seem to show that this Gospel was written in independence of the Synoptics. It is not in contradiction of them, but had John had their statement before him he would scarcely have left his own account in just this form.

The solution to the difficulty is probably that there was a sense in which John was Elijah and a sense in which he was not. He fulfilled all the preliminary ministry that Malachi had foretold (*cf.* Luke 1 : 17), and thus in a very real sense Jesus could say that he was Elijah. But the Jews remembered that Elijah had left the earth in a chariot of fire without passing through death

---

[13] The word "Christ" is the transliteration of the Greek Χριστός, "anointed". This in turn is a translation of the Hebrew מָשִׁיחַ which we transliterate as "Messiah" (*cf.* v. 41). Since Χριστός is a translation, not a transliteration of the Hebrew, it can be argued that we should translate it here and read "Anointed". But we are so used to the term "Christ" that it is probably best to retain it.

[14] See further my *The Lord from Heaven* (London and Grand Rapids, 1958), pp. 29–32.

[15] This is John's first use of οὖν, a particle he employs in all 194 times, far more than any other New Testament writer (next is Acts with 62 times). It is so much a mark of style that we cannot always insist on an inferential sense.

(II Kings 2 : 11), and they expected that in due course the identical figure would reappear.[16] John was not Elijah in this sense, and he had no option but to deny that he was.[17] And, of course, we must bear in mind the possibility that John may not have known that he was Elijah.[18] No man is what he is in his own eyes. He really is only as he is known to God. At a later time Jesus equated John with the Elijah of Malachi's prophecy, but that does not carry with it the implication that John himself was aware of the true position. It is further proper to point out that, whereas the Synoptists give something of a biography of the Baptist, this Evangelist does not. Instead he concentrates on John's theological significance, and derives this rigorously from his relationship to Jesus. Jesus confers on John his true significance. No man is what

---

[16] LXX reads "Elijah the Tishbite" and not simply "Elijah" in Mal. 4 : 5 (LXX, 3 : 22), which would have encouraged the idea. The animal vision in Enoch 90 appears to depict Elijah's return before the judgment (En. 90 : 31; cf. 89 : 52). The contemporary Jewish expectation is attested in Mark 8 : 28; 9 : 11. We read of the functions of Elijah in the Mishnah (e.g. Eduy. 8 : 7). See also LT, II, pp. 706–9, SBk, IV, pp. 764–98. Justin reports the Jewish view that the Messiah "is unknown, and does not even know Himself, and has no power until Elias come to anoint Him, and make Him manifest to all" (Dial. Try., viii; ANF, I, p. 199). Augustine had the idea that Elijah is to come before Christ's second advent, so that John was not he (NPNF, I, vii, p. 27). This idea has been taken up in modern times by J. C. Ryle, who cites Chrysostom, Jerome, Theophylact, and Gregory in support of the theory of two advents of Elijah, or more accurately of two Elijahs, an Elijah in the spirit and an Elijah in the flesh.

[17] It is objected that if this was John's meaning he should have explained himself further. But John was in no mood for long discourses about himself as his severely curtailed answers show. His desire was to bear witness to Christ, not talk about himself. In any case in his modesty he may not have dared to claim that he was Elijah in any sense. He thought of himself as no more than "a voice". That this Evangelist did not deny that the Baptist was Elijah in any sense is perhaps indicated by his description of John in 5 : 35 in terms which recall the description of Elijah in Sir. 48 : 1.

[18] C. F. D. Moule points out that it is too simple to see a straight contradiction between John's account and that of the Synoptists. "We have to ask by whom the identification is made, and by whom refused. The Synoptists represent Jesus as identifying, or comparing, the Baptist with Elijah, while John represents the Baptist as rejecting the identification when it is offered him by his interviewers. Now these two, so far from being incompatible, are psychologically complementary. The Baptist humbly rejects the exalted title, but Jesus, on the contrary, bestows it on him. Why should not the two both be correct?" (The Phenomenon of the New Testament, London, 1967, p. 70).

he himself thinks he is. He is only what Jesus knows him to be.

John's denial provoked a third question, "Art thou the prophet?" The Jews appear to have expected all sorts of prophets to appear before the coming of the Messiah (*cf.* Matt. 16 : 14; Mark 6 : 15; Luke 9 : 19).[19] More particularly they thought of the prophet spoken of in Deut. 18 : 15ff. But John was not that prophet either, so he briefly answered[20] "No".[21] It is not without its interest that from the days of the very earliest Christian preaching it was held that "the prophet" was identical with the Christ (see Acts 3 : 22). But the Jews distinguished between the two as we see from this passage and from 7 : 40f.[22] The increasing curtness of John's successive utterances should not be missed. It appears to stem from a dislike for answering questions about himself. He had come to bear witness to Another.

---

[19] Yet this should not blind us to the startling effect on them of a man who looked and acted like a prophet. For them prophecy was dead. It was congealed in parchment and ink. John stabbed them into a new awareness of what prophecy really is.

[20] "Answered" is ἀπεκρίθη, a verb of which John is fond. He uses it 78 times (Matthew 55 times, Mark 30 times, Luke 46 times). In the great majority of instances he has the aorist passive as here, the aorist middle being found twice only (5 : 17, 19), and the present, which might be either middle or passive, four times (12 : 23, where see note; 13 : 26, 38; 18 : 22).

[21] The form is the accented οὔ, which is the negative answer, "No" (see AG). John uses it again only in 7 : 12; 21 : 5. In all three places the negative is a very firm one.

[22] The Jews seem to have made little use of the prophecy in Deut. 18. When they did use it they do not seem to have identified the prophet with the Christ. Sometimes they thought that Jeremiah was meant (see SBk on Acts 3 : 22). F. J. Foakes Jackson and Kirsopp Lake suggest that the application of the prophecy to the Christ came into Christianity from Samaritan sources (*The Beginnings of Christianity*, I, London, 1920, pp. 404–8). In the Qumran Scrolls the prophet and the Christ seem to be distinguished. Thus in the *Manual of Discipline* we read, "Until the coming of the Prophet and of both the priestly and the lay Messiah" (*SDSS*, p. 67). Millar Burrows renders "a prophet" (*DSS*, p. 383), but M. Black accepts the reference to the prophet of Deut. 18 : 15 (*SJT*, VI, 1953, p. 6). J. T. Milik points out that the Qumran texts display a concern for the due recognition of this prophet as a true prophet, but apart from this show little interest in him. "Once it becomes clear that the Priestly Messiah's functions include the proclamation of the eschatological law, it is hard to see what the Prophet can be except a precursor of the Messiah" (*Ten Years of Discovery in the Wilderness of Judaea*, London, 1959, p. 126). The Christian (and Samaritan) view is thus distinctive. For Jewish speculations about the coming of prophets see SBk on John 6 : 14.

22 The questioners were in a difficult position. So far all that they had elicited from John was a string of denials. They had no positive statement to put in their report. Yet John was preaching, drawing crowds in the wilderness, and baptizing. They must have something to say about him. So they turn the matter over to John. Instead of making another suggestion they ask him what he thinks about himself. They must[23] have some answer to take back to those who had sent[24] them.

23 John's reply is given in words from Isa. 40 : 3 which are applied to him in each of the four Gospels (Matt. 3 : 3; Mark 1 : 3; Luke 3 : 4). In each of the others the words are applied to John by the Evangelist: here John uses them himself. The point of the quotation is that it gives no prominence to the preacher whatever. He is not an important person, like a prophet or the Messiah. He is no more than a voice (contrast the reference to Jesus as "the Word"). He is a voice, moreover, with but one thing to say. John's ethical teaching is not large in amount, nor striking in content (see Luke 3 : 10–14). As T. W. Manson says, "It is an anticlimax and it is important to realise why. It is because it is *Interimsethik*, the genuine article: telling men how to make the best of a bad job till the new day dawns."[25] John's real function was not to teach ethics, but to point men to Jesus. "Make straight the way of the Lord" is a call to be ready, for the coming of the Messiah is near. The imagery is that of preparing a roadway by clearing away the obstacles.[26] This was an important process in ancient times, especially for roads in the wilderness country.

It is not without its interest that the Qumran sect made use

---

[23] For the suggestion that ἵνα is imperatival see on v. 8. An imperative here would yield the sense, "let us give an answer" which seems improbable. The meaning is surely "(Tell us) so that we may give an answer".

[24] The verb is πέμψασιν. For the alleged distinction of this verb from ἀποστέλλω see on 3 : 17.

[25] *The Servant-Messiah* (Cambridge, 1953), p. 45.

[26] εὐθύνω was used not only in the literal sense, "to straighten", but also with the derived meaning, "to correct". Thus in the papyri the passive participle, "the corrected ones" has the meaning, "the culprits" (see MM, *s.v.*). Similarly the active participle is used of the steersman of a ship, "the one guiding straight". The word does not occur in the Synoptic parallels, nor in LXX from which they quote (all read ἑτοιμάσατε). John may be making his own translation from the Hebrew. And he may, as Edwin D. Freed thinks, have been attracted to this verb because of its frequent use in an ethical or moral sense (*Old Testament Quotations in the Gospel of John*, Leiden, 1965, pp. 1–7).

of the same passage from Isaiah. We read: "they shall be separated from the midst of the session of the men of error to go to the wilderness to prepare there the way of the Lord; as it is written, 'In the wilderness prepare the way of the Lord; make straight in the desert a highway for our God.' This is the study of the law, as he commanded through Moses".[27] But they understood it to apply to themselves as they sat down quietly reading their Bibles in the desert. Whatever happened to people outside, *they* would be ready when Messiah came. John, by contrast, understood the words as a clarion call to the nation. He was not concerned with himself and his own safety at all. He was trying to prepare the way of the Lord by getting people ready to meet Him. He was only a voice. But he *was* a voice, proclaiming the Lord's message.[28]

24 The meaning of this verse is not quite clear. Traditionally it has been understood as "they which were sent were of the Pharisees" (AV). But this involves the inclusion of an article which most textual critics agree should be omitted.[29] If we omit it, we are still left with different ways of taking the words. They could mean, "they had been sent from the Pharisees" (so Bernard). But this implies that the whole delegation was Pharisaic, which is most unlikely (see on v. 19). Alternatively we could take the words as "Some Pharisees who were in the deputation asked him" (NEB), which makes part of the delegation Pharisaic, or, "Now some of the Pharisees had been sent to John" (Phillips), which gives the Pharisees a delegation of their own in addition to the official one.[30] It is difficult to be sure, but I incline to the sense of NEB. I do not see that the words point to two delegations, but they do seem to indicate that there were some Pharisees who were not content

---

[27] 1 QS, viii. 13ff. (*DSS*, p. 382).

[28] *Cf.* W. H. Brownlee: "John's ministry is well explained as that of a 'voice' not in any vague sense that adheres to Is. 40 : 3 itself, but in the dynamic sense that here was a neglected function which the Essenes had not been performing as they sought to prepare the Lord's way in the wilderness" (*SNT*, p. 47).

[29] It is lacking in P66א*A*B syrᵖ co. See the note in Field, p. 84.

[30] Dodd sees significance in the difference in the kind of questions asked by the two groups: "The official deputation, as such, is content with obtaining from the Baptist a disavowal of any dangerous pretensions; its Pharisaic members (or the Pharisaic deputation) wish to probe more deeply into the theoretical basis of his baptism. There is nothing here inconsistent with what we know of conditions at the time. At this point the evangelist seems to be following a well-informed tradition" (*HTFG*, pp. 264f.).

with the progress made by the official delegation, and who accordingly added some questions of their own. The Pharisees[31] were a religious party, dating from the time of John Hyrcanus and Alexander Jannaeus. They seem always to have represented the ordinary people as against the aristocracy, and pure religion over against the ecclesiastical politics so characteristic of the Sadducees.[32] They made a great deal of the study of the Law (for "law" see on v. 17). But they tended to surround it with a mass of their own interpretations. In practice this meant that the keeping of their traditions loomed larger than the Law. On occasion, as Jesus pointed out, the traditions hindered men from living in accordance with the spirit of the Law (Mark 7 : 6ff.). Some of the Pharisees were men of noble spirit, but all too often their multitudinous regulations led to an emphasis on the outward, and this in turn to spiritual pride. This was accentuated by the fact that ordinary men did not have the time (nor the inclination!) to learn, let alone practise, the host of traditions which the Pharisees valued so highly. On this occasion their inquiry was the natural outcome of the position they had arrogated to themselves in the Jewish religion. A man was preaching and baptizing. He was drawing crowds in the name of religion. The Pharisees must know all about it. 25 John had given them an answer as to his view of his activities. But it could not have satisfied them. What had they really discovered of a positive nature? Nothing. So they try a new tack. Since John does not claim to be either the Messiah or a messianic person why does he baptize? Baptism was not a new practice in

---

[31] The name "Pharisee" is usually said to derive from a root which means "to separate", so that the name basically means those who have separated themselves from all loose religious practices and live in strict accordance with the Law. This may indeed be the correct way of understanding it. T. W. Manson, however, suggests that the name derives from the word for "Persian": "The word Pharisee originally meant simply 'Persian'; and it was applied to the innovators in theology in much the same way that the term 'Romaniser' has been used in theological controversy in our own day. The name stuck, and at a later date was furnished with an edifying etymology. It was explained that it was really connected with a Hebrew root meaning 'to separate', and so signified that those who bore it were separated from all that is abominable in God's sight" (*op. cit.*, pp. 19f.). Whatever be the truth about the origin of the name the Pharisees were the party of strict orthodoxy.

[32] "In theology" the Sadducees "are the representatives of an ossified orthodoxy with no guiding principle except *quod semper, quod ubique, quod ab omnibus*" (T. W. Manson, *op. cit.*, p. 20).

Judaism. It was the regular rite in the admission of converts from other religions.[33] When such a conversion took place the males of the family were circumcised. But all, of both sexes, were baptized. In this way they removed ceremonially the pollutions contracted in the Gentile world. The novelty in John's case and the sting behind his practice was that he applied to Jews the ceremony which was held to be appropriate in the case of Gentiles coming newly into the faith.[34] All Jews were prepared to accept the view that Gentiles were defiled and needed cleansing. But to put *Jews* in the same class was horrifying. The Jews were God's people already. It is true that on the basis of certain Old Testament passages (Ezek. 36 : 25; Zech. 13 : 1) some expected that there would be baptizing when the messianic age dawned. But John had denied being the Messiah. It was all very perplexing, and the Pharisees wanted to know more about it.

26, 27 John's reply points them to Jesus in accordance with his characteristic role. "I" is emphatic (as is "ye"). All that he does is to baptize in water.[35] After this we expect a reference to another kind of baptism, like the baptism in the Holy Spirit to which in fact all three Synoptists refer in a corresponding statement. But instead our Evangelist passes on to the greatness of Jesus and drops the subject of baptism. This should not be taken as indicating that he did not regard his baptism as important. He did. He does not depreciate it. But his baptism is not an end in itself. Its purpose is to point men to Christ (v. 31). John's interest is in the Christ

---

[33] Some deny that proselyte baptism is as old as this period. But see SBk, I, pp. 102–13; G. F. Moore, *Judaism*, I (Harvard, 1958), pp. 323–53, III (Harvard, 1959), pp. 107–14; T. W. Manson, *op. cit.*, pp. 43f.

[34] Perhaps it was also new that he baptized men (as his title "the Baptist" indicates). Previously people seem to have baptized themselves before witnesses. E. Stauffer thinks that John was "an apocalyptist of levitical stamp". He raises the question whether John may not have expected "a levitical Messiah" (*New Testament Theology*, London, 1955, p. 24). T. W. Manson devotes ch. II of *The Servant-Messiah* to John the Baptist. *Inter alia* he says, "John was not the first to preach repentance and moral reformation: he was not the first to make washing a ritual act charged with religious significance: he was not the first to indulge in Messianic propaganda. But he was the first to bring all three things together in an organic unity" (*op. cit.*, p. 39). See also W. H. Brownlee, "John the Baptist in the New Light of Ancient Scrolls" (ch. III of *SNT*).

[35] We ought to notice that John is interested in water, both literally and symbolically. He uses the term 21 times. It is found 4 times in 1 John and 18 times in Revelation, but no more than 7 times in any other book.

and in nothing less. So he proceeds to tell his inquisitors that the Great One stands among them, though not known by them (*cf.* v. 11).[36] Then he repeats the words about His coming after him (v. 15). Finally be brings out the greatness of the One who was to come by referring to his own personal unworthiness. A "latchet" is a leathern thong, in this case one used to tie on a sandal (not "shoe" as ARV). Loosing the sandal was the task of a slave. A disciple could not be expected to perform it. To get the full impact of this we must bear in mind that disciples did do many services for their teachers. Teachers in ancient Palestine were not paid (it would be a terrible thing to ask for money for teaching!). But in partial compensation disciples were in the habit of performing little services for their Rabbis instead. But they had to draw the line somewhere, and menial tasks like loosing the sandal thong came under this heading. There is a Rabbinic saying (in its present form dating from *c.* A.D. 250, but probably much older): "Every service which a slave performs for his master shall a disciple do for his teacher except the loosing of his sandal-thong."[37] John selects this task which the Rabbinic saying stresses as too menial for any disciple, and declares himself unworthy to perform it. He is unworthy to perform the most menial of tasks for the One who was to come after.[38] Humility could scarcely take a lower place.

---

[36] Among the Qumran Thanksgiving Psalms is one which says:
"this tree which is planted in Truth
puts forth upon its boughs
blossoms of Holiness,
keeping its secret hidden, unknown,
sealed and unsuspected" (*SDSS*, p. 165).
If, as a number of scholars believe, this refers to the Messiah, we have a striking parallel to the thought of this verse, though the language is very different.

[37] SBk, I, p. 121.

[38] ἵνα (in the expression ἄξιος ἵνα λύσω) has lost most of its telic force and is practically equivalent to the infinitive, as often in John. Yet Abbott points out that it is used only in sentences when it is preceded by words like "good" or "command", never words like "evil" or "forbid". He proceeds, "The reason is that 'goodness' and 'command' suggest *a positive object to be attained or a positive object in commanding; and object suggests purpose*" (2094). Note further the use of the redundant pronoun αὐτοῦ, complementing the relative pronoun οὗ. Burney points out that in Semitic languages a statement like "I saw the man *to whom* I gave the book" would appear as "I saw the man *who* I gave the book *to him*". He sees this construction again in 1 : 33; 9 : 36; 13 : 26; 18 : 9 (*AO*, pp. 84f.). Each of these is in direct speech and this reinforces the view that an Aramaic source lies behind the sayings of this Gospel.

28 The section closes with a note of place. These things happened at John's normal spot for baptizing on the other side of the Jordan (*i.e.* from Jerusalem). The name of the place varies in the MSS. Some read "Bethabarah" and some "Betharabah". But both these seem due to Origen, who early in the third century visited the land and reported that he could find no town called "Bethany" on the other side of the Jordan. He says that the ancient manuscripts read "Bethany".[39] But because he thought the place must be Bethabarah he adopted that reading. Origen was a great scholar, but for once it appears that he is not to be relied on. Close attention to his words shows that he did not actually go to Jordan, but only that "they say that Bethabara is pointed out". He appears to have been misinformed.[40] It seems clear that "Bethany" is the right reading. But quite early the location was lost sight of. The Evangelist adds "beyond the Jordan" to distinguish this locality from the better known Bethany, which was near Jerusalem.[41]

---

[39] His words are, "We are aware of the reading which is found in almost all the copies, 'These things were done in Bethany.' This appears, moreover, to have been the reading at an earlier time; and in Heracleon we read 'Bethany.' We are convinced, however, that we should not read 'Bethany,' but 'Bethabara.' We have visited the places to enquire as to the footsteps of Jesus and His disciples, and of the prophets. Now Bethany . . . is fifteen stadia from Jerusalem, and the river Jordan is about a hundred and eighty stadia distant from it. Nor is there any other place of the same name in the neighbourhood of the Jordan, but they say that Bethabara is pointed out on the banks of the Jordan, and that John is said to have baptized there" (*Commentary on John*, VI, 24; ANF, X, p. 370).

[40] *Cf.* the comment of R. D. Potter: "How did the name disappear in 100 or 150 years? The answer is that Origen, despite his pious assertion about visiting the scenes of our Redemption, had never been there. He is reporting hearsay (δείκνυσθαι δὲ λέγουσιν). He never discovered Bethany beyond Jordan because he never went to look. He did not even get to Bethabara on this side of Jordan" (*SE*, I, p. 332).

[41] Pierson Parker has put forward the interesting suggestion that the Bethany meant is the one near Jerusalem. He thinks a correct paraphrase would be, "These things took place in Bethany, which is across from the point of the Jordan where John had been baptizing" (*JBL*, LXXIV, 1955, pp. 257–61; *cf.* also the adaptation of this by Dr. Harold Greenlee, *BT*, IX, 1958, pp. 137f.). His argument is interesting, but I am unconvinced that the Bethany near Jerusalem could naturally be described as "across from" a point on the Jordan. The distance is more than 15 miles, and there are hills in between.

(b) John and Jesus, 1 : 29–34

29 On the morrow he seeth Jesus coming unto him, and saith,
Behold, the Lamb of God, that [1]taketh away the sin of the
world! 30 This is he of whom I said, After me cometh a man
who is become before me: for he was [2]before me. 31 And I
knew him not; but that he should be made manifest to Israel,
for this cause came I baptizing [3]in water. 32 And John bare
witness, saying, I have beheld the Spirit descending as a dove
out of heaven; and it abode upon him. 33 And I knew him
not: but he that sent me to baptize [3]in water, he said unto
me, Upon whomsoever thou shalt see the Spirit descending,
and abiding upon him, the same is he that baptizeth [3]in the
Holy Spirit. 34 And I have seen, and have borne witness that
this is the Son of God.

[1] Or, *beareth the sin* [2] Gr. *first in regard of me* [3] Or, *with*

On the second day of this momentous week John publicly
pointed out Jesus as the Messiah to whom he had given his
witness. He went on to tell how he had come to know that Jesus
was He.
29 For the note of time see on vv. 19–28. "Coming" will here
mean "approaching", not "coming to him for the first time".
Vv. 26, 32f. show that John had recognized Jesus[42] as the Christ
on an earlier occasion. "Behold" is a favourite expression in this
Gospel and John uses it more often than all the rest of the New
Testament writers put together.[43] The expression "the Lamb of
God"[44] has passed into the general Christian vocabulary. But for
all that it is very difficult to know exactly what it means. It is
not found elsewhere in the New Testament (though Jesus is

[42] There is an article with Ἰησοῦν as often. For this construction see
Richard C. Nevius, "The Use of the Definite Article with 'Jesus' in the Fourth
Gospel" (*NTS*, XII, 1965–66, pp. 81–85); also the note in Bernard.
[43] The word is ἴδε which John uses 15 times out of its 29 New Testament
occurrences. Matthew has it 4 times and Luke 9 times (the other occurrence
is in Galatians). By contrast ἰδού is found in Matthew 62 times, in Mark 7
times, in Luke 57 times, and in John only 4 times. There seems little difference
in meaning, both forms being originally imperatives from εἶδον. But they have
become conventionalized particles and, for example, both may be followed by
the nominative (ἴδε here, ἰδού in 19 : 5).
[44] The nominative Ἀμνός shows that ἴδε is no longer a real imperative
("Look at – "), but an exclamation ("Behold!").

sometimes spoken of as "the Lamb", especially in Revelation[45]),
nor in any previous writing known to us. Thus we are not able
to appeal to some other writing as John's source. The genitive
"of God" may mean "provided by God" (*cf.* Gen. 22 : 8), or
"belonging to God".[46] Perhaps in his usual manner the Evangelist
wants us to combine both meanings. But to what does "the Lamb"
refer? Many suggestions have been made, among which we notice
the following: (i) *The Passover Lamb*, a suggestion supported by
the apparent identification of Christ's sacrifice with the Passover
in 19 : 36. Against it are two main points, the one that the Passover
victim was not necessarily a lamb at all,[47] and the other that the
proper term in use at the time for the Passover victim was not
"lamb", but "Passover" *(pascha)*.[48] Another objection sometimes
urged that the Passover was not an expiatory sacrifice (and thus
could not be said to take away the world's sin) is not valid. All

---

[45]   The word used in Revelation (and in John 21 : 15) is ἀρνίον, whereas
that used here is ἀμνός (elsewhere in the New Testament only in v. 36; Acts
8 : 32; I Pet. 1 : 19). There does not appear to be any real difference of meaning
between the two. MacGregor thinks it "likely that the Evangelist is throwing
back into John's words a title which, as applied to Christ, had in his own day
become stereotyped". So far from this being the case it is very difficult to find
any evidence for the use of the term which does not depend on this passage.
As far as I know the expression is found nowhere before its occurrence here.
Nor is it attested in later times other than in passages dependent on this one.
There is evidence for referring to Christ as "the Lamb", but this is with a
different word and the qualifier, "of God", is not added.

[46]   It may possibly also be a Hebraism which describes anything great by
referring it to God (*e.g.* Nimrod was a very mighty hunter, literally "a mighty
hunter before Jehovah", Gen. 10 : 9). In that case it would describe Jesus as
"that eminent, great, divine, and most excellent Lamb" (Ryle).

[47]   It might be a kid. I am not convinced by the contention that, while
a kid was possible, a lamb was more usual. This may well have been the case
(though I have never seen it proved). But it fails to deal with the main point,
namely that "the Passover Lamb" is a modern expression, not an ancient one.
Even if a lamb was offered most often the term "the Passover Lamb" was not
used of it (τὸ πάσχα was the term). We are looking for the source of an expression which explicitly mentions a lamb.

[48]   G. Buchanan Gray says, "the Paschal victim was . . . neither as a matter
of fact necessarily a lamb, nor in the usage of the time was it called a lamb;
the proper term for it was 'Passover', and it is only reasonable to suppose that
had the author of the Fourth Gospel intended this he would, like St. Paul,
have used the correct and unambiguous designation" (*Sacrifice in the Old Testament*, Oxford, 1925, p. 397).

sacrifice was held to be expiatory,[49] and specifically, the Passover was sometimes viewed this way.[50] (ii) *The "lamb that is led to the slaughter"* (Isa. 53 : 7). This is possible. But there is nothing in the context that points to it, and we can hold this reference probable only if we can feel that there was a widespread acceptance of the view that Isa. 53 applied to the Messiah. If this was the case, then when John was referring clearly enough to the Messiah and using the term "lamb" the allusion could be detected. But unless there was such a widespread acceptance of the view it is not easy to see how the allusion could be picked up. The evidence seems to be against this interpretation of Isa. 53,[51] and the suggested explanation is thus unlikely. (iii) *The Servant of the Lord.* This is another way of seeing the origin of the expression in Isa. 53. Some scholars think that an ambiguous expression in Aramaic, meant

---

[49] SBk cite evidence that even the meal offering was regarded as having atoning value (III, p. 699; notice that Lev. 14 : 20 regards the burnt and meal offerings as making atonement). Lev. 17 : 11 connects atonement with "the blood" simply, not the blood of any particular sacrifice or sacrifices. Johs. Pedersen can say: "Everything in any way connected with sacrifice acquired an expiatory power" (*Israel*, III–IV, London, 1947, p. 364). Similarly C. R. North: "By the close of the OT period, too, all sacrifices were believed to have atoning value" (*TWBB*, p. 206).

[50] G. Dalman cites ExR 15 (35b), "I see the Paschal blood and propitiate you", and again (35a), "I mercifully take pity on you by means of the Paschal blood and the blood of circumcision, and I propitiate your souls" (*Jesus-Jeshua*, London, 1929, p. 167). Josephus says of the Passover, that the Israelites "in readiness to start, sacrificed, purified the houses with the blood" (*Ant.* ii, 312).

[51] See the authorities cited by H. H. Rowley, *BJRL*, XXXIX, 1950-51, p. 103, n. 4. Those who accept this view usually agree that other ideas are present also. For example Vincent Taylor says, "The dominant conception appears to be that of the Servant, freely used in association with other sacrificial ideas" (*Jesus and His Sacrifice*, London, 1939, p. 227). But Rowley's arguments seem conclusive that the association of Isa. 53 with the Messiah was not made in pre-Christian times. He says specifically, "There is no serious evidence, then, of the bringing together of the concepts of the Suffering Servant and the Davidic Messiah before the Christian era" (*The Servant of the Lord*, London, 1952, p. 85). Similarly H. Wheeler Robinson: "There has been no success in all the endeavours made to find previous or contemporary identification of the Messiah with the suffering servant of Yahweh" (*Redemption and Revelation*, New York and London, 1942, p. 199).

as "the Servant of the Lord", was mistranslated.[52] The difficulties
here are linguistic. It is not easy to think that so well known an
expression as "the Servant of the Lord" should be unrecognized,
and should be translated by so difficult and unusual a phrase as
"the Lamb of God".[53] (iv) *The lamb of the daily sacrifices* offered
morning and evening in the Temple.[54] Once more we must admit
the possibility. But we must add that there is nothing that clearly
indicates it. We have no knowledge of the daily sacrifice being
called "God's Lamb". (v) *The "gentle lamb"* of Jer. 11 : 19. This
should probably be dismissed, for that lamb was apparently not
thought of as taking away sins. (vi) *The scapegoat.* This accords
well with the thought of the taking away of sin. But it suffers
from the fatal defect that the scapegoat was not a lamb. (vii) *The
triumphant Lamb* of the apocalypses. This is undoubtedly the
meaning of "the Lamb" in Revelation, and Dodd accepts the
idea in this passage.[55] But is it difficult to see this as the reference.
The thought here appears to be not so much that of victory over
enemies, as of sacrifice for sin. (viii) *The God-provided Lamb* of Gen.

---

[52] J. Jeremias says, "the expression ὁ ἀμνὸς τοῦ θεοῦ conceals both a
factual and a linguistic difficulty. (1) The description of the Saviour as a lamb
is unknown to late Judaism. (2) The expression is an unparalleled genitive
combination. Both difficulties are solved if we refer to the Aramaic where
טַלְיָא means (*a*) the lamb, (*b*) the boy, the servant. Probably behind the phrase
ὁ ἀμνὸς τοῦ θεοῦ lies an Aramaic טַלְיָא דֵאלָהָא in the sense of עֶבֶד יהוה "
(*The Servant of God*, by W. Zimmerli and J. Jeremias, London, 1957, p. 82).

[53] Dodd puts the criticism of Jeremias's view succinctly: "ἀμνός in the
LXX never translates טָלֶה. No examples are adduced of טַלְיָא as a rendering
for עֶבֶד ... Thus we lack evidence in support of the view either that the
Aramaic-speaking Church (or John the Baptist) could have spoken of the
עבד יהוה as טליא דאלהא, or that a bilingual translator who took טַלְיָא
in the sense of 'lamb' would have chosen ἀμνός as its equivalent" (*IFG*, pp.
235f.). (A Palestinian Syriac text is now known to have טַלְיָא for עֶבֶד
"servant" in Isa. 52 : 13, as also in Gen. 18 : 3; Jer. 30 : 10; cf. J. Jeremias
in *TDNT* VI, p. 679, n. 156; p. 702, n. 356.)

[54] Hoskyns is one of few commentators who adopt this view. He speaks
of John as declaring "Jesus to be the property of God, by whose complete
obedience the normal sacrifices in the Temple – a lamb without blemish was
offered daily both morning and evening (Exod. xxix. 38–46) and even during
the siege of Jerusalem these sacrifices were maintained in spite of very great
difficulties ... – were fulfilled and superseded (ii. 18–22)."

[55] *IFG*, pp. 230-38.

146

22 : 8. This draws attention to one important aspect of Christ's sacrifice, the divine initiative.[56] But it does not help with the others. And in any case there is no indication in Gen. 22 that the lamb was considered to effect or foreshadow the far-reaching atonement of which the Baptist speaks.[57] (ix) *A guilt-offering*, since sometimes this was a lamb (passages suggested are Lev. 14 : 12ff., 21, 24f.; Num. 6 : 12; *cf.* the expression "the lamb of the trespass-offering", Lev. 14 : 24).[58] The objection to this view is that a guilt offering was not characteristically a lamb. Since the victim was so often another animal (*e.g.* a ram) the allusion would be almost impossible to detect.

From all this it is clear that there is no agreement (though many would be found to accept one or other of two or three of these views). The fact is that a lamb taking away sin, even if it is distinguished as God's Lamb, is too indefinite a description for us to pin-point the reference. If the writer really had in mind an allusion to one particular offering we are not able any longer to detect it with certainty. But it seems more probable that of set purpose he used an expression which cannot be confined to any one view. He is making a general allusion to sacrifice. The lamb figure may well be intended to be composite, evoking memories

---

[56] A. Richardson sees more than one allusion here, but certainly this one among others. He says, "St John would seem (as is his way) to have caught the subtle allusion to the sacrifice of Isaac implicit in the (Synoptic) tradition of the Baptism of Jesus, and he is emphasizing the truth in his own way: Christ is the Lamb of sacrifice promised by God to Abraham, the father of many nations, and thus he is the God-given universal Sin Bearer" (*An Introduction to the Theology of the New Testament*, London, 1958, p. 228).

[57] Yet we should not overlook the tremendous importance assigned in Jewish thought to the Binding of Isaac. This was held to be a supremely significant sacrifice (see the evidence cited by G. Vermes, *Scripture and Tradition in Judaism*, Leiden, 1961, pp. 193–229; H. J. Schoeps, *Paul*, London, 1961, pp. 141–9). Vermes maintains that in the light of this the Johannine passage ceases to be a *crux:* "For the Palestinian Jew, all lamb sacrifice, and especially the Passover lamb and the Tamid offering, was a memorial of the Akedah with its effects of deliverance, forgiveness of sin and messianic salvation" (*op. cit.*, p. 225).

[58] *Cf.* J. Morgenstern: "Here, beyond all doubt, Jesus is conceived of, precisely as was the Servant, as an אשם, 'a guilt-offering', sacrificing himself for the redemption of mankind from its iniquity and thus effecting its salvation" (*Vetus Testamentum*, XI, 1961, p. 425).

of several, perhaps all, of the suggestions we have canvassed.[59] All that the ancient sacrifices foreshadowed was perfectly fulfilled in the sacrifice of Christ.[60]

The verb "taketh away" conveys the notion of bearing off.[61] It is perhaps not specific enough to point to any one particular means of atonement, but it does signify atonement, and that by substitution. "Jesus bears the consequence of human sin in order that its guilt may be removed" (Hoskyns). It is removed completely, carried right off. John speaks of sin,[62] not sins (*cf.* I John 1 : 9). He is referring to the totality of the world's sin, rather than to a number of individual acts. The expression "the sin of the world" does not appear to be used prior to this passage. The reference to "the world" is another glance at the comprehensiveness of Christ's atonement. It is completely adequate for the needs of all men. Right at the beginning of his Gospel John points us forward to the cross and to the significance of the cross.

---

[59] Feliks Gryglewicz argues that, in accordance with John's habit, the expression is used with a double meaning, the Servant of the Lord, and the Passover Lamb (see "*Das Lamm Gottes*", *NTS*, XIII, 1966–67, pp. 133–146). This is all right as far as it goes, but it seems to me that the meaning is more likely to be multiform than dual in this case.

[60] The complex background is stressed by C. K. Barrett in his article "The Lamb of God" (*NTS*, I, 1954–55, pp. 210–218). He gives a special place to the eschatological element. See further my *The Apostolic Preaching of The Cross*, 3rd edition (London and Grand Rapids, 1965), pp. 129–143.

[61] The verb is αἴρω, which John uses more than any other New Testament writer (26 times). It is found with the object ἁμάρτημα in I Sam. 15 : 25, and ἀνόμημα in I Sam. 25 : 28, both times in the sense "forgive". The idea of bearing sin in Heb. 9 : 28; I Pet. 2 : 24 is conveyed by ἀναφέρω, but there is not likely to be a great difference in meaning. MacGregor, agreeing that the verb αἴρω means not "take upon oneself", but "take out of the way", yet says, "But the latter thought, while enriching the former, also includes it, for a lamb can only 'remove' sin by vicariously 'bearing' it, and this Christ did". J. Jeremias sees two possible meanings of the verb in this passage: "to take up and carry" and "to carry off". He says, "In both cases it is a matter of setting aside the guilt of others. In the former, however, the means of doing this is by a substitutionary bearing of penalty; in the latter sin is removed by a means of expiation" (*TDNT*, I, pp. 185f.). In the Johannine manner probably both meanings are in mind. For the concept of sinbearing see my *The Cross in the New Testament* (Grand Rapids, 1965), pp. 322ff.

[62] John's interest in the sins of men should not be missed. He uses the noun ἁμαρτία 17 times, the same total as in 1 John. The only New Testament books which use the term more are Romans (48 times) and Hebrews (25 times).

Objection has been made to the authenticity of this saying. It is pointed out that the Synoptic Gospels (as well as general probability) show that Jesus was not held to be Messiah till some considerable time later than this. But this is to overlook the significance of Zacharias and Simeon and Anna. Luke tells us that, even before Jesus' ministry started, "all men reasoned in their hearts concerning John, whether haply he were the Christ" (Luke 3 : 15). Messianic expectations were in the air, and there is no reason why the man whom Jesus called the greatest of those born of women (Luke 7 : 28) should not have had the prophetic insight to have greeted Jesus thus.[63] Again, it is urged that the disciples found difficulty to the very end in accepting the truth that Jesus must suffer. Yet before His ministry has begun the Baptist is here depicted as referring to His sacrificial death. To this there is a threefold answer. In the first place what John knew of the Christ he knew by way of revelation, as the succeeding verses make clear. It is not a matter of what the unaided human reason or intuition could discern in Jesus of Nazareth, but what God had made known. He would be a bold man who would set limits in advance to what God can reveal to His prophets. That John's words made little impression on the followers of Jesus need cause no surprise. Neither did the Master's own predictions of His passion.[64] In the second place, the Qumran scrolls have made acceptance of the saying "not so impossible as it once seemed" as Brownlee puts it. He points out that the scrolls link suffering, and specifically the Suffering Servant, with messiahship, and he sees "important Essene conceptions in John's messianic expectation."[65] They have not

---

[63] *Cf.* Vacher Burch: "He is a man of uncommon powers, and his words flash out from his intuitive genius which owes nothing to the teaching method of his abrogator" (*The Structure and Message of St. John's Gospel*, London, 1928, p. 58).

[64] *Cf.* C. F. Burney: "From these considerations we deduce the conclusion that the fact that our Lord was to fulfil the rôle of the ideal Servant, though not understood by the Apostles, *was in some measure realized by the Baptist*" (*AO*, p. 106; Burney's italics).

[65] *SNT*, pp. 50,51. He goes on to speak of "the validation of the Fourth Gospel as an authentic source concerning the Baptist" (*op. cit.*, p. 52). This is not in contradiction of n. 51 above. There the point was that the linking of the Messiah with Isa. 53 was not widely made: here it is that the link was occasionally made, and specifically that this was done in circles to which John was apparently indebted.

been taken over unaltered, but the point is that the Qumran evidence indicates that a saying like this on the part of a man like John no longer looks improbable. In the third place, if it is not authentic it is difficult to see where the saying comes from. It possesses none of the characteristic marks of a Johannine construction.[66]

30 For the most part this verse repeats the thought of v. 15 (where see note). There is a change from the participles of that verse and of v. 27 to the indicative, which states the fact with greater directness. There is also the use of the word "man".[67] While the Christology of this Gospel is of the highest the writer never loses sight of Jesus' genuine manhood. Before leaving this verse we should perhaps also notice that, though the Baptist says he is quoting words he spoke on a previous occasion, there is no record of that occasion in this Gospel.

31 The "And" with which the sentence begins should not be overlooked. The linking of sentences with "and" (or parataxis, to give the construction its technical name) is very common in John, especially in speeches. The construction is found in all languages, but it is much more common in Aramaic than in most, certainly than it is in Greek. John's fondness for the construction is further evidence of the fact that Aramaic lies behind this Gospel, more particularly the speeches.[68] "I" is emphatic.[69] John had been looking for the Messiah, but he did not know who He was. Yet the whole purpose of his baptism was to make Him manifest to

---

[66] Thus ἀμνός does not occur in John outside this saying, nor does this Evangelist use αἴρω of the removal of sin, nor, though he uses both ἁμαρτία and κόσμος often, does he speak elsewhere of "the sin of the world". It is worth pointing out that C. H. Dodd concludes his discussion of this passage with, "There seems no real reason why the whole expression, ὁ ἀμνὸς τοῦ θεοῦ ὁ αἴρων τὴν ἁμαρτίαν τοῦ κόσμου, should not have been used by John the Baptist, or in a traditional account of his preaching" (*HTFG*, pp. 270f.).

[67] ἀνήρ. "Of whom" is ὑπὲρ οὗ, "on behalf of whom". Many MSS read περί, but this preposition, besides giving a somewhat easier sense, is very common in John, and is not likely to have been altered. The Baptist thinks of himself as an ambassador speaking "on behalf of" Christ.

[68] See *AO*, pp. 56ff.; *AA*, pp. 44ff.

[69] κἀγώ. John uses this form 30 times, just three times as often as in any other New Testament book (I Corinthians, with 10 times). Clearly he finds this form of emphasis congenial.

150

Israel. The Greek construction emphasizes this point.[70] One might have thought that John's baptism was concerned largely with leading men to repent. But this was not its final purpose. John baptized in view of the coming of the Messiah. He baptized in order that the Messiah should be "made manifest to Israel". The verb indicates a bringing into clear light. "In water" may perhaps be another small depreciation of the Baptist, for in v. 33 we are to read of One "that baptizeth in the Holy Spirit". This, however, is not a necessary inference and the manifestation of the Messiah to Israel is no mean task for a man to perform.

32 For "witness" see on v. 7. This second act of witness is to make clear how John had come to know Jesus for what He was (*cf.* Rieu: "John gave proof"). "I have beheld" renders a Greek perfect, which should be given its full force. John is not thinking of something he saw once and which soon passed away. What he saw had continuing effects. The verb is used in this Gospel of seeing with the bodily eye.[71] John is not talking about a vision. He actually saw the Holy Spirit come down[72] upon Jesus in a form like that of a dove.[73] Not only did the Spirit descend, but

---

[70] ἵνα has its full telic force, and it is reinforced by διὰ τοῦτο. The thought of making Christ manifest to Israel is given prominence by putting the ἵνα clause first.

[71] It is sometimes alleged that John uses several verbs for seeing with distinctive meanings and that the verb θεάομαι, which is used here, has the notion of spiritual insight. But it is impossible to see this in some of its occurrences (*e.g.* v. 38; 6 : 5). Brown has a good note on John's verbs for seeing (pp. 501-3). He agrees that there are different kinds of sight in John, but not that these are conveyed by different verbs. He concludes, "Those scholars who think that the verbs are synonymous have almost as many texts to prove their point as do the scholars who would attribute specific meanings to the verbs" (p. 503). John uses θεάομαι 6 times, the most in any New Testament book.

[72] It is uncertain whether ἐξ οὐρανοῦ should be taken with καταβαῖνον ("descending from heaven like a dove") or with περιστεράν ("descending like a dove from the sky").

[73] The symbolism is puzzling and perhaps inexplicable. The dove was not, as is sometimes said, a recognized symbol of the Holy Spirit (see, for example, *LT*, I, pp. 286f.; C. K. Barrett, *The Holy Spirit and the Gospel Tradition*, London, 1947, pp. 35-39). It sometimes stood for Israel, but it is not easy to see the force of this here. Perhaps Jesus is being regarded as the true, ideal Israelite at the very time that He received the Spirit.

"it abode[74] upon him" (a detail not in the Synoptists). We should probably understand that the Spirit remained with Him permanently.

33 John repeats his statement that until the time of this descent of the Spirit he did not know Him. This does not necessarily mean that he did not know Jesus at all, though some have taken this to be the meaning of his words.[75] It is, of course, quite possible that this is his meaning, for Jesus was brought up in Galilee and John in the lonely parts of Judea. They may never have met until now, though they were related. But it seems more probable that John means that he did not know Jesus to be the Messiah who would baptize with the Holy Spirit until he saw the sign. Recognition came not from prior knowledge, but from supernatural revelation. John does not tell us how and when he had been given the sign. But he says that he had it from God[76] who had sent him to baptize that the Spirit would descend and abide upon the One whom he awaited.[77] He does not say whether the sign of the dove was included in the original revelation, or whether he simply recognized the dove for what it was when he saw it alight on Jesus. But what is clear is that he had a divinely appointed sign, and that he knew Jesus by that sign. He goes on to describe Him as "he that baptizeth in the Holy Spirit." All three Synoptists make this point. Jesus came that men might be brought into contact with the divine Spirit. But baptism is a figure which stresses

---

[74] The verb is ἔμεινεν, aorist of μένω, a characteristic word of this Evangelist, here denoting the beginning of the Spirit's permanent dwelling in Jesus and the inception of the new order: the whole of Jesus' ministry is accomplished in the power of the Spirit.

[75] Chrysostom held that Jesus was quite unknown to John until this moment, the reason being that the latter "had passed all his time in the wilderness away from his father's house" (XVII, 2; p. 60). Godet follows the same line of reasoning, and thinks he would have known from the birth stories that Jesus was the Messiah (on v. 31). It is possible, as Brownlee points out (*SNT*, p. 35) that John's aged parents died while he was very young, and that he was brought up by a community of Essenes (who frequently adopted children according to Josephus, *Bell.* ii, 120). Origen thinks the reference is to the pre-incarnation period, with the added thought that "perhaps he is here learning something new about Him", namely that He is to baptize with the Holy Spirit (*Commentary on John*, I. 37; ANF, X, p. 317).

[76] The use of the emphatic ἐκεῖνος should not be missed: "he that sent me to baptize with water, he (and none less) said. ..." For ἐκεῖνος in this Gospel see on v. 8.

[77] For the significance of the redundant pronoun αὐτόν see on v. 27.

abundant supply. So John will mean that the Spirit leads men into the infinite divine spiritual resources. This had not been possible previously, for there is a quality of life that Christ and none other makes available to men. This life is a positive gift coming from the Spirit of God. Baptism with water had essentially a negative significance. It is a cleansing from – . But baptism with the Spirit is positive. It is the bestowal of new life in God. [78]

34 Again the Greek perfects must be allowed their full force. "I have seen" means much the same as "I have beheld" in v. 32. [79] "Have borne witness" points to the continuing effect of the Baptist's words. They were not the idle utterance of the moment, said and then over. They continued with full effect. The meaning of the end of the verse is affected by a textual difficulty. If we follow the text favored by ARV we have a certain stress on the deity of Christ. Each of the Evangelists in his own way brings out the deity of Christ at the beginning of his Gospel. Matthew and Luke do it with the birth stories, Mark with his reference to Jesus as "the Son of God" in his opening sentence. John has already done this in the Prologue, but with this reading he does it again. The climax of the Baptist's testimony is that "this is the Son of God". [80] This is all the more important to him in that his Gospel was written to bring men to a knowledge of this truth (20 : 31). "Son of God" is, of course, an expression that might mean much or little. Men who believe and are thus admitted to the heavenly family address God as "Father" and are said to be "sons of God" (though John never uses that term of them; see on v. 12). But here the expression will have its fullest force. It will point to the closest personal relationship to the Father. It will be an assertion

---

[78] For the idea of baptism with the Spirit *cf.* the *Manual of Discipline*, "Like waters of purification (God) will sprinkle upon him the spirit of truth" (1 QS, iv. 21; *SDSS*, p. 55).

[79] The verb is ἑώρακα. For John's use of verbs of seeing see n. 71 above.

[80] See further the article " 'Son of God' in the Fourth Gospel" (*NTS*, X, 1963–64, pp. 227–237). In it Dom J. Howton argues that "Whereas God of old chose a nation to work out his purpose in the world, and in that nation raised up prophets to direct his people, now he has chosen only one individual who in himself represents God active in the world (cf. Heb. i. 1–2). It is this meaning of the title 'son of God' that is primary for the Evangelist" (*op. cit.*, p. 233).

of the deity of the Messiah.[81] It seems to me, however, that we should probably read "God's Chosen One" (so NEB).[82] This reading is fairly well attested and it is unlikely that an original "the Son of God" would have been altered into it, whereas the reverse process is quite intelligible. If we accept this reading John is saying that Jesus is the object of the divine call. The choice of none less than God has fallen upon Him.

2. THE FIRST DISCIPLES, 1 : 35–51

(a) Andrew and Peter, 1 : 35–42

35 Again on the morrow John was standing, and two of his disciples; 36 and he looked upon Jesus as he walked, and saith, Behold, the Lamb of God! 37 And the two disciples heard him speak, and they followed Jesus. 38 And Jesus turned, and beheld them following, and saith unto them, What seek ye? And they said unto him, Rabbi (which is to say, being interpreted, Teacher), where abidest thou? 39 He saith unto them, Come, and ye shall see. They came therefore and saw where he abode; and they abode with him that day: it was about the tenth hour. 40 One of the two that heard John speak, and followed him, was Andrew, Simon Peter's brother. 41 He findeth first his own brother Simon, and saith unto him, We have found the Messiah (which is, being interpreted, [1]Christ). 42 He brought him unto Jesus. Jesus looked upon him, and said, Thou art Simon the son of [2]John; thou shalt be called Cephas (which is by interpretation, [3]Peter).

[1]That is, *Anointed*. Comp. Ps. 2.2   [2]Gr. *Joanes:* called in Mt. 16.17, *Jonah* [3]That is, *Rock* or *Stone*.

---

[81] Brown notes the christological richness of this section of the Gospel: "When we look back on the wealth and depth of the material contained in the intervening verses (*i.e.* vv. 19–34), we appreciate John's genius at incorporating a whole christology into one brief scene."

[82] ὁ υἱός has far and away the best attestation, P66, P75 ℵcABC Θ boh *etc.* But ὁ ἐκλεκτός is read by P5vid ℵ* itb.e syrc.s Ambrose, a strong combination. Two other readings ὁ ἐκλεκτὸς υἱός and ὁ μονογενὴς υἱός appear secondary. There would be every reason for scribes to alter another reading before τοῦ Θεοῦ to υἱός, but it is difficult to see how ἐκλεκτός could have been derived if υἱός was original. R. V. G. Tasker gives an additional reason for preferring ἐκλεκτός, namely that it "is in harmony with what would appear to have been the early tradition about the significance of the heavenly voice at Jesus' baptism" and he refers to Matt. 3 : 17; Mark 1 : 11 (*GNT*, p. 425).

It was the Baptist's mission to point men to Jesus. In the previous section we have seen him bearing his witness. Now we find him sending some of his followers after the Lord. There is an account of a "call" in the Synoptists (*e.g.* Mark 1 : 16–20), but it differs greatly from this. Despite Barrett's hesitation we should not fear to accept both as authentic. The Fourth Gospel tells of a call to be disciples; the Synoptists of a call to be Apostles. "John's theme is not the calling of the apostles into office; it is their congenial association with Christ."[83] Strictly speaking there is no "call" in this Gospel (except in the case of Philip, v. 43). Neither does Jesus call, nor John send. The disciples of John recognize the Messiah and spontaneously attach themselves to Him. A minor confirmation is that John tells us that Simon was given the name "Peter" when Jesus first met him (v. 42), whereas in the Synoptists, who do not recount this meeting, there is no indication of when the name was bestowed. Psychologically it may well be that some such contact as is here recorded is almost the necessary prelude to the far-reaching call narrated by the Synoptists, with its requirement that the called abandon everything for Jesus. See further Godet's note on v. 43.

35, 36 Once again there is a precise note of time (see on vv. 19–28). One of the two disciples (*i.e.* "learners"; the word meant those who had attached themselves to a given teacher) is subsequently named as Andrew, but the other's name is not given. From early times it has been thought that he was the beloved disciple, and, while this is not proven, it may well be the case.[84] It would accord with this that we have some touches of an eyewitness, the picture of John "standing", and the look[85] he gave Jesus as He walked. For "the Lamb of God" see on v. 29.

---

[83] Luther, vol. 22, p. 182.

[84] J. A. T. Robinson finds "little to set against the traditional view that the unnamed disciple of the pair was the actual source of this material (*i.e.* the material in this Gospel) – whether or not he was also the author of the Gospel" (*NTS*, IV, 1957–58, p. 264, n. 2).

[85] The verb is ἐμβλέπω. *Cf.* Swete on Mark 10 : 21, " Ἐμβλέπειν ... is to fix the eyes for a moment upon an object, – a characteristically searching look turned upon an individual". But see n. 71 above.

37 The Baptist on this occasion said[86] nothing about following Jesus. But his whole ministry was forward-looking, and he had instructed his disciples well. Thus when this pair heard Jesus acclaimed as "the Lamb of God" they knew what was expected of them. They immediately left John and followed Jesus. The verb "followed" is in the tense appropriate to once-for-all action, which may be meant to indicate that they cast in their lot with Jesus. They did not mean to make a tentative inquiry but to give themselves to Him. We should also notice that the verb has both a general sense of "follow", and a more specific sense of "follow as a disciple". In this place it may be used in both senses. They walked down the path after Jesus and thus followed. But they also symbolically committed themselves to Him.

Let us not overlook the light all this sheds on John's greatness. It is not particularly easy to attach disciples firmly to oneself when one is calling for a strenuous following of the right. But when this has been done it is the mark of a truly great man that he can gently, but firmly, detach them, so that they may go after a greater.

38 As the two approached Jesus He turned and asked, "What seek ye?" It is a very natural touch that they did not know what to say, for "where abidest thou?" (Knox: "where dost thou live?") is not really an answer to the question. They may have felt shy. Their words also probably imply that what they wanted with Him could not be settled in a few minutes by the wayside. They

---

[86] John's verb is λαλοῦντος, present participle of λαλέω. This verb is unusually frequent in John, where it occurs 60 times. Matthew has it 26 times, Mark 21 times and Luke 31 times (Acts 60 times). We see the significance of these figures by comparing them with those for λέγω, where John shows no special preference: Matthew 289 times, Mark 202 times, Luke 217 times (Acts 102 times), John 266 times. John's use of λαλέω is thus unusual. His reason is another matter. LS give the meaning of this verb as "talk, chat, prattle", while AG points out that in the classics it usually means "chatter, babble". This, however, is certainly not the meaning in John. MM cites examples from the papyri, which, it claims, "all bear out the usual distinction that, while λέγω calls attention to the substance of what is said, the onomato-poetic λαλέω points rather to the outward utterance". However it does not seem possible to find a real difference between the two verbs in John. This evangelist seems to use them interchangeably. His unusual use of λαλέω appears to be no more than a mark of style.

looked for a long talk.[87] They address Him as "Rabbi", the custo-
mary form of address for disciples speaking to their teacher.[88] The
Evangelist explains the Aramaic word for the benefit of his non-
Jewish readers.

39 Jesus welcomed them. "Come, and ye shall see" is equivalent
to "Come and see" (v. 36, where see note). This invitation implies
more than that they should see for themselves the place where He
was lodging. It is an invitation to visit Him. It led to their staying
with Him that day. This probably means that they spent the night
with Him. The time is given as "about the tenth hour",[89] *i.e.*
about 4 p.m. on our time scale. The Jews measured their days
from sunset to sunset, and divided both night and day into twelve

---

[87] Calvin sees in the words a rebuke to those who are satisfied "with a
bare passing look . . . For there are very many who merely sniff at the Gospel
from a distance, and thus let Christ suddenly disappear, and whatever they
have learned about Him slip away."

[88] רַבִּי means literally "my great one". But the personal pronoun tended
to become conventional as in *monsieur* or *madame*. The word was used very
much like our "Sir". Some maintain that John's statement is anachronistic,
on the grounds that the title was not in use before A.D. 70. Brown, however,
cites Sukenik who discovered an ossuary on the Mount of Olives which he
dates several generations before the destruction of the temple and which uses
διδάσκαλος as a title. This may well indicate that "Rabbi" was in use in this
way (though it is not absolutely conclusive, for διδάσκαλος does not always
represent רַבִּי. W. D. Davies has no doubt about the usage in Jesus' day,
for he devotes a section of his great work on the Sermon on the Mount to
Jesus as "The Rabbi", and he says explicitly: "He was called rabbi. While
in his day the title did not have the exact connotation of one officially ordained
to teach that it later acquired, it was more than a courtesy title: it did designate
a 'teacher' in the strict sense" (*The Setting of the Sermon on the Mount*, Cambridge,
1964, p. 422).

[89] A reads ἕκτη, "sixth", but this is difficult to accept without support.

hours.[90] John's habit of noticing the time of day is one of the small touches which point to an eyewitness (see 4 : 6, 52; 18 : 28; 19 : 14; 20 : 19). Coming to Jesus in the late afternoon and then having the kind of conversation that the circumstances indicate almost requires us to understand "abode" as "remained overnight". This means that the Evangelist is regarding the coming

---

[90] Some date the incident around 10 a.m. They suggest that John follows the Roman system of reckoning the day from midnight to midnight (so Westcott). But it is not at all clear that this Roman usage is relevant. It is true that the Romans counted from midnight when reckoning the legal day on which leases or contracts were dated (see Dods), but for all other purposes they appear to have reckoned from sunrise. For example, they marked noon on their sundials with VI not XII. *The Oxford Companion to Classical Literature* (compiled and edited by Sir P. Harvey, Oxford, 1959), makes it clear that both Greeks and Romans measured from sunrise: "The Romans when they spoke of 'the first hour' meant as a rule the point of time when the first *hora* from sunrise was completed" (*op. cit.*, p. 88). J. Carcopino gives a table showing the hours of the day and comparing them with our time (*Daily Life in Ancient Rome*, Penguin Books, 1962, pp. 167f.). The tenth hour at the summer solstice according to him lasted from 3.46 p.m. to 5.02 p.m. on our reckoning. Similarly Gepp and Haigh's *Latin-English Dictionary* defines *prima hora* as "daybreak, sunrise" and defines other hours accordingly. It notes no other usage. For Jewish use there is an instructive passage concerning evidence in which R. Judah accepts the evidence of two witnesses when one speaks of the third hour and another of the fifth, but rejects it if one spoke of the fifth hour and the other of the seventh, "since at the fifth hour the sun is in the east and at the seventh it is in the west" (*Sanh.* 5 : 3). H. R. Stroes has a full examination of the biblical evidence in an article entitled, "Does the Day Begin in the Evening or Morning?" (*Vetus Testamentum*, XVI, 1966, pp. 460–75). As the title indicates, Stroes sees just two ways of viewing things, and does not even mention as a possibility that the day might begin at midnight. In New Testament times he thinks the day was regarded as beginning at sunset when precision was required; otherwise at sunrise (*op. cit.*, p. 462). It is difficult to see why this Evangelist alone should have such an unusual mode of reckoning time as the Roman legal use. The early commentators seem to have accepted without question that John used the same method as the other Evangelists. Thus Chrysostom speaks of "the tenth hour" here as when "the sun was already near its setting" (XVIII. 3; p. 65). Augustine sees only an allegorical reference to the law "because the law was given in ten commandments" (VII. 10; p. 51)! MacGregor also adopts an allegorical explanation, " 'the tenth hour,' the number of perfection, would mark the beginning of the Christian era." Bultmann is another who sees allegory. J. Edgar Bruns has a note in which he regards all the Johannine time references as symbolic (*NTS*, XIII, 1966–67, pp. 285–290). But this seems to me to be going beyond the evidence and the probabilities. It certainly seems preferable to regard this (and other such passages) as a straightforward note of time. See further on 19 : 14.

of the two to Jesus as the events of one day. The next happenings belong to the following day.

40 The name of one of the two is given as Andrew. He came from the city of Bethsaida (v. 44). Although his brother has not yet appeared on the scene, nor been given the name "Peter" by Jesus, the full name "Simon Peter"[91] is used and Andrew is identified with reference to him. When the Gospel was written the great Apostle was well known and this way of writing is both intelligible and natural. The more obscure Andrew is described in terms of his relationship to his famous brother.

41 There is a difficulty about the word rendered "first". First there is a textual problem for the manuscripts yield a number of different readings.[92] One reading is the nominative of an adjective, which gives the meaning, "Andrew was the first to find. . . ." This probably would imply that the unnamed disciple also found *his* brother, but Andrew did it first. A second reading could be taken in either of two ways. It might be an adverb, when it will mean that Andrew found his brother before he did anything else. Or it might be the accusative of the adjective, when the meaning will be that Andrew found his brother before he found anyone else. A third reading, not very well attested, means "in the morning" (Bernard accepts this, and so Moffatt, Schonfield, *etc.*). It seems to me that the second of these is most likely to be correct, and in the sense of the adverb. This probably means that next morning Andrew promptly went in search of his brother. When he found him he told him that they had found the Messiah[93] (an expression which occurs only here and in 4 : 25 in the New Testament). In his customary manner the Evangelist explains that this word means "Christ" (see on v. 20). This early recognition of Jesus as the Messiah puzzles some in view of the indications in

---

[91] John uses the compound name Simon Peter seventeen times (Matthew 3 times, Mark 1 time, Luke 2 times). He also uses both Simon and Peter, but his fondness for the compound is noteworthy. See further on 21 : 15.

[92] The readings are $\pi\varrho\tilde{\omega}\tau\varrho\varsigma$ in $\aleph$*KLW, $\pi\varrho\tilde{\omega}\tau\varrho\nu$ in P66, P75 $\aleph$c ABΘ f1 f13, and $\pi\varrho\omega\ell$ in some MSS of the Old Latin. The attestation of $\pi\varrho\tilde{\omega}\tau\varrho\nu$ is thus superior. Some hold that the use of $\tau\grave{\varrho}\nu$ $\ell\delta\iota\varrho\nu$, "his own", favours $\pi\varrho\tilde{\omega}\tau\varrho\varsigma$. But this argument is worth little, for in late Greek $\ell\delta\iota\varrho\varsigma$ often means no more than "his" (though Moulton denies that it applies here, M, I, p. 90).

[93] The transliteration of a Hebrew word meaning "anointed". See further n. 13 above. "In Jewish lips 'we have found the Messiah' was the most comprehensive of all Eurekas" (Dods).

159

the Synoptic Gospels that it was a long time before the disciples had anything like an adequate view of His Person. But, as Hoskyns puts it, "the Evangelist does not, as is often supposed, idealize the first disciples, since it is precisely the title Christ which requires interpretation." There is no great mystery about the disciples' thinking of Jesus as the Messiah. There seem to have been many claimants to messiahship in that period. It was the content put into the term that mattered. All the evidence is that it was quite some time before any of Jesus' followers reached anything like an adequate understanding of the term. But that does not mean that they did not use it. It was easy to call Jesus "Messiah". It was quite another thing to understand what this should mean as He interpreted His vocation. Part of John's purpose appears to be to refute erroneous ideas about messiahship. It would be quite in accordance with this that he should record the disciples' first inadequate recognition of Jesus as Messiah, preparatory to un- folding in his Gospel the true meaning of the messianic office. Messiahship means a good deal to John. He writes his whole Gospel to make us see that Jesus is the Messiah. For the further development of the thought see vv. 45, 49; 3 : 28f.; 4 : 25f., 29, 42; 5 : 45f.; 6 : 15; 7 : 26f., 31, 40–43; 9 : 22; 10 : 24; 11 : 27; 12 : 34; 17 : 3; 20 : 31.

42 Andrew brought his brother to Jesus, an act of which Temple says "perhaps it is as great a service to the Church as ever any man did". Each time we meet Andrew in this Gospel he is bringing someone to Jesus (6 : 8; 12 : 22), a consistency that is worth noting. Jesus gave the newcomer a searching glance ("gazed at him", Moffatt), and proceeded to re-name him. This must be understood in the light of the significance attaching to the "name" in antiquity (see on v. 12). It stood for the whole man. It summed up his whole personality. The giving of a new name when done by men is an assertion of the authority of the giver (*e.g.* II Kings 23 : 34; 24 : 17). When done by God it speaks of a new character in which the man henceforth appears (*e.g.* Gen. 32 : 28). There is something of both ideas here. Simon is from this time Jesus' man. But he is also a different man, and the new name points

to his character as "the rock man".[94] Peter appears in all the Gospels as anything but a rock. He is impulsive, volatile, unreliable. But that was not God's last word for Peter. Jesus' words point to the change that would be wrought in him by the power of God.

(b) Philip and Nathanael, 1 : 43–51

43 On the morrow he was minded to go forth into Galilee, and he findeth Philip: and Jesus saith unto him, Follow me. 44 Now Philip was from Bethsaida, of the city of Andrew and Peter. 45 Philip findeth Nathanael, and saith unto him, We have found him, of whom Moses in the law, and the prophets, wrote, Jesus of Nazareth, the son of Joseph. 46 And Nathanael said unto him, Can any good thing come out of Nazareth? Philip saith unto him, Come and see. 47 Jesus saw Nathanael coming to him, and saith of him, Behold, an Israelite indeed, in whom is no guile! 48 Nathanael saith unto him, Whence knowest thou me? Jesus answered and said unto him, Before Philip called thee, when thou wast under the fig tree, I saw thee. 49 Nathanael answered him, Rabbi, thou art the Son of God; thou art King of Israel. 50 Jesus answered and said unto him, Because I said unto thee, I saw thee underneath the fig tree, believest thou? thou shalt see greater things than these. 51 And he saith unto him, Verily, verily, I say unto you, Ye shall see the heaven opened, and the angels of God ascending and descending upon the Son of man.

The process of adding to the number of followers of Jesus continues. Jesus Himself seeks out Philip and calls him, and Philip repeats the earlier pattern by going out and bringing Nathanael. Very little is known of this man, but the story of his coming to Jesus is full of interest.

43 For the note of time see on 1 : 19–28. In the previous section Jesus is not said to have done anything to draw Andrew and the others. They heard the Baptist's words and followed or were brought by one another. Here Jesus takes the initiative. He deter-

---

[94] Cephas is our transliteration of the Aramaic כֵּיפָא meaning "rock". Peter is from the Greek πέτρος with the same meaning. Cephas does not occur in any of the other Gospels. It points to an Aramaic-speaking author, as anyone else would use the common form, Peter. Simon's father is called John, though in Matt. 16 : 17 the name is Jonah. This is John's only use of the name Cephas. Indeed, apart from this passage the term is found only in Paul.

mined[95] to leave for Galilee, and sought out Philip. No reason is
given for this, nor any explanation of how He knew Philip. It is
not even said where He found him. There is nothing to determine
whether it was in the same general area as the preceding, or
somewhere on the way to Galilee, or even in Philip's city of Bethsaida.[96] We are not told whether Philip was a disciple of John
the Baptist, though this seems likely. The name "Philip" is Greek
(and means "lover of horses"). It is, however, found among the
Jews, so we need not reason that its bearer was of Greek descent.
It has been conjectured that he was named after Philip the tetrarch
(mentioned in Luke 3 : 1), who rebuilt Bethsaida Julias. The Synoptists mention Philip in lists of the Apostles, but give us no further
information about him. John brings him before us on a number
of occasions. Each time he seems somewhat out of his depth, and
it is probable that he was of limited ability. His contribution to
feeding the multitude is the information that they could not be
fed even with "two hundred shillings' worth of bread" (6 : 7).
When the Greeks came to him asking to see Jesus he did not
know what to do. He had to consult with Andrew before the men
were brought to Jesus (12 : 21f.). And it was Philip who requested
Jesus in the upper room to show them the Father – that is all
they ask! (14 : 8f.). The fact that on this occasion he did not seek
Jesus, but Jesus went to find him may indicate some lack of initiative. If so it is encouraging to reflect that Jesus went out of His
way to find this perfectly ordinary Philip and to enlist him in
the apostolic band. Some of the apostles were undoubtedly men
of great ability, but Philip compels us to reflect that others were
perfectly ordinary people. Christ had and has use for such followers.
The verb "Follow" will be used here in its full sense of "follow
as a disciple". The present tense has continuous force, "keep on
following".

44 Philip's home city is given as Bethsaida. Andrew and Peter
were also natives of this place (though they had a house in Capernaum at the time of Jesus' ministry which may mean that they

[95] The meaning of the aorist ἠθέλησεν is probably "he resolved". Grammatically its subject could be "Peter" (who was last mentioned). But the sense
of the passage plainly requires us to understand "Jesus".
[96] Barclay understands the passage to mean that the event took place in
Galilee. He translates, "and there He found Philip".

lived there then, Mark 1 : 21, 29).[97] Not much is told us in the
Gospels of the city (Mark 6 : 45; 8 : 22; Luke 9 : 10), but Jesus'
denunciation of it as one of the cities wherein "most of his mighty
works were done" (Matt. 11 : 20ff.; Luke 10; 13f.) shows that He
exercised a considerable ministry there. We are reminded that
there is much that is not recorded in our Gospels (*cf.* 21 : 25).
The exact site of the city is not known, and there is dispute as to
whether there was a Bethsaida "of Galilee" (12 : 21) in addition
to Bethsaida Julias.[98] This latter had been rebuilt by Philip the
tetrarch, and named Julias after the daughter of the Emperor.
45 The process of one disciple finding another is repeated, as
Philip seeks out Nathanael. "One lighted torch serves to light
another" (Godet). The plural "we" shows that Philip had already
identified himself with the little group about Jesus. Of Nathanael
nothing is recorded other than this incident and his presence
among the fishermen in 21 : 2 (which verse also adds the information than he came from Cana). The name means "God has given"
(and is thus equivalent to our Theodore). This has led some to
conjecture that the passage is allegorical and that an ideal disciple
is meant (one "given by God"). There seems little to be said for

---

[97] There is a change of preposition, Philip being ἀπὸ Βηθσαϊδά, and ἐκ
τῆς πόλεως Ἀνδρέου καὶ Πέτρου. Some find a distinction between them, with
ἀπό signifying place of residence and ἐκ place of origin (Abbott, 2289). But
the two prepositions are used more or less interchangeably. In this Gospel
we read of Christ as both ἐκ and ἀπό heaven (6 : 33, 38), as ἐκ Galilee and
ἀπό Bethlehem (7 : 41f.). There is no real difference. For John's habit of variation see *SFG*, ch. 5. John is much more fond of ἐκ than of ἀπό. He uses the
former 165 times, which is more than in any other New Testament book (next
is Revelation 134 times, then Luke 87 times). But he uses ἀπό only 40 times,
whereas Matthew has it 113 times, Mark 47 times, Luke 127 times and Acts
114 times).

[98] There is good evidence that Bethsaida was to the East of Jordan (Josephus, *Bell.* ii, 168, locates it in lower Gaulanitis, and in *Bell.* iii, 515 it appears
to be near the place where the Jordan flows into the lake of Galilee; Pliny and
Jerome are also cited in support of this view). Mark 6 : 45 is urged by some
as indicating that there was a Bethsaida in the general region of Capernaum,
and this is supported by the expression, "Bethsaida of Galilee" (John 12 : 21).
But George Adam Smith cites evidence that by the time of the War of 66–70
the term "Galilee" had extended its meaning to include territory round the
lake. He thinks that even earlier the jurisdiction of Galilee's ruler extended
to the East of the Lake (*EB*, 566). On the whole it seems probable that there
was but one Bethsaida, perhaps with a suburb across the river. The name
incidentally means "House of fishing".

this. While the name is not a common one among the Jews, it is found. There is no reason for doubting that a real person is meant. The incident reads like the record of an actual happening rather than a pious fiction. Others think that Nathanael is another name for Matthew the Apostle, since the two names are of similar meaning. Others again suggest that Nathanael is to be identified with Bartholomew, an apostle who is never mentioned in John, just as Nathanael is never mentioned in the Synoptists. Bartholomew is coupled with Philip in all three Synoptists (Matt. 10 : 3; Mark 3 : 18; Luke 6 : 14), while another link is that he is mentioned immediately after Thomas in Acts 1 : 13 and Nathanael is in the same position in John 21 : 2. Moreover Bartholomew is not really a personal name, but a patronymic meaning "son of Tolmai" (*cf.* Barjona = "son of Jona"). The man who bore it almost certainly had another name. The other disciples mentioned in this chapter all became apostles, and it is suggested that Nathanael is, accordingly, likely to have done so too. If he is to be identified with one of the apostles Bartholomew is probably our man. But why should we so identify him with an apostle? Jesus had many disciples outside the Twelve, and there seems no reason for holding that Nathanael was anything other than one of them. It is certain that John wants us to think of him as attaching himself firmly to Jesus, but this does not make him an apostle.

Philip speaks of Jesus as the object of prophecy. Both Moses and the prophets have spoken of Him.[99] This is, of course, another way of calling Him Messiah. In an unobtrusive, but very definite way John, in accordance with his declared aim (20 : 31), is emphasizing that Jesus is the Messiah. Andrew and his friend recognized Him and now Philip does the like. Philip does so in terms which show that the messianic ministry of Jesus was to fulfil the purposes of God from of old as they have been recorded in Holy Writ. Westcott thinks that the form of the sentence, with "we have found" coming last in the Greek, implies that Philip and Nathanael "had often dwelt on the Old Testament portraiture of the Messiah". When Philip speaks of Jesus as "the son of Joseph"

---

[99] The prominent position of Ὅν ἔγραψεν may indicate that Philip and Nathanael had previously discussed the fulfilment of these scriptures. Philip cites no specific passage. Edersheim notes that the Rabbis interpreted no less than 456 passages messianically (*LT*, II, pp. 710–41). For Jesus' messiahship see on v. 41.

this must not be taken as a denial of the Virgin Birth.[100] Joseph was the legal father of Jesus, and the Lord would accordingly be known as Joseph's son. In any case it is unlikely that the Virgin Birth would have been already communicated to such a new disciple as Philip. This is a good example of "the irony of St. John". Again and again he allows his characters to state, without refutation, ideas which Christian people would know to be false.[101]

46 Nathanael's sceptical question[102] does not reflect, as far as is known, a widely held opinion of Nazareth. It was not a famous city, but we have no reason for thinking it was infamous. We should probably understand Nathanael's words as the utterance of a man who could not conceive of the Messiah as coming from such an insignificant place.[103] Moreover, as Nathanael himself came from Cana, it is not at all improbable that we have here a trace of the rivalry that often grips small centres (and bigger ones!) not far from one another. Philip was not a particularly resourceful man (see on v. 43), and he did not attempt to convince his friend by argument. Instead he invited him to see for himself, which, in the circumstances, was probably as wise an answer as he could have given. It is good advice still. "Come and see" was a formula common among the Rabbis.[104] They used it

---

[100] "It is in accord with (John's) ironical use of traditional material that he should allow Jesus to be ignorantly described as 'son of Joseph' while himself believing that Jesus had no human father" (Barrett). Godet vigorously exclaims, "as if it were the evangelist who was here speaking, and not Philip! And that disciple, after exchanging ten words with Jesus, must have been already thoroughly acquainted with the most private circumstances of His birth and infancy!"

[101] For this characteristic of the evangelist *cf.* G. Salmon, *A Historical Introduction to the Study of the Books of the New Testament* (London, 1892), pp. 280ff. As Salmon says, "no one understands better the rhetorical effect of leaving an absurdity without formal refutation, when his readers can be trusted to perceive it for themselves" (*op. cit.*, pp. 281f.).

[102] G. D. Kilpatrick points out that the adjective $\dot{\alpha}\gamma\alpha\vartheta\acute{o}\varsigma$ is used predicatively here and at 7 : 12, while it is pronominal at 5 : 29. $\varkappa\alpha\lambda\acute{o}\varsigma$ he finds is always attributive (*BT*, 11, 1960, pp. 173f.). The difference between the two then appears to be purely grammatical. In this Gospel there is no difference in meaning in the two terms. John uses $\dot{\alpha}\gamma\alpha\vartheta\acute{o}\varsigma$ three times and $\varkappa\alpha\lambda\acute{o}\varsigma$ seven times.

[103] "Nathanael uses intelligent human observation to set a firm limit to the power of God" (Hoskyns).

[104] See SBk, II, p. 371.

to show that a solution to the particular problem was possible and that it should be sought together. The expression might also point to something new or important or the like.

47 As Nathanael approached Jesus described him as "an Israelite indeed, in whom is no guile". This last word is used in earlier Greek writers as a "bait" (for catching fish). Hence it comes to signify *"any cunning contrivance for deceiving or catching*, as the net in which Hephaestus catches Ares ... the Trojan horse ... Ixion's bride ... the robe of Penelope".[105] It thus has the notion of "deceit" or "craft". It is used in the Bible of Jacob before his change of heart (Gen. 27 : 35), which is the point of Temple's translation, "an Israelite in whom there is no Jacob!" (Morgan also gives this as the sense of the verse.) Jesus salutes Nathanael as a straightforward person. "Israelite" is used here only in this Gospel, though "Jew" (especially in the plural) is common as we have noted. It means here a true son of Israel (*cf.* Rom. 2 : 29) The most frequent use of the term in the New Testament is as an address in the speeches in Acts.

48 Nathanael's reaction is a surprised question as to the source of Jesus' knowledge of him, a reaction incidentally which shows the accuracy of Jesus' description. A more guileful man would have "modestly" asserted his unworthiness. Jesus' reply[106] was evidently convincing to His questioner, but it is not at all clear to us. He said that He had seen Nathanael before ever Philip called him,[107] and the time is specified as "when thou wast under the

---

[105] LS, *sub δόλος*.

[106] Burney claims ἀπεκρίθη (or ἀπεκρίθησαν or ἀποκρίνεται) without a connecting particle (which is found 66 times in John, elsewhere in the New Testament once only) as pointing to Aramaic. He also suggests that ἀπεκρίθη καὶ εἶπεν is a literal rendering of an Aramaic idiom (*AO*, pp. 53f.).

[107] Note the use of the articular infinitive, πρὸ τοῦ ... φωνῆσαι, a construction rare in this Gospel. Abbott takes from Bruder the information that it is found four times only, namely, here, 2 : 24; 13 : 19; 17 : 5 (1995*a*). It occurs in Matthew *c.* 24 times, Mark *c.* 15 times, Luke *c.* 70 times, so that John's use is exceptional.

fig tree".[108] There is no further explanation and no other reference to the incident. We are left to conjecture. The fig tree was almost a symbol of home (*cf.* Isa. 36 : 16; Mic. 4 : 4; Zech. 3 : 10). Its shade was certainly at a later time used as a place for prayer and meditation and study,[109] and there is no reason for thinking that the practice does not go back as far as this. It seems probable that Nathanael had had some outstanding experience of communion with God in the privacy of his own home, and that it is this to which Jesus refers. Whatever it was, Nathanael was able to recognize the allusion. It is difficult to explain Jesus' knowledge of the incident on the level of merely human knowledge.[110] Nathanael had never met Him before this moment. We are required to understand that Jesus had some knowledge not generally available to the sons of men (*cf.* 2 : 24f.).

49 The effect on Nathanael of these simple words is more than surprising. His immediate response is to salute Jesus in terms implying divinity. "Nathanael capitulated for ever to the man who read and understood and satisfied his heart" (Barclay). For the respectful "Rabbi" (which Nathanael did not use at first) see on v. 38, and for "Son of God" on v. 34 (*cf.* 11 : 27). Here, as there, the article is important. It indicates that the expression is to be understood as bearing a full, not a minimal content. While Nathanael could not as yet have understood all that Jesus' sonship involved, Jesus' knowledge of the fig tree incident impressed him.

---

[108] ὑπὸ τὴν συκῆν. If ὑπό (with the accusative here only in this Gospel) has the idea of motion towards it may imply that Nathanael had withdrawn to the fig tree. There is probably no significance in the change to ὑποκάτω τῆς συκῆς in v. 50, for John often repeats an expression with slight variations (see *SFG*, ch. 5). Grammatically it is possible to take "when thou wast under the fig tree" with "called thee" (as Chrysostom, for example, does). This would mean no more than that Nathanael had been under a fig tree when Philip called him. But there seems little to be said for this view, and it is contradicted by v. 50. Calvin draws a lesson from this: "We should also gather from this passage a useful lesson, that when we are not even thinking of Christ we are observed by Him; and this must needs be so, that He may bring us back when we have withdrawn from Him."

[109] See the passages in SBk.

[110] It is likely that we should understand the passage as meaning not only that Jesus had knowledge of some incident, but of what went on in Nathanael's thinking. "His surprise is not merely that Jesus in some clairvoyant way saw him in his own home, but that He knew what was going on in his mind" (Strachan).

Here was someone who could not be described in ordinary human terms. He could be described in terms which indicate the closest possible relationship to God. "King of Israel" is an unusual expression. In the New Testament it is used, apart from this passage, three times only. In Matt. 27 : 42 Jesus is saluted as "King of Israel" and invited to come down from the cross (so that Nathanael uses sincerely at the very beginning of Jesus' ministry a title which is to recur in mockery at the very end!). In Mark 15 : 32 "the Christ" and "the King of Israel" are almost synonyms. Finally in John 12 : 13 at the triumphal entry Jesus is hailed in these words by the multitude.[111] In the Old Testament God is the King of His people, and it is clear that in the intervening period the Messiah came to be thought of as exercising the divine prerogative of rule. Nathanael is speaking in the highest terms open to him.[112] In recording this estimate of Jesus John is adding to the evidence accumulated throughout this chapter that He is indeed the Messiah. Nathanael expresses it differently from the others, but the essential meaning is the same (see further on v. 41). Nor should we overlook the fact that Nathanael has just been called "an Israelite". In calling Jesus "the King of Israel" he is acknowledging Jesus to be his own King. He submits to Him. John uses the term "King" sixteen times, and on almost every occasion it refers to Jesus (the exceptions being at the trial when Pilate and the Jewish leaders both use the term; but even here the use is brought about solely because of Jesus' claim). The royalty of Jesus is important, even though it is veiled by His lowly life and death.

---

[111] There is an article with "king" in 12 : 13, but not here, and Abbott sees a difference: " 'The Son of God' *reigns over, or is 'king of,' all the nations of the earth including Israel.* David, or Hezekiah, or a merely Jewish Messiah, might naturally be called '*the king of Israel*,' i.e. the king for the time being. Nathanael is made to utter a confession much more inclusive than that of 'the great multitude' " (1966). This must, however, be rejected in the light of the rule established by E. C. Colwell, that where a definite predicate noun precedes the verb it does not have the article (see on 1 : 1). βασιλεύς here is surely just as definite as υἱός.

[112] "Note the strongly Hebraic mentality for which it is in the order of climax to pass from *Son of God* to *King of Israel*" (Temple).

50 Jesus' words,[113] "believest thou?" (alternatively the words might be taken as a statement, "thou believest") mark Nathanael as the first man explicitly said to believe in this Gospel (though *cf.* vv. 7, 12 and the notes there). The previous exchange had led Nathanael to put his trust in Jesus, with all that that implies. From this time forth he was a "believer". It was Jesus' statement that He had seen Nathanael underneath the fig tree that had brought this about. Now the Master promises that His new disciple will see greater things.[114] The Master's ministry was only beginning. There would be many more examples of His power to reveal.

51 "Verily" is not a translation of a Greek word, but the transliteration of an Aramaic (or Hebrew) word, namely *Amen*. It is the participle of the verb meaning "to confirm", and it was used to give one's assent. For example, it was (and still is) the response of the congregation to a prayer uttered by him who leads their worship. In this way they make it their own (1 Cor. 14 : 16). Very occasionally it is the conclusion to one's own prayer (*e.g.* Tobit 8 : 7f.), when it has the nature of a wish. But this use is rare. Characteristically it is one's assent to words uttered by another. In the Gospels it is used only by Jesus, and always as a prefix to significant statements. Presumably this is to mark them out as solemn and true and important. This use of Amen to introduce one's own words appears to be Jesus' own, no real Jewish parallel being adduced.[115] In view of the associations of the term it almost certainly has religious significance. It marks the words as uttered before God, who is thus invited to bring them to pass.

---

[113] The use of causal ὅτι introducing a clause preceding the main clause is to be noted. This construction is not common, and Prof. G. D. Kilpatrick in a private communication says it is completely absent from Matthew, Mark, Ephesians, the Pastorals, Hebrews *etc.* There is no certain example in Luke-Acts and the Pauline Epistles, but he finds six examples in John, namely here, 8 : 45; 15 : 19; 16 : 6; 19 : 42; 20 : 29 (of which 15 : 19 is textually uncertain), and at least one in Revelation. For John's fondness for ὅτι see on 1 : 15.

[114] This may be another reference to Nathanael as an Israelite (as Bernard, for example, thinks). The name "Israel" was widely held to be derived from אִישׁ רֹאֶה אֵל "the man seeing God". Thus Jacob was thought of as the man of vision *par excellence*.

[115] See the note by D. Daube, *JThS*, XLV, 1944, pp. 27–31 and the literature there cited. Also H. Schlier, *TDNT*, I, pp. 335–38; also G. Ebeling, *Word and Faith* (London, 1960), pp. 236–38.

There are also probably christological implications. Jesus identifies Himself with the words and also with the God to whom He appeals.[116] A small point is the fact that in the Synoptic Gospels the word always occurs singly, whereas in John it is invariably doubled.[117] No satisfactory explanation of this has been put forward. But it certainly marks what follows as important.[118]

The change from "thee" to "you" shows that the saying is meant for a wider circle, though addressed in the first place to Nathanael. There is no subsequent reference in this Gospel to the heavens being opened (the verb is used mostly of the opening of the eyes of the blind, and once of the opening of a door). In the rest of the New Testament we read of the heavens being opened only in the accounts of the baptism of Jesus (Matt. 3 : 16; Luke 3 : 21), and in the visions in Acts 10 : 11; Rev. 19 : 11, none of which is likely to be in mind here. That the expression points to some vision of the divine is clear enough, but beyond that it is not easy to go. The ascent and descent of the angels seems to be a reference to the vision of Jacob (Gen. 28 : 10ff.). But there is no mention in the Patriarch's dream of the heavens being opened, while conversely there is no mention here of the ladder Jacob saw. However in both passages there is the thought of communication between heaven and earth. In both the angels are spoken of as ascending first, which may imply their presence on earth already. In this passage the place of the ladder is taken by "the Son of

---

[116] Schlier thinks that in ἀμήν used in this way "we have the whole of Christology *in nuce*. The one who accepts His word as true and certain is also the one who acknowledges and affirms it in his own life and thus causes it, as fulfilled by him, to become a demand to others" (*TDNT*, I, p. 338). Ebeling is of opinion that Jesus' use of ἀμήν gives expression "to the fact that Jesus identifies himself entirely with his words, that in the identification with these words he surrenders himself to the reality of God, and that he lets his existence be grounded on God's making these words true and real" (*op. cit.*, p. 237). G. E. Ladd says, "Jesus used the expression as the equivalent of an oath, paralleling the Old Testament expression, 'As I live, saith the Lord.' Jesus' usage is without analogy because in his person and words the Kingdom of God manifested its presence and authority" (*Jesus and the Kingdom*, London, 1966, p. 163).

[117] Matthew uses the single ἀμήν 31 times, Mark 13 times, Luke 6 times. John has the doubled ἀμήν ἀμήν 25 times. Clearly he is fond of the expression.

[118] The translators adopt a variety of devices to bring out the meaning: "Truly, truly" (Moffatt, RSV), "in all truth "(Rieu), "Believe me" (Knox), "in most solemn truth" (Weymouth), "for a positive fact" (Schonfield), "most assuredly" (Wuest), "in truth, in very truth" (NEB).

man".[119] Jesus Himself is the link between heaven and earth (3 : 13). He is the means by which the realities of heaven are brought down to earth. Nathanael will see this for himself. The expression then is a figurative way of saying that Jesus will reveal heavenly things to men, a thought which is developed throughout this Gospel. Philip's view of Jesus (v. 45) is true, but inadequate. Jesus is indeed the fulfiller of prophecy, but He is also the Son of man, the revealer of God, the means of establishing communication between earth and heaven. The force of the perfect, "opened", should not be overlooked. They would see the heavens opened and remaining opened. For "the Son of man" see Additional Note C, pp. 172f. Strachan regards this verse as "the key to the Evangelist's whole conception of Jesus".[120] His conclusion is, "The wide open heaven, and the ascending and descending angels symbolize the whole power and love of God, now available for men, in the Son of man".[121]

In this chapter Jesus has been accorded several titles: the *Logos* (1), God (1), the light of men (4), the true light (9), the only begotten from the Father (14), a greater than John the Baptist (15, 26f., 30), Jesus Christ (17), the only begotten God (or Son, 18), the Lord (23), the Lamb of God (29, 36), he that baptizeth with the Holy Spirit (33), probably God's Chosen One (34), the Son of God (49), Rabbi (38, 49), the Messiah (41), he of whom Moses and the prophets wrote (45), the King of Israel (49). We may fairly comment that by recording all these John makes a beginning on the picture of the Lord that he is to paint throughout

---

[119] Yet it is possible to take בּוֹ in Gen. 28 : 12 as meaning "on him" (*i.e.* Jacob), not "on it" (the ladder). This interpretation was actually held by some Rabbis (though not until after New Testament times as far as our present knowledge goes). Burney thinks that John is accepting this point of view (*AO*, pp. 115f.), as does Odeberg. See also the notes in Bernard and Barrett. It should be noted that the Rabbinic tradition is that the angels "ascended and descended on Jacob: they raised him up and put him down, they leapt on him, ran on him, teased him . . . They ascended on high and found (beheld) his image, they descended on earth and found him sleeping" (*FG*, pp. 33f.). The thought in John is not this, but rather that the Son of man is the means of bridging the gap between earth and heaven. He takes the place of the ladder. Bernard has a valuable Additional Note in which he cites the patristic interpretations of Gen. 28 : 13, and John 1 : 51. He shows that Augustine is the first to connect the two.

[120] P. 6. His whole note is important (pp. 5–11).

[121] P. 11.

the Gospel. He wants to show Him as the Christ, and this is how he begins to do it. But one more comment is fitting. All these titles have been used by others. Jesus calls Himself simply, "the Son of man".

ADDITIONAL NOTE C: THE SON OF MAN.

"The Son of man" is a curious expression, and just as unusual in Greek as in English. It is a literal translation of the Aramaic בַּר־נָשָׁא which means "man" or "the man". In the Gospels it is used by Jesus as His favourite self-designation, occurring in this way over eighty times. Nobody else ever uses it of Him[122] except Stephen (Acts 7 : 56) and the people in this Gospel who inquire who Jesus means by the term (12 : 34). The fact that they do so inquire shows that the term was not an accepted messianic designation. In general we can say that Jesus uses the expression in a threefold way: (i) as a periphrasis for "I", (ii) of the heavenly Son of man, who will come in glory, and (iii) of the Son of man who suffers to bring men salvation. The origin of the term is probably to be sought in Dan. 7 : 13f., where a heavenly Being is so designated.[123] I have discussed the expression in my *The Lord from Heaven* (London and Grand Rapids, 1958), pp. 26–9, and perhaps I may repeat my conclusion: Jesus adopted the term, "firstly because it was a rare term and one without nationalistic associations. It would lead to no political complications. 'The public would . . . read into it as much as they apprehended of Jesus already, and no more.'[124] Secondly, because it had overtones of divinity. J. P. Hickinbotham goes as far as to say, 'the Son of Man is a title of divinity rather than humanity.'[125] Thirdly, because of its societary implications. The Son of man implies the redeemed people of God. Fourthly, because it had undertones of humanity. He took upon Him our weakness."[126] It was a way of alluding

---

[122] *Cf.* Th. Preiss: "The title which Jesus himself prefers and remarkably enough, as in the Synoptics, is found only on his lips – is that of Son of Man. Do we not see there another proof, indirect but very substantial, of the definitely ancient character of the Johannine tradition?" (*Life in Christ*, London, 1954, p. 24).

[123] B. Vawter argues convincingly that Ezekiel's use of the term is one of the influences behind the significance of "the Son of man" in this Gospel (*CBQ*, XXVI, 1964, pp. 451–455).

[124] R. H. Fuller, *The Mission and Achievement of Jesus* (London, 1954), p. 106.

[125] *The Churchman*, LVIII, 1944, p. 54.

[126] *Op. cit.*, p. 29.

to and yet veiling His messiahship, for His concept of the Messiah differed markedly from that commonly held.

In the Fourth Gospel there are one or two additions that should be made to the above. Here the term is always associated either with Christ's heavenly glory or with the salvation He came to bring. Thus there are references to Him as having access to heaven or even as being in heaven (1 : 51; 3 : 13; 6 : 62). The first of these (1 : 51) carries the idea that He brings heaven to men. He is the only One who has ascended into heaven and come down (3 : 13). He will be the Judge of men at the last day (5 : 27; here the term lacks the article – it is "Son of man", not "the Son of man"). Twice Jesus refers to the Son of man as being lifted up (3 : 14; 8 : 28; *cf.* 12 : 34), and twice to His being glorified (12 : 23; 13 : 31). The Son of man gives the living bread, that food that abides for ever (6 : 27), and those who receive it eat His flesh and drink His blood (6 : 53). His gift of eternal life is probably implied also in His demand on the man born blind that he believe on the Son of man (9 : 35). In the typical Johannine manner there is sometimes a combination of the themes of suffering and of glory (12 : 23; 13 : 31). The true glory lies precisely in His sufferings. The term, "the Son of man", then points us to Christ's conception of Himself as of heavenly origin and as the possessor of heavenly glory. At one and the same time it points us to His lowliness and His sufferings for men. The two are the same.

The literature on the subject is enormous. Particular reference may perhaps be made to N. B. Stonehouse, *The Witness of Matthew and Mark to Christ* (Philadelphia, 1944), pp. 110ff., 249ff.; E. Stauffer, *New Testament Theology* (London, 1955), pp. 108–111; T. W. Manson, *The Teaching of Jesus* (Cambridge, 1937), pp. 211–234; *The Servant-Messiah* (Cambridge, 1953), pp. 72–4; H. E. W. Turner, *Jesus Master and Lord* (London, 1957), pp. 196–205; C. H. Dodd, *According to the Scriptures* (London, 1953), pp. 116–8; *IFG*, pp. 241–9; Bernard, pp. cxxii–cxxxiii; also to articles by M. Black, *ExT*, LX, 1948–49, pp. 11–15, 32–36, *SJT*, VI, 1953, pp. 1–11; J. Bowman, *ExT*, LIX, 1947–48, pp. 283–8; E. Schweizer, *NTS*, IX, 1962–63, pp. 256–61; and for the expression in the Fourth Gospel, E. M. Sidebottom, *ExT*, LXVIII, 1956–57, pp. 231–5. There is a useful list in C. F. D. Moule, *The Birth of the New Testament* (London, 1962), p. 63.

CHAPTER II

III. THE SIGNS AND PUBLIC DISCOURSES OF THE CHRIST, 2 : 1 – 12 : 36

1. The First Sign – Water into Wine, 2 : 1–11[1]

1 And the third day there was a marriage in Cana of Galilee; and the mother of Jesus was there: 2 and Jesus also was bidden, and his disciples, to the marriage. 3 And when the wine failed, the mother of Jesus saith unto him, They have no wine. 4 And Jesus saith unto her, Woman, what have I to do with thee? mine hour is not yet come. 5 His mother saith unto the servants, Whatsoever he saith unto you, do it. 6 Now there were six waterpots of stone set there after the Jews' manner of purifying, containing two or three firkins apiece. 7 Jesus saith unto them, Fill the waterpots with water. And they filled them up to the brim. 8 And he saith unto them, Draw out now, and bear unto the [1]ruler of the feast. And they bare it. 9 And when the ruler of the feast tasted the water [2]now become wine, and knew not whence it was (but the servants that had drawn the water knew), the ruler of the feast calleth the bridegroom, 10 and saith unto him, Every man setteth on first the good wine; and when men have drunk freely, then that which is worse: thou hast kept the good wine until now. 11 This beginning of his signs did Jesus in Cana of Galilee, and manifested his glory; and his disciples believed on him.

[1]Or, *steward* [2]Or, *that it had become*

It is often suggested that this miracle is not historical, but that, when the wine ran out, Jesus commanded water to be used. The "ruler of the feast", entering into the spirit of the thing, made a merry quip about this being the best wine of all. Someone who did not understand, heard the remark and thus a story of a

---

[1] Bultmann sees this section of the book as the beginning of the manifestation of the glory of Jesus. Chapters 3–12 set forth its manifestation before the world and chapters 13–17 before believers (p. 77).

miracle originated.[2] Others think that John has adapted a heathen legend in order to set forth Christian truth.[3]

Such reconstructions founder on verses 9 and 11. In the first place John says that the water became wine. He records a miracle. And in the second place it was a miracle which had profound effects on those who had begun to follow Jesus. It is impossible to maintain that "his disciples believed on him", and that He "manifested his glory", on the basis of nothing more than a good

---

[2] See, for example, Leslie D. Weatherhead, *It Happened in Palestine* (London, 1944), pp. 43–54. Weatherhead imagines the scene: "The wine runs out. Water is served. Why, that's the best joke of all! They lift their wine-cups, as we do in fun when we shout, 'Adam's ale is the best of all.' The bridegroom is congratulated by the master of ceremonies, who carries the joke farther still. 'Why you've kept the best wine until now.' It requires only a servant going through the room into the kitchen for a wonderful rumour to start" (*op. cit.*, pp. 50f.).

[3] J. Estlin Carpenter draws attention to the parabolic nature of the miracle: "It is a parable in action. The wine that failed was the old wine of Judaism" (*The Johannine Writings*, London, 1927, p. 377). He goes on to note the rites associated with the god Dionysos and he suggests that the Fourth Evangelist has transformed the miracles of Dionysos "into an imaginative symbol of the glory of Christ" (*op. cit.*, p. 380). Similarly Bultmann thinks that the story is doubtless (*zweifellos*) from heathen legend. But this is pure assumption. The parallels are not close enough to carry conviction. "No part of this legend as we know it bears any very close resemblance to the miracle at Cana" (F. E. Williams, *JBL*, LXXXVI, 1967, p. 312, n. 1). John gives the impression that he is telling what happened and recording it for its meaning. That the story may well have been used to show the superiority of Christ to Dionysos is likely. But that its origin is in pagan legend does not follow. Hoskyns rejects the idea. "Neither in the actual narrative of the miracle of Cana nor anywhere else in the rest of the Gospel" can he find any hint of the transformation of a Greek story (Detached Note 3, p. 191). See also the notes in Barrett, who, while being ready to allow for the possibility of some Dionysiac elements, concludes, "there can be little doubt that (John) meant to show the supersession of Judaism in the glory of Jesus. It is possible that in doing so he drew material from Dionysiac sources; but it was Jewish purificatory water which stood in the water pots and was made the wine of the Gospel." Strachan brings out another valuable point when he says, "The whole style of the Johannine narrative of the Cana miracle is itself sufficient to disprove this (*i.e.* Carpenter's view). In addition, the Evangelist in his battle with the Docetists could not afford to 'transform' mythical stories into allegedly historical incidents". Wright also rejects Carpenter's view, but himself suggests that "some incident and some words of Jesus are fused in the creative imagination, and by the spiritual insight, of the author, into a kind of parable. The incident and the words are treated by the Evangelist with the utmost freedom." This is no improvement on Carpenter, and is just as subjective. It is one thing to

joke.[4] Nor is it easier to think that John would say this about a heathen legend. Plainly he records the miracle because he believes that it happened. But for him the miracles are all "signs". They point beyond themselves. This particular miracle signifies that there is a transforming power associated with Jesus. He changes the water of Judaism into the wine of Christianity,[5] the water of Christlessness into the wine of the richness and the fulness of eternal life in Christ, the water of the law into the wine of the gospel.[6] While this "sign" is recorded only in this Gospel, it should not be overlooked that there are partial parallels in the Synoptics. Thus the imagery of the wedding feast is used with reference to

---

say that John saw a symbolic meaning in this story; it is quite another to say that he constructed a parable.

Others derive the story from Philo who says, "But let Melchizedek instead of water offer wine, and give to souls strong drink, that they may be seized by a divine intoxication, more sober than sobriety itself" (*Leg. alleg.* III. 82). But again the parallels are not nearly close enough.

Barclay sees the narrative this way: "So to the Jews John said: 'Jesus has come to turn the imperfection of the law into the perfection of grace.' And to the Greeks John said: 'Jesus has come really and truly to do the things you only dreamed the gods could do.'" This may well be the point of John's telling the story. But it does not imply that he derived it from either his Jewish or his Greek predecessors. He recounts a Christian story which is valuable in both contexts.

[4] Bailey rejects the jest idea, going on to say: "no event in the Gospel bears stronger evidence of personal observation." *Cf.* Murray: "It is morally incredible that 'the beginning of signs' can have been a conjuring trick"; and again, "I cannot help feeling that the statement of the effect of the sign on the faith of the disciples comes straight from the personal experience of one of them."

[5] A. R. Vidler has a sermon on this story in which he says that John is trying to drive home a contrast, "the contrast between the old Jewish order of things, which was based on trying to observe the Law, and the new Christian order of things which springs from the grace and truth brought into the world by Jesus the Messiah, and which consists not in trying to be good but in rejoicing in the generosity of God" (*Windsor Sermons*, London, 1958, p. 68). F. F. Bruce speaks succinctly of "Christ's changing of the water of Jewish purification into the wine of the new age" (*Second Thoughts on the Dead Sea Scrolls*, London and Grand Rapids, 1956, p. 135).

[6] Ryle sees eschatological significance in the story. "To attend a marriage feast, and cleanse the temple from profanation were among the first acts of our Lord's ministry at His first coming. To purify the whole visible Church, and hold a marriage supper, will be among His first acts, when He comes again."

176

the kingdom of God (Matt. 22 : 1–14; 25 : 1–13; Luke 12 : 36), and the disciples in the presence of Christ are likened to wedding guests rejoicing with the bridegroom (Mark 2 : 19). Again, the contrast of Jesus' message with Judaism is illustrated by the wine and the wineskins (Luke 5 : 37ff.).

J. Duncan M. Derrett has a very valuable discussion of this miracle.[7] He points out that in the ancient Near East there was a strong element of reciprocity about weddings, and that, for example, it was possible to take legal action in certain circumstances against a man who had failed to provide the appropriate wedding gift. This is quite foreign to our wedding customs and we are apt to overlook such possibilities. But it means that when the supply of wine failed more than social embarrassment was involved. The bridegroom and his family may well have become involved in a heavy pecuniary liability. The gift made by Jesus was thus doubly important.

1, 2 For "the third day" see on 1 : 19–28. The expression occurs here only in this Gospel. Verses 43–51 of the first chapter have given us the events of day 5 of the momentous week John describes. Nothing is said of day 6. "The third day", by the inclusive mode of reckoning then current, brings us to day 7. Cana is mentioned in this passage, in 4 : 46; 21 : 2, and nowhere else in the New Testament. On each occasion it is qualified by "of Galilee". Evidently it was not a well known place.[8] John does not disclose the identity of the happy couple, but the presence of the mother of Jesus (neither here nor anywhere else does he make use of her name[9]), and the invitation extended to Jesus shows that friends of the family were involved. The whole attitude of Mary, her

---

[7] *Biblische Zeitschrift*, N.F., VII, 1963, pp. 80–97. To the literature there cited for information about wedding customs we should add, H. Granquist, "Marriage Customs in a Palestinian Village", in *Commentationes Humanarum Litterarum* III, 8 (Helsingfors, 1931), pp. 1–200; VI, 8 (1935), pp. 1–366.

[8] Josephus says that he once had his quarters there (*Vit.* 86). But it is certainly not mentioned often in ancient literature.

[9] This is puzzling, all the more so since this Evangelist is usually so explicit with names. A. H. N. Green-Armytage links this with the absence of all mention of the Apostle John by name. "If, as described in the Gospel, she was committed to the care of the beloved disciple and thereafter treated by him as his own mother, this way of referring to her is exactly what we should expect" (*John Who Saw*, London, 1952, p. 85 n.). For John's use of names see further *SFG*, pp. 237ff.

taking action when the wine ran out, and her giving instructions
to the servants accords with this.[10] It is sometimes said that Jesus
and His disciples[11] were unbidden guests, being "invited" only
when they turned up unexpectedly. It is inferred that it was
their presence that caused the supply of wine to be inadequate.
There is nothing in the narrative to show that this was in fact
the state of affairs. The Greek may well mean that they had been
invited earlier.[12] We should perhaps comment on the absence of
any mention of Joseph (he is not mentioned anywhere in this
Gospel other than in the expression, "son of Joseph"). It may be
that he had died before these days, though against this the natural
inference from 6 : 42 is that he was alive then.

Our information about the details of marriage ceremonies (as
distinct from marriage regulations) in first century Jewry is far
from complete. It may be filled out by assuming that customs
did not alter greatly, so that earlier and later references may help
us. We know that marriage was preceded by a betrothal which
was a much more serious matter than is an engagement with us.
It meant the solemn pledging of the couple, each to the other,
and was so binding that to break it divorce proceedings were
necessary. At the conclusion of the betrothal period the marriage
took place. According to the Mishnah the wedding would take
place on a Wednesday if the bride was a virgin and on a Thursday
if she was a widow (*Ket.* 1 : 1). The bridegroom and his friends
made their way in procession to the bride's house. This was often
done at night, when there could be a spectacular torchlight procession. There were doubtless speeches and expressions of goodwill
before the bride and groom went in procession to the groom's
house, where the wedding banquet was held. It is probable that

---

[10] It may be significant that Mary "was ($\tilde{\eta}\nu$)" there, while Jesus and the
others were "bidden ($\dot{\epsilon}\varkappa\lambda\dot{\eta}\vartheta\eta$, aorist)". She had apparently taken up residence.

[11] Bernard points out that the the expression οἱ μαθηταί αὐτοῦ (Jesus'
disciples as distinct from those of other Rabbis) was the earlier designation,
οἱ μαθηταί, "*the* disciples" being later. It is a mark of John's acquaintance
with the primitive state of affairs that he usually employs the former expression,
as here.

[12] Taking the aorist $\dot{\epsilon}\varkappa\lambda\dot{\eta}\vartheta\eta$ in the sense of the pluperfect. See Abbott,
2461. Schonfield renders "Jesus had also been invited to the wedding with
his disciples" (Knox and Moffatt are similar). This verb is found in John
only here and in 1 : 43, which is somewhat curious as it is used often by Matthew
and Luke (though four times only in Mark).

there was a religious ceremony, but we have no details. The processions and the feast are the principal items of which we have knowledge. The feast was prolonged, and might last as long as a week.[13]

3 On this occasion the wine was all used up before the end of the feast.[14] This meant more than the disruption of the feast.[15] There was also something of a slur on those who had provided it, for they had not fully discharged the duties of hospitality. This may indicate that they were poor and had made the minimum provision hoping for the best. It is also possible that the lack of wine involved another embarrassment, in that it rendered the bridegroom's family liable to a lawsuit.

Up till this time Jesus had never performed a miracle (v. 11), but His mother's words to Him[16] show that she reposed trust in His resourcefulness. They may show more. Godet suggests that there was a "state of extraordinary exaltation" as a result of the events recorded in the first chapter. Mary would have shared in this. In addition she knew that angels had spoken about Jesus before His birth. She knew that she had conceived Him while still a virgin. She knew that His whole manner of life stamped Him as different. She knew Jesus, in short, to be the Messiah, and it is likely that she now tried to make Him take such action

---

[13] For information about marriage in New Testament times see SBk, I, pp. 500–17, II, pp. 372–99, the articles on "Marriage" in *HDB*, *ISBE*, *etc.*, and the works cited in n. 7 above.

[14] John says ὑστερήσαντος οἴνου. This is the sole occurrence of this verb in this Gospel. It is unusual, for ὑστερέω in the active more often means "lack" than "be lacking".

[15] It did mean this. The Rabbis could say, "there is no rejoicing save with wine" (*Pes.* 109a). This does not point to carousing, for drunkenness was severely reprobated, and wine was usually well watered (according to the Soncino Talmud, *Pesahim*, p. 561, n. 7 the normal dilution was one part wine and three parts water). But wine was a symbol. Its absence would mar so joyous an occasion as a wedding feast.

[16] πρὸς αὐτόν. G. D. Kilpatrick finds πρός used in this way after λέγω 8 times in all in this Gospel, after εἶπον 10 times (including two *v.l.*), and after κατηγορέω and ἀποκρίνομαι once each (the latter a *v.l.*). The dative is much more common. But there appears to be no real difference in meaning (*BT*, 11, 1960, pp. 176f.).

179

as would show Him to all as the Messiah she knew Him to be.[17]
4 Jesus' address to her, "Woman", is not as cold in the Greek as
in English. He uses it, for example, in His last moments as He
hangs on the cross and tenderly commends her to the beloved
disciple (19 : 26).[18] LS informs us that the vocative is "a term of
respect or affection". Yet we must bear in mind that it is most
unusual to find it when a son addresses his mother. There appear
to be no examples of this cited, other than those noticed in this
Gospel. It is neither a Hebrew nor a Greek practice. That Jesus
calls Mary "Woman" and not "Mother" probably indicates that
there is a new relationship between them as He enters on His
public ministry.[19] And if the form of address is tender, the rest
of Jesus' words make it clear that there was something of a barrier
between them.[20] Evidently Mary thought of the intimate relations

---

[17] Calvin suggests that Mary may have been trying to get Jesus "to allay the
guests' annoyance with some godly exhortations, at the same time relieving the
embarrassment of the bridegroom." But her words seem to mean more than this.

[18] Jesus used it also in addressing women for whom He was performing
miracles (Matt. 15 : 28; Luke 13 : 12), the woman at the well (John 4 : 21),
the adulteress (8 : 10), and Mary Magdalene at the tomb (20 : 15). In none
of these can we detect any harshness.

[19] *Cf.* Hoskyns, "before her request, He first makes it plain that He is no
longer able to act under her authority (contrast Luke ii. 51) or in response
to her wishes. The time of her authority is over: she must lose her son: this
is the destiny that has been laid upon her (Luke ii. 35)." Derrett says, "The
appellation 'woman' causes no difficulty: it is universally recognised that it
implies no hostility or rudeness, though the correct explanation, namely that
a religious devotee or ascetic will speak to a woman, if unavoidable, only in
the most formal terms, seems not to have attracted attention" (*op. cit.*, pp.
89f.). The trouble with this is that the Gospels picture Jesus as anything but
a "religious devotee or ascetic". After all He was described as "a gluttonous
man, and a winebibber, a friend of publicans and sinners!" (Luke 7 : 34).
And He did talk with women (*e.g.* ch. 4).

[20] Barclay translates "Lady, let me handle this in my own way." The
expression is found in Judg. 11 : 12; I Kings 17 : 18; II Kings 3 : 13; II
Chron. 35 : 21; Matt. 8 : 29; Mark 1 : 24; Luke 8 : 28. Vincent Taylor (on
Mark 1 : 24) understands the Old Testament expression to mean, "Why dost
thou meddle with us?" but this is too strong for the present passage. Godet
gives its force as, "This formula signifies, that the community of feeling to
which one of the interlocutors appeals is rejected by the other, at least in the

of the home at Nazareth as persisting. But Jesus in His public ministry was not only or primarily the son of Mary, but "the Son of man" who was to bring the realities of heaven to men (1 : 51). A new relationship was established. Mary must not presume.²¹ The meaning of "mine hour is not yet come"²² in the context is surely "It is not yet time for Me to act". Yet we should notice a remarkable series of passages throughout this Gospel which refer to the "hour" or the "time" of Jesus. This is said not to have come in 7 : 6, 8, 30; 8 : 20, as well as in the present passage. But when the cross is in immediate prospect Jesus says, "The hour is come that the Son of man should be glorified" (12 : 23; *cf.* also 12 : 27; 13 : 1; 16 : 32; 17 : 1; the same idea may be present in Matt. 26 : 18, 45; Mark 14 : 41). If we are right in linking the present passage with the later ones Jesus is thinking of His Messianic

---

particular point which is in question." *Cf.* Morton Smith, "Jesus is asking his mother why she intrudes in his affairs, why she bothers him" (*JBL*, LXIV, 1945, p. 513). Sometimes Roman Catholic scholars see Mary as asking for a miracle. Thus J. Cortés sees Jesus' words as meaning: "What has changed between us? Why do you hesitate to ask me for a miracle? The hour of my Passion, in which you will not be able to ask me for miracles nor will I work them, has not come yet. You are as always my mother and I am your son. Therefore I will gladly accept your petition" (*New Testament Abstracts*, III, 1958–59, p. 247). The difficulty with this position is that there *was* a change. Jesus had never previously worked a miracle (v. 11), so Mary might well hesitate to ask for one. The beginning of the public ministry altered all Jesus' relationships, but Mary was apparently slow to grasp this.

²¹ There is a valuable note on this passage by Edgar J. Goodspeed (*BT*, 3, 1952, pp. 70f.). He thinks there is no adequate English translation for γύναι and counsels that it be left untranslated. He sees Jesus' words as suggesting "his independence of action", and he translates, "Do not try to direct me. It is not yet time for me to act." See also the note of Harry M. Buck (*BT*, 7, 1956, pp. 149f.). He advocates the rendering, "Madam, why is that our concern?" Perhaps Goodspeed's position is better.

²² It is possible to take the expression as a question, "Has not my hour now come?" and Brown cites Gregory of Nyssa and Theodore of Mopsuestia in ancient times and Boismard and Michl in recent days as adopting this view. But it should almost certainly be rejected. Where οὔπω introduces a question (*e.g.* Mark 4 : 40; 8 : 17, 21) the answer expected is "No" not "Yes". Moreover Johannine usage is against it. In all John's eleven other uses of the word the meaning is negative (*cf.* especially 7 : 30; 8 : 20).

function. At the threshold of His ministry He looks forward to its consummation.[23]

5 Clearly Mary did not understand Jesus' words as a sharp rebuke. She doubtless realized that things between them were not the same as they had been hitherto. But she realized also that Jesus was not unmindful of the present difficulty, and that He would take what action was necessary. So she commanded the servants to obey His instructions.

6 John now draws attention to the presence of six large waterpots made of stone. A "firkin"[24] was about 8–9 gallons, so that each of these vessels held something like 20 gallons. The half dozen represented a good store of water for the carrying out of the kind of purification that we read of in Mark 7 : 1–4. Before the meal servants would have poured water over the hands of every guest. If there was any large number of guests a good deal of water would have been required. John does not elaborate, but says sufficient to enable his Greek readers to understand why so much water was provided. "Containing" means "having space for". It refers to capacity not actual content. Some see symbolism in the number six. The Jews regarded seven as the perfect number and six accordingly was short of perfection, lacking, incomplete.[25] The six pots are then held to point to Judaism as imperfect. There may

---

[23] O. Cullmann discusses the miracle in *Early Christian Worship* (London, 1954), pp. 66–71. He takes these words to point to the cross. He lays down the principle that "it belongs to the very essence of John's Gospel that words are used in a double sense, that they signify on the one hand something material, and on the other hand point to something quite different" (*op. cit.*, p. 68). The wine then is "a pointer to the wine of the Lord's Supper" (*op. cit.*, p. 69), while the water is a reference to Jewish rites of purification. "In place of all these rites there comes now the wine of the Lord's Supper, the blood of Christ" (*op. cit.*, p. 70; see p. 69, n. 1 for others who see a reference to the Lord's Supper). There are interesting and suggestive points in this approach, but it does seem to be reading a good deal into the text. That John often uses words with a double meaning is undoubted, but we cannot go on to say that a reference to "the hour" plus one to wine compels us to discern an allusion to the Eucharist. Cullmann sees one or other of the sacraments almost everywhere in John. Bultmann, by contrast, doubts whether there are any references to the sacraments in this Gospel (p. 360).

[24] μετρητής is found here only in the New Testament. AG draws attention to its wide use as a measure for wine.

[25] Yet it should not be overlooked that Philo can regard six as "the perfect number". His reason is that it is "equal to the sum of its factors, 3, 2 and 1" (*De Decal.*, 28).

be something in this, but a strong objection is that the narrative contains nothing that would symbolize completeness, which would surely be required to correspond to the incomplete. Jesus does not create or produce a seventh pot.

7 Jesus tells "them", evidently the servants, to fill the pots.[26] This they do, "up to the brim". This detail is possibly to indicate that there could be no addition to the contents. These pots at the time of the miracle contained nothing but water.

8 Jesus' next command is "Draw out" and then "bear unto the ruler of the feast". This evidently means to draw water from the big waterpots. Since, however, the verb is the normal one for drawing water from a well,[27] some (e.g. Westcott) have thought that Jesus means that they should draw from the well and take the water direct to the chief table. This is within the range of possibility. But it is open to the not inconsiderable objection that, if it be accepted, there seems no reason at all for mentioning the waterpots or for the command to fill them up. That they were filled right up to the brim surely indicates that they have some part to play in the story. As the verb can be used of drawing water from a large vessel we need not doubt that that is what was done.[28] "The ruler of the feast" (an official mentioned here only in the New Testament) is apparently one of the guests charged with the duty

---

[26] Ryle comments: "Duties are ours. Events are God's. It is ours to fill the water-pots. It is Christ's to make the water wine."

[27] It should, however, be quite clear that the verb has no original or necessary connection with wells. ἀντλέω is connected with ἄντλος, "bilge-water", and LS gives its first meaning as "bale out bilge-water, bale the ship". The word is used quite generally of drawing water, and not infrequently it is employed in metaphorical senses (see LS). There is no linguistic reason for insisting on a well. The word is peculiar to John in the New Testament. He uses it 4 times.

[28] Westcott objects to the view we have adopted on the ground that "It seems most unlikely that water taken from vessels of purification could have been employed for the purpose of the miracle." But surely that is just its point. It is not simply "purification", but "*Jewish* purification". It is precisely Judaism that is transformed by the power of God in Christ. More recently S. H. Hooke has maintained the position that the water was drawn from the well (*NTS*, IX, 1962–63, pp. 374f.). But he adds little to what the earlier commentators have said on this point.

Is there perhaps a connection with the thought that Jesus gives that water which "shall become in him a well of water springing up unto eternal life"?

of being "master of ceremonies". He presided over the gathering.²⁹
9, 10 John does not say how or when the miracle took place.
He simply speaks of "the water now become wine".³⁰ He does
not even tell us how much water was changed into wine. It is usually
held that it was all the water in the six waterpots, in which case
Jesus was making a bountiful wedding gift to the couple, who
were evidently poor. Not only did He rescue them from what
might have been a crippling liability but He provided that they
began their married life with an unexpected asset. There will be
spiritual significance also, for the "sign" points to the truth that
Christ abundantly supplies all the need of His people (*cf.* 1 : 16).
This interpretation is, however, not certain. It is possible that
John refers to the water actually drawn out (somewhat in the
manner of the lepers who found themselves cleansed as they went
to report to the priests, Luke 17 : 12–14). On this view, however,
it is hard to see a reason for mentioning the size of the pots. It is
probably better accordingly to accept the first-mentioned view.
Either way what happened was startling. The ruler of the feast
did not know the origin of the wine he was tasting, but he recognized its quality. He summoned the bridegroom (who was
responsible for the feast), and commented on his departure from
common custom. Men universally put out the better wine at the
beginning of a feast, while palates are still sensitive. It is only
when their guests³¹ are somewhat affected (the word rendered

---

²⁹ There is a difficulty in that the ἀρχιτρίκλινος (which is the title used
here) was rather like a headwaiter, not an honoured guest. His duty was "to
arrange the tables and food" (AS). In this story, however, he is clearly not
a servant, for he can summon the bridegroom (v. 9). He is a guest and an important one. His function appears to be much like that usually designated with
the term συμποσιάρχης, "toast master". In Sir. 32 (35) : 1f. the guest with this
responsibility is called the ἡγούμενος.

³⁰ *Cf.* Augustine: "even as that which the servants put into the water-pots
was turned into wine by the doing of the Lord, so in like manner also is what
the clouds pour forth changed into wine by the doing of the same Lord. But
we do not wonder at the latter, because it happens every year: it has lost its
marvellousness by its constant recurrence. And it suggests a greater consideration
than that which was done in the water-pots. For who is there that considers
the works of God, whereby this whole world is governed and regulated, who
is not amazed and overwhelmed with miracles?" (VIII. 1; p. 57).

³¹ The verb μεθυσθῶσιν is without a subject, a construction which John
employs from time to time. Here he can scarcely mean the indefinite "people"
(which is what the construction would normally signify). But there is no real
difficulty. The context shows that "their guests" is meant.

"drunk freely" means "are drunken"[32]), that they produce the worse wine.[33] This bridegroom however, has kept the good[34] wine until the end. We are thus left in no doubt as to the quality of the wine that resulted from the miracle.[35]

11 John rounds off the narrative with a reminder of the nature of the event, and of its effect on the disciples. He gives a precise note of locality ("in Cana of Galilee") in accordance with his general tendency to stress the factuality of the events he records. This is the first[36] of Jesus' miracles which John, as often, calls "signs".[37] It is characteristic of them not so much that they arouse wonder and are hard to explain, nor even that they are demonstrations of the divine power, but rather that they point us to something beyond themselves. They show us God at work. They are meaningful. (See further Additional Note G, pp. 684ff.)

John tells us further that Jesus "manifested his glory" (for "glory" see on 1 : 14). This is very important for the Evangelist. His declared intention in writing his Gospel is to show that "Jesus is the Christ" (20 : 31). This involves the clear recognition that He is fully man, it is true, but it also involves bringing out the truth that He is more. Throughout the first chapter he has shown us both aspects. Jesus is the Logos who was with God and was

---

[32] Schonfield translates, "when everyone is drunk". Barrett reminds us that "There is of course no ground here for conclusions regarding the degree of intoxication of the guests at this wedding; John finds the remark a neat way of emphasizing the superior quality of the wine provided by Jesus – the new faith is better than the old."

[33] *Cf.* the term ἑωλοκρασία defined by LS as "*mixture of dregs, heel-taps, etc.*, with which the drunken were dosed at the end of a revel by their stronger-headed companions". This is, of course, not a parallel, and John does not use this word. But it shows what could happen at a banquet.

[34] The word is καλός which in John probably does not differ in meaning from ἀγαθός. See note on 1 : 46.

[35] P. W. Meyer argues that this verse brings out an important symbolical meaning. He sees in the story a reference to the Christian salvation in contrast to Hellenistic ideas. According to the latter the best came first, the heavenly man before the earthly, the divine before the deterioration we see in the world. Salvation then was a reversal of the process, with the recovery of the original. But Christ brings men a salvation that is miraculously new. God has kept the best wine until last (*JBL*, LXXXVI, 1967, pp. 191–97).

[36] The Greek reads Ταύτην ἐποίησεν ἀρχὴν κτλ. The absence of the article gives a meaning like "this he did (as) a beginning of signs". See Abbott 2386(i).

[37] σημεῖα. John never uses δύναμις, the Synoptists' favourite word for the miracles, which stresses the element of power.

God. He is also the "Teacher" to whom Andrew and his friend came (1 : 38). Neither aspect should be overlooked. So now he tells us that the "sign" he has described displayed the glory of Jesus.[38] This might be hid from the casual observer. Indeed John says nothing at all of the effect of the "sign" on the ruler of the feast or on the guests generally or on the servants who certainly knew what had happened. But His disciples saw His glory and they "believed on him" (Rieu: "his disciples' faith in him was fixed"). The glory of the Messiah was revealed to some and hid from others. The disciples are now said to have "believed" on Him. Nathanael has already been recorded as a believer (1 : 50), and now others join him. They had known enough about Jesus before this to follow Him. Now in this miracle they saw His glory, and despite His outward lowliness they put their trust in Him.[39]

INTERLUDE, 2 : 12

12 After this he went down to Capernaum, he, and his mother, and his brethren, and his disciples; and there they abode not many days.

12 After the wedding[40] Jesus and those with Him went down to Capernaum[41] for a short stay. The verb is appropriate, for Cana was on the uplands whereas Capernaum was by the sea of Galilee. No reason is given for going to this city. Jesus has already been described as "of Nazareth" (1 : 45), but it may be that His

---

[38] *Cf.* Bultmann: "that he manifested his δόξα is nothing other than that he manifested the ὄνομα of the Father (17.6)." Richardson points out that John "records no scene of Transfiguration, as do the three Synoptists; he regards the whole of Christ's incarnate life as an embodiment of the δόξα of God, though the glory is revealed only to believing disciples and not unto 'the world' " (*An Introduction to the Theology of the New Testament*, London, 1958, p. 65).

[39] For πιστεύω εἰς see on 1 : 12 and Additional Note E, pp. 335ff.

[40] "After this" translates μετὰ τοῦτο. John uses this expression again in 11 : 7, 11; 19 : 28, and the plural μετὰ ταῦτα in 3 : 22; 5 : 1, 14; 6 : 1; 7 : 1; 19 : 38; 21:1. Bernard thinks that when the singular is used it is always implied that the time interval is short, whereas the plural is much more general (p. cviii). Barrett and Bultmann, however, deny that there is a distinction, and in view of John's habit of making slight variations in similar statements but without distinction of meaning (see on 3 : 5) they may well be right.

[41] The spelling favored by most authorities is Καφαρναούμ (Kapharnaoum). This is equivalent to כפר נחום, "village of Nahum". The exact location is not known, but Tell Hum and Khan Minyeh have been strongly supported. In any case it must have been on the northern shore of the sea of Galilee.

family had now moved to Capernaum[42] (though against this is the expression, "not many days", which looks like a reference to a short visit). From the Synoptists we know that Capernaum was Jesus' centre throughout most of His ministry and it might even be called "his own city" (Matt. 9 : 1). "His mother" is mentioned here for the last time until the passion narrative. The expression, "his brethren" has been variously understood. The most natural way of taking it is to understand children of Joseph and Mary. This is called the "Helvidian" view (from Helvidius, a fourth century theologian who advocated it). The expression occurs several times in the Synoptic Gospels, and never with any qualification such as would be expected if the words were to bear any other meaning. The view is supported by appealing to the statements that Joseph "knew her not till she had brought forth a son" (Matt. 1 : 25) and that Jesus was Mary's "firstborn son" (Luke 2 : 7). The most natural interpretation of both these passages is that Joseph and Mary had children after the birth of Jesus.

However, in the second century of our era the idea of Mary's perpetual virginity appeared. Where this was held the possibility of any other children was, of course, excluded. Two alternative explanations of "his brethren" were proposed. One saw them as the children of Joseph by a former marriage (the view of Epiphanius) and the other regarded them as Jesus' cousins (the view of Jerome). This last-mentioned view is almost universally rejected nowadays (except by some Roman Catholics). There seems nothing in its favor and much against it (*e.g.* "brother" does not mean "cousin", the correct word for which existed and was in use in the New Testament, *viz.*, Col. 4 : 10). The Epiphanian view can claim the support of many writers of antiquity and some in modern times. The principal evidence in its favor is the very appearance of the tradition of Mary's perpetual virginity. But this can scarcely outweigh the natural sense of Matt. 1 : 25; Luke 2 : 7; expressions which, as even J. B. Lightfoot (who favored the Epiphanian view) admits, would have been avoided by men who thought the idea of Mary's perpetual virginity of paramount importance. It seems

---

[42] It may support this that in Mark 3 : 31ff. our Lord's mother and brothers appear at Capernaum, and that in Mark 6 : 3, while Jesus' brothers are named, only his sisters are spoken of as remaining at Nazareth. This would be natural if the sisters had married, and later the rest of the family had moved to Capernaum.

to me that the Helvidian view is much the most probable.[43]

No indication is given as to which disciples accompanied Jesus. Probably we should understand those mentioned in ch. 1.

2. CLEANSING THE TEMPLE, 2 : 13–17

13 And the passover of the Jews was at hand, and Jesus went up to Jerusalem. 14 And he found in the temple those that sold oxen and sheep and doves, and the changers of money sitting: 15 and he made a scourge of cords, and cast all out of the temple, both the sheep and the oxen; and he poured out the changers' money, and overthrew their tables; 16 and to them that sold the doves he said, Take these things hence; make not my Father's house a house of merchandise. 17 His disciples remembered that it was written, [1]Zeal for thy house shall eat me up.

[1] Ps. lxix. 9.

There are accounts of a cleansing of the temple in Matt. 21 : 12f.; Mark 11 : 15–17; Luke 19 : 45f. The Markan account is the fullest, but even so it is shorter than this one. John differs from Mark in the references to the oxen and sheep, the scourge of cords, the word for "changers of money" in v. 14,[44] the "pouring out" of the money, and the command, "Take these things hence". John's word for "overthrew" is different from that in any of the Synoptics,[45] and whereas they tell us that Jesus quoted Isa. 56 : 7

---

[43] See further J. B. Lightfoot, *Saint Paul's Epistle to the Galatians* (London, 1902), pp. 252–91; J. B. Mayor, *The Epistle of St. James* (London, 1910), pp. v–lv; R. V. G. Tasker, *The General Epistle of James* (London, 1956), pp. 22–4; V. Taylor, *The Gospel according to St. Mark* (London, 1959), pp. 247–9; Godet, *in loc.* Taylor concludes, "There can be little doubt that the Helvidian view stands as the simplest and most natural explanation of the references to the brothers of Jesus in the Gospels" (*op. cit.*, p. 249). He points to the significance of this: "The fact that Jesus had blood brothers and sisters, it may be held, underlines the reality and completeness of the Incarnation" (*ibid.*). Those who oppose the Helvidian view stress the fact that it is almost universally held that James of Jerusalem was one of "the brethren of the Lord". Many hold that the Epistles of James and Jude likewise emanate from the "brethren". If these prominent Christians were really sons of Mary, they urge, it would have been impossible for the tradition of Mary's perpetual virginity to have arisen so early. This must be treated with respect, but it can scarcely outweigh the natural meaning of the language of Scripture. The Helvidian view is to be preferred.

[44] κερματιστής. The Synoptists use κολλυβιστής (which John employs also in v. 15).

[45] John has ἀνέτρεψεν; Matthew and Mark have κατέστρεψεν.

followed by Jer. 7 : 11, John does not speak of Him as citing any Scripture. But he does say that the disciples remembered the words of Ps. 69 : 9, which none of the Synoptists recalls. He does not mention, as Mark does, Jesus' prohibition of carrying anything through the temple, *i.e.* making a short cut out of it. Mark says that Jesus overturned the seats of the sellers of doves, John only that he told them to take "these things" away. Finally, the most important difference is one of time. In this Gospel the cleansing of the temple is the first great public act of Jesus' ministry: in the other Gospels it is the last.

The usual solution of the problem is to say that there was but one cleansing, and that it took place, as the Synoptists allege, at the climax of the ministry.[46] It was probably the event which sparked off the opposition of the high priests and led to the arrest of Jesus. John's placing of the incident on this view is regarded as due to his general approach. It was fitting that Jesus should begin His ministry in this way, and thus John depicts it.[47] If we

---

[46] Some scholars accept the Johannine dating, pointing out that, as Mark records but one visit to Jerusalem, he had to place the cleansing then. Ivor Buse is of opinion that "The explanation of the most complicated series of facts seems to be that both John and Mark were dependent upon an earlier account of the Temple Cleansing and that the influence of this earlier account led Matthew and Luke to make the same corrections in the Marcan story" (*ExT*, LXX, 1958–59, p. 24). I find his argument ingenious but unconvincing. R. H. Lightfoot devotes two chapters to the incident (*The Gospel Message of St. Mark*, Oxford, 1950, pp. 60–79). He finds himself unable to say whether the cleansing came early or late, though he inclines towards the Markan date. He does not discuss the possibility of two cleansings. E. B. Redlich argues for displacement, thinking that the passage 2 : 13 – 3 : 21 was removed by an editor from an original position after 12 : 36 (*ExT*, LV, 1943–44, pp. 89–92). His arguments are answered by G. Ogg (*ExT*, LVI, 1944–45, pp. 70–72).

[47] *Cf.* Barclay: "John, as someone has said, is more interested in the truth than in the facts" (cf. B. W. Bacon, "He aims to give not *fact* but *truth*", *The Making of the New Testament*, London, n.d., p. 223); "He was not interested to tell men *when* Jesus cleansed the Temple; he was supremely interested in telling men that Jesus *did* cleanse the Temple." But this is not the impression left by a reading of this Gospel. John *was* interested in facts. He speaks much more often, for example, of "*witness*" (a means of attesting facts) than does any of the other Evangelists. He includes notes of time and place. I see no reason for holding that he saw any conflict between truth and facts. He cared about both. It is further the case that the point of view put forward by Barclay, though widely held, does not face the very real difficulty of seeing how John could confront opponents of a Docetic type while holding such a light-hearted attitude to facts.

hold that there could have been only one cleansing this is probably the way to understand it.

But why should we make this assumption? The Johannine narrative is firmly embedded in a great block of non-Synoptic material. Apart from the work of the Baptist (which is manifestly different from anything in the Synoptics[48]) nothing else in the first five chapters of this Gospel is to be found in any of the Synoptics. Of course, it is not impossible that John took one lone Synoptic episode and bound it firmly into his own framework as far from its correct historical setting as he could make it. But in view of the major differences in wording and in setting, as well as in time, we will require more evidence than a facile assumption that two similar narratives must refer to the same event.[49] The words in common are very few, "sellers", "tables", "doves", "moneychangers", and without them it would be practically impossible to tell a story of temple-cleansing.

Moreover the evil in question was one which was likely to recur after a check. Jesus' action, though salutary, is not likely to have put a permanent end to the practice.[50] Nor can it be said that the authorities would certainly have taken such action after one incident as would effectively prevent a recurrence. At the time indicated in John Jesus was quite unknown. His strong

---

[48] *Cf.* the discussion in ch. I of P. Gardner-Smith, *Saint John and the Synoptic Gospels* (Cambridge, 1938). See also *SFG*, pp. 23ff.

[49] Most recent scholars do simply assume the point. Thus Dodd says: "The suggestion that the temple was twice cleansed is the last resort of a desperate determination to harmonize Mark and John at all costs. The only legitimate question is whether the (single) cleansing is to be placed early or late in the Ministry" (*HTFG*, p. 157, n. 2). But with all respect, this is rhetoric, not reasoned argument. The question is to be resolved by evidence, not dogmatism. The reason some scholars see two cleansings is not "a desperate determination to harmonize", but the number and character of the differences between the two accounts. Despite the assertions of some critics there are practically no resemblances between the two narratives, apart from the central act.

[50] Plummer thinks it "incredible that anyone who had contemporary evidence could through any lapse of memory transfer a very remarkable incident indeed from one to the other. On the other hand the difficulty of believing that the Temple was twice cleansed is very slight. Was Christ's preaching so universally successful that one cleansing would be certain to suffice? He was not present at the next Passover (vi. 4), and the evil would have a chance of returning. And if two years later He found that the evil had returned, would He not be certain to drive it out once more? Differences in the details of the narratives corroborate this view."

action would have aroused a furore in Jerusalem, but that is all. The authorities may well have been disinclined to go to extremes against Him, especially if there was some public feeling against the practices He opposed.[51] It was quite otherwise at the time indicated in Mark. Then Jesus was well known and vigorously opposed by the high-priestly party. His action would inevitably lead to strong counter-action.

Again, Murray makes the point that, at the trial before Caiaphas, there was difficulty in establishing the words used by Jesus on this occasion (v. 29; Mark 14 : 56-9). This is intelligible if the reference is to an event which occurred some three years earlier;[52] scarcely so if it had taken place within the week. The differences in the wording of Jesus' protests in the two accounts may also well point to two occasions, especially if Murray is right in seeing in "Ye have made it 'a brigands' cave' " a reference to the determination of the authorities to kill Jesus. This would have been true on the second occasion, but not on the first.[53] Tasker sees two cleansings and thinks of this one as explaining the mission of scribes sent to Galilee to oppose Jesus. The mission is mentioned, but no reason given for it in Mark 3 : 22.[54]

13 John refers to three Passovers (or four if 5 : 1 be taken of a Passover). The first is that mentioned here and in v. 23. There

---

[51] *Cf.* Bailey: "I cannot see that it is unlikely that Jesus should have repeated His action, though it is surprising that He should not have been immediately arrested on the first occasion. But the Temple authorities were not popular, and *v.* 23 suggests that He had popular support for what He did."

[52] It is quite possible that Jesus' saying was repeated during His ministry (see n. 74 below). Even so Murray's point will hold. If there was only one cleansing Jesus' words must have been spoken then, and if it was only a few days before the trial it would be very remarkable indeed if the authorities could find no witnesses who could agree on what He said.

[53] See also Westcott's careful comparison of the accounts, yielding the conclusion that there were two cleansings.

[54] Tasker says, "it may be suggested that it was because Jesus made this early attack upon traditional Pharisaic worship at the capital, that the mission of scribes was sent from Jerusalem to Galilee, when they entered upon what was virtually a 'counter-attack' by asserting that Jesus was possessed by Beelzebub. This mission is mentioned, without any explanation of its origin, in Mark iii. 22." Tasker has earlier said that "we may reasonably suppose" that this was a cleansing "which the Synoptic writers had no occasion to relate, for it did not form part of the Petrine, Galilaean tradition which they were embodying."

is a second in 6 : 4, while the third is referred to several times, 11 : 55; 12 : 1; 13 : 1; 18 : 28, 39; 19 : 14. If, as seems probable, we take 5 : 1 to refer to another feast we are left with three Passovers, which will give us a minimum of two years for Jesus' ministry, and possibly something approaching three years. Each of these feasts John speaks of as "the passover of the Jews". For "the Jews" see on 1 : 19. Some (*e.g.* Westcott, Barrett) think the expression points to the existence of a Christian Passover distinct from that of the Jews. This is intrinsically unlikely, for at this period the Christians were not noted for the production of liturgical feasts. There is not much evidence in the New Testament even for the observance of Sunday (though enough to show that the day was kept). Again, I Cor. 5 : 7 speaks of the Christian Passover as already sacrificed, which would be a strange mode of speech if the Christians observed an annual festival with that name. There is also the difficulty that the feast of Tabernacles is referred to in a similar fashion in 7 : 2. Are we to think of a Christian feast of Tabernacles also? Where is this to stop? It is best to take the expression as John's usual explanation inserted for the benefit of his Gentile readers. The Passover commemorated the great deliverance of the people from Egypt (Exod. 12). John mentions the festival much more than do the Synoptists and this may well be part of his plan to bring out the messianic significance of Jesus. What was foreshadowed in the great Passover deliverance of old was brought to its consummation in the sacrifice of Jesus.[55]

The Passover was one of the three occasions in the year when the Law required all the males to "appear before Jehovah" (Deut. 16 : 16). Not all Jews went up to Jerusalem for this feast, but many did. "Went up" is the usual word for going up to the capital, or to a feast. It does not necessarily denote ascent from lower to higher ground (though Jerusalem is, of course, fairly high up). **14** The "temple" signifies the whole of the temple precincts, in-

---

[55] See R. H. Lightfoot, Appended Note (pp. 349–56), for a discussion of the extent to which the idea of the Lord as the Passover Victim pervades this Gospel. Hendriksen gives a brief account of the Passover ritual, and there is a fuller one in Edersheim's *The Temple* (London, n.d.), ch. XII. See also my article, "The Passover in Rabbinic Literature" (*ABR*, IV, 1954–55, pp. 59–76).

cluding the various courts as well as the holy place.[56] Here clearly
one of the courts is meant.[57] It is certain that the selling[58] referred
to here took place in the outer courtyard, the court of the Gentiles.
The reason for the practice was, of course, the convenience of
having at hand a supply of the victims required for the prescribed
sacrifices. People who came to worship from a distance could
scarcely bring their offerings with them. If they were to sacrifice
at all they must have some way of purchasing the appropriate
victims when they reached Jerusalem. The "changers of money"[59]
plied their trade because it was permitted to make money offerings
in the temple only in the approved currency. Men from other
countries would bring all sorts of coinage with them and this had
to be changed into acceptable coinage. An astonishing number
of commentators affirm that the reason for the unacceptability of
other currencies was that the coins bore the Emperor's image or

---

[56] The word is ἱερόν. By contrast ναός signifies "the shrine", "the holy
place", "the sanctuary". The former is not used metaphorically in the New
Testament, but the latter is used of the body of Christ (v. 21), and is also
applied to believers (I Cor. 3 : 16f.; 6 : 19; II Cor. 6 : 16).

[57] At first sight it seems unlikely that animals would be allowed into any
of the temple courts, because of the risk of their getting loose and defiling the
sanctuary. But V. Eppstein ("The Historicity of the Gospel Account of the
Cleansing of the Temple", ZNTW, 55, 1964, pp. 42ff.) infers from Rosh ha-Shanah
31a and other passages in the Babylonian Talmud that there was a dispute
between Caiaphas and the Sanhedrin, as a result of which the high priest
allowed merchants to set up animal stalls within the temple precincts.

[58] The present participle τοὺς πωλοῦντας will denote the habitual practice.

[59] The word κερματιστής properly denotes one who changes large money
into small (κερματίζω = "to cut small"). In the next verse the word is
κολλυβιστής from κόλλυβος, originally a small coin, and then the fee for
exchange. Weymouth renders the former term "money-changers" and the latter
"brokers". But in this passage there is surely no difference in meaning. Both
terms apply to those who carried on the business of money-changing.
A certain charge was legitimate. But the temple money-changers had a
monopoly and often charged exorbitant rates. They have been estimated to
have made an annual profit of about £stg. 9,000 a year, while the temple tax
brought the temple authorities about £stg. 75,000 a year. The enormous wealth
of the temple is illustrated by the fact that the Roman Crassus is said to have
taken from it a sum equal to about two and a half million pounds sterling.
See A. Edersheim, LT, I, pp. 367ff., for details. He relates that on one
occasion the action of Simeon, the grandson of Hillel, caused the price of a
pair of pigeons to fall from the equivalent of 15s. 3d. to 4d.

some heathen symbol. But, as Israel Abrahams long ago pointed out, Tyrian coinage was not only permitted but expressly prescribed (Mishnah, *Bekh.* 8 : 7), and this bore heathen symbols.[60] He thinks that the reason for the prescription was that this coinage was "of so exact a weight and so good an alloy". Whatever the reason, men had to change their money before making their offerings and this required that money-changers should be at work somewhere. **15, 16** Jesus made a whip[61] of "cords" (more probably "rushes"[62]), and proceeded to drive all the traders[63] from the temple with their goods. It is clear that it was not so much the physical force as the moral power He employed that emptied the courts. "It was surely the blazing anger of the selfless Christ rather than the weapon which He carried which really cleared the Temple Courts of its noisy, motley throng."[64] He overturned the tables used by the money-changers and poured out their money. He commanded the dove-sellers to take their birds away. His words to them are important, for they give the reason for His whole action: "make

---

[60] *Studies in Pharisaism and the Gospels*, I (Cambridge, 1917), pp. 83f. He says: "It is strange enough that while the bronze coins circulated in Judaea should conform scrupulously to the tradition and represent nothing but inanimate objects, the payment of Temple dues should not only be accepted but required in coins containing figures on them. Reinach meets this objection by the suggestion that 'once thrown into the Temple treasury, all gold and silver coins were melted down and transformed into ingots'" (*op. cit.*, p. 84).

[61] There is some support for the reading ὡς φραγέλλιον, "as it were a whip" (notably P66, P75 f1 and some MSS of the OL). But this reading is probably not original, and in any case it does not give us a significantly different meaning. The term is found here only in the New Testament, and it is not so far attested in earlier writings.

[62] The expression is φραγέλλιον ἐκ σχοινίων. Yet it should be noted that in the only other place where σχοινίον occurs in the New Testament, namely Acts 27 : 32, it denotes ropes on a ship. Schonfield renders, "a lash of twisted rushes".

[63] This is the most natural way of understanding the masculine πάντας even though the following τά τε πρόβατα καὶ τοὺς βόας means "both the sheep and the oxen". If the animals only had been meant πάντα would have been more natural (see also Field, pp. 85f.).

[64] H. E. W. Turner, *Jesus Master and Lord* (London, 1957), p. 325. *Cf.* also Hengstenberg, "Christ had a powerful confederate in the consciences of the offenders" (cited by Reynolds).

not[65] my Father's[66] house a house of merchandise"[67] (Moffatt, "My Father's house is not to be turned into a shop!"). Note the play on the word "house". In the Markan story the traders are stigmatized as making the temple "a den of robbers", but here the objection is not to their dishonesty, but to their presence. Jesus is objecting to the practice, and not merely to the way it is conducted. It is sometimes said that this represents an attack on the whole sacrificial system, inasmuch as it would not have been possible to maintain the sacrifices unless people from afar could purchase the necessary victims in a convenient place. But that is just the point. A "convenient" place need not necessarily be within the temple precincts. It is to this that Jesus makes His objection, and not to anything else.[68]

---

[65] The force of the present, $\mu\dot{\eta}$ $\pi o\iota\epsilon\tilde{\iota}\tau\epsilon$ is "stop making". It implies that the action is going on. Moulton has a long note in which he shows that in the New Testament the distinction between the present and aorist tenses in prohibitions is observed, and specifically is this the case with John (M, I, pp. 122–26).

[66] Not "our Father's house". Jesus never joins men with Himself in such a way as to indicate that their sonship is similar to His (*cf.* 20 : 17). Bernard says that Jesus uses "my Father" 27 times in John, 16 times in Matthew and 4 times in Luke. The temple is often called "the house of God" in the Old Testament. Jesus' words are a claim to deity. *Cf.* Dalman: "In Jewish parlance it is unusual to refer to God in common discourse informally as Father without adding the epithet 'heavenly' " (*The Words of Jesus*, Edinburgh, 1902, p. 190). He examines Jesus' usage and concludes, "The usage of family life is transferred to God: it is the language of the child to its father" (*op. cit.*, p. 192).

[67] *Cf.* R. H. Lightfoot: "The word 'merchandise' suggests a reference to the messianic passage Zech. 14[21-end], if it is translated 'In that day (the day of the Lord) there shall be no more a trafficker in the house of the Lord of hosts'." It is quite in the Johannine manner to introduce in this way a subtle allusion to Jesus' messiahship, his great theme (20 : 31).

[68] *Cf.* Strachan: "It is erroneous to suppose that Jesus' action is an attack on the whole sacrificial system. His motive was one of reverence for *my Father's house*, and of deep concern that the spirit of worship should thus be dissipated at its very door." The court in which all this noisy and boisterous traffic took place was the only court to which Gentiles might go when they wished to pray or meditate in the temple. They ought to have been able to worship in peace. Perhaps we could go so far as to say that they had the right to worship in peace. Instead they found themselves in the midst of a noisy bazaar. "A place that should have stood as a symbol for the freedom of access of all nations in prayer to God, had become a place associated with sordid pecuniary interests" (Wright). On the necessity for sternness in the face of evil Wright quotes Ruskin, that it is "quite one of the crowning wickednessess of this age that we have starved and chilled our faculty of indignation."

17 The effect on the disciples is to remind them of Ps. 69 : 9.[69] The action of Jesus gave evidence of a consuming zeal for the house of God. The ancient Scriptures found their fulfilment in what He did. "The action is not merely that of a Jewish reformer: it is a sign of the advent of the Messiah" (Hoskyns). We should not miss the way this incident fits in with John's aim of showing Jesus to be the Messiah. All His actions imply a special relationship with God. They proceed from His messianic vocation. The citation from Scripture is important from another point of view, for it accords with another habit of this Evangelist's. While John does not quote the Old Testament as frequently as do some other New Testament writers it is still the case, as Richard Morgan says, that "the *Old Testament is present at every crucial moment in the Gospel*".[70] It is one of John's great themes that in Jesus God is working His purposes out. Every critical moment sees the fulfilment of Scripture in which those purposes are set forth.

3. Destroying and Raising the Temple, 2 : 18–22

18 The Jews therefore answered and said unto him, What sign showest thou unto us, seeing that thou doest these things? 19 Jesus answered and said unto them, Destroy this [1]temple, and in three days I will raise it up. 20 The Jews therefore said, Forty and six years was this [1]temple in building, and wilt thou raise it up in three days? 21 But he spake of the [1]temple of his body. 22 When therefore he was raised from the dead, his disciples remembered that he spake this; and they believed the scripture, and the word which Jesus had said.

[1]Or, *sanctuary*

The Synoptics tell of a cleansing of the temple, but they have nothing equivalent to this section. John records a cryptic

---

[69] The formula of citation is γεγραμμένον ἐστίν. The participial construction is usual in this Gospel (see 6 : 31, 45; 10 : 34; 12 : 14, 16; 15 : 25). The Synoptists prefer γέγραπται, as does Paul, and this form is found in 8 : 17 (though even here ℵ has the more usual Johannine formula and it could be right). No real difference of meaning appears to attach to these two formulae. Whichever way Scripture is cited it is regarded as authoritative.

[70] *Interpretation*, XI, 1957, p. 156 (Morgan's italics).

saying of our Lord's, and goes on to give both a Jewish mis-understanding of it and his own interpretation.[71] Characteristically he rounds it off with the effect of all this on the faith of the disciples. **18** The cleansing of the temple was a startling act. It had its implications not only for the condemnation of the temple traders, but also for the Person of Jesus (see on v. 17). It was a messianic action. The Jews (for this term see on 1 : 19) demanded[72] that Jesus authenticate the implied claim by producing a "sign" (see on v. 11 and Additional Note G, pp. 684ff.). Interestingly they do not dispute the rightness of His action. They were not so much de-fending the temple traffic as questioning Jesus' implied status. Their demand arose from the facts that the Jews were a very practical race and that they expected God to perform mighty miracles when the messianic age dawned.[73] Thus their test for a messianic claimant was, Can he do the signs of the Messiah? Paul could think of the Jews as seekers after signs just as typically as the Greeks were pursuers of wisdom (I Cor. 1 : 22). In the temple cleansing the Jews discerned a messianic claim (note again how faithfully John records anything that bears on Jesus' messiah-ship), and they demanded accordingly that He authenticate Him-self by a sign.

---

[71] See the excellent discussion in Dr. Alan Cole's Tyndale Lecture for 1950 published under the title *The New Temple*. Cole argues that the temple references in the First Gospel "necessitate and indeed presume the Saying and interpretation found in Jn. ii. 19" (*op. cit.*, p. 21). He sums up his conclusions in these terms: "(1) There was a certain amount of truth in the charge of the two witnesses at the trial of the Lord, as in that of the witnesses at Stephen's trial. (2) The fuller Marcan version of the Saying, especially in respect of its pair of correlated adjectives, represents what the early Church fully believed to be the teaching of the Lord. (3) These points are inexplicable unless the Saying recorded in the fourth Gospel at the account of the Temple purge (Jn. ii. 19) be accepted. (4) The interpretation there given is not merely 'Johannine mysticism,' but corresponds to the primitive post-resurrection belief of the Church at large" (*op. cit.*, p. 52).

[72] John says that they "answered", and Morgan sees significance in the verb: "It is quite significant. The rulers recognized the startling challenge in what He had done in cleansing the Temple courts. As He stood in lonely dignity, coins scattered, animals dispersed in every direction, and with the animals those who owned them gone, they gathered about Him and they 'answered' Him. It was an answer to what He had done."

[73] See Edersheim, *LT*, II, pp. 68f. for examples of this tendency in the Rabbinic literature.

19 Despite the hesitation of some critics the genuineness of this saying is beyond reasonable doubt, as is shown by the persistence of references to it. At the trial of Jesus one of the charges brought against Him was that He had said He would destroy the temple and raise it up again (Matt. 26 : 60f.; Mark 14 : 57–9). The mockers flung the same accusation at the dying Sufferer on the cross (Matt. 27 : 40; Mark 15 : 29).[74] Stephen's opponents said, "we have heard him say, that this Jesus of Nazareth shall destroy this place, and shall change the customs which Moses delivered unto us" (Acts 6 : 14; *cf.* Acts 7 : 48; 17 : 24). There is possibly another echo of the same accusation in the charge that Paul taught men "against . . . this place" (Acts 21 : 28), all the more so since the detailed charge against Stephen is an elaboration of the simple "This man ceaseth not to speak words against this holy place, and the law" (Acts 6 : 13). It is clear that the charge was persistent and repeated. It is idle to deny that there was any reality behind it at all, and to put the whole thing down to the malice of false witnesses.[75] While there is no reason to doubt that those who witnessed against Jesus at His trial were ready to say almost anything to have Him condemned, yet the evidence before us is that they used a distorted version (or rather, versions – their witness did not agree, Mark 14 : 59) of a genuine saying of Jesus. What was this saying? There is nothing that seems adequate in the teaching recorded in the Synoptic Gospels.[76] But this saying does meet the conditions. It has the necessary references to the

---

[74] It is possible that the present participles, ὁ καταλύων . . . καὶ οἰκοδομῶν in both accounts point to a repeated claim by Christ. At the very least they do not look like a reference to a single, isolated saying.

[75] It may be significant that Matthew does not call those who brought this charge "false" witnesses (AV is based on an inferior reading). There was a measure of truth in their words. Mark does call them false, but his meaning is probably not that Jesus did not utter the saying, but that He did not mean it in the sense claimed.

[76] *Cf.* C. F. D. Moule: "Putting the synoptic and the Johannine evidence together – and the two appear to be independent – we have a strong presumption that Jesus did say something about the destruction and replacement of the temple. This is important, because (apart from this saying) there seems to me to be no direct evidence that Jesus ever said anything which might have exposed him to the charges popularly levelled against him and brought with more formality against his follower Stephen" (*JThS*, n.s., I, 1950, p. 30; the whole article, "Sanctuary and Sacrifice in the Church of the New Testament", is important).

destruction and raising again of the temple, and it is not easy to understand. It would readily be misunderstood and misremembered.

Jesus usually refused to give a sign when asked for one (Mark 8 : 11f.; *cf.* His refusal to answer the question of John 6 : 30). He complains that, though His enemies could discern the weather signs in the heavens they were unable to recognize the real signs, "the signs of the times", when they were before them (Matt. 16 : 3). But in the Synoptic Gospels He regularly pointed to His resurrection as the only sign that would be given to these people (Matt. 12 : 39f.; 16 : 4; Luke 11 : 29). "Destroy" is literally "loose".[77] The verb is often used of untying and the like. It can refer to the loosing of the component parts from one another, and so "to destroy" (*cf.* its use for the breaking up of part of a ship, Acts 27 : 41, and the breaking down of "the middle wall of partition", Eph. 2 : 14). It can also be used of the dissolution of life, or killing. The imperative here seems equivalent to a conditional, "If you destroy ... I will raise up", though Howard equates it with the future tense, "You will destroy" *(IB)*. It is possible also that we should discern something of the prophetic method wherein the spoken word initiates the action in which the purpose of God is worked out. There is irony in the fact that ultimately the Jews themselves were to be the means of bringing about the sign they asked the Christ to produce, and which they did not recognize when it came. There is further irony in that to put Jesus to death was to offer the one sacrifice that can truly expiate sin, and thus doom the temple as a place for the offering of sacrifice. Jesus' word for "temple" denotes the shrine, the sanctuary, the very dwelling place of deity.[78] It may be applied to the believer (as in I Cor. 6 : 19), but Jesus' use of the word probably

---

[77] Λύσατε. Abbott points to Ecc. 11 : 9 as a parallel construction for it contains an imperative which implies a threat (2439 (iv)). Temple understands the word as "not an empty challenge, but a judgement on their mentality and policy which will involve the destruction of the Temple". Christ will then raise up "what shall thereafter be the habitation of God among men, that Risen Body which after the Ascension and Pentecost finds its earthly manifestation in that 'holy temple in the Lord, in whom ye also are builded together for a habitation of God in the Spirit' (*Ephesians* ii, 21–22)."

[78] His word is ναός. For its distinction from ἱερόν see above, n. 56.

implies that God dwelt in Him in a very special way.[79] "In three days" means "within the space of three days" and does not pinpoint the event.

20 The Jews explode in an incredulous question. Their temple was a magnificent structure. Herod had commenced its rebuilding partly to satisfy his lust for building, and partly in an attempt to stand well with his Jewish subjects, among whom he was very unpopular.[80] Work was still going on at his death, and for that matter, for long after. The temple was not completed until A.D. 64. The Jews accordingly mean here that work has been proceeding for forty-six years.[81] The fact that it was still not complete would heighten their amazement at a statement which they understood to mean that Jesus claimed the power to erect its like in a mere three days. "Thou" is emphatic. Though they had asked Jesus for a sign they mocked the suggestion that *he* of all people could do such a thing. Incidentally the pattern we see in these verses,

---

[79] *Cf.* Matt. 12 : 6, "a greater thing than the temple is here" (ARV mg.) However we interpret the neuter it is clear that the "greatness" exceeding that of the temple is closely connected with Christ. If we take it as equivalent to the masculine Cole's words bring out the meaning: "Why is Christ 'greater than the Temple'? There can be only one all-embracing answer. It is because God's presence is more manifest in Him than in the Temple. On Him, not on the Temple, now rests the Shekinah" (*op. cit.*, p. 12). Similar thoughts are brought out in the Prologue to this Gospel where the very Word of God "became flesh" in Jesus, He "tabernacled" among men, and the glory of God was manifest in Him (1 : 14). On v. 21 Barrett comments, "the human body of Jesus was the place where a unique manifestation of God took place and consequently became the only true Temple, the only centre of true worship". Luther explains that when Christ calls Himself a temple this means that "in him dwelleth all the fulness of the Godhead bodily" (Col. 2 : 9; Luther, vol. 22, p. 250).

[80] Josephus says that the work was begun in the eighteenth year of Herod's reign (*Ant.* xv, 380). This would be 20–19 B.C., and if the Jews' statement is accurate the date of this incident will be A.D. 27 or 28.

[81] Τεσσαράκοντα καὶ ἓξ ἔτεσιν οἰκοδομήθη ὁ ναὸς οὗτος is difficult. Robertson explains the case of ἔτεσιν as instrumental, though it might be regarded as locative, "the whole period regarded as a point of time" (*A Grammar of the Greek New Testament in the Light of Historical Research*, London, n.d., p. 527). Barrett thinks it a combination of the two. The aorist is constative, the lengthy process being viewed as one whole. Yet the application of this tense to an edifice that was not to be completed for many years is not easy. There is, however, a parallel in LXX II Esdras 5 : 16 (= Ezra 5 : 16), καὶ ἀπὸ τότε ἕως τοῦ νῦν ᾠκοδομήθη καὶ οὐκ ἐτελέσθη. It is not unlikely that the words in John refer to the completion of a definite stage of the work and perhaps no building was going on at the time they were uttered. Some think that the

a saying of Jesus, a complete misunderstanding, and an explanation, recurs in this Gospel (*e.g.* 3 : 3ff.; 4 : 10ff., 32ff.; 6 : 41ff., 51ff.; 11 : 11ff.; 14 : 7ff.). It is not, of course, confined to this Gospel (see, for example, Mark 7 : 15ff.; 8 : 15ff.), and we may see in it one of the ways in which Jesus instructed His hearers. **21** The Evangelist gives his own comment. Jesus[82] was not talking about the temple of stones and mortar that they saw about them. He was talking about His body. It is possible to understand "his body" of the church, which in Paul's writings is explicitly called the body of Christ (Eph. 1 : 23; 4 : 16; Col. 1 : 18). On this view the saying would mean that Jesus would presently establish His church[83] (*cf.* Matt. 16 : 18). There is little to be said for this, however. Such a saying would be far more cryptic than a reference to the resurrection. And there is no evidence for the application of the term "body" to the church for many years after this time. A somewhat similar suggestion is that Jesus referred to the destruc-

---

ναός as against the ἱερόν had been completed. The problem of the aorist would be solved if we could think with Abbott (2021–24) that the reference is to the temple of Zerubbabel, begun in 559 B.C., and completed in 513 B.C. But Herod's rebuilding was so extensive that this seems most unlikely. The problem is discussed in detail by G. Ogg, *The Chronology of the Public Ministry of Jesus* (Cambridge, 1940), pp. 153–67. He concludes that the reference gives us no firm date. Nevertheless it does indicate within a year or two the time of Jesus' ministry. J. B. Lightfoot in an important note has shown that it is difficult to square this reference with the idea of a late writer who sat loose to accurate historical writing. It would have involved some abstruse research, both into Jesus' life and Herod's building program. And it is impossible to think of anyone doing all this work and then not drawing attention to it. See E. Abbot, A. P. Peabody, and J. B. Lightfoot, *The Fourth Gospel* (London, 1892), pp. 158–60.

[82] Note the emphatic ἐκεῖνος (see on 1 : 8). In contrast to the Jews (who did not understand) *He* spoke.

[83] *Cf.* Wright: "The symbolism of Jesus was misunderstood in His day, as in every age it has been misunderstood. What He meant was that if they succeeded in destroying the true worship of Him whom he know to be the Father, in this place, he would raise another 'temple' in the lives of His followers. This would be the true 'temple of his body.' God's temple is where He is known and worshipped." Similarly Cullmann says that the reference to the temple not made with hands (Mark 14 : 58) "can only refer to the community of disciples" (*op. cit.*, p. 72, n. 3). R. H. Fuller dissents. John, he thinks, "does not speak of the church as the body of Christ: John 2 : 21 is often expounded in a Pauline sense, but it probably refers to the literal body of Jesus which passed through death to resurrection" (*The New Testament in Current Study*, London, 1963, p. 129). This view is surely correct.

tion of the temple as a living force, *i.e.* He spoke of the abolition of the sacrifices in the new system He would set up.[84] It is not easy to see this as His meaning.

More commonly scholars think that Jesus was referring to the literal temple. But since we can scarcely think of Him as undertaking to raise up the material temple in three days they feel that John is not giving us the saying exactly, and that its original form is lost. Jesus said something about the temple, possibly about its being superseded in the new covenant He had come to establish, and the saying was misunderstood.

Such explanations, however, are in no way superior to that put forward by John. These factors are relevant.

(i) Jesus did predict the resurrection, though the disciples did not understand what He meant (Matt. 12 : 40; 16 : 21; 17 : 9, 23; 20 : 19, 26, 32; Mark 8 : 31; 9 : 9, 31; 10 : 34; Luke 9 : 22; 18 : 33). One such prediction with its specific mention of "three days and three nights in the heart of the earth" (Matt. 12 : 40) comes in the same chapter as the reference to the "greater than the temple" (Matt. 12 : 6).

(ii) Jesus said something about the temple which referred in some way to its destruction. But the saying was not clear and straightforward. At His trial it was felt to be a useful charge to level at Him, but the witnesses could not agree on the form of it (Mark 14 : 59). This argues for some such cryptic saying as we have here.

(iii) In our Lord's teaching "three days" almost always refers to the period leading up to the resurrection. It is not easy to see how this expression could have been attached to a saying about the temple unless Jesus Himself had connected the two. The explanations mentioned above ignore the three days, or explain them as "a short time". This meaning is found in the Old Testament, but it is not common in the Gospels.

---

[84] Barclay thinks that Jesus meant that He would put an end to the temple and to temple worship: "He had come to show men a way to come to God without any Temple at all." He proceeds: "That must be what Jesus actually said; but in the years to come John saw far more than that in Jesus' saying. He saw in it nothing less than a prophecy of the Resurrection; *and John was right*. He was right for this basic reason, that the whole round earth could never become the temple of the living God until Jesus was released from the body and was everywhere present". Granted that the saying contains all this, why could not Jesus have meant it so? Why should John see in it more than his Master who uttered the saying?

(iv) The persistence of the saying in accusations levelled at Jesus and afterwards at His followers shows that He must have said something of the sort, and said it in such a way that it was impressed on the minds of His hearers, more especially of His opponents. Such a saying as this, made immediately after the cleansing of the temple, meets the requirements. It would be easy for His foes to misinterpret it, their attention being focussed on the material temple at that moment. And it would not be inappropriate for Jesus to be thinking at that time of the real nature of His mission.

While then the primary reference of the saying is surely to the resurrection of Jesus it would be quite in the Johannine manner to see a double meaning in the words. It may well be that they point us also to the ultimate abolition of the temple and of the temple sacrifices. The words about rebuilding will in that case refer to their replacement by the spiritual temple[85] and the new covenant effected by the death and resurrection of Christ.[86] This is all the more likely in that all these events are inseparably bound up with one another.[87] Such a double meaning would link the saying on the one hand with the Matthean passages noted above, and on the other with the "temple without hands" of Mark 14 : 58 (*cf.* Acts 7 : 48; 17 : 24).

[85] Bertil Gärtner has shown that there are affinities with and differences from the teaching of Qumran (*The Temple and the Community in Qumran and the New Testament*, Cambridge, 1965). The sectarians rejected the worship of the Jerusalem Temple and thought of themselves as the new temple. But they lacked any equivalent to Christ. Gärtner says, "the temple symbolism of the New Testament is built on the work of Christ; this it was believed had replaced the temple and its sacrifices once and for all. In short, the boundary between Qumran and the New Testament, in this matter of the content and function of temple symbolism, goes through the person of Christ" (*op. cit.*, pp. 104f.).

[86] *Cf.* R. H. Lightfoot: "there is in this story, thus set before us here, a triple depth of meaning. First, the Lord performs an act by which He condemns the methods and the manner of the existing Jewish worship. Secondly, this act, as set forth by St. John, is a sign of the destruction of the old order of worship, that of the Jewish Church, and its replacement by a new order of worship, that of the Christian Church, the sanctuary or shrine of the living God. And thirdly, intermediate between the old order and the new order is the 'work' – the ministry, death, and resurrection – of the Lord, which alone makes possible the inauguration and the life of the new temple."

[87] *Cf.* Hoskyns: "The rejection and putting to death of Jesus, His resurrection, the destruction of the temple and the end of animal sacrifice, the presence of God in the midst of the community of those who believe in Jesus, and the removal of sin – these are not isolated, separable occurrences. The sign that is given to the Jews is, therefore, the sign of the resurrection".

22 John does not say that the saying was luminous to His disciples (for this expression see on v. 2). But when Jesus was raised[88] they remembered it, and it was then a strengthening of faith for them. John tells us that they then "believed the scripture". In the singular "scripture" usually refers to a single passage.[89] If this is the case it is not easy to identify the passage in mind. It may perhaps be Ps. 16 : 10, which is interpreted of the resurrection in Acts 2 : 31; 13 : 35. Or it may be Isa. 53 : 12, which is not unfairly understood of the resurrection for it speaks of the activity of the Servant after His death. There is a reference to being raised on the third day in Hos. 6 : 2, but this does not seem at all relevant to the resurrection of Christ.

The disciples believed not only "the scripture" but also "the word[90] which Jesus had said". This placing of Jesus' saying alongside Scripture is interesting and its christological implications should not be overlooked. Notice also that the disciples are not said to have believed this saying until they saw it fulfilled. Jesus was fond of parabolic language and evidently they took this to be another example of it. They may well have reasoned, "Obviously He cannot mean a rising from the dead in a literal sense. What then does He mean?" But when the resurrection took place

---

[88]   In accordance with the usual New Testament usage the resurrection is ascribed to the Father as the passive, $\mathring{\eta}\gamma\acute{\epsilon}\varrho\vartheta\eta$, shows. Bernard, however, is incorrect when he says, in objection to the preceding saying's being understood of the resurrection, "by the N.T. writers God the Father is *always* designated as the Agent of Christ's Resurrection ... Jesus is not represented as raising Himself" (on v. 19; Bernard's italics). Similarly Strachan: "The Resurrection is never regarded in the New Testament as the act of Christ Himself. It is the supreme act of God's almighty power." While it is true that the New Testament generally refers to the Father's action, Jesus Himself said on a number of occasions that He would rise (Mark 8 : 31; 9 : 9, 31; 10 : 34; Luke 18 : 33; 24 : 7, 46; some MSS also in Matt. 17 : 9, 23; Luke 9 : 22; *cf.* also John 10 : 17f.). It is also said that He rose (Acts 10 : 41; 17 : 3; I Thess. 4 : 14).

[89]   In John this is clear enough in passages like 10 : 35; 13 : 18; 17 : 12; 19 : 24, 28, 36, 37, and this creates a presumption that other occurrences of $\mathring{\eta}$ $\gamma\varrho\alpha\varphi\acute{\eta}$ also have a single Old Testament passage in mind, even though we are not able to identify it with certainty (namely 7 : 38, 42; 20 : 9). But the possibility remains that sometimes the general sense of the Old Testament may be meant. It is perhaps no coincidence that the two most difficult to pin down are this verse and 20 : 9, both of which refer to the resurrection. John may mean that this is the general tenor of Old Testament teaching.

[90]   For John's use of $\lambda\acute{o}\gamma o\varsigma$ see Additional Note A, pp. 115ff. John uses $\gamma\varrho\alpha\varphi\acute{\eta}$ 12 times, the most in any New Testament book (next come Acts and Romans each with 7).

they saw the meaning of the words, and they believed them. May we not see in this a fulfilment of Jesus' later words, "the Holy Spirit ... shall ... bring to your remembrance all that I said unto you" (14 : 26)?

4. JESUS AND MEN, 2 : 23–25

23 Now when he was in Jerusalem at the passover, during the feast, many believed on his name, beholding his signs which he did. 24 But Jesus did not trust himself unto them, for that he knew all men, 25 and because he needed not that any one should bear witness concerning ¹man; for he himself knew what was in man.

¹Or, *a man; for ... the man*

John inserts a short section to show the success that attended the ministry of Jesus in Jerusalem[91] at this time, and also to show Jesus' knowledge of and independence of men. When many came to believe on Him He did not commit Himself to them. He was not dependent on man's approval. The Master went His own way, unswayed by the passing enthusiasms of men. He knew men thoroughly. **23** For "the passover" see on v. 13,[92] and for believing on the name see on 1 : 12. The verb "believed" is in the aorist tense. Many came to the point of decision. Yet we should probably not regard them as having a profound faith. They believed because they saw[93] the "signs" (*cf.* 6 : 2, and see Additional Note G). While

---

[91] ἐν τοῖς ʽΙεροσολύμοις (for this form see on 1 : 19). The article is found with this name elsewhere in the New Testament only in 5 : 2; 10 : 22; 11 : 18. It is difficult to see the reason for it. Perhaps as Bernard suggests, it means "the precincts of Jerusalem". The form with the article is found also in II Macc. 11 : 8; 12 : 9; III Macc. 3. 16.

[92] John adds ἐν τῇ ἑορτῇ, this being his first use of the noun. It is indicative of his interest in the feasts generally that he uses the term 17 times, whereas Matthew and Mark use it but twice each and Luke 3 times.

[93] John is fond of the verb θεωρέω which he uses 24 times. In the whole New Testament it is found 58 times so he has nearly half its occurrences. The verb is often said to denote a more concentrated gaze than say, βλέπω, but it is difficult to see this consistently carried through (though it may be present on some occasions). It can be used for the deepest and most perceptive sight (6 : 40), but on the other hand there is no such connotation here. In the note on 1 : 32 we drew attention to R. E. Brown's examination of John's words for seeing, in which he finds that while John certainly does have different kinds of sight in mind these are not consistently linked with particular words. We conclude that θεωρέω is a favourite word with John and is used of a variety of kinds of seeing.

such faith is better than none (see 6 : 26) it is not the deepest faith (*cf.* 20 : 29).[94] It is no more than a beginning. R. H. Lightfoot points out that it is "only a first attraction to the Lord (cf. 4[45, 48]), and does not yet know Him as the Son of man, still less as the unique Son of God, and is therefore imperfect and liable to be overthrown; and of this He, the Word become flesh, is well aware". Strachan brings out the unsure basis of this faith by translating, "So long as they were beholding". The reference to Jesus' "signs", and the imperfect tense of the verb "did" (showing that Jesus continued to do signs), are somewhat perplexing, for John records no sign in Jerusalem unless the cleansing of the temple be called such. But he disclaims any attempt at being exhaustive (20: 30; 21 : 25). There is no doubt that he wants us to think of Jesus as continually manifesting His glory but he does not go into details. **24** Jesus is set in emphatic contrast to those who saw His signs.[95] There is an interesting word play, for the verb "trust" in this verse is the same as that rendered "believed" in the previous one. Because of what they knew of Jesus from His signs many came to put their trust in Him. But because He knew[96] all men Jesus

---

[94] Luther speaks of this as a "milk faith". This he explains as "a young faith of such as enthusiastically accede, give in, and believe but just as quickly withdraw when they hear something unpleasant or unexpected" (*op. cit.*, p. 251).

[95] As we see from the emphatic αὐτός which opens the clause, and the adversative δέ.

[96] The verb is γινώσκω. For the use of the articular infinitive see on 1 : 48. Some differentiate this verb from οἶδα, suggesting that it denotes acquired knowledge, the knowledge that comes from observation and reasoning, whereas οἶδα points to immediate, intuitive knowledge. The former is said to be partial and growing, the latter complete and absolute. But it is very doubtful whether the distinction can be pressed especially in this Gospel. Bernard has a helpful comment (on 1 : 26): "Both verbs are used of Christ's knowledge of the Father; γινώσκω at 10[15] 17[25], οἶδα at 7[29] 8[55]. Both are used of the world's knowledge (or ignorance) of God, or of that possessed by the Jews: γινώσκω at 1[10] 17[23, 25] 8[55] 16[3], I Jn. 3[1, 6]; οἶδα at 7[28] 8[19] 15[21]. Both are used of man's knowledge of God and Christ: γινώσκω at 14[7, 9] 17[3], I Jn. 2[4, 13, 14] 4[6, 7, 8] 5[20], and οἶδα at 1[31, 33] 4[22] 14[7]. Both are used of Christ's knowledge of men or of ordinary facts, *e.g.* γινώσκω at 2[25] 5[6, 42] 6[15] 10[14, 27], and οἶδα at 6[64] 8[37] 13[3]. The word used for the Father's knowledge of the Son is γινώσκω (10[15]), and not οἶδα as we should have expected. With this array of passages before us, we shall be slow to accept conclusions which are based on any strict distinction in usage between the two verbs." The view that the two verbs can be differentiated is argued by J. B. Lightfoot, *Notes on Epistles of St Paul* (London, 1904), pp. 178f. But

put His trust in none of them. The verb used of His action is in the imperfect tense. It denotes His habitual attitude.[97] Those who had been attracted by the miracles would have been ready to try to make an earthly king of Him (*cf.* 6 : 15). But He did not trust Himself to them. He looked for genuine conversion, not enthusiasm for the spectacular.[98]

25 The idea of witness is a prominent one in this Gospel (see on 1 : 7), but John tells us that there was one form of witness that was not required, namely a witness that would inform Jesus about mankind. "He himself" is emphatic. John leaves us in no doubt as to the fact of Jesus' knowledge. This is to be understood in the light of the Old Testament view that God alone knows what is in man ("thou, even thou only, knowest the hearts of all the children of men", I Kings 8 : 39). It involves an unobtrusive, but not unimportant, claim as to the Person of Jesus.[99]

Bernard's case is strong. And it may be reinforced by the reflection that John habitually uses minor variations without significant difference of meaning (see on 3: 5), John never uses the noun γνῶσις but the importance he attaches to knowledge is perhaps indicated by the fact that he uses γινώσκω 56 times and οἶδα 85 times. As we have seen, both verbs are used of a variety of aspects of knowledge. But the really significant thing is the knowledge of Christ and of God, which are interconnected. To know Christ is to know the Father (14 : 7).

[97] John quite often draws attention to unusual knowledge possessed by Jesus (4 : 17; 5 : 42; 6 : 61, 64; 13 : 1, 11; 18 : 4).

[98] Loyd makes a comparison between this chapter and the temptation narrative: "(i) He will not turn stones into bread to satisfy His own hunger; but He turns water into wine to meet the needs of others. (ii) He will not leap from the pinnacle of the Temple in order to capture the popular imagination; but He does the unpopular thing of cleansing the Temple. (iii) He will not fall down and worship Satan in order to gain wordly power; but insists upon the need of individual conversion."

[99] It is probably significant that "what is in the heart of his neighbour" is one of the seven things the Rabbis thought of as hidden from man (Mekhilta Exod. 16 : 32). John assigns this knowledge explicitly to Jesus. Odeberg points out that in one place or another John attributes to Jesus knowledge of the other six as well (*FG*, p. 45). John clearly regards Jesus as possessed of a knowledge that is more than human, but just as clearly he does not regard this as vitiating His real humanity. Jesus' knowledge is derived from His close communion with the Father (8 : 28, 38; 14 : 10).

CHAPTER III

5. THE FIRST DISCOURSE – THE NEW BIRTH, 3 : 1–36

John pursues his aim of showing that Jesus is "the Christ, the Son of God" (20 : 31) chiefly in two ways: he narrates some of the signs Jesus did, and he records some of the discourses Jesus delivered. Sometimes the "sign" and the discourse are intimately connected, sometimes not. The first "discourse" is a private talk to a single listener, Nicodemus, a member of the ruling class. The conversation brings out the means of attaining eternal life, and, in typical Johannine fashion, this leads on to reflections of the Evangelist and to further incidents.

(a) The New Birth, 3 : 1–15

1 Now there was a man of the Pharisees, named Nicodemus, a ruler of the Jews: 2 the same came unto him by night, and said to him, Rabbi, we know that thou art a teacher come from God; for no one can do these signs that thou doest, except God be with him. 3 Jesus answered and said unto him, Verily, verily, I say unto thee, Except one be born [1]anew, he cannot see the kingdom of God. 4 Nicodemus saith unto him, How can a man be born when he is old? can he enter a second time into his mother's womb, and be born? 5 Jesus answered, Verily, verily, I say unto thee, Except one be born of water and the Spirit, he cannot enter into the kingdom of God. 6 That which is born of the flesh is flesh; and that which is born of the Spirit is spirit. 7 Marvel not that I said unto thee, Ye must be born [1]anew. 8 [2]The wind bloweth where it will, and thou hearest the voice thereof, but knowest not whence it cometh, and whither it goeth: so is every one that is born of the Spirit. 9 Nicodemus answered and said unto him, How can these things be? 10 Jesus answered and said unto him, Art thou the teacher of Israel, and understandest not these things? 11 Verily, verily, I say unto thee, We speak that which we know, and bear witness of that which we have seen; and ye receive not our witness. 12 If I told you earthly things and ye believe not, how shall ye believe if

[1]Or, *from above* See ver. 31; ch. 19.11; Jas. 1.17; 3.15, 17 [2]Or, *The Spirit*

I tell you heavenly things? 13 And no one hath ascended
into heaven, but he that descended out of heaven, even the
Son of man, ³who is in heaven. 14 And as Moses lifted up
the serpent in the wilderness, even so must the Son of man
be lifted up; 15 that whosoever ⁴believeth may in him have
eternal life.

breatheth ³ Many ancient authorities omit *who is in heaven.* ⁴Or, *believeth in
him may have*

Right from the opening verse of this Gospel John has been
concerned to impress on his readers the surpassing excellence of
Jesus. He is the Word become flesh. But He did not become flesh
so to speak on general principles. He had a purpose. He came
specifically in order that men might have the abundant life (10 :
10). In this chapter John furthers his purpose by recording a conversation between Jesus and Nicodemus, a typical representative
of Pharisaic Judaism. As such Nicodemus would have stressed the
careful observance of the Law and the traditions of the elders.
For the loyal Pharisee this was the way of salvation. John uses
this conversation to show that all such views are wide of the mark.
Not a devout regard for the Law, not even a revised presentation
of Judaism is required, but a radical rebirth.¹ The demand is
repeated three times (vv. 3, 5, 7). Nicodemus and all his tribe of
law-doers are left with not the slightest doubt but that what is
asked of a man is not more law, but the power of God within him
to remake him completely. In its own way this chapter does away
with "works of the law" every bit as thoroughly as anything in
Paul.
1 Jesus' visitor is introduced as "a man² of the Pharisees" (for

---

¹ *Cf.* L. S. Thornton: "The Christian doctrine of a new life stands in
contrast to the contemporary Jewish expectation of a new world. Doubtless
the two doctrines overlap in the New Testament. But the relation between
them might be not inappropriately described in terms of kernel and husk.
Within the sheltering husk or shell of Jewish apocalyptic expectations there
appeared first the gospel revelation and then the pentecostal gift of the Spirit
and the new life in Christ" (*The Common Life in the Body of Christ*, London, n.d.,
p. 188).
² The expression "a man of the Pharisees" is as unusual an expression in
Greek as in English. The use of ἄνθρωπος is probably meant to link the opening
words of this chapter with the closing words of the preceding, and so bring out
Jesus' knowledge of man. This will also be behind the use of αὐτόν rather
than 'Ιησοῦν in the first reference to the Lord.

this latter term see on 1 : 24). The Pharisees had no vested interest in the temple (which was rather the prerogative of the Sadducees). A Pharisee would, accordingly, not have been unduly perturbed by the action of Jesus in cleansing the temple courts. Indeed, he may possibly have approved it, partly on the general principle that anything that put the Sadducees in their place was laudable and partly in the interests of true religion. So there is no problem about a leading Pharisee coming to Jesus just after the temple cleansing (though, of course, we have no means of knowing how long after the events of ch. 2 Nicodemus came to Jesus). The name "Nicodemus" is Greek, but it occurred among the Jews. There was a well known Nicodemus who survived the destruction of Jerusalem in A.D. 70, and whom some identify (improbably) with this Nicodemus. "A ruler of the Jews"[3] means that he was a member of the Sanhedrin. For "the Jews" see on 1 : 19. The use of the expression is doubtless intended to convey to us that Nicodemus stands as the representative of the old religion. We hear of Nicodemus only in this Gospel. He comes before us again raising a hesitant (and apparently ineffectual) voice on behalf of Jesus when He was being discussed by the authorities after the abortive attempt to arrest Him during the Feast of Tabernacles (7 : 50–52). He is not recorded as saying anything at the trial of Jesus, but he assisted Joseph of Arimathea at the burial (19 : 39). We may, I think, fairly infer that he had a love for the truth, but that he was a rather timid soul. In the end he came right out for Jesus, and that at a time when all the disciples forsook Him. Which is saying a lot for a timid man.

2 Anyone in Nicodemus' position would be an unlikely candidate for the position of Jesus' follower. But Jesus' "signs" had impressed this Pharisee, and he wanted to know more. But prudently he came "by night". This is usually taken to mean that he had a fear of men, or at least a careful regard for their opinions. Nicodemus was a prominent man. As "the teacher of Israel" (v. 10), it would never do for him to commit himself to the unofficial Teacher from Galilee, not at any rate until he was absolutely sure

---

[3] John often speaks of "the Jews", and he uses the expression "ruler" (ἄρχων) not infrequently (e.g. 7 : 26, 48). But this is the only place where he links the two. There seems little doubt that by the expression he means a member of the Sanhedrin, for it is difficult to see any other reasonable explanation.

of his ground. If this is the explanation it is not without its interest
that Jesus says nothing in condemnation. He was content to receive
Nicodemus just as he was. But it is not at all certain that the reason
for the night visit was fear. The Pharisee may have chosen this
time in order to be sure of an uninterrupted and leisurely
interview. During the day Jesus would be busy and there would
be crowds (crowds of common people!). Not so at night. Then
there could be a long private discussion. Others associate the late
visit with the Rabbinic commendation of those who pursued their
studies into the night hours.[4] Perhaps most scholars today think
that the words should be taken symbolically. Jesus is the Light
of the world, and it was out of the darkness in which his life had
been lived that Nicodemus came to that light.[5] It would be quite
in his manner for John to have more than one of these meanings
in mind.[6]

Nicodemus begins with a courteous, even flattering address (for
the respectful "Rabbi" see on 1 : 38). He hails Jesus as a teacher[7]
"come from God".[8] We must notice that he sees Jesus as a teacher
only, and that he has as yet no perception of the real nature of
Him whom he sought out. He has come as one teacher to another

---

[4] B. Gerhardsson cites examples, *Memory and Manuscript* (Lund, 1964), p.
237. As is well known the men of Qumran provided that the Law should be
studied by night as well as by day. Bultmann notices the view that night study
lies behind the present passage, but thinks it even more probable that John
is simply creating an atmosphere of mystery.

[5] Thus Barrett thinks "it is perhaps more probable that he intended to
indicate the darkness out of which Nicodemus came into the presence of the
true Light (cf. vv. 19–21)". *Cf.* also Augustine: "because he came by night,
he still speaks from the darkness of his own flesh" (XI. 5; p. 76).

[6] But we should not overlook the timidity which marks Nicodemus in 7 : 50f.
Even in 19 : 39 he simply follows Joseph of Arimathea. The repetition of the
statement that he came "by night" (19 : 39) perhaps indicates that it is to be
taken literally. It may connect up with the fact that Joseph is said to have
been a secret disciple for fear of the Jews.

[7] T. H. Gaster sees a reference to the "Teacher of Righteousness" of the
Qumran scrolls: "The spiritual leader of the community is called 'teacher'
or 'right-teacher'. In John 3.2, Jesus is hailed as the teacher sent by God –
that is, as the teacher who, it was held, would arise in the last days" (*The
Scriptures of the Dead Sea Sect*, London, 1957, p. 23). The absence of the article
in the Greek is, however, against such a specific identification.

[8] The word order ἀπὸ Θεοῦ ἐλήλυθας διδάσκαλος perhaps puts an emphasis
on "from God".

to discuss matters of mutual interest.[9] Indeed, there may even be a trace of condescension in that he, an honoured Pharisee, had come to talk to a teacher who had never been through the schools (7 : 15).[10] Though he comes alone he speaks in the plural: "we know". Evidently he is associated with others and feels that he can speak for them. The continuous tenses he uses[11] perhaps are meant to indicate that Jesus habitually did the signs of which he speaks. Nicodemus has a true perception that such signs point to God (see Additional Note G, pp. 684ff., for the significance of the "signs").

3 Jesus declines to carry on with courteous exchanges that get nowhere. He plunges immediately into the very heart of the subject. Clearly Nicodemus is seeking instruction in the way to life. Jesus' first words tell him about it. He underlines the importance of His words by introducing them with the solemn "Verily, verily" (see on 1 : 51). Then in one sentence He sweeps away all that Nicodemus stood for, and demands that he be re-made by the power of God.[12] The word rendered "anew" might equally be

---

[9] Plummer, commenting on οἴδαμεν, remarks: "there is a touch of Pharisaic complacency in the word: 'some of us are quite disposed to think well of you.' "

[10] In Egerton Papyrus 2 the words of Nicodemus are linked with some from the quotation about paying tribute to Caesar (Matt. 22 : 15–22): "...came to him to put him to the proof and to tempt him, whilst they said: 'Master Jesus, we know that thou art come from God, for what thou doest bears a testimony to thee which goes beyond that of all the prophets. Wherefore tell us: is it admissible to pay to the kings the charges appertaining to their rule? Should we pay them or not?" (cited from E. Hennecke: *New Testament Apocrypha*, ed. W. Schneemelcher, trans. R. McL. Wilson, I, London, 1963, p. 97). This appears to indicate a view that Nicodemus' words may be regarded as part of an attempt to trap Jesus. But I know of no other evidence for this interpretation.

[11] He says ταῦτα τὰ σημεῖα ποιεῖν ἃ σὺ ποιεῖς. This looks like the doing of a number of signs, a reference, probably, to those mentioned comprehensively in 2 : 23. Although thus far John has recorded no specific signs in Jerusalem, we must bear in mind that he expressly tells us that he has omitted many things (21 : 25).

[12] We may discern something of the force of this passage by noticing what is possibly the closest Jewish parallel, the passage which tells us that Wisdom "guided (Jacob) on straight paths; she showed him the kingdom of God" (Wis. 10 : 10). But the thought here does not go beyond an increase of knowledge. In the Johannine passage we have something quite different, a rebirth brought about by the very Spirit of God.

212

translated by "from above".[13] Both senses are true, and in the
Johannine manner it is likely that we should understand both
here (as Barclay does; he gets the best of both worlds with his
"unless a man is reborn from above"). The man who would enter
the kingdom of God must be born[14] in a radically new fashion,
and this second birth is from heaven. Entry into the kingdom
is not by way of human striving (*cf.* 1 : 13), but by that re-birth
which only God can effect. "The kingdom of God" is the most
common topic of Jesus' teaching in the Synoptic Gospels. As such
it has attracted a great deal of attention, and the literature on
the subject is enormous.[15] Most modern students hold that the

---

13 Abbott argues for the meaning "from above" (1903–08). So also SBk,
II, pp. 420f. There it is pointed out that there is no Aramaic adverb with the
meaning "again". Westcott, by contrast, has an additional note in which he
urges "anew" as the meaning. He thinks that "The reality of the new birth
has to be laid down first, and then its character (v. 5)." It must be borne in
mind that ἄνωθεν means "from above" in every other place where it occurs
in this Gospel, *viz.*, 3 : 31; 19 : 11, 23. Against this is the fact that Nicodemus
evidently took the term to mean "again", for he speaks of entering his mother's
womb a second time (v. 4). Yet this is a clear misunderstanding. If the meaning
"from above" be rejected we must translate "anew" rather than "again". It
is a new thing, not the repetition of an old one, of which Jesus speaks. Yet we
should probably not try to pin John down exclusively to either meaning. This
seems to be another example of his habit of using expressions which may be
understood in more ways than one with a view to both senses being accepted.
We should perhaps notice that ἄνωθεν can also mean "from the beginning"
(as it does in Luke 1 : 3), though this can scarcely be the meaning here.
14 The verb is γεννάω which properly signifies the action of the male parent,
when it should be rendered "be begotten". However, it is used also of the female
parent (*e.g.* 16 : 21) so the translation "be born" is certainly possible. But it
is somewhat more probable that John means "be begotten" (*cf.* the use of
the same imagery in I John 3 : 9). The verb is a favourite one. Matthew uses
it freely in his genealogy, but apart from that uses it only 5 times, Mark once,
Luke 4 times, Acts 7 times, and Paul 7 times. John's 18 uses are thus significant.
The same essential idea is found in Tit. 3 : 5; I Pet. 1 : 23. But John is more
fond of this imagery than any other New Testament writer.
15 See, for example, R. Otto, *The Kingdom of God and the Son of Man* (London,
1938); C. H. Dodd, *The Parables of the Kingdom* (London, 1938); T. W. Manson,
The Teaching of Jesus (Cambridge, 1939), pp. 116ff.; V. Taylor, *Jesus and His
Sacrifice* (London, 1939), pp. 6ff.; N. B. Stonehouse, *The Witness of Matthew
and Mark to Christ* (Philadelphia, 1944), ch. VIII; W. Manson, *Jesus the
Messiah* (London, 1944); R. Bultmann, *Theology of the New Testament* (London,
1952), I, pp. 4ff.; E. Stauffer, *New Testament Theology* (London, 1955), ch. 28;
A. M. Hunter, *The Work and Words of Jesus* (London, 1956), pp. 68ff.; H. E.
W. Turner, *Jesus Master and Lord* (London, 1957), pp. 239ff.; SBk, I, pp. 172ff.;
TDNT sub βασιλεία; G. E. Ladd, *Jesus and the Kingdom* (London, 1966).

term "kingdom" is to be understood in a dynamic sense. It is "reign" rather than "realm".[16] It is God's rule in action. We are probably not meant to put much difference between seeing and entering (v. 5) the kingdom. But it will be appropriate that Jesus speaks here of seeing it. So far from entering into all that its privileges mean the man who is not reborn will not even see the kingdom.[17] This passage incidentally is the only one in this Gospel which mentions the kingdom of God (though Jesus speaks of "my kingdom", 18 : 36).[18] But John frequently speaks of eternal life, and for him the possession of eternal life appears to mean very much the same thing as entering the kingdom of God as the Synoptists picture it.

4 Nicodemus answers[19] in a way which shows that he takes Jesus' words to refer to physical birth (for similar misunderstandings see on 2 : 20). It seems so obvious that the words are not meant to be taken literally that we must ask why Nicodemus adopted this curious interpretation. Perhaps it is a case of hurt dignity. There are references to proselytes who entered the Jewish religion as being like children new born.[20] Nicodemus may have felt that the term appropriate to the Gentile as he entered the ranks of the chosen people was the last word that should be applied to one who was not only a Jew, but a Pharisee, and a member of the Sanhedrin.[21] So, not liking the way the conversation is going, he

---

[16] This is disputed, however, by S. Aalen in an important article, " 'Reign' and 'House' in the Kingdom of God in the Gospels" (*NTS*, VIII, 1961–62, pp. 215–240).

[17] *Cf.* Barrett: John "set out from an exceptionally clear perception of the two 'moments' of Christian salvation, that of the work accomplished and that of the work yet to be consummated; and he perceived that the language of Judaism (the kingdom of God) and the language of Hellenism ($\gamma \varepsilon \nu \nu \eta \theta \tilde{\eta} \nu \alpha \iota$ $\ddot{\alpha} \nu \omega \theta \varepsilon \nu$) provided him with a unique opportunity of expressing what was neither Jewish nor Hellenistic but simply Christian."

[18] It has been suggested that the reason for the omission of any emphasis on the Kingdom in this Gospel is the fact that John had earlier so thoroughly misunderstood its nature and tried to get the best place in it (Mark 10 : 35ff.). Now he was ashamed of his previous conduct and preferred not to dwell on what reminded him of it.

[19] For $\lambda \acute{\varepsilon} \gamma \varepsilon \iota \pi \varrho \grave{o} \varsigma \alpha \grave{v} \tau \acute{o} \nu$ see on 2 : 3.

[20] SBk, II, p. 423.

[21] *Cf.* Findlay: "as though in modern times an Anglican dignitary or eminent Nonconformist divine were told to go and get converted in an evangelical mission hall!" (p. 57).

chooses to misunderstand. It is perhaps more likely that he is wistful rather than obtuse. A man, Nicodemus might have said, is the sum of all his yesterdays. He is the man he is today because of all the things that have happened to him through the years. He is a bundle of doubts, uncertainties, wishes, hopes, fears and habits good and bad built up through the years. It would be wonderful to break the entail of the past and make a completely fresh beginning. But how can this possibly be done?[22] Can[23] physical birth be repeated?[24] Since this lesser miracle is quite impossible how can we envisage a much greater miracle, the remaking of man's essential being? Regeneration is sheer impossibility!

5 Once again Jesus prefaces His remarks with the solemn and emphatic "Verily, verily". This invites Nicodemus' undivided attention to the words which follow for they are important. Jesus explains being born "anew" as being born "of water[25] and the Spirit". There is no article with either noun in the Greek, but ARV can be defended for supplying one by the consideration that Jesus is undoubtedly referring to the regenerating activity of the Holy Spirit of God.[26] On this occasion, however, He does not speak of being born "of the Spirit" simply (as He does in vv. 6, 8), but of being born "of water and the Spirit". The explanations of this unusual and arresting expression are many, but most of them fall into one or other of three main groupings.

(i) "Water" stands for purification (cf. 2 : 6). If this is the correct

---

[22] Cf. Strachan: "His question is not hopeless so much as wistful. Can human nature be changed?"

[23] Though John does not use the noun δύναμις at all he employs the verb δύναμαι more often than any other book in the New Testament (Matthew 27 times, Mark 33 times, Luke 26 times, John 36 times). He is quite interested in what is and is not possible.

[24] The question introduced by μή expresses his incredulity: "Surely he cannot . . . .?"

[25] Some exegetes (e.g. Bultmann) regard ὕδατος καί as a later insertion. Interestingly Brown is able to cite a group of learned Roman Catholics who take this line, as well as certain Protestants. But there are no textual grounds for the omission, and the doctrinal and contextual considerations adduced seem inadequate. We should take the text as it stands.

[26] A Jewish parallel sometimes cited is Wis. 9 : 17, "Who has learned thy counsel, unless thou hast given wisdom and sent thy holy Spirit from on high?" But in this passage the thought is that of enlightenment whereas John speaks of regeneration.

explanation there is probably a backward look at the baptism of John. This was a "baptism of repentance" (Mark 1 : 4). It was concerned with purifying (v. 25), and it could be explicitly contrasted with the baptism of the Spirit (1 : 33). The meaning then will be that Nicodemus should enter into all that "water" symbolizes, namely repentance and the like, and that he should also enter into the experience which is summed up as "born of . . . the Spirit", namely the totally new divine life that Jesus would impart.[27] Both demands were radical. The Pharisees refused John's baptism (Luke 7 : 30), and they consistently opposed Jesus. It was asking a lot that Nicodemus should accept both.

(ii) "Water" may be connected with procreation. This conception is quite foreign to us and we find it difficult at first to make sense of it. But Odeberg has gathered an impressive array of passages from Rabbinic, Mandaean, and Hermetic sources[28] to show that terms like "water", "rain", "dew", and "drop" are often used of the male semen. If "water" has this meaning here there are two possibilities. Being born "of water" may point to natural birth, which must then be followed by being born "of the Spirit", *i.e.* spiritual regeneration. Or better, we may take "water" and "Spirit" closely together to give a meaning like "spiritual seed".[29]

---

[27] *Cf.* Morgan: "Mark the continuity. You have been attending the ministry of one who baptized you in water, and told you Another would baptize you in the Spirit. Except you are born of all that the water baptism signified, repentance; and that which the Spirit baptism accomplishes, regeneration, you cannot enter into the Kingdom of God." J. A. T. Robinson says forthrightly, "If the words have a setting in the life of Jesus, then the allusion must be to the teaching of John", and he proceeds to cite Armitage Robinson: "the whole of John's mission lies behind the saying" (*NTS*, IV, 1957–58, p. 273). Notice also that Ezek. 36 : 25f. combines the ideas of water purification and the giving of "a new spirit". *Cf.* also Isa. 44 : 3.

[28] *FG*, pp. 48–71. Here we may take notice of the fact that the mystery religions make use of the terminology of rebirth. But any connection between them and this Gospel is purely verbal. In them the worshipper may be brought more surely into relationship with his god, but there is no idea of a transformation of his whole nature such as the Christian conception signifies. In this Gospel, as MacGregor notes, "The entrance upon eternal life is conditioned not by a magical renewal of the physical nature to be obtained by prescribed rites, but by a birth *from above*, from God" (on v. 3).

[29] This is rendered the more likely in that neither noun has the article and the one preposition governs both.

In this case being born "of water and the Spirit" will not differ greatly from being born "of the Spirit".[30]
(iii) "Water" may refer to Christian baptism.[31] The strong argument in favour of this view is that baptism may well have been the natural association that the term would arouse among Christians at the time the Gospel was published.[32] John could scarcely have been unmindful of this. The weak point is that Nicodemus could not possibly have perceived an allusion to an as yet non-existent sacrament. It is difficult to think that Jesus would have spoken

---

[30] *Cf.* Odeberg: "One may even venture the hypothesis, that γεννηθῆναι ἐξ ὕδατος καὶ πνεύματος is identical in sense with the γεννηθῆναι ἐκ πνεύματος" (*FG*, p. 48). He argues that this view is also favored by the contrast between physical birth (3 : 4) and birth "of water and the Spirit". It is of interest that this was the view of Calvin: "he used the words *Spirit* and *water* to mean the same thing ... By water ... is meant simply the inward cleansing and quickening of the Holy Spirit."
It must be borne in mind that it is John's habit in repeating a statement to make minor variations. This happens in twofold variation (compare 7 : 30 and 44; 3 : 17 and 12 : 47). For threefold variation with two the same see 6 : 35, 48, 51, and with all three different 1 : 32, 33, 34 (three different Greek verbs for seeing), or 5 : 8, 11, 12. For multiple variation consider the references to Judas Iscariot in 6 : 71; 12 : 4; 13: 2, 26, 29. The variations are unimportant, but no two of these are identical. Even when he is expressly quoting, John does this kind of thing as we see by comparing 1 : 48 and 50, or 6 : 44 and 65. Many more examples could be cited. It is clearly a mark of Johannine style. It is fair to say that the sense is not distorted by the stylistic variations, but the variations are real. See further *SFG*, ch. 5. In this chapter the four references to rebirth, vv. 3, 5, 6, 7, all probably mean much the same thing.
[31] Luther says: "here Christ is speaking of Baptism, of real and natural water such as a cow may drink ... Therefore the word 'water' does not designate affliction here; it means real, natural water, which is connected with God's Word and becomes a very spiritual bath through the Holy Spirit or through the entire Trinity" (vol. 22, p. 283).
[32] This does not necessarily mean a doctrine of "baptismal regeneration" in the sense that baptism effects an operation of the Spirit within man. The whole passage emphasizes the work of the Spirit, not the performance of any rite (there is no other expression in the whole passage that can be construed as a reference to baptism). Wright, who accepts the reference to baptism, says, "it is clear that while the Evangelist is probably thinking of the symbolic rite of baptism, his thought is at the farthest possible remove from any magical sacramentalism. In other words, he does not mean that the physical act of immersion in water is indispensable to spiritual quickening. Those who so interpret this reference isolate it from the whole context of the mind of Jesus as expressed in this Gospel. The passage does not say that the Spirit necessarily comes to those who are immersed in water."

in such a way that His meaning could not possibly be grasped. His purpose was not to mystify but to enlighten.[33] In any case the whole thrust of the passage is to put the emphasis on the activity of the Spirit, not on any rite of the church.[34]

It seems to me that the second explanation is the most likely, and in the sense of taking "water" and "spirit" closely together. Nicodemus was a Pharisee. He was used to this way of speaking. The allusion would be natural for him. We should accordingly take the passage to mean being born of "spiritual water", and see this as another way of referring to being born "of the Spirit". Jesus is referring to the miracle which takes place when the divine activity re-makes a man. He is born all over again by the very Spirit of God. As John is fond of using expressions which may be taken in more ways than one, it is, of course, not impossible that he wants us to think of the other meanings as well. But the main thrust of the words surely has to do with the divine re-making.

In v. 3 Jesus has spoken of "seeing" the kingdom of God, whereas here He speaks of "entering" it. There is probably no great difference of meaning.[35] In both places Jesus is stressing the truth that spiritual regeneration is indispensable if we would be God's. It is the perennial heresy of the natural man to think that he can fit himself by his own efforts for the kingdom of God.

---

[33] D. W. B. Robinson examines and refutes the idea that baptism is in mind (*RThR*, XXV, 1966, pp. 15–23).

[34] See, for example, the discussion by Brown. He finds the argument that "of water" was not in the original text inconclusive. But accepting it still leaves him with uncertainties: "Accepting 'water' at its face value, we do not think there is enough evidence in the Gospel itself to determine the relation between begetting of water and begetting of Spirit on the level of sacramental interpretation. Begetting of Spirit, while it includes accepting Jesus by faith, is primarily the communication of the Holy Spirit" (p. 144). In other words, though Brown inclines to seeing a reference to baptism he puts his emphasis on the activity of the Spirit. This is surely the significant thing.

[35] Westcott, it is true, sees a "marked contrast" between the two. He equates "see" with "outwardly apprehend" (on v. 3), and "enter" with "become a citizen of the kingdom, as distinguished from the mere intelligent spectator" (on v. 5). Barrett, by contrast, finds it impossible to distinguish between the two. Among the witness of antiquity Hermas distinguishes sharply between the two (though not by way of a comment on the present passage). He says that those bearing certain names ("Faith", "Continence", *etc.*) will enter the kingdom, while others ("Unbelief", "Intemperance", *etc.*) "shall see the kingdom of God, but shall not enter into it" (*Sim.* 9 : 15).

Jesus makes it clear that no man can ever fit himself for the kingdom. Rather he must be completely renewed, born anew, by the power of the Spirit. These solemn words for ever exclude the possibility of salvation by human merit. Man's nature is so gripped by sin that an activity of the very Spirit of God is a necessity if he is to be associated with God's kingdom.

6 The teaching of this verse is succinctly paraphrased by Hoskyns: "There is no evolution from flesh to Spirit".[36] While John does not use the term "flesh"[37] in the same way as does Paul, to denote mankind's sinful nature, he yet uses it in such a way as to make clear that it is, so to speak, of the earth earthy. It cannot give rise to anything other than what is earthy. But Jesus has been speaking of a spiritual kingdom, the kingdom of God. For entrance into that kingdom a spiritual birth is required.[38] It is perhaps worth adding that Jesus' statement is couched in quite general terms.[39] This is a truth of general application and is not meant only for Nicodemus and his friends.

7 In the light of the principle He has just enunciated Jesus urges Nicodemus not to be astonished at the teaching on the new birth. It is only what is to be expected. Notice that Jesus now says "you", whereas earlier He has spoken about "one" being reborn. The plural may be a recognition that Nicodemus had associates (*cf.* his own "we", v. 2). At any rate it makes the application of the words wider than to the Pharisee only. "Must" is a strong

---

[36] P. 204.

[37] John uses σάρξ 13 times (more than the three Synoptists put together). Most of the examples come from ch. 6 where Jesus speaks of giving His flesh for the life of the world. John does not use the term to convey the notion of moral frailty as does Paul. For him it may denote the physical weakness inseparable from human existence, but not wickedness or sinfulness. It may point to limitations on vision (8 : 15), but on the other hand it may refer to the Incarnation (1 : 14) or to the gift of God (6 : 51).

[38] "There are two levels of existence; the one is the sphere of flesh and the other of spirit. On each level like produces like. A man can only pass from the lower order, the realm of flesh, into the higher order, the realm of spirit, by being born again" (G. Appleton, *John's Witness to Jesus*, London, 1955, p. 29).

[39] In both cases He uses the neuter participle τὸ γεγεννημένον "that which" rather than the masculine, "he who".

expression.[40] There is no other way but that of rebirth. **8** The interpretation of this verse is complicated by the fact that the word which has been uniformly translated "spirit" in its occurrences hitherto in this chapter has more than one meaning. In Greek (as, for that matter, in several other languages) the one word may mean "spirit" or "breath" or "wind". The spirit of a man is that immaterial principle of life within him. It was a matter of observation for men in early days that when the breath ceases the life ceases also. What more natural, then, than to apply the same word to both? And, since wind is nothing more than a lot of breath moving in a hurry, it was equally natural to use the word of the wind.[41] The word used here might then mean "wind" or it might mean "Spirit". Since the term was used earlier in the chapter we would expect the meaning to be unchanged. This would give the meaning "Spirit" here as earlier. The passage then would mean that man cannot predict the movements of the Spirit. The Spirit breathes where He wills. And just as man cannot comprehend the Spirit neither can he comprehend him that is born of the Spirit. This gives us a consistent interpretation and a very natural one.

But it suffers from the considerable disadvantage that it is more than difficult to see how the man who cannot comprehend the Spirit or him that is born of the Spirit can be said to hear "the voice" of the Spirit. The impossibility of giving this a satisfactory meaning inclines most translators and commentators to take the word in the sense of "wind". The meaning then is that the familiar wind has its mysteries. It can be heard (did Nicodemus and Jesus hear a gust of wind at this point?). Yet man knows neither its origin nor its destination. As is the wind, so is he who has been born of the Spirit. The natural man may have contact with him, but he knows neither the origin of the life that is in him, nor his final destiny. This latter seems to me the preferable interpretation of the passage.[42]

---

[40] John uses it again of the necessity of the crucifixion (v. 14; 12 : 34), of the resurrection (20 : 9), of the things Jesus did in the execution of His ministry (4 : 4; 9 : 4; 10 : 16), and of the eclipse of John the Baptist before Jesus (3 : 30). The term is also used of worship (4 : 20, 24).

[41] Yet it should be borne in mind that elsewhere in the New Testament πνεῦμα does not seem to have its primitive meaning "wind" (ἄνεμος is used where this sense is required).

[42] The verb πνέω always refers to the blowing of the wind in its other six New Testament occurrences.

9, 10 Nicodemus confesses himself baffled by all this. His puzzled question elicits the gentle reminder that a man in his position ought not to find it all so very difficult. "The teacher of Israel" points at the very least to preeminence as a teacher. The article ("the" not "a" teacher) may indicate that Nicodemus held some official position, but if so we do not know what it was.[43] But this leading Pharisee professed to know the things of God, and even to teach them to others. Under these circumstances he ought to have known that no man is able to come to God in his own strength or righteousness. Even if the information that he as well as others must be reborn was new to him he should not have greeted it with such astonishment.

11 For the third time in this conversation Jesus uses the solemn "Verily, verily" (vv. 3, 5). This time it is not the truth that one must be reborn that is underlined, but that other truth that Jesus can be relied on. He has said[44] nothing but that of which He has knowledge (Goodspeed: "we know what we are talking about"). Notice the twofold reference to witness (see on 1 : 7). It emphasizes the reliability of what Nicodemus has heard. "Witness" does not point to opinions which may be debated, but to objective fact. Jesus is not hazarding an opinion, but is telling Nicodemus about things of which He has perfect knowledge. The plural "we" is curious, all the more so since Jesus so rarely associates men with Him.[45] Moreover this passage must refer, at least primarily, to the Master's own knowledge and witness. But it may well be that He is here associating His disciples with Himself. Westcott thinks that some of them may even have been present.[46] None is mentioned but it is not impossible. Those who have learned from Jesus

---

[43] For this curious expression see the note by E. F. F. Bishop, *BT*, 7, 1956, pp. 81–3.

[44] The verb is λαλοῦμεν for which see note on 1 : 37.

[45] According to A. G. Hebert this is done only here, 9 : 4; Mark 9 : 40 and parallels; and Matt. 17 : 27 (*The Form of the Church*, London, 1944, p. 46n.).

[46] Hoskyns understands it differently: "Jesus is no isolated person (v. 11). There are, and have been, men who speak because they know, and bear witness because they have seen. There have been prophets: there is a man named John baptizing in the desert: and there are men who have left all and followed Jesus. These all say the same thing; and it is with their testimony that Nicodemus and his like must first concern themselves" (p. 204). Abbott thinks that the plural means "the Father and I" (2428).

and have experienced the rebirth of which He speaks can speak to others of the necessity for the new birth. In doing so they testify to what they know. But whether it is of Jesus or His followers. the witness is not received. "Ye" is another plural which takes us beyond Nicodemus. The Jews at large did not receive the witness. The present tense must be given its full force. This was no occasional thing, but the regular habit.

12 Jesus reverts to the first person singular and draws attention to what He Himself is doing. He has borne witness to "earthly things" without being believed.[47] The simplest way of understanding this is to see a reference to the present discourse. It was taking place on earth and concerned a process with effects discernible on earth. In contrast with this, Jesus can impart "heavenly things", *i.e.* higher teaching. But if men like Nicodemus will not believe the simpler things they cannot be expected to believe what is more advanced.[48] Another suggested way of taking the words is to see in the "heavenly things" a reference to the present discourse, when "earthly things" would apply to some previous teaching of Jesus. It is urged that "heavenly things" is a better description of this discourse than is "earthly things", and that if this meaning is taken it gives an excellent reason for the unbelief mentioned in the previous verse. Against it, however, is the fact that we have no evidence of any previous contact between Jesus and Nicodemus. Indeed, the opening words seem clearly to imply that this is a first meeting. This being so there is no previous occasion to which we may refer the "earthly things", and they must accordingly describe the conversation in this chapter. A reference to previous teaching seems quite out of the question. Thus we adopt the first-mentioned interpretation.[49]

13 Jesus now makes it clear that He can speak authoritatively

---

[47] In the expression καὶ οὐ πιστεύετε we have another example of καί in the sense καίτοι "and yet" (see on 1 : 5).

[48] Notice the difference between the two conditional clauses. εἰ τὰ ἐπίγεια εἶπον implies fulfilment. It refers to what has actually happened, whereas ἐὰν εἴπω ὑμῖν τὰ ἐπουράνια has no implications about the fulfilment of the condition. It refers to what is as yet future.

[49] For the contrast between earthly and heavenly things *cf.* Wis. 9 : 16, "We can hardly guess at what is on earth . . . but who has traced out what is in the heavens?"

about things in heaven, though no one else can. No man has ever ascended[50] into heaven (Prov. 30 : 4). But He has come down from there.[51] Throughout the Gospel John insists on Jesus' heavenly origin. This is one way in which he brings out his point that Jesus is the Christ. Here the heavenly origin marks Jesus off from all the rest of mankind.[52] Men are, as Paul puts it, "of the earth, earthy" (I Cor. 15 : 47). But He is from heaven. Men cannot raise themselves to heaven[53] and penetrate divine mysteries. It was part of the sin of the "son of the morning" that he said in his heart, "I will ascend into heaven" (Isa. 14 : 12f.). But he could not do it. It remained a boast and an ambition. Jesus, however, really has been in heaven and He has brought

---

[50] The perfect ἀναβέβηκεν is unexpected. Perhaps the meaning is "no man has gained the heights of heaven". There is the thought of continuing possession. But the primary reference of the words may well be spiritual rather than physical. *Cf.* Godet: "No one has *entered into* communion with God and possesses thereby an intuitive knowledge of divine things, in order to reveal them to others, except He to whom heaven was opened and who dwells there at this very moment."

[51] "The reference to the descent out of heaven, which preceded the ascent, is noteworthy. It is the first hint of our Lord's consciousness of pre-existence" (Murray).

[52] Bultmann explains the present passage in terms of the Gnostic myth of the descent of the Redeemer (in addition to his Commentary see his *Theology of the New Testament*, II, London, 1955, p. 37; see I, pp. 166ff. for an outline of the myth). He cites no evidence, and takes the truth of his assumption for granted. But weighty objections may be urged against it. First, it is not certain that the Gnostic myth existed at the time this Gospel was written. As Alan Richardson says, "the only first-century literature to which Bultmann appeals is the NT itself, and this is capable of a simpler explanation. There is no real evidence for the existence of 'the Gnostic myth' in the first century A.D." (*An Introduction to the Theology of the New Testament*, London, 1958, p. 143). Secondly, the picture John gives is not that of the myth. As Theo Preiss says, the setting "radically differentiates from the oriental and gnostic idea of the *anthropos* and the mystical body, the Jewish and Christian figure of the Son of Man and the Body of his Church. The difference can be summed up very briefly: in the gnostic myth, Man is the divine principle substantially and eternally identical with the sum of the souls of men scattered but predetermined to salvation. In the thought of Jesus the Son of Man freely identifies himself with each of the wretched ones by an act of substitution and identification, and he will gather them together at the last day" (*Life in Christ*, London, 1954, p. 53). Thirdly, the heavenly origin of Christ is brought out by John with terminology which is not Gnostic. His idea is independent of Gnosticism.

[53] "It is well to note this text, which hurls a thunderbolt against all the work-saints (*werckheilige*)" (Luther, *op. cit.*, p. 330).

heavenly realities to earth (see on 1 : 51). The words may possibly have a polemical aim and be directed against those Jews who taught the possibility of great saints attaining heaven.[54] Since in the context there is the thought of the new birth, and since there are references to seeing and entering the kingdom of God we should probably understand the passage to mean that ascent into heaven is in fact possible. But this can be done only by the new birth which is "of the Spirit" and which the Son of man in some sense effects. It is not a human possibility. For "the Son of man" see Additional Note C, pp. 171ff. The words "who is in heaven" are absent from some of the most reliable manuscripts[55] and they should probably be omitted. If they are included they will point to the eternal being of the Son of man. The Incarnation represents not a diminution of His functions, but an addition to them.[56] Only a crassly literal localization of heaven would require us to think that Jesus had to leave heaven to come to earth.

14, 15 This section of the Gospel concludes with an impressive statement of the purpose of the death of Jesus.[57] Jesus recalls the incident related in Num. 21 wherein, when fiery serpents bit the Israelites, Moses was told to make a serpent of bronze and set it

---

[54] See Odeberg, *FG*, pp. 72–98 for details.

[55] *E.g.* P66, P 75 ℵ B L sah boh.

[56] Augustine puts this succinctly: "Born of a mother, not quitting the Father" (XII. 8; p. 84). *Cf.* Calvin: "Christ, who is in heaven, put on our flesh that, by stretching out a brotherly hand to us, He might raise us to heaven along with Himself."

[57] To the objection that Jesus could not have known of the cross as early as this, and that the Synoptists do not represent Him as speaking of it until the incident at Caesarea Philippi, Murray replies: "If Jesus knew what was coming six months or six hours before it came to pass, it is clearly possible that He was Himself familiar with the thought from the first, and was only waiting to communicate it to His disciples till their faith was strong enough to bear the revelation." There are hints in the Synoptists even before Caesarea Philippi (*e.g.* Matt. 9 : 15; 10 : 38). Murray has a long note on Jesus' foreknowledge of the cross. He stresses the courage of our Lord in living out His ministry with the knowledge of what lay before Him.

An impressive, though unobtrusive witness to the factuality of this saying is the effect on Nicodemus of the crucifixion. When all the disciples fled it was this hesistant and timid man who assisted Joseph of Arimathea at the burial. If, when Jesus died, he was able to recall that in his first contact with Him Jesus had prophesied that He would die in this way the situation is easier to understand.

on a pole. Whoever looked[58] at the bronze serpent was healed.[59] And, just as[60] that serpent was "lifted up" in the wilderness, so, says Jesus, must[61] the Son of man be "lifted up". This must refer to His being "lifted up" on the cross, as the context here and John's use of the verb elsewhere[62] plainly show. But this does not

---

[58] T. F. Glasson points out that the idea of looking is central in Num. 21. It is not mentioned explicitly here, but Glasson thinks it is implied, all the more so since the idea of seeing is so pronounced in this Gospel (*Moses in the Fourth Gospel*, London, 1963, pp. 34f.).

[59] The Jewish understanding of this passage insisted that Jehovah, not the serpent, brought deliverance. Thus Wis. 16 : 7 says: "he who turned toward it was saved, not by what he saw, but by thee, the Savior of all". So also, Mishnah, *R. H.* 3 : 8, "But could the serpent slay or the serpent keep alive! – it is, rather, to teach thee that such time as the Israelites directed their thoughts on high and kept their hearts in subjection to their Father in heaven, they were healed; otherwise they pined away." T. W. Manson points out that this saying is ascribed in other Jewish writings to R. Eliezer b. Hyrcanus and comments: "Since Eliezer is a first-century Palestinian Rabbi, it seems clear that we have to do in John iii. 14 and Mishnah *R. H.* iii. 8 with Palestinian Christian proofs and Palestinian Jewish rebuttals. So, whatever we may think about the authorship, date, and place of writing of the Fourth Gospel, here is one more piece of evidence of its dependence on Palestinian materials" (*JThS*, XLVI, 1945, p. 132). The *R. H.* passage understands the incident in which Israel prevailed while Moses' hands were held up in the same fashion. Interestingly Justin Martyr also joins these two passages, but he understands them of Jesus: "And shall we not rather refer the standard to the resemblance of the crucified Jesus, since also Moses by his outstretched hands, together with him who was named Jesus (Joshua), achieved a victory for your people?" (*Dial. Try.* 112; ANF, I, p. 255). They are also linked in Ep. Barnabas, 12 : 2–7. Dodd cites from the Hermetic tractate called *The Bowl* a passage in which the author speaks of "the image of God *(τοῦ θεοῦ εἰκών)*, which if you behold exactly and contemplate with the eyes of the heart ... you will find the way to the higher sphere *(τὴν πρὸς τὰ ἄνω ὁδόν)*; or rather, the image itself will guide you" (*IFG*, p. 307). Even Hellenistic thinkers who would not perceive the allusion might well comprehend the essential meaning of the words.

[60] John uses *καθώς* 31 times which compares with Matthew 3 times, Mark 8 times, Luke 17 times. Clearly he is fond of making comparisons.

[61] See on v. 7; 4 : 4 for the use of "must" with respect to Jesus' mission.

[62] John uses the verb *ὑψόω* again in 8 : 28; 12 : 32, 34. Particularly important is 12 : 32 where Jesus says, "I, if I be lifted up from the earth", and John explains: "this he said, signifying by what manner of death he should die." There can be no doubt as to the significance John attaches to *ὑψόω*. Black notes and rejects the view that this points to Syriac influence. He cites G. Kittel as pointing out that the equivalent verb is used in this sense in Ezra 6 : 11 and the Targums on I Chron. 10 : 10; Esther I. 9 : 13; II. 7 : 10. He concludes, "The Johannine use is therefore an Aramaism" (*AA*, p. 103).

exhaust the meaning of the expression. It is almost certainly another example of John's use of words of set purpose to convey more than one meaning. The verb can refer to exaltation in majesty. It is used of Christ's exaltation to heaven in Acts 2 : 33, and (in a compound form) in Phil. 2 : 9. It is part of John's aim to show that Jesus showed forth His glory not *in spite of* His earthly humiliations, but precisely *by means of* those humiliations.[63] Supremely is this the case with the cross. To the outward eye this was the uttermost in degradation, the death of a felon. To the eye of faith it was (and is) the supreme glory.[64]

The purpose of Jesus' death was to give life to believers. For the importance of faith in this Gospel see on 1 : 12 and Additional Note E, pp. 335ff. The man who has faith has (the present tense points to a present possession) eternal life in Christ.[65] This associates the life very closely with Christ. The life Christians possess is not in any sense independent of Christ. It is a life that is "hid with Christ in God" (Col. 3 : 3). This is the first mention in this Gospel

---

[63] This is a very different idea from that of the Qumran sectarians who looked for a "prince of the congregation" who would "tread down peoples like the mire of the streets" (1 Q Sb. v. 28; *ML*, p. 398).

[64] *Cf.* Vincent Taylor: "There could be no vainer controversy than the dispute whether in these passages (*i.e.* John 3 : 14; 8 : 28; 12 : 32) the crucifixion or the exaltation is meant. The death *is* the exaltation" (*The Atonement in New Testament Teaching*, London, 1946, p. 147). The cross of shame is the throne of glory. *Cf.* H. Blair: "the suffering and struggle of Jesus are only alternative names for his glory. In fact, glory hurts. It is when it hurts and is accepted that it becomes glory" (*The Ladder of Temptations*, London, 1960, p. 100). Odeberg strangely does not see a reference to the cross. He thinks instead of the spiritual experience which leads towards the spiritual birth: "*this spiritual experience is described as an elevation of the Son of Man, scil.* by earthly man, and *a directing of man's spiritual gaze towards that lifted-up Son of Man by believing in him*" (*FG*, p. 111). Admittedly the passage may profitably be employed to start us on such a meditation, but that is not to say that that was John's meaning. Wherever he uses ὑψόω he has the cross in mind (see n. 62 above).

[65] It is almost certain that we should take πᾶς ὁ πιστεύων ἐν αὐτῷ ἔχῃ ζωὴν αἰώνιον in this fashion. John never elsewhere follows the verb πιστεύω with ἐν so that ἐν αὐτῷ is to be taken with ἔχῃ. πιστεύω is often used absolutely in this Gospel. See Additional Note E, pp. 335ff. There is a valuable note on ἐν in the New Testament by N. Turner (*BT*, 10, 1959, pp. 113–20). There are variant readings ἐπ' αὐτῷ, ἐπ' αὐτόν, and εἰς αὐτόν. These are probably due to the difficulty caused by what scribes deemed to be the construction πιστεύω ἐν. This is rendered all the more probable since some MSS have imported μὴ ἀπόληται ἀλλ' from v. 16, and have placed it between ἐν αὐτῷ and ἔχῃ.

of eternal life (for "life" see on 1 : 4), a concept which means much to the Evangelist. He gives it a good deal of emphasis before his Gospel is through. In the Prologue he has informed us that life is "in" the Logos, and it is much the same thought here, with the addition that the lifting up of the Son of man is an integral part of the process whereby the life is mediated to men. The word rendered "eternal" (always used in this Gospel of life) basically means "pertaining to an age".[66] The Jews divided time into the present age and the age to come, but the adjective referred to life in the coming age, not the present one. "Eternal life" thus means "the life proper to the age to come". It is an eschatological conception (cf. 6 : 40, 54). But as the age to come is never thought of as coming to an end the adjective came to mean "everlasting", "eternal". The notion of time is there. Eternal life will never cease. But there is something else there, too, and something more significant. The important thing about eternal life is not its quantity but its quality.[67] In Westcott's phrase, "It is not an endless duration of being in time, but being of which time is not a measure."[68] Eternal life is life in Christ, that life which removes a man from the merely earthly. As we see from the earlier part of this chapter it originates in a divine action, in a man's being born anew. It is the gift of God,[69] and not the achievement of man.

---

[66] The word is $\alpha i \dot{\omega} \nu \iota o \varsigma$. John employs the term 17 times, nearly three times as often as it is used in any other book of the New Testament.

[67] Salmond says that "eternal" is used "not in order to add to the 'life' the idea of *perpetuity*, but to express more fully the quality which belongs to the 'life' itself. In John's writings 'death' is an ethical condition, the condition of failure and evil in which men exist by nature, and out of which they are raised by Christ. The 'life' is the new condition – the spiritual order of being, the existence of fellowship with God into which Christ brings men; and the 'eternal life' is this 'life' in its quality of the divine order of life, the life which fulfils the whole idea of life, the good of life, the perfection of life, the satisfaction of life in God." He is careful to add, "It lies in the nature of the 'life' as *eternal*, a life of the divine order, that it is superior to change, decay, or extinction" (*The Christian Doctrine of Immortality*, Edinburgh, 1907, p. 391).

[68] *The Epistles of St John* (London, 1892), p. 215.

[69] "Eternal life" is always in this Gospel the life of the believer. Neither the Father nor the Son is said to have it. The Father "hath life in himself" (5 : 26), and He has granted this also to the Son (*ibid.*). The Son is "the life" (11 : 25; 14 : 6). But "eternal life" is reserved for the life bestowed on believers.

(b) Reflection, 3 : 16–21

16 For God so loved the world, that he gave his only begotten Son, that whosoever believeth on him should not perish, but have eternal life. 17 For God sent not the Son into the world to judge the world; but that the world should be saved through him. 18 He that believeth on him is not judged: he that believeth not hath been judged already, because he hath not believed on the name of the only begotten Son of God. 19 And this is the judgment, that the light is come into the world, and men loved the darkness rather than the light; for their works were evil. 20 For every one that [1]doeth evil hateth the light, and cometh not to the light, lest his works should be [2]reproved. 21 But he that doeth the truth cometh to the light, that his works may be made manifest, [3]that they have been wrought in God.

[1]Or, *practiseth* [2]Or, *convicted* [3]Or, *because*

All are agreed that from time to time in this Gospel we have the meditations of the Evangelist. But it is difficult to know where these begin and end. In the first century there were no devices such as inverted commas to show the precise limits of quoted speech. The result is that we are always left to the probabilities, and we must work out for ourselves where a speech or a quotation ends. In this passage Jesus begins to speak in v. 10, but John does not tell us where this speech ends. The dialogue form simply ceases. Most agree that somewhere we pass into the reflections of the Evangelist. Perhaps the dividing point comes at the end of v. 15. The sentence which ends there has a reference to "the Son of man", an expression used by Jesus only in all four Gospels. We are on fairly safe ground in maintaining that these are His words. But in v. 16 the death on the cross appears to be spoken of as past, and there are stylistic indications that John is speaking for himself.[70] It would seem that the Evangelist, as he records Jesus' words about His death, is led to some reflections of his own on the same subject. That death is God's gift to deliver men from perishing. If, after all, they do perish it is because they prefer darkness to light. They bring it upon themselves.

---

[70] The term μονογενής (16, 18) is applied to Christ elsewhere in the New Testament only by John (1 : 14, 18; I John 4 : 9). The expressions πιστεύω εἰς τὸ ὄνομα (18) and ποιέω τὴν ἀλήθειαν (21) are not found elsewhere in speeches of Jesus, but are Johannine. The repeated use of γάρ while not conclusive (it is found in speeches of Jesus) is quite in the Johannine manner.

16 God loved[71] "the world" (see Additional Note B, pp. 126ff.). The Jew was ready enough to think of God as loving Israel, but no passage appears to be cited in which any Jewish writer maintains that God loved the world.[72] It is a distinctively Christian idea that God's love is wide enough to embrace all mankind. His love is not confined to any national group or any spiritual elite. It is a love which proceeds from the fact that He is love (I John 4 : 8, 16). It is His nature to love. He loves men because He is the kind of God He is. John tells us that His love is shown in the gift of His Son. Of this gift Odeberg finely says, "the Son is God's gift to the world, and, moreover, it is *the* gift. There are no Divine gifts apart from or outside the one-born (*sic*) Son".[73] In typical Johannine fashion "gave" is used in two senses. God gave the Son by sending Him into the world, but God also gave the Son on the cross. Notice that the cross is not said to show us the love of the Son (as in Gal. 2 : 20), but that of the Father. The atonement proceeds from the loving heart of God.[74] It is not something wrung from Him. The Greek construction puts some stress on the actuality of the gift: it is not "God loved so as to give", but "God loved so that He gave".[75] His love is not a vaguely sentimental feeling, but

---

[71] This is John's first use of ἀγαπάω, a verb he is to use 36 times, more than twice the number in any other book of the New Testament except I John (which has it 31 times; next is Luke with 13 times). He also uses φιλέω more than anyone else, though the figures are smaller (John 13 times, out of 25 times in the New Testament; next is Matthew with 5 times). It is interesting that John uses both verbs more than twice as often as anyone else. For the supposed distinction between the two verbs see on 21 : 15. Clearly love matters a good deal to this author.

[72] *Cf.* Odeberg: "The relation of the Holy One to 'his world' is, as far as we know, never expressed by the term 'love' " (*FG*, p. 116).

[73] *FG*, p. 130.

[74] *Cf.* Dodd: "The statement in iii. 16 is quite fundamental to our author's position, and the reader is intended to bear it in mind during the following discussions, though little further is said about the love of God until with ch. xiii it becomes a dominant theme" (*IFG*, p. 307).

[75] John uses the indicative ὥστε . . . ἔδωκεν (not the infinitive ὥστε . . . δοῦναι which might have been expected). This is John's only use of ὥστε so we have no means of knowing how often he would have used the one construction in preference to the other. But ὥστε is found in the New Testament 84 times, of which only 21 times have the indicative (15 times in Paul). Outside the Pauline Epistles it is thus infrequent. John's use accordingly is rather unusual and probably emphatic.

a love that costs. God gave what was most dear to Him.[76] For "only begotten" see on 1 : 14, and for "believeth on" see on 1: 12 (also Additional Note E, pp. 335ff.). The death of the Son is viewed first of all in its revelatory aspect. It shows us the love of the Father. Then its purpose is brought out, both positively and negatively. Those who believe on Him do not "perish". Neither here nor anywhere else in the New Testament is the dreadful reality behind this word "perish" brought out. But in all its parts there is the recognition that there is such a reality awaiting the finally impenitent.[77] Believers are rescued from this only by the death of the Son. Because of this they have "eternal life" (see on v. 15). John sets perishing and life starkly over against one another. He knows no other final state.

17 Now John uses the thought of judgment to bring out God's loving purpose, and once again he employs the device of following a negative statement with the corresponding positive. God did not send[78] the Son[79] into the world, he tells us, in order to judge[80] it.

---

[76] "This is the heart of the Gospel. Not 'God is Love' – a precious truth, but affirming no divine act for our redemption. *God so loved that He gave*" (Temple).

[77] See further my *The Biblical Doctrine of Judgment* (London, 1960), pp. 69ff; *The Cross in the New Testament* (Grand Rapids, 1965), pp. 146ff., 385f.

[78] The verb is ἀποστέλλω. Westcott distinguishes this from πέμπω in that it "conveys the accessory notions of a special commission, and so far of a delegated authority in the person sent. The simple verb πέμπω marks nothing more than the immediate relation of the sender to the sent" (Additional Note to 20 : 21; Rengstorf makes a similar distinction, *TDNT*, I, pp. 398ff.). Abbott reverses the distinction: "we are perhaps justified in thinking that ἀποστέλλω means 'sending away into the world at large,' but πέμπω 'sending on a special errand' " (*Johannine Vocabulary*, London, 1905, 1723g). It may be doubted whether a sharp distinction between the two words is legitimate. C. C. Tarelli has pointed out that John uses ἀποστέλλω in the aorist and perfect indicative and the perfect passive participle, whereas he uses πέμπω in the aorist participle active, the present and the future (*JThS*, XLVII, 1946, p. 175). The difference is not one of meaning but of John's consistent choice of certain parts only of these verbs. That there is no difference of meaning is further to be seen in the way the verbs are used. Both are used of purely human sending (ἀ. in 1 : 24; π. in 1 : 22), of the sending of John the Baptist (ἀ., 1 : 6; π., 1 : 33), of Christ's sending of the disciples (ἀ., 17 : 18; π., 13 : 20). In both the preponderance is for the Father's sending of the Son (ἀ. 17 times out of 28 occurrences; π. 24 times out of 32). The verbs occur together in 7 : 28f.; 20 : 21 and both roots in 13 : 16. No real difference of meaning is apparent. Both words occur in John more often than in any other New Testament book, ἀποστέλλω 28 times, as against Matthew 22 times, Mark 20 times, Luke 25 times, πέμπω 32 times,

Elsewhere, however, he tells us that Jesus did come into the world "for judgment" (9 : 39). The resolution of the paradox demands that we see salvation as necessarily implying judgment. These are the two sides to the one coin. The very fact of salvation for all who believe implies judgment on all who do not. This is a solemn reality and John does not want us to escape it. Judgment is a recognized theme in contemporary Jewish thought, but it is the judgment of God, and it is thought of as taking place at the last day. John modifies both these thoughts. He does, it is true, speak of judging sometimes in much the normal Jewish way (8 : 50). But it is quite another matter when he says that God has committed all judgment to Christ (5 : 22, 27). He goes on to speak of Christ as judging (5 : 30; 8 : 16, 26) or not judging (8 : 15 [but *cf.* 16]; 12 : 47), and of His word as judging men (12 : 48). His judgment is just (5 : 30) and it is true (8 : 16). How men fare in the judgment depends on their relation to Him (5 : 24; 3 : 19). As the cross looms large Jesus can even speak of the world as judged (12 : 31) and of Satan likewise as judged (12 : 31; 16 : 11). Clearly John sees the whole traditional doctrine of judgment as radically modified in the light of the Incarnation. The life, and especially the death of Jesus have their effects on the judgment. So far we have referred to future judgment, the judgment of the last day. But this is not all of John's teaching. He sees judgment also as a present reality (v. 18). What men are doing now determines what will happen when they stand before Christ on judgment day. All this has obvious Christological implications. Clearly John has a high view of Jesus' Person. His teaching on judgment is yet another way in which he brings out the messiahship of Jesus, his great central aim.

In this verse "judge" has a meaning much like "condemn" (AV), as the contrast with "be saved" shows.[81] Some men will,

---

as against Matthew 4 times, Mark once, Luke 10 times. These statistics show that the thought of mission is important to John.

[79] "It will be observed also that the title *Son (the Son*, not *his Son)*, which is that of dignity, takes the place of *only begotten Son*, which is the title of affection" (Westcott).

[80] John uses the verb κρίνω 19 times, as against 6 times each in Matthew and Luke, and none at all in Mark. The only New Testament book to use the term more often than John is Acts, where it is found 21 times. John also uses the nouns κρίσις (11 times) and κρίμα (once). Such statistics show that the idea of judgment interested him more than it did most writers.

[81] This is all the more likely in that John never uses the word κατακρίνω (though it is found in the story of the woman taken in adultery, 8 : 10, 11).

in fact, be condemned, and that as the result of Christ's coming into the world (v. 19). But the purpose of His coming was not this.[82] It was on the contrary "that the world should be saved". So John brings out his positive corresponding to the negative at the beginning of the verse. Salvation was central to the mission of Jesus, a truth which is brought out also in the Synoptists (Matt. 27 : 42; Mark 8 : 35; Luke 19 : 10, etc.). We should not overlook the "through him" at the end of the verse, for this attributes the salvation in question ultimately to the Father. It is also worth noticing that in this verse we have another example of John's habit of giving emphasis to certain words by the simple device of repetition. He uses "world" three times in this verse.

18 John proceeds to bring out the importance of faith. He has said that Christ died for men. But that does not automatically bring salvation. No man is saved unless he believes. John asserts this with yet another example of a favourite construction, the same truth being put both positively and negatively.[83] The man who exercises faith is not condemned (or "judged"; see on previous verse). For him judgment is not to be feared. But the man who does not believe (persistence in unbelief is meant) does not have to wait until Judgment Day. He is condemned already. His unbelief has shut him up to condemnation. John goes on to remove all doubts as to why this should be. He has not believed[84] "on the name of the only begotten Son of God". For believing "on the name" see on 1 : 12, and for "only begotten" on 1 : 14. Notice

---

[82] MacGregor cites Holtzmann that Christ comes to judge the world "as little as the sun comes to throw a shadow". But "judgment like the shadow is the natural consequence of the world's constitution and circumstances."

[83] Godet cites H. Jacottet: "Here is justification by faith, and condemnation by unbelief."

[84] Note the perfects κέκριται and πεπίστευκεν. He has passed into a continuing state of condemnation because he refused to enter a continuing state of belief. On μὴ πεπίστευκεν, which may be contrasted with οὐ πεπίστευκεν in I John 5 : 10, Abbott comments: ὅτι μή "states it *subjectively*, as the judgment pronounced by the Judge, 'This man is guilty *in that he hath not believed*,' so that the meaning is almost 'hath been pronounced guilty *of not believing*' " (2187). Moulton puts it this way: the present passage "states the charge, *quod non crediderit*", whereas I John 5 : 10 states "the simple *fact*, *quod non credidit*" (M, I, p. 171).

another example of emphasis by repetition, this time the verb "believe" being mentioned three times in one verse. It is important. John goes on to bring out the enormity of a refusal to believe with his description of Jesus as "the only begotten Son of God". Though "only begotten" does not in itself refer to metaphysical relationship, there can be no doubt but that here John is affirming emphatically that Jesus has community of nature with the Father. When men do not believe on such a Person they condemn themselves. The coming of Jesus divides men into the saved and the condemned. This verse is of the utmost importance for the understanding of the paradox (noted in the comment on the preceding verse) that Jesus both came to judge and did not come to judge. His coming gives men the opportunity of salvation and challenges them to a decision. To refuse His good gift is to be judged.

19 The word translated "judgment" here denotes the *process* of judging, not the *sentence* of condemnation.[85] Faced with the light (see on 1 : 4) that has come into the world men usually prefer the darkness.[86] John is not saying that God has decreed that men who do such and such things are condemned. It is not God's sentence with which he is concerned here. He is telling us rather how the process works. Men choose the darkness and their condemnation lies in that very fact. They shut themselves up to the darkness. They cut themselves off from the light. Why do they do this? Because "their works were evil". Immersed in wrongdoing they have no wish to be disturbed. They refuse to be shaken out of their comfortable sinfulness. So they reject the light that comes to them. They set their love (aorist tense) on darkness. In this way they condemn themselves. There is a certain emphasis on "light" in this section of the meditation. In characteristic fashion John makes the concept prominent by the simple device of repeating the word (it occurs five times in vv. 19–21). We should probably give it a twofold meaning in this verse. There is the usual metaphorical meaning whereby "light" stands for "good" over against "darkness" which means "evil". But in this Gospel Christ is the light (1 : 9; 8 : 12; 9 : 5), and John is here speaking

---

[85] κρίσις not κρίμα. LS gives the meaning of the word as "separating, distinguishing". E. Stauffer says, "History is *krisis*, is separation of souls" (*NTT*, p. 42).

[86] This is John's one use of σκότος. He prefers σκοτία. See on 1 : 5.

of Christ's coming to men. The supreme condemnation of the men
of his day, John says, was that when Christ, the Light of the world,
came to them they rejected Him. For they loved the darkness.

This is one of the points at which the teaching of the Qumran
texts diverges from that of this Gospel. In the scrolls there is a
rigid and hopeless determinism. The men of darkness belong to
the spirit of error. Their fate deprives them of any power of choice.
Willy nilly they belong to the spirit of error. But John is concerned
with meaningful moral choice, not blind fate. Men preferred
darkness to light. And in that lies their condemnation.

20 John amplifies his explanation. Why did the men who do evil[87]
not come to the light? Because all who make a practice of wrong-
doing hate the light. John does not hesitate to use the strong term
"hateth". He employs this verb 12 times, almost a third of all its
New Testament occurrences. This is accounted for largely because
he so often sees the sinful world as hating God or Christ or, as
here, what they stand for. The strife between good and evil is no
tepid affair, but one which elicits the bitter hatred of the forces
of evil. One reason for this is brought out here. To come to the
light means to have one's darkness shown for what it is, and to
have it rebuked for what it is. No one likes this uncomfortable
process, persistent wrongdoers least of all. The fear of salutary
reproof keeps them away from the light. There is a moral basis
behind much unbelief.

21 Not so he that "doeth the truth". For "truth" see Additional
Note D, pp. 293ff. "He that doeth the truth" is an unusual expression.[88] We generally speak of "telling the truth". It may be
that John's choice of verb is partly due to the need for a contrast

---

[87] "That doeth evil" is ὁ φαῦλα πράσσων. Both adjective and verb are
found again in 5 : 29 and nowhere else in John. In strictness φαῦλος expresses
that which is worthless (we might render "paltry" or "mean"), and πράσσω
has the thought of "practise". But probably the meanings should not be pressed
unduly. John is fond of small variations without significant change of sense
(see on v. 5). In 5 : 29 the expression used here is set in contrast with τὰ ἀγαθὰ
ποιέω as here with ποιέω τὴν ἀλήθειαν.

[88] It is found, however, more than once in the Dead Sea Scrolls, see 1
QS 1 : 5; 5 : 3; 8 : 2. But the Qumran covenanters connected truth with the
Law as when they explain Hab. 2 : 3: "This means the men of truth, the doers
of the law, whose hands do not grow slack from the service of the truth" (*DSS*,
p. 368).

with "doeth evil" (v. 20).[89] But there are actions that are true as well as words. The man who habitually performs the actions that can be described as true comes to the light. This man's works are not such as must be reproved. They are "wrought in God",[90] and the light will but make this clear to all. John does not, of course, mean that there are some men who by nature do what is right. He is not teaching salvation by works or by nature. In this very chapter he has reported the words of Jesus which emphasize that not good works, but rebirth is the way to God. The man John has in mind here is the man who responds to the gospel invitation, the man who has life in Christ (v. 15). Perhaps we could bring out his meaning by saying that the truth conveyed elsewhere in the New Testament by the doctrine of election underlies this verse. It is only the man on whom God has laid His hand who can truly say that his works are "wrought in God". And he will not avoid the light.

(c) Jesus and John the Baptist, 3 : 22–36

(i) A Question about Purifying, 3 : 22–26

22 After these things came Jesus and his disciples into the land of Judaea; and there he tarried with them, and baptized. 23 And John also was baptizing in Aenon near to Salim, because there [1]was much water there: and they came, and were baptized. 24 For John was not yet cast into prison. 25 There arose therefore a questioning on the part of John's disciples with a Jew about purifying. 26 And they came unto John, and said to him, Rabbi, he that was with thee beyond the Jordan, to whom thou hast borne witness, behold, the same baptizeth, and all men come to him.

[1] Gr. *were many waters.*

It is often suggested that vv. 22–30 are out of their proper place. Some advocate transferring them to a position after 2 : 12, others after 3 : 36. The arguments usually revolve round their

---

[89] But against this is the fact that the Greek verbs are different: "doeth" is πράσσων in v. 20 and ποιῶν here.

[90] The expression is ὅτι ἐν Θεῷ ἐστιν εἰργασμένα. This puts an emphasis on "in God". The perfect participle may point to the permanence of such works.

suitability to the the context in which we find them. There are suggestions of displacement at various points in this Gospel, and more or less plausible arguments are produced to support such theories. But we must always bear in mind that what we think an appropriate sequence is not necessarily the one that the compiler of this Gospel would have adopted. And in any case our first duty is to see whether the verses in question fit into the Gospel where they are traditionally found. Only if we find compelling reason should we place them elsewhere. In the case of the present passage examination does not appear to disclose any such compelling reason.[91]

In vv. 1–21 John has recorded a conversation in which Jesus sets forth the way of salvation. Then he has added some comments of his own. Already, in his opening chapter, he has insisted that John the Baptist regarded his function as that of bearing witness to Jesus. Now, after making plain what Jesus stands for, the Evangelist returns to the Baptist to show that he still bears witness to Jesus. The readers of the Gospel now know what Jesus wants of men. They know that He demands a radical rebirth. They know that He will die for man's salvation. They know that those who believe in Him have eternal life while those who do not are condemned already. Now John wants them to see that in the light of all this the Baptist maintains his unswerving support. He is still a witness to Jesus.

22 After the events previously recorded[92] Jesus moved with His disciples from Jerusalem into the country districts of Judaea.[93] The locality is not closely specified, but it appears to be somewhere in the Jordan plain, perhaps not so very far from Jericho. "Tarried"[94] is another word that is not very specific, but we get

---

[91] V. 31 does not really follow very smoothly on v. 21. *Cf.* Dodd: "It is pretty certain that if our MSS. had given verse 31 immediately after verse 21, critics would have pointed out a disjuncture; for there is no immediate connection between the thought of judgment by the light in verses 17–21 and the supremacy of Christ as the One who descends from heaven and bears witness to what He has seen, which is the theme of 31–2" (*IFG*, p. 309).

[92] For μετὰ ταῦτα see on 2 : 12.

[93] εἰς τὴν Ἰουδαίαν γῆν. The expression is found nowhere else in the New Testament. It may denote the country districts as contrasted with Jerusalem itself.

[94] διέτριβεν. John uses the verb again in 11 : 54, but otherwise it occurs only in Acts in the New Testament.

the impression of an unhurried period during which Jesus and
His followers got to know each other better. We do not read of
Jesus as baptizing in any other Gospel than this, and from 4 : 2
we learn that the actual baptizing was carried out by the disciples,
not by Jesus in person. It is difficult to think of this as Christian
baptism in the later sense. More probably it represents a continuation of the "baptism of repentance" that was characteristic
of John the Baptist. Both Jesus and His first disciples had come
from the circle around John, and it may well be that for some
time they continued to call on men to submit to the baptism that
symbolized repentance. We know that Jesus' first preaching was
the same as that of John, "Repent ye" (Matt. 3 : 2; 4 : 17). It may
well be that the symbol of repentance was retained for a time also.

23 From Jesus the spotlight moves to John. At that time he was
at work[95] at Aenon, which is located as "near to Salim".[96] Neither
place can now be identified with certainty. One suggestion for
Aenon is a site about seven miles south of Beisan.[97] If this is correct
there is a striking accuracy in the statement that there was "much
water", or better "many waters", there, for in this locality there
are seven springs within a radius of a quarter of a mile.[98] In some
such place John pursued his activities. The tense of the last two
verbs is continuous and we might give the force of it as "they
kept coming and being baptized".

---

[95] "Was baptizing" is $\tilde{\eta}\nu \ldots \beta a\pi\tau\iota\zeta\omega\nu$. There is probably no great difference
from $\dot{\epsilon}\beta\dot{a}\pi\tau\iota\zeta\epsilon\nu$ of the previous verse. John is fond of the periphrastic construction. If the two are differentiated the thought will be that John gave himself
to baptizing more continuously than did Jesus.

[96] The meaning of the former name is "fountains", and of the latter "peace".
Those who delight to allegorize have not failed to point out the significance
of "fountains near to peace". The work of the Baptist leads men near to that
peace which Christ alone can give. This is edifying, but it is quite another
thing to maintain that John's meaning is wholly symbolic. He appears to be
using the terms because they were in fact the names of the places in question.

[97] This is accepted, for example, by R. D. Potter (*SE*, I, p. 333). He objects
to Albright's idea of a site three miles to the East of Sychem on the ground
that there is not much water there (for Albright's position see *BNT*, p. 159).
The Westminster Historical Atlas mentions both sites and says, "no decision is
possible" (p.8 5). *The Rand McNally Bible Atlas* likewise leaves the question open.

[98] Bernard cites Sir C. W. Wilson for this information.

24 The Evangelist tells us nothing about the imprisonment of John the Baptist apart from this laconic statement. Apparently he regarded this as so well known that he had no need to do other than simply mention it. We must turn to the fuller accounts in the Synoptists for information about it (Matt. 14 : 1–12; Mark 6 : 14–29; Luke 3 : 19f.). John is concerned to give us information about Jesus, not the Baptist. The latter is mentioned for his witness to Jesus and for that alone. His imprisonment does not clarify his witness in any way, so it does not fit in with our Evangelist's plan. But the present incident does, so he records it. He adds to the information given in the Synoptic Gospels by indicating that between the temptation of Jesus and the arrest of the Baptist there was an interval during which Jesus and John worked side by side. We should not have known this from Mark 1 : 13f. and the parallels.

25 The particular incident which triggered off John's statement was a dispute his disciples[99] had with a Jew[100] about purifying. This verse is compressed to the point of obscurity. A little light may be shed on it however, by the Qumran scrolls. These show us that there were Essene-type sects with a deep interest in ceremonial purifications. If the suggestions that John the Baptist had had contacts with such a sect and had broken with it are well grounded, such a dispute as the one mentioned here would be very natural. It is also a natural touch that the dispute concerned John's disciples and not John himself. They would probably be more aggressive than their master, and possibly more accessible for such a dispute.

26 The discussion must have taken a curious turn, for when John's disciples bring it to him there is no question of differing views about purification. It is a complaint that Jesus was having great

---

[99] It is possible to take ἐκ τῶν μαθητῶν ᾽Ιωάννου as a partitive genitive, "some of John's disciples". But it is better to see in it an indication that the dispute originated with these disciples.

[100] μετὰ ᾽Ιουδαίου seems to be the correct reading, though there is strong support for the plural. Some have conjectured μετὰ τῶν ᾽Ιησοῦ but there seems little in favor of this. While it would suit the context admirably it is difficult to think that, if original, it would have no support in the MSS.

success.[101] For "Rabbi" see on 1 : 38. Jesus is not mentioned by name, but described as "he that was with thee beyond the Jordan, to whom thou hast borne witness". This perhaps indicates that Jesus stayed with John rather longer than we would have gathered from a cursory reading of chapter one. We should also notice that John's disciples recognize the place that witness (see on 1 : 7) to Jesus occupied in their master's teaching.[102] At a later time disciples of John might refuse to give allegiance to Jesus, but his immediate disciples knew what he had said about Him. "Thou" is emphatic and stands in sharp contrast with "the same". John's disciples believe that John has behaved generously in bearing his witness to Jesus. They find it intolerable that Jesus should then act in independence, so to speak, and gather more disciples than His illustrious predecessor. "All men" is an indignant exaggeration, very natural in the circumstances.

(ii) *The Reply of John the Baptist, 3 : 27-30*

27 John answered and said, A man can receive nothing, except it have been given him from heaven. 28 Ye yourselves bear me witness, that I said, I am not the Christ, but, that I am sent before him. 29 He that hath the bride is the bridegroom: but the friend of the bridegroom, that standeth and heareth him, rejoiceth greatly because of the bridegroom's voice: this my joy therefore is made full. 30 He must increase, but I must decrease.

27 John's reply is an immediate justification of Jesus' success. His first words are very general. They may be applied to John himself. He has what God has given[103] him, that and no more.

---

101   Godet comments: "Perhaps in response to the disciples of John who invited him to have himself baptized, reminding him of the promises of the Old Testament (Ezek. xxxvi. 25, etc.), he answered ironically that one knew not to whom to go: 'Your master began; here is a second who succeeds better than he; which of the two says the truth?' The question was embarrassing. The disciples of John decide to submit it to their master." The difficulty about this is that it scarcely gives sufficient weight to the statement that the dispute originated with John's disciples. But if we can picture them as taking the initiative, perhaps as picking an argument with a Jew who was rather impressed by Jesus, we may have the situation.

102   The perfect μεμαρτύρηκας may well be meant to indicate the continuing effects of John's witness.

103   John uses the verb δίδωμι 76 times, which is more often than any other New Testament writer. He has a specially interesting number of things the Father gives the Son (see on v. 35).

He cannot be anything more than the forerunner. God has not given it to him to intrude on the place of the Messiah.[104] They apply also to Jesus. He has had this success given Him (the verb is a perfect with the idea of a permanent gift) from God Himself ("heaven" was a common circumlocution to avoid the use of the divine name). John sees the hand of the Father in everything. If people were flocking to Jesus, that was because the Father willed it so. The words also apply to the believer. The salvation he enjoys is given him by God. He could never have acquired it otherwise. It is unlikely that the Baptist meant the words in this way. His intention is to show the reason for Jesus' greater success. But the language he uses is certainly capable of this further application.

28 John is able to appeal to what was well known about his preaching. "Ye yourselves" is emphatic. "You", John is saying, "have the answer already if you will only think of the significance of what you have already heard." He had spoken on this subject before and had explicitly disclaimed being the Christ.[105] They should have remembered that. His "I" is also emphatic. He wants there to be no doubt about his disclaimer. "I am sent" is in the perfect tense, which may be meant to indicate that his permanent character was that of a man sent from God (1 : 6) to be the forerunner of the Messiah. Nothing can alter that. The success of Jesus is not at all difficult to explain if John was truly sent from God. On the contrary, it was the most natural thing in the world. For Jesus is the One before whom[106] John came, and to prepare whose way John came.

29 So far from being downcast at what is happening, John rejoices. He now employs the illustration of a wedding to bring this out. At a wedding the bridegroom is the important man. His friend may stand by him, and rejoice with him. Indeed in the Jewish scene he could do more. "The friend of the bridegroom"

[104] *Cf.* Calvin: "he denies it is in his power or theirs to make him great, because the stature of us all is that we are what God wanted us to be." For John's development of the messianic idea see on 1 : 41.

[105] Characteristically there are small variants from the former statement. He reverses the order of ἐγώ and οὐκ εἰμί from that in 1 : 20. Again, the statement, "I am sent before him", does not seem to occur previously, though the sense of it is there (*e.g.* 1 : 15, 30).

[106] For ἐκεῖνος see on 1 : 8.

was an important person.[107] He was responsible for many of the details of the wedding, and in particular it was he who brought the bride to the bridegroom. But when he had done this his task was over. He did not expect to take the centre of the stage.[108] "He that hath the bride is the bridegroom". But a wedding is a happy occasion for others than the bridegroom. The bridegroom's friend also "rejoiceth greatly".[109] The joy of his friend brings joy to him, too. In the same way, says John, his own joy,[110] not simply that of Jesus, is filled to the very brim. The news his disciples brought him was what he had been longing to hear. It filled his cup of joy to the full. Elsewhere Jesus used the wedding illustration to explain why His disciples did not fast (Mark 2 : 19). The present passage shows that the joy of His coming was not confined to His immediate circle. There may be more to the present passage than a happy illustration. The Baptist would have been well aware that in the Old Testament Israel is regarded as the bride of Jehovah (Isa. 54 : 5; 62 : 4f.; Jer. 2 : 2; 3 : 20; Ezek. 16 : 8; Hos. 2 : 19f.). This imagery made its appeal as a way of referring to the Messiah, and we find it, for example, applied to Christ in II Cor. 11 : 2; Eph. 5 : 32. "In some real sense the Baptist testified that God Himself was in Christ betrothing His bride to Himself afresh" (Murray). At the time the Evangelist records the saying it would be impossible to miss the overtones that Jesus,

---

[107] See I. Abrahams, *Studies in Pharisaism and the Gospels*, II (Cambridge, 1924), p. 213; SBk, I, pp. 500ff. He was the שׁושׁבִין, "the best man". Abrahams cites Mishnah, *Sanh.* 3 : 5, "A friend is his *shoshbin*." He also says, "There was anciently a *shoshbin* for the bridegroom and another for the bride . . . but, adds the Talmud, this was not the custom in Galilee."

[108] Calvin draws out the implication for the Christian teacher: "Those who win the Church over to themselves rather than to Christ faithlessly violate the marriage which they ought to honour."

[109] χαρᾷ χαίρει, "rejoices with joy", is probably a Semitism reflecting the use of the infinitive absolute (though the construction is sometimes found in the classics).

[110] The expression ἡ ἐμή is probably not emphatic. G. D. Kilpatrick has shown that this is the normal way of denoting possession in John. When emphasis is required the possessive goes between the article and the noun (*e.g.* 4 : 42; 5 : 47; 7 : 16). See *BT*, 11, 1960, p. 173. The form used here carries more emphasis than the genitive of the personal pronoun, but it is not John's emphatic form. John uses ἐμός 40 times, and, as no other book has it more than 9 times (I Corinthians; next is Matthew, 5 times) it is quite a feature of Johannine style. *Cf.* his frequent use of ἐγώ (see on 1 : 20).

not the Baptist, is the Bridegroom. The church is His bride, not that of His forerunner.[111]

30 The last words of John to be recorded in this Gospel form surely one of the greatest utterances that ever fell from human lips. It is not particularly easy in this world to gather followers about one for a serious purpose. But when they are gathered it is infinitely harder to detach them, and firmly insist that they go after another. It is the measure of John's greatness that he did just that. Jesus, he says, "must" increase. It is not merely advisable, nor is it the way events have happened to turn out. There is a compelling divine necessity behind the expression (*cf.* v. 27). John sets "he"[112] and "I" over against one another in emphatic contrast. They are not cast for identical or even similar roles. It is God's plan that the Messiah must continually increase. The servant, however, must of necessity decrease. It is never the part of the servant to displace the Master. Which is something that must be learned in every age.

(iii) *Reflection, 3 : 31–36*

> 31 He that cometh from above is above all: he that is of the earth is of the earth, and of the earth he speaketh: ¹he that cometh from heaven is above all. 32 What he hath seen and heard, of that he beareth witness; and no man receiveth his witness. 33 He that hath received his witness hath set his seal to this, that God is true. 34 For he whom God hath sent speaketh the words of God: for he giveth not the Spirit by measure. 35 The Father loveth the Son, and hath given all things into his hand. 36 He that believeth on the Son hath eternal life; but he that ²obeyeth not the Son shall not see life, but the wrath of God abideth on him.
>
> ¹Some ancient authorities read *he that cometh from heaven beareth witness of what he hath seen and heard.* ²Or, *believeth not*

Once again we are confronted with the difficulty of knowing exactly where a speech ends. Some hold that John the Baptist is the speaker to the end of the chapter (*e.g.* Murray). Others think the words were spoken by Jesus (usually, as Bultmann, they

---

[111] See further the chapter on "The Bridegroom" in V. Taylor, *The Names of Jesus* (London, 1953), pp. 87f.

[112] For ἐκεῖνος see on 1 : 8.

think of a transposition of order of some of the verses). It seems
to me more probable that vv. 31–36 are from the Evangelist.[113]
They come more naturally as his reflection on the significance of
Jesus in the light both of the Baptist's words and of subsequent
happenings, than as a comment of the forerunner or of the Master.
There are some stylistic points of a minor nature which perhaps
indicate the hand of the Evangelist. There is also the difficulty
of seeing how the Baptist could say, "no man receiveth his witness"
(v. 32) in the very speech in which he is answering the affirmation
that "all men come to him" (v. 26). Whoever originated them
the words bring out the community of Jesus with the Father and
the importance of being in right relationship with Him.

31 "He that cometh from above"[114] is another reference to the
heavenly origin of Jesus, in which this Evangelist delights (others,
of course, also remind us of this as Paul in I Cor. 15 : 47). It may
even be a title of Jesus, but in view of the later "he that is of the
earth" it is probably not. It is John's plan in writing this book
to show "that Jesus is the Christ" (20 : 31), and one way he does
this is to emphasize that Jesus does not take His origin from the
earth.[115] Being "from above" He is superior to all on earth.[116]
"He that is of the earth"[117] is a general term which has its application to all mankind. None such can ever do other than speak

---

[113] See the note in Lagrange, p. 96.

[114] The expression is ὁ ἄνωθεν ἐρχόμενος. Jesus is called ὁ ἐρχόμενος in
the Synoptists (*e.g.* Mark 11 : 9; Luke 7 : 19f.), as also in this Gospel (*e.g.*
11 : 27; *cf.* 1 : 15). The expression is a title of the Messiah. Notice John's habit
of small variations (see on v. 5). Jesus is called "he that descended out of
heaven" (v. 13), "he that cometh from above" (v. 31), and "he that cometh
from heaven" (v. 31).

[115] Chrysostom makes the point that His accreditation is not earthly: "it
is impossible for One who cometh from heaven to have His credit strengthened
by one that inhabiteth earth" (XXX. 1; p. 103).

[116] πάντων is ambiguous. It might be masculine, with the meaning, "above
all men" (*i.e.* superior to all teachers), or it might be neuter, "above all things".
Perhaps John would not care to be tied exclusively to either meaning.

[117] Black maintains that the present passage is a translation of sayings
which originally formed an Aramaic poem. He points out that " 'he that is
of the earth is of the earth' is pure tautology and has no meaning" in Aramaic,
as in Greek or English. He suggests that there has been a misreading of an
expression meaning "he that is of the earth *is inferior to Him*" (*AA*, pp. 109f.).
This makes sense and completes the parallelism required by the poem. Yet we
should bear in mind that John loves to repeat words for emphasis, and this
may be the significance of the threefold "of the earth".

"of the earth" ("of" denotes origin;[118] it must not be understood, as the English would allow, as though it meant "about"; he may speak "about" heavenly realities, but it still remains that what he says originates on earth). But there is particular reference to John the Baptist. His followers may think of him as the Messiah. The Evangelist cannot but contrast him with the Messiah. The Baptist is "of the earth".[119] He does not come "from above". His teaching is important (cf. the stress placed on John's "witness"), but it must always be borne in mind that it is of earthly origin. The repeated affirmation that Christ is "above all"[120] is impressive. He is absolutely preeminent. The words refer to all things and all men.

32 Jesus earlier assured Nicodemus that He (and those with Him) speak only of what they know and have seen. John now gives us a similar statement about the Master. "What he hath seen and heard"[121] is another way of expressing certainty. The teaching of

---

[118] εἶναι ἐκ is a common Johannive construction. Besides being ἐκ τῆς γῆς men may be said to be ἐκ τοῦ κόσμου (15 : 19), ἐκ τῆς ἀληθείας (18 : 37), ἐκ τοῦ Θεοῦ (8 : 47), ἐκ τοῦ πατρὸς τοῦ διαβόλου (8 : 44), or ἐκ τῶν κάτω (8 : 23). By contrast with the latter, Jesus is ἐκ τῶν ἄνω. In I John men may be ἐκ τοῦ διαβόλου (3 : 8) or ἐκ τοῦ πονηροῦ (3 : 12), while certain ἐπιθυμίαι are not ἐκ τοῦ Πατρός but ἐκ τοῦ κόσμου (2 : 16). The construction is occasionally found in other parts of the New Testament, but nowhere is it characteristic as it is in John.

[119] Note that John does not use γῆ in a derogatory sense as he does κόσμος. To be "of the earth" is very different from being "of the world".

[120] The expression is ἐπάνω πάντων. Paul similarly speaks of Christ as ὁ ὢν ἐπὶ πάντων (Rom. 9 : 5, and cf. Eph. 1 : 21). An important group of MSS omits the words (ℵ* D f1 565 it syr). This would give the sense: "He who comes from heaven testifies to what he has seen and heard." A decision is difficult, but perhaps the retention of the words is slightly more probable. The sense then will be as ARV.

[121] The change of tense from the perfect ἑώρακεν to the aorist ἤκουσεν is unexpected. Perhaps, as Westcott thinks, the former points us to "that which belonged to the existence" and the latter to "that which belonged to the mission" of the Son. Abbott thinks a similar explanation possible, but he points out that in this Gospel ἀκούω is in the aorist when Christ is described as "hearing" from the Father, and that "(apart from forms of ὀφθῆναι, ὄψομαι, etc.) the perfect of ὁρᾶν is the only part of the verb used by John" (2451). BDF thinks that the combination "puts the chief emphasis on seeing". In 5 : 37; I John 1 : 1,3 the same two verbs occur, but both tenses are perfect. In these cases BDF thinks that hearing is equally essential with seeing and the coordinated verbs bring this out (342 (2)).

the Master is not a hypothesis put forward as a basis for discussion. He teaches what He knows. The particular form in which John casts this certainty agrees with the heavenly origin referred to in the previous verse. It is of what He has seen and heard in the heavenly sphere that He bears His witness among men (for witness, see on 1 : 7). But though what He says is thus seen to be supremely reliable, men in general do not accept it. "No man" is not to be taken literally as the very next verse shows. The passage is reminiscent of 1 : 11f., where a statement that might be understood to mean that nobody at all received Jesus is immediately explained. John has already made it clear in this chapter that a man must be reborn. The natural man will not accept Christ's witness. The world, as a whole, is not interested in the truth that Jesus came to bring. John sorrowfully makes it plain that men do not receive His witness.

33 "He that hath received" is an aorist participle. John is thinking not of a continuous, day-by-day receiving of the witness of Jesus (though that, too, is important), but of a decisive act whereby a man decides to accept Jesus and Jesus' witness.[122] When he does this he does more. He sets his seal on the proposition that God is true. The seal was used a great deal in antiquity when there were many who could not read. A design imprinted by a seal conveyed a clear message even to the illiterate. Great men used distinctive seals which stamped articles as belonging to them. The seal came to be used not only to denote ownership, but to authenticate, to give a man's personal guarantee.[123] It is something of the sort that is meant here (Moffatt: "certifies to the truth of God").[124] When a man accepts Christ he is not merely entering

---

[122] Abbott thinks that the reference is not general, but to a particular person, probably John the Baptist (2501). If the reference must be confined to one person there is no more likely candidate. But there is nothing in the context to limit it to any one person. It seems more probable that the verse applies to any who receives the testimony.

[123] AG gives as one of the meanings of $\sigma\varphi\rho\alpha\gamma\iota\zeta\omega$ "*attest, certify, acknowledge* (as a seal does on a document)". The most common use of the verb in the New Testament is for God's marking out of people as His own (*cf.* 6 : 27).

[124] *Cf.* Luther: "Among men nothing is safer and more certain than that which is given under one's hand and seal. I feel sure when I have a sealed document . . . Anyone who really accepts the message of the Gospel resolutely sets his seal to it and says: 'This seal and document mean that I can stake life and limb and all I possess on this.' His heart is certain and harbors no doubts" (*op. cit.*, pp. 471f.).

into a relationship with a fellow-man (as he would be doing, for example, if he attached himself to John the Baptist). He is accepting what God has said. He is recognizing the heavenly origin of Jesus. He is acknowledging the truth of God's revelation in Christ. He is proclaiming to all his deep conviction that God is true. This probably means more than would "God is truthful". Elsewhere John reports that Jesus said, "I am . . . truth" (14 : 6). It is something like this that is in mind here. Truth is rooted in the divine nature. But there is also an emphasis on Jesus who bears the decisive witness to God. The God who is true will not mislead men, and He has not misled them in the witness borne by Jesus.[125]

34 This is brought out with the express assertion that Jesus (note the change from "he that cometh from above" to "he whom God hath sent"; for this last expression see on v. 17) speaks "the words of God". His words are not human words but divine. Therefore to receive His witness is the same thing as to receive the words of God. It is to agree that God is true. "He giveth not the Spirit by measure"[126] has been understood variously.

(i) The Father gives the Spirit to the Son without measure. There is perfect communion between them, and no limit to the gift[127] (*cf.* Rieu, "God bestows the Spirit on him with no grudging hand"). His perfect endowment with the Spirit guarantees the truth of His words. For the Father's various gifts to the Son see on v. 35.

(ii) The Son gives the Spirit to believers without measure. The verse is often understood in this way, but caution must be exercised. It is true that believers receive the Spirit in abundant measure

---

[125] It is possible that the text should be amended, in which case these comments would not stand. Black thinks that the original Aramaic has been misread and that the passage originally read
  "He that hath received his testimony
  Hath set to his seal *('ashar)* that God *sent him*" (*AA*, p. 110).
This would give an excellent sense, but it scarcely seems that the amendment is required.

[126] ἐκ μέτρου is an unusual expression, which does not appear to occur elsewhere. Probably it is correctly understood as "by measure" (which is usually simply μέτρῳ).

[127] *Cf.* the saying in *The Gospel according to the Hebrews* (described by M. R. James as "a divergent yet not heretical form of our Gospel according to St. Matthew", *The Apocryphal New Testament*, Oxford, 1926, p. 1): "And it came to pass when the Lord was come up out of the water, the whole fount of the Holy Spirit descended and rested upon him" (James, *op. cit.*, p. 5).

and that their consequent illumination enables them to speak aright (*cf.* 16 : 14 where Christ says of the Spirit: "He shall glorify me: for he shall take of mine, and shall declare it unto you"). But it is not true that the New Testament regards believers as receiving the Spirit without measure. In the first place no one else has the Spirit in any way comparable to Jesus.[128] And in the second, there is an implied limitation when we are told that "unto each one of us was the grace given *according to the measure* of the gift of Christ" (Eph. 4 : 7; both Augustine and Calvin draw attention to the importance of this verse).

(iii) The Spirit does not give by measure, *i.e.* when the Spirit gives He does so liberally. This is a barely possible interpretation of the Greek.

The first of these seems preferable, though there is probably also a hint that Jesus gives the Spirit to His followers. Elsewhere John speaks of the Spirit as given by the Father (14 : 26), but also by the Son (15 : 26).

35 The mutual love of the Father and the Son means much in this Gospel. John pictures for us a perfect unity in love. Here the point is that the love of the Father for the Son guarantees the Son's plenipotentiary powers. Men may trust the Son in all things, for the Father "hath given all things into his hand".[129] In the context this refers especially to the gift of life in the Spirit. Men may come to Christ as they would come to God. Christ, with the full authority of the Father, gives the Spirit bountifully, as the previous verse hints, and gives life eternal, as the following verse

---

[128] *Cf.* the Rabbinical saying attributed to R. Acha (*c.* 320), "The Holy Spirit, who rests on the prophets, rests (on them) only by weight במשקל (= by measure)" (SBk, II, p. 431). If this view is as early as the Fourth Gospel there may be in mind a deliberate contrast between Jesus and the prophets.

[129] We read again of the Father as having given "all things into his hands" (13 : 3; *cf.* Matt. 11 : 27; Luke 10 : 22). Specifically the Father gave Christ the Spirit (v. 34), the work He accomplished (17 : 4), and the works He did (5 : 36; *cf.* 14 : 31), His message (12 : 49; 17 : 8), His authority (17 : 2), His name (17 : 11), His glory (17 : 22–24), His disciples (6 : 37–39; 10 : 29; 17 : 6, 9, 12, 24; 18 : 9), the cup He must drink (18 : 11), "all judgment" (5 : 22), "to have life in himself" (5 : 26), and power over all flesh (17 : 2). In these passages the perfect is the usual tense (17 times), the aorist being used less than half as often (8 times), and the present twice only. This may point to the permanence of the gifts. John uses the verb $\delta i \delta \omega \mu \iota$ 76 times, which is more than any other New Testament writer (next is Luke with 60 times).

makes clear. The words also indicate the dependence of the human Jesus on the Father. This is one of John's great themes,[130] and he lays great stress on it. While he is sure of Jesus' preeminent place (He is the *Logos*, the Son, *etc.*), he is also sure of His real humanity. As a man Jesus depended on the Father as other men do. In this we see His lowliness, and His perfect example to us. **36** For "believeth on" see on 1 : 12, and for "eternal life" see on v. 15. Notice that eternal life is, as often, regarded as the present possession of the believer. When he puts his trust in Christ and is reborn from above he enters a new life. The decisive thing has happened. He will in due course pass through the portal of death, but that does not alter the fact that abiding eternal life is his already. In the things that matter he is alive eternally. The present participle indicates a continuing trust. "The Son" is used absolutely, as often in this Gospel. Men may in some sense become children of God (1 : 12), but Christ is "the" Son.[131] The absolute use emphasizes the uniqueness of His position. In typical Johannine fashion the positive is followed by the negative. We might have expected "he that believeth not", and, indeed, some hold that the verb John uses should be translated that way.[132] It seems that "obeyeth not" is the meaning, but this is not so markedly different. For those who believe do in fact obey the Son, and those who do not believe do not in fact obey Him. The verb is a present participle indicating a continuing attitude. This verse is important in view of the idea held by some that John's concept of faith is an intellectual one, the assent to certain truths.

---

[130] L. Hodgson speaks of this dependence as the "keynote of our Lord's thought" (*And Was Made Man*, London, 1933, p. 198). J. E. Davey puts great emphasis on John's treatment of the theme of dependence (*The Jesus of St. John*, London, 1958, ch. 5).

[131] As we have noted before John never uses υἱός when he speaks of men as sons of God. He reserves this word for Jesus, and the terminology points to his view that the nature of Jesus' sonship is different from that of ours.

[132] Thus AG says: "since, in the view of the early Christians, the supreme disobedience was a refusal to believe their gospel, *ά.* may be restricted in some passages to the mng. *disbelieve, be an unbeliever*. This sense, though greatly disputed (it is not found outside our lit.), seems most probable in J 3 : 36. . . ." Bernard thinks the meaning is "strictly, 'to be disobedient,' . . . but rather implies a rebellious mind than a series of disobedient acts." Godet says that it "brings out the voluntary side in unbelief, that of revolt." F. F. Bruce in his commentary on Acts (London, 1951) under 14 : 2 says, "unbelief and disobedience are both involved in the rejection of the Gospel".

This verse shows that for him faith and conduct are closely linked. Faith necessarily issues in action. The thought is like that in vv. 18ff., where those who are not saved are the men who choose darkness rather than light, who hate the light, and do not come to it. Of such a man it is now said that he "shall not see life" (see on vv. 3, 5 for "seeing" and "entering" the kingdom). His disobedience cuts him off from that life which is life indeed. Far from seeing life ("but" is a strong adversative) he can look for nothing but the continuing wrath of God.[133] "The wrath of God" is a concept which is uncongenial to many modern students, and various devices are adopted to soften the expression or explain it away. This cannot be done, however, without doing great violence to many passages of Scripture and without detracting from God's moral character. Concerning the first of these points, I have elsewhere pointed out there that are literally hundreds of passages in the Bible referring to God's wrath, and the rejection of them all leaves us with a badly mutilated Bible.[134] And with reference to the second, if we abandon the idea of the wrath of God we are left with a God who is not ready to act against moral evil. It is true that the wrath of God has sometimes been understood in crudely literal fashion, but of which of God's attributes and activities is this not true? The remedy is not to abandon the conception, but to think it through more carefully. It stands for the settled and active opposition of God's holy nature to everything that is evil.[135]

---

133 This is John's one use of ὀργή. But the idea is expressed in other terms which show the certainty of the punishment of the finally impenitent (cf. the use of the concepts of perishing and of judgment earlier in this chapter).

134 *The Apostolic Preaching of the Cross* (London and Grand Rapids, 1955), chs. IV and V. Cf. also the note on I Thess. 1 : 10 in NICNT; R. V. G. Tasker, *The Biblical Doctrine of the Wrath of God* (London, 1951); the Addendum in P. T. Forsyth, *The Work of Christ* (London, 1946); art. on ὀργή in *TDNT*; C. S. Lewis, *The Problem of Pain* (London, 1943), pp. 46ff.; A. Richardson, *op. cit.*, pp. 75ff. For the contrary view see C. H. Dodd, *The Bible and the Greeks* (London, 1935), and his Moffatt commentary on Rom. 1 : 18.

135 Strachan quotes from Westcott that God's wrath "is not an arbitrary sentence, but the working out of a moral law", and objects: "This tends to make us think that moral laws are forces which come automatically into operation when men do wrong, or cherish wrong aims ... The New Testament writers ... think in much more personal terms of the nature and consequences of wrong-doing ... God is not thought of as handing over the wrong-doer to an impersonal blind force which automatically punishes. The 'wrath of

We may not like it but we should not ignore it. John tells us that this wrath "abideth". We should not expect it to fade away with the passage of time. If a man continues in unbelief and disobedience he can look for nothing other than the persisting wrath of God. This is basic to our understanding of the gospel.[136] Unless we are saved from real peril there is no meaning in salvation.

God' is an expression of God's holy personality." Our God is active in opposing the wrong. *Cf.* also L. Hodgson: "The wrath of God and divine punishment are essential elements in a doctrine which is to face the facts of evil and retain a fundamental optimism. The belief that God has sworn in His wrath that men who do certain things shall not enter into His rest enables the Church to open its worship each day with the words, 'Come, let us sing unto the Lord, let us heartily rejoice in the strength of our salvation' " (*The Doctrine of the Atonement,* London, 1951, p. 60). The latter reference is to the use of Ps. 95 in the worship of the Anglican church.

[136] F. V. Filson maintains that "verse 36 is as basic as the famous 3 : 16". A little later he says, "The wrath of God, the divine judgment, immediately and relentlessly rests on the unrepentant sinner who stubbornly rejects the offer of grace and life. There is no place for neutrality. Man was made as a moral being who can really live only by being obedient to his Father. He must either believe, obey God, and find eternal life, or refuse and so suffer the ruin that his evil choice makes inevitable".

CHAPTER IV

6. THE SECOND DISCOURSE – THE WATER OF LIFE, 4 : 1–42

(a) Jesus' Departure for Galilee, 4 : 1–3

1 When therefore the Lord knew that the Pharisees had heard that Jesus was making and baptizing more disciples than John 2 (although Jesus himself baptized not, but his disciples), 3 he left Judaea, and departed again into Galilee.

Jesus had been at work in Judea. The next incident took place in Samaria. John inserts a brief section to explain how Jesus came to be there.

1 "Therefore" is at first sight a little curious, for in the immediately preceding section John has not mentioned the Pharisees, nor, of course, how they came to know what Jesus was doing. We can take it only as marking a stage in Jesus' journeyings.[1] "The Lord"[2] is an expression which might be used as an ordinary polite form of address (much like our "Sir"). It could also be used with reverence and awe, as when applied to the Deity. After the resurrection it was used of Jesus habitually. But during His lifetime it was apparently not often used of him other than in the ordinary polite sense. He was usually referred to by name as "Jesus", or else as "Teacher" (Rabbi), and this whether in direct address or in the third person. In this Gospel He is often called "Sir" (vv. 11, 15, 19, 49, etc.), or "Rabbi", by people who have not come to understand the significance of His Person. At first the disciples do this as well as others. But in 6 : 68 Peter calls Him "Lord", which we may not unfairly associate with the heightened appreciation shown in the words which follow. After this the disciples sometimes use "Rabbi" (9 : 2; 11 : 8), but they also use "Lord" (11 : 3, 21; 13 : 6; 14 : 5, etc.; of course some of these may well be examples of "Sir" rather than "Lord"). The

---

[1] See on 1 : 21 for John's use of οὖν. It is so much a mark of his style that we cannot insist on an inferential sense. It simply links this stage of the narrative loosely with the preceding.

[2] ὁ Κύριος is the reading of P66, P75 ABCf13 syrˢ co etc., and should probably be accepted. But ὁ 'Ιησοῦς is found in ℵD Θ fl syrᶜ bo, and some regard it as the true reading.

climax is reached in Thomas's magnificent exclamation "My Lord and my God" (20 : 28). After the resurrection the disciples habitually use "Lord". It is also worth noticing that the Evangelist himself speaks of Jesus as "the Lord" only here and in 6 : 23; 11 : 2; 20 : 20; 21 : 12. His reserve may be a mark of acquaintance with the primitive state of affairs.[3] We should, however, notice that while the title "Lord" was not characteristic during the earthly ministry the lordship of Christ was there. The relationship established during the days of His flesh prepared the way for the full use of the title in later times.

The Pharisees[4] have already been mentioned as taking a close interest in John the Baptist (1 : 19, 24). It is not surprising that they took steps to acquaint themselves with Jesus' activities. The situation reflected in 3 : 26 (where see note) is continued here. Jesus drew many more adherents than did John.

2 In an aside the Evangelist makes it clear that, though[5] baptism was practised in Jesus' circle and with His approval,[6] He Himself did not perform[7] the rite. That was left to the disciples.[8]

---

[3] See further J. Gresham Machen, *The Origin of Paul's Religion* (Grand Rapids, 1947), pp. 293-317; G. Vos, *The Self-Disclosure of Jesus* (Grand Rapids, 1954), pp. 118-140; and my *The Lord from Heaven* (London and Grand Rapids, 1958), pp. 55-8, and the literature there cited.

[4] Westcott comments: "It is worthy of notice that St. John never notices (by name) the Sadducees or the Herodians. The Pharisees were the true representatives of the unbelieving nation."

[5] This is John's only use of καίτοι. See on 1 : 5 for his use of καί in the sense of καίτοι.

[6] W. F. Flemington examines the doubt cast by some on the authenticity of this statement *(The New Testament Doctrine of Baptism*, London, 1948, pp. 30f.). He thinks the association of both Jesus and His disciples with the Baptist to be significant. The silence of the Synoptists is understandable for they have nothing to say about this early ministry in Judea, while John does not speak of such baptism as is here recorded at any later period.

[7] The imperfect tense may indicate the habitual practice. *Cf.* Barclay: "although it was not Jesus Himself who was in the habit of baptizing". Godet comments on the significance of Jesus' practice: "By baptizing, He attested the unity of His work with that of the forerunner. By not Himself baptizing, He made the superiority of His position above that of John the Baptist to be felt."

[8] Calvin comments on the significance of baptism by Christian ministers: "He calls Christ's Baptism that which He administered by the hands of others, to teach us that Baptism is not to be valued from the person of the minister, but that its whole force depends on its author, in whose name and by whose command it is administered . . . our Baptism has no less efficacy to cleanse and renew us than if it had been given directly by the Son of God ".

3 John does not say that the Pharisees took any action against Jesus, or even that they were planning any such action.[9] But it is not likely that they would view with equanimity the rapid increase in the number of Jesus' followers. Jesus, however, fore-stalled any action on their part by withdrawing from Judea and setting out for Galilee. He would not precipitate a clash until the right time. Probably also He did not wish to enter into a controversy on baptism. John's word for "left" is unusual in the sense of leaving a place. It often has the meaning "abandon" (as in v. 28 of the woman's waterpot), and there may be something of this meaning here.[10]

(b) Living Water, 4 : 4–14

4 And he must needs pass through Samaria. **5** So he cometh to a city of Samaria, called Sychar, near to the parcel of ground that Jacob gave to his son Joseph: **6** and Jacob's [1]well was there. Jesus therefore, being wearied with his journey, sat [2]thus by the [1]well. It was about the sixth hour. **7** There cometh a woman of Samaria to draw water: Jesus saith unto her, Give me to drink. **8** For his disciples were gone away into the city to buy food. **9** The Samaritan woman therefore saith unto him, How is it that thou, being a Jew, askest drink of me, who am a Samaritan woman? [3](For Jews have no dealings with Samaritans.) **10** Jesus answered and said unto her, If thou knewest the gift of God, and who it

---

[9] E. Stauffer even thinks that the Pharisees were friendly. They had never liked the Baptist, but they "could see an ally in Jesus, the man who observed the sabbath so conscientiously, and who enforced so strictly the prohibitions against carrying anything in the temple area; they spoke amongst themselves with satisfaction of his unparalleled success at his baptism . . . to Jesus this was a sign that he should retire" (*Jesus and His Story*, London, 1960, pp. 62f.). But this seems to me an unlikely reading of the evidence.

[10] The verb is ἀφίημι. Morgan comments: "We should not misinterpret the thought if we said He abandoned Judaea. He did go back, but very seldom. He had been to Judaea. He had gone to the Temple. He had exercised His ministry in the surrounding country with marvellous success; but hostility was stirring there, and He left Judaea; He broke with it". So also Plummer: "First the Temple, then Jerusalem, and now Judaea has to be abandoned, because He can win no welcome." Loyd goes on from this position to notice the relevance of Rom. 11 : 15, "the casting away of them is the reconciling of the world." Jesus goes to Galilee, and goes by way of Samaria. John's use of the verb is unusual in another respect. He employs it with the meaning "forgive" (relatively common elsewhere) only in 20 : 23 in the whole Gospel.

253

is that saith to thee, Give me to drink; thou wouldest have asked of him, and he would have given thee living water. 11 The woman saith unto him, [4]Sir, thou hast nothing to draw with, and the well is deep: whence then hast thou that living water? 12 Art thou greater than our father Jacob, who gave us the well, and drank thereof himself, and his sons, and his cattle? 13 Jesus answered and said unto her, Every one that drinketh of this water shall thirst again: 14 but whosoever drinketh of the water that I shall give him shall never thirst; but the water that I shall give him shall become in him a well of water springing up unto eternal life.

[1]Gr. *spring:* and so in ver. 14; but not in ver. 11, 12 [2]Or, *as he was* Comp. ch. 13. 25. [3]Some ancient authorities omit *For Jews have no dealings with Samaritans.* [4]Or, *Lord*

Nicodemus was an eminent representative of orthodox Judaism. Now John records an interview Jesus had with one who stood for a class which was wholeheartedly despised by orthodox Judaism.[11] The rivalries and hatreds which were meat and drink to the Jews of His day mattered not all at to our Lord. His was a ministry for all men. In the former incident Jesus spoke of the importance of the new birth. Here His theme is the living water which He came to bring to men. The terminology is different, but the basic message is the same.[12] A feature of this story is the way the woman persistently attempts to avoid the issues that Jesus raises. But just as persistently Jesus brings her back to them until finally He secures the desired result.[13]

[11]   There is a useful bibliography on the Samaritans in John Macdonald, *The Theology of the Samaritans* (London, 1964).

[12]   I cannot follow Cullmann when he asserts that this conversation is "concerned in the first instance with worship" *(Early Christian Worship*, London, 1954, p. 80), and in particular with baptism. The references to baptism he regards as "certain" *(op. cit.,* p. 84). It is much more probable that the living water refers to the Holy Spirit (7 : 38f.), and the life He brings. There is a reference to worship, but this is secondary, and, in fact, it is a result of the divine nature and activity.

[13]   Findlay appositely cites Ephrem the Syrian's summary of this incident: "Jesus came to the fountain as a hunter . . . He threw a grain before one pigeon that He might catch the whole flock . . . At the beginning of the conversation He did not make Himself known to her . . . but first she caught sight of a thirsty man, then a Jew, then a Rabbi, afterwards a prophet, last of all the Messiah. She tried to get the better of the thirsty man, she showed her dislike of the Jew, she heckled the Rabbi, she was swept off her feet by the prophet, and she adored the Christ" (Findlay, p. 61).

R. H. Lightfoot points out that there are parallels with the passion narrative. In both we read of Jesus' physical distress (4 : 6; 19 : 1f.), and of His thirst (4 : 7; 19 : 28). In both there is a time note mentioning "the sixth hour" (4 : 7; 19 : 14), and a reference to the completion of His work (4 : 34; 19 : 30; the Greek verbs are related). There may be nothing to all this. Yet in 4 : 42 Jesus is called "the Saviour of the world", and John may accordingly be recalling of set purpose incidents which point to the Passion, wherein man's salvation was wrought out.

4 The necessity for Jesus to pass through Samaria[14] was not absolute. Strict Jews, like the Pharisees, disliked the Samaritans so intensely that they avoided their territory as much as possible.[15] Their route from Jerusalem to Galilee lay through the region beyond the Jordan. This was considerably longer, but it avoided contact with the Samaritans. Those who were not so strict went through Samaria.[16] For those in a hurry the shorter way was a necessity. Josephus uses exactly the expression rendered "must needs" when he says, "for rapid travel, it was essential to take that route (*i.e.* through Samaria)".[17] John may possibly wish us to take the expression in this fashion. More probably the necessity lies in the nature of the mission of Jesus. John often uses the word "must" of this mission (3 : 14; 9 : 4; 10 : 16; 12 : 34; 20 : 9; see

---

[14] There is practically no mention of Samaria in the first two Gospels, but Luke speaks of a journey of our Lord through this region (Luke 9 : 51f.), and of the gratitude of the Samaritan leper (Luke 17 : 15-19), as well as recording the parable of the Good Samaritan. Both Luke and John were very sensitive to the place of the Gentiles, and it is significant that they record Jesus' activities in Samaria. For a very useful account of the Samaritans in general and of the references to them in this Gospel in particular see the article "Samaritan Studies" by J. Bowman, *BJRL*, 40, 1957-58, pp. 298-327; also Macdonald, *op. cit.*

[15] Morgan says that "Those of Judaea practically never travelled to Galilee through Samaria." He thinks that Jesus chose His road "as a protest against their reason for not taking it". This is attractive and may be right. But unfortunately Morgan cites no evidence that the Jews avoided Samaria as a general rule. That strict Jews did so is clear, but the general practice may not have been the same. Less fussy people may not have been prepared to go the extra miles involved.

[16] Josephus says that it was the custom of the Galileans to pass through Samaria when they went up to Jerusalem for the feasts (*Ant.* xx, 118).

[17] *Vit.*, 269.

on 3 : 7). The expression points to a compelling divine necessity. Jesus had come as "the light of the world" (9 : 5). It was imperative that this light shine to others than Jews.

The reason for the hostility of the Jews to the Samaritans goes back a long way. When the Assyrians took Samaria captive they deported large numbers of the inhabitants and replaced them by men from all over their empire (II Kings 17 : 23f.). These people brought their own gods with them (II Kings 17 : 29–31), but they added the worship of Jehovah to their other worships (II Kings 17 : 25, 28, 32f., 41). In time their polytheism disappeared, and they worshipped Jehovah alone, though their religion had its peculiarities. For example, they acknowledged as sacred Scripture only the Pentateuch. They thus cut themselves off from the riches in the Psalms and the Prophets and other books. Their religion was also marked by a pronounced bitterness towards the Jews. When the Jews returned from exile in Babylon the Samaritans offered to help them rebuild their temple but the offer was refused (Ezra 4 : 2f.). This naturally engendered great bitterness. One might have expected that the Jews would have appreciated the fact that the Samaritans worshipped the same God as they did. But it did not work out this way. The Samaritans refused to worship at Jerusalem, preferring their own temple built on Mt. Gerizim c. 400 B.C. When this was burned by the Jews c. 128 B.C. relations between the two groups worsened. Occasions of friction were not lacking, and by New Testament times a settled attitude of hostility had resulted.[18] At the time with which we are dealing then hostility between Jews and Samaritans was bitter and widespread (though not universal). Properly "Samaria" was the name of the capital city, but the term was used also of the territory of which the city was capital. Here the latter, of course, is the meaning. "A woman of Samaria" (v. 7) means a member of the race that inhabited the general area, and not a lady from the city of Samaria (which was many miles away).

---

[18] Something of the feeling between the two groups may be gauged from the words of Ben Sira: "With two nations my soul is vexed, and the third is no nation: those who live on Mount Seir, and the Philistines, and the foolish people that dwell in Shechem" (Sir. 50 : 25f.).

5 Sychar is perhaps to be identified with the village called Askar, near Shechem.[19] There is a reference to Jacob's buying of a piece of ground in this vicinity (Gen. 33 : 19). He also gave some land to Joseph (Gen. 48 : 22), and he was buried there (Josh. 24 : 32). There is no Old Testament reference to his having dug a well there, but there is nothing improbable about it.

6 The word for "well"[20] is not the usual one (which is used later, vv. 11, 12). It signifies rather a spring or fountain. As applied to a well it may mean a well fed by a spring. But probably we should not look for too great precision. Some think that the choice of word is linked with the "well of water springing up unto eternal life" (v. 14), where the other word would be impossible. But as this water is contrasted with that the reason is not exactly impressive.

The well top was apparently furnished with a wooden or stone surround, which formed a seat for the weary traveller. In speaking of the weariness of Jesus our Evangelist points to His true humanity. While he consistently depicts the full deity of Jesus, he is insistent

---

[19] Biblical Shechem is the modern Balata, near Nablus. Some suggest that Sychar was really Shechem, Sychar being a mocking corruption, meaning either "drunken-town" (שִׁכָּר) or "lying-town" (שֶׁקֶר). Against this are the facts that *(a)* we know of nothing to justify either title, and *(b)* from early times Sychar has been distinguished from Shechem. W. F. Albright argues that the town was Shechem and that the corruption into Sychar was accidental (so also Brown). He regards the evidence of the Old Syriac as significant and accounts for the differentiation between the two places by the fact that Shechem was destroyed *c.* A.D. 67 and rebuilt a few miles away under the name Neapolis (corrupted to the modern Nablus). See *The Archaeology of Palestine* (Harmondsworth, 1949), pp. 247f.; *BNT*, p. 160. R. D. Potter favors Askar. Of the topographical references in this chapter he says, "No passage could show better that our author knew this bit of Samaria well" *(SE*, I, p. 331). *The Westminster Historical Atlas* opposite "Sychar" has " 'Askar?" On the whole it seems as though Askar is the most probable site.

[20] πηγή. The other word is φρέαρ. On the difference between the two Loyd comments: "A spring is a God-given thing. God creates the spring; man only digs the well". It is a curiosity that such a deep well should have been dug in a country where there are many springs. (Godet says that there are as many as eighty springs in the region.) The well must originally have been well over a hundred feet deep, so that digging and lining it was no small task. This has been worked into an argument that the well really was dug by Jacob. Only "a stranger in the land" would have gone to all the trouble to construct such a well in a land as plentifully endowed with springs! Many commentators give the depth of the well as about seventy-five feet, but according to Hendriksen a great deal of debris has been cleaned out and the well restored to its original depth.

also that He really became man, with all that that means in terms of human limitation. "Thus" may mean "being thus tired", or possibly, "thus as He was", *i.e.* without selecting a good place. Chrysostom explains it as "Not upon a throne, not upon a cushion, but simply, and as He was, upon the ground."[21] The note of time is quite in the Johannine manner (see on 1 : 39). The sixth hour is noon on our reckoning, which seems an unusual time for a woman to be drawing water, for sunset seems to have been the favored hour. However, we should not overlook the fact that Josephus speaks of the damsels that Moses helped (Exod. 2 : 15ff.) as coming to draw water at noon,[22] so the custom was not unknown. Another strange feature in the present narrative is that the woman should have come to this well at all. There was plentiful water nearer her home. It may be that the water at Jacob's well was thought to be of better quality. More likely there was some superstitious veneration for a place hallowed by associations with the patriarch. But the woman had a bad reputation, and the explanation may be very simple – she chose the time and the place to avoid other women.

7-9 It was probably Jesus' weariness that led the disciples to leave Him while they went into the village to buy food. He was thus at the well, possibly alone, when the woman came to draw water. He asked for a drink (the impossibility of His providing for His own need is brought out in v. 11[23]). On this request Godet sagely remarks, "He is not unaware that the way to gain a soul is often to ask a service of it". Yet we should not think of this as simply a device to get into conversation. Jesus really was thirsty. But His request startled the woman into asking, "What? You are a Jew, and you ask me for a drink – me, a Samaritan!" (Moffatt). That He should ask a woman for water is perhaps not so very surprising, since it was women who generally drew water.[24] But this particular request involved using the Samaritan woman's utensil, and Jews could be very scrupulous about contracting defilement. The words, "For Jews have no dealings with Samar-

---

[21] XXXI. 3; p. 109.
[22] *Ant.* ii, 257ff.
[23] Any band of travellers would probably have an ἄντλημα or skin-bucket for drawing water. But in this case the disciples would have had it with them.
[24] Yet the Rabbinic attitude to talking with women was very strict. See on v. 27.

itans", are probably the Evangelist's comment and not part of the
woman's speech. The expression seems to refer to the use of vessels
for food or drink.[25] The customary rendering "have no dealings
with" is difficult to sustain. For the narrative informs us that the
disciples had gone into the village to buy food.[26] It is hard to see
what meaning we are to put into "have dealings with" if it does
not cover buying food, all the more so in view of the importance
attached to food laws by the Jews.

10 Jesus immediately lifts the conversation to a higher plane by
speaking of God's gift, and of seeking "living water". His word

---

[25] The verb συγχράομαι has usually been understood here in the sense "to
have familiar intercourse with". However D. Daube has shown that this sense
is not found elsewhere and that it is highly unlikely in the present passage (*JBL*,
LXIX, 1950, pp. 137-47). The verb means properly, "to use with", and this
appears to be the meaning in the present passage. Jews do not use (utensils) with
Samaritans. This was built into a regulation in A.D. 65 or 66: "The daughters of
the Samaritans (deemed unclean as) menstruants from their cradle"
(Mishnah, *Nidd.* 4 : 1), *i.e.* they are all regarded as ceremonially unclean. Barrett
finds a difficulty in the date of promulgation. However, such regulations do not
spring from thin air, and the saying before us indicates that there must have been
widespread Jewish scruples in Jesus' time. But it is difficult to be sure of exactly
how Jews viewed Samaritans. On the one hand if three men eat together we are
told that they must say the Common Grace and a Samaritan may be included
in the number (*Ber.* 7 : 1). Similarly "They may answer 'Amen' after an Israelite
who says a Benediction, but not after a Samaritan until they have heard the
whole Benediction" (*Ber.* 8 : 8). This presupposes that Jews and Samaritans eat
together. Samaritans and the '*Am-ha'aretz* are classed together as distinct from
Gentiles, even if not completely acceptable (*Dem.* 3 : 4). On the other hand,
R. Eliezer used to say: "He that eats the bread of the Samaritans is like to one
that eats the flesh of swine" (*Shebi.* 8 : 10). Again, Samaritans may offer free will
offerings, but not any statutory offering (*Shek.* 1 : 5); and further, "No writ is
valid which has a Samaritan as witness excepting a writ of divorce or a writ of
emancipation" (*Gitt.* 1 : 5). Danby summarizes the complicated situation as
"*(a)* a Samaritan conveys uncleanness by what he lies, sits, or rides on, by his
spittle (including the phlegm of his lungs, throat, or nose) and by his urine; and
(b) the daughters of the Samaritans even from their cradles (convey uncleanness
in like manner), as also do the gentiles" (Danby, p. 803; see also SBk, I, pp.
538-60).

[26] τροφάς. This is the only place in the New Testament where the word is
used in the plural, though the singular is common. We cannot conclude from the
fact that the disciples were buying food that the laws about uncleanness were
being disregarded, for certain dry foods did not convey defilement. It was otherwise with water and wet foods.

for "gift" (here only in the Gospels) stresses the freeness of it all.[27] It is a matter of bounty. Jesus is referring to the new life He brings. Had the woman been aware of the realities of the situation in which she found herself, and especially of the fact that she was speaking to Him whom God had sent to give life to the world, the asking would have been the other way round.[28] This is indicated by the use of the emphatic "thou". In the ordinary usage of the time "living water" was water that flowed. It was water in a river or stream as against water in a pond or cistern, which did not flow. This usage is almost invariable. And it is worth noting that, while the Rabbis freely use "water" in a metaphorical sense,[29] they rarely employ "living water" in this way.[30] For the meaning of the present passage there may possibly be significance in the fact that "living water", water that flowed, was greatly preferred for purposes of ritual purification. It was "living water" that took away defilement and made acceptable worshippers out of unclean men. But Jesus is giving the expression a deeper meaning than that. In 7 : 38f. the living water that flows from within the believer is explained in terms of the Holy Spirit. Something similar is required here. Jesus is speaking of the new life that He will give, a life connected with the activity of the Spirit. Notice that, although Jesus calls Himself "the bread of life" (6 : 35), He does not refer to Himself as the living water. Living water rather symbolizes the Spirit,[31] whom He would send, than the Christ Himself. Odeberg shows that in a number of

[27] δωρεά. The accusative δωρεάν occurs elsewhere as an adverb with the meaning "freely", but this is the only place in any of the Gospels where the noun is found in the sense "free gift".

[28] *Cf.* Stauffer: "The spiritual man understands the wisdom of God's way, he recognizes the hidden plan of salvation which comes to its climax in the cross, and he lays hold of the *beneficia* of God" (I Cor. 2. 1–16; John 4. 10)" *(NTT,* p. 173). But the woman was not in this sense "spiritual".

[29] For the Rabbinic use see SBk, II, pp. 433–36. The Rabbis sometimes refer to the Holy Spirit when they use "water" metaphorically, but more often to the Torah.

[30] Actually we sometimes come quite close to it in the Old Testament, *e.g.* "The law of the wise is a fountain of life" (Prov. 13 : 14); "The words of a man's mouth are as deep waters; the wellspring of wisdom is as a flowing brook" (Prov. 18 : 4). Macdonald informs us that "living water" is common in a sense like that in John in Samaritan writers *(op. cit.,* p. 425).

[31] *Cf.* the Qumran teaching, "Like purifying waters He will sprinkle upon him the spirit of truth" (1 QS, iv, 21).

Jewish writings water symbolizes teaching or doctrine.[32] It seems likely that the primary meaning here is the Holy Spirit. But, in the manner so typical of this Gospel, there may be also a reference to Jesus' teaching. If so, it will be to His teaching as issuing forth in spiritual life.[33]

In the Old Testament living water is sometimes associated with Jehovah. He is called "the fountain of living waters" (Jer. 2 : 13; 17 : 13). Again, an invitation can be issued in these terms: "Ho, every one that thirsteth, come ye to the waters" (Isa. 55 : 1). We should also bear in mind the waters that issued from the temple in Ezekiel's vision (Ezek. 47 : 1-12; perhaps the application of "a fountain of gardens" and "a well of living waters" to the bride is also relevant, Song 4 : 15). With Jehovah "is the fountain of life" (Ps. 36 : 9). We should not miss the claim implied in Jesus' words.

11, 12 Up to this point the woman has no desire to talk about profound spiritual realities. She accordingly chooses to understand Jesus' words as referring to nothing more than water of the kind that she came to draw (for similar misunderstandings see on 2 : 20). "Sir" (see on v. 1) is a respectful form of address, and may be meant to put a polite barrier between them. The well[34] is so deep (about a hundred feet) that it would be impracticable to secure water from it without some implement for drawing it up. And, as the woman points out, Jesus has nothing of the sort.

---

[32] *FG*, pp. 149-69. Some of the passages are striking, *e.g.* "And speaking *waters* . . . drew near my lips from the *fountain of the Lord* . . . plenteously. And I *drank* and was inebriated with *living water* that *doth not die*" *(Od. Sol.,* xi. 6f.; *op. cit.,* p. 156). The Qumran covenanters say explicitly "The well is the law", but they add, "and those who dug it are the captivity of Israel, who went out from the land of Judah and sojourned in the land of Damascus" *(DSS,* p. 353). They can also speak of apostates who "departed from the well of living water" *(DSS,* p. 356). R. E. Brown can say, "For Qumran the water of life comes from the community's discipline and lore; for John it is given by Christ to those who believe in him " *(SNT,* p. 200).

[33] Water was widely connected with life in antiquity, and this is rooted in the very language. Thus ἀλίβας, "a dead body", was apparently derived from ἀ-privative and λιβάς, "a stream", "water" (see LS), while σκελετός, "skeleton", has the notion of "dried up" *(cf.* σκέλλω, "to parch"). Jesus' symbolism is very natural and would have a wide appeal.

[34] The word is φρέαρ, a change from πηγή in v. 6. There is a similar change in Gen. 16 : 7, 14, where the source of water is first called "a fountain" and then "the well". So also with Gen. 24 : 11, 13, 16, where we have "well", "fountain", "fountain". In all these passages where the English has "well", LXX has πηγή and where the English has "fountain" LXX has φρέαρ, the same two Greek words as in our passage.

She sees a further reason for scepticism in the unimportance of her acquaintance. To her way of thinking there was nothing extraordinary about Him. So she asks whether He is greater than Jacob, renowned as the great progenitor of the race,[35] and particularly important in the present connection, since he was responsible for the well. "Thou" is emphatic. The woman is incredulous. The people of the day had a deep reverence for Abraham (*cf.* 8 : 53, where Jesus is similarly asked whether He is greater than Abraham), Isaac, and Jacob. The claims Jesus made sometimes seemed to them to imply that He was greater than these patriarchs. In their eyes this was impossible. If He made the claim He was automatically wrong. In the woman's attitude there appears to be something of a sense of outrage. She was content with her patriarchal well. How dare a mere stranger claim to produce anything better than that? "The woman does not know, as the readers of the gospel do (and the irony of the situation is characteristic of John), that Jesus is greater than Jacob because he gives water better by far".[36]

13, 14 Jesus' response contrasts the impermanent result of drinking water from the well with the permanent consequences of receiving water from Him.[37] Water from Jacob's well might quench a

[35] Josephus tells us that the Samaritans claimed to be descended from Joseph, through Ephraim and Manasseh (*Ant.* xi, 341). Jesus, however, referred to the Samaritan leper as ἀλλογενής, "of another race" (Luke 17 : 18). Yet it should not be overlooked that neither here nor in v. 20 where the woman refers to "our fathers" does Jesus deny the claim as He does that of the Jews in 8 : 39ff. Odeberg comments: "The Samaritan woman, who is ready, seemingly, to desert her traditional religion (vs. 15b), is in reality faithful towards the element of truth received from the fathers, whereas the Jews, who were apparently unswervingly loyal to the inheritance from their father Abraham and to the Tora of Moses, in opposition to the demands of J (*i.e.* Jesus), had already severed themselves spiritually and intrinsically from the way of Abraham and the Tora of Moses" (*FG*, pp. 178f.). On the appeal to a great one of the past Ryle pungently remarks, "Dead teachers have always more authority than living ones" (on 6 : 31).

[36] Barrett. MacGregor thinks that the woman came to this well, "Possibly because of 'the fondness of tradition which . . . drew Jacob's fanatic children to its scantier supplies' (G. A. Smith, p. 374); for the same reason, John may have felt, that men cling to dead ritual when they might draw from the Spirit of the living Christ "(on v. 7).

[37] Note the contrast between the present participle, πᾶς ὁ πίνων ("everyone who drinks continually"), and the aorist subjunctive, ὃς δ'ἂν πίῃ ("whoever has drunk once for all"). Abbott sees the contrast between "the multitude of those that go wrong" and "the individual that goes right" (2574).

thirst, but it could not prevent thirst from rising again. The living water that Jesus gives is such that those who receive it are permanently satisfied (*cf.* Matt. 5 : 6).[38] The living water becomes in them a vigorous stream (the word for "well"[39] is that used in v. 6, where see note) issuing forth in eternal life (see on 1 : 4; 3 : 15). The movement of a fountain is brought out in the vigorous "springing up"[40] (or "leaping"; the word in a compound form is used of the formerly lame man leaping up, Acts 3 : 8). The life that Jesus gives is no tame and stagnant thing. It is much more than merely the entrance into a new state, that of being saved instead of lost. It is the abundant life (10 : 10), and the living Spirit within men is evidence of this. It is more than possible that the words are also an indication that the life within believers goes forth (*cf.* 7 : 38; Isa. 58 : 11). Life has a way of begetting life.

(c) The Woman and her Husbands, 4 : 15-19

15 The woman saith unto him, ¹Sir, give me this water, that I thirst not, neither come all the way hither to draw. 16 Jesus saith unto her, Go, call thy husband, and come hither. 17 The woman answered and said unto him, I have no husband. Jesus saith unto her, Thou saidst well, I have no husband: 18 for thou hast had five husbands; and he whom thou now hast is not thy husband: this hast thou said truly. 19 The woman saith unto him, ¹Sir, I perceive that thou art a prophet.

¹ Or, *Lord*

---

38 Calvin notes that this does not exclude a legitimate thirsting after God: "Christ's words do not contradict the fact that believers to the very end of their lives ardently desire more abundant grace. For He does not mean that we drink so that we are fully satisfied from the very first day, but only that the Holy Spirit is a constantly flowing well. So there is no danger of those who are renewed by spiritual grace becoming dry."

39 On the contrast between φρέαρ and πηγή Strachan comments: "A contrast is intended which goes deeper than the natural one between 'spring' and 'pit'. It is between the 'water of life', and the human labour that is spent on conserving it by means of traditional institutions." R. H. Lightfoot asks, "Is it possible, therefore, that in St. John's thought Jacob's Well can be described by the more living word until the coming of the Lord, but that with His arrival it becomes no better than a cistern, in contrast to the fount of springing water which His coming brings?"

40 The verb is ἅλλομαι, which does not appear to be used elsewhere of the action of water. There may be here the thought of the Spirit as working violently within a man.

Up till this point it is probable that the woman was not serious. Perhaps she thought of the Stranger as a little mad, and humored Him accordingly. But there is no indication that she took seriously the important things He has been saying. Jesus now proceeds to show such knowledge of her and her affairs that she is startled into the recognition that He is more than He seems.

15 If the woman has any inkling of the meaning Jesus is giving the living water she chooses not to display it (*cf.* the way Nicodemus took the new birth literally, 3 : 4). She understands His words with a crass literalism, and asks for the water "that I thirst not, neither come all the way hither to draw." Her concern is with her own personal convenience. It would be a pleasant thing not to have the necessity for frequent journeys to the well nor for the labor of drawing. Though the thing is impossible it is a pleasant thought to play with.

16-18 Jesus' request that she go and fetch her husband has no apparent connection with what precedes.[41] It is best taken as His way of bringing the woman's sin into the open. He is met with the curt response that she has no husband. "Her volubility is checked: in the fewest possible words she tries to stop a dangerous subject at once" (Plummer). Jesus' reply is devastating.[42] It shows that He knows all about her misadventures. He knows that she has had five husbands and that the man with whom she now lives is not her husband. This may mean that she had availed herself liberally of the provisions for divorce, but that after all that she was living with a man who was not legally her husband.[43]

---

[41] Temple, however, does find a logical sequence. He connects Jesus' words with the woman's request for the water for her own convenience (v. 15): "But the *gift of God* (10) cannot be received to be merely enjoyed. It must always be shared ... If we are not sharing with others the gift of God, that is proof that we have not received it. So the Lord tells this woman to call the person with whom she would naturally share first."

[42] Although the woman had said, $O\mathring{v}\varkappa\ \mathring{\varepsilon}\chi\omega\ \mathring{a}\nu\delta\varrho a$, Jesus reports her words as $"A\nu\delta\varrho a\ o\mathring{v}\varkappa\ \mathring{\varepsilon}\chi\omega$, thus putting an emphasis on $\mathring{a}\nu\delta\varrho a$. Similarly $\pi\acute{\varepsilon}\nu\tau\varepsilon$ is stressed.

[43] A woman could not divorce her husband in Jewish law. But under certain circumstances she could approach the court which would, if it thought fit, compel the husband to divorce her (see, for example, Mishnah, *Ket.* 7 : 9, 10). Or she might pay him or render services to induce him to divorce her (*Git.* 7 : 5, 6). In theory there was no limit to the number of marriages that might be contracted after valid divorces, but the Rabbis regarded two, or at the most three marriages as the maximum for a woman (SBk, II, p. 437).

Or it may mean, in accordance with the standards taught by Jesus (*e.g.* Matt. 19 : 3-9), that the last union that the woman had contracted was not really a marriage. In either case the woman recognized that she was in the wrong. How did Jesus know all about her? Some maintain that the conversation is not reported in full, and that she told Him herself. While it is not likely that John has recorded everything that was said, this inference is precarious, especially in view of v. 29, "Come, see a man, who told me all things that ever I did." It is more likely that we have here an example of Jesus' more than human knowledge which John reveals to us from time to time. This does not cast any reflection on His genuine humanity, but it does indicate that there was revealed to Him all that was needful for His ministry.[44]

Some interpret the five husbands allegorically and see a reference to the false gods brought to Samaria by the colonists of II Kings 17 : 24. They suggest that Samaria now professed to worship Jehovah, but He was not "thy husband".[45] But this interpretation will scarcely hold. In the first place, though it is true that five nations are mentioned in II Kings 17 : 24, the fact is that when their gods are listed in II Kings 17 : 30f. there are seven

---

[44] Similar to this passage are those telling us that Jesus knew that Lazarus was dead (11 : 14), and that Peter would deny Him (13 : 38). Not very different is His foreknowledge of the feeding of the multitude (6 : 6) and of what would befall Him after the arrest (18 : 4). He knew the truth of witness borne of Him (5 : 32). He knew His sheep (10 : 14, 27). He knew who did not believe, and who would betray Him, and He knew this "from the beginning" (6 : 64). He knew the extent of the Father's gift to Him (13 : 3). Above all He had such a knowledge of the Father as no one else could have (7 : 29; 8 : 55; 10 : 15; 17 : 25). Plainly the knowledge John attributes to Jesus is part of the way in which he shows us the divine Christ.

[45] *Cf.* Wright: "What, therefore, the Evangelist wishes to say here, is to remind his readers of the 'religious adultery' of Samaria's past, personified in this 'woman of Samaria,' and of the 'irregular' union of Samaria in the time of our Lord to the service and worship of Jehovah." J. Estlin Carpenter thinks that "the figure may outwardly imply the supernatural knowledge of the Incarnate Son; but inwardly it points (as has long been recognised) to the gods brought by the five groups of settlers transported from Mesopotamia by the Assyrian conquerors". He rejects the reference of "the contemporary who was no true husband" to Jehovah, and favors "some representative of false teaching." As possible candidates he cites Dositheus (mentioned by Jerome) and Simon Magus (*The Johannine Writings*, London, 1927, p. 245). Augustine reports that some interpret the passage of the five books of Moses. He himself understands it of the five senses of the body (XV. 21; p. 104).

of them.[46] The number is wrong. Moreover the false gods in II
Kings are not worshipped one after another (as the husbands
followed one another), but simultaneously. Again, it is impossible
to think that Jesus (or John) thought of the false gods as the
legitimate husbands of the Samaritans and held that Jehovah,
the one true God, was no "husband" at all, but a paramour.
Moreover it is difficult to see how John's readers could have been
expected to detect such an allusion. It is much better to take the
passage literally, as a factual statement[47] about the men with
whom the woman had lived.

19 What Jesus has just said has forced on the woman the realization that He is no ordinary being. She gives expression to this
conviction by calling Him a "prophet". The function of a prophet
in the Scriptures was usually to tell forth a message he had from
God. But there is evidence that among the people of this time a
prophet was sometimes held to have special insight into men's
condition (*cf.* Luke 7 : 39, "This man, if he were a prophet, would
have perceived who and what manner of woman this is that
toucheth him"). It is also possible that the woman was already
groping towards the recognition that Jesus was the Christ. The
Samaritans acknowledged no prophet after Moses other than the
one spoken of in Deut. 18 : 18, and him they regarded as the
Messiah (see further on 1 : 21). For her to speak of Jesus as a
prophet was thus to move into the area of messianic speculation.

(d) True Worship, 4 : 20–26

20 Our fathers worshipped in this mountain; and ye say,
that in Jerusalem is the place where men ought to worship.
21 Jesus saith unto her, Woman, believe me, the hour cometh,

---

[46] It is often said that Josephus refers to the number of gods as five. This
is not so. He says that there were five tribes and that each brought its own
god (*Ant.* ix, 288). It might be inferred that there were five gods, but Josephus
does not say so. We could draw the same inference from II Kings 17 : 29.
But when we turn to v. 30 we find not five gods, but seven. This kind of inference
is precarious.

[47] Abbott says that τοῦτο ἀληθὲς εἴρηκας is quite different from τοῦτο
ἀληθῶς εἴρηκας. The latter might mean, "*Truly*, i.e. *in truth*, thou hast said
this", or, "Thou hast said this *truly*, i.e. *with truth*." John's expression, however,
means " '*This*, *at all events*, among all that thou hast said, is true' – implying
that hitherto the woman has talked in a reckless and trifling way" (1894).

when neither in this mountain, nor in Jerusalem, shall ye
worship the Father. 22 Ye worship that which ye know not:
we worship that which we know; for salvation is from the
Jews. 23 But the hour cometh, and now is, when the true
worshippers shall worship the Father in spirit and truth: ¹for
such doth the Father seek to be his worshippers. 24 ²God
is a Spirit: and they that worship him must worship in spirit
and truth. 25 The woman saith unto him, I know that Messiah
cometh (he that is called Christ): when he is come, he will
declare unto us all things. 26 Jesus saith unto her, I that
speak unto thee am he.

¹Or, *for such the Father also seeketh* ²Or, *God is spirit*

The woman may have been genuinely interested in the topic
she now raises. She is clearly impressed by Jesus. She has recognized Him as a prophet. The right place for worship was a
prominent topic of dispute between Samaritans and Jews. She
may have been genuinely interested in what a prophet would say
about this ancient and bitter controversy. But it seems more
probable that she is simply trying to change the subject. She
wants to steer the conversation away from the unpleasant subject
of her sin. So she introduces a distraction. She points to the different
ideas held by Jews and Samaritans about the place God has
chosen in which men may worship Him. But this gambit serves
to open up the way for Jesus to speak of the essential nature of
God and of the worship that should be offered Him. Genuine
worship is spiritual. It is not dependent on places and things.⁴⁸
20 The woman introduces her controversial topic. As we saw
earlier (on v, 4), there was bitter division between Jews and
Samaritans over the rival claims of Jerusalem and Gerizim as

---

⁴⁸ In these verses the verb προσκυνέω is used absolutely (v. 20), with the
dative (vv. 21, 23), and with the accusative (v. 23; this is unusual). It seems
that these variations are stylistic only. Abbott thinks that there is a difference
between the last two, the construction with the dative signifying prostration
(before God or man), bowing down *to*, and that with the accusative indicating
adoration, worship proper to God alone (*Johannine Vocabulary*, London, 1905,
1640–51). Moulton also sees a distinction (M, I, p. 66). But few recent writers
agree. In view of John's habit of introducing slight variations without distinction
of meaning (see on 3 : 5) the differences should not be pressed.

places for worship. Both the building of the temple on Mt. Gerizim (which the Jews regarded as an illegitimate rival to the only temple there could be, that in Jerusalem) and its destruction increased the bitterness between the two peoples. The woman, now convinced that Jesus was a prophet, but unwilling to apply His message to herself, refers to this great religious division. "Our fathers" points back to the building of altars in this region by Abraham (Gen. 12 : 7), and Jacob (Gen. 33 : 20). Mt. Gerizim was the scene of the blessing of the people (Deut. 11 : 29; 27 : 12). The Samaritans also read in their Bibles that an altar was commanded to be set up in this mountain (Deut. 27 : 4ff.).[49] They had a tradition that Abraham's offering of Isaac took place on this mountain. They held that it was here that Abraham met Melchizedek. In fact, most of the blessed events in the time of the patriarchs seem to have been linked with Gerizim! The Samaritans were assisted in this by seeing references to their holy mountain in such expressions as "the house of God", "the goodly mount", *etc.*[50] All these associations, added to the building of the temple on this height, made it a place especially holy for the Samaritans.[51] "Ye" is in emphatic opposition to "our fathers". Far from accepting all this the Jews held that men must (so, rather than "ought to") worship in Jerusalem.[52] They held that

---

[49] It is usually agreed that MT is correct in reading "Mount Ebal", and that the Samaritans have altered the text to suit their own purposes. This may well be the case. But it should not be overlooked that the reverse procedure is also possible. If Gerizim were original it might well have been altered by the Jews as part of an anti-Samaritan polemic.

[50] The Samaritans thought there were thirteen different names for their holy mountain. Where any of them occurs in Scripture they applied the passage to Gerizim. See J. Macdonald, *op. cit.*, pp. 327–33 for Samaritan views about Gerizim.

[51] The feelings aroused by controversy may be gauged from the following incident: "R. Ishmael b. Jose was going up to Jerusalem to pray. He was walking past a plane tree (by Gerizim) where a Samaritan found him. He said to him, 'Where are you going?' He answered, "I am going up to Jerusalem to pray.' The former said, 'Would it not be better for you to pray in this blessed mountain rather than in that dunghill?' " (SBk, I, p. 549).

[52] SBk cite a midrash on Ps. 91: "He who prays in Jerusalem is as one who prays before the throne of glory; for there is the gate of heaven and the open door to the hearing of prayer" (II, p. 437).

the Law teaches that there can be only one place for the temple (Deut. 12 : 5). Though it is not specifically said in the Pentateuch that Jerusalem was this one place, this is laid down in other parts of Scripture (II Chron. 6 : 6; 7 : 12; Ps. 78 : 68). These passages carried conviction to Jews. But they meant nothing to the Samaritans, for they acknowledged no writings as sacred save the Pentateuch.

21 For "Woman" as a form of address see on 2 : 4. Jesus refuses to be drawn into an argument. Rather He solemnly predicts that a time is coming when worship will be possible in neither place. There may be a reference to the troubled times that lay ahead for the whole region of Palestine (*cf.* Luke 21 : 20ff., *etc.*). God is often called "the Father" in this Gospel (see on 1 : 14). Usually, however, it is the Father of Jesus Christ that is meant. Here He is thought of as the Father of all. The woman had appealed to the example of "our fathers". Jesus points her to the one Father.

22 Jesus' concern is with the essential nature of worship. He accordingly points out to the woman the inadequacy of Samaritan worship. Though they worshipped the true God the Samaritans did so very imperfectly. When we consider that they rejected the writings of the prophets, the psalms, the historical books of the Old Testament and much more we see that their knowledge of God was, of necessity, very limited. Jesus says that they do not know what they worship (*cf.* Acts 17 : 23).[53] Both His "ye" and His "we" are emphatic. He sets Jews and Samaritans in sharp contrast. And He associates Himself quite definitely with the Jews.[54] They do know what they worship. Jesus uses the neuter,

---

[53] *Cf.* Calvin: "we are not to essay anything in religion rashly or unthinkingly. For unless there is knowledge present, it is not God that we worship but a spectre or ghost. Hence all so-called good intentions are struck by this thunderbolt, which tells us that men can do nothing but err when they are guided by their own opinion without the Word or command of God." On v. 20 he has said, "The Samaritans took the example of the fathers as a precedent; the Jews were grounded on the commandment of God."

[54] *Cf.* Bernard: "Jesus, here, definitely associates Himself with the Jews; He *is* a Jew. Their God is His God. Nowhere in the Gospels is there another passage so emphatic as this, in its assertion of the common nationality of Jesus and the Jews who rejected Him". In passing we may notice that John possibly recorded this saying with a certain form of heretical teaching in mind. Some held that the God of the Old Testament was an inferior being. Jesus fully accepts the Old Testament and rules out any such interpretation.

"that which", and not the masculine, "him whom", as might have been expected.[55] This may point to the whole system of worship (*cf.* Goodspeed: "You worship something you know nothing about"), and not confine itself specifically to the knowledge of God. The reason for the superior knowledge of the Jews is that salvation comes from among them. This might perhaps be understood to mean that men enter salvation by following the Jewish system rather than that of the Samaritans. But, quite apart from the difficulty of fitting this into Jesus' teaching as a whole, there is an article with "salvation" which is probably significant. It is "the" salvation of which Jesus speaks. That is to say, the messianic salvation comes from this nation. The Messiah is a Jew.[56]

23 It is probable that in this verse Jesus is pointing to the new way that He would inaugurate. "The hour cometh, and now is" is a reference to a crisis, to something new. It cannot be taken simply as the enunciation of a principle that was always true (though this, in fact, in this instance is the case; but that is not what Jesus is emphasizing). Disputes between Jews and Samaritans will fade away. Men will worship on neither pattern. Jesus has already spoken of the destruction of the temple (2 : 19ff.). Primarily He referred to the destruction of the temple of His body, but, as we saw there, there is probably also a reference to the new system of worship which Jesus would inaugurate, a system not tied to any particular holy place. So here He teaches that the distinction of which the woman speaks is outmoded.

True[57] worshippers worship "in spirit and truth". It is not likely that "spirit" refers to the Holy Spirit (though the Spirit does help our worship, Rom. 8 : 26ff.). It is the human spirit that Jesus means. A man must worship, not simply outwardly by being in the right place and taking up the right attitude, but in

---

[55] Murray thinks that the significance of this is that "In neither case did worship rise to the height of personal communion."

[56] *Cf.* Lenski: "Though in the Greek abstract nouns may have the article as a matter of course, here 'the salvation' denotes the specific and only salvation contemplated in God's promises and to be realized in his incarnate Son. This salvation is in no way promised to the Samaritans, so that it would emanate from their midst, but to the Jews alone. The Messiah could not be a Samaritan, he had to be a Jew."

[57] For ἀληθινοί see on 1 : 9. On only two occasions in this Gospel does attributive ἀληθινός precede its noun, so it must be regarded as emphatic in these two places (here and at 17 : 3).

his spirit. For "truth" see Additional Note D, pp. 293ff. The combination "spirit and truth"[58] points to the need for complete sincerity and complete reality in our approach to God. There is an important point in the concluding statement that the Father seeks such[59] "to be his worshippers".[60] It is not simply that He accepts such worship when it is brought to Him. He is a God of love, a God who seeks the best for men, and therefore a God who actively seeks men out.[61]

24 We should omit the indefinite article before "Spirit" (with Moffatt, Goodspeed, Rieu, *etc.*; Knox curiously retains it). Greek has no such article, and we insert it or not in English as the sense requires. Here Jesus is not saying, "God is one spirit among many". Rather His meaning is, "God's essential nature is spirit". The indefinite article is no more required than it is in the similar statements, "God is light" (I John 1 : 5), and "God is love" (I John 4 : 8). We must not think of God as material, or bound in any way to places or things. The word order puts an emphasis on "Spirit". The statement is emphatic. Since He is essentially spirit it follows that the worship brought to Him must be essentially of a spiritual kind. Notice the "must". Jesus is not speaking

---

[58] Both here and in v. 24 the expression is ἐν πνεύματι καὶ ἀληθείᾳ. The linking of the two nouns under a single preposition shows that they belong together. There is one complex idea. E. C. Blackman sees the expression as demanding worship "conformable to the divine nature which is spirit, and determined by the truth which God has made available concerning himself. Here again the thought of Jesus as the personal embodiment of truth is not far away . . . in so far as men see the truth in Jesus they will both worship and live acceptably to God, but such worship and conduct are not possible apart from Jesus" (*TWBB*, p. 270). *Cf.* Westcott: "Worship is necessarily limited by the idea of the being worshipped. A true idea of God, even if still διὰ κατόπτρον, is essential to a right service of Him."

[59] There is an ambiguity connected with τοιούτους. The meaning might be, "the Father seeks such to be his worshippers", or, "The Father seeks that his worshippers be such". Most take the former meaning, but Phillips translates, "Indeed, the Father looks for men who will worship Him like that."

[60] For the unusual accusative after προσκυνέω see n. 48 above.

[61] That God seeks men is a new and distinctively Christian idea. *Cf.* C. G. Montefiore's comment on the parable of the lost sheep: "The virtues of repentance are gloriously praised in the Rabbinical literature, but this direct search for, and appeal to, the sinner, are new and moving notes of high import and significance. The good shepherd who searches for the lost sheep, and reclaims it and rejoices over it, is a new figure" (*The Synoptic Gospels*, II, London, 1909, p. 985).

merely of a desirable element in worship. He is speaking of something that is absolutely necessary. In view of the references to living water (which symbolizes the life-giving Spirit) in the context it is probable that this verse contains an allusion to the life-giving activity of God. This is all the more likely in that when the Old Testament refers to the Spirit of God, the usual idea is that of divine activity, not of opposition to things material. John not infrequently combines the ideas of Spirit and life (*cf.* 6 : 63). God is a living God. Since He is ceaselessly active as the life-giving Spirit He must be worshipped in a manner befitting such a Spirit. Man cannot dictate the "how" or the "where" of worship. He must come only in the way that the Spirit of God opens to him.[62] 25 This appears to be the woman's last attempt to evade the challenge Jesus is forcing upon her. She does not dispute what He has been saying. But her "He" is emphatic. It suggests that these are matters which really come within the province of none but Messiah (for this term see on 1 : 20, 41). There are messianic prophecies in the Pentateuch, and thus the Samaritans expected the Messiah. But their rejection of the rest of the Old Testament meant that their information about Him was meagre.[63]

---

[62] *Cf.* G. S. Hendry: "it has commonly been taken to mean that God, being Spirit, is present everywhere and can be worshiped anywhere; the important thing is not where men worship, but how they worship." This he vigorously denies. The saying "means the precise opposite; it means that God is present in his own realm, to which man as such has no access. To worship God in spirit is not a possibility that is always and everywhere open to man . . . But this is just the gospel of Christ, that this possibility has now been opened to men . . . The meaning is that the location has been redefined, and God is now to be worshiped in the place where he is present, i.e., in Him who is the truth incarnate" (*The Holy Spirit in Christian Theology*, London, 1957, pp. 31f.).

[63] The Samaritan name for the Messiah was Taheb (תהב), "He who returns", or "He who restores". According to Odeberg, "A prominent feature in the *Taëb*-traditions was that the Redeemer, in accordance with Deut 18[18] would teach the faithful concerning all things" (*FG*, p. 183). Dodd reminds us that we should not build too much on this figure, for our information about him is late and we do not know whether or not the *Taheb* was known in New Testament times (*IFG*, p. 240, n. 2). But Josephus recounts an incident wherein a man gathered armed men to Mt. Gerizim, saying that he would show them sacred vessels hidden there by Moses (*Ant.* xviii, 85). This looks very much like messianic expectation during the New Testament period.

But the woman recognized His authority and looked to Him to tell men "all things".[64]

26 In words of simple dignity Jesus discloses the truth of His Person (*cf.* 9 : 37). This is the one occasion on which He admitted His messiahship prior to the trial (though *cf.* Mark 9 : 41). He knew that He was the Messiah, but to affirm it openly in Jewish circles would have been to arouse associations of that political Messiah that so many people expected. But in places like this country district of Samaria the term could be used with safety.[65] Jesus' "I am" raises problems. It may be that we have here nothing more than a simple affirmation. On the other hand, the use of the emphatic pronoun in this expression is in the style of deity (see on 8 : 58).[66] There is no "he" in the Greek. Jesus says, "I that speak to thee, I am." Hoskyns comments, "Jesus is more than either Jew or Samaritan had comprehended in the word 'Christ'. He is the answer of God to the sin of the world." But if this is so it is also the case that in this context the words cannot be only an affirmation of greatness. They are a challenge to respond. As Strachan puts it, they "are really another form of the invitation 'Come unto me' ".

(e) The Woman's Witness, 4 : 27–30

27 And upon this came his disciples; and they marvelled that he was speaking with a woman; yet no man said, What seekest thou? or, Why speakest thou with her? 28 So the woman left her waterpot, and went away into the city, and saith to the people, 29 Come, see a man, who told me all things that ever I did: can this be the Christ? 30 They went out of the city, and were coming to him.

---

[64] For the Messiah as a teacher *cf.* Enoch 49 : 3, and *cf.* SBk, II, p. 438. "All things" may refer to Deut. 18 : 18. This incidentally is John's only use of ἅπας.

[65] There is no reason for thinking that Samaritan ideas of the Messiah were without nationalistic aspects. But the *Taheb* was primarily a teacher, a restorer of true worship, a priest. Macdonald says, "no king was looked for and no royal prerogatives" (*op. cit.*, p. 362). Clearly to accept the title "Messiah" in Samaritan surroundings in a discussion with a woman about worship was a very different matter from accepting the title among Jews.

[66] E. Stauffer gives six reasons for affirming that Jesus' words are "to be understood as the theophanic formula *ANI HU*" (*Jesus and His Story*, London, 1960, p. 152). He later says, "There is no doubt that the evangelist wishes this to imply that Jesus pronounced the first significant, but as yet half-veiled, words concerning the secret of his person not in Judea or Galilee, but on that occasion in Samaria" (*op. cit.*, p. 153).

With the affirmation of Jesus' messiahship the conversation has been brought to its climax. There remains to be recounted only the effect of all this on others. John shows us both the surprise of the disciples and the evangelistic zeal of the woman. She bore such an effective testimony that people went out of the village to meet Jesus.

27 "Upon this" indicates that the disciples returned just as Jesus made His great affirmation. For "his disciples" see on 2 : 2. They were astonished[67] to find Him carrying on a conversation with a woman. Whatever might be thought of the propriety of asking for a drink (see on v. 7), no Rabbi would have carried on a conversation with a woman. One of their sayings ran: "A man shall not be alone with a woman in an inn, not even with his sister or his daughter, on account of what men may think. A man shall not talk with a woman in the street, not even with his own wife, and especially not with another woman, on account of what men may say."[68] Yet, though the disciples were astonished, they did not question the action of the woman (the first hypothetical question) or that of their Master (the second). They had learned enough to know that, while Jesus did not always respect the con-

---

[67] The verb "marvelled" is $\vartheta\alpha\nu\mu\acute{\alpha}\zeta\omega$ which denotes "incredulous surprise" (MM).

[68] SBk, II, p. 438. Nor was it only discourse in public places that was discountenanced. "Jose b. Johanan of Jerusalem said: Let thy house be opened wide and let the needy be members of thy household; and talk not much with womankind. They said this of a man's own wife: how much more of his fellow's wife! Hence the Sages have said: He that talks much with womankind brings evil upon himself and neglects the study of the Law and at the last will inherit Gehenna" (*Ab.* 1 : 5). R. Jose the Galilean once asked a woman, "By what road do we go to Lydda?" only to be rebuked by her: "Foolish Galilean, did not the Sages say this: Engage not in much talk with women? You should have asked: By which to Lydda?" (*Erub.* 53b; Soncino trans., p. 374). Perhaps the greatest blot on the Rabbinic attitude to women was that, though the Rabbis held the study of the Law to be the greatest good in life, they discouraged women from studying it at all. When Ben Azzai suggested that women be taught the Law for certain purposes R. Eliezer replied: "If any man gives his daughter a knowledge of the Law it is as though he taught her lechery" (*Sot.* 3 : 4). The Rabbis regarded women as inferior to men in every way. A very ancient prayer (still found in the Jewish prayer book) runs, "Blessed art thou, O Lord . . . who hast not made me a woman." The equivalent prayer for a woman was "Blessed art thou, O Lord, who hast fashioned me according to thy will." Temple comments, "If we now feel that the women had the best of the exchange, that is a Christian and not an ancient Jewish sentiment!"

ventions of the Rabbis, He had good reasons for what He did.
28, 29 The woman had come to the well expressly to obtain water.
It is thus an indication of the deep impression that had been
made upon her that she left her waterpot there.[69] She completely
abandoned the business in hand (though the abandoned waterpot
meant that she would certainly return). She set about telling what
had happened to her instead. She went back to the village and invited
the men there to come and meet Jesus.[70] Her recommendation is
couched in the terms, "see a man,[71] who told me all things that
ever I did." This pardonable exaggeration indicates the profound
impression that Jesus' knowledge of her private life had made on
her. The question, "can this be the Christ?" is put tentatively.
It is as though a negative answer might be expected, but a positive
one is hoped for.[72] For Messiah, see on 1 : 20, 41.
30 Her news and her invitation evoked a response. The people
went out from the city, and kept on coming to Jesus ("The tense
is vividly descriptive", Westcott). No indication is given of the

---

[69] Barrett thinks the reason "presumably in order that Jesus might drink"
(so Hendriksen and others). This seems most unlikely. Hoskyns' view is better,
namely that it was partly as I have indicated in the text, and partly "in order
to contrast her behaviour with that of the disciples (*vv.* 31-3). She went as
quickly as possible, unencumbered by having to carry a pot full of water on
her head, and without difficulty persuaded the Samaritans to come and see
the man whom she had good reason to suppose was the Christ." It is, of course,
also possible that the woman had not yet filled the pot. She would then leave
it to save carrying it back and forth. But my point still stands. She abandoned
the bringing of water for the bringing of men. Temple comments: "The water-
pot is a little bit of sheer realism. As Scott Holland used to say 'You cannot
allegorise that water-pot. It is a perfectly empty water-pot. No one ever found
the old Law at the bottom of it.' "
[70] "And it is the nature of faith that we want to bring others to share eternal
life with us when we have become partakers of it. The knowledge of God
cannot lie buried and inactive in our hearts and not be made known to men.
For that word must be true: 'I believed, and therefore will I speak' (Ps. 116. 10)"
(Calvin).
[71] That she should call Jesus "a man" is not remarkable. But John often
uses ἄνθρωπος of Jesus, as in 5 : 12; 8 : 40; 9 : 11, 24; 10 : 33; 11 : 47, 50;
18 : 14, 17, 29; 19 : 5. He may wish to stress the real manhood of Jesus, to
depict Him as "the Man".
[72] The question is introduced by μήτι, and BDF gives the force of it as
"that must be the Messiah at last, perhaps this is the Messiah" (427(2)).

275

number who came, but the impression is that a considerable group was involved.[73]

(f) Christ's Meat, 4 : 31–38

31 In the mean while the disciples prayed him, saying, Rabbi, eat. 32 But he said unto them, I have meat to eat that ye know not. 33 The disciples therefore said one to another, Hath any man brought him aught to eat? 34 Jesus saith unto them, My meat is to do the will of him that sent me, and to accomplish his work. 35 Say not ye, There are yet four months, and then cometh the harvest? behold, I say unto you, Lift up your eyes, and look on the fields, that they are [1]white already unto harvest. 36 He that reapeth receiveth wages, and gathereth fruit unto life eternal; that he that soweth and he that reapeth may rejoice together. 37 For herein is the saying true, One soweth, and another reapeth. 38 I sent you to reap that whereon ye have not labored: others have labored, and ye are entered into their labor.

[1]Or, *white unto harvest. Already he that reapeth &c.*

The disciples' suggestion that Jesus should eat some of the food they had brought becomes the occasion for Him to teach them something of His priorities. It was meat and drink to Him to do the divine will, and the urgent task is not to be postponed.[74]
31 While[75] the woman was about her business another scene was being enacted at the well. The disciples' suggestion that Jesus eat was eminently natural. The whole purpose of their trip into the village had been to buy food. They had left the Master weary, and presumably hungry. Now they brought food and asked Him to eat. For "Rabbi" see on 1 : 38.
32 Jesus' reply puts a distance between them. His "I" and "you"

---

[73] S. D. Gordon has a suggestive comment: "The disciples had just been down to the town – they who knew the Master much longer and better. They brought back some *loaves*. That was all. The woman went down; she brought back some *men*" (*The Sychar Revival*, London, n.d., p. 25).

[74] The words remind us of the temptation narrative where Jesus refused to use His powers to satisfy His physical hunger. It is worth pointing out that John has parallels to the other two temptations also, namely Jesus' refusals to be made a king (6 : 15), and to do the kind of sign that His brothers demanded (7 : 3ff.). He does not have a specific temptation narrative, but he makes the point in his own way.

[75] μεταξύ is not a common adverb and it may well be used to put some stress on the idea of the interval: " *'During the interval'* Jesus utters His doctrine about the *interval* between the sowing and the harvest" (Abbott, 2668).

are in emphatic contrast. "Meat" is not meat in our sense of the term, but "food" generally.[76] Jesus declares that He has sustenance of which the disciples have no knowledge.

33 Following a pattern that we have seen in the conversations with the Jews after the Temple cleansing (2 : 20, where see note), with Nicodemus (3 : 4), and with the woman (4: 15), the disciples misunderstand Jesus by taking His words in a literal and material fashion.[77] Their question expects the answer, "No". "Surely no one has brought Him anything to eat?" But the point is that they think only in terms of material food.[78] However, their complete misunderstanding opens up the way for Jesus to impart valuable truths.

34 "My" is emphatic. Whatever be the case with others, Jesus' meat (*i.e.* food, see on v. 32) is to do[79] the divine will.[80] The words are eloquent of a sense of mission and devotion. They speak, too, of the satisfaction it was to the Son to do the will of the Father. Notice that God is characterized as "him that sent me" (as often in this Gospel). The work that Jesus did was no mere human work. It was that of One sent by God. Quite often in this Gospel Jesus declares that the work He does is that which the Father has for Him to do (*e.g.* 5 : 30; 6 : 38; 7 : 18; 8 : 50; 9 : 4; 10 : 37f.; 12 : 49, 50; 14 : 31; 15 : 10; 17 : 4). Obedience to the divine will is for Him the major concern. Singlemindedly He presses on. Here He

---

[76] The word is $\beta\varrho\tilde{\omega}\sigma\iota\varsigma$. Strictly it denotes the process of eating, but here (and elsewhere in John) it is used in the sense of $\beta\varrho\tilde{\omega}\mu\alpha$ (which occurs in v. 34), *i.e.* of food in general.

[77] Augustine comments: "What wonder if that woman did not understand about the water? See; the disciples do not yet understand the meat" (XV. 31; p. 107).

[78] They think also in terms of someone bringing Him food. Their question throws light on Jesus' use of His miraculous powers. As Wright says, "It never entered their minds that He would or could work a 'miracle' in order to feed Himself; as, for example, that he could or would turn stones into bread." The miracles were never wrought for selfish ends.

[79] Moulton cites this clause as one of his examples which "will show anyone who is free from predisposition that *ἵνα* can lose the last shred of purposive meaning" (M, I, p. 208).

[80] "Jesus, whose hunger is to do the Father's will, sees the satisfaction of His hunger in the prospect of the universal Church foreshadowed by the conviction of the Samaritan woman. But His words are not only to be taken symbolically. Everyone knows how the enthusiasm of achievement can make a man rise superior to his bodily needs" (Bailey).

adds the thought of "accomplishing" His work (for "work" see Additional Note G, pp. 684ff.). The verb is cognate with that used on the cross, when Jesus cried "It is finished" (19 : 30).[81] It reminds us of the awful cost of that work, and underlines the devotion implied in the whole expression. There is a sense in which each stage of His work may be regarded as perfect and complete. And there is a deeper sense in which nothing is complete without the cross.

35 It is not easy to interpret the saying Jesus quotes. "Ye" is emphatic, which shows that it is not a saying of His. At first sight we would take it for a proverb. It is objected that such a proverb is nowhere attested, and that in fact it takes longer than four months for a harvest to ripen in Palestine. Accordingly the suggestion is made that Jesus is referring to a chance remark of the disciples as they looked at the fields green with the crops in their early stages. But it is even more difficult to think of this incident as taking place four months before harvest. Jesus' request for water points to a time of heat. Moreover, four months before harvest there would be plenty of surface water. A weary traveller would not depend on the charity of a chance acquaintance. A proverbial saying is rendered the more likely in that the introduction "Say not ye" is not suited to a casual remark about the state of the crops.[82] It is favored also by the metrical form of the saying. Its lack of attestation might be due to a rustic provenance. How many literary people today can cite all the rural adages now current? Modern rural sayings exist which are not embodied in formal literary works and we have no reason for thinking it was otherwise in the first century. There is evidence, moreover, that the agricultural year was divided into six two-month periods, seed-time, winter, spring, harvest, summer, and the time of extreme

---

[81]   The verb used here is $\tau\epsilon\lambda\epsilon\iota\acute{o}\omega$ and in 19 : 30, $\tau\epsilon\lambda\acute{\epsilon}\omega$.

[82]   A rather similar expression is used to introduce a proverbial saying in Matt. 16 : 2. Knox translates here: "Is it not a saying of yours, It is four whole months before harvest comes?" In a footnote he comments, "this may have been a proverb, meaning that there was no hurry, like our 'Rome was not built in a day'." Cf. also Dodd: "That it is to be understood as a banal remark upon the time of the year (as many commentators have assumed, in their anxiety to discover data for a calendar of the Ministry of Jesus) I find entirely incredible; such remarks did not find a place in the gospel tradition" (HTFG, p. 394).

heat.[83] Thus four months elapsed between the end of seed-time and the beginning of harvest. This might well have given rise to a proverbial saying indicating that there is no hurry for a particular task. The seed may be planted, but there is no way of getting round the months of waiting. Growth is slow and cannot be hurried.[84] But Jesus did not share this view when applied to spiritual things. He had an urgent sense of mission and these words convey something of it to the disciples. They must not lazily relax, comfortable in the thought that there is no need to bestir themselves. The fields are even now ready for harvest.[85] There may even be the thought that in the kind of harvest in which they were engaged

---

[83] See John Lightfoot, *HHT*, p. 277. He cites a Talmudic saying: "Half Tisri, all Marchesvan, and half Chisleu, is זרע the seed's time", and so on for the periods called "the winter", "the winter solstice", "the harvest", "the summer", and "the great heat". There is support for this also in the Gezer Calendar, our oldest Hebrew inscription. Between its "Two months of sowing" and its month for the general harvest it has "Two months of late sowing (*or* spring growth). Month of pulling flax. Month of barley harvest" (translation by J. Mauchline, in *Documents from Old Testament Times*, ed. D. Winton Thomas, London, 1958, p. 201). Again there is a period of four months between the end of sowing and the beginning of harvest.

[84] Calvin sees a hint "at how much more careful men's minds are for earthly things than for heavenly. For they are so consumed with looking for harvest that they carefully count up the months and days. But it is surprising how lazy they are in reaping the wheat of heaven."

[85] The use of λευκαί is somewhat puzzling, because few crops are white at harvest time, and certainly not wheat (*cf.* "the golden grain"; Stauffer thinks that rye is meant, *op. cit.*, p. 63). The expression clearly means "ready to reap". H. V. Morton tells of an incident at this spot: "as I sat by Jacob's Well a crowd of Arabs came along the road from the direction in which Jesus was looking, and I saw their white garments shining in the sun. Surely Jesus was speaking not of the earthly but of the heavenly harvest, and as He spoke I think it likely that He pointed along the road where the Samaritans in their white robes were assembling to hear His words" (*In the Steps of the Master*, London, 1935, p. 154). This may well be the explanation of it. Incidentally the same explanation was given long ago by John Lightfoot, who depicts our Lord as "pointing without doubt towards that numerous crowd of people, that, at that time, flocked towards him out of the city" (*HHT*, p. 277). Morgan comments on this verse: "If those disciples had been appointed a commission of enquiry as to the possibilities of Christian enterprise in Samaria I know exactly the resolution they would have passed. The resolution would have been: Samaria unquestionably needs our Master's message, but it is not ready for it. There must first be ploughing, then sowing, and then waiting. It is needy, but it is not ready."

(unlike those in farms and the like) there is no necessary interval between sowing and reaping. The disciples must acquire a sense of urgency in their task.[86]

36 It seems likely that "already" should be taken with this verse and not the preceding.[87] Already the man who is keen and active in his reaping is receiving his wage. As payment was commonly given only for work completed (or at least with a stage completed) this indicates something of the urgency of the task. The disciples should not delay, when others are so far ahead that they are already receiving wages. Just who these reapers are is not said, and it is difficult to identify them. Perhaps Jesus does not mean that others are actually at work, but is simply continuing the thought of the previous verse. The harvest is ready. The wages are there. Let no man hang back. A harvest will not wait. Unless it is reaped while it is ripe it will spoil, and there will be no harvest.

Jesus is not thinking only of the wages. The reaper "gathereth fruit unto life eternal." The man who wins souls for Christ is at work on something with lasting consequences. His work is for eternity. In doing it he is not in any way competing with the sower. He is in fact cooperating with the sower, for he is completing the work that the other commenced. So it is that his work is done in order that the two may rejoice together. Sometimes when there is a distinction between sower and reaper there is the thought that the sower has lost all his labor (*e.g.* Deut. 28 : 33; Judg. 6 : 3; Mic. 6 : 15). But here there is cooperation. Sowing was hard and wearisome work, and it could be contrasted with reaping, which was joyful (Ps. 126 : 5f.). But here the interval between seed-time and harvest is done away (*cf.* Amos 9 : 13). Sower and reaper rejoice together.

37, 38 Another proverb is pressed into service.[88] In farming, while

---

[86] There is a fine sense of urgency in a saying attributed to R. Tarfon (*c.* A.D. 130) and which reminds us of the present passage: "The day is short and the task is great and the labourers are idle and the wage is abundant and the master of the house is urgent" (Mishnah, *Ab.* 2 : 15).

[87] There are, of course, few or no punctuation marks in the oldest MSS, and we are dependent on our sense of the fitness of things. It seems to me that the note of urgency throughout the passage requires us to take "already" with "he that reapeth" (as in ARV mg.).

[88] For ἀληθινός, "true", see on 1 : 9. G. D. Kilpatrick argues that we should read here ὁ ἀληθινός with the meaning, "the true saying consists in this" (*BT*, 11, 1960, p. 174).

it is usually the case that the sower looks forward to reaping, it also sometimes happens, as we have just seen, that "one sows and another reaps".[89] This is also true in a wide variety of situations outside agriculture, not least in the field of Christian service.[90] It must be almost always the case that those who reap precious souls profit from the work of those who have been before them. Each Christian worker is dependent for success on the labors of his predecessors. This general truth is clear enough. But its detailed application is not so clear. One difficulty concerns the particular reaping Jesus had in mind. One would most naturally take it to refer to what the disciples were then doing. But the trouble is that they are not represented as doing anything at all about the reception of the Samaritans. Perhaps they did something that is not recorded. Or Jesus may be referring to such activities as those recorded in v. 2.

Again, the meaning of "others" is not clear. It may be that the plural is not meant to be significant, and that Jesus refers to Himself only.[91] If the saying refers only to the contemporary scene the "others" will be Jesus and the woman.[92] J. A. T. Robinson has argued, convincingly to my mind, that the reference is primarily to the work of John the Baptist and his followers. Their work in

---

[89] Notice the double use of ἄλλος. John is fond of this word, which he uses 34 times.

[90] "This world is not merely directed and guided by those of us who happen to be alive. We inherit not only the sins of the dead, but their faith and sacrifice also as a spiritual heritage. It is ours to bear the one without murmuring as our opportunity, and to thank God for the other" (Strachan).

[91] Plummer takes this view. The plural, ἄλλοι, he thinks, is used to balance the plural ὑμεῖς. Similarly, he argues, in v. 37 "both are in the *singular* for the sake of harmony; ὁ σπείρων, Christ; ὁ θερίζων, His ministers." An objection to the latter part of his interpretation is that Jesus was simply quoting a current proverb (or so it would seem). It may not be without significance that we have the same verb and the same tense as that which tells us that Jesus sat weary, κεκοπιακώς, by the well (v. 6).

[92] *Cf.* Bernard: "Primarily, Jesus and the woman were the ἄλλοι into whose labours the disciples had entered, not to speak of every prophet and pious teacher of the past who had prepared the way in Samaria for the message of Christ." The difficulty in the way of interpreting the words too strictly of the Samaritans is that it is hard to see how the disciples reaped at all in this case. All the work, sowing and reaping, seems to have been done by Jesus and the woman (unless we look forward to Acts 8).

this very area had prepared the way for Jesus and His band.[93] Another possibility is that the labors of the prophets in days of old and of men like John the Baptist in more recent times are taken together as the basis for the work of the disciples. What is clear is that Jesus expected them to be reapers. The time spent with Him was not only a time of training. It was a time in which they were meant to be rendering significant service.[94]

The Christian will necessarily read this saying in the light of the cross. It was there, above all, that Christ sowed the seed (*cf.* 12 : 24). It is only because He so sowed the seed that eternal life may be reaped by anyone.

(g) Samaritan Believers, 4 : 39–42

39 And from that city many of the Samaritans believed on him because of the word of the woman, who testified, He told me all things that ever I did. 40 So when the Samaritans came unto him, they besought him to abide with them: and he abode there two days. 41 And many more believed because of his word; 42 and they said to the woman, Now we believe, not because of thy speaking: for we have heard for ourselves, and know that this is indeed the Saviour of the world.

---

[93] "The 'Others' of John 4, 38" (*SE*, I, pp. 510–15). Robinson takes this passage as a test of exegetical method. He refutes Cullmann's view that the passage is to be understood, not of any situation in the life of Jesus, but of the mission of the apostolic church. Cullmann, who is supported by M. Simon (*St Stephen and the Hellenists*, London, 1958, pp. 36ff.), sees in the "others" the Hellenists of Acts 8 (pre-eminently Philip), who took the gospel to Samaria after which the apostles Peter and John entered the fruits of their labors. Robinson shows that the connection between Jesus and the Baptist movement, and between the Baptist movement and the location of this chapter, make it reasonable to infer that Jesus was speaking of the way His followers were reaping the fruits of the earlier work. (This argument might be used in support of Albright's identification of "Aenon near to Salim" in 3 : 23; cf. p. 237, n. 97.)

[94] "The parable of sower and reaper is so narrated as to cross various planes of interpretation. First, no doubt, the seed sown in the woman bears fruit in the harvest of the advancing Samaritans; then the work of the prophets, and especially of John the Baptist, is embraced by and completed in the work of Jesus; then the Samaritans disappear in the thought of the apostolic mission to the world based upon the mission of Jesus; and finally, the Evangelist addresses his contemporaries and exhorts them to reap the harvest, so that the *others* who have laboured become, as Bauer has noted, less Jesus and the prophets of Israel than Jesus and the apostolic generation" (Hoskyns).

John rounds off the section dealing with the Samaritans with a short statement of the effect of the woman's witness, and of Jesus' short stay. There is a magnificent climax as the Samaritan believers acclaim Jesus as "the Saviour of the world".

39 For "believed on him" see on 1 : 12, and for "testified" (= "witnessed") on 1 : 7. Because the woman bore her testimony[95] to Jesus faith was enkindled within the Samaritans. Many came to believe. The particular words which impressed them form a pardonable overstatement. But it certainly indicates that Jesus' unexpected knowledge of the intimate details of the woman's life had made a profound impression on her. Through her it was passed on to others.[96] It is an example of John's irony that he lets the words which reflect such a limited conception of messiahship pass, without drawing attention to what is really involved (*cf.* vv. 31ff.).

40 The new believers did not part readily with their new-found Lord. They pressed Jesus to remain with them ("besought" is in a continuous tense: they kept on asking Him). Nor was their insistence without result. Jesus stayed with them for two days.

41, 42 The result of this stay was an increase in the number of the followers of Jesus. Notice the absolute use of the verb "believe". So fundamental to Christianity is faith that it is not necessary to specify the object (see further Additional Note E, pp. 335ff.). "His word" here means something very much like "the gospel" (as in Mark 2 : 2). It is the whole message for which Jesus stands. Even in the case of those who believed because they heard Jesus for themselves there was some influence stemming from the woman, as their "no longer"[97] indicates. They had been impressed by

---

[95] "Who testified" is not an ideal translation for μαρτυρούσης (there is no article). It means rather, "as she testified". There is the thought of persistence in testifying rather than the designation of the woman as the one "who" testified.

[96] "She spoke a word, the word, to them; and we have already noticed that this confession or *word* (4[25, 29, 39]) was very far from perfect; but such as it was, for its purpose and at that moment it was adequate; and it brought many of her countrymen to belief in Him" (Lightfoot).

[97] οὐκέτι means "no longer" and not simply "not" as ARV. In the note on 1 : 5 we saw that John uses οὐ and οὐδέ more than any other New Testament writer. The same is true of οὐκέτι which he uses 12 times; next come Mark and Romans each with 7 times.

what she had said[98] though their faith was not fully formed. The woman might introduce them to Jesus, but faith is not faith as long as it rests on the testimony of another. There must be personal knowledge of Christ if there is to be an authentic Christian experience. The incident forms something of an exemplification of Jesus' words in vv. 37 f.

Their belief about Jesus is crystallized in the expression "the Saviour of the world" (for "world" see Additional Note B, pp. 126ff., and for Jesus' messiahship see on 1 : 41). This expression occurs again in I John 4 : 14 and nowhere else in the New Testament. The word "Saviour" is applied to the Father (Luke 1 : 47; I Tim. 1 : 1, *etc.*) as well as to the Son, though John never uses it of either outside the passages mentioned. It is used in the Septuagint of God the Father. Secular Greek writers employ it of a multitude of deities.[99] "Saviour" is a very general word, but it certainly contains the idea of deliverance, of saving from serious disaster. Jesus is more than our perfect example.[100] He really saves. The

---

[98] The expression is $\delta\iota\grave{a}\ \tau\grave{\eta}\nu\ \sigma\grave{\eta}\nu\ \lambda a\lambda\iota\acute{a}\nu$ which Findlay renders "not because of your chatter". Calvin also comments severely: "the Samaritans seem to be claiming that they now have a stronger support a woman's tongue – which is usually untrustworthy." The word $\lambda a\lambda\iota\acute{a}$ undoubtedly often denotes speech that is not to be taken seriously, gossip. Thus Thorlief Boman dismisses the term when he is studying the concept of "the word" in Greek, saying "$\lambda a\lambda\iota\acute{a}$ signifies disorderly utterance, mere prattle" (*Hebrew Thought compared with Greek*, London, 1960, p. 67). Yet not too much should be read into this, for in the New Testament the unfavorable sense is not marked, if present at all. The word may even be used of Jesus' speech (8 : 43). See further on 1 : 37 for the cognate verb $\lambda a\lambda\acute{\epsilon}\omega$. $\sigma\grave{\eta}\nu$ is emphatic. G. D. Kilpatrick has shown that in John the normal order for personal possessives with the article is article, noun, article, possessive (see on 3 : 29). The order in the present passage is found three times only, and in each case there is emphasis (5 : 47; 7 : 16). It should, perhaps, be noted that P75 supports B and Origen in reading $\lambda a\lambda\iota\acute{a}\nu\ \sigma ov$. But even with this reinforcement the reading will scarcely commend itself.

[99] Deissmann cites "Saviour of the world" as a title frequently used with reference to the Emperor (*LAE*, p. 364; *cf.* also *TDNT*, III, p. 892, n. 88). That such an expression was common in the Hellenistic world is clear. But John does not derive it from such a milieu. Its Old Testament roots are sufficient to show this.

[100] *Cf.* Barclay: "A great example can be merely a heart-breaking and frustrating thing when we find ourselves powerless to follow it. Jesus was *Saviour*. That is to say, He rescued men from the evil and hopeless situation in which they found themselves; He broke the chains that bound them to the past and gave them a power and a presence which enabled them to meet the future."

addition, "of the world", elevates the title to one of infinite grandeur. Jesus is not concerned simply with petty, minor issues. Nor is He the Saviour of a few unimportant individuals. He is the Saviour of the world.[101]

INTERLUDE. IN GALILEE, 4 : 43–45

43 And after the two days he went forth from thence into Galilee. 44 For Jesus himself testified, that a prophet hath no honor in his own country. 45 So when he came into Galilee, the Galilaeans received him, having seen all the things that he did in Jerusalem at the feast: for they also went unto the feast.

The scene of action shifts to Galilee, and John inserts a verse or two to explain this. He brings out two points: the one that a prophet is not honored in his own land, the other that the Galileans who had been in Jerusalem at the feast gave Jesus a welcome.

43, 44 These two verses are joined by "for", but it is not easy to see how the second gives the reason for the first. V. 43 simply tells of the completion of Jesus' brief ministry in Samaria and the the resumption of His journey to Galilee (*cf.* v. 3). The saying about a prophet being without acceptance in his own country is reported in all three Synoptists (Matt. 13 : 57; Mark 6 : 4; Luke 4 : 24), and in connection with Jesus' visit to Nazareth. Perhaps the "for" is meant to indicate that Jesus must show that this is, indeed, the case.[102] He had come unto His own, not under a delusion that He would be welcomed, but knowing full well that He must expect a rejection. This would not take Him by surprise, for it was in the divine plan. So, to fulfil all this implies, He went to Galilee.

Some, it is true, argue that "his own country" refers to Judea which He was just leaving. "Both by fact and the current inter-

---

[101] The expression "sums up the main point of this chapter – that the conversion of Samaritans is the first sign of the universality of salvation in Christ" (Bailey).

[102] "It was not in accord with the mind of Jesus, says the Evangelist, to stay where the welcome was greatest, or the difficulties least" (Wright). "He had to go on and get on with the business of being rejected by the many and accepted by only the few ... He goes on into Galilee, to receive the kind of welcome which He knew so well to be hollow and worthless" (Loyd).

pretation of prophecy, Judaea alone could receive that title" (Westcott). Similarly Hoskyns maintains that Jerusalem was the home of every Jew. Preeminently must it be so in the case of the Messiah. It is often added that only this interpretation accords with the circumstances. Jesus had been rejected in Judea, His own country, so He turned to another region, Galilee. Against this is the fact that the reason given for His leaving Judea was not failure but success (v. 1). Moreover, John nowhere indicates that Jesus is "of Judea", whereas several times he links Him with Galilee where He had been brought up (2 : 1; 7 : 3, 41, 52, and especially 1 : 46; 19 : 19). This agrees with the witness of the Synoptists. It is also the case that if Judea were meant the words ought to be found when Jesus left that land and not between His Samaritan and Galilean visits.[103] Brown makes the further point that "there is an implication in this explanation that Jesus was disappointed with the reception he had received in Judea and had come back to Galilee to be accorded the honor denied him in Judea. Such a search for human praise is abhorrent to the ideals of the Fourth Gospel (ii 24–25, v 41–44)." R. H. Lightfoot argues powerfully that heaven is meant. He asks "Does not St. John perhaps wish to teach that, if the Lord's *patris* is sought anywhere on earth, nowhere does He receive the honour due to Him, even as a prophet? For He is not of this world (8^{23}) and His *patris* is in heaven".[104] This view is much to be preferred to that which sees John as locating Jesus in Judea.

45 When He reached Galilee Jesus was welcomed[105] by the Galileans. Large numbers of them habitually went up to Jerusalem

---

[103] Bernard finds both interpretations so difficult that he thinks the verse a gloss, the meaning of which is not clear. This seems no better an explanation. It also poses the question why a straightforward text should be complicated by a perplexing gloss. Other suggestions are that "his own country" is Palestine in general as opposed to Samaria, or upper as opposed to lower Galilee. For a thorough discussion see J. Willemse, "La Patrie de Jésus selon Saint Jean iv. 44" (*NTS*, XI, 1964–65, pp. 349–364). Willemse thinks that Judea or Jerusalem is meant.

[104] Lightfoot, p. 35.

[105] ἐδέξαντο, "received", has about it the air of welcome. It is used, for example, of welcoming guests. Hoskyns cites Quesnel: "To have believed without miracles was the excellency of the faith of the Samaritans; to believe, as the Galileans did, because of them is, at least, to yield to the authority of God and to advance further than did the generality of the Jews."

at the feasts. Some had been there for the events narrated in 2 : 13–25. "The feast" is the Passover mentioned in that passage. Once again we are reminded that Jesus did many things which are not recorded. He cleansed the temple, but the record is incomplete as 2 : 23 plainly shows. It is not John's purpose to attempt a complete chronicle, but only to select such events and teachings as will bring out his thesis that Jesus is the Christ, the Son of God (20 : 31). So now he does not mention what the things were that so impressed the Galileans, but contents himself with pointing out that their attitude to Jesus was conditioned by what they had seen in Jerusalem. This is not quite what we would have expected after the words about a prophet having no honor (v. 44). This is probably another example of the Evangelist's irony. He does not stay to explain that the enthusiasm of the Galileans was not soundly based. It was dependent on the wonder arising from their sight of the signs, not on a realization that Jesus was indeed the Christ, the Saviour of the world. Their very acceptance of Him was thus in its way a rejection. They gave Him honor of a sort, but it was not the honor that was due to Him. [106]

7. THE SECOND SIGN – HEALING THE NOBLEMAN'S SON, 4 : 46-54

46 He came therefore again unto Cana of Galilee, where he made the water wine. And there was a certain [1]nobleman, whose son was sick at Capernaum. 47 When he heard that Jesus was come out of Judaea into Galilee, he went unto him, and besought him that he would come down, and heal his son; for he was at the point of death. 48 Jesus therefore said unto him, Except ye see signs and wonders, ye will in no wise believe. 49 The [1]nobleman saith unto him, [2]Sir, come down ere my child die. 50 Jesus saith unto him, Go thy way; thy son liveth. The man believed the word that Jesus spake

---

[106]   It is perhaps significant that John's word for "honor" here is τιμή, a term he uses nowhere else. When he refers to the honor due to Jesus he prefers δόξα.

287

unto him, and he went his way. 51 And as he was now going down, his [3]servants met him, saying, that his son lived. 52 So he inquired of them the hour when he began to amend. They said therefore unto him, Yesterday at the seventh hour the fever left him. 53 So the father knew that it was at that hour in which Jesus said unto him, Thy son liveth: and himself believed, and his whole house. 54 This is again the second sign that Jesus did, having come out of Judaea into Galilee.

[1]Or, *king's officer*   [2]Or, *Lord*   [3]Gr. *bondservants*.

The second sign of which John gives a report is a miracle of healing. It has some interesting features, notably that it is a case of healing at a distance. Jesus spoke the healing word in Cana and the boy was cured at Capernaum. It is quite in John's manner that the wonderful happening is spoken of as eliciting faith (53). It is a "sign", which effects the divine purpose. Some have held that this is a variant of the story of the healing of the centurion's slave (Matt. 8 : 5–13; Luke 7 : 2–10). But about the only things in common are some interesting verbal parallels (noted, for example, by Barrett and by Hoskyns), and the healing at a distance. There it is a centurion (probably a heathen), here an officer of Herod (probably a Jew[107]); there a slave, here a son. There Jesus speaks His word of power in Capernaum, here in Cana; there the centurion's faith evokes Jesus' praise, here the father's faith is weak; there the centurion asks Jesus not to come to his home, here the father begs Him to come. There the illness is paralysis, here a fever. There the elders plead for the man, here he pleads in person. This story takes place just after Jesus' return from Judea, that is evidently much later.[108] Despite the verbal parallels the two stories are distinct.[109]

---

[107] This is not certain. But *(a)* there is nothing in the story that hints at the presence of a Gentile, and *(b)* in v. 48 the man appears to be included in the crowd of miracle-seeking Jews.

[108] E. Haenchen maintains that "the story which John used" is identical with that in the Synoptics on the grounds that it "differs only in one, though most important point" (*SE*, I, p. 497). The hollowness of this position is demonstrated by the list of differences.

46 In Galilee Jesus made His way once more to Cana (see on 2 : 1). The statement that it was "where he made the water wine" is a further indication that John means the earlier narrative to be taken as fact, and not simply as an allegory constructed to to convey helpful spiritual truths. "Nobleman"[110] denotes one of the king's officers. He would have been an official attached to Herod's court. Evidently he had heard of the previous "sign" at Cana, so that when his son became ill with a fever (v. 52) he sought Jesus out.

47 The officer heard of Jesus' arrival and went to Him. "Besought" is in a continuous tense, conveying the thought of a persistent request. The man's need was great. He pressed his plea. John makes the situation quite plain by telling us that the boy was "at the point of death".[111] "Come down" is a minor mark of

---

[109] Many draw attention also to a Rabbinical story. "Once the son of R. Gamaliel fell ill. He sent two scholars to R. Ḥanina b. Dosa to ask him to pray for him. When he saw them he went up to an upper chamber and prayed for him. When he came down he said to them: Go, the fever has left him. They said to him: Are you a prophet? He replied: I am neither a prophet nor the son of a prophet, but I learnt this from experience. If my prayer is fluent in my mouth, I know that he is accepted: but if not, I know that he is rejected. They sat down and made a note of the exact moment. When they came to R. Gamaliel, he said to them: By the temple service! You have not been a moment too soon or too late, but so it happened: at that very moment the fever left him and he asked for water to drink" (*Ber.* 34b; Soncino edn. pp. 215f.). This is a typical Rabbinic story, the purpose being to excite wonder at the extraordinary power exercised by the man of God. The story John narrates has quite a different purpose. It is a "sign". It shows us God at work. At the same time v. 48 vigorously opposes the view that faith should be bound up with miracles. In this Gospel the faith elicited by miracles is never despised. But it is not the highest kind of faith.

[110] βασιλικός is the adjective "royal". It could denote a man of royal blood, but the present passage seems to rule this out. More likely is the meaning "royal officer", *i.e.* one who serves the king. Some have conjectured that he was Manaen, "the foster-brother of Herod the tetrarch" (Acts 13 : 1), or Chuzas, "Herod's steward" (Luke 8 : 3). But there is no evidence for either identification. Strictly speaking Herod was not a king at all, but a tetrarch. However, he was of the royal house, and exercised rule, so on occasion could be called King (*e.g.* Mark 6 : 14). The word probably denotes, then, one of Herod's officers.

[111] ἤμελλεν γὰρ ἀποθνῄσκειν. The auxiliary μέλλω conveys the thoughts of imminence and certainty. It is worth noticing that ἀποθνῄσκω is used in John more frequently than in any other book in the New Testament, namely 28 times (next is Romans 23 times).

accuracy. Cana was on high ground and Capernaum by the lake.
48 Jesus' reply is at first sight rather harsh. But it is addressed
to a wider audience than the officer as the plural "ye" indicates.
It is not so much Jesus' answer to the nobleman's request as "a
reflection which He makes on the occasion of that request" (Godet).
This is the typical attitude of Galileans. "Signs" (see on 2 : 11,
and Additional Note G, pp. 684ff.) is the usual word in this Gospel
to bring out the truth that Jesus' miracles have meaning. They
point men to God. In this context, however, this thought is not
prominent. The word here means little more than "miracles".
"Wonders"[112] directs attention to the sheerly miraculous. The
word denotes a portent, something beyond explanation, at which
men can but marvel. Jesus is affirming that people such as the
man who had come to Him were lacking in that deep trustful
attachment which is of the essence of faith. They looked for the
spectacular, and were linked to Him only by a love for the sen-
sational. "In no wise" renders an emphatic double negative.[113]
For the people of whom He speaks signs and wonders are an
absolute necessity. In this Gospel it is clear that Jesus accepted
people who came only because of the miracles (*cf.* 6 : 26; 14 : 11).
But such faith is not the highest kind of faith (*cf.* 2 : 23f.).
49 The nobleman's deep concern comes out in this plea. He does
not defend himself. He does not argue. He simply urges Jesus to
do something before the child dies. The word for "child" is not

---

[112] τέρατα. The word is always plural in its sixteen New Testament occurrences, and it is always linked with σημεῖα. The miracles of which the New
Testament treats are never merely wonders. They have meaning and point
men to God.

[113] Moulton has a valuable note on the use of the emphatic οὐ μή in the
New Testament (M, I, pp. 187–92). He disagrees with the contention of such
scholars as Gildersleeve that "the stress" of this construction "has been lost by
overfamiliarity" (*op. cit.*, p. 189). He points out that it occurs in all 93 times, of
which 12 are citations from LXX, 60 are in the Gospels, 4 in Paul, 1 in the
Catholic Epistles and 16 in Revelation. Apart from the last-mentioned (where
special factors operate) the construction is thus uncommon outside the Gospels.
Of the 60 Gospel occurrences 54 are in words of Jesus and they are distributed
over all the Gospels and all the sources postulated by critics. It is clear that
the New Testament writers used the construction sparingly apart from passages
coming from the Old Testament and words of the Master. Moulton concludes:
"Since these are just the two elements which made up 'Scripture' in the first
age of Christianity, one is tempted to put it down to the same cause in both
– a feeling that inspired language was fitly rendered by words of a decisive
tone not needed generally elsewhere."

that used in vv. 46, 47, but a term more expressive of affection (Barclay, "my little lad").[114] The father is so deeply anxious for the welfare of his son that no other consideration weighs with him. **50** Jesus' reply[115] must have been totally unexpected. The man had been urging Him to come down to Capernaum, evidently thinking that the Master's presence was necessary if He were to perform a cure (contrast the centurion of Matt. 8 : 5ff. who asked Jesus not to come to his house, since He could easily heal without doing so). Jesus' words impose a stiff test. He gives the man no sign. The officer has nothing but Jesus' bare word. But this is enough. He rises to the implied demand for faith. He believes what Jesus says and goes his way.
51-53 As he journeyed[116] his slaves (this is the meaning of "servants") met him with the good news that the lad was well. On inquiring[117] when[118] the boy "began to amend"[119] (though "got

114 The word is παιδίον. Although the diminutive is often used conventionally, here it is a real term of affection. υἱός is used in vv. 46, 47, 50, and παῖς (according to the better reading) in v. 51. On the latter verse Godet comments: "The servants, in their report, use neither the term of affection (παιδίον), which would be too familiar, nor that of dignity (υἱός), which would not be familiar enough, but that of family life: παῖς, *the child.*" G. D. Kilpatrick argues that παῖς is "a harmonization to Matthew and Luke" and that υἱός is to be preferred (*JThS*, n.s., XIV, 1963, p. 393). But the MS evidence is strong against this reading, and further, it scarcely seems as though Kilpatrick does justice to John's love of variation, as Edwin D. Freed points out (*JThS*, n.s., XVI, 1965, pp. 448f.).

115 Translations like "Your son is going to live" (Goodspeed), "your son will live" (RSV, Schonfield), or "thy son is to live" (Knox) miss the point that Jesus is not simply prophesying the outcome of the disease. He is speaking a word of power, a healing word. It is a "sign" that John is recording.

116 αὐτοῦ καταβαίνοντος is a somewhat free use of the genitive absolute in view of the following αὐτῷ. But such constructions are found elsewhere in the New Testament and in other writings of this period. No special significance attaches to it.

117 The verb is ἐπύθετο. Normally the imperfect of this verb is used where an answer is sought, and BDF goes as far as to say that the aorist here is "incorrect" (328). This seems to be going too far. The aorist will give a touch of peremptoriness to the question.

118 We might have expected the dative (as in v. 53) to express the point of time instead of the accusatives, τὴν ὥραν and ὥραν ἑβδόμην. But Moulton points out that the accusative was encroaching on this section of the sphere of the dative (M, I, p. 63). BDF sees the construction as classical with ὥρα (161(3)). Perhaps we should notice that in place of παρ' αὐτῶν P75 and B read ἐκείνην.

119 κομψότερον ἔχω appears to be a colloquialism (like our "He is doing nicely!"). MM cite the expression from the papyri. It occurs here only in the New Testament.

better" would be a better rendering of the aorist[120]) he was given a precise time: "Yesterday at the seventh hour". This presents us with something of a difficulty. If John is using the normal method of computing time this will be about one o'clock in the afternoon. But as it is only twenty miles or so between Cana and Capernaum many feel that it is unlikely that the officer would still be on his way as late as this. They suggest accordingly that John was using the alleged Roman time system and the time meant is 7 p.m. If the man reached Jesus at such a time he might well delay his return until the next day, but, they ask, Why would he do this if the encounter took place in the early afternoon? This suggestion is attractive, but there are strong objections to the view that John ever uses the "Roman" system (see on 1 : 39). In the present case the man is expressly said to have believed Jesus, so that his anxiety was relieved and he may have been in no hurry to return. Practical considerations may also have weighed, such as the need to rest his horse (he would certainly have ridden the animal hard on the way to Jesus). Or the delay may have been accidental. In any case sunset would bring him into a new day, though admittedly "yesterday" would sound a little strange if used in the evening of an event which had occurred around midday.[121]

At any rate the statement of the time coincided with the time when Jesus had told the nobleman that his son lived. This is the third time we have been told that the boy "lives". John does not want his readers to miss the emphasis on life, that life that Jesus gives. The servants' words were sufficient to cause the nobleman and his household to believe. In v. 50 this verb had been used of giving credence to Jesus' words. Here it is used in the sense of becoming a Christian. Previously the man had known enough about Jesus to regard Him as a talented wonder-worker. But the "sign" pointed him beyond that. He plainly saw the hand of God in it, and his whole attitude was modified accordingly. He became a believer. The "sign" transformed his faith into a greater faith.

---

[120]   So also MM.
[121]   MacGregor comments: "it is certain that John is not the least concerned with problems of time and distance. It is enough for him that the healing occurred simultaneously with the word of Jesus". Plummer examines the various possibilities and decides that the balance is in favor of the normal Jewish method of reckoning time.

54 This cannot mean the second[122] of all Jesus' signs, for in 2 : 23 John has spoken of other signs. The sense is as Rieu, "Thus once again Jesus wrought a miracle after leaving Judaea for Galilee." John has described two signs and both took place after a visit to Judea. Evidently he intends to link this sign with the preceding. In both cases there is divine power at work, but there is a progression. There there was a mighty miracle where Jesus was: here a healing at a distance. There there was a transformation in *things* (water to wine); here life is given to *a boy* as good as dead. (See further Additional Note G, pp. 684ff.)

ADDITIONAL NOTE D: TRUTH

In Greek writings generally the basic idea of truth is much like our own. It is truth as opposed to falsehood, reality as opposed to mere appearance.[123] But in the New Testament the use of the term is complicated by the fact that it has imported some features from the Old Testament as well. There words like אֱמֶת, אֱמוּנָה refer to truth, but they also refer to faithfulness, reliability, trust-worthiness, sureness, and the like. Especially are they used of God, and it is probably not too much to say that they derive part of their meaning from the connection with God. He may in fact be called "the God of truth" (Ps. 31 : 5; Isa. 65 : 16). Truth is characteristic of God, and it is only as we know God that we know truth. But men may know truth, for God has revealed it to them. Thus Jacob can speak of "all the lovingkindnesses, and of all the truth, which thou hast showed unto thy servant" (Gen. 32 : 10). Such a prayer as "Destroy thou (mine enemies) in thy truth" (Ps. 54 : 5) is perplexing until we remember that truth includes the complete reliability and the complete integrity of God. He will certainly act in accordance with the highest conceivable morality.

In the New Testament truth is associated with God (Rom. 3 : 7; 15 : 8). In a very interesting passage Paul refers to idolatry as exchanging the truth of God for a lie (Rom. 1 : 25), which makes truth very close to God's essential nature. Truth is also associated with Christ (II Cor. 11 : 10), and significantly in the expression,

---

[122] The construction is unusual: τοῦτο . . . δεύτερον σημεῖον ἐποίησεν, "This he did (as) a second sign" (*cf.* 2 : 11).

[123] *Cf.* Bultmann: "As in judicial language the ἀλήθεια is the actual state of affairs to be maintained against different statements, so historians use it to denote real events as distinct from myths, and philosophers to indicate real being in the absolute sense" (*TDNT*, I, p. 238).

"as truth is in Jesus" (Eph. 4 : 21). This is often misquoted as "the truth as it is in Jesus" (and even translated in this way in RSV, NEB). But Paul is not talking about that aspect of truth which he finds in Jesus. He is saying that the very truth of God, truth itself resides in Him. It is but a step to what Christ has done, and so we read of "the truth of the gospel" (Gal. 2 : 5), while "the word of the truth" can be explained as "the gospel of your salvation" (Eph. 1 : 13). Many passages could be cited here. Now all this affects the conduct of the believer. He girds his loins with truth (Eph. 6 : 14). He keeps the feast "with the unleavened bread of sincerity and truth" (I Cor. 5 : 8). Truth must be as characteristic of the saved as it is of the Saviour.

The summit of this development is reached in the Fourth Gospel. Truth for John is a very important concept. He uses the noun $\dot{\alpha}\lambda\dot{\eta}\vartheta\varepsilon\iota\alpha$ 25 times, over against once in Matthew and 3 times each in Mark and Luke (47 times in Paul, and 20 times in the Johannine Epistles). There is a similar disparity with the adjectives $\dot{\alpha}\lambda\eta\vartheta\dot{\eta}\varsigma$ (14 times in John, once each in Matthew and Mark, not in Luke, 4 times in Paul), and $\dot{\alpha}\lambda\eta\vartheta\iota\nu\dot{o}\varsigma$ (9 times in John, not in Matthew or Mark, once each in Luke and Paul). Plainly this concept matters to John.

Bultmann sees "the basic meaning of 'truth' in John" as "God's reality, which, since God is the Creator, is the only true reality".[124] Especially important is the fact that truth may be linked with Jesus. He is "full of grace and truth" (1 : 14), and the source of grace and truth to men (1 : 17). John the Baptist bore witness to the truth (5 : 33), and, as he is depicted simply as a witness to Jesus (see on 1 : 7), this may also link the truth closely with Jesus. The Master could say, "I am ... the truth" (14 : 6). "So truth is not the teaching about God transmitted by Jesus but is God's very reality revealing itself – occurring! – in Jesus."[125] Truth understood in this way has a special connection with the cross. As the Gospel comes to its climax Pilate asks, "What is truth?" (18 : 38). No answer is given in words, but the Passion narrative gives the answer in deeds. As A. Corell puts it, "There can only be one meaning of $\dot{\alpha}\lambda\dot{\eta}\vartheta\varepsilon\iota\alpha$ in the Fourth Gospel: it is the truth about the death and resurrection of Jesus, to which witness is borne in 16.7 and 17.19. This is in accordance with the whole

---

[124] *Theology of the New Testament*, II (London, 1955), p. 18.
[125] Bultmann, *op. cit.*, p. 19.

theology of the Fourth Gospel, the central point of which is the 'lifting-up' of Jesus."[126] Truth as Jesus understood it was a costly affair.

All this has consequences for men. "If ye abide in my word, then are ye truly my disciples; and ye shall know the truth, and the truth shall make you free" (8 : 31f.). To know the truth is not to enter intellectual freedom as such, but it is to enter into the liberating experience of being a disciple of the Lord, with all that that means in terms of freedom from sin and guilt, and of fellowship with and knowledge of God. Jesus is not describing truth as an ethical virtue or a philosophical concept. [127] The thought is close to that of 17 : 3 which describes eternal life in terms of the "true" God and of Jesus Christ. We should probably consider here, too, the fact that "grace and truth came through Jesus Christ" (1 : 17), for this indicates a close link between truth and the gospel of God's grace. The whole of Jesus' ministry was exercised in order that He might bear His witness to the truth (18 : 37; cf. 8 : 40, 45, 46; 16 : 7). By contrast the evil one does not stand in the truth, and, indeed, there is no truth in him (8 : 44).

Truth can be associated with the Spirit (who was to continue Christ's work). Indeed, this forms a distinctive feature of the teaching of this Gospel. The Spirit is "the Spirit of truth" (14 : 17; 15 : 26; 16 : 13; John can even say, "the Spirit is the truth", I John 5 : 7). Part of the work of the Spirit is to guide men "into all the truth" (16 : 13).

So significant for believers is truth that they can be said to be "of the truth" (18 : 37). Only those who are "of the truth" hear Christ's voice (18 : 37). They are sanctified "in the truth" (17 : 17). Indeed, Christ's sanctification of Himself (which most agree involves a reference to setting Himself apart for a sacrificial death)

---

[126] *Consummatum Est* (London, 1958), p. 161.

[127] G. E. Wright says, "the 'grace and truth' of Jesus Christ (John 1 . 14) are not abstract virtues but the active *ḥesed* and *'emeth*, rooted in the covenant conception" (*God Who Acts*, London, 1954, p. 114). It is valuable to be reminded that these are dynamic concepts, rooted in the Old Testament. But we should not overlook the fact that they are not simply Old Testament ideas re-stated. They have a new content, and that content comes from Jesus Christ. There is a valuable note on truth in E. Hoskyns and N. Davey, *The Riddle of the New Testament* (London, 1931), pp. 35–43. Their conclusion is: "Truth, in short, is knowledge of God through Jesus; such knowledge of God as through Jesus makes men veritably Sons of God."

was "that they themselves also may be sanctified in truth" (17 : 19). They "do" the truth (3 : 21; contrast I John 1 : 6). Truth is a quality of action, and not simply an abstract concept. Believers worship "in spirit and truth" (4 : 23f.). So important is this that the Father seeks such worshippers (4 : 23). Worship must be in conformity with the divine reality as revealed in Jesus.

The connection with Jesus is essential to the idea of truth as we see it in this Gospel. It starts from the essential nature of God, it finds its expression in the gospel whereby God saves men, and it issues in lives founded on truth and showing forth truth.[128]

---

[128] See also the note in Strachan, pp. 141–3, and that by S. Aalen, *SE*, II, pp. 3–24.

CHAPTER V

THE ORDER OF CHAPTERS FIVE AND SIX

Of the various suggested rearrangements of the text of this Gospel none has more probability than the transposition of chs. 5 and 6. The opening words of ch. 6 read strangely after a chapter set in Judea, but naturally after ch. 4. The Passover is near in 6 : 4, and may be present in 5 : 1. The reference in 7 : 1 to Jesus' walking in Galilee because the Jews sought to kill Him reads strangely after a narrative set in Galilee, but would be in place after ch. 5. Such a transposition must be held to be possible.

Against it is the point made by MacGregor (who nevertheless accepts the transposition): "the crisis of the Galilean ministry described at the end of chapter 6 comes too early if placed before chapter 5, its appropriate setting being immediately before Jesus' final departure from Galilee at 7 : 10, in which position it provides a fitting conclusion to the first Section of the Gospel." Moreover it must be borne in mind that John is not giving a complete history.

We ought not to expect everything to fit into a neat geographical or chronological picture. John draws his incidents from where he chooses. It may not be without relevance that in 21 : 1 there is an abrupt and unexplained transition from Judea to Galilee, so that the phenomenon is found elsewhere. We have no manuscript evidence for any other order than the traditional one. Nor is it easy to see how such a transposition could have taken place despite the claims of those who advocate displacement so strenuously. There is also the point made by Godet (on ch. 6) that a removal to Galilee would follow naturally on the conflict mentioned in ch. 5. Finally there is the theological point that in ch. 6 Jesus speaks of Himself as the bread of life, the bread which came down from heaven, the living bread, and makes it clear that men have eternal life only through Him. The establishment of Jesus' position as the Divine Son in 5 : 19–47 seems to be required as the basis for the claims made in ch. 6.[1] It is best to suspend judgment,[2] for certainty in such a matter is not attainable.

8. The Third Sign – The Healing of the Lame Man, 5 : 1–18

(a) The Healing, 5 : 1–9a

1 After these things there was [1]a feast of the Jews; and Jesus went up to Jerusalem. 2 Now there is in Jerusalem by the sheep gate a pool, which is called in Hebrew [2]Bethesda, having five porches. 3 In these lay a multitude of them that were sick, blind, halt, withered [3] 5 And a certain man was there, who had been thirty and eight years in his infirmity. 6 When Jesus saw him lying, and knew that he had been now a long time in that case, he saith unto him, Wouldest thou be made whole? 7 The sick man answered him, [4]Sir, I have no man, when the water is troubled, to put me into the pool: but while I am coming, another steppeth down before me. 8 Jesus saith unto him, Arise, take up thy [5]bed, and walk. 9 And straightway the man was made whole, and took up his [5]bed and walked.

[1]Many ancient authorities read *the feast*. (Comp. ch. 2. 13?) [2]Some ancient authorities read *Bethsaida*, others *Bethzatha*. [3]Many ancient authorities insert, wholly or in part, *waiting for the moving of the water: 4 for an angel of the Lord went down at certain seasons into the pool, and troubled the water: whosoever then first after the troubling of the water stepped in was made whole, with whatsoever disease he was holden.* [4]Or, *Lord* [5]Or, *pallet*

Up till this point John has been almost exclusively concerned with Jesus' dealings with individuals. There is still individual contact, but the healing of the lame man leads to a conflict with the Pharisees, the religious leaders. We are thus introduced to a theme which is important in the rest of this Gospel. Jesus does His mighty works, His "signs". But, instead of faith, strenuous opposi-

---

[1] *Cf.* Dodd: "It is God alone of whom it can properly be said that through union with Him (mutual indwelling) man enjoys eternal life (vi. 53, 56). Here therefore, as unequivocally as in v. 17 sqq., specifically divine functions and prerogatives are ascribed to Christ. We see therefore how important it is for our author's argument that the discourse in ch. v should precede the present discourse" (*IFG*, p. 340). D. M. Smith, Jr., argues that Bultmann has not made out his case for reversing the order of the two chapters (*The Composition and Order of the Fourth Gospel*, Yale University Press, 1965, pp. 128ff.).

[2] Wright is impressed by the absence of external evidence and thinks a verdict must be "not proven". He also says, "The conjecture is interesting, but it may well be dictated by a desire to confer a chronological accuracy and concern to the Evangelist of which there are few signs in his Gospel."

tion is aroused among the national religious leaders. The conflict grows and intensifies. Eventually as a result of it Jesus will meet His death.[3] Here we see the first example of this motif, the emergence of an implacable hostility. This has, of course, been foreshadowed in the Prologue ("He came unto his own, and they that were his own received him not", 1 : 11), and it will be developed in chs. 8, 12, 13 especially.[4]

1 Some time later[5] came a feast which is not further defined in this verse. If this chapter be held to follow ch. 6 it will most certainly refer to the Passover mentioned in 6 : 4. If not, there seems no way of identifying it with certainty.[6] John commonly adds "of the Jews" to such a reference for the benefit of his Gentile readers. Jesus followed the practice of the pious men of His day by going up to Jerusalem to observe festivals. Indeed John's indefinite reference to "a feast "may be intended to convey as much (it may imply that it was not only for specific, outstanding feasts that Jesus went up).

2 If the present tense "is" is significant it points us to a time before the destruction of Jerusalem.[7] This cannot be pressed, but

---

[3] *Cf.* Morgan: "On the human level, what Jesus did that day, and what He said that day, cost Him His life. They never forgave Him."

[4] Cullmann sees in the incident a reference to Baptism (*Early Christian Worship*, London, 1954, pp. 84ff.). But he admits that "It may seem at first sight that we are forcing a system" (*op. cit.*, p. 84). It does so seem, all the more so in that the only evidence he offers is: "After the previous chapters which refer explicitly or implicitly to Baptism in the Christian community, the connexion with Baptism here too is quite compelling" (*op. cit.*, p. 86).

[5] For μετὰ ταῦτα see on 2 : 12.

[6] For a discussion of the whole question see Westcott's Additional Note (pp. 204–7). He favors the Feast of Trumpets but few have been found to support him. Most commentators favor Purim or Passover. The theological context of John's treatment of the theme does not help us for the thought of judgment, which is prominent in this chapter, is associated with no less than four of the feasts. Thus we read: "At four times in the year is the world judged: at Passover, through grain; at Pentecost, through the fruits of the tree; on New Year's Day all that come into the world pass before him like legions of soldiers, for it is written, *He that fashioneth the hearts of them all, that considereth all their works;* and at the Feast (of Tabernacles) they are judged through water" (Mishnah, *RH* 1 : 2). Some manuscripts have the article, "the feast", notably KCL fl co. If it be accepted the feast will probably be Tabernacles, *cf.* 7 : 2 (though some think the Passover). The article is however omitted by P66, P75, ABDWΘ f13 *al.* There seems little doubt that we should read "a feast". But it does not seem possible to identify the feast with any certainty.

[7] For the article with Ἱεροσολύμοις see on 2 : 23.

neither should it be overlooked. "Sheep" is an adjective, which we should probably take with "pool" to give the meaning "There is by the sheep-pool, (the pool) which is called. . . ." The alternative is to supply "gate" as ARV (*cf.* Neh. 3 : 1; 12 : 39),[8] or perhaps "market" (AV). The name of the pool is likewise beset with difficulty. This may be due in part to the fact that the name is given "in Hebrew", which would have been unfamiliar to the Greek scribes who copied out the Gospel. It would be easy for them to make mistakes in a strange language. "In Hebrew" is usually understood to mean, "in the language spoken by the Jews" *i.e.* "in Aramaic". This is probably the way to take it, but the matter is not simple.[9] "Bethsaida", "Bethzatha", and "Bethesda"

---

[8] The problem is complicated by the fact that κολυμβήθρα might be either nominative or dative. The most ancient manuscripts do not differentiate. Some manuscripts read "in the sheep" (ἐν τῇ προβατικῇ) for "by the sheep", others omit the expression. But it is attested by P66, P75, BCK Wsupp fl f13 28 33 565 700 sa bo and should be accepted. Both nominative and dative are difficult, as in either case a noun must be supplied. If we take it as nominative we must supply a noun to go with προβατικῇ (most have "gate" as ARV and Goodspeed, but other suggestions have been made). If we view the term as dative it must be taken with προβατικῇ, "sheep pool", but then we must supply a subject for the verb (*e.g.* "Now at the Sheep-Pool in Jerusalem there is a place with five colonnades", NEB). In either case we could, of course, supply "pool" ("There is in Jerusalem by the Sheep Pool, a pool which is called . . ."), as do a number of translators, some (*e.g.* Berkeley) particularizing with "bathing pool". On the whole it seems as if we should take the word as dative and regard the widespread acceptance of "gate" with "sheep" as mistaken. Barrett may well be right in regarding as perhaps decisive the fact that "the whole ancient tradition takes together προβατικῇ κολυμβήθρα, and that no ancient writer (none in fact before A.D. 1283) supplies πύλη with προβατικῇ." Abbott finds no evidence anywhere for the ellipsis of "gate" (2216). He points out that in Nehemiah, for example, the word "gate" is added. Moulton and Howard cite a Christian amulet, possibly of the 5th century, which appeals to "the God of the sheep pool" ὁ θς τῆς προβατικῆς κολυμβήθρας (M, II, p. 85 n.). A κολυμβήθρα would be quite a large pool. The word is cognate with κολυμβάω "to swim" (used in Acts 27 : 43), and is defined in AS as "a swimming-pool".

[9] See the articles, "Did Jesus speak Hebrew?", by J. A. Emerton (*JThS*, n.s. XII, 1961, pp. 189–202); "The Words of Jesus according to St. John", by A. J. B. Higgins (*BJRL*, XLIX, 1966–67, pp. 363–86); "Hebrew as the Spoken and Written Language in the Last Days of the Second Temple", by Jehoshua M. Grintz (*JBL*, LXXX, 1961, pp. 32–47). These writers show that there is no certainty in the matter. Some hold that a variety of Hebrew was spoken in first century Palestine, and this may well have been the case. Scripture was read in Hebrew and the learned at any rate understood it. But Aramaic seems, on the evidence, to have been in all probability the language in common use, and thus the language meant here.

are all well attested, and "Belzetha" is also found.[10] The textual problem is a complicated one, and none of these variants can be ruled out as impossible. However, the copper scroll found at Qumran reads "Beth Eshdatain", which makes "Bethesda" almost certainly correct.[11] The clue that the pool had five "porches"[12] (better "colonnades") makes it probable that it is correctly identified as the double pool now known by the name of St. Anne.[13] There

---

[10] Probably the last mentioned is a variant of "Bethzatha". The strongest attestation appears to be that of "Bethsaida" (P66, P75, BW *pc c ff²z* vg co Tert), but it is not strong enough to be decisive. "Bethesda" appears to be a Greek form of בת חסדה, meaning "House of mercy". "Bethzatha" may be a corruption of "Bezetha" which Josephus tells us was the name of the quarter of the city in which the pool lay, or it may come from בית זית, "House of olives". Schonfield thinks it probably means "Place of Alkaline Salt". As, however, John gives no indication of attaching significance to the meaning of the name this does not help us in our quest for the original reading. David J. Wieand points out that Bethsaida, the best attested reading, probably means "House of Fish" or "House of the Fisher", and that there was a good deal of fish symbolism in the early church ("John v. 2 and the Pool of Bethesda", NTS, XII, 1965–66, pp. 392–404). This would favor the acceptance of this reading once it was introduced. He thinks Bethesda is likely to be the original reading, that this was corrupted into Bethsaida, and that the fish symbolism assisted the acceptance of the reading once established.

[11] 3 Q 15, col. 11, l. 12. J. M. Allegro, *The Treasure of the Copper Scroll* (London, 1960), pp. 165f.; M. Baillet, J. T. Milik, et R. De Vaux, *Les "Petites Grottes" de Qumran* (Oxford, 1962), p. 297; J. Jeremias, *ExT*, LXXI, 1959–60, p. 228. Calvin favored this etymology, "a place of pouring out".

[12] Augustine interprets the passage allegorically. He sees in the five porches a reference to the five books of Moses, utterly unable to bring healing (XVII. 2; p. 111).

[13] This identification is accepted by *The Westminster Historical Atlas to the Bible* (see p. 99 and plate XVII: B), the Rand McNally Bible Atlas (pp. 392f.), *et al.* See especially the discussion by E. J. Vardaman (*BT*, 14, 1963, pp. 27–29). He points out the importance of the discovery of a reference to this pool in the copper scroll at Qumran. Not only does the discovery point to the true name as Bethesda, but the fact that the form is dual points to twin pools. Wieand discusses six suggested sites and agrees that the identification of the twin pools of St. Anne with Bethesda is "virtually established" (*op. cit.*, p. 397). This site is now several feet below ground level, the natural result of the rebuilding which has taken place through the centuries. Many commentators point out that the identification is apparently ancient, for a Crusader church built over the pool has a mural depicting an angel arising out of the pool. G. Adam Smith is rather doubtful of the identification and inclines to the Virgin's spring (*Jerusalem*, II, London, 1908, pp. 564–7). St. Anne's twin pools, however, seem most likely.

would have been a colonnade along each side and a fifth on the area between the two pools.

3 There were many sick people gathered there. The true text says nothing as to why they so came. Vv. 3b–4 form a very ancient explanation which has somehow crept into the text. The manuscript evidence makes it certain that it is not part of the original Gospel.[14] But there is no reason for doubting that it explains the presence of the people (*cf.* v. 7). They held that a periodic disturbance of the waters was due to an angel. The first to enter the pool at such a time, they thought, would be healed. Accordingly they lay there each hoping to be the speedy one and thus to receive healing. The disturbance may have been caused by the intermittent bubbling up of a natural spring.[15]

5 John speaks of a certain man among the unwell. He does not tell us what his trouble was, but from v. 8 it would appear to have been some form of paralysis or lameness.[16] It was a complaint of long standing, thirty-eight years in fact.[17] The supposedly

---

[14]   It is omitted by P66, P75, ℵ BC* DW 33 157 *f l q* syr^c co *etc.* The authorities which include it (the more important being AC³ KL Θ f1 f13 Tert) differ among themselves.

[15]   R. D. Potter says that there is no spring there now. He argues from fragments of stone piping that water was piped in from the Temple area or elsewhere. "Then the 'moving of the water' would be the necessary renewals" (*SE*, I, p. 336).

[16]   As we ponder the question of why John selected this particular "sign", it may not be without significance that in the Old Testament the leaping of lame men is sometimes associated with the end time when the Messiah should come (*e.g.* Isa. 35 : 6). This miracle would help bring out the messiahship of Jesus.

[17]   Those who delight in allegories have not failed to point out that this is the number of years wherein Israel wandered in the wilderness (Deut. 2 : 14). They see in the man a symbol of the Jews at the time of Christ, paralysed in their lack of faith. Or, with Wright, they ask: "Is it not that the author inserts this period of time because it symbolises to him a period of spiritual impotency prior to the full enrichment of life which Jesus is now bringing to those who have faith in Him: a period of 'homelessness' prior to the unveiling of the Father's heart which constitutes the Mission of Jesus?" But while John may not have been unmindful of symbolic meanings, his mention of the thirty-eight years seems primarily to be a way of emphasizing the intractability of the complaint. Perhaps also he means us to infer that it was the years of suffering that aroused the compassion of Jesus. Chrysostom uses the persistence of the man in seeking a cure through all those years to point a moral: "while we if we have persisted for ten days to pray for anything and have not obtained it, are too slothful afterwards to employ the same zeal" (XXXV. 2; p. 126). For the use of an accusative after ἔχω to denote the length of time *cf.* 5 : 5, 6; 8 : 57; 9 : 21; 11 : 17.

healing water in all those years had effected no cure. It is against this background that John sets Jesus' healing word of power.

6 John does not say how Jesus knew of the length of time the man had suffered. He may wish us to understand it as another example of Jesus' supernatural knowledge (see on 4 : 17).[18] But it would have been quite possible for Jesus to have asked the man or someone else. John simply takes up the story at the point where the Lord asks the question, "Wouldest thou be made whole?" It is noteworthy that Jesus takes the initiative (as in the case of all the "signs" in this Gospel save the healing of the nobleman's son). He does not wait for this man to approach Him. He begins by inquiring as to his willingness to be cured.[19]

7 The man does not regard Jesus as a possible Healer.[20] This is not surprising for he did not even know who He was (v. 13). His thoughts were all on the curative properties of the pool. He explains that his failure to be cured during the long years of illness arises from his inability to get to the water quickly enough when the waters are disturbed. He really needs some one to help him down (the pool is deep, and lacks a shallow end). Because he lacks such assistance he is always beaten by someone else.

8-9a Jesus commands the man to rise, take up his pallet[21] and walk.[22] Immediately[23] he does so. The cure is instantaneous and

---

[18]   The aorist, γνούς, is rather against this. It would be better understood as "having come to know", "having found out".

[19]   Barclay has a helpful comment: "The first essential towards receiving the power of Jesus is the intense desire for it. Jesus comes to us and says: 'Do you really want to be changed?' If in our inmost hearts we are well content to stay as we are there can be no change for us. The desire for the better things must be surging in our hearts." Findlay reminds us that "an eastern beggar often loses a good living by being cured of his disease."

[20]   *Cf.* Calvin: "This sick man does what we nearly all do. He limits God's help to his own ideas and does not dare promise himself more than he conceives in his mind."

[21]   The word is κράβαττος (also spelt κράββατος; in א it is usually κράβακτος). It is apparently Macedonian in origin and denotes a camp-bed, a pallet (*cf.* Latin *grabatus*). Moffatt translates it "mat". MM speak of it as "the poor man's bed or mattress". It is a late word. Dods comments, "He was commanded to take up his bed that he might recognise that the cure was permanent."

[22]   Notice the significance of the tenses ἆρον, ἦρεν, of the single action of rising, περιπάτει, περιεπάτει, of his continuing to walk.

[23]   The immediacy of the cure is stressed by the use of εὐθέως. This word is common in Matthew and the very similar εὐθύς is frequent in Mark. But both are rare in this Gospel (three times each), and the rarity puts all the greater emphasis on the present passage.

complete. This healing differs from many others in that, not only is there no mention of faith on the part of the man, but there seems no room for it. The man did not even know Jesus' name (v. 13). Moreover right up till Jesus uttered the critical words his thoughts were centered on healing through getting into the pool (v. 7). We must feel that, while faith was commonly the prerequisite of healing, it was not absolutely necessary. Jesus is not limited by man as He works the works of God.

(b) Dispute over the Sabbath, 5 : 9b–18

Now it was the sabbath on that day. 10 So the Jews said unto him that was cured, It is the sabbath, and it is not lawful for thee to take up thy [1]bed. 11 But he answered them, He that made me whole, the same said unto me, Take up thy [1]bed, and walk. 12 They asked him, Who is the man that said unto thee, Take up thy [1]bed, and walk? 13 But he that was healed knew not who it was; for Jesus had conveyed himself away, a multitude being in the place. 14 Afterward Jesus findeth him in the temple, and said unto him, Behold, thou art made whole: sin no more, lest a worse thing befall thee. 15 The man went away, and told the Jews that it was Jesus who had made him whole. 16 And for this cause the Jews persecuted Jesus, because he did these things on the sabbath. 17 But Jesus answered them, My Father worketh even until now, and I work. 18 For this cause therefore the Jews sought the more to kill him, because he not only brake the sabbath, but also called God his own Father, making himself equal with God.

[1]Or, *pallet*

This is the first open hostility to Jesus recorded in this Gospel. As in the Synoptists the cause is Jesus' attitude to the sabbath. Those Gospels contain several references to disputes between Jesus and His Jewish opponents on the question of sabbath keeping. It is a little curious that the issue should loom so large in Galilee, where, on the whole, Jews were not as strict as those in Jerusalem. But sometimes we read of religious men from Jerusalem appearing in Galilee (Matt. 15 : 1; Mark 3 : 22; 7 : 1), and this may be the explanation. Some such incident as the one John relates here aroused the vehement opposition of the religious leaders, and they sent their emissaries into Galilee seeking evidence of similar breaches of the law. The Jews regarded the sabbath as a joyful day,[24] but nevertheless they hedged it about with a multitude of restrictions, which cannot but have been burdensome. Work of all kinds was prohibited, and the attempt to define work exactly so as to be certain of what was disallowed was sometimes fantastic.[25] Jesus persistently maintained that it is lawful on the sabbath to do good. He ignored the mass of scribal regulations, and thus inevitably came into conflict with the authorities.

9b, 10 John draws attention to the fact that the day of this cure was the sabbath.[26] Jesus' act of compassion had not been inhibited because there were scribal regulations forbidding works of healing on that day. Perhaps He even chose the day for His deed in order that the issues might be made clear. At any rate the reaction was not long in coming. The leaders of the opposition are called, as is John's wont, simply "the Jews" (see on 1 : 19). As the healed man was a Jew clearly the term is used in a sense other than ethnic. They will probably have been mostly Pharisees. They reminded the man who had been cured[27] that it was the sabbath (their word order stresses this word), and that therefore it was not lawful for

---

[24]   *Cf.* C. G. Montefiore: "in spite of the many restrictions and regulations, the Sabbath was upon the whole a joy and a blessing to the immense majority of Jews throughout the Rabbinic period" (*The Synoptic Gospels*, I, London, 1909, p. 93).

[25]   Some of the detailed regulations are passing wonderful. For example, "(On the Sabbath) a man may borrow of his fellow jars of wine or jars of oil, provided that he does not say to him, 'Lend me them' " (*Shab.* 23 : 1). This would imply a transaction, and a transaction might involve writing, and writing was forbidden. Or again, "If a man put out the lamp (on the night of the Sabbath) from fear of the gentiles or of thieves or of an evil spirit, or to suffer one that was sick to sleep, he is not culpable; (but if he did it with a mind) to spare the lamp or to spare the oil or to spare the wick, he is culpable" (*Shab.* 2 : 5). The attitude to healing on the sabbath is illustrated by a curious provision that a man may not put vinegar on his teeth to alleviate toothache. But he may take vinegar with his food in the ordinary course of affairs, and the Rabbis philosophically concluded, "if he is healed he is healed" (*Shab.* 14 : 4)!

[26]   There is no article with $\sigma\acute{\alpha}\beta\beta\alpha\tau o\nu$ (nor is there one in vv. 10, 16, though one appears in v. 18). John does not so much draw attention here to the sabbath, as to the fact that this was a sabbath kind of day, a day when certain regulations applied. $\dot{\varepsilon}\nu$ $\dot{\varepsilon}\varkappa\varepsilon\acute{\iota}\nu\eta$ $\tau\tilde{\eta}$ $\dot{\eta}\mu\acute{\varepsilon}\varrho\alpha$ is also hardly what we would have expected. Westcott finds the whole expression "very remarkable". It "suggests the idea that the sabbath was a day of rest other than the weekly sabbath."

[27]   The perfect $\tau\tilde{\omega}$ $\tau\varepsilon\vartheta\varepsilon\varrho\alpha\pi\varepsilon\nu\mu\acute{\varepsilon}\nu\omega$ puts some stress on the permanence of the cure. By contrast in v. 13 $\acute{o}$ $\iota\alpha\vartheta\varepsilon\acute{\iota}\varsigma$ points to the single act of healing.

him to lift up his pallet, let alone carry it. They probably had
in mind such passages as Jer. 17 : 21ff., and Neh. 13 : 15.[28] These
were in origin protests against the tendency to secularize the sabbath. It is not just another day of business. It is God's day. It
must be kept free from worldly pursuits.[29] So the regulations began
in the laudable attempt to safeguard the holiness of the day.
But in time they became so many, and drew so many absurd
distinctions that the true character of the day was lost in the
manner of its observance. Jesus' attitude recalled men to the real
meaning of the sabbath.

11-13 The man was not of the stuff of which heroes are made.
He put the whole blame on the shoulders of Him who had healed
him.[30] He did not know His name (v. 13). But he managed to
put a certain emphasis on the fact that it was the One who had
spoken the healing word and not himself that was to blame. Not
unnaturally the authorities immediately sought to know who this
was.[31] Their reference to "the man" is significant. It implies "a
contemptuous contrast with the law of God" (Plummer). But their
informant could not oblige them. He did not know the name.[32]

---

[28]   Mishnah, *Shab.* 7 : 2 lists thirty-nine classes of work forbidden on a sabbath,
the last being "taking out aught from one domain into another". An interesting
regulation provides that if a man took out "a living man on a couch he is
not culpable by reason of the couch, since the couch is secondary" (*Shab.* 10 : 5).
This clearly implies that the carrying of the "couch" by itself is culpable.

[29]   *Cf.* Strachan: "The rabbinic legal regulations were dealing with what
is also a modern social problem. The religious authorities were aware that
destruction of the Sabbath rest-day created a real danger to the higher values
of human life. It is as well that we should remember this when we criticize
their methods."

[30]   "Whole" is ὑγιής, an adjective meaning "healthy". It is curious that
John uses the word five times in this chapter and once only in the rest of his
Gospel. It is not a very common word, being found five times in the rest of the
New Testament.

[31]   McClymont comments: "The very form of the question showed how
entirely their thoughts were occupied with the infringement of their rule to
the exclusion of the miracle of healing. They put the question for the purpose
of dealing with the offender".

[32]   *Cf.* Temple: "Christianity founds hospitals, and atheists are cured in
them, never knowing that they owe their cure to Christ. Prisons are reformed
under the influence which flows from the Gospel; and the prisoners never know
– sometimes the reformers themselves do not know – that Christ is the Author
of the reform."

Nor could he point Jesus out, for He had "conveyed[33] himself
away." The multitude in the place would certainly have thronged
around the healed man, and made concealment easy.[34]
14 "Afterward" is an indefinite term.[35] It does not mean immediately afterward, but leaves the time uncertain. Jesus sought the
man out and found him in the temple. We may not unfairly
conjecture that the man had gone there to offer thanks to God
(*cf.* Mark 1 : 44; Luke 17 : 14). Jesus first drew attention to the
cure. "Thou art made whole" employs the perfect of the verb,
indicating that the cure was permanent. No doubt some of the
"cures" that were reported from the pool did not last very long.
Jesus' healing of the man was not in such a category. "Sin no
more" means "sin no longer" (Goodspeed: "Give up sin").
There is the implication that the man has sinned, and continues
in his sin.[36] Jesus enjoins him to break with it and be reconciled
to God. In 9 : 1ff. Jesus repudiates the idea that disasters like
blindness are inevitably caused by sin. But He does not say that
they are never caused by sin. In this present verse He seems to
imply that the man's sin had brought about his infirmity. Sinning
again may bring a worse fate. Jesus may mean a worse physical
fate. But it is more likely that He is referring to the eternal consequences of sin. They are indeed "a worse thing" than any
physical handicap.
15 The man who had been healed seems to have been an unpleasant
creature. It is obvious from the attitude of the Jews in v. 10 that
they were incensed at a breach of the sabbath. Yet as soon as
he found out the identity of his Benefactor he betrayed Him to
the hostile authorities.[37] There is an interesting difference between

---

[33] The verb ἐκνεύω (only here in the New Testament) means "to bend
the head aside" (AS), and so "to dodge".

[34] The genitive absolute, ὄχλου ὄντος, is ambiguous. It may give the reason
for the withdrawal, or the means of the withdrawal. Augustine has an interesting
comment on this verse: "It is difficult in a crowd to see Christ: a certain
solitude is necessary for our mind; it is by a certain solitude of contemplation
that God is seen" (XVII. 11; p. 115). Of the man he says, "He did not see
Jesus in the crowd, he saw Him in the temple" *(ibid.)*.

[35] For μετὰ ταῦτα see on 2 : 12.

[36] For this use of the present tense see on 2 : 16.

[37] Yet we should not overlook the fact that there was a certain amount
of danger to the man. He was still under the accusation of sabbath breaking,
an offence for which the death penalty was possible. His defence was that his
Healer had told him to carry his pallet. By producing the name, he made his case.

307

question and answer. The Jews had asked the man who it was who told him to take up his bed (v. 12). He answers that it was Jesus who made him whole. They emphasize the offence, he the healing.

16 The result was inevitable. The Jews took action against Jesus,[38] though we are not told exactly what form their "persecution" took. In v. 11 there was an emphasis on Jesus as the One who had caused the action. Here there is stress on the fact that it was the sabbath on which the deed was done. It was this that caused the opposition. "He did" is in a continuous tense. John may imply that there were other sabbath incidents he has not recorded, or that the Jews discerned what Jesus' habitual attitude was. *Cf.* NEB: "It was works of this kind done on the Sabbath that stirred the Jews to persecute Jesus."[39]

17 There are no words which Jesus is said to "answer".[40] He answered their deed of persecution. In the Synoptic tradition in such a situation Jesus defended His action by saying, "the Son of man is lord even of the sabbath" (Mark 2 : 28). This is often taken as indicating that any man is entitled to do as he wishes on the sabbath. This is almost certainly a misunderstanding. Jesus is there laying it down that He, the Son of man, is lord over even the divinely instituted sabbath.[41] Here His defence rests on His

---

[38] *Cf.* Augustine: "They sought darkness from the Sabbath more than light from the miracle" (XXI. 6; p. 140).

[39] Similarly C. B. Williams renders: "because He persisted in doing such things. . . ." The imperfect, $\dot{\varepsilon}\pi o\acute{\iota}\varepsilon\iota$, may of course signify "began to do". Even so, it implies continuity. However we understand it, the verb indicates more than a single action.

[40] Here and in verse 19 the verb is in the aorist middle, the only examples in 78 occurrences of $\dot{a}\pi o\varkappa\varrho\acute{\iota}\nu o\mu a\iota$ in this Gospel (there are a few places where the present might be either middle or passive). Abbott suggests that the middle here has something of a legal force "made answer to the charge", "made his defence" (2537). MM say that examples of the aorist middle are frequent in the papyri "but they are without exception legal reports".

[41] In Mark 2 : 27f. the word "man" occurs both simply and in the expression "Son of man". On this Moffatt says, "Had the original Aramaic simply meant 'man' in both sentences of Mark, it would have been translated as such uniformly, and, besides, Jesus would not have claimed that man was master of the sabbath which God had instituted" (*The Theology of the Gospels*, London, 1928, p. 152). Cullmann agrees that an Aramaic *barnasha*, meaning "man", might be mistranslated $v\acute{\iota}\dot{o}\varsigma$ $\tau o\tilde{v}$ $\dot{a}\nu\vartheta\varrho\acute{\omega}\pi o\nu$, "son of man", but he points out that Mark cannot have given the expression a meaning different from that he employs elsewhere. "He himself has thought, in any case, of Jesus as Lord of the Sabbath" (*op. cit.*, pp. 88f.).

intimate relationship to the Father. In the end both defences come to much the same. But it is interesting to see that Mark reports the saying with the emphasis on the position of authority that belongs to the heavenly Son of man, and John that which brings out the close personal fellowship between Jesus and His Father. The expression "My Father" is noteworthy. It was not the way Jews usually referred to God. Usually they spoke of "our Father", and while they might use "My Father" in prayer they would qualify it with "in heaven" or some other expression to remove the suggestion of familiarity. Jesus did no such thing, here or elsewhere. He habitually thought of God as in the closest relationship to Himself. The expression implies a claim which the Jews did not miss.[42] Jesus points to the unceasing activity of the Father.[43] Without Him this whole created universe would cease.[44] Unless He works continually no man could survive. And because of His close relationship with the Father Jesus works in the same way. The sabbath cannot interfere with the work of such an One. This has its implications for Christian service. The basic reason given in the Fourth Commandment for keeping the sabbath is that on that day God rested. God's people must rest as He rests. But Jesus "repudiates the thought that the divine rest from Creation took the form of idleness" (Temple). The compassion of God must be reflected in compassion in God's people.[45]

18 The Jews did not miss the significance of Jesus' words. He had called God "his own Father",[46] and this meant that He was

---

[42] I have dealt with this more fully in *The Lord from Heaven* (London and Grand Rapids, 1958), pp. 33–36.

[43] It is somewhat curious that He says, "even until now" (ἕως ἄρτι), rather than "continually" or the like. Godet gives the force of it by supposing Jesus at work in the carpenter's shop at Nazareth with Joseph. Should some suggest that He cease He might well reply: "My Father works until now, and I also (consequently) cannot cease to work."

[44] Dodd cites a Hermetic saying, "God is not idle, else all things would be idle, for all things are full of God" (*IFG*, p. 20).

[45] *Cf.* Plummer: "to cease to do good is not to keep the Sabbath but to sin."

[46] Πατέρα ἴδιον.

"making himself equal with God" (*cf.* 10 : 33).[47] "His own" confirms what we have said on the previous verse. Jesus was not teaching men that God is the Father of all. The Jews would have accepted this. He was claiming that God was *His* Father in a special sense. He was claiming that He partook of the same nature as His Father. This involved equality. So the Jews held that He was guilty of blasphemy as well as of sabbath breaking.[48] They discerned that the sabbath breaking was no isolated rootless phenomenon. It proceeded from Jesus' view of His person and was consistent with it.[49] But to them this was nothing less than blasphemy. It led them to unremitting efforts ("sought"[50] is in a continuous tense) to secure His death.[51] For other references to attempts to kill Jesus *cf.* 7 : 19, 25; 8 : 37, 59. "Brake" and "called" are both in continuous tenses. The Jews looked to the habitual attitude, not one isolated act and word.

---

[47] *Cf.* Stauffer: "Jesus does not displace God, he represents him, he can make himself equal, indeed identical, with God (John 5. 18; 10. 30). The incarnate Word is the completely valid bearer of divine revelation in the form of this world" (*NTT*, p. 122). Odeberg sees the words as corresponding to a Rabbinic expression "which to a Rabbinic ear is equivalent to 'makes himself independent of God', *i.e.* by usurping for himself the Divine power and authority . . . From the Rabbinic point of view the profanation of the Holy One . . . consisted not in his calling the Holy One his Father, but in his presuming upon a peculiar sonship in virtue of which he had the right of performing the same 'continual work' as his Father" (*FG*, p. 203).

[48] "Brake" is ἔλυεν. This verb has a meaning like "destroy", so that AG say, "Jesus is accused not of breaking the Sabbath, but of doing away w. it." In their view His attitude means the abolition of the sabbath.

[49] Hoskyns comments on the importance of the Jews' accusation: "The Evangelist recognizes that the accusation of the Jews is a thrust at the very heart of the mission of the Church; for their accusation overthrows the work of Jesus by making of it a thing to be set beside, and compared with, the work of God."

[50] ἐζήτουν. The verb is a favorite one with John and he uses it 34 times (Matthew 14 times, Mark 10 times, Luke 25 times). He uses it, as here, of seeking to kill Jesus 8 times and of seeking to arrest Him twice more.

[51] μᾶλλον is usually rendered "the more" which is a little strange as there has been no thought of killing Jesus up till this point. We should probably take it in the sense "rather". Up till now they had been "persecuting" him in a fairly mild way. Now that they realized what His claims were they sought rather to kill him.

9. THE THIRD DISCOURSE – THE DIVINE SON, 5 : 19–47

(a) The Father and the Son, 5 : 19–24

¹⁹ Jesus therefore answered and said unto them, Verily, verily, I say unto you, The Son can do nothing of himself, but what he seeth the Father doing: for what things soever he doeth, these the Son also doeth in like manner. 20 For the Father loveth the Son, and showeth him all things that himself doeth: and greater works than these will he show him, that ye may marvel. 21 For as the Father raiseth the dead and giveth them life, even so the Son also giveth life to whom he will. 22 For neither doth the Father judge any man, but he hath given all judgment unto the Son; 23 that all may honor the Son, even as they honor the Father. He that honoreth not the Son honoreth not the Father that sent him. 24 Verily, verily, I say unto you, He that heareth my word, and believeth him that sent me, hath eternal life, and cometh not into judgment, but hath passed out of death into life.

The third discourse turns attention explicitly to the person of Christ. This is a passage of critical importance, the significance of which is not always realized. It perhaps lacks striking expressions like "the bread of life" or the "I am" sayings. But its central theme is crucial. "Nowhere else in the Gospels do we find our Lord making such a formal, systematic, orderly, regular statement of His own unity with the Father, His divine commission and authority, and the proofs of His Messiahship, as we find in this discourse" (Ryle).[52] In the end it was this kind of claim that aroused the implacable hostility of the Jewish hierarchy, and brought about Jesus' death.[53] And it is only because His relationship to the Father is what He said it was, only because He is what He claimed to be that He is able to bring the new birth and the water of life that were the subjects of the preceding discourses.

---

[52] Ryle adds: "To me it seems one of the deepest things in the Bible." Similarly Phillips in his translation inserts a sub-heading "Jesus makes His tremendous claim."

[53] It is, as Barclay says, "an act of the most extraordinary and unique courage . . . He must have known that to speak like this was to court death. It is His claim to be King; and He knew well that the man who listened to words like this had only two alternatives – the listener must either accept Jesus as the Son of God, or he must hate Him as a blasphemer and seek to destroy Him. There is hardly any passage where Jesus appeals for men's love and defies men's hatred as He does here."

Similarly His claim to be the living bread, the Good Shepherd, and much beside depends on the truth here set forth. All this gives peculiar interest to this discourse.

We may divide it into three sections (though these divisions are not hard and fast): in the first Jesus speaks of His relationship to the Father, in the second of His function as Judge of men, and in the third of the witness borne to Him which establishes His claims.

19 The introduction to the discourse underlines its importance. There is the "answered[54] and said" and the solemn "Verily, verily" (see on 1 : 51, and notice its recurrence in vv. 24, 25). The language Jesus uses is thoroughly Rabbinic.[55] He begins with a very strong affirmation of community of action with the Father. It is not simply that He does not act in independence of the Father. He cannot act in independence of the Father. He can do only the things He sees the Father doing.[56] There is a continual contemplation of the Father by the Son,[57] an uninterrupted commu-

---

[54] For ἀπεκρίνατο see n. 40 above.

[55] *Cf.* Odeberg: "This is exactly how one versed in Rabbinic thought would try to make his compeers understand the relation between the Father and the Son. The expressions reflect, as has been pointed out already by Schlatter, characteristic Rabbinic thought and language" (*FG*, p. 203).

[56] Dodd sees here a genuine parable, "In John v. 19–20a (down to . . . αὐτὸς ποιεῖ) we have a perfectly realistic description of a son apprenticed to his father's trade. He does not act on his own initiative; he watches his father at work, and performs each operation as his father performs it. The affectionate father shows the boy all the secrets of his craft" (*HTFG*, p. 386, n. 2). It is possible that the words have their origin in such a situation, but if so the meaning has been transformed and deepened.

[57] Of the absolute use of ὁ υἱός Westcott says: "The idea is simply that of the absolute relation of the Divine Persons, of the Son to the Father, and consequently this term is used (19–23), and not (as below vv. 30ff.) 'I' – the Christ whom you reject – or 'the Son of God' (v. 25), or 'Son of man' (v. 27), which emphasise the divine or human nature of the Lord relatively to man." Murray points out that the Jews recognized the divine sonship of the Messiah, "But, somehow, they had never regarded it as more than an honorific title, familiar enough on the lips of the courtiers of an oriental despot, but never meant to be taken literally. They were, therefore, not a little startled when Jesus refused to regard it as a mere metaphor, and declared that His divine Sonship, so far from being a mere adjunct of His earthly sovereignty, was in fact the living root and ground of it." It is noteworthy that Jesus uses ὁ υἱός absolutely eight times in verses 19–26 and only five times in all the rest of this Gospel. His usual self-designation is "the Son of man". But here he is giving strong emphasis to His divine Sonship. See further on v. 25.

nion. The result of this is that it is the things that the Father[58]
does that the Son does, too,[59] "not in imitation, but in virtue of
His sameness of nature" (Westcott).[60] The verse contains the
thought of subordination, for the Son is pictured as completely
obedient to the Father. But there is also a mighty claim, for the
Son does "what things soever" the Father does.[61] Neither the lowly
obedience, nor the implication of deity should be overlooked.
John often reverts to the thought of Jesus' close relationship to the
Father (6 : 57; 7 : 16; 8 : 26, 38; 10 : 30; 14 : 9f., etc.). The implication is that the authority with which He teaches and acts is
nothing less than the authority of God.

20 The disclosure of the relationship between the Father and the
Son is taken a step farther. The Father loves[62] the Son (the tense
denotes a continuing habitual love; the Father never ceases to
love the Son). Now love ever gives. Love does not withhold. Thus
the Father shows (again the tense is present denoting continuous
action) the Son all the things He does. This carries the implication
that the Son does the things He is shown. Jesus' actions do not

---

[58] For the emphatic ἐκεῖνος see on 1 : 8.

[59] Abbott sees significance in the use of καί here. John "dwells on the principle of *correspondence* between the visible and the invisible, between the incarnate
Son below and the Father above" (2148).

[60] Schonfield misses the point with his translation, "What he does the Son
copies". It is not a question of copying: the Son does the same deeds as the
Father does. *Cf.* Barclay: "The things that God does are the things that Jesus
does; and the things that Jesus does are the things that God does. The great,
salient truth about Jesus is that in Jesus we see God." R. H. Lightfoot comments: "The union, therefore, is absolute. It is not, for instance, as though
the Son reveals the Father in certain particular ways or in certain remarkable
actions; no moment of His life, and no action of His, but is the expression of
the life and action of the Father".

[61] Chrysostom points out that " 'cannot do anything of Himself' is the
expression of One not taking away His (own) authority, but declaring the
unvarying resemblance of His Power and Will (to those of the Father)"
(XXXVIII. 4; p. 136). Augustine goes from the thought that the Father
and Son are inseparable to the thought of the eternal generation of the Son.
"The generating flame is coeval with the light which it generates: the generating
flame does not precede in time the generated light; but from the moment the
flame begins, from that moment the light begins. Show me the flame without
light, and I show thee God the Father without Son. Accordingly, 'the Son
cannot do anything of Himself, but what He seeth the Father doing,' implies,
that for the Son *to see* and *to be begotten* of the Father, is the same thing" (XX.
8; p. 135).

[62] For φιλέω see on 3 : 16.

proceed from merely human motivation. He acts only in accordance with the divine revelation.[63] Thus He looks forward to doing greater works, for He will be shown greater works. The result will be that His hearers[64] will be astonished.[65] The following verses show that these "greater works" are the Son's activities in giving life and in judging.

21 The thought moves on to judgment. The Father (He and no other) raises men from the dead and gives them life.[66] This is the teaching of the Old Testament (Deut. 32 : 39; I Sam. 2 : 6; II Kings 5 : 7). It would have been accepted without question by Jesus' hearers. There was no matter for marvel in this. What is marvellous is the next assertion that the Son also[67] gives life. This should be understood in the first place of the present gift of life that is the result of Jesus' activity. He is to go on and speak of Himself as the Judge of men at the last day (vv. 28f.), and this is not out of mind in the present verse also. He will raise men

---

[63] In 14 : 10 the works Jesus does can even be said to be done by the Father. Notice that John often uses the term "works", ἔργα, to denote the miracles (*cf.* 5 : 36; 7 : 3, 21; 10 : 25, 32, 37f.; 14 : 10f.; 15 : 24). The word does not denote something spectacular, but normal daily work. What passes with us as miracle is to Christ no more than a "work". The term is wider than the miracles, and includes all that Jesus does. But its application to the miracles is the important thing. See Additional Note G, pp. 684ff.

[64] ὑμεῖς is emphatic. There will be nothing astonishing to Jesus in all this, but His attitude is in sharp contrast to that of His unbelieving hearers.

[65] Jesus does not often speak of arousing wonder. But wonder may lead to faith (14 : 11), and thus be commended. Clement of Alexandria has recorded a statement attributed to Jesus: "he that wondereth shall reign, and he that reigneth shall rest" (*Strom.* I, 9,45; cited from M. R. James, *The Apocryphal New Testament* (Oxford, 1926), p. 2. James also cites an amplified version of the saying from Clement himself, and from the Oxyrhynchus Sayings; it occurs also in the *Gospel of Thomas*, saying 1.

[66] The idea was accepted throughout Judaism. SBk cite a Rabbinic saying: "Three keys are in the hand of God and they are not given into the hand of any agent, namely that of the rain (Deut. 28 : 12), that of the womb (Gen. 30 : 22), and that of the raising of the dead (Ezek. 37 : 13)" (I, p. 523). *Cf.* also the *Shemoneh Esreh* (one of the most ancient Jewish forms of prayer): "Blessed art Thou, O Lord, the shield of Abraham. Thou art mighty for ever, O Lord; Thou restorest life to the dead ... who sustainest the living with beneficence, quickenest the dead ... who can be compared unto Thee, O King, who killest and makest alive again ...? And faithful art Thou to quicken the dead. Blessed art Thou, O Lord, who restorest the dead" (E. Schürer, *A History of the Jewish People*, II, ii, Edinburgh, 1885, pp. 85f.).

[67] For this use of καί see n. 59 above.

314

up. But in this Gospel the thought recurs that there is a sense in which judgment takes place even now. Men's condemnation is that they love darkness rather than light (3 : 19). He that believes on the Son has (present tense) life (3 : 36). Just as the Father takes dead bodies and raises them into new life, so the Son takes men who, though their bodies are alive, are yet in a state of death, and raises them into spiritual life. Notice the significance of "whom he will". Men may not command the miracle. The Son gives life where He, not man, chooses.

22, 23 The thought moves on to that of judgment. Arising out of the lifegiving activities of the Son comes the thought that the Father does not judge men.[68] This was something new to Jews. They held that the Father was the Judge of all men,[69] and they expected to stand before Him at the last day. Jesus tells them now that the Father will exercise His prerogative of judging through the Son (*cf*. Acts 17 : 31). This has implications for the Person of Jesus. The Father has given Him this function of judging for the express purpose of ensuring that men give the Son the same honor as they do to Himself (see on 3 : 35 for the things the Father gives the Son). This is very close to an assertion of deity. Those who fail to honor Him fail to honor the Father that sent Him (for the "sending" of the Son see on 3 : 17). This probably means more than that the Sender is dishonored if His messenger is dishonored. The whole stress of this present passage is on the unity of the Father and the Son. What is done to one is done also to the other. The inherent dignity of the Son and His intimate relationship to the Father make the dishonoring of Him a very serious matter indeed.

24 The unity of Father and Son is seen also in the way men are saved. This very important saying is introduced with the doubled "verily" (see on 1 : 51). The man who receives the blessing is the one who hears Christ and believes the Father, in itself a striking way of affirming the unity between the two. "Word", as often in

---

[68] There is a double negative $o\dot{v}\delta\dot{\varepsilon} \ldots \varkappa\varrho\acute{\iota}\nu\varepsilon\iota \ o\dot{v}\delta\acute{\varepsilon}\nu a$ to emphasize the point. Similarly there is an air of finality about the perfect $\delta\acute{\varepsilon}\delta\omega\varkappa\varepsilon\nu$.

[69] *Cf*. SBk: "According to the Rabbinic view it is exclusively God who will judge the world ... In Rabbinic literature there is no passage which unambiguously places the judgment of the world in the hand of the Messiah" (II, p. 465). S. Mowinckel stresses the point (*He that Cometh*, Oxford, 1959, pp. 313, 319, 336, *etc*.).

the New Testament, stands for the whole of the message of Jesus. "Believeth him that sent me" is unusual. It is more common to have a reference to believing "in"[70] than simply to believing, in the sense of giving credence to, accepting as true. And it is more usual to have Christ as the object of faith than the Father. Yet the form of the expression here is important. All those who believe the Father, who really believe the Father, accept Christ. It is not possible to believe what the Father says and to turn away from the Son. The theme of this whole passage is the unity of the Father and the Son. Consequently it is natural to refer faith to the Father, the ultimate Object, with whom the Son is one. (See further Additional Note E, pp. 335ff.) The man who gives heed to the Son and the Father in this way "hath" eternal life. The life is his present possession. For "eternal life" see on 1 : 4; 3 : 15. The implications of the present possession of eternal life are brought out in the assurance that its possessor "cometh not into judgment." This is the usual Johannine thought that judgment is something that takes place here and now. The man who accepts the way of darkness and evil has already been judged. His judgment lies in that fact.[71] So with the man who has eternal life. His vindication is present in the here and now. He has already passed right out of the state of death, and has come into life. Though this is a present state it has future implications. The man who does not come into judgment will not come into judgment on the last great day either (Moffatt translates with a future: "he will incur no sentence of judgment"). The saying points to his permanent safety. To have eternal life now is to be secure throughout eternity.

The words of this verse should not be taken simply as a statement of fact. They are that. He who hears and believes has eternal life. But the words also constitute an invitation, a challenge.

---

[70] Phillips actually translates "believes in. . . ." But this obscures the construction used.

[71] Wright brings out the force of this. "To stop the ears is *one* way of listening: it is to pass a sentence of judgement upon oneself.

> Still, as of old,
> Man by himself is priced.
> For thirty pieces Judas sold
> Himself, not Christ."

They are a call to hear Christ and to take the step of faith.[72]

(b) The Son and Judgment, 5: 25–29

25 Verily, verily, I say unto you, The hour cometh, and now is, when the dead shall hear the voice of the Son of God; and they that [1]hear shall live. 26 For as the Father hath life in himself, even so gave he to the Son also to have life in himself: 27 and he gave him authority to execute judgment, because he is a son of man. 28 Marvel not at this: for the hour cometh, in which all that are in the tombs shall hear his voice, 29 and shall come forth; they that have done good, unto the resurrection of life; and they that have [2]done evil, unto the resurrection of judgment.

[1]Or, *hearken* [2]Or, *practised*

It is not possible to insist on a hard and fast division here, and some would take v. 25 closely with v. 24. It certainly repeats much the same thought, but the "Verily, verily" seems to indicate a new start. Some hold that this whole section is no more than a repetition of the thought of the last, arguing that the raising of the dead means the raising of the spiritually dead.[73] But the language of vv. 28f. seems too strong for this. Jesus has been thinking of His close relationship to the Father, culminating in the statement that whoever heeds His word and believes the Father has everlasting life. From that He proceeds to the thought foreshadowed in v. 22, that the Father has given Him the prerogative of judg-

---

[72] Bultmann points out that "Jesus' words are not didactic propositions but an invitation and a call to decision" (*Theology of the New Testament*, II, London, 1953, p. 21). He sees this not only in constructions like the present one with a participle stating the condition (see also 6 : 35; 8 : 12, *etc.*), but also in sayings where an if-clause precedes (*e.g.* 6 : 51; 7 : 16f.; 8 : 51, *etc.*).

[73] Wright, for example, says forthrightly, "It should be manifest to every reader, not wholly devoid of the historical imagination, that by the 'dead' the Evangelist neither means those who are physically dead nor the completely annihilated... The Evangelist – true to his Hebrew mentality – is giving expression to *the fact* of the life-giving mission of Jesus; he is not indulging in *speculations* about a problematical future... Those who are 'in the tombs' are those who are in need of spiritual quickening." But this ignores the language used. As Plummer points out (on v. 29), "A passing from spiritual death to *judgment* is not spiritual resurrection."

317

ment.[74] The plain meaning of His words is that He will be men's Judge on the great Day of Judgment.

25 For "Verily, verily" see on 1 : 51. It marks the statement following as emphatic and important. We might understand it of the raising of the dead at the last day were it not for the "and now[75] is". This shows that what is primarily in mind is the present giving of life that characterizes the ministry of the Son. In Him the last age is vividly present. Men's eternal destiny is determined by their attitude to Him. Those who are spiritually dead hear His voice, and those who have heard it live. "Hear", of course, means "hear with appreciation", "take heed".[76] Notice that Jesus refers to Himself here as "the Son of God", this being one of only three places in this Gospel where He uses this title (the others are 10 : 36; 11 : 4; cf. also 19 : 7). Apart from this chapter where "the Son" is so common (5 : 19 bis, 20, 21, 22, 23 bis, 26; elsewhere 6 : 40; 8 : 35, 36; 14 : 13; 19 : 1) Jesus' favourite way of referring to Himself is as "the Son of man" (1 : 51; 3 : 13, 14; 5 : 27; 6 : 27, 53, 62; 8 : 28; 9 : 35; 12 : 23, 34; 13 : 31; see Additional Note C, pp. 171ff.). In view of John's declared aim in writing, "that ye may believe that Jesus is the Christ, the Son of God" (20 : 31), the sparing use of "the Son of God" by Jesus is noteworthy. John prefers to make his point by the events that occurred rather than by Jesus' express claim.

26 The Old Testament makes it clear that life derives from the Father. It is He who breathes life into men (Gen. 2 : 7), and life

---

[74] Hoskyns emphasizes the eschatological significance of all this: "In the Fourth Gospel the history of Jesus possesses its proper, final, eschatological form – son of man, good and evil, death and life, judgement and salvation. But this form has not been imposed upon Jesus or upon the earlier tradition by the Evangelist: it is the meaning which the Father has impressed upon His Son and which Jesus, the son of man, understood, accepted, obeyed, and made known."

[75] Note that when the reference is to the future judgment in v. 28 the expression is ἔρχεται ὥρα. Here there is added, by contrast, καὶ νῦν ἐστιν. A similar expression is found in 4 : 23 where the reference is clearly present, while in 4 : 21 ἔρχεται ὥρα applies to the future.

[76] John to a large extent follows the usual custom of employing an accusative after ἀκούω where a thing is heard, and a genitive when a person is heard. But ten times he uses the genitive of the thing (here; 5 : 28; 6 : 60; 7 : 40; 10 : 3, 16, 27; 12 : 47; 18 : 37; 19 : 13). It is likely that this construction means "to hear with appreciation". Bernard (on 3 : 8) accepts this use wherever the genitive is found, but he does not notice that the genitive is *always* used with persons.

is always thought of as His gift (Job 10 : 12; 33 : 4). With Him "is the fountain of life" (Ps. 36 : 9). It is He who shows men "the path of life" (Ps. 16 : 11) and who "holdeth our soul in life" (Ps. 66 : 9). Moses can go so far as to say "he is thy life" (Deut. 30 : 20). The Psalmist speaks similarly, "Jehovah is the strength of my life" (Ps. 27 : 1), and he makes his prayer "unto the God of my life" (Ps. 42 : 8). Jesus' words must be understood against this background. The Jews accepted unhesitatingly the thought that all life takes its origin from the Father, all life save His own. His own life is inherent in His being. Goodspeed translates "the Father is self-existent".[77] But it is characteristic of this Gospel to bring out the thought that the Son has been given (see on 3 : 35) a share in this life. To Him it is given to have the same kind of life within Himself that the Father has within Himself.[78] John's interest is in that life which is associated with the Son. Again and again he records sayings and incidents that bring this home (see on 1 : 4). Cf. I John 5 : 11, "God gave unto us eternal life, and this life is in his Son."

27 In the Old Testament judgment is so typical of God that He can be spoken of as "the Judge of all the earth" (Gen. 18 : 25), or as "Jehovah, the Judge" (Judg. 11 : 27). While He commits present aspects of judging to men so that they are frequently exhorted to do just judgment and the like, yet the final verdict on men is in the hands of one Judge alone. It is this which makes the present passage startling. It is like the earlier expression which spoke of the Father as granting to the Son that He might have life within Himself. Both point to divine prerogatives in the Son. For the giving of judgment to the Son cf. v. 22, and for authority

---

[77] This seems to reflect the meaning of the Greek better than such translations as those of Knox, "the Father has within him the gift of life", or Rieu, "the Father, being as He is the source of Life."

[78] Augustine says that God "does not, as it were, borrow life, nor, as it were, become a partaker of life, of a life which is not what Himself is; but 'hath life in Himself,' so that the very life is to Him His very self... God lives, and the soul also lives; but the life of God is unchangeable, the life of the soul is changeable" (XIX. 11; p. 126). He illustrates from light. Men require an external source of light, "but since you remain in darkness when the candle is withdrawn, you have not light in yourselves" (ibid.). He concludes his discussion with the point that there is equality between the Son and the Father, with only this difference, "that the Father hath life in Himself, which none gave Him, whilst the Son hath life in Himself which the Father gave" (ibid.).

cf. 17 : 2. Judgment is committed to Him "because[79] he is a son of man." There is a difficulty about the indefinite article which ARV inserts before "son of man". Greek has no such article. We insert it or omit it in English according as the sense requires. If we insert it here the expression reflects a common Semitic idiom and means no more than "man". Jesus would then be saying that He will be the final judge of men because He, too, is man.[80] He shares their nature. This is not impossible. But one would have expected more than this as a qualification to be men's final Judge. On the whole it seems likely that we should understand the expression as equivalent to the frequently occurring "the Son of man" (see Additional Note C, pp. 172ff.). This is Jesus' favourite self-designation. Moreover it gives an excellent reason for judgment being committed to Him. He is the heavenly figure of Dan. 7 : 14 to whom is given "dominion, and glory, and a kingdom, that all the peoples, nations, and languages should serve him: his dominion is an everlasting dominion, which shall not pass away, and his kingdom that which shall not be destroyed."[81]

---

[79] Chrysostom refuses to take ὅτι as meaning "because" ("since then what hindered all men from being judges?"). He understands it to mean "that", giving the sense "That He is the Son of Man, marvel not at this" (XXXIX. 3; p. 140). He has not convinced very many, however, either in the meaning he assigns to ὅτι or in his sentence division.

[80] Dods accepts this meaning. He lists several ways in which the passage has been interpreted: the judgment is to take place with human publicity, Christ redeems men as man, men should be judged by the lowliest and most loving, the Judge must share the nature of the judged, only a man could enter the sphere of judicial office and have the compassion a judge of men ought to have, the judgment is an act of homage to God and must proceed from within humanity. He finally accepts the view of Beyschlag that men judge themselves by their attitude to the man, Jesus.

[81] Bernard thinks that the reason for the omission of the definite article is that "Official titles have a tendency to become anarthrous". But this tendency is not marked in connection with the present title. It may be better to see in it an emphasis on the nature rather than the personality of the Son of man. The expression is anarthrous also in Heb. 2 : 6; Rev. 1 : 13; 14 : 14, but these seem all to be quotations from or, at least, references to LXX. But almost certainly we are to see the real reason in the rule formulated by E. C. Colwell that if a predicate noun precedes the verb (as is the case in the present passage) it usually does not take the article even though it is definite (see on 1 : 1). This supports the view that we should understand the expression here as meaning "*the* Son of man". It is also worth noting that the expression is anarthrous in LXX of Dan. 7 : 13 (which is usually taken as the origin of the expression "Son of Man"), and in the original כְּבַר אֱנָשׁ.

28, 29 The climax to this section is reached with the explicit declaration that it is the voice of the Son that will call the dead from their graves.[82] The Johannine emphasis is on the present aspect of judgment. Here and now those who love darkness receive their condemnation. Here and now those who believe on Christ enter into eternal life. But this does not mean that the concepts of a future resurrection of the dead and of a judgment day are done away. John may perhaps not emphasize that future day, but he recognizes that it will come.[83] This passage is most explicit. At the consummation of the age the voice of the Son will usher in the resurrection.[84] All the dead will rise. Judgment, as always in Scripture, is on the basis of works. It is those who "have done good" who attain "the resurrection of life" (*cf.* 6 : 39f.), while those who "have done evil"[85] rise only to "the resurrection of judgment" (or "condemnation"; see on 3 : 17f.). This does not mean that salvation is on the basis of good works, for this very Gospel makes it plain over and over again that men enter eternal life when they believe on Jesus Christ. But the lives they live form

---

[82]   There is an ambiguity about the ὅτι. If we take it as "that" the passage will mean "Marvel not at this, that an hour is coming when all in the tombs will hear his voice." If we understand it as "because" then τοῦτο will refer to the preceding, "marvel not at what I have just said because an hour is coming...." The second alternative is preferable.

[83]   *Cf.* Bernard: "Such a doctrine, no doubt, has its roots in Jewish eschatology, but the Fourth Gospel cannot be understood unless it be realised that Jn. has not abandoned this, while he lays his emphasis on the spiritual conceptions of eternal life and judgment in the present". Similarly Barrett: "There is no reason whatever for regarding vv. 28f. as a supplement to the original Johannine discourse unless it is held incredible that John should have thought of resurrection and judgement under both present and future aspects." S. D. F. Salmond discusses John's teaching on life and judgment (*The Christian Doctrine of Immortality*, Edinburgh, 1907, pp. 387–95). He concludes that "Though they occupy a smaller place in John's writings, and are subordinate to other truths, the Second Coming, the Resurrection, the Judgment, the Life Eternal appear in John's teaching as they do in that of the New Testament generally" (*op.cit.*, p. 395).

[84]   Mowinckel points out that there is not much evidence in Jewish writings to link the Messiah with the raising of the dead: "the thought that the Son of Man will raise the dead is overshadowed by the more theocentric view, that God himself will work the miracle; and we never find a clear and emphatic statement that the Son of Man will raise the dead" (*op.cit.*, pp. 400f.). It is distinctly Christian doctrine which is set forth here.

[85]   For οἱ τὰ φαῦλα πράξαντες see on 3 : 20.

the test of the faith they profess.[86] This is the uniform testimony of Scripture. Salvation is by grace and it is received through faith. Judgment is based on men's works.

(c) Witness to the Son, 5: 30–47

30 I can of myself do nothing: as I hear, I judge: and my judgment is righteous; because I seek not mine own will, but the will of him that sent me. 31 If I bear witness of myself, my witness is not true. 32 It is another that beareth witness of me; and I know that the witness which he witnesseth of me is true. 33 Ye have sent unto John, and he hath borne witness unto the truth. 34 But the witness which I receive is not from man: howbeit I say these things, that ye may be saved. 35 He was the lamp that burneth and shineth; and ye were willing to rejoice for a season in his light. 36 But the witness which I have is greater than that of John; for the works which the Father hath given me to accomplish, the very works that I do, bear witness of me, that the Father hath sent me. 37 And the Father that sent me, he hath borne witness of me. Ye have neither heard his voice at any time, nor seen his form. 38 And ye have not his word abiding in you: for whom he sent, him ye believe not. 39 [1]Ye search the scriptures, because ye think that in them ye have eternal life; and these are they which bear witness of me; 40 and ye will not come to me, that ye may have life. 41 I receive not glory from men. 42 But I know you, that ye have not the love of God in yourselves. 43 I am come in my Father's name, and ye receive me not: if another shall come in his own name, him ye will receive. 44 How can ye believe, who receive glory one of another, and the glory that cometh from [2]the only God ye seek not? 45 Think not that I will accuse you to the Father: there is one that accuseth you, even Moses, on whom ye have set your hope. 46 For if ye believed Moses, ye would believe me; for he wrote of me. 47 But if ye believe not his writings, how shall ye believe my words?

[1]Or, Search the scriptures [2]Some ancient authorities read the only one.

---

[86] Cf. Calvin: "He marks out believers by their good works, just as elsewhere He says that a tree is known by its fruit... The Papists' inference from these passages, that eternal life repays the merits of works, may be refuted without any difficulty. For Christ is not here treating of the cause of salvation, but only distinguishing the elect from the reprobate by their own mark."

The thought of witness is a prominent one in this Gospel (see on 1 : 7). John insists that what he writes is well attested. Here he records some words of Jesus which stress the witness borne to Him. Jesus speaks of a five-fold witness. Witness is borne to Him by (i) the Father (32, 37); (ii) the Baptist (33); (iii) His works (36); (iv) Scripture (39); and (v) Moses (46). The Evangelist has earlier put some emphasis on the witness borne by John the Baptist. Here Jesus mentions this witness, but puts little stress on it. He is not interested in human witness of any kind (v. 34). He refers His hearers rather to the witness of His own works, and most of all, to that of the Father. He does not expect them to respond to this witness, for, although they profess a profound reverence for the Scriptures, they do not in their heart of hearts believe them. For this reason they do not accept the testimony that they afford to Jesus.

This stress on the witness borne by God has implications which should not be overlooked. Witness commits. As we pointed out in the note on 1 : 7, when a man gets into a witness box and bears his witness he commits himself. He no longer has freedom to come down on either side of the question at issue. He has burned his bridges. He has destroyed his freedom. Now it is something like this that God has done in Christ. Jesus is the supreme revelation of God. If we want to know what God is like we must look to Jesus. God, so to speak, has gone on record that this is what He is like. He has committed Himself in Jesus.

30 Once again Jesus stresses His dependence on the Father. As in v. 19, He confesses His inability to do anything completely on His own volition.[87] There He spoke of "seeing" the Father, here of hearing Him. There is no essential difference between these.[88]

---

[87] Both here and in v. 19 "the order of words lays great stress on οὐδέν. If he were to act independently of God (supposing such a thing to be possible), Jesus would be completely powerless. The whole meaning and energy of his work lie in the fact that it it not his work but God's" (Barrett).

[88] *Cf.* Bultmann: "The varying turns of phrase, namely that the Son does or speaks what He has seen in the Father or heard from Him express exactly the same thoughts: He is the Revealer in whom God Himself makes encounter in action and speech" (on v. 20).

In both places the language is metaphorical and points us to the Son's complete dependence on the Father. In the present context the activity being discussed is judging. So Jesus says that His judgment is "righteous" (or "just"; the same Greek word does duty for both meanings). He is always in touch with the Father. His perfect obedience means that His judgment is divine.[89] As in the earlier section, there is the combination of a great claim and the taking of a lowly place. Nothing more could be said for His judgment. But the reason that He exercises this "righteous judgment" is that He does not seek His own will, but that of the Father (the Father being characterized in typical fashion as "him that sent me").[90]

31, 32 Jesus points to the impossibility of a man's being accepted on the basis of his own word. Witness to a man must always be borne by someone else. Two or three witnesses are demanded by Deut. 19 : 15.[91] So in His own case he agrees that if He[92] bears witness to Himself, that witness is not to be accepted. By saying "my witness is not true" He does not mean that it is, in fact, false. It is, in fact, true, but it is true because it is witness borne in conjunction with the Father. Some modern translators, *e.g.* Rieu, Moffatt, translate "valid", but this seems to miss some, at any rate, of Jesus' point. He is not discussing the terms on which witness may be held to be legally valid. He is asserting that if of Himself He

---

[89] Chrysostom gives Christ's meaning thus: "As therefore none could object to the Father judging, so neither may any to Me, for the sentence of Each is given from the same Mind" (XXXIX. 4; p. 141).

[90] There is a noble saying attributed to Rabban Gamaliel: "Do his will as if it was thy will that he may do thy will as if it was his will. Make thy will of none effect before his will that he may make the will of others of none effect before thy will" (*Ab.* 2 : 4). Yet there is a suspicion of using God to secure one's ends in the Rabbinic saying that is quite absent from the Gospel saying. For Jesus' concern to do God's will see on 4 : 34.

[91] *Cf.* the Rabbinic sayings in *Ket.* 2 : 9, "none may be believed when he testifies of himself... None may testify of himself".

[92] The ἐγώ is emphatic. This is the case also in the preceding verse "I can of myself do nothing" and in v. 34 "the witness which I receive." In the present verse the force of the emphasis is, "If I alone and in fellowship with no other" (Westcott). To attempt to assert Himself (were that conceivable) would be to break the harmony between Himself and the Father.

were to bear witness to Himself that would make it untrue.[93] The
kind of witness He is bearing is true only if it is supported by the
Father. In 8 : 13f. the Jews maintain that His witness is in fact
false. This He denies. His witness is indeed true. But here the
point is rather that in view of the kind of witness He is bearing
with its stress on oneness with the Father (*cf.* vv. 19ff., 30) the
witness cannot possibly be true if it is unsupported. Independent
confirmation is required.[94] And that independent confirmation is
available. Jesus does not name that Other[95] that bears witness,[96]
but it is plain enough that He is referring to the Father. Jesus'
consciousness of mission, and of His relationship to the Father do
not rest simply on His own convictions. The Father bears witness
to Him. The witness of the Father may not be acceptable to the
Jews. It may not even be recognized by them. But it is enough
for Jesus. He knows that this witness is "true". His word order
puts emphasis on the word "true". For Him it is important that
there is a witness quite apart from Himself. His ministry does not

---

[93] *Cf.* Odeberg, "**self**-*testimony is not only not valid, but it is eo ipso* **not true**...
the very existence of J's (*i.e.* Jesus's) μαρτυρία is conditioned by his absolute
unity with and dependence on his Father. Thus *self-testimony*, in the sense in
which it is spoken of in 5³¹, means not merely testimony concerning oneself
but an act of severance from the centre and fountain-head of the spiritual
world, the establishment of oneself as an independent or self-dependent being;
such an act of self-assertion in the spiritual realm at once relegates the subject
of that act to the class of beings 'who are of the lie', 'who hate the light' or,
to use another technical expression of Jn for this category, '*who seek their own
glory*' (8⁵⁰), or who 'come in their own name' (5⁴³ ctr 5³⁰)" (*FG*, p. 219).

[94] *Cf.* Temple: "if His word stood alone, it would not be true at all. For
divine revelation did not begin and end in Him, though it reached its crown
and finds its criterion in Him. There must be other evidence, not only to support
His own, but because the nature of His claim is such that it can only be true
if all the work of God – the entire universe so far as it is not vitiated by sin –
attests it."

[95] It is uncertain whether we should regard the use of ἄλλος rather than
ἕτερος as significant. Many maintain that the former denotes "another of the
same kind", the latter "another of a different kind" (see on 14 : 16). If this
distinction holds the meaning here will be " '*another of the same kind as myself*'...
by which the evangelist suggests Christ's unique unity with the Father" (Abbott,
2730). But many writers do not observe the distinction, and, as John employs
ἕτερος once only (in 19 : 37), we do not have enough information to be sure that
he did. See further on v. 43. Chrysostom understands ἄλλος to refer to John
the Baptist (XL. 1; p. 144). There is little to be said for this view.

[96] ὁ μαρτυρῶν and μαρτυρεῖ indicate that the witness is a present fact,
and that it continues.

arise from any human volition. And the witness is such that He can rely on it. "I know that the witness . . . is true." It is the witness of the Father and nothing else that brings conviction to Him.

33-35 The Jews did not receive this witness that meant so much to Jesus. But He goes on to make it plain that they could have done so. They had not been overlooked. A witness had been given to them that they could understand and appreciate. They had even regarded him highly. But they had not in the end accepted his witness to Jesus. "Ye" is emphatic, as though to say, "You yourselves had a witness. My position is not so strange after all." "Have sent" (rather than simply "sent") is somewhat unusual. The Greek perfect puts the stress not so much on their act of sending as on its continuing result. Not only did they send to John, but the result of their embassy remained permanently with them. Yet they did nothing with it. Similarly when it is said of John "he hath borne witness" the thought is of a continuing message (Weymouth: "and he both was and still is a witness to the truth"). John's words were not spoken into empty air and forgotten. He bore his witness and it continued (*cf.* 1 : 15 and note). There is a note of permanence about it. John's witness was to "the truth".[97] This will have its full meaning here and point to Christ as the very embodiment of truth (*cf.* 14 : 6).

Now comes a little aside, in which Jesus explains His reason for referring to John's witness. It is not because He Himself bases His position on it. His "I" is emphatic. It sets Him in contrast to them. The [98] witness He receives is not from man (*cf.* 2 : 24f.). The whole emphasis of this passage is on the divine attestation of Jesus. His purpose in referring to John, then, is not to adduce further confirmation of what He already knows from God. It is to direct the attention of His hearers to that which might bring them to salvation. John's witness, if heeded, could start them out on the path that leads to salvation. This had, in fact, happened

---

[97]   The Qumran sect regarded themselves as "witnesses of truth" (IQS, VIII,6). As the idea of bearing witness to the truth occurs in the New Testament only in this Gospel (here and 18 : 37; though *cf.* III John 3, 12) this is a further example of the kinship between John and Qumran.

[98]   Godet explains the article thus: " '*the* testimony,' means here: 'that of which I have need, the only one which I would allege as confirmation of my own.' "

to some of the Twelve. They had been numbered among John's followers, but had left him to follow Jesus, in accordance with John's own witness (*cf.* 1 : 35–37).

Jesus, in His turn, bears witness to John. The past tense, "was", may indicate that John was now dead, or at the least that he was in prison. His work was past. Jesus likens him to a lamp[99] which "burneth". There is a hint here at "burning up". John's witness was costly to himself.[100] But the verb is used also in the sense of "kindle".[101] John's lamp was not self-sufficient (as was Jesus, *cf.* 1 : 4; 8 : 12). It was kindled from on high. "Shineth" points to John's unwavering testimony. A lamp shows men the way. John bore clear and consistent witness to Jesus. And Jesus recalls them to their reaction to John ("ye" is emphatic – this was what *you* did). "Rejoice" is a word denoting an overflowing, enthusiastic happiness, not simply "joy". They had exulted for a time in his light.[102] It may be that there is an idea of light-hearted merrymaking[103] where there should have been serious purpose. The Jews never did take John seriously. They never got to grips with his message. John was steadily, unflickeringly, pointing the way in his stern call to seriousness of purpose. And these Jews, who professed to be the people of God and to be seeking the way of

---

[99] The article, ὁ λύχνος, may point to a definite, well-known lamp. If so it will probably be the lamp prepared by the Lord for His anointed (or, "Christ", Ps. 132 : 17).

[100] "The lamp is exhausted by shining; its illuminating power is temporary, and sensibly consumed" (Westcott). There may possibly be a reference to Elijah whose word ὡς λαμπὰς ἐκαίετο (Sir. 48 : 1). We should also refer to our Lord's words, "Even so let your light shine before men; that they may see your good works, and glorify your Father who is in heaven" (Matt. 5 : 16). There is also a Talmudic injunction, "Let thy light shine forth like a lamp" (*Shab.* 116b), though this may conceivably depend on the Matthean passage.

[101] The verb is καίω. The meaning "kindle" is plain in Matt. 5 : 15, "Neither do men light a lamp...." Knox translates here, "He... was the lamp lit...."

[102] Josephus tells us that the people "were aroused (a variant reads 'overjoyed') to the highest degree" by John's sermons (*Ant.* xviii, 118).

[103] "Like children, they were glad to disport themselves in the blaze, instead of seriously considering its meaning. And even that only for a season: their pilgrimages to the banks of the Jordan had soon ended" (Plummer). Dods comments: "the expression seems intended to suggest the thoughtless and brief play of insects in the sunshine or round a lamp." He cites Hausrath, "As gnats play in the sunshine," and concludes, "the type of sentimental religionists revelling in their own emotions."

God, just as steadily ignored his essential message. Instead they
took him to be part of their ecclesiastical furniture, so to speak.
They exulted in God's gift of a prophet to their generation. And
promptly turned their backs on him.

36 Jesus' emphatic "But I" with which the verse begins in the
Greek stresses His separation from men. There is all the majesty
of His person in it. Great though John was, gladly though Jesus
attested his worth, his witness could not establish the position of
such a one as the Son.[104] "I", He says, "have the witness greater
than that of John."[105] In fact He has a twofold witness. Jesus
begins with His "works" (see on v. 20, and Additional Note G,
pp. 684ff.). He did this before when John sent messengers to ask
whether He were the Messiah (Matt. 11 : 4; Luke 7 : 22). These
works are not simply the product of His own assessment of what
is required. They are "given" Him by the Father (see on 3 : 35).
And they are tremendously important. Jesus repeats the word to
fasten attention on it. The works which He does are no ordinary
works. They are "the works which none other did" (15 : 24).
They are the Father's works, and, indeed, it is the Father abiding
in Him who does them (14 : 10). These works bear upon them
the hallmark of their divine origin. They show that Jesus is not
of human origin, but that the Father has sent Him (for "sent"
see on 3 : 17). Jesus' words have particular force, set as they are
in the context of the healing of the lame man. Before the very
eyes of the Jews there was evidence of divine power. And they
rejected it!

37, 38 From the works, the product of the Father, Jesus turns to
the Father Himself, who is described in terms of His sending of
the Son. He has borne His witness to the Son (*cf.* I John 5 : 9).
The past tense shows that this witness is no new thing.[106] The

---

[104] This seems better than understanding it in the sense, "I have witness
(pointing to me) greater than that which John had (pointing to him)", though
this is grammatically possible.

[105] There is no "that of" in the Greek, which reads "greater than John".
The meaning is certainly as ARV, but Black discerns a Semitic idiom (*AA*, p. 87).
Once again, words of Jesus reflect the Aramaic.

[106] *Cf.* R. H. Lightfoot: "all life, in and from the beginning onwards, when
rightly understood, has borne witness, as the activity of the Father, to the
Lord... But the Jews throughout have proved deaf and blind to the Father's
revelation of Himself."

entire revelation of the Father from the very beginning has prepared the way for the coming of the Son. Rightly understood it bears witness to Him. This is the witness that means so much to Jesus. Because He has the witness of God He is not troubled by the opposition of man. But though this witness is so clear and so valuable to Him, He does not anticipate that the Jews will respond to it. Their ignorance is threefold. (i) They have never heard God's voice. Moses heard that voice (Exod. 33 : 11), but they are no true followers of Moses, otherwise they would have heard God's voice in Jesus (3 : 34; 17 : 8). (ii) They have never seen God's form.[107] Israel saw that form (Gen. 32 : 30f.),[108] but they are no true Israelites. Were they, they would have seen God in Jesus (14 : 9). (iii) They have not God's word abiding in them.[109] The Psalmist laid up God's word in his heart (Ps. 119 : 11), but they do not share his religious experience. Had they done so they would have received that word from Jesus (17 : 14). "For" may give the evidence or the cause of the foregoing. The evidence is plain and simple. They do not believe Him whom the Father sent. Their unbelief excludes the possibility of intercourse with God. But their unbelief is also the reason why they do not have the word abiding in them. Both senses are true and probably both are meant. There is a contrast between emphatic pronouns: *He*[110] sent the Son, but *you* do not believe. (For "believe" see Additional

---

107   Knox renders, "You have always been... blind to the vision of him".

108   LXX translates both פְּנִיאֵל and פְּנוּאֵל as Εἶδος Θεοῦ (Gen. 32 : 30, 31; in the latter case both nouns have the article; in both Hebrew and LXX the verses are 31,32), "the form of God". Both Hebrew words mean "the face of God", the second form apparently representing the survival of the old nominative ending וּ (see Gesenius, *Hebrew Grammar*, ed. E. Kautzsch, rev. A. E. Cowley, Oxford, 1946, pp. 251f.).

109   In 15 : 7 Christ speaks of His own word abiding in men (though with the use of τὰ ῥήματά μου, not τὸν λόγον αὐτοῦ as here): "If ye abide in me, and my words abide in you, ask whatsoever ye will". Closely allied is the saying in 8 : 31, "If ye abide in my word (ἐν τῷ λόγῳ τῷ ἐμῷ), then are ye truly my disciples". In such passages the word stands for the whole message. Whether the word abides in the person or the person in the word, either way there is the thought of a continuing commitment to the totality of the message. In the present passage there is probably also a glance at the thought that Jesus is the true Word. *Cf.* Dodd: "λόγος is never merely a 'word'. It is in the widest sense God's self-disclosure, in word or deed, or in silent operations within the mind of man" (*IFG*, p. 330).

110   For the emphatic ἐκεῖνος see on 1 : 8.

Note E, pp. 335ff.) From all this we see that the Father's witness is accessible only to those who believe on the Son. As Barrett says, "the observer cannot sit in judgment upon it and then decide whether or not he will believe in Jesus. He must believe in Jesus first and then he will receive the direct testimony from God ... What John means is that the truth of God in Jesus is self-authenticating in the experience of the believer; but no such convenient phrase lay to his hand."[111]

39, 40 The Greek here is ambiguous. It could mean "Ye search the scriptures" or "Search the scriptures."[112] We should almost certainly take it as indicative.[113] Jesus throughout this section is taken up with the Jews and their attitude. Here He points out that they search the scriptures constantly (which we know from other sources they did, most diligently), thinking[114] in this way to find eternal life.[115] And, indeed, they might have found it thus, for the Scriptures, like the "works" (36) and the Father (37), bear witness to Him. Had they rightly read the Scriptures they would

---

[111] *Cf.* Bernard: "The believer has an internal witness, which is in reality the witness of God. We are not to think of voices from heaven or visible epiphanies... It is the confident assurance of the believer which is here in question."

[112] Goodspeed, Phillips, and other modern translators bring out the idea of diligent search implied in ἐραυνάω with "You pore over the Scriptures...." Chrysostom points out that it is not "read" but "search", and he thinks the word means "dig down with care that they might be able to discover what lay in the depth below" (XLI. 1; p. 147). This is the only place in this Gospel where the plural, γραφαί, is found.

[113] "And yet, when this is said, an imperative lurks behind the indicative, for the Saying encourages the steady investigation of the Scriptures" (Hoskyns). For a discussion of the textual evidence see Dodd, *IFG*, p. 329, n.1, and for a cogent argument in favor of the imperative see Field, pp. 89f.

[114] The subordinate clause is cited as an evidence of an underlying Aramaic. The Aramaic דִּ could be translated into Greek by ὅτι, as in most texts here, or by a relative as in some Old Latin texts, the Curetonian Syriac and the Armenian. The relative is also found in the apocryphal Gospel in the Egerton Papyrus, which is generally held to depend on John at this point. All this strengthens the evidence for an Aramaic source behind the sayings in this Gospel.

[115] *Cf.* the saying attributed to Hillel: "the more study of the Law the more life... if he has gained for himself words of the Law he has gained for himself life in the world to come" (*Ab.* 2 : 7). There are several sayings like Baruch 4 : 1f., "This is the book of the commandments of God, and the law endureth for ever: all they that hold it fast are appointed to life."

no doubt have come to recognize the truth of His claims.[116] But
they read them with a wooden and superstitious reverence for the
letter,[117] and they never penetrated to the great truths to which
they pointed. The result is that in the presence of Him to whom
the Scriptures bear witness,[118] in the presence of Him who could
have given them life, they are antagonistic. The words convey a
rebuke for the wrong attitude of the Jews to Scripture, coupled
with a profound respect for the sacred writings. *Cf.* Moffatt: "You
search the scriptures, imagining you possess eternal life in their
pages – and they do testify to me – but[119] you refuse to come to
me for life." "Ye will not come to me" stresses the activity of the
will. The Jews set themselves against Him. It is like Luke 13 : 34:
"O Jerusalem, Jerusalem, that killeth the prophets, and stoneth
them that are sent unto her! how often would I have gathered
thy children together, even as a hen gathereth her own brood
under her wings, and ye would not!" There is the same thought
of a tender eagerness to save, met by a stubborn refusal to be
saved.

41 In v. 34 Jesus disclaimed receiving witness from men. In the
same spirit He now disclaims receiving "glory" from men. The
word "glory" is patient of several meanings. Here Jesus means
something like "esteem" or "praise". His thought is that He does
not set before Himself the idea of pleasing men, but that of pleasing
the Father. Therefore it is nothing to Him whether men praise

---

[116] *Cf.* Morgan: "There is no life in the Scriptures themselves, but if we
will follow where they lead, they will bring us to Him, and so we find life,
not in the Scriptures, but in Him through them."

[117] In the early centuries of our era this reverence for the letter of Scripture
was taken to extreme lengths. Sir Frederic Kenyon says that scribes "numbered
the verses, words, and letters of every book. They calculated the middle word
and the middle letter of each. They enumerated verses which contained all the
letters of the alphabet, or a certain number of them" (*Our Bible and the Ancient
Manuscripts*, London, 1939, p. 38). In copying out the Scriptures the scribe
was not to do more than one letter before looking at his exemplar again (*Meg.*
18b). This kind of thing cannot be attested for the New Testament period,
but it undoubtedly had its roots there. It leads to a profound reverence for
the letter of the Scripture, coupled with a failure to grapple with its thought.

[118] The present, αἱ μαρτυροῦσαι, carries a double meaning. The Scriptures
now bear witness of Me. The Scriptures always bear witness of Me.

[119] Notice Moffatt's rendering of καί as "but". John often uses this coor-
dinating conjunction in an adversative sense, yielding the meaning "and yet".
See, for example, vv. 43,44; 6 : 36; 7 : 36.

Him or not. He does not receive the glory that they might wish to bestow on Him.

42 This verse is connected closely with the preceding. Some editors make it part of the same sentence. Be that as it may, Jesus' refusal to accept glory from the Jews is bound up with His intimate knowledge of them (see on 2 : 24). This intimate knowledge enables Him to say that they do not really love God.[120] They make a profession of loving Him. But in fact there is no real love. This is always the case where men's religion is basically self-willed. The Jews had worked out their pattern of religion and tried to fit God into it. They did not seek first the way of God and then try to model their religious practices on it.[121] They succumbed to the perennial temptation of religious men.

43, 44 Jesus returns to the thought of His rejection by the Jews, though in a form which connects it closely with the preceding sentence dealing with the Jewish love for the glory of men. It arises from this that they would receive a man who came in his

---

[120] $\tau\dot{\eta}\nu$ $\dot{\alpha}\gamma\dot{\alpha}\pi\eta\nu$ $\tau o\tilde{v}$ $\vartheta\varepsilon o\tilde{v}$ might denote love from God, or love for God. In this passage it seems more likely to be the latter. But we should not forget that "God is at once the Author and the Object of this love" (Westcott). Abbott argues at length for the meaning "the love *that proceeds from God*" (2032–40). It may incidentally be worth pointing out that John uses $\dot{\alpha}\gamma\dot{\alpha}\pi\eta$ seven times (here, 13 : 35; 15 : 9, 10bis, 13; 17 : 26). A. Nygren in his classic *Agape and Eros* (trans. P. S. Watson, London, 1953) has shown that the basic idea of $\dot{\alpha}\gamma\dot{\alpha}\pi\eta$ is that of self-giving love for the unworthy. His linguistics have been assailed by some, and it may be that he has drawn the distinction between two types of love too finely, and equated it too narrowly with the use of particular Greek words. But that there is such a love as he describes as *Agape* and that it is the Christian understanding of love seems clear. God's love to us is evoked by God's own inner nature, not by anything worthy in man. God loves us despite our unworthiness and we see the cost of His love in the cross. Moreover, this love of God is creative. It evokes a corresponding love within man. But the Jews were so engrossed in their own self-love, their own darling ideas about religion, that they did not react to God's love.

[121] "They did not really love God; they loved their own ideas about God" (Barclay); "They valued themselves on what they presented to Him, and yet they presented not that which most of all He sought, – the love in which self is lost" (MiM).

own name.[122] Such a one they would understand and appreciate.
He came from their world, and spoke of their world. But Jesus
is not of this type. Again His "I" is emphatic. It differentiates
Him from His hearers and all their ilk. He takes His origin from
the Father. He comes "in the name" of the Father (for "the
name" see on 1 : 12). This means that He was intimately connected
with the Father, that He in some way expressed what the Father
stood for. It is an affirmation of community of purpose, and it roots
His mission squarely in the will of God. But despite all this He
knows that He will not be acceptable to the men of His generation.
"How can *you* (the pronoun is emphatic) believe?"[123] He asks.
The thing is impossible with men whose habit it is to receive
glory from each other,[124] and who do not make a practice of seeking

---

[122] Attempts to identify this "other" seem futile. Some have seen a reference
to Bar-Koseba (*c.* A.D. 132), and find this evidence, accordingly, for a late
date for the Gospel. This allusion, however, is rightly rejected by nearly all
commentators. Jesus' words are very general, and are probably meant so.
McClymont and others say that Jewish historians enumerate no less than sixty-
four messianic claimants. There was a tendency for the Jews to accept such
men, and it is to this tendency that the words apply. If one figure is specially
in mind it is the anti-Christ. If we are to attach significance to the use of
ἄλλος (we might have expected ἕτερος) the meaning will be, as Abbott, " 'If
another come (*professing to be of the same kind as myself*),' like the Pauline (2 Cor.xi.4)
ἄλλον Ἰησοῦν" (2677). Odeberg thinks the reference is to the devil (*FG*, p. 226).

[123] The aorist πιστεῦσαι points to the act of putting one's trust in, rather
than the continuing belief, which we see in the present πιστεύειν in 12 : 39.

[124] Strachan understands this of the rabbinical schools: "Scripture study
had become a world in which men sought fame by showing their intellectual
prowess. One big authority was set over against another, and the result was
barren logomachy where men sought *honour one of another*." We might cite John
Masefield (as Strachan does in another connection):
> "The trained mind outs the upright soul,
> As Jesus said the trained mind might,
> Being wiser than the sons of light,
> But trained men's minds are spread so thin
> They let all sorts of darkness in;
> Whatever light man finds they doubt it,
> They love not light, but talk about it"

(*The Everlasting Mercy*, 1936 edn., p. 47).

the glory of the one God.[125] The issue is the glory of self or the glory of God. It is an issue which divides men still.

45-47 The discourse closes with an unexpected twist. The Jews prided themselves on their knowledge of Scripture, and Jesus had dealt with that (v. 39). Now He turns to their pride in Moses. They were proud of their connection with the great lawgiver. But Moses, not Jesus, is their accuser before God. Notice the present tense. Moses is a standing witness against them, a present accuser. They thought that they followed Moses, and could even make this their point of departure when disputing with the man born blind (9 : 28). They had "set (their) hope" on him.[126] But just as they misunderstood the scriptures in general, so they perverted the writings of Moses in particular. "The law of Moses is not a religion of salvation, it is the categorical imperative of God by which men are accused and exposed as sinners" (Hoskyns). Had they really paid heed to Moses they would have been convicted of their sin, and eager to recognize the Saviour. If they had really believed (notice the change from "set your hope" of the previous verse) what Moses said they would have believed what Jesus said, too. Moses' writings were prophetic. They pointed forward to Christ (*cf.* 1 : 45). Therefore those who rejected the Christ did not really believe what Moses had written.[127] And if these people, who professed to be Moses' disciples, who honored Moses' writings as sacred Scripture, who gave an almost superstitious reverence to the letter of the law, if these men did not really believe the things that Moses had written, and which were the constant objects of

---

[125] *Cf.* Calvin: "the door of faith is shut against all whose minds are filled with a vain desire for earthly glory." So also Ryle: "If a man is not thoroughly honest in his professed desire to find out the truth in religion, – if he secretly cherishes any idol which he is resolved not to give up, – if he privately cares for anything more than God's praise, – he will go on to the end of his days doubting, perplexed, dissatisfied, and restless, and will never find the way to peace. His insincerity of heart is an insuperable barrier in the way of his believing."

[126] The perfect ἠλπίκατε points to a continuing state. Their hope is a present hope, and not simply a past state.

[127] "Every true disciple of Moses is on the way to becoming a Christian; every bad Jew is on that towards rejecting the Gospel" (Godet).

their study, then how could they possibly believe the words,[128] the spoken words of Jesus?[129]

ADDITIONAL NOTE E: BELIEVING[130]

One of the mysteries of the Fourth Gospel is that while the verb πιστεύω is found 98 times, the corresponding noun πίστις is completely absent. The reason for this is uncertain. It is usually held that the use of the noun in some of the pre-Gnostic systems of the day gave it unhealthy associations and rendered the word suspect with John. This may be so, but if it is the case it still remains curious that he makes such a large use of the verb. Matthew uses it but 11 times, Mark 10 (plus 4 more in the ending of ch. 16), and Luke 9 times, so that John's use is remarkable.

Broadly we may say that he uses the word in four ways. He uses it of believing facts and the like 12 times, of believing people (or Scripture, *etc.*) 19 times, and of believing "in" Christ 36 times, while 30 times he uses it absolutely (the remaining passage is that wherein Christ refused to "trust" Himself to men, 2 : 24). There is nothing unusual about believing "that" such and such things happened, nor in believing people (dative). More significant is the use of the verb with the preposition εἰς to believe "into".[131] While it may be overpressing the use of the preposition to insist on its literal meaning yet John's idea is not unlike that of Paul

---

[128] ἐμοῖς is emphatic (see on 4 : 42). Jesus' words are set in strong contrast with Moses' writings.

[129] Loyd reminds us that the fault of not discerning the drift of Bible teaching is not confined to the Jews: "When we read the Bible, how little compunction and honest heart-searching it often arouses in us! When we hear sermons, how much more apt we are to apply their rebukes and warnings to our neighbours than to ourselves! And therefore the sermon is only just one more sermon, and not Jesus Himself speaking in our heart."

[130] See the important discussion in Dodd, *IFG*, pp. 179–186.

[131] Dodd finds no parallel to this construction either in profane Greek or in the LXX (*IFG*, p. 183).

when he speaks of men as being "in" Christ.[132] Faith, for John, is an activity which takes men right out of themselves and makes them one with Christ. It is important to notice that the construction is a literal translation of the Hebrew בֿ הֿאמין. This strengthens the hand of those who see a Semitic original behind this Gospel. But it also points us to an important aspect of the subject on which Dodd has well commented, "It would seem that πιστεύειν with the dative so inevitably connoted simple credence, in the sense of an intellectual judgment, that the moral element of personal trust or reliance inherent in the Hebrew and Aramaic phrase – an element integral to the primitive Christian conception of faith in Christ – needed to be otherwise expressed."[133] This "moral element of personal trust" is of the first importance for any understanding of Christianity and there had to be some way of bringing it out. πιστεύειν εἰς is the construction which does this.

It may be no coincidence that it is this Gospel which speaks so much of believing which also speaks much of "abiding" in God or in Christ. While believing and abiding are not connected in so many words (though *cf.* 12 : 46) they clearly mean much the same. In fact it might be held that the abiding in Christ which is stressed in the opening verses of ch. 15 is practically equivalent to believing, and that it is this fact that explains the otherwise strange absence of the verb "believe" from that passage.

---

[132] *Cf.* Moulton: "εἰς recalls at once the bringing of the soul *into* that mystical union which Paul loved to express by ἐν Χριστῷ" (M, I, p. 68). He does not see a great deal of difference between πιστεύειν εἰς and πιστεύειν ἐπί, but insists on the important difference between both of these on the one hand and πιστεύειν with the dative on the other. Bultmann thinks that πιστεύειν εἰς Χριστὸν Ἰησοῦν and similar expressions mean nothing else than πιστεύειν ὅτι Ἰησοῦς ἀπέθανεν καὶ ἀνέστη (I Thess. 4 : 14). He takes πιστεύειν εἰς to be an abbreviation, taken from the vocabulary of missionary preaching, for "to be converted from (Jewish or) heathen faith to Christian faith" (*TWNT*, VI, p. 204). Later he says of this expression that it is understood as "the reception of the Christian kerygma, and thereby as the saving faith which recognizes God's saving work effected in Christ, and makes it its own. Naturally πίστις here too contains the sense of *to give credence to;* and the concepts of obedience, trust, hope and loyalty can also be conveyed with it" (*ibid.*, p. 209). Burney, of course, is greatly attracted by Moulton's suggestion that this Greek idiom reflects the Hebrew בֿ הֶאֱמִין, Aramaic בֿ הֵימִין and that it thus signifies personal trust (*AO*, p. 34).

[133] *IFG*, p. 183.

So important is this conception of believing "in" Christ that the verb can be used absolutely, with no object expressed. There is no need in this Gospel to say who is in mind when "believing" is spoken of. Believing and Christ are so much part of one another that the former inevitably implies the latter. This is well illustrated in Jesus' conversation with the man born blind. To Jesus' question "Dost thou believe on the Son of God?" the man replies, "And who is he, Lord, that I may believe on him?" But when he finds the answer to his question he says not, "I believe on him" but simply, "I believe".[134] Again, there is not really a great deal of difference between believing the facts about Christ (really believing them) and believing, as we see from John's reason for writing his Gospel, "that ye may believe that Jesus is the Christ, the Son of God; and that believing ye may have life in his name" (20 : 31). In the same way simple credence of the Father is connected with the gift of eternal life (5 : 24).

The conclusion to which we come is that, while each of the various constructions employed has its own proper sense, they must not be too sharply separated from one another. Basic is the idea of that activity of believing which takes the believer out of himself and makes him one with Christ. But really to believe the Father or really to believe the facts about Christ inevitably involves this activity. Whichever way the terminology is employed it stresses the attitude of trustful reliance on God which is basic for the Christian.[135]

---

[134] In view of the warm tone of this passage and the fact that believing here cannot be separated from personal trust we must reject the contentions of those who maintain that for John believing means "intellectual assent" or the like (cf. E. F. Scott, *The Fourth Gospel*, Edinburgh, 1906, pp. 52, 267).

[135] Cf. C. H. Dodd commenting on πίστις in I John 5 : 4: "The way to victory is not a confident assertion of our own better selves, but *faith*, and faith necessarily refers us to something beyond ourselves. The victorious faith of the Christian is trust in God as He is revealed in Jesus Christ His Son. It means committing ourselves to the love of God as it is expressed in all that Jesus Christ was and all that He did" *(in loc.)*.

CHAPTER VI

10. THE FOURTH SIGN – FEEDING THE MULTITUDE, 6 : 1–15

1 After these things Jesus went away to the other side of the sea of Galilee, which is the sea of Tiberias. 2 And a great multitude followed him, because they beheld the signs which he did on them that were sick. 3 And Jesus went up into the mountain, and there he sat with his disciples. 4 Now the passover, the feast of the Jews, was at hand. 5 Jesus therefore lifting up his eyes, and seeing that a great multitude cometh unto him, saith unto Philip, Whence are we to buy [1]bread, that these may eat? 6 And this he said to prove him: for he himself knew what he would do. 7 Philip answered him, Two hundred [2]shillings' worth of [1]bread is not sufficient for them, that every one may take a little. 8 One of his disciples, Andrew, Simon Peter's brother, saith unto him, 9 There is a lad here, who hath five barley loaves, and two fishes: but what are these among so many? 10 Jesus said, Make the people sit down. Now there was much grass in the place. So the men sat down, in number about five thousand. 11 Jesus therefore took the loaves; and having given thanks, he distributed to them that were set down; likewise also of the fishes as much as they would. 12 And when they were filled, he saith unto his disciples, Gather up the broken pieces which remain over, that nothing be lost. 13 So they gathered them up, and filled twelve baskets with broken pieces from the five barley loaves, which remained over unto them that had eaten. 14 When therefore the people saw the [3]sign which he did, they said, This is of a truth the prophet that cometh into the world. 15 Jesus therefore perceiving that they were about to come and take him by force, to make him king, withdrew again into the mountain himself alone.

[1]Gr. *loaves.* [2]The word in the Greek denotes a coin worth about eight pence halfpenny, or nearly seventeen cents. [3]Some ancient authorities read *signs.*

This is the one miracle, apart from the resurrection, that is recorded in all four Gospels. We can only conjecture why this story was thus singled out, but obviously it made a strong appeal to the Gospel writers. In this account we see that the reason for the multitude's presence was the attraction of the "signs" that

Jesus wrought.[1] John also records Philip's perplexity as to the
feeding of the great crowd, and his little piece of mental arithmetic
which showed so clearly the impossibility of a solution out of the
disciples' own resources. And he tells us that it was Andrew who
brought the boy forward. It is in this Gospel that we read of the
proximity of the Passover, of the bread as "barley loaves", of the
reason for gathering up the fragments, of the effect on the people,
and of Jesus' dismissal of the disciples and of the people in general.
Clearly John has quite a lot of information not derived from the
Synoptists. Characteristically, John describes what happened as a
"sign". The effect of the sign is to make some people think of
Jesus as a prophet, and some to wish to make a king out of Him.

There are three principal ways of understanding what happened.
Some hold that a "miracle" took place in men's hearts. Christ
induced the selfish to share their provisions, and when this was
done there proved to be more than enough for them all. Others
think that the feeding should be understood as a sacramental
meal, rather like Holy Communion, wherein each received a tiny
fragment. This view has been severely criticized by G. H. Boob-
yer.[2] Though it is defended by Alan Richardson,[3] for example,
it seems to me untenable. Indeed, both the views we have noticed
seem to rely too much on presupposition, and to overlook what
the writers actually say. It is much better, accordingly, to hold to
the third view, that Jesus, the Son of God incarnate,[4] did do
something that we can describe only as miracle. Undoubtedly,
it inculcates spiritual truth (it is a "sign"). But this does not alter
the fact that the Gospel writers speak of something wonderful that
actually happened.

---

[1] Augustine marvels at the blindness of those who discern God's miracles
only in the unusual: "For certainly the government of the whole world is a
greater miracle than the satisfying of five thousand men with five loaves; and
yet no man wonders at the former; but the latter men wonder at, not because
it is greater, but because it is rare. For who even now feeds the whole world,
but He who creates the cornfield from a few grains?" (XXIV. 1; p. 158).

[2] *JThS*, n.s., III, 1952, pp. 161–171.

[3] *The Miracle Stories of the Gospels* (London, 1952), pp. 96f.

[4] Temple brings out the implications of the narrative for Christology: "It
is clear that every Evangelist supposed our Lord to have wrought a creative
act; and for myself I have no doubt that this is what occurred. This, however, is
credible only if St. John is right in his doctrine of our Lord's Person. If the Lord was
indeed God incarnate, the story presents no insuperable difficulties. But of course
such a creative act is quite incredible if He is other or less than God incarnate."

For the significance of this story we must bear in mind that the figure of eating and drinking is widely used in the Old Testament. It is a figure of prosperity ("a man hath no better thing under the sun, than to eat, and to drink, and to be joyful", Ecc. 8 : 15; *cf.* also Ecc. 3 : 13; 5 : 18), and it is often used of the blessings the people of God would enjoy in the Promised Land (Deut. 8 : 9; 11 : 15; Neh. 9 : 36, *etc.*). Contrariwise not to be able to eat is disaster (Ecc. 6 : 2). The metaphor of eating is used also of spiritual blessing. There are some interesting passages where men are said to eat God's word (Jer. 15 : 16; Ezek. 2 : 8; 3 : 1, *etc.*), but these are probably not the most apposite for our purpose. Eating is sometimes associated with the vision of God (perhaps because it was so characteristic of the sacrificial system), as when Moses and his companions "beheld God, and did eat and drink" (Exod. 24 : 11; *cf.* also Deut. 12 : 7; 15 : 20; 27 : 7; Ezra 6 : 21; Neh. 8 : 10; Ezek. 44 : 3). There may also be some link with the experiences of Israel in the wilderness at the time when God "rained down manna upon them to eat, and gave them food from heaven" (Ps. 78 : 24). So the prophet holds out before the people the promise of God: "If ye be willing and obedient, ye shall eat the good of the land" (Isa. 1 : 19; *cf.* Ezra 9 : 12). Contrariwise disobedience to God will lead to the absence of satisfaction in eating (Lev. 26 : 23–6). So also the gracious invitation goes forth: "come ye, buy, and eat . . . Wherefore do ye spend money for that which is not bread? and your labor for that which satisfieth not? hearken diligently unto me, and eat ye that which is good" (Isa. 55 : 1f.). So too, the Psalmist can look forward to the day when "The meek shall eat and be satisfied" (Ps. 22 : 26). From all this it is not surprising that the messianic banquet was one of the ways in which the delights of the age to come were set forth (*e.g.* Enoch 62 : 14).[5]

This "sign" then shows Jesus to be supplier of man's need. John's mention of the Passover (v. 4) is evidently meant to awaken associations of the wilderness as well as to locate the event in time. Later in the chapter the references to "living bread" (v. 51), "the true bread out of heaven" (v. 32), "the bread of God" (v. 33), *etc.*, are clearly to bring the same things before us. What the manna in the wilderness foreshadowed is perfectly given to men in Jesus. He is the Messiah who gives men the richest banquets

---

[5] *Cf.* also the passages cited in SBk, IV, pp. 1154ff.

to enjoy. The "sign" has to do with the Kingdom. The Jews misinterpret it, and think in terms of a prophet (v. 14) and of an earthly kingdom (v. 15). Both times they were on too low a plane. The miracle, rightly understood, pointed them to the Messiah, not a prophet, and to the heavenly Kingdom, not a kingdom on earth. There is probably another thought. Paul tells us that in the wilderness the Israelites "did all eat the same spiritual food; and did all drink the same spiritual drink: for they drank of a spiritual rock that followed them: and the rock was Christ" (I Cor. 10.3f.). It is likely that John has a similar thought in mind. Christ always has been the perfect provider of His people's need. It was He who was their "bread of God" in the wilderness, and it is He who is the bread of God now.

There are one or two coincidences of language in John's account with the story in II Kings 4 : 32-44 of the feeding of a hundred men.[6] But with the Synoptic narratives before us we will be slow to accept any theory of dependence on the Old Testament story. While we need not think of John as necessarily dependent on them,[7] they show us that a story of miraculous feeding was current in Christian circles.[8]

1 "After these things" is an indefinite note of time.[9] It does not pinpoint the following narrative. If we follow the text behind ARV the name of the lake is given twice. "Galilee" was probably the name by which it was known locally, and referred to in the Christian church. But it was officially called "Tiberias" from the town on its shores named after the Emperor. This town was founded about A.D. 20, so it is unlikely that the lake was called "Tiberias" during Jesus' ministry.[10] John then adds the name by which it was known

---

[6] Thus in II Kings and in John the loaves are said to be of barley bread (which Richardson sees as evidence that John saw Jesus as "the new Elijah-Elisha", *An Introduction to the Theology of the New Testament*, London, 1958, p. 101), whereas the synoptists do not specify any kind of bread. The word for "servant" in the LXX of II Kings 4 : 41 (immediately before our incident) is παιδάριον, which John uses of the boy with the loaves.

[7] Edwin D. Johnston discusses the relationship between the Markan and the Johannine accounts and finds five items in John but not in Mark which have every appearance of being historical. He concludes that John's account is not derived from that of Mark, but is independent (*NTS*, VIII, 1961-62, pp. 152ff.).

[8] For a full discussion of this miracle see H. van der Loos, *The Miracles of Jesus* (Leiden, 1965), pp. 619-37.

[9] For μετὰ ταῦτα see on 2 : 12.

[10] Josephus refers to τῆς πρὸς Τιβεριάδι λίμνης (*Bell.* iii, 57; Loeb notes as v. 1. πρὸς Τιβεριάδα and Τιβεριάδος).

when his Gospel was written. There is some support for reading "to the region of Tiberias" after "sea of Galilee",[11] and Brown, for example, thinks this may be original. ARV, however, has much greater support and is to be preferred.

2 The important thing about this verse is the use of the imperfect tense, denoting continuous action. The multitude "kept following" Jesus because they "continually saw" the signs that He "habitually did" on the sick. John does not record a great number of miracles, but such a statement as this makes it clear that he knew of a good number. Notice his characteristic word "signs" (see Additional Note G, pp. 684ff.).

3 The place of these happenings is defined as "the mountain". This expression occurs several times in the Gospels (e.g. Matt. 5 : 1; Mark 3 : 13), and raises the question whether there was a particular mountain which Jesus and His immediate followers familiarly knew as "the" mountain. If so, we have no means of identifying it. In any case the expression may mean no more than "the hill country".

4 Here we have a number of Johannine characteristics: an interest in feasts,[12] and in time notes, and the reference

---

[11]   εἰς τὰ μέρη is read by DΘ, some cursives, it[b.d.e.r¹] geo Chry. If accepted, this reading would place the feeding to the southwest of the Lake, whereas Luke 9 : 10 locates it near Bethsaida, on the north east.

[12]   Dodd thinks the mention of the Passover significant: "the Christian reader could hardly fail to remember that the Christian Passover was the Eucharist, and it is probable that the evangelist intended at the outset to give a hint of the eucharistic significance of the narrative which follows" (*IFG*, p. 333). But the Christian Passover was not the Eucharist, but Christ (I Cor. 5 : 7). There is no more reason for thinking that the Passover points to the eucharist here, than in 2 : 23. It is much simpler to hold that John mentioned the Passover because it was, in fact, near. Strachan wonders whether John represents the crowd "as receiving what the Passover could not give them?" This is probably justified for John seems to use the feasts to show how Jesus supplies what the feasts point to. *Cf.* Lucetta Mowry: "Christ in his signs, discourses, and religious ideas associated with each of the Jewish feasts finds a higher and absolute meaning in them. Thus Jesus is the bread of life and not the mazzah or unleavened bread" (*The Biblical Archaeologist*, XVII, Dec. 1954, p. 88). Similarly Richard Morgan points out that John "sets the content of his message within the *framework of Jewish feasts*. The long discourses on manna in the sixth chapter of John find their meaning within the perspective of the Jewish Passover" (*Interpretation*, XI, 1957, pp. 155f.). Bertil Gärtner has worked out in detail the points of connexion between the Passover and this chapter (*John 6 and the Jewish Passover*, Copenhagen, 1959). P. Borgen criticizes Gärtner (along with others) on the grounds that he does not reckon with the Torah and the theophany on Sinai as an important part of the background of this chapter (*Bread from Heaven*, Leiden, 1965, pp. 152f.).

to "the Jews" (see on 1 : 19).[13]

5-7 John does not record that Jesus and the disciples had withdrawn to a deserted place to be alone, and that the multitude sought Him out. Nor that He spent the day teaching and healing. Nor that it was in the evening that the multitudes were fed. It may be that he presumed that these facts would be known. For whatever reason he takes up the story at the point when Jesus sees[14] a large number of people coming towards Him. Philip is the natural person to ask where the food might be found to feed them all, for he was a native of nearby Bethsaida (1 : 44). John makes it clear that the question was by way of testing Philip out,[15] not because Jesus did not know (for Jesus' knowledge see on 4 : 18).[16] Philip's reply stresses the hopelessness of the situation judged from the meagre resources of the little band. Two hundred denarii's worth of bread would not suffice to give all this crowd a little taste.[17] Philip does not point to a solution, but to an impossibility.

8, 9 For Andrew see on 1 : 40, 42. Here, as there, he is introduced as "Simon Peter's brother" (he was clearly a subordinate person), and there as here he is bringing someone to Jesus. It is possible that his knowledge of the lad came as the result of a reconnaissance

---

[13] So too ἐγγύς is a Johannine word, occurring 11 times in this Gospel (the largest number elsewhere is 3 each in Matthew, Luke and Acts). John uses πάσχα 10 times (7 times in Luke), and ἑορτή 17 times (3 times in Luke).

[14] He says, Jesus "lifting up his eyes. . . ." Elsewhere in this Gospel Jesus is said to have lifted up His eyes only in prayer, at the tomb of Lazarus (11 : 41) and at the beginning of His high priestly prayer (17 : 1).

[15] πειράζω is used here (John's one use of the verb) in its earlier neutral sense of testing. It was so often used of testing in a bad sense, testing with a view to failure, that it came to mean "tempt". By contrast δοκιμάζω was used of testing in a good sense, testing with a view to commendation, so that it came to mean "prove", "approve".

[16] Notice the way Jesus' certainty is brought out: αὐτός sets Him in contrast to Philip, ᾔδει speaks of knowledge, not optimistic speculation, while ἔμελλεν gives a note of definiteness lacking in the simple future.

[17] Westcott, working on the facts that a denarius was a day's wage (Matt. 20 : 2), and that in normal times its purchasing power was known (eight choenixes of wheat), concludes that two hundred denarii would buy 4,800 quarts of barley, or 1,600 quarts of wheat. Attempts to render the amount of money into modern currency produce curious results. Goodspeed, RSV and *Amplified* make it forty dollars, but *Berkeley* renders fifty dollars and *Good News for Modern Man* two hundred dollars. In the sterling area the divergence is also marked. Barclay and Weymouth have £7, Schonfield £8, Rieu, Lightfoot and Phillips £10, *Twentieth Century* and NEB £20 (presumably the devaluation of the pound would affect these figures!).

with a view to finding out what food resources could be mustered, for he definitely relates the boy's small supply (evidently provisions for his own personal use) to the needs of the multitude. But, like Philip, Andrew is baffled by the emergency. The word for "lad" is a double diminutive, probably meaning "little boy".[18] Barley bread[19] was bread of a cheap kind, so that the boy was probably poor. The two fishes were something of a titbit[20] which would make the coarse barley bread more palatable.

10,11 Jesus now takes charge. He instructs the disciples to get the people[21] seated (strictly the word means "recline"). John tells us that there was a good deal of grass (so that reclining would present no difficulty), and mentions the number[22] as five thousand. Then he tells how Jesus took the loaves and gave thanks ("said grace").[23] After this He distributed to the people. John lets us understand that the disciples were the medium of this act of distribution, and does not mention them explicitly in this con-

---

[18] παιδάριον (here only in the New Testament). The strict meaning cannot be insisted upon, for the word is used in LXX at Gen. 37 : 30 to describe Joseph at the age of seventeen, and several times in Tobit 6 of a young man of marriageable age. MM say it is often used in the papyri with the meaning "slave", and Moffatt translates in this passage, "servant".

[19] κρίθινος, "made of barley", is found elsewhere in the New Testament only in v. 13.

[20] The word is ὀψάριον, diminutive of ὄψον. Both signify what is eaten with bread, "cooked food". ὀψάριον thus has the meaning of a special delicacy, a titbit (see MM), and sometimes it denotes fish. The parallel passages in the Synoptic Gospels, which have ἰχθῦς, show that it means "fish" here. In the New Testament the word is used only by John (five times).

[21] Notice the change from τοὺς ἀνθρώπους ("the people") to οἱ ἄνδρες ("the men"). It is unlikely that men only sat, the women and children remaining standing. Abbott suggests dropping οἱ, with W. H. margin, to give the meaning, "they sat down therefore, *(being) men* (exclusive of women) to the number of five thousand" (2009). This would agree with Matt. 14 : 21. Weymouth translates, "the adult men numbering about 5,000."

[22] The use of the accusative, τὸν ἀριθμόν, is given by Moulton as a survival of the classic use of the accusative of specification, whereas in the papyri and the New Testament the dative is more usual (M, I, p. 63).

[23] There is probably no great significance in the fact that John uses the verb εὐχαριστέω, whereas the Synoptists employ εὐλογέω in the parallels. Apart from a quotation in 12 : 13 John never employs εὐλογέω. Matthew and Mark use εὐχαριστέω in their accounts of the feeding of the four thousand (Matt. 15 : 36; Mark 8 : 6). Though in later times εὐχαριστέω came to be associated especially with the eucharist, John's use does not express this as we see from 11 : 41.

nection as the Synoptists do. "As much as they would" indicates
that this was a satisfying repast, not simply a token meal.
12, 13 The thought of plentiful supply is continued in the reference
to their being "filled" (*cf.* Mk. 6 : 42). But though there was
abundance there was no waste, for Jesus commanded the fragments
to be gathered up.[24] MiM think that the reason for this was "to
bring out the preciousness of the food which Jesus had given".
Twelve baskets[25] were filled in this way, from the pieces of loaves
that remained after the people had eaten.[26]
14 Once more John refers to a "sign" (see Additional Note G,
pp. 684ff.). It pointed men to God. But these men saw only a reference to a prophet, though admittedly the prophet that they
held would be the greatest of all, namely the one foretold in Deut.
18 : 15. It is somewhat curious that they thought of this prophet
rather than the Messiah, unless, contrary to usual Jewish opinion,

---

[24] Those who like to see a symbolical meaning sometimes draw attention
to the gathering of believers into the unity of the church as expressed in the
Didache 9 : 4, "As this broken bread was scattered upon the mountains and
being gathered together became one, so may Thy Church be gathered together
from the ends of the earth into Thy kingdom". If John does wish to express
a symbolical meaning in recording this detail it is perhaps more likely that
he is thinking of the "abiding" bread which Christ supplies: "the pieces which
are to be collected symbolize the bread which 'abides' and is not 'lost' " (Dodd,
HTFG, p. 207).
[25] The word is κόφινος, which is used in all four accounts of this miracle.
It is usually thought of as a small wallet, such as might be used by a traveller
to carry his provisions. σπυρίς (or σφυρίς), used in the accounts of the feeding
of the four thousand, could certainly be large, for it could hold a man (Acts
9 : 25). But the real difference between the two words, as MM maintains,
"is one of material rather than of size." The κόφινος was more rigid, probably
of wicker, whereas the σπυρίς was of hemp or similar material and thus flexible.
Hort has a lengthy note on the words κόφινος, σπυρίς and σαργάνη (*JThS*,
X, 1909, pp. 567–71) in which he denies that a distinction is to be made on
account of size. "The distinction appears to lie in the material, consistency,
and use. κόφινος is a word of very comprehensive use, but seems always to
denote a stiff wicker basket, σπυρίς always a flexible mat-basket made of such
materials as rushes" (*op. cit.*, p. 567). Juvenal apparently regards the κόφινος
as typical of the Jew (3 : 14; 6 : 542). This might well arise from a Jewish
habit of carrying food from reasons of ceremonial purity.
[26] The perfect, τοῖς βεβρωκόσιν, is a little surprising. Perhaps it is used
to reinforce the earlier indication of a satisfying meal. The plural, ἐπερίσσευσαν,
after a neuter plural subject is unusual. It may be meant to emphasize the
multiplicity of the fragments.

they thought of this prophet as the Messiah.[27] But perhaps this
is part of the confused state of mind of so many at that time.
Various ideas about the Messiah were current, and various prophets were expected (see further on 1 : 20f.), some being linked
with nationalist, militaristic views.[28]

15 Jesus saw the effect on the crowds, and perceived that they
would try and make a king of Him. There were fierce nationalistic
longings among the Jews of that period. Doubtless many of the
people who saw the miracle felt that here was a divinely accredited
leader, who was just the person to lead them against the Romans.
So they set themselves to make Him king. Like many others since,
they wanted to use Him to further their own ends. But to Jesus
the prospect of an earthly kingdom was nothing else than a temptation of the devil, and He decisively rejected it (Luke 4 : 5-8).
So, on this occasion He simply withdrew[29] into the mountain
until He was alone,[30] thus effectively stopping the enthusiasm of
the would-be king-makers.[31] Bailey points out that there is "much
of S. John's irony in the passage; He who is already King has

---

[27] Lagrange points out that the Pharisees were the ones who distinguished
between the Christ and the prophet in 1 : 21, whereas here the reference is
to a group of Galileans. This may point to the explanation. The Galileans
may well have had ideas different from those of the men of Jerusalem, and
perhaps influenced by the Samaritans (see on 1 : 21; for Jesus' messiahship
see on 1 : 41). Wayne A. Meeks maintains that "the prophetic and royal elements
in the Johannine christology are not to be understood separately, but exactly
in their combination and mutual interpretation" (*The Prophet-King*, Leiden, 1967,
p. 25). For John Jesus' prophetic and kingly functions were closely connected.

[28] See SBk, II, pp. 479f.

[29] πάλιν is difficult if it to be understood as "again". Abbott points out
that the word can mean "back" locally as well as "again" temporally. He
explains this passage as " 'he *retreated* (lit.) back . . . to the mountain.' He had
not 'retreated' before; He had 'sat' there; now He retires '*back*' to the mountain"
(2649 (i)). Similarly AG take the word to mean here "go back, return". John
uses the word 43 times, which is considerably more than any other New Testament writer (Mark has it 28 times).

[30] αὐτὸς μόνος coming at the end of the sentence is very emphatic. Knox
renders "all alone". μόνος is another Johannine word. It occurs in this Gospel
9 times, which is more than in any other New Testament book.

[31] Some find contradictions with the Synoptists. Matthew and Mark
tell us that Jesus withdrew to pray. But, as Bernard points out, such a motive
is not at all inconsistent with that given by John. Again Matthew and Mark
both say that Jesus dismissed the crowds. This, however, does not exclude the
possibility that "some, more obstinate and excited than the rest, would not
leave" (Bernard).

come to open His kingdom to men; but in their blindness men try to force Him to be the kind of king they want; thus they fail to get the king they want, and also lose the kingdom He offers."[32]

11. THE FIFTH SIGN – WALKING ON THE WATER, 6 : 16–21

16 And when evening came, his disciples went down unto the sea; 17 and they entered into a boat, and were going over the sea unto Capernaum. And it was now dark, and Jesus had not yet come to them. 18 And the sea was rising by reason of a great wind that blew. 19 When therefore they had rowed about five and twenty or thirty furlongs, they behold Jesus walking on the sea, and drawing nigh unto the boat: and they were afraid. 20 But he saith unto them, It is I; be not afraid. 21 They were willing therefore to receive him into the boat: and straightway the boat was at the land whither they were going.

This incident is recounted also in Matt. 14 : 22–33; Mark 6 : 45–52. In both cases the account is somewhat fuller than here (Chrysostom thinks of two different miracles, but the evidence does not indicate this). Matthew speaks of Peter's attempt to walk on the water, a detail not found in either of the other two accounts. Some have thought that John is not giving an account of a miracle. They hold that he thought that Jesus was walking by the shore. In the uncertain light the disciples, who in any case were scared by the storm, thought that He was walking on the water. However I do not think that that is the way the narrative reads. The disciples' terror at the sight of Jesus is inexplicable if He were on the shore, and they were thus safe. Some of them, at least, were used to the lake and its storms, and there is no indication that they were afraid before they saw Jesus. It seems clear enough that John recounts this as one of the "signs" of which he is so

---

[32] This is another indication that the Gospel is early, or at least that it is faithful to the facts. At the end of the first century, when Christianity was coming into conflict with the State, there would be no temptation to invent and little inclination to record that one result of Jesus' "signs" was that people wished to make a king out of Him.

fond,[33] even though he does not apply that word to it. In fact he makes no comment on the story at all. He apparently records it because it happened at this juncture, and not because he wants to point an edifying moral. This does not mean that it is without significance in this place. Its appropriateness as an introduction to the discourse that follows has been noted by many.[34]

16, 17 John's account is highly compressed. We do not learn from him, as we do from Matthew and Mark, that Jesus had sent the disciples away. Clearly He preferred to deal with the would-be king-makers without the presence of His own close followers. But this has to be inferred. John says nothing of the reason for the embarkation. He simply tells of the journey.[35] He mentions the coming of darkness,[36] which is understandable. But it is not easy

---

[33] *Cf.* Barrett: "That he meant to record a miracle, and not that Jesus waded into the sea a few yards from the beach, seems certain." And again: "there can be little doubt that both Mark and John, whether or not they used the best possible Greek, intended to record a miracle."

[34] For example MacGregor comments on the story's "fitness to serve as an introduction to the sacramental discourse on 'the bread of life.' The miracle in part meets the objection of verses 52 and 60, by hinting that Jesus' corporeality was of a peculiar kind which transcended the limits both of gravity and of space." Similarly Wright: "If . . . in the discourse that follows, the author is seeking to express the real mind of Jesus as to wherein true eucharistic feeding consists, it is exceedingly suggestive that he prefaces it with a narrative pregnant with the allegorical thought that Jesus is to be found when least expected." Even if one has doubts about the application of the discourse to the eucharist it still follows that this passage makes a suitable introduction to the later part of the chapter. Morgan points out that it was a miracle seen by the disciples only. He suggests that it is Jesus' way of answering the disappointment they must have felt when He refused to be made king. "So He gave them a demonstration of His present Kingship, and that in the realm of Nature. It was as though He had said, I have refused to be crowned King upon the basis of bread, but make no mistake, I am King in every realm; King in the realm of Nature, contrary winds cannot hinder Me; the tossing sea cannot overwhelm Me. I am King."

[35] ἤρχοντο points to a continuity, "they were in process of crossing", unless it is conative, "they were trying to cross".

[36] The impression left is that the voyage began shortly before or after darkness set in. Mark 6 : 48 refers to the walking on the sea as taking place "about the fourth watch of the night", *i.e.* towards dawn (the fourth watch was about 3 a.m. – 6 a.m.). The storm had made the four mile crossing so difficult that it took practically all night.

to see why he tells us that "Jesus had not yet come to them". They hardly expected Him to come walking on the sea, as their subsequent terror shows. Probably, with Westcott, we should take the meaning to be: "Jesus had directed the apostles to wait for Him at some point on the eastern shore on their way to Capernaum, but not beyond a certain time." The statement of Mark 6 : 45, that Jesus sent them "before him unto the other side to Bethsaida, while he himself sendeth the multitude away", is not irreconcilable with this view. The disciples were sent away by ship, but Jesus might well have rejoined them at some point further along the shore. His delaying is related to the dismissal of the crowd. The disciples knew this and may have expected Christ accordingly.[37]

18 John indicates something of the difficulties of the mariners. A storm was rising.[38] The Synoptists tell us that the wind was contrary. John merely says it was "a great wind".

19 Rowing under these circumstances was very hard work,[39] but they made fairly good progress. Twenty-five to thirty furlongs[40] must have taken them the best part of the way across the lake.[41] Then they see Jesus. John's language becomes vivid with the use

---

[37] Hendriksen thinks the reason for this way of expressing it is that the Evangelist, writing long after the event, presupposes that his readers will have in their minds the story of Jesus' coming to the disciples: "that coming of Jesus about which you have read in the other Gospels happened later during this same night." But Godet, writing of a similar view, says, "this sense seems quite unnatural."

[38] For the way in which sudden storms arise on the lake, and for a description of one such, see W. M. Thomson, *The Land and the Book* (London, 1880), pp. 374f.

[39] ἐληλακότες may possibly imply this. It is used in Luke 8 : 29 of a demon "driving" a demoniac into the wilderness. There is the thought of a compulsion. LS give the meaning "drive, set in motion".

[40] A στάδιον was about 600 feet (according to LS, 606¾ English feet). The greatest breadth of the lake is 61 στάδια but they were not crossing at the greatest breadth. They apparently were going from the N.E. to the N.W., and the distance, depending on their exact points of departure and arrival, would have been much less.

[41] Mark says "the boat was in the midst of the sea" (Mark 6 : 47). But this does not pinpoint the location as the center of the lake. It simply indicates that they were some distance from the shore.

of the present tense. The sight of Jesus walking on the sea[42] and nearing their boat filled them with fear. Again we must supplement this narrative by that of the Synoptists to find the reason – they thought that they saw a phantom.

20 Jesus immediately reassured them. His well known voice with its words of comfort identified Him to them. What they saw was real. It is possible that His words are meant to give a hint of deity.[43] Certainly spoken in these circumstances at the culminating point of the miracle they must have been impressive, and it is probably no coincidence that all three accounts tell us that He said "It is I; be not afraid" (the Synoptists prefix "Be of good cheer"). **21** The narrative ends rather curiously. They wanted to take Jesus into the boat. This is natural enough. But did they actually do so? John's words may be intended to mean this (as translations like AV, RSV, Knox, Phillips, Schonfield imply). The choice of expression may be dictated by the wish to show that their attitude was completely changed from the fear of a little time back. Bernard thinks the meaning is that they were so close to the shore that they were not able to translate their wish into action. They finished the voyage before this could happen. But it may well be that

---

[42] It is most natural to take ἐπὶ τῆς θαλάσσης as meaning "on the lake", and not "by the shore" as Bernard, Barclay and others understand it. Bernard understands the incident this way: "when the boat got into the shallow water near the western shore, the disciples saw Jesus in the uncertain light walking by the lake, and were frightened, not being sure what they saw." He thinks that "to read ἐπὶ τὴν θαλάσσαν would indicate beyond question that Jesus literally 'walked on the sea.' " This latter point is contradicted by the use of this construction in v. 16 where the meaning is that the disciples came to the sea shore. That the construction with the genitive can mean "by the lake" is clear from its occurrence in 21 : 1. But that is not its only meaning, and here the context puts it beyond reasonable doubt that the meaning is "on" and not "by" the lake. Mark employs the same expression as John, and there the context leaves no doubt that it means "on" the lake. Moule takes the genitive here to mean much the same as the accusative in Matt. 14 : 25 (*IBNTG*, p. 50). In a similar construction in John 17 : 4 ἐπὶ τῆς γῆς can mean only "on" (not "by") the earth.

[43] Ἐγώ εἰμι is often the style of deity, especially in the Greek Old Testament. Undoubtedly such a meaning is conveyed in some places in this Gospel (*e.g.* 8 : 58). But here it is primarily a means of self-identification. What else would He say? However, Dodd can say, "it seems more than probable that it is to be understood here as elsewhere as the equivalent of the divine name אני הוא, I AM" (*IFG*, p. 345). Abbott denies that the expression means "It is I", and brings evidence to support the meaning "I am the Saviour" (2220–22).

John's very short account is intended to be understood in the same
way as that of Mark, who tells us that Jesus was received into the
ship, and that there was then a lull in the wind. This could
facilitate the speedy end of the voyage,[44] which John tells us
actually came to pass. Or John may wish us to think of a second
miracle, as Barrett suggests, in the spirit of Ps. 107 : 23-32
(especially v. 30, "he bringeth them unto their desired haven"). This is
brought out in Moffatt's version, "so they agreed to take him on board,
and the boat instantly reached the land they were making for."[45]

12. THE FOURTH DISCOURSE – THE BREAD OF LIFE, 6 : 22–66

There are three main lines of interpretation of this discourse.[46]
Most expositors today apply it to the Lord's Supper. Unlike the
Synoptists, John does not mention the institution of this sacrament.
He has a lengthy account of Jesus' farewell discourses, but gives
no hint of the institution of the Supper though this occupied an
important place in the life of the church at the time the Gospel
was written.[47] However, in this chapter John uses language which

---

[44] McClymont thinks the meaning may be "that the vessel went straight
to its destination, and that the remaining mile or two seemed as nothing to
the astonished and rejoicing disciples."

[45] Cf. Godet: "One can scarcely imagine, indeed, that, after an act of
power so magnificent and so kingly as Jesus' walking on the waters, He should
have seated Himself in the boat, and the voyage should have been laboriously
continued by the stroke of the oar? At the moment when Jesus set His foot
on the boat, He communicated to it, as He has just done for Peter, the force
victorious over gravity and space, which had just been so strikingly displayed
on His own person."

[46] Some scholars prefer to think of various strata in the narrative and regard it
as it stands as self-contradictory. Of such views Hoskyns says: "The dislocation of
the discourse on the assumption that it is possible to separate an original stratum
from later interpolations is only a learned method of saying that a scholar is
unable to penetrate the author's meaning, and prefers to substitute two or
more disjointed fragments for one homogeneous whole" (Detached Note, p. 305).

[47] The reason for this omission is far from clear. J. Jeremias thinks that
John "consciously omitted the account of the Last Supper because he did not
want to disclose the sacred formula to the heathen" (The Eucharistic Words of
Jesus, Oxford, 1955, p. 73). He rejects other explanations such as that John
wrote "before it was possible to speak of a Christian Eucharist" (G. Kittel),
or that he "rejected the Eucharist or regarded it as superfluous" (R. Bultmann),
or that he "did not connect the institution of the Eucharist with the Last Supper,
but with the feeding of the five thousand" (H. Windisch and E. Lohmeyer).
Perhaps better than any is the possibility that John was confronted with Christians who overstressed participation in the sacrament, and that he accordingly did
not even mention the institution. But there is no evidence, and all this is conjecture.

many feel applies to the sacrament as it applies to nothing else. They hold accordingly that John, for reasons of his own, has omitted all mention of the sacrament at the point where one would have naturally expected it, and has instead given us his sacramental teaching in the form of a discourse of our Lord inserted at this point.[48] Little evidence is cited for this view. It is accepted as axiomatic that language like that used here (especially vv. 53ff.) refers to the sacrament.[49]

But there are some strong arguments against it. There is firstly the setting. Jesus is speaking in the synagogue at Capernaum to a crowd which includes opponents and lukewarm disciples. It is difficult to hold that John intends us to think that to such an audience Jesus gave teaching about a sacrament whose institution lay well in the future. References to such a sacrament could not possibly have been discerned by this audience. The only result could have been profound mystification. Secondly, there is the very strength of the language used. Take as an example v. 53, "Except ye eat the flesh of the Son of man and drink his blood, ye have not life in yourselves." This language is absolute. No qualification is inserted. No loophole is left. But it is impossible to think that Jesus (or for that matter the Evangelist) should have taught that the one thing necessary for eternal life is to receive the sacrament. Those who think of the discourse as referring to the sacrament usually do not face the logic of their position at this

---

[48] It is perhaps worth noting that this interpretation is not early. *Cf.* M. Wiles: "The Eucharistic interpretation of this passage is so familiar to us that it comes as something of a surprise to find that it takes a comparatively subordinate place in the earliest exegesis, especially from Alexandria" (*The Spiritual Gospel*, Cambridge, 1960, p. 52). Brown cites Clement of Alexandria, Origen and Eusebius as specific examples of patristic exegetes who interpreted the whole passage spiritually, not with reference to the Eucharist.

[49] Oscar Cullmann regards the chapter as practically a demonstration of the truth of his method (*Early Christian Worship*, London, 1954, pp. 93ff.). The discourse refers to the Lord's Supper, the miracle points to the discourse, but without mentioning the sacrament, therefore other miracles should be taken as pointing to the sacraments. Characteristically Cullmann does not cite evidence for and against. He treats the sacramental reference as axiomatic (though he does notice some who disagree with his view). In particular he does not notice the implications of taking v. 53 as applying to the sacrament.

point, but introduce some qualification.[50] Thirdly, the consequences of the eating and drinking spoken of here are also said by
John, both elsewhere and in this very context (see vv. 35, 40, 47),
to follow from receiving Christ and believing on Him. Fourthly,
the words, considered as the utterance of a first-century Jew,
would most naturally have quite a different meaning. The metaphor of eating and drinking was quite common among the Jews
as Odeberg, for example, has shown. It points to a taking within
one's innermost being. Westcott can say that language like that
used here "cannot refer primarily to the Holy Communion; nor
again can it be simply prophetic of that Sacrament. The teaching
has a full and consistent meaning in connexion with the actual
circumstances, and it treats essentially of spiritual realities with
which no external act, as such, can be co-extensive."[51]

Such considerations have led some commentators to hold that
the sacramental view is untenable. They hold to the second view,
namely, that the chapter refers to purely spiritual realities. Eating
Christ's flesh and drinking His blood point to that central saving act
described otherwise in, say, 3 : 16. Christ's death opens the way
to life. Men enter that way by faith. So in this chapter Christ
speaks of giving His flesh (v. 51), which points to the same act

---

[50] The Eastern Church, showing an unexpectedly logical attitude
at this point, has carried on the practice of infant communion. But I do not
think that even that Church goes as far as to say that no one who has not
received communion can be saved. Yet Jesus says bluntly that apart from the
eating and drinking of which He speaks, there is no salvation. Richardson is
one who does carry to its logical conclusion the view that the chapter refers
to the sacrament, saying that the Eucharist "is the indispensable means of
salvation (John 6. 53; 15. 4f.). It is constitutive of the Christian community
itself, and where there is no Eucharist there is no Church of Christ" (op. cit.,
p. 377); "In the Eucharist, St John is saying, the life-giving Spirit of Christ
is received; that is why the Eucharist is necessary to salvation" (op. cit., p.
372). This is more than difficult to reconcile with the testimony of the New
Testament (e.g. John 3 : 16). And it excludes from salvation infants, and whole
communions like the Quakers and the Salvation Army. It is a pity that Richardson does not examine the catastrophic implications of his position.

[51] Additional Note, p. 256. Later he adds: "But, on the other hand, there
can be no doubt that the truth which is presented in its absolute form in these
discourses is presented in a specific act and in a concrete form in the Holy
Communion; and yet further that the Holy Communion is the divinely appointed
means whereby men generally may realise the truth." Cf. also W. H. Griffith
Thomas, The Principles of Theology (London, 1930), pp. 389f.

as God's giving His Son.[52] But men must appropriate this gift by faith (v. 47). Eating the flesh and drinking the blood represent a striking way of saying this. The Son of man "must enter into and be assimilated with the *spiritual organism* of the believer."[53] Men must take Christ into their innermost being if they would have the life He died to bring them.

The third line of interpretation (which seems to me preferable) is a mediating one. It sees in the words primarily a teaching about spiritual realities (as outlined in the preceding paragraph), but does not deny that there may be a secondary reference to the sacrament.[54] This teaching about spiritual feeding on Christ must be seen to have its first reference to something other than any liturgical observance. It refers to the spiritual appropriation of Christ, however that takes place, whether in sacraments or in any other way. But in a secondary sense the discourse may well have as one of its aims showing us how we should receive the holy communion.[55] It is not at all impossible that Christ should have had some thought of the sacrament in His mind. He certainly did not institute it on the spur of the moment, and we have no

---

[52] *Cf.* C. H. Dodd: "the 'flesh and blood' of Christ (all that He is, offered in complete self-sacrifice) are given to nourish the inner life of men. His gift of bread to the hungry was a 'sign,' or symbol, of the greater gift of spiritual life" (*How to Read the Gospels*, London, 1944, p. 26).

[53] Odeberg, *FG*, p. 239. He goes on to say, "with this understanding of the meaning of the discourse it is obvious, that no part of the discourse, – still less the whole of it – can *primarily* refer to the sacrament of the Eucharist. In fact, one who understands the words of the eating and drinking of the flesh and blood to refer to the bread and wine of the Eucharist takes exactly the mistaken view of which Nicodemus in ch 3 and the 'Jews' here are made the exponents, viz. that J's (*i.e.* Jesus') realistic expressions refer to objects of the terrestrial world instead of to objects of the celestial world."

[54] C. F. Nolloth speaks of Jesus in this discourse as having "laid down the meaning and necessity of that union with Himself of which the Sacrament was to be the chief effectual sign and means" (*The Fourth Evangelist*, London, 1925, p. 120).

[55] Wright cites F. D. Maurice: "If you ask me, then, whether he is speaking of the Eucharist here, I should say, 'No.' If you ask me where I can learn the meaning of the eucharist, I should say, 'Nowhere so well as here' " (p. 180).

means of knowing how long He premeditated it.[56] John, moreover, may have had in mind some who gave undue emphasis to the externals of sacramental religion. So he left out all formal mention of holy communion, which would certainly discourage over-emphasis. But communion is important, so he included a discourse of the Lord Jesus that sets out the principles governing worthy reception.[57] But to agree with this is not to see the main thrust of the passage in sacramental teaching. It lies elsewhere.[58]

(a) The Audience Gathers, 6 : 22–25

22 On the morrow the multitude that stood on the other side of the sea saw that there was no other [1]boat there, save one, and that Jesus entered not with his disciples into the boat, but that his disciples went away alone 23 (howbeit there came [2]boats from Tiberias nigh unto the place where they ate the

---

[56] "Are we to suppose that just a year before the Eucharist was instituted, the Founder of this, the most distinctive element of Christian worship, had no thought of it in His mind? . . . That the audience at Capernaum could not thus understand Christ's words is nothing to the point: He was speaking less to them than to Christians throughout all ages" (Plummer). The writer goes on to say, however, "But while it is incredible that there is no reference to the Eucharist in this discourse, it is equally incredible that the reference is solely or primarily to the Eucharist . . . Rather the discourse refers to all the various channels of grace by means of which Christ imparts Himself to the believing soul: and who will dare to limit these in number or efficacy?" Bailey argues for the historicity of the discourse: "if we believe that Jesus often spoke words which He knew were too deep for all His hearers, or even for any of them at the time of utterance (see xvi. 13), and if we believe, with S. John, that the whole divine plan of salvation lay open to His thoughts from the beginning, we cannot categorically deny that we are given the discourse just as it was first delivered."

[57] "Without minimizing the value of the Sacrament, the Evangelist rejects a conception of it that would isolate the presence of Christ in the Sacrament from His presence in the everyday life of the believer" (Strachan).

[58] It is usually said that the Fathers unanimously interpret this chapter of the sacrament. But long ago Daniel Waterland conducted a thorough examination of the teaching of the Fathers on John 6 (A Review of the Doctrine of the Eucharist, ch. 6). His conclusion is that, while there is some variety, "what prevailed most, and was the general sentiment wherein they united, was, that Christ himself is properly and primarily our bread of life, considered as the Word made flesh, as God incarnate, and dying for us" (edn. of Oxford, 1880, p. 123). Any reference to "sacraments, or doctrines or any holy service" he finds to be of secondary importance. See also the discussion in ch. II of The Evangelical Doctrine of Holy Communion, ed. A. J. MacDonald (London, 1936).

bread after the Lord had given thanks): 24 when the multitude therefore saw that Jesus was not there, neither his disciples, they themselves got into the ²boats, and come to Capernaum, seeking Jesus. 25 And when they found him on the other side of the sea, they said unto him, Rabbi, when camest thou hither?

¹Gr. *little boat.* ²Gr. *little boats.*

The multitude next day looked for Jesus. They discerned that He was no longer on the same side of the lake as they (though they could not see how He could have crossed it). So they followed the disciples across the lake, and sought Him. We do not know where they found Him. It may have been in the synagogue (v. 59). But it is not at all impossible that the discourse took place in stages, with only the concluding section in the synagogue.[59]

22 The crowd had been very anxious to make Jesus king, so it is not surprising that with the morning light those that remained of them once again sought Him. The meaning of the reference to the boat[60] is not quite clear. The usual interpretation is that the crowd, on reflection, recalled that there had been but one boat there the previous night and that Jesus had not sailed in it (the boats of v. 23 were driven in during the night by the gale). But it is also possible to understand "no other boat" to mean that only one boat had been at the disposal of Jesus and His party, and He had not travelled in that. Again, it may be that they had one boat before them on the shore, as Lightfoot holds. Jesus had not entered that (it was still there), nor had He gone with the disciples. Our inability to determine which of these is correct need

---

[59] Thus Ryle holds it unnatural to think of the crowd as greeting Jesus in the synagogue in the way reported here. He thinks of the first part of the address as delivered at the landing place or somewhere else near the city, a break at v. 40, and the remainder in the synagogue. This is possible, but there is no evidence.

[60] It is possible, as Bernard thinks, that we are to distinguish between πλοιάριον and πλοῖον (both translated "boat" in ARV). He speaks of the πλοιάριον as "the skiff or dinghy belonging to the πλοῖον", the latter being "the big fishing boat, able to carry Jesus and the Twelve". MM however think that πλοιάριον is "hardly to be distinguished from the ordinary πλοῖον." Most commentators agree. Rieu manages to get three translations out of the two words: "only one dinghy was there ... Jesus did not board the ship ... small boats from Tiberias."

not trouble us. The main point is that the crowd saw no way by which Christ could have crossed the lake.

23 The boats from Tiberias may have come before the miracle, and have been still there. More probably they arrived after the disciples left, probably blown in by the storm. The miracle is described in an unusual fashion. Indeed it is not described as a miracle at all. There are simply references to eating the bread, and to the Lord's giving of thanks.[61] Jesus is not commonly referred to as "Lord" (see on 4 : 1). Indeed there are several unusual features in the Greek of verses 22f., and we may conjecture that this long sentence was not revised by the author into what would otherwise have been its final form.

24, 25 The crowds, seeing neither Jesus nor the disciples, and seeing that there were boats there, decided to sail across the lake to Capernaum, looking for Jesus. There was apparently little difficulty in finding Him once they reached Capernaum (it was a small town). They greet Him as "Rabbi" which may be significant in the context. John has just described happenings which show that Jesus was far removed from the ordinary. But the crowds have no knowledge of the events nor of His person. They think of Him as a teacher (which is curious after their recent attempt to make Him a king), not as the divine Son. Somewhat strangely they ask Him when He came[62] there. After their puzzlement about the ships we might have expected them to ask "How?" which we know to be the significant question.[63]

(b) Food that abides, 6 : 26, 27

26 Jesus answered them and said, Verily, verily, I say unto you, Ye seek me, not because ye saw signs, but because ye ate of the loaves, and were filled. 27 Work not for the food

---

[61] The words εὐχαριστήσαντος τοῦ Κυρίου are omitted by some MSS, D 69 pc *a d e* syr[s.c.] These are mostly Western. As the Western text tends to insert rather than to omit, and as there seems no reason for omitting these words, if original, it may be that they are not part of the true text.

[62] The perfect γέγονας is somewhat unexpected after πότε. We might have anticipated an aorist. Perhaps there is a conflation of two thoughts "When did you come?" and "How long have you been here?"

[63] Murray says, "When they find Jesus they naturally ask how He had got there." Barclay makes a similar assumption. It does seem to us the natural question. But it is not the one they ask. Chrysostom sees in their failure to ask the right question an indication that they did not seek "to understand so great a sign" (XLIII. 1: p. 156).

357

which perisheth, but for the food which abideth unto eternal life, which the Son of man shall give unto you: for him the Father, even God, hath sealed.

The long discourse is broken several times by interjections of the Jews. At first these interjections are close together, though later there are more considerable sections of exhortation. Jesus begins by putting His interrogators in the wrong, and urging them to mend their habits.

26 Jesus totally ignores the opening question of the multitude (as He had earlier done with Nicodemus' courtly greeting, 3 : 1-3). With an emphatic "Verily, verily" (for this expression see on 1 : 51) He moves straight into the important thing. He recognizes the real motive of these fellow-travellers and speaks sharply. Had they come even on the basis of the "signs" (see Additional Note G, pp. 684ff.) they had seen, it would have betokened some faith, however small. Faith which rests on the miracles is not the highest kind of faith, but it is better than no faith at all. But these people were crass materialists. They had not reflected on the spiritual significance of the sign they had seen.[64] "Instead of seeing in the bread the sign, they had seen in the sign only the bread."[65] They came because their hunger had been satisfied.[66] They were moved not by full hearts, but by full bellies.[67]

---

[64] Barrett points out that Jesus' hearers had certainly perceived that a miracle had taken place. They "are happy to obtain unexpected supplies of free bread, and willing to accord the highest honours to the supplier as a miracle worker; but they do not perceive the parabolic significance of what he does, that the loaves he distributes are the sign of heavenly food, the bread of eternal life . . . a sign is not a mere portent but a symbolic representation of the truth of the Gospel." So Morgan: "They had seen the wonder wrought, and the power put forth; but they had not caught the significance of the thing." Calvin goes a little further: "Just as today many would eagerly embrace the Gospel if it were empty of the bitterness of the cross and only brought carnal delights."

[65] Lange (cited in Godet).

[66] The verb χορτάζω applied originally to the gross feeding of animals. It came to be used of men (as in the Synoptic accounts of the feeding of the multitude, Matt. 14 : 20; Mark 6 : 42; Luke 9 : 17). But John earlier used ἐνεπλήσθησαν of the multitude's satiety (v. 12), and his change of word may be significant.

[67] Ryle comments on this motive: "Perhaps those only can thoroughly understand it who have seen much of the poor in pauperized rural parishes. They can understand the immense importance which a poor man attaches to having his belly filled".

27 So Jesus bids them set their labor on the right sort of food.[68]
The food they were seeking would perish. There is another kind
of food, that which remains for ever and issues in eternal life.[69]
This Gospel habitually associates life with Christ. If they seek
this food, then the Son of man (see Additional Note C, pp. 171ff.)
will give[70] them eternal life. Life is not the reward for work. Life
is always His gift. They may seek the more confidently because
the Father ("even God" is added with emphasis to ensure that they
would not misunderstand) has "sealed" Him.[71] The affixing of a
seal in antiquity was common as a mark of ownership. In an age
when many were illiterate the seal attested ownership as a label
could not. But a seal could also authenticate a document or the
like. The seal showed that the seal's owner approved. This is the
meaning here. The Father has set the seal of His approval on the
Son.[72]

(c) The Works of God, 6 : 28, 29

28 They said therefore unto him, What must we do, that we
may work the works of God? **29** Jesus answered and said unto

---

[68] The word used is $\beta\rho\tilde{\omega}\sigma\iota\varsigma$, which properly denotes the act of eating.
Here, however, it is equivalent to $\beta\rho\tilde{\omega}\mu\alpha$, that which is eaten, food (see on
4 : 32). On the whole expression Chrysostom compares Matt. 6 : 34, "Take
no thought for the morrow", and this he says in a picturesque phrase means,
"not to be nailed to the things of this life" (XLIV. 1; p. 158).

[69] $\tau\grave{\eta}\nu$ $\mu\acute{\epsilon}\nu o\upsilon\sigma\alpha\nu$ $\epsilon\grave{\iota}\varsigma$ $\zeta\omega\grave{\eta}\nu$ $\alpha\grave{\iota}\acute{\omega}\nu\iota o\nu$ is an unusual expression, which seems
to contain two meanings: that the food, in contrast to that which perishes,
remains for ever, and that it also has the effect of producing a life that lasts
for ever.

[70] Eternal life is usually viewed in this Gospel as a present possession. The
future here may point to the action of the Son on the last day (cf. v. 40). Or,
as Hoskyns thinks, it may point to the atoning death of Christ, as yet in the
future. If the giving refers not to life, but to the food that abides, then that
food being His flesh (v. 51), the giving is naturally thought of as yet future.
See further on 1 : 4; 3 : 15.

[71] If the aorist points to a particular act it will probably be Jesus' baptism.
It is worth noting that in the early church the baptism of Christians was often
described as a seal.

[72] Westcott suggests that "the thought of Christ as an accepted sacrifice"
may be what is meant. His reason is that "In the Jewish ritual the victims
are examined and sealed if perfect" and he gives as reference Mishnah *Shek.*
1 : 5. He is followed by Hoskyns who adds no other Rabbinic reference. The
view is attractive, but the passage cited says nothing about sealing perfect
victims.

them, This is the work of God, that ye believe on him whom
[1]he hath sent.

[1]Or, *he sent*

28 Perhaps in view of Jesus' reference to working, the question
in terms of human endeavour is natural enough. Nevertheless
"What must we do?" shows that the questioners had not grasped
Jesus' point about life being His gift. They looked, as the natural
man always looks, for salvation as the result of their own effort.
They simply inquire what is the particular work that God requires
of them. The present subjunctive denotes continuity: "What is to
be our regular course of action?" Moreover there are Rabbinic
passages in which heavenly food is taken to symbolize the Torah,
the Law.[73] The Jews may have taken Jesus' words about the food
which abides to eternal life as pointing to the Law. What then,
does Jesus think, ought they to do by way of law works? "The
works of God" is an unusual expression, but there seems little
doubt we should take it in the sense "godly works", "works
pleasing to God".[74]

29 Jesus replaces their "works of God" with the singular, "work
of God". But one thing is needful. And this one thing, He makes
plain, is faith.[75] They must believe[76] on Him (for the construction
see on 1 : 12; the present tense here denotes the continuing
attitude, not the once-for-all decision). In view of the controversy
over faith and works reflected in the Epistle of St. James it is
interesting to find Jesus describing "work" as believing. The "work
of God" means that which God requires of men. "There is a sense

---

[73] See Odeberg, *FG*, pp. 242f.

[74] It is found in the *Manual of Discipline* (IQS, iv, 4; *DSS*, p. 375), but
in the sense "works done by God".

[75] Hoskyns comments: "it would be to misunderstand what the Evangelist
has here said, if it were supposed that the Act of faith were an act grounded
in an independent, individual decision to believe. The Act of faith is itself the
work of God (*v.* 44, cf. Rom. xii. 3). Neither the fourth Evangelist nor Saint
Paul is driven finally to a Pelagian or even semi-Pelagian conception of faith."
Cf. also Bernard: "The answer of Jesus contains, in small compass, the gist
of the Pauline teaching about faith."

[76] *Cf.* Augustine: "This is then to eat the meat . . . which endureth unto
eternal life. To what purpose dost thou make ready teeth and stomach? Believe,
and thou hast eaten already" (XXV. 12; p. 164).

in which 'to believe' is to perform a work" (MacGregor). The object of faith is spoken of in terms of mission. Jesus is sent by the Father ("he" is emphatic[77] – none less than He!), and this makes faith in Him eminently reasonable.

(d) The Bread of Life, 6 : 30–40

30 They said therefore unto him, What then doest thou for a sign, that we may see, and believe thee? what workest thou? 31 Our fathers ate the manna in the wilderness; as it is written, He [1]gave them bread out of heaven to eat. 32 Jesus therefore said unto them, Verily, verily, I say unto you, It was not Moses that gave you the bread out of heaven; but my Father giveth you the true bread out of heaven. 33 For the bread of God is that which cometh down out of heaven, and giveth life unto the world. 34 They said therefore unto him, Lord, evermore give us this bread. 35 Jesus said unto them, I am the bread of life: he that cometh to me shall not hunger, and he that believeth on me shall never thirst. 36 But I said unto you, that ye have seen me, and yet believe not. 37 All that which the Father giveth me shall come unto me; and him that cometh to me I will in no wise cast out. 38 For I am come down from heaven, not to do mine own will, but the will of him that sent me. 39 And this is the will of him that sent me, that of all that which he hath given me I should lose nothing, but should raise it up at the last day. 40 For this is the will of my Father, that every one that beholdeth the Son, and believeth on him, should have eternal life; and [2]I will raise him up at the last day.

[1]Neh. ix. 15; Ex. xvi. 4, 15; Ps. lxxviii. 24; cv. 40. [2]Or, *that I should raise him up*

This section of the discourse is to be understood against the background of a Jewish expectation that, when the Messiah came, He would renew the miracle of the manna. Comfortably filled with the loaves Jesus has provided, the multitude challenge Him to give them a permanent supply of bread. Jesus turns their

---

77 For ἐκεῖνος see on 1 : 8.

attention to "the true bread" (32), "the bread of God" (33), "the bread of life" (35). Their thoughts are hopelessly earthbound. He seeks to raise them to heaven and to that eternal life which is inextricably linked with himself. A. M. Farrer sees the central thought of the chapter here. "The whole of ch. vi is a homily on v. 31b, 'He gave them bread from heaven to eat.' It must be shown *(a)* that Christ is true Bread, *(b)* that He came down from the true Heaven, whereas the manna was earthly bread from the visible sky."[78]

30 "Jews ask for signs" wrote Paul (I Cor. 1 : 22),[79] and we could hardly wish for a better example (see on 2 : 18). At the same time their demand is rather curious in that they have just seen one sign, and had they been spiritually aware would probably have known of another. Indeed, the plural in v. 26 implies that they had seen several signs. But they had not penetrated to the spiritual significance of what they had seen.[80] They observed only the wonders, and for some reason, these did not satisfy them. They dared to impose on God the sign they must have before they would believe.[81] "Thou" is emphatic. They are incredulous about *Jesus* producing the sign that they sought. "See, and believe" puts the priority on sight. They do not understand the nature of faith.

31 The kind of sign they want is illustrated by the manna in the wilderness. In a way this is a strange choice, for the multiplication of the loaves in the early part of this chapter seems to be a sign of exactly the same type. But it took place on one occasion: Moses

---

[78] *The Parish Communion*, ed. A. G. Hebert (London, 1957), p. 85n.

[79] SBk cite a rabbinic saying that if a prophet gives "a sign אות and wonder מופת then one must listen to him; but if not, then one need not listen to him."

[80] Dodd sees the Johannine irony: "The 'signs' which the people expect from the Messiah are mere miracles; yet when they see a miracle they fail to see the 'sign'; for to the evangelist a σημεῖον is not, in essence, a miraculous act, but a significant act, one which, for the seeing eye and the understanding mind, symbolizes eternal realities" (*IFG*, p. 90).

[81] "Christ could produce no credential so conclusive but that the Jews would demand one more conclusive still" (MacGregor). "They were always deceiving themselves with the idea that they wanted more evidence, and pretending that if they had this evidence they would believe. Thousands in every age do just the same . . . The plain truth is that it is want of heart, not want of evidence, that keeps people back from Christ" (Ryle).

gave the manna for forty years. Jesus gave bread to five thousand: Moses supplied manna to a whole nation. Jesus gave them ordinary bread, bread such as they ate every day: Moses gave "bread out of heaven", and goodness knows what phantasies they had about this (in Matt. 16 : 1 they asked for a sign "from heaven"). Add to this a Jewish expectation that when the Messiah came He would give men manna once more,[82] and we see that there was much that might arouse speculation. Jesus had done something wonderful in multiplying bread. Could He go on from there and produce manna? They support their plea with a quotation apparently from Ps. 78 : 24 (it is also like Neh. 9 : 15, and has some resemblances to Exod. 16 : 4, 15; Ps. 105 : 40, but agrees exactly with neither). Though they do not mention his name they apparently apply the quotation to Moses. The manna accredited Moses.

32 For the second time in this chapter Jesus prefaces His remarks with the solemn "Verily, verily". What follows is important. He begins by dispelling their illusion about Moses. It is difficult to find an English translation that will bring out the two meanings of what follows. These are firstly, that the gift of manna was not Moses' gift. It came from God (which is the real meaning of the words they have quoted; *cf.* Exod. 16 : 13ff.). Secondly, it was

---

[82] "It shall come to pass . . . that the treasury of manna shall again descend from on high, and they will eat of it in those years" (II Baruch 29 : 8). Similarly in the Sibylline Oracles we read of those who inherit life in the new age "feasting on sweet bread from the starry heaven" (Frag. 3 : 49). A Midrash expresses the idea in terms of Moses: "As the former redeemer (*i.e.* Moses) caused manna to descend, as it is stated, *Behold, I will cause to rain bread from heaven for you* (Ex. XVI, 4), so will the latter Redeemer cause manna to descend, as it is stated, *May he be as a rich cornfield in the land* (Ps. LXXII, 16)" (Ecc. R., 9; Soncino edn., p. 33). Peder Borgen shows that there is quite a complex of Jewish ideas behind this chapter, with thoughts of the Law, of the events on Mt. Sinai, and of the wisdom literature underlying much that is said (*Bread from Heaven*, Leiden, 1965, especially ch. 6). "In John the bread from heaven has been given the life-giving functions of Torah and wisdom" (*op. cit.*, p. 157). Jesus does perfectly what the others foreshadow. Borgen rejects the idea that the reference here is adequately explained on the basis of Jewish expectation of the manna in the messianic age, "since it ignores or minimizes the distinction between the external bread and the spiritual bread" (*op. cit.*, p. 174). That Jesus gives spiritual bread is one of the leading thoughts of this discourse.

not the true "bread from heaven", but an earthly, material type of that bread.[83] "My Father" indicates a consciousness that Jesus stood in a relation to the Giver that His hearers did not. He assures them not that God once gave the gift of the manna, but that He continually gives. This would provide a difficulty if it were the manna that He continually gives. But it is something more. The word order puts emphasis on "true".[84] The crowd had followed Jesus because of the loaves they had eaten. But they were quite unmindful of the much more important fact that the Father keeps on giving that bread which is bread indeed.

33 The statement is explained a little further. The bread is now "the bread of God", which fastens attention on another aspect of the gift. It originates with God, and is connected with Him in a special fashion. It is His bread. "That which" might be understood as "he who".[85] It is not likely that John wants us to think that Jesus' hearers took it that way (they immediately say, "Lord, evermore give us this bread"). But Jesus did. He knew Himself to be the bread of God. In accordance with this He speaks of this bread not as sent, but as coming down. It has life. And it gives life. The present tense denotes continuing action, and "the world" indicates the scope. Here is no narrow particularism but a concern for all mankind.[86] This is to be interpreted against the background of the grossly materialistic way in which the messianic age was commonly understood.[87] Jesus did not come to bring manna or satisfy any other materialistic expectation of the people. His dis-

---

[83] There may be yet other meanings. Among the Rabbis "bread" often symbolizes the Law (see SBk on v. 35), and there could be a reference to Jesus as the true bread in contrast to the Law as the Jews understood it. Barrett notices also Torrey's suggestion that the words are a question, "Did not Moses give you bread from heaven? (Yes, indeed, But the Father gives you the true bread from heaven)".

[84] For the use of ἀληθινός in this Gospel see on 1 : 9.

[85] Or as "that (bread) which".

[86] There are Jewish sayings which parallel this in part. They refer to the giving of the Law on Sinai as the giving of life to Israel or even to the world, e.g. "If the earth trembled when He gave life to the world" (Ex. R. XXIX. 9; Soncino edn., p. 343).

[87] This may be illustrated from the prophecy concerning the messianic age in II Baruch 29 : 5, "The earth also shall yield its fruit ten thousandfold and on each (?) vine there shall be a thousand branches, and each branch shall produce a thousand clusters, and each cluster produce a thousand grapes, and each grape produce a cor (about 120 gallons) of wine".

course is a vigorous protest against unworthy views of messiahship, and a strong affirmation of the essentially spiritual character of the life He came to bring.[88]
34 Like the woman at the well who wanted the living water (4 : 15) these people want the bread of God. They may have much the same materialistic reason. She had wanted the water to be relieved of the task of drawing from the well. They had been fed from the loaves, and they probably wanted some permanent gift of this kind. And they, like her, were ironical. They did not really think that He could provide this bread.[89] We should probably translate "Sir" rather than "Lord" (see on 4 : 1). Their greeting is respectful, but they do not regard Jesus as their Lord. They request Him to provide them with this gift "evermore".[90]
35 In a supremely majestic statement Jesus removes this misconception. The bread of which He speaks is not something like the manna, which they can pick up and eat. It is nothing less than Himself (*cf.* vv. 48, 51). His "I am" is a solemnly emphatic statement, and in this context has overtones of divinity.[91] This is the first of seven such emphatic statements in this Gospel.[92] Each one brings home an important aspect of the person and the ministry of Jesus. "The bread of life" is another way of linking life in the closest fashion with Christ. He Himself is the food, the

---

[88] J. Jeremias maintains that "The passages in the Fourth Gospel where Jesus calls Himself the bread of life (John 6.33, 35, 41, 48, 50, 51) and his Gospel bread (6.35; cf. Mark 7.27 par.) and water (John 4.10, 14; 6.35; 7.37-8), are to be understood similarly in an eschatological sense" (*op. cit.*, p. 156). They point forward to life in the age to come.
[89] *Cf.* Calvin: "Thus unhappy men are not satisfied simply with the sin of rejecting God's promises, but throw the guilt of their unbelief on Christ."
[90] πάντοτε is unexpected with the aorist. The verb implies a once-for-all gift, the adverb that it will be with them always (there may be a glance at the gift of the manna every morning).
[91] Morgan is reminded of the "I AM" that Moses heard from the burning bush. He thinks that Jesus "took the name of the burning bush, and linked it with the symbol of perfect sustenance for human life. 'I am the Bread of life.' Thus He employed the simplest of terms, with sublimest significance."
[92] ἐγώ εἰμι is repeated with "the bread of life" in v. 48, and with similar statements about bread in vv. 41, 51; with "the light of the world" (8 : 12); with "the door" (10 : 7, 9); with "the good shepherd" (10 : 11, 14); with "the resurrection and the life" (11 : 25); with "the way, and the truth, and the life" (14 : 6); with "the (true) vine" (15 : 1,5).

sustenance that nourishes spiritual life. It is only from this bread that men really obtain life.[93]

Becoming a Christian may be described in various ways. Here Jesus speaks of coming to Him, which stresses the movement away from the old life with its beggarly famine and its total inability to satisfy, and into all that association with Christ means. The thought of coming to Christ recurs (vv. 37, 44, 45, 65). They must come, as Wright puts it, "not as they have now come, in physical presence, but *come* with the whole needy personality" (*cf.* Matt. 11 : 28ff.). The expression is parallel to "he that believeth on me" in the latter part of the verse (*cf.* vv. 64f.; 7 : 37f.), and it indicates another facet of the same essential process. "Not" and "never" are both emphatic (*cf.* Weymouth, "shall never, never thirst"). No room is left for spiritual hunger and thirst[94] after receiving Christ. This does not exclude a further desire for spiritual things, but it rules out for ever the possibility of that unsatisfied hunger for it knows not what that is typical of the world even at its best.[95] This verse should not be regarded as an abstract statement. It constitutes an appeal. Since Jesus is the bread of life men are invited to come to Him, and to believe on Him.

36 "But"[96] introduces a strong contrast with what Jesus would have wished to see, perhaps also, with what might have been expected. His hearers had seen Him, and were still seeing Him. Yet they were far from appreciating the significance of what they

---

[93] As Hendriksen points out, the use of the article in $\tau\tilde{\eta}\varsigma\ \zeta\omega\tilde{\eta}\varsigma$ indicates not life in general, but "the" life, *i.e.* everlasting life. "Bread of life" means primarily "bread that gives life" (Goodspeed), though there will be the secondary meaning, "living bread" (*cf.* v. 51).

[94] The subjunctive is used of not hungering, $o\dot{v}\ \mu\dot{\eta}\ \pi\varepsilon\iota\nu\acute{\alpha}\sigma\eta$, and the indicative of never thirsting, $o\dot{v}\ \mu\dot{\eta}\ \delta\iota\psi\acute{\eta}\sigma\varepsilon\iota$. But there does not seem to be significance in the change.

[95] In Sirach 24 : 21 Wisdom by contrast says, "Those who eat me will hunger for more, and those who drink me will thirst for more." That passage goes on to identify wisdom with the Law (v. 23), which may support the contention that Jewish ideas about the Law underlie this chapter. Jesus is superior to the Law and gives men a satisfaction which the Law cannot. But unless we see such a reference to the Law there is no contradiction between the two sayings. Jesus is saying that men will not hunger after anything else once they have tasted of His good gift, the son of Sirach that men can never have too much of wisdom.

[96] $'A\lambda\lambda'$.

366

saw.[97] They did not believe. Their attitude is the very reverse of that which Jesus looks for in 20 : 29. The occasion to which "I said" refers is not clear. It may point to v. 26, but it is more likely that it refers to a saying on some other occasion altogether.[98] **37** "All" is neuter, which makes it very general, "everything", although persons are certainly meant. The words stress the sovereignty of God.[99] People do not come to Christ because it seems to them a good idea. It never does seem a good idea to natural man. Apart from a divine work in their souls (*cf.* 16 : 8) men remain contentedly in their sins. Before men can come to Christ it is necessary that the Father give[100] them to Him. This is the explanation of the disconcerting fact that those who followed Jesus to hear Him, and who at the beginning wanted to make Him a king, were nevertheless not His followers in the true sense. They did not belong to the people of God. They were not among those whom God gives Him. The second part of the verse brings us Jesus' warm welcome to all. He rejects none. "In no wise" is emphatic (*cf. Amplified*, "I will never, no never reject . . ."). There are difficulties as we try to reconcile the two parts of this verse.

---

[97] "They ask again for bread, the earth still and nothing but the earth, while He had desired, by means of this figurative repast, to offer them *life*, to open to them heaven!" (Godet).

[98] Bernard favors the omission of με after ἑωράκατε with ℵ A *a b e q* syr[s.c.]. Then the words refer to v. 26. If the με be read, he sees an allusion to some unrecorded saying, as in 10 : 25; 11 : 40. Tasker also favors the omission, thinking that "The addition of the word would have seemed very natural; but the implied object of the verb in the context would appear to be the 'sign' which the disciples had recently witnessed" (*GNT*, p. 426). There is force in this but it does not carry complete conviction. P. Borgen sees the explanation in terms of current modes of exegesis. In v. 32 Jesus has substituted ὑμῖν for αὐτοῖς in the passage quoted in v. 31. He has authoritatively interpreted this Old Testament verse. Borgen thinks we should accordingly translate v. 36, "But I said '*you*', because *you* have seen me and yet do not believe" (*Bread from Heaven*, Leiden, 1965, p. 74). This is very attractive and may well be right.

[99] MacGregor speaks of "a comprehensive neuter, the thought of the believer's individuality being thus subordinated to that of the Father's grace". Westcott reminds us that "The unbelief of the people was not a proof that the purpose of God had failed. Rather it gave occasion for declaring more fully how certainly the Son carried out the Father's will."

[100] The present tense is used here where the Son awaits. In v. 39 the perfect δέδωκεν expresses the gift as completed in the will of the Father. For the things the Father gives the Son see on 3 : 35.

But whether we succeed in that or not we dare not abandon the truth in either part.

38 In this whole work of salvation Jesus is in the most perfect harmony with the Father. He came down from heaven specifically to do the will of the Father (see on 4 : 34). The thought of His coming down from heaven is repeated seven times in this chapter (vv. 33, 38, 41, 42, 50, 51, 58). Notice the characteristic statement of a proposition in both the negative and the positive forms. The perfect unity with the Father ensures that Christ will accept all that the Father gives. It underlines the certainty of the process of the previous verse. For "sent" see on 3 : 17.

39 The will of God is not left in general terms. The particular aspect of His will that Jesus came to perform has to do with that which the Father gives Him. Again we have the negative and the positive sides. Jesus is to lose none of what[101] He is given (and at the end of His life He could affirm that He has lost none of them, 17 : 12). But His keeping of them is not concerned with this life only. Those who are His He will raise[102] at the last day (*cf.* 5 : 25ff.). This is a kind of refrain that runs through this address (vv. 40, 44, 54). The salvation He brings is no ephemeral thing. It is ultimate and final. This thought is of the greatest comfort to believers. Their assurance is based not on their feeble hold on Christ, but on His sure grip of them (*cf.* 10 : 28f.). "The last day" is an expression found only in John in the New Testament.

40 For the third consecutive verse the subject is God's will. By a characteristic Johannine construction we have a slight change from the way the thought has been expressed before. Jesus has spoken of men coming to Him and believing on Him. Now He refers to beholding Him and believing (contrast the attitude of His hearers in v. 36). "Beholding" is not commonly used in connexion with salvation. It reminds us of the necessity for seeing the

---

[101] The neuter $\pi\tilde{a}\nu$ $\ddot{o}$ (as in v. 37), where we should have expected the masculine.

[102] $\dot{a}\nu\alpha\sigma\tau\acute{\eta}\sigma\omega$ may be an aorist subjunctive dependent on $\ddot{\iota}\nu\alpha$ (and thus giving us part of the Father's will, *cf.* Schonfield, "must raise him up"), or future indicative in an independent clause ("I will raise him up"). Concerning this raising Stauffer says, "The coming of Christ is no isolated event for John, but an historical fact which reaches out beyond itself to an explication at the end of history" (*NTT*, p. 43).

heavenly vision, and for seeing it with a steady, constant gaze.[103]
And once again Christ insists that the life He brings a man is
eternal. None other than He ("I" is emphatic) will raise him up
at the last day. The close connexion of this with eternal life should
not be overlooked. So far from the present possession of eternal life
excluding the idea of a future resurrection it demands it in the
Johannine understanding of things. It is unthinkable that death
should blot out for ever the life that Christ gives. Because He is
what He is, He will assuredly raise up those to whom He gives life.[104]

(e) Christ and the Bread, 6 : 41–51

41 The Jews therefore murmured concerning him, because he
said, I am the bread which came down out of heaven. 42 And
they said, Is not this Jesus, the son of Joseph, whose father
and mother we know? how doth he now say, I am come down
out of heaven? 43 Jesus answered and said unto them, Mur-
mur not among yourselves. 44 No man can come to me,
except the Father that sent me draw him: and I will raise
him up in the last day. 45 It is written in the prophets, [1]And
they shall all be taught of God. Every one that hath heard
from the Father, and hath learned, cometh unto me. 46 Not
that any man hath seen the Father, save he that is from God,
he hath seen the Father. 47 Verily, verily, I say unto you,
He that believeth hath eternal life. 48 I am the bread of life.
49 Your fathers ate the manna in the wilderness, and they
died. 50 This is the bread which cometh down out of heaven,
that a man may eat thereof, and not die. 51 I am the living
bread which came down out of heaven: if any man eat of
this bread, he shall live for ever: yea and the bread which I
will give is my flesh, for the life of the world.

[1] Is. liv. 13; (Jer. xxxi. 34?)

---

[103] Bailey translates "contemplateth," and says that it "implies not mere
vision but grasping the significance of a thing, and so it is the precursor of
faith".

[104] *Cf.* Westcott: "So far from the doctrine of the Resurrection being, as
has been asserted, inconsistent with St. John's teaching on the present reality
of eternal life, it would be rather true to say that this doctrine makes the necessity of the Resurrection obvious. He who feels that life *is* now, must feel
that after death all that belongs to the essence of its present perfection must
be restored, however much ennobled under new conditions of manifestation."
A minor point is that in v. 39 all believers are included collectively, whereas
in vv. 40, 44, 54 the reference is more individual.

369

Jesus' words were not what the crowd expected or wanted. They rebel against the claims implied in them, feeling that they know very well who Jesus is. In the face of this Jesus emphatically repeats what He has said, and takes the thought a stage further by speaking of the bread which He will give as His flesh.

41 "The Jews" is a change of subject, and may indicate a change of scene. There is nothing unlikely in the supposition that the earlier words were spoken near the lake, and that the scene now shifts to the synagogue. Yet as the dialogue flows on it seems that Jesus' opponents are the same as in the previous section. It is unusual to find the expression "the Jews" used of Galileans. More usually it is the Jews of Jerusalem (see on 1 : 19). But the primary idea is that of the Jews, especially the leading Jews, in opposition to Jesus, so, while it is unusual, it is not out of place to have the expression used of Galilean Jews. "Murmured" indicates discontent.[105] It is the confused sound that runs through a crowd when they are angry and in opposition. Their words are not an accurate quotation of what Jesus has said,[106] but they do give His meaning.

42 The first question is another example of the Evangelist's irony. Had the Jews known the truth about Jesus' parentage,[107] as they claim, they would have perceived that it illustrates vividly the truth He is here expounding. "We" is emphatic. These people feel that whatever be the case with others, out of their own personal knowledge they can show that Jesus' statement is false. They do not stop to question their assumptions that because Jesus was lowly, and because He was well known to them, therefore, He

---

[105] We are reminded of the "murmuring" of the Israelites in the wilderness (Exod. 15 : 24; Num. 14 : 2, *etc.*). These people "preserve the genuine succession of unbelief" (Hoskyns). The imperfect ἐγόγγυζον indicates that "they kept murmuring".

[106] Where Jesus used the perfect indicative καταβέβηκα, they have the aorist participle, ὁ καταβάς, and they link "I am the bread" directly with the reference to coming down from heaven as He does not when He identifies Himself with the bread (v. 35); though *cf.* v. 33. Such differences are not important. See further *SFG*, ch. 5. It is worth noting the tenses used of Jesus' descent. The aorist (3 : 13; 6 : 41, 51, 58) points to the decisive action of the incarnation, the present (6 : 33, 50) to Jesus' character as the One from heaven, the perfect (6 : 38, 42) to the continuing result of the past act of incarnation.

[107] The expression is Ἰησοῦς ὁ υἱὸς Ἰωσήφ. In a similar expression in 1 : 45 there is no article. Its meaning here is probably, as Abbott suggests, "the (well-known) son of Joseph" (1970).

could not have been from heaven.[108] They fasten their attention on His claim to have come from heaven,[109] and not on that to give life. "Now" means "after all the years He has lived like anyone else." For the pattern of misunderstanding see on 2 : 20.

43, 44 Jesus bids them cease their murmurings among themselves. That is not the way to learn divine truth. Then He repeats the saying of v. 37, but in a slightly stronger form. Now He says that no man "can" come unless the Father draws him. The thought of the divine initiative in salvation is one of the great doctrines of this Gospel,[110]

---

[108] Odeberg draws attention to the Jewish idea of the divine $n^e\check{s}\bar{a}m\bar{a}$ descending from heaven and joining itself to man. He goes on to state with precision the Jewish objection: "(1) The Jews do not reject the idea that a man appearing on earth as an earthly being could be descended from heaven; they maintained that Elijah and other celestial figures appeared on earth and dwelt among men as earthly beings; (2) neither do they reject the idea, that a man, born of known parents, of 'woman', of 'earthly semen', could receive a Divine calling, be a messenger from God, obtain revelations from the Divine world; (3) but they rejected the idea that a man born of earthly semen could at the same time be a celestial being, of celestial origin, could have 'descended from heaven' " (*FG*, p. 264, n. 3).

[109] Their word order puts stress on ἐκ τοῦ οὐρανοῦ. This is contrary to Jesus' word order in the earlier verses (33, 38; His word in the latter is ἀπό not ἐκ though the difference does not seem significant). But He follows it subsequently (50, 51, 58).

[110] "Here is a fundamental doctrine of the Fourth Gospel, viz. that the approach of the soul to God or Christ is not initiated by the man himself, but by a movement of Divine grace" (Bernard). Barclay gives a number of examples of the use of the verb ἑλκύω in the New Testament to show that "Always there is this idea of resistance." This is surely true, and indicates that God brings men to Himself although by nature they prefer sin. But curiously Barclay adds, "God can and does draw men, but man's resistance can defeat the pull of God." Not one of his examples of the verb shows the resistance as successful. Indeed we can go further. There is not one example in the New Testament of the use of this verb where the resistance is successful. Always the drawing power is triumphant, as here. Calvin speaks of "an effectual movement of the Holy Spirit, turning men from being unwilling and reluctant into willing." Luther has an interesting note on the verse in *The Bondage of the Will*, trans. J. I. Packer and O. R. Johnston (London, 1957), pp. 310f. The verb is used in one of the sayings of Jesus in the Oxyrhynchus Papyri, but the text is mutilated. It is impossible to be sure whether it is used in the same sense as here, or not. See *LAE*, pp. 426–28. Borgen sees the verb as a legal term, equivalent to the Hebrew משׁך (which it often renders in LXX), and which means "to take possession of" (*i.e.* by drawing the object to oneself). Borgen sees Jesus as the agent of the Father and sees this verse as meaning, "only those of whom the sender (through the agent) takes the actual possession are received by the agent, and nobody else" (*op. cit.*, p. 161). Apart from one example in Acts, the verb is confined to this Gospel in the New Testament (5 times).

371

and indeed of the Christian faith. Men like to feel independent. They think that they come or that they *can* come to Jesus entirely of their own volition. Jesus assures us that this is an utter impossibility. No man, no man at all can come unless the Father draw him. The impossibility was implied in the former statement, but it is explicit here. And even when talking of this subject Jesus refers to the Father as sending Him.[111] Not for one moment does He lose His sense of mission. For the third time He refers to His future activity of raising up His people at the last day.

45 The same truth is put in another way. To show that this is something in the plan of God Jesus quotes from Isa. 54 : 13 (or perhaps Jer. 31 : 34).[112] God will teach His people Himself, *i.e.* He will teach them within their hearts.[113] Only those who are taught in this fashion come to Jesus. But He makes it quite clear that all those who are taught in this way, who hear God, and learn what they hear, do come to Him.

46 This might be misunderstood as implying that those who have heard God have also seen Him.[114] All the more is this the case

---

[111] *Cf.* Godet: "the God who sends Jesus for souls, on the other hand, draws souls to Jesus. The two divine works, external and internal, answer to and complete each other. The happy moment in which they meet in the heart, and in which the will is thus gained, is that of the *gift* on God's part, of *faith* on man's part."

[112] The Isaiah passage seems the more likely source. Perhaps both are in mind, for "the prophets" is an unusual way to cite a passage (though *cf.* Matt. 2 : 23; 26 : 56, rec. text of Mark 1 : 2; Acts 13 : 40). It may signify the general tenor of what is written in more than one prophet, no one passage being singled out. Or the plural may be meant to point us to "the prophets" as a division of the Old Testament. In my judgment the reference is to Isa. 54 : 13, though whether to the Hebrew or LXX is uncertain.

[113] *Cf.* Paul's statement that the Thessalonian Christians were θεοδίδακτοι (I Thess. 4 : 9). Odeberg maintains that this term "points to the fact that no real knowledge exists of the Divine world, that does not proceed from God, it points to the internality versus the externality; διδακτοὶ θεοῦ is to be subsumed under the general γεννηθέντες ἐκ θεοῦ" (*FG*, p. 258).

[114] The previous verse "must not be taken to mean that any man might enjoy a direct mystical experience of God and then, enlightened, attach himself to Jesus. Jesus only has immediate knowledge of God (τὸν πατέρα ἑώρακεν), and to others he is the mediator, since he has come forth from the presence of God (ὢν παρὰ τοῦ θεοῦ)" (Barrett). Temple speaks of "an error that must be at once repelled, the alluring peril of mysticism, according to which a man may have direct experience of unmediated communion with the infinite and eternal God. That is not so; and any experience taken to be this is wrongly interpreted. Only the Son has that direct communion with the Father."

in the light of 5 : 37, "Ye have neither heard his voice at any time, nor seen his form." This saying might perhaps have been understood to mean that hearing and seeing are firmly linked. To hear Him would then guarantee seeing Him. This is not the case. As in 1 : 18, it is insisted that no man has ever seen God. There the exception is described as "the only begotten God" (or "only begotten Son"), here as "he that is from God". Both expressions point to an intimate relationship between the Father and the Son shared by none else. No man has the vision of God, apart from the Son. The reality of intimate intercourse is stressed by the addition, "he hath seen the Father".

47 For the third time in this discourse there is the solemn "Verily, verily" (previously vv. 26, 32; see on 1 : 51). Jesus' main concern is with life and how men obtain it, not with His own person. Now He solemnly repeats the way to life. For "believeth" see Additional Note E (pp. 335ff.), and for "eternal life" see on 3 : 15.

48 See on v. 35. The statement stands here in an isolation and simplicity which makes it very impressive. Jesus wants His claim to be seen in all its stark grandeur.

49 The crowd had earlier introduced the subject of the manna, and had intimated that they would like to have such a gift from Jesus. It was this that brought forth the great saying, "I am the bread of life". Now as Jesus repeats His majestic claim He goes on to point out that the manna had its limitations. It was food for the body, but it was no more. Those who ate it died in due course.

50 By contrast Jesus is offering them food which brings that life for which there is no death. This bread is not of earthly origin, but of heavenly. And when a man once takes it ("eat" is in the aorist tense, of the once-for-all action of receiving Christ) he will not die. "Die" in the previous verse referred to physical death, here to spiritual. The man who partakes of Christ has within him that life which is eternal.

51 Once again Jesus refers to Himself as bread, this time as "living bread" (*cf.* 1 : 4; 5 : 26). "Came down" is in the aorist, pointing to the single act of the incarnation. As in the previous verse "eat" (aorist tense) refers to the act of appropriating Christ.[115] Any man who takes this decisive action will live for ever, the positive state-

---

[115] This aorist makes it difficult to understand the word as referring to the Holy Communion as some suggest.

ment balancing the negative of the previous verse. In the manner of v. 35 this constitutes an invitation to eat. In a very startling statement Jesus defines the bread that He will give as His flesh. The future takes it out of the realm of the general, and looks to the gift that would be made on Calvary.[116] Those who understand the verse of the incarnation or the like usually ignore the tense. It is difficult to see how it can fit into their theories. "Flesh" is a striking word. In distinction from "body" or "myself" it puts marked emphasis on the physical side of life. It is a strong word and one bound to attract attention. Its almost crude forcefulness rivets attention on the historical fact that Christ did give Himself for man. He is not speaking simply of a moving idea. Many commentators speak as though the word "flesh" self-evidently marked a reference to Holy Communion.[117] It, of course, does nothing of the sort. It is not found in the narratives of the institution, nor in I Cor. 10, nor in I Cor. 11 in connexion with the

---

[116] "For" is ὑπέρ. Barrett examines the use of this preposition in other contexts in John, ὑπὲρ τῶν προβάτων (10 : 11, 15), ὑπὲρ τοῦ λαοῦ (11 : 50f.), ὑπὲρ τοῦ ἔθνους (11 : 52; actually, it is ἔθνους not λαοῦ which is repeated), ὑπὲρ τῶν φίλων αὐτοῦ (15 : 13), and ὑπὲρ αὐτῶν ἐγὼ ἁγιάζω ἐμαυτόν (17 : 19). He concludes: "These passages show conclusively that a reference to the death of Jesus is intended – he will give his flesh in death – and suggest a sacrificial meaning." For the substitutionary force in ὑπέρ in such contexts see my *The Apostolic Preaching of the Cross* (3rd edn., London and Grand Rapids, 1965), pp. 62–4. R. H. Lightfoot points to another important aspect of this saying, *viz.* that it "will make clear that the Lord's language in 6³²⁻³⁵ is not to be understood in a sense which would imply that the true bread, the bread of life which He gives, costs nothing to the Giver. On the contrary, His gift involves His death." John's use of ὑπέρ is noticeably more frequent than is that of the other evangelists, the figures being: Matthew 5 times, Mark twice, Luke 5 times, John 13 times. John's fondness for the word is due to his references to Jesus' death (this is the case in all but four of his references). It mattered to him that Jesus died ὑπὲρ ἡμῶν.

[117] *E.g.* MacGregor: "no explanation is adequate which fails to recognize that John's main purpose in thus identifying the life-giving bread with Christ's *flesh* is at last to bring into prominence the sacramental bearing of the whole discourse." By contrast Plummer sees in the use of this term evidence that the reference is *not* primarily sacramental: "But that the reference is not exclusively nor even directly to the Eucharist is shewn from the use of σάρξ and not σῶμα." Later he says, "The primary reference therefore is to Christ's propitiatory death; the secondary reference is to *all* those means by which the death of Christ is appropriated, especially the Eucharist."

sacrament. Nor is it common in the Fathers[118] in this sense. The usual word in sacramental usage is "body". The last words of the verse bring before us once more the truth that the mission of Jesus is universal. He had not come to minister to the Jews only. When

---

[118] Ignatius is usually said to use σάρξ in this way, but his words need careful examination. In Rom. 7 : 3 he says, "I desire the bread of God, which is the flesh of Christ who was of the seed of David". This might be understood of the sacrament except that he immediately adds, "and for a draught I desire His blood, which is love incorruptible" (the blood is love also in Trall. 8 : 1). Moreover the words occur in a section in which Ignatius is seeking martyrdom ("I write to you in the midst of life, yet lusting after death"). He appears to be using a highly coloured way of referring to death, when he would enter heavenly blessing. To refer the words to the sacrament, besides ignoring the context, is to make them a commonplace, hardly worth saying. What Christian is there who does not desire to receive the sacrament? Philad. 4 : 1 is clear enough, "Be ye careful therefore to observe one eucharist (for there is one flesh of our Lord Jesus Christ...)", but Philad. 11 : 2 (which Hoskyns, for example, cites) has nothing to do with the sacrament, the words being "Jesus Christ, on whom their hope is set in flesh and soul and spirit". Smyrn. 6 : 2 speaks of allowing that "the eucharist is the flesh of our Saviour Jesus Christ", but immediately goes on to say, "which flesh suffered for our sins, and which the Father of His goodness raised up." Ignatius, moreover, refers to the gospel as "the flesh of Jesus" (Philad. 5 : 1), and again of faith as "the flesh of the Lord" (Trall. 8 : 1). It is clear that "flesh" for him is far from a technical term pointing to the sacrament. In any case we must bear in mind the verdict of such scholars as Helmut Koester, "Σάρξ does not mean the same to John and Ignatius" ("The Bultmann School of Biblical Interpretation: New Directions?" *Journal for Theology and the Church*, I, 1965, p. 114). Justin Martyr speaks of Christ as "having been made flesh by the Word of God... the food which is blessed by the prayer of His word, and from which our blood and flesh by transmutation are nourished, is the flesh and blood of that Jesus who was made flesh" (*Apol.* 1 : 66). But writers like Irenaeus consistently use "body" not "flesh" of the sacrament, and so do ancient liturgies like those of Hippolytus, Serapion, St. James, *etc.* J. Jeremias suggests that the Aramaic behind the words of institution recorded in the Gospels was בִּשְׂרִי דֵן which might readily be rendered in Greek by σάρξ. He regards John 6 : 51c as "the Johannine tradition of the word of interpretation over the bread" (*op. cit.*, p. 141 and n. 13). The possibility that Jesus used the Aramaic, בִּשְׂרָא, and that this may be rendered in Greek by σάρξ, is undoubted. All that I am contending is that in point of fact, with reference to the eucharist, the custom was to use σῶμα (whatever the original Aramaic may have been), so that the occurrence of σάρξ in itself cannot be held to point to the sacrament.

375

He gave His flesh it would be "for[119] the life of the world."[120]

(f) Eating the Flesh and Drinking the Blood, 6 : 52–59

52 The Jews therefore strove one with another, saying, How can this man give us his flesh to eat? 53 Jesus therefore said unto them, Verily, verily, I say unto you, Except ye eat the flesh of the Son of man and drink his blood, ye have not life in yourselves. 54 He that eateth my flesh and drinketh my blood hath eternal life; and I will raise him up at the last day. 55 For my flesh is ¹meat indeed, and my blood is ²drink indeed. 56 He that eateth my flesh and drinketh my blood abideth in me, and I in him. 57 As the living Father sent me, and I live because of the Father; so he that eateth me, he also shall live because of me. 58 This is the bread which came down out of heaven: not as the fathers ate, and died; he that eateth this bread shall live for ever. 59 These things said he in ³the synagogue, as he taught in Capernaum.

¹Gr. *true meat.* ²Gr. *true drink.* ³Or, *a synagogue*

This is the section of the discourse which above all is claimed confidently as referring to the holy communion. The language of eating the flesh and drinking the blood is said to be explicable only, or at least most naturally, in terms of the sacrament. But is this so? I think not. The objections already urged remain. The very strength of the language is against it. The eating and drinking spoken of are the means of bringing eternal life (v. 54), and they are absolutely unqualified. Are we to say that the one thing necessary for life is to receive the sacrament? Again, "flesh"[121] is not commonly used with reference to the sacrament. In every

---

[119] Considering the wide range of meaning of ὑπέρ it is interesting to notice the way John so often uses it of death. See 10 : 11, 15; 11 : 50, 51, 52; 13 : 37, 38; 15 : 13; 17 : 19; 18 : 14 (elsewhere he has it only in 1 : 30; 11 : 4). See also n. 116 above.

[120] This is another expression not easy to reconcile with the sacramental reference. On Calvary Christ gave Himself "for the life of the world", but in the sacrament His gift is to the communicants there present, not to the world. The words are perhaps not impossible to understand of the sacrament, but they refer much more naturally to the cross.

[121] See n. 118 above. In an Appendix on vv. 51b–58 Godet suggests that the broken loaf at the institution of the Lord's Supper corresponds to "His *body* as an *organism* (σῶμα) broken. In the discourse at Capernaum where the question is only of *nourishment*, according to the analogy of the multiplication of the loaves, Jesus was obliged rather to present His body as *substance* (σάρξ) than as an organism. This perfect propriety of the terms shows the originality and authenticity of the two forms" (II, p. 41).

other New Testament passage referring to it the word is "body". Ryle further points out that to take the view we are opposing "is to interpose a bodily act between the soul of man and salvation. This is a thing for which there is no precedent in Scripture. The only things without which we cannot be saved are repentance and faith." I am not contending that there is no application to the sacrament. But I very strongly doubt whether this is the primary meaning. It seems much better to think of the words as meaning first of all the appropriation of Christ.[122]

52 Not unnaturally the Jews are perplexed, for the saying is not an easy one. "Strove"[123] (*Berkeley* and Moffatt, "wrangled"; Weymouth, "This led to an angry debate") is not quite the word we would have expected. It implies that some were strongly for Jesus, though the following narrative makes it clear that they must have been outnumbered. Their question indicates that they do not see how it is possible for Jesus to give His flesh. The mechanics of it bother them.[124] For the pattern of misunderstanding a saying of Jesus see on 2 : 20.

[122] *Cf.* Strachan: "Whilst the Evangelist in *vv.* 52–57 is using sacramental language, the emphasis and intention of his thinking is to reassert his main central theme in the Gospel, that only through faith in the risen Christ, once an historical personality, is life obtained." Or again: "The *primary* reference of *flesh* and *blood* is not to the sacrament, but to the demand for faith in a Christ, who became 'flesh and blood', *i.e.* truly man." McClymont sees a reference to the sacrificial death of Jesus and adds: "To go further than this, however, and apply the passage exclusively to the sacrament of the Lord's Supper is not warranted by anything in the discourse or its circumstances, though it is quite true that in the Lord's Supper we have the symbolic representation of the eating and drinking which is here described." Augustine maintains that our Lord "would have this meat and drink to be understood as meaning the fellowship of His own body and members, which is the holy Church in his predestinated, and called, and justified, and glorified saints and believers." Again: "This it is, therefore, for a man to eat that meat and to drink that drink, to dwell in Christ, and to have Christ dwelling in him" (XXVI. 15, 18; p. 173). Those who apply the words to the sacrament sometimes think of this section as no part of the original discourse but as an interpolation. See J. Jeremias, *op. cit.*, p. 73.

[123] ἐμάχοντο. The verb is translated "fight" in Jas. 4 : 2. It is found in II Tim. 2 : 24, "the Lord's servant must not strive".

[124] So does the Person. οὗτος probably is used in a somewhat contemptuous sense, "This fellow". It stands in sharp contrast to ἡμῖν. Bailey denies that they took the words literally. "They mean (in our language) 'How can one human personality be incorporated into another?'" This is very difficult to accept. It is much more likely that they thought of the words as meant literally, but could not see how they could be put into operation.

53 Jesus does not retract one iota of His statement. He prefixes
His reply with the solemn "Verily, verily" (used for the fourth
time in this chapter; see vv. 26, 32, 47, and note on 1 : 51). What
He says is thus shown to be deliberate and important. He wants
there to be no doubt about it. He adds to what He has said before.
He has spoken about eating bread which is Himself, and as giving
His flesh. Now He speaks explicitly of eating His flesh, and He
adds the thought of drinking His blood,[125] an idea that would be
especially abhorrent to Jews because they were forbidden to
partake of the blood (Gen. 9 : 4, *etc.*).[126] Both "eat" and "drink"
are aorists, denoting once-for-all action. It is not a repeated
eating and drinking, such as would be appropriate to the sacrament. And this eating and drinking are absolutely necessary for
eternal life. Those who do not eat and drink have no life. Eating
and drinking thus appear to be a very graphic way of saying that
men must take Christ into their innermost being. There is moreover a reference to the death of Christ, as we saw on v. 51. Flesh

---

[125] Temple is of the opinion that "The blood is the life; especially is it
the life released by death that it may be offered to God . . . Blood . . . when
poured out, is the life released by death and given to God." Such positions are
commonly advocated, though usually with no attempt to adduce evidence.
It is true that Gen. 9 : 4f.; Lev. 17 : 11, 14; Deut. 12 : 23 associate blood
and life very closely (though it is not true, as Temple claims, that there are
"many similar passages", at least in the Old Testament). It is also true that
many primitive peoples regard blood with superstitious awe. But this is a
flimsy foundation for the edifice that is built upon it by such writers as S. C.
Gayford, *Sacrifice and Priesthood* (London, 1924), or F. C. N. Hicks, *The Fullness
of Sacrifice* (London, 1930). A close examination of the biblical evidence shows
clearly that "blood" points to a violent death, not the release of life at all.
See A. M. Stibbs, *The Meaning of the Word 'Blood' in Scripture* (London, 1947),
or my *The Apostolic Preaching of the Cross* (London and Grand Rapids, 3rd edn.
1965), ch. 3 (this embodies material in my articles "The Biblical Use of the
Term 'Blood'" in *JThS* n.s. III, 1952, pp. 216–227; VI, 1955, pp. 77–82).
It is not without its interest that, whereas Temple sees in the blood a reference
to life and in the flesh a reference to death, McClymont reverses the process.

[126] References to drinking blood are rare in Jewish literature. Josephus
once says "it was still possible to feed upon the public miseries and to drink
of the city's life-blood" (*Bell.* v, 344). But this sheds no light on the present passage.

and blood in separation point to death.[127] The words, then, are a cryptic allusion to the atoning death that Christ would die, together with a challenge to enter the closest and most intimate relation with Him.[128] They are to be interpreted in the light of v. 47.

54 What has been put negatively is now stated positively in a way typical of this Gospel. The man who does eat Christ's flesh and drink His blood has eternal life,[129] and he will be raised up by Christ at the last day. The word for "eat" is different[130] from that used previously, and it is used again in the following verses (56, 57, 58; elsewhere in the New Testament only in Matt. 24 : 38; John 13 : 18). It properly applies to somewhat noisy feeding (like "munch" or "crunch"). There is often the notion of eating with enjoyment (so in Matt. 24 : 38). It is a startling word in this context, and stresses the actuality of the partaking of Christ that is spoken of. Some suggest that it points to a literal feeding and therefore to the sacrament. But this does not follow. There is no logic in saying, "The verb is used of literal eating. Therefore eating the flesh of Christ must mean eating the communion

---

[127] *Cf.* Dodd: "the expression δοῦναι τὴν σάρκα, however figuratively it is taken, can hardly fail to suggest the idea of death. And the expression πίνειν τὸ αἷμα, again, can hardly fail to suggest shed blood, and therefore violent death. In such veiled terms the evangelist suggests that it is through death that Christ becomes bread of life to the world" (*IFG*, p. 339). He cites Wetstein, *Ubi sanguinis a carne separati fit mentio, violenta morte mortuus intelligitur.*

[128] *Cf.* Westcott: "To 'eat' and to 'drink' is to take to oneself by a voluntary act that which is external to oneself, and then to assimilate it and make it part of oneself. It is, as it were, faith regarded in its converse action. Faith throws the believer upon and into its object; this spiritual eating and drinking brings the object of faith into the believer." The Midrash on Ecc. 2 : 24, "There is nothing better for a man than that he should eat and drink", says, "All the references to eating and drinking in this Book signify Torah and good deeds" (Soncino edn., p. 71; so also on Ecc. 8 : 15).

[129] *Cf.* the statements of Augustine, cited in n. 122 above.

[130] The tense is different also. The present, ὁ τρώγων, points to a continuing appropriation. Indeed Ryle sees the whole point of the verb in this. He cites Leigh, that the word "noteth a continuance of eating, as brute beasts will eat all day, and some part of the night" and adds, "our Lord meant the habit of continually feeding on Him all day long by faith. He did not mean the occasional eating of material food in an ordinance."

bread."[131] On any showing there is a symbolic element in the "eating", and it is better to understand it, as the earlier references, to receiving Christ. The continuing reference to Christ's raising up the believer at the last day is interesting. There may be more to eternal life than life in the age to come, but life in that age is certainly prominent.

55 Other things were not food in the true sense. Jesus has already pointed out that the fathers ate the manna in the wilderness and they died (v. 49). His opponents had altogether the wrong idea of what constituted true bread. With Christ's signs before them they still sought their sustenance apart from Him. This verse is an emphatic statement that true food and drink for men's deepest needs are to be found in Christ, and by implication in Him alone.

56 The close connexion between fellowship with Christ and the activity of eating the flesh and drinking the blood is stressed. The man who eats and drinks "abideth" (the tense is continuous; it denotes more than a fleeting contact) in Christ. There is the closest possible relationship so that the eater is in Christ and Christ is in him. The thought of abiding is a prominent one in John. It reminds us that the believer enters into no temporary state, but a permanent one, with fellowship with his Lord as the predominant note.

57 Jesus comes back to His sense of mission. He had been sent by "the living Father", the participle stressing the active quality of life that inheres in the Father. "On account of" is patient of two meanings[132] and probably both are in mind here. Firstly, the life of the Son is bound up with that of the Father (it is 5 : 26 in another form): the Son has no life apart from the Father. And secondly, the Son lives for the Father. To do the Father's will is His very meat (4 : 34). This forms an analogy whereby the effect of feeding on Christ may be gauged. Notice that no longer does He speak of eating the flesh and drinking the blood, but simply of eating Him. The tense is continuous. This way of putting it

---

[131] That τρώγω does not differ significantly from ἐσθίω is indicated by the fact that in their reports of the activity of the men of Noah's generation Matthew uses the former (Matt. 24 : 38) and Luke the latter (Luke 17 : 27). Similarly in the quotation from Ps. 41 : 9 in John 13 : 18 we find τρώγω but the LXX has ἐσθίω.

[132] The Greek is διὰ τὸν πατέρα. Many draw attention to Alexander's dictum that he owed life to his father, but good life to Aristotle, δι' ἐκεῖνον μὲν ζῶν, διὰ τοῦτον δὲ καλῶς ζῶν (Plut., Vit. Alex., VIII).

makes it clearer than ever that it is the taking of Christ within oneself that is meant by the metaphor of eating and drinking.[133] The man[134] who so receives Christ will have the life that comes only from Christ. And he will live only for Christ. Nought else will matter for him. Notice that Christ alone has direct access to the Father. Believers receive life only mediately through Christ. **58** The thought of vv. 49f. is repeated in another form. Jesus' opponents had expressed their respect for the manna, and, indeed, had challenged Him to produce it. Jesus now reminds them that, wonderful though the manna had been, there had been no life-giving quality in it. Those who ate of it died like other men. But the bread of which He has been speaking, the bread which really came down from heaven,[135] is different. The man who eats of it will not die like other men. He will, to be sure, pass through the gateway of death, but he will live eternally. It is likely that the singular "he that eateth" in contrast with the plural "the fathers" is significant. At any rate throughout the discourse the singular is regularly used to denote him who is in right relationship with Jesus. Faith must be personal. There is more to it than being a member of a group.
59 John adds a note locating the speech he has just recorded. It took place "in synagogue" (*cf.* our "in church") as Jesus taught in Capernaum. The absence of the article in the Greek seems to indicate an assembly for worship, and not simply the building.

(g) Words that are Spirit and Life, 6 : 60-66

60 Many therefore of his disciples, when they heard this, said, This is a hard saying; who can hear ¹it? 61 But Jesus knowing in himself that his disciples murmured at this, said

---

[133] Notice the variation from the preceding verses: "He that eateth my flesh and drinketh my blood" is repeated in vv. 54, 56. But the third time it is "he that eateth me." John has the habit in a threefold repetition of introducing slight variants without appreciable change of meaning (see on 3 : 5). It is unlikely that eating the flesh and drinking the blood are to be understood in any other sense than "he that eateth me". For the meaning Strachan aptly cites the Talmud (*Sanh.* 99a) for a saying which speaks of "eating" the Messiah. The Soncino translation (p. 669) employs the verb "enjoy" which is what the passage must signify.

[134] κἀκεῖνος is emphatic.

[135] This is the tenth reference in this chapter to coming down from heaven. In the earlier nine οὐρανοῦ is invariably preceded by the article. There is no article here, though the meaning appears the same.

unto them, Doth this cause you to stumble? 62 What then if ye should behold the Son of man ascending where he was before? 63 It is the spirit that giveth life; the flesh profiteth nothing: the words that I have spoken unto you are spirit, and are life. 64 But there are some of you that believe not. For Jesus knew from the beginning who they were that believed not, and who it was that should ²betray him. 65 And he said, For this cause have I said unto you, that no man can come unto me, except it be given unto him of the Father. 66 Upon this many of his disciples went back, and walked no more with him.

¹Or, him ²Or, *deliver him up*

During the first part of the ministry of Jesus people were attracted by His teaching and flocked round Him. Many attached themselves to Him, some of them wholeheartedly, some very loosely. But then came a time when their allegiance was tested. The real nature of the claims of Jesus became apparent. The true disciples were sifted from the false, and the deep from the shallow. We see something of this process beginning at this point of the Fourth Gospel. Hitherto there has been the dominant theme of witness. Christ has been attested in one way and another and many have come to hear Him. But in this last discourse it has become obvious that He is not simply another Rabbi. His claims for Himself and His claims on His followers are such that it is no longer possible to follow Him unreflectively, and without committing oneself. So John tells us of what happened, not now among His enemies, but among His professed adherents, His disciples (v. 60) and the Twelve (v. 67).

60 For "his disciples" see on 2 : 2. A wider circle than the twelve is meant. The reference is to those who had attached themselves loosely to Jesus, but without giving much consideration to the implications. "Hard"¹³⁶ means not so much that the saying is hard to understand as that it is hard to accept. The following words make this clear. "Hear" means "hear with appreciation",

---

¹³⁶ σκληρός is derived from σκέλλω, "to dry". It means "hard to the touch", "rough". In the Bible it is applied metaphorically to Abraham's view of the command to cast out Hagar (Gen. 21 : 11), to men (Matt. 25 : 24), and to things, including it being "hard" for Saul of Tarsus to kick against the goad (Acts 26 : 14), and the "rough winds" of Jas. 3 : 4. Here (as in Jude 15) the meaning is something like "harsh". Calvin comments, "the hardness was in their hearts and not in the saying."

"take in" (see on 5 : 25).[137] The disciples no doubt found the discourse mysterious. But it was the part they could understand rather than the part they could not that bothered them.[138]
61 This is the occasion of another demonstration of Jesus' unusual powers of knowledge (see on 2 : 24; 4 : 18). Jesus knew what was going on in His disciples. Notice that whereas earlier the murmurers were the opponents of Jesus, "the Jews" (v. 41), now they are His own followers. They do not like the sound of what He is saying at all. So He asks them, "Doth this cause you to stumble?"[139] (RSV: "Do you take offense at this?"). His choice of word indicates that He knew exactly how it was with them.
62 The sentence is unfinished and there is no certainty as to how it should be completed. The meaning might be "If, then, you behold the Son of man ascending where He was before, will you not be convinced?" Or we could supply as the last clause: "will you not then be even more offended?" On the former view the ascension will be the means of ending the difficulty for those who see it. When they see Christ ascend they will know that the eating and drinking are spiritual phenomena, to be interpreted in the light of Jesus' heavenly status. To this it is objected that John does not record the ascension (though he does allude to it, 20 : 17). In any case in the Lukan account the ascension was witnessed by only a very small band of intimate associates. It was evidently not meant to be witnessed by a large group as a means of comfort and a help to them. The other view is that "ascending" is not to be isolated from the thought of the cross. John's previous reference to Christ as ascending (3 : 13) led immediately to one to the "lifting up" on the cross. On this view the ascension stands for all that series of events that was inaugurated by the crucifixion.

---

[137] αὐτοῦ I have taken to refer to the saying. But it could refer to Jesus, "who can hear him?"

[138] Barclay comments: "Here we come upon a truth that re-emerges in every age. Time and again it is not the intellectual difficulty of accepting Christ which keeps men from becoming Christians; it is the height of Christ's moral demand." There is mystery in religion, of necessity. But "Any honest thinker will accept the mystery . . . to this day many a man's refusal of Christ comes, not because Christ puzzles and baffles his intellect, but because Christ challenges and condemns his life."

[139] σκανδαλίζει. The σκάνδαλον was the bait stick which triggered off a trap when an animal or bird touched it. The verb, then, used metaphorically, signifies to be caught in a difficulty. It is frequent in Matthew and Mark, but only here and 16 : 1 in this Gospel.

If men stumbled at the discourse, much more would they stumble at the cross! To them it would seem like defeat, like a going down to Sheol. In reality it would be victory, the first in a series of events which would bring Him back to His Father. Difficulties here are the word used for "ascending"[140] and John's later reference to ascension subsequent to the cross (20 : 17). Neither view is really satisfactory, and it may well be that both are required. The form of the question does seem to favor the view that a severe testing is in store,[141] and this will be the cross. But the cross does not stand alone. The crucifixion and resurrection and ascension are linked in an unbreakable sequence. The one implies the others. And that which is to the shallow-minded a cause of stumbling and going away becomes to the man of faith the deepest cause of comfort and assurance.[142] Notice that "where he was before" implies Christ's pre-existence. It is one and the same Person who was with the Father, who became incarnate, and would in due course return whence He came.

63 The thought of this verse is complex. There is a contrast between "the spirit that giveth life"[143] and the flesh that does not

---

[140] Elsewhere in the New Testament ἀναβαίνω is never used of the crucifixion. Bernard accordingly rejects the view. He thinks that the use of this verb "provides a notable illustration of Jn.'s manner of writing, that here and at 20[17] he introduces an allusion to the Ascension of Christ, whilst he does not state explicitly that it took place."

[141] A minor point supporting this is the use of οὖν, "therefore". If Jesus were proceeding to treat of something that would comfort rather than offend, "but" would be more natural. οὖν is very frequent in this Gospel, but not in the words of Jesus. Abbott points out that of 195 occurrences of οὖν only eight are in sayings of Jesus (2191). We are justified in seeing significance in these few occurrences. Here the meaning will be, "You are scandalized at this? The logical, inevitable consequence is. . . ."

[142] *Cf.* Westcott: "You are troubled, the Lord seems to say, by words which cannot be interpreted according to the laws of material, phenomenal existence. How then will you bear the last revelation of the Ascension, when that which is truly human will be seen to be transfigured and to rise beyond the conditions of earthly life? This will be at once the severest trial and the highest reward of faith."

[143] ζωοποιέω occurs in 5 : 21, seven times in Paul and once in I Peter. Especially interesting are I Cor. 15 : 45, ἐγένετο . . . ὁ ἔσχατος Ἀδὰμ εἰς πνεῦμα ζωοποιοῦν, and II Cor. 3 : 6, τὸ γὰρ γράμμα ἀποκτείνει τὸ δὲ Πνεῦμα ζωοποιεῖ. This New Testament insistence that life comes from the Father or the Son (John 5 : 21) or the Spirit (here) should be contrasted with the Rabbinic view: "Great is the Law, for it gives life to them that practise it both in this world and in the world to come" (*Ab.* 6 : 7). But no Law can give life. Only the life-giving Spirit can do that.

profit.[144] The antithesis between flesh and spirit would lead us to think that the spirit of man is meant. But the human spirit is not life-giving. There is unquestionably a reference to the Holy Spirit, the Life-giver. This is the case in John's previous contrast between flesh and spirit in 3 : 6 (*cf.* also the reference to the Spirit in the discourse on living water in ch. 4, and in 7 : 38f.). Probably there is also in the manner of II Cor. 3 : 6 a contrast between the letter of the words and the spirit. A woodenly literal, flesh-dominated manner of looking at Jesus' words[145] will not yield the correct interpretation. That is granted only to the spiritual man, the Spirit-dominated man. Such words cannot be comprehended by the fleshly, whose horizon is bounded by this earth and its outlook. Only as the life-giving Spirit informs him may a man understand these words. This applies to much more than the words of this discourse. In His teaching as a whole Jesus emphasizes the Spirit, though specific references to the Spirit are not frequent. He is not concerned with the good that men may produce by the best efforts of the flesh. All His teaching presupposes the necessity for a work of the divine Spirit within man. Jesus goes on to equate His words with spirit and with life.[146] This does not mean that we should indulge in thorough-going allegory by way of interpretation. It means that Jesus' words are creative utterances (*cf.* the words of God in Gen. 1). They bring life. They do not only tell of life (*cf.* 5 : 24). Some see a contradiction in that life is here connected with Christ's words, whereas earlier in the chapter it comes from eating the flesh and drinking the blood. But we must not separate the words and deeds of Christ.[147] His words point us to the deed on Calvary whereby life is won for believers. Those words and that deed are one.

---

[144] "Profiteth nothing" contains an emphatic double negative, οὐκ ὠφελεῖ οὐδέν.

[145] ῥῆμα is always used in the plural in this Gospel, and it always refers to the words of God or of Christ. λόγος (used in v. 60) is usually singular (plural, 7 : 40; 10 : 19; 14 : 24; 19 : 13). For this term see Additional Note A, pp. 115ff.

[146] The repetition of ἐστιν in the expression πνεῦμά ἐστιν καὶ ζωή ἐστιν means that πνεῦμα and ζωή are not blurred; they are regarded as distinct. There is also some emphasis on the verb, "spirit they *are*, and life they *are*."

[147] *Cf.* Lightfoot: "The Lord's work and the Lord's word are one; and both must be received and assimilated by the believing disciple."

64 Despite the life-giving quality of Jesus' words there are some who do not accept them (or Him). In contrast with what would have been expected ("but" is a strong adversative[148]) some of the hearers, though in some sense disciples, do not believe (see Additional Note E, pp. 335ff.; and notice that in vv. 64, 65 as in v. 35, believing and coming to Jesus are parallel expressions). The truths of which Jesus has been speaking are accessible only to faith. They are hid forever from such as Judas. Human wisdom can never win an understanding of them for only those in whom God works come to Christ. John uses this as the opportunity to tell us that Jesus knew those who would believe and those who would not. This was not simply a matter of observation, but right from the beginning[149] He knew. It is a little curious that John should mention also that Jesus knew that Judas would be[150] His betrayer.[151] Perhaps this arises from a combination of Jesus' more than human knowledge and the reference to the passion which underlies the preceding discourse (see v. 51). It is in keeping with John's picture of Jesus as going on His serene way well aware of all that concerned Him, and of the crucifixion as divinely predestined.

65 The predestinarian strain continues. Jesus has already told them that it is only as the Father draws a man that he can come

---

[148] ἀλλ'. See on 1 : 8.

[149] ἐξ ἀρχῆς is found elsewhere in the New Testament only in 16 : 4. But John does not seem to put much difference between ἐκ and ἀπό, and ἀπ' ἀρχῆς occurs in 8 : 44; 15 : 27 and often in I John. The expression here probably means from the beginning of their professing discipleship, though in view of the strongly predestinarian strain in this Gospel it is not impossible that there is the thought of a knowledge going back to before the incarnation. For Jesus' knowledge see on 4 : 18, and for the use of οἶδα and γινώσκω on 2 : 24.

[150] τίς ἐστιν is read by most MSS here, but G. D. Kilpatrick points out in a private communication that τίς ἦν is read by P66 ℵ a e q and he suggests that this is an example of an infrequent construction (noted by Goodwin and occasionally found in the classics and elsewhere) when the imperfect replaces the present of direct speech. τίς ἐστιν then is a correction to the more usual construction.

[151] παραδίδωμι is used in a variety of ways of the "delivering up" of Jesus. Here Judas was responsible, but He was also "delivered up" by the Jewish nation and their high priests (18 : 35), by Pilate (19 : 16), for our sins (Rom. 4 : 25), and by the Father (Rom. 8 : 32). In the most moving passage of all Christ is said to have delivered Himself up (Gal. 2 : 20). ὁ παραδώσων here is the only example in John of a future participle with the article (Abbott, 2510, citing Bruder).

to Him (v. 44). He explains now[152] that He had told them this so
that they might not be perplexed when some did not believe.
Unbelief is to be expected apart from a divine miracle. It is impossible for anyone to come to Christ without the Father's giving
him the grace to do so. Left to himself the sinner prefers his sin.
Conversion is always a work of grace.

66 "Upon this", which may mean "from this time" or "for this
reason"[153] (or John may mean both), a large number of people
ceased to follow Jesus. They went away, not only from the
synagogue where Jesus had been teaching, but from all that
discipleship means.[154] The events of this chapter had made it all
too clear that following Him meant something different from
anything they had anticipated. Nothing is said to give us a clear
idea of their views, but the probability is that they were interested
in a messianic kingdom in line with the general expectation.
Instead they are invited to believe, to receive Christ, to eat His
flesh and drink His blood, to enter into that eternal life that He
proclaimed. It was too much for them. They rejected these words
of life. They went back. "Walked" is a revealing little glimpse of
the wandering nature of Christ's ministry.

13. PETER'S CONFESSION, 6 : 67–71

67 Jesus said therefore unto the twelve, Would ye also go
away? 68 Simon Peter answered him, Lord, to whom shall
we go? ¹thou hast the words of eternal life. 69 And we have
believed and know that thou art the Holy One of God. 70
Jesus answered them, Did not I choose you the twelve, and
one of you is a devil? 71 Now he spake of Judas the son of

---

[152] If the imperfect tense *(ἔλεγεν)* is significant the meaning will be that
this is the kind of thing that Jesus said repeatedly. Barclay renders, "So that
was why He often said."

[153] "For this reason" contains a further ambiguity in itself. It may refer
to the words of the previous verse (they went back because the Father did not
draw them to Jesus), or to the discourse as a whole (they were repelled by the
"hard" sayings).

[154] ἀπῆλθον εἰς τὰ ὀπίσω, "they went away to the things they had left
behind." Godet sees in the words "more than simple defection; they denote
the return of these people to their ordinary occupations, which they had
abandoned in order continuously to follow the Lord."

Simon Iscariot, for he it was that should [2]betray him, being one of the twelve.

[1]Or, *hast words* [2]Or, *deliver him up*

This is a passage of tremendous importance. So far in this Gospel enough of the claims of Jesus has been brought out to make it clear that He was no run-of-the-mill claimant to messianic honors. His claims for Himself and His claims on men are becoming clearer. At first men tended to flock around Him (2 : 23). He had chosen to withdraw from Judea because of the problem posed by the number of those who associated themselves with His band (4 : 1-3). It had looked as though He might become the head of a very popular movement. But then men began to see what Jesus really stood for and they did not like it. The preceding sections of this chapter have shown how first the multitude and then some of His disciples were repelled. Now comes the big test. What will the Twelve do? And here Peter becomes their spokesman in a magnificent declaration of allegiance and acceptance. The passage is paralleled in the Synoptics with the crisis at Caesarea Philippi (Matt. 16 : 13ff.).[155] John has a typical addendum with Jesus'

---

[155] It is often said that John's narrative is no more than a variant of the Synoptic story, *e.g.* "The confession of Peter in *vv.* 68 and 69 is the Fourth Evangelist's account of the confession of the Apostle at Caesarea Philippi, recorded by the Synoptists . . . Here, he feels, is a dramatic setting too good to be missed, too allegorically appropriate to be lost. So he takes the confession of Peter out of its historical setting and places it against the denial that is growing within the soul of Judas" (Wright). The principal reasons for holding such views (other than "insights" into the Evangelist's method) are two: the setting and the nature of the confession. In Matthew and Mark the incident is related not long after the feeding of the four thousand, in Luke it follows immediately on the feeding of the five thousand. The decisive nature of the confession, it is felt, means that it would have been uttered once only. Against the identification are (i) The difference in place. The Synoptics refer to an incident in the vicinity of Caesarea Philippi, John to one at Capernaum. (ii) The difference in Jesus' approach. The Synoptists record that He asked their opinion of His Person, John that He challenged them to continue following Him. (iii) The difference in circumstances. In the Synoptists outsiders are recognized as venerating Jesus, though with imperfect knowledge. In John outsiders have opposed Him and even disciples have left Him. The Synoptists are talking about a more complete as against a less complete understanding of His Person. John is dealing with following as against desertion. (iv) The difference in the confession. In the Synoptists the wording differs, but it is concerned with "Christ" in one way or another, "Thou art the Christ" (Mark

knowledge of Judas's role. Jesus knew what was in man (2 : 25), even at the moment that Peter made his great confession on behalf of them all.

67 It is a dramatic moment as Jesus challenges the Twelve.[156] They have heard the Sermon. They have seen the reaction of the Jews. They have seen the defection of many disciples. Now Jesus puts the question to them: "Will *you* go away too?" The form in which the question is put shows that a negative answer is expected. Jesus confidently looks for loyalty from these men.

68, 69 The question is addressed to them all. But it does not surprise us that Peter is the spokesman. He often appears in this role in the Gospels. He is impetuous, ready sometimes to jump to conclusions, and capable of incredible ineptitude (for example, his rebuke of Jesus, Matt. 16 : 22). But he is also capable of reaching astonishing heights. He does so now. "Lord" could mean much or little (see on 4 : 1). It might be no more than a polite form of address, but it might also be the proper form of referring to deity. In this context there can be no doubt that the word has the maximum, not the minimum meaning. Peter shows the impossibility of their forsaking Jesus by asking to whom could they go.[157] Then

---

8 : 29), "The Christ of God" (Luke 9 : 20), "Thou art the Christ, the Son of the living God" (Matt. 16 : 16). In John Peter says, "Lord, to whom shall we go? thou hast the words of eternal life." The differences are marked. Though the two come from the same period the evidence indicates that they should be regarded as different confessions. Murray thinks of John's account as "in striking contrast, in spite of many points of similarity, with the account given in the Synoptists of a challenge made by Jesus somewhat later at Caesarea Philippi. Here the challenge is addressed directly to their sense of personal loyalty, and the confession is a confession of a consciousness of personal indebtedness. There the challenge relates to the place that they were prepared to assign to their Master in the working out of the purpose of God for the nation and the world." Temple does not deal with the question directly but assumes a distinction. Peter's epithet, "the Holy One of God", he says, "points to the spiritual character rather than the official status of the Messiah. That will be affirmed at Caesarea Philippi." P. Gardner-Smith says bluntly, "The only real point of contact is the belief that Peter understood the Lord's Person best" (*Saint John and the Synoptic Gospels*, Cambridge, 1938, p. 36).

[156] John assumes that his readers will be familiar with the Twelve, for, though this is the first time this group is mentioned in the Gospel (it is implied in v. 13), he does not explain the term. Matthew adopts a similar procedure. He introduces the Twelve without explanation (Matt. 10 : 1).

[157] The very word for "go" used here (ἀπέρχομαι) is used also of Judas's going to the chief priests to betray Jesus in Mark 14 : 10.

he shows that he has correctly understood v. 63 by saying that Jesus has "words[158] of life eternal". No one who has come to know Jesus' life-giving word would ever forsake Him. When a man once knows Jesus, none else can satisfy. "And we", Peter goes on, using the emphatic pronoun. Whatever be the case with the others the Twelve have made their decision. The verbs "have believed" and "know"[159] are both in the perfect tense and this should be given its full force. "We have come to a place of faith and continue there. We have entered into knowledge and retain it." "Thou" is also emphatic. Peter stresses Christ's place and person. "The Holy One of God" is not a usual description of Jesus. In fact it is applied to Him on only one other occasion in the New Testament, when the demon-possessed man addressed Him in the synagogue at Capernaum (Mark 1 : 24; Luke 4 : 34). It is rare in the Old Testament (used of Aaron in Ps. 106 : 16 and *cf.* "thy holy one", Ps. 16 : 10), but it does remind us of the frequently occurring "the Holy One of Israel". There can be not the slightest doubt that the title is meant to assign to Jesus the highest possible place. It stressess His consecration and His purity. It sets Him with God and not man.[160]

70, 71 Jesus did not allow Himself to be carried away by Peter's enthusiasm. He knew what was in man. He knew that, well meant as they were, Peter's words overstated the case. He Himself had chosen the Twelve. And of this inner circle, one would not merely go away as the fringe disciples had gone. He was "a devil". In the spirit of Satan he would actively oppose what Christ stood for.

---

[158] ARV reads "the words" but the article is lacking in the better MSS. Barrett points out that "τὰ ῥήματα would imply a formula." Moulton says, "For exegesis, there are few of the finer points of Greek which need more constant attention than this omission of the article when the writer would lay stress on the quality or character of the object. Even the RV misses this badly sometimes, as in Jn.6⁶⁸" (M, I, p. 83).

[159] Richardson points out that "one cannot know if one will not believe . . . 'To know' in the Johannine usage, as generally in the Bible, means to enter into relations with someone and thus to have personal experience of him, as distinct from mere knowledge by description; it is first-hand or 'I-thou' knowledge, not scientific-objective knowledge" (*op. cit.*, pp. 45f.). See further on 2 : 24.

[160] Vincent Taylor is of opinion that, while the expression "does not appear to have been an accepted Messianic title," it is used by Peter as "a Messianic designation" (*The Names of Jesus*, London, 1953, p. 80).

John adds an explanatory note. The words apply to Judas, whose name is given in full with solemnity.[161] "Should"[162] adds a little touch of certainty. For "betray" see on v. 64. The poignancy of it all is underlined with the addition "being one of the twelve". It is worth noticing that none of the Evangelists indulges in invective when they speak of Judas's act of treachery. They simply record the fact and let it speak for itself. At most, as here, they mention that he was one of the inner circle, but even then they let their readers work out for themselves how that adds to the enormity of his crime.

---

[161] This verse names his father as Simon Iscariot. Ἰσκαριώτης, which is applied to Judas also in 12 : 4, is usually accepted as a place name, signifying אִישׁ קְרִיּוֹת, "man of Kerioth". It would thus apply equally to father and son. Kerioth may be the Kerioth-hezron of Josh. 15 : 25 (in Judah), or Kerioth in Moab (Jer. 48 : 24). Judas was thus the only one of the Twelve who was not a Galilean. Schonfield and others think the title might mean "One of the Sicarii" (or "Assassins"; the name was given to a group of desperate rebels with a bitter hatred of Rome and Roman sympathizers), citing Jos. *Bell*. II. xiii, 3. But this view has little to commend it, and has not attracted many. Goguel rejects both views and finds it impossible to discover a satisfactory meaning (*The Life of Jesus*, London, 1958, p. 495, n. 1).

[162] ἔμελλεν. The verb may denote simple futurity, but it can also convey the thought of inevitability, as when it is used in Matt. 17 : 22 of the certainty of the passion.

CHAPTER VII

14. The Fifth Discourse — The Life-Giving Spirit, 7 : 1-52

The opposition to Jesus grows. At first it might have been thought possible that men would in time come to make Jesus their Leader. The events of the preceding chapters show that this will not be the case. From now to the end of the public ministry John depicts a steadily deepening hostility. In this chapter and the next John has a good deal to tell us about the arguments used by the enemies of Jesus. This may well be his way of saying that the objections raised to Jesus' messianic claims all had their answers.[1]

It had now become dangerous for Jesus to appear in Judea (v. 1), so that His appearance at Jerusalem at the Feast of Tabernacles must be carefully arranged. Even so it was a feat of courage, and an attempt was actually made to arrest Him. But though danger was in the air Jesus continued on His appointed path. He went up to the feast in due course, and there He gave the teaching that was appropriate to the occasion. The great advance was in His teaching on the Spirit. Some aspects of this have occupied us before, but on this occasion Jesus brings out the point that when the Spirit is within a man He overflows in abounding life. The Spirit-filled man cannot but be a blessing to other people.

The Feast of Tabernacles was a feast of thanksgiving primarily for the blessings of God in the harvest, but it was also observed with special reference to the blessings received during the wilderness wanderings, the time when God was pleased to manifest Himself in the tabernacle. It may be this which gives significance to John's

---

[1] C. H. Dodd points out that in chs. 7, 8, there is a strongly polemical tone, with the enemies of Jesus having more to say than at any other place in the four Gospels. This is doubtless, as he says, in order to bring out the constant pressure of the opposition that Jesus met (note the repeated statements that Jesus' life was in danger, 7 : 1, 13, 19, 25, 30, 32, 44; 8 : 37, 40, 59). It should also be noted that "The evangelist has brought together here most of what he has to say in reply to Jewish objections against the messianic claims made for Jesus" (*IFG*, p. 346). Messiahship is central for John. This section of his Gospel is one in which he shows that objections to the messiahship of Jesus can all be met.

392

recording of the happenings in this chapter. Neither in the tabernacle in the wilderness, nor in the temple which replaced it, was God fully manifested. The final and perfect manifestation of God was in Jesus, whose ministry would result in God's dwelling neither in a tent nor in a temple, but in men's hearts by His Spirit.

(a) Jesus' Discussion with His Brothers, 7: 1–9

1 And after these things Jesus walked in Galilee: for he would not walk in Judaea, because the Jews sought to kill him. 2 Now the feast of the Jews, the feast of tabernacles, was at hand. 3 His brethren therefore said unto him, Depart hence, and go into Judaea, that thy disciples also may behold thy works which thou doest. 4 For no man doeth anything in secret, ¹and himself seeketh to be known openly. If thou doest these things, manifest thyself to the world. 5 For even his brethren did not believe on him. 6 Jesus therefore saith unto them, My time is not yet come; but your time is always ready. 7 The world cannot hate you; but me it hateth, because I testify of it, that its works are evil. 8 Go ye up unto the feast: I go not up ²unto this feast; because my time is not yet fulfilled. 9 And having said these things unto them, he abode still in Galilee.

¹Some ancient authorities read *and seeketh it to be known openly.* ²Many ancient authorities add *yet.*

The hatred of His opponents meant that Jesus could no longer move openly. He must be circumspect lest He run into the kind of trouble that would hinder His mission. Thus He rejected the invitation of His unbelieving brothers to go up to Jerusalem for the Feast of Tabernacles. To do as they suggested would be to provoke trouble. While He was ready to die when the time came,² He was not ready to rush into precipitate action. He awaited the proper time for any action that He took.
1 "After these things" is an indefinite note of time.³ It gives no indication of how much time had elapsed. The time between Passover (6 : 4) and Tabernacles, however, shows that the interval is about six months. This is instructive for John's method. He

---

² Calvin reminds us that "it was not right for Him to rush headlong into danger", but that also, "He did not turn aside a hair's-breadth from the course of His duty". From this he draws the moral, "We must always beware that we do not for the sake of life lose the purpose for living".

³ For μετὰ ταῦτα see on 2 : 12.

records nothing at all that happened during this period. He is not writing a complete history, but making a selection for a definite purpose, that of bringing out the messiahship of Jesus and of bringing men to faith. Despite the passage of months, the hostility of Jesus' opponents persisted. So forbidding was their attitude ("sought" does not denote a solitary action; the tense is continuous, "they kept on seeking") that Jesus withdrew from Judea altogether. He "walked" in Galilee. The verb expresses the itinerant ministry of a Rabbi moving among the people with his disciples. "Would not" signifies that He set His will against walking in Judea.[4] For "the Jews" see on 1 : 19.

2 John is fond of time notes and fond of references to feasts. We see both here. Notice that "the" feast is defined as the Feast of Tabernacles, a usage that is paralleled in the Mishnah and elsewhere.[5] The name "tabernacles" refers to the custom of building leafy booths to be inhabited during the festival, a feature to which Goodspeed's rendering, "the Jewish camping festival", draws attention (though this translation obscures the fact that the feast had also deep religious significance).

3-5 For "his brethren" see on 2 : 12. Jesus' brothers did not believe

---

[4] Abbott points out that θέλω with the present infinitive here and in v. 17 stresses continuity, "he did not wish *to continue teaching (περιπατεῖν)* . . ."; "If any one be willing *to continue doing (ποιεῖν)* his will", whereas the aorist πιάσαι in v. 44 refers to a particular act (2498).

[5] See *Maas.* 3 : 7; *Bikk.* 1 : 6, 10; *Shek.* 3 : 1; 6 : 3, *etc.* Similarly Josephus *Ant.* viii, 100 refers to Tabernacles as ἑορτῆς σφόδρα παρὰ τοῖς ῾Εβραίοις ἁγιωτάτης καὶ μεγίστης, while in xv, 50 he says ἑορτὴ δέ ἐστιν αὕτη παρ' ἡμῖν εἰς τὰ μάλιστα τηρουμένη. The place the feast held is shown by the choice of it and not one of the others as the test in Zech. 14 : 16–19. Knox's rendering, "one of the Jewish feasts, the Feast of Tabernacles" misses the emphasis. This was not "a" feast. It was "the" feast. Tabernacles was the great feast held when the harvest was finally gathered in (Exod. 23 : 16 calls it "the feast of ingathering, at the end of the year, when thou gatherest in thy labors out of the field"; see also Lev. 23 : 33ff., 39ff.; Deut. 16 : 13ff.). There are references to the feast as lasting for seven days (*e.g.* Lev. 23 : 34), and also to the eighth day (as Lev. 23 : 36), from which the conclusion is drawn that an original feast of seven days had been extended by one day. Together with the note of thanksgiving for harvest the feast commemorated the goodness of God to His people during the wilderness wanderings. The tents, or leafy bowers, which gave the feast its name, were erected in the courts of houses or on the roofs. Plummer points out that this custom "involved much both of the discomfort and also of the merriment of a picnic". He goes on to remark that distinctions between rich and poor were thus largely obliterated for the duration of the merrymaking.

on Him (v. 5; the imperfect tense gives the continuing attitude). But they challenge Him to appear publicly at the feast. "That thy disciples also may behold[6] thy works" is somewhat puzzling. It appears to mean that the brothers had seen Jesus perform miracles, and that they now wish that His disciples should see this sort of thing. But there is no indication in the previous narrative that the brothers had seen any sign which the disciples (or some of them) had not. It may be that the brothers are pretending to superior knowledge. It may be that they are ironic. It may be that they are thinking primarily of disciples in other places than Galilee, or perhaps His disciples as a whole. Such would be gathered in Jerusalem for the feast and Jesus could make contact with them then. It may be that they have in mind the defections mentioned in 6 : 66, and suggest that Jerusalem is the best place to try to retrieve the situation. More likely they mean that the signs wrought by a messianic claimant must be wrought in the holy city,[7] and not simply in remote places. It is only as the Messiah openly performs the messianic signs that He is the Messiah.[8] They point out that no one who claims to be a public[9] figure (*Berkeley*, "to be in the lime-

---

[6] The construction is ἵνα with the future indicative, which may put a slight emphasis on the actuality of the beholding. Abbott thinks that "there may be an intention to blend purpose with assured result" (2690).

[7] *Cf.* Jesus' remark, "it cannot be that a prophet perish out of Jerusalem" (Luke 13 : 33). The brothers were right in seeing Jerusalem as the proper centre for the manifestation of the essence of the Messiah's work. They were wrong in their conception of what that work was and how it should be manifested.

[8] For this Jewish idea *cf.* S. Mowinckel: "they mean, come forward, and perform openly the Messianic works and miracles ... According to Jewish thought, it is only then that He will become Messiah in the full sense of the term. Before that time we may say that He is but *Messias designatus*, a claimant to Messianic status" (*He that Cometh*, Oxford, 1959, p. 303).

[9] The expression translated "openly" is ἐν παρρησίᾳ. The noun is often used in the New Testament with the meaning "boldness", and its use here may be meant to indicate that Jesus' conduct was not courageous. In John the word is mostly used of speech (7 : 13, 26; 10 : 24; 11 : 14; 16 : 25, 29; 18 : 20), and the meaning is "open", "not obscure". But John also uses the word in the sense "public", as here (11 : 54; it is not impossible that some of the references to speech should have this meaning). In 18 : 20 Jesus denies that He has taught in secret. The basic idea in the word (πᾶν compounded with ῥῆσις) is freedom of speech, the attitude of being completely at home, when the words flow freely. This may lead to the idea of boldness, or confidence, or openness. In all John uses the word 9 times, and it is found 4 times in I John. As the New Testament total is 31 times it is clear that it is a Johannine word. The highest total in any other book is 5 times in Acts.

light") can establish himself by working in secret. There is no implication that Jesus had hidden Himself of set purpose. But Galilee was far from the capital, and anything done there would be "secret" as far as the dwellers in the metropolis were concerned. And such things as messianic claims must be established in the capital city before the religious leaders.[10] To act in Galilee accordingly was to act "in secret". The brethren challenge Jesus to produce miracles in the nation's heart and centre. Their action is like that of Mary in chapter 2, and even more like that of the multitude who tried to make a king of Him (6 : 15).[11] It implies a belief that He could work miracles,[12] coupled with a thoroughgoing misunderstanding of His mission, a complete lack of faith in the only sense that matters.[13] They had no idea that Jesus' mission, in its very nature, must be unpopular.[14] We should not overlook the importance of this for an understanding of the difficulties under which Jesus labored. Many

---

[10] "Certainly, speaking absolutely, they were right: the Messianic question could not be decided in Galilee" (Godet).

[11] Brown points out that in this section of the Gospel there are parallels to the Synoptic temptation stories. In 6 : 15 they try to make Him King, just as Satan tempted Him with the offer of all the kingdoms of the world. In 6 : 31 they ask for miraculous bread, which is not unlike Satan's suggestion that He turn stones into bread. Now they want Him to go to Jerusalem and show His power, which reflects the same spirit as the suggestion that He jump from the pinnacle of the Temple. We are justified in concluding that the temptations narrated so graphically by Matthew and Luke recurred throughout Jesus' ministry.

[12] Bernard strangely understands the passage as ironical. He thinks the brothers were sceptical about Jesus' power. By contrast MacGregor comments: "The brothers' challenge does not so much imply doubt concerning the reality of Jesus' works as a hint that a change of method is necessary".

[13] "Their supreme misunderstanding lies in their distinction between secret and public, which covers a false distinction between glorious and inglorious (v. 41-4), bold and cowardly. There will be a public ministry of Jesus in Jerusalem . . . but it consists in the public exposition of the sin of the world and the provocation of its hatred . . . There is also a glorious display of power, but it consists in secret obedience to the will of the Father and in the transmission of the truth to the disciples in private . . . and is displayed completely in the death of the Christ" (Hoskyns). Bultmann comments that there is always an ambiguity in the revelation, so that the very works which the world finds insufficient are the fulfilment of its demand. It is, of course, still the case that the world is unable to discern the hand of God in the events in which it is concerned.

[14] "His destiny was not popularity but the hatred of the world, a hatred such as no one else could experience, since he alone brought the world into judgment" (Barrett).

a man faced with cruel opposition in public life has been sustained by the faith and the faithfulness of his kith and kin. Jesus was denied this solace.

"These things" are not explained. But the expression points to the works wherein Jesus showed forth His glory, and by implication if no more claimed a special position for Himself. If He claims to be the Messiah, the brothers are saying, then let Him tell it to the world. This may be another example of John's irony. Jesus was indeed the Messiah, and would in due course be manifested to the world and that in a way far fuller than they could comprehend. But their words arose from unbelief. "Did not believe" denotes a continuing attitude. They had no faith and their words must be understood in the light of that.

6 Greek has two words for "time", and that used here[15] often refers to time not simply in its chronological sequence, but with reference to the events which take place in it. Used in this way, it is time in its qualitative rather than its quantitative aspect. It points to the suitable time, the right time, the favorable opportunity. In the present context it must refer to the time for going up to the feast. It was not the right time for Jesus to go up. He would not get the opportunity He sought if He went up with the brothers at the beginning of the feast. It was better for Him to wait till the crowds assembled so that He could suddenly come among them (in the spirit of Mal. 3 : 1). *Cf.* Barclay: "to arrive with the crowds all assembled and expectant

---

[15] The word is καιρός which occurs in this Gospel only in this passage (here and in v. 8) and in the spurious 5 : 4. The other word is χρόνος. In much recent literature there is a determined attempt to differentiate between them as in J. A. T. Robinson, *In the End God* (London, 1950), or J. Marsh, *The Fulness of Time* (London, 1952). This has been subjected to a very critical examination by J. Barr in *The Semantics of Biblical Language* (Oxford, 1961), and in *Biblical Words for Time* (London, 1962). He makes it clear that the differences have been exaggerated but he does not deny them altogether. Thus, in the latter book he sums up: "In many contexts the two words are interchangeable, apart from the stylistic preference for καιρός. For the lapse of time, with an adjective of quantity, χρόνος is usual; for cases like 'the time for figs', and for 'opportunity', καιρός is used. The strong eschatological expectation, and the sense of fulfilment of past eschatological promises, produces frequent contexts like 'the time is coming', in which ὁ καιρός is usual. The sense of 'season', both for natural and sacred seasons, appears a few times for καιρός. In two passages both χρόνος and καιρός appear together, probably with no appreciable difference in meaning" (*op. cit.*, p. 121). In the present passage καιρός is clearly the appropriate word.

gave Him a far better opportunity than to go at the very beginning. This simply shows us Jesus choosing His time with careful prudence in order to get the most effective results." It is not impossible that John saw more in it than this. John's picture of Jesus is of One steadily moving on to meet His divinely-appointed destiny. If this is in mind here the meaning will be that Jesus' time, His God-appointed time, was not yet come (see on 2 : 4). Yet we should not overlook the facts that John normally uses the word "hour", not "time", to express this thought, and that the context at least in part is against it.[16] But there is one feature of the context which strongly favors it, namely the following verse which speaks of the world as hating Jesus but not the brothers. Odeberg points out that "To the Jews it was a self-evident truth that every man had his time".[17] To affirm that they had no particular "time", but that their "time" was always present was accordingly striking and novel teaching. What gives it point is the fact that the world as such did not recognize Jesus. It was not interested in His "time". In this respect the brothers joined with the world. Since the world (and the brothers) have cut themselves off from the divinely appointed "time" all times are alike to them. The brothers are set in strong contrast to Jesus.[18]

---

[16] Wright expressly differentiates this verse from those referring to the "hour". Those refer to "the end of the Ministry of Jesus on the Cross", but καιρός means that "the occasion did not seem as yet opportune to Jesus to *manifest Himself to the world* (v. 4)." Similarly Bernard thinks that καιρός "stands for the moment of opportunity, the fitting occasion, rather than for the 'predestined hour' *(ὥρα)*, on which the Fourth Gospel dwells with such insistence ... The fitting time had not yet come ... and by this is meant not the hour of His Passion, but rather the best time for that public manifestation of Himself as Messiah, which He would make when He went up the Feast of Tabernacles". A. Guilding is another to draw attention to the distinction from ὥρα. She thinks that the words of this verse "bring instantly to mind the Markan summary of the Lord's preaching Πεπλήρωται ὁ καιρός, καὶ ἤγγικεν ἡ βασιλεία τοῦ θεοῦ (Mark 1. 15) ... The time, then, is the time of the coming of the Messiah predicted by the prophets" (*The Fourth Gospel and Jewish Worship*, Oxford, 1960, p. 99). But καιρός is by no means as specific as this. There are many occurrences of καιρός in the New Testament, and there seems no reason for thinking that Mark 1 : 15 is in mind here. Moreover this interpretation overlooks the fact that the καιρός in Mark 1 : 15 is fulfilled, whereas that in the present passage is not.

[17] *FG*, p. 279.

[18] "My" is ὁ ἐμός, and "your" is ὁ ὑμέτερος. The use of the possessive adjective rather than the genitive for the pronoun may be significant. See on 3 : 29 for John's use of possessives.

They had no divine commission to discharge. Their only duty was to be faithful Jews. For this there was little point in a careful choice of time. One time was as good as another. The brothers' "time" was that when they would show themselves faithful Jews by going up to the feast. Their advice came out of their own situation and was completely irrelevant to the situation of Jesus accordingly.

7 The contrast with the brothers continues.[19] Jesus takes up their word "world", but uses it in a very different sense. The world not only does not, but cannot hate them. How could it? They belong to it. Its hate is not for such (cf. 15: 19). But Jesus is in a different position. Him it does hate. The reason is the unfailing testimony that He bears against it ("testify" is in a continuous tense, as is "hateth"; both point to continuing attitudes). Jesus marks Himself off from the world by His continual testimony that the world's deeds are evil. The evil-doer does not care to have his sin rebuked, and the hatred of which Jesus speaks is the inevitable result.

8 The difference in the "times" of Jesus and of His brothers, and that in the attitude of the world to Him and to them, lead to a difference in conduct. Jesus tells the brothers to go up to the feast. That is the natural thing to do in their position. But He is not in their position. Therefore He is not[20] going up. There is a difficulty here, for after saying this Jesus does later go to Jerusalem. It is important accordingly to notice that the use of the present tense does not exclude subsequent action of a different kind. Jesus simply says that the brothers should go (the implication being "go now"[21]), and He separates Himself from them. He is refusing to go up at their request and with a view to accomplishing what they set before

---

[19] ὑμᾶς and the emphatic ἐμέ are set in immediate juxtaposition. The opposition is not to be missed.

[20] οὐκ is read by ℵ DK Lat syr[s.c] boh arm eth geo *etc.*, οὔπω "not yet", by P66 P75 BLTW ΓΔΘ f1 f13 *etc.* The third century neo-Platonist, Porphyry, spoke of an inconstancy at this point, and this may have given rise to the variant οὔπω (so *IB*). Hendriksen argues that the context so strongly favors the meaning "not yet" that the attestation of οὔπω (which is by no means meagre to say the least) should be accepted. It is doubtful whether he allows sufficient weight to the maxim *difficilior lectio potior*. If the original read οὔπω why should anyone alter it to οὐκ? I cannot see any convincing answer so I incline to the reading οὐκ. *Cf.* also *GNT*, p. 426.

[21] *Cf.* Chrysostom: " 'How then,' saith some one, 'went He up after saying, "I go not up"?' He said not, once for all *(καθάπαξ)*, 'I go not up,' but, 'now,' that is, 'not with you' " (XLVIII. 2; p. 174).

Him, but He is not refusing to go up.[22] He is working out the implications of His messiahship in His own way, not in theirs. Moreover what they are urging Him to do is to go up to keep the feast. This Jesus did not do, either then or later. He was absent for a good part of the ceremonies, perhaps for all of them. He went up to give certain teaching, not to observe the feast in the manner of the typical pilgrim. He tells His brothers that His time "is not yet fulfilled".[23] This means that the events in the time of which He speaks have not yet approached their consummation. Until they do He will not act.[24] And much will happen before He can make that public claim that His brothers seek to foist on Him at this moment.

[22] Several commentators draw attention to the parallels in 2 : 4 where Jesus refuses to be constrained to perform a miracle, though subsequently He does perform it, and 11 : 6, when, on being told of Lazarus' illness He goes up at what is the wrong time as men would think. On the present passage Barrett says, "John's οὐκ ἀναβαίνω merely negatives the request of the brothers, and does not negative absolutely the intention of Jesus to go to Jerusalem at the proper time." *Cf.* Godet: "Jesus begins here by refusing to go up to Jerusalem in the sense in which He was urged to do so (that of manifesting Himself to the world), in order to go up afterwards in a wholly different sense." Temple says, "when He appears at the feast it is not as one of the pilgrim-worshippers but as a Prophet." It is plain that Jesus' words refer specifically to the suggestion made by the brothers and to the whole of that suggestion. He is refusing to go up in the way they suggest, *i.e.* with a view to manifesting Himself openly. At the next Passover this would happen. In the meantime Jesus declines to do as the brothers suggest. Hoskyns thinks there is a subtle play on words. ἀναβαίνω is used not only of going up to Jerusalem to feasts, but also for Jesus' going up to the Father (3 : 13; 6 : 62; 20 : 17), and Hoskyns relates this to the use of ὑψόω for the lifting up of Jesus on the cross (3 : 14, *etc.*). "In the Evangelist's thought the death and resurrection form one act of ascension or lifting up to the Father . . . Jesus does not go up to Jerusalem to the Feast of Tabernacles, but His ascent for the salvation of the world is deferred by the will of the Father until the Time of the more significant feast of the Passover." This, however, seems too subtle. If that is what Jesus meant He certainly misled the brothers.

[23] Harold Blair sees a reference to Jesus' rejection by the people: "Jesus had something to say which by its very nature must rouse hatred and antagonism; not only must his message be said, it must be acted out stage by stage until his people had seen the whole picture. There would come the inevitable end: he would be rejected. But he must be rejected on his own terms, no less. Above all he must not be rejected on a misunderstanding. 'My time', he said, 'is not yet fulfilled' " (*The Ladder of Temptations*, London, 1960, p. 96).

[24] Notice the repetition from v. 6, "My time is not yet come . . . my time is not yet fulfilled", and for similar repetitions of the negative in this Gospel see 5 : 19, 30; 5 : 30 and 6 : 38; 5 : 34, 41; 13 : 33, 36. Similarly the Jews take up a negative of Christ and repeat it in 7 : 34–6; 8 : 21f.

9 Jesus has made His position clear. And having done so, He acts in accordance with it. When the brothers go up to the feast He stays where He is, in Galilee.

(b) The Reaction of the Multitudes, 7 : 10-13

10 But when his brethren were gone up unto the feast, then went he also up, not publicly, but as it were in secret. 11 The Jews therefore sought him at the feast, and said, Where is he? 12 And there was much murmuring among the multitudes concerning him: some said, He is a good man; others said, Not so, but he leadeth the multitude astray. 13 Yet no man spake openly of him for fear of the Jews.

It is apparent that the brothers were not alone in the thought that it would be natural for Jesus to be in Jerusalem for this feast. There was comment on His absence, or rather on the fact that He was not known to be present, for John introduces the section in which he tells us of the discussion by informing us that Jesus did go up to Jerusalem. It is apparent that His ministry is having an effect. The people are divided. They do not know what to say. But the hostility of the hierarchy is now plain and serious, so that open discussion is inhibited.

10 Jesus has differentiated Himself from His brothers. Thus they go up to the feast but He does not go up with them. But after they have gone He goes up, too. But He does not go up in the way they have outlined. John is clear that others do not lay down the pattern for Jesus. He is supremely the master of every situation. So now He goes up when He is ready, and in the way He chooses. "Not publicly" takes up the "manifest thyself" of v. 4, and rejects it.[25] Jesus' going up is not the going up that the brothers had counselled. "As it were in secret" is not quite as definite as "in secret" would have been, and probably indicates that, though He took care to avoid undue publicity, Jesus did not go up in such a way that His presence was completely unknown to all others (*cf.* Kleist and Lilly, "not so as to attract attention, but incognito"). Mark also tells us that Jesus' last journey to Jerusalem was without publicity (Mark

---

[25] "Not publicly" is οὐ φανερῶς, recalling φανέρωσον σεαυτόν of v. 4. It does not mean "furtively", but "without being a member of a pilgrim cavalcade". It is interesting to notice that the first time John records Jesus as going up to a feast it is as purifier of the temple (2 : 13ff.), then as one of the pilgrims (5 : 1ff.), here alone for the purpose of giving a prophetic message, and finally as King (12 : 12ff.).

9 : 30). What John is saying is that Jesus did not go up with the pilgrim caravan. We see how large such a group might be from the incident in Luke 2 wherein Joseph and Mary looked for the child Jesus throughout an entire day. Nothing could be more public than to journey in such a company. Jesus eschewed such a conspicuous method of travel and went up privately.

11 For "the Jews" see on 1 : 19. Here the expression denotes particularly the enemies of Jesus. "Sought" and "said" are continuous tenses. They kept on looking for Him and asking where He was. John does not tell us why they were so sure that He would be there. Possibly they discerned a fitness for His message about this feast; possibly they reasoned that He had been absent from the city on some previous feasts and thus might be expected to be present this time.

12, 13 "Murmuring" usually indicates discontent, but here it probably denotes rather quiet discussion, "'whispering,' suppressed discussion in low tones, in corners, and among friends" (Dods). The crowds[26] were divided in their opinions, but it was not safe to speak up about Jesus, so they kept their voices low.[27] "He is a good man" indicates an awareness of His character and a lack of perception of His Person. Those who thought of Him as leading the multitude astray did not go into details. Presumably they held that His signs and His preaching, while ostensibly setting forth the divine, cloaked sinister designs. Those who followed such teaching could not but be led astray. The role of "the crowd" throughout this chapter should not be overlooked. Except in chapter 12 there is nothing like it in this Gospel. The term denotes the uninformed majority, wanting to do the right thing but not sure what it was. They are distinguished from "the Jews" (which here must mean the religious leaders, for the crowds were Jews themselves), and also from the disciples of Jesus (see further on v. 25). Some of them differed sharply[28] from the view that Jesus was a good man. John concludes this part of his narrative with the information that "fear

---

[26] The plural ὄχλοι (if this is the right reading) is found here only in John. It may denote groups of pilgrims from various places.

[27] *Amplified* renders, "There was . . . much whispered discussion *and* hot disputing". There is nothing in the Greek corresponding to the last two words, and they represent an unlikely interpretation. There were varied opinions, but the discussion was guarded.

[28] οὔ, ἀλλά represents a radical contradiction, "Not at all", "on the contrary". For οὔ see on 1 : 21.

7 : 1-52 FIFTH DISCOURSE - THE LIFE-GIVING SPIRIT

of the Jews" prevented free and open discussion.[29] This represents the high point of hostility so far reached. The opposition is rising.

(c) Righteous Judgment, 7: 14-24

14 But when it was now the midst of the feast Jesus went up into the temple, and taught. 15 The Jews therefore marvelled, saying, How knoweth this man letters, having never learned? 16 Jesus therefore answered them, and said, My teaching is not mine, but his that sent me. 17 If any man willeth to do his will, he shall know of the teaching, whether it is of God, or whether I speak from myself. 18 He that speaketh from himself seeketh his own glory: but he that seeketh the glory of him that sent him, the same is true, and no unrighteousness is in him. 19 Did not Moses give you the law, and yet none of you doeth the law? Why seek ye to kill me? 20 The multitude answered, Thou hast a demon: who seeketh to kill thee? 21 Jesus answered and said unto them, I did one work, and ye all marvel because thereof. 22 Moses hath given you circumcision (not that it is of Moses, but of the fathers); and on the sabbath ye circumcise a man. 23 If a man receiveth circumcision on the sabbath, that the law of Moses may not be broken; are ye wroth with me, because I made [1]a man every whit whole on the sabbath? 24 Judge not according to appearance, but judge righteous judgment.

[1]Gr. *a whole man sound.*

When the feast was at its height Jesus came out of His seclusion and taught in the temple.[30] His opening address is a call to make

---

[29] Note that παρρησία, which the crowd did not attain here, is the very word used in v. 26 of Jesus' way of speaking.

[30] *Cf.* C. H. Dodd: "Choosing His own time, He goes up μεσούσης τῆς ἑορτῆς. What does this mean but a fulfilment of the prophecy, 'The Lord whom ye seek shall suddenly come to His temple' (Mal. iii. 1)? It is the Day of the Lord, which, according to Zech. xiv, the Feast of Tabernacles foreshadows. We have here a striking instance of the characteristic Johannine irony. On the surface, we are reading about a rustic prophet who leaves the obscurity of the provinces to appeal to the great public of the metropolis. But the words φανέρωσον σεαυτὸν τῷ κόσμῳ have a weight disproportionate to the ostensible situation. In their deeper meaning they are an appeal to the Messiah to manifest Himself to Israel. But if we go deeper still, they speak of the manifestation of the eternal Logos, as life and light, to the world of human kind" (*IFG*, p. 351). Dodd goes on to point out that here we have the Logos, in the world unknown, coming to and being rejected by His own. Lightfoot also sees a reference in this passage to Mal. 3 : 1, and finds in this the reason that Jesus did not go up with the pilgrims.

403

serious judgments, and not simply snap decisions on the basis of surface appearance. He points out that if anyone is really in earnest he will know whether Jesus' teaching is divine in origin or not. But in this situation the people are trying to kill him and thus break the very law they profess to uphold.[31] Their consideration for the outward letter of the law (as shown in their concern for circumcision) contrasts sharply with their carelessness toward the deeper things to which the law points (as shown in their attitude toward Jesus' healing on the sabbath). Their values are wrong. They are superficial. They do not understand the meaning of the law they profess to honor, and therefore they do not recognize that the authority of Jesus is the very authority of God.

14 Jesus waited until the feast was half way through[32] before going up to the temple. No reason is given for this choice of time. We may conjecture that He wished to teach at the climax of the festivities but not to be involved in the whole of the celebrations. When He went up there was no attempt at concealment or at remaining in semi-seclusion. He taught[33] in the temple which was just about as public an activity as was possible. Nothing is said about the subject of His discourse.

15 His hearers were surprised. This seems to indicate that many of them had never heard Jesus teach before this, and indeed, John has not recorded any previous teaching of Jesus in Jerusalem. He has told us that Jesus had been in the capital before, that He had done "signs" there, and that He had defended Himself when accused of making Himself "equal with God". But in any case many of His audience on this occasion would be pilgrims from centres where Jesus had never been. They express astonishment at Jesus' knowl-

---

[31] Wayne A. Meeks sees the nature of Jesus' prophetic activity as the point at issue: "The whole argument of 7.15–24 turns on the question whether Jesus is the true prophet like Moses or whether he is the false prophet . . . Jesus' hearers are placed before a dramatic decision, for while they are commanded to heed the true prophet upon pain of divine judgment (Deuteronomy 18. 19), they are also commanded to put the false prophet to death (Deuteronomy 18. 20; 13. 6). The crowd therefore divides" (*The Prophet-King*, Leiden, 1967, p. 56).

[32] τῆς ἑορτῆς μεσούσης is not definite. It may mean the exact centre of the feast, *i.e.* the fourth day. Or it may be a vague way of saying that Jesus came up some time between the beginning (when the brothers wanted Him to go up) and the last day, when He made His great proclamation (vv. 37ff.).

[33] The imperfect ἐδίδασκεν is probably ingressive, "He began to teach".

edge of the "letters" (basically the Bible[34]) when He had never[35] "learned", *i.e.* been a disciple attached to a Rabbi (*cf.* the reference to Peter and John as "unlearned", Acts 4 : 13). They would not have been surprised at His knowing a little Scripture. The Bible was read regularly in the synagogues, and the *Shema*ʿ (Deut. 6 : 4f.) at any rate was memorized by all. So probably most people could quote some parts of the Bible. The surprise would be connected with the fact that Jesus could carry on a sustained discourse apparently in the manner of the Rabbis, and perhaps also with the amount of Scripture Jesus could quote. "This man" is contemptuous (Moffatt renders, "this uneducated fellow"). MacGregor points out that "The Evangelist would see something intensely dramatic in this picture of the Jews confronted by the Incarnate Logos and yet treating him as an *'uneducated fellow'*!" It is a highly ironical situation.

16, 17 Jesus assures them that the origin of His message is divine. Had He said that He was self-taught, or that He needed no teacher, or the like, He would have been discredited immediately. The age did not prize originality. The Rabbinic method was to cite authorities for all important statements. So Jesus does not claim to be the originator of His[36] message. That does not stem from any earthly source. It stems from Him who sent Him (notice once again the thought John so often repeats, that Jesus was sent from God, and see note on 3 : 17). Jesus goes on to affirm that any really sincere person would know this. It is not something that can be learned only by those who are expert in the theological niceties. Any man who really wills to do the will of God (*i.e.* whose whole will is bent in this direction; it is the set of the life that is

---

[34] γράμματα will denote primarily "sacred letters", *i.e.* scripture. The term could apply to learning in general, and the article is required to make a reference to scripture unambiguous; *cf.* τὰ ἱερὰ γράμματα in II Tim. 3 : 15, or αἱ γραφαί, John 5 : 39. But there is no reason for thinking there is an allusion to learning in general here, for the meaning the context demands is clearly concerned with teaching the meaning of scripture. *Berkeley* renders "literature", and Ferrar Fenton "theology", but neither quite meets the situation.

[35] The use of μή with this participle will not be to throw doubt on the proposition, but μή here is really equivalent to οὐ. μή encroaches on the territory of οὐ in Hellenistic Greek, and there are few examples of οὐ with participle in John (BDF 430 (1)).

[36] ἐμή is emphatic (see on 4 : 42) which makes the disclaimer that He Himself is responsible for the message all the more effective.

meant) will have the spiritual discernment required. This means more than ethical determination. It involves faith (as in 6 : 29).[37] Such a one will know whether this teaching is divine in origin or whether it bears the stamp, "Manufactured in Nazareth".[38] His hearers had raised the question of His competence as a teacher. He raises the question of their competence as hearers.

18 The Jews can verify Jesus' statement from their own observation. The man whose message originates with himself seeks his own advancement. He can do no other. But the Man who is concerned with the interests of One who sent Him is different (see on 4 : 34 for Jesus' concern with the Father's will). He that seeks the glory of God is true.[39] Notice that Jesus does not say that He speaks the truth, but that He *is* true (*cf.* 14 : 6). And of Him that is true He further says that there is no unrighteousness in Him. The negative way of putting it may be meant to point a contrast with the Jews in whom there certainly was unrighteousness.

19 Jesus develops this thought. It was a favorite cause for self-congratulation among the Jews that they were the recipients of the Law (*cf.* Rom. 2 : 17). But now our Lord points out that there is a difference between receiving and keeping the law. Moses gave them the law. But none of them keeps it (Paul points out that the only profit in circumcision is when the law is kept; being a Jew is not simply a matter of pride of race, Rom. 2 : 25-29). Far from keeping the law they are seeking to put Jesus to death (*cf.* v. 1). Or Jesus may mean that from time to time all of them break the law because of conflicting regulations of the type He is about to cite (v. 22). He has done no more than they all do, yet they seek

---

[37] Augustine emphasizes the place of faith in understanding this saying: "understanding is the reward of faith. Therefore do not seek to understand in order to believe, but believe that thou mayest understand ... what is 'If any man be willing to do His will'? It is the same thing as to believe" (XXIX. 6; pp. 184f.).

[38] *Cf.* C. J. Wright: "It does not mean that if a man really centres his whole personality on doing the Divine will as it is known to him, he will arrive at a perfectly articulated doctrinal position, or at dogmatic statements which will answer every perplexity of the logical intellect. It means that the truthful spirit comes to those truths of eternity by which Jesus lived and died. In other words, it is the truthful who recognise Him who is Truth".

[39] ἀληθής is applied to God in 3 : 33; 8 : 26, and these are the only other places in this Gospel where a person is said to be true. This is another unobtrusive indication, then, of the very high place John assigns to Jesus. He alone shares with God this quality.

to kill Him. Against this interpretation is the fact that the example which substantiates the point is not cited until three verses later, so the first interpretation is to be preferred.

20 The "multitude" will be largely the crowd of pilgrims who came up from various places for the feast, and not the Jerusalem mob. This multitude professes to know nothing of the plot,[40] and it attributes Jesus' words to demon possession. It is not without its interest that the demon possession that we meet so frequently in the Synoptic Gospels is quite absent from John.[41] But John mentions a number of accusations, like this present one, that Jesus is demon-possessed and that this is the explanation of what He says (8 : 48-52; 10 : 20f.).[42] The accusation is made, of course, in the Synoptics also (Mark 3 : 22, *etc.*).

21 Jesus answers by referring them to "one work" (see Additional Note G, pp. 684ff.) which He did. This does not, of course, mean that He had done only one miracle, but it singles out one for attention. He does not specify more exactly, but as He goes on to refer to the sabbath there is no doubt but that He is referring to the curing of the man by the pool Bethesda which caused such a discussion about Jesus' attitude to the sabbath (5 : 1-9). He recalls the astonishment with which they had greeted this miracle. "Because

---

[40] "This is a lifelike touch. It was not the 'people,' but the 'Jews,' who had begun the plot; the people knew nothing of it" (Bernard).

[41] It is possible that this is due to the fact that the ancient world knew large numbers of "exorcists". John writes with singleminded concentration on his theme, that Jesus was the Christ. To have written of His casting out of demons would scarcely have set forward this aim, and it might have had the disadvantage of causing some, at any rate, to class Jesus with those who cast their spells and muttered their enchantments in the endeavor to obtain power over demons. A similar motive, it might be countered, would inhibit John from recounting miracles lest Jesus be classed with the thaumaturgists. But here John does not speak of "wonders", but of "signs". He is not interested in miracles as such, but in the spiritual significance of those he recounts. He relates incidents which point men to God, incidents pregnant with spiritual meaning. It is not immediately obvious how exorcisms are to be fitted into this pattern.

[42] δαιμόνιον is the word used in these passages (δαιμονίζομαι in 10 : 21). John used διάβολος of Satan (8 : 44), of Judas (6 : 70), and of Satan's putting the thought of betrayal into Judas's heart (13 : 2).

thereof" should probably be taken with the next verse.[43] It indicates that the true meaning of the institution of the sabbath and of circumcision is seen in Jesus' action. He is not transgressing the Law of Moses, but fulfilling its deepest meaning.

22, 23 Jesus has spoken of Moses as giver of the Law (v. 19), and He now goes on to speak of him in connection with circumcision. He immediately adds that circumcision did not originate with Moses, but with the patriarchs. But it was included in the Law of Moses and it was in accordance with the precepts of that Law that the Jews governed their practice in circumcising. So binding did they regard the command of Leviticus 12 : 3 to circumcise on the eighth day that they held this to override the sabbath (Mishnah, *Shab.* 18 : 3; 19 : 1, 2; *Ned.* 3 : 11). Thus, though they would scrupulously avoid all manner of things that even remotely looked like work lest the sabbath be profaned, they had no hesitation in carrying out the ritual requirement of circumcision on that day. Had they understood the significance of what they were doing they would have seen that a practice which overrode the sabbath in order to provide for the ceremonial needs of a man justified the overriding of the sabbath in order to provide for the bodily healing of a man. This is a most important point for an understanding

---

[43] Grammatically διὰ τοῦτο could be taken with either verse, but most recent commentators favor v. 22. "It is contrary to Johannine usage to connect διὰ τοῦτο (v. 22) with θαυμάζετε, equating τοῦτο with ἐν ἔργον; and the suggestion of confusion in Aramaic (Torrey, 5) is not convincing" (Barrett). John often uses διὰ τοῦτο to begin a new section (*cf.* 5 : 16, 18; 6 : 65; 8 : 47; 10 : 17; 13 : 11; 16 : 15), but he never ends a section with it. Bernard prefers to take the expression with the preceding, and (on 9 : 23) he cites 9 : 23; 13 : 11; 15 : 19; 16 : 15; 19 : 11 in support. But in all these cases διὰ τοῦτο heads a clause or sentence. There is no example of John's using it to end a sentence (as, indeed, Bernard admits). Lenski argues very strongly for taking the expression with v. 21, but he does not look at the decisive argument that John never uses διὰ τοῦτο in this way elsewhere. Moreover he does not notice what seems to be the probable meaning. If the words be taken with v. 22 he thinks the meaning would be "*For this reason* has Moses given you circumcision, not because it originates with Moses, but with the fathers; and you circumcise". But this is surely not the meaning. Rather Jesus is saying that the reason for Moses' prescribing of circumcision on the sabbath was to give a precedent for such sabbath activities as He had just engaged in. Alternatively, the words may mean that the circumcision Moses enjoined foreshadows the perfecting of man ("every whit whole") that Jesus accomplishes. Godet sees here "the most piquant irony: 'Moses has in advance pleaded my cause before you, by making you all jointly responsible for the crime with which you charge me. . . .' "

of the sabbath controversy between Jesus and His legalistic oppo·
nents. He was not arguing simply that a repressive law be
liberalized. Nor did He adopt an anti-sabbatarian attitude, opposing the whole institution. He pointed out that His action
fulfilled the purpose of the original institution. Had they understood
the implications of the Mosaic provision for circumcision on the
sabbath they would have seen that deeds of mercy such as He had
just done were not merely permissible but obligatory. Moses quite
understood that some things should be done even on the sabbath.
The Jews had his words but not his meaning. They misinterpreted
the significance of the sabbath. Jesus draws them back to the basic
reason for its institution. He inquires why, if a ritual act must be
performed, they should be wrathful when He has done a deed of
mercy. "Made a man every whit whole" puts some emphasis on
the completeness of the cure. The man had been in need. Jesus
fully met his need. Some emphasize "every whit whole" to make it
include the moral cleansing implied in 5 : 14 in contrast with the
purely ritual requirement of circumcision. There may be something
in this though we must not press the latter part of the proposition.
The Jews did not regard circumcision as "purely ritual", but as
having profound significance. The Greek seems rather to mean,
"made an entire man healthy", *i.e.* circumcision is concerned
primarily with one member, whereas Jesus has made a complete
man healthy.[44]

24 In the light of their practice Jesus calls on them to judge, not
in accordance with the outward appearance (C. B. Williams,
"Stop judging superficially"), but in accordance with right. The

---

[44] *Cf.* Ryle: "Is it then just and fair to be angry with Me, because I have
done a far greater work to a man on the Sabbath, than the work of circumcision?
I have not wounded his body by circumcision, but made him perfectly whole.
I have not done a purifying work to one particular part of him, but have
restored his whole body to health and strength. I have not done a work of
necessity to one single member only, but a work of necessity and benefit to
the whole man." Field takes the view that " 'the whole of a man,' in contrast
to a single member" is the meaning (p. 93). Jesus may well be contrasting the
cure wrought on the whole man with a work on but one of the members of the
body, of which the Jews counted 248. *Cf.* the Rabbinic saying, "If circumcision,
which attaches to one only of the two hundred and forty-eight members of
the human body, suspends the Sabbath, how much more shall (the saving of)
the whole body suspend the Sabbath!" (*Yoma* 85b, Soncino edn., p. 421).
It is possible also that there is in mind the thought that the foreskin was the
seat of corruption in accordance with the adage *praeputium est vitium in corpore*.

present imperative, "Judge not", means "stop judging". It implies that they were guilty of wrong judgment and urges them to mend their ways. Again, the aorist imperative, "but judge", directs urgent attention to the specific example.[45] Jesus is not laying down a general rule (though admittedly the words may well be applied generally). He is telling them how they should estimate this specific case.

(d) Is This the Christ? 7: 25-31

25 Some therefore of them of Jerusalem said, Is not this he whom they seek to kill? 26 And lo, he speaketh openly, and they say nothing unto him. Can it be that the rulers indeed know that this is the Christ? 27 Howbeit we know this man whence he is: but when the Christ cometh, no one knoweth whence he is. 28 Jesus therefore cried in the temple, teaching and saying, Ye both know me, and know whence I am; and I am not come of myself, but he that sent me is true, whom ye know not. 29 I know him; because I am from him, and he sent me. 30 They sought therefore to take him: and no man laid his hand on him, because his hour was not yet come. 31 But of the multitude many believed on him; and they said, When the Christ shall come, will he do more signs than those which this man hath done?

Jesus' teaching made a favorable impression, such a favorable impression, indeed, that some of His hearers wondered whether the rulers' failure to arrest Him was due to a recognition that He really was the Christ. This leads to some discussion of the origin

---

Jesus was doing more even than the removal of the foreskin signified when He made a man "every whit whole".

I. Abrahams regards Jesus' defence of His position here as "yet another instance of the Fourth Gospel's close acquaintance with Hebraic traditions" (*Studies in Pharisaism and the Gospels*, First Series, Cambridge, 1917, p. 135). He says, with respect to the whole method of Jesus' teaching as recorded in this Gospel: "My own general impression, without asserting an early date for the Fourth Gospel, is that the Gospel enshrines a genuine tradition of an aspect of Jesus' teaching which has not found a place in the Synoptics" (*op. cit.*, p. 12). Dodd also agrees that this passage shows a familiarity with Rabbinic methods of reasoning (*IFG*, p. 79).

[45] Moule keeps open the possibility that the two imperatives in this verse are not used with strict regard for the tense (*IBNTG*, p. 135), though in a footnote he allows the interpretation I have adopted. Incidentally some MSS read κρίνετε in both places.

of the Christ. It is clear that there was much uncertainty about Jesus, and a variety of reactions to His message.

25, 26 In this chapter a number of groups of people is referred to. "The Jews" (vv. 1, 11, *etc.*; see on 1 : 19) denotes the leaders of the nation, Jesus' enemies. These men were seeking to be rid of Him, apparently quite openly. Then there is "the multitude" (vv. 20, 31, *etc.*). These are the pilgrim crowds, not knowing a great deal about either the plans of the authorities or the teachings of Jesus. But they are ready to listen to Him and even to believe on Him (v. 31). The reference in the present verse to "them of Jerusalem" (actually "some of the Jerusalemites"; the word is found only here and in Mark 1 : 5 in the whole New Testament) apparently is to a third group, the Jerusalem mob. They were not the instigators of the plot to arrest Jesus, but they knew about it as their words here show. Their question, "Is not this he . . .?" looks for an affirmative answer. They were sure that this was the man. Why then was no action taken? They were impressed by Jesus' words and by His manner. He spoke openly[46] despite the plan to kill Him. So they put two and two together. He was apparently immune from arrest, for no one even spoke to Him, let alone took action against Him (*cf.* Phillips: "It's amazing – he talks quite openly and they haven't a word to say to him"). They began to wonder whether this indicated that their leaders really[47] knew that Jesus was the Christ (for this term see on 1 : 20, 41). At the same time their question expects the answer "No". They suggest the possibility only to dismiss it.

27 They do a little reasoning on their own account. "But[48] this fellow," they say, "we know where he comes from." And they proceed to lay it down that the origin of the Christ is a mystery.[49] This was not universally held. The scribes in Matthew 2 do not

---

[46] For παρρησία see n. 9 above. Here the thought is that Jesus is quite at home and unafraid.

[47] "Indeed" before "know" is ἀληθῶς, "know truly", "know for a certainty".

[48] "Howbeit" of ARV renders ἀλλά, the strong adversative (a very common conjunction in this Gospel; see on 1 : 8). Abbott points out that "in most instances, a negative is expressed or implied in the context of a Johannine ἀλλά (2055). In the present passage he says, "ἀλλά implies something quite different from that which has been suggested by the preceding context" (2057).

[49] If we can insist upon the force of the present tense in ὅταν ἔρχηται it will signify that at the very time that the Christ is coming men still will not know where He comes from.

seem to have been at a loss when Herod asked them where the Christ should be born. They were able to assure him on the basis of prophecy that Bethlehem was the spot. Yet it must be borne in mind that they could tell him no more. Family, circumstances and all the rest remained completely unknown so that this knowledge did not really take them very far. Later in this chapter some of the crowd show a similar knowledge of the prophecy about Bethlehem (vv. 41f.; Jesus' association with Galilee puzzled them). But there were divergent ideas in this matter. While some appealed to prophecies like that cited by Herod's scribes others must have interpreted these same scriptures differently, for they ascribed to the Christ a mysterious supernatural origin and a sudden appearance on the scene. Passages like Daniel 9 : 25 and Malachi 3 : 1 might be interpreted of a sudden appearance, and this line is developed in some of the apocryphal books.[50] It is typical of John's irony that he leaves the objection without comment. Those who know the truth about Jesus' origin know that it is baseless.[51]

[50] Thus IV Ezra 7 : 28; 13 : 32; II Baruch 29 : 3, picture the Messiah as "revealed", and IV Ezra 13 : 1ff. sees Him as arising out of the sea (which, of course, implies a sudden appearance). The idea appears among the Rabbis, for R. Zera taught that "Three come unawares: Messiah, a found article and a scorpion" (*Sanh.* 97a; Soncino edn., p. 659). Justin in his *Dialogue* reports Trypho as saying, "But Christ – if He has indeed been born, and exists anywhere – is unknown, and does not even know Himself, and has no power until Elias come to anoint Him, and make Him manifest to all" (*Dial.* VIII; ANF, I, p. 199; this appears to be the only reference to an anointing of the Messiah by Elijah). The apocryphal texts are discussed by R. H. Charles, *A Critical History of the Doctrine of a Future Life* (London, 1899), V. H. Stanton, *The Jewish and the Christian Messiah* (Edinburgh, 1886). Notice that while the sudden appearance of the Messiah is the most natural understanding of the apocryphal texts cited, they do not actually say in set terms that the origin of the Messiah is unknown. But the Jews expected the Messiah's work to begin suddenly when God willed it. Thinking as they did of the Messiah as a man, this involved that he be in the world, a grown man and ready for his task, before anyone knew him for what he was. Plummer thinks that the present passage means only that the Messiah's parentage "immediate and actual" would be unknown.

[51] Lightfoot points out that their declaration had implications they were not prepared to face. "To admit the truth of the doctrine of the secret origin of the Messiah is, or should be, equivalent to the admission that all human judgement about it is, and is bound to be, inadequate; and this admission the Lord's opponents are not prepared to make." Lenski comments on their whole position, "This type of reasoning has often been followed by men who imagine themselves to be superior to others. They pick some flaw, and fasten on that and refuse to consider the real and decisive facts, however great and convincing these may be."

28 Jesus uses their comment for some further teaching on His mission. It is probable that we should understand John's "therefore" to refer back to the immediately preceding "no one knoweth whence he is" rather than to "he speaketh openly" in the face of the desire of His enemies to kill Him. "Cried" indicates a loud shout. Jesus is giving the greatest publicity to this piece of teaching. The verb, as John uses it, always seems to introduce with emphasis a saying of some importance (1 : 15; 7 : 37; 12 : 44). It may also indicate here that Jesus spoke with some emotion. He agrees that they know Him and that they know where He came from, but this is almost certainly ironical: "So you know me and my origin!" While there is a sense in which this is true (they knew that He came from Nazareth), there is a more important sense in which it is not true (they did not know that He came from God and this is the important point).[52] Jesus proceeds to enlighten them. As in v. 16 He has disclaimed originality for His teaching, so here He disclaims responsibility for His mission. He did not set out on any self-chosen task. On the contrary, He was sent (see on 3 : 17) and that by One who is true. These last words should not be overlooked. The Jerusalemites did not accept Jesus' divine mission. In their minds He has no Sender. They thought of Him as going forth on His own initiative. Jesus insists that He is sent by a real Person (cf. Goodspeed: "someone who is very real, whom you do not know, has sent me"; C. B. Williams: "the One who has sent me exists as the Real One"). As often in this Gospel, a word will have a deeper meaning than appears on the surface. God is "true" with all that that means (see on v. 18).[53] But the Jerusalemites cannot be expected to know all this because they do not really know God. Had they known God they would have recognized Him whom God sent. The thought is repeated elsewhere that they

---

[52] That this is the correct understanding of it appears from the fact that elsewhere Jesus explicitly denies that they know Him (8 : 19), and apparently His origin also (8 : 41ff.). Some commentators think the statement here is not ironical, but that Jesus is simply agreeing that His opponents do know that He comes from Nazareth. This is possible, but hardly seems adequate. Some take Jesus' words as questions, e.g. Moffatt, "You know me? you know where I come from?", or Phillips, "So you know Me and know where I have come from?" (so also RSV, Torrey, etc.).

[53] See on 1 : 9 for ἀληθινός. This is one of the places where Kilpatrick thinks ἀληθής should be read (with P66 ℵ 544).

do not know the Father (8 : 19, 55). The implication is plain: if they do not know the Father who sent Him, how can they be expected to know the Christ whom the Father sent?

29 Jesus' "I" is emphatic and in sharp contrast with the preceding "ye". He does not share their ignorance. He knows the Father (see on 4 : 18). He gives a twofold account of this, namely in connection with His origin and His mission. He came out from a state of existence with the Father, and He was sent[54] by the Father to accomplish the Father's purpose. Here once more we have a reference to one of the dominant ideas of this Gospel.

30 This saying aroused varied reactions.[55] On account of it ("therefore") His enemies sought to arrest[56] Him. But God is over all. His purpose is worked out. Men cannot interfere with it. The time for Jesus' death was not yet and[57] His enemies could not bring that time forward no matter how they might try.[58] For Christ's "hour" see on 2 : 4.[59]

31 But (there is a contrast with the preceding) among the uncommitted multitude all this had an effect precisely the opposite of that on His enemies. Many of them came to believe on Jesus (see on 1 : 12, 41). The reason for their faith was not a profound one. They could not conceive that when the Christ came He

---

[54] The change from πέμψας in the previous verse to ἀπέστειλεν is not significant. See on 3 : 17.

[55] Barclay reminds us that it still does: "Either, what Jesus said about Himself is false, in which case He is guilty of such blasphemy as no man ever dared to utter; or, what He said about Himself is true, in which case He is what He claimed to be and can be described in no other terms than the Son of God. Jesus leaves us with the definite choice – we must accept Him fully or reject Him absolutely. That is precisely why every man has to decide for or against Jesus Christ."

[56] The verb πιάζω is not found in the other Gospels, but John uses it 8 times.

[57] "And" in the expression, "and no man laid his hand on him", is καί, here equivalent to καίτοι, "and yet".

[58] Calvin reasons from Christ's death to ours: "From this a general doctrine must be gathered; for though we live unto the day, the hour of every man's death has nevertheless been fixed by God . . . we are safe from all dangers until God wishes to call us away."

[59] Goodspeed emphasizes Jesus' mastery of the situation with his rendering: "and yet no one laid hands on him, because he was not yet ready." Cf. the comment of Augustine: "that is, because He was not willing . . . He meant not therefore an hour in which He should be forced to die, but that in which He would deign to be put to death" (XXXI. 5; p. 190).

would do more miracles than Jesus (their question "will he do more signs . . .?" expects the answer "No"). But throughout this Gospel it is better to believe on the basis of miracles than not to believe at all. So there is no condemnation of this faith as inadequate.

(e) An Attempt at Arrest, 7: 32

32 The Pharisees heard the multitude murmuring these things concerning him; and the chief priests and the Pharisees sent officers to take him.

32 It is not without its interest that the Pharisees heard all this and that "the chief priests and the Pharisees" took action. The Pharisees would have their finger on the public pulse more than the chief priests who were more remote. And the Gospels indicate that the Pharisees were more active in opposing Jesus, and therefore more likely to be taking an interest in what He said and did. But the chief priests were in the place of power. More effective action was possible by combining with them. So the band of police sent to arrest Jesus came from them as well as the Pharisees.[60] The combination points to the Sanhedrin as usually in John (cf. v. 45; 11 : 47, 57; 18 : 3). In view of the sequel it is likely that the command was not to arrest Jesus straight away, but to watch for a favorable moment. The authorities may well have hesitated to provoke a riot among the pilgrims who supported Jesus. There was, of course, only one "chief priest". But since the Romans had taken to deposing and appointing the principal ecclesiastic there were quite a few ex-chief priests who apparently retained the courtesy title. The title also seems to have been extended to others of the chief-priestly families, so that it came to denote quite a party. This is John's first use of the term. MacGregor maintains that for John "the 'high-priests' practically correspond to the Synoptic Sadducees". "Murmuring" usually has the thought of a

---

[60] On the combination Strachan comments: "This is a significant combination. The *chief priests* belong to the sect of the Sadducees and concerned themselves with the Temple worship and revenues . . . They were not closely in touch with the common people. The Pharisees were the popular religious leaders and concerned themselves with the synagogue, which was the real religious centre. They were in close touch with the popular mind. It is they who hear the 'murmurs' of popular opinion regarding Jesus. These two parties combine, when ecclesiastical and religious interests are threatened, to arrest Jesus."

muttered complaint, but here, as in v. 12, the thought will be simply that of lowered voices. It was not prudent to speak openly of Jesus, especially if one's opinion of Him was favorable. So those who believed spoke softly. The "officers" will be members of the temple police. The word is used a good deal more by John than by the other evangelists.[61] Nothing more is said of these officials until v. 45, and in particular John does not tell us whether they had any direct contact at all with Jesus.

(f) The Return to the Father, 7: 33-36

33 Jesus therefore said, Yet a little while am I with you, and I go unto him that sent me. 34 Ye shall seek me, and shall not find me: and where I am, ye cannot come. 35 The Jews therefore said among themselves, Whither will this man go that we shall not find him? will he go unto the Dispersion [1]among the Greeks, and teach the Greeks? 36 What is this word that he said, Ye shall seek me, and shall not find me; and where I am, ye cannot come?

[1]Gr. of.

This whole section is redolent of the thought that Jesus will be taken from among men one day. John thus includes some teaching from Jesus on the subject, teaching which, as might be expected, is misunderstood by the crowds.

33 It is not clear to what John's "therefore" refers. It may follow on from the threat of arrest. Because He was being threatened Jesus spoke of His removal in due course to a place beyond the reach of His persecutors. Or it may be that v. 32 is to be taken as a parenthesis. The multitudes were talking about Jesus' miracles (v. 31). He turns the discussion to His death which was the most significant topic for faith. Or again, it may be that the words refer back to the last recorded words of Jesus (in v. 29). There He spoke of the Father as having sent Him. Now He goes on to the

---

[61] John uses ὑπηρέτης 9 times, while each of the Synoptists uses it twice. It is also found 4 times in Acts and once in I Cor., so that John's use of the term is unusual.

thought of His return to the Father.[62] But, whatever be the connection, Jesus is expressing His unconcern at the plot. His life (and His death) are determined by the Father, not the Pharisees. It is true that in due course He will return to Him that sent Him. The thought is that of the accomplishment of His mission, with a hint also that His proper and natural abode is not here. But any suggestion that His enemies are in control is excluded.

34 Enigmatically Jesus refers to His death. When He is[63] with the Father they will look for Him, but He will be secure from their approaches. Lenski cites Amos 8 : 11ff.; Prov. 1 : 24ff., and adds: "This terrible seeking comes when the day of grace is past." There is a sharp contrast between the "I" and the "ye". Jesus and His opponents are of different order. They cannot reach Him when He is in His natural place.

---

[62] John uses the word ὑπάγω. The word simply means "go" or "go away". But John uses it quite often of Jesus' "going" to the Father. He does this in all 17 times, which accounts for the fact that he uses this verb far more often than does anyone else (32 times; Matthew has it 19 times, Mark 15 times and Luke 5 times). Here Jesus speaks of going to Him who sent Him (again in 16 : 5). Or He may speak of going to the Father (16 : 10), or to God (13 : 3). Or He may use the term absolutely and speak simply of going away (8 : 21). He can speak of knowing where He is going (8 : 14), or of the impossibility of being followed there (8 : 21). Again He links the thought of His departure with that of a return (14 : 28).

[63] It is possible to accent εἰμι and get the sense "go", here and in other passages, viz., v. 36; 14 : 3; 17 : 24, but in no case does this seem likely. εἰμι is an obsolete form (there is no certain example of its use in the New Testament), and few take the possibility seriously. "Where I am" is surely the meaning. Temple puts emphasis on the present tense: "It is not merely where He will be that they cannot come, but where He is now, that is, *in the bosom of the Father* (i, 18). When He *came down out of heaven* (vi, 38), He did not leave Heaven, but all the while *is in heaven* (iii, 13). For Heaven is fellowship with the Father; from that fellowship He came down, or forth, into the world, yet He was never without it." Similarly Augustine: "He came in such wise that He departed not thence; and He so returned as not to abandon us" (XXXI. 9; p. 192). Lightfoot reminds us that this expression recurs at 12 : 26; 14 : 3; 17 : 24, and that "whither I go" is found in 8 : 14, 21; 13 : 33. He thinks it probable "that a spiritual truth is being expressed both in terms of motion ('whither I go') and in terms of rest ('where I am'). Even now, when the Lord is standing before His opponents, they cannot come where He is, because they do not share His mind. For, in spite of what He has just said in 7[33], it is also true that separation from Him is caused not by distance in space, but by unlikeness of heart and mind and spirit." But this thought should not be held in such a way as to obscure the reference to His death.

35 The Jews wonder among themselves. The saying puzzles them. Their "we" is emphatic. "Where can he possibly go that we won't find him?" They suggest as a hypothetical possibility in Jesus' mind a journey to the Dispersion. This was a technical term for the large number of Jews who at this time were dispersed throughout the Roman Empire and beyond.[64] Ever since the exile to Babylon there had been Jews living outside Palestine. When permission to return was given many availed themselves of it, but many also did not. This evidently set something of a precedent, for in later days quite large numbers of Jews were to be found in cities throughout the Empire. Those in Alexandria were especially numerous.[65] Notice that they speak of going to the Dispersion, but of teaching not the Dispersion but the Greeks. This would seem to mean going to the Jewish synagogues and making them the springboard for a mission outward to the Greeks. It is, of course, the method that according to Acts the first Christian preachers actually employed. These Jews, however, dismiss the method as too fantastic to be considered a proper activity of the Messiah. This is another example of John's irony.[66] It is not without its interest that John has recorded a misunderstanding as to the origin of the Messiah on the part of some (vv. 26f.). Now he matches it with a misunderstanding as to His departure.

---

[64] In I Pet. 1 : 1 Διασπορά is used of Christians (also Jas. 1 : 1). But this is an unusual usage and there is nothing to indicate anything of the same sort here.

[65] With Jews dispersed in many countries it is curious that the dispersion "among the Greeks" is singled out. It may be, as W. C. van Unnik thinks, that this gives a clue as to the circle for which the Gospel was intended: "The Jewish Diaspora was spread over all the world: It would have been possible to speak about the dispersion in general; why is not Babylon, Egypt or Rome mentioned? There is only one explanation possible: because the writer was specially interested in this part of the world" (*SE*, I, p. 408). If this Gospel was written with a synagogue in a Greek environment specially in mind, there would be a natural interest in preserving any saying which referred to the Greeks.

[66] "It is as if he would say: the Jesus who in the days of His flesh transcended the divisions of Judaea, Samaria, and Galilee, accomplished in spiritual presence with His Church an even wider liberation, an even more signal breaking down of racial barriers. What seemed so absurd to 'the Jews' was accomplished when Jesus returned to the Father" (Wright). *Cf.* also N. A. Dahl: "As often in the Fourth Gospel, the misunderstanding conveys the truth: Jesus was, indeed, going to the Father, and thus also going to the Greeks – through the word of his missionary witness" (*Current Issues in New Testament Interpretation*, ed. W. Klassen and G. F. Snyder, London, 1962, p. 126).

36 The Jews repeat Jesus' words of v. 34, this being noteworthy as one of the very few places in this Gospel where words are repeated exactly (see on 3 : 5 for John's habit of variation). It is clear that the saying puzzled them greatly. And it not only puzzled them. It made them uneasy. Was there perhaps some meaning in it that still eluded them? Was the Man from Nazareth mocking them? Should they have understood more?[67]

(g) A Prophecy of the Spirit, 7: 37-39

37 Now on the last day, the great day of the feast, Jesus stood and cried, saying, If any man thirst, let him come unto me and drink. **38** He that believeth on me, as the scripture hath said, [1]from within him shall flow rivers of living water. **39** But this spake he of the Spirit, which they that believed on him were to receive: [2]for the Spirit was not yet *given*; because Jesus was not yet glorified.

[1]Gr. *out of his belly.* [2]Some ancient authorities read *for the Holy Spirit was not yet given.*

Jesus kept His great saying for the climax of the Feast. Chrysostom thought that more people were gathered together then, and this is not unlikely. Tabernacles was a festival rich in symbolism and popular appeal, and the symbolism forms the background to our Lord's saying. The principal features of the observance, in addition to the erection of the leafy bowers in which the people camped out and the offering of the sacrifices, appear to have been these.[68] The people carried with them bunches of leaves, called *lulabs*.[69] There was apparently a disagreement between the Sadducees and the Pharisees over the correct interpretation of Lev. 23 : 40, "And ye shall take you on the first day the fruit of goodly trees, branches of palm-trees, and boughs of

---

[67] As Westcott says, "In spite of all, Christ's words cannot be shaken off. They are not to be explained away. A vague sense remains that there is in them some unfathomed meaning." *Cf.* also Strachan: "Sarcasm, however, often conceals a deep perplexity. The speakers are still haunted by Jesus' words."

[68] For the ceremonies of Tabernacles *cf. TDNT*, IV, pp. 277f.

[69] A. Edersheim describes the *lulab* thus: "the *lulav*, or palm, with myrtle and willow branch on either side of it, tied together on the outside with its own kind, though in the inside it might be fastened even with gold thread" (*The Temple*, London, n.d., p. 238; ch. 14 of this work gives a description of the way the feast was observed). R. Ishmael laid down the requirement in these terms, "Three myrtle-branches (are needful) and two willow-branches and one palm-branch and one citron" (*Sukk.* 3 : 4).

thick trees, and willows of the brook. ...." The former took the words to refer to the material out of which the booths for the observance of the feast were to be constructed, while the latter held them to mean that the worshippers were actually to carry branches of the trees named as they entered the temple. The Pharisaic interpretation prevailed among the people, and accordingly each worshipper, as he marched in procession, would carry a *lulab* in his right hand and a citron in his left. The *lulab* symbolized the stages of the wilderness journey (marked by different kinds of vegetation), and the fruit the fruit of the goodly land that God had given His people. As certain Psalms were recited the worshippers shook their *lulabs*.[70] The rejoicing was marked further by the flute-playing and dancing that went on for most of the feast and by bringing in young willow branches and arranging them round the altar (*Sukk.* 4 : 5). The tops thus were bent over the altar forming a leafy canopy for it. The reciting of the words, "Save now, we beseech thee, O Jehovah: O Jehovah, we beseech thee, send now prosperity" (Ps. 118 : 25), is probably to be understood as a prayer for rain and fruitful season. On each of the seven days of the feast a priest drew water from the pool of Siloam in a golden flagon and brought it in procession to the temple with the joyful sounding of the trumpet. There the water was poured into a bowl beside the altar from which a tube took it to the base of the altar. Simultaneously wine was poured through a similar bowl on the other side of the altar. These symbolic ceremonies were acted thanksgivings for God's mercies in giving water in past days (probably looking right back to the smiting of the rock in the wilderness and then on to the giving of rain in recent years). They were also an acted prayer for rain for the coming year.[71] It is also significant that the words of Isaiah are associated with these ceremonies, "with joy shall ye draw water out of the wells of salvation" (Isa. 12 : 3).[72] The Jerusalem Talmud connects the

---

[70] *Sukk.* 3 : 9 records a division of opinion, with the school of Hillel advocating the shaking at the beginning and end of Ps. 118 and at Ps. 18 : 25, while the school of Shammai favored shaking also at Ps. 118 : 25.

[71] Bernard cites a saying of Rabbi Akiba: "Bring the libation of water at the Feast of Tabernacles, that the showers may be blessed to thee. And accordingly it is said that whosoever will not come up to the Feast of Tabernacles shall have no rain."

[72] So R. Ena (*Sukk.* 48b). Some say that the words were sung during the procession.

ceremonies and this scripture with the Holy Spirit: "Why is the name of it called, The drawing out of water? Because of the pouring out of the Holy Spirit, according to what is said: 'With joy shall ye draw water out of the wells of salvation.' "[73]

Jesus' words are to be understood against this background. Up till now nothing has been recorded of His teaching at this feast, for all His words in this chapter hitherto have been replies to the accusations of His foes. But now, at the culmination of the greatest feast of the Jewish year, He unfolds its significance in terms of the life that He came to bring. He takes the water symbolism of the feast and presses it into service as He speaks of the living water that He will bestow. The people are thinking of rain, and of their bodily need. He turns their attention to the deep need of the soul, and to the way He would supply it. In chapter 4 we have had references to the living water, but here only is the explanation given of its significance in terms of the Holy Spirit.

37 From Deut. 16 : 13 it would appear that the feast at one time went for seven days, but Lev. 23 : 36 makes it plain that there was also an eighth day (even though it is mentioned separately from the seven). It is not quite clear whether it was the seventh day or this eighth day which was the climax of the whole celebration, and of which John speaks as "the great day of the feast".[74]

---

[73] J *Sukk.* 5 : 1 (cited from A. Guilding, *The Fourth Gospel and Jewish Worship*, Oxford, 1960, p. 2).

[74] It is possible that the eighth day was not reckoned as part of the feast at all, in which case the seventh day would be "the great day". This is supported by the consideration that the ceremonies with water and lights seem not to have continued after the seventh day (*Sukk.* 4 : 1); the Talmud, however, cites R. Judah as saying that the ceremony of water libation continued for eight days (*Sukk.* 48b). But against it is the difficulty of seeing how the seventh day could be called "the last day" if the eighth day was observed at all. Further the eighth day seems in Lev. 23 : 36 to be a special day, like a sabbath, and *Sukk.* 5 : 6 with its mention of special sacrifices for this day supports the idea that the day was marked off from the others in New Testament times. Josephus speaks of this feast as lasting eight days (*Ant.* iii, 245), as does II Macc. 10 : 6, and this may bear on the problem. The fact that there was no water poured on the eighth day may better explain Jesus' words to them that lack water. On the whole it seems that the eighth day is more probable (though Edersheim favors the seventh). Incidentally the eighth day was the last festival day in the Jewish calendar and is called "the last good day" in *Sukk.* 4 : 8. Similarly Philo speaks of it as "a sort of complement $(\pi\lambda\acute{\eta}\varrho\omega\mu\alpha)$ and conclusion of all the feasts in the year" (*De Spec. Leg.*, II. 213; Loeb edn. p. 439).

Once again he tells us that Jesus "cried" (see on v. 28). The word indicates that importance is attached to the saying. It is proclaimed loudly and emphatically, perhaps also with emotion, so that all might hear and all might heed. Jesus is also said to have stood (the verb means "was standing", rather than "rose to His feet"). A teacher usually sat with his disciples, so that the Master's posture as well as His voice called attention to His words as important. Moreover He was thus in a position to make the maximum number of people see and hear Him. In words reminiscent of those of 4 : 10 Jesus gives the invitation to the thirsty to come to Him and drink. There is the implication that the thirsty soul will find supplied in Him that need which could not be supplied elsewhere. The appropriateness of the words at this feast is that throughout the seven days libations were made in the temple with water brought from the pool of Siloam (*Sukk.* 4 : 9). But on the eighth day no water was poured, and this would make Jesus' claim all the more impressive. At the same time His primary reference may be not to the temple rite, but to the supply of water from the rock in the wilderness. The water supplied the physical needs of the Israelites, whereas no one drank from the water poured out of the golden ewer.[75]

38 There is uncertainty as to the sentence division here and this affects the sense. Some hold that the full stop at the end of v. 37 should be deleted, and the passage made to read, "If any man thirst, let him come unto me, and let him that believeth on me drink."[76] These usually hold that the next section, "as the

---

[75] Godet favors this view and he points out that it accords with the symbolism of this Gospel in terms of Old Testament figures: "In chap. ii. He had presented Himself as the true temple, in chap. iii., as the true brazen serpent, in chap. vi., as the bread from heaven, the true manna; in chap. vii., He is the true rock; in chap. viii., He will be the true luminous cloud, and so on, until chap. xix. where He will finally realize the type of the Paschal lamb."

[76] *IB* says that this punctuation "alone makes sense", but this is far too cavalier. It ignores the difficulties in the way of this view and magnifies those of the other. Hoskyns points out that part of our difficulty is that both ways of dividing the text are Johannine. He thinks the reference to Jesus as the source of the water of life is primary, but he sees the believer as becoming "a well of water springing up unto eternal life" (4 : 14; strictly it is not the believer but the water Jesus gives that is so described). "The explanation of the possibility of a double punctuation and of the consequent obscurity both of the grammar and of the application of the citation is that the subsidiary meaning presses upon the primary meaning in the author's mind and this jostling causes a disturbance in the construction of the Saying."

scripture hath said, from within him shall flow rivers of living water", refers not to the believer, but to Christ. Indeed, part of the reason for preferring this punctuation is the desire to refer these words to the Lord. Two main reasons are given for this way of taking the words: (a) it is hard to find a scriptural passage which refers the source of the living water to the believer, and (b) Christ, not the believer, is in fact the source of the living water. This position cannot be ruled out as absolutely impossible, but the punctuation of ARV seems preferable.[77] The statement about thirst calls for one about drinking but it does not call for one about faith. The words about faith go better with what follows.[78] It does not seem to me that any really satisfactory reason has been given for separating "and drink" from the previous words. It is the thirsty, not the faithful who need to drink. In fact to come to Jesus and drink is to believe. There is no difference in meaning. To invite the believer to drink is thus tautology. It is also worth noting that the construction "he who believes" is common in John and it seems always to indicate the present possession of life (3 : 18, 36; 6 : 35, 47; 11 : 25; 12 : 44; 14 : 12).

But the biggest difficulty is in accepting the change of subject involved if we take the words, "from within him shall flow rivers of living water", to refer to Christ. However we punctuate, it does seem as though the "him" is the same person as the preceding "he". We need strong reasons for taking it otherwise. Again, while it is true that the living water comes from Christ as the

---

[77] The punctuation of ARV has the weighty support of P66. Patristic evidence is divided, but modern critical editions of the Greek text seem all to favor ARV. So do translations like AV, RV, RSV. In fact NEB seems the only major translation to agree with the new suggestion.

[78] In a private communication Professor G. D. Kilpatrick points out that καθώς clauses show a strong tendency to follow their main clause though this is less marked in John than elsewhere. Thus the rule is invariable in Matthew and Mark; in Luke it is followed 13 times out of 17 and in Acts 13 times out of 15; whereas in John it is followed 19 times (including one v. l.) and transgressed 13 times (though in several of the exceptions there is a resumptive word). When καθώς introduces a quotation there is no certain example of its not following the main clause, and it is never inserted in the middle of a quotation. From this he reasons that the main clause ends at εἰς ἐμέ, and that the quotation begins with ποταμοί. The latter point may be accepted without separating off ὁ πιστεύων εἰς ἐμέ. It is true that this means having the καθώς clause precede, but the usage in John is not so regular, it would seem to me, as to preclude this.

ultimate source, yet the believer is mediately a source to others.[79] And, while it is true that it is hard to find an Old Testament passage which unambiguously prophesies that rivers of living water will flow from the believer, it is also true that it is harder still to find one which says this of Christ. Exod. 17 : 6; Ps. 105 : 41; Ezek. 47 : 1 and Joel 3 : 18 are adduced, but a good imagination is required to see in any of these a prophecy that Christ would become the source (some see significance in the reference to water, as well as blood, proceeding from the Saviour's side, 19 : 34, but this is far-fetched). And, if the Old Testament does not speak explicitly of living water as proceeding from the believer, at least there are passages which speak of spiritual blessing for God's people under the symbolism of water. Some regard the water as outgoing, which is consonant with the view that the blessing is passed on. The most relevant is perhaps Isa. 58 : 11, "thou shalt be like a watered garden, and like a spring of water, whose waters fail not" (see also Prov. 4 : 23; 5 : 15; Isa. 44 : 3;[80] 55 : 1; Ezek. 47 : 1ff.; Joel 3 : 18; Zech. 13 : 1; 14 : 8).[81] The meaning of our passage then, in accordance with such Old Testament prophecies appears to be that when any man comes to believe in Jesus the scriptures referring to the activity of the Holy Spirit are fulfilled.[82] On the day of Pentecost Peter claimed the fulfilment of the prophecy of Joel (Acts 2 : 16ff.). It is something like that we should understand here. Verse 38 carries on the thought of v. 37. The drinking of which Jesus there spoke is possible only to him who comes in faith. And faith has its results. When the believer[83] comes

---

[79] For a roughly contemporary parallel Brown cites a saying of R. Akiba from Midrash Sifre on Deut. 11 : 22: "The disciple who is beginning is like a well who can give only the water it has received; the more advanced disciple is a spring giving living water."

[80] The parallelism in this verse connects water and the Spirit:"I will pour water upon him that is thirsty, and streams upon the dry ground; I will pour my Spirit upon thy seed, and my blessing upon thine offspring".

[81] See also the discussion by Juan B. Cortés, *CBQ*, XXIX, 1967, pp. 75–86.

[82] There is a further ambiguity as to whether we should take the words "as the scripture says" with the preceding or the following. Chrysostom adopted the former course, but most commentators the latter. And they are surely right. There does not appear to be an Old Testament passage which explicitly foretells faith in Jesus, and in any case the emphasis is on the flowing of living water. It is this to which the words most naturally refer, and we need scarcely take the alternative seriously.

[83] ὁ πιστεύων is a nominative absolute.

to Christ and drinks he not only slakes his thirst but receives such
an abundant supply that veritable rivers flow from him.[84] This

---

[84] The Greek is ἐκ τῆς κοιλίας αὐτοῦ, "out of his belly", *i.e.* "from his
innermost being". Some find great difficulty in seeing such a prophecy in
Scripture and understand the passage to refer to Jerusalem. Thus I. Abrahams
says that Zech. 14 : 8 is read in the synagogues in connection with the Feast
of Tabernacles (on the first day). This speaks of waters going out from Jerusalem:
"But as in Rabbinic tradition (T. B. Sanhedrin 37a, Ezekiel xxxviii. 8, Jubilees
viii.) Jerusalem was situated in the *navel* of the earth, John may be using
belly as a synonym for Jerusalem" (*op. cit.*, p. 11). C. F. Burney sees a mistranslation of the original Aramaic. He points out that מְעִין "fountain", and

מְעִין "belly", are identical if unpointed, and gives the meaning as,
  "He that thirsteth, let him come unto Me;
  And let him drink that believeth in Me.
As the Scripture hath said, Rivers shall flow forth from the fountain of living
waters" (*AO*, p. 110).
    C. C. Torrey denies that the two Aramaic words suggested by Burney could
have been confused, and he says that Burney's reconstruction "is neither good
Aramaic nor comes anywhere near accounting for our Grk." (*Our Translated
Gospels*, New York and London, 1936, p. 110). He thinks that confusion has
arisen between the Aramaic *gawwah* ("the midst of her"), and the masculine
gawweh (which leads to the reading "out of his belly") (*op. cit.*, p. 111; unpointed these forms would be identical). His translation runs, "As the scripture
says, Out of the midst of Her shall flow rivers of living water", and he appends
a note explaining that "Her" is Jerusalem, and the scripture is Ps. 46 : 4f.
Against the whole idea is the difficulty that the New Testament sees Christ,
not Jerusalem, as the source of blessing. The linguistics are not convincing
enough to counter-balance this. See further Hendriksen's criticism of Torrey,
and W. F. Howard's note (M, II, p. 475). SBk cite Rabbinic evidence for the
use of גּוּף "body" (which they say is equivalent to κοιλία) to mean "person".
This may be significant, though it is fairly objected that this would more naturally be translated σῶμα than κοιλία. "Belly" is used in the Old Testament
of the innermost feelings of a man, *cf.* Prov. 20 : 27. In Ps. 40 : 8 (LXX 39 : 9)
Rahlfs accepts the reading κοιλίας (the Law is "in the midst of my belly"),
though noting that B has καρδίας; *cf.* v. 10. Chrysostom says of the present
passage, "By 'belly' he here meaneth the heart" (LI. 1; p. 183; he proceeds
to cite Ps. 40 : 10). So also Augustine: "The belly of the inner man is the conscience of the heart. Having drunk that water then, the conscience being purged
begins to live; and drinking in, it will have a fountain, will be itself a fountain"
(XXXII. 4; p. 194). Recent translations as RSV and Goodspeed have "heart",
Phillips, "inmost heart", Knox, "bosom". J. Behm also supports "heart"
(*TDNT*, III, p. 788). Barclay gives Jesus' meaning as "Come to me; accept
me; trust me; and I will put into you through my Spirit a new life which will
give you purity and satisfaction, and which will take away all your frustrations
and unsatisfied hungers and give you the kind of life you have always longed
for and never had." This is true, but the words also point to the outgoing of

425

stresses the outgoing nature of the Spirit-filled life. In contrast with the men of Qumran there is nothing of the piety of the pond about Christianity. The covenanters (of this very period) had withdrawn into the wilderness to become the people of the Lord. They became ingrown. They seem to have made no effort to influence others and so to bring the blessing to them. Just as the Dead Sea receives the Jordan, but gives nothing out and thus becomes lifeless and arid, so the Dead Sea sect sought to receive the blessing of the law of God and to keep it for themselves.[85] And in the process they became sterile. Not so the true Christian.[86] The believer is not self-centred. As he receives the gift of God, so he passes it on to others. Or to put the same thought in another way, when a man believes he becomes a servant of God, and God uses him to be the means of bringing the blessing to others.[87] "Living water" is the gift of Christ in 4 : 14. Here we must think

---

this life. Not only does the believer receive blessing, but he becomes the source of blessing to others.

Thus the "innermost being" or the "life" is understood by many, both ancient and modern. It seems to meet the requirements of the passage better than any other suggestion thus far made.

[85] Wright quotes from Bunyan,
> "There was a man, the world did think him mad,
> The more he gave away, the more he had."

Against this he sets the " 'rule' of the stagnant pool"
> ". . . the good old rule
> Sufficeth them, the simple plan,
> That they should take who have the power,
> And they should keep who can."

He adds: "This 'plan' defeats itself. The pool that only receives eventually dries up. The living waters that flow for the healing of others do not dry up, for their source is in the Divine life – in that 'Spiritual Rock' which is Christ".

[86] Not so either, Judaism at its best. There is a saying of R. Meir: "He that occupies himself in the study of the Law for its own sake merits many things . . . And it gives him kingship and dominion and discernment in judgment; to him are revealed the secrets of the Law, and he is made like to a never-failing spring and like to a river that flows ever more mightily" (*Ab.* 6 : 1). But it is significant that, whereas the Rabbi speaks of the Law, Jesus speaks of the Spirit-filled life.

[87] *Cf.* J. Behm: "the basic thought is that he who is touched by Jesus in the innermost recesses of his personal life will from thence send forth saving powers in superabundant measure (cf. v. 39, also Mt. 5 : 13ff.)" (*TDNT*, III, p. 789). In a footnote he says that the view which sees αὐτοῦ as referring to Jesus and the blessing as proceeding from Him "has the text very definitely against it" (n. 17).

426

of the gift as divine in origin, but as channelled through the
believer.

39 John explains Jesus' cryptic utterance. It concerns the Spirit,
and the Spirit would be given to them that should put their trust
in Christ. The explanation is important. "Living water" is not
elsewhere explained, and the expression is not a common one
(other than in its use for running water as against the stagnant
water of a pool or the like).[88] This explanation helps us interpret
passages like chapter 4. The expression translated "for the Spirit
was not yet given" is difficult. There is nothing in the Greek
corresponding to "given", and a more literal rendering would be
"for it was not yet Spirit".[89] This probably points us to the period
after Pentecost. The gift of the Holy Spirit to the infant church
that day transformed everything, so that all that followed might
be called the era of the Spirit. The Bible does not speak of the
Spirit as totally inactive up till that point. There is much about
Him in the Old Testament and the Gospels. But there is nothing
that we can compare with the activity of the apostolic age. Then it
"was Spirit" in a way it had never been before. John tells us that
it was the work of Jesus that made the difference. It was not yet
Spirit because Jesus was not yet glorified.[90] Calvary is the necessary
prelude to Pentecost. Notice that the cross is referred to in terms
of glory, not of shame. Once again John sees the cross and the
glory as one. And he sees the atoning work of Christ as the necessary
prelude to the work of the Spirit. Without trying to divide up the
believer's experience too minutely it is yet plain that his sin must
be dealt with before he can enter on the life of the Spirit. It is
a point repeated in this Gospel that the Spirit could not come

---

[88] Perhaps we should notice that water and spirit are combined in a number
of places in the Dead Sea Scrolls, *e.g.* IQS, iv, 20f.

[89] For a careful study of these words *cf.* S. H. Hooke, *NTS*, IX, 1962–63,
pp. 372–380. His conclusion is: "never until the Son of Man had ascended
up where he was before, and the last Adam had become a life-giving spirit,
had it been possible for the Spirit to enter into and become the life of the
believer, producing in him the life of Jesus, as Paul says 'That the life of Jesus
may be manifested in our mortal flesh' (II Cor. iv. 11)" (*op. cit.*, p. 380).

[90] For John's idea of glory see on 1 : 14. This is his first use of $\delta o \xi \acute{a} \zeta \omega$,
a verb he uses in all 23 times. In no other book of the New Testament does
it occur more than 9 times (Luke), so it can be seen that it is an important
concept for John. He invariably uses it of the glorifying of the Son or of the
Father, and he sees this glorifying particularly in the cross.

during the time of Christ's earthly ministry (16 : 7). But when that work was consummated the Spirit was given (20 : 22; Acts 2).[91]

(h) Division, 7 : 40–44

40 Some of the multitude therefore, when they heard these words, said, This is of a truth the prophet. 41 Others said, This is the Christ. But some said, What, doth the Christ come out of Galilee? 42 [1]Hath not the scripture said that the Christ cometh of the seed of David, and from Bethlehem, the village where David was? 43 So there arose a division in the multitude because of him. 44 And some of them would have taken him; but no man laid hands on him.

[1]2 S. vii. 12 ff.; Mic. v. 2.

As throughout this chapter, there is division over Christ's words. Here John records a tendency to accept Jesus on account of His words and a tendency to reject Him on account of His connection with Galilee.

40 John returns to the opinions of the multitude. Some[92] of them were impressed by Jesus' words (for the plural see on 14 : 24) so much that they affirmed Him to be "the prophet", *i.e.* the prophet of Deut. 18 : 15. The persistence of references to this prophet in this Gospel is remarkable (*cf.* 1 : 21, where see note; 1 : 25; 6 : 14). Evidently there was a considerable section of the Jews who looked for the prophet's appearance. The attitude recorded here is more logical than that of 6 : 14. There the men saw the prophet in Jesus on account of the "sign" they saw Him perform, whereas here it is His words which impress. The words of a prophet are more characteristic than any doing of miracles.

41 Others in the multitude took the further step of seeing in Jesus none less than the Christ (see on 1 : 41). But the first group (or perhaps a third group) countered with a question as to the origin of the Christ. Their question is so phrased as to expect the answer "No". It was agreed that the Christ did not come from Galilee (in v. 52 it is accepted that not even a prophet came from Galilee;

---

[91] Though there is nothing like this statement in the Synoptic Gospels G. W. H. Lampe reminds us that it "is implicit in all the records" (*SJT*, V, 1952, p. 168).

[92] ἐκ τοῦ ὄχλου is a partitive genitive, "some of the multitude".

how much less then the Christ?). This confidence is interesting in contrast with the attitude behind Matt. 2 : 23, which speaks of scripture as being fulfilled in the fact that "he should be called a Nazarene". Though this passage has difficulties of its own it certainly does not rule out the possibility of a Galilean Christ. **42** The objectors back up their case with an appeal to the Bible. "The scripture" usually refers to a specific passage, but there is no place where the Old Testament says precisely this. It seems that here it is the general tenor of several Old Testament passages that is in mind (*e.g.* I Sam. 20 : 6; II Sam. 7 : 12ff.; Ps. 89 : 3f.; Mic. 5 : 2, *etc.*). The expectation shows that the Exile was not held to have put an end to the possibilities of the Davidic line. In due course, when God sent His Messiah, He would be of that line, and, indeed, come from the very town of Bethlehem. Incidentally the description of Bethlehem as "the village where David was" rather overstates the case. David was born there and grew up there, but after he left Bethlehem we have no record of his returning at any time. Nearly all of the significant events of his life took place elsewhere. It is not without its interest that these members of the crowd could cite such scriptures spontaneously. There must have been some quite strong messianic expectations, such that messianic predictions were eagerly sought out. The verse is another example of the Johannine irony.[93] How strange that these people were citing as an objection to Jesus' messiahship just that fact that they required to attest it, had they but known the facts of the case.[94]

43, 44 There was thus a "division".[95] The crowd of pilgrims was

---

[93] "John often takes pleasure in reporting objections which, for his readers who are acquainted with the Gospel history, turn immediately into proofs" (Godet).

[94] "But John's irony goes far deeper than this. The birth place of Jesus is a trivial matter in comparison with the question whether he is ἐκ τῶν ἄνω or ἐκ τῶν κάτω (8. 23), whether he is or is not from God. Cf. 7. 28 where though Jesus admits that his hearers know whence he came he emphasizes that human origins are irrelevant (ἀπ' ἐμαυτοῦ οὐκ ἐλήλυθα), and 8.14 where Jesus denies that the Jews (truly) know whence he came – they judge κατὰ τὴν σάρκα. See also 3.8 – no one knows whence comes and whither goes one who has been born of the Spirit. This refers primarily to Christians, but *a fortiori* to Jesus himself. It follows that all disputes about the birth place of the Messiah, the heavenly Man, are far wide of the point" (Barrett).

[95] σχίσμα does not denote anything as thoroughgoing as a "schism" in our sense of the term. It is rather a party, or a faction, and it is used in the plural, for example, of the parties in the Corinthian church (I Cor. 1 : 10).

not unanimous in its views of Jesus. Some of them thought Him
to be a prophet, some the Christ, and as v. 44 shows, some of
them wanted to arrest Him (it would appear that this refers to
the crowd and not to the police spoken of in vv. 32, 45f.). No
actual attempt at arrest is described, but simply the will[96] to do
it. John leaves us in no doubt as to the intention of this group.
But nothing came of it. Though he does not repeat the reason
he has given in v. 30 concerning an earlier attempt we must
understand that to operate here also. No arrest could take place
before His "hour" was come.

(i) The Failure to Arrest Jesus, 7 : 45–52

45 The officers therefore came to the chief priests and Pharisees; and they said unto them, Why did ye not bring him?
46 The officers answered, Never man so spake. 47 The Pharisees therefore answered them, Are ye also led astray? 48 Hath
any of the rulers believed on him, or of the Pharisees? 49 But
this multitude that knoweth not the law are accursed. 50
Nicodemus saith unto them (he that came to him before,
being one of them), 51 Doth our law judge a man, except it
first hear from himself and know what he doeth? 52 They
answered and said unto him, Art thou also of Galilee? Search,
and [1]see that out of Galilee ariseth no prophet.

[1]Or, see: for out of Galilee &c.

The abortive attempt of the temple police to arrest Jesus
brings Nicodemus before us once more, this time in discussion
with the Sanhedrin. His defense of Jesus is not exactly spirited,
but it is a defense of sorts. And it induces his colleagues to give
expression to the objection to Jesus' messiahship based on His
supposed Galilean origin (mentioned for the third time in this
chapter!). It would seem that this objection must have been
widely bruited, and John, in pursuance of his declared aim of
showing that Jesus is the Messiah, notes that it is not new, and
he goes on to provide material for its refutation.

45 The "officers" referred to in v. 32 now return to the Sanhedrin[97]

---

[96] "Would" translates $\check{\eta}\vartheta\varepsilon\lambda o\nu$.

[97] There is but one article in the expression $\tauo\grave{\upsilon}\varsigma$ $\grave{\alpha}\varrho\chi\iota\varepsilon\varrho\varepsilon\tilde{\iota}\varsigma$ $\varkappa\alpha\grave{\iota}$ $\Phi\alpha\varrho\iota\sigma\alpha\acute{\iota}o\upsilon\varsigma$,
which points to the official body on which they sat together.

with their mission unfulfilled. We are driven to think that their orders had been not simply to make an arrest (for then they would surely have pressed through the crowd and been stopped only by physical force), but to look for a favorable opportunity of apprehending Jesus. The authorities wanted an arrest but not a riot. They had waited for some time (v. 37 points to a time later than does v. 14, the previous time note, which apparently covers v. 32). But no such opportunity as they sought presenting itself, they now returned to the Sanhedrin. Nothing is recorded of any report they may have made. But it was obvious that they had no prisoner, so they were met with a question as to the reason.

46 The officials' reply stresses the effect Jesus' teaching had on them. No man ever spoke like this.[98] It is curious that they do not mention the crowd, the hostility of a section of which was presumably a big factor in their failure to make the arrest. They simply tell of the effect of Jesus' words on them and let it go at that. This must have taken some courage, as they must have known that it would leave them subject to the rebuke (and the disciplinary action) of the Sanhedrin. Some mention of the hostility of the crowd, or a section of it, would have served as an excuse, palliating their offence to some extent. But they had been deeply impressed by Jesus and they say so.[99] That, and that alone, was the basic reason for their failure to carry out their orders. If the shorter reading in this verse be the true one[100] we have a typical Johannine double meaning. The officers will mean, "Never did another man speak like this", while John will understand it as, "Never did one who was no more than a man speak like this".[101]

---

[98] οὕτως puts the emphasis on the manner rather than the content of His teaching. *Cf.* Lenski: "The authority, majesty, and power of the speaker restrained these officers".

[99] Dods draws attention to two remarkable things about this: "The testimony is notable, because the officers of a court are apt to be entirely mechanical and leave all responsibility for their actions with their superiors. Also it is remarkable that the same result should have found place with them all; for in view of the divided state of public feeling, probably five or six at least would be sent."

[100] This is the text presupposed by ARV, "Never man so spake", and supported by P66cP75, א^c BLTW boh Or Chrys Cyr. The longer text adds "as this man speaks". The shorter text seems preferable.

[101] *Cf.* Barrett: "The stress appears to lie on the last word (*i.e.* ἄνθρωπος). The speech of Jesus is not the speech of a *man*. The constables were cowed by his superhuman authority...."

47-49 The Pharisees were apparently irritated by this answer, and took the initiative in replying (the chief priests might have been expected to be the ones to rebuke their servants). Their question expects the answer "No". "Surely you also are not deceived?" is the sense of it. The "also" indicates that they know that some were deceived, and they are trying to separate their officers from those who have gone astray (RSV: "Are you led astray, you also?"). The perfect tense in the verb "led astray" points to a continuing state. A further question implying the negative answer shows how unthinkable it is that any leading person should believe on Jesus[102] ("any" is singular; not so much as one has believed). The "rulers" are here distinguished from the Pharisees and will denote the Sadducees in general or the high-priestly party in particular. The explicit rejection of the idea that any of the Pharisees believed may give us something of Nicodemus's reason for coming at the first by night. Plainly the Pharisees were set in opposition to Jesus and this supports the thought that his motive then was one of timidity. The multitude is contrasted with the rulers and the Pharisees. It is characterized as not[103] knowing the Law. This does not mean either that it was not interested in the Pentateuch, or that it did not have a good working knowledge of Scripture (in v. 42 some at least show acquaintance with passages of Scripture which do not immediately strike the casual reader). It means that they did not know the Law in the way the Pharisees did. These students discerned 613 commandments in the Law, and they set themselves the task of earning their salvation by trying to keep them all. Even this was not the whole task, for they added the entire corpus of oral tradition concerning the Law (which governed the interpretation of

---

[102] *Cf.* Barclay: "Their plea was: 'Nobody who is spiritually and academically of any account has believed on this Jesus. Only ignorant fools accept him.' It is indeed a terrible thing when a man thinks himself either too clever or too good to need Jesus Christ – and it can happen yet." It is worth noting moreover that in the light of 12 : 42 their statement is premature.

[103] The choice of μή as negative is regarded by Abbott as significant: "John could not have used οὐ without limiting the assertion to a particular crowd pointed out, whereas the meaning is 'This multitude (these and their like, this rabble) that knoweth not the law are accursed' " (2253).

biblical passages). It was small wonder that ordinary pious people, like the crowd of pilgrims, simply gave up the task. Their knowledge of the Bible could not be compared with that of the Pharisees. And because it could not, their practice could not be the same as that of these zealous exponents of the traditions. Inevitably then the crowds failed to comply with what the Pharisees thought of as necessary rules, and thus they came under severe condemnation. They were "accursed"[104] (Deut. 27 : 26 speaks of him "that confirmeth not the words of this law to do them" as "cursed").[105]

50, 51 Apparently there was no dissentient voice, and this provoked Nicodemus into saying something. There is something dramatic in the way John introduces this. The leaders denied that any important person believed on Jesus, and Nicodemus immediately spoke up. They condemned the multitude for not knowing the Law, and Nicodemus puts his finger straightway on their own disregard for the Law. John characterizes Nicodemus in two ways, as having formerly come to Jesus and as being one of the Pharisees. It is this double character which causes him to speak in this situation. But though he speaks up in defense of Jesus it is a very cautious line that he takes. He does not commit himself. He does not bear witness as do so many in this Gospel.[106] Yet the temper of the meeting must be borne in mind. Plain testimony to Jesus would undoubtedly have enraged the majority further. Nicodemus may have judged that Christ's cause would best be served by pointing these angry men to a legal weakness in their position. His question looks for a negative answer. He is sure of his point. He reminds them that according to their law the accused must

---

104 It is interesting that, while the participle $\gamma\iota\nu\dot{\omega}\sigma\varkappa\omega\nu$ is singular to agree with $\ddot{o}\chi\lambda o\varsigma$, the verb and predicate are plural, $\dot{\epsilon}\pi\dot{\alpha}\varrho\alpha\tau o\dot{\iota}$ $\epsilon\dot{\iota}\sigma\iota\nu$. This will put some emphasis on the thought that each and every individual is included as accursed. Phillips translates $\dot{\epsilon}\pi\dot{\alpha}\varrho\alpha\tau o\iota$ as "damned". This is the one use of the word in the New Testament.
105 For the contempt in which those expert in the Law held "the people of the land" see the passages cited in SBk, II, pp. 494–519.
106 Ryle is among those who commend rather than condemn Nicodemus: "Slow work is sometimes the surest and most enduring. Nicodemus stood firm, when Judas Iscariot fell away and went to his own place. No doubt it would be a pleasant thing, if everybody who was converted came out boldly, took up the cross, and confessed Christ in the day of his conversion. But it is not always given to God's children to do so . . . Better a little grace than none! Better move slowly than stand still in sin and the world!"

first be heard in person.[107] The judges must "know" what he does. The implication is clear that these judges do not really know what Jesus does. Nicodemus is of opinion that they ought not to give sentence until they do.

52 But the Sanhedrin is in no mood for legal niceties. "Surely you are not from Galilee, too?" they ask, and they exhort their colleague to make a search. He will see that no prophet came from Galilee. They were angry men, and men who had been baulked of their prey, so their answer is not a careful one. They ignore Jonah,[108] who was a Galilean (other prophets may also have come from there; there is uncertainty about the origin of some). And they ignore the power of God to raise up His prophets where He will. [109]

For commentary on 7 : 53–8 : 11 see Appendix.

---

[107] The rule is thus expressed by R. Eleazar b. Pedath, "Unless a mortal hears the pleas that a man can put forward, he is not able to give judgment" (Ex. R., XXI. 3).

[108] It is possible that emphasis should be placed on the present tense, "ariseth". The Pharisees would surely have known where Jonah came from, and it may be that they are belittling the inhabitants of Galilee in their own day: "Search them out. See for yourself that a prophet never comes from people like these Galileans." It is clear that the Galileans were commonly despised. See, for example, *Erub.* 53b for a series of stories holding them up to mockery for their inexact speech. Yet the Rabbis, too, could be more just than this. In the Talmud there is recorded the saying of R. Eliezer: "There was not a tribe in Israel from which there did not come prophets" (*Sukk.* 27b.; Soncino edn., p. 121).

[109] P66 has a singular reading. It inserts ὁ before προφήτης. If this were accepted there would be no difficulty, for the rulers would then be saying that *the* prophet, the Messiah does not come from Galilee. Bultmann had already conjectured that the article should be supplied, a conjecture regarded with some favor by C. K. Barrett (*ExT*, LXVIII, 1956–57, pp. 176, 177). The Nestle text says that Owen made this conjecture. J. R. Michaels thinks this "almost certainly the correct text, or at the very least a true interpretation of what John really meant" (*BT*, 8, 1957, p. 154). G. D. Fee thinks the scribe tried to delete it (*JBL*, LXXXIV, 1965, p. 68). E. R. Smothers argues for accepting this reading (*HThR*, LI, 1958, pp. 109–111). The evidence of P75 is not clear, for there is a lacuna. The editors think the article was there originally but B. M. Metzger is not convinced (*ExT*, LXXIII, 1961–62, p. 202). The reading is attractive, but in view of the overwhelming evidence of the rest of the MSS we can scarcely say more.

CHAPTER VIII

15. THE SIXTH DISCOURSE – THE LIGHT OF THE WORLD, 8 : 12-59

It is usually held that the background of this chapter, as of the last, remains the Feast of Tabernacles. In the Jewish celebration of that feast the imagery of water and of light were both very important, and light continues to occupy attention in this section. But it is not always noticed that, though the crowd is mentioned eight times in chapter 7 it is not mentioned at all in this chapter (in fact it is not mentioned again until 11 : 42). Throughout this section of the Gospel Jesus is confronted by His adversaries, not by the people at large. All this appears to indicate that the Feast was over and the crowd had gone home. Perhaps it was not long over, and the significance of the ceremonies had not yet faded from men's minds.

The discussion is triggered off by Jesus' statement that He is "the light of the world". The first reaction of His enemies is to attack the witness borne to Him. Then the discussion goes on to the fate of dying in sins (21–24), the relationship between the Father and the Son (25–30) and the fact that the opponents of Jesus are slaves to sin (31–47). It concludes with a section on the glory the Father gives the Son (48–59). It thus covers a wide range.

(a) The Witness of the Father, 8 : 12–20

12 Again therefore Jesus spake unto them, saying, I am the light of the world: he that followeth me shall not walk in the darkness, but shall have the light of life. 13 The Pharisees therefore said unto him, Thou bearest witness of thyself; thy witness is not true. 14 Jesus answered and said unto them, Even if I bear witness of myself, my witness is true; for I know whence I came, and whither I go; but ye know not whence I come, or whither I go. 15 Ye judge after the flesh; I judge no man. 16 Yea and if I judge, my judgment is true; for I am not alone, but I and the Father that sent me. 17 Yea and in your law it is written, [1]that the witness of two men is true. 18 I am he that beareth witness of myself, and the Father that sent me beareth witness of me. 19 They said therefore unto him, Where is thy Father? Jesus answered, Ye

know neither me, nor my Father: if ye knew me, ye would know my Father also. 20 These words spake he in the treasury, as he taught in the temple: and no man took him; because his hour was not yet come.

¹Comp. Dt. xix. 15; xvii. 6.

Jesus makes a great claim. This provokes the Pharisees into vigorous opposition, and they choose to oppose Him on the grounds of invalid witness. Witness is not a new theme. Jesus has already claimed that the Father bears witness to Him (5 : 37). He has said that it is this witness that carries conviction to Him, so that He rejects all other witness (5 : 34), though He has also made it clear that this witness will not be received by His enemies. Here He is not going back on the position He there took up. But, in reply to the accusation that no witness is borne to Him other than His own (which is legally invalid witness), Jesus insists that there is in fact Another who witnesses to Him. Whether the Pharisees accept the witness of the Father or not it is a fact. And the fact is important. John does not confine his attention to legal niceties, but he wants it to be clear that the witness borne to Jesus is completely valid.

12 The discussion of chapter 7 is resumed.¹ John does not say when this happens, but he does indicate the place, namely "the treasury" (20). Jesus' opening words, "I am the light of the world", are very impressive. "I am" is emphatic. It is the very style of deity which we have seen employed before in this Gospel (see on 6 : 35). There has been a good deal of speculation about the origin of the expression, "the light of the world" (*cf.* 9 : 5; 12 : 46 for the repetition of the thought in slightly different wording²). Many draw attention to the ceremonies with lights at the Feast of Tabernacles and suggest that Jesus was consciously fulfilling the symbolism suggested by them. There is nothing unlikely in this, especially if the words were uttered reasonably close to the time of the Feast. The feasts were very important

---

¹ The aorist ἐλάλησαν signifies "uttered a discourse" rather than "was teaching".

² For John's habit of introducing variations in repetitions though without substantial difference of meaning see on 3 : 5. Here and in 9 : 5 Jesus is called "the light of the world" but the word order in the Greek is different and the emphatic ἐγώ is lacking from 9 : 5. In 12 : 46 we read that He came "a light into the world".

to the Jews. They delighted in their observance and rejoiced in their symbolism.[3] And it was important to the Christians that the Christ fulfilled all the spiritual truths to which the feasts pointed. Now the brilliant candelabra were lit only at the beginning of the Feast of Tabernacles. There is dispute as to the number of nights on which the illumination took place, but none as to the fact that at the close of the Feast it did not. In the absence of the lights Jesus' claim to be the Light would stand out the more impressively. In favor of this view there is also the fact that the candelabra were lit in the Court of the Women, the most frequented part of the temple, and the very place in which Jesus delivered His address.

Yet, just as the reference to the water in ch. 7 seems to point us back to the rock in the wilderness rather than to the pouring of water from the golden pitcher, so the light may refer us to the pillar of fire in the wilderness. We have noted the reference to the manna in ch. 6, so that in three successive chapters the wilderness imagery seems consistently used to illustrate aspects of Jesus' Person and work.[4] It must always be borne in mind that light is a common theme in both Old and New Testaments, so that it is not necessary for us to find the source of Jesus' great saying in any non-biblical place.[5] Elsewhere we read that God is

---

[3] It is worth noting that Philo sees the time at which the Feast of Tabernacles was observed as significant. On the first day of the feast the moon succeeded the sun without interval so that there was no dark interlude (*De Spec. Leg.*, II, 210). This kind of symbolism may have suggested "the light of the world".

[4] *Cf.* the chapter headed "The Light of the World and the Three Gifts" in T. F. Glasson, *Moses in the Fourth Gospel* (London, 1963), pp. 60ff.

[5] Barrett has a lengthy and important note in which he shows that the background of the saying is complex. He sees it in the ceremonies of the feast of Tabernacles, in pagan religions (notably the Hermetic literature), in Judaism, and in the synoptic Gospels. He concludes: "John stands within the primitive Christian tradition . . . Nevertheless, it remains very probable that in the formulation of his statement he was influenced both by Hellenistic religion and by Jewish thought about Wisdom and the Law . . . yet for John 'the light of the world' describes what is essentially a soteriological function rather than a cosmological status." MacGregor sees in the expression an echo of the Prologue and specifically rejects a reference to the symbolism of Tabernacles. Some draw attention to the fact that light is one of the major themes of the Qumran scrolls. The good spirit may there be called "the prince of lights" and good men are designated "sons of light". There is even a reference to looking at "the light of life" (IQS, iii, 7; *DSS* p. 373). As often there is similarity in terminology and even ideas, but difference in basic concept. The scrolls have nothing like Christ's statement that He is "the light of the world".

light (I John 1 : 5) and Jesus Himself said that His followers were
"the light of the world" (Matt. 5 : 14; the expression is identical
with that used here[6]). Paul can also speak of Christians as "lights
in the world" (Phil. 2 : 15[7]). It is, of course, plain that such terms
must be applied to believers in a sense different from that in which
they are applied to Christ. He is the fundamental source of the
world's illumination. They, having kindled their torches at His
bright flame, show to the world something of His light.

Bultmann sees the emphasis not in the fact that Jesus is distinguished from other claimants to give light, but from that human
certainty that it already has the light. Light is not a natural
human possession. It comes only from Christ. And it is not a
separable entity which may be possessed in itself. It is not an objective revelation which men may receive and hug to themselves.
Jesus *is* the light. To have the light is to have Jesus. There is no
light apart from a right relationship to Him.[8]

This is the supreme example of John's interest in light which
we have seen from the Prologue on (see on 1 : 4). In the opening
verses of the Gospel he associated both life and light with the
Logos. Now the whole world[9] draws its light from Him, and light
and life are again connected. This saying does not mean that all
men indiscriminately receive the light. It does not belong to
mankind as such. Only "he that followeth me" is delivered from
darkness and has the light. We should not overlook the present
participle with its idea of a continuous following. Jesus is speaking
of whole-hearted discipleship, not of casual adherence (*cf.* 1 : 37
and note). The follower of Jesus will not "walk in the darkness".
This may refer to the darkness of this world or the darkness of

---

[6] This should not blind us to the significance of Christ's claim. The assertion
that He is the Light of the world gives Him a unique place and sets Him apart
from all others. To say that His followers are collectively the light of the world
is to say that, in contrast to outsiders, the church mediates light to the world.
But its light is derivative. It comes from Christ and is a reflection of Him.

[7] Paul's word is $\varphi\omega\sigma\tau\tilde{\eta}\varrho\varepsilon\varsigma$, whereas here and in Matthew the term is $\varphi\tilde{\omega}\varsigma$.
$\varphi\omega\sigma\tau\acute{\eta}\varrho$ is used primarily of the heavenly bodies, and seems to mean "light-
bearers", though it has "light" as a secondary meaning.

[8] The Rabbis sometimes used "Light" as a name for the Messiah, which
may point to the same truth (SBk, I, p. 67).

[9] The implications of the use of $\varkappa\acute{o}\sigma\mu o\varsigma$ should not be overlooked. John is
not writing about a parochial salvation, a gospel for a restricted group. Jesus
is the light of nothing less than the world.

Satan. Perhaps we are not meant to distinguish sharply between them, for the believer is delivered from both. By contrast with the darkness he will have "the light of life".[10] "The light of the world" does not give men a fugitive glimpse of light. A man's whole life is illuminated. "Shall have" points to something that continues. The coming of the light transforms him permanently. For "life" see on 1 : 4; 3 : 15.

13 The leaders of the opposition to Jesus are the Pharisees. They do not address themselves to the main question. Indeed, they do not speak of light and darkness at all. Typically, they fasten on a legal technicality. Jesus is bearing witness (see on 1 : 7) of Himself, they say, and therefore His witness is not "true". This does not necessarily mean that it is false.[11] It means that it is not valid. It has no legal worth.[12] There is no reason to accept it. Cf. 5 : 31. The Pharisees' reaction to Jesus' claim to be light is at base the answer men always make when they do not wish to be convinced: "I do not see it that way. The evidence is not sufficient to establish the claim." But light establishes its claim. It does so, not by arguments, but by shining. Light must always be accepted for itself, and that notwithstanding the objections of the blind.[13]

---

[10] The meaning of the genitive τὸ φῶς τῆς ζωῆς is not obvious. It might signify "the light which gives life" or "the light which is life" or "the light which springs from life" or "the light which illuminates life". Probably in the Johannine manner all the meanings are included. The expression is found in the Qumran scrolls, where we read that the man whose sins are atoned "will look at the light of life" (IQS, iii, 7; DSS, p. 373). This would favor the first of the suggestions.

[11] The Pharisees would, of course, have affirmed that Jesus' witness was false. This may be another of John's many uses of a word with more meanings than one. But the main thrust of the passage is clearly that the witness of Jesus has not complied with the legal requirements for valid testimony.

[12] Cf. Mishnah Ket. 2 : 9, "none may be believed when he testifies of himself . . . None may testify of himself."

[13] Cf. C. J. Wright: "there are types of so-called religious apologetic, which, distrusting the intrinsic claims of religion itself, seek to put in its place 'external evidences' and 'institutional safeguards.' How can light convince us that it is light except by what it does for us? We do not demonstrate that light is light by treatises, or by analyses of its constituent rays. It is only light to us when it illumines and quickens us." He also says, "Anyone can, to his own satisfaction, confute the claim which Beauty makes, by saying, I do not see it; or the claim inherent in Goodness, by saying, I do not hear it; or the self-evidencing nature of Truth, by saying, I do not know it. But man does not create Goodness, or Truth, or Beauty; and to say that he cannot see them is to condemn himself, not them." So with Light.

439

THE GOSPEL ACCORDING TO JOHN

14 Jesus insists that His witness is true (*cf.* Rieu: " 'What if I am?' said Jesus. 'My evidence is sound' "). In 5 : 31 He has said, "If I bear witness of myself, my witness is not true", by which He meant that His witness had to be supported to be accepted (see note). He agreed there with the Pharisees that unsupported testimony has no legal value. He did not mean that His words were not in fact true. They were true. But if His testimony was unsupported it was not to be received. In the present passage He has two points to make, the one that He is qualified to bear witness though His enemies are not, and the other that in any case His testimony is not unsupported. The Father bears witness of Him. Here Jesus is contrasting Himself with the Pharisees. He knows both His origin and destination,[14] but they know neither.[15] They are not in a position to comment on His witness. They are totally unaware of the great heavenly verities.

15 Their disqualification is further emphasized. They[16] judge, and they can judge, only "after the flesh". Now it is the nature of the flesh to be weak and incomplete,[17] so the expression draws attention to the weakness and imperfection of their judgment. It cannot but be imperfect and partial. After such a statement we expect something like "I do not judge after the flesh". But Jesus says, "I judge no man". The statement is a strong one, with an emphatic double negative. A difficulty is posed by its obvious meaning

---

[14] *Cf.* Westcott: "In the past lie the manifold elements out of which the present grew; in the future lies the revelation of what the present implicitly contains. He can bear witness to himself who has such knowledge of his own being." For John's use of ὑπάγω see on 7 : 33.

[15] There is a change from the aorist, ἦλθον, "I came", to the present, ἔρχομαι, "I come". It may be that Jesus is contrasting His own knowledge of a definite event, with the continuing uncertainty of the Pharisees. MiM comments, "The past fact ('I came') is not one which the Pharisees could know, except by inference: His present mission from the Father ('I come') should have been discerned by all who saw His works and heard His words". Notice also the change from καί (of Christ) to ἤ (of the Pharisees). He knows both, but they know neither.

[16] ὑμεῖς and ἐγώ are set in emphatic contrast.

[17] NEB renders "You judge by worldly standards." This paraphrase brings out the error of the Pharisees, but not the weakness and incompleteness that seem to be implied. Torrey renders "You judge from outward appearance"; Rieu, "You judge superficially"; Phillips, "You are judging by human standards" (similar is *Berkeley*); Knox, "You set yourselves up to judge, after your earthly fashion".

together with the fact that in succeeding verses it is clear that Jesus does judge. But Jesus did not come to judge men. That was not His purpose. And in any case the kind of judging that He engages in is not the same thing at all as that which the Pharisees envisage by the term. The two activities are so different that the same word does not describe them both. Judgment "after the flesh" is not really judgment at all. As the Pharisees understand judgment Jesus makes no judgment whatever.[18] The contradiction with "For judgment came I into this world" (9 : 39) is no more than apparent. There judgment is the natural consequence of the coming of Jesus. Being what He is He must divide men. Some accept Him, some reject Him. His coming is in itself a judgment. But here it is quite another truth that comes before us. Jesus is pointing out in the firmest manner that He does not practise the kind of judgment that the Pharisees practised. He came for salvation, not for judgment (3 : 17; 12 : 47).

16 Jesus turns now to the sense in which He does judge,[19] and the justification for it. "If I judge" could be understood of the judgment at the last day. But, as often in this Gospel, the context has to do with present judgment and the words should be taken in this sense. Jesus is continuing the thought that His judgment is unlike that of the Pharisees. It is not "after the flesh" but "true" judgment, for it arises from His relationship to the Father. It is to sustain this point that Jesus insists that He is not alone. To the Jews He may appear a solitary figure, but the truth is that the Father is with Him.[20] *Cf.* v. 29; 16 : 32. This validates His judgment, for any judgment carried out by One who is in the very presence of the Father and in harmony with Him must be valid judgment. Characteristically Jesus adds a reference to His mission. He is "sent" (see on 3 : 17), but sent in such a way that the Father who sent Him has not left Him but is with Him still. Some very good

---

[18] Bernard reminds us that Jesus did not set Himself up as a Judge during His earthly life. In fact men charged Him with not judging enough, for He mingled with publicans and sinners (Mark 2 : 16; Luke 15 : 2), He did not repulse the sinner in Simon's house (Luke 7 : 39), and even when confronted with the adulteress whose guilt was clear He refused to condemn (John 8 : 11).

[19] Notice that δέ comes unusually late in the sentence (fourth word). It supports καί to give a meaning like "*even* if".

[20] There is no verb in the last part of the verse. "I" and "the Father that sent me" are set side by side in impressive simplicity.

manuscripts omit "the Father" in this verse.[21] If (as is probable) this is the correct way to take the verse the emphasis is not on the Father-Son relationship, but rather on the mission of Jesus. He is the "sent" One. He is not forsaken by the Sender. His judgment is informed by His intimate contact with the Sender.

17 Jesus now appeals to the Law which the Jews admitted to be binding. "Your"[22] sets Him apart from them. The expression is that by which Gentiles refer to the Law in dialogues reported in the Rabbinic literature.[23] The Law applied to them in a way that it did not apply to Him. He stands with God and they with men. Yet this must not be overpressed for Jesus was Himself a Jew. The primary emphasis then is on the fact that this is the Law to which they made their appeal (*cf.* Nicodemus's "our law", 7 : 51). It is the Law which is binding on them and which they must accept. Now this Law provided that the agreement of two witnesses was sufficient to establish testimony (Deut. 19 : 15), even in so serious a case as an execution (Deut. 17 : 6).[24] "True" here means, of course, "valid". In view of what follows it may be significant that Jesus does not cite Deuteronomy exactly. That book speaks of "two witnesses", but He of "two men", which He puts in an emphatic position. The Law accepts the testimony of two *men*. What shall we say then of the testimony of the Father and the Son?

18 Jesus asserts that He has the required twofold testimony. He is emphatic. "I am" may be meant to recall the style of deity.

---

[21] The words are omitted by ℵ* D syr$^{s.c.}$.

[22] The expression is ἐν τῷ νόμῳ δὲ τῷ ὑμετέρῳ. The following γέγραπται signifies "it stands written" (see on 2 : 17 for John's method of citation). "Your law" is very unusual (though *cf.* 10 : 34; 15 : 25). It must not be taken as though Jesus repudiated the authority of the Law. Rather it is an *argumentum ad hominem*. By their own principles, by the Law they invoked and so proudly claimed as their own, they were shown to be in the wrong. We see here a further example of the Johannine irony. The Jews sought conformity to the Law they accepted. Jesus offers the testimony, not merely of one under the Law like themselves, but of the very Giver of that Law. But they cannot accept it.

[23] *IFG*, p. 82.

[24] Num. 35 : 30 provides that one witness is not sufficient. The Jews took this so seriously that they interpreted Scripture to mean "two witnesses" wherever a witness is mentioned unless it is specifically laid down that only one is required (SBk, I, p. 790).

At the very least it adds solemnity and grandeur to the statement.[25] Both verbs expressing witness are in continuous tenses. There is a continuing witness which Jesus bears to Himself[26] and which the Father bears to Him. In the light of His claims no other witness is possible. If Jesus really stands in the relationship to God in which He says He does, then no mere man is in a position to bear witness. No human witness can authenticate a divine relationship. Jesus therefore appeals to the Father and Himself,[27] and there is no other to whom He can appeal. Notice that once again the Father is described in terms of His sending of the Son.

19 Not unnaturally the Jews want to know where this Father of whom Jesus speaks is. Jesus' reply indicates that the Father is inaccessible to them. A man can know the Father[28] only as He knows Jesus. It is a key doctrine of this Gospel that it is in the Son and in the Son alone that the Father is revealed. No one has ever seen God. It is the Son who has "declared" Him (1 : 18). This is fundamental. If a man really comes to know Jesus then he will know the Father also, and acknowledge the Father's testimony to the Son. The two go together (*cf.* Weymouth: "You know my Father as little as you know me"). But to reject Jesus is to place oneself out of reach of the divine testimony. There is a sense in which the Pharisees know Jesus, but it is not the significant sense (see on 7 : 28). Their failure to understand the significance of Jesus and to enter into an appreciation of His mission and message meant that they were quite unable to perceive the witness of the Father to Him. They prided themselves on their knowledge of their God. Jesus tells them that they have no knowledge of Him at all.

---

[25] This expression is found in Isa. 43 : 10 (when it is used of Jehovah) as is the thought of witness.

[26] Field prefers AV to RV here. He rejects the latter as ungrammatical and says: "In making out the *two* witnesses, we should say in English: 'There is I (or myself) that bear witness of myself, and there is the Father,' &c. But the Greek idiom for 'There is I,' or 'It is I,' is not ἐστὶν ἐγώ, but ἐγώ εἰμι (Ch. vi. 20). Hence the A.V. (only italicizing *one*) exactly expresses what is intended" (p. 93).

[27] Among the Jews the combined witness of a father and son was not acceptable, at least for some purposes (Mishnah, *RH*, 1 : 7). But this is not laid down in the Law, and it is the Law to which Jesus appeals, not tradition.

[28] Abbott points out that in this Gospel ἄν always follows an emphatic word, so that "my Father" is more emphatic than is "know" (2566*b*).

20 John adds another of those little notes which indicate an exact knowledge of the circumstances. Jesus spoke these things, he says "in the treasury". It is most unlikely that Jesus taught in the actual treasure chamber, so the expression will mean that part of the Temple precincts into which people came to cast their offerings into the chests (*cf.* Mark 12 : 41, 43; Luke 21 : 1). This was part of the court of the women (which got its name from the fact that women as well as men were permitted to enter it). There were thirteen trumpet-shaped collection boxes there, each with its inscription showing the use to which its contents would be put.[29] In no other writing does the name "the treasury" appear to be applied to a section of the court of the women, but it is difficult to give John's words any other meaning. This court was a place to which people resorted and where teaching could take place accordingly. It is not without its interest in view of the attitude of the authorities to Jesus that it was quite near to the hall where the Sanhedrin met. Yet[30] no one arrested Him. Following the open enmity between the Pharisees and Jesus an arrest might have been expected. John explains that its failure to materialize was due, not to any lack of desire or opportunity, but to the will of God. Jesus' "hour" (see on 2 : 4) had not yet come. Until it did His enemies were entirely powerless to harm Him.

(b) Dying in Sins, 8 : 21-24

21 He said therefore again unto them, I go away, and ye shall seek me, and shall die in your sin: whither I go, ye cannot come. 22 The Jews therefore said, Will he kill himself, that he saith, Whither I go, ye cannot come? 23 And he said unto them, Ye are from beneath; I am from above: ye are of this world; I am not of this world. 24 I said therefore unto you, that ye shall die in your sins: for except ye believe that I am he, ye shall die in your sins.

The previous verse appears to denote a break in proceedings. It is impossible to say when what follows was spoken. It follows on naturally enough, but this does not necessarily mean that it

---

[29] The inscriptions are quoted in the Mishnah, *Shek.* 6 : 5.
[30] καί is used in the sense καίτοι, "and yet" (see on 1 : 5).

was spoken on the same occasion. There is no note of the time of the year between 7 : 37, when it is still the season of Tabernacles, and 10 : 22 when it is the Feast of the Dedication. The interval is two months, and there is no way of knowing to what point in this period any of the intervening matter should be dated. This section appears somewhat later than the previous section but how much later cannot be determined.

The ideas here set forth are important. Indeed, Wright says of vv. 21-30: "These profound verses develop and unfold the key thought of Jesus in this Gospel, and cannot, therefore, be understood apart from the Gospel as a whole." John is all the time writing of One who stands in unique relationship to the Father, who is the supreme revelation of the Father. In this passage this relationship is the dominating thought.

21 "Therefore again" links what follows rather loosely with the preceding. It does not mean that it follows on immediately. Jesus begins by telling the Jews that He will leave[31] them and that they will not be able to follow Him where He goes (*cf.* 7 : 33f., where see note). The words are mysterious, but we need not doubt that Jesus is referring once more to His departure to be with the Father. His death is set in contrast to theirs. They will die in their sin[32] and this will prevent them from going where He goes. Dying in sin is not further defined. It is an Old Testament expression, but there, as here, it is not explained (Prov. 24 : 9 LXX; Ezek. 3 : 18; 18 : 18). It points to a horror which is all the more terrible for being unexplained. To die with one's sin unrepented and unatoned is the supreme disaster. *Amplified* renders, "(under the curse of) your sin". Why the Jews should seek Him Jesus does not say. It may be understood as their implacable pursuit of Him which would continue even after He has "gone away". Or Jesus may mean that their moment of insight will come too late. Only after they have crucified Him will they realize who He is. Then their

---

[31] When John uses ὑπάγω of Jesus it most commonly refers to His going to the Father, *i.e.* it is a reference to His death.

[32] If there is significance in the singular ἁμαρτία as against the plural ἁμαρτίαις of v. 24 it will be to concentrate attention on the sin of all sins, that of rejecting Jesus (so Barrett). It is placed before the verb for emphasis, whereas in v. 24 it is the thought of death that is more prominent. But it is a habit of John's to introduce small variants in his threefold repetitions and this could be another example (see on 3 : 5).

seeking of Him will be in vain. Throughout this entire section the emphatic personal pronouns are used freely. Jesus and the Jews are set in emphatic opposition.

22 The form in which the question is cast shows that the answer "No" is expected.[33] "Surely He will not kill Himself?" is the force of it. The Jews do not think of Jesus as a likely suicide[34] but they correctly catch a reference to death. The parting of which He is speaking is final. Some think the Jews are jesting, their meaning being, "If you are going to lowest Hades, we certainly will not be able to follow you!" Their quotation of the words of Jesus at the end of the verse is noteworthy for being exact, and the saying is quoted accurately once more in 13 : 33.[35] The similar words in 7 : 34 are also quoted accurately in 7 : 36. In this Gospel the more usual habit is for slight variation (*e.g.* 1 : 48, 50; 16 : 14, 15, *etc.*; see on 3 : 5) so we cannot but feel that John attached especial importance to these sayings.

23, 24 Jesus differentiates Himself from the Jews with a pair of contrasts.[36] "He has to remind them that there are other gulfs dividing men besides the gulf of death" (Murray). His opponents are closely tied up with this world. They are "from beneath" and "of this world".[37] In a sense this can be said of all men. But there is a sense in which the attitude is all-important. These Jews were not only members of the human race. They were of the earth, earthy. Their attention was concentrated on this world

---

[33] Μήτι ἀποκτενεῖ ἑαυτόν;

[34] The Jews had a very severe attitude toward suicide. Thus Josephus says, "But as for those who have laid mad hands upon themselves, the darker regions of the nether world receive their souls, and God, their father, visits upon their posterity the outrageous acts of the parents" (*Bell.* iii, 375). Occasional exceptions, such as Samson (Judges 16 : 30), were regarded as praiseworthy, but the general attitude was one of abhorrence.

[35] This is the only threefold repetition in this Gospel with all three members identical that I have been able to find. See *SFG*, ch. 5.

[36] The imperfect ἔλεγεν suggests to Bernard that this was a habitual saying of the Lord's. Lagrange sees in the use of καὶ ἔλεγεν rather than ἔλεγεν οὖν an indication that Jesus does not reply to the Jews' question but merely continues with what He had in mind to say to them.

[37] There is a variation in word order here. "This world" is τούτου τοῦ κόσμου when used of the Jews, but τοῦ κόσμου τούτου at the end of the verse. As the latter is John's normal order the former may well be emphatic. Indeed this is the only place in the whole New Testament where οὗτος precedes the noun in the expression "this world". There is emphasis on *this* world.

instead of on doing the Father's will (contrast Col. 3 : 1f.). However, Jesus' meaning here does not appear to centre on this aspect (though it will be included) as much as on the fact that He and they differ in their essential being. He comes "from above", He is "not of this world".[38] He is a Being of a different order, and thus their pursuit of Him when He chooses to leave them will be futile. It is because of this essential nature of theirs that He has told them they will die in their sins. They belong to the world, the world where Satan is supreme (*cf.* I John 5 : 19). Therefore,[39] when they die they will die in their sins. There is but one way of avoiding this fate, namely by coming to believe[40] in Jesus. And this involves a right estimate of His person. It is important to believe "that I am".[41] This expression is in the style of deity. There is no predicate expressed. The same Greek expression occurs in 6 : 20; 18 : 6, neither of which is difficult to understand (and, of course, it is found several times with a predicate; see on 6 : 35). But it is not easy to see what predicate could be supplied here. The answer of the Jews shows some mystification. We should probably understand it along the lines of the similar expression in LXX, which is the style of deity (*cf.* Is. 43 : 10).[42] Its use here involves the very highest estimate of Christ's Person (see further on v. 58). It is worth noting also that this gives a certain intellectual content to faith. Basically faith is trust. But in our reaction against the view that faith means no more than a firm acceptance of certain intellectual propositions we must not go so far as to say that it is entirely a matter of personal relations. It is impossible to have the kind of faith that John envisages without having a certain high view of Christ. Unless we believe that He is more than man we can never trust Him with that faith that is saving faith.

---

[38] The preposition ἐκ denotes origin in each case. For εἶναι ἐκ see on 3 : 31.

[39] This is one of the few examples in this Gospel of the use of οὖν in speeches of Jesus (see on 6 : 62). It links the saying that they will die in their sins very closely with the foregoing.

[40] The aorist πιστεύσητε means "make an act of faith", "come to believe".

[41] Temple maintains that this "cannot be reproduced in English, for it combines three meanings: (*a*) that I am what I say – *sc.* the Light of the World; (*b*) that I am He – the promised Messiah; (*c*) that I am – absolutely, the divine Name. All these are present; none is actually indicated".

[42] See n. 116 below.

(c) The Father and the Son, 8 : 25–30

25 They said therefore unto him, Who art thou? Jesus said unto them, [1]Even that which I have also spoken unto you from the beginning. 26 I have many things to speak and to judge concerning you: howbeit he that sent me is true; and the things which I heard from him, these speak I unto the world. 27 They perceived not that he spake to them of the Father. 28 Jesus therefore said, When ye have lifted up the Son of man, then shall ye know that [2]I am he, and that I do nothing of myself, but as the Father taught me, I speak these things. 29 And he that sent me is with me; he hath not left me alone; for I do always the things that are pleasing to him. 30 As he spake these things, many believed on him.

[1]Or, *Altogether that which I also speak unto you.* [2]Or, *I am he: and I do*

This leads on to a discussion of Christ's Person and of His relation to the Father. There is a strong affirmation of the unity between them, and a reference to Christ's death. This concept of the death on the cross of One who was one with the Father is the great central thought of this Gospel.

25 It is unlikely that the Jews perceived the full implications of Jesus' words. There is mystery in them, and the mystery is open only to faith. But they caught enough to discern that Jesus was making a large claim and the outrageousness of this claim (as it seemed to them) caused them to explode into the question "Who are you?" The pronoun "is scornfully emphatic" (Plummer) and placed first. "You, who are you to be saying such things?" is the force of it. The meaning of Jesus' answer is not clear.[43] ARV may be correct, but the expression rendered "from the beginning" is not the usual one.[44] It really means "at first", "at the beginning" and it is not easy to see how this fits in. Barrett takes this as the significance of the expression, but when he gives the meaning of the whole clause he substitutes "from the beginning", which is

---

[43] There is a good discussion of this passage by E. R. Smothers, *HThR*, LI, 1958, pp. 111–122.

[44] The expression is $\tau\grave{\eta}\nu\ \mathring{\alpha}\varrho\chi\acute{\eta}\nu$. It is more normal in the New Testament to find $\mathring{\alpha}\pi$' $\mathring{\alpha}\varrho\chi\tilde{\eta}\varsigma$ which means "from the beginning"; sometimes $\mathring{\varepsilon}\nu\ \mathring{\alpha}\varrho\chi\tilde{\eta}$ or $\mathring{\varepsilon}\xi\ \mathring{\alpha}\varrho\chi\tilde{\eta}\varsigma$ is preferred. This is the only place in the New Testament where $\tau\grave{\eta}\nu\ \mathring{\alpha}\varrho\chi\acute{\eta}\nu$ is used adverbially though the accusative is not uncommon elsewhere as LS shows. This lexicon gives the meaning as "to begin with, at first". It is not usual to have a present tense with such an expression, and this increases the difficulty of the present passage.

not the same thing as "at the beginning" at all. He says, "We must choose between the renderings (*a*) I am from the beginning what I tell you, and (*b*) I am what I tell you from the beginning." He thinks (*a*) is probably right. His (*b*) is the way RSV and Phillips take it. But nobody appears to have shown that the expression is used in the sense "from the beginning".[45] If we substitute Barrett's "at the beginning" neither of his suggestions is felicitous. With this rendering the present tense is really difficult. One way of avoiding the difficulty is to go back to an understanding of the expression favored by the Fathers, namely, as "altogether" or the like.[46] It is the "at all" in our phrase "not at all". On this view Jesus' reply may be regarded either as a question or an exclamation. The favorite way of taking it in recent translations is as a question (RSV mg., NEB, Weymouth, Goodspeed, Knox, *etc.*). "To begin with, why do I even speak to you?" or "Why do I talk to you at all?" This yields a good sense. In the face of the Jews' continued refusal to recognize Jesus for what He was He wonders what is the point of continuing to talk with them. They are wilfully obtuse. However this meaning does not fit in very well with the context, particularly with verse 26, where He says He has much to say about them. And it involves an interrogative which is not common anywhere in the New Testament and does not occur at all elsewhere in John.[47] This may be avoided by taking the expression as an exclamation, "That I speak to you at all!" But the difficulty of the context remains. Others retaining the "at all", "altogether", significance suggest a meaning like that of ARV mg., "Altogether that which I also speak unto you" (*cf. Berkeley:* "I am exactly what I tell you"). Jesus is then saying that He is altogether what His words show Him to be.

---

[45] It may be possible to derive this meaning from the adverbial accusative. So, for example, BDF, 160, but the meaning "from the beginning" is there bracketed with "at all", and in 300(2) the latter appears to be favored.

[46] *Cf.* Chrysostom, "What He saith, is of this kind; 'Ye are not worthy to hear My words at all, much less to learn who I am'" (LIII. 1; p. 191).

[47] ὅ τι is, of course, used in indirect questions. But it is not common in direct questions. BDF cites examples from LXX, from Mark, and from early Christian literature, and sees the construction as "a piece of 'biblical Greek'". In the present passage he favors the reading of P66 (εἶπον ὑμῖν τὴν ἀρχήν) though noting that this is rejected by Barrett (300(2)). Abbott rejects the idea that ὅ τι is interrogative here (2155). If ὅ τι is read as introducing a question it will, of course, have the meaning "why?" (unless it is read as ὅτι, "that").

But our expression seems to be used with this meaning only when there is a negative. As we have noticed, it is the "at all" in "not at all". It does not appear to be used often, if ever, in this positive sense.[48] Hoskyns is of opinion that "beginning" is such an important word for John that he would never allow it to be lost completely, as in some of the above suggestions. Both the beginning of creation and the beginning of Jesus' ministry are important to him, and if he has both in mind at the same time (and we must bear in mind John's fondness for double meanings) this may well have complicated the grammar. A further suggestion arises from the unique reading of the great Bodmer papyrus (P66): "I told you at the beginning what I am also telling you."[49] This is so much better than the other readings that the only difficulty lies in seeing how, if it was original, it has affected the manuscript tradition so little. Barrett rejects it as secondary.[50]

The question is thus a very complicated one. It is not surprising that many exegetes think it incapable of solution with the information at our disposal. If we could accept the reading of P66 all would be well. Failing that, Hoskyns' suggestion seems to be best, that there is a complication due to the double meaning in the writer's mind. If neither of these be acceptable then it would seem that we are in the presence of a primitive corruption of the

---

[48] See Abbott, 2154, 2154c. Hendriksen accepts this meaning ("Exactly what I am also telling you"), but cites no example of this use without a negative (he says it is "not without parallel elsewhere", but he does not cite any parallel). Dods takes up the same position, but again cites no examples. Jacob Elsner cites a few, but himself prefers to understand the expression in the sense *initio, a principio* (*Observationes Sacrae*, Jacob van Poolsum, 1720, pp. 319–21). Clearly this construction is very rare, and that is the objection. It is not a natural way of understanding the expression.

[49] In the text of P66 there is a mark to show an omission just before $\tau\dot{\eta}\nu$ $\dot{a}\varrho\chi\dot{\eta}\nu$ and in the margin is written $\varepsilon\tilde{i}\pi\sigma\nu$ $\dot{\upsilon}\mu\tilde{i}\nu$. Prof. V. Martin, who edited this papyrus, thinks the marginal correction was made by the original scribe and he says that there are many examples of this throughout this papyrus. R. W. Funk argues for accepting this reading (*HThR*, LI, 1958, pp. 95–100), and J. R. Michaels favors it (*BT*, 8, 1957, p. 154).

[50] *ExT*, LXVIII, 1956–57, pp. 176f. He translates it, "I told you in the beginning that which also I am speaking to you (now), since I have many things to speak and judge concerning you." His conclusion is, "It seems doubtful whether this is an improvement on the current text, of which it is probably a secondary development."

text such that the original is irrecoverable without further evidence.[51]

26 Then Jesus goes on to point out that He has much to say "about" (not "to") them, and that these things concern judgment. Judgment is necessarily involved in all right teaching and action, and preeminently is this the case where the mission of the Son is concerned. In His function as Judge of mankind He cannot overlook such conduct as that of His antagonists. But the right place and the right time to say such things are not yet. There are things that Jesus says now, and a consideration of them leads to His close connection with the Father.[52] Once more He thinks in terms of mission. The Father is "he that sent me" (see on 3 : 17). And once more He thinks of His message as thoroughly reliable because it rests on His contact with the Father. The Father is "true" (see Additional Note D, pp. 293ff.; elsewhere Christ also speaks of Himself as "the truth", 14 : 6), and the things Jesus speaks are only the things that He has heard from Him.[53] Notice that His message is to "the world".[54] It is not restricted in its scope.

27, 28 The Jews did not catch the allusion. As they did not recognize Jesus' heavenly origin it meant nothing to them that Jesus could trace His message to Him that sent Him, nor that

---

[51] Other meanings have, of course, been suggested. Thus Rieu renders, "So we go back to our starting-point!" and Barclay, "Anything I am saying to you is only the beginning." Black sees a mistranslation of an Aramaic expression. But he has to do a considerable rearrangement of the text, and he offers no explanation of how such disorder is possible (*AA*, pp. 172ff.). Torrey thinks an original ἔτι has been corrupted to ὅτι and translates "I am even yet in the beginning of my word to you." But I have not found a solution which carries conviction.

[52] This is introduced by ἀλλ'. It is not easy to see why this emphatic adversative is chosen. Perhaps a contrast is intended between what the Jews understood to be Christ's origin and the facts of the case. Or perhaps the thought is "But now is not the time. That must await the Father's time."

[53] κἀγώ is an emphatic aligning of Jesus with the Father's message. The aorist ἤκουσα is in accordance with the custom in this Gospel when reference is made to Christ's hearing anything from the Father (3 : 32; 8 : 26, 40; 15 : 15). It may be that John has in mind "that message which He heard (when He came down from the Father to save mankind)" (Abbott, 2451 on 3 : 32). *Cf.* also Deut. 18 : 18.

[54] Unless we take εἰς τὸν κόσμον as equivalent to ἐν τῷ κόσμῳ. The construction λαλέω εἰς is found only here in John (elsewhere I Cor. 14 : 9). λέγω is occasionally followed by εἰς as in Luke 22 : 65; Acts 2 : 25; Eph. 5 : 32, but the meaning then is "with reference to".

that Sender was "true". What they did think of it is not said. So Jesus went on. "Lifted up" is a curious expression, but it must point to the cross here as in other places where it occurs in this Gospel (see on 3 : 14).[55] It is not a natural expression to use for crucifixion. No other New Testament writer uses it with this meaning. Elsewhere it always signifies "to exalt". John probably uses it to convey a double meaning. Jesus was "lifted up" on the cross, and He was also exalted in a deeper sense, for His greatest glory consists in His accepting the shame and the humiliation of the cross in order that thereby He might bring salvation to sinful men. Here Jesus is saying that the Jews will not understand who He really is before they have crucified Him.[56] There is a revelatory aspect to the cross, and after the crucifixion those who reflect on it will be in a position to appreciate that Jesus is indeed more than man.[57] It is probable that we should put a stop after "I am he", so that what follows is not a statement of what the Jews will come to realize, but of what Jesus constantly does (there is nothing in the Greek corresponding to the second "that" of ARV). He does not act as an isolated individual. He does nothing on His own initiative. He repeats from v. 26 that what He speaks to men is what God has spoken to Him. His message is not of human origin, but divine.

29 This is followed by a statement of the intimate communion that always exists between Jesus and the Father. Again there is the thought of mission. It is He that sent Jesus that is with Him, and this may perhaps be regarded as part of the consequence of the sending. God does not and will not forsake His messenger. Jesus is not abandoned. The words which follow may give the reason for this in His continual doing of the Father's will. Or we may think of an ellipsis "(I can say this) because I do always...."

---

[55] "Here it is a grim suggestion that the Jews will help him on his upward way – by killing him" (Hunter).

[56] Bultmann reminds us that these words have their significance for all men, and not only for Jesus' contemporaries: "all who identify themselves with the Jews by their unbelief have brought Jesus to the cross. The cross was the Jews' last and definitive answer to Jesus' revelation (*Offenbarungswort*), and the world always, when it lets its unbelief be its last answer, 'lifts up' the Revealer, and at the same time makes him its Judge."

[57] Dodd sees a possible reference to Isa. 43 : 10 and adds, "It is difficult not to see here an allusion to the divine name אֲנִי הוּא" (*IFG*, p. 95).

The deeds that Jesus did were evidence that the Father was indeed with Him. Sometimes objection is taken to the whole idea of "the sinlessness of Jesus" on the grounds that it is a negative conception. Here we have the glorious positive. Jesus is active in doing what pleases the Father. Always.

30 John briefly gives us the result of this. As Jesus was speaking[58] these things many came to put their trust in Him (see on 1 : 12 for the significance of this construction). We are not told who the "many" were. They may have come from the opponents who disputed, or they may have been bystanders. But they caught enough of the significance of all this to take up their stand with Jesus.

(d) Slaves of Sin, 8 : 31–47

31 Jesus therefore said to those Jews that had believed him, If ye abide in my word, then are ye truly my disciples; 32 and ye shall know the truth, and the truth shall make you free. 33 They answered unto him, We are Abraham's seed, and have never yet been in bondage to any man: how sayest thou, Ye shall be made free? 34 Jesus answered them, Verily, verily, I say unto you, Every one that committeth sin is the bondservant of sin. 35 And the bondservant abideth not in the house for ever: the son abideth for ever. 36 If therefore the Son shall make you free, ye shall be free indeed. 37 I know that ye are Abraham's seed, yet ye seek to kill me, because my word [1]hath not free course in you. 38 I speak the things which I have seen with [2]my Father: and ye also do the things which ye heard from your father. 39 They answered and said unto him, Our father is Abraham. Jesus saith unto them, If ye [3]were Abraham's children, [4]ye would do the works of Abraham. 40 But now ye seek to kill me, a man that hath told you the truth, which I heard from God: this did not Abraham. 41 Ye do the works of your father. They said unto him, We were not born of fornication; we have one Father, even God. 42 Jesus said unto them, If God were your Father, ye would love me: for I came forth and am come from God; for neither have I come of myself, but he sent me. 43 Why do ye not [5]understand my speech? Even

---

[58] Note the genitive absolute αὐτοῦ λαλοῦντος, though the participle might have agreed with αὐτόν.

because ye cannot hear my word. 44 Ye are of your father the devil, and the lusts of your father it is your will to do. He was a murderer from the beginning, and standeth not in the truth, because there is no truth in him. ⁶When he speaketh a lie, he speaketh of his own: for he is a liar, and the father thereof. 45 But because I say the truth, ye believe me not. 46 Which of you convicteth me of sin? If I say truth, why do ye not believe me? 47 He that is of God heareth the words of God: for this cause ye hear them not, because ye are not of God.

¹Or, *hath no place in you.* ²Or, *the Father; do ye also therefore the things which ye heard from the Father.* ³Gr. *are.* ⁴Some ancient authorities read *ye do the works of Abraham* ⁵Or, *know* ⁶Or, *When* one *speaketh a lie, he speaketh of his own: for his father also is a liar*

This section of discourse is addressed to those who believe, and yet do not believe. Clearly they were inclined to think that what Jesus said was true. But they were not prepared to yield Him the far-reaching allegiance that real trust in Him implies. This is a most dangerous spiritual state.⁵⁹ To recognize that truth is in Jesus and to do nothing about it means that in effect one ranges oneself with the enemies of the Lord. It means also that there is some powerful spiritual force holding back the would-be believer from what is recognized as the right course of action. The man in that position is not free but a slave. Jesus makes it plain that his adversaries are slaves to sin and in the closest possible relationship to the Evil One. True freedom is to be found in the liberty which Christ gives. By setting themselves in constant opposition these Jews did but proclaim their servitude to the Enemy of men's souls.⁶⁰

31 There is a puzzle in the meaning to be attached to "believed

---

⁵⁹ *Cf.* W. Temple: "As we read the stern words that follow, let us not ask so much how He the Lord of Love should so speak to the Jews, as whether we have deserved that the Lord of Love should so speak to us. Above all, let us remember, and here observe, how resistance on grounds of self-will to what we recognise as right and noble, has a hardening and embittering effect on those in whom it is found which involves mortal peril to the soul."

⁶⁰ Wright points out that "The answers of Jesus deepen the perplexity, for that is grounded, not in serious and anxious inquiry, but in the blind determination of the whole nature. The perplexity hardens into exasperated hostility, and then, at the end of the chapter, into open violence".

him".[61] Normally John uses this verb of trust in Jesus, such trust as brings men out of death into life. Especially is this so when the construction signifies "believe on" (as in v. 30), but, as we saw in Additional Note E (pp. 335ff.), it is usually not possible to make a sharp differentiation between the various constructions used with this verb. We should expect a discourse introduced in this fashion to be addressed to genuine disciples. But as it unfolds it appears that these Jews are nothing of the sort. Therefore many commentators look for a change of subject. Some think v. 30 refers to genuine believers and v. 31 to those who made an outward profession simply. Others think of real believers in both places, but think the "they" of v. 33 to refer to a different group, the enemies of Jesus.[62] But there is no indication in the narrative that different groups of people are meant. Some are so impressed with the difficulty that they think the passage composite and ascribe some of the words to a redactor. This, however, introduces a further difficulty, namely the problem of the mind of a redactor who would take a reasonably straightforward narrative and produce this result, not being concerned about a difficulty which has troubled commentators through the centuries. It is best to think that John is speaking of men who had made an outward profession, but that in this particular case it did not go very deep. Jesus' words then are meant to drive home to formal and casual adherents something of the meaning of true discipleship. If men in any sense believe in Him it is important that they be led to see what real faith means. While "therefore" in this Gospel often denotes a very loose connection, there may be point in the use of the word here. Since many attached themselves to Jesus He proceeded to unfold what their attachment should mean. The key word here is "abide". It is easy enough to be attracted in a superficial fashion,

---

[61] τοὺς πεπιστευκότας αὐτῷ 'Ιουδαίους. The perfect may, as Abbott suggests (2506), be due to the fact that there is no pluperfect participle active, and John wants something to indicate more than the simple past. Certainly the context rules out the possibility of taking it to mean a continuing belief. The use of the dative often denotes simple credence rather than trust in a person, and the change to this construction from εἰς + accusative of the previous verse may be significant. But John does not appear to put much difference between the two (see Additional Note E, pp. 335ff.), and in any case it appears to be the same persons who are spoken of. Nor should we overlook the fact that εἰς + accusative may apparently be used of a defective faith (*cf.* 2 : 23f.; 12 : 42).

[62] Augustine, for example, thinks of a change here (XLI. 2; p. 230).

but the test is "abiding". It is only those who continue who are genuine disciples. There is some emphasis on "ye", as though to say, "ye, ye who have believed, even ye can become true disciples by abiding". "My word" will stand for the whole of Jesus' teaching (cf. 5 : 24; 14 : 23, etc.). The thought is repeated several times in this chapter (vv. 37, 43, 51, 52, cf. 55). It is probably significant that Jesus does not say "you will be", but "you are" disciples. He is not laying down a condition of discipleship, but telling them in what discipleship consists. When a man abides in Christ's word, then he *is* a true disciple.[63]

32 Now Jesus does move into the future. When a man is a true disciple there are consequences. He then will know the truth. This discourse is specially concerned with truth, which is mentioned seven times over (twice here, vv. 40, 44 *bis*, 45, 46). Truth is closely connected with the Person of Christ (1 : 17; 14 : 6), so that knowledge of the truth is naturally associated with being His disciple. What is essentially part of Himself He communicates to His followers. See further on 1 : 14. Jesus goes on to say that the truth in question liberates. This must be understood in the context of this whole Gospel. The meaning is not that truth in a philosophical sense exercises a liberating function, and that adherence to the school of Jesus procures such intellectual insight that men are delivered from the bonds of ignorance. There is, of course, a sense in which it is true that only by surrender to the facts is genuine freedom possible, be it in philosophy, science, or what you will. But that is not the point here.[64] The truth of which

---

[63] Of the kind of conditional clause used here Burton says, "The thought would be expressed more fully but less forcibly by supplying some such phrase as *it will appear that* or *it will still be true that*" (*Moods*, 263). It says nothing about whether the condition is fulfilled or not, but explains what would be the case were it to be realized.

[64] For this reason parallels sometimes adduced from the Stoics and others to the effect that wisdom or the like liberates are misleading. Even Prov. 25 : 10a (**LXX**: not in Hebrew) χάρις καὶ φιλία ἐλευθεροῖ is not really parallel. Perhaps the nearest approaches are in Epictetus. That philosopher says to the tyrant, "How can *you* be my master? Zeus has set me free" (1, 19, 9; Loeb edn. I, p. 131): "no one has authority over me. I have been set free by God, I know His commands, no one has power any longer to make a slave of me" (4, 7, 16f.; Loeb edn. II, p. 367). But this is simply the expression of a proud self-sufficiency. Epictetus also says, "I pay attention only to myself. But if you wish me to say that I pay attention to you too, I tell you that I do so, but only as I pay attention to my pot" (1, 19, 10; Loeb edn. I, pp. 131f.). This is far from the spirit of Jesus.

John writes is the truth that is bound up with the Person and the work of Jesus. It is saving truth. It is the truth which saves men from the darkness of sin, not that which saves them from the darkness of error (though there is a sense in which men in Christ are delivered from gross error; this Gospel has a good deal to say about knowledge). Luke tells us that Jesus saw fulfilled in His ministry the prophecy that "He hath sent me to proclaim release to the captives" (Luke 4 : 18). It is this kind of freedom of which John writes. Men do not always, or even usually, realize that they are in bondage. They tend to rest in some fancied position of privilege, national, social, or religious. So these Jews, proud of their religion, did not even know their need to be free.

33 They retort by pointing to their relationship with Abraham. Connection with the great ancestor of the race was a high privilege and in their view it was inconsistent with bondage. With a superb disregard for the facts of the situation as typified by the Roman yoke they maintain emphatically[65] that they have never been in a state of subjection.[66] So they ask triumphantly how those who have never been in slavery can possibly be made free.[67]

---

[65] $οὐδενί$ is placed in an emphatic position. $δεδουλεύκαμεν$ is perfect, pointing to a continuing state of bondage. If the word is pressed their claim was technically correct. They had not been made slaves. (Yet notice that Jesus has not yet used the term $δοῦλος$.) But their detestation of the Romans was evidence that they were not unmindful of the pressure from their overlords. There is possibly significance also in their use of the emphatic pronoun $σύ$, "How do *you* of all people, say . . . ?"

[66] Ryle comments: "The power of self-deception in unconverted man is infinite. These Jews were not more unreasonable than many now-a-days, who say, 'We are not dead in sin; we have grace, we have faith, we are regenerate, we have the Spirit,' while their lives show plainly that they are totally mistaken."

[67] Some suggest that their meaning is "We have never lost our freedom of spirit", rather than "We have never been in subjection to a conqueror", the latter being so patently false. Moreover, "truth" would not set free from such bondage. Yet if this is the meaning it is rather curiously expressed. The most natural way of taking their words is with reference to outward bondage. But in any case Jesus' reply will stand. A proud assertion of self-sufficiency is itself evidence of the bondage of which He speaks. It is worth noticing that Josephus quotes a speech of Eleazar in which he says, "Long since, my brave men, we determined neither to serve $(δουλεύειν)$ the Romans nor any other save God" (*Bell.* vii, 323; he also cites the followers of Judah the Galilean as holding that God is their only Ruler and Lord, *Ant.* xviii, 23-5). The Talmud records a saying that "R. Simeon b. Gamaliel, R. Simeon, R. Ishmael, and R. Akiba, all hold that all Israel are royal children" (*Shab.* 128a; Soncino edn., p. 637).

34 Jesus' answer is prefaced by the solemn "Verily, verily" (see on 1 : 51), which shows that the saying is important. "Every one that committeth sin" is a participial construction which points us to a continuing state (*cf.* I John 3 : 6). Jesus is not saying that every individual act of sin represents slavery (though in a sense that, too, is true). What He is saying is that every man who continues in sin, who is a sinner, is thereby a slave.[68] We should not minimize the force of "bondservant". It does not mean a person who is paid wages and who has a considerable area of freedom. It means a slave.[69] The man who sins is a slave to his sin and this whether he realizes it or not. This means also that he cannot break away from his sin.[70] For that he needs a power greater than his own.

35, 36 Jesus draws attention to the difference between the slave's relationship to the home and that of the son in order to show that He can bring men the freedom they need but cannot procure for themselves. The Jews held themselves to be sons in God's household. They presumed accordingly on rights that, being really slaves, they did not possess. The slave's position is temporary. He may in fact remain in a particular house all his life, but he has no rights, no security. He can at any time be sold or transferred to some other part of the property.[71] A son may in fact leave

---

[68] The words τῆς ἁμαρτίας are omitted by D b d syrˢ Cl Cypr. If this is the true reading we have a very terse and pointed epigram. But whether the shorter or longer reading be accepted the meaning is essentially the same.

[69] Calvin brings out the point that men may not realize their true position by saying, "the greater the mass of vices anyone is buried under, the more fiercely and bombastically does he extol free will."

[70] Augustine points out that slavery to sin is worse than other forms of slavery: "at times a man's slave, worn out by the commands of an unfeeling master, finds rest in flight. Whither can the servant of sin flee? Himself he carries with him wherever he flees. An evil conscience flees not from itself; it has no place to go to; it follows itself. Yea, he cannot withdraw from himself, for the sin he commits is within. He has committed sin to obtain some bodily pleasure. The pleasure passes away; the sin remains. What delighted is gone; the sting has remained behind. Evil bondage!" (XLI. 4; p. 231).

[71] This interpretation assumes the correctness of ARV. But in the New Testament οὐ . . . εἰς τὸν αἰῶνα means "never". If we take the normal meaning of this expression the passage, after saying that the sinner is a slave, goes on to affirm that, being a slave, he has no security in the household and never can have it. It is a household of God's people, of God's free men. No slave, specifically no slave of sin, can ever have place there.

home or be expelled (though either would be the unusual thing). But he has the position of a son, and nothing can alter that. He belongs. He has rights. In the Johannine manner we have a passing over to another meaning. John's interest is not in *a* son, but in *the* Son.[72] And He "abideth for ever" in the sense of eternal existence. It is because He is what He is that He can give the freedom of which He speaks.[73] He has His rights, and they concern a heavenly, not merely an earthly home. Because He is what He is He is able to give real freedom.[74] It is possible that we have here an allusion to I Chron. 17 : 13f., "I will be his father, and he shall be my son ... I will settle him in my house and in my kingdom for ever; and his throne shall be established for ever."[75] If so there is a hint at Christ's high majesty, as well as His rights in the house.

37 Jesus concedes their claim to be of Abraham's line. But over against that He sets their attempt to kill Him, which stamps them as being of another spirit than Abraham (*cf.* Luke 3 : 8). The reason for their hostility is given in terms of Jesus' "word", *i.e.* His whole message (*cf.* v. 31), which finds no place in them (or perhaps, among them). They have no room for it.[76] Religious privilege does not guarantee a right attitude to the things of God.

38 There is a series of contrasts in this verse. Jesus is set over against the Jews, "seen" stands over against "heard", His Father

---

[72] John, of course, habitually uses υἱός of Christ, not the believer (for whom he prefers τέκνον). *Cf.* Heb. 3 : 5 for a contrast between Moses as a servant *(θεράπων)* and Christ as the Son of the house.

[73] This is another example of John's rare use of οὖν in speeches of Jesus (see on 6 : 62). It is *because* it is the Son who frees that they will indeed be free.

[74] ὄντως occurs here only in John. Westcott sees it as appearing to express "reality in essence from within, as distinguished from reality as seen and known *(ἀληθῶς...)*".

[75] S. Aalen takes this allusion as "something beyond doubt" (*NTS*, VIII, 1961–62, p. 237).

[76] The verb χωρεῖ, often transitive (as in 2 : 6), is here used intransitively. Tasker rejects the translation "hath not free course in you" and says: "The meaning, however, is not that these Jews have received the word but not allowed it to make progress, but that they have never really made room for it at all."

against theirs,[77] His speaking against their doing.[78] Jesus insists, as always, that His message is derivative. It is from the Father. He has unclouded vision of God and He speaks accordingly of the things He has seen in Him. They by contrast have no vision. They are children of darkness. But they have heard certain things from their father, and these are the things they do. "Speak" and "do" are both continuous tenses. Jesus is referring to His consistent message and their persistent practice. This assumes that ARV has translated correctly. But "do" might also be an imperative. In this case we must take "Father" in both parts of the verse as referring to God. Jesus is then enjoining His opponents to do what the heavenly Father tells them. This, while not an impossible understanding of the text, seems to me out of harmony with the general drift. It does away with several of the contrasts of the verse and is not the natural understanding of the Greek.[79]

39, 40 Their reply is to reiterate their relationship to Abraham, This is a little strange, since Jesus admitted that (v. 37). But probably they discern in His latest words an assertion that they have another kinship, a spiritual kinship, which negates their physical descent from the great patriarch. Abraham was called "the Friend of God" (*cf.* Isa. 41 : 8 *etc.*, and for Moses, Exod. 33 : 11), and the Jews are implying that they are aligned with him and are also friends of God. Jesus' reply is that deeds count for more than impressive ancestry (*cf.* Luke 3 : 8; Rom. 9 : 6f.).

---

[77] ὑμῶν is read after τοῦ πατρός by ℵ CKΘ f1 f13 *etc.*, but is to be omitted with P66, P75, BLW Or *etc.* Hellenistic Greek proliferates personal pronouns, but sometimes the New Testament follows classical usage by employing only the article. This does not lead to ambiguity. In this verse, for example, there is no suggestion that Jesus' Father is identical with the father of the Jews. The whole sentence structure seems to show that there is a contrast, not an identity. Moulton argues from the absence of a possessive pronoun that "*the* Father" (*i.e.* God) is meant (M, I, p. 85), but this scarcely seems evidence enough.

[78] There is also a contrast of cases, παρὰ τῷ Πατρί of God, and παρὰ τοῦ πατρός of the devil. Abbott sees a contrast "between the distinctness with which the Son 'sees' the things *in* the House of the Father and the indistinctness with which men receive promptings *from* the invisible, whether for good or for evil" (2359).

[79] For the rare use of οὖν in the words of Jesus see on 6 : 62. Abbott argues that this particle here means "that there is a *correspondence* between the conduct of Christ and that of His persecutors. They are as consistent in evil as He in good" (2194).

If they were Abraham's children they would do the kind of deeds that Abraham did.[80] These deeds are summed up in their attempt to kill Jesus. Their murder plot arises out of their fundamental hostility to God.[81] At this point He characterizes Himself as "a man[82] that hath told you the truth". Truth receives a good deal of emphasis in this chapter (see on v. 32). And, as is characteristic, Jesus roots His message in God. He is not enunciating truth of Himself. The truth He speaks to them He first heard from God. Abraham's conduct was not that of His descendants.

41 Jesus repeats that His enemies do the works of their father, but again He does not say who this father is. It is plain, both from this verse and from v. 38, that He is thinking of someone other than Abraham, but in neither place is this explicit. The implication in both places is that their evil deeds are the result of their paternity. There is a family likeness. It is possible to take "Ye do" as imperative ("Do") and to understand "your father" as God. But this involves the idea that the Jews know what His works are and this scarcely seems consistent with the context (cf. v. 43; their whole failure to recognize Jesus as sent by God shows that they do not know the ways of God). It is better to take the verb as indicative and "your father" as referring to the devil. In v. 44 it is explicitly said that their father is the devil and it would be perverse to understand this verse differently. They answer that they were not born "of fornication" (Moffatt: "We are no bastards"). This is a very curious response. They may be reviling

---

[80] Both the text and the interpretation are difficult. In the first clause the verb is certainly ἐστε though ἦτε is read in some MSS. The big difficulty is whether to read in the second clause ποιεῖτε with P66 B* 700 lat syrˢ, ἐποιεῖτε with P75 (vid) ℵ*DWΘ 070 13 22 28 etc., or even, ἐποιεῖτε ἄν with ℵᶜ C KL. Grammatically we should expect either ἐστε ... ποιεῖτε, or ἦτε ... ἐποιεῖτε ἄν. Transcriptional probability accordingly favors ἐστε ... ἐποιεῖτε, for there would be every temptation to scribes to alter this, and each of the other readings is explicable on this basis. As there is really good MSS attestation it seems that this is the reading we should accept. The meaning then will be "If you are ... you would do. ..." If we were to read ποιεῖτε it would be possible to take it as imperative. But the indicative is more likely. The following νῦν δέ would perhaps also accord better with an indicative.

[81] Dods paraphrases: "this has not only the guilt of an ordinary murder, but your hostility is roused against me because I have spoken to you the truth I heard from God. It is murder based upon hostility to God."

[82] For John's use of "man" with respect to Jesus see on 4 : 29.

Jesus. While they would not have given countenance to the Christian doctrine of the Virgin Birth, the Jews may well have known that there was something strange about the birth of Jesus, and have chosen to allude to it in this way.[83] Their emphatic "we" sets them over against someone else who they imply was born this way. By contrast with the unfortunate manner of birth of which they speak they maintain that they themselves are children of God. They dimly perceive the drift of Jesus' discourse. He was not speaking of physical paternity when He spoke of their father. They apparently now realize this, and proceed to claim the highest spiritual paternity. Not only are they Abraham's seed, but, they say, in spiritual things they are closely related to God. Their spiritual, as their physical, descent is impeccable (*cf.* Knox: "God, and he only, is the Father we recognize"). Alternatively it is possible to take the words in the sense often found in the Old Testament, where the forsaking of Jehovah is frequently likened to fornication or adultery. The Jews would then be asserting that they are not apostate, that they retain a firm hold on true religion.[84]

42 The form of the conditional denies both propositions. "If God were your Father (as He is not), you would love me (as you do not)". Jesus finds evidence for this in their attitude to Him. He came out from[85] God (the tense points to a moment of time, the incarnation) and has come (this time the tense indicates a continuing state). His was not a self-originated mission. It was the

---

[83]   There was, of course, a Jewish slander that Jesus was born out of wedlock (see the passages cited in R. Travers Herford, *Christianity in Talmud and Midrash*, London, 1903, pp. 35ff.), though, as far as our information goes, it was later than this.

[84]   Odeberg sees this as the explanation: "The Jews are blind to J's (*i.e.* Jesus') Divine origin: this shows that they are directed away from God's world to the world of 'another one'. Quite naturally such an utterance would to a Rabbinic mind imply an accusation of idolatry ... Thence the vehemence of their retort: 'We be not born of fornication, we have *one* Father, even God' " (*FG*, p. 302; in a footnote he explains further, "Fornication is the Rabbinic as well as O.T. simile for idolatry").

[85]   The preposition is ἐκ which denotes origin. Dodd sees a distinction from οὐδὲ γὰρ ἀπ' ἐμαυτοῦ ἐλήλυθα, for ἀπό expresses no more than mission: "Christ's coming was not initiated by Himself – He came, not ἀπ' ἐμαυτοῦ but ἀπὸ τοῦ θεοῦ, since the Father sent Him; but not only so – He had His origin in the being of the Father" (*IFG*, p. 259). This may well be the meaning, but we must bear in mind John's penchant for slight variations in vocabulary without real difference of meaning (see on 3 : 5).

Father[86] that sent Him (see on 3 : 17). Once more we get this concept of mission. John is full of it. There is the thought of dependence. **43** Everything in this verse depends on the contrast between "speech" and "word".[87] The former term will denote the form of expression, the outward shape of the discourse. The latter signifies rather its content. Rieu renders, "Why do you not understand my language? Because you cannot comprehend my thought." It is a constant charge that the Jews do not hear Christ's teaching. They are so wrapped up in their preconceptions that they cannot perceive its truth. It repels them. *Cf.* Phillips: "you cannot bear to hear what I am really saying." And, because the essential content is alien to them, they do not understand the discourse in which the message is set forth. But Jesus is speaking basically of spiritual incomprehension, not of any failure of intellect. The Jews take no notice of what Jesus says because they have no notion of what He stands for. This has to be borne in mind in interpreting the frequent misunderstandings of Jesus recorded in this Gospel. If there is a lack of sympathy and comprehension of the basic position then all manner of details will inevitably be misunderstood. **44** Now comes Jesus' explicit assertion of the kinship of His enemies with Satan. He has previously hinted at it, but now He affirms it in set terms. They take their origin from the devil their father.[88] Consequently they set their will on doing his evil desires. They voluntarily choose to do His will. "To do" is continuous and points to an attitude. Their difficulty was not primarily intellectual, but spiritual. The word rendered "lusts" may on occasion denote good desires (*e.g.* I Thess. 2 : 17), but this is rare in the New Testament. The basic idea is that of very strong desire, and usually of strong desire directed in the wrong way. Here it is plainly evil desire. Specifically Jesus has charged them with trying to murder Him (v. 40; *cf.* 7 : 25), and indeed, has said that in the end they will succeed (v. 28). This He puts down to Satan's proclivity for this kind of thing. "From the beginning" will possibly refer to the murder of Abel (*cf.* I John 3 : 12), more probably to the fact that it was through Satan that Adam became mortal (Rom. 5 : 12ff.; *cf.* Wis. 2 : 24). Satan thus became the murderer

---

[86] "He" is the emphatic ἐκεῖνος, for which see on 1 : 8.
[87] λαλιά and λόγος.
[88] ἐκ denotes origin here as it does in vv. 23, 42. For εἶναι ἐκ see on 3 : 31.

of the whole human race. Though the devil existed before that time men did not, so there was no opportunity for him to show himself as a "man-killer". Once again there is a reference to truth.[89] Truth is associated with God and with Christ. Satan has no interest in them or in their truth. His habitat is falsehood.[90] When he speaks a lie he is at home.[91] That is what we expect from him. Basically he is a liar, and the father of lying.[92] Therefore those who live in a false way, as Jesus' opponents were doing, do but reflect their kinship with the devil. There is a change of tense in this verse. Satan was from the beginning a murderer, and was not standing in the truth. But then comes "there is no truth in him". That is his present and continuing characteristic.[93]

[89] Of the devil it is said, $οὐκ\ ἕστηκεν$, i.e. he was not standing fast in the truth. The smooth breathing is to be noted. It will point us to the imperfect of $στήκω$ rather than the perfect of $ἵστημι$, and thus to the meaning "he was not standing fast" rather than "he does not stand".

[90] Canon Harold Blair points to this passage as indicating that the fundamental sin is not so much pride, as is often asserted, as falsehood (*The Ladder of Temptations*, London, 1960, p. 79).

[91] $ἐκ\ τῶν\ ἰδίων\ λαλεῖ$ = "he speaks from his own family" or "he speaks from his own things" according as we take $ἰδίων$ to be masculine or neuter. ARV, "he speaketh of his own", is not a very natural rendering and is liable to be misunderstood as though it meant "he speaks about his own". $ἐκ$, of course, does not have this meaning. The meaning is somewhat like that of Matt. 12 : 34, "out of the abundance of the heart the mouth speaketh" where we also have $ἐκ$. $ὅταν\ λαλῇ$ earlier in the verse points to simultaneous action. Whenever he speaks the lie, at that very time he shows himself to be. . . ."

[92] This seems the probable meaning of $αὐτοῦ$. Torrey finds support for this view in the Aramaic: " 'Liar' was *b'el sh'qar*, 'master of falsehood'; which explains the pronoun, 'The father of *it*,' at the end of the verse." It is possible to take the expression to mean, "he is a liar and so is his father" from which some scholars conclude that there is a reference to the Gnostic idea that the God of the Old Testament was the father of the devil. But there is no real reason for seeing an allusion to such speculations, let alone an acceptance of them. Scripture never refers to such a being as Satan's father. There are those who hold that we should understand "anyone" as the subject of $λαλῇ$, with the meaning, "whenever anyone speaks . . . he is a liar and so is his father (*i.e.* the devil)." It is not at all certain that this is grammatically permissible, but in any case it is simpler to take $αὐτοῦ$ as referring to the thing that is false. Others again take the meaning to be that the devil is a liar and the father of the liar. Again this is possible, but it does not seem as probable as the meaning adopted.

[93] The Qumran Scrolls oppose "the spirit of truth" to "the spirit of error" (IQS, iii, 19). The former expression is found very rarely outside these scrolls and John, which is one of the pieces of evidence pointing to a connection of some sort (see on 14 : 17). John does not have the other expression, "the spirit of error", but this verse shows that he thinks of Satan as diametrically opposed to truth.

45 This essential relationship of His foes with the devil and that of the devil with falsity made it impossible for the Jews to believe Jesus. He and they were in opposite camps. They had opposed presuppositions. Notice that He says, "because"[94] not, "*although* I say the truth". They being what they were, it was not to be expected that they would respond to the truth.

46 The hollowness of their attitude is exposed. The first part of the verse is a staggering assertion of sinlessness and they do not take it up. We are often so interested in the fact that they found no charge to lay that we overlook that other fact that the really striking thing is the making of the challenge.[95] It betokens a clear and serene conscience. Only one who was in the closest and most intimate communion with the Father could have spoken such words. It is impossible to envisage any other figure in history making such a claim. In the light of their inability to point to any sin at all in Him their continuing failure to believe in Him is shown for the sham it was. If there was no sin, then He was indeed speaking the truth, and if He was speaking the truth then they should have believed.

47 Jesus gives the answer to His own questions. A man must be "of God" really to hear "the words of God".[96] His opponents are not "of God". He has already pointed out that they are of their father the devil (v. 44). And because they lack the necessary kinship with heaven they do not heed the things He says.

---

[94] For causal ὅτι see on 1 : 50.

[95] *Cf.* Godet: "The *perfect* holiness of Christ is proved in this passage, not by the silence of the Jews, who might very well have ignored the sins of their interlocutor, but by the assurance with which Jesus lays this question before them. Without the immediate consciousness which Christ had of the perfect purity of His life, and on the supposition that He was only a more holy man than other men, a moral sense so delicate as that which such a state would imply, would not have suffered the least stain to pass unnoticed, either in His life, or in His heart; and what hypocrisy would there not have been in this case in addressing to others a question with the aim of causing them to give it a different answer from that which, in His inmost heart, He gave Himself!"

[96] *Cf.* Barclay: "it is quite possible that a man may lack the something essential which will enable him to have the experience. A man who is tone deaf cannot ever experience the thrill of music. A man who is colour blind cannot ever appreciate a picture ... unless the spirit of God is in a man's heart he *cannot* recognize God's truth when he sees it."

(e) The Glory the Father gives the Son, 8 : 48–59

48 The Jews answered and said unto him, Say we not well
that thou art a Samaritan, and hast a demon? 49 Jesus
answered, I have not a demon; but I honor my Father, and
ye dishonor me. 50 But I seek not mine own glory: there is
one that seeketh and judgeth. 51 Verily, verily, I say unto
you, If a man keep my word, he shall never see death. 52
The Jews said unto him, Now we know that thou hast a
demon. Abraham died, and the prophets; and thou sayest,
If a man keep my word, he shall never taste of death. 53 Art
thou greater than our father Abraham, who died? and the
prophets died: whom makest thou thyself? 54 Jesus answered,
If I glorify myself, my glory is nothing: it is my Father that
glorifieth me; of whom ye say, that he is your God; 55 and
ye have not known him: but I know him; and if I should
say, I know him not, I shall be like unto you, a liar: but
I know him, and keep his word. 56 Your father Abraham
rejoiced [1] to see my day; and he saw it, and was glad. 57 The
Jews therefore said unto him, Thou art not yet fifty years
old, and hast thou seen Abraham? 58 Jesus said unto them,
Verily, verily, I say unto you, before Abraham was born,
I am. 59 They took up stones therefore to cast at him:
but Jesus [2] hid himself, and went out of the temple[3].

[1]Or, *that he should see* [2]Or, *was hidden, and went &c.* [3]Many ancient authorities add *and going through the midst of them went his way and so passed by.*

John brings this section of his Gospel to its close by leading
up to a resounding climax – Jesus' claim to deity. This is recognized
by the Jews for what it is and rejected with decision. The logical
result is their attempt to stone Him. But John has always before him
the thought that no harm can come to Jesus until His "hour" is come.
So He was concealed from them, and went away from the temple.

48 The Jews remain totally unconvinced by what Jesus says.
Their accusation that He was a Samaritan is somewhat puzzling.[97]
But clearly it points to a laxity, as they would see it, in the observance of the tenets of Judaism. Possibly they have in mind Jesus'
failure to observe the traditions of the elders. In their view this

---

[97] Some see a reference to Samaritans like Simon Magus and Dositheus,
but these are too late. Hoskyns thinks that II Kings 17 : 24ff. could naturally
be interpreted of unions between Gentiles and Israelite women and that the
Jews are thus contrasting their legitimate birth with "the irregularity of the
birth of Jesus". This seems to be reading a good deal into the words.

is being disloyal to the faith. He is observing only those parts of
their religion which the heretical Samaritans observed and is thus
to be classed with them. Or His refusal to agree with the Jews
that they had an exclusive right to be called Abraham's children
may be the point (*cf.* vv. 39f.). The Samaritans disputed this
with some vigour, and Jesus' enemies may be saying "You are
no better than a Samaritan!"[98] "Say we not well . . ." appears to
indicate that this is a standing accusation, but we have no information about its being levelled on any previous occasion.[99] The
charge of demon possession is found in 7 : 20; 8 : 52; 10 : 20. It
is also reported in the Synoptic Gospels, where it is regarded as
particularly heinous, being linked with the unforgivable sin (Matt.
12 : 24ff.; Mark 3 : 22ff.; *cf.* Matt. 9 : 34; 11 : 18, *etc.*).

49 Jesus ignores the charge that He is a Samaritan (which in
any case probably counted for less to Him than it did to them),
and quietly denies that He has a demon. Against this He sets the
contrasting thought[100] that it is His practice to honor His Father,
which, of course, is as far removed from demon possession as is
possible. With that is to be taken the fact that they are dishonoring
Him. Rieu's "you insult me" appears to be too strong. Jesus is
saying that He gives honor where it is due while they do not.
This failure on their part is the reason why they make such erroneous statements.

---

[98] Edersheim thought that the word may have been misunderstood. *Shomroni*,
he says, means "Samaritan", but it is also used as the equivalent of '*Ashmedai*',
a name of the chief of the demons. "Samaritan" on this view means much the
same as "hast a demon" (*LT*, II, pp. 174f.). This would be supported by the
fact that Jesus refuted the charge that He was demon-possessed but said nothing
about being a Samaritan. It is an attractive hypothesis, but the evidence for
this use of *Shomroni* does not appear to be early enough to carry complete
conviction. Matthew Black thinks that "the word 'Samaritan' had become
practically equivalent in meaning to 'schismatic' or 'heretic', and appears to
have passed almost as a term of abuse" (*The Scrolls and Christian Origins*, London,
1961, p. 70).

[99] There is a passage in the Talmud which says, "It has been reported,
If one has learnt Scripture and Mishnah but did not attend upon Rabbinical
scholars, R. Eleazar says he is an '*Am ha-arez*; R. Samuel b. Naḥmani says he
is a boor; R. Jannai says he is a Samaritan" (*Sot.* 22a; Soncino edn., pp. 109f.).
It is just barely possible that there is a connection with 7 : 15 where it is mentioned that Jesus had never learnt in the schools.

[100] Jesus sets Himself and His opponents in contrast with ἐγώ and ὑμεῖς.
Note also the strong adversative ἀλλά, which sets the thought of His honoring
the Father in strong opposition to their suggestion of demon possession.

50 Immediately Jesus goes on to disclaim self-seeking. His words just spoken might perhaps be misinterpreted as meaning that He sought glory for Himself. This was not His aim at all. He reminds them that there is One that seeks. In this context this must mean "seeks glory". Jesus is not concerned that men should give Him the glory that is His due. God is looking after that. God seeks out the glory that men bestow, and not only seeks what they do, but judges it. Jesus' hearers may act as though they are supreme and dispense justice. Actually they are men under judgment. It is therefore not a matter indifferent where they give glory. God searches out what they do and judges accordingly. Notice the present tense. As elsewhere in this Gospel, judgment is regarded as a present process. There is possibly some of John's irony here. The Jews were continually "seeking" Jesus in their mistaken zeal for God's glory, and their seeking was aimed at, and would ultimately issue in, Jesus' death (5 : 18; 7 : 1, 19, 25, 30; 8 : 37, 40; 10 : 31, 39; 11 : 8; 18 : 3). But in a deeper sense the real seeking was done by God. And He sought not the treatment of Jesus which the Jews sought, but His glory. Further, this seeking of His means judgment for those men who, for all their zeal, are so hopelessly opposed to God's purposes. A further ironical touch is seen in the fact that while the Jews sought the death of Jesus, this when it was eventually accomplished would turn out to be His real glory.
51 Now comes the climax of this short speech as the solemn "Verily, verily" (see on 1 : 51) shows. As earlier in this chapter, "word" signifies the whole of Jesus' message (vv. 31, 37, 43). There is some emphasis on "my".[101] The Jews are ready to classify Him as a demon-possessed Samaritan. Yet it is His word that a man must keep[102] if he is to enter into life. Jesus chooses to put

---

[101] The expression is τὸν ἐμὸν λόγον. John's normal habit is to place the possessive after the noun with a repeated article, as in v. 43 (and in *v.l.* here). The form here is much less common and appears to be used for the purpose of adding emphasis. For John's use of possessives see on 3 : 29.

[102] Calvin puts emphasis on this verb: "Therefore in this passage, Christ promises eternal life to His disciples, but demands disciples who will not merely nod their assents like donkeys, or profess with the tongue that they approve His teaching, but who will keep it as a precious treasure." The verb is used in this Gospel 18 times, in I John 7 times, and in Revelation 11 times, while no other book of the New Testament has it more often than Acts with 8 times. This is accounted for very largely by the emphasis in all the Johannine writings on keeping the commandments of God or of Christ. A minority of passages in all three speaks of God or Christ as keeping believers.

His statement into the negative form "he shall never see death". "Death" is in an emphatic position: "Death he will not see". This is possibly occasioned by the preceding thought that the Jews are under judgment. The outcome of this judgment is death for such as they. But death is not the lot of the man who keeps Jesus' message.[103] 52 The Jews think that their previous statements about Jesus are now proved. None but such as they held Him to be could make such statements. They point out that Abraham (and he the great forbear of the race) died. The prophets (the spiritual giants of the race) died. Yet in the face of these facts Jesus ("thou" is scornfully emphatic) says that keeping His "word" is the way to avoid death.[104] Obviously, their reasoning runs, this claim is something bigger than anything accomplished by the greatest of the ancients. It does not occur to them that therefore it is not necessarily false. 53 So they ask Jesus to reflect on the implications of His words. Their question is so framed as to look for the answer "No". This is another example of John's irony. The true situation is the very opposite of that presupposed by their words. Is He greater than Abraham who[105] died? And the prophets died. The use of the aorist tense in both clauses points to the actuality of these happenings. Death comes to all men and it came to these men. What

---

[103] Temple admits to some exaggeration when he translates "he shall not notice death". He explains that if a man's mind "is turned towards (Jesus') word it will not pay any attention to death; death will be to it irrelevant. It may truly be said that such a man will not 'experience' death, because, though it will happen to him, it will matter to him no more than the fall of a leaf from a tree under which he might be reading a book. It happens to him, but he does not in any full sense see or notice it." I think it better to interpret "death" here as spiritual death, but I cite this as a notable statement of the attitude of the believer to physical death.

[104] Note the small changes between what Jesus said and their report of His words – τὸν λόγον μου for τὸν ἐμὸν λόγον, γεύσηται for θεωρήσῃ and θανάτου in a less emphatic position than θάνατον. Probably these changes are not significant as John often has small changes when sayings are repeated (see on 3 : 5). Abbott, however, refers "seeing" death to spiritual death and "tasting of" death to physical death (2576).

[105] There is probably point in the use of the relative of quality ὅστις (here only in this Gospel; the neuter occurs a number of times). It brings out the truth that Abraham (and by inference all men, even the greatest) was of such a quality as to die. BDF sees this as an example of ὅστις correctly used "with reference to a definite person where the relative clause expresses the general quality . . .' who nevertheless was a man who died' " (293).

then does it mean to say that Jesus can deliver other men from death? Clearly it means a claim to superhuman power. They imply that to expose the claim for what it is is to show it to be impossible of fulfilment. They do not face the fact that Jesus is aware of the implications and still makes the claim. It is worth noticing that the Jews constantly accuse Jesus of "making" Himself divine (5 : 18; 10 : 33; 19 : 7). But this Gospel stresses Jesus' continual dependence on the Father (5 : 19, *etc.*). He is aware of His high dignity, but speaks of it in terms of obedience and service. He does not see dignity as enhanced or even brought out by the making of exaggerated claims.

54 For the moment Jesus leaves Abraham and returns to the thought of glory. If He were to glorify Himself (which He has just disclaimed, v. 50) that would be nothing. All self-glorification is to be discounted. But that does not mean that Jesus is not glorified. The Father glorifies Him. The Jews are attempting to make nothing of Jesus. Before dealing specifically with the case of Abraham which they have raised Jesus points out that He is not without His glory. But it is God-given, not self-given. He speaks of God as "my Father", and then differentiates His relationship from theirs by pointing out that Him whom He calls "Father" they call not "Father" but "God".[106]

55 And yet He is not really their God at all. They have not known Him. This probably includes the thoughts that they have never known Him in the past and that they do not know Him in the present. In this their case is different from that of Jesus. He really does know Him (see on 4 : 18), and to say otherwise would be to reduce Himself to the class of liars to which they belong. In their case it means saying that they know God whereas in fact they do not. In His it would be the opposite error, but error for all that. Facts must be faced. Jesus does more than know Him. He keeps His word. That is to say He acts in accordance with all that God has revealed of Himself.

56 Now Jesus returns to the case of Abraham on which they built so much. Abraham, so far from being opposed to Jesus,

---

[106] This is so even if we read ἡμῶν (P75 A B² WΘ) and not ὑμῶν (ℵ B* D; G. D. Fee shows that P66 supports this reading, *JBL*, LXXXIV, 1965, p. 69). The significant thing is the noun rather than the possessive.

rejoiced at His "day".[107] Notice that Abraham is characterized as "your father". His relationship to the Jews is noticed at the same time as His joy in Christ is brought out. The Jews were being false to their great ancestor. Their reliance on Abraham was baseless. "Rejoiced" is a wholehearted word, and signifies something like "exulted", "was overjoyed".[108] There are two points to be considered here – the occasion of Abraham's rejoicing and the meaning of Christ's "day". Taking the latter first, "my day" is not defined. Elsewhere "the day of Christ" points to the second coming and to final judgment (Phil. 1 : 10; 2 : 16). Here a reference to the incarnation is more probable. The whole of Christ's work for men seems in mind. The occasion of Abraham's rejoicing is difficult. Some take it as present, and think of Abraham as rejoicing in Paradise over Christ's work on earth. This, however, ignores the use of the past tenses (*cf.* the similar statement about Isaiah which is definitely located in the prophet's lifetime, 12 : 41). The rejoicing must be taken as occurring in Abraham's lifetime. There are various possibilities suggested by Jewish thought about Abraham, though it should be noted that the Rabbis were more concerned about Abraham's foresight of later events than about his rejoicing. Thus some apparently pointed to the promise, "in thee shall all the families of the earth be blessed" (Gen. 12 : 3), and held that Abraham then rejoiced at the prospect of the Messiah being born from his descendants.[109] Others concentrated on the vision of Genesis 15, thinking that Abraham then foresaw the future of the nation, and thus of Messiah.[110] A view which seems to involve misinterpretation of Scripture saw in the laughter of Gen. 17 : 17 not incredulity but happiness that the birth of this

---

[107] ἵνα ἴδῃ is difficult for ἵνα seems to have no telic force. Abbott thinks that "this exultant and ecstatic belief was a gift from God *with a view to* (ἵνα) the fulfilment of divine purpose" and he cites Rom. 4 : 18 (2689). BDF prefers the meaning, "he longed with desire, rejoiced that he was to . . ." (392(1a); *cf.* RSV, "rejoiced that he was to . . ."). Moule sees it as denoting content (*IBNTG*, pp. 145f.), and this seems the preferable view.

[108] ἠγαλλιάσατο.

[109] Barclay gives this as a Jewish interpretation though he does not cite authorities. Wright adopts it as his understanding of this verse.

[110] SBk cite R. Eleazar and R. Nathan and others for views of this type (II, pp. 525f.).

child would lead on to God's Chosen One.[111] And there is a very curious piece of Rabbinic exegesis in connection with Gen. 24 : 1, "Abraham was . . . well stricken in age", which is literally "gone into the days". This was understood to mean that Abraham entered into all the days of the future.[112] Though much of this seems fanciful to us it shows that among the Jews the idea that Abraham looked forward to the day of the Messiah and rejoiced in it was not strange. We cannot, however, feel confidence in any of the proposed occasions, and it may be significant that Jesus does not specifically refer to any.[113] In other words He may well mean that Abraham's general attitude to this day was one of exultation, rather than refer to any one specific occasion in the life of the patriarch.

57 The Jews' incredulity breaks out in a reference to the age of Jesus. A man not yet fifty years old could not have seen Abraham, they imply. It is curious that they use the number "fifty". Luke tells us that Jesus was "about thirty years of age" (Luke 3 : 23) at the beginning of His ministry and all the indications are that the ministry occupied no more than about three years. It is not likely that John is presenting us with another tradition as to the age of Jesus.[114] More probably fifty is thought of as a good age, possibly as the completion of a man's working life and the entrance on to old age. It is the age at which the Levites completed their service (Num. 4 : 3). Or it may be meant to contrast one short life-time with the centuries that had elapsed since Abraham's day. In any case we must bear in mind Lagrange's reminder that they thought of Jesus as being out of His mind. They were certainly not

---

[111] Jubilees 16 : 19 says that Abraham and Sarah rejoiced "with exceeding great joy" at the prospect of Isaac's birth. Philo sees joy in the very name Isaac, which name "is that of the best of the good emotions, joy, the Isaac who is the laughter of the heart, a son of God" (*De Mutat. Nom.*, 131). Eb. Nestle pointed out that the Targum on Gen. 17 : 17 renders Heb. צחק "to laugh" "not by הוך, *laugh*, as in 18[12.13.15] 19,[14] but by חדי, to rejoice, to be *glad;* likewise in 21[9]" (*ExT*, XX, 1908–09, p. 477).

[112] SBk cite *Tanch. B* for this view *(loc. cit.)*.

[113] *Cf.* Lagrange: "Jésus n'argumente pas le livre à la main et ne cite ici aucun texte."

[114] Strachan thinks that "the words suggest His youthfulness. The Jewish objectors interpret Jesus' reply prosaically and ironically as meaning that Abraham had actually seen one who still had his reputation to make, and was as yet undistinguished."

discussing his age with any precision accordingly. They simply gave good measure.[115] Jesus was still a young man. He could not claim even to be one of the elders. How then could He possibly have seen Abraham? Notice that the Jews do not repeat Jesus exactly. He speaks of Abraham seeing His day, they of His seeing Abraham.
58 So we reach the climactic point in this chapter with Jesus' magnificent affirmation, "before Abraham was born, I am". John began his Gospel by speaking of the pre-existence of the Word. This statement does not go further than that. It could not. But it brings out the meaning of pre-existence in more striking fashion. Before the great patriarch, who lived centuries before, Jesus' existence went on. His "Verily, verily" marks this out as an important and emphatic statement (see on 1 : 51). Whether we translate "before Abraham was" (as AV), or "was born" (as ARV, NEB, etc.) the meaning will be "came into existence", as the aorist tense indicates. A mode of being which has a definite beginning is contrasted with one which is eternal. "I am" must have the fullest significance it can bear. It is, as we have already had occasion to notice (see on vv. 24, 28) in the style of deity.[116] It is not easy to render into Greek the Hebrew underlying passages like Exod. 3 : 14. The LXX translators did so with the use of the form we have here.[117] It is an emphatic form of speech and one that would not normally be employed in ordinary speech. Thus to use it was recognizably to adopt the divine style.[118] In passages like vv. 24,

---

[115] Chrysostom reads: "thou art not yet forty years old" (LV. 2; p. 198). Irenaeus argues that Jesus must have been over forty, for had he been less they would have said "thou art not yet forty years old" (*Adv. Haer.* II, 22. 6).

[116] ἐγώ εἰμι in LXX renders the Hebrew אֲנִי הוּא which is the way God speaks (*cf.* Deut. 32 : 39; Isa. 41 : 4; 43 : 10; 46 : 4, *etc.*). The Hebrew may carry a reference to the meaning of the divine name יהוה (*cf.* Exod. 3 : 14). We should almost certainly understand John's use of the term to reflect that in the LXX. It is the style of deity, and it points to the eternity of God according to the strictest understanding of the continuous nature of the present εἰμι. He continually IS. *Cf.* Abbott: "taken here, along with other declarations about what Jesus IS, it seems to call upon the Pharisees to believe that the Son of man is not only the Deliverer but also one with the Father in the unity of the Godhead" (2228).

[117] LXX has 'Εγώ εἰμι ὁ ὤν for the Hebrew rendered "I am that I am" in Exod. 3 : 14, ARV; and ὁ ὤν for "I am" in the last clause of the verse.

[118] "That is a supreme claim to Deity; perhaps the most simple and sublime of all the things He said with that great formula of old, the great 'I AM' . . . These are the words of the most impudent blasphemer that ever spoke, or the words of God incarnate" (Morgan).

28 this is fairly plain, but in the present passage it is unmistakable. When Jesus is asserting His existence in the time of Abraham there is no other way of understanding it.[119] It should also be observed that He says "I am", not "I was". It is eternity of being and not simply being which has lasted through several centuries that the expression indicates.

59 The Jews could interpret this as nothing other than blasphemy. Therefore they took up stones to stone Him, this being the proper punishment for that offence (Lev. 24 : 16). In their angry state they felt that there was no other course. They could, of course, have chosen to proceed by legal means. This would have meant trying Jesus on this count and stoning Him only when He was duly sentenced by a proper authority.[120] But their passions were aroused. They were incensed. So they took the law into their own hands. Incidentally we should notice that the reason they found stones ready to hand in the temple area is likely to be that building operations were still in progress. "Hid himself" is really a passive "was hidden".[121] John is perhaps hinting that God protected His Son. It is not so much that Jesus by superior cleverness was able to conceal Himself from them. It was rather that He was concealed by Another, and so passed out of the temple. It may well be that we are to discern a symbolism in this action. "At this point Jesus symbolically abandons his own people (the temple) and goes out to humanity (the man born blind; chap. 9)" (MacGregor).

---

[119] E. Stauffer has an important examination of the I AM formula in *Jesus and His Story* (London, 1960), pp. 142–159. The mention of Abraham, he thinks, "recalls the insertion of the figure of Abraham in God's speeches in the rabbinic Targum on Isa. 40–55. This is certainly not an accident. It agrees with the evangelist's report that the opponents only at this point grasp the monstrous meaning and claim of Jesus' ANI HU – and at once set about to do away with the blasphemer by stoning him on the spur of the moment" (*op. cit.*, p. 154). Of the I AM formula he says, "It is Jesus' boldest declaration about himself. 'I AM'. This means: *where I am, there is God, there God lives, speaks, calls, asks, acts, decides, loves, chooses, forgives, rejects, hardens, suffers, dies*. Nothing bolder can be said, or imagined" (*op. cit.*, p. 159). See also N. Walker, *ZATW*, 74, 1962, pp. 205f.

[120] The difficulty in the way of carrying out the sentence even if it were imposed by a Jewish court would also have been a deterrent. *Cf.* 18 : 31 and note.

[121] The aorist passive ἐκρύβη is used in the sense of the middle in the LXX and most understand it so here. But the New Testament usage is rather to take the form as passive. *Amplified* renders, "Jesus by mixing with the crowd concealed Himself", but this is based on inferior manuscripts and in any case includes a large element of interpretation.

CHAPTER IX

16. THE SIXTH SIGN – HEALING THE MAN BORN BLIND, 9 : 1–41

It would not be true to say that there are no accounts of the healing of the blind in antiquity other than those of Jesus, but there are remarkably few in canonical scripture. There is no story of the giving of sight to the blind anywhere in the Old Testament. Nor is this function anywhere attributed to the followers of Jesus. The nearest we come to it is when Ananias laid hands on Saul of Tarsus and that Pharisee's temporary blindness disappeared (Acts 9 : 17f.). But this exceptional case is not on all fours with the giving of sight as Jesus gave it. There are more miracles of giving of sight to the blind recorded of Jesus than healings in any other category (see Matt. 9 : 27–31; 12 : 22f.; 15 : 30f.; 21 : 14; Mark 8 : 22–6; 10 : 46–52; Luke 7 : 21f.). In the Old Testament the giving of sight to the blind is associated with God Himself (Exod. 4 : 11; Ps. 146 : 8). It is also a messianic activity (Isa. 29 : 18; 35 : 5; 42 : 7), and this may be its significance in the New Testament. It is a divine function, a function for God's own Messiah, that Jesus fulfils when He gives sight to the blind. This chapter then has significance in John's plan for showing Jesus to be the Messiah.[1] This story has features all its own, notably in the character of the healed man. He is no lay figure, but a colorful personality with a mind of his own and a readiness to say what he thinks before the highest in the land if need be. His argument with the Pharisees is lively and very true to life. The narrative brings in the motif of judgment. Jesus is the Light of the world, and light is always in conflict with darkness. When

---

[1] Cullmann sees in the story a reference to baptism, but, as in the case of his other alleged references to the sacraments he proceeds by the way of dogmatic assertion rather than by that of adducing evidence. Indeed on this occasion he appears to realize this and says: "The opponents of the method of examination which we apply in this study to the Fourth Gospel will not fail to stress the questionable character of the observations made by us on this passage, and we can only repeat here that each detail taken by itself does not in fact amount to much" (*Early Christian Worship*, London, 1954, p. 105). Exactly. And nothing else that he says removes this impression.

men walk in darkness the coming of light always represents judgment. Indeed Jesus can say that He came "for judgment" (v. 39). This particular miracle was performed on the sabbath, which opened up the way for a controversy. There were those so firmly in the grip of darkness that they saw only a technical breach of their law and could not discern a spectacular victory of light over darkness.[2] They disputed with the man and in the process revealed their inward blindness. The incident takes us one step further in the dispute between Jesus and the authorities. In the end they take action against the healed man. Whether this is rightly understood as excommunication or not it marks the first definite action taken by way of persecution of Jesus' followers.

Jesus' method of dealing with the man is not to be overlooked. First He healed him, then He left him to debate the situation with the Pharisees, and only after they had taken disciplinary action against the man did Jesus approach him to deal with his spiritual need. The result was that the man came to believe (v. 38). In His ministry to the souls of men Jesus adopted no stereotyped approach. He dealt with each man as his peculiar need required.

(a) The Healing, 9 : 1–7

1 And as he passed by, he saw a man blind from his birth. 2 And his disciples asked him, saying, Rabbi, who sinned, this man, or his parents, that he should be born blind? 3 Jesus answered, Neither did this man sin, nor his parents: but that the works of God should be made manifest in him. 4 We must work the works of him that sent me, while it is day: the night cometh, when no man can work. 5 When I

---

[2] Barrett thinks that "This short chapter expresses perhaps more vividly and completely than any other John's conception of the work of Christ. On the one hand, he is the giver of benefits to a humanity which apart from him is in a state of complete hopelessness . . . The illumination is not presented as primarily intellectual (as in some of the Hermetic tractates) but as the direct bestowal of life or salvation . . . On the other hand, Jesus does not come into a world full of men aware of their own need. Many have their own inadequate lights . . . which they are too proud to relinquish for the true light which now shines. The effect of the true light is to blind them, since they wilfully close their eyes to it. Their sin abides precisely because they are so confident of their righteousness." Hoskyns acutely remarks "To become a Christian is not to recover what has been lost, but to receive a wholly new illumination".

am in the world, I am the light of the world. 6 When he had thus spoken, he spat on the ground, and made clay of the spittle, ¹and anointed his eyes with the clay, 7 and said unto him, Go, wash in the pool of Siloam (which is by interpretation, Sent). He went away therefore, and washed, and came seeing.

¹Or, and with the clay thereof anointed his eyes

There are unique features about this healing. The man is said to have been blind from birth, there is a discussion as to the reason for this, there are means used for the healing, namely spittle to make clay, and the washing in the pool of Siloam.

1 There is no time note. John does not relate this incident to others in his story and we are left to guess at its place in the sequence. Hoskyns says the incident took place on the last day of the Feast of Tabernacles, but this is pure assumption. It is likely that some time has elapsed since the attempt on Jesus' life (8 : 59), but more than this we cannot say. John simply tells us that Jesus passed by (where?) and saw a man blind from birth.³ Nothing is said as to how it was known that the man had been blind from birth, which argues that he was a well known figure. The Synoptic Gospels mention a number of cases of restoration of sight to the blind, but they do not include any mention of a man blind from birth. One might have expected some mention of the disciples, in view of the following question, but John appears to mean that it was Jesus who first took notice of the man. The initiative was His.

2 The man's plight provoked the disciples⁴ into asking Jesus the reason for it.⁵ It was widely held that suffering, and especially

---

3 τυφλὸν ἐκ γενετῆς signifies congenital blindness, but John may also have in mind the truth that from birth men are spiritually blind. The man blind from birth symbolizes every man. All men need the illumination that Christ alone can give. This is the only occurrence of γενετή in the New Testament.

4 For "his disciples" see on 2 : 2. The exact meaning of the term here is not clear. We do not read of Jesus' disciples as being with Him in chs. 7, 8. If the Twelve are meant, as seems probable, this is our first indication that they were with Him in Jerusalem. The alternative is to hold that there were followers of Jesus who lived in Jerusalem (cf. 7 : 3) and who were with Him on this occasion.

5 ἵνα here seems to express result, an unusual but not unparalleled use (see J. H. Greenlee in BT, 6, 1955, p. 14).

such a disaster as blindness, was due to sin. The general principle was laid down by R. Ammi: "There is no death without sin, and there is no suffering without iniquity."[6] The disciples evidently accepted this, but in the present case were perplexed as to the application of the dogma. There were grave difficulties in seeing how a man could have sinned before his birth.[7] And it is not much easier to think that a man should bear such a terrible punishment for the sin of his parents.[8] So the disciples put the matter to Jesus.

3 Jesus decisively rejects both alternatives.[9] Suffering is not always due to sin and this blindness is not the result of sin either in the man or in his parents. "But" marks a strong adversative. On the contrary, far from that. It happened[10] so that God's works might be shown in the man.[11] It is perhaps worth noticing the significance

---

[6] *Shab.* 55a (Soncino edn., p. 255). The latter point is proved from Ps. 89 : 33 (32).

[7] Yet the Rabbis did not find the difficulties insurmountable. SBk cite a few passages, mostly based on Gen. 25 : 22, which show that it was held that a child could sin in the womb (II, pp. 528f.). An alternative is to think of the soul as pre-existent (a belief which appears in Wis. 8 : 20), and as sinning in the pre-existent state. But views like this do not appear to have been held widely in Judaism.

[8] Yet the Rabbis held such things to be possible. There are sayings which speak of children as being born epileptic or leprous on account of the sins of their parents (SBk, II, p. 529). The untimely death of a scholar can be ascribed to his mother's dalliance with idolatry while pregnant with him (Ruth R., VI. 4; Soncino edn., p. 79).

[9] *I.e.* in this particular case. "Sin no more, lest a worse thing befall thee" (5 : 14) indicates that there are times when sin and suffering are connected.

[10] The construction is elliptical and it is not certain what should be supplied before ἵνα. It is usually taken as "but (he was born blind) that . . .", though it is quite possible to understand something like "but (all was ordained) that..." C. J. Cadoux thinks this is a possible example of the imperatival ἵνα with the meaning "but the works of God had to be made manifest . . . in his case" (*JThS*, XLII, 1941, p. 169). This however, is not an imperative, which would be rather, "let the works of God be made manifest", which does not seem correct. See further on 1 : 8 for this construction. Richardson sees the ἵνα as expressing result. It is, of course, possible to change the punctuation and read ". . . nor his parents. But that the works of God should be made manifest in him we must work the works of Him that sent me. . . ." Morgan, for example, adopts this punctuation. The construction seems to hint at the divine purpose, and it seems best to adopt one or other of the two first-mentioned suggestions.

[11] *Cf.* Brown: "Jesus was asked about the cause of the man's blindness, but he answers in terms of its purpose."

of the use of the term "works". What was to happen is to man a miracle, but to God no more than a normal "work" (see Additional Note G, pp. 684ff.).

4 Both "we"[12] and "must" are important. Jesus is not speaking only of what He must do. His followers share with Him the responsibility of doing what God directs (specifically Jesus has said that it is "the work of God" for men to believe on Him whom God sent, 6 : 29). And "must" reminds us that this is not simply what is advisable or expedient. There is the thought of a compelling necessity (see on 4 : 4, and for Jesus' obedience on 4 : 34). As happens so often in this Gospel God is characterized in terms of His sending of Jesus (see on 3 : 17). That is the critical event, and John does not let us lose sight of it. It is a reminder in this context also of the fact that the works in question do not originate here on earth. They are heaven-sent works that we must do. And there is an urgency about the doing of them, for the opportunity will not always be present. "The night cometh" speaks of the remorseless passage of time removing the present opportunity.[13]

5 There is particular appropriateness in Jesus doing the works of which He speaks and doing them while it is day because He is "the light of the world" (*cf.* 8 : 12).[14] For "light" see on 1 : 4.

---

[12] There are textual uncertainties but it seems that we should read ἡμᾶς with P66, P75, א* BDW Or *etc.* rather than ἐμέ אa A Θf1 f13 lat syrs. After πέμψαντος P66, P75, א* W* read ἡμᾶς but here the singular is to be preferred, with אaABCDΔΘf1 f13 *etc.* It would seem that the variants are different ways of removing the difficulty posed by the use of both plural and singular. For Jesus' associating others with Himself see on 3 : 11.

[13] Odeberg understands "night" to signify "the period beginning with the discursive judgement for those who, although having the possibility of seeing, condemn themselves to blindness because they do reject the light that comes to them" (*FG*, p. 312). This would accord well with John's use of "light" and "darkness". The difficulty is in seeing how this can be said to be coming. Jesus' statement envisages a time now when work may be done, followed by another time when it will be too late to work. Odeberg's view does not safeguard this thought.

[14] Westcott argues from the absence of an article with φῶς as compared with 8 : 12 that "Christ is 'light to the world' as well as 'the one light of the world'." But E. C. Colwell has shown that in the New Testament definite predicate nouns which precede the verb usually lack the article (see on 1 : 1) and that would cover this case. The expression will mean "the light of the world".

"When" is the indefinite "whenever".[15] It is a little strange to find this expression, and we might have expected something general as in 8 : 12. But here there is a sense of urgency, and Jesus may well be saying that the time of the incarnation is limited. His stay in this world is short. Therefore He must work quickly, and in accordance with His character as the world's light.

6 Jesus proceeds to cure the man. He chooses to do this by making clay of His spittle, putting it on the man's eyes[16] and bidding him wash it off.[17] Questions arise like "Why clay?" "Why spittle?" "Why wash in Siloam?" In most other cures Jesus wrought such things are not mentioned. It is known that the the ancient world often attributed curative powers to saliva.[18] And it may have helped this particular man to have something that he might do himself. But in any case Jesus performed His miracles with sovereign hand and He cannot be limited by rules of procedure. He cured how He willed. Mark once relates a cure in which Jesus "had spit on his eyes" and later laid His hands on the eyes (Mark 8 : 22–25), but there is no mention of clay there. Some of the patristic writers saw in the mention of clay a reference to Gen.

---

[15]   ὅταν. In a context like this the meaning will not be repetition or continuity, but coincidence of time: "during the time I am in the world". Plummer, however, says, "ὅταν is important; it shews the comprehensiveness of the statement. The Light shines at various times and in various degrees, whether the world chooses to be illuminated or not." Dods thinks ὅταν is used rather than ἕως to suggest a time when Jesus would not be in the world.

[16]   The meaning of αὐτοῦ before τὸν πηλόν is uncertain. It may mean "His clay" *i.e.* the clay Jesus had made, or "its clay" *i.e.* the clay from the spittle.

[17]   There are several technical breaches of the sabbath here. The making of clay represents a breach of the prohibition of kneading (one of the thirty-nine classes of work forbidden in the Mishnah, *Shab.* 7 : 2), probably also of mixing (*Shab.* 24 : 3). The placing of it on the eyes would come under the class of prohibited anointings (*Shab.* 14 : 4), for one may anoint on the sabbath only with what one employs for this purpose on other days. This section provides that if a man's loins pain him "he may not rub thereon wine or vinegar, yet he may anoint them with oil but not with rose-oil. King's children may anoint their wounds with rose-oil since it is their custom so to do on ordinary days". Healing on the sabbath was forbidden unless the life was in danger (see the passages in SBk, I, pp. 623ff.). Barrett cites a specific prohibition of the application of fasting spittle to the eyes on the sabbath.

[18]   The curative value of spittle was highly esteemed in antiquity, especially in connection with the eyes it would seem. There is a well known incident in which a blind man sought a cure from the Emperor Vespasian by means of his spittle. Mark twice records that Jesus used spittle (Mark 7 : 33; 8 : 23). For a general account see art. "Saliva" in *ERE*.

2 : 7 where man is made out of the dust of the earth. If this is the right way of viewing the passage then we are to discern in Christ's action a work of creation.

7 Jesus told the man to go and wash in[19] the pool of Siloam.[20] "Pool" denotes quite a large pool, one big enough to swim in (see on 5 : 2). This pool is mentioned here only in the New Testament (though *cf.* Luke 13 : 4). According to his custom John explains the meaning of the Hebrew word, giving the Greek equivalent.[21] Originally the name will have had to do with the fact that this water was "sent" into the pool by a channel. Actually the Hebrew is active and in the first place will have referred to the channel, the "sender". But the pool was given the name quite early (Neh. 3 : 15; Isa. 8 : 6). For John such a name has obvious spiritual significance, and is not to be overlooked. So he draws attention to the meaning. In this Gospel the thought of being sent is very prominent. Again and again John refers to Jesus as having been "sent" by the Father. So now blindness is removed with reference to and with the aid of the "sent". John describes the actual miracle in the simplest possible fashion. The man washed as he was told, "and came seeing". Nothing could be more concise or less flamboyant.

(b) The Effect on the Neighbours, 9 : 8–12

8 The neighbours therefore, and they that saw him aforetime, that he was a beggar, said, Is not this he that sat and begged? 9 Others said, It is he: others said, No, but he is like him. He said, I am he. 10 They said therefore unto him, How then were thine eyes opened? 11 He answered, The man that is called Jesus made clay, and anointed mine eyes, and said

---

[19] εἰς is a little curious. It may be an example of the encroachment of this preposition on the territory of ἐν. But AG cite a similar construction with νίπτω in Epictetus. In the blind man's account of the incident in v. 11 it is attached to ὕπαγε not νίψαι.

[20] The genitive τοῦ Σιλωάμ is rather strange. Probably the whole system, spring, conduit and pool, is being thought of as a unit and it is the pool *of* this complex is meant.

[21] The Hebrew is שִׁלֹחַ. Hezekiah cut a tunnel through the rock to bring waters from Gihon (the "Virgin's Fountain") into the city. It flowed into the Upper Pool *(Birket Silwan)* and probably from there to the Lower Pool *(Birket el-Ḥamra)*, though it is not possible to verify this archaeologically owing to the buildings on the site. See further the article in *NBD*.

unto me, Go to Siloam, and wash: so I went away and washed, and I received sight. 12 And they said unto him, Where is he? He saith, I know not.

The first result John records is the effect of the miracle on the neighbors of the formerly blind man. They were so astonished at such a cure that some of them refused to believe that this was the man who had been blind.

8, 9 The mention of the neighbors probably indicates that the man went home (*cf.* Moffatt: "he . . . went home seeing", v. 7). There are two groups here, the man's neighbors and those who knew him as a beggar.[22] This is the first mention of his being a beggar, but it is almost implied in the earlier statement that he was blind. There was little that a blind man could do in the ancient world apart from beg, so that the one presupposes the other. The people who had lived near him and those familiar with him from his begging are probably singled out as those who knew him best. Their amazement at his cure is expressed in a question, "Surely this is he . . .?" The question expects an affirmative answer, but the putting of it shows the great difficulty they had in accepting the evidence of their senses. Others, who perhaps knew him but not quite so well, kept talking.[23] Some said that it was the man, others that it was not, though those of the latter opinion admitted a resemblance. The man himself put an end to this form of speculation by saying emphatically "I am he."[24]

10, 11 This excites the eager question, "How therefore were your eyes opened?". The man responds with a succinct account of the miracle.[25] He apparently knows little about Jesus and expects

---

[22] In the expression ὅτι προσαίτης ἦν Burney claims that ὅτι is a mistranslation of an Aramaic 7, rendered ὅτι instead of ὅτε (*AO*, p. 78). But this is not necessary. The ὅτι may well mean "because" *i.e.* they noticed him because he was a beggar (so Bernard).

[23] Note the large number of imperfect tenses. John is describing a situation in which excited people keep talking.

[24] Ἐγώ εἰμι. The occurrence of the expression in such a context makes it plain that it does not necessarily convey the divine overtones we saw in 8 : 24, 28, 58.

[25] His word for receiving sight is ἀνέβλεψα which strictly means "I saw again". The point may be, as Westcott suggests, that "sight by nature belongs to a man even though he has been born blind." The word also means "to look up" and John may use it with the idea in mind that the man came to look up to Jesus.

that his hearers will likewise know little, for he speaks of Him as "The man that is called Jesus".[26] He expects that Jesus will be known, but no more. That he speaks of Him as no more than a man shows that he has, as yet, little understanding of His Person.[27] It is interesting to observe as the chapter progresses how his awareness of the significance of Jesus grows.

12 The interrogators want to know the whereabouts of Him who had done such a miracle. But the healed man does not know where Jesus is.

(c) The Healed Man and the Pharisees, 9 : 13–34

This miracle, no more than any of the others, serves to induce faith in Jesus' bitter opponents. Rather it stimulates them into more vigorous opposition. John evidently wants us to see that the activity of Jesus as the Light of the world inevitably results in judgment for those whose natural habitat is darkness. They oppose the Light and they are condemned thereby.

The man now enters into a spirited discussion with the Pharisees, which may be divided into three sections, the first in which the position is made clear (vv. 13–17), the second in which the Pharisees concentrate on the man's parents (vv. 18–23), and the third in which they turn to the man himself (vv. 24–34).

(i) Preliminary Discussions, 9:13–17

13 They bring to the Pharisees him that aforetime was blind. 14 Now it was the sabbath on the day when Jesus made the clay, and opened his eyes. 15 Again therefore the Pharisees also asked him how he received his sight. And he said unto them, He put clay upon mine eyes, and I washed, and I see. 16 Some therefore of the Pharisees said, This man is not from God, because he keepeth not the sabbath. But others said, How can a man that is a sinner do such signs? And there was a division among them. 17 They say therefore unto the blind man again, What sayest of him, in that he opened thine eyes? And he said, He is a prophet.

---

[26] For John's use of ἄνθρωπος of Jesus see on 4 : 29.

[27] Augustine is interested that the man straightaway speaks out so clearly: "see, he preaches the gospel; endowed with sight, he becomes a confessor. That blind man makes confession, and the heart of the wicked was troubled; for they had not in their heart what he had now in his countenance" (XLIV. 8; p. 247).

In this section the lines are drawn. It is established that it was the sabbath, and that the man claimed to have been cured of blindness. The division of opinion among the Pharisees is indicated with some impressed by the miracle and others by the sabbath breach. And the man's own emphatic declaration for Jesus is recorded.

13 There is no note of time, but it seems plain that this is on a day subsequent to that of the cure. It is not said who the "they" were, nor why they should have brought the man[28] to the Pharisees. The expression may be indefinite (like the French *on*) and mean no more than "he was brought". But perhaps it is more likely that the disputants of the previous verses are in mind. Not being able to make up their own minds they decide to lay the matter before the recognized religious leaders. They probably felt that there must be a religious aspect to the cure (was not Jesus a religious teacher?), and the Pharisees would be the ones to pronounce on such an aspect. It is possible that the Pharisees were acting as official representatives of the Sanhedrin. Hendriksen argues cogently that they were an official body, possibly even "the minor Sanhedrin or synagogue-court, of which there are said to have been two in Jerusalem." If this is the case it will explain such things as the fear of the parents in the face of interrogation. But neither the proceedings nor the sentence read like the account of formal proceedings and it may be better to think of an influential but unofficial inquiry.

14 John interpolates an explanation of his own which is important in the light of the coming discussion. It was sabbath (no article) when Jesus made the clay and performed the cure. Calvin is of opinion that Jesus purposely wrought this miracle on the sabbath in order that the resultant offence to the orthodox would give more publicity to the matter and so "the truth of the miracle shines more brightly".

15 The Pharisees question the man. The verb denotes a continuing process, and not simply an invitation to rehearse the matter. They were evidently persistent. Again the man relates what happened.

---

[28] τόν ποτε τυφλόν receives emphasis from being thrown in at the end of the sentence with no syntactical link with the preceding. Notice that John, as is his habit in repetition, describes the man in different ways. In v. 17 he is "the blind man" and in v. 18 "him that had received his sight".

He has a gift for succinct statement, and puts the essence of the matter in one terse sentence.

16 The man's statement divides the Pharisees. The more doctrinaire seize on the breach of the sabbath as they saw it. If a man[29] did not keep the sabbath according to their understanding of sabbath-keeping he could not possibly be from God. It was as simple as that. Others, however, were more open-minded. They took their stand on another principle, a principle neatly stated by the formerly blind man in v. 31. Jesus was doing "signs" (note the plural; they were not confining their attention to this one miracle) of such a kind that they could not envisage Him as being a sinner.[30] One group starts from the sabbath breach. Since the Pharisaic rule has been broken Jesus cannot be from God. The other starts from the miracle. Since He has performed such signs He must be from God. So the Pharisees were divided.[31] The group speaking tentatively in favor of Jesus must have been a small one. We do not hear of them again after this verse, and throughout the rest of the chapter the narrative proceeds as though the other group were the only one to be considered.

17 It is a measure of their perplexity and division that they ask the man what he thinks of Jesus. Normally they would not have dreamed of putting a question on a religious issue to such a man. But after all he did know what happened. So they request his opinion. The request is the measure of their embarrassment. Their "thou" is emphatic. The man is in a special position. He does

---

29 In the expression "this man" $o\tilde{v}\tau o\varsigma$ is separated from $\acute{o}$ $\check{a}\nu\vartheta\varrho\omega\pi o\varsigma$ by $\pi a\varrho\grave{a}$ $\vartheta\varepsilon o\tilde{v}$. This unusual order may be intended to put some emphasis on "man". This is probably meant contemptuously (cf. NEB: "This fellow"). John possibly wants also to indicate their ignorance of the incarnation.

30 $\acute{a}\mu a\varrho\tau\omega\lambda\acute{o}\varsigma$ occurs four times in this chapter (vv. 16, 24, 25, 31) and nowhere else in this Gospel. Notice that the principle stated by these Pharisees does not fit in with the teaching of some facts of Scripture. Thus Pharaoh's magicians were able to imitate some of the miracles performed by Aaron (Exod. 7 : 11, 22; 8 : 7; but cf. 8 : 18f.). A continuing possibility, against which the men of Israel are warned, is the appearance of a prophet or dreamer who should perform "a sign or a wonder" to lead men astray (Deut. 13 : 1ff.). Jesus spoke of the same kind of thing (Matt. 24 : 24). A reconciliation might perhaps be sought in the nature of Jesus' miracles. They were not simply "wonders". They were "signs" pointing men to God. Such miracles could not proceed from a deceiver.

31 $\sigma\chi\acute{\iota}\sigma\mu a$ does not denote a schism in our sense of the term, but rather a dissension. It is a division within the group not a splitting off from the group.

not hesitate. "He is a prophet" (*cf.* the verdict of the Samaritan woman, 4 : 19). Knox renders "Why, he must be a prophet" but this is not strong enough. The man is definite. "He is a prophet". If this seems to us inadequate we must remember that the man had no way of knowing that Jesus was more. His contact with the Lord had been very brief. And for him "prophet" was probably the highest place he could assign to a man of God. His answer puts Jesus in the highest place he knew.[32] It is interesting to notice his progressive apprehension of the significance of Jesus. He passes from thinking of Him as a man (v. 11) to seeing Him as a prophet (here). Then he advances to the thought of one to whom allegiance may fitly be given (vv. 27f.), then to one "from God" (v. 33), and finally he comes to believe in the Son of Man to whom worship should be given (vv. 35–38). By contrast the Pharisees, starting with the view that Jesus is not from God (v. 16), question the miracle (v. 18), speak of Jesus as a sinner (v. 24), are shown to be ignorant (v. 29), and finally are pronounced to be blind and sinners (v. 41).

(ii) *The Man's Parents Examined, 9 : 18–23*

18 The Jews therefore did not believe concerning him, that he had been blind, and had received his sight, until they called the parents of him that had received his sight, 19 and asked them, saying, Is this your son, who ye say was born blind? how then doth he now see? 20 His parents answered and said, We know that this is our son, and that he was born blind: 21 but how he now seeth, we know not; or who opened his eyes, we know not: ask him; he is of age; he shall speak for himself. 22 These things said his parents, because they feared the Jews: for the Jews had agreed already, that if any man should confess him to be Christ, he should be put of the synagogue. 23 Therefore said his parents, He is of age; ask him.

The first tack attempted by Jesus' enemies is that of discrediting the miracle. They held that Jesus did not come from God. For them it followed that He could not have done a miracle.

---

[32] McClymont cites Maimonides as attesting a common Jewish belief that a prophet had authority even over the law of the sabbath. If this is as early as New Testament times it will make the man's rejoinder very significant.

Therefore this miracle did not happen. They do not examine the evidence with open minds, but in the light of their firmly held prejudices seek to discover the flaw which they feel must surely be present. They begin by trying to establish that the man who now saw had not been born blind.

18 The opposition is now called by the usual name "the Jews". "The Pharisees" are mentioned in this chapter again only in v. 40. The Jews did not believe that the man really had been cured. So they called the man's parents.

19 They put two questions to the parents. The first is natural enough. They want to know whether this man is really their son. But when they ask as the second, "how then doth he now see?" they give their case away. They concede that the man was blind and now sees.

20, 21 The parents were evidently of a very different temper from that of their sturdily minded son. Their reply is characterized by timidity and a complete readiness to submit to the authority of their questioners. They testify out of their own knowledge to the identity of the man as their son, and to the fact that he was born blind. But they say they know nothing of how or by whom he received his sight. In avowing their ignorance of the identity of the Healer they use the emphatic pronoun. Evidently this was the tricky question. In saying "ask him" they also put emphasis on "him", and they have the emphatic pronoun when they say "*he* shall speak...." All this emphasis shows their determination not to get mixed up in the affair any more than they can help. There is no reason to think that they had been present when the cure was performed, so it was inevitable that they should give negative answers here. What was not inevitable was that they should manifest such an indecent concern for thrusting the matter back on their son, with their "ask him", and their "he is of age",[33] and their "he shall speak for himself". It is plain that they discerned danger, and had no intention of being caught up in it with their son.[34]

---

[33] Among the Jews this would be thirteen years and one day (SBk, II, p. 534). But the expression may perhaps mean "he is old enough to reason" rather than "he is legally of age".

[34] Strachan suggests that their fear was not for themselves but for their son, and that accordingly they rightly leave the ultimate decision to him. But this is not the impression that the passage leaves.

22 John explains the predicament in which the parents found themselves. It is interesting that the authorities had agreed as early as this to take action against the followers of Jesus. There is difficulty in seeing exactly what meaning is to be attached to "confessing" Christ (for "Christ" see on 1 : 20, 41). The meaning scarcely appears to be, as ARV, "that if any man should confess him to be Christ", for there seems no possibility of these people being accused of that. "Confess" seems rather to be interpreted in a broad sense, as of giving support to Jesus. "Put out of the synagogue" will refer to something like excommunication.[35] The

---

[35] ἀποσυνάγωγος γένηται is found in the Greek Bible only here, 12 : 42 and 16 : 2 (cf. Luke 6 : 22). The exact significance of the term is uncertain, as is the nature of and procedure for excommunication among the Jews of the day. At a later time there were two forms of excommunication: the נִדּוּי, a temporary exclusion lasting 30 days, and the חֵרֶם, which was a permanent ban. Both were at the discretion of the elders of the congregation. Excommunication cut a man off from all normal dealings with the Jewish community, but apparently not from worship (Mishnah, *Midd.* 2 : 2). But whether this applied in New Testament times is far from certain. The Mishnah speaks of excommunication, but without giving details, and assumes the possibility of readmission (*MK* 3 : 1, 2: see also *Taan.* 3 : 8; *Ned.* 1 : 1; *Eduy.* 5 : 6; *Midd.* 2 : 2). The practice of excommunication is undoubtedly old (Ezra 10 : 8). *Taan.* 3 : 8 contains a saying threatening excommunication, which was said to have been uttered by Simeon b. Shetah, *c.* 80 B.C. But we have practically no information as to how it was carried out in New Testament times. See further E. Schürer, *A History of the Jewish People in the time of Jesus Christ*, II, ii (Edinburgh, 1885), pp. 59ff.; SBk, IV, pp. 293–333; *TWNT*, VII, pp. 845–50. Barrett regards the present passage as anachronistic: "That the Synagogue had already at that time applied a test of Christian heresy is unthinkable." In view of our ignorance of much surrounding the subject this may be a little too confident. Dodd points out that "We have therefore no means of testing the accuracy of the evangelist's representation of the trial." He goes on: "But there are certain expressions in the narrative which do suggest knowledge of Jewish ideas and procedure" (*IFG*, p. 80). C. F. D. Moule questions "whether there is any inherent reason for declaring this to be unhistorical" (*The Birth of the New Testament*, London, 1962, p. 107). In any case we do not know of a formal ban on Christians (as opposed to a general curse on heretics included in the prayers) until later than the date of this Gospel. Long ago Lagrange expressed his astonishment at Loisy's assurance that such excommunication did not exist in the time of Jesus, but did exist when the Fourth Gospel was written. Lagrange adds: "Plainly the excommunication of the Christians as such did not exist in the time of Jesus; but excommunication existed, and the Jews continued to employ it to stop the spread of Jesus' teaching while He lived as well as after His death." It seems best to accept the evidence of John that some form of excommunication was in use at this time as a means of opposing Jesus and all that He stood for, but that it was not a firm policy, permanently binding.

term is not found in LXX nor in secular writers, and it is not clear as to exactly what it covered. But any deprivation of synagogue privileges was something to be feared. That Christians did not suffer excommunication in the full sense as a matter of course is evidenced by the fact that Acts depicts them as moving freely in the synagogues. But the precise meaning to be attached to the word used here is not certain. Unless we hold that John is anachronistically reading the conditions of a later day back to this period it seems best to understand the term of a temporary withdrawal of the privileges of membership in the community. But this was not yet a settled policy and it was not continued. "Had agreed already" does not necessarily indicate a formal decree of the Sanhedrin. It could well mean that some of the leading men had agreed among themselves to take action, perhaps to initiate proceedings in the Sanhedrin.

23 John simply repeats in abbreviated form the reply of the parents, and gives the threat of excommunication as the reason for it.[36]

(iii) *The Man Examined and Excommunicated, 9 : 24-34*

24 So they called a second time the man that was blind, and said unto him, Give glory to God: we know that this man is a sinner. 25 He therefore answered, Whether he is a sinner, I know not: one thing I know, that, whereas I was blind, now I see. 26 They said therefore unto him, What did he to thee? how opened he thine eyes? 27 He answered them, I told you even now, and ye did not hear; wherefore would ye hear it again? would ye also become his disciples? 28 And

---

[36] In this verse ἐπερωτήσατε (if this is the right reading), is used in place of ἐρωτήσατε in the parents' statement in v. 21. But probably no significance is to be attached to this in view of John's habit of making small alterations in repetition (see on 3 : 5). But there is good attestation for the reading ἐρωτήσατε, and this may be considered the preferable reading in view of John's marked preference for the uncompounded verb (27 times elsewhere, whereas ἐπερωτάω occurs only here and in 18 : 7 and in both places ἐρωτάω has support). It is clear at least that John used ἐπερωτάω considerably less than some other New Testament writers (and ἐρωτάω more than any of them; Luke comes a long way behind with 15 times).

they reviled him, and said, Thou art his disciple; but we are disciples of Moses. 29 We know that God hath spoken unto Moses: but as for this man, we know not whence he is. 30 The man answered and said unto them, Why, herein is the marvel, that ye know not whence he is, and yet he opened mine eyes. 31 We know that God heareth not sinners: but if any man be a worshipper of God, and do his will, him he heareth. 32 Since the world began it was never heard that any one opened the eyes of a man born blind. 33 If this man were not from God, he could do nothing. 34 They answered and said unto him, Thou wast altogether born in sins, and dost thou teach us? And they cast him out.

This is the most spirited part of the chapter. The Jews press the healed man, and he withstands them with some vigor. They take their stand on their preconceived ideas, he on the simple facts that he knows. It is not possible to argue a man out of his position when he can say, "one thing I know, that, whereas I was blind, now I see." Indeed, far from shaking him, their arguments caused him to clarify his position, and he finished the interrogation with a deeper appreciation of Jesus than he had had at the beginning. We should not miss this further example of John's irony. He depicts those who thought of themselves as enlightened trying to badger the once blind man into denying his certainty that he now had light.

24 "So" is significant here. They perceive that further interrogation of the parents will be fruitless. So they switch their attack back to the son. They begin with the pious exhortation to give glory to God. This may be understood in more ways than one. It may be taken, in the spirit of Joshua 7 : 19, as an exhortation to tell the truth[37] and confess one's misdeeds. "Remember that God sees you" is the thought, "and give Him due honor by speaking the truth." If this is the way of it the man is being told that he has not been completely frank up till now. He has held back something which would show Jesus[38] to be a sinner. Alternatively the saying may imply that all Jesus did was put clay on the man's eyes and tell him to wash. No glory is due for that. Glory is due

---

[37] Rieu renders "the Jews ... swore him in" which gives the sense of it according to this view, even though it is scarcely a translation.

[38] For John's use of ἄνθρωπος of Jesus see on 4 : 29.

rather to God who wrought the miracle. Jesus had nothing to do with it, and the man should ascribe the glory where it is due (*cf.* Phillips: "You should give God the glory for what has happened to you"). They, the religious experts, can indeed assure him that this is the case. Their "we" is emphatic. "We, the religious leaders, know" (Moffatt: "we know quite well") and therefore others ought to follow the lead we give. Significantly they leave their accusation that Jesus is a sinner in general terms and do not attempt to demonstrate their point with an example.

25 The man has a sturdy independence as his answer shows. He does not go into the theoretical question of whether Jesus was a sinner or not. He sticks to the facts of which he has certain knowledge, and thus produces an answer which is a classic. No fine-spun web of airy theory can budge a man who is able to say with conviction "one thing I know". The man had sight. No mere words could alter that.

26 But the restless questioning continues. It may be that there is matter for accusation in the circumstances of the cure. So the interrogators begin to go over the whole ground again.

27 This is not to the taste of the healed man. Forthrightly he reminds them that he has already answered these questions. The questioners can therefore scarcely be seeking information by asking such things. What is the point of it all?[39] The question, "would ye also become his disciples?" is asked in such a way as to expect the answer, "No" but the asking of it is the significant thing. The man did not really expect that these men who were so plainly opposed to Jesus were changing their minds. But he was quite ready to bait them. His "also" is significant. He was now counting himself among Jesus' disciples.[40]

28, 29 They stop arguing and abuse the man. Then they contrast their position with his. He, they say, can claim to be only Jesus'[41]

---

[39] θέλετε ἀκούειν is interesting because θέλω is usually followed by the aorist infinitive (as in the second half of the verse). The meaning will be "Why do you want to keep on hearing?"

[40] Some hold that the expression does no more than draw attention to the known band of Jesus' disciples, and inquire whether the Pharisees wish to join them. But this seems pointless, and not at all in accord with the healed man's frank espousal of Jesus' cause. The next verse indicates that the inquisitors understood the man to be Jesus' disciple.

[41] ἐκεῖνον is probably used here with a touch of contempt (so BDF, 291(1)), "that fellow".

disciple; they are Moses' disciples. This gives them a sure basis, they think. They speak out of a certainty. Whatever be the case with the rabble, such men as they know that God spoke to Moses. The perfect tense "hath spoken" implies that these words stand. "This man" will be used contemptuously. They regard their ignorance of Jesus' origin as damaging to His cause. But in 7 : 27 it was said that when the Christ comes no one will know whence He comes. Their argument was thus less convincing and less consistent than they may have thought.[42] Had they considered its implications they might have been led to the truth.

30 The man continues his independent line. So far from being impressed with their argument he launches out on one of his own designed to lead to the opposite conclusion. He finds it astonishing that they do not know whence Jesus is. The article before "marvel" may well signify "this is the really marvellous thing; your unbelief in the face of the evidence is more of a miracle than my cure!" His "ye" is emphatic and may carry some sly irony: "You, the religious experts, cannot work out a simple thing like this?"

31 The man lays down his basic proposition negatively and positively. He matches their "we know" with one of his own, and thus claims to share with his questioners, and perhaps with the community at large, the knowledge that God does not hear sinners. This should have been accepted by the second group mentioned in v. 16 at any rate. *Cf.* Ps. 66 : 18; Prov. 15 : 29; Isa. 1 : 15. Then comes the positive. If a man is a worshipper,[43] and if he does the will of God, then he will be heard.

32, 33 He goes on to point out that restoration of sight to the blind is most uncommon. Indeed it was never been heard since the age began[44] that a man born blind has received sight. His chain of reasoning is complete. Jesus could not possibly have done such a thing,[45] a thing unparalleled in all history, unless He were

---

[42] Filson comments here: "they admitted and took pride in the fact that they did not know the origin of Jesus (vs. 29). Just so! This was their basic failure: Jesus had come to them from God, and they did not face this fact".

[43] θεοσεβής is found here only in the New Testament.

[44] The expression ἐκ τοῦ αἰῶνος is found here only in the Greek Bible (Gal. 1 : 4 is different, the expression there being qualified; ἐξ αἰῶνος occurs in LXX, *e.g.* Prov. 8 : 21; Jer. 7 : 7; Sir. 1 : 4). ἀπὸ τοῦ αἰῶνος or ἀπ' αἰῶνος is much more common.

[45] Note the emphatic double negative, οὐκ ἠδύνατο ποιεῖν οὐδέν.

from God (*cf.* 3 : 2). For the man the proposition is incontestable. It is not a bad chain of reasoning for one who had hitherto been a beggar all his life, and presumably a stranger to academic and forensic argument.

34 But it is wasted on men like these. They pay no attention to the argument, but concentrate on the person of the man who presumed to teach them. In sins, they maintain, he was altogether born. And that ends that. They probably imply that his blindness was the punishment of sin (*cf.* v. 2). If so, their answer gives away their case, for they are then admitting the point they had questioned (vv. 18f.) namely that the man really had been blind, though now he could see. They cast the man out, which probably means much the same as "put out of the synagogue" in v. 22. It is possible that the latter is a technical term, and that the expression used here by contrast means no more than that they expelled the man from their assembly and from the building in which they were (*cf.* Barclay: "they ordered him to get out"). But it is more probable that this represents a stronger disciplinary action against a stubborn heretic.

(d) Faith in the Son of God, 9 : 35–38

35 Jesus heard that they had cast him out; and finding him, he said, Dost thou believe on [1]the Son of God? 36 He answered and said, And who is he, Lord, that I may believe on him? 37 Jesus said unto him, Thou hast both seen him, and he it is that speaketh with thee. 38 And he said, Lord, I believe. And he [2]worshipped him.

[1]Many ancient authorities read *the Son of Man.* [2]The Greek word denotes an act of reverence, whether paid to a creature (as here) or to the Creator (see ch. 4. 20).

John is always interested in the way the coming of Jesus divides men. Throughout this chapter we have seen the process in operation. At the close we see the natural conclusion, first a confession of faith, and then a plain statement of the condemnation of those who have been resisting the light.

35 The interesting thing here is the simple "and finding him" (*cf.* 5 : 14). It would have been common knowledge that the Jews had taken action against the healed man, and Jesus heard this in due course. John does not find it necessary to say that He sought him out. When the man had been persecuted for Jesus' sake it could be assumed that Jesus would not remain indifferent. So John simply tells us that He found him. (Moffatt's "on meeting him" is inadequate.)[46] Jesus' "thou" is emphatic. He asks how it is with the man personally, whatever may be the case with others. Faith is an essentially personal thing. For "believing on" see on 1 : 12. For "the Son of God" many of the best manuscripts read "the Son of man", and it seems probable that this reading should be accepted.[47] Whichever text we adopt, faith in Christ is meant.[48]

36 The man evidently recognizes the voice, for he clearly knows that Jesus is his benefactor, though up till now he has not seen Him. He responds[49] respectfully, though whether we should translate "Lord" as ARV, or "Sir" is not so clear. As the man does not yet know who Jesus is it seems preferable to give the term the lesser significance (see on 4 : 1). The man's gratitude to Jesus comes out in his readiness to believe. He wants to know who the

---

[46] *Cf.* Chrysostom: "The Jews cast him out from the Temple, and the Lord of the Temple found him" (LIX. 1; p. 212). Calvin points out that an excommunication can have good results. "If he had been kept in the synagogue, he would have run the danger of becoming gradually alienated from Christ and plunged into the same destruction as the ungodly ... We have known the same thing in our own time. For when Luther, and others like him, were beginning to reprove the grosser abuses of the Pope, they had scarcely the slightest taste for pure Christianity. But after the Pope had fulminated against them and cast them out of the Roman synagogue by terrifying bulls, Christ stretched out His hand and made Himself fully known to them. So there is nothing better for us than to be far away from the enemies of the Gospel so that He may come near to us."

[47] ἀνθρώπου is read by P66, P75 ℵ BDW syrˢ sa, and θεοῦ by AΘ f1 f13 lat. Both expressions are Johannine. We do not elsewhere find "the Son of man" directly connected with believing (though *cf.* 3 : 14f.; 12 : 34ff.), but "the Son of God" is used in connection with confessions of faith (1 : 34, 49; 3 : 18; 11 : 27; 20 : 31). It is thus unlikely that an original θεοῦ would be altered to ἀνθρώπου but the reverse process may readily be envisaged (this carries conviction to Tasker; *GNT*, p. 427). As the attestation of ἀνθρώπου is superior there seems no reason why it should not be accepted. A further confirmatory consideration is that the passage moves on to the thought of judgment, a topic with which "the Son of man" is connected (*cf.* 5 : 27).

[48] The question may indicate an affirmative answer. *Cf.* Bailey: "Thou puttest thy trust on the Son of Man dost thou not?" So also Bernard.

[49] BDF note the use of καί to introduce an apodosis when the apodosis is a question with the meaning "who then" (442(8)).

Son is so that[50] he may believe.[51] He has gathered from Jesus' question that Jesus wants him to believe. He for his part is ready to do what is right.[52]

37 Jesus discloses His identity. His use of the verb "thou hast seen" must have meant a good deal to the man who up till that day had seen nothing.

38 The man's instant response is "Lord, I believe", and this time there is little reason for thinking that "Lord" has less than the maximum content. Several translations (*e.g.* RSV, NEB) have "sir" in v. 36 but "Lord" here and this seems to be right. *Twentieth Century*, Goodspeed, *etc.*, have "Sir" in both places but the second is incongruous in view of the immediately following reference to worship. This is the climax for the man of a process that has been going on throughout the chapter. His insight into the Person of Jesus has been growing, and now this final revelation puts the coping stone on what has gone before. The man sees that Jesus is the one object of a right faith and accordingly puts his trust in Him. This is the only place in this Gospel where anyone is said to worship Jesus. The verb occurs several times in ch. 4 of worshipping God, and it is found in the same sense in 12 : 20. It can be used of paying very high respect to men,[53] but in John it is more natural to understand it of paying divine honors. The man has already recognized that Jesus came from God (v. 33). Now

---

[50] Burney cites this verse as an example of the Semitic use of the redundant pronoun (εἰς αὐτόν) after the relative (*AO*, p. 85; for the construction in John see on 1 : 27). But this example is not convincing for it rests on the view that ἵνα is a mistranslation of the relative, a view which is far from established (*cf.* Black, *AA*, pp. 58f.).

[51] Jesus' question uses the present: "Do you habitually, continually believe?" The man's reply employs the aorist: ". . . that I may come to believe".

[52] Some suggest that we should take ἵνα here as imperatival. This would give the meaning "Would that I might believe!" See on 1 : 8. More probably, we should postulate an ellipsis: "(Tell me) in order that. . . ."

[53] AG says that προσκυνέω is "used to designate the custom of prostrating oneself before a person and kissing his feet, the hem of his garment, the ground, etc.; the Persians did this in the presence of their deified king, and the Greeks before a divinity or someth. holy". Of the use with regard to people it says, "to human beings who, however, are to be recognized by this act as belonging to a supernatural realm". LS show that in later times this meaning was weakened considerably, but in the New Testament it is plain that the word is used with a very full meaning which the occasional use of men (Matt. 18 : 26; Rev. 3 : 9) does little to weaken.

he goes a step further. He gives to Jesus that reverence that is appropriate to God.

(e) The Condemnation of the Pharisees, 9 : 39–41

39 And Jesus said, For judgment came I into this world, that they that see not may see; and that they that see may become blind. 40 Those of the Pharisees who were with him heard these things, and said unto him, Are we also blind? 41 Jesus said unto them, If ye were blind, ye would have no sin: but now ye say, We see: your sin remaineth.

The light has had its effect on the man who was ready to receive it. It remains for us to notice its effect on those who closed their eyes to it.

39 Were these words said on the same occasion? John says nothing to indicate a change of scene. But the conversation with the formerly blind man seems unlikely to have been held before hostile witnesses, and it is difficult to think that the Pharisees would have witnessed the man's act of worship without some protest. It seems more probable accordingly that Jesus' words are spoken a little later. They represent His account of the principle at work. In one sense Jesus did not come to judge men (3 : 17; 12 : 47). But for all that His coming represents a judgment,[54] for men divide according to the way they react to that coming (see on 3 : 18; 8 : 15). In this passage the thought is worked out in terms of sight and blindness. The result of Jesus' coming is that blind men see.[55] This has obvious relevance to the happenings of this chapter, and it must be understood to include the recovery of spiritual sight as well as of physical sight. Indeed it is especially spiritual sight that is in mind now. We must understand the concluding words to mean "that those who claim to have spiritual sight (apart from Me) may be shown up for the blind men that they really are" (cf. also Isa. 6 : 10).

40 We are not told how and why some[56] of the Pharisees were

---

[54] This is the only place in this Gospel where $\varkappa \varrho \iota \mu \alpha$ is found. John prefers $\varkappa \varrho \iota \sigma \iota \varsigma$.

[55] $\beta \lambda \epsilon \pi \omega$ is used here in the sense of $\dot{\alpha} \nu \alpha \beta \lambda \epsilon \pi \omega$.

[56] John uses the partitive $\dot{\epsilon} \varkappa$, as often, to give the meaning "Some of the Pharisees", rather than "Those of the Pharisees", as ARV.

with[57] Jesus, but they heard these things. Their reaction was an incredulous question:[58] "Are we also blind?" They are the embodiment of the condemnation of which Jesus has been speaking. It never occurs to them that they can possibly be blind.

41 Jesus' answer is paradoxical and probably highly unexpected. The Pharisees doubtless expected Jesus to say that they were blind. That was only to be anticipated from One they had opposed so vigorously. Instead He says that blindness would have been an excuse. If the Pharisees had been really blind, if they had had no understanding of spiritual things at all, they would not have sinned in acting as they did (*cf.* Rom. 5 : 13). They could not be blamed for acting in ignorance. They would not have been acting in rebellion against their best insights. But they claim to see. They claim spiritual knowledge. They know the Law. And it is sin for men who have spiritual knowledge to act as they do. Jesus does not say that they really do see, but that they claim to see. If they really had spiritual sight in the full sense they would act differently towards Him. Yet they are not completely blind. His meaning is that they have enough spiritual knowledge to be responsible. Had they acted on the best knowledge they had they would have welcomed the Son of God. But they did not act on this. They claimed to have sight, but acted like the blind. Therefore their sin is not taken away. It remains with them.[59]

---

[57] Westcott speaks of these Pharisees as in some sense followers of Jesus. This, however, seems to be going beyond the meaning of μετ' αὐτοῦ which in itself signifies no more than "with". In 3 : 25 μετὰ 'Ιουδαίου is even used of antagonism.

[58] The question is introduced by μή thus expecting the answer, "No", and their καὶ ἡμεῖς registers surprise at the suggestion that they, of all people, are blind.

[59] *Cf.* Temple: "It is a crushing, overwhelming retort. Can we escape its impact? Only in one of two ways. Either we must confess our blindness and seek the opening of our eyes; or else we must accept the light and walk by it. What we may not do, yet all strive to do, is to keep our eyes half-open and live by half the light. That kind of sight holds us to our sin and our sin to us. But the only way of avoiding it is to look with eyes wide open upon ourselves and the world as the full light reveals it; but this is the surrender of faith, and pride resists it." For the concept of "having" sin see on 15 : 22.

497

CHAPTER X

17. THE SEVENTH DISCOURSE – THE GOOD SHEPHERD, 10 : 1–42

In this, the last public address of Jesus that John records, a further aspect of His ministry is unfolded in an allegory of great power. Jesus uses the figure of the Good Shepherd to differentiate His ministry from that of false shepherds, and to stress the voluntary nature of His sacrifice for men. This chapter should be read in the light of Old Testament passages which castigate shepherds who have failed in their duty (see Jer. 23 : 1–4; 25 : 32–8; Zech. 11, and especially Isa. 56 : 9–12[1] and Ezek. 34). God is the Shepherd of Israel (Ps. 80 : 1; *cf.* Ps. 23 : 1; Isa. 40 : 10f.), which gives us the measure of the responsibility of His under-shepherds. Those entrusted with this duty must be faithful, and it is a heinous crime when they are not. But Israel's shepherds on more than one occasion did fail in their responsibility. It is this which calls forth the prophecy that a shepherd after God's own heart will in due time appear: "I will set up one shepherd over them, and he shall feed them, even my servant David; he shall feed them, and he shall be their shepherd" (Ezek. 34 : 23). It is this shepherd who is depicted in this chapter.

Nowadays we think of the shepherd in terms of tender care and concern for the flock, thoughts which are legitimate for the ancient world as for the modern. But we should not overlook the fact that for men of biblical times other associations were also aroused by the term. The shepherd was an autocrat over his flock, and passages are not wanting where the shepherd imagery is used to emphasize the thought of sovereignty.[2] Jesus is thus set forth in this allegory as the true Ruler of His people[3] in contrast to all false shepherds.

---

[1] In this passage the leaders are spoken of as both "shepherds" and "watchmen" (*cf.* the "porter" of this passage) and they are castigated as "blind" and "without knowledge" (*cf.* 9 : 40f.; 10 : 6).

[2] For the significance of the role of shepherd *cf.* Rev. 2 : 27, ποιμανεῖ αὐτοὺς ἐν ῥάβδῳ σιδηρᾷ. The same verb is used in Matt. 2 : 6 (in a quotation from Mic. 5 : 2) to describe the activity of the messianic ruler (ἡγούμενος).

[3] *Cf.* Richardson: "We must, however, clearly understand that 'shepherd' in biblical phraseology means 'ruler', and St John is claiming that Jesus is the ideal ruler of prophetic expectation".

Some have felt that there is little connection between the opening of this chapter and the end of the preceding one. Various reconstructions have been proposed. But these are not necessary. It is likely that John saw a link in the Old Testament passages noted above.[4] There are many of them, and it is clear that the Jews delighted in this particular imagery. It is apt, accordingly, that, immediately after Israel's shepherds have failed so conspicuously in the case of the man born blind, we should have set forth the nature and functions of the Good Shepherd. The sequence is tolerably plain.

The main teaching here is clear enough but there are difficulties in detail, and the passage is far from simple. Jesus is spoken of both as the Door and as the Shepherd (who goes in by the door), statements not easy to harmonize formally.[5] Then the force of the Good Shepherd is not always the same, for He is contrasted first with thieves and later with hirelings. Again, the meaning of the sheep does not seem to be always exactly the same. Nor is the discourse itself perfectly straightforward, for literal and symbolic sayings are closely interwoven.[6]

There are references to the shepherd and the sheep in the Synoptic Gospels, notably in the parable which speaks of a shepherd leaving ninety-nine sheep while he searches through the wilderness for one that was lost (Matt. 18 : 12f.; Luke 15 : 3–7). In the Synoptics the shepherd is seen in his relationship to the sheep; he provides for them and cares for them. In John this concern is clear. Indeed, it is taken further than in the Synoptics, for the Good Shepherd provides for the sheep even to the extent of laying down His life for them. But John also sounds a distinctive note.

---

[4] R. H. Lightfoot thinks 10 : 1–21 "to be closely connected with ch. 9" and finds grounds for this in the Old Testament use of the shepherd-sheep imagery.

[5] But such statements are not uncommon in this Gospel. Jesus is the bread of life (6 : 35), and He gives it (6 : 51). He speaks the truth (8 : 45f.), and He is the truth (14 : 6). Throughout the Gospel He is depicted as showing men the way, and He is the way (14 : 6).

[6] Brown sees the explanation in the presence of more than one parable: 1–3a forms a parable dealing with the proper approach to the sheep, through the gate opened by the gatekeeper, 3b–5 is a separate parable concerned with the relationship of sheep to shepherd. It is possible to understand the passage this way, but it does not seem necessary in the light of the facts adduced in n. 5 above.

Here the Good Shepherd is seen also in contrast to false shepherds.[7]
He is the rightful shepherd, whose voice the sheep know.[8]
Finally let us notice that the shepherd imagery was common
in many parts of the ancient world. Kings and gods alike were
described as shepherds. Thus whenever this Gospel was read
language like this would strike a chord. In contrast to whatever
false shepherds John's readers may have known Jesus would stand
forth as the Good Shepherd who makes genuine provision for His
sheep.

(a) The Parable, 10 : 1–6

1 Verily, verily, I say unto you, He that entereth not by the
door into the fold of the sheep, but climbeth up some other
way, the same is a thief and a robber. 2 But he that entereth
in by the door is [1]the shepherd of the sheep. 3 To him the
porter openeth; and the sheep hear his voice: and he calleth
his own sheep by name, and leadeth them out. 4 When he
hath put forth all his own, he goeth before them, and the
sheep follow him: for they know his voice. 5 And a stranger
will they not follow, but will flee from him: for they know
not the voice of strangers. 6 This [2]parable spake Jesus unto
them: but they understood not what things they were which
he spake unto them.

[1]Or, a shepherd. [2]Or, proverb

Jesus begins with an allegory[9] in which He sets forth the
main facts of herding sheep in ancient Palestine. His audience no

---

[7] Cullmann sees in this chapter and especially in v. 18 an intentional
contrast with the Teacher of Righteousness of the Qumran scrolls. He says
of the reference to the voluntary nature of Jesus' death in v. 18, "The emphasis
with which this is said makes clear that Jesus' death is being interpreted in
intentional contrast to another conception" (*SNT*, p. 31). But this is too
specific. As W. S. LaSor says, it would be just as easy to make out a case for a
polemic against Socrates or Lao-tze (*Amazing Dead Sea Scrolls*, Chicago, 1956,
p. 212). The words are general and must be understood so.

[8] J. A. T. Robinson finds this parable stands the test of genuineness, and
he points out that it is significant that this would be so in a passage which
obviously is not derived from the Synoptists (*Twelve New Testament Studies*,
London, 1962, pp. 67–75).

[9] It is difficult to class this section exactly. It is called a παροιμία in v. 6
(where see note), which may indicate a proverb, or, more generally, a "dark
saying" of some sort. It differs from the Synoptic parables in that there is no
connected story. Most people call it an allegory but Lagrange objects that in

doubt is familiar enough with the general pastoral picture, but it does not discern the spiritual meaning behind the words.

1 There is no introductory explanation of the occasion or the like. The chapter opens with Jesus fairly launched on His discourse. This indicates that there is no great break with the previous section, a conclusion which is reinforced by the reference to opening the eyes of the blind in v. 21. Moreover the blind man, so ready to heed the voice of Christ, clearly belongs among the sheep of this discourse, while the Pharisees are the very embodiment of the false shepherds. The opening "Verily, verily" (for the expression see on 1 : 51) agrees with this, for elsewhere it never begins a discourse. It always follows up some previous teaching. It indicates that the following statement is important, but also that it has a connection with the preceding. This passage then must be understood in the closest of connections with the story of the blind man. Sheep were commonly herded in a walled enclosure, mostly open to the sky, but providing protection from the worst of the elements, and from beasts of prey. The word used here is the usual word for a courtyard,[10] and thus may denote that the sheep are herded close alongside the house. Whatever be the truth about this, the fold envisaged was one with stout walls and one door guarded by a door-keeper. If a man does not enter by the door in the normal way but climbs over[11] the wall, then it is clear that he is there for no good purpose. He is castigated as a robber.[12]

2, 3 By contrast if a man enters by the door he is seen to be the

---

an allegory the one person can scarcely be represented by two figures, as here Jesus is both shepherd and door. He prefers to call it *un petit tableau parabolique*. The name we give it matters little, but in our interpretation we must bear in mind that it does not fit neatly into any of our usual categories. It is basically an allegory, but with distinctive features of its own.

[10] αὐλή is used for the court adjacent to a house in Matt. 26 : 58, *etc*. LS note its use to denote "*steading* for cattle" as far back as Homer. This might be the courtyard of a house, or it might be a special fold.

[11] This is an unusual use of ἀναβαίνω for this Gospel. Elsewhere John uses it of going up to Jerusalem for feasts 9 times, of ascending to heaven 5 times, and in 21 : 11 of Peter's going up and dragging the net to land.

[12] In strictness κλέπτης denotes something like a sneak-thief (it is used of Judas, 12 : 6), and λῃστής a brigand (it is used of Barabbas, 18 : 40). The combination may denote a readiness to engage in violence as well as dishonesty (*cf.* v. 10), though we should not make too sharp a distinction between them. Incidentally we find the same two words employed in Obadiah 5.

shepherd.[13] He has the right to enter[14] and this is recognized when the door-keeper opens to him. In the case of a small flock there would be no such official, but what is apparently in mind is a large fold where several flocks find shelter. One door-keeper can thus look after a large number of sheep. Various attempts have been made to find a meaning for the door-keeper but none has won wide acceptance, and none, it would seem, should. The point is that in an allegory not all details are significant. Some are inserted as necessary parts of the picture even though they have no part to play in the symbolism. So here with the door-keeper. When the shepherd comes in he calls the sheep, who know his voice. The Eastern shepherd often has an individual call for each of his sheep and it is this that is in mind here. The sheep know their shepherd and they recognize[15] the call he gives his own.[16] More, they respond to it,[17] and in this way he leads them out.

---

[13] ARV mg. reads "a shepherd", but this is erroneous. This is another example of the definite predicate preceding the verb and therefore lacking the article (see on 1 : 1). We should translate "the shepherd". Some commentators treat ποιμήν as more or less adjectival owing to the absence of the article. But this is to overlook New Testament usage in this grammatical point.

[14] Augustine connects this passage with ch. 9 by emphasizing that there is one right way of entering, and the Pharisees did not use it. He also says, "there are many who, according to a custom of this life, are called good people, – good men, good women, innocent, and observers as it were of what is commanded in the law; paying respect to their parents, abstaining from adultery, doing no murder, committing no theft, giving no false witness against any one, and observing all else that the law requires – yet are not Christians . . . Pagans may say, then, We live well. If they enter not by the door, what good will that do them, whereof they boast?" (XLV. 2; p. 250).

[15] For ἀκούω with the genitive of the thing heard see note on 5 : 25. It denotes that the sheep hear the shepherd's voice with understanding and appreciation.

[16] Note the significance of ἴδια. The shepherd does not call sheep in general. He calls his own sheep, and he has a call that they recognize.

[17] H. V. Morton gives a account of this sort of thing: "Early one morning I saw an extraordinary sight not far from Bethlehem. Two shepherds had evidently spent the night with their flocks in a cave. The sheep were all mixed together and the time had come for the shepherds to go in different directions. One of the shepherds stood some distance from the sheep and began to call. First one, then another, then four or five animals ran towards him; and so on until he had counted his whole flock" (In the Steps of the Master, London, 1935, p. 155). George Adam Smith similarly tells of three or four shepherds separating out their flocks solely by their peculiar calls (The Historical Geography of the Holy Land, London, 1931, pp. 311f.).

4 When he has put all his own sheep out[18] of the fold the shepherd takes them to their destination by walking before them. This is a very different picture from that of driving the sheep which is more familiar in lands like Australia in these days. The sheep follow, we are told, because they know[19] their shepherd's voice.
5 The case is different when a stranger attempts to take them. They certainly will not (double negative) follow[20] a stranger. The reason is given in terms of the voice again. They do not know the voice of strangers[21] and therefore they run away. Travellers in Palestine in modern times have sometimes been able to document this. It appears that strangers, even when dressed in the shepherd's clothing and attempting to imitate his call, succeed only in making the sheep run away. The sheep know their shepherd's voice but do not know and do not respond to that of a stranger.
6 "Parable" translates a word which is not often found in the New Testament, and which appears to mean "proverb" in its

---

[18] Some points of language are worth noting. $\ddot{\iota}\delta\iota\alpha$ reminds us of the particular relationship of these sheep to the shepherd. They belong. $\pi\acute{\alpha}\nu\tau\alpha$ indicates that he secures them all. $\dot{\epsilon}\varkappa\beta\acute{\alpha}\lambda\eta$ is somewhat puzzling. It is the word used of expelling the formerly blind man from the synagogue in 9 : 34 and may form a link between the two narratives. But not too much can be made of this as the sense is different. There the false leaders expelled the men. Here the rightful shepherd compels the sheep to leave the fold, but for their good. The word does have about it the air of force. Left to themselves the sheep might not go in the right way, but the shepherd constrains them. He uses force if necessary to ensure that their best interests are served.

[19] Note the plural verb, though the subject is neuter plural, and two previous verbs with the same subject are singular ($\dot{\alpha}\varkappa o\acute{\nu}\epsilon\iota$, v. 3, and $\dot{\alpha}\varkappa o\lambda o\nu\vartheta\epsilon\tilde{\iota}$, v. 4). Singular and plural are found with this subject throughout the chapter and it is difficult to assign a reason for this. The singular occurs in vv. 3, 4, 12, 16, and the plural in vv. 4, 5 (three times), 8, 10, 14, 16, 27 (twice), 28, while the textual evidence is divided on this verb in v. 16 ($\gamma\epsilon\nu\acute{\eta}\sigma\epsilon\tau\alpha\iota$ and $\gamma\epsilon\nu\acute{\eta}\sigma o\nu\tau\alpha\iota$).

[20] This is one of only three examples in this Gospel of a future indicative with $o\dot{\nu}$ $\mu\acute{\eta}$ (the others are 4 : 14; 6 : 35). This construction is not common in the New Testament anywhere. J. H. Moulton speaks of it as "a possible, though moribund, construction" and he finds no apparent difference in meaning from the usual aorist subjunctive (M, I, p. 190).

[21] There is probably some emphasis intended by the placing of $\tau\tilde{\omega}\nu$ $\dot{\alpha}\lambda\lambda o\tau\varrho\acute{\iota}\omega\nu$ before $\tau\grave{\eta}\nu$ $\varphi\omega\nu\acute{\eta}\nu$.

only non-Johannine occurrence, 2 Peter 2 : 22.[22] In John (elsewhere, 16 : 25, 29) it signifies something like "figure of speech". It denotes language of which the meaning is not obvious, but which conveys to those who probe deeply enough spiritual truths of importance. So here Jesus spoke indeed to His hearers, but they did not understand[23] the spiritual truth He was conveying.

(b) The Application to Christ, 10 : 7–18

7 Jesus therefore said unto them again, Verily, verily, I say unto you, I am the door of the sheep. 8 All that came [1]before me are thieves and robbers: but the sheep did not hear them. 9 I am the door; by me if any man enter in, he shall be saved, and shall go in and go out, and shall find pasture. 10 The thief cometh not, but that he may steal, and kill, and destroy: I came that they may have life, and may [2]have it abundantly. 11 I am the good shepherd: the good shepherd layeth down his life for the sheep. 12 He that is a hireling, and not a shepherd, whose own the sheep are not, beholdeth the wolf coming, and leaveth the sheep, and fleeth, and the wolf snatcheth them, and scattereth them: 13 he fleeth because he is a hireling, and careth not for the sheep. 14 I am the good shepherd; and I know mine own, and mine own know me, 15 even as the Father knoweth me, and I know the Father; and I lay down my life for the sheep. 16 And other sheep I have, which are not of this fold: them also I must [3]bring, and they shall hear my voice; and [4]they shall become one flock, one shepherd. 17 Therefore doth the Father love me, because I lay down my life, that I may take it again. 18 No one [5]taketh it away from me, but I lay it down of myself. I have [6]power to lay it down, and I have [6]power to take

---

[22] The word is παροιμία. This is not found in the Synoptic Gospels while παραβολή, so frequent there, is not found in John. It is difficult to put a real difference of meaning between them, and both probably reflect something of the Hebrew מָשָׁל. Either can be used of a short saying (παραβολή in Luke 4 : 23; παροιμία in II Pet. 2 : 22), or of a more extensive passage like the present. Either way it may require careful thought or an explanation before its meaning is grasped. This is not to say that there is no difference between the parables so characteristic of the Synoptic Gospels and such a passage as the present one. The differences are plain. All that I am saying is that it is difficult to make a hard and fast distinction between the meanings of the two words. The two terms are found together in Sir. 39 : 3; 47 : 17.

[23] The verb is ἔγνωσαν. There is a certain emphasis on "knowing" in these verses (cf. οἴδασιν, vv. 4, 5).

it again. This commandment received I from my Father.

¹Some ancient authorities omit *before me.* ²Or, *have abundance* ³Or, *lead* ⁴Or, *there shall be one flock* ⁵Some ancient authorities read *took it away.* ⁶Or, *right*

In this section of the discourse Jesus applies the parable to Himself. There are two ways of viewing Him, as the Door and as the Good Shepherd, and He deals with them successively. Both have to do with salvation. As the Door He is the one way of entrance into salvation. As the Good Shepherd He is the One who cares for the sheep and provides for their salvation at the cost of His life. The two figures lend themselves to different contrasts. When Jesus considers Himself as the Door He stigmatizes those who do not use the Door as thieves and robbers. When He thinks of Himself as the Good Shepherd He thinks rather of hireling shepherds. But both have in common a stress on personal gain on the part of the persons opposed and an absence of interest in the well-being of the sheep. In all this Jesus is not engaging in an exposition of animal husbandry. He is showing what it means to see Him to be the Good Shepherd. The essential thing is the laying down of His life. But while the earthly shepherd is a useful illustration there is a difference from anything earthly, for Jesus insists that He has power both to lay down His life and to take it again.

7 Jesus resumes His discourse. "Therefore" may indicate that this is an explanation given in the light of His hearers' failure to understand what He has been saying. "Again" is resumptive.²⁴ For "Verily, verily" see on 1 : 51. It introduces a solemn and important statement, and this is continued in the emphatic "I am" (see on 6 : 35). We might have expected some explanation of Christ's function as the Shepherd, but instead we have the new thought introduced that He is the door.²⁵ "Door" is used metaphorically in other places in the New Testament (*e.g.* Luke 13 : 24;

---

²⁴ John uses πάλιν for repetition (as in 4 : 3, 13), and with the thought of going "back" (6 : 15, where see note). But sometimes it is little more than a connective (*e.g.* 16 : 28). It has such a sense here.

²⁵ Instead of ἡ θύρα the Sahidic and Achmimic and now the recently discovered P75 read ὁ ποιμήν. Despite the adoption of this reading by Moffatt it is difficult to take it seriously. It would seem an obvious correction to a scribe who was concentrating on the thought of the Good Shepherd and did not discern that another thought is being expressed here.

Acts 14 : 27; I Cor. 16 : 9, *etc.*) but this is the only passage in which Jesus Himself is regarded as the door.[26] The thought is not unlike that of 1 : 51, where Jesus is the ladder connecting heaven and earth, or 14 : 6, where Jesus is the Way, but here it gets its force from the imagery of the sheepfold. There is but one door to a fold, and sheep and shepherds alike must enter by this door. There is no other way for them. But Jesus does provide the way. It seems that the thought here is primarily that Jesus provides the door by which the *shepherd* must enter (see next verse). In verse 9 the emphasis is rather on the door as the way by which the *sheep* go in.

8 Jesus contrasts Himself with His predecessors. "All that came before me" must signify the Jewish religious leaders, but the expression is strangely comprehensive.[27] It cannot mean the prophets and the like,[28] for they were anything but thieves and robbers (for this expression see on v. 1). Jesus' attitude to the men of the Old Testament is clear in 5 : 46; 8 : 56. He must have in view the whole Jewish hierarchy of His day. They were not interested in the wellbeing of the sheep but in their own advantage. The Sadducees in particular were known to make quite a lot of

---

[26] Barrett proposes a very complicated background for the saying including the thought of a door in heaven in Greek literature from Homer downwards, "the gate of heaven" (Gen. 28 : 17) and similar Old Testament expressions, the use of such terms in apocalyptic literature, the Synoptic Gospels, and early Christian theology. He also ranges forward to Ignatius and Hegesippus. On the Synoptics he says: "These synoptic passages have for the most part an eschatological reference, which John has characteristically transformed, using Old Testament material which the earlier tradition had already selected, but applying it with special reference to the person of Jesus (rather than to the Kingdom) and in such a way as to make it appropriate to the intellectual atmosphere in which he lived." All this seems unnecessarily complicated. The very fact that "door" turns up in such varied literatures is evidence that it comes naturally to man to use it, and there is no need to postulate a complicated dependence. The figure is used a good deal in early Christian writings, *e.g.* Ignatius, *Philad.* 9 : 1; Hegesippus (Eus. *H. E.* ii. 23. 8); Hermas *Sim.* 9. 12. 1; Clem. Rom. 48 : 4. Hippolytus finds a similar reference in a Naassene writer (*Refut.* 5. 3; ANF, V, p. 54). *Cf.* also Acts of John, 95; Clem. Hom. 3. 52 (ANF, VIII, p. 248).

[27] This may be the reason for the omission of the words $\pi\varrho\grave{o}\ \grave{\epsilon}\mu o\tilde{v}$ by P45vid P75 ℵ* Δ28 lat syrs.p sah. But as they are read by P66 ℵc ABDW f13 33 700 boh they should be accepted. Bultmann emphasizes the exclusiveness and the absoluteness of the claim Jesus is making. He brooks no rival.

[28] Some of the Gnostics appear to have used the expression to discredit the entire Old Testament, including the God who speaks there. Hippolytus says that Valentinus held this view (*Refut.* 6. 30; ANF, V, p. 89).

money out of temple religion and there are denunciations of the
Pharisees (Luke 16 : 14) and the scribes (Mark 12 : 40) for covet-
ousness. Some understand the words of revolutionaries like Judah
the Galilean, and if this is right the references to violence are
much in point.[29] We should almost certainly take "before me" as
part of the imagery, rather than as indicating Jesus' predecessors
as religious leaders. The shepherd comes to the fold for his sheep
(vv. 2f.) first thing in the morning. All who preceded him accordingly must be thieves and the like working in the darkness. All
the more is this likely to be the case in that Jesus does not say
that they "were" but that they "are" thieves and robbers. The
emphasis is on His own day. It is perhaps a little strange to have
this reference to religious leaders when Jesus is speaking of Himself
as the door. We would have anticipated it rather when He is
developing the idea of the Good Shepherd. The meaning appears
to be that if men are to bring other men into God's fold they
must first enter it themselves (cf. I Tim. 4 : 16). And the only
way of entrance is through the one door. These men declined to
come to God through Christ. They therefore stamped themselves
as impostors. All who seek to bring men life, but themselves do
not enter into life through Christ, stand condemned. Jesus has
already pointed out that the sheep will take no notice of strangers.
Now He says that the sheep did not hear these robbers. Those
who really are the sheep, given by the Father, have spiritual
discernment. They await the voice of their true Shepherd.

9 Jesus repeats that He is the door.[30] This time "of the sheep"

---

[29] For the view that the Teacher of Righteousness of the Qumran Scrolls
is meant see n. 7 above.

[30] Morgan cites a story told him by Sir George Adam Smith to illustrate
this point. "He was one day travelling with a guide, and came across a shepherd
and his sheep. He fell into conversation with him. The man showed him the
fold into which the sheep were led at night. It consisted of four walls, with a
way in. Sir George said to him, 'That is where they go at night?' 'Yes,' said
the shepherd, 'and when they are in there, they are perfectly safe.' 'But there
is no door,' said Sir George. 'I am the door,' said the shepherd. He was not
a Christian man, he was not speaking in the language of the New Testament.
He was speaking from the Arab shepherd's standpoint. Sir George looked at
him and said, 'What do you mean by the door?' Said the shepherd, 'When
the light has gone, and all the sheep are inside, I lie in that open space, and
no sheep ever goes out but across my body, and no wolf comes in unless he crosses
my body; I am the door.' " If this is the understanding of it (as several commentators think) the expression points to the absolute safety of the sheep in the care of
the Good Shepherd. But such a sheepfold is difficult to reconcile with v. 3.

is lacking and the words stand forth in impressive simplicity. The stress is on Jesus' function. The words "by me" are in an emphatic position. It is He and no other who enables men to enter salvation. There is a certain exclusiveness about "the door". If there is one door then men must enter by it or stay outside.[31] They cannot demand another door. John does not often use the verb "to save", and he never explains exactly what he means by it.[32] But he makes it clear that salvation was the purpose of Jesus' coming (3 : 17; 5 : 34; 12 : 47). It is the comprehensive term for the whole process whereby men are delivered from the consequences of their sin and brought into the blessing of God. Here the blessing is described in terms of secure pasturage, the supreme good for the sheep. The sheep that enters the fold through Christ will then be able to go in and out and have all its need met. We should not attempt to find some esoteric meaning for "go in and go out". It is simply an expression to indicate free and secure movement (*cf.* Knox: "he will come and go at will").

10 The thought is further developed by a contrast with the thief. His interest is entirely selfish. He steals or kills for food[33] or even

---

[31] *Cf.* Murray: "The door, however, has characteristics which are not conveyed under the image of the way. First, the door suggests, even more distinctly than the way, a certain exclusiveness of function. There may conceivably be more ways than one of getting to a goal. In the fold of which our Lord is speaking, He has already made it clear that there is but one door." Bultmann has an interesting note in which he draws attention to the exclusiveness and the intolerance which attend all genuine revelation. When the true way is revealed it is impossible to be tolerant of the various false ways which can lead only to error and disaster.

[32] It is found in 3 : 17; 5 : 34; 10 : 9; 11 : 12; 12 : 27, 47. Matthew uses it 15 times, Mark 15 times, Luke 17 times, so that John's use is much less marked. He also lacks the frequent Synoptic use of the verb for healing (except for 11 : 12 and even this is not quite the same; it does not refer to a healing activity of Jesus). With John it signifies much the same as having eternal life, and indeed the two ideas lie close together in 3 : 16f. and here (*cf.* v. 10).

[33] θύσῃ is usually understood as though it meant simply "kill" and were little more than a synonym for the following ἀπολέσῃ. But the word means "to sacrifice". As "to sacrifice" generally meant also to provide a meal for the worshippers, the secondary meaning developed, "to kill for food". These are the two normal meanings of the verb, "to sacrifice" or "to kill for food". In the New Testament, apart from this passage, there is no occasion when the verb does not have one or other of these meanings. G. D. Kilpatrick examines the word, and concludes that in the present passage "the three verbs have each a proper meaning and none is otiose, 'steal, kill for food, and destroy' " (*BT*, 12, 1961, p. 132).

destroys the sheep. He comes only for harm to the flock and with no interest in its welfare. Christ by contrast ("I" is emphatic) came for the benefit of the sheep. He came that they might have life (for this term see on 1 : 4), and not only life, but a more abundant life (*cf.* 20 : 31). There is nothing cramping or restricting about life for those who enter His fold.

11 Now comes another of Jesus' resounding declarations. For the "I am" sayings see on 6 : 35. That He is the Good[34] Shepherd[35] has meant much to every generation of Christians. It makes an instant appeal to the depths within man, even though man may be a citydweller and have never seen a shepherd in his life. But the thought of the care for the sheep that is involved in the title is plain enough. It is interesting to bear in mind that while there are many things that a shepherd does for his flock, when Jesus speaks of Himself in the capacity of Good Shepherd He immediately goes on to say "the good shepherd layeth down his life[36] for[37] the sheep". This must have been a fairly rare occurrence among Palestinian shepherds.[38] But for Jesus it is the characteristic thing.

---

[34] καλός of course means "beautiful" as well as "good", and Rieu translates "I am the shepherd, the Shepherd Beautiful". Temple also translates "beautiful" but he adds: "Of course this translation exaggerates. But it is important that the word for 'good' here is one that represents, not the moral rectitude of goodness, nor its austerity, but its attractiveness. We must not forget that our vocation is so to practise virtue that men are won to it; it is possible to be morally upright repulsively!" This comment is attractive and draws attention to an important truth, but we must bear in mind John's penchant for variation. In particular it is difficult to see a difference in meaning between καλός and ἀγαθός in this Gospel (see on 1 : 46).

[35] Notice John's habit of introducing variation in statements repeated three times. Here and in v. 14 there are three closely similar statements about the Good Shepherd. In the second, however, "the good shepherd" is not given simply as a title of Jesus, but as the subject of "layeth down his life for the sheep".

[36] τὴν ψυχὴν τιθέναι is a peculiarly Johannine turn of phrase, and one he uses a number of times (vv. 15, 17, 18 (twice); 13 : 37, 38; 15 : 13; I John 3 : 16 (twice)). We might have expected τὴν ψυχὴν δοῦναι as in Mark 10 : 45. John's expression is not found in LXX, the nearest to it being ἐθέμην τὴν ψυχήν μου ἐν τῇ χειρί μου (Judg. 12 : 3; *cf.* I Sam. 19 : 5; 28 : 21; Ps. 118 (119): 109; Job 13 : 14). But there the meaning is *risk* the life, here it is *give* it. The verb is used with τὴν ψυχήν μου in I Kings 19 : 2. The expression does not appear to be classical, LS citing only this Gospel.

[37] For ὑπέρ see on 6 : 51.

[38] Though David, at least, put his life in jeopardy (I Sam. 17 : 34–37; *cf.* also Gen. 31 : 39). David was, of course, remembered as the shepherd-king (Ps. 78 : 70–72).

It is that for which the metaphor is chosen. The great act of care for the sheep which He is impressing on His hearers by this figure is that of laying down the life. Moreover when the Palestinian shepherd did die in defence of his sheep that was an accident. He planned to live for them, not die for them. With Jesus, however, death for the sheep was the set purpose. There is an element of voluntary acceptance of death in the expression "layeth down his life" which ought not to be missed (*cf.* v. 18). One may cavil at Moffatt's translation, "a good shepherd . . .", for Jesus is not classing Himself as one among many shepherds. He is speaking of His own distinctive activity. "A" good shepherd does not characteristically give his life for the sheep. "The" Good Shepherd does. Finally the death of the Palestinian shepherd meant disaster for his sheep. The death of the Good Shepherd means life for His sheep.

12 Jesus contrasts the behaviour of the man who is not really the shepherd at all, but simply a servant, paid to do his work.[39] His interest is in his wages, not the sheep. "Hireling" is perhaps a little too strong for the word, as this has connotations in the English that are missing from the Greek. In the only place where the word is used in the New Testament apart from this verse and the next it refers to fishermen working for pay (Mark 1 : 20; MM cite its use for men paid to carry bricks). But certainly it indicates someone other than the owner. It speaks of a man whose interest is in what he is paid for doing his job rather than in the job itself. So Jesus says explicitly "whose own the sheep are not". Such a man lacks pride of ownership and the care that proceeds from possession. When he sees the wolf coming he does not go into danger. He abandons the sheep and runs. The result is that the

---

[39] The expression ὁ μισθωτὸς καὶ οὐκ ὢν ποιμήν is unusual. The single article links the two members closely together. Our attention is also caught by οὐκ since μή is more usual with participles. This carries some emphasis on factuality. This man is certainly not a shepherd. One is reminded of names in the Old Testament compounded with "not" like "Lo-ammi". Perhaps the meaning here is that a hireling is a "no-shepherd". Moulton includes this passage in a list in many of which "we can distinctly recognise, it seems, the lingering consciousness that the proper negative for a statement of a downright fact is οὐ . . . The closeness of the participle to the indicative in the kinds of sentence found in this list makes the survival of οὐ natural" (M, I, p. 232). BDF notes a preference for καὶ οὐ over καὶ μή but also sees an emphasis on the negation (430(1)).

wolf seizes and scatters the sheep. Presumably this means that he seizes some of the sheep and the rest run in all directions. The Mishnah lays down the legal responsibility of the hired shepherd. An interesting provision is that if one wolf attacks the flock he is required to defend the sheep, but "two wolves count as unavoidable accident" (*i.e.* no blame attaches to the hired man for any damage they may cause).[40] Jesus, however, gives His life for the sheep without condition.

13 The hireling runs away not fortuitously, but because he is what he is, because he is a hireling. His interest is in wages, not sheep. He is not deeply concerned for the sheep.[41] He is not involved in their situation. His passions are not aroused. The interests of the sheep are not a lively concern with him.

14, 15 Again comes the majestic assertion that Jesus is the Good Shepherd, this time not directly linked with His laying down of His life. Instead there is first put forward the relationship between the Good Shepherd and His sheep and arising from that a reiteration of His determination to lay down His life for them. Being the Good Shepherd He knows His sheep. And His sheep know Him (*cf.* v. 4). There is a relationship of mutual knowledge. And this reciprocal knowledge is not superficial but intimate. It is likened to the knowledge wherewith Jesus knows the Father and the Father knows Him.[42] It may be that the love implied in this relationship elicits the following statement that Jesus lays down

---

[40] The quotation is from *B.M.* 7 : 9. The responsibility of the hired shepherd is laid down in *B.M.* 7 : 8, "a paid guardian or a hirer may take an oath if the beast was lamed or driven away or dead, but he must make restitution if it was lost or stolen."

[41] I do not see how *Berkeley* makes a question out of this: "what does he care about the sheep?" If it were a question the $o\dot{v}$ would look for a positive answer. There is moreover nothing to correspond with "what".

[42] This assumes the correctness of the punctuation of ARV. It is, however, possible to put a full stop after $\tau\grave{a}$ $\grave{\epsilon}\mu\acute{a}$ and begin a new sentence with $\varkappa\alpha\vartheta\grave{\omega}\varsigma$ $\gamma\iota\nu\acute{\omega}\sigma\varkappa\epsilon\iota$ $\mu\epsilon$ $\acute{o}$ $\Pi\alpha\tau\acute{\eta}\varrho$. The difficulty is in seeing the point of inserting a reference to the mutual love of the Father and the Son in this way. A difficulty urged against the view I have adopted is that it implies that the knowledge disciples have of Christ is comparable to that between the Father and the Son. But this is reading too much into $\varkappa\alpha\vartheta\grave{\omega}\varsigma$. It does not necessarily denote a very close parallelism. In any case it is not so much the degree of knowledge that is being compared as its reciprocal character. For Jesus' knowledge see on 4 : 18.

His life for the sheep.[43] Or it may be a simple addition. Either way it is the culmination of this part of the discourse. Jesus here speaks directly in the first person, "I lay down my life", whereas in v. 11 He has used the third person, "the good shepherd layeth down his life".

16 Now Jesus looks beyond the immediate circle of His followers to "other sheep". It is difficult to interpret "not of this fold" other than as indicating those who are not to be found within Judaism. The words look to the world-wide scope of the gospel. "I have" shows that these already belong to Christ, even though they have not yet been "brought" (*cf.* Acts 18 : 10, where "I have much people in this city" is used of the Corinthians prior to their conversion). But the bringing of them is an urgent task and Jesus says He "must" perform it. There is a compelling necessity here (see on 4 : 4). Throughout this discourse there is an emphasis on the voice of the shepherd (vv. 3, 4, 5) and thus it is said of these other sheep that are to be brought that they, too, will hear the shepherd's voice. Again the thought is that they will hear with appreciation. The end result is one flock and one shepherd.[44] The other sheep are not to remain distinct from the existing sheep, as though there were to be a Jewish church and a separate Gentile church. They are to become united in one flock. And they all stand under the leadership of one shepherd. The unity is not a natural unity but one brought about by the activity of the Shepherd in "bringing" them.

17 Throughout the discourse the thought that Jesus will lay down His life recurs (vv. 11, 15). Here it is given as the reason for the Father's loving the Son. One might perhaps have expected rather the thought that the Father loves the Son for what He is and that this leads to the cross (*cf.* 3 : 16). But the meaning here is that the death of Jesus is the will of God for Him. And because He is in perfect harmony with the will of God He goes forward to that death. Thus the Father's love is the recognition from the Father's side of the perfect community between them in this

---

[43] Notice that we have here one of John's threefold repetitions with variation. There are references to Christ's laying down His life in vv. 15, 17, 18 and each differs slightly from the others.

[44] We cannot reproduce the play on words in English, μία ποίμνη, εἰς ποιμήν. AV renders "one fold", a reading which goes back to Jerome's Vulgate. But the MSS evidence is solidly against it, and we must read "one flock".

matter.[45] With the death is linked the thought of the resurrection. Christ dies in order[46] that He may rise again. The death is not defeat but victory. It is inseparable from the resurrection.

18 Nowhere is John's view of Jesus as in complete command of every situation brought out more strongly than here. The Lord's death does not take place as the result of misadventure or the might of His foes or the like. No man takes[47] His life from Him. Far from this being the case, He Himself lays it down and does so completely of His own volition. He claims authority[48] both to do this and also to take it again.[49] And, characteristically, the whole is linked with the Father. He gave commandment[50] to this effect and Jesus accordingly is but doing His will.

---

[45] Loyd explains it in these words: "The love of God must needs express itself; and therefore the Father could not love the Son, or know Him, if that Son did not express the Father's love."

[46] If ἵνα is used with full telic force there will be emphasis on the thought that the death of Christ was with a view to the triumph of the resurrection. The resurrection is not simply a happening that chanced to occur, but is as necessary as the crucifixion. The crucifixion led inevitably to the resurrection. But in view of the variety in the usage of ἵνα the point cannot be insisted upon.

[47] It is likely that the more difficult reading ἦρεν is to be preferred, though read only by P45 ℵ*B (P75 is defective, but the editors think the space indicates ἦρεν). In this case Jesus is looking on His death as so certain that it may be regarded as already accomplished.

[48] "Authority" is given some emphasis by the repetition of ἐξουσίαν. The same word is repeated in similar fashion by Pilate (19 : 10).

[49] Notice that Jesus affirms that He Himself has power to take it again. Strachan says: "In the New Testament Jesus is never represented as rising again by His own power." Cf. also Hoskyns: "Elsewhere throughout the New Testament (i.e. apart from here and 2 : 19) the Resurrection of Jesus is always referred to as an act of God." It is undoubtedly the case that the New Testament prefers to speak of God as raising up Jesus, but Jesus several times predicted that He would rise (e.g. Mark 8 : 31; Luke 24 : 7) and there are some passages which say that He did rise (Acts 10 : 41; 17 : 3; I Thess. 4 : 14). We ought not to put any opposition between the Father and the Son in this matter, nor should we doubt that the habitual New Testament form of expression is that the Father raised the Son. But we should not overlook the fact that there is also a strand of New Testament teaching which says that the Son "rose". The present passage fits in with this strand.

[50] John is notably interested in the commandments of God or Christ. He uses ἐντολή 11 times (all but one referring to the divine commandments). The Johannine Epistles use the word 18 times, but no other writing contains the word more often than Romans with 7 times.

(c) The Reaction of the Jews, 10 : 19–21

19 There arose a division again among the Jews because of these words. 20 And many of them said, He hath a demon, and is mad; why hear ye him? 21 Others said, These are not the sayings of one possessed with a demon. Can a demon open the eyes of the blind?

As always, Jesus' words cause division. Some reject Him altogether, repeating the Synoptic canard that he is demon-possessed. Others reject this view on the grounds that a demon can scarcely open the eyes of the blind.

19 "Again" may indicate that the pattern is repeated. Once more there is division[51] among the Jews over words of Jesus. For the plural "words" see on 14 : 24.

20 First, John gives us the view of the opposition party. They put "demon" in an emphatic position: "A demon he has", as indeed they did on three previous occassions (7 : 20; 8 : 48, 52). It is not without its interest that the only occasions in this Gospel when the word "demon" occurs are when the Jews are accusing Jesus of being demon-possessed or when He is defending Himself from the charge (or others are doing so, as v. 21). A further point to be noted is that on this occasion having a demon and being mad are apparently equated. At the least they are thought of in the closest possible connection. In other places (e.g. Matt. 4 : 24)[52] they appear to be distinguished. Those who hold that Jesus has a demon are able to dispense with the evidence. He is mad, they say, and therefore there is no point in taking notice of Him.[53]

21 Others were impressed both by Jesus' words and by His deeds. The words, they affirmed, are not the words of a demon-possessed man. And a demoniac would not have been able to open the eyes of a blind man.[54] Their respect for the facts prevented this

---

[51] The word is σχίσμα, as in 7 : 43 (where see note); 9 : 16.

[52] ARV, it is true, renders σεληνιαζομένους with "epileptic". But the word is equivalent to our "lunatic". Its meaning is given by LS as "to be moonstruck" (though they explain this as epileptic). AV, Phillips and others have translations like "lunatic" or "insane".

[53] For ἀκούω with the genitive see on 5 : 25.

[54] The question introduced by μή looks for a negative answer.

group from prejudging the case. So they refused to condemn Jesus. Yet their position remains entirely a negative one. They say what Jesus is not, but they make no attempt to say what He is.

(d) The Jews' Final Rejection of Jesus, 10 : 22-42

There follows a section introduced by the note that it was the feast of the Dedication. The reference to sheep (vv. 26ff.) connects it with the preceding and marks it as in some sense a continuation. But there is also an advance, notably in the teaching on the unity of the Father and the Son. The question of the Person of Jesus dominates the section. It becomes clear that men must recognize Jesus as standing in such a relation to the Father as none other ever did, or else reject Him entirely.[55] John's account of the public ministry of Jesus ends accordingly with the final breach with the Jews, after which Jesus retires beyond the Jordan.

(i) *The Unity of the Father and the Son, 10 : 22-30*

22 ¹And it was the feast of the dedication at Jerusalem: 23 it was winter; and Jesus was walking in the temple in Solomon's ²porch. 24 The Jews therefore came round about him, and said unto him, How long dost thou hold us in suspense? If thou art the Christ, tell us plainly. 25 Jesus answered them, I told you, and ye believe not: the works that I do in my Father's name, these bear witness of me. 26 But ye believe not, because ye are not of my sheep. 27 My sheep hear my voice, and I know them, and they follow me: 28 and I give unto them eternal life; and they shall never perish, and no one shall snatch them out of my hand. 29 ³My Father, who hath given them unto me, is greater than all; and no one is able to snatch ⁴them out of the Father's hand. 30 I and the Father are one.

¹Some ancient authorities read *At that time was the feast.* ²Or, *portico* ³Some ancient authorities read *That which my Father hath given unto me.* ⁴Or, *aught*

Using the symbolism of the feast of the Dedication John brings us to the last act in Jesus' offer of salvation to the Jews. This feast commemorated the rededication of the temple by Judas Macca-

---

[55] *Cf.* Barrett: "John brings out the point that the issue between Jesus and the Jews is in the last resort Christological, and makes clearer the absolute relation between Jesus and the Father."

baeus in 165 B.C. after its profanation by Antiochus Epiphanes.[56] It was the last great deliverance that the Jews had known and therefore it must have been in men's minds a symbol of their hope that God would again deliver His people. It was an occasion for gratitude to God whose mercy had resulted in renewed opportunity for temple worship and that at a time, as Josephus says, when the people scarcely dared to hope for it.[57] In this present passage John is presenting us with the last act in Jesus' public ministry, and with the Jews' final rejection of all that He stood for. In some aspects the passage is not unlike those in which Matthew and Luke recall that when the messengers of John the Baptist asked Jesus, "Art thou he that cometh?" He replied by pointing to the works that attested His messiahship (Matt. 11 : 2ff.; Luke 7 : 19ff.). It is not otherwise here. There are the thoughts of Jesus' works as bearing witness to His messiahship (v. 25), of the eternal life He gives His sheep (v. 28), of His unity with the Father (v. 30), and of the Father's consecration of Jesus for His work of salvation (v. 36)[58] leading up to the final appeal for faith (v. 38).[59] Perhaps we should also discern the thought of the dedi-

---

[56] For a full discussion of this feast see O. S. Rankin, *The Origins of the Festival of Hanukkah* (Edinburgh, 1930). On the present passage he says: "That this theme, the divine sovereignty in the New Age, should be selected by the author of the Fourth Gospel as the topic for the days of the enkainia may not appear to be accidental if it be recognized that in other instances his mention of a festival serves a wider purpose than merely that of connecting the ministry of Jesus with Jerusalem" (*op. cit.*, p. 278).

[57] Josephus gives a account of the institution of the festival (*Ant.* xii, 316–325). He concludes, "And from that time to the present we observe this festival, which we call the festival of Lights, giving this name to it, I think, from the fact that the right to worship appeared to us at a time when we hardly dared hope for it."

[58] *Cf.* Strachan: "Here he makes use of another feature of the ceremonial of the Feast of Dedication. The altar was rededicated. Here Jesus dedicates Himself to death (*v.* 36)." Similarly Lightfoot maintains that "here the Lord's ministry, which will reach its climax in the passion, is set forth as the true dedication, which is to supersede and replace the Jewish festival."

[59] W. Lüthi reminds us that it is all too easy to repeat the mistake of the Jews. "Nowadays we can understand only too well these people, in their militant mood, rejecting a Shepherd who lets Himself be crucified. A God who fights His battles like a shepherd, and with sheep, is no more popular today than at the feast of the dedication of the Temple. That is where the hidden danger lies for us: it is so easy to whip up a crusading mood over the shameful wrongs of the world and, in so doing, to deny the Shepherd and no longer hear His voice" (pp. 144f.).

cation of a new temple (cf. 2 : 19ff.). All this may well be held to embody the great truths behind that feast of Lights wherein men recalled that the sovereign God, against all the human probabilities, wrought deliverance for His people, brought them out of their darkness, and enabled them to offer real worship.

Let us notice the sequence of thought. Jesus' works bear witness, but the witness is appreciated only by the "sheep". These are eternally safe. No one can take them from His hand. No one can take them from His Father's hand. The justification for two such statements together is the unity between the Father and the Son, to which this whole paragraph leads up. The statement on unity is noteworthy, as is the fact that Jesus links it with the care both have for the sheep.

22 The passage is introduced by mentioning that it was then[60] "the feast of the dedication at Jerusalem".[61] This could possibly be simply a time note, somewhat like 6 : 59, where John has inserted a similar note into a section of discourse, though there the note is one of place. But, as we have already noticed, it is more likely that John means us to see in Jesus the fulfilment of all that the feast stands for. The feast began on 25th Chisleu, and thus took place about November-December in our calendar. It lasted for eight days. The manner of its observance resembled that for the feast of Tabernacles (II Macc. 10 : 6), and indeed, it could be called "the feast of Tabernacles in the month of Chisleu" (II Macc. 1 : 9).

23 For the benefit of those not familiar with the time of this feast John adds that "it was winter". This may be no more than another time note, though some commentators see symbolical

---

[60] $τότε$ is read by P66^c P75 BW etc. and should probably be accepted. Bernard maintains that this word "indicates here that some time had elapsed since the last date mentioned, viz. the Feast of Tabernacles (7^{37})." We should gather the lapse of time however from other things than the use of $τότε$ which does not necessarily indicate any such thing (cf. Acts 17 : 14). Wright in fact argues that the word "suggests a close connexion with the preceding passage". So also Tasker and others. The lapse of time would be more probable if the alternative reading $δέ$ be accepted with P66* $\aleph$ADΘ f13 etc.

[61] For the article with ῾Ιεροσόλυμα see on 2 : 23. The point of mentioning Jerusalem may be that this feast could be observed anywhere. It was not like the three great festivals when men were required to go up to the capital. There is point accordingly in mentioning that Jesus was at Jerusalem for this feast.

importance. They suggest that in John's mind is the thought that it was winter, grim winter, in the relations between Jesus and the Jews. "Porch" should rather be rendered "colonnade". The term denotes a roofed structure supported on pillars. It would have given a certain amount of shelter from the wintry weather. The reference is to a colonnade in Herod's temple. It appears to have been a very old structure, and was popularly thought to have been part of Solomon's temple, though this belief, of course, was not well founded. It is mentioned again in Acts 3 : 11; 5 : 12. It seems to have stretched along the east side of the temple,[62] and apparently was the place where the scribes normally held their schools. Jesus is not depicted as engaging in any formal teaching on this occasion, but simply as walking in this colonnade.

24 As He walked the Jews (see on 1 : 19) crowded round Him. The act of encirclement may indicate a determination to get an answer. They hemmed Him in (*cf.* Phillips: "The Jews closed in on Him"). They are serious and really want a clear reply. Their question[63] as ARV translates it implies that Jesus has not been quite fair to them.[64] He has not made His position plain. They are kept in suspense. So they demand plain[65] speech. But it is possible that we should understand their words to mean "Why dost thou plague us?"[66] In this case the Jews are not quite so

[62] See the note by Kirsopp Lake, *The Beginnings of Christianity*, V (London, 1933), pp. 483ff. See also J. Simons, *Jerusalem in the Old Testament* (Leiden, 1952), pp. 401f. Simons gives reason for thinking that part, at any rate, of this portico was pre-Herodian, and was simply incorporated into Herod's plan (*op. cit.*, p. 421).

[63] ἔλεγον probably indicates persistence. They pressed their question. *Cf.* Weymouth: "kept asking Him".

[64] The Greek is Ἕως πότε τὴν ψυχὴν ἡμῶν αἴρεις; The meaning of ARV may well be possible, but few passages appear to be adduced in which τὴν ψυχὴν αἴρω has the meaning "hold in suspense" (AG cites one). In the LXX the expression is used of religious aspiration, of lifting up the soul to God (Ps. 25 : 1; 86 : 4; 143 : 8), but this is an impossible meaning here. Similar to LXX is Josephus' reference to certain Israelites who "*with hearts elated* at the peril, were ready to face the horror of it" (*Ant.* iii, 48).

[65] παρρησία has the meaning "boldly" as well as "plainly". The choice of word may contain the hint of an accusation of timidity.

[66] A. Pallis argues persuasively for this translation from the usage in modern Greek, which, he thinks, has retained something of the idiom. He cites ὡς πότε θὰ μᾶς βγάζεις τὴν ψυχή, "how long will you plague us?" (*A Few Notes on the Gospels according to St. Mark and St. Matthew*, Liverpool, 1903, pp. vf.; so also in *Notes on St John and the Apocalypse*, Oxford, n.d., pp. 23f.). This must remain a possible interpretation of the passage.

friendly and their demand for plain speaking will have been made
in a hostile spirit. They may also mean "Why dost thou take away
our life?"[67] in which case the Jews appear to be discerning,
somewhat in the manner of Caiaphas in 11 : 48, that the drift
of Jesus' teaching meant the end of Judaism. He has warned
them that they will die in their sins unless they believe in Him
(8 : 21, 24), and He appears to be looking for followers outside
Judaism (v. 16). The logical outcome of such a program is the end
of exclusivism. They rightly discern that the critical question is
that of Jesus' messiahship and accordingly they proceed to interrogate Him on the matter. This makes the present passage important for the understanding of this Gospel, the aim of which
is to show that Jesus is the Messiah and to bring men to believe
on Him as such (20 : 31). The basic question is whether Jesus is
or is not the Messiah (see on 1 : 41). As the passage unfolds it
becomes clear that messiahship is not something that can be
recognized by all, but only by the "sheep" (v. 26). It becomes
clear also that the work of the Messiah is to bring eternal life, a
life which can never be lost because the Messiah is one with God.[68]
Their "thou" is emphatic, perhaps implying that He is far from
being the glorious being that the Christ should be.

25 In view of the erroneous ideas of messiahship held by His
questioners, to answer either "Yes" or "No" would have been
misleading. But Jesus' assertion that He has already told them
raises a problem, for no answer to this question has been given
in specific terms in this Gospel. Jesus has spoken unequivocally
to the Samaritan women (4 : 26), and He has also disclosed Himself
to the man born blind (9 : 35ff.), but He has not said to any of
the Jews in set terms that He is the Christ. He may mean that
the general drift of His teaching is so clear that if they had come
in the right attitude they would have believed,[69] just as His disciples

---

[67] The cogent argument in favor of this is that the nearest parallel to the
expression, which is no further away than v. 18, is οὐδεὶς ἦρεν αὐτὴν ἀπ'
ἐμοῦ, where αὐτήν refers back to ψυχήν and the expression signifies death.
This is the case also with αἴρεται ... ἡ ζωὴ αὐτοῦ in Acts 8 : 33 (a quotation
from LXX).

[68] *Cf.* Dodd: "With complete dramatic appropriateness the Jews ask 'Are
you the Messiah?' Jesus's avowal is all but explicit, but in the course of the
dialogue we learn what the Messiah really is: He is the Son who being one
with the Father is the Giver of eternal life" (*IFG*, p. 361).

[69] *Cf.* Calvin: "they accuse His teaching of obscurity, when it was abundantly
plain and distinct but for falling on deaf ears."

did (*cf.* 6 : 68f.). Or He may mean that such statements as "before Abraham was born, I am" (8 : 58) are the answer. Or, as the rest of the verse indicates, He may mean that His works and His whole manner of life are such that the answer to the question is plain for all who really want to know. Notice His "ye believe not". It denotes a present attitude, and not simply a past state, and it indicates the root trouble. These people had no faith. The "works" will mean particularly the miracles, but the term is broad enough to embrace other things as well, and may include all His deeds of kindness (see Additional Note G, pp. 684ff.). These works were done "in my Father's name" (for "the name" see on 1 : 12), *i.e.* they accord with all that the Father stands for, they fit in with His revealed character. And these works "bear witness" (see on 1 : 7 for "witness", and *cf.* 5 : 36 for Jesus' works bearing witness). They are not empty, though spectacular. They are meaningful and they point men to the truth of God. The trouble with these men is that they do not pay attention to the significance of what is going on before their very eyes. The very recent healing of the blind man is in their minds (v. 21), and this should answer their question. Such works do indeed bear a vivid witness.[70]

26 "But" is the strong adversative.[71] Far from their heeding the witness, their habitual attitude is one of unbelief. The predestinarian strain in this Gospel comes out in the reason given for their failure: "ye are not of my sheep". Christ's "sheep" know Him (v. 14), but the knowledge of Christ is not the natural possession of any man. Faith is always a gift of God.

27 Christ's sheep hear His voice, an aspect of the sheep-shepherd relationship that has been stressed in this chapter (vv. 3, 4, 5, 16). One might have expected "and they know me", but the proposition is reversed. It is the knowledge Christ has of the sheep that is the important thing, and accordingly it is this that receives the emphasis. The result of this knowledge is that they follow Him, the present tense denoting a habitual following.

---

[70] Ryle has an interesting note: "We should observe how our Lord always and confidently appeals to the evidence of His miracles. Those who try to depreciate and sneer at miracles, seem to forget how often they are brought forward as good witnesses in the Bible. This, in fact, is their great object and purpose." The general attitude toward miracles in modern times should not blind us to the significance such "works" held for the New Testament writers.

[71] Ἀλλά (see on 1 : 8).

28 Eternal life is His gift. It is often emphasized that the important thing about eternal life is its quality rather than its quantity. It is life of a certain kind, and not simply life that goes on for ever. While there is truth in this, yet we should not overlook the point that in fact eternal life does not end. It is this aspect that is prominent here. Those to whom Christ gives the gift will "never perish".[72] This perhaps points to the impossibility of a steady decay setting in which would end in total loss. At the end of the verse the thought is rather that of active evil. No one whatever will snatch[73] them from Christ. It is one of the precious things about the Christian faith that our continuance in eternal life depends not on our feeble hold on Christ, but on His firm grip on us. We should notice that the teaching of this verse is not that believers will be saved from all earthly disaster, but that they will be saved, no matter what earthly disaster may befall.

29 This is a very difficult verse. The true text appears to be as ARV mg., "That which my Father hath given unto me is greater than all",[74] but the sense of the passage seems to require something

---

[72] Barrett argues that in John $εἰς$ $τὸν$ $αἰῶνα$ does no more than strengthen the negative $οὐ$ $μή$: "not 'They shall not perish eternally' but 'They shall never perish' " and he cites 11 : 26. That passage, however, seems to prove the very opposite. Jesus, surely, is not saying to Martha that the man who believes in Him "will never die". There is a sense in which he will die (unless he is alive at the Second Coming). Jesus is saying "He will not die eternally". And so here. In any case it is difficult to see what " They shall never perish" means if we exclude "They shall not perish eternally".

[73] There is a notion of violence in $ἁρπάζω$. But even this will not suffice to remove them from Christ's hand.

[74] $ὅ$ ... $μεῖζον$ is read by B*latt bo Ambr Hier; the masculine $ὅς$ ... $μείζων$ by P66 f1 f13 syr sa ac ac²; the combination $ὅ$ ... $μείζων$ by ℵ W and $ὅς$ ... $μεῖζον$ by AΘ (P75 has $ὅς$, but a gap prevents our knowing whether it had $μείζων$ or $μεῖζον$). D has the reading $ὁ$ $δεδωκώς$ $μοι$ $πάντων$ $μείζων$. This is a confused picture, but the best explanation appears to be that the first reading is original and that the others represent attempts to make better sense of it. The neuter is undoubtedly difficult (cf. Matt. 12 : 42; Luke 11 : 31), but cf. 1 : 4; 6 : 39; 17 : 2, and the somewhat similar $Πάτερ$, $ὅ$ $δεδωκάς$ $μοι$, $θέλω$ ... (17 : 24). Hoskyns refuses to see much difference in meaning. All the readings, he says, mean that "The Father is the only source of the ultimate security of the believers in Jesus. They belong to Jesus because they have been given to Him by the Father." Those who reject the neuter and take the masculine, at least in the pronoun, do not always face the difficulties of this reading. Neither $δέδωκεν$ nor $ἁρπάζειν$ has an object on this view and this is an unlikely piece of Greek. For the Father's gifts to the Son see on 3 : 35.

like ARV text, "My Father, who hath given them unto me, is greater than all". But the suspicion remains that the popularity of the latter reading is because the former was found so difficult. Taking the former as original the meaning appears to be that the flock that the Father has given the Son is greater in His eyes[75] than anything else on earth. Since He thus attaches the highest value to it He will look after it to the end. Or the meaning may possibly be that the quality of life, the life of eternity which the Father has given is greater than anything else. Or again, it may be the divine plan for salvation, the charge given by the Father to the Son, as Stephen M. Reynolds argues.[76] But it seems to me that the more probable reference is to the church. *Cf.* I John 5 : 4: "whatsoever is begotten of God overcometh the world". The context seems to demand that it is the "sheep" that are given.[77] Notice that the statement here is more far-reaching than that in the previous verse. There we had a future, "no one *shall* snatch them"; here it is "no one *is able to* snatch them".[78] This Shepherd is all-powerful and the sheep in His hand have nothing to fear.

30 The bracketing of "I" and "the Father" is significant in itself quite apart from the predicate. Who else could be linked with God the Father in this fashion? "One" is neuter, "one thing" and not "one person".[79] Identity is not asserted, but essential unity is. These two belong together. The statement does not go beyond the opening words of the Gospel, but it can stand with them. It

---

[75] For the use of μείζων in this sense *cf.* Matt. 23 : 17, 19.

[76] *Westminster Theological Journal*, XXVIII, 1965–66, pp. 38–41.

[77] *Twentieth Century* renders: "What my Father has entrusted to me is more than all else". *Cf.* also Knox: "This trust which my Father has committed to me is more precious than all else".

[78] This assumes that the generally accepted text is correct. A difficulty is the use of the present infinitive ἁρπάζειν after δύναται, whereas, unless there were some stress on continuity, we would anticipate the aorist, ἁρπάσαι. This is actually read by a few cursives, but it seems to be only an attempt to improve the grammar. The Sinaitic Syriac omits δύναται (see Burkitt's edition), and presupposes ἁρπάζει. Abbott cites this reading also from Origen and thinks it probably correct (2767). But this, too, looks like an attempt to tidy up the grammar. It seems much more likely that δύναται ἁρπάζειν is original.

[79] ἕν not εἷς. There is a similar expression in I Cor. 3 : 8, ὁ φυτεύων δὲ καὶ ὁ ποτίζων ἕν εἰσιν, and this should warn us against reading too much into the expression. We should also notice the usage in 17 : 11 where our Lord prays ἵνα ὦσιν ἓν καθὼς ἡμεῖς. Cf. also 17 : 22f., ἵνα ὦσιν ἓν καθὼς ἡμεῖς ἕν . . . ἵνα ὦσιν. τετελειωμένοι εἰς ἕν.

is another statement which puts Jesus Christ with God rather than with man. It may be true that this ought not to be understood as a metaphysical statement, but it is also true that it means more than that Jesus' will was one with the Father's.[80] As Hoskyns remarks, "the Jews would not presumably have treated as blasphemy the idea that a man could regulate his words and actions according to the will of God". But they did regard this as blasphemy as the next verse shows. They had asked Jesus for a plain assertion of His messiahship, and they got more than they had bargained for.

(ii) *A Charge of Blasphemy Rebutted, 10 : 31-39*

31 The Jews took up stones again to stone him. 32 Jesus answered them, Many good works have I showed you from the Father; for which of those works do ye stone me? 33 The Jews answered him, For a good work we stone thee not, but for blasphemy; and because that thou, being a man, makest thyself God. 34 Jesus answered them, Is it not written in your law, [1]I said, Ye are gods? 35 If he called them gods, unto whom the word of God came (and the scripture cannot be broken), 36 say ye of him, whom the Father [2]sanctified and sent into the world, Thou blasphemest; because I said, I am the Son of God? 37 If I do not the works of my Father, believe me not. 38 But if I do them, though ye believe not me, believe the works: that ye may know and understand that the Father is in me, and I in the Father. 39 They sought again to take him: and he went forth out of their hand.

[1]Ps. lxxxii. 6. [2]Or, *consecrated*

The Jews' reaction to Jesus' great assertion is the extreme one of trying to stone Him. But He stays them with an argument based on Ps. 82 : 6. If there is a sense in which the term "gods"

---

[80] Augustine is often quoted in order to be refuted. He comments "when He says, 'I and the Father are one,' hear both, both the *one, unum*, and the *are, sumus*, and thou shalt be delivered both from Charybdis and from Scylla. In these two words, in that He said *one*, He delivers thee from Arius; in that He said *are*, He delivers thee from Sabellius. If *one*, therefore not diverse; if *are*, therefore both Father and Son" (XXXVI. 9; p. 211). It is, of course, true that our Lord was not speaking with respect to the controversies that excited the church in later times. But it is also true that His words have implications, and it was natural for those embroiled in the controversies to seek out the implications.

may be legitimately applied to men, then much more may Jesus assert His unity with His Father.

31 The Jews could regard Jesus' words only as blasphemy, and they proceeded to take the judgment into their own hands.[81] It was laid down in the Law that blasphemy was to be punished by stoning (Lev. 24 : 16). But these men were not allowing the due processes of law to take their course. They were not preparing an indictment so that the authorities could take the requisite action. In their fury they were preparing to be judges and executioners in one.[82] "Again" will refer back to their previous attempt at stoning (8 : 59).

32 But they did not actually throw their stones. Before this happened Jesus "answered" them with a question (for this use of "answered" cf. 2 : 18; 5 : 17). We should not miss the calm courage He displayed. He did not run away, nor apparently show any signs of fear or the like. In the face of stoning He quietly resumed the discussion, and pointed out that He had done[83] many good works.[84] Notice that He adds, "from the Father". He is not acting in isolation. Then He inquires which[85] of these good works is the

---

[81] "Took up" is ἐβάστασαν, "carried". There would be no stones in Solomon's colonnade, and they would have to bring them there.

[82] Yet we should not overlook the fact that in certain cases lynch law was encouraged rather than the reverse. "If a man stole a sacred vessel or cursed by Kosem or made an Aramean woman his paramour, the zealots may fall upon him. If a priest served (at the Altar) in a state of uncleanness his brethren the priests did not bring him to the court, but the young men among the priests took him outside the Temple Court and split open his brain with clubs" (*Sanh.* 9 : 6). The last mentioned practice is all the more curious in that the legal penalty for the offence was apparently no more than scourging (*Makk.* 3 : 2).

[83] He actually says "showed". The miracles were "signs" pointing out the way. The use of the aorist is perhaps a little curious but it must be borne in mind that the perfect of δείκνυμι is not common. It is not found anywhere in the New Testament (where the verb occurs 32 times).

[84] The word order puts some emphasis on καλά and also on ἔργα. The works He did were *good* works from the Father. They were about to stone Him, but what He had done was work, not blasphemy. Notice that the adjective καλός is that used of the Shepherd (vv. 11, 14). As is the Shepherd, so are His works.

[85] "Which" translates ποῖον, "of what kind". It refers to the quality of the action, a quality Jesus has in this case characterized as καλά. It is the quality of the actions which shows their divine origin, and the choice of word invites the Jews to consider their significance.

cause of the attempt at stoning.[86]

33 The reply rejects any thought that they are stoning Jesus for a good work. It is blasphemy[87] to which they object. They particularize.[88] Jesus, they affirm, is a man,[89] yet makes Himself God.[90] This shows that they had discerned accurately enough what His teaching meant. What they did not stop to consider was whether it was true. This is the first occasion on which the charge of blasphemy is made, though we may fairly say that it is presupposed elsewhere (*e.g.* 8 : 59).

34 Jesus' answer is to direct them to Scripture. He uses the term "law", which strictly applied only to the Pentateuch, but which was extended in meaning to embrace the whole Old Testament, and this is the use here, for the passage He cites is from the Psalms. For the expression "your law" see on 8 : 17. Jesus points out that in Ps. 82 : 6 it stands written,[91] "Ye are gods" (the citation is exact, agreeing both with the Hebrew and LXX). The passage refers to the judges of Israel, and the expression "gods" is applied to them in the exercise of their high and God-given office.[92]

---

[86] BDF see in λιθάζετε here an example of a "conative present", explained as "an attempted but incomplete action". They translate *"want to stone me?"* (319).

[87] It is sometimes said that this charge can scarcely be historical since according to the Mishnah it was necessary to pronounce the sacred name for a man to be guilty of blasphemy (*Sanh.* 7 : 5), and there is no evidence that Jesus did this. But this ignores the facts that (*a*) the Mishnah represents Pharisaic Judaism and does not give the views of the Sadducees who were important in this connection; (*b*) Jesus' enemies were anxious to be rid of Him and would not boggle at legal niceties; (*c*) in any case there was a broader interpretation of blasphemy, based on passages like Num. 15 : 30f.; Deut. 21 : 22, as SBk show (I, pp. 1008–19). They regard the present passage as coming under this broader heading based on Deut. 21 : 22 (*op. cit.*, p. 1017).

[88] καὶ ὅτι does not introduce a new charge, "and that", but explains and amplifies the charge already made, "even that".

[89] For John's use of ἄνθρωπος of Jesus see on 4 : 29.

[90] McClymont neatly comments: "In reality He, being God, had become man (Phil. ii. 5–8)."

[91] For John's formula of citation see on 2 : 17.

[92] I have discussed the passage in Ps. 82 in *The Biblical Doctrine of Judgment* (London, 1960), pp. 34ff. Since then J. A. Emerton's discussion has appeared (*JThS*, n.s., XI, 1960, pp. 329–32). He takes "gods" in Ps. 82 to refer to beings who "were regarded as angels by the Jews, but as gods by the gentiles." He concludes that Jesus "does not find an Old Testament text to prove directly that men can be called god. He goes back to fundamental principles and argues, more generally, that the word 'god' can, in certain circumstances, be applied

35 Now Jesus unfolds the implication of this statement. If we translate "If he . . ." (as ARV) the words will be regarded as the utterance of God, but it is also possible to render "If it . . ." when the law will be the subject. Either way a very high authority is being recognized in Scripture, for Jesus goes on "and the scripture cannot be broken".[93] Notice that he says this, not in connection with some declaration which might be regarded as among the key declarations of the Old Testament, but of what we might perhaps call without disrespect a rather run-of-the-mill passage.[94] The singular is usually held to refer to a definite passage from the Old

---

to beings other than God himself, to whom he has committed authority" (*op. cit.*, pp. 330, 332). Emerton's discussion, in my opinion, suffers from the defect that it makes no allowance for the context in which the expression occurs in Ps. 82. It is very difficult to see how this can refer to either angels or gods. It refers to men, to human judges. A better explanation than Emerton's is that of A. T. Hanson who takes seriously the Rabbinic view that the Psalm was spoken to Israel by God at Sinai (*NTS*, 11, 1964–65, pp. 158–62). He thinks that John thought of the pre-existent Word, rather than God, as addressing the Jews, and that this gives the citation relevance: "if to be addressed by the pre-existent Word justifies men in being called gods, indirect and mediated though that address was (coming perhaps through Moses, certainly written down only through David), far more are we justified in applying the title Son of God to the human bearer of the pre-existent Word, sanctified and sent by the Father as he was, in unmediated and direct presence" (*op. cit.*, p. 161). M. de Jonge and A. S. van der Woude draw attention to a recently discovered Qumran Scroll in which Melchizedek is regarded as the speaker of Ps. 82 and evil angels as the addressees (*NTS*, 12, 1965–66, pp. 301–26). They disagree with Hanson's interpretation but do not offer one of their own. Emerton claims the scroll as support for his position (*JThS*, n.s., XVII, 1966, pp. 399–401), but Hanson disputes the correctness of this and vindicates his own position in the face of the criticisms offered (*NTS*, 13, 1966–67, pp. 363–67).

[93] It is possible to take καὶ οὐ δύναται λυθῆναι ἡ γραφή as a parenthesis. But it is perhaps better to regard it as depending also on εἰ, which then introduces two certainties – that the passage calls men "gods", and that the Scripture cannot be broken.

[94] B. B. Warfield has a valuable note on this passage (*The Inspiration and Authority of the Bible*, London, 1951, pp. 138ff.), in which he stresses this point: "Now, what is the particular thing in Scripture, for the confirmation of which the indefectible authority of Scripture is thus invoked? It is one of its most casual clauses – more than that, the very form of its expression in one of its most casual clauses. This means, of course, that in the Saviour's view the indefectible authority of Scripture attaches to the very form of expression of its most casual clauses. It belongs to Scripture through and through, down to its most minute particulars, that it is of indefectible authority" (*op. cit.*, p. 140).

Testament and not to Scripture as a whole. Even so, what was true of this passage could be true only because it was part of the inspired Scriptures and showed the characteristics of the whole. Jesus puts all His emphasis on the exact word used. The argument would fall to the ground if any other word for "judge" had been employed. Yet Jesus not only appeals to the word, but says in connection with it that Scripture cannot be broken. The term "broken" is not defined, and it is a word which is not often used of Scripture or the like (though it is so used in 7 : 23 and *cf.* 5 : 18; Matt. 5 : 19). But it is perfectly intelligible. It means that Scripture cannot be emptied of its force by being shown to be erroneous. Jesus' point here is that the Bible calls "gods" those who were no more than men. They were themselves the recipients of "the word of God", *i.e.* they were required to hear and heed and obey the word of God, primarily of course in connection with their calling as judges. Yet these men were on this occasion called "gods".

36 In the light of this word of Scripture Jesus asks whether they can say[95] that He blasphemes[96] when He calls Himself the[97] Son of God (for this term see on 5 : 25). It is sometimes said that this verse classes Jesus as a man among men, and shows that His claims to divinity are not to be taken seriously. But notice that His argument runs not, "Psalm 82 speaks of men as gods; therefore I in common with other men may use the term of Myself", but rather, "If in any sense the Psalm may apply this term to men,

---

[95] There is an air of incredulity about the question. Notice the emphatic ὑμεῖς – you, who regard yourselves as the keepers and expounders of the Law. Abbott points out that it is only in special circumstances that ὑμεῖς λέγετε can be used interrogatively at the beginning of a clause, and he includes this passage as one of two in John in which "a conditional clause ('if... as you cannot deny') prepares the way for something incongruous with that condition, which incongruity is expressed by an interrogative or exclamation of amazement" (2244).

[96] BDF select this as "a characteristic example" of the tendency of the New Testament narrators, and especially Mark and John, to use direct rather than indirect speech. They point out that βλασφημεῖν "would connect up much better with the preceding ὅν etc." (470(1)). Notice that though direct speech is used the quotation does not give us the exact word used, at least as John reports it. He is giving us the sense of their words, rather than a transcript.

[97] Υἱός is anarthrous and sometimes this is pressed, but wrongly. This is surely another example of the definite predicate preceding the copula and therefore being without the article (see on 1 : 1).

then much more may it be applied to Him whom the Father
sanctified and sent into the world." Jesus is not classing Himself
among men. He calls Himself "him, whom the Father sanctified
and sent into the world" (for "sent" see on 3 : 17). He separates
and distinguishes Himself from men. His argument is of the "How
much more –" variety. A minor difficulty arises from the fact
that Jesus has not previously in this Gospel told the Jews that He
is "the Son of God". But this is no more than a question of terminology. He has spoken of Himself as "the Son", and referred to
God as His Father in such a way as to leave no doubt that He
claims a special relationship. It is His way of accepting the charge
made against Him in v. 33. He does not deny the charge, but
He denies that the Jews are right in their understanding of the
situation. They thought He was making Himself God. He held
that He was not making Himself anything. He was what He was,
and it was the Father who in the first instance sent Him into the
world, and in the second instance testified of Him (5 : 37).

37, 38 Jesus tells them to let His works (see Additional Note G,
pp. 684ff.) be the criterion. They show the reality of the situation.
He is ready to stand or fall by the works. If He does not do[98] "the
works of the Father", then He is ready for them not to believe[99] Him
(the dative denotes simple credence, not trust; see Additional Note
E, pp. 335ff.). But if He does do such works the situation is different.
If[100] they are not prepared to believe Him let them believe the works
(simple credence both times). He suggests that they do this so
that[101] they may come into important knowledge. The expression
translated, "that ye may know and understand" contains the

---

[98] εἰ οὐ ποιῶ is used rather than εἰ μὴ ποιῶ, which probably signifies
that the negative is more or less equivalent to the á-privative, as though negative
and verb were one: "if I were to leave undone . . .", "if I were to omit to do. . . ."

[99] The present imperative is curious, for we would naturally understand
μὴ πιστεύετε to mean "stop believing". Such a meaning is impossible here
and we must take it to mean "do not have a continual trust".

[100] Burton classes this among concessive clauses referring to the future.
Where the subjunctive is used it is to denote "a future possibility, or what
is rhetorically conceived to be possible". He goes on "Καὶ ἐάν introduces an
extreme case, usually one which is represented as highly improbable" (*Moods*,
285(b)).

[101] ἵνα will here have its full telic force.

528

same verb twice over,[102] the tense only being changed. The two verbs in ARV are an attempt to bring out the significance of this change of tense. The first verb is in the aorist with the meaning, "That ye may come to know", whereas the second is in the present signifying, "and keep on knowing". Jesus is looking for them to have a moment of insight and then to remain permanently in the knowledge that that moment has brought them. The knowledge to which a right perception of the works would bring them is that of the mutual indwelling of the Father and the Son. Such works could not be done by a mere man, acting of himself (as the blind man had so clearly stated, 9 : 30ff.). For Jesus' obedience to the Father, see on 4 : 34.

39 This brought the discussion to an end. But instead of renewing their attempt to stone Him His enemies now tried to arrest[103] Him (though possibly they simply wanted to take Him out for stoning; we do not know for certain, but it looks more like judicial proceedings this time). But their attempt was not successful. John does not say why, but contents himself with registering their failure. It is not necessary to think of a miracle, but it is necessary to see that until His "hour" came Jesus was safe from men. It is possible that the singular "hand" reflects a Semitic usage, for Greek often has the plural.[104] It is also not unlikely that John has in mind a contrast between the "hand" of the enemy, impotent to arrest, and the "hand" of the Father, mighty to protect (v. 29).

(iii) *Retirement beyond Jordan, 10 : 40–42*

40 And he went away again beyond the Jordan into the place where John was at the first baptizing; and there he abode. 41 And many came unto him; and they said, John indeed did no sign: but all things whatsoever John spake of this man were true. 42 And many believed on him there.

The result of the Jews' hostility was that Jesus withdrew to the land on the other side of the Jordan. But this did not mean

---

102 ἵνα γνῶτε καὶ γινώσκητε. Some MSS read πιστεύσητε, as ℵA f13 *etc.*, but this seems to be no more than a scribal variant arising because of the difficulty of γινώσκητε after γνῶτε. The same is perhaps true of the omission of the second verb by D syrˢ *etc.*

103 Notice the change of tense: ἐζήτουν, "they kept on seeking"; πιάσαι, "to lay hold on Him once and for all". ἐξῆλθεν also points to a single action: "He went on out".

104 See the discussion by Turner (M, III, pp. 23ff.).

the end of His influence. People sought Him out there, particularly people who had been influenced by John the Baptist's witness to Him. **40** Jesus went away from Jerusalem to the far side of the Jordan.[105] The locality is stated with some precision as the place where John the Baptist was baptizing[106] at first. This is a small touch, but it shows us that the author knew what he was describing. Jesus remained there for some time ("abode"),[107] but the length of stay is not closely defined.

41 The change of scene did not mean a diminution of activity. If Jesus was no longer moving among the people the people sought Him out where He was. It is interesting that the reason they gave[108] was the ministry of John the Baptist, for he has not been mentioned since 5 : 36, when his activity was referred to as though already past. But his influence lived on. Men still treasured his words, and acted on them. It is not without significance that this, the final mention of John in this Gospel, at one and the same time sounds a note of high praise and puts a definite stress on his subordinate position. It is high praise, for it affirms that his witness to Jesus was true, and true in its entirety. But there is subordination, for John did no miracle.[109] His function was solely to bear witness to Jesus (see on 1 : 7).[110]

---

[105] It seems probable that we should translate πάλιν as "back" rather than "again" (see on 6 : 15). Jesus went back to the early scenes of His ministry, the place where John had been as he baptized. *Cf.* Moffatt: "went across the Jordan, back to the spot. . . ."

[106] It is a question whether we are to understand ἦν . . . βαπτίζων as a periphrastic tense or not. If so there will be stress on the continuous nature of John's activities. But the context does not require anything of the sort, and it seems better to take the expression as signifying "where John was at first, baptizing".

[107] ἔμεινεν read by the MS tradition as a whole, but ἔμενεν by B it. If the former reading be adopted the aorist may be constative, regarding the stay as a completed whole, or perhaps ingressive, "he settled down". In its favor is the fact that it is John's habit to use the aorist rather than the imperfect of this verb (apart from this verse the imperfect does not occur in this Gospel). Against is the possibility that he chose the less usual tense here to stress the length of Jesus' stay.

[108] ἔλεγον is a continuous tense: "they kept saying".

[109] σημεῖον in John denotes "miracle". See on 2 : 11, and Additional Note G, pp. 684ff.

[110] Notice that the grammatical construction is a little unusual. After Ἰωάννης μέν we would anticipate οὗτος δέ. Alternatively πάντα δέ might have been preceded by σημεῖον μέν. It is difficult to see how πάντα δέ answers to Ἰωάννης μέν.

42 The result was that many came to believe on Jesus (see Additional Note E, pp. 335ff., for "believing"). The addition of "there" is probably significant. It may envisage a process similar to that at Samaria. There the woman brought men to Jesus, but they believed, not because of her words, but because they heard Him themselves (4 : 39ff.). So here John's testimony led these people to seek out Jesus, but faith came because of their contact with the Lord. They believed, not at home reflecting on what John had said, but "there". The word may also contain an implied contrast with Judea. In the place where one might have thought He would be welcomed men tried to stone Him. Now in despised Perea men believed on Him.

CHAPTER XI

18. The Seventh Sign – The Raising of Lazarus, 11 : 1–57

In a sense the problems of the Fourth Gospel may be said to be summed up in miniature in this chapter. John narrates here a stupendous miracle – the raising of a man who had been dead for four days. Moreover he says that this was done in circumstances which necessarily involved publicity and that in Bethany, a little village no more than a couple of miles from Jerusalem. The miracle was witnessed by some of "the Jews" who told the Pharisees what had been done (v. 46). It was on account of this that the chief priests and Pharisees consulted about how Jesus could be destroyed and thus was instituted the chain of events that was to lead to His death.

All this is perfectly straightforward. Critics might be expected to boggle at the thought of a dead man's being raised, but had this been the only Gospel we possessed, it is likely that the discussion would have centred on the type of event which lay at the heart of the story. But we possess also the three synoptic Gospels and none of them so much as mentions this miracle.[1] It may be

---

[1] *Cf.* A. Richardson: "The reason for thinking that the Lazarus story is not literally true is not that it is difficult to believe ... The difficulty about accepting it as literally true is that it cannot be reconciled with the Synoptic tradition." Earlier he has said, "St John expresses the truth of history by means of a story that is not literally true." But, though he is thus alert to the difficulties of the traditional view, he totally ignores the difficulty involved in his own. For example he never attempts to show how such an attitude to historical truth is compatible with the aim of combating opponents of a "Docetic" type, an aim which almost all admit to have been one of John's motives. These men rejected the historical fact of the Incarnation, while accepting Christ as the supreme revelation of truth. But Richardson's evaluation of John's method rather classes him with such men than sets him in opposition to them. Westcott pinpoints another difficulty: "No explanation of the origin of the narrative on the supposition that it is unhistorical, has even a show of plausibility. Those who deny the fact are sooner or later brought to maintain either that the scene was an imposture, or that the record is a fiction. Both of these hypotheses involve a moral miracle." In any case it is to be noted that the kind of critic who rejects the historicity of this story because it is not in the Synoptics is usually not ready to accept what is there, the feeding of the multitude, for example. On this Richardson himself says, "it is clear to us that in the Feeding

fairly argued in many cases that there was no reason why the synoptists should include some of the things that John narrates. They had plenty of material of their own and in any case no-one expects them to have known all the information that was at the disposal of the Fourth Evangelist.

But in the case of the raising of Lazarus things are said to be different. The publicity of which John speaks makes it difficult to see how this miracle should not have been known to the synoptists. And if they did know it, and if it had the consequences that John says it had, it is difficult to see why they should have omitted it.[2] They seem to give to the events associated with the triumphal entry and the cleansing of the temple the role of initiating the events that were to issue in the crucifixion, whereas for John it seems to be the raising of Lazarus which does this.

It is not surprising accordingly that quite a battle has raged round the interpretation of this chapter. Of those who do not see the story as historical[3] some have suggested that it is inspired by the scattered references in Luke. There we read of Martha and Mary (Luke 10 : 38–42), of an unnamed woman who anointed Jesus (Luke 7 : 36–50), of a character called Lazarus in a parable and a resurrection parable at that (Luke 16 : 19–31). But in the

---

stories, even in St Mark's version, we do not have simple straightforward historical accounts of 'what happened', but elaborately theological interpretations which have turned the historical facts into profound parables of the significance of the person of Christ and of the Eucharist in his Church" (*An Introduction to the Theology of the New Testament*, London, 1958, p. 102). There appears to be something other than the absence of synoptic attestation which causes the hesitation.

[2] Yet possibly we are unconsciously expecting the Evangelists to see things as we see them. *Cf.* E. M. Sidebottom: "it must be remembered that in the world of those days tales of marvels and omens, rivers running blood and stones gushing out water were of everyday occurrence ... The 'tremendous miracle' of the raising of a dead man would not be such a sensation to a first-century writer as to necessitate its inclusion by Mark; Luke's widow of Nain and her son are tucked away into a corner" (*The Christ of the Fourth Gospel*, London, 1961, p. 179).

[3] Hamilton finds it impossible to say what happened. He goes on: "We can, of course, decide on principle that this did not happen, merely because this kind of thing cannot happen. But perhaps it should not be quite so easy for us to make our peace with these difficult portions of the New Testament. If God is really doing something in Jesus Christ that is unique, can we decide on the impossibility of incomprehensible or improbable events with assurance?"

first place, it is difficult to see how such material could give rise to
our story, and in the second, it is a fallacy to suppose that John had
no information other than that contained in the Synoptics. Others
see in it no more than a dramatic illustration of Jesus' words "I
am the resurrection, and the life" (v. 25; *cf.* also 5 : 21, 25), a
kind of acted parable.[4] It is difficult to reconcile this with John's
method, however, and few find this really satisfactory. It seems
clear that John believed he was narrating something that had
actually happened. The multiplicity of factual details he includes
is evidence of that.[5] In a symbolic narrative there would be no
need for details like the names of the persons and the village,
the distance from Jerusalem, and so on. We are faced with the
straight choice between accepting what he says, and refusing to
accept the story as credible because of our regard for the synoptic
tradition. Yet it must be borne in mind that the Synoptists do
speak of Jesus as claiming to raise the dead (Matt. 11 : 5; Luke
7 : 22), and they give two specific examples, the daughter of Jairus
(Matt. 9 : 18ff.; Mark 5 : 22ff.; Luke 8 : 41ff.), and the son of
the widow of Nain (Luke 7 : 11ff.). It is possible that they saw
no need to add to these.

It is also to be borne in mind that, if the traditional view that
the reminiscences of St. Peter lie behind the Second Gospel is
true, the silence of the Synoptists may be explicable. Peter is not
mentioned in John between 6 : 68 and 13 : 6, and there is a
similar, though not so pronounced, gap in Matthew (19 : 27 and
26 : 33) and Luke (18 : 28 and 22 : 8). The gap in Mark is between
10 : 28 and 11 : 21, but there is nothing in that Gospel against
the view that Peter remained behind (in Galilee?) when the others
went up to Jerusalem, and that he came up to the capital only
for the week prior to Passover. If so the reason he said nothing

---

[4] The point made by Lagrange with respect to the view that John was
concerned not with facts but with the teaching that Christ confers on believers
a life which would triumph over death, should be borne in mind: "To prove
it by a symbolical narrative would be plain childishness; it must be an actual
happening" (p. 311).

[5] Hunter is impressed by these. He does not underestimate the seriousness
of the problem posed by the Synoptic silence and thinks it may never be solved.
He adds: "But in view (*a*) of the vivid and lifelike detail of the narrative, and
(*b*) of the abundant evidence that John had access to good independent sources
of information about Jesus, the one thing we should not do is to dismiss this
famous story as fiction."

about the raising of Lazarus was that he did not see it. It did not belong to his personal reminiscences. All the more is this possible in that it does not seem that this miracle took place immediately before the events leading to the Passion.[6] One small piece of evidence supporting the view that Peter was absent is the fact that Thomas is the spokesman for the Twelve in v. 16. Normally we should expect Peter to fill that role. As Matthew seems dependent on Mark at this stage in his narrative, the absence of the story from the First Gospel follows from its absence from the Second. Its absence from Luke is more serious, but it has to be borne in mind that Luke's special source (or sources) appears to be episodic rather than a full chronological narrative. I do not maintain that this clears up all the difficulty, but it must be borne in mind so that the difficulty is not exaggerated.[7] We must also remember that the miracles in Jerusalem form no part of the Synoptic tradition. Not only this one, but those concerning the lame man at Bethesda and the blind man at Siloam are not mentioned in the Synoptists. For whatever reason they treat only

---

[6] In v. 8 the disciples say that the Jews "but now" tried to stone Jesus. This appears to refer to the attempt recorded in 10 : 31, at the feast of the Dedication (10 : 22). This was on 25th Chisleu (November-December). Thus the events of ch. 11 took place close to the feast of the Dedication (even allowing for the stay in Perea, 10 : 40), and hence at some distance from Passover. It accords with this that John says, "from that day forth they took counsel that they might put him to death" (v. 53). This does not appear to mean that the Passion followed within a few days. It suggests rather that there was plotting over a period.

[7] Such considerations induce Temple to say: "I accept the Johannine narrative as correct". He adduces also the placing of the cleansing of the temple in Mark. Since this Evangelist records but one visit to Jerusalem the cleansing had to be included at the end of Jesus' life and it gave a motive for the chief priests to intervene. It is difficult then to find a place and a reason for the Lazarus story. Holding John to be substantially later than Mark, Temple thinks a further motive for not mentioning the incident was possible embarrassment to a still living Lazarus. He concludes: "Of course all this is mere conjecture, and by no means satisfactory. All I contend is that the origins of *Mark* are such that the omission of this story there is not at all decisive; and to accept, as I do, the Johannine narrative is in no way false to the principles of evidence. The story is singularly vivid and has all the characteristics of the record of an eye-witness." Bailey similarly accepts the story despite its difficulties for he finds it "still more difficult to believe that the fourth evangelist is either misinformed about, or deliberately misplacing or inventing an incident which bears such strong evidence of personal observation."

of the last week at Jerusalem and omit all that goes before. As this miracle must apparently be dated an appreciable time before that week,[8] they naturally do not mention it.

Yet this is not to deny that the story has spiritual meaning. We should not overlook the fact that this Gospel has a good deal to say about life, from the Prologue on, and that John loves to convey the revelation by Jesus' deeds as well as His words. There can be no doubt but that He attaches spiritual significance to this story, placing it as he does as the climax of Jesus' ministry. John wants us to see that Jesus does give life[9] and that it is this aspect of Jesus' ministry which brought Him into the final clash with the authorities.

(a) The Death of Lazarus 11 : 1–16

1 Now a certain man was sick, Lazarus of Bethany, of the village of Mary and her sister Martha. 2 And it was that Mary who anointed the Lord with ointment, and wiped his feet with her hair, whose brother Lazarus was sick. 3 The sisters therefore sent unto him, saying, Lord, behold, he whom thou lovest is sick. 4 But when Jesus heard it, he said, This sickness is not unto death, but for the glory of God, that the Son of God may be glorified thereby. 5 Now Jesus loved Martha, and her sister, and Lazarus. 6 When therefore he heard that he was sick, he abode at that time two days in the place where he was. 7 Then after this he saith to the disciples, Let us go into Judaea again. 8 The disciples say unto him, Rabbi, the Jews were but now seeking to stone thee; and goest thou thither again? 9 Jesus answered, Are there not twelve hours in the day? If a man walk in the day, he stumbleth not, because he seeth the light of this world. 10 But if a man walk in the night, he stumbleth, because the light is not in him. 11 These things spake he: and after this he saith unto them, Our friend Lazarus is fallen asleep; but I go, that I may awake him out of sleep. 12 The disciples therefore said unto him, Lord, if he is fallen asleep, he will

---

[8] See n. 6 above.

[9] *Cf.* Tasker: "Jesus raises Lazarus not solely out of sympathy with Martha and Mary the bereaved friends of Jesus, though His sympathy was great, nor merely because Lazarus was especially dear to Him, though that was equally true, but because through the miracle of his restoration Jesus desires to manifest Himself as *the resurrection, and the life*".

[1]recover. 13 Now Jesus had spoken of his death: but they thought that he spake of taking rest in sleep. 14 Then Jesus therefore said unto them plainly, Lazarus is dead. 15 And I am glad for your sakes that I was not there, to the intent ye may believe; nevertheless let us go unto him. 16 Thomas therefore, who is called [2]Didymus, said unto his fellow-disciples, Let us also go, that we may die with him.

[1]Gr. *be saved.* [2]That is, *Twin.*

In this introduction the scene is set for the miracle. Jesus' friends inform him of Lazarus' sickness, but the Lord makes no immediate move. After a couple of days He suggests going into Judea and tells the disciples that Lazarus is dead. The disciples recognize the danger but agree to go with Him.

1 Without a time note Lazarus of[10] Bethany is introduced to us and we are told that he was a sick man. It is curious that in this introduction his relationship to Mary[11] and Martha is not mentioned. That comes in the next verse. Here it is simply said that they lived in the same village. Lazarus (the name is the same as Eleazar[12]) is mentioned in the New Testament only in this chapter and the next (though the name is found also in the parable in Luke 16 : 19–31). The two sisters are mentioned in both these chapters and also in Luke 10 : 38ff. It seems that Martha was the elder of the two (she is the hostess in the Lukan passage), and if this is so it is interesting that Mary is mentioned before her here, and is alone mentioned in v. 45. She was probably the more important in Christian tradition, and she had probably entered more deeply into the mind of Christ.

2 Mary is now identified as the one who anointed the Lord with unguent and wiped His feet with her hair. It is curious that John

[10] Some see a difference of meaning between ἀπό (with Βηθανίας) and ἐκ (with τῆς κώμης), the former denoting domicile and the latter origin. Johannine usage, however, is against such a distinction between the prepositions (see on 1 : 44). It is, of course, quite possible that the family had changed its place of residence, all the more so since Luke 10 : 38ff. appears to locate them in Galilee. But the prepositions do not prove this.

[11] The name is given here in the form Μαρία, but elsewhere in this Gospel the form is the indeclinable Μαριάμ.

[12] אֶלְעָזָר is the Old Testament form, but this was later sometimes abbreviated to לְעָזָר. The name means "God has helped".

identifies her in this fashion for he has not yet described the incident (he relates it in the next chapter). But clearly it was well known in the church and he could presume that his readers would be familiar with it.

3 The sisters sent to let our Lord know that Lazarus was ill, neither of them being specially mentioned as taking the initiative. For "Lord" we should probably read "sir" (see on 4 : 1). They do not name Lazarus but refer to him simply as "he whom thou lovest". If this was sufficient identification the ties between Jesus and this family must have been very close indeed. We are reminded that our knowledge of the events in the life of Jesus is at best meagre. There is no request that Jesus should come to them. Doubtless the sisters were well aware of the dangers that would beset Jesus if He were to visit them, and they refrain from asking Him to imperil Himself. Nevertheless their words are in effect a plea for help. Jesus was resourceful and they look to Him for aid without specifying ways and means.

4 In 9 : 3 Jesus has denied that a certain man was born blind on account of sin saying that it was rather "that the works of God should be made manifest in him". Now He gives a similar reason for Lazarus' sickness. It is not a sickness "unto death".[13] This does not mean that Lazarus would not die (a few verses later Jesus says plainly that he has died). It means that the ultimate issue of this sickness would not be death. Rather it would be the revelation of "the glory of God" (for "glory" see on 1 : 14). The glory of the Father and the glory of the Son are always in close connection in this Gospel. It is not surprising accordingly that Jesus adds that the sickness is that the Son might be glorified through it. Once again we have the close relation between the Father and the Son, and the thought of glory, both favorite themes in this Gospel. And it is likely that we should understand the glorification of the Son in two ways in the Johannine manner.

---

[13] $\pi\varrho\grave{o}\varsigma$ $\vartheta\acute{a}\nu\alpha\tau o\nu$, "with a view to death", an unusual construction (found again I John 5. 16f.). By contrast it is $\acute{v}\pi\grave{e}\varrho$ $\tau\tilde{\eta}\varsigma$ $\delta\acute{o}\xi\eta\varsigma$ $\tau o\tilde{v}$ $\vartheta\varepsilon o\tilde{v}$, "on behalf of God's glory". Barrett understands $\acute{v}\pi\acute{e}\varrho$ here as "for revealing", "in order to reveal": "V. 40 shows that the meaning is not 'in order that God may be glorified'; here as elsewhere the glory of God is not his praise but his activity." For the confident attitude in the face of death we may compare Jesus' words concerning the daughter of Jairus, "the child is not dead, but sleepeth" (Mark 5 : 39).

538

Jesus was seen to be at one with the Father, and many came to believe on Him (v. 45). But the true glory is in the cross, and this incident led right on to Calvary (v. 50).

5 Now John tells us that Jesus loved[14] all three in the family. It is not without its interest that Martha is named first and Mary is not named at all. She is simply defined by her relationship to Martha. It is likely that Martha was the elder of the two. The separate mention of the three persons is probably meant to put some stress on Jesus' affection for each one individually. He did not simply love the family. He loved Martha and He loved Mary and He loved Lazarus. It may be that John has prefaced v. 6 with this note so as to make it clear that Jesus' failure to move immediately was not due to any lack of affection for the family.

6 This verse is really rather curious. We would have expected Jesus to take some action on receipt of the news of Lazarus' sickness. The message of the sisters is a plea for help, even though they do not in set terms ask Jesus to do anything. But Jesus simply remained, indeed "therefore"[15] remained where He was for two days. John gives no indication of any urgency in the work that He was doing. Indeed he does not so much as mention what that work was. But his "therefore" cannot mean that Jesus deliberately waited for Lazarus to die. Indeed the death must have already taken place when the messengers arrived. In v. 39 we find that Lazarus had been dead for four days when Jesus reached Bethany, and the journey would scarcely have taken more than a day. The four days are accounted for by allowing a day for the journey of the messengers, the two days that Jesus remained where He was, and a day for Jesus' journey. Lazarus must have died shortly after

---

[14] The verb is ἠγάπα, whereas φιλεῖς was used in v. 3 of Jesus' love for Lazarus. It is difficult to see a difference between the two verbs. φιλέω is used again in v. 36. See further on 21 : 15.

[15] Abbott draws attention to the fourfold οὖν in this story (vv. 6, 17, 33, 38): "the intention of the narrative as a whole is to represent the Raising of Lazarus as foreordained; and this repetition of 'therefore' may be intended, in particular, to show how the Son, step by step, moved forward in a regular and predetermined sequence to do the Father's will in performing the last and greatest of His 'signs'" (2198). This may be so, but we must bear in mind the fact that οὖν is used frequently in this chapter (in addition to the verses named by Abbott, in 3, 12, 14, 16, 20, 21, 31, 32, 36, 41, 45, 47, 53, 54, 56). In view of this list we may not be able to insist on a strict significance for Abbott's four verses. But the word certainly has its normal significance in the present passage.

the messengers started on their way. The delay would certainly heighten the miracle but we cannot think that Jesus permitted His friends to suffer bereavement simply in order that He might perform a more spectacular miracle. It is much more probable that John means us to see Jesus as moved by no external forces, but solely by His determination to do the will of God. As on the occasion of the Feast of Tabernacles (7 : 3–10) Jesus went up to Jerusalem as and when He Himself determined, not at the dictates of others. At the marriage in Cana (2 : 1ff.) Jesus had been urged by His mother to take action. In all three cases the urge to action came from those near or dear, in all three their request was refused, in all three Jesus in the end did what was suggested, but in all three only after it had been made clear that what He did He did in God's time, and according to God's will. He was not to be coerced, even by His dearest friends. All the more is this the case in the present instance, because Jesus was going up to Jerusalem to His death, the climax of His mission.

7 The double time note "then" and "after this"[16] puts some emphasis on the delay. It was only after the two days that Jesus suggested action. He invites the disciples to go[17] with him once more into Judea. He says "into Judaea" not "into Bethany", for it was the entrance into unbelieving Judea, which would crucify Jesus, that was the significant thing.

8 The suggestion provokes an immediate protest. The disciples have not forgotten the Jews' attempt to stone Jesus (10 : 31). They speak of it as happening "but now". The incident was vivid in their memory and they were fully alive to the danger. So they ask Jesus whether He goes there again.[18] Notice that they address Him as "Rabbi", this being the last occasion in this Gospel on which this term is used. The courage of Jesus is brought out in their comment. To go up to Judea clearly meant to run considerable risk. But He went up.

9 "Twelve hours" stands for the whole day. The men of antiq-

---

[16] ἔπειτα and μετὰ τοῦτο. The latter expression recurs in v. 11. As used by John there seems to be no great difference in meaning from the more frequently occurring μετὰ ταῦτα (see on 2 : 12).

[17] Note the intransitive use of ἄγωμεν. The verb of course is usually transitive. When intransitive the 1st person plural, ἄγωμεν, as here, is most common (cf. vv. 15f.).

[18] καί is used here in the sense of καίτοι, "and yet".

uity did not have time-pieces as we have and twelve hours did not stand for any precisely calculated period. Their procedure was to divide the whole of the daylight period into twelve, so that one hour stood for one twelfth of the available day. The actual amount of time in twelve hours would thus vary from one part of the year to another.[19] When Jesus then directs attention to the "twelve hours" He is reminding His followers that this is all the time there is in a day. It is during these hours that a man may walk without stumbling. He has "the light of this world" to guide him. In the context this expression must refer to the sun, and Jesus must be talking about his intention of going up to Jerusalem. For Him, as for others, it is true that He must do His work while He has the opportunity (cf. 9 : 4f.). But in view of Jesus' repeated statement that He is "the light of the world" (8 : 12; 9 : 5) we should probably discern a deeper meaning, in the Johannine manner. Men should make the most of the presence of Christ, the Light of the world. For when He is withdrawn from them there is no possibility of their "walking" without stumbling. It is not impossible in view of the use of "hour" in this Gospel that the reference here to "hours" contains also an allusion to the work that Jesus, the Light of the world, came to do. The disciples need not fear to go up with Him, because He cannot die before the appointed time, and there is still a little time left.[20] There will also be the thought that to be with Him is to be in the light, and the next verse brings out the reverse – if they are away from Him they will certainly stumble in the darkness.

10 This is the corollary of the previous statement. The man who walks in the night stumbles. The metaphorical element is plain in this verse for Jesus says, "the light is not in him" rather than, "he has no light" or the like.[21] The saying is true with regard

---

[19] The variation in Palestine was between 14 hours, 12 mins. and 9 hours, 48 mins. (SBk).

[20] Barclay points out that this has its relevance to our own situation: "If there are twelve hours in the day there is time enough for everything a man should do. There is no need for a rushed haste. If a man uses these twelve hours all that he ought to do can be done in them . . . But, even if there are twelve hours in the day, there are *only* twelve hours. They cannot be extended. And, therefore, time cannot be wasted. There is time enough, but there is not too much time."

[21] D misses this point, and actually reads "the light is not in it (αὐτῇ, i. e. the night)".

to physical events. A man will stumble if he walks in darkness. But the real concern here is with the deeper darkness which may be within a man. When darkness is in his soul, then will he stumble indeed.

11 Now[22] John gives attention to the sickness of Lazarus. He carefully separates Jesus' words about walking in the day or the night, words which have a mystical and spiritual as well as a literal application, from the words which have to do with the sickness of Lazarus. Jesus speaks specifically of His friend and tells the disciples that he "is fallen asleep". In the New Testament death for the believer is characteristically spoken of as "sleep".[23] In passing it is worth noticing that few things illustrate more graphically the difference the coming of Christ made than this. Throughout the ancient world the fear of death was universal. Death was a grim adversary that all men feared and no man could defeat. But Christ's resurrection altered all that for His followers. For them death no longer was a hateful foe. Its sting was drawn (1 Cor. 15 : 55). Of course this development was as yet future. But in the words of Jesus we may see the manner of speech that was to become characteristic of His followers. Death is no more now than sleep. So He speaks of Lazarus as sleeping. He adds that He is going to wake Lazarus from this sleep. In view of the disciples' unwillingness to go it may be significant that Jesus here uses the singular and not the plural as in v. 7. Yet in v. 15 He again associates them with Him.

12 There is a common pattern in this Gospel wherein Jesus' hearers misunderstand something He has said, usually taking in literal fashion what He means metaphorically, and this opens the way for further teaching on His part (see on 2 : 20). This may be an example of this pattern, but the mistake is natural. The disciples think not of death but of natural sleep and they affirm

---

[22] For $\mu\varepsilon\tau\grave{\alpha}$ $\tauo\widehat{\upsilon}\tauo$ see on 2 : 12.

[23] Thus the verb $\varkappa o\iota\mu\acute{\alpha}o\mu\alpha\iota$ (used here) denotes literal sleep 4 times and death 14 times. It is worth noting that the Christian word for a burial place, "cemetery", $\varkappa o\iota\mu\eta\tau\acute{\eta}\varrho\iotao\nu$, is connected with this root, and denotes "a place of sleep". The use of "sleep" for death is not, of course, an invention of the Christians. It is to be found in secular writers. But it is not characteristic of them, and it is characteristic of the Christians.

that if Lazarus is sleeping it is a good sign. "He will recover".[24]
They were probably all the more ready to reach this conclusion
because it removed the necessity for the dangerous journey into
Judea.
13 John makes the situation clear. Jesus has spoken[25] of Lazarus'
death. The disciples however misunderstand. They[26] are thinking
in terms of rest from slumber.
14 Therefore at this point Jesus removes their uncertainty. He
says plainly,[27] "Lazarus is dead". The aorist tense, which incidentally is somewhat abrupt, indicates that the action has taken place.
"Lazarus died" gives the sense of it.[28] We might contrast the
perfect tense in v. 11 where the continuing state is meant. This
statement of Jesus implies supernatural knowledge (see on 4 : 18).
The messengers had spoken only of illness, and there was no other
human source of information.
15 Yet Jesus regards this as a matter for rejoicing. We should
not take this too calmly, for "The same shock that the disciples
would have felt we also are intended to feel, when we hear Jesus
say, 'Lazarus is dead, and I rejoice.' "[29] He is aware of what He
will do and He has already said that the death of Lazarus is "for
the glory of God" (v. 4). Now He says that His joy is for the
disciples "to the intent ye may believe" (cf. vv. 42, 45, 48). The
aorist tense used here would naturally indicate the beginning of
faith and this is curious in the case of the disciples who had so
trusted Jesus that they left all they had to follow Him. Without

---

[24] We should notice that the word for "he will recover" is σωθήσεται, "he
will be saved". The verse may be intended to convey a secondary meaning
pointing to a truth of salvation. If a believer "sleeps" (the word in use among
the Christians for "dies") he will be saved. P75 reads ἐγερθήσεται, but this
can scarcely be right.
[25] The verb is εἰρήκει, the only example of the pluperfect of this verb in
John. Abbott thinks this tense "takes the reader, as it were, behind the scenes
– after some mention of deeds or words – to tell him what *really had been the
cause* of the result" (2481).
[26] ἐκεῖνοι δέ gives the subject emphasis. *They* in distinction from Him.
[27] παρρησίᾳ often has the meaning "boldly" and this may be in mind here.
Jesus boldly spoke the truth, trusting that His disciples would not fail, but
would receive it. If this is correct, the reaction of Thomas (v. 16) is an immediate
vindication of the Lord's action.
[28] Unless with Black we take it as the rendering of a Semitic perfect (*AA*,
p. 93) when the continuing state will be in mind.
[29] Abbott, 2102. He has a long note on the passage (2099–2102).

a doubt they were already "believers", yet their faith was not strong, for at the critical hour they were all to forsake Him.[30] The meaning will be that faith is a progressive thing. There are new depths of faith to be plumbed, new heights of faith to be scaled. The raising of Lazarus would have a profound effect on them and would give their faith a content that it did not have before. Faith would be strengthened (cf. Luke 17 : 5). "Nevertheless" will connect with "I was not there". Jesus had not been there when Lazarus died but now He calls on His followers to accompany Him thither.

16 It is somewhat curious to find Thomas taking the lead in this matter. He is not usually the spokesman for the Twelve. But here he takes the initiative. John identifies him by giving the meaning of his name. "Didymus" is the Greek equivalent of the Hebrew "Thomas", both of which mean "twin".[31] Thomas then said to his fellows,[32] "Let us also go, that[33] we may die with him[34]". Thomas is usually known to us as the doubter. It is good

---

[30] Cf. Temple: "It is hard to know what one's faith is worth till some severe test comes. I believe – in some measure; of that I am quite sure. But in what measure I do not know. I pray God to do for me, or to me, or in me, whatever will have the result that I *may believe*."

[31] The Greek $\Delta i\delta \nu \mu o \varsigma$ and the Hebrew תְּאֹם. It is not said to whom Thomas was twin, and in some of the apocryphal literature he is even said to have been the twin of Jesus (*e.g. Acts of Thomas*, 31), and to have resembled Him (*Acts of Thomas*, 11). His personal name may have been Judas (*Acts of Thomas*, 1). Plummer thinks he may have been twin to Matthew, with whom he is linked in all the lists of the apostles in the Gospels. MM, however point out that $\Delta i\delta \nu \mu o \varsigma$ was quite capable of standing alone. One brother might have a name and the other be called simply "Twin". In the Synoptic Gospels he is mentioned only in the lists of the Twelve. But in this Gospel, in addition to the present incident, he is mentioned in connection with a question asked in the upper room (14 : 5), and twice in the resurrection narratives (20 : 24f., 26–9). The name does not appear to be attested before the New Testament (*EB*, IV, 5058: *i.e.* the Hebrew name is not; $\Delta i\delta \nu \mu o \varsigma$, is, of course, much earlier).

[32] τοῖς συμμαθηταῖς. The noun is used here only in the New Testament. The choice of the unusual word may possibly be meant to hint that Thomas and the rest had a fellow-feeling. Thomas was not isolated in his view.

[33] ἵνα expresses purpose: "Let us go in order that. . . ."

[34] Some have taken μετ᾿ αὐτοῦ to mean "with Lazarus". Grammatically this is possible, but it is a highly improbable interpretation. Thomas is seeking to avoid a situation in which Jesus would die alone, not seeking to rejoin Lazarus.

accordingly to see this act of leadership and courage.[35] In a way it fits in with his doubting, for it is a gloomy saying and one not marked by any abundance of faith. And in a sense too it expressed more than Thomas (or the others for that matter) could perform. When it came to the critical point Thomas like all the others forsook Jesus and ran away. Nevertheless we should not overlook the present situation. Thomas looked death in the face and chose death with Jesus rather than life without Him.[36] His words, in the Johannine manner, may also have a further meaning. They should probably be read in the light of 12 : 24–26: the follower of Christ must die if he would truly live.

(b) Jesus' Meeting with Martha, 11 : 17–27

17 So when Jesus came, he found that he had been in the tomb four days already. 18 Now Bethany was nigh unto Jerusalem, about fifteen furlongs off; 19 and many of the Jews had come to Martha and Mary, to console them concerning their brother. 20 Martha therefore, when she heard that Jesus was coming, went and met him: but Mary still sat in the house. 21 Martha therefore said unto Jesus, Lord, if thou hadst been here, my brother had not died. 22 And even now I know that, whatsoever thou shalt ask of God, God will give thee. 23 Jesus saith unto her, Thy brother shall rise again. 24 Martha saith unto him, I know that he shall rise again in the resurrection at the last day. 25 Jesus said unto her, I am the resurrection, and the life: he that believeth on me, though he die, yet shall he live; 26 and whosoever liveth and believeth on me shall never die. Believest thou this? 27 She saith unto him, Yea, Lord: I have believed that thou art the Christ, the Son of God, even he that cometh into the world.

John takes this story in stages. He does not move immediately to the central miracle, but describes Jesus' meetings first with

---

[35] *Cf.* Loyd: "Here is a sufficient rule to walk by, whether our faith be dim or clear; namely, sheer loyalty."

[36] Torrey translates, "Let us also go, to mourn with him", and asks, "Is it not probable that ἵνα πενθῶμεν was mistakenly copied as ἵν᾽ ἀποθάνωμεν?" This presupposes an unlikely mistake (which appears to have left no trace in the MS tradition) and his further suggestion that even if Jesus were to be executed the disciples had no cause for fear is unrealistic.

Martha, then with Mary, and he makes these meetings the vehicle of important teaching.
17 We have no description of the journey. John simply tells us that when Jesus arrived He found that Lazarus had already been buried for four days.[37] We do not know how long before that he died, but probably not long. Burial was not usually delayed and for example Ananias and Sapphira were buried immediately they died (Acts 5 : 6, 10). The four days may be significant. There was a Jewish belief that the soul stays near the grave for three days, hoping to be able to return to the body.[38] But on the fourth day it sees decomposition setting in and leaves it finally. If this view was as early as the time of which we are thinking (it is attested *c.* A.D. 220 but is probably a good deal earlier) it will mean that a time had been reached when the only hope for Lazarus was a divine act of power.[39]
18 John inserts a typical topographical note. It is interesting to notice that he locates Bethany with precision as "about fifteen furlongs"[40] from Jerusalem.[41] By contrast, when he is speaking about this family Luke speaks only of "a certain village" (Luke 10 : 38), giving neither the name nor the location. John's note

---

[37] For the accusative of time after the verb ἔχω see on 5 : 5.
[38] "R. Abba b. R. Pappai and R. Joshua of Siknin said in the name of R. Levi: For three days (after death) the soul hovers over the body, intending to re-enter it, but as soon as it sees its appearance change, it departs . . . Bar Kappara said: The full force of mourning lasts for three days. Why? Because (for that length of time) the shape of the face is recognisable" (Lev. R. 18 : 1; Soncino edn., p. 226; see also Ecc. R. 12 : 6). In line with this the Mishnah provides that evidence of the identity of a corpse may be given only during the three days after death (*Yeb.* 16 : 3).
[39] See SBk, II, p. 544 for the relevant passages. On the significance *cf.* Strachan: "The conception that the mourning reaches its height on the fourth day implies that all hope of any restoration to life by what might be called natural means, is banished. Restoration can only be accomplished by a new creative act of God. Such a creative act, Jesus is represented as accomplishing."
[40] A στάδιον measured 606¾ feet so that it was somewhat shorter than our furlong. Fifteen στάδια come to rather less than two miles.
[41] The Greek order is rather curious, for he says, ἐγγὺς τῶν Ἱεροσολύμων ὡς ἀπὸ σταδίων δεκαπέντε. We should expect ἀπό to precede τῶν Ἱεροσολύμων (*cf.* Luke 24 : 13). But our translation certainly gives the sense correctly. *Cf.* 21 : 8 for this construction again. We should probably understand the measurement to be thought of as beginning "from" Jerusalem. Some suggest that this is a Latinism but BDF deny this (161 (1)). So does Moulton (M, I, p. 102). For the article with Ἱεροσόλυμα see on 2 : 23.

about distance serves a twofold purpose: it explains how "many of the Jews" could be there to comfort the sister, and it proclaims that Jesus has practically reached Jerusalem for the climax. Some have seen in the use of the past tense "was" an indication that John was writing after Bethany had been destroyed. This however seems to be reading too much into a natural use of the past tense.

19 "The Jews" in this Gospel usually denotes the enemies of Jesus, and consequently of His adherents (see on 1 : 19). Its use here accordingly is a little unusual. Perhaps John means to imply that though the mourners could bring themselves to sympathize with Martha and Mary[42] they were hostile to Jesus. They apparently came[43] with the intention of staying for some time and not simply of paying a passing visit. A fairly prolonged stay to comfort the bereaved was apparently usual at a time of bereavement.[44] At the funeral itself the mourners were left alone with their sorrow and their friends refrained from speaking to them. But later it was expected that visits for consolation would be made, and the Jews rated this duty highly.

20 There is a difference in the attitude of the two sisters, and it is not unlike the difference we see in the incident recorded in Luke 10 : 38–42. Then Martha was occupied with the duties of hospitality, while Mary simply "sat at the Lord's feet, and heard his word". So here, when it was told that Jesus was approaching, Martha was the one who went out to welcome Him. It is not said

---

[42] The received text reads τὰς περὶ Μάρθαν καὶ Μαριάμ (with P45 (vid) A Θ f1 f13 etc.) making the Jews come not so much to Martha and Mary, as to their (feminine) friends or perhaps their household. This is inherently unlikely, and the better texts read τήν. Bernard suggests that τὰς περί may have come from (αὐ)τὰς περί in the next line. We should have anticipated either that there would be no article or that it should be repeated before Μαριάμ. The expression τὴν Μάρθαν καὶ Μαριάμ is possibly meant to indicate something of a unity. The two sisters now made up the household.

[43] Note the use of the pluperfect ἐληλύθεισαν to denote previous action. The Jews "had come" before Jesus made His appearance.

[44] A. Edersheim speaks of a threefold division in the time of mourning. The first three days were days of weeping, then deep mourning lasted for the rest of the week, and lighter mourning for the remainder of thirty days (*Sketches of Jewish Social Life*, London, n.d., p. 174; see also *LT*, II, p. 320; SBk, IV, pp. 592–607). The regulation is given in the Talmud: "Three days for weeping and seven for lamenting and thirty (to refrain) from cutting the hair and (donning) pressed clothes" (*MK* 27b; Soncino edn., p. 180).

that Jesus summoned her, nor indeed, that He sent any message.
Yet we must bear in mind that no words of His summoning Mary
are recorded, but from v. 28 we learn that He did so. A similar
call to Martha may have gone unrecorded. But it is perhaps more
likely that Martha simply heard He was near, and that was
enough for this busy and active soul. It would be natural for
anyone giving information to give it first to Martha, as the mistress
of the household. Clearly she was the one who was likely to take
the initiative, especially in the duties of hospitality. Mary remained
sitting where she was in the house.[45] Incidentally sitting appears
to have been the usual posture in which mourners received
their comforters (*cf.* Job 2 : 13).[46]

21 Martha's greeting is an expression of faith. She was sure that
if Jesus had been present her brother would not have died. The
Lord who had healed so many others would surely have healed
Lazarus. In the story in Luke's Gospel Martha rebuked the Lord
because He did not tell Mary to assist her with the housework.
Some see an implied rebuke here. Why had Jesus not been there?
Martha knew when the message had been sent to Jesus and she
knew how long it had taken Him to get there. If we are right in
our explanation of the four days (see on v. 6) He could not have
arrived in time, but Martha may have been upset about His two
days' delay. Yet she does not say "If only you had come —". On
the whole it is more likely that her remark expresses regret rather
than rebuke. It probably echoed what she and Mary had said
often to each other (*cf.* v. 32) during the past few days.[47]

---

[45] Ryle thinks that Martha comes off best in this incident: "There is such
a thing as being so crushed and stunned by our affliction that we do not adorn
our profession under it. Is there not something of this in Mary's conduct
throughout this chapter? There is a time to stir, as well as to sit still; and here,
by not stirring, Mary certainly missed hearing our Lord's glorious declaration
about Himself. I would not be mistaken in saying this. Both these holy women
were true disciples; yet if Mary showed more grace on a former occasion than
Martha, I think Martha here showed more than Mary." Strachan also commends Martha here above Mary.

[46] *Cf.* Edersheim: "Immediately after the body is carried out of the house
all chairs and couches are reversed, and the mourners sit (except on the
Sabbath, and on the Friday only for one hour) on the ground or on a low stool"
(*loc. cit.*).

[47] It is probable that for ἀπέθανεν at the end of the verse we should read
ἐτεθνήκει. See the discussion on v. 32.

22 The meaning of this verse is puzzling. On the surface of it it seems to mean that Martha knew that Jesus even now could perform the miracle, that He could raise Lazarus from the sleep of death. But the subsequent narrative shows that she cannot have meant that, or at any rate that if she did mean it she was not able to sustain the high faith it implies. When Jesus commanded the stone to be taken away from the tomb it was Martha who objected in the strongest of terms (v. 39). Her attitude there is so clear that it seems impossible to reconcile it with any real hope of a resurrection here. The words may be an expression of faith to make up for any lack of warmth in the previous verse. The "even now" may perhaps point to the thought of a resurrection. But equally the expression may be logical rather than temporal, *i.e.* the meaning may be: "If you had been here my brother might not have died, for I know that God gives the things you ask." "Whatsoever" is plural. It does not point to any one gift, but to whatever things Jesus should at any time ask.[48]

23 Jesus turns Martha's thoughts to resurrection. Lazarus will rise. The words could be taken as a perfectly general reference to the final resurrection for Jesus does not mention His own part. He gives no indication that the rising is imminent.

24, 25 Martha unhesitatingly takes the words to refer to the final resurrection at the end of the age.[49] Her words show that she had no idea of an immediate raising of Lazarus to life; but they do represent a certainty about the resurrection at the last day. Many commentators think that they also show that she thought of Jesus' words as a commonplace of consolation, as the sort of thing others had doubtless been saying to her frequently, and in which

---

[48] Martha uses the verb αἰτέω. It is not without its interest that, while Jesus uses this verb of the prayers of men (14 : 13; 15 : 7, 16 *etc.*) He never uses it of His own prayers. Instead He employs ἐρωτάω (14 : 16; 16 : 26; 17 : 9 (twice), 15, 20), which, with the exception of I John 5 : 16, is used of prayer to God only in this Gospel, and always of the prayers of Jesus (unless 16 : 23 is an exception). But too much ought not to be built on this. It is hard to establish a consistent difference between the two verbs in late Greek. Perhaps there is a slight hint at equality, or at least of less inequality, in ἐρωτάω which originally meant "to ask a question" rather than to make a request. But we must not overlook the fact that the verb is once used of the prayers of men, as we noted (I John 5 : 16). See also on 1 : 19.

[49] This, of course, was the accepted teaching of the Pharisees, but was denied by the Sadducees.

she found but cold comfort. Be that as it may, her words open the way for one of the great declarations of Jesus which mark this Gospel.[50] For these "I am" sayings see on 6 : 35. Jesus does not say simply that He will give resurrection[51] and life.[52] So much are resurrection and life associated with Him that He says that He *is* the resurrection and the life.[53] The linking of resurrection and life perhaps points to the truth that the life He brings is the life of the age to come. It is the "eternal life" of which He speaks elsewhere (see on 1 : 4; 3 : 15). The man who believes on Jesus (the construction signifies personal trust; see Additional Note E, pp. 335ff.) will live even though he dies. The paradox brings out the great truth that physical death is not the important thing. For the heathen or the unbeliever death may be thought of as the end. Not so for the man who believes in Christ. Such a man may die in the sense that he passes through the door we call physical death, but he will not die in the fuller sense. Death for him is but the gateway to further life and fellowship with God. This transcends the Pharisaic view of a remote resurrection at the end of time. It means that the moment a man puts his trust in Jesus he begins to experience that life of the age to come which cannot be touched by death. Jesus is bringing Martha a present power, not the promise of a future good.

26 Everyone who lives and believes on Jesus (one article ties the two closely together; life and faith must be understood in the closest of connections) will never die. Jesus does not of course

---

[50] And according to Godet they were meant to lead up to something of the sort: "If she speaks only of the *final* resurrection which is to her mind certain, it is that she may give to Jesus the opportunity to explain Himself, and to declare expressly what she scarcely dares to hope for in the present case."

[51] ἀνάστασις is not a common word in this Gospel, being found only in 5 : 29 and twice in the present passage. Similarly the verb ἀνίστημι occurs only in 6 : 39, 40, 44, 54; 20 : 9 outside this chapter. ζωή by contrast is one of the great concepts of this Gospel, being found throughout (36 times).

[52] The words καὶ ἡ ζωή are omitted by P45 (vid) *a l* syrˢ Cyp Or. This is scarcely sufficient to establish the shorter reading as original, and in any case in the context the meaning will be much the same.

[53] Calvin comments: "First, He calls Himself the resurrection; for restoration from death to life precedes the state of life. But the whole human race is plunged in death. Therefore, no man will possess life unless he is first risen from the dead. Hence Christ teaches that He is the beginning of life. Afterwards He adds that the continuity of life is also the work of His grace."

mean that the believer will not die physically. Lazarus was dead even then, and millions of Jesus' followers have died since. But He means that he will not die in the sense in which death has eternal significance. He will not[54] die with reference to the age to come.[55] He has eternal life, the life of the age to come. Jesus rounds this off with a challenge: "Believest thou this?" His words about faith and life are not a philosophical dictum to be critically argued. They are a saving truth to be received and acted on.

27 These words of Martha do not always receive the attention they should. When Martha and Mary are spoken of, Martha is apt to be characterized as the lady of whom Jesus said, "Martha, Martha, thou art anxious and troubled about many things: but one thing is needful: for Mary hath chosen the good part . . ." (Luke 10 : 41f.). But Martha with all her faults was a woman of faith. Hers is a significant declaration. First, she agrees with what Jesus has said. She is not choosing her own way but accepting His. She may not understand fully the implications of what He has just said, but as far as she can she accepts it. Then she puts her faith in her own words: "I have believed" indicates a faith once given and permanently remaining.[56] Her "I" is emphatic. Whatever may be the case with others she has put her trust in Jesus. And she believes *that* —. Her faith is not a vague, formless credulity. It has content, and doctrinal content at that. She brings out three points. First, Jesus is "the Christ" *i.e.* the Messiah of Jewish expectation (see on 1 : 20, 41). Secondly, He is "the Son of God" (for this expression see also the confessions of John the Baptist,

---

54 "Not" is the emphatic double negative, $o\dot{v}\ \mu\dot{\eta}$.

55 As in 10 : 28 (where see note) Barrett argues that the meaning is "shall never die" and denies that it is "shall not die eternally". His idea appears to be that there is a kind of death which believers do not die ("The only death that is worth regarding cannot affect those who believe in Christ") and that this is all that is in view here. But I do not see how this is to be separated from the idea that the life believers have is eternal life. It may well be true that Jesus is saying there is a kind of death believers do not die, but to say that this does not refer to dying eternally seems to me to misrepresent the situation. The wonderful truth that He is enunciating is that the believer "to all eternity cannot die" (Knox). He has eternal life. He will not undergo the worst of deaths, eternal death.

56 This is the force of $\pi\varepsilon\pi\acute{\iota}\sigma\tau\varepsilon v\varkappa\alpha$. *Cf.* the use of the perfect also in 3 : 18; 6 : 69; 8 : 31; 16 : 27; 20 : 29. Martha's use of this tense is all the more noteworthy in that the present would have been the natural tense to use in reply to Jesus' question.

1 : 34, and Nathanael, 1 : 49; and for Jesus' own use of the term see note on 5 : 25). It is an expression which can mean little more than that the person so described is a godly man, but it can also point to a specially close relation to God. It is in the latter sense that it is used throughout this Gospel, and, indeed, John writes explicitly to bring men into faith in Jesus as the Son of God (20 : 31). There can be no doubt but that Martha is giving the words their maximum content. Thirdly, she speaks of Jesus as "he that cometh into the world" (see on 3 : 31), *i.e.* the long awaited Deliverer, the One sent by God to accomplish His will perfectly. Taken together these three affirmations give us as high a view of the person of Christ as one well may have. Martha should be known to us from this moving declaration rather than from her worst moment of criticism and fretfulness.

(c) Jesus' Meeting with Mary, 11 : 28-32

28 And when she had said this, she went away, and called Mary [1]her sister secretly, saying, The Teacher is here, and calleth thee. 29 And she, when she heard it, arose quickly, and went unto him. 30 (Now Jesus was not yet come into the village, but was still in the place where Martha met him.) 31 The Jews then who were with her in the house, and were consoling her, when they saw Mary, that she rose up quickly and went out, followed her, supposing that she was going unto the tomb to [2]weep there. 32 Mary therefore, when she came where Jesus was, and saw him, fell down at his feet, saying unto him, Lord, if thou hadst been here, my brother had not died.

[1]Or, *her sister, saying secretly* [2]Gr. *wail.*

John describes Jesus' meeting with Mary much more shortly. There is no outstanding declaration on the part of Mary corresponding to that of Martha (v. 27), nor is there any resounding statement of our Lord's.

28 Having made her great declaration of faith Martha calls her sister unobtrusively.[57] Why she does it this way is not said. Possibly

---

[57] λάθρᾳ may go either with the preceding or the following: "called Mary secretly and said" or "called Mary and said secretly". But there is no very great difference in meaning.

she wanted Mary to have the opportunity for a few minutes'
private conversation with Jesus, as she apparently had had. And
this may be the reason that Jesus remained for a time outside
the village. She speaks of Jesus as "The Teacher" and the article
is probably important. Among His followers Jesus was designated
primarily by His teaching activities.[58] But He is recognized as
incomparable. He is "*the* Teacher". It is important to notice this
use of the term by a woman. The Rabbis refused to instruct women,
but Jesus took a very different view. John does not record any
words of Jesus asking for Mary, so that he is not giving us a complete account of everything that took place. He tells us sufficient,
and leaves the rest to be understood.

29 "When she heard it" indicates an action performed without
delay. Mary was quick to act on her sister's word. It is possible
that we should read "rises" rather than "arose"[59] in which case
John is introducing a vivid touch. He sees Mary in the act of
rising. "Went" is in a continuous tense: "she began to go" or "she
was going" (this too may even be a present,[60] "she is going").

30 A brief explanation of the situation is given. John tells us
why Mary was going to Jesus. Martha in her eagerness had gone
right outside the village to meet the Lord (v. 20). He was still in
the same place, Martha having probably suggested that she should
go and fetch Mary. Some think that an additional reason for Jesus'
remaining outside the village was that He was nearer to the
cemetery where His real business lay. This however is speculation.
We do not know where the cemetery was, but Jesus was certainly
at some distance from it, and in any case can scarcely have chosen

---

[58] $\delta\iota\delta\acute{a}\sigma\varkappa\alpha\lambda o\varsigma$ is used by Matthew 12 times, by Mark 12 times, by Luke
17 times and by John 8 times, and with the exception of the general statement
of the relationship of $\mu\alpha\vartheta\eta\tau\acute{\eta}\varsigma$ to $\delta\iota\delta\acute{a}\sigma\varkappa\alpha\lambda o\varsigma$ (Matt. 10 : 24f. and parallels),
the statement about the child Jesus sitting among the teachers (Luke 2 : 46),
and the statement that Nicodemus was "the teacher of Israel" (John 3 : 10)
all refer to Jesus. In addition $\dot{\varrho}\alpha\beta\beta\varepsilon\acute{\iota}$ is used of Him by Matthew twice, Mark
3 times, John 8 times (excluding the fuller $\dot{\varrho}\alpha\beta\beta o\upsilon\nu\varepsilon\acute{\iota}$, found in Mark 10 : 51;
John 20 : 16).

[59] Many MSS do read $\dot{\eta}\gamma\acute{\varepsilon}\varrho\vartheta\eta$, but the present, attested by P45, P66,
AC^c Θ f1 f13 *etc.*, is perhaps preferable.

[60] The present is found in P45, P66 AD Θ f1 f131 at *etc.* It is possible that
past tenses were substituted in some MSS for original presents in the case of
this verb and $\dot{\varepsilon}\gamma\varepsilon\acute{\iota}\varrho\varepsilon\tau\alpha\iota$ on account of the preceding $\mathring{\eta}\varkappa o\upsilon\sigma\varepsilon\nu$.

His stopping point with reference to the cemetery for He did not know exactly where it was (v. 34).

31 The Jews of v. 19 had remained with Mary and not accompanied Martha when she went out to meet Jesus. John tells us that they "were consoling" Mary though we do not know exactly what form that took. When they saw that Mary quickly[61] got up and left they followed, telling themselves that she was going to wail at the tomb (for lamentation at the tomb *cf.* Wis. 19 : 3). They may have intended to share in this activity. This action meant that what followed would have many witnesses and so receive wide publicity.

32 Mary now came to the spot where Jesus was waiting. She greeted Him by falling at His feet in homage. She seems to have been more emotional than her rather matter-of-fact sister. For "Lord" see on 4 : 1. In this context it will have its full meaning. Mary's words, which are almost identical with those of Martha in v. 21,[62] are eloquent of a firm conviction that Christ's power could have saved Lazarus from death. They reveal Mary's certainty that Jesus could overcome sickness. But they reveal no more. It is possible that her quick action (vv. 29, 31) gained her a short respite from the attentions of her comforters, who did not realize at first where she was going. Her prostration and greeting may accordingly have been private. But her companions speedily rejoined her as the next verse shows.

(d) Lazarus is Raised, 11 : 33–44

33 When Jesus therefore saw her ¹weeping, and the Jews also ¹weeping who came with her, he ²groaned in the spirit, and ³was troubled, **34** and said, Where have ye laid him? They

---

[61] "Quickly" here is ταχέως, while in v. 29 it is ταχύ. There seems no difference in meaning, this being another of John's little variants. BDF speak of ταχέως as "the more literary" (102(2)), but this will hardly be significant in the present passage, where indeed they think it "likely an interpolation". John uses neither form elsewhere in the Gospel.

[62] Martha's verb is probably ἐτεθνήκει, and Mary's ἀπέθανεν, while μου is differently placed. In view of John's habit of making slight alterations when statements are repeated these variations should not be regarded as significant (see on 3 : 5). Most MSS read ἀπέθανεν in v. 21, but this seems an assimilation to the present passage and ἐτεθνήκει is to be preferred, with A C³ ΓΔΛΘΨ. John uses ἀποθνήσκω 28 times and θνήσκω but twice, so there would be a tendency for scribes to replace the less familiar verb with the more common one.

say unto him, Lord, come and see. 35 Jesus wept. 36 The Jews therefore said, Behold how he loved him! 37 But some of them said, Could not this man, who opened the eyes of him that was blind, have caused that this man also should not die? 38 Jesus therefore again ⁴groaning in himself cometh to the tomb. Now it was a cave, and a stone lay ⁵against it. 39 Jesus saith, Take ye away the stone. Martha, the sister of him that was dead, saith unto him, Lord, by this time ⁶the body decayeth; for he hath been dead four days. 40 Jesus saith unto her, Said I not unto thee, that, if thou believedst, thou shouldest see the glory of God? 41 So they took away the stone. And Jesus lifted up his eyes, and said, Father, I thank thee that thou heardest me. 42 And I knew that thou hearest me always: but because of the multitude that standeth around I said it, that they may believe that thou didst send me. 43 And when he had thus spoken, he cried with a loud voice, Lazarus, came forth. 44 He that was dead came forth, bound hand and foot with ⁷grave-clothes; and his face was bound about with a napkin. Jesus saith unto them, Loose him, and let him go.

¹Gr. *wailing.* ²Or, *was moved with indignation in the spirit* ³Gr. *troubled himself.* ⁴Or, *being moved with indignation in himself* ⁵Or, *upon* ⁶Gr. *he stinketh.* ⁷Or, *grave-bands*

John brings out the point that nobody expected an act of resurrection. He has let us see that both Martha and Mary were confident in Jesus' power to cure sickness. He goes on to bring out the same point for the Jews who were with them (v. 37). But none of them expected resurrection. John proceeds to describe just that. **33** The previous verse has said nothing about Mary's tears but they were to be expected and this verse makes it clear that she was wailing in her grief, as were the Jews who had accompanied her. The word signifies a loud weeping, a wailing.⁶³ It was the habit of the day to express grief in a noisy, rather unrestrained fashion and this is what these mourners were doing. With a crowd of people engaged in this activity there must have been quite a scene of confusion and sorrow. The sight of it caused Jesus deep

---

⁶³ κλαίω is defined by LS in this way: "*cry, wail, lament,* of any loud expression of pain or sorrow".

emotion. The verb rendered "groaned"[64] is an unusual one. It signifies a loud inarticulate noise, and its proper use appears to be for the snorting of horses. When used of men it usually denotes anger. Here it clearly points to some deep emotion (RSV, "he was deeply moved in spirit"). "In the spirit" does not, of course, refer to the Holy Spirit, but to the human spirit of Jesus.[65] It signifies that His feeling was no light emotion. Many feel that the word must be taken to mean anger,[66] and if so it is probably anger against death that is meant.[67] But the word may not be so specific. It is difficult to read anger into either of the other passages where it is used of Jesus. Both times it is used of His attitude to men He cured, namely two blind men (Matt. 9 : 30) and a leper (Mark 1 : 43). John probably means no more than that Jesus

---

[64] $\dot{\varepsilon}\nu\varepsilon\beta\varrho\iota\mu\dot{\eta}\sigma\alpha\tau o$. Elsewhere in the New Testament it is found only in v. 38 and in Matt. 9 : 30; Mark 1 : 43; 14 : 5. LS give the meaning of the verb as "*snort in* . . . of horses".

[65] Chrysostom takes the dative $\tau\tilde{\omega}$ $\pi\nu\varepsilon\dot{\upsilon}\mu\alpha\tau\iota$ as the object of the verb (as the dative is in Matt. 9 : 30; Mark 1 : 43) and thinks that Jesus rebuked His spirit for feeling so troubled: "He weepeth, and is troubled; for grief is wont to stir up the feelings. Then rebuking these feelings, (for He 'groaned in spirit' meaneth, 'restrained His trouble,')" (LXIII. 1; p. 232).

[66] Thus Barrett says: "It is beyond question that $\dot{\varepsilon}\mu\beta\varrho\iota\mu\tilde{\alpha}\sigma\vartheta\alpha\iota$ . . . implies anger. This is suggested by biblical . . . and other . . . usage of the word itself, by the use of the simple form $\beta\varrho\iota\mu\tilde{\alpha}\sigma\vartheta\alpha\iota$ . . . of which $\dot{\varepsilon}\mu\beta\varrho\iota\mu\tilde{\alpha}\sigma\vartheta\alpha\iota$ is here only an intensive and by the usage of the cognates". This view may be supported by appealing to the Greek commentators.

[67] This view has nowhere been better put than by B. B. Warfield: "It is death that is the object of his wrath, and behind death him who has the power of death, and whom he has come into the world to destroy. Tears of sympathy may fill his eyes, but this is incidental. His soul is held by rage: and he advances to the tomb, in Calvin's words again, 'as a champion who prepares for confict.' The raising of Lazarus thus becomes, not an isolated marvel, but – as indeed it is presented throughout the whole narrative . . . – a decisive instance and open symbol of Jesus' conquest of death and hell. What John does for us in this particular statement is to uncover to us the heart of Jesus, as he wins for us our salvation. Not in cold unconcern, but in flaming wrath against the foe, Jesus smites in our behalf" (*The Person and Work of Christ*, Philadelphia, 1950, p. 117). There is little to be said for Plummer's idea that it wrath against the Jews for their hypocritical wailing, for, as we shall see, there is no reason to accuse them of insincerity.

was profoundly moved.[68] This is meant also by "was troubled."[69]
Rieu translates, "he gave way to such distress of spirit as made
his body tremble". All this is somewhat curious. Jesus was about
to raise Lazarus and we cannot interpret His perturbation as an
act of mourning for the deceased. It must refer to His deep concern
and indignation at the attitude of the mourners. They so completely misunderstood the nature of death and of the Person of
the Son.[70] Even Mary, who from what we know of her elsewhere

---

[68] Thus Bernard can say: "anger is not primarily suggested by the verb
$\dot{\varepsilon}\mu\beta\varrho\iota\mu\tilde{a}\sigma\vartheta a\iota$, nor does the idea of Jesus being angry enter into the story of the
Raising of Lazarus." Lagrange points out that the ancient versions such as the Lat-
in, Syriac and Sahidic do not take the word to mean anger. Black sees in the expression a Syriacism meaning "he was deeply moved in his spirit" (*AA*, pp. 174ff.).

[69] $\dot{\varepsilon}\tau\dot{a}\varrho a\xi\varepsilon\nu$ $\dot{\varepsilon}a\nu\tau\dot{o}\nu$. Later Jesus says, "Now is my soul troubled" $\dot{\eta}$ $\psi\nu\chi\dot{\eta}$
$\mu o\nu$ $\tau\varepsilon\tau\dot{a}\varrho a\varkappa\tau a\iota$ (12 : 27), and the Evangelist says, "he was troubled in the
spirit" $\dot{\varepsilon}\tau a\varrho\dot{a}\chi\vartheta\eta$ $\tau\tilde{\omega}$ $\pi\nu\varepsilon\dot{\nu}\mu a\tau\iota$ (13 : 21). These references form another
example of John's habit of variation in repeated statements (see on 3 : 5). The
present passage is the one example of the active voice in this Gospel, "He
troubled Himself". Cf. R. H. Lightfoot: "the expression used here implies that
He now voluntarily and deliberately accepts and makes His own the emotion
and the experience from which it is His purpose to deliver men." For the last
point cf. 14 : 1, 27. The expression is a way of showing that Jesus of His own
free will entered fully into man's lot, identifying Himself with the griefs of
His friends. As Morgan puts it, "He made Himself responsible, and gathered
up into His own personality all the misery resulting from sin, represented in
a dead man and broken-hearted people round about Him. This was voluntary
identification with the sorrow that issues from sin, and was the outcome of
righteous wrath against the sin that caused the sorrow. It is a most remarkable
unveiling of the heart of Jesus".

[70] Barrett understands it thus: "Jesus perceives that the presence and grief
of the sisters and of the Jews are almost forcing a miracle upon him, and as
in 2.4 the request for miraculous activity evokes a firm, almost rough, answer,
here, in circumstances of increased tension, it arouses his wrath. This miracle
it will be impossible to hide (cf. vv. 28, 30); and this miracle, Jesus perceives,
will be the immediate occasion of his death (vv. 49–53)." Richardson's view is
similar. I find such interpretations impossible to accept. I do not see how the
presence of grief almost forced a miracle on Jesus. This would be quite out
of harmony with the position taken up consistently throughout this Gospel
that Jesus is supremely the Master of every situation and that He is not
coerced by any. In this very chapter He has refused to move when informed
of Lazarus' illness and has awaited God's time for action (v. 6, where see
note). And in this very sentence John says not "He was troubled", but "He
troubled Himself". Nor is it any easier to think of the anger as caused by the
prospect of death. Throughout this Gospel Jesus moves majestically to the
appointed consummation, and there seems no reason for His rebelling now.
It is moreover completely out of character for Jesus to give way to anger
against friends who, even if misguided, sought Him no harm.

might have been expected to have understanding, had her thoughts firmly fixed on earth. The words will also probably mean that to work this miracle cost Jesus something (*cf.* Mark 5 : 30). **34** Jesus now inquires the location of the tomb. Instead of directing Him they invite Him to come and see. "They" is not defined, but apparently it means the two sisters.

35 In this shortest verse in the Bible the noteworthy thing is that a different word is used for weeping from that used of Mary and the Jews. The word used of them denotes a loud demonstrative form of mourning, a wailing. That used here (and here only in the New Testament) points rather to a quiet weeping.[71] Jesus did not wail loudly but He was deeply grieved. As in v. 33 this will not be owing to the death of His friend, for He was about to raise him. It will be because of the misconception of those round about Him.[72] We are reminded of that other occasion when Jesus wept over Jerusalem (Luke 19 : 41). There as here it was the wrong attitude of the Jews that aroused His deep emotion.[73]

36 As always the Jews fail to enter into the mind of Christ. They take His tears to be no more than a mark of the love He bore to Lazarus. They do not discern the deeper reason.

37 Some of them now reach a position much like that of Martha and Mary. They remember Jesus' ministry to the sick and specifically His opening of the eyes of the blind man. So they ask: "Could not One who could do this have somehow prevented the death of His friend?" There is no reason for thinking of the words as spoken in mockery. These people seem quite sincere, and, while they are not quite as definite as Martha and Mary, they

---

71 δακρύω means "to shed tears". Though the verb is found here only in the New Testament the cognate noun δάκρυον occurs ten times. The aorist here should probably be taken to signify "burst into tears".

72 R. H. Lightfoot comments: "He Himself, in His first words recorded in this gospel, at 1[35-42], had invited two of John's disciples, who were following Him, to 'come and see' where He abode; and this had resulted in their own discipleship and that of others; in other words, by following Him, they had themselves received 'the light of life' (8[12]). But now He is Himself invited by the mourners round Him to leave the place and the light which are His by nature and by right, and to 'come and see' (11[34]) – and so, if the analogy with 1[38, 39] may be pressed, to become associated with – darkness and death, since those around Him regard darkness and death as being in control of the situation; and the strain upon Him finds expression in an outburst of tears."

73 See Hoskyns for a succinct account of the great variety of interpretations that have been given this passage in both ancient and modern times.

think that Jesus' power might somehow have been exercised. He might have done[74] something. They misinterpret His tears as though they meant frustration. But there is no reason for doubting their sincerity.

38 Jesus comes to the burial place. He is still in the grip of the deep emotion described in v. 33. "Groaning" is the same verb as that used in v. 33 (where see note).[75] Tombs might be of various kinds[76] and John supplies the information that this one was a cave with a stone against the opening. This type of burial place was not uncommon in Palestine of the day, especially for people of some importance. There is no indication here of whether the cave is thought of as vertical with the stone lying on top of it, or as horizontal with the stone up against it. Both types were used. From the later statement that Lazarus came out (v. 44) it is probable that this was the horizontal type.

39 This verse is of the greatest importance for John's understanding of what took place. The Evangelist puts some stress on the actuality of the death of Lazarus. He leaves no doubt but that he is describing a miracle of resuscitation. First comes Jesus' command to remove the stone. Then there is Martha's astonished protest based on the certainty that the body would certainly be decomposing for it had already been buried for four days.[77] If the reading, the sister of "him that was dead", is the true one[78] John also conveys the idea of death by the use of the perfect participle. This points us to the permanence of the state into which Lazarus had entered. Martha is described as "the" not "a" sister of Lazarus, perhaps because she was the elder. At any rate throughout this narrative she takes the leading place. Mary consistently remains in the background.

---

[74] Note the aorist infinitive ποιῆσαι. They looked for some particular act, not for an attitude.

[75] Calvin sees in this something of the cost of the miracle: "Christ does not come to the sepulchre as an idle spectator, but like a wrestler preparing for the contest. Therefore no wonder that He groans again, for the violent tyranny of death which He had to overcome stands before His eyes."

[76] μνημεῖον is "a memorial" and so a monument to the memory of the dead. It was used of burial places in general. σπήλαιον, "a cave", might be used of a robbers' haunt (Mark 11 : 17) or a place of refuge (Heb. 11 : 38). But a natural cave might also be used for a burial place, as here.

[77] τεταρταῖος: "he is a fourth day man".

[78] The words are omitted by Θ it syr[s] ac². This is an interesting combination but the strong probability is that the words are genuine.

40 Jesus firmly rejects the protest. He reminds Martha of His earlier words. This however introduces a small difficulty for these exact words have not previously been recorded. As we noted earlier (see on 3 : 5) there is a tendency in this Gospel for slight variations to be introduced when statements are repeated and this may be another example of the same sort of thing. Alternatively Jesus may be referring to a saying uttered on some other occasion and not recorded. The words are not unlike those of v. 4, but those were not spoken to Martha (though Jesus may be assuming that they have been reported to her). Some see a reference to v. 26 but this is improbable for the critical words about "the glory of God" are absent from that verse. His words are a challenge to faith ("if thou believedst"; *cf.* 2 : 11) and a reminder of Jesus' unfailing aim – the glory of God. What was going to happen would be a spectacular miracle, it would be a display of the power of Jesus, it would be an inestimable gift to the sisters, and so on. But typically Jesus speaks of none of these aspects. For Him the glory of God was the one important thing. The real meaning of what He would do is accessible only to faith. All there, believing or not, would see the miracle. But Jesus is promising Martha a sight of the glory. The crowd would see the miracle, but only believers would see its real significance, the glory.

41, 42 After Jesus' words they removed the stone. Who actually did it is not said but presumably it was "the Jews" who accompanied Martha and Mary.[79] Jesus raised His eyes in the attitude of prayer (*cf.* 6 : 5; 17 : 1). He addresses God simply as "Father" (*cf.* 12 : 27f.; 17 : 1). He does not say "Our Father" or the like. His relationship to the Father is not the same as that of others. The first words of the prayer are a thanksgiving that the Father has heard Him. The aorist might conceivably refer to some past and unrecorded prayer. More likely it is a thanksgiving for a present prayer. None such is actually recorded. Jesus may have uttered a prayer which John does not mention (he does not mention

---

[79] Chrysostom thinks that our Lord made the Jews move the stone, rather than simply raising Lazarus without their aid, so that they would know for a certainty that it was indeed Lazarus who had been raised. They would not, he says, be like those who disputed in the case of the blind man with some saying "It is he" and others "It is like him" (LXIII. 2; p. 233). Similarly he thinks that later Jesus commanded the Jews to release Lazarus from the grave clothes for the same reason (LXIV. 3; p. 239).

560

everything in this story, for example Jesus' request for Mary to
come to Him, v. 28). Or he may want us to think that Jesus prayed
within the recesses of His soul so that God heard, though men
did not. The aorist will more naturally refer to a particular prayer
than to God's habitual hearing of Jesus. The habitual hearing
comes out in the next words "thou hearest me always". "But" is
the strong adversative.[80] It was not on His account but because
of the crowd standing round that Jesus had spoken. The emphasis
is on Jesus' concern for the people. This does not mean that His
prayer was primarily for the crowd to hear. That would make it
an artificial thing, and in any case, as we do not know when it
was spoken, we have no reason for thinking the crowd heard. As
Wright says, "The Evangelist does not say that *Jesus's prayer* was
for the sake of the multitude; but that *His thanksgiving* was for their
sakes. Jesus, in other words, would always have people know that
He did nothing of Himself." "That"[81] introduces the thought of
purpose. Jesus spoke "in order that" the crowd might believe (the
aorist tense points to the beginning of faith) that He had been
sent by God. Once again we notice that faith has content and that
that content is concerned with the mission of the Son. It includes
the conviction that He is indeed God's "Sent One" (for "sent"
see on 3 : 17). John consistently depicts Jesus as dependent on the
Father and interested in His glory. He is not like the ordinary
popular wonder-workers who sought to magnify themselves. So
here Jesus acts not of His own volition but in dependence on the
Father to whom He addresses His prayer.

43 Jesus summoned the dead man. He cried out in a loud voice[82]
and addressed Lazarus directly by name, calling him to come[83]

---

[80] ἀλλά. Abbott cites this as an instance of the usage "where, without a
negative in the context, it introduces something different from the past,
something for which the past has not prepared us, but which *nevertheless* will
take place" (2058).

[81] ἵνα.

[82] κραυγάζω of itself means "cry loudly" and it is reinforced here with
φωνῇ μεγάλῃ. This is the one place (out of six occurrences) when John uses
the verb of Jesus. E. K. Lee thinks that the word often indicates passion and
want of self-control and that it is significant that the one place where Jesus
uses it is when He is concerned for others (*ExT*, LXI, 1949–50, pp. 146f.).

[83] δεῦρο is an adverb of place which may be used as an imperative like
our "Here!" This is the only place where it occurs in this Gospel. Jesus'
command is wonderfully succinct: "Here! Outside!"

out of the tomb. The loud voice was not, of course, because a loud voice was needed to make the dead hear. Probably it was in part at least so that the crowd could know that this was no work of magic, but the very power of God. Wizards muttered their incantations and spells (*cf.* Isa. 8 : 19). Not so the Son of God.

44 John records that the man who had been dead[84] came out. He notes that he was still bound hand and feet with the graveclothes.[85] It is difficult to see how he could walk under such circumstances and it is possible that we are to understand what Hoskyns calls "a miracle within a miracle. Lazarus does not walk out of the grave; he is rather drawn out tightly bandaged." It is however quite possible that the legs were bound separately, in which case there is no insuperable difficulty. John makes special mention of the sweat band[86] over the face. It must have been a strange sight indeed. John concludes his narrative of the miracle with Jesus' command to loose Lazarus and let him go. We are reminded of synoptic incidents which show a similar thoughtfulness, as when He commanded that something to eat be given to the daughter of Jairus (Mark 5 : 43). Jesus was never so carried away by the wonder of His miracles that He forgot the needs of the person.

(e) The Reaction of Faith, 11 : 45

45 Many therefore of the Jews who came to Mary and beheld [1]that which he did, believed on him.

[1]Many ancient authorities read *the things which he did.*

The result of the miracle, as always, is division. Because Jesus is what He is inevitably He divides men. John first brings before us those who believed. These were some "of the Jews" and John

---

[84] ὁ τεθνηκώς. In v. 39 ὁ τετελευτηκώς is used. No difference of meaning is apparent and we must regard this as another example of John's love of variation. Burton sees the perfect here as used "to denote a state existing antecedent to the time of the principal verb. The action of which it is the result is, of course, still earlier" (*Moods*, 156).

[85] κειρίαις. The word denotes "bandages" (see LS), so that we are to think of narrow strips wound round the body.

[86] σουδαρίῳ. The word is a transliteration of the Latin *sudarium*, defined by AG as "*face-cloth* for wiping perspiration, corresp. somewhat to our *handkerchief*".

makes it clear that there were many of them. Interestingly he describes them as those "who came to Mary".[87] Throughout this narrative the emphasis has been on Martha and it is curious that the Jews are said to have come to the less prominent sister. They were associated with her also in vv. 31, 33. It may be that they were more concerned for Mary than for the bustling Martha. Mary appears to have been more emotional, and may perhaps have been in greater need of consolation. Whatever the reason they are associated with Mary here once more. Linked with "came" is "beheld. . . ."[88] It was the sight of the miracle[89] which brought the effect. "Believed on him" is John's favorite construction for genuine trust (see Additional Note E, pp. 335ff.). A faith which is based on the miracles is not the highest faith but it is accepted throughout this Gospel as better than no faith at all (see on 2 : 23).

(f) The Reaction of Unbelief, 11 : 46–57

46 But some of them went away to the Pharisees, and told them the things which Jesus had done. 47 The chief priests therefore and the Pharisees gathered a council, and said, What do we? for this man doeth many signs. 48 If we let him thus alone, all men will believe on him: and the Romans will come and take away both our place and our nation. 49 But a certain one of them, Caiaphas, being high priest that year, said unto them, Ye know nothing at all, 50 nor do ye take account that it is expedient for you that one man should die for the people, and that the whole nation perish not. 51 Now this he said not of himself: but being high priest that year, he prophesied that Jesus should die for the nation; 52 and not for the nation only, but that he might also gather

---

[87] We might have expected τῶν ἐλθόντων. The expression is difficult, but οἱ ἐλθόντες must be taken as in apposition with πολλοί and explanatory of it: "many of the Jews, namely the ones who came . . ." or as Rieu, "many of the Jews, those who had visited Mary and witnessed what he did".

[88] There is one article linking ἐλθόντες and θεασάμενοι. The same people performed both actions.

[89] This assumes the reading ὅ with P66* (vid) AᶜBC*D f1 sa acᴾ. ἅ is read by P6, P45, ℵ A*WΘ 28 33 f13 lat. The attestation for ἅ is perhaps slightly stronger, but this reading may well have crept into the text to make it agree with the next verse. On the whole the singular is more likely here. The thing that carried conviction was the great stupendous miracle, a single act. But when some went to report to the Pharisees they spoke of a number of things.

together into one the children of God that are scattered abroad.
53 So from that day forth they took counsel that they might
put him to death. 54 Jesus therefore walked no more openly
among the Jews, but departed thence into the country near
to the wilderness, into a city called Ephraim; and there he
tarried with the disciples. 55 Now the passover of the Jews
was at hand: and many went up to Jerusalem out of the country
before the passover, to purify themselves. 56 They sought
therefore for Jesus, and spake one with another, as they stood
in the temple, What think ye? That he will not come to the
feast? 57 Now the chief priests and the Pharisees had given
commandment, that, if any man knew where he was, he
should show it, that they might take him.

Following his brief account of the birth of faith in some who
saw the miracle John goes on to speak of those who were repelled.
This leads on to the effect of the report. The chief priests and others
were so hardened that they plotted against Jesus' life. This in turn
gives the opening for reporting Caiaphas's unconscious prophecy
of the substitutionary death of Christ.[90]

46 In contrast with those who believed there were others[91] who
simply went away to the Pharisees, known to be the enemies of
Jesus, and told them the things that Jesus had done. While John
makes no explicit declaration about their motive, in the context
there can be little doubt but that they acted in a spirit of hostility.
They were bearing the latest news to the enemy, not trying to
win them over.

47 The result was the gathering of a council of chief priests and
Pharisees.[92] Apparently an informal meeting is meant, and not

---

[90] C. H. Dodd examines the pericope, vv. 47-53, in the Cullmann *Fest-schrift* (*Neotestamentica et Patristica*, Leiden, 1962), pp. 134ff. He decides that the many primitive touches show that the Evangelist "was in a position to draw, directly or indirectly, upon a source of information deriving from a very early Jewish Christian circle still in close association with the synagogue" (*op. cit.*, p. 143).

[91] *τινὲς ἐξ αὐτῶν* could mean "some of the Jews" or "some of the Jews who had come to Mary. . . ." The former seems to be required, for the language of v. 45 *(οἱ ἐλθόντες κτλ.)* implies that all who had come to Mary and seen what Jesus did believed. These people are distinguished from those.

[92] The separate articles with "chief priests" and "Pharisees" possibly point to two groups as combining for the purpose.

the official Sanhedrin.[93] In convening it the chief priests apparently take the initiative. It is noteworthy that from this point on the Pharisees are not mentioned often and the opposition to Jesus is firmly in the hands of the chief priests. In all four Gospels the Pharisees are Jesus' principal opponents throughout His ministry, but in all four they are rarely mentioned in connection with the events associated with the Passion. The discussion that took place apparently included much heart-searching. Notice that they say "What do we?" not: "What shall we do?" (RSV, "What are we to do?" misrepresents the Greek). They are not at this point planning a course of action but wondering how effective their efforts are. Their words may also imply that they are in fact doing nothing in contrast to Jesus with His miracle after miracle. We should not miss their clear recognition of the fact of the miracles. Jesus,[94] they say, "doeth (= 'is doing'; the tense indicates continuous action) many signs" (see Additional Note G, pp. 684ff.). It has always been the case that those whose minds are made up to oppose what Christ stands for will not be convinced by any amount of evidence. In this spirit these men recognize that the miracles have taken place, but find in this a reason for more wholehearted opposition, not for faith. In their hardness of heart they continue on their own chosen line and refuse to consider the evidence before their eyes.

48 They see it as certain that many will put their trust in Jesus if they let him alone. Indeed they go as far as to say that "all men" will do so, an exaggeration which indicates the strength of their fears. The Romans would not stand by indifferent if there were popular tumult stirred up by messianic expectations.[95] They would certainly take strong action and the speakers feared the

---

[93] This is the only occurrence of συνέδριον in this Gospel, and the only place in the New Testament where the singular is found without the article (the plural is so found, giving the sense "councils"). It is thus "a" sanhedrin or council, rather than "the" Sanhedrin. This is supported by the fact that Caiaphas is called "a certain one of them" (v. 49), whereas in the Sanhedrin he would have been president.

[94] For John's use of ἄνθρωπος of Jesus see on 4 : 29.

[95] There is evidence from Jewish sources that the authorities were rather nervous for some time before the Jewish War. Thus Josephus speaks of all manner of portents which occurred in Jerusalem (*Bell.* vi, 288ff.). It is clear that the leading men would not have tolerated anything that looked like provoking disorder.

destruction of all they stood for. "Our[96] place"[97] probably means the temple (so in Acts 6 : 13f.; 21 : 28). It was in a special sense *the* place for the Jews (though the NEB goes too far when it translates by "our temple"). And the nation, too, they feared, would cease to exist, and with it, of course, their own special place.

49 John singles out the reaction of Caiaphas. This man was high priest from about A.D. 18 to A.D. 36. John describes him as "high priest that year", which some have drawn into an argument for the view that John had little idea of what went on in Palestine. They suggest that he was ignorant of the fact that the high priesthood was normally conferred for life, and that he thought that it was an annual appointment. This however is reading too much into the expression. There is a good deal of evidence that John was familiar with Palestine and that with pre-A.D. 70 Palestine. It is not without significance that he twice repeats the statement (v. 51; 18 : 13). It is difficult to think that in as careful and theologically minded a writer as John such solemn repetition would be given to a minor piece of administrative information, information moreover which he could not have checked for it was erroneous. What he means is "that fateful year".[98] That was the year when the world's salvation was wrought out. In that year of all years it was Caiaphas who was the high priest. The information is the more relevant in that, though the office was not an annual one, the Romans did change the high priest quite often. Caiaphas's first words "Ye know nothing at all"[99] show a rudeness which is

---

[96] ἡμῶν stands before καὶ τὸν τόπον καὶ τὸ ἔθνος. Abbott finds in this possibly the one example in the Gospels of "the precedent unemphatic possessive with ἡμῶν" (2559a). Other pronouns as μου and σου are used much more often in this way. So also BDF (473(1)). Hoskyns and Bernard think ἡμῶν here to be emphatic, but perhaps wrongly.

[97] *Cf.* Mishnah *Bikk.* 2 : 2, "(Second) Tithe and First-fruits require to be brought to the Place. . . ." Both here and in the passage we are discussing the "place" could be Jerusalem, though the Temple seems more likely. In II Macc. 5 : 19 the reference is plainly to the Temple: "the Lord did not choose the nation for the place's sake, but the place for the nation's sake."

[98] "As E. A. Abbott well says, 'Luke dates the coming of "the word of God" about Jesus from *(inter alia)* "Annas and Caiaphas." John dates Caiaphas from Jesus' " (*FGRCI*, p. 187).

[99] There is an emphatic double negative οὐκ οἴδατε οὐδέν. Barclay translates: "You are witless creatures."

alleged to have been typical of the Sadducees.[100] The "ye" is
emphatic and probably contemptuous. He himself clear-sightedly
and ruthlessly discerns a line of action which he accounts desirable
and he contemptuously dismisses the whole assembly of the
Sanhedrin as ignorant because its members do not see things in
the same way.

50 Caiaphas continues with his rebuke. "Take account" is a
word used of reckoning up accounts[101] and the like. He is saying
that they cannot even calculate, cannot even work it out that
such and such a course of action is the expedient one. "It is expedient for you" concentrates attention on their own position.
Neither Caiaphas nor the others were basically concerned for
abstract right and wrong, nor yet for the nation as a whole. But
the position of the privileged class was threatened and it is action
that would save that privileged class that he advocates. "That one
man should die for the people"[102] is a simple prophecy of the
meaning of the cross. But on Caiaphas's lips it is sheer cynicism.
Better that one man, however innocent, should die than that the
nation as a whole should perish is how this worldly-wise politician
reasons. This is, of course, another example of John's irony. The
leaders did adopt the course of slaying the innocent, but so far
from saving the nation this, on John's view, initiated the events
that would lead up to its destruction.

51, 52 John adds his own reflection on these words. They did
not originate with Caiaphas.[103] On the contrary[104] he spoke this
way because he was the high priest, and because on account of

---

[100] *Cf.* Josephus: "The Sadducees ... are, even among themselves, rather
boorish in their behaviour, and in their intercourse with their peers are as
rude as to aliens" (*Bell.* ii, 166).

[101] λογίζεσθε. MM say this verb "is common in the sense of 'reckon,' 'put
down to one's account' ".

[102] In Gen. R. XCIV. 9 there is a discussion about whether one man
should be given up to save the lives of others, based on the incident in II Sam.
20 when Sheba was slain and the city of Abel spared. Most agree that one
man should die and thus save others.

[103] But Rieu's "These words, it must be noted, were put into his mouth"
is probably too strong. John does not mean that Caiaphas had no control
over his words. He was not speaking like Balaam. He had thought the matter
out and gave his verdict. But God so overruled that, while Caiaphas meant
one thing his words had another, and a deeper and a more important meaning.

[104] He uses the strong adversative ἀλλά (see on 1 : 8).

his office God spoke through him.[105] What Caiaphas uttered as a piece of cynical political realism, God meant to be understood in a deeper, more significant way. John repeats the important part, namely, "that Jesus should[106] die for the nation".[107] His death was a death for others, not a death for Himself. We should not overlook the fact that this way of putting it means a definitely substitutionary death.[108] Either the nation dies or Jesus dies. But if He dies the nation lives. It is His life instead of theirs. And John sees a wider purpose in the death of Jesus than the salvation of the Jewish nation. This death would be the means of gathering together the children of God wherever they might have been scattered[109] (they are called "children" even before they are gathered together). Caiaphas's words are not big enough. John has a world-wide vision. And those who are gathered are gathered into a unity, "into one" (*cf.* 10 : 16). Sin scatters men, but salvation in Christ brings them together. The New Testament always thinks of a very real unity as linking all who are truly Christ's. "The children of God that are scattered abroad" would normally be taken on the lips of a Jew to mean the Jews of the Dispersion, but here they will point to Gentile Christians.

53 Having concluded his own aside John returns to the Sanhedrin. Caiaphas's words mark a turning point. From that day (John

---

[105] Prophecy was associated with the high priest as in the manipulation of the oracle (Num. 27 : 21). David calls Zadok a seer (II Sam. 15 : 27). Philo can speak of the true priest as necessarily a prophet (*de Spec. Leg.* IV, 192), and Josephus claims that since he was of priestly descent he was himself able in some measure to foretell the future (though his emphasis is on knowledge of the prophetical books, *Bell.* iii, 352). It was held among the Jews that prophecy was often, perhaps even usually, unconscious as a number of passages testify (SBk, II, p. 546).

[106] ἔμελλεν adds a touch of certainty.

[107] John's interpretation twice uses ἔθνος for "nation". In v. 50 Caiaphas has used both λαός and ἔθνος. The former word is that usual for the people of God, whereas ἔθνος is the general word for a nation, and in the plural is the ordinary expression for "the Gentiles". John's avoidance of λαός in his interpretation of Caiaphas's remarks may be due to an unwillingness to use an expression which might imply that the Jews were the people of God. Yet this cannot be pressed, because John is prone to slight alterations when he repeats, and in any case Caiaphas applies both words to the Jews.

[108] Moule lists this as one of the passages in which there is not much difference between ὑπέρ and ἀντί (*IBNTG*, p. 64). For ὑπέρ see on 6 : 51.

[109] The perfect διεσκορπισμένα may perhaps indicate the permanence of the scattering, apart from Christ's saving work.

has the habit of noting the time when events took place) they looked out for ways and means of killing Jesus. The high priest's words had had the effect of clarifying their ideas. They now knew what they must do. Schonfield: "So that day they decided to kill him."

54 "Therefore" will denote a much stricter sequence of thought than often in this Gospel. Because of the plot of the chief priests and their allies Jesus used no more to walk openly among the Jews. Far from it, He went away to the district near the wilderness country. With His customary precision John tells us that He went to a city whose name was Ephraim. The site of this city is not known for certain, but if its identification with Ophrah be accepted it was about fifteen miles from Jerusalem.[110] Jesus then did not retire to a very great distance. But He went to a place lonely enough for Him to be undisturbed. John adds the note that He stayed there with His disciples. In this difficult period the little band stuck together.

55 It is John's habit to note the feasts and once again he draws attention to the approach of the Passover. As in 2 : 13; 6 : 4, he characterizes it as "of the Jews". Well before the feast many went up out of the countryside in order to purify themselves ceremonially.[111] The point of mentioning this is to make it clear that well before the actual feast itself Jerusalem would be crowded with pilgrims.

56 After the resolve taken in v. 53 Jesus' enemies were looking for Him. "Sought" carries the implication of "kept on seeking". And as they sought they kept asking one another whether Jesus would come to the feast. The second of their questions seems to

---

[110] This town is mentioned in II Chron. 13 : 19 with Bethel in the immediate context. Josephus also links it with Bethel (*Bell.* iv, 551). Most are inclined to identify it with the modern El-Tayibeh.

[111] Ceremonial defilement disqualified a man from keeping the Passover (Lev. 7 : 21; Num. 9 : 6; *cf.* II Chron. 30 : 17f.). Depending on what was involved the rites for purification might last as long as a week so that, with large numbers involved, it might be well to come to the city early. The "whited sepulchres" of which Jesus spoke (Matt. 23 : 27) were whitewashed to make them conspicuous so that people at festival time would not contract defilement accidentally.

show that they expected as answer "No"[112] (Phillips: "Surely he won't come to the Festival?"). They considered it unlikely that in view of circumstances He would be so foolhardy as to put in an appearance.

57 A further reason for this view appears. In furtherance of their plan the authorities had commanded[113] that anyone who knew Jesus' whereabouts should disclose it. This would make anyone who came to know where He was but did nothing about it an accessory, and would thus constrain people to supply information and facilitate arrest.[114]

---

[112] See Moulton (M, I, pp. 188ff.) for a valuable note on the use of οὐ μή in the New Testament. He combats the view that it is used so often as to have lost its emphatic sense, pointing out that most examples are in quotations from LXX or in the words of Christ. Apart from these the expression is rare, and when it does occur, as here, must be given its full weight of emphasis.

[113] The pluperfect δεδώκεισαν may be meant to indicate the permanent nature of the order. The command was given and remained in force. BDF points out that the pluperfect includes the idea of lasting consequence; otherwise the aorist is used (347). This is John's one use of "commandment" for anything other than a command of God or of Christ (see on 10 : 18).

[114] ὅπως πιάσωσιν αὐτόν is the one example of the use of ὅπως in this Gospel. Interestingly Mark also has it once, but Matthew 17 times and Luke 7 times. ὅπως here may be used simply for the sake of variety as John has just used ἵνα, which is his usual conjunction for expressing purpose.

CHAPTER XII

19. THE CLOSE OF THE PUBLIC MINISTRY, 12 : 1-50

John has practically concluded his account of the public ministry of Jesus. Chapter 13 begins the section on the final discourses addressed to the disciples in the upper room after which John goes on to the events surrounding the Passion. This chapter then contains Jesus' last words and acts before the general public. John selects three incidents: the anointing at Bethany, the triumphal entry, and the visit of the Greeks to Jesus. Then he rounds the section off with an appeal to prophecy showing why it was that some did not believe, followed by a rousing call to faith, spoken by Jesus Himself.

(a) The Anointing at Bethany, 12 : 1-8

1 Jesus therefore six days before the passover came to Bethany, where Lazarus was, whom Jesus raised from the dead. 2 So they made him a supper there: and Martha served; but Lazarus was one of them that ¹sat at meat with him. 3 Mary therefore took a pound of ointment of ²pure nard, very precious, and anointed the feet of Jesus, and wiped his feet with her hair: and the house was filled with the odor of the ointment. 4 But Judas Iscariot, one of his disciples, that should ³betray him, saith, 5 Why was not this ointment sold for three hundred ⁴shillings, and given to the poor? 6 Now this he said, not because he cared for the poor; but because he was a thief, and having the ⁵bag ⁶took away what was put therein. 7 Jesus therefore said, ⁷Suffer her to keep it against the day of my burying. 8 For the poor ye have always with you; but me ye have not always.

¹Gr. *reclined.* ²Or, *liquid nard* ³Or, *deliver him up* ⁴See marginal note on ch. 6. 7. ⁵Or, *box* ⁶Or, *carried what was put therein* ⁷Or, *Let her alone:* it was *that she might keep it*

There are accounts of an anointing of Jesus by a woman in all four Gospels and the question of the relationship between them is rather complicated. The first is found in Mark 14 : 3-9 (= Matt. 26 : 6-13). It tells of an anointing in Bethany in the house of Simon the leper by a woman who poured "ointment of pure nard" over Jesus' head. This provoked great indignation among some who thought the ointment might well have been sold and the money given to the poor. But Jesus defended the woman saying, "She hath done what she could; she hath anointed my body beforehand for the burying" (Mark 14 : 8). The second story is in Luke 7 : 36–50. It appears to take place in Galilee earlier in the ministry and is located in the house of "one of the Pharisees". His name is given as Simon, but he is not spoken of as a leper (as in Mark), nor indeed could he be such under the circumstances. In any case Simon was one of the commonest of names, so we need not think of these two persons as identical. The woman who carried out the anointing is described as "a sinner". She first wet our Lord's feet with her tears, then wiped them with her hair, kissed them and finally anointed them. This led the Pharisee to think that Jesus could not even be a prophet and opened the way for our Lord to speak of the greatness of the woman's love. The story in this chapter seems clearly distinct from that in Luke. There is no reason for equating Mary of Bethany with Luke's "sinner". Though the anointing is of the feet, and the hair is used to wipe them, the time, the circumstances, the discussion are all different.[1]

---

[1] Yet some argue that all three anointings refer to the same incident. A variant is that put forward by, for example, Bernard. He argues that Mark and John describe the same incident, and that Luke describes an earlier incident with the same woman. He identifies Mary of Bethany with Mary Magdalene and thinks of her as saved from a life of sin by Jesus. The first anointing expresses her penitence and gratitude. The second recalls the first, and this is why the feet are anointed, and why the hair is used. But this time there are no tears, for Mary cannot go back to her earlier emotions. Perhaps the strongest argument for this view is the fact that the present passage clearly betokens an interest in Jesus' burial on the part of Mary of Bethany, yet none of the Gospels speak of her at the tomb, whereas all mention Mary Magdalene. Bernard further points out that the identification of Mary as the one who anointed Jesus' feet and wiped them with her hair (11 : 2) demands that only one woman had done this. If two did the same thing it would not identify her.
Temple, Bailey, and others take up similar positions.
Strachan thinks that John is working on oral tradition which included details from the traditions underlying both the Marcan and the Lukan stories. Dodd thinks that Mark, Luke and John all worked on oral tradition, "each evangelist used independently a separate strand of tradition, and the strands overlapped" (*HTFG*, p. 172). Brown holds that Luke tells of a woman who wiped tears from Jesus' feet and Mark and John of Mary as anointing Jesus' head, but that during the period of oral transmission details were transferred from each story to the other. The strength of this case is the difficulty of seeing in the one story why feet should be anointed, and in the other why ointment should be wiped off.

It is otherwise with the Markan story. There the similarities are great. Both use the most unusual expression "pistic nard"[2] for the perfume. Both locate the incident in Bethany, and if Mark says the house belonged to Simon the leper[3] John does not say to whom it belonged. Some infer that he means the house of Lazarus and the sisters, but more probably he omits to say whose it was for he knew it belonged to another who had no part in his story. Particularly strong are the resemblances in the reaction aroused by the anointing. In both the suggestion is made that the unguent should have been sold. In both a sum of three hundred denarii is mentioned (in Mark the price is "more than" this), and in both the suggestion is made that the money be given to the poor. In both Jesus' answer includes a "Let her alone" and a reference to His burial. The chief differences are first that Mark appears to place the incident after the triumphal entry,[4] John before, and second that Mark speaks of an anointing of the head[5] and John of an anointing of the feet.[6] There are also minor differences of wording and word order, while Mark's words about

---

[2] νάρδου πιστικῆς. This highly unusual expression is nowhere attested before the Gospels. H. E. Edwards refuses to see in it evidence of literary dependence. "We might compare it to the phrase 'a mess of pottage', which, as nine people out of ten will tell you, was the price for which Esau sold his birthright. The phrase is not to be found in Scripture at all, either in Genesis, where the story is told, or in Hebrews, where allusion is made to it. It has come down to us orally, preserved in our memories by its pithy and unusual form" (*The Disciple who Wrote These Things*, London, 1953, p. 98).

[3] A. Cole thinks that Simon the leper was the father of Lazarus and the sisters. Thus the house was his, but for practical purposes belonged to the children. He reminds us of Uzziah living in isolation while his son Jotham reigned (*Tyndale Commentary on the Gospel according to St. Mark*, London, 1961, p. 208). This is possible, but there is no evidence.

[4] Yet it is to be borne in mind that neither Matthew nor Mark dates this incident with precision. They simply recount it in immediate juxtaposition to Judas's betrayal. The place where they insert it may be due to a desire to draw a sharp contrast with the traitor rather than to put it in its correct chronological position.

[5] The anointing of the head is probably to be understood as a recognition of Jesus' royal place as Messiah. *Cf.* R. V. G. Tasker: "she pours the fragrant perfume, her most costly possession, over His head as though she were anointing a king" (*Tyndale Commentary on the Gospel according to St. Matthew*, London, 1961, p. 242).

[6] Anointing the feet is most unusual, to say the least. There appear to be no parallels to the Gospel stories. In neither incident is a reason given for such an anointing but it appears to indicate the taking of a very lowly place.

the woman's having done a good work are absent from John as is the reference to being able to do good to the poor when you will. Mark does not name the woman, but John says it was Mary. Mark speaks of the woman as breaking an alabaster cruse to release the unguent, and he reports Jesus as saying that wherever the gospel is preached the story will be told in memory of the woman, neither of which is in John. He also refers generally to some of those present as being indignant, whereas John speaks of Judas.

It is not without its interest that in some points John's account is nearer that of Matthew than of Mark. Thus Matthew says it was "the disciples" who were indignant (John specifically names Judas), and he omits Jesus' words about being able to do good to the poor at any time.

It is difficult to escape the conclusion that Matthew, Mark and John all refer to the same incident. But Luke's story appears to be different.

1 "Therefore" ties this section of the narrative in with the preceding. The chief priests and the Pharisees were seeking to put Jesus to death. He had no intention of rushing needlessly into danger, and therefore He had retired to a quiet spot (12 : 54). But this Gospel is written out of a deep conviction that Jesus came to die for men. It was in the purpose of God that He should lay down His life for others. "Therefore" at the set time Jesus came up to the city where He would be delivered up to death. Notice John's interest in precise detail. He tells us exactly when Jesus came to Bethany, locating His arrival characteristically by a reference to one of the great feasts. Six days before Passover[7]

---

[7] He does not say "six days before the Passover", but $\pi\varrho\grave{o}$ $\overset{\centerdot}{\varepsilon}\xi$ $\mathring{\eta}\mu\varepsilon\varrho\tilde{\omega}\nu$ $\tauο\tilde{\nu}$ $\pi\acute{a}\sigma\chi\alpha$, i.e. six days before, beginning from the Passover. Some think the construction a Latinism, but Moulton points out that the earliest Greek examples are pre-Roman, and he finds "the hypothesis of Latinism utterly improbable" (M, I, p. 101). The construction is certainly like *ante diem tertium Kalendas*, but in view of the early occurrence of the Greek all that we can say is that the similar Latin may have stimulated its use. A similar expression is found in Amos 1 : 1, $\pi\varrho\grave{o}$ $\delta\acute{\nu}o$ $\overset{\centerdot}{\varepsilon}\tau\tilde{\omega}\nu$ $\tauο\tilde{\nu}$ $\sigma\varepsilon\iota\sigma\muο\tilde{\nu}$. P66, according to G. D. Fee, instead of $\overset{\centerdot}{\varepsilon}\xi$ has the singular reading $\pi\acute{\varepsilon}\nu\tau\varepsilon$, "five" (*JBL*, LXXXIV, 1965, p. 71).

would be the sabbath, presuming that 14th Nisan that year fell on a Friday. Jesus may have arrived on the Friday after sunset, or alternatively not have travelled very far so as not to exceed the sabbath day's journey. John proceeds to characterize Bethany by the great miracle he has just described. It was the place "where Lazarus was, whom Jesus raised from the dead." The repetition of the name Jesus in this verse is interesting, and it may be a means of stressing the personal activity of the Lord.

2 The result of Jesus' visit was a supper.[8] "They" is not defined. It probably means the people of the village who have been impressed by the miracle, though it could mean the people of the household. Martha is mentioned first which may indicate that she was acting as hostess. She was active in serving (Moffatt: "waited on him"; the imperfect tense denotes a continuing activity). This agrees with Luke's portrait of her on another occasion when Jesus visited the family (Luke 10 : 40; "serving" in that verse is cognate with "served" in this).[9] Lazarus is placed among the guests. He was one of those who reclined at table with[10] the Lord. This is perhaps a more natural remark if the feast were in another house than Lazarus's own. His presence among the guests could be assumed in his own home.

3 Once more John begins a verse with "therefore".[11] The anointing is closely tied in with the preceding circumstances.

---

[8] δεῖπνον can denote a meal at any time of the day (see LS). In the New Testament, however, it appears to mean the main meal of the day, held towards evening. Elsewhere in this Gospel it is used only of the Last Supper.

[9] Morgan makes the interesting point that in the Lukan passage where she served a meal for four people Martha was distracted; here she probably had seventeen, but "there is not a word here about being distracted. Martha had learned something on that sad, dark day . . . Her service had not ceased, but some secret had been learned, which kept her from distraction."

[10] "With" is σύν, a preposition found only at 18 : 1; 21 : 3 elsewhere in this Gospel. If, as is generally held, its use is a mark of literary rather than spoken Greek, it is of interest that it occurs 4 times in Matthew, 6 times in Mark, but 23 times in Luke and 52 times in Acts.

[11] This is the third verse running introduced by οὖν.

575

Mary now took a pound[12] of very costly unguent.[13] "Ointment" perhaps gives the wrong impression. It is not a healing preparation that is meant, nor a solid of any kind, but a scented oil which might be poured on the head as a mark of festivity. Phillips renders "perfume", and this is the sense of it. A pound of it was a considerable amount, and spikenard was an expensive perfume, so that Mary's was a very costly action. John goes out of his way to emphasize the cost involved. The use of unguents was very common in the first century especially on festive occasions. But the oil was normally poured on the head and the peculiar thing about this anointing was that Mary poured it on the feet of the Lord. This is probably to be taken as an act of utter humility. Mary is taking the lowliest possible place. A little later in this Gospel there is an incident wherein Jesus rebuked the disciples by washing their feet, a menial task which none of them would willingly undertake (13 : 2ff.). To attend to the feet was the task of the most lowly slave. Thus Mary's action denoted great humility as well as great devotion. This is emphasized by her using her hair to wipe the feet. It is curious that the oil was wiped off at all. In the case of the incident in Luke 7 it is understandable that the tears be wiped off before the oil was applied, but it is difficult to think of a reason for wiping off the unguent. Be that what it may, the use of the hair rather than the employment of a towel or the like may also indicate something of personal involvement. The act is all the more striking in that a Jewish

---

[12] λίτρα is a Latin loan word = *libra*. It denotes a Roman pound *i.e.* 12 ozs, or 327.45 grams (AG). It is found again in the New Testament only in 19 : 39.

[13] There are some difficulties about this perfume. νάρδος is fairly straightforward, referring in the first place to the plant; and in the second to the perfumed oil it yields. But the adjective πιστική is more difficult. It is not found before the Gospels, so there are no other passages with which to compare it. There seem four possibilities. The word may derive from πίστις with a meaning like "faithful", "trustworthy", hence "genuine" (ARV "pure"). Nard was apparently adulterated on occasion, and this would mean that this specimen was of the pure type. A second view (favored by LS) is that it derives from πίνω, and means "drinkable" *i.e.* "liquid". AG is surely right in regarding this as "very improbable". The third view connects the word with πιστάκια, "pistachio tree". The fourth sees in it a place name (so Augustine) or a trade name "pistic nard", the significance of which now eludes us. A small point in favor of the last is the absence of καί before πολυτίμου, for this may indicate that νάρδου πιστικῆς is being treated as something like a compound noun (so Abbott, 2168).

lady never unbound her hair in public. That apparently was a mark of loose morals.[14] But Mary did not stop to calculate public reaction. Her heart went out to her Lord and she gave expression to something of her feelings in this beautiful and touching act. The repetition of "feet" may be a way of stressing Mary's willing acceptance of the lowliest place. R. H. Lightfoot reminds us that Jesus' words to Peter in connection with the feet washing imply that the washing of the feet "is equivalent to a complete washing" (13 : 9f.). He adds, "possibly the same principle may hold good here. If so, the reader is invited to see in Mary's action a symbolical embalming of His body for burial, as though He were already dead." Calvin thinks the reference to the feet means that the "whole body was anointed down to the feet." John recalls that "the house was filled with[15] the odor of the ointment." This looks like the reminiscence of someone who was there. It is possible also that it has a further significance. There is a rabbinic saying: "(The scent of) good oil is diffused from the bed-chamber to the dining-hall while a good name is diffused from one end of the world to the other."[16] If some such thought is in mind this may be John's equivalent of the saying that the action would be spoken of throughout the world (Mark 14 : 9).

4 Mark simply tells us that "there were some that had indignation among themselves" (Mark 14 : 4). John, however, singles out Judas for mention in this connection. He characterizes the man in three ways: he gives his surname, Iscariot (see on 6 : 71), he speaks of him as one of Jesus' disciples, and he reminds us that he would betray Jesus.[17] Notice that he does not launch out on

---

[14] In Num. 5 : 18 the priest loosed the hair of the woman suspected of adultery. *Cf.* also *Sot.* 8a where the priest undoes the hair of the adulteress. J. Lightfoot cites a Rabbinic passage: "Kamitha had seven sons, who all performed the office of high-priests: they ask of her, how she came to this honour? she answered, The rafters of my house never saw the hairs of my head" (*HHT*, p. 361). A respectable woman always kept her hair covered.

[15] This is the one place in the New Testament where $\pi\lambda\eta\varrho\delta\omega$ is followed by $\grave{\epsilon}\varkappa$. This preposition follows $\gamma\acute{\epsilon}\mu\omega$ in Matt. 23 : 25 and $\gamma\epsilon\mu\acute{\iota}\zeta\omega$ in Luke 15 : 16; Rev. 8 : 5, but it is rather rare with all verbs of filling.

[16] Ecc. R. VII. 1. 1 (Soncino edn., p. 166).

[17] John has a similar statement about Judas in 6 : 71, but characteristically in repeating it he makes slight changes. The word order is different, in the earlier passage $\grave{\epsilon}\varkappa$ is used before $\tau\tilde{\omega}\nu$ $\delta\acute{\omega}\delta\epsilon\varkappa\alpha$ but here it is not (some MSS have it also here, but it does not appear to be the true text); there we have $\tau\tilde{\omega}\nu$ $\delta\acute{\omega}\delta\epsilon\varkappa\alpha$, here $\tau\tilde{\omega}\nu$ $\mu\alpha\vartheta\eta\tau\tilde{\omega}\nu$, to which $\alpha\grave{\upsilon}\tau o\tilde{\upsilon}$ is added; while the former has $\check{\epsilon}\mu\epsilon\lambda\lambda\epsilon\nu$ this passage reads $\acute{o}$ $\mu\acute{\epsilon}\lambda\lambda\omega\nu$.

a tirade against the traitor. The only way he brings out the enormity of the offence is by setting side by side the statements that he was a disciple and that he would betray the Lord.

5 Judas points out that nard was valuable. He asks why the unguent was not sold for 300 denarii and the proceeds given to poor folk.[18] The sum is a large one. A laborer was paid a denarius a day (Matt. 20 : 2), so that, allowing for sabbaths, it amounts to about a year's wages for a laboring man.

6 Such a gift would have been a worthwhile benefaction especially considering the small size of the apostolic group. But John now vouchsafes the information that Judas did not speak in this way out of concern for the poor[19] but from motives of dishonesty. This is the one place in the four Gospels wherein Judas is shown to be of bad character prior to the betrayal. John characterizes him as "a thief", his word indicating something like a sneak-thief.[20] He also gives us the information that Judas was "treasurer"[21] of the little band, which argues that he was a man of some ability. It also meant that he would be in a position to help himself from time to time.[22] It further opens up the possibility that disappointed avarice may have been one of the motives leading Judas to betray Jesus. This is specially clear in the arrangement of the narrative

---

[18] There is no article with πτωχοῖς, so that the meaning is "to poor people" rather than "to the poor".

[19] The construction is impersonal, οὐχ ὅτι περὶ τῶν πτωχῶν ἔμελεν αὐτῷ. The only other example of this construction in John is in 10 : 13 where it is used of the hireling who "careth not for the sheep". This may be more than a coincidence.

[20] κλέπτης.

[21] τὸ γλωσσόκομον ἔχων. The noun denoted a small box or case, originally one for the mouthpiece of a flute (γλῶτται). From its proper use for the flute it appears to have been used of any small case, but in the New Testament its two occurrences (here and 13 : 29) both refer to a money box. MM comment: "This out-of-the-way-looking word proves to be decidedly vernacular, and quite in place in Jn 12[6], 13[29], where it is 'money-box' (cf. RV marg.): its original meaning, as 'receptacle' (κομίζω) for the 'tongues' or mouthpieces of flutes, had been long forgotten, and influenced it only by stamping on it generally the sense of small size and portability." They cite numerous examples. See also Field, p. 97. What is clear is that it referred to a box made of wood or other rigid material, not a "bag" as ARV, or "purse" as Phillips.

[22] βαστάζω is a word with a double meaning, not unlike the English word "lift". It signifies "to carry" (as AV, "bare"), but it may also mean "to carry away" and thus "to pilfer" (see MM). Judas not only "carried" what was put in the box, but "carried it off".

in Matthew and Mark. These two Evangelists speak of Judas as going away to the chief priests and making his agreement with them immediately at the close of this incident. The impression left is that Judas, seeing one source of personal enrichment lost, hastened to create another. And if this is the character of the man we may well feel that he was dissatisfied with the way the mission of Jesus was turning out. Certainly he would have hoped for better pickings when he first attached himself to the little band.

7 Jesus immediately took Mary's part. He would have nothing to do with the criticism brought against her. But there is difficulty in seeing the precise bearing of His defence. In the first place it is curious that He should refer to His "burying" [23] at all. Anointing was usually a mark of festivity. Its omission was an act of discourtesy towards a guest (Luke 7 : 46). When men were engaged on solemn activities such as fasting they sometimes refrained from anointing as a way of drawing attention to what they were doing, a practice which Jesus discouraged (Matt. 6 : 16f.). Anointing was thus associated with revelry rather than with funerals. A remark concerning a burial is not at all what we should have expected. We must take this as a measure of the extent to which the Passion was in the mind of our Lord at this time. It loomed large in His thoughts and therefore an action which at another time might arouse very different associations, He immediately associated with His death. Here He associates Mary with this view. He may mean that she had entered more fully into His mind than others and knew that the end could not be far off. Or He may mean that she had procured the perfume with a view to His final anointing. Probably the former. The other difficulty is in seeing what meaning we are to put into the word "keep", [24] for Mary had just done the very opposite of "keeping" the unguent. She

---

[23] ἐνταφιασμός refers properly not so much to the burial as to the "laying out" of the corpse, the preparation for burial (MM). In 19 : 40 the wrapping in linen with spices is described as the Jewish custom ἐνταφιάζειν.

[24] There is some difficulty with the construction ἄφες αὐτήν, ἵνα τηρήσῃ. Moulton points out that ἄφες is possibly used more or less as an auxiliary which would here give the meaning "let her keep it". The accusative αὐτήν, however, and the similar expression in Mark 14 : 6 are against the auxiliary idea, and favour "Let her alone: let her keep it" (M, I, pp. 175f.). The former interpretation is behind ARV "Suffer her to keep it", but the latter seems preferable with Phillips, Rieu, FF, C. K. Williams, C. B. Williams *etc.* Barrett sees another possible meaning as "Let her alone; (it was, *or* this took place) that she might keep it. . . ." So ARV mg., *Amplified.*

had poured it out and it was irrevocably lost. Perhaps the meaning is that Mary should "keep" the unguent for the use she had in mind, and not devote it to the use of which Judas had spoken. That is to say she had kept the unguent for a special purpose. In view of the Lord's imminent death now was the time to discharge that purpose.[25] There seems little to be said for the view of Bernard, Richardson, and others that part only of the unguent was used and the rest kept until the burial (*cf.* v. 3; Mark 14 : 3).[26] Such a view is difficult to reconcile, for example, with Judas's remarks. He was complaining that the perfume had been wasted, not that it was being reserved for a wrong purpose.[27]

8 Opportunity is to be seized while it is there. The poor are always present (*cf.* Deut. 15 : 11). But Jesus[28] is not. He will not live to old age but will soon be taken from among them. The time for actions of devotion toward Him is much shorter than those at the table think.[29] Our Lord accordingly welcomes the action of Mary.

(b) The Triumphal Entry, 12 : 9–19

9 The common people therefore of the Jews learned that he was there: and they came, not for Jesus' sake only, but that they might see Lazarus also, whom he had raised from the dead. **10** But the chief priests took counsel that they might put Lazarus also to death; **11** because that by reason of him many of the Jews went away, and believed on Jesus. **12** On the morrow [1]a great multitude that had come to the feast, when they heard that Jesus was coming to Jerusalem, **13** took the branches of the palm trees, and went forth to meet him, and cried out, Hosanna: Blessed is he that cometh in

---

[25]   This accords with the view of Lagrange who points out that τετήρηκεν of the received text, while not the true reading, has yet preserved the true sense.

[26]   Jesus does not refer to part of it, but to "it" *(αὐτό)*. Moreover Mark refers to the alabaster cruse as having been broken (Mark 14 : 3) which makes it unlikely that any significant amount could have been retained.

[27]   Torrey makes the words a question: "should she keep it for the day of my burial?"

[28]   Note the use of the emphatic ἐμέ set at the beginning of the clause. Jesus is placed in the sharpest contrast with τοὺς πτωχούς.

[29]   There are Jewish expressions which indicate that the care of the dead takes precedence over almsgiving. Thus *Sukk.* 49b praises *Gemiluth Ḥasadim* ("the practice of kindness") above charity, among other reasons because it can be done both to the living and the dead, the latter of which is explained as: "By attending to their funeral and burial" (Soncino ed., p. 233, n. 8).

the name of the Lord, even the King of Israel. 14 And Jesus,
having found a young ass, sat thereon; as it is written, 15
²Fear not, daughter of Zion: behold, thy King cometh,
sitting on an ass's colt. 16 These things understood not his
disciples at the first: but when Jesus was glorified, then
remembered they that these things were written of him, and
that they had done these things unto him. 17 The multitude
therefore that was with him when he called Lazarus out of
the tomb, and raised him from the dead, bare witness. 18
For this cause also the multitude went and met him, for that
they heard that he had done this sign. 19 The Pharisees
therefore said among themselves, ³Behold how ye prevail
nothing; lo, the world is gone after him.

¹Some ancient authorities read *the common people*. See ver. 9. ²Zech. ix. 9.
³Or, *Ye behold*

The narrative of the triumphal entry is found in all four
Gospels. At this point accordingly John's story links up with that
in the Synoptic Gospels. John does not include all the details
that we find elsewhere, and, for example, says little about the
procuring of the ass, saying only that Jesus "having found a young
ass, sat thereon" (v. 14). But John tells enough to bring out the
royalty of Jesus. Characteristically he does not think of this as a
glorification of Jesus (for that he looks to the cross, v. 16). But
he leaves no doubt but that the challenge of Jesus was felt and
appreciated. He has some touches of his own. He alone dates the
incident on the Sunday preceding the Passover. He alone mentions
the palms, the reference to the raising of Lazarus, the fact that
the disciples did not understand the significance of these happenings
until after Jesus "was glorified", and the pessimistic utterance of
the Pharisees.

9 It was not difficult to make the journey from Jerusalem to
Bethany, and a great crowd of people came. The expression is
similar to that rightly rendered "the common people" in Mark
12 : 37 but the word order is different[30] and it would seem that

---

30 Mark has ὁ πολὺς ὄχλος and John appears to read ὁ ὄχλος πολύς with
the adjective in the predicate position. This is the reading of אּ B* *al*, and, though
most authorities omit the article, it should probably be accepted. A text without
it would read smoothly and there seems no reason for inserting it, whereas
the omission from a text containing it would seem a fairly obvious correction.
There is a division of authorities again over the same expression in v. 12. If
we accept the reading ὁ ὄχλος πολύς, we have another problem. The expression
ought to mean "the crowd is great", but the context makes it clear that "the

John's meaning is "the great crowd". While obviously this will include many of the "common people" yet this is not what John says and his intention should be respected. The crowd is described as "of the Jews", an expression which in this Gospel naturally applies to Jesus' enemies rather than to those who were disposed to be friendly towards Him. They came to know[31] that Jesus was there and so they came. John makes it plain that Lazarus was a great attraction for them. They came not simply to see Jesus but on account of Lazarus. To this man's name John adds "whom he had raised from the dead". He does not want us to lose sight of the stupendous miracle.

10, 11 John now records the effect on the high priests. They took counsel together in order that they might kill Lazarus[32] (the construction indicates purpose). This seems a strange desire since death had not been able to hold him in the face of Jesus' command. But the "also" is significant. They wanted to destroy both Lazarus and the Man who had raised him. Perhaps too they felt that the raising had not been genuine so that if they could really secure Lazarus's death it would be an end to the mischief that the reports of his raising were causing. It is interesting to reflect that Caiaphas had said, "it is expedient for you that one man should die for the people" (11 : 50). But one was not enough. Now it had to be two. Thus does evil grow. For the Sadducees Lazarus was a double embarrassment. Not only did he cause men to go over to the side of Christ, but he was also a standing condemnation of their doctrine. They denied that there would be a resurrection and here was a man who had lived through death. "Many of the Jews", *i.e.* of the group normally opposed to Jesus, were departing,[33] and were believing on Jesus. John uses the imperfect tense, which may indicate continuity, in which case he sees the process as going on for quite some time. Or it may be inceptive "they began to

---

great crowd" is meant. Lightfoot thinks the unusual expression may be meant to recall the crowd of 6 : 2, 5 (ὄχλος πολύς and πολὺς ὄχλος), for that crowd had followed Jesus in Galilee and sought to make Him King. Westcott regards ὄχλος πολύς as a "compound noun". This would simplify the situation, but he gives no reasons.

[31] Ingressive aorist.

[32] The καί before Lazarus looks back to 11 : 53 where they plotted to kill Jesus. Now they include Lazarus *also* in their plans.

[33] ὑπῆγον. The verb is common in John. It may be used here with something of the meaning "depart from one's allegiance" (*i.e.* to the chief priests). *Cf.* its use in 6 : 67.

582

go away", "they began to believe". The construction used for "believed on Jesus" is that which John habitually uses for a deep and genuine faith (see Additional Note E, pp. 335ff.).

12, 13 "On the morrow" is a typical Johannine note of time, and refers back to v. 1. "A great multitude"[34] is the same expression as that rendered "the common people" in v. 9 (where see note), but it does not refer to the same people. There it referred to the people from Jerusalem who went out to Bethany. Here it refers to the country people who were coming up to Jerusalem for the feast, probably most of them from Galilee.[35] These would accordingly be the men among whom the greater part of Jesus' ministry had been exercised, a fact which perhaps explains their enthusiasm. Doubtless many of them had felt for some time that Jesus' teaching and miracles showed Him to be the Messiah. But up till now He would not make the claim. He would never set Himself up as King. When on this occasion He did not reject their acclamation, their enthusiasm knew no bounds. He was doing, they thought, what they had always wanted Him to do. As John tells it these people did not happen to be in the way as Jesus came. They heard[36] that He was coming and went out of set purpose to meet Him.[37]

They took palm branches and they cried out (the imperfect tense means that they cried out persistently; cf. Berkeley: "shouting all the while"). Both the actions and the words expressed their

---

[34] The article is read by P66* BL Θ fl syrˢ boh. As in v. 9 it should probably be accepted.

[35] Great numbers assembled at Jerusalem at Passover time. Josephus speaks of a crowd exceeding 2,700,000 (Bell. vi, 425). Even allowing for some exaggeration it is clear that large numbers were to be expected at this feast. J. Jeremias estimates that on such occasions the city could accommodate 150,000 persons (Jerusalem in the Time of Jesus, E.T., London, 1969, pp. 82 ff.).

[36] The plural, ἀκούσαντες, coming as it does after the singular noun ὄχλος and the singular participle ἐλθών is to be noted. It would not be so strange if it came after the plural verb ἔλαβον. Perhaps John is putting some emphasis on plurality in the crowd, which may also be in mind in the adjective, πολύς.

[37] εἰς ὑπάντησιν αὐτῷ. Moulton has a note on the expression in which he denies that it is a Semitism, and regards it as synonymous with εἰς ἀπάντησιν. Of the latter he says, "It seems that the special idea of the word was the official welcome of a newly arrived dignitary" (M, I, p. 14, n. 3). Similarly MM speaks of it as "a kind of t.t. for the official welcome of a newly arrived dignitary". This, of course, is very much in place in the present context.

praise. John's word for "branches"[38] is found only here in the New Testament. It is not clear why the Synoptists do not indicate the kind of branches that were used on this occasion, but it is to John that we owe the information that they were from palm trees. The Law provided that palms should be used at the Feast of Tabernacles (Lev. 23 : 40). Later they were used on other festal occasions also (I Macc. 13 : 51; II Macc. 10 : 7).[39] In keeping with this we read in Revelation of a multitude before the throne with palms in their hands (Rev. 7 : 9). Palms were an emblem of victory, and in John's mention of them here we must detect a reference to the triumph of Christ. The word Hosanna is the transliteration of an Aramaic or Hebrew expression with the meaning, "Save, I pray" (Torrey translates "God save him!").[40]

---

[38] βαΐα. His phrase is τὰ βαΐα τῶν φοινίκων, which is peculiar in that either βαΐα or φοινίκων could denote palm branches (though the latter might also mean "palm-trees"), so that the whole means "palm branches of palm trees". βαΐον is apparently taken over from the Coptic bai (AG). Some suggest that what is meant is the *lulab* or branch of palm, willow and myrtle used at the Feast of Tabernacles. But no sufficient reason is given for their use at Passover. It is better to think of palm branches used in a spontaneous expression of joy as a royal Person is acclaimed. Some see an inaccuracy in that palms do not grow near Jerusalem, but John does not say where the people got them from. They may have been carrying them for general festal purposes. The references cited from Maccabees and Revelation show that palms were used on occasions of festal rejoicing. See further the note by W. R. Farmer, *JThS*, n.s., III, 1952, pp. 62–66.

[39] Lightfoot points out that the palm is also found on Jewish coins of the period 140 B.C.–A.D. 70, sometimes with the inscription "the redemption of Zion".

[40] Aramaic נָא הוֹשַׁע; Hebrew נָּא הוֹשִׁיעָה. It is found in Ps. 118 : 25 where ARV renders "Save now". It apparently became a familiar liturgical expression, though our evidence for this is later than the New Testament. The Greek form ὡσαννά is not found in LXX, and may be a Christian coinage (so Edwin D. Freed, *Old Testament Quotations in the Gospel of John*, Leiden, 1965, pp. 71f.). It is not easy to see why words which have meaning in connection with supplication should be used in this way of acclamation. It is possible that we should take the expression as addressed to Jesus. He is then being implored as Messiah to bring salvation. Against this is the difficulty of taking this meaning with a following ἐν τοῖς ὑψίστοις (Matt. 21 : 9; Mark 11 : 10). Others have suggested that the words should be understood as a prayer addressed to God for His Messiah (*cf.* "God save the king"), or that it had become conventionalized and meant something like "Hail" or "Praise" (so, for example, Augustine, who thought it indicates "rather a state of mind than having any positive significance" (LI. 2; p. 283) *i.e.* it is an interjection. On the whole the last-mentioned seems most probable. See further E. Werner, *JBL*, LXV, 1946, pp. 97–122; G. Dalman, *The Words of Jesus* (Edinburgh, 1902), pp. 220–23; Edwin D. Freed, *op. cit.*, pp. 66–73.

It is not likely that the multitude used the term with a clear understanding of its etymological significance (any more than we do when we say "Good-bye"). But John was probably mindful of the meaning, and thought of Jesus as entering the city on a mission of salvation, indeed on a royal, triumphant mission of salvation. The verb to be supplied after "blessed" might be "be" or, as ARV, "is". Usually "be" is to be preferred as the expression is used in calling down blessing on a man. But here "is" is just as possible and seems preferable. The multitude are proclaiming the blessedness of Jesus rather than praying that he might be blessed. "He that cometh in the name of the Lord" is almost certainly John's meaning, though the Hebrew of Psalm 118 : 26 should probably be understood as "Blessed in the name of the Lord is he that comes". The expression here is a messianic title.[41] There is evidence that the Jews looked for "a coming one". The Messiah might be spoken of in various ways. Here the thought is that He comes in God's name. To this the crowd adds the thought that He is "the King of Israel"[42] (this expression is not found in the prophecy; it is their addition). In the first chapter Nathanael had greeted Jesus as Israel's king (see on 1 : 49). Now John brings out the royalty of Jesus by ascribing the same conviction to the multitude at large. In the Synoptics the acclamation is given after the mention of Jesus' being seated on the ass and riding into the city, whereas here it is before. But it is not likely that John is in essential contradiction. It may be that it was the fulfilment of prophecy that drew forth the acclamation and that John's mention of the ass is left till late in order to leave room for emphasis on the acclamation, and not with the meaning that the ass was found late. Phillips translates: "For Jesus had found a young ass". Moreover it is not at all impossible that both accounts are needed to give us the complete picture. We need not think that Jesus sent

---

[41] See Vincent Taylor, *The Names of Jesus* (London, 1953), pp. 78f. He cites Cadbury, that "There is no evidence that it was a Jewish or Christian technical term", but notes that it is used of Jesus quite a number of times. He thinks that "the title had only a brief and restricted currency in certain circles. It has a marked eschatological tone".

[42] The text is in some doubt. ὁ βασιλεύς is read by P66 DΘ f1 *al*, but καί is prefixed by P75 *(vid.)* ℵ BW and it seems to be right. We should understand it in the sense, "even the king. ..."

the disciples for the ass before there was any indication at all of the crowd's enthusiasm. When this enthusiasm began to be manifested Jesus chose to accept it. But He rode into Jerusalem on a donkey to symbolize a conception of messiahship very different from that of the crowds. They hailed Him as the messianic King.[43] He came as the Prince of peace.

There is of course no great significance in the fact that the shouts of the multitude are differently reported in the several accounts. People in a crowd shout many things.

14, 15 Nothing is said as to the way Jesus obtained the ass.[44] John simply tells us that He found[45] it and sat upon it. The other Gospels tell how Jesus sent disciples into a village with minute instructions for finding the animal. They also tell us that when the ass was brought the disciples sat Jesus on it, using their garments as a saddle. John says nothing of these things. But he does go on to speak of fulfilment of Scripture. For him it is important that the will of God was done. The citation is from Zechariah 9 : 9.[46]

---

[43] A. Schweitzer says, that the Entry was messianic for Jesus, but not for the people (*The Quest of The Historical Jesus*, London, 1945, pp. 391f.). He is followed by, for example, J. W. Bowman, *The Intention of Jesus* (London, 1945), pp. 133f. But such a position fails to account for the enthusiasm of the crowds. Not so were prophets hailed. They thought of Him as a prophet indeed, but also as "he that cometh".

[44] The word is ὀνάριον, found here only in the New Testament. It is a diminutive in form, but it is not certain whether this should be pressed, as the word often seems to mean simply a "donkey".

[45] Some see a contradiction between εὑρών here and the Synoptic accounts of the way the disciples brought the ass to Jesus. But this is to be unnecessarily precise. John's εὑρών does not mean that Jesus personally went searching for an ass until He found one. It is his way of passing over the details entirely, and concentrating on the main event. In any case the verb could well mean "found by the agency of others".

[46] It does not agree exactly, notably in the opening words. The Hebrew גִּילִי מְאֹד is rendered by LXX Χαῖρε σφόδρα, so that John agrees with neither. Some suggest that his Μὴ φοβοῦ is from Isa. 40 : 9, but there it is the plural μὴ φοβεῖσθε. In any case it is hardly necessary to find a Scriptural source for so simple an expression or to imagine that John is using a text different from any known to us. It is quite natural to prefix such words, words moreover which were frequently on the lips of Jesus, to a prophecy telling how Jesus comes as the Prince of peace.

Zion appears originally to have denoted either the citadel at Jerusalem or the hill on which it stood. But the word was used poetically as a designation of the city itself. "Daughter of Zion" is a collective, referring to the inhabitants of Jerusalem as a whole. The words of this prophecy point to a distinctive mark of Christ's kingship. The ass was not normally used by a warlike person. It was the animal of a man of peace, a priest, a merchant or the like. It might also be used by a person of importance but in connection with peaceable purposes.[47] A conqueror would ride into the city on a war horse, or perhaps march in on foot at the head of his troops. The ass speaks of peace. John sees accordingly not only a fulfilment of prophecy, but such a fulfilment of prophecy as indicates a special kind of king.

16 Later John tells us that when the Holy Spirit came He would lead believers into all the truth. In this verse he gives us an example of this. At first the disciples did not understand what these things[48] meant, things which they themselves had done.[49] It was only when Jesus was "glorified" that they recalled these events and their significance. It was only then that they recalled these prophecies[50] and saw how they had been fulfilled[51] (*cf.* 2 : 22). The meaning of the happenings of the life of Jesus are not open for every unregenerate man to see. They are revealed only by the

---

[47] But the ass also had lowly associations. *Cf.* the dictum: "Fodder and a stick and burdens for an ass" (Sir. 33 : 24).

[48] Note the threefold repetition of ταῦτα in this verse. Such a multiplication of pronouns is not common in John (he much prefers to use nouns). It is likely that he wants to lay some stress on the way the events fulfilled prophecy.

[49] The subject of ἐποίησαν will be the same as that of the earlier verbs. John is not talking accordingly about what others, the crowd in general, had done, but about what the disciples themselves had done.

[50] The preposition ἐπί is somewhat unexpected in the expression ταῦτα ἦν ἐπ᾿ αὐτῷ γεγραμμένα (AG cite Herodotus 1 : 66 as a parallel). This is all the more the case in that John frequently uses περί with the genitive in the sense "about". John is not fond of ἐπί, which he uses 33 times (and only 5 times with the dative) out of a New Testament total of 878, whereas he uses περί twice as often, namely 66 times out of a New Testament total of 331. His use of ἐπί here is thus far from usual.

[51] Note that John does not repeat ὅτι before ταῦτα ἐποίησαν. It may be that he is hinting at a unity, in that the prophecy and the fulfilment are in some sense one. But this is perhaps too subtle.

Holy Spirit of God. Barrett sees the narrative as self-contradictory. The multitude recognized that Jesus was the messianic King (v. 13), but it was not possible for the disciples to recognize this until after the glorification of Jesus. But what John appears to be saying is that the disciples did not understand the real significance of these events. They did not comprehend the nature of Jesus' kingship (though they may well have thought of Him as in some sense the messianic King). John is not affirming that the multitude correctly evaluated the Person of the Lord. They thought of Him as King in a wrong sense. After the glorification the disciples thought of Him as King in a right sense. There is no contradiction.

17 John now introduces us to a different group, "the multitude that was[52] with him when he called Lazarus out of the tomb, and raised him from the dead". Notice that mention is made both of the calling of Lazarus from the tomb and of his being raised from the dead. The latter was the important thing, but the way Jesus had done it, in calling the dead man to come out of the tomb, had evidently made a profound impression. The multitude is described as bearing witness (see on 1 : 7), the imperfect tense denoting a continuing process. In the middle of the scenes of enthusiasm, with Jesus being hailed on all sides as king, those who had seen the stupendous miracle, were moved to tell others of what they had seen.

18 For this reason "the multitude" met [53] Him. This it would seem is a different multitude from that mentioned in v. 17[54] though the same expression is used of them. What John evidently means is that those who had seen the miracle bore their witness as a result of which those who had not seen it but now heard[55] of it went out to meet Him. They wanted to see for themselves the one who had done such a stupendous thing. In v. 12 the multitude that went with

---

[52] Burton notices ὤν here as an example of the present participle used to denote action prior to that of the main verb (*Moods*, 127).

[53] The significance of καὶ ὑπήντησεν is sometimes overlooked. The position of καί shows the meaning to be "For this reason the crowd (besides doing other things) also met Him", not "For this cause also (*i.e.* in addition to other causes)" of ARV.

[54] Swete commenting on the Markan narrative sees two crowds, one pouring out from Jerusalem and the other coming from Bethany (on Mark 11 : 9).

[55] ἤκουσαν is used in much the same sense as the pluperfect, "they had heard".

Jesus was clearly the pilgrim crowd streaming into Jerusalem. In this verse it seems rather to be the Jerusalem mob coming out to meet the procession. Notice that the reason given is "that they heard that he had done this sign."[56] The last word is significant (see Additional Note G, pp. 684ff.).

19 The scene provoked the Pharisees to pessimism.[57] "Behold" is clearly addressed to one another, but it is not at all certain whether it is to be taken as imperative, as ARV, or as indicative, "Ye behold", as ARV mg. Perhaps the latter is a little more probable, but we cannot be sure. The first part of their statement points to a complete lack of success. They had no profit at all in what they were doing against Jesus, The second part points to the great success attending Jesus' efforts. In a magnificent hyperbole they speak of "the world" as going after Him. John may wish us to see in this an unconscious prophecy of the effects of the preaching of the gospel (*cf.* Acts 17 : 6). It is ironical. They are concerned that a few Judeans were being influenced. But their words express John's conviction that He was conquering the world.

(c) The Greeks, 12: 20-36a

20 Now there were certain Greeks among those that went up to worship at the feast: 21 these therefore came to Philip, who was of Bethsaida of Galilee, and asked him, saying, Sir, we would see Jesus. 22 Philip cometh and telleth Andrew: Andrew cometh, and Philip, and they tell Jesus. 23 And Jesus answereth them, saying, The hour is come that the Son of man should be glorified. 24 Verily, verily, I say unto you, Except a grain of wheat fall into the earth and die, it abideth by itself alone; but if it die, it beareth much fruit. 25 He that loveth his ¹life loseth it; and he that hateth his ¹life in this world shall keep it unto ²life eternal. 26 If any man serve me, let him follow me; and where I am, there shall also my servant be: if any man serve me, him will the Father honor. 27 Now is my soul troubled; and what shall I say? Father, save me from this ³hour. But for this cause came I unto this

---

⁵⁶ τοῦτο is separated from σημεῖον possibly for greater emphasis: "They heard that He had done this thing – the sign". There is a similar separation of this adjective from its noun in 9 : 16 (where see note).

⁵⁷ Black takes πρὸς ἑαυτούς as a reflection of an Aramaic *dativus ethicus* (*AA*, p. 77). This, if correct, would strengthen the conviction that an Aramaic source or Aramaic thinking lies behind this Gospel.

hour. 28 Father, glorify thy name. There came therefore a voice out of heaven, saying, I have both glorified it, and will glorify it again. 29 The multitude therefore, that stood by, and heard it, said that it had thundered: others said, An angel hath spoken to him. 30 Jesus answered and said, This voice hath not come for my sake, but for your sakes. 31 Now is [4]the judgment of this world: now shall the prince of this world be cast out. 32 And I, if I be lifted up [5]from the earth, will draw all men unto myself. 33 But this he said, signifying by what manner of death he should die. 34 The multitude therefore answered him, We have heard out of the law that the Christ abideth for ever: and how sayest thou, The Son of man must be lifted up? who is this son of man? 35 Jesus therefore said unto them, Yet a little while is the light [6]among you. Walk while ye have the light, that darkness overtake you not: and he that walketh in the darkness knoweth not whither he goeth. 36 While ye have the light, believe on the light, that ye may become sons of light.

[1][2]*life* in these places represents two different Greek words [3]Or, *hour*? [4]Or, *a judgment* [5]Or, *out of* [6]Or, *in*

This rather curious incident is peculiar to John. I say "rather curious" because it is unusual that we should encounter Greeks in a narrative of important events at Jerusalem, because the other Evangelists do not mention the incident at all, and because the Greeks simply say, "Sir, we would see Jesus" and then disappear from the narrative. Clearly John regards their coming as significant. But he does not treat their presence as important. Jesus recognizes in their coming an indication that the climax of His mission has arrived. Immediately he hears of them he says "The hour is come", and goes on to speak of His glorification and of death.[58] In this Gospel we see Jesus as the world's Saviour, and evidently John means us to understand that this contact with the Greeks ushered in the climax. The fact that the Greeks had reached the point of wanting to meet Jesus showed that the time had come for Him to die for the world. He no longer belongs to Judaism, which in any case has rejected Him. But the world whose Saviour He is, awaits Him and seeks for Him.

---

[58] A. Cole sees a link with the saying about the destruction of the Temple (2 : 19), for the abolition of the Temple and the inclusion of the Gentiles are closely linked (*The New Temple*, London, 1950, p. 31).

20 John introduces us now[59] to certain Greeks. As these men had come up[60] to worship it is likely that they were "God-fearers". They may have been proselytes but if so they would scarcely have been described simply as "Greeks".[61] The "God-fearers" were men who were attracted by the lofty morality and the monotheism of Judaism, but did not care to become full proselytes by circumcision. They might visit Jerusalem for the great feasts, but they could not pass beyond the court of the Gentiles when they went to the temple.[62] These men would not necessarily have come from Greece itself. There were many Greeks in Decapolis, for example, and they could have come from such a place. At Passover time worshippers came from widely scattered places throughout the Roman Empire to join in the festivity.

21 It is not clear why they came to Philip. Possibly being Greeks they were attracted by his Greek name (though Andrew, to whom Philip came in perplexity, also has a Greek name). If so they could easily have been misled for the name signified little. Many Jews bore this Greek name. But if this is not the reason we have no means of knowing why they selected Philip. Notice John's habit of particularizing. This Philip was the one from Bethsaida of Galilee (see on 1 : 44). John says that they "asked" (the tense is continuous, "they kept asking him") but no question is recorded. However one is implied in "Sir, we would see Jesus". "See", of course, means

---

[59] His δέ may indicate a contrast with the preceding. The Pharisees set themselves in opposition to Jesus *but* the Greeks came up to Jerusalem and to Jesus.

[60] The present participle, ἀναβαινόντων, may indicate habitual practice, "among those who used to go up...." The verb is often used for "going up" to celebrate festivals.

[61] Ἕλλην of course does not necessarily indicate a person of the Greek race. It can stand for the cultured over against the non-cultured (Rom. 1 : 14), or for Gentiles over against Jews (Acts 14 : 1). In Mark 7 : 26 a woman is described as Ἑλληνίς and then as Συροφοινίκισσα. But if proselytes are meant some further descriptive word would be natural. The fact that they came to Jerusalem to worship does not mean that they were necessarily proselytes, for the Ethiopian eunuch did this (Acts 8 : 27), and he could not be a proselyte. The word is to be distinguished from Ἑλληνιστής (Acts 6 : 1 etc.), though this word does not denote Greek-speaking Jews as certainly as some suggest (see the note by H. J. Cadbury, *The Beginnings of Christianity*, V, London, 1933, pp. 59ff.). Josephus speaks of many Greeks, Ἕλληνες, as being attracted to Judaism (*Bell.* vii, 45).

[62] See SBk, II, pp. 548-51, for the status and limitations of these "half-proselytes".

something like "interview". Anyone could "see" Jesus as He moved among the people, but the Greeks clearly wanted more than that. They wanted to talk to Him and get to know Him. They give no reason for this. Up to this point John has given no indication that Jesus' reputation was such that Greeks would have heard of him (though, of course, in a place like Decapolis this would not be difficult). But the general tone of his Gospel leaves us in no doubt as to the point of the inquiry. Jesus was the Saviour of the world and this group of Gentiles symbolically represents the world seeking its salvation from Jesus.

22 Philip did not know what to make of their request. (Philip seems frequently to be in difficulties; see on 1 : 43.) Now in his perplexity he sought out Andrew. He is mentioned along with Andrew also in 1 : 44; 6 : 7f.; *cf.* Mark 3 : 18. Andrew, as might have been expected, joins Philip in telling[63] the Master (we find Andrew bringing people to Jesus in 1 : 42; 6 : 8f.).

23 Jesus' answer is surprising. He totally ignores the Greeks and neither immediately nor subsequently makes any reference to them whatever. His words are apparently addressed to Andrew and Philip,[64] but it is impossible to confine the reference to them. Clearly the words are addressed to a wider audience, possibly including the Greeks also. Plainly their coming is important. Jesus sees it as evidence that His mission has reached its climax and that he is now to die for the world, Greeks included. Barrett comments: "Here John does not represent Jesus in direct conversation with the Greeks; this however is not careless writing, for the rest of the chapter winds up the ministry of Jesus to the Jews in order that the true and spiritual 'conversation' of Jesus with the Greeks may begin – on the other side of the crucifixion". The gospel is a gospel for the whole world only because of the cross. "The hour is come"[65] reminds us

---

[63] The rule appears to be that where a verb precedes more than one noun which together constitute its subject it is singular, but where the verb follows it is plural. Thus we have the singular ἔρχεται and the plural λέγουσιν.

[64] This is the significance of ἀποκρίνεται αὐτοῖς. This verb occurs in John 78 times, the almost invariable form being the aorist passive. The present is found only here, 13 : 26, 38; 18 : 22. It may be meant to make these passages specially vivid. See also on 1 : 21.

[65] The reference to the hour as come is probably another example of John's habit of introducing slight variations in repetitions. Here and in 17 : 1 we have ἐλήλυθεν ἡ ὥρα, but in 13 : 1 Jesus knew ὅτι ἦλθεν αὐτοῦ ἡ ὥρα. Then in 16 : 32 we read ἔρχεται ὥρα καὶ ἐλήλυθεν (though in this last-mentioned passage the meaning of "hour" is slightly different).

of the series of references to "the hour" throughout the Gospel (see on 2 : 4). Though unobtrusive, this is one of the important ideas in John's Gospel. This is that for which Jesus is destined. The verb "is come" is in the perfect tense, "the hour has come and stays with us". There is no going back on it. In referring to His "hour" there is no doubt but that Jesus is referring to His death (see next verse). But He speaks not of tragedy but of triumph. He is not to be dishonored. He is to be glorified (for "glory" see on 1 : 14), and that by the way of the cross.[66] "The Son of man" is Jesus' way of referring to Himself, especially in connection with His mission. Its use in this verse accordingly is significant (see further Additional Note C, pp. 171ff.).

24 The solemn "Verily, verily" (see on 1 : 51) introduces a statement of importance. The[67] grain of wheat introduces us to a paradox, namely, that the way to fruitfulness lies through death. Unless the wheat falls into the ground and "dies" it will not bear.[68] It is only through "death" that its potentiality for fruitfulness becomes actual. This is a general truth. But it refers particularly to our Lord Himself.[69]

25 The application of the analogy from the grain of wheat is made plain. The man who loves his life loses it (*cf.* Mark 8 : 35 and parallels). By the very fact of his love for it he loses the possibility of real life. The verb translated "loseth" often means "destroys" (Phillips translates, "The man who loves his own life will destroy it"). John means us to understand that loving the life is a self-defeating process. It destroys the very life it seeks to retain. This may be involved also in the use of the present tense, where we might expect a future to match "shall keep". The man who loves his life is destroying it right now. "Hateth" is of course not to be taken literally, but "hating the life" is the natural antithesis of loving it (*cf.* Matt. 6 : 24 = Luke

---

[66] *Cf.* Barclay: "When He said that, the listeners would catch their breath. They would believe that the trumpet call of eternity had sounded, and that the might of heaven was on the march, and that the campaign of victory was on the move. But Jesus did not mean by *glorified* what they meant. By *glorified* they meant that the subjected kingdoms of the earth would grovel before the conqueror's feet; by *glorified* He meant *crucified.*"

[67] The article with κόκκος denotes the class.

[68] αὐτὸς μόνος puts emphasis on the aloneness of the grain that does not "die".

[69] As Augustine long since pointed out, "He spake of Himself. He Himself was the grain that had to die, and be multiplied; to suffer death through the unbelief of the Jews, and to be multiplied in the faith of many nations" (LI. 9; p. 285).

16 : 13; Luke 14 : 26). It points to the attitude that sets no store by this life in itself. The man whose priorities are right has such an attitude of love for the things of God that it makes all interest in the affairs of this life appear by comparison as hatred. This man will keep his life "unto life eternal"[70] – unto the life of the age to come (see on 1 : 4; 3 : 15).

26 The outcome of all this is the service of Christ. Throughout this verse there is emphasis on the first-personal pronoun.[71] It is personal relationship to Christ which is important. The servant must follow the Lord. He is to be where his Lord is.[72] This is to be understood in the light of the previous verse. Being where the Lord is entails suffering. It means losing the life for the Master's sake. There is no other way of Christian service. But the verse concludes on a different note. Any man who serves Christ in this fashion will be honored by the Father.

27 Christ feels His soul troubled (NEB: "my soul is in turmoil").[73] The perfect points to a continuous state. He first asks "what shall I say?". It may be important that His verb is "say" rather than "choose" or the like. There was no question as to His doing the Father's will. The question was, "What is the Father's will?" The next words look like a question about a possible answer to the first

---

[70] Notice the change from ψυχήν of loving or hating the life, i.e. this present, earthly life, to ζωήν of the life proper to the age to come. It may be entered on here and now, but its characteristics concern eternity. McClymont comments on ψυχήν here that it denotes "the natural life of man, with all its appetites, desires, and affections, which seek their gratification irrespective of the will of God. The loving of this life is another name for the spirit of selfishness which is unwilling to spend or be spent for any higher object than self-enjoyment and self-aggrandisement, while the hating of it denotes that spirit of self-sacrifice which counts nothing in this world too dear to be given up in obedience to the Divine will".

[71] The first ἐμοί is specially emphatic; it precedes τις (Rieu prints "me" in italics), whereas the third (the second to go with a τις) follows it (but before we put too much emphasis on this difference we should remember John's habit of making small changes in repetitions). Notice also ἐγώ and ἐμός. The first person is prominent throughout the verse.

[72] Hunter aptly comments: "It has been said that follow me is the whole of a Christian's duty, as to be where Christ is is the whole of his reward."

[73] For the verb ταράσσω see on 11 : 33. Jesus is to use this verb of the disciples' not being troubled (14 : 1, 27). But the price of their peace is His trouble of spirit.

question: "(shall I say) Father, save me from[74] this hour?" All the more is this the case in view of the preceding deliberative subjunctive. It is hard to see the point of this if it is to be followed by a positive prayer. It is also difficult to see the point of the strong adversative which begins the next clause unless this be a question.[75] The whole structure of the verse points to a hypothetical rather than an actual prayer. The words are taken this way by R. H. Lightfoot, Strachan, Godet, Lagrange, Torrey, Rieu, Phillips, Moffatt, etc. Is Jesus to pray to be saved from this hour? The question is immediately answered. This is the very reason for which He has come.[76] This "hour" must be faced and passed through. Others take the words as a positive prayer (so Bernard, Hendriksen, Barclay, Goodspeed, etc.). But this is very difficult. If this is the sense Jesus immediately repudiates His prayer, recognizing that He came to "this hour" in order to undergo it. It seems clear that the words represent a rhetorical question, a hypothetical prayer at which Jesus looks, but which He refuses to pray. The words reveal the natural human shrinking from death. John does not record the agony in Gethsemane, and this is his equivalent of the Synoptic prayer in the Garden, "not what I will, but what thou wilt" (Mark 14 : 36).[77] The

---

[74] ἐκ does not always signify "out of" a state one is already in. It may mean, as here, "keep me from being in the hour". Westcott accepts the meaning "bring me safely out of the conflict" (citing Heb. 5 : 7) rather than "keep me from entering into it". Cf. *Twentieth Century*: "Father, bring me safe through this hour". But Heb. 5 : 7 does not really seem to support Westcott. It says, "Who in the days of his flesh, having offered up prayers and supplications with strong crying and tears unto him that was able to save him from death...." The meaning appears to be that God had the power to save Him even from death.

[75] Godet stresses the importance of this strong adversative. "Here Westcott proposes an absolute *tour de force*. 'But to what purpose say this? The favorable issue is not doubtful.' This sense of *but* is altogether forced; and there is no more opposition between: to come forth from the struggle, and: to have come for it. However we may turn this phrase, we are always brought back to see in it a hypothetical prayer."

[76] Strachan comments: "The best commentary ever made on this utterance are the terse words of Bengel. *Concurrebat horror mortis et ardor obedientiae;* 'horror of death and ardour of obedience are fused together.'"

[77] MacGregor says of this verse: "John thus tacitly corrects the Synoptic tradition that Jesus was ever subject enough to human weakness to pray 'My Father, if it is possible, let this cup pass me' (Mt. 26 : 39)." But in the first place it is unlikely that John had the Synoptists before him, and in the second it is astonishing to have a reference to "human weakness" rejected in a passage in which Jesus says, νῦν ἡ ψυχή μου τετάρακται.

"hour" in this Gospel has about it the air of inevitability. It represents the doing of the Father's will. So[78] Jesus affirms that this is the reason for His coming to this "hour". "Here 'for this cause' looks back to 'this hour,' and forward to a phrase in which 'hour' is repeated for emphasis ('to [meet] this hour')."[79]

28 Jesus prays that the Father's name be glorified, or, more exactly, that the Father Himself will glorify it. The overruling sovereignty of God is implied. The aorist tense in the verb perhaps indicates a single act and if so it will be the cross that is in mind. There supremely the name of God was glorified. The response to this prayer is a voice from heaven, the voice of God Himself.[80] "I have glorified it" is another aorist tense, but it is hard to know which action is particularly in mind. The baptism of Jesus with the voice from heaven, or the transfiguration with the similar phenomenon would meet the situation. But unfortunately John records neither. It may be that we should attach little significance to this aorist. The perfect active of the verb is never used in the New Testament, and the aorist may well be used here with something of the meaning of the perfect. The future "will glorify" is a little easier. In this text it will refer to the cross.

29 We do not know where all this took place. There appears to be a break between verses 19 and 20 and it is impossible to say whether this event immediately followed the triumphal entry or not. So we do not know whether "the multitude" is the same as that referred to in verses 9, 12 or a different group. The crowd is described as standing and as hearing the voice from heaven. This voice was var-

---

[78] ἀλλά indicates that, far from being saved from the "hour", this was the very purpose of His coming.

[79] Abbott, 2389a.

[80] In Rabbinical literature we read of a heavenly voice, the קוֹל בַּת, lit., "the daughter of a voice". This is explained by the Tosaphist on *Sanh.* 11a in this way: "One would not hear the sound which went out from heaven, but another sound went out of this sound, as when a man strikes a blow with violence and one hears a second noise which goes out from it (the blow) in the distance. One would hear such a sound; therefore it is called 'Daughter of the sound'." (SBk, I, p. 125). That is to say, it is an echo. Among the Rabbis the *bath qol* was thought of as inferior to prophecy. God no longer spoke to men directly. But in the New Testament on each occasion when a voice is heard from heaven it is the voice of God Himself. Thus it is not true that the New Testament reproduces the Rabbinic idea of *bath qol*. The New Testament idea is something different. It is the very voice of God.

iously interpreted. Some thought it was thunder (in the Old Testament thunder is sometimes the voice of God, as in Ps. 29 : 3). Others thought an angel had spoken directly to Jesus.[81] Clearly John wants us to think of a sound audible to all (even if the meaning was not). He is not talking of a subjective vision.[82] We are reminded of the various accounts of the heavenly voice that spoke to Saul of Tarsus, from which it seems clear that Saul's companions heard a sound, but did not understand what was said (Acts 9 : 7; 22 : 9).

30 Jesus responded to their perplexity. He explained that the voice did not come for His sake but for theirs. But if this removes one difficulty it introduces another. It is now plain that the voice was not intended primarily for Jesus but for the crowds. Why then did they not understand it? Perhaps because they lacked the spiritual perception to recognize the voice of God. Jesus was aware of His intimate communion with the Father. He did not need to be reassured.[83] But the voice would be of the greatest value to those of His followers who could take in its significance, though it required some spiritual perception to understand it.

31 The connection of this with the preceding verse is not clear. But Jesus is now plainly proceeding to the meaning of the cross. The cross represents the judgment of the world. The world will condemn itself by its treatment of the Son (*cf.* 3 : 18f. and the notes there). "The prince of this world" is, of course, Satan (the expression recurs in 14 : 30; 16 : 11 and *cf.* II Cor. 4 : 4; Eph. 2 : 2; 6 : 12).[84] So much

---

[81] R. H. Lightfoot comments: "Unhappily the multitude, owing to the half-light in which it lives, cannot discern or appreciate the import of the utterance from heaven."

[82] Bernard points out that neither here, nor on the occasion of the voice at the baptism or the transfiguration, is it said that others than Jesus understood the voice, "and if we put this into our modern ways of speech, we should say that their messages were *subjective* in the sense that they conveyed a meaning to none but Him to whom they were addressed, while *objective* in the sense that He was not deluded or deceived, for they were truly messages from God" (on v. 28). But this does not do justice to the present passage. The people did hear something objective, and Jesus said it was spoken not on His account, but on theirs (v. 30).

[83] Tasker however understands this expression as "probably an example of the Semitic way of expressing comparison, rather than a strict contrast – i.e. 'more for your sake than Mine'. It is clear that on this occasion the voice had considerable significance for Jesus Himself."

[84] SBk cites examples of this designation of Satan from Jewish sources (II, p. 552). κοσμοκράτωρ is transliterated and used also in this sense (the same authority also notes that the Rabbis often have in mind not Satan but a leading angel).

is he the ruler of men's minds that he may be spoken of as their "prince".[85] But if the expression stresses his power in this world it may also be meant to convey a hint of his powerlessness in the other world. And just as the cross represents the judgment of this world so it represents the defeat of Satan. To men it appeared his victory. It seemed to be the triumph of evil. But in fact it was the source of the world's greatest good. Satan was defeated in what appeared outwardly to be the very moment of his triumph. "Cast out" is not the verb that we expect here. It probably conveys a reference to something like a being cast into the outer darkness of which we read in the Synoptic Gospels (Matt. 8 : 12; 22 : 13; 25 : 30).

32 "And I" is emphatic. This is a work for Christ and no other. "If" has something of the force of "when". It does not throw doubt on the certainty of the crucifixion. In this Gospel "lifting up" always refers to the cross (see on 3 : 14). In this particular passage the reference is made indisputable by the next verse. But here Jesus is concerned with the effect rather than the simple fact of his death. "Draw" is used elsewhere in this Gospel to emphasize the truth that the natural man does not come to Christ. It is only as God works a work in a man's soul and "draws" him that a man can come to Christ (6 : 44 where see note). "All men" is something of a problem. In fact not every man is drawn to Christ and this Gospel envisages the possibility that some will not be. We must take the expression accordingly to mean that all those who are to be drawn will be drawn. That is to say Christ is not affirming that the whole world will be saved. He is affirming that all who are to be saved will be saved in this way. And He is speaking of a universal rather than a narrowly nationalistic religion.[86] The death of Christ would mean the end of particularism. By virtue of that death "all men" and not

---

[85] The word is ἄρχων, "ruler". K. G. Kuhn sees equivalents in the Qumran texts, and that with a good reference as well as a bad one. He says, "God as well as Satan has such in his army, or (in another image) in his court, always with specific duties. In the Qumran texts and in Jewish apocalyptics – and not in the gnosis – is the place of origin of this idea" (*SNT*, p. 266, n. 11). Raymond E. Brown reminds us that John never describes Satan as "the leader, spirit, or angel of the forces of darkness" as do the scrolls, but he sees a similarity in the struggle between Christ and "the prince of this world" (*SNT*, p. 188).

[86] *Cf.* Calvin: "When He says *all* it must be referred to the children of God, who are of His flock. Yet I agree with Chrysostom, who says that Christ used the universal word because the Church was to be gathered from Gentiles and Jews alike".

the Jews alone would be drawn. And they would be drawn only by virtue of that death.[87]

33 John adds a typical explanatory note. These words of Jesus are to be understood as indicating the kind of death that He would die. This, of course, is not to be understood as though the exaltation were excluded. As we pointed out in the note on 3 : 14 the two thoughts of death and exaltation are combined in John's use of this word. But this verse makes it quite plain that the verb points us to the cross. It was there that the "lifting up" took place.

34 The crowd sets itself in contrast with Jesus. Their "we" and their "thou" are both emphatic. They are saying that the Scripture teaches certain things about the Christ (see on 1 : 20, 41) and they are sure that they are right. Jesus, however, is teaching something different and they seek an explanation. They base their retort on "the law" but it is difficult to find in the Pentateuch a passage which says "that the Christ abideth for ever".[88] The passages in mind are probably such as Ps. 89 : 36; 110 : 4; Isa. 9 : 7; Dan. 7 : 14. This means that "law" is being used in the wide sense of "Scripture". The crowd evidently discerned that "lifting up" referred to death.[89] If "the Son of man" (see Additional Note C, pp. 171ff.) was the Messiah they could not reconcile this with their understanding of Scripture. They thought the Messiah would live for ever. Their minds were probably full of thoughts aroused by the Triumphal Entry. They were expecting Jesus to be the triumphant Messiah of popular expectation. But now He speaks of death. So they inquire who this Son of man is. Perhaps he is not the Messiah after all. As John does not say that Jesus used this term this represents a difficulty. Perhaps He has not given us Jesus' exact words but rather the substance of what He said. More likely the crowd knew "the Son of man" to be Jesus' habitual self-designation. Their question then does not mean, "Which individual is the Son of man?" but rather,

---

[87] "This saying contains the whole of the Fourth Gospel's 'Church-theology'. The Church is anchored in the death and resurrection of Christ. She is thus founded not on myth but on historical reality, called into being not by human hands but by the intervention of God Himself" (A. Corell, *Consummatum Est*, London, 1958, p. 13).

[88] The view was, however, held within Judaism, and apparently fairly widely. *Cf.* I Enoch 49 : 1; 62 : 14; Orac. Sib. 3 : 49f.; Ps. Sol. 17 : 4. In other places, however, we find the idea that the Messiah will die, so that this is not the only Jewish teaching on the subject.

[89] For "must" in relation to the ministry of Jesus see on 4 : 4.

"What is the function of the Son of man? Is He distinct from the Messiah?" John may have here one of his many double meanings. The question was natural enough on the lips of the people. But also it is the really significant question in all religion. We should not overlook the fact that this is the last mention of the crowd in Jesus' ministry. It is significant that to the end they remain confused and perplexed, totally unable to appreciate the magnitude of the gift that is offered them, nor the significance of the Person who offers it.
35 Jesus does not answer the question directly. His reply directs them to the urgent necessity for acting on the light they have.[90] It is reasonable to infer that to do this is to enter into a knowledge of the Son of man. Let them give up their preconceived notions of messiahship and act on the revelation Jesus is giving them and their question will be answered. The light is there only for "a little while". This applies primarily to Jesus' presence. He is about to be taken from the earth. But is also points to the timeless truth that if we do not use the light we lose it.[91] So Jesus enjoins His hearers to walk (the present imperative means "keep on walking") while they have the light "lest darkness overtake"[92] (or perhaps "overcome"; see on 1 : 5) them. The man in darkness does not know where he is going and this applies to the spiritual realm as to the physical. Notice the stress on "light". The noun occurs five times in these two verses (*cf.* 3 : 19-21, and see on 1 : 4). It is perhaps worth noting that walking in the light or the darkness is not dissimilar to the thought in the Qumran scrolls that there are two ways in which men may walk, light and darkness being used of them, though the terminology is

---

[90]   It is usual to take ὡς here in the sense of ἕως, "while", though elsewhere John does not use it in this fashion (unless those MSS are right which read ὡς at 9 : 4). But it makes quite good sense to take it in its more usual sense of "as", to yield the meaning, "walk as you have the light", *i.e.* "Live and act according to the light that you have" (Weymouth). *Cf.* Col. 2 : 6. BDF prefer to read ἕως, "as long as", in this verse and ὡς, "now while" in the next (455(3)).

[91]   *Cf.* Hans Urs von Balthasar: "As long as God's presence in the world and for the individual is regarded more or less as a universal philosophical sun which is always available because it neither rises nor sets and is without time and without history, being of the same nature as Ideas, it will scarcely be possible to grasp the quality of the Johannine 'light' which is always just rising *now*, always shining *just for this present time*, and whose dawn always carries with it (even for us!) the threat of decline and withdrawal" (*A Theology of History*, London and New York, 1964, p. 69).

[92]   καταλάβῃ.

not quite that of this Gospel. Perhaps both are indebted to Isa.
50 : 10, which refers to him "that walketh in darkness, and hath no
light".

36a We should expect "while you have light, *walk* in the light".
Instead we get "while[93] you have the light, believe...." This reminds
us that throughout this discussion Jesus Himself must be understood
as the Light (*cf.* 8 : 12; 9 : 5). Therefore there is not only the question of illumination, but also of faith. Men must put their trust in
Him. This makes an important difference from the Qumran texts.
There there is a good deal about light and "the sons of light". But
men there are not called upon to perform an act of faith in their
Lord in order to become "sons of light". They are apparently such
because they belong to the good spirit. The major difference between the scrolls and the New Testament is Christ. This is not periph-
eral but central. Men must believe on Him. There is an interesting change of tense. "Believe" in the present tense gives the thought
of a continuous belief, whereas "become" in the aorist points us to a
once-for-all becoming sons of light. While faith is an activity to be
practised without ceasing one does not become a son of light by
degrees. One passes decisively out of death into life (5 : 24). In
Semitic idiom to be a "son of" is to be characterized by the quality
in question.[94] "Sons of light" are accordingly not merely men with
a slight interest in light, but men whose lives have been so revolu-
tionized that they may be characterized with reference to light (*cf.*
Luke 16 : 8; Eph. 5 : 8; I Thess. 5 : 5). One cannot be a follower of
Jesus and be half-hearted about the light.

(d) The Witness of Prophecy to Jesus 12: 36b-43

36b These things spake Jesus, and he departed and ¹hid
himself from them. 37 But though he had done so many signs
before them, yet they believed not on him: 38 that the word
of Isaiah the prophet might be fulfilled, which he spake,
²Lord, who hath believed our report? And to whom hath the

---

93 For ὡς see n. 90 above. Weymouth here renders: "In the degree that
you have light...."

94 The form of expression is Semitic but this exact expression is not common.
In fact SBk does not find it attested (II, p. 219). It is, however, used in the
Qumran scrolls to describe the members of the community, a further indication
that there may be some connection between Qumran and this Gospel. It must
also be borne in mind, that such an expression is not difficult in Greek, where
it would be equivalent to "enlightened ones".

arm of the Lord been revealed? 39 For this cause they could not believe, for that Isaiah said again, 40 ³He hath blinded their eyes, and he hardened their heart; Lest they should see with their eyes, and perceive with their heart, And should turn, And I should heal them. 41 These things said Isaiah, because he saw his glory; and he spake of him. 42 Nevertheless even of the rulers many believed on him; but because of the Pharisees they did not confess ⁴it, lest they should be put out of the synagogue: 43 for they loved the glory that is of men more than the glory that is of God.

¹Or, *was hidden from them* ² Is. liii. 1. ³ Is. vi. 10. ⁴Or, him

The unbelief of the Jews has been a recurring theme throughout this Gospel. As John brings his account of the public ministry of Jesus to a close he brings out this point once more, and this time he gives something of an explanation of it by pointing us to prophecy. Even the fact of unbelief is not beyond the power and even the purpose of God. After centuries of Christian history, during which the church has been almost exclusively Gentile, we have come to accept it as quite normal that there should be very few Jews in it. But this was not the way it seemed to the men of the New Testament. For them the Jews were the people of God and Jesus was the Messiah of Jewish expectation. The Jews accordingly ought to have welcomed Him. The way Paul agonized over the problem of his people is revealed in the well-known discussion in Romans 9-11. John's contribution to the solution we see here. The Old Testament again and again denounces the Israelites for their failure to recognize the messengers of God and to heed their message. And the same Old Testament shows that God overrules the designs of evil men to work out His purpose. So John looks to prophecy and sees the Jews' rejection of Jesus foretold there.⁹⁵

---

⁹⁵ Hoskyns goes so far as to say: "The fact of the unbelief of the Jews is, however, only superficially a scandal to Christian faith (*cf.* Rom. ix – xi). Rightly understood in the light of the Old Testament Scriptures it is the ground of the manifestation of the inevitable judgement of God upon unbelief. The unbelief of the Jews is not a problem; it is the precise fulfilment of prophecy". Later he says, "The Jews are manifestly culpable, since the Evangelist has recorded the mission of Jesus in such a manner as to exclude the thought that it was impossible for them to recognize Him as the Son of God. The purpose of his final summary of the public ministry of Jesus is not to deny the whole tenor of his narrative, but to point out that the rejection of the Messiah by His own people ought not to surprise those familiar with the Old Testament Scriptures."

36b When He had completed the discourse just reported Jesus went away and was hidden[96] from them. The previous narrative has made it quite plain that He will certainly die. But He will die when He wills. He will not be seized before the time.

37 John's form of expression draws attention both to the intrinsic quality of the miracles and to their abiding effects. As often he refers to them as "signs" (see Additional Note G, pp. 684ff.). They are not simply displays of power. The event may pass into history but the abiding meaning does not. It remains. It is probable that his word for "so many"[97] also contains a hint at the quality. It is not only the number but the kind of signs that he has in mind (Barclay translates, "such great signs", and Knox, "such great miracles"). "Had done"[98] renders a perfect participle which again points to the permanent character. John is drawing attention to the continuing quality of the actions of Jesus, a quality which ought to have induced faith. The perfect makes it all in some sense present. The guilt of the opponents of Jesus was present and not simply past. But John records that "they were not believing", where the continuous tense points to their state. They might give occasional evidence of a transitory belief but that is not saving faith (*cf.* 8 : 30ff.). See further Additional Note E, pp. 335ff.

38 The basic cause of unbelief is now traced to prophecy.[99] John has already made it clear that it is only as God draws a man that he can believe. Now we have the further thought that what is written in prophecy must be fulfilled.[100] The prophecy cited (Isa. 53 : 1) speaks both of failure to believe and of a revelation of "the arm of the Lord". In other words faith and the divine activity are connected.

---

[96] ἐκρύβη is passive, but most take it as equivalent to a middle. See on 8 : 59.

[97] τοσαῦτα. The word is used of quality as well as of quantity (see AG *etc.*). Yet we should not overlook the fact that elsewhere John always uses it of quantity (6 : 9; 14 : 9; 21 : 11).

[98] πεποιηκότος. Notice the genitive absolute, a construction not found in this Gospel in words of Jesus (Abbott, 2031).

[99] This is the first occurrence in this Gospel of the formula ἵνα πληρωθῇ with respect to prophecy. The formula is frequent in Matthew, but John has not used it hitherto. It occurs a number of times in subsequent chapters (13 : 18; 15 : 25; 17 : 12; 19 : 24, 36).

[100] ἵνα, as usually in John, denotes purpose.

39, 40   John is explicit that they were not able[101] to believe[102] because of another Scripture. The divine sovereignty is strongly insisted upon.[103] The quotation is from Isa. 6 : 9f., words which are cited by our Lord Himself (Matt. 13 : 14f.; Mark 4 : 12, Luke 8 : 10), and by Paul (Acts 28 : 26f.). In Isaiah the verbs are imperative and might be thought of as indicating a punishment for past evil. In the Synoptics they are the illustration of a principle: people who are unbelieving hear the outward words of the parable but they do not discern the inner meaning. Paul sees it as the reason that "this salvation of God is sent unto the Gentiles" (Acts 28 : 28). The present passage ascribes everything to the will of God. Unless His hand is in it nothing is possible. But when John quotes "he hath blinded their eyes . . ." he does not mean that the blinding takes place without the will or against the will of these people. So with the hardening[104] of their heart. These men chose evil. It was their own deliberate choice, their own fault. Make no mistake about that. Throughout his Gospel John has insisted upon the seriousness of the decision forced on the Jews by the presence of Jesus, on their responsibility, and on their guilt. He is not now removing all that. What he is now saying is that the hand of God is in the consequences of their choice (*cf.* the threefold "God gave them up" in Rom. 1 : 24, 26, 28). The ultimate cause of all there is, in a genuinely theistic universe, must be found in the will of God. The passage is very thoroughgoing. John makes it clear that the hand of God is in the whole process, even though this means that men do not "see" nor "perceive"[105] nor "turn" nor are they "healed".[106] God's purposes are not frustrated by the opposition of evil men. They are

---

[101]   *Cf.* Plummer: "Grace may be refused so persistently as to destroy the power of accepting it. 'I will not' leads to 'I cannot' ".

[102]   The present, "to believe continuously" or "habitually", not the aorist, "to come to believe".

[103]   *Cf.* Murray: "We must never forget that it is by God's appointment that if His word does not quicken, it must deaden."

[104]   ἐπώρωσεν αὐτῶν τὴν καρδίαν. The verb originally has to do with the forming of a callus and thus is very expressive. *Amplified* renders "hardened and benumbed".

[105]   The aorist here might be constative, of complete knowledge, or ingressive, "come to realize" (*cf.* Moulton, M, I, p. 117).

[106]   Notice the future indicative though apparently still governed by ἵνα. In this context the subject of the verb will be Jesus.

accomplished.[107] In this particular case, while there is certainly an element of the mysterious it is also true that we can discern a little of the divine purpose. Had the Jews accepted the gospel it is difficult to see how it could have gone out to all the nations. But when the Jews rejected it, it became a world religion. We cannot think that this took place apart from the will of God.

41 John sees in the words of the prophet primarily a reference to the glory of Christ. Isaiah spoke these things "because[108] he saw his glory". The words of Isaiah 6 : 3 refer to the glory of Yahweh, but John puts no hard and fast distinction between the two. To him it is plain that Isaiah had in mind the glory revealed in Christ.[109] Again we have the complex idea of glory. It points at once to the supreme greatness of Christ and the cross as the supreme illustration of His greatness. Here it includes the thought of His rejection, for that, too, is part of His real glory. He being what He is stooped to a position where men might and did reject Him. Only as we see this can we see what His glory implies. Notice that John says Isaiah "spoke of him". Whatever other application the words of the prophet might have, for John the supremely important thing is that they point to Jesus.

42 But John does not want to leave us with the impression that none of the leaders believed. On the contrary[110] many from among them did just this. They "believed on him", where the construction points to a genuine faith. Nicodemus and Joseph of Arimathea are the only ones of whom we have knowledge, but evidently they were but two of a much greater number. The ministry of Jesus was not without its effect even in the highest circles. But by now the opposition to Jesus on the part of the Pharisees was so great that it meant

---

[107] *Cf.* Augustine: "God thus blinds and hardens, simply by letting alone and withdrawing His aid: and God can do this by a judgment that is hidden, although not by one that is unrighteous" (LIII. 6; p. 293).

[108] ὅτι, "because", is read by P66, P75, ℵ AB L Θ fl 33 cop *etc.*, and is to be preferred to ὅτε, "when" with D f13 565 *etc.* W reads ἐπεί.

[109] In the Targum on Isa. 6 : 1 instead of "I saw the Lord" we read, "I saw the glory of the Lord".

[110] "Nevertheless" renders ὅμως μέντοι, an expression found here only in the New Testament. The combination forms a very strong adversative.

excommunication[111] to confess Him.[112] So they were silent.[113]

43 John puts the condemnation of these men in one crisp memorable phrase "they loved the glory of men more than[114] the glory of God". "Glory" here has the meaning "praise", "esteem" (Phillips: "approval"), but John is also looking back to v. 41. The glory of Christ sets the standard. To love the glory of men above the glory of God is the supreme disaster.[115]

(e) A Final Challenge to Believe, 12 : 44-50

44 And Jesus cried and said, He that believeth on me, believeth not on me, but on him that sent me. **45** And he that beholdeth me beholdeth him that sent me. **46** I am come a light into the world, that whosoever believeth on me may not abide in the darkness. **47** And if any man hear my sayings, and keep them not, I judge him not: for I came not to judge the world, but to save the world. **48** He that rejecteth me, and receiveth not my sayings, hath one that judgeth him: the word that I spake, the same shall judge him in the last day. **49** For I spake not from myself; but the Father that sent me, he hath given me a commandment, what I should say, and what I should speak. **50** And I know that his commandment is life eternal; the things therefore which I speak, even as the Father hath said unto me, so I speak.

---

[111] For ἀποσυνάγωγοι see on 9 : 22.

[112] Calvin comments: "We must also notice, that rulers have less courage and constancy, because ambition almost always reigns in them, and there is nothing more servile than that. To put it in a word, earthly honours may be called golden shackles binding a man so that he cannot freely do his duty."

[113] There is an interesting variation of tenses in this verse. ἐπίστευσαν denotes the definite act of faith, the imperfect ὡμολόγουν the continuing failure to confess, while with γένωνται we return to the aorist and the decisive act of expulsion from the synagogue.

[114] ἤπερ is found here only in the New Testament. Abbott thinks it implies that they loved the glory of God not at all (2092).

[115] Godet denies that this verse refers to men such as Nicodemus and Joseph of Arimathea. Rather those "who remained outwardly attached to the Jewish system, such as Gamaliel and many others, the Erasmuses of that time." Westcott is scathing: "Such ineffective intellectual faith (so to speak) is really the climax of unbelief."

John finishes off his account of the public ministry of Jesus with
one last appeal to men to believe. He has had some stern things to
say about the Pharisees and their ilk. But his last word is not one
of condemnation. It is one of tender appeal. Jesus came that men
might believe and be saved. It is interesting to notice that in this
brief concluding section some of the important themes which run
right through this Gospel find expression. Faith, Jesus as the One
sent by the Father, light and darkness, judgment now and at the
last day, eternal life, all are caught up in this final summary and
appeal.

44 The occasion is not indicated,[116] and it is not important. These
words of Jesus form the conclusion to John's account of the ministry
as a whole. In the light of v. 36 it is probable that they were spoken
earlier, but are inserted here as a fitting summary of Jesus' message.
While we need not doubt that they were spoken on some specific
occasion or occasions, yet for John it is not the occasion that is important but the challenge to men to believe. The words are spoken
loudly[117] (Moffatt: "And Jesus cried aloud") which probably is a
way of indicating their importance. The closeness of the Father and
the Son is brought out. The man who puts his trust in Christ puts
his trust not simply in the Man of Galilee but in God the Father.
The two are so close that to trust the One is to trust the Other.
Characteristically the Father is not referred to by name, but as
"him that sent" the Son (for "sent" see on 3 : 17).

45 Similarly the man who steadily contemplates the Son contemplates Him who sent Him (*cf.* 1 : 18; 13 : 20; 14 : 9).

46 "I" is emphatic. Whatever be the case with others Christ's own
activities and purpose are clear. "Am come"[118] in the perfect tense

---

116 ARV's "and" represents the Greek δέ which is probably to be taken
as adversative. In contrast to those who kept quiet about their real beliefs
Jesus cried out loudly.
117 The verb is κράζω. It is used of Jesus in 7 : 28 (where see note), 37,
and of John the Baptist, 1 : 15. On each occasion when Jesus is the subject
the verb is in the aorist, but the perfect is used of John the Baptist. The verb
used of the multitude in verse 13 is κραυγάζω.
118 ἐλήλυθα. John three times has this perfect with εἰς τὸν κόσμον (16 : 28;
18 : 37), and there is the usual slight variation in repetition. The perfect is found
also in other contexts with reference to His coming (3 : 19; 5 : 43; 7 : 28; 8 : 42),
though the aorist is also common (1 : 11; 8 : 14; 9 : 39; 10 : 10; 12 : 27, 47). It
is interesting that after the perfect in this verse John immediately moves to
the aorist in the next. He is fond of such variation.

denotes a coming forth and remaining. For Christ as "the Light" see on 8 : 12. Once again we have the duality of light[119] and darkness (see on 1 : 4). Darkness is the state of the natural man but Christ came in order to deliver men from such a state. It is not His purpose that men should continue in darkness. In view of the preceding section with its strong emphasis on the hand of God even in the unbelief of sinful men this verse is important. The purpose of Christ's coming was salvation. He came to deliver men from darkness, not to imprison them within it.

47 The same truth now receives emphasis from another direction. Those who have an intelligent understanding of Jesus' teaching[120] and yet do not keep it, are certainly condemned. But Jesus can say "I judge him not". We are not to think of Him as standing over men as a judge. There is indeed a sense in which Christ judges (5 : 22, 27, 30; 8 : 16, 26; 9 : 39). But in a very real sense men judge themselves (3 : 18f.). Jesus did not come for the purpose of judging the world (*cf.* 8 : 15). Notice the repetition of "the world" (the pronoun "it" might easily have been used). John puts a certain stress on the word by the repetition (*cf.* 3 : 17).

48 As always in this Gospel there is another side to the saving action. Where the saving word is spoken and where a man despises the Speaker and persistently rejects[121] His sayings, that man does not go scatheless. He has a judge, and that judge is the very saving word itself. In the last day his judgment will be that the word of salvation came to him and he rejected it.[122]

49 "For" introduces the reason for the foregoing. It is because Jesus' message is divine in origin that it is the fitting judge of men on the last day. "I spake not from[123] myself" is an emphatic dis-

---

[119] φῶς is emphatic from its position: "I light have come. . . ."

[120] The genitive after ἀκούω signifies "hear with appreciation and understanding" (see on 5 : 25). In John ῥῆμα always refers to the words of Christ or of God. Here the expression stands for Christ's whole teaching.

[121] ὁ ἀθετῶν is a strong expression. Barclay translates, "He who completely disregards me as of no account". *Cf.* Luke 10 : 16.

[122] Brown points out that in the first part of this verse we have realized eschatology, and in the latter part final eschatology. But the last "is offered as an explanation of the first part – an indication that the sharp contradiction drawn today between realized and final eschatology was not so apparent in NT times."

[123] The expression is ἐξ ἐμαυτοῦ. The expression is found here only in this Gospel, but seven times John has ἀπ' ἐμαυτοῦ. There seems no difference in meaning.

claimer of personal responsibility for the message. Jesus is not, of course, saying that He disagrees with it. It is the word He has always proclaimed. What He is saying, and saying in the strongest possible terms, is that the saving word did not originate in any human source. It is the Father who gave[124] the commandment (see on 4 : 34). Once again the Father is spoken of in terms of the Son's mission, "the Father that sent me". That is to say the Father is bound up with the mission of the Son. He has, so to speak, committed Himself in the Son. "He" is emphatic.[125] It emphasizes that it is the Father and no other who gives the commandment. "Hath given" in the perfect tense shows that the gift is permanent. It is not withdrawn. It is difficult to put a difference between "say" and "speak".[126] But the two words together stress the totality of Jesus' message. For the thought *cf.* Deut. 18 : 18f.

50 The final words of Jesus' public ministry contain a renewed note of certainty. The Father's commandment is no harsh restriction. On the contrary, it "is life eternal". It does not simply speak of life eternal, nor is it the case that keeping it leads to life eternal (as *Twentieth Century:* "Immortal Life lies in keeping his command"). The commandment *is* life eternal. It is God's great love acting upon us, and acting upon us for our salvation.[127] "Therefore" (the word is important) the things that Jesus speaks He speaks just as the Father has spoken to Him. "Hath said" in the perfect tense stresses the permanence while the present "speak" indicates that Jesus continues right to this moment to speak in this way. The whole verse puts stress on the permanent relation between the Father and the Son. This is a striking note on which to end the account of the ministry of Jesus. "Jesus is not a figure of independent greatness; he is the Word of God, or he is nothing at all" (Barrett).

---

[124] For the various things said to have been "given" to the Son by the Father in this Gospel see on 3 : 35. The tense is most commonly the perfect, as here, indicating the permanence of the gift.

[125] The pronoun αὐτός follows ὁ πέμψας με Πατήρ.

[126] εἴπω and λαλήσω.

[127] *Cf.* Temple: "His commandment is not a stark precept given by supreme authority; it is direction given by almighty love ... it is the impact of His holy love upon our consciences and wills."

CHAPTER XIII

IV. THE FAREWELL DISCOURSES, 13 : 1–17 : 26

The public ministry of Jesus is over. John tells us nothing more of any words spoken by Jesus to the multitude. There are a few words addressed to those who arrested Him. There are a few to those who examined Him. But apart from these the whole of the rest of the Gospel concerns Jesus' final ministry to His own disciples, and the events surrounding the Passion. The section on the farewell discourses is noteworthy. There is nothing like it in the Synoptic Gospels. From those Gospels we learn that Jesus ate a final meal with His disciples in the upper room and that He instituted the Lord's Supper there. Curiously John says nothing about this. The reason is by no means clear. It will not do, as some suggest, to affirm that he has given us his eucharistic teaching in the sixth chapter for, as we saw when we were dealing with that chapter, the hypothesis that Jesus was there talking primarily about the eucharist is not soundly based. It is more likely that to John "the *inner significance* of what happened in that upper room was in danger of being overlaid by materialistic beliefs" (Wright). He is concerned more with meaning than with ceremonial, so gives us teaching which brings out the significance of the rite everywhere practised by Christians. R. H. Lightfoot draws attention to the fact that after 13 : 2 John "avoids mention of any particular place or time in connexion with the events and instruction of chs. 13 to 17, until 18[1] is reached." He thinks that John wants his readers to have in mind "not only the original disciples, but all the future members of the Lord's body", and that it may be for this reason that he avoids mentioning the institution of the Lord's Supper, "a narrative describing a unique event." In these chapters John is concerned with principles and significance rather than specific events. Many have attempted to locate the point in the Johannine narrative at which the institution took place. This seems to me impracticable. John does not mention it and he is thus not concerned to provide us with clues as to when it took place.

But if the Synoptists tell us of the institution of the Lord's Supper which John omits John has much more which they omit. Their narrative leaves the way open for us to think of a discourse as being delivered, for they speak of a Passover meal and there was usually an address on this occasion. But it is to John that we owe the priceless teaching which Jesus gave then.[1]

1. TWO SIGNIFICANT ACTIONS, 13 : 1-30

Before the sustained instruction begins there are two significant actions performed by our Lord. The first, that of washing the disciples' feet, is pregnant with meaning, the meaning of the cross which now loomed before Jesus. The second, that of giving the sop to Judas, taken with Jesus' words to the traitor, set in motion the events leading to the passion.

(a) The Feet Washing, 13:1-11

1 Now before the feast of the passover, Jesus knowing that his hour was come that he should depart out of this world unto the Father, having loved his own that were in the world, he loved them [1]unto the end. 2 And during supper, the devil having already put into the heart of Judas Iscariot, Simon's son, to [2]betray him, 3 Jesus, knowing that the Father had given all things into his hands, and that he came forth from God, and goeth unto God, 4 riseth from supper, and layeth aside his garments; and he took a towel, and girded himself. 5 Then he poureth water into the basin, and began to wash the disciples' feet, and to wipe them with the towel wherewith he was girded. 6 So he cometh to Simon Peter. He saith unto him, Lord, dost thou wash my feet? 7 Jesus answered and said unto him, What I do thou knowest not now; but thou shalt understand hereafter. 8 Peter saith unto him, Thou shalt never wash my feet. Jesus answered him, If I wash thee not, thou hast no part with me. 9 Simon Peter saith unto him, Lord, not my feet only, but also my hands and my head. 10 Jesus saith to him, He that is bathed needeth not [3]save to wash his feet, but is clean every whit:

---

[1] T. F. Glasson points out that Deuteronomy is the farewell discourse of Moses, and that in these chapters there are many allusions to Deuteronomy (*Moses in the Fourth Gospel*, London, 1963, pp. 74–78). This is another of the ways in which John sees Moses as a helpful way of understanding the significance of Jesus.

and ye are clean, but not all. 11 For he knew him that
should ²betray him; therefore said he, Ye are not all clean.
¹Or, *to the uttermost.* ²Or, *deliver him up* ³Some ancient authorities omit
save, and *his feet.*

In the Synoptic account of the events of this evening we read of
a dispute among the disciples as to which of them would be the
greatest. John does not record this. But he does tell of an action of
our Lord's which rebuked their lack of humility more strikingly
than any words could have done. Yet we should not take the feet-
washing, standing as it does at the head of the long section of the
Farewell Discourse, as no more than a reaction to the petty-minded-
ness of the disciples. It is a significant action, setting the tone for all
that follows. "It foreshadows the cross itself: the voluntary humility
of the Lord cleanses his loved ones and gives to them an example
of selfless service which they must follow" (Richardson). All the
more is this the case in that it takes place during the meal (v. 2),
not on arrival when the feet would normally be washed. This shows
that it was an action undertaken deliberately, and not simply
the usual act of courtesy.² It is a parable in action, setting out that
great principle of lowly service which finds its supreme embodiment
in the cross,³ setting out also the necessity for the disciple to take the

---

² Hoskyns protests against views which stress the sacraments, or which
reduce the action to a lesson in humility. John "is not preoccupied with two
sacraments, as Loisy seems to be; he is preoccupied with the Jesus of History,
with His life, death, and resurrection . . . the washing of the disciples' feet rests
upon and interprets the death of the Lord, and is not a detached action containing in itself a merely ethical lesson." *Cf.* also the important treatment of
the incident by J. A. T. Robinson in *Neotestamentica et Patristica: Eine Freundesgabe
Herrn Professor Dr. Oscar Cullmann* (Leiden, 1962), pp. 144ff. For a notice of
the variety of interpretations of this passage see A. Corell, *Consummatum Est*
(London, 1958), pp. 69ff.
³ Literal foot-washing has been practised from time to time in the Christian
Church. For a good account both of the practice and its significance see Hoskyns,
Detached Note 7 (pp. 443–6). See also the article "Feet-washing" in *ERE.*
Calvin's comment should be heeded by all who take the practice as one to be
perpetuated: "Every year they hold a theatrical feet-washing, and when they
have discharged this empty and bare ceremony they think they have done
their duty finely and are then free to despise their brethren. But more, when
they have washed twelve men's feet they cruelly torture all Christ's members
and thus spit in the face of Christ Himself. This ceremonial comedy is nothing
but a shameful mockery of Christ. At any rate, Christ does not enjoin an annual
ceremony here, but tells us to be ready all through our life to wash the feet
of our brethren." This is a continuing warning against externality. More than
an action is enjoined. It is a spirit, an attitude to others.

Lord's way, not his own. It is important that we see this. Many take the story as no more than a lesson in humility, quite overlooking the fact that, in that case, Jesus' dialogue with Peter completely obscures its significance! But those words, spoken in the shadow of the cross, have to do with cleansing, that cleansing without which no man belongs to Christ, that cleansing which is given by the cross alone. As Hunter says, "The deeper meaning then is that there is no place in his fellowship for those who have not been cleansed by his atoning death. The episode dramatically symbolizes the truth enunciated in I John 1 : 7, 'We are being cleansed from every sin by the blood of Jesus'."[4]

1 The chapter opens with a mark of time in the characteristic Johannine manner, though "before the feast of the passover" (the expression looks back to 12 : 1) is not as precise as most such notes. John thinks of Jesus as in complete command of the situation. "His hour" (see on 2 : 4) did not take him by surprise. He knew that it was this that had come[5] and acted accordingly. The "hour" is thought of now not in terms of glory (as in 12 : 23), but of leaving this world and going to the Father. It marks the decisive end of Jesus' ministry. This leads John to a characteristic emphasis on the love[6] Jesus had for His own.[7] They were in the world and he had

---

[4] Hunter adds: "Many people today would like to be Christians but see no need of the cross. They are ready to admire Jesus' life and to praise the sublimity of his moral teaching, but they cannot bring themselves to believe that Christ died for their sins, and that without that death they would be lost in sin. This, as Brunner has said, is one of the prime 'scandals' of Christianity for modern man – and the very heart of the apostolic Gospel."

[5] The aorist ἦλθεν signifies "came". It points to the moment of arrival. Moulton sees in it probably "one of the most ancient uses of the aorist . . . expressing what has *just happened*" (M, I, p. 135).

[6] Dodd draws attention to an interesting change in the Johannine vocabulary from this point on. The earlier part of the Gospel is marked by the use of words like life *(ζωή, ζῆν, ζωοποιεῖν)* and light *(φῶς, φωτίζειν; σκότος, σκοτία)*. In chs. 1–12 words of the former group occur 50 times and the latter 32 times whereas in chs. 13–17 the "life" words occur but 6 times and the "light" words not at all. By contrast ἀγάπη, ἀγαπᾶν are found 6 times in chs. 1–12, and 31 times in chs. 13–17 *(IFG,* p. 398). Clearly love takes on a new prominence in the Farewell Discourses.

[7] Moulton notes that ὁ ἴδιος without a noun expressed is used in the papyri "as a term of endearment to near relations" (M, I, p. 90). He cites only the singular, but the plural here has a similar warm content. In 15 : 19 we have the parallel thought that the world loves its own.

loved them there. "He loved them unto the end" does not give the meaning as well as "now he showed how utterly he loved them"[8] (Rieu; similarly Knox, NEB). The whole verse with its emphasis on love may be meant to set the tone for the lengthy section it heads. Up till now Jesus has had a ministry to men in general. From this point He concentrates on those He loves intimately.

2 According to the best text John locates the event he is about to describe as taking place "during supper".[9] The exact meaning of the second half of the verse is not clear, and again there is textual difficulty. But the best text appears to read, "the devil had already made up[10] his mind that Judas . . . ." It is not unlikely that we should take "his" as meaning "the devil's", which gives us a very graphic expression, though some prefer to understand it as "Judas's". The reading has been altered in the later MSS to give unambiguous expression to the idea that the devil put the thought into Judas's mind.[11] Whichever reading we adopt, it is, of course, part of the truth that at some time the devil did this. But to say that he did it at this point appears to be in contradiction of v. 27. Here John is rather discussing the devil's thoughts than those of Judas. For "betray" see on 6 : 64.[12]

---

[8] εἰς τέλος (this noun only here in this Gospel) is ambiguous, meaning both "to the end" and "to the utmost". It is likely that here we have a typical Johannine double meaning, with both meanings intended. But the aorist, ἠγάπησεν, is more consistent with love shown in a single act than with the continuance of love (imperfect).

[9] γινομένου is read by ℵ*BLW etc. and γενομένου by P66 ℵ^c AD Θf1 f13 etc. The former clearly means "during supper", the latter probably means "after supper" (as AV; Field however accepts it and takes it to mean "a supper was holden"). An action like the footwashing would seem more likely after a meal than as an interruption during the course of a meal, which might explain γενομένου. The reverse alteration is more difficult to understand. That the incident took place before the end of the meal is plain from v. 26. For δεῖπνον see on 12 : 2.

[10] βάλλω is normally used in the New Testament with more of a sense of moving something physical. AG however are able to cite classical parallels for the idea of putting something into the heart or mind. For τίθημι in a similar construction cf. Luke 21 : 14.

[11] The latter reading requires the genitive 'Ιούδα which is read by AD Θ f1, but the nominative 'Ιούδας is to be preferred with P66 ℵ B etc.

[12] The verb is παραδοῖ which Moulton describes as "An obviously vernacular form . . . Though a late form of the opt. coincides with it, there is not the slightest reason for doubt that in NT it is always subj." (M, II, p. 211).

3   The subject is not expressed but it must be "Jesus" as ARV.
Again John stresses Jesus' command of the situation. He knew what
was taking place (see on 2 : 24; 4 : 18). Here we have an unexpected
twist. Instead of something like "knowing what Judas would do"
we have "knowing that the Father had given all things into his
hands."[13] The threshold of Calvary seems an unlikely place for a
statement of this sort. But John does not see the cross as the casual
observer might see it. It is the place where a great divine work was
wrought out and the divine glory shown forth. So he describes it in
terms of the Father's giving of all things to the Son (see on 3 : 35 for
the things the Father gives the Son). The reference to the Father is
important. He is no idle spectator at the Passion, but He works out
His will there. John further refers to what is about to take place as a
return to God of Him who had gone out from God.[14] This is the
consummation of His mission. Both "from God" and "unto God"
receive a certain emphasis from their position. John is about to
describe an act in which Jesus takes a very lowly place. But he does
not lose sight for one moment of the truth that the highest possible
place is His by right.
4, 5   The present tense, "riseth" is vivid. The writer sees the scene
taking place before his very eyes. The preparations are detailed:
the rising from the table, the putting off of the garments,[15] the taking

---

[13]   In 3 : 35 the Father gave all things ἐν τῇ χειρὶ αὐτοῦ. Here the expression
is αὐτῷ εἰς τὰς χεῖρας. Again we see John's habit of introducing small variants
without great difference of meaning.

[14]   This is one of two places in this Gospel where ἐξέρχομαι is followed by
ἀπό, the other being 16 : 30. The construction occurs fairly often in Luke,
somewhat less so in Matthew, and once only in Mark. John prefers to use ἐκ.
See on 1 : 44 for John's use of ἀπό and ἐκ. It is worth noticing that the disciples
do not use either of the prepositions employed by Jesus to describe His coming
from the Father, namely παρά (16 : 27) and ἐκ (16 : 28), and they alter "Father"
to "God". This is another example of John's habit of minor alterations in
repetitions, though without appreciable difference of meaning. For ὑπάγω see
on 7 : 33.

[15]   Though the word is plural, τὰ ἱμάτια, it is possible that a single garment
is meant. But it seems more likely that we should take the plural seriously.
Elsewhere John uses the singular for one outer garment in 19 : 2,5 and the
plural for all the garments in 19 : 23, 24. If ἱμάτια here has the same meaning
as in the latter passages then Jesus stripped to a loin cloth, just like a slave.
τίθησιν, "layeth aside", is used of Christ's laying down His life in 10 : 17f.

of a towel,[16] the girding of Himself,[17] the pouring of water into the basin.[18] Then Jesus began[19] to wash the disciples' feet and to wipe them with the towel about His waist.[20] We are reminded of the words recorded by St. Luke as having been spoken on this occasion, "I am in the midst of you as he that serveth" (Luke 22 : 27), which he tells us were spoken after a quarrel among them as to which of them was to be the greatest. Our Lord's action is a sharp rebuke to their attitude. For the significance of the action *cf.* I Sam. 25 : 41. Barclay quotes some words of T. R. Glover concerning certain clever intellectuals: "They thought they were being religious when they were merely being fastidious." There was nothing of this about our Lord.

6 There is no mention of any comment until Jesus came to Peter. Apparently there was dead silence. But Peter expostulates. His

---

[16] λέντιον (only in this passage in the New Testament and not attested in earlier writings) is a loan word from the Latin *linteum*. It denoted a long towel, so that Jesus could gird Himself with it and still use the free end to dry the disciples' feet. *Cf.* I Pet. 5 : 5.

[17] John changes to the aorist διέζωσεν after a succession of presents, but the reason is not apparent. He is the only New Testament writer to use this verb (13 : 4, 5; 21 : 7).

[18] It is not certain what the rare word νιπτήρ means. We are not helped by the fact that it does not appear to occur before this passage. Washing would not be in a basin as with us, but water would be poured over the feet from one vessel and presumably caught in another, and it is not clear which was the νιπτήρ. Rieu renders "jug", but most translators, "basin". In view of the occurrence of the compound ποδανιπτήρ it is perhaps more likely to refer to the basin, for it is difficult to see the relevance of the compound to a ewer. This is the only New Testament use of the term. The cognate verb νίπτω, "to wash", used here, is employed by John 13 times out of 17 New Testament occurrences.

[19] The verb is often used in the Synoptic Gospels practically as an auxiliary (a Semitic use). But in this, the only place where it occurs in John (though *cf.* 8 : 9), it means "began". The order in which He washed the feet is not given. Chrysostom thinks that the Greek indicates that He washed someone else (namely "the traitor") before coming to Peter (LXX. 2; p. 258).

[20] Temple comments: "We rather shrink from this revelation. We are ready, perhaps, to be humble before God; but we do not want Him to be humble in His dealings with us. We should like Him, who has the right, to glory in His goodness and greatness; then we, as we pass from His presence, may be entitled to pride ourselves on such achievements as distinguish us above other men . . . man's humility does not begin with the giving of service; it begins with the readiness to receive it. For there can be much pride and condescension in our giving of service."

"Thou" is emphatic, and in the Greek is followed immediately by "my", thus placing the two in sharp contrast. "Lord, dost Thou my feet wash?"

7 Jesus' reply puts "I" and "thou" in emphatic contrast. Peter is far from having a sympathetic understanding of his Lord. "Hereafter" is an indefinite time note.[21] Jesus does not say when it will be. But He does prophesy that one day Peter will understand that which at the present moment is hidden from him (*cf.* 2 : 22; 12 : 16). In part Jesus may be referring to the explanation that He was about to give (vv. 12ff.). But in view of the later teaching in this section of the Gospel we may fairly infer that the primary reference is to the illumination of the Holy Spirit which was necessary, and which would be given (*cf.* 14 : 26; 16 : 13).

8 Peter's reaction is characteristically vigorous.[22] He brushes aside Jesus' suggestion that something is going on whose significance he does not yet know. To him it is unthinkable that Jesus should ever engage in the menial activity of washing His servant's feet.[23] So he says that this will never happen. He will have no part in such an activity. "Peter is humble enough to see the incongruity of Christ's action, yet proud enough to dictate to his Master" (MacGregor). His words evoke the reply that if our Lord does not wash Peter then Peter has no part with Him. "Wash" in the Johannine manner will have a double meaning. In the context it must refer to the washing of the feet. Unless Peter submits to the feet-washing he may not eat with Jesus. But Jesus means more. A literal washing of the feet is not necessary before a man can be a Christian. The words point us to a washing free from sin which only Christ can give. Apart from this a man will have no part in Christ.

9 Now we have a characteristic Petrine touch. Convinced by Jesus' words, Peter will not do the thing by halves. Hands and head must be washed as well as feet. Peter may not have meant the

---

[21] μετὰ ταῦτα. The plural probably points to all the events associated with the Passion.

[22] He uses the emphatic double negative οὐ μή (except on the lips of Jesus only 11 : 56; 20 : 25 elsewhere in this Gospel), and backs it up with εἰς τὸν αἰῶνα.

[23] It is sometimes pointed out that this task was so menial that a Hebrew slave was not required to perform it, though a Gentile slave might be. This is so, but the point must not be exaggerated. After all a wife was obliged to wash her husband's feet, and children those of their father (see SBk, II, p. 557). For Christian practice *cf.* I Tim. 5 : 10.

617

words to be taken literally, but as a wholehearted renunciation of his previous refusal to be washed at all. But we should not overlook the fact that the answer is still the product of self-will. Peter is reluctant to let Jesus do what He wants. He prefers to dictate the terms. There is also a misunderstanding of the meaning of the action. It is not a way of cleansing the disciples, but a symbol of that cleansing. It is not the area of skin that is washed that matters but the acceptance of Jesus' lowly service.

10 Jesus gently discourages excess. The imagery is that of a man going to a feast. He will bathe at home. Then when he arrives he needs only to wash his feet to sit at table wholly clean. Jesus applies this to the spiritual situation of His followers. "He that is bathed" points to permanent character: he is not simply one who once upon a time was washed, but one who continues in the character of "the washed one".[24] Such a man has no need for washing except with respect to the feet.[25] He is "clean every whit". GT gives the meaning thus: "he whose inmost nature has been renovated does not need radical renewal, but only to be cleansed from every several fault into which he may fall through intercourse with the unrenewed world".[26] This may be true though I doubt whether the language of this verse will yield all of it. Perhaps the meaning is "such a cleansing as you indicate is not necessary. The one who has thrown in his lot with Me, who has identified himself with Me, who has been washed by Me, has no need to supplement that washing. He is wholly cleansed." Some see a reference to Christian baptism.[27] But, apart from the fact that this appears to be reading something

---

[24] Such appears to be the force of the perfect ὁ λελουμένος. The verb properly applies to the bathing of the whole body as against νίψασθαι, which is rather the washing of a part.

[25] There is a shorter reading which omits εἰ μὴ τοὺς πόδας. This is supported chiefly by ℵ vg Tert Or. It gives the sense, "He that is bathed does not need to wash". The strong MS preponderance for the longer reading should probably be respected. All the more is this the case in view of the difficulty of giving a satisfactory meaning to "bathed" in the context if the shorter reading be accepted. Further, the shorter reading contradicts v. 8. It is interesting that Hoskyns, Barrett, and most modern commentators decide for the shorter reading, whereas Phillips, Rieu, RSV, and most modern translations accept the longer text.

[26] Sub καθαρός.

[27] Corell even discerns a reference to "the Sacrament of Penance"! (op. cit., p. 72).

into the narrative, there is the further point that we have no evidence for thinking the apostles were baptized (unless with John's baptism). But Jesus goes on to affirm that the apostolic band ("ye" is plural, showing that Jesus is now looking beyond Peter) are clean in the sense meant, *i.e.* clean from sin (*cf.* 15 : 3). But He immediately adds "but not[28] all."

11 John brings out the meaning of the last expression by noting once again that Jesus knew His betrayer.[29] That was the reason that He said not all were clean. We should not overlook the fact that Jesus does not tell the disciples who the unclean person is. The reader of the Gospel knows, but right up until the arrest the disciples know no more than that there is a traitor in their midst.

(b) Lowly Service, 13:12-20

12 So when he had washed their feet, and taken his garments, and ¹sat down again, he said unto them, Know ye what I have done to you? 13 Ye call me, Teacher, and, Lord: and ye say well; for so I am. 14 If I then, the Lord and the Teacher, have washed your feet, ye also ought to wash one another's feet. 15 For I have given you an example, that ye also should do as I have done to you. 16 Verily, verily, I say unto you, A ²servant is not greater than his lord; neither ³one that is sent greater than he that sent him. 17 If ye know these things, blessed are ye if ye do them. 18 I speak not of you all: I know whom I ⁴have chosen: but that the scripture may be fulfilled, ⁵He that eateth ⁶my bread lifted up his heel against me. 19 From henceforth I tell you before it come to pass, that, when it is come to pass, ye may believe that I am he. 20 Verily, verily, I say unto you, He that receiveth whomsoever I send receiveth me; and he that receiveth me receiveth him that sent me.

¹Gr. *reclined.* ²Gr. *bondservant.* ³Gr. *an apostle.* ⁴Or, *chose* ⁵Ps. xli. 9. ⁶Many ancient authorities read *his bread with me.*

---

28 Notice the strong negative, $o\dot{v}\chi\acute{\iota}$. Abbott points out that in this Gospel the construction $o\dot{v}\ldots\pi\tilde{a}\varsigma$ in the sense "not any" does not occur, but that three times in this passage we have it in the sense "not all", namely, verses 10, 11, 18 (2262–63). $o\dot{v}\chi\acute{\iota}$ is most commonly used in this Gospel in questions, so that the use here is noteworthy. Abbott finds no parallel (2265(i)).

29 For $\pi a \varrho a \delta \acute{\iota} \delta \omega \mu \iota$ see on 6 : 64. The present here may possibly signify "him that was betraying him". For Jesus' knowledge see on 2 : 24.

Jesus proceeds to bring out the implications of His symbolic action. It points to the importance of observing in daily life the principle that underlay His action. Characteristically the paragraph concludes with a reference to the position of Jesus and to His status as One sent by the Father.

12 Jesus completed His task. Evidently He washed the feet of all including Peter (and including Judas!). Then He resumed His garments and returned to His seat.[30] He challenged them to think of the significance of what He had done.[31]

13, 14 He reminds them of the way in which they addressed Him.[32] "Teacher", which is equivalent to "Rabbi", was the ordinary respectful way of addressing a religious leader. "Lord" was not nearly so common (though *cf.* 20 : 28; Rev. 4 : 11; see on 4 : 1). It expresses a very high reverence, perhaps even having overtones of divinity. Jesus proceeds to endorse this way of speaking. He commends the disciples, for these expressions point to His true position. But precisely because of this there are implications.[33] His repetition of "the Lord and the Teacher" (the reversed order may be significant) emphasizes His dignity. This exalted Person has washed their feet.[34] They[35] ought therefore to wash one another's feet. It is unlikely that this is to be taken as a regulation promulgated in the interests of pedal cleanliness. Though on occasion disciples ought to

---

[30] ἀνέπεσεν. Plummer points out that this verb (confined to the Gospels in the New Testament) "always implies a *change* of position".

[31] Γινώσκετε is usually taken as interrogative, but it might well be imperative: "Understand what I have done" (so Rieu).

[32] The nominative ὁ Διδάσκαλος καὶ ὁ Κύριος is equivalent to a vocative. BDF reminds us that "Attic used the nominative (with article) with simple substantives only in addressing inferiors, who were, so to speak, thereby addressed in the 3rd person . . . The NT (in passages translated from a Semitic language) and the LXX do not conform to these limitations, but can even say ὁ θεός, ὁ πατήρ etc., in which the arthrous Semitic vocative is being reproduced by the Greek nominative with article" (147(3)).

[33] οὖν is used with full meaning.

[34] ἐγώ (see on 1 : 20) puts emphasis on the subject and stresses Christ's place, which is further brought out with ὁ Κύριος καὶ ὁ Διδάσκαλος. The insertion of these words without any connecting word poses a problem. Does Jesus mean, "If I washed your feet *although* I am your Lord and Teacher" or "*because* I am your Lord and Teacher"? Most understand the former sense, but the latter is not at all impossible. It would stem from the idea, so plain in this Gospel, that true greatness is seen in lowly service.

[35] καὶ ὑμεῖς puts emphasis on the apostles. They too must act in the spirit so challengingly demonstrated by their Lord.

perform this needful service for one another, the point of Jesus'
saying is rather that they should have a readiness to perform the
lowliest service. Nothing was more menial than the washing of the
feet (*cf.* the reference to loosing the sandal thong, 1 : 27, where see
note). No act of service should be beneath them.

15 Jesus makes it clear that His action was no casual event. It set
them an example[36] which they were to follow. Temple aptly remarks
"We would gladly wash the feet of our Divine Lord; but He dis-
concertingly insists on washing ours, and bids us wash our neighbour's feet."

16 For the solemn "Verily, verily" see on 1 : 51. It marks the
following statement as important. Jesus reminds His followers of
their status as "slaves" and "men sent".[37] They are not to stand on
their dignity or think too highly of themselves. If their Master and
their Sender does lowly actions, then they the slaves and the sent
ones should not consider menial tasks beneath their dignity. This
saying (with variants) is found on four occasions: here, Matt.
10 : 24; Luke 6 : 40; John 15 : 20 (and *cf.* Luke 22 : 27). It was
evidently a saying that Jesus loved to repeat.

17 The construction "If ye know these things" carries the implication that in fact they did know them.[38] But it is one thing to
know and another to do. The disciples (and we) are reminded of the
importance of acting on what is known. The precise meaning to be
attached to "these things" is not clear. One would naturally refer
it to the previous verse, with its teaching that a servant is not greater than his master, nor an agent than his principal. But one cannot
"do" these things. Yet the meaning is not really in doubt. The pre-

---

[36] ὑπόδειγμα is a word rejected by the Atticists, who preferred παράδειγμα
(which is not found in the New Testament). It may refer to an example to
be avoided (Heb. 4 : 11), but more usually one to be followed. καθώς ... καί
shows how closely they are to follow the example given. At the same time we
should notice that this is not identical with "what I have done". It is the
spirit and not the action which is to be imitated.

[37] The use of ἀπόστολος for "one sent" and πέμψαντος for the "one sending"
is an illustration of the impossibility of seeing a distinction between ἀποστέλλω
and πέμπω in this Gospel. See further on 3 : 17. This is the one place in John
where the term ἀπόστολος is found.

[38] εἰ with the indicative. It is interesting that the further protasis, ἐὰν
ποιῆτε αὐτά, though connected with the same apodosis puts the condition
with less certainty. Christ implies that the disciples do know these things, but
He leaves it an open question whether they act on their knowledge.

vious passage sets out principles of conduct and Christ's followers
are to act on them.

18 Once again the tragedy of Judas is brought to the fore. It must
have made a big impression on John for he mentions it so often.
Here he records Jesus' explicit denial that His words refer to all of
them.[39] He knows whom[40] He chose. The implication is that the
choosing is the decisive thing. Once again we have the divine initiative. And once again there is an appeal to Scripture to clinch the
argument.[41] The passage quoted is from Ps. 41 : 9. The eating[42] of
bread together signifies close fellowship. Most commentators understand "lifted up his heel" as a metaphor derived from the lifting
up of a horse's hoof preparatory to kicking, and this is probably
correct. We should not, however, overlook the possibility that it is
the shaking off of the dust from the feet that is meant (*cf.* Luke
9 : 5; 10 : 11). The point of the quotation is that Judas's action was
unnatural. It represented a betrayal not of an acquaintance but of
an intimate friend.

19 "From henceforth"[43] seems a little strange. "At" rather than
"from" this moment seems required. Perhaps the expression is
meant to indicate an on-going movement. The prediction is not
separated from the fulfilment.[44] And the prediction is given expressly to strengthen the disciples' faith. When it all happens they

---

[39] For the construction οὐ ... πᾶς see on v. 10.

[40] τίνας may mean "what kind of men", as in Barclay's translation: "I
know the kind of men whom I have chosen" (so also Rieu and others).

[41] For the ellipsis of a principal verb before ἵνα see on 1 : 8. Phillips sees
imperatival ἵνα with, "But let this Scripture be fulfilled". Goodspeed is similar.
It seems better, however, to supply some such words as "it will happen"; *cf.*
"it is that the scripture may be fulfilled" (RSV).

[42] For the verb τρώγω see on 6 : 54. It is not found in LXX of Ps. 41 : 9.
The end of the quotation also differs from LXX and it seems clear that John
has made his own translation from the Hebrew.

[43] ἀπ' ἄρτι. A number of translators take it to mean "from now onwards"
and understand λέγω in a future sense (Phillips, Goodspeed, Weymouth,
Twentieth Century, C. B. Williams). This does seem to be stretching the Greek
a little and it seems better to understand ἀπ'ἄρτι as "now" (Barrett, Rieu,
Amplified, Torrey, Knox, *Berkeley*, C. K. Williams, Lagrange). BDF cites A.
Fridrichsen as supporting the meaning, "exactly, certainly", and Debrunner
"definitely" (12(3)). For Debrunner see *Coniectanea Neotestamentica* xi (1947), p.
47.

[44] The articular infinitive (πρὸ τοῦ γενέσθαι) is to be noted, for the construction is rare in this Gospel. See on 1 : 48.

are to believe[45] "that I am". The expression almost certainly has overtones of deity as in 8 : 28 (where see note). The faith that Jesus looks for is one with a full content. We should not miss the tender concern implied in this prediction. The disciples might well have been seriously shocked and their faith shattered had the betrayal taken them completely unawares. They would have thought Jesus' enemies too resourceful for Him. The prediction altered all that. It ensured that, on reflection, they would continue to see His mastery of the situation. When He was betrayed into the hands of His enemies it was just what He had foretold. He was not the deceived and helpless Victim of unsuspected treachery, but One sent by God to effect God's purpose going forward calmly and unafraid, to do what God had planned for Him to do.

20 Again the solemn introduction (*cf.* v. 16) as the dignity of Christ's messengers is brought out. To receive the messenger is to receive the Sender[46] and to receive the Sender is to receive the Father. The supreme dignity of Christ is in mind as is the importance of aligning oneself with Him. Earlier in this Gospel the thought of Jesus as being sent is common (see on 3 : 17). Later, as here, there is also the thought that He sends His people (Matt. 10 : 40 expresses a similar thought though the language is different; *cf.* also Mark 9 : 37; Luke 9 : 48; 10 : 16). Jesus' followers are men with a mission. This verse is to be taken with vv. 14, 16. There the disciples are warned not to have too high an opinion of themselves, nor to stand on their dignity. To serve Jesus is to take the way of the cross and it necessarily leads men into lowly paths. But it is not to be lightly esteemed. It has a high and holy dignity. Those sent by Christ are brought close to God.

(c) A Prophecy of the Betrayal, 13:21-30

21 When Jesus had thus said, he was troubled in the spirit, and testified, and said, Verily, verily, I say unto you, that one of you shall [1]betray me. 22 The disciples looked one on another, doubting of whom he spake. 23 There was at the table reclining in Jesus' bosom one of his disciples whom Jesus loved. 24 Simon Peter therefore beckoneth to him, and

---

[45] The present subjunctive πιστεύητε may be meant to indicate a continuing faith (though we should add that the aorist is read by many MSS).

[46] ἐμέ is emphatic, both from its form and its position.

saith unto him, Tell us who it is of whom he speaketh. 25
He leaning back, as he was, on Jesus' breast saith unto him,
Lord, who is it? 26 Jesus therefore answereth, He it is, for
whom I shall dip the sop, and give it him. So when he had
dipped the sop, he taketh and giveth it to Judas, the son of
Simon Iscariot. 27 And after the sop, then entered Satan
into him. Jesus therefore saith unto him, What thou doest,
do quickly. 28 Now no man at the table knew for what
intent he spake this unto him. 29 For some thought, because
Judas had the ²bag, that Jesus said unto him, Buy what
things we have need of for the feast; or, that he should give
something to the poor. 30 He then having received the sop
went out straightway: and it was night.

¹Or, *deliver me up.* ²Or, *box*

Immediately after the explanation of the footwashing there
comes a prophecy that one of those present will betray Jesus. Jesus
has already intimated twice that something was amiss in the apostolic band (vv. 10, 18), and the Evangelist has explained that the
first of these refers to the betrayal (v. 11). But nothing has been said
which makes clear to the disciples what is about to take place. Even
now nobody, the traitor excepted, really knows what Jesus is speaking about. The reader of the Gospel knows that Judas is to betray
Him. The apostles know only that one of them is false in some undefined way.
21 A very human Jesus is described as "troubled in the spirit"
(see on 11 : 33). Though John pictures Jesus as in control of the
situation he does not want us to think of Him as unmoved by the
events through which He is passing. The words of Jesus are invested
with a special solemnity as we see from the introduction "testified,⁴⁷
and said" and from the introductory "Verily, verily" (see on 1 : 51).
This is the third time that Jesus has referred to the traitor (vv. 10,
18). Previously however the reference has been very general. Now
Jesus specifically assures the apostolic band (in the same words as
in Mark 14 : 18) that from among them will come a betrayer. For
"betray" see on 6 : 64.
22 The announcement brought consternation. The disciples

---

⁴⁷ μαρτυρέω is most commonly used in this Gospel with reference to the
witness borne to Jesus (see on 1 : 7). Its use here marks the following statement
as a solemn affirmation, one not lightly made.

looked at one another in perplexity.[48] It is clear that the news took them completely by surprise. It is interesting that neither here nor elsewhere does anyone express suspicion of Judas. He had covered his duplicity very well.

23 One of the disciples is singled out with the description "whom Jesus loved" (so also 19 : 26; 20 : 2; 21 : 7, 20). Neither here nor elsewhere is this disciple named but there seems no reason for doubting that it was the apostle John (so Bailey, Bernard, Barclay and others).[49] This disciple was reclining in Jesus' bosom.[50] The usual arrangement at a meal[51] was to have a series of couches each for three persons arranged in a U round the table. The host, or the most important person reclined in the centre of the chief couch placed at the junction of the two arms of the U. The guests reclined with their heads towards the table and their feet stretched out obliquely away from it. They leaned on the left elbow, which meant that the right hand was free to secure food. The place of honor was to the left of, and thus slightly behind the principal person. The second place was to his right, and the guest there would have his

---

[48] ἀπορούμενοι is middle in form (as usually in the New Testament), but active in meaning, though the active also occurs (*e.g.* Mark 6 : 20). The verb signifies perplexity rather than doubt.

[49] Some suggest that the beloved disciple is to be identified with Lazarus on the grounds that John specifically tells us that Jesus loved this man (11 : 3, 5, 36). This is an attractive hypothesis, but it is not easy to fit Lazarus into all the evidence. Nothing in the Gospels leads us to think that Lazarus had entered into the mind of Jesus as fully as the beloved disciple had. Moreover Mark 14 : 17 appears to mean that it was the Twelve who were with Jesus at the Last Supper and this rules Lazarus out. No explanation which rules out John the son of Zebedee appears to give a satisfying explanation of the omission of all reference to that apostle from this Gospel. From the Synoptists it is plain that he was a prominent member of the apostolic band. It is intelligible that he would omit all reference to himself from his Gospel, but why should anyone else do this? The evidence indicates that he was close to Peter (*e.g.* 13 : 24; 20 : 2; 21 : 7; *cf.* 18 : 15; Acts 3). Tradition unanimously supports John. No other name is suggested in antiquity. See further *SFG*, pp. 246ff.

[50] ἐν τῷ κόλπῳ τοῦ Ἰησοῦ. In the only other place where John uses κόλπος it refers to the Son's being in the bosom of the Father (1 : 18, where see note). It may be that this passage is meant to evoke memories of that, and that we are to regard the expression as hinting at the tender regard Jesus had for this disciple. But it is going too far to say, "the specially favoured disciple is represented as standing in the same relation to Christ as Christ to the Father" (Barrett).

[51] For the conduct of a meal at this period see SBk, IV, 2, pp. 611–639.

head on the breast of the host. Plainly this was the position occupied by the beloved disciple.

24 Peter's position is not given. From our knowledge of the apostles we might have thought he would be on Jesus' other side, the place of honor. If this were the case however he could just as easily ask the question himself. It would also be more than difficult to make signs to the beloved disciple from such a position. So he probably was elsewhere.

We have no means of knowing how seating would be arranged in the apostolic band. But Peter was somewhere where he could be observed by the beloved disciple and he made signs indicating that he would like to know who it was.[52] It seems not unlikely that Judas was in the chief place. From Matthew's account it seems clear that Jesus could speak to him without being overheard by the others (Matt. 26 : 25). His position as treasurer would give him a certain status in the little group, and thus make the seat of honor not inappropriate. It is also possible that the giving to Judas of this place was part of Jesus' last appeal to the traitor.

25 The verb translated "leaning back" is the ordinary one for reclining at a meal, and it is used for example of Jesus resuming his place in verse 12. The aorist tense here probably means a change of position (see on v. 12). This disciple leaned back as he was,[53] on Jesus' breast and asked "Lord, who is it?" By leaning back in this way he could speak very quietly and still be heard by Jesus.

26 Jesus answers[54] that He will point the traitor out by an action. It is implied, though not actually stated, that the words could be heard only by him to whom they were spoken. It is clear that Jesus did not want the group as a whole to know the identity of the traitor. The giving of the "sop" would not do this. Indeed it would probably be interpreted as a mark of honor, and thus help to keep his identity

---

[52] We might have expected an indirect question, but, as is usual in this Gospel, we have the direct form: "Say 'Who is it...?' " The majority of MSS do read πυθέσθαι τίς ἂν εἴη, but most agree that this is unlikely to be correct. The direct question has the support of ℵ B lat, and it is most unlikely that an original indirect question would be altered to this form. The reverse procedure is much more likely.

[53] On οὕτως Abbott remarks, "The meaning probably is, that the beloved disciple, instead of turning round to speak to Jesus (which would have attracted attention) merely 'leaned back a little, *keeping the same attitude*' " (1917).

[54] For the rare ἀποκρίνεται see on 12 : 23.

secret. "The sop" was a small piece of bread, or meat.[55] Jesus proposed to dip it in the common dish and then pass it on.[56] This He did and gave it to Judas (who must accordingly have been seated fairly close to Jesus). "He taketh and giveth" is more complicated than need be, and perhaps is meant to bring out the solemnity of the action. It may be for the same reason that Judas's full name is given (see on 6 : 71).

27 Satan (mentioned by name here only in this Gospel) now entered Judas. John is under no delusion as to the magnitude of the issues involved or the real source of Judas's inspiration. It was Satan who entered him and inspired his actions. John sees this as the critical moment. If the giving of the sop was a mark of favor or the like[57] it would be in the nature of a final appeal to Judas from Jesus. But Judas did not respond. He gave himself the more fully to Satan's leading. "Therefore" indicates that Jesus realized how it was. He accordingly urged Judas to do what he has to do quickly.[58] But His words are general and the real import of them remains hidden from the eleven.

28 John makes this latter point clear. Of those who reclined at the table none knew the reason for Jesus' words. This seems to imply that the beloved disciple did not grasp the significance of the sop at the time. It will also explain why he did not denounce the traitor to

---

[55] Lagrange thinks that in this case it was meat: "The bread being at the disposal of each of them, one would rather offer a portion of meat." The term $\psi\omega\mu\acute{\iota}o\nu$ is used 4 times in this narrative and nowhere else in the New Testament.

[56] For the significance of the redundant $a\grave{\upsilon}\tau\tilde{\wp}$ see on 1 : 27.

[57] Most commentators assert that the giving of a morsel in this fashion was a gracious compliment from the host to one of the guests. This may indeed be the case, but no evidence from antiquity appears to be cited (John Lightfoot says that it "was a very unusual thing to dip a sop *(buccellam)* and reach it to any one", *HHT*, p. 378). Hendriksen interestingly denies this significance and sees it as "a warning for Judas". But he does not explain how Judas was to know that it was a warning, nor does he say of what Judas was being warned.

[58] $\tau\acute{a}\chi\iota o\nu$ is comparative in form and strictly means "more quickly". John uses both $\tau a\chi\acute{\epsilon}\omega\varsigma$ (11 : 31) and $\tau a\chi\acute{\upsilon}$ (11 : 29), while in the only other place where he employs $\tau\acute{a}\chi\iota o\nu$ (20 : 4) it is a true comparative. It seems probable that we should take the word in its proper sense. John may want us to think of Judas as not originally intending to consummate the betrayal that night. Jesus made him do it "more quickly" than he wished. It is Jesus, not Judas, who determines the time of the passion. It is, of course, possible to take the comparative as equivalent to a superlative and understand it in an elative sense, "very quickly" or the like (*cf.* Rieu: "The quicker you act the better"). *Cf.* Luke 12 : 50 for the state of mind behind the saying.

the others. Barrett says: "To say that he failed to grasp the meaning of the sign is to make him an imbecile". But this is less than fair. There is nothing in the narrative to show that Jesus meant that betrayal was imminent. For all that has been said so far it may well have been far in the future. John as well as the rest thought that Judas's departure was concerned with other things. There seemed no reason for taking immediate action. We should also remember that the Synoptists inform us that when Jesus predicted the betrayal the disciples asked "Lord, is it I?" This seems to indicate that they had no thought at the time of a deliberate act of treachery. They were thinking of an involuntary betrayal. It should also be borne in mind that they were still ignorant of Christ's purpose in going to the cross. We are so used to reading the Gospels with this in mind that we do not always stop to reflect that on the other side of Calvary it must have seemed incredible that Jesus should urge Judas to do his work of betrayal quickly. Any understanding of His words other than that must have seemed preferable to the apostles.

29 John gives us two interpretations which the disciples placed on the words. Why does he do this? It is not necessary for his narrative. Probably he wants us to see that the disciples had no idea of what was going on and in this matter they stand in sharp contrast with their Master. Judas was the treasurer of the little band. For "the bag" see on 12 : 6. Being treasurer Judas might be expected to buy what was necessary for the feast or to give alms. The former expression may indicate that the Passover still lay ahead. But the words could equally mean the seven days of the feast of unleavened bread.

30 This verse tells us two things. Judas went out immediately after he had received the sop. And it was night. Both details point to an eye-witness. "Night" is more than a time note. In view of the teaching of this Gospel as a whole it must be held to point us to the strife between light and darkness and to the night, black night, that was in the soul of Judas (*cf.* 11 : 10). He had cut himself off from the light of the world and accordingly shut himself up to night.

2. The Disciples' Questions, 13 : 31–14 : 31

It was not until Judas had left them that the discourse proper could begin. The first section of it is interrupted by a series of questions from the disciples, not always the kind of question we might have anticipated. Jesus uses the questions as a means of bringing out further teaching. He answers the questions, but He usually goes far beyond them.

(a) The New Commandment, 13:31-35

31 When therefore he was gone out, Jesus saith, Now ¹is the Son of man glorified, and God ¹is glorified in him; 32 and God shall glorify him in himself, and straightway shall he glorify him. 33 Little children, yet a little while I am with you. Ye shall seek me: and as I said unto the Jews, Whither I go, ye cannot come; so now I say unto you. 34 A new commandment I give unto you, that ye love one another; ²even as I have loved you, that ye also love one another. 35 By this shall all men know that ye are my disciples, if ye have love one to another.

¹Or, *was* ²Or, *even as I loved you, that ye also may love one another.*

There is a good deal of discussion among commentators as to whether the discourse that follows should be thought of as coming from Jesus or as the reflections of the author. While few would be prepared to say that there is nothing in these chapters which comes from the narrator, yet the words of Wright should be heeded: "every reader must feel that here he is in touch with the mind of our Lord. Here One is speaking, greater than the Evangelist. If these be the words of the Evangelist, he cannot be less than another Jesus." If Jesus is not speaking to us in these passages we must despair of finding His words anywhere.

A further topic which arouses controversy is as to whether we have here the original order of these chapters. The end of ch. 14 contemplates an immediate departure, but there are three more chapters before the little band is said to be elsewhere. Many urge, accordingly, that chs. 15, 16 should be transferred to a position in the middle of 13 : 31. This helps us over some difficulties but introduces others (17 : 1 does not really follow well on 14 : 31; the reference to the "new" commandment in 13 : 34 does not sound as though it were originally spoken after 15 : 12, and there are other difficulties). Some think the departure did take place at the end of ch. 14, and that the following chapters represent words spoken as they walked to Gethsemane. This is not impossible, though of course it cannot be proved. Another suggestion is that 13 : 31-14 : 31

and 15-17 give us alternative versions of the same discourse. Both are Johannine in style, so it is necessary to say the original author wrote both. Then either he was removed from the scene before he could decide which to use and someone else included both, or else he could not bring himself to drop either. Even the great names which support such views cannot make them plausible.

The fact is that all these discussions rest upon the basic premise that these chapters do not conform to our canons of tidy and logical arrangement. But why should they? The writer did not think like a twentieth-century man and it is too much to ask him to arrange his material according to our tastes. He does not do it elsewhere ("dislocations" are found by some critic or other in practically every part of the Gospel), and we ought not to look for it here. There is no MS evidence for any of the suggested rearrangements, nor any support in ancient writers. It is much the best course to take the writing as it stands, recognizing the fact that the author is not concerned to arrange his work in accordance with modern conventions.

The first part of the instruction in the upper room now begins. It is significant that Jesus begins with love. The new thing that Christianity brought to men was "that ye love one another". It is also worth noticing that the themes of "going" and "coming" are prominent throughout the discourse. These terms refer to Jesus' death and resurrection. Dodd reminds us that in the section 13 : 31-14 : 31 "the longest passage without direct reference to going and coming is no more than five verses. This dialogue in fact is occupied with the interpretation of the death and resurrection of Christ."[59] It is the death and resurrection which really show us what love is.
31 The further time note indicates John's interest in the order of events. The departure of the traitor was a significant happening. It meant that the little company was purged of its evil element. It meant also that the betrayal was under way and that therefore the great saving act to be consummated on Calvary was fairly launched. In these changed circumstances Jesus immediately[60] begins His teaching. "Now" points to present circumstances. Now that the betrayal is under way the glorification of the Son has begun. Indeed

[59] *IFG*, p. 403.
[60] Moulton sees here another example of the aorist to express what has just happened (see on v. 1).

this verse regards it as already completed.[61] For "the Son of man" (used here for the last time in this Gospel) see Additional Note C, pp. 172ff. We have here some characteristic Johannine ideas. The glorification of Christ is connected with what appears to men as the very opposite of glory. Jesus is looking to the cross as He speaks of glory. Origen employs the striking phrase "humble glory" to express this idea of glory.[62] And the glory of the Father is intimately connected with the glory of the Son. The two are one in the essential purpose of saving mankind. The glory of Christ as He stoops to save mankind is the glory of the Father whose will He is doing. The cross shows us the heart of God as well as that of Christ.

32 The text in the opening part of this verse is uncertain. Most MSS read "if God be glorified in him" before "God shall glorify him in himself" of ARV.[63] They were possibly omitted by an important group of MSS by homoioteleuton[64] or because their retention makes an exceedingly complicated sentence. Even without these words the sentence is not straightforward. If they be retained the conditional construction implies that the condition has been fulfilled.[65] No doubt is being thrown on God's being glorified in Christ. Rather Jesus is expressing three certainties. The first is that God is glorified in Him (*i.e.* in His passion; see on v. 31). The second is that God will glorify Christ in Himself[66] (*i.e.* in heaven; *cf.* 17 : 5). The meaning of this appears to be that the resurrection will follow the crucifixion, and that it will be the Father's seal on the work of the Son. Since the Father is glorified in the Son the Father will certainly vindicate the Son and glorify Him. The future tense points beyond the passion to the eternal glory of the Father which the Son will share. "As God is glorified in the Messianic

---

[61] The aorist ἐδοξάσθη contemplates the glorification as a completed whole. It also lends a note of certainty to the saying. Nothing can prevent the complete accomplishment of this glorification. For δοξάζω see on 7 : 39.

[62] Cited in M. F. Wiles, *The Spiritual Gospel* (Cambridge, 1960), p. 82.

[63] The words are read by ℵ^c AΘ f13 Or. But they are omitted by important MSS like P66 ℵ* BC*DW f1 it syr^s.

[64] Note the repeated ἐν αὐτῷ ... ἐν αὐτῷ. It is countered, however, that, apart from the εἰ, the insertion could be explained by dittography. But the εἰ does remain a stumblingblock to any theory of accidental addition.

[65] εἰ with the indicative.

[66] Reading ἐν αὐτῷ or ἐν ἑαυτῷ as most agree. Some however take ἐν αὐτῷ and understand it to refer to Christ, *i.e.* God will glorify Him in His own human person: "God will also give him glory of his own" (Rieu).

631

work of the Son, so the Son shall be glorified in the eternal blessedness of the Father" (Plummer). The third is that God will do this
without delay. Jesus is looking into the immediate future, not discussing a remote prospect.

33 "Little children" is a diminutive expressing affection.[67] Jesus
knows that this teaching is difficult, but He wants them to be sure
of His tender concern for them. He proceeds to unfold a little more
of the meaning of the preceding words. He will be with them only
for a little while[68] longer, and then, as He has already said to the
Jews (7 : 33f.; 8 : 21), they will look for Him and will not be able to
follow Him. He does not add, as He did to the Jews on the first
occasion, "ye shall not find me", and this may be significant. The
words puzzled the Jews when they were spoken to them, and they
puzzle the disciples now (v. 36). This saying is noteworthy in that it
occurs in exactly the same words in 8 : 21, 22 (where see note). It is
the only saying I have been able to find in this Gospel which is
repeated exactly in three occurrences (see on 3 : 5 for John's habit
of introducing slight variations). Obviously John attached significance to it. It is possibly also another example of this Evangelist's
habit of using expressions to which more than one meaning might
be attached, for it might refer to Jesus' death or to His ascension. If
both meanings are in mind then Jesus is affirming that the disciples
as they are go with Him neither to death nor to the glory beyond.

34 "A new commandment" (*cf.* I John 2 :8) is in an emphatic
position in the Greek. It is important. This is the one place in this
Gospel where our Lord uses the term "new".[69] The content of the

---

[67] τεκνίον is found here only in the Gospels. It appears in a variant reading
in Gal. 4 : 19, and elsewhere in the New Testament only in I John where it
is found 7 times. It is thus a Johannine word, and one not used excessively.
Since John has τέκνον on three occasions the diminutive should be regarded
as significant. Jesus is speaking with tenderness, like a father to his little children.
The word incidentally is always in the plural in the New Testament.

[68] This is the first example of μικρόν used substantively in this Gospel,
but the term recurs in the following chapters (14 : 19; 16 : 16 *bis*, 17 *bis*, 18,
19 *bis*). It is clear that this thought of a short interval sounded through the
final discourse. The expression χρόνον μικρόν is found in 7 : 33; 12 : 35.

[69] καινός is used also of the tomb, 19 : 41. Perhaps we should mention
also that the risen Lord once uses the comparative of νέος, 21 : 18. Turner
sees the present passage as an example of the predicative use of the adjective,
with the meaning, "I give you it anew" (M, III, p. 225). This, however,
scarcely seems to be justified.

commandment is given very simply: "that ye love one another". Jesus is not speaking here of love to all men but of love within the brotherhood. Love itself is not a new commandment, but an old one (Lev. 19 : 18). The new thing appears to be the mutual affection that Christians have for one another on account of Christ's great love for them.[70] A brotherhood has been created[71] on the basis of Jesus' work for men, and there is a new relationship within that brotherhood. "It was 'new,' because the love of Christ's friends for Christ's sake was a new thing in the world" (Dods). Jesus Himself has set the example.[72] He calls on them now to follow in His steps. He is not asking them to do any more than He Himself has done.[73]

35 This is to be the distinguishing mark of Christ's followers. All men will know that they are Jesus' disciples if, and only if, they have love to one another (*cf.* I John 3 : 23; 4 : 7f., 11f., 19ff., *etc.*).[74]

---

[70]   *Cf.* Plummer: "The commandment to love was not new, for 'thou shalt love thy neighbour as thyself' (Lev. xix. 18) was part of the Mosaic Law. But the motive is new; to love our neighbour because Christ has loved us. We have only to read the 'most excellent way' of love set forth in 1 Cor. xiii., and compare it with the measured benevolence of the Pentateuch, to see how new the commandment had become by having this motive added."

[71]   The men of Qumran were very fierce towards outsiders, but they had a high regard for love within the brotherhood (see, for example, IQS i. 10; v. 26). John cannot parallel their hatred for outsiders but the love within the fellowship forms another point of contact.

[72]   It may be significant that in speaking of His own love Jesus uses the aorist tense ἠγάπησα, but on both occasions when He speaks of the disciples loving one another, the present ἀγαπᾶτε (*cf.* also v. 35; 15 : 12). His love was strikingly set forth in the cross: they are to keep on loving.

[73]   Note the significance of καθώς ... καὶ ὑμεῖς. The second ἵνα will not depend on the first, but rather be coordinate with it, so that the second clause reaffirms and amplifies the first. It is in accordance with John's method that there are slight differences between the two ways the thought is expressed in this verse, and that 15 : 12 differs from both (see on 3 : 5). It is also quite Johannine in that the saying here is ambiguous (Christ's love may be the measure or the ground of ours) and that both meanings are probably intended.

[74]   Tertullian tells us that the heathen commented on the Christians: "See, they say, how they love one another" (*Apol.* XXXIX; ANF, III, p. 46). Chrysostom, however, complains that in his day Christian men show all too little love: "even now, there is nothing else that causes the heathen to stumble, except that there is no love ... Their own doctrines they have long condemned, and in like manner they admire ours, but they are hindered by our mode of life" (LXXII. 5; pp. 266, 267). For ἀγάπη in John see on 5 : 42.

(b) A Prophecy of the Denial, 13: 36-38

36 Simon Peter saith unto him, Lord, whither goest thou? Jesus answered, Whither I go, thou canst not follow me now; but thou shalt follow afterwards. 37 Peter saith unto him, Lord, why cannot I follow thee even now? I will lay down my life for thee. 38 Jesus answereth, Wilt thou lay down thy life for me? Verily, verily, I say unto thee, The cock shall not crow, till thou hast denied me thrice.

All the Gospels tell us that Jesus prophesied Peter's threefold denial (Matt. 26 : 33-35; Mark 14 : 29-31; Luke 22 : 31-34). There cannot be any doubt but that it made a profound impression on the early church.

36 The full name Simon Peter is used as this apostle ignores the words about love and reverts to the subject of Jesus' departure. He speaks respectfully ("Lord"; for this term see on 4 : 1), and inquires where the Master is going. Jesus' reply retains the element of mystery. He repeats His earlier statement, though in the singular, making it personal to Peter: "Where I am going you, Peter, cannot follow now".[75] But to this He adds a further point: "You will follow afterwards".

37 Peter appears astounded, and his pride in his discipleship is hurt. Still using the respectful "Lord" in his address,[76] he goes on to inquire why he cannot follow. He affirms his readiness to lay down his life for[77] Jesus. The words Peter uses are almost exactly the same as those used of the Good Shepherd (10 : 11). John may well be indulging here in some more of his irony. Peter affirms his readiness to die for Jesus. The exact opposite is true and that in two ways. In the first place Peter was not really ready as the sequel would show. And in the second Jesus was about to lay down *His* life for Peter.

---

[75] It may be significant that this time the personal pronouns are omitted. In v. 33 ἐγώ and ὑμεῖς put Jesus and the disciples in strong contrast. When Jesus repeats the words to Peter this contrast is not stressed. Instead we find νῦν inserted. The stress appears to be on present circumstances.

[76] According to the usual text. Κύριε is omitted by a few important MSS such as ℵ* 33 565 vg syr^s, and it may possibly have crept in by scribes imitating v. 36.

[77] For ὑπέρ see on 6 : 51.

38 Jesus' reply[78] queries His follower's confident assumption. Peter's readiness to die for Jesus is not quite what he thinks it is. His use of the sword in the garden shows that he was ready in certain circumstances to face death boldly. There was truth as well as error in his words. But he was not ready to stand for Christ when all seemed lost. That demanded a different brand of courage and devotion. Now comes Jesus' prediction of the denial (for Jesus' knowledge see on 4 : 18). It is introduced with the solemn "Verily, verily" (see on 1 : 51). This is no casual remark. It is a solemn pronouncement made in full awareness of its gravity. Jesus assures Peter that a cock will not crow[79] until he has three times denied[80] Him (see 18 : 27 for the fulfilment). The prediction must have come as a shock to Peter. It evidently quite subdued him, and this may be the reason why he remained silent throughout the rest of the time in the upper room, though the others apparently spoke freely. We do not hear of him again until 18 : 10.

---

[78] For the rare $\dot{a}\pi o\varkappa\varrho\acute{\iota}\nu\varepsilon\tau a\iota$ see on 12 : 23.

[79] There is some evidence that the cock was held to crow at a set time (*cf.* Mark 13 : 35 for cock-crow as fixing one of the four watches of the night). *NBD* says that "in many countries the domestic cock was regarded as an alarm clock" (p. 156). However in this place it seems that an actual crowing is meant, as the words recording the fulfilment indicate.

[80] The subjunctive after $\check{\varepsilon}\omega\varsigma$ $o\check{v}$ indicates that the time is indefinite.

CHAPTER XIV

(c) Christ, The Way, 14: 1-7

1 Let not your heart be troubled: [1]believe in God, believe also in me. 2 In my Father's house are many [2]mansions; if it were not so, I would have told you; for I go to prepare a place for you. 3 And if I go and prepare a place for you, I come again, and will receive you unto myself; that where I am, there ye may be also. 4 [3]And whither I go, ye know the way. 5 Thomas saith unto him, Lord, we know not whither thou goest; how know we the way? 6 Jesus saith unto him, I am the way, and the truth, and the life: no one cometh unto the Father, but [4]by me. 7 If ye had known me, ye would have known my Father also: from henceforth ye know him, and have seen him.

[1]Or, *ye believe in God* [2]Or, *abiding-places* [3]Many ancient authorities read *And whither I go ye know, and the way ye know.* [4]Or, *through*

Jesus looks beyond the trouble the disciples are about to enter and reassures them. They need not be troubled in heart. He is preparing a place in heaven for them. And He is the means of bringing them to the Father.

1 If the present imperative[1] is significant its meaning will be "stop being troubled". Jesus is not urging trouble-free men not to start worrying. He is talking to men whose hearts[2] are far from tranquil. We should not be misled by the chapter division. These words are to be taken in close connection with the preceding. Peter has been

---

[1] Μὴ ταρασσέσθω. The verb is used of Jesus' trouble of soul (11 : 33; 12 : 27; 13 : 21) and of the "troubling" of the waters of Bethesda (5 : 7). It is found later in another exhortation to the disciples not to be troubled in heart (14 : 27). John uses it 6 times, but outside this Gospel it is not common (Acts 3 times is the next most frequent use).

[2] Turner has an interesting table to illustrate his point that "Contrary to normal Greek and Latin practice, the NT sometimes follows the Aram. and Heb. preference for a distributive sing. Something belonging to each person in a group of people is placed in the sing." (M, III, pp. 23f.). It is interesting that John uses καρδία in this way in the singular 5 times (including one quotation from LXX), but never in the plural. His only other appearance in the table is also a singular (χείρ, 10 : 39).

thrown into consternation at the prediction of the threefold denial, and we cannot doubt that this had its effect on the others also. If Peter was to deny Jesus did not that mean that some great trial was imminent? Moreover Jesus had spoken of His impending departure, a departure to a place where they could not follow. To men who have left everything for their Leader to be told that He is about to leave them is shattering.[3] They are all very disturbed. And Jesus knows that within a few short hours they will be even more disturbed. So he tells them to be calm. The meaning of the second part of the verse is not certain because of the ambiguity of the Greek twice rendered "believe".[4] This can be either imperative or indicative in each case. Thus the expression might be translated in any one of a bewildering variety of ways. It could mean "you believe in God, you believe also in me"; or "believe in God, believe also in me"; or "you believe in God, believe also in me"; or "believe in God, you also believe in me" (though the "also" makes this last rather difficult). It is moreover possible to take some of these as interrogatives, e.g. "Do you believe in God? Believe also in me". Or a comma might be placed after the first word thus: "Believe, believe in God and also in me" (cf. Moffatt: "you believe – believe in God and also in me"). Against the rendering of AV, "ye believe in God, believe also in me", it may be urged that, as John understands it, faith in Jesus is not something additional to faith in God, to be exercised by those who choose so to do. Rather, since Jesus is the revelation of God, and there is no way to the Father but through Him (v. 6), faith in the Father in any meaningful sense is impossible apart from faith in Him. But this still leaves us with quite a few possibilities. In view of the preceding imperative it is in my judgment best to take both forms as imperative. Jesus is urging His followers to continue to believe in the Father and to continue to believe also in Him, and in this way not to let their hearts be troubled. Yet it must be admitted that other ways of taking the

---

[3] Lüthi brings out the significance of this: "Peter and Thomas and the others are thoroughly shocked, and with good reason. They have followed Jesus, burning their boats, and blowing up the bridges behind them, so to speak ... And now He has disclosed to them that He is about to go where they cannot follow Him as yet. That means that they must part from Him. The reason why they are so deeply shocked is that separation from their Lord is absolutely unthinkable to them."

[4] πιστεύετε.

words are possible. Perhaps we have here another example of John's habit of using expressions which can be understood in more ways than one, with a view to calling to mind what each means. We should not miss the challenge implied in the call to have faith in Jesus Himself. It is one thing for the disciples to have faith in the God who acted in days of old. It is another to have faith in the Jesus who stands before them, especially when He is about to be betrayed by one of His followers, denied three times by the chief of them, abandoned by the rest, and crucified by His enemies. To call for faith in these circumstances is not to utter a platitude.

2 "My Father's house" clearly refers to heaven.[5] The meaning of "mansions"[6] is not so clear. It seems better understood as "permanent residences" than as "steps along the way of development". The idea of continuing development in the next world, though attractive and possibly true, is not taught in Scripture. The bliss and permanence of heaven, however, are taught, and it seems that it is this to which Jesus is now referring. Some suggest that the reference is to progress in this life. Christ has provided many a resting place and place of refreshment for those who move along life's way. The objection to this is that "my Father's house" is scarcely a recognizable description of this world. Moreover the imagery of temporary resting places, or stages upon a journey, within a "house" is very difficult. It is much more likely to be "rooms", "places of residence". "Many" should not be misinterpreted as though it signified for all. "The phrase means that

---

[5] Unless, with S. Aalen, we take "house" to mean the people of God in the manner of Heb. 3 : 2ff. He thinks the present passage to be dependent on the Targum of I Chron. 17 : 9, "And I will make (or, appoint) *for my people a prepared place,* and they shall *dwell in their places,* and they shall *not tremble more*" (*NTS,* 8, 1961–62, p. 238). The words in italics indicate the close resemblances. Very attractive is the suggestion of MiM, that "my Father's house" includes earth as well as heaven, so that wherever we are we are in that house. But on this this view it is not easy to see why Jesus should "go" in order to prepare a place for us.

[6] μονή (only here and v. 23 in the New Testament) is cognate with μένω, which occurs so frequently in this Gospel. It is used both of temporary and permanent abiding. AG cites μονὴν ποιεῖσθαι in the sense "live, stay". In later times the noun is used for "monastery" (MM). In the present chapter on both occasions it is the sense of permanence that is required. The translation "mansions" is derived from the Vulgate *mansiones* ("lodging-places") but the modern associations of the term make this misleading. Robert H. Gundry stresses the connection with μένω, and sees a reference to "spiritual positions in Christ, much as in Pauline theology" (*ZNTW,* 58, 1967, p. 70).

there is room and to spare for all the redeemed in heaven" (Richardson). "If it were not so"[7] underlines this point. There is not the slightest doubt about it, otherwise Jesus' teaching would have been much different. The punctuation of ARV is favored by many. Some however delete the semicolon after "you" and understand the passage as Rieu:[8] "Were this not so, should I have told you that I am on my way to prepare a place for you?" (so Phillips, Knox, RSV *etc.*). The big difficulty with this way of taking the passage is that Jesus is not recorded as having previously said this. This is not a fatal objection as many sayings of Jesus have not been recorded (*cf.* 21 : 25). But we ought not to call on this possibility if a better one lies ready to hand, as it does here. Probably we should take the words, "if it were not so, I would have told you", as a parenthesis. The verse will then read "In my Father's house are many rooms (if it were not so, I would have told you), for I go to prepare a place for you." All the preceding is shown to be true in that now Jesus goes[9] to prepare their place.[10]

3 This has consequences. If Jesus goes for such a purpose He returns (the use of the present introduces a note of greater certainty).[11] The reference to the second advent should not be missed. It is true that John does not refer to this as often as do most other New Testament writers, but it is not true that it is missing from his pages. This is not to deny that John uses the idea

---

[7] εἰ δὲ μή is found in John only here and in v. 11. In both cases it follows πιστεύετε.

[8] Taking ὅτι to mean "that" rather than "because".

[9] πορεύομαι is used here and in verse 3, but ὑπάγω in 13 : 33, 36; 14 : 4, 5. Some draw a distinction between the two verbs, but Johannine usage does not appear to warrant this. See also on v. 28, and for John's use of ὑπάγω on 7 : 33.

[10] The term "place" is used in almost a technical sense in the so-called *Gospel of Thomas*. Thus in Saying 60 we read, "He said to them: You too seek for yourselves a place within for rest" (cited from R. M. Grant and D. N. Freedman, *The Secret Sayings of Jesus*, London, 1960, p. 157). But here, as elsewhere, the "place" is within the believer. It is an inward state of peace. John is concerned with something quite different. His concept is eschatological. Of His preparing T. D. Bernard says, "We understand how men are prepared for the place; but not how the place is prepared for men" (*The Central Teaching of Jesus Christ*, London, 1900, p. 134). Jesus is engaged on some activity for us that passes our comprehension.

[11] BDF class this among the presents of which they say, "In confident assertions regarding the future, a vivid, realistic present may be used for the future (in the vernacular; a counterpart to the historical present . . .)" (323).

of "coming" in more senses than one, nor that in a very real sense Jesus comes to His followers in the here and now. But the thought is not confined to this life. Now and then John does look forward to the Parousia. Nothing is said about the nature of the place that Christ prepares. It is sufficient for the believer that he will be with His Lord.[12]

4 The shorter text of ARV is almost certainly correct.[13] The longer reading "and whither I go ye know, and the way ye know" (ARV mg.), is more sonorous. The shorter almost invites expansion, but the longer is not naturally abbreviated. Jesus is asserting[14] that they know how to follow Him. He has been showing them the way in the whole body of His teaching. If they follow that way they will come where He is.

5 This leads Thomas (see on 11 : 16) into an expression of perplexity. He wants the position to be clear, and will not let our Lord's words stand as though he understands them when he really does not. The man's fundamental honesty stands revealed. He says that he and his companions do not know where Jesus is going (cf. Peter's question, 13 : 36). Has He Himself not said that they cannot come there (13 : 33, 36)? How then do they know the way? The whole thing is impossible.

6 Jesus now introduces a somewhat different topic. He has been talking about leaving the disciples and it is with this that Thomas has been concerned. But Jesus is to go to the Father (13 : 3; 16 : 5, 10, 17) and He now speaks of the way[15] to God (cf. Ps. 27 : 11) as the end of the verse shows. Jesus is Himself the way (notice how

---

[12] ἵνα will be fully telic here. This is the purpose of Christ's going away and coming again. For ἵνα see on 1 : 8. John uses ὅπου twice as often as any one else in the New Testament (30 times; next is Mark with 15 times; John has more than one third of the New Testament total of 82).

[13] Some texts stop at οἴδατε, but τὴν ὁδόν should be read with P66 ℵ BW etc. The addition καὶ τὴν ὁδὸν οἴδατε is found in P66 A D Θ fl f13 syrˢ sa but this can scarcely outweigh the testimony of the important MSS which omit the words, together with the probability of an addition being made to the shorter text.

[14] MacGregor takes the words as a question: "And do you know the way to the place where I am going?" But there seems no good reason for taking them this way.

[15] For the seven "I am's" of this Gospel see on 6 : 35. For Jesus as the Way, cf. Heb. 10 : 20. In Acts "the Way" is sometimes used of Christianity (e.g. Acts 9 : 2; 19 : 9, 23; 24 : 14, 22).

"way" receives emphasis through repetition, vv. 4, 5, 6). He not only shows men the way (*i.e.* by revealing it), but He *is* the way (*i.e.* he redeems men). "The truth" (see Additional Note D, pp. 293ff.) in this connection will have saving significance. It will point to Jesus' utter dependability, but also to the saving truth of the gospel. "The life" (see on 1 : 4) will likewise take its content from the gospel. Jesus is both life, and the source of life to men.[16] All this is followed by the explicit statement that no man comes to the Father other than through Christ. "Way", "truth", and "life" all have relevance,[17] the triple expression emphasizing the many-sidedness of the saving work. "Way" speaks of a connection between two, the link between God and man. "Truth" reminds us of the complete reliability of Jesus in all that He does and is. And "life" stresses the fact that mere physical existence matters little. The only life worthy of the name is that which Jesus brings, for He is life itself. Jesus is asserting in strong terms the uniqueness and the sufficiency of His work for men. We should not overlook the faith involved both in the utterance and in the acceptance of those words, spoken as they were on the eve of the crucifixion. "I am the Way", said One who would shortly hang impotent on a cross. "I am the Truth", when the lies of evil men were about to enjoy a spectacular triumph. "I am the Life", when within a few hours His corpse would be placed in a tomb.

7 The conditional construction implies that the disciples have not really known[18] Christ and accordingly that they have not known

---

16 The threefold article is something of a puzzle. Moule sees that with ὁδός as required by the context, but are the others simply accommodation to this one? Or the use with the abstract noun? He asks whether we should translate "I am the Way, I am Truth, I am Life" (*IBNTG*, p. 112). Turner cites Zerwick as finding these articles inexplicable unless the reference "is to Christ as the real truth, life, light, etc.; all other truths, lives, lights, being transitory" (M, III, p. 178). This seems the best suggestion.

17 Some see in the three nouns a construction which John Lightfoot quaintly calls "a Hebrew idiotism" signifying "true and living way" (*HHT*, p. 382). *Cf.* Moffatt: "I am the real and living way". This is possible but does not carry conviction since this Gospel elsewhere uses other forms for "true" and for "living".

18 There is a natural tendency to put the emphasis on "Me" which we then contrast with "My Father". But the enclitic με cannot be emphatic. The stress in the first clause is rather on ἐγνώκειτε. The stress in the second is on τὸν Πατέρα μου as its position in the clause and its relationship to ἄν shows. The whole thus means: "If you had really *known* Me (with all that that knowledge implies) you would have known (no less than) *My Father*."

the Father.[19] In a sense, of course, they had known Jesus. They had known him well enough to leave their homes and friends and livelihood to follow him wherever He went. But they did not know Him in His full significance. Really to know Him is to know His Father. Up till now all has been preparation. They have not really come to the full knowledge of Jesus and His significance. But from now on it is to be different. From now they know[20] Him and they have seen Him.[21] This is to be understood in terms of 1 : 18, "No man hath seen God at any time; the only begotten Son, who is in the bosom of the Father, he hath declared him." God cannot be seen in the literal sense. But to know Jesus fully is to see the heavenly Father. We should not miss the advance on Old Testament teaching. Throughout the Old Testament, as Dodd has pointed out,[22] the knowledge of God is not normally claimed. It is looked for as a future blessing, or men may be urged to know God, but it is very rare indeed to find assertions that men know God (as Ps. 36 : 10). John sees this whole situation as changed in Christ. As a result of what He has done ("from henceforth") His followers really know God. It is a revolution both in religious experience and in theological understanding.

(d) The Father and the Son, 14 : 8-14

8 Philip saith unto him, Lord, show us the Father, and it sufficeth us. 9 Jesus saith unto him, Have I been so long time with you, and dost thou not know me, Philip? he that hath seen me hath seen the Father; how sayest thou, Show us the Father? 10 Believest thou not that I am in the Father, and the Father in me? the words that I say unto you

---

[19] εἰ with a past tense of the indicative in the protasis and ἄν with the indicative in the apodosis. The words are a rebuke. There is another reading, found, for example, in P66 ℵ D* which has εἰ ἐγνώκατε . . . γνώσεσθε (without ἄν). This would make the words a promise: "If (as is the case) you have come to know Me, you will know my Father also." The attestation of this reading is inferior, and the context makes the rebuke more likely.

[20] It is possible to take γινώσκετε as imperative: "From now onwards you are to recognize him" (Knox). But the indicative seems more likely.

[21] Barclay comments: "It may well be that to the ancient world this was the most staggering thing that Jesus ever said. To the Greeks God was characteristically *The Invisible*. The Jew would count it as an article of faith that no man has seen God at any time."

[22] *IFG*, pp. 163ff.

I speak not from myself: but the Father abiding in me doeth his works. 11 Believe me that I am in the Father, and the Father in me: or else believe me for the very works' sake. 12 Verily, verily, I say unto you, He that believeth on me, the works that I do shall he do also; and greater works than these shall he do; because I go unto the Father. 13 And whatsoever ye shall ask in my name, that will I do, that the Father may be glorified in the Son. 14 If ye shall ask ¹anything in my name, that will I do.

¹Many ancient authorities add *me*.

A question from Philip opens the way for some teaching on the intimate relation existing between Jesus and the Father. The two are so closely connected that anyone who has seen the Son has seen the Father. This has consequences for the prayer life of the disciples and Jesus proceeds to bring out some of them.
8 Philip (see on 1 : 43) is attracted by the words about seeing the Father. It seems to him that really to see the Father might well be the end of many a difficulty. So he asks Jesus to show them the Father. "That is all we want", he says. He is apparently looking for a theophany such as we find from time to time in the Old Testament (Exod. 24 : 10; 33 : 17ff.; Isa. 6 : 1). See on 2 : 20 for John's habit of using misunderstandings as a way of introducing further explanation.
9 Jesus' reply is a gentle rebuke. Though Jesus has been with them all ("you" is plural) for "so long time" Philip has not really known Him. "So long time" ²³ is not defined with precision, but it indicates a ministry of some duration. Philip²⁴ might have been expected to know more about Jesus than he did. His question reveals the limitations of his knowledge. And now comes the explanation, staggering in its simplicity and its profundity. To see

---

²³ τοσοῦτον χρόνον. (א* D read τοσούτῳ χρόνῳ, but the meaning is not essentially different.) The verb εἰμί also gives the thought of duration, regarding the action as continuing through past time right up to the moment of speaking.
²⁴ It is not certain whether we should attach "Philip" to the preceding or the following. Most take it in the former way, but it makes quite good sense to read, "Have I been so long time with you, and dost thou not know me? Philip, he that hath seen me...."

Jesus is to see the Father (*cf.* 12 : 45; 13 : 20).[25] This means that
Jesus is the revelation of the Father. In 1 : 18 Jesus is said to have
declared the Father. If anything this goes further. It is difficult to
interpret it without seeing the Father and the Son as in some sense
one. These are words which no mere man has a right to use. There
is some emphasis on "thou" ("how sayest *thou*"). Philip, being one
of the apostolic band, one of Jesus' intimates, might have been
expected to know better.

10 Now comes a statement about the mutual interpenetration
of the Father and the Son. Each is "in" the other, and this is put
as something that Philip might have been expected to believe.
The question "believest thou not...?" looks for the answer "yes".
In 10 : 38 this was something which even "the Jews" ought to come
to know. Much more an intimate disciple. Apparently it was
Jesus' teaching that should have brought this home to Philip, for
He goes on immediately to speak of His words. These are not
merely of human origin (*cf.* 7 : 17 *etc.*). Jesus says "I speak[26] not
from myself". Then, when we expect something like, "but the
Father abiding in me speaketh the words", we have instead, "the
Father doeth his works" (see Additional Note G, pp. 684ff.).
Throughout this Gospel the deeds are "signs", and the words
are God in action. The words and the deeds of Jesus are alike a
revelation of God. Alike they proceed from the Father and reveal
what the Father is like. Notice that though from a human point
of view Jesus does them they are said to be done by the Father
and they are called "his" works. "Abiding" points to a permanent
relation (*cf.* Phillips: "lives"). The argument is much like that in
10 : 38 and forms yet another example of John's habit of minor
variations in repeated statements.

11 "Believe me that" should be noted. In modern times it is
often stressed that faith is not merely adherence to certain intellectual propositions, but rather trust in a living person. This may
be conceded without any implication that the content of faith is

[25] This may well be another example of John's habit of introducing slight
variations in repetitions (see 12 : 45; 13 : 20). 13 : 20 has to do with receiving
rather than seeing, and if this be excluded we have a twofold variation, for
12 : 45 differs slightly from this verse. But it may be included as all three deal
with the intimate relationship between Christ and the Father such that what
is done to one is done also to the other.

[26] There appears to be no appreciable difference between $\lambda\acute{\epsilon}\gamma\omega$ and $\lambda\alpha\lambda\tilde{\omega}$
(some MSS read $\lambda\alpha\lambda\tilde{\omega}$ in both places). See on 1 : 37.

644

unimportant. While it is true that the New Testament looks for a vital faith in a living person, it is also true that this is not a blind credulity. Faith has an intellectual content. So here Jesus calls on Philip and the others (note the change to the plural) to believe Him,[27] not only to believe in Him. Faith includes a recognition that what Jesus says is true. Jesus also calls on Philip to believe "that". We might well ask where faith in Christ would be without the basic idea that Jesus is worthy of faith? Faith that there is a mutual indwelling of the Father and the Son[28] is part of the faith whereby a man commits himself to Christ. If there is no such indwelling there can scarcely be full commitment.

The latter part of the verse draws attention to the miracles (for the appeal to the miracles *cf.* 5 : 36; 10 : 25,38). As elsewhere in this Gospel, faith on the basis of miracles is regarded as better than no faith at all. This is not really a contradiction of the temptation narrative that we see in the Synoptics. There Jesus resisted the temptation to be a miracle worker performing wonders that would bludgeon men into belief. In John the characteristic of the miracles is not that they are wonders, nor that they show mighty power, but that they are "signs". For those who have eyes to see they point men to God. Notice also that the miracles are spoken of here as "works". What for us is a miracle is for Him nothing more than a normal work. See further Additional Note G, pp. 684ff.

12 For the solemn "Verily, verily" see on 1 : 51. It underlines the following statement as important. "He that believeth on me" (for the construction see on 1 : 12) stresses personal commitment. Jesus is not talking about the merely formal believer. He goes on to say that the man who really trusts will do the works that Jesus does and greater things than these.[29] The reason for this is that Jesus goes[30] to the Father, *i.e.* His saving work is consummated.

---

[27]   Reading μοι with P75 AB Θ f1 f13 it boh *etc.* The word is omitted by P66 ℵ DW lat, but should probably be read. The attestation of the word is strong and it would moreover be easy to omit it and thus get a smoother sentence.

[28]   In the repetition of the statement from v. 10 there is in the Johannine manner a slight variation, namely the omission of ἐστιν.

[29]   ἐγώ (see on 1 : 20) and κἀκεῖνος are both emphatic. Notice that ἔργα is not repeated with μείζονα. It is possible that ARV is correct in supplying "works", or perhaps we should understand "things" (so NEB, Knox). Jesus is not speaking of the doing of miracles, but of service of a more general kind.

[30]   For this use of the present to denote a future certainty see on v. 3.

This is probably to be explained in terms of the coming of the Holy Spirit. The Spirit will not come until the Son goes away (16 : 7; cf. 7 : 39). What Jesus means we may see in the narratives of the Acts. There there are a few miracles of healing, but the emphasis is on the mighty works of conversion.[31] On the day of Pentecost alone more believers were added to the little band of believers than throughout Christ's entire earthly life. There we see a literal fulfilment of "greater works than these shall he do". During His lifetime the Son of God was confined in His influence to a comparatively small sector of Palestine. After His departure His followers were able to work in widely scattered places and influence much larger numbers of men. But they did it all on the basis of Christ's return to the Father. They were in no sense acting independently of Him. On the contrary in doing their "greater works" they were but His agents.

13 This leads us directly into the importance of prayer. Whatever[32] the disciples ask[33] in His name[34] Christ will do. This does not mean simply using the name as a formula. It means that prayer is to be in accordance with all that the name stands for. It is prayer proceeding from faith in Christ, prayer that gives expression to a unity with all that Christ stands for, prayer which seeks to set forward Christ Himself. And the purpose of it all is the glory of God. Yet notice that this glory is "in the Son". The two are inseparable, as throughout this paragraph. That is why prayer may be addressed to either. It is a characteristic Johannine thought that the Father and the Son are so intimately related that what one does the other does also. We should not overlook the importance of the fact that Christ says that He Himself will answer prayer.[35]

---

[31] Cf. Ryle: " 'greater works' mean more conversions. There is no greater work possible than the conversion of a soul."

[32] ὅ τι ἄν is indefinite and includes anything at all. Similarly τι in the next verse sets no limit.

[33] For αἰτέω and ἐρωτάω in prayer see on 11 : 22.

[34] Notice the sevenfold occurrence of ἐν τῷ ὀνόματί μου: here, 14 : 14, 26; 15 : 16; 16 : 23, 24, 26. The Father's "name" is also referred to seven times, though not always in the same words: 5 : 43; 10 : 25; 12 : 13; 17 : 6, 11, 12, 26. For "the name" in antiquity see on 1 : 12.

[35] Bernard can comment: "The difference between δώσει, 'He will give,' of 16²³, and ποιήσω, 'I will do,' of 14¹³ is the difference between the Jewish and the Christian doctrine of prayer."

14 There is no object to the verb "ask" in the preceding verse, so that it is not certain whether it is Christ or the Father who is to be asked (though it is Christ who will "do" the response). As the subject is prayer it is perhaps more natural that we should think of the Father as the object. We expect the same to be true of this verse. However the true text appears to be "if ye shall ask me anything in my name". Prayer may be addressed to the Son as well as to the Father. But it is still "in my name". The basic condition is the same. Some object to the idea of praying to Christ in His own name, but there is good Old Testament precedent for this in that the Father is appealed to "for his name's sake" (*e.g.* Ps. 25 : 11; 79 : 9). As in the previous verse, the prayer will be answered by Christ Himself. Indeed there is some emphasis on this.[36] "Anything" makes this promise very wide indeed. There is no limit to the power of prayer. Passing from v. 13 to this verse we notice the characteristic Johannine habit of introducing slight variations when a statement is repeated.[37]

(e) The Coming of the Spirit, 14 : 15-17

15 If ye love me, ye will keep my commandments. 16 And I will ¹pray the Father, and he shall give you another ²Comforter, that he may be with you for ever, 17 even the Spirit of truth: whom the world cannot receive; for it beholdeth him not, neither knoweth him: ye know him; for he abideth with you, and shall be in you.

¹Gr. *make request of.* ²Or, *Advocate* Or, *Helper* Gr. *Paraclete.*

This passage introduces the first of an important series of references to the Holy Spirit (14 : 26; 15 : 26; 16 : 7-15). There is little said about Him in the earlier part of the Gospel but in

---

[36] The pronoun ἐγώ is used, as it was not in the preceding verse. τοῦτο, it is true, is read by some authorities (ABL *etc.*), but most agree that ἐγώ is the true text.

[37] The whole of this verse is omitted by some authorities (XΛ f1 565 syrˢ·ᶜ *etc.*). με is omitted by some which do read the verse (A D it co *etc.*). It seems likely that the verse is original and that the omissions are different attempts to deal with the problem posed by the addressing of prayer to Christ in His own name immediately after a reference to praying to the Father. Or the omission of the whole verse may be due to homoioteleuton, the eye passing from the first ἐάν to the second.

each of chs. 14, 15, 16 His work is spoken of. The important point made in this passage is that when Jesus goes away the Spirit will be with His followers. They will not be left without resource.

15 Jesus' previous words have given the disciples a tremendous promise as to what they might receive through prayer. But Jesus follows that immediately with a reminder of the ethical implications of being His follower. If anyone really loves Christ then that love will be shown in the keeping of His commandments. There is a certain emphasis on "my commandments".[38] It is a thought to which Jesus returns (v. 21). The present tense is probably significant. Jesus is talking about a continuing attitude of love.[39]

16 For those who are serious about their commitment to Him, those who both love Him and keep His commandments, Jesus promises that He[40] will pray.[41] And the effect of His prayer is that the Father will give the disciples "another[42] Comforter".

---

[38] It comes first in the clause, and the form τὰς ἐντολὰς τὰς ἐμάς is used. This is more emphatic than τὰς ἐντολάς μου though, as John uses it, less so than τὰς ἐμὰς ἐντολάς (see on 3 : 29). But we should not put much weight on this form in the light of τὰς ἐντολάς μου a few verses later (v. 21). The position of τὰς ἐντολάς is more significant.

[39] For ἀγαπάω see on 3 : 16.

[40] κἀγώ is emphatic (see on 1 : 31): "no less than I".

[41] This is the first example in this Gospel of the use of ἐρωτάω in Jesus' prayers (up till now it has been used of men asking questions). For the difference between αἰτέω and ἐρωτάω see on 11 : 22. The latter is the commoner word in John being found 27 times, whereas αἰτέω occurs 11 times.

[42] ἄλλον is said to mean "another of the same kind", whereas ἕτερον would mean "another of a different kind". Thus J. B. Lightfoot affirms that ἕτερον "implies a difference of kind, which is not involved in ἄλλο. The primary distinction between the words appears to be, that ἄλλος is another as 'one besides,' ἕτερος another as 'one of two.' . . . ἄλλος adds, while ἕτερος distinguishes. Now when our attention is confined to two objects, we naturally compare and contrast them; hence ἕτερος gets to signify 'unlike, opposite' . . . while ἄλλος is generally confined to a negation of identity, ἕτερος sometimes implies the negation of resemblance" (*Saint Paul's Epistle to the Galatians*, London, 1902, p. 76; he adds that on some occasions the two terms are interchangeable). The Spirit is thus said to be a Comforter like Christ. This may well be so, but not all writers observe the difference between the two terms. And as John uses ἕτερος only once (19 : 37), we cannot be sure whether he employs the words strictly or not. Abbott points out that Christ has not called Himself a παράκλητος. He feels accordingly that we should take ἄλλον to mean not "another than myself", but "other than yourselves", i.e. "The Father will send you *Another*, a Spirit like yours but beyond yours, (as) *Paraclete* (to you)" (2793). Similarly W. Michaelis understands the passage to signify, "another, and to be sure as

Jesus' bodily presence was about to be withdrawn from them. Never again would they know the warm intimate companionship of the days of His earthly ministry. But this does not mean that they will be bereft. "Another" will be with them. "Comforter" is the traditional translation.[43] But its modern associations render this word unsuited to conveying the meaning of the Greek term. The thought is rather that of the advocacy of one's cause than of comforting in our sense of the term. "Advocate" (as Rieu, NEB *etc.*) is a more satisfactory rendering, but the word really means a friend, especially a legal friend. See further Additional Note F, pp. 662ff. The Advocate will be with the disciples "for ever".[44] The new state of affairs will be permanent. The Spirit once given will not be withdrawn.

17 More information is given about the Advocate. He is first described as "the Spirit of truth" (*cf.* 15 : 26; 16 : 13).[45] It is

---

a Paraclete" (*Coniectanea Neotestamentica*, xi, 1947, p. 153). Against this it can be contended that though Christ has not used the word *Paraclete* of Himself He has spoken of performing actions which a Paraclete might well perform. H. B. Swete is definite. The Spirit is "a second of the same and not of a different order." He further says, "It is impossible to conceive of ἕτερον παράκλητον standing in this context" (*The Holy Spirit in the New Testament*, London, 1910, p. 300, and n. 2). It seems best to understand Jesus as a Paraclete and the Spirit as another, all the more so since this term is actually used of Him (I John 2 : 1).

43 The Greek is παράκλητος which means rather an advocate than a comforter. "Comforter" as an English equivalent appears to be due to Wycliffe.

44 Black draws attention to the *qui* which is a variant to ἵνα in the Old Latin MSS *m* and *q*. He sees in these variants different ways of understanding the Aramaic דְּ and concludes: "we have here a piece of valuable evidence for an Aramaic tradition behind a Johannine saying of Jesus" (*AA*, p. 59).

45 In the Qumran scrolls we read of "the spirits of truth and of error (or 'perversity')" (1QS, iii, 18f.). This is a striking coincidence of language as the expression is not at all common. But it is a coincidence of language, not thought. Where John thinks of "the Spirit of truth" as a Being to be associated with the Father and the Son, the scrolls think of two spirits, one good and one evil, and fairly evenly matched, which strive for mastery within men. Again, the scrolls equate the "prince of lights" with the spirit of truth, whereas John prefers to associate light with Christ. See further my *The Dead Sea Scrolls and St. John's Gospel* (London, 1960), pp. 5–7. "The spirit of truth" is referred to in Test. Jud. 20 : 1, 5, but again the coincidence is in language, not thought. The passage in the Testaments appears to be a development of the Jewish doctrine of the two Yetzers (which makes it unlikely that this is a Christian interpolation).

interesting to see the Spirit associated with truth, for we have just
had Jesus describe Himself as "the truth" (v. 6), and those who
worship the Father must do so "in truth" (4 : 23f.). Clearly truth
is regarded as very closely associated with the Godhead. The
expression probably means "the Spirit who communicates truth"
(Barrett). Jesus then proceeds to contrast the world with the
disciples in their attitudes to the Spirit. First he tells them that
the world (see Additional Note B, pp. 126ff.) "cannot[46] receive" the
Spirit. This is a strong expression. It is further explained as that
the world neither sees nor knows Him. "Beholdeth" is equivalent
to "perceiveth". The world is quite unaware of the Spirit's
workings. Therefore it does not know Him. It enters into no
personal relations with Him. But it is not so with the disciples.
They[47] do know Him. The present "he abideth with[48] you", points
to a continuing reality,[49] just as "shall be in you" indicates a
future certainty.[50]

(f) The Manifestation of Christ to the Disciples, 14 : 18–24

18 I will not leave you [1]desolate: I come unto you. 19 Yet
a little while, and the world beholdeth me no more; but ye
behold me: because I live, [2]ye shall live also. 20 In that
day ye shall know that I am in my Father, and ye in me,
and I in you. 21 He that hath my commandments, and
keepeth them, he it is that loveth me: and he that loveth
me shall be loved of my Father, and I will love him, and
will manifest myself unto him. 22 Judas (not Iscariot) saith

---

[46] For John's interest in what can and cannot be done see on 3 : 4.

[47] ὑμεῖς is emphatic. They stand in sharp contrast to the world.

[48] In this passage three prepositions are used to describe the Spirit's
association with believers. μεθ' ὑμῶν (v. 16) does not seem to differ much
from παρ' ὑμῖν. It is possible that both point to the Spirit's presence in the
church whereas ἐν ὑμῖν stresses rather His indwelling in the Christian (as
Barrett, for example, thinks). But the three forms may result simply from
John's love of variety of expression.

[49] That is if it is a present. μένει could be accented μενεῖ, which would
make it a future (so Torrey, Knox). But the present seems more likely.

[50] Just as there is a slight uncertainty whether μένει should not be read
as a future, so there is doubt, this time textual, as to whether we should read
"shall be" or "is". ἔσται is read by nearly all MSS, but BD*W f1 565 syrᶜ
and a few others have ἐστιν. In this place the present seems to be due to a
desire to harmonize this verb with the two preceding presents, γινώσκετε and
μένει.

unto him, Lord, what is come to pass that thou wilt manifest thyself unto us, and not unto the world? 23 Jesus answered and said unto him, If a man love me, he will keep my word: and my Father will love him, and we will come unto him, and make our abode with him. 24 He that loveth me not keepeth not my words: and the word which ye hear is not mine, but the Father's who sent me.

¹Or, *orphans* ²Or, *and ye shall live.*

Arising out of the thought that the Spirit will be within the disciples though the world does not even recognize His existence, Jesus goes on to speak of the way He will manifest Himself to the disciples but not to the world. The relationship of Jesus to His followers is one that worldly men cannot appreciate. Christians may "know" Christ with the fullest meaning that that word will take. But the world has no knowledge of Him at all.

18 Jesus has several times spoken of going away from the disciples (13 : 33, 36; 14 : 2ff.). He has also said that He will come back again (v. 3), though as we have seen the thought there is primarily that of the second coming. Now Jesus takes up the thought of a return to the disciples which will meet their immediate need. "Desolate" is literally "orphans".[51] The expression harmonizes with the address "Little children" (13 : 33). Jesus will not[52] leave[53] the disciples to battle their way through the world alone. He assures them that He will come to them, the present tense giving greater certainty (see on v. 3). It is true, as many commentators point out, that He comes in the coming of the Holy Spirit. But here Jesus is surely referring to the post-resurrection appearances.[54]

---

[51] ὀρφανούς. In the only two other places where it occurs in the New Testament it is used in the literal sense (Mark 12 : 40 *v.l.* ; Jas. 1 : 27). Berkeley renders "I shall not leave you orphans".

[52] It is worth noticing that John makes more use of this negative than the other Evangelists. οὐ is found in Matthew 204 times, Mark 117 times, Luke 174 times, John 286 times. But John often uses his negative as a means of introducing an important positive as he does here. See further on 1 : 5.

[53] ἀφήσω is a strong term. It can be used in the sense "abandon".

[54] *Cf.* Hoskyns: "This advent of the Christ is not an interpretation of the coming of the Spirit, as many commentators ancient and modern have supposed . . . It is, rather, a distinct appearance, and the primary reference is to the Resurrection appearances." So also Barrett, who, however, thinks that John may have deliberately used language "applicable to both the resurrection and the *parousia*".

19 "A little while" (see on 13 : 33) is a further reminder that Jesus is not speaking of events in the remote future. The crucifixion is very near now. It will mean a sharp distinction between "the world" and "the disciples". After Jesus' death the world will see Him no more. Physically He will be removed from them, and spiritually they had never approached Him. With the disciples it will be different. The crucifixion will indeed separate them from Him. But this will only be for a little while. "Ye behold me" is difficult. The crucifixion meant the same separation for them as for the world. They then saw Jesus no more than the world did. Probably we should understand the saying to look right through the crucifixion to the resurrection. Certainly that is in mind at the end of the verse. After being taken from them Christ will "live". And His living has implications for them.[55] His resurrection is the guarantee that they will not be overcome of death.[56] His life means life for them (*cf.* 6 : 57). In the Johannine manner the saying probably has a deeper reference. Throughout history it has always been the case that the world has not "seen" Christ, though His followers have done so.

20 "In that day" is not defined but it seems that we must understand it of the day of the resurrection of Christ. Some prefer to see a reference to the coming of the Holy Spirit, but if this is done it must be in the sense of 20 : 22, when the Spirit was in some sense given on the day of resurrection. All this will give the apostles certainty. This certainty is expressed not in terms of the greatness of Christ, nor of the rightness of their position or the like. Rather it concerns the indwelling of Christ in God and the mutual indwelling of Christ in believers. When He is risen and when the Spirit is come then they will know the truth of His relationship to the Father, and they will know that He dwells in them and they in Him.

21 Once again love to Christ is expressed in ethical terms (see

---

[55] Note the emphatic pronouns ὑμεῖς (setting the disciples over against the world), and then ἐγώ and ὑμεῖς.

[56] Taking ὅτι to mean "because", and καί "also". Others prefer to make them mean "that" and "and" respectively, to give the meaning: "the world taketh note of me no more, but ye take note of me that I live and ye shall live" (Temple). It is also possible to take ὅτι as "because", but to run the sentence on thus: "the world will see Me no more but you will see Me, because I am really alive and you will be alive, too" (Phillips).

v. 15). The man who loves Christ is the one who "has" His commandments and keeps them. To "have" commandments is an unusual expression and does not seem to be exactly paralleled (though *cf.* I John 4 : 21). The meaning appears to be to make the commandments one's own, to take them into one's inner being. Jesus speaks not only of "having" the commandments but also of "keeping" them, *i.e.* to observe them in daily life is more than to have a firm intellectual grasp of their content.[57] Obedience is the mark of true love. The man who truly loves Christ in this way will be loved of the Father.[58] It might be possible to understand from this that the Father's love is thus merited. But this is not the thought of the passage. Jesus is saying in the first place that love to Him is not a thing of words. If it is real it is shown in deeds. The lover keeps the commandments of the loved one. He is also saying that the Father is not indifferent to the attitude men take to the Son. This does not mean that He hands out rewards on the basis of merit. It means rather that love calls to love. Not only will the Father love such a man, but Jesus also will love Him. He further says that He will "manifest"[59] Himself to them. He does not explain what this means. He simply says that in some undefined way He will reveal Himself to the man who loves Him.

22 This provokes a question from Judas, who is expressly distinguished from Iscariot. This is the one place where this apostle is mentioned in this Gospel. He is mentioned once in Luke and

---

[57] Augustine describes the man who fulfils this saying as one "who hath them orally, and keepeth them morally" (LXXV. 5; p. 336).

[58] This is the one place in this Gospel where John uses ὑπό with the genitive. It is a fairly common construction and his avoidance of it is evidently due to a preference for using the active (though perhaps we should note that he uses ὑπό very rarely, only twice in fact, whereas Matthew has it 28 times, Mark 12 times and Luke 30 times). Why he should have departed from his normal practice in this passage is not clear unless it is that he wished to repeat ὁ ἀγαπῶν με. Westcott thinks that the passive "seems to bring out the idea of the conscious experience of love by the object of it."

[59] ἐμφανίζω, found only here and in the next verse in this Gospel. It is not the usual word for "manifest" (φανερόω). AG defines it as "make visible", while MM speaks of it as used in the papyri in a "quasi-technical sense" for "make an official report". Obviously that is not the use here, which is rather, as Westcott puts it, "presentation in a clear, conspicuous form". It is used of Moses' desire for a visible manifestation of God (Exod. 33 : 13, 18). But it can also be used of God's manifesting Himself to those who do not distrust Him (Wis. 1 : 2). It is in somewhat this sense that the word is used here.

once in Acts, from which we learn that he was the son (or perhaps brother) of James (Luke 6 : 16; Acts 1 : 13). He may be, as some think, the same person as Thaddeus (Matt. 10 : 3; Mark 3 : 18). Very little is known about him. Incidentally the repeated interruptions of this solemn discourse, as the disciples put the questions that puzzle them, illustrates graphically the fact that they were indeed the "friends" of Jesus (15 : 14f.) and were perfectly at home with Him. Judas now voices what must have been the perplexity of the whole band. He asks what has happened (in view of Christ's words we might perhaps have anticipated a future) that Christ will manifest Himself to the disciples[60] and not[61] to the world. Evidently He is understanding "manifest" in terms of physical manifestation. Like the Jews in general he expects the Messiah to stand forth in all His glory before all mankind. The way he puts it seems to imply that he now thinks that something has happened to disrupt our Lord's planned program.

23 The answer to Judas's question is love. As in vv. 15, 21, Jesus insists that love to Him will be expressed in deeds. If a man truly loves Christ He will keep Christ's word (*cf.* 8 : 51; 17 : 6). This leads to the further thoughts that the Father will love that man and that both the Father and the Son will come to make[62] their dwelling with Him.[63] "Abode"[64] will have its full force. Jesus is not speaking of a temporary lodgment, but of a permanent dwelling. Elsewhere we read that God is love, that no-one has ever seen God, but that if a man abides in love He abides in God (I John 4 : 12, 16). The thought here is akin to that. John is not thinking of the second coming, nor of the post-resurrection appearances, but of that state of the believer by which he experiences the immediate presence of the Deity.[65]

24 The negative side of the same thing now receives expression.

---

[60] ἡμῖν is emphatic from its position: "to *us*, not to the world".

[61] The use of the strong negative οὐχί puts emphasis on *not* to the world.

[62] "Make" is ποιησόμεθα, apparently the only example in this Gospel of the middle of this verb. It appears, however, to be used in much the sense of the active.

[63] παρ' αὐτῷ is literally "beside him", but from v. 17 we see that it does not differ greatly from ἐν αὐτῷ.

[64] For μονή see on v. 2.

[65] Morgan paraphrases neatly: "Now He said in effect: You ask Me, Jude, why I have abandoned the world? I have not abandoned the world. My Father and I are coming to dwell in you, and in all who shall, like you, love Me."

The man who does not love Christ does not keep His teaching.[66] Love is not regarded in this Gospel as an abstract emotion. It is something intensely practical. It involves obedience. The seriousness of this is brought out with the reminder that the word Jesus preaches is not His own but that of the Father (*cf.* 7 : 16; 8 : 28; 12 : 49). There can be no higher authority.

Characteristically the Father is spoken of as the one who sent the Son (see on 3 : 17). The mission of Christ is never far from view in this Gospel. And it points to the permanence of God's purpose of love.

(g) I go unto the Father, 14 : 25–31

25 These things have I spoken unto you, while yet abiding with you. 26 But the [1]Comforter, even the Holy Spirit, whom the Father will send in my name, he shall teach you all things, and bring to your remembrance all that I said unto you. 27 Peace I leave with you; my peace I give unto you: not as the world giveth, give I unto you. Let not your heart be troubled, neither let it be fearful. 28 Ye heard how I said to you, I go away, and I come unto you. If ye loved me, ye would have rejoiced, because I go unto the Father: for the Father is greater than I. 29 And now I have told you before it come to pass, that, when it is come to pass, ye may believe. 30 I will no more speak much with you, for the prince of the world cometh: and he hath nothing [2]in me; 31 but that the world may know that I love the Father, and as the Father gave me commandment, even so I do. Arise, let us go hence.

[1]Or, *Advocate* Or, *Helper* Gr. *Paraclete* [2]Or, *in me.* 31 *But that &c . . . I do, arise &c.*

This section of the discourse closes with a renewed emphasis on Jesus' going away and its consequences to the disciples. These consequences are not put in terms of sorrow and the like, as we might have anticipated, but of blessing. The Holy Spirit will be

---

[66] We should probably not distinguish sharply between λόγους and λόγον. It is John's habit to use the singular as a summary of Jesus' teaching (2 : 22; 5 : 24, *etc.*), but the plural is found with reference to it on two other occasions (7 : 40; 10 : 19). This is the one place in this Gospel where Jesus Himself uses the plural. It apparently means much the same as does ἐντολαί in v. 21.

active in the believers. Christ's peace will remain among them. They should rejoice at the prospect of Christ's being with His Father.

25 "These things" will mean the words of this discourse rather than the whole of the teaching of Jesus.[67] "While yet abiding with you" indicates that the earthly abiding was near its end. There may also be something of a contrast with "we will . . . make our abode with him" (v. 23).

26 Here we have the fullest description of the Spirit to be found in this Gospel. For "the Comforter" see Additional Note F, pp. 662ff. In the previous passage He was called "the Spirit of truth". Now He is entitled "the Holy Spirit".[68] This characteristic designation, found throughout the New Testament, does not draw attention to the power of the Spirit, His greatness, or the like. For the first Christians the important thing was that He is holy. His character mattered most of all. This verse shows Him to be closely related to both the Father and the Son. He is to be sent by the Father, but in the name of the Son. In 15 : 26 He is sent by the Son from the Father. Probably no great difference should be put between these. We have noticed a tendency in John to vary statements a little when they are repeated. What he is saying in both places is that the Spirit's mission derives exclusively neither from the Father nor the Son. It comes from both. For "in my name" see on v. 13. Here it can scarcely mean that the disciples ask in Christ's name. It may mean that He Himself will ask (as in v. 16), or perhaps that the Spirit will be sent to continue the work of Christ, to be in His place.[69] The particular function of the Spirit here stressed is that of teacher.[70] "All things" is comprehensive and probably means "all that you will need to know." The Spirit is to be the guide and teacher of the church. In addition

---

[67] The perfect λελάληκα may be meant to indicate the permanence of the words spoken. The expression ταῦτα λελάληκα ὑμῖν is found 7 times in the farewell discourse and nowhere else in this Gospel (here, 15 : 11; 16 : 1, 4, 6, 25, 33).

[68] This is the one place in this Gospel where the full form τὸ Πνεῦμα τὸ Ἅγιον occurs. It puts a certain stress on the quality of the Spirit as holy.

[69] C. B. Williams translates: "whom the Father will send to represent me".

[70] Note the pronoun ἐκεῖνος. It is not grammatically necessary, and, especially following the neuter πνεῦμα, it reminds us of the personality of the Spirit. Cf. Westcott: "The emphatic masculine pronoun brings out the personality of the Advocate".

to this he will bring back to the disciples' memory all the things that Jesus[71] had told them. John has made it clear that the disciples did not grasp the significance of a good deal that their Master taught them. It seems likely that they let slip some of the things they did not understand. Jesus is now saying that the Holy Spirit will supply their lack. Notice that the things of which He will remind them are the things that Jesus has spoken[72] to them. In other words the Spirit will not dispense with the teaching of Jesus. The teaching to be recalled is His.

27 In a way this verse introduces a new subject. There has been no talk of peace up till now. But in another way there is nothing new, for the peace that Jesus gives men is the natural result of the presence within them of the Holy Spirit, of whom Jesus has been speaking. Peace is Jesus' bequest[73] to His disciples. Peace was commonly used at this period as a word of greeting (so in 20 : 19, 21, 26) or of farewell. It thus comes in aptly in this final discourse of our Lord's. But the expression used here is not the usual formula of farewell. Jesus is using the term in His own way for His own purpose. The repetition of "peace" is impressive.[74] The concept is important. Having stated positively what He gives, Jesus goes on to differentiate this gift from anything that the world can give. When the world uses "Peace" in a greeting it expresses a hope. It can do no more. And even that it usually does in no more than a conventional sense like our "Good-bye" (= "God be with you"). But Christ effectually gives men peace.

---

[71] ἐγώ (see on 1 : 20) is emphatic, both from its form and its position. The dispensation of the Spirit will not be radically new in the sense of dispensing with what Jesus has taught. Rather it will emphasize that teaching.

[72] The aorist εἶπον gives an air of finality to the expression. Jesus' teaching has come to its end.

[73] ἀφίημι will have the sense here of "leave behind", "leave as a bequest". (For this use of ἀφίημι cf. Ps. 17 : 14.) "Peace" was commonly used as a form of salutation, but here Jesus refers to it as a special gift of His own and to His own. Cf. Col. 3 : 15; II Thess. 3 : 16 etc. Apart from the greetings in 20 : 19, 21, 26, εἰρήνη is used only here and in 16 : 33 in this Gospel. In both places it is the gift of Christ.

[74] We would expect the article with the second εἰρήνην, all the more so as it is followed by τὴν ἐμήν. Its absence may mean that attention is drawn to the quality of the peace in question. It is not the usual peace, but Christ's own peace. BDF sees this as an example of a construction in which "the definitiveness of the substantive is supplied only as an afterthought through the additional phrase" (270(3)).

Moreover, the peace of which He speaks is not dependent on any outward circumstances, as any peace the world can give must necessarily be. Because He gives[75] men such a peace Jesus can enjoin them not to be troubled in heart[76] nor cowardly.[77] A Christ-given serenity excludes both. It is worth noting that in the Bible "peace" is given a wider and deeper meaning than in other Greek writings. For the Greeks (as for us) peace was essentially negative, the absence of war. But for the Hebrews it meant positive blessing, especially a right relationship with God. This is to be seen in the Old Testament, and it is carried over into the New.[78] The word here has its fullest content.

28 Jesus recalls His teaching of v. 3 that He will go away[79] and come again. This had perturbed the disciples at the time and the Lord had dealt with their question and perplexities. Now He returns to the thought of His impending departure. If they really loved Him this would have been a matter for rejoicing (the Greek conditional implies that they neither loved nor rejoiced[80]), not for consternation. The thought that Jesus goes to the Father is not one to cause sorrow. It is a joyful thought. "The Father is greater than I" presents difficulties to those who hold a trinitarian faith. The reference, however, is not to Christ's essential Being, but rather to His incarnate state. The incarnation involved the acceptance of a certain subordination as is insisted throughout the New Testament. The saying must be understood in the light of "I and

---

[75] The multiplication of $\delta i \delta \omega \mu \iota$ in this verse is a characteristic Johannine way of driving a point home. It is a *gift* of Jesus.

[76] For the singular $\kappa \alpha \varrho \delta i a$ see on v. 1.

[77] This is the significance of $\delta \epsilon \iota \lambda \iota \acute{a} \tau \omega$. The verb is defined by AG as "be cowardly, timid". It is found only here in the New Testament.

[78] The Hebrew שָׁלוֹם has a fuller content than the Greek $\epsilon i \varrho \acute{\eta} \nu \eta$, but when in LXX the latter term was used to translate the former it acquired this fuller meaning. The New Testament writers then used it in the LXX sense rather than in that of contemporary Greek writers in general. See further my *The Apostolic Preaching of the Cross* (London and Grand Rapids, 3rd edn., 1965), pp. 237-44, and the literature there cited.

[79] The use of $\acute{v} \pi \acute{a} \gamma \omega$ and $\pi o \varrho \epsilon \acute{v} o \mu a \iota$ in this verse shows that John puts little difference between the two. Some assert that in this Gospel the former means "go home" and the latter "go on a journey". But the evidence will not sustain this. See also on v. 2.

[80] $\epsilon i \ \mathring{\eta} \gamma a \pi \tilde{a} \tau \epsilon \ldots \mathring{\epsilon} \chi \acute{a} \varrho \eta \tau \epsilon \ \mathring{a} \nu$. It is possible, as some commentators think, that Jesus is being gently playful with the disciples. But He is certainly showing the limitations of their love.

the Father are one" (10 : 30).[81] John is not asserting, as the Arians maintained, that Jesus was a created being. He is talking about the departure of the human Jesus from this earth to be with the Father. In the light of this Jesus sees it as a matter for rejoicing that He returns to the Father. True love will recognize this.

29 Jesus' words will have a greater effect in the future. When the things of which He speaks actually come to pass the disciples will recall the words and believe. This last verb probably means more than give credence to the words of Jesus. They will trust[82] their Master all the more when they see His words verified. For the thought of this verse *cf.* 13 : 19.

30 The end of Jesus' words is approaching. This would suit the close of His discourse, but it does not, as some advocates of rearranging these chapters maintain, require it.[83] As a matter of fact He could have put these words at the very beginning of the entire final discourse. The reason given for the cessation of Jesus' teaching is the coming of Satan. The human agents are not forgotten, but they are given no stress. In the coming of Judas and the soldiers Jesus saw the coming of the evil one. He was especially active in the crucifixion. There the forces of good and evil were engaged. For "the prince of the world" see on 12 : 31. The meaning of "He hath nothing in me" in detail is not easy to see,

---

[81] Westcott has an excellent note in which he sets out the principal patristic views on this passage. See also the valuable note in Hoskyns. Godet sagely remarks: "our passage breathes, in Him who thus speaks, the most lively feeling of His participation in divinity. God alone can compare Himself with God".

[82] The aorist πιστεύσητε may well mean, "come to trust".

[83] Advocates of rearrangement might well heed some wise words of Wright: "The only real objection to the present order is that it is felt to involve an illogical or unchronological sequence. Such an objection, in our own judgement, is in large measure dictated by the demand that the Evangelist *ought* to have conformed to more modern standards of writing. Our study of the Gospel up to this point has already made it abundantly clear that the author had a mind of his own, and a way of writing which is not that of us moderns. Is it not possible that he would have been, shall we say, mildly surprised and perhaps a little amused, at our modern endeavours to achieve a logical harmony for his writings? A little of the grace of humour would have saved many critics from their dogmatic pronouncements on the *original* order of the discourses" (p. 295). Dodd has some scathing criticism: "This is an example of precisely the kind of wooden criticism which ought never to be applied to the work of a mind like our evangelist's. However long these discourses may be, they are burdened from beginning to end with the sense of parting, and the time is short" (*IFG*, p. 407, n. 1).

though the general sense is clear enough. It is sin which gives Satan his hold on men, but there is no sin in Jesus as in others. Perhaps "There is no point at which He can take hold" is somewhere near it.[84]

31 There is dispute as to the correct punctuation of this verse. Some would place a comma instead of a full stop after "even so I do" to give the sense, "but that the world may know . . . arise, let us go hence."[85] This cannot be ruled out as impossible but ARV seems to give the better sense and we follow it accordingly. In other places Jesus lays on His followers the necessity for obedience if they are to show their love (vv. 15, 21, 23). Now He says that He does the same thing Himself (see on 4 : 34). "Even so I do" might refer to the whole of Christ's life. It was characterized from first to last by obedience to the commandments of the Father.[86] But in the context we should probably think particularly of the cross. Jesus is about to die in obedience to the commandment of the Father[87] and this will demonstrate to the world[88] that He loves the Father.[89] "Arise, let us go

---

[84] *Amplified* gives the various possibilities, "he has no claim on Me – he has nothing in common with Me, there is nothing in Me that belongs to him, he has no power over Me." The disadvantage, of course, is that it gives no indication which is to be preferred.

[85] Plummer sees in this arrangement of the words "a want of solemnity, if not a savour of 'theatrical effect' " and he proceeds, "Moreover it is less in harmony with S. John's style". Dodd, however, argues strongly for this division (*IFG*, pp. 406–9). He sees ἄγωμεν as used in the military sense of advancing to meet the enemy, so that ἐγείρεσθε ἄγωμεν ἐντεῦθεν means, "let us go to meet the advancing enemy". The whole verse he takes in this way: "In order that the world may learn (*a*) that Jesus loves the Father, since (*b*) He is obedient to His command . . . He goes to meet His assailant." He suggests such a translation as: "The Ruler of this world is coming. He has no claim upon me; but to show the world that I love the Father, and do exactly as He commands, – up, let us march to meet him!" (*IFG*, p. 409). This is a very attractive understanding of the words, though it does seem to rest heavily on a particular interpretation of ἄγωμεν.

[86] For the things the Father "gave" the Son see on 3 : 35.

[87] This is the 23rd occurrence of "Father" in this chapter. The concentration of references is unusual, and puts a strong emphasis on the nature of God as Father. See on 1 : 14.

[88] For ἵνα with the omission of the preceding principal verb see on 1 : 8.

[89] This is the one place in the New Testament in which Jesus' love for the Father is explicitly mentioned. There are, of course, many passages in which the love of the Father for the Son is referred to. And the love of the Son is implied everywhere. But this is the one place where it comes to expression.

hence''[90] is curious at this stage of the discourse. It has been a major factor in inducing certain scholars to think of a dislocation of the material in these chapters. But this does not necessarily follow. It is not impossible that the words were followed immediately by action, and that the following two chapters were spoken as the little band walked to Gethsemane, or, as some think, at a halt somewhere along the way, possibly at the temple. But such hypotheses are not necessary. Anyone who has tried to get a group of a dozen or so to leave a particular place at a particular time will appreciate that it usually takes more than one brief exhortation to accomplish this. There is nothing at all unlikely in an interval between the uttering of the words and the departure of the group. And if an interval, then there is no reason why Jesus should not have continued to speak during it.

But it is more likely, as R. H. Lightfoot thinks, that we should take the words about departing as referring to a stage in the teaching. The stages leading up to the passion "consist, on one side, of the external events of the passion, and, on the other, of internal resolution and self-dedication by the Lord, as He increasingly imparts Himself to His disciples. This paragraph will then represent the close of one such stage, on the internal side; and it is noteworthy that, whereas at its close, in His devotion and obedience to the Father, He invites the disciples to arise and act along with Him, the first person plural being used, at the close of the next instruction He is the only Agent in the conquest of the world (16[33]); the first person singular alone is used." Hoskyns and Dodd are others who see in the words a pause in the discourse rather than a change of scene. Most of our trouble is caused by our natural inclination to expect the writer to arrange his material in accordance with our modern standards of logic and coherence. But John has his own standards, and he arranges his work to produce effects in his own way. All theories of dislocation and rearrangement come up against the difficulty that the final redactor must have seen the meaning of the words at the end of this chapter just as clearly as we do. Yet he retained (or created!) the present order. By far the simplest proceeding appears to be to take the

---

[90]   Matthew and Mark relate that at the end of the scene in Gethsemane after rebuking the disciples for sleeping Jesus used these words, ἐγείρεσθε ἄγωμεν (Matt. 26 : 46; Mark 14 : 42).

narrative as it stands, and recognize a major division in the discourse at the end of this chapter.[91]

ADDITIONAL NOTE F: THE PARACLETE

The Greek adjective παράκλητος being passive in form should have the meaning, "called to the side of" (*i.e.* for the purpose of helping). As a substantive it was used (though not often[92]), like its Latin equivalent *advocatus*, as a legal term indicating the counsel for the defense. Thus LS define the word in this way: "*called to one's aid*, in a court of justice: as Subst., *legal assistant, advocate*" (the other meanings given are "summoned" and "intercessor"). Westcott in a valuable Additional Note (II, pp. 188ff.) points out that the form of the word is "unquestionably passive", and that the classical use "is equally clear. The word is used technically for the 'advocates' of a party in a cause, and specially for advocates for the defence." He finds a similar usage in Rabbinic writers,[93] and in early Christian writings like the *Epistle of Barnabas*. Strangely, however, the Greek Fathers normally seem to have used the word in the active sense, "consoler", "comforter". No reason appears to be given for this, and, though one must always pay due respect to the Greek Fathers in their interpretation of a Greek word, in this particular case it is hard to escape the impression that they are not correct. Neither Greek use in general, nor that in the Greek Bible, supports them.

In the New Testament the word is applied to Christ on one occasion (I John 2 : 1), and perhaps by implication on another, namely in the expression, "another παράκλητος" (John 14 : 16). In the former passage the legal aspect of the word is clearly prominent, so that the translation "Advocate" is in order. Christ

---

[91] C. C. Torrey points out that, apart from the three words ἐγείρεσθε, ἄγωμεν ἐντεῦθεν, "the connection here is perfect". He postulates a misreading of an Aramaic original which was singular: "I will arise and go hence" (*HThR*, XVI, 1923, p. 342).

[92] "But the technical mng. 'lawyer', 'attorney' is rare" (AG *sub voce*). Behm also denies this usage (*TWNT*, V, p. 799).

[93] The Greek word is simply taken over and transliterated, פרקליט, a fact which is of interest. There appears to be no Semitic word of which παράκλητος is the translation. We must get our information from Greek, not Hebrew sources.

ADDITIONAL NOTE F: THE PARACLETE

is thought of as pleading His people's cause before the Father.

All the other New Testament references employ the word of the Holy Spirit (John 14 : 16, 26; 15 : 26; 16 : 7). The παράκλητος is described as "the Holy Spirit" in 14 : 26, and as "the Spirit of truth" (15 : 26). No one aspect of the Spirit then appears to be in mind when παράκλητος is used. Yet these two descriptions remind us that there is an important moral aspect to the work of the Spirit.[94] This may be in mind also when "the world" is opposed to the Spirit as neither seeing nor understanding Him (14 : 17).

The word is always in this Gospel used by Jesus, who speaks of the Spirit as sent to supply the need of His followers after His departure. The Spirit is to be with the disciples continually, and, indeed, to be in them (14 : 16f.). He is to be their teacher, and to remind them of all that Jesus has said (14 : 26). He bears witness to Christ (15 : 26). He has one work to do in unbelievers, namely to convict the world of sin, righteousness, and judgment (16 : 8). He can come only when Jesus goes away (16 : 7). This appears to mean that the work of the Spirit in the believer is a consequence of the saving work of Christ and not something separate from it. The same truth may be implied in the statement that the Spirit is sent in the name of Jesus (14 : 26). It is only because Christ has died for us and put away our sin that the Holy Spirit can be found at work within our hearts.

It is worth noticing that, without exception, these functions assigned to the Spirit are elsewhere in this Gospel assigned to Christ. Thus He is in the disciples (14 : 20; 15 : 4, 5), He is their teacher (7 : 14; 13 : 13). As the Paraclete bears witness, so does Jesus (8 : 14). Much more could be cited.[95] There is point in Jesus referring to "another" Paraclete (14 : 16).

What then are we to say is the fundamental idea in παράκλητος? There is fairly general agreement that "Comforter" is not the idea, but not so very much agreement on anything else. "Comforter",

---

[94] Cf. Abbott: "emphasis is laid on the Paraclete, or Advocate, as not being one of the ordinary kind – the kind that takes up a client's cause, good or bad, and makes the best of it – but as being 'holy,' and – which is twice repeated – 'a Spirit of truth' " (1932).
[95] See R. E. Brown, NTS, 13, 1966–67, pp. 126f.

which we owe in the English translation to Wycliffe,[96] can be defended it would seem only if the word be taken in its etymological sense (Latin, *con*, "with" and *fortis* "strong"). It will then denote "Strengthener", "Helper", and there are several modern translators who adopt this last-mentioned as the best rendering. But in modern times "comfort" has come to have a meaning like "consolation". It points to a making the best of a difficult situation, whereas the idea in παράκλητος is not so much this as that of providing the assistance that will deliver from the difficult situation. "Helper" is rather better, but it does not really face the fact that the word is not active in meaning.

N. H. Snaith argues strongly for the meaning " 'Convincer,' *i.e.* He who convinces men of the things of God, and accomplishes in them a change of heart."[97] This seems to me to be going too far in one direction (for the Spirit does not necessarily convince in every one of the relevant passages, or even in most of them), and not far enough in another (for this does not cover, for example, the case of reminding the disciples of Christ's teaching).

C. K. Barrett contends that "the Paraclete is the Spirit of Christian paraclesis."[98] He sees the expression as John's way of bringing together "the Church's doctrine of the Spirit . . . and the gospel tradition." To make this combination "was to surrender any attempt to represent historically the words of Jesus."[99] It is tempting to link the Paraclete with the general Christian *paraclesis*. But the price paid is too high. John's method throughout his Gospel will not allow us to think that he surrendered "any attempt to represent historically the words of Jesus." Rather the reverse. Nor can a good case be made out for linking παράκλητος with

---

[96] For an excellent summary of the various English translations of the word see E. J. Goodspeed, *Problems of New Testament Translation* (Chicago, 1945), pp. 110f. He concludes: "The best opinion seems to be that the word meant one called to someone's aid in court, a helper, intercessor, pleader; a character witness . . . 'Defender' is a very close equivalent, yet more than a defense witness seems intended. The work of teaching and reminding them seems to go far beyond this meaning and calls for a looser and broader word, as it is used in the gospel" (*op. cit.*, p. 111). He suggests "another Helper" for the translation in the Gospel, and "one who will intercede for us" in the Epistle.

[97] *ExT*, LVII, 1945–46, p. 50; see also *The Distinctive Ideas of the Old Testament* (London, 1950), pp. 180f.

[98] *JThS*, n.s., I, 1950, p. 14.

[99] *Op. cit.*, p. 15.

παρακαλέω in general. Though superficially attractive this hypothesis will not really meet the case.

Some feel that "Advocate" is the best English equivalent, and this is the translation adopted, for example, by NEB, Rieu, and Weymouth. Plummer argues that this is the fundamental idea in the use of the term in the Fourth Gospel as well as in I John: "the idea of pleading, arguing, convincing, instructing, is prominent in every instance . . . In short, He is represented as the Advocate, the Counsel, who suggests true reasonings to our minds and true courses for our lives, convicts our adversary the world of wrong, and pleads our cause before God our Father" (on 14 : 16). In this connection it may be relevant to notice the frequent references to keeping the commandments in the context, at any rate of the first sayings (14 : 15, 21, 23, 24). This is to be understood in the light of the fact that judgment is one of the great themes of this Gospel. There is a high standard, set before Christians and one that they do not meet. Precisely because of the standard expected and the certainty of judgment, they need a παράκλητος.

Yet when all is said this fails to carry complete conviction. To take the last point, though it is true that the Christian needs an Advocate on account of his failure to keep the commandments, yet παράκλητος in John is never connected with such a failure. Again, while the παράκλητος engages in activities like arguing and instructing it is not clear that these are always those associated with an Advocate. Such a person would certainly argue, but on behalf of his client. He would instruct, but not the client. He would instruct the court. In John the παράκλητος is found instructing those whose παράκλητος He is.

We may be helped by reflecting that the παράκλητος as the Greeks knew this legal functionary was not as precisely defined as our counsel for the defence. There might be more than one παράκλητος, and he was not necessarily a trained legal personage, in sole charge of the conduct of the defendant's case. Any friend who would take action to give help in time of legal need might be called a παράκλητος. It is interesting to see that C. K. Williams translates the word, "Friend", while Knox has renderings like "another to befriend you". It seems that it is something like this that is needed, though the legal background of the term is not to be overlooked. John is thinking of the Friend at court, but characteristically he fills the word with a specifically Christian content. The One who stands for us as the Friend at the heavenly court will perform functions that would not be required in any earthly court. Thus He will remind us of what Christ has said (14 : 26). For heavenly purposes in certain circumstances this may well be the most important thing that can be done. So with His teaching of us, of His bearing witness to Christ, His convicting of the world, and the rest. In all these things He is the legal helper, the friend who does whatever is necessary to forward their best interests. But it is impossible to find one English word that will cover all that the παράκλητος does. We must content ourselves with a term which stresses a limited aspect or aspects, or else use such a term as "Paraclete".[100] There is an extensive literature. The following may perhaps be noted: C. K. Barrett, *JThS*, n.s., I, 1950, pp. 1–15; J. G. Davies, *ibid.*, IV, 1953, pp. 35–8; *LAE*, p. 336; *HDB*, art. "Paraclete"; *TWBB*, art. "Spirit"; MM *s.v.*; N. H. Snaith, *ExT*, LVII, 1945–46, pp. 47–50; Westcott's Additional Note (II, pp. 188–91); SBk, II, pp. 560–62; *TWNT*, V, pp. 798–812; W. F. Howard, *Christianity according to St. John* (London, 1943), pp. 71–80; AG, *s.v.*; J. B. Lightfoot, *On a Fresh Revision of the English New Testament* (London, 1872), pp. 50–56; B. S. Brown, *Theolog Review* (Melbourne) vol. 3, no. 3 (1966) pp. 1–10; R. E. Brown, *NTS*, 13, 1966–67, pp. 113–132.

---

[100] *Cf.* R. E. Brown: "the Paraclete is a *witness* in defence of Jesus and a *spokesman* for him in the context of the trial of Jesus by his enemies; the Paraclete is a *consoler* of the disciples; more important, he is their teacher and guide and thus, in an extended sense, their *helper*. No one translation captures the complexity of these functions ... Christian usage has given a peculiar connotation and status to παράκλητος – a connotation not entirely independent of related Hebrew concepts and of the secular Greek meaning of the words, but a connotation that is unique just the same" (*op. cit.*, p. 118).

CHAPTER XV

3. THE TRUE VINE, 15 : 1–16

1 I am the true vine, and my Father is the husbandman. 2 Every branch in me that beareth not fruit, he taketh it away: and every branch that beareth fruit, he cleanseth it, that it may bear more fruit. 3 Already ye are clean because of the word which I have spoken unto you. 4 Abide in me, and I in you. As the branch cannot bear fruit of itself, except it abide in the vine; so neither can ye, except ye abide in me. 5 I am the vine, ye are the branches: He that abideth in me, and I in him, the same beareth much fruit: for apart from me ye can do nothing. 6 If a man abide not in me, he is cast forth as a branch, and is withered; and they gather them, and cast them into the fire, and they are burned. 7 If ye abide in me, and my words abide in you, ask whatsoever ye will, and it shall be done unto you. 8 Herein [1]is my Father glorified, [2]that ye bear much fruit; and so shall ye be my disciples. 9 Even as the Father hath loved me, I also have loved you: abide ye in my love. 10 If ye keep my commandments, ye shall abide in my love; even as I have kept my Father's commandments, and abide in his love. 11 These things have I spoken unto you, that my joy may be in you, and that your joy may be made full. 12 This is my commandment, that ye love one another, even as I have loved you. 13 Greater love hath no man than this, that a man lay down his life for his friends. 14 Ye are my friends, if ye do the things which I command you. 15 No longer do I call you [3]servants; for the [4]servant knoweth not what his lord doeth: but I have called you friends; for all things that I heard from my Father I have made known unto you. 16 Ye did not choose me, but I chose you, and appointed you, that ye should go and bear fruit, and that your fruit should abide: that whatsoever ye shall ask of the Father in my name, he may give it you.

[1]Or, *was* [2]Many ancient authorities read *that ye bear much fruit, and be my disciples.* [3]Gr. *bondservants.* [4]Gr. *bondservant.*

The allegory of the vine[1] brings before us the importance of fruitfulness in the Christian life and the truth that this is the result, not of human achievement, but of abiding in Christ. There is a stern side to this. Branches which are not fruitful are purged out. Jesus is not simply issuing some comforting advice. He is outlining the difficult, but important way of service. There seems little doubt that Jesus has in mind passages in the Old Testament which regard Israel as a vine (Ps. 80 : 8-16; Isa. 5 : 1-7; Jer. 2 : 21; Ezek. 15; 19 : 10; Hos. 10 : 1). Indeed in time the vine became a symbol of Israel, and it is found, for example, on coins of the Maccabees.[2] Interestingly all the Old Testament passages which use this symbol appear to regard Israel as faithless or as the object of severe punishment. Jesus' description of Himself as the "true" vine is to be seen against this background. The passage is the Johannine counterpart of the Pauline view of the church as the body of Christ and of believers as "in" Christ. Both are ways of bringing out the vital connection that exists between Christ and His own.

1 Jesus begins by laying it down that He Himself is "the true vine".[3] For the "I am" sayings see on 6 : 35. Jesus does not say that the church is the vine but that He is. The church is no more than the branches which are "in" the vine. And not only is Jesus the vine, but He is the "true"[4] vine. As we have seen, the vine is often the symbol of Israel, and this adjective may point to Israel as the degenerate vine (Jer. 2 : 21) now replaced by the

---

[1] A surprising number of commentators see in the vine a reference to the eucharist. This seems to me far-fetched. A vine is not wine, let alone the wine of the eucharist. And if it were there is nothing in the passage to compare to the bread. But the biggest objection is the subject matter of the whole section. Jesus is clearly talking about the life of the Christian and his relationship to his God, not about a liturgical observance.

[2] See SBk, II, pp. 563f., for evidence that the vine symbolism continued to be used among the Jews.

[3] John uses ἄμπελος three times only, vv. 1, 4, 5. Characteristically there are slight variants in the repetition. MM cite evidence from the papyri that this word was sometimes used in the sense of ἀμπελών, "vineyard", but there is no reason for thinking that this is the meaning here. A few commentators do accept this meaning, including Calvin, who sees κλῆμα as meaning "vine". The meaning then would be that Christ is the vineyard and His disciples the vines. Pallis argues to the same effect from the usage in modern Greek. But this usage has not been shown to be common in the ancient world, and the usual interpretation remains far more probable.

[4] For ἀληθινός in John see on 1 : 9.

true.[5] In a way characteristic of the Fourth Gospel there is an immediate reference to the Father. Father and Son are never regarded as separate entities each going His way regardless of the other. John sees them at work together. So when he reports Jesus as speaking of Himself as the true vine he immediately goes on to the thought that the Father is the vine-dresser.[6]

2 The part of the Father here is decisive. He watches over the vine and takes action like that of a vine-dresser to secure fruitfulness. Every fruitless branch[7] he takes away (*cf.* Matt. 3 : 10).[8] We should not regard this as a proof that true believers may fall away. It is part of the viticultural picture, and the point could not be made without it. The emphasis is on the bearing of fruit.[9] Pruning is resorted to to ensure that this takes place. Left to itself a vine will produce a good deal of unproductive growth. For maximum fruitfulness extensive pruning is essential. This is a suggestive figure for the Christian life. The fruit of Christian service is never the result of allowing the natural energies and inclinations to run riot. "Cleanseth"[10] where we might have expected "pruneth" shows that we have now moved into the spiritual sphere. The interest is in what happens with people rather than vines. The

---

[5] There are several linguistic connections with Jer. 2 : 21 where Yahweh says to Israel, ἐγὼ δὲ ἐφύτευσά σε ἄμπελον καρποφόρον πᾶσαν ἀληθινήν.

[6] γεωργός is a more general word than vine-dresser and denotes "one who tills the soil", *i.e.* a farmer. Thus some translators prefer expressions like "Cultivator" or "Gardener". The context rather than the word shows that here it is activity in connection with vines that is meant. This activity of the Father is not unlike that ascribed to Him in Psalm 80 : 8ff. where the vine is Israel.

[7] κλῆμα is found only in this passage in the New Testament (vv. 2, 4, 5, 6). The term denotes not a branch in our sense of the term (κλάδος), but a cane or shoot of a vine.

[8] The redundant pronoun in the expression πᾶν κλῆμα ... αἴρει αὐτό is Semitic. The construction is repeated in the next clause.

[9] John uses καρπός 8 times in vv. 1–16, and twice only in all the rest of his Gospel.

[10] As we pass from αἴρει to καθαίρει (here only in the New Testament) there is a play on words which it is impossible to reproduce in English. MM incidentally cites an example of the use of this latter verb in a papyrus of third century B.C. for an agricultural process, ". . . on condition that Heron shall measure out and winnow the produce annually for the State" (it is rendered "winnow"). It cites no example of the verb with the meaning "prune",

669

action of the Father is such as to cleanse His people so that they will live fruitful lives. The "fruit" is not defined here. But we need not doubt that qualities of Christian character are in mind as elsewhere in the New Testament (Matt. 3 : 8; 7 : 20; Rom. 6 : 22; Gal. 5 : 22; Eph. 5 : 9; Phil. 1 : 11, *etc*.).

3 The disciples are not to think that they are being singled out for criticism. They are already clean[11] on account of Jesus' word (*i.e.* His whole message) spoken[12] to them. He is not reproaching them, but encouraging them. He is pointing out the way in which they may continue to progress spiritually.

4 But they must not presume. Let them take care that they abide in Christ.[13] "And I in you" could conceivably be an imperative directed by Jesus to Himself with the meaning, "You must abide in me and I must abide in you". It could be a promise: "Abide in me, and I will abide in you." But it is perhaps more probable that it is a continuation of the command to the disciples. "Abide in me, and see that I abide in you." Jesus means that the disciples should live such lives that He will continue to abide in them. The two "abidings" cannot be separated, and "abiding" is the necessary prerequisite of fruitfulness. No branch bears fruit

---

and the same is true of LS (which cites only this passage). It is often said that the word can mean "prune", but Lagrange denies this. He points out that the thought is otherwise conveyed by the context in the passage from Philo usually cited to prove the point. Dodd is also sceptical about its use for pruning. He does not find the word in a number of documents referring to viticulture and he concludes, "I do not think it was a word which a vinegrower would naturally have used" (*IFG*, p. 136 n.). The connection between καθαίρει and καθαροί of the next verse should also not be missed. This incidentally helps us to see the meaning of the branches that are taken away. The term was applied to the disciples in 13 : 10 with Judas explicitly excluded: "ye are clean, but not all". The branches cut off are people like Judas. This man had had contact with Jesus, even close contact, but was not a real disciple. He was "the son of perdition" (17 : 12).

[11] The word is καθαροί, used elsewhere in John only in the incident of the foot-washing (13 : 10f.).

[12] The perfect λελάληκα may be meant to indicate that the word remains with them. For this verb see on 1 : 37.

[13] E. M. Sidebottom regards "abide" as "a technical term with the rabbis" and he cites as typical "When ten sit together and occupy themselves with the Torah, the Shekinah abides among them" (*The Christ of the Fourth Gospel*, London, 1961, p. 37).

in isolation. It must have vital connection with the vine. So to abide in Christ is the necessary prerequisite of fruitfulness for the Christian.[14]

5 For "I am the vine" see on v. 1. "I" and "ye" are set over against each other (the emphatic pronouns are used). The roles of Christ and of His followers are not to be confused. But there is a mutual indwelling and this is the condition of fruitfulness. The man who so abides in Christ and has Christ abide in him keeps on bearing fruit in quantity. And the verse concludes with an emphatic declaration of human helplessness apart from Christ.[15] In isolation from Him no spiritual achievement is possible. For the complementary truth *cf.* "I can do all things in him that strengtheneth me" (Phil. 4 : 13).

6 Thus should anyone not abide in Christ he is thrown out[16] like a branch.[17] The fate of such branches is known. They wither away, they are gathered (it is not said who does the gathering, and this may simply be equivalent to a passive[18]) and burnt. These are strong words which emphasize the necessity of remaining in vital contact with Christ if fruitfulness is to continue.[19]

7 From fruit-bearing in general Jesus moves on to prayer. The passage has to do with abiding, so here the condition of prevailing prayer is abiding in Christ. But whereas before He has spoken of His own abiding in believers, now He speaks of His words abiding

---

[14] Abbott points out that ἐὰν μή with the present subjunctive is rare in the New Testament, being found twice in this verse, and again only in v. 6, and Luke 13 : 3 in the Gospels. In the Lukan passage there is plainly the thought of retribution, and he thinks this would make good sense here also, "except a man be (found) abiding" (2521). This is probably too subtle. But the present is certainly unusual.

[15] χωρὶς ἐμοῦ is reinforced with the double negative οὐ... οὐδέν. For δύναμαι see on 3 : 4.

[16] The aorist ἐβλήθη views the action as completed. Moule adds the point that it suggests immediacy, "he has forthwith been thrown out" (*IBNTG*, p. 13). ἔξω seems to mean "out of the vineyard".

[17] The article in the expression τὸ κλῆμα points to a definite branch, the one not in vital contact with the vine. In strict grammar the following αὐτά should be αὐτό but the meaning is not in doubt.

[18] Some see in the expression an indication of a Semitic background, since this type of indefinite plural is more common in Semitic languages than in Greek (see Black, *AA*, pp. 91f.).

[19] *Cf.* Strachan: "Unfruitfulness alone separates men from Christ and His Church. The Church without a sense of mission is no church."

in them (*cf.* 14 : 21, 23). This is not a different attitude to prayer from that in the previous chapter. There prayer must be offered "in the name" of Christ (14 : 14) and obedience is strongly insisted on. The same spiritual attitude is in mind here, but from a different standpoint. If a man is truly abiding in Christ then his prayers will certainly be "in the name" of Christ, *i.e.* in accordance with all that Christ stands for. And if he is really abiding in Christ he will live in obedience to the words of Christ. We should not overlook the importance of the reference to "my words". The teaching of Christ is important[20] and is not lightly to be passed over in the interests of promoting religious feeling. When the believer abides in Christ and Christ's words abide in him then he lives as close to Christ as well may be. Then his prayers will be prayers that are in accord with God's will and they will be fully answered.

8 "Herein" is forward-looking. The Father is glorified[21] in the fact that the disciples bear much fruit. In 13 : 31f. God is said to have been glorified in the work of the Son. Now we have the other truth that God is also glorified in the work of believers who abide in the Son. There is an air of completeness and of certainty about it. The disciples will surely glorify the Father by their continual fruit-bearing. The last part of the verse is difficult. One would have thought that those Jesus was addressing were already disciples. It is possible, with ARV, to supply "so" (the italics show that this word is not in the Greek). The meaning then will be that the bearing of fruit shows that they are disciples. It is also possible that we should not supply "so". The meaning then is that the Father is glorified both in the bearing of fruit and in their continuing to be disciples.[22] In either case there is also the thought

---

[20] *Cf.* Loyd: "the Lord Jesus can only live and express Himself in us, if we are constantly meditating on His words which we have treasured up for us in the Gospel." Profound piety and study of the words of Jesus go together.

[21] The aorist ἐδοξάσθη views the glorification as complete as in 13 : 31f. For this verb see on 7 : 39.

[22] In this understanding of it ἵνα is followed by the future indicative, a construction not common in John (though *cf.* 7 : 3, and some MSS of 17 : 2). The change of tense and mood will give this second proposition a certain independence of the first (*cf.* BDF, 369(3)). It is partly to avoid this construction that "so" is supplied. The second verb in that case is not governed by ἵνα. Some MSS read γένησθε (P66 (vid) BDΘ), thus plainly carrying on the construction. But this looks like a scribal emendation. For ἵνα see on 1 : 8.

that discipleship is not static, but a growing and developing way of life. Always the true disciple is becoming more fully a disciple.
9 From the obligations resting on His disciples Jesus turns to His love for them. That inspires them. He first tells them that His love for them is like the Father's love for Him. Then He commands them to continue in His love.[23] It is possible for men to live without being mindful of Christ's love[24] for them and so break the closeness of the fellowship. They are enjoined not to do this.
10 It is interesting to see the way the obligations resting on the disciples intertwine with the thought of the blessings that there are in Christ. So now Jesus returns to the thought of keeping the commandments. Notice that this is done as an explanation of the means of abiding in His love.[25] This is not some mystical experience. It is simple obedience. It is when a man keeps Christ's commandments that he abides in Christ's love. And once again appeal is made to Christ's own example. He kept[26] the Father's commandments and thus abides continually in the Father's love.
11 For "These things have I spoken unto you" see on 14 : 25. The purpose[27] of Jesus' words is now defined in terms of joy. He has spoken these things in order that His joy might be in them. This may mean that Jesus looks for their conduct to be such that He can rejoice in them (Schonfield: "that I may have joy in you"). More probably He means that He had the joy of living the completely fruitful life and He wants the joy that He already has to be in them too as they live fruitfully (*Twentieth Century:* "so that my own joy may be yours"). He looks for their joy to be filled, *i.e.* be complete. It is no cheerless barren existence that Jesus plans for His people. But the joy of which He speaks comes

---

[23] It is possible to punctuate with a comma instead of a colon after ἠγάπησα to give the sense: "As the Father loved me and I loved you, abide in my love". But this would give an unusual sense to κἀγώ (see on 1 : 31) and also overlook the fact that the normal continuance of that construction would refer to "our" rather than "my" love. ARV is to be preferred.

[24] For ἀγάπη in John see on 5 : 42.

[25] Notice the characteristic slight change when the thought of abiding in Christ's love is repeated from the previous verse. μου replaces τῇ ἐμῇ and the verb is future.

[26] There is emphasis on completion in the pronoun and the perfect tense, ἐγώ . . . τετήρηκα. See on 4 : 34 for Jesus' obedience.

[27] ἵνα is fully telic.

only as they are wholehearted in their obedience to His commands. To be halfhearted is to get the worst of both worlds. The note of joy is a new one, for the word "joy" has been used in this Gospel hitherto only in 3 : 29.[28] But in the upper room we find it seven times (in this verse twice, 16 : 20, 21, 22, 24; 17 : 13). In his comment on 17 : 13 Strachan reminds us that "joy" and "pleasure" must not be confused. "The *joy* of Jesus is the joy that arises from the sense of a finished work. It is creative joy, like the joy of the artist. It produces a sense of unexhausted power for fresh creation. This joy in the heart of Jesus is both the joy of victory (xv. 11), and the sense of having brought His Church into being." It is an inspiring thought that Jesus calls His followers into *joy*. The Christian life is not some shallow, insipid following of a traditional pattern. It is a life characterized by "unexhausted (and inexhaustible) power for fresh creation".

12 The "commandments" of v. 10 are reduced to one, the commandment to love one another as Christ has loved them.[29] This is the "new commandment" of 13 : 34 (where see note).

13 Now comes the reference to the greatest love of all. There is no love greater than that of him who lays down his life for[30] others. Anything else must be less. This is the supreme test of love. In the context this must refer primarily to the love of Jesus as shown in the cross. There He laid down His life on behalf of His friends. Some have raised the question whether the love that dies for enemies is not greater than that which is concerned for friends. But that is not before us here. In this passage Jesus is not comparing the love which sacrifices for enemies with that which sacrifices for friends. He is in the midst of friends and is speaking only of friends. With respect to them he is saying that one cannot have greater love than to die for them. When it is a

---

[28] The cognate verb χαίρω is found more often in the intervening section (3 : 29; 4 : 36; 8 : 56; 11 : 15). But in none of these passages does it refer to the joy of the disciples as it does in 16 : 22; 20 : 20. Clearly joy receives special stress in the upper room. John uses χαρά in all 9 times, which is more than in any other New Testament book (Luke has it 8 times).

[29] The present ἀγαπᾶτε is used of the disciples' love, but the aorist ἠγάπησα of Christ's. They are to love habitually. His love is shown strikingly in the cross. When the thought is repeated in v. 17 ταῦτα ἐντέλλομαι ὑμῖν replaces αὕτη ἐστὶν ἡ ἐντολὴ ἡ ἐμή of this verse. See also 13 : 34.

[30] For ὑπέρ see on 6 : 51.

question of enemies Christ in fact did die for them (Rom. 5 : 10). And as Loyd says, "in truth love has sunk below its proper level if it begins to ask who is my friend and who my enemy. Love gives, and gives everything, for all men". That is the thought of this verse. Jesus gives everything, even life itself, for others. There is no greater proof of love.[31]

14 Jesus makes it clear that the members of the apostolic band are His friends (*cf.* Luke 12 : 4). But friendship depends on common aims and outlook and thus Jesus qualifies "Ye are my friends" by "if ye do the things which I command you".[32] Once again obedience is the test of discipleship. The friends of Jesus are those who habitually obey Him.[33]

15 Jesus will no longer call them "servants", *i.e.* "slaves". He has not actually used this term of them previously, though 13 : 16 comes very near it, and 13 : 13 certainly implies it. The characteristic of the slave which Jesus picks out is that he "knoweth not what his lord doeth". The slave is no more than an instrument. It is not for him to enter intelligently into the purposes of his owner. His task is simply to do what he is told. But this is not the pattern of relationship between Jesus and His disciples. He has called them "friends". He has kept nothing back from them. He has revealed to them all that the Father has made known[34] to Him. There is no contradiction with 16 : 12. Here Jesus denies that He has treated them like slaves – He has taken

---

[31] W. D. Davies finds this passage of central importance: "For the author of the Fourth Gospel the words of Jesus do not, explicitly at least, constitute a court of appeal. Rather they are summed up in one commandment – prominent also in Matthew and Paul, as elsewhere – which finds its connotation, primarily at least, not in what Jesus said, but in what he did, and especially in the Cross" (*The Setting of the Sermon on the Mount*, Cambridge, 1964, p. 413).

[32] As often in this discourse the emphatic pronouns bring out the sense. ὑμεῖς marks the disciples off as a definite, significant group, "you, and not the world in general". ἐγώ reminds them whose commands are important: "I and no other" (see on 1 : 20).

[33] Many commentators draw attention to the fact that a small group of specially favored people were called "Friends" of the Emperor. It is not likely that Jesus' words owe anything to this. Perhaps more important is the fact that Rabbinic teachers spoke of the Jews as friends of God (see SBk, II, pp. 564f.). This, of course, is found in the Old Testament in the case of Abraham (II Chron. 20 : 7; Isa. 41 : 8).

[34] Some contend that the aorist ἐγνώρισα points to a single decisive act, probably the foot-washing. But against this is the preceding πάντα, and also

them fully into His confidence. There the thought is rather that their knowledge is not as yet exhaustive. They still have much to learn and Jesus will disclose it in due time through the Spirit. **16** Man always tends to feel that the initiative is with him. Jesus now assures His followers that this is not the case. It was not they who chose Him, as was normally the case when disciples attached themselves to a particular Rabbi.[35] Students the world over delight to seek out the teacher of their choice and attach themselves to him. But Jesus' disciples did not hold the initiative. On the contrary it was He who chose them.[36] And not only did He choose them but He appointed[37] them to their task. This is first, to go. The idea of mission is frequent in this gospel. The first function then of the disciple is that he is the emissary of Christ. The second thing is that he should "bear fruit" (see on v. 2). The fruit that he bears is not transient but abiding. It is possible that here the bearing of fruit includes the thought of service leading to the conversion of others (why else should they "go"?), as in 4 : 36. It is perhaps unexpected that this is subordinate to the aim of prevailing prayer. The disciples are to bear fruit, so that their fruit may abide, so that whatever they ask God in Jesus' name He may give it (the latter thought is repeated with slight variations in 16 : 23). "Whatsoever" is very thoroughgoing. Nothing is held back. For "in my name" see on 14: 13. Notice that here it is the Father who answers prayer, not Christ Himself as in 14 : 14.

---

the fact that the perfect of this verb never occurs in the New Testament. It seems as though the aorist is used here in the sense of the perfect. The earlier aorist ἤκουσα agrees with the fact that in this Gospel the aorist rather than the perfect is always used of what Jesus heard from the Father (3 : 32; 8 : 26, 40).

[35] *Cf.* the dictum of Rabbi Joshua b. Peraḥyah: "Provide thyself with a teacher . . ." (*Ab.* 1 : 6).

[36] John puts some emphasis on this. οὐχ negates ὑμεῖς not ἐξελέξασθε, i.e. "it was not you that chose", rather than "you did not choose". ἀλλ' is the strong adversative, "on the contrary" (see on 1 : 8), and this is followed by the pronoun ἐγώ (see on 1 : 20). Perhaps this is the place to notice that the Qumran scrolls frequently have the idea of election. It mattered to the covenanters that God had chosen them.

[37] The verb rendered "appointed" is ἔθηκα which is the verb used also of Christ's laying down of His life for His people (10 : 11, 15, 17f.; 15 : 13). R. H. Lightfoot comments: "If this is no accident, it emphasizes, indirectly, that it is the Lord's redemptive death which enables and empowers the disciples to undertake their work in His name." Hoskyns attempts to convey something of this in English with "He *set aside* His life and *set* them to their work."

676

4. Persecution, 15 : 17–25

Jesus foresaw that when He left the disciples they would not find life easy. The gospel they propagated would bring them into collision with the worldly-minded, and indeed with the religious men of the day. So now He gives them counsel, warning them of persecution to come. For the true Christian opposition is inevitable.

(a) Suffering for Christ's Sake, 15 : 17–21

17 These things I command you, that ye may love one another. 18 If the world hateth you, [1]ye know that it hath hated me before it hated you. 19 If ye were of the world, the world would love its own: but because ye are not of the world, but I chose you out of the world, therefore the world hateth you. 20 Remember the word that I said unto you, A [2]servant is not greater than his lord. If they persecuted me, they will also persecute you; if they kept my word, they will keep yours also. 21 But all these things will they do unto you for my name's sake, because they know not him that sent me.

[1] Or, know ye [2] Gr. bondservant.

It is not certain whether we should take v. 17 as the conclusion of the previous section (in which case Jesus rounds it off with the command to love), or whether it begins this new section on persecution. Somewhat hesitantly I adopt the latter course. This views the words as a renewal of the command to love as characteristic of the Christian life. And it is precisely because this life is what it is that it attracts the persecution of the world. Jesus points out first that the world will hate His followers as it has hated Him (vv. 18–20), then that it will hate them because it hated Him (vv. 21–25). He reminds them that there is a sharp distinction between themselves and the world. And because they are identified with Him His followers will be treated by the world in much the same way as He was. The world does not know God, therefore the world illtreats God's men.

17 The plural "These things" is somewhat surprising (RSV, NEB, and, surprisingly, *Amplified* render, "This" as though the pronoun were singular). The singular would give an easier sense, looking forward to the single command to love one another. The plural may mean that all the injunctions in the preceding discourse really amount to this, love for one another. Or, more probably, it may signify that all the commandments contained in the discourse are for a single purpose,[38] that the disciples may engage in mutual love.

18 Now the world is set in sharp contrast. "If the world hateth you" does not imply that there is any doubt about the matter. Rather the reverse. The world will certainly hate them.[39] But when that happens they have the knowledge[40] that no new and surprising thing has befallen them. The world hated Jesus[41] first.[42] And because it hated[43] Him it is not in the least strange that it came to hate His followers (cf. Matt. 10 : 25). It is not without its significance that the disciples are to be known by their love, the world by its hatred.[44]

19 This last point is made clear. "If ye were of the world" implies that in point of fact they are not. Therefore they do not share the world's love, for the world loves its own. The disciples

---

[38] In this case ἵνα will be fully telic. This ἵνα is omitted by D e and Nonnus. This is not a powerful group of authorities, but Barrett thinks it may give the true text. The ἵνα would be due to assimilation to v. 12. He thinks that "without it the sentence is harsher, but stronger. 'These things I charge you: Love one another.' " This is attractive and may well be right. NEB, Phillips, *Berkeley*, take it in this way.

[39] This is the implication of εἰ with the indicative.

[40] γινώσκετε may be indicative or imperative: "You know" or "know".

[41] ἐμέ is emphatic, both from its form and its position.

[42] Abbott finds no precedent in Greek literature for rendering πρῶτον ὑμῶν "before (it hated) you". He proposes to take it in the sense, "It hath hated me, your *First*, i.e. *your Chief*" (1901, 2666). Calvin anticipated this with his view that the expression denotes primacy in rank rather than time. MM, however, argues from the papyri that the similar words in 1 : 15 mean "before me" and accordingly this is the meaning here (*sub* πρῶτος). Dods sees it as meaning "not only 'before' in point of time, but as the norm or prototype." There is a similar expression in 1 : 15 (where see note). The situation is difficult, as the expression is not the usual one, but it seems best to take it as "before you".

[43] The perfect μεμίσηκεν should not be overlooked. It points to a permanent attitude. The world's hatred of Christ was no passing phenomenon.

[44] This is in contrast with the men of Qumran. They stress the importance of love within the brotherhood, but also of hatred towards outsiders. Thus in the *Manual of Discipline* we read: "These are the regulations of the way for the wise man in these times, for his love together with his hate, eternal hate for the men of the pit" (*DSS*, p. 384). There is no equivalent in the New Testament.

are not "of the world",[45] for Christ has chosen them out of it[46] (incidentally a further indication of the divine initiative: divine election means a good deal throughout this Gospel). The necessary consequence is that the world hates them. The present tense in this last verb indicates a continuing attitude. This verse is a good example of the way John can give emphasis by repeating a word. Here he makes "world" linger in the mind by using the word five times in a single verse. And the world being what it is and Christians being what they are it is inevitable that the world reacts against Christians as it did against their Master. It is important to realize this for we sometimes act as though it is surprising that upright worldly men oppose the things of God. On the contrary it is inevitable.[47]

20 Jesus now recalls an earlier saying of His (13 : 16, where see note), and calls on them to remember it.[48] The quotation is exact, which is fairly rare in this Gospel (see on 3 : 5). We may be meant to think of the saying as specially important. The saying reminds them that the treatment given the Master determines that accorded the servant. They persecuted Jesus. They will persecute Jesus' followers.[49] They will keep the "word" of Jesus' followers only to the extent they kept His.[50] Basically this, of course, points to rejection. But the positive aspect should not be overlooked.

---

[45] For causal ὅτι which introduces this clause see on 1 : 50.

[46] ἐκ is used in two senses in this verse. On both the first two occasions it denotes origin, but on this third occasion the thought is rather that of separation from. For εἶναι ἐκ see on 3 : 31.

[47] *Cf.* Ryle: "It is not the weaknesses and inconsistencies of Christians that the world hates, but their grace." So also Barclay: "It is dangerous to have and to practise a higher standard than the standard of the world." He adds: "Nowadays a man can be persecuted even for working too hard or too long."

[48] μνημονεύετε may be imperative or indicative. The imperative seems more likely here. Phillips makes it a question: "Do you remember . . . ?"

[49] Loyd has an interesting reflection on this statement: "How good it would be for us sometimes, when we are worrying about our feelings and about our 'prayer-life,' if an angel were to appear to us and say, 'Don't waste time worrying about these things. What you need to do is to get on with the business of being persecuted'! Not that we are to go out of our way to invite persecution; but we should examine our lives more seriously to see if they are free from compromise with the world."

[50] BDF points out that this verse contains an example of μου "in a contrast (probably not intended at first)" (284(1)).

Some had in fact kept Christ's words, and some would keep theirs.

21 The root cause of persecution is now traced to the world's ignorance of God.[51] This is characteristic Johannine teaching (*cf.* 16 : 3). It is not, as might have been expected, the rejection of the Father, who, however, is spoken of as "him that sent me" (see on 3 : 17). The Father is known in the mission of the Son. The accusation then is that the world rejects the Father who is made known in Jesus Christ. And when the world rejects the God who is thus revealed the world rejects and illtreats the ministers of that God. Persecution accordingly will come to Jesus' followers "for my name's sake" (for "the name" see on 1 : 12 and 14 : 13).

(b) Christ Reveals Men's Sin, 15 : 22–25

22 If I had not come and spoken unto them, they had not had sin: but now they have no excuse for their sin. 23 He that hateth me hateth my Father also. 24 If I had not done among them the works which none other did, they had not had sin: but now have they both seen and hated both me and my Father. 25 But this cometh to pass, that the word may be fulfilled that is written in their law, [1] They hated me without a cause.

[1] Ps. xxxv. 19; lxix. 4.

Jesus takes up the theme of opposition to Himself. He points out now that this opposition underlines the guilt of the people. The greatness of the revelation made in Christ is the measure of the guilt of those who rejected Him.

22 The seriousness of rejecting Christ is brought out. Jesus does not mean, of course, that the Jews would have been sinless had He not appeared.[52] But He does mean that the sin of rejecting

---

[51] The ἀλλά which begins the verse is rather strange as there is no contrast with the preceding. There may be an implied contrast with what might have been expected.

[52] *Cf.* Temple: "Jews who were loyal to their tradition, the noblest religious tradition in the world, might still be involved in what theologians call 'material sin' so far as that tradition was less than the perfect will of God; but they were not involved in 'formal sin', which is deliberate action in opposition to that will made known. Now that it is made known and they refuse it, the sin becomes inexcusable."

God as He really is would not have been imputed to them[53] had
they not had the revelation of God that was made through Him.
But now, as things are, they have no excuse.[54] There is no way
of covering up their sin.

23 Both "me" and "my Father" are emphatic. Jesus wants there
to be no doubt as to the seriousness of the conduct of the men
of His day. He lays down the general principle that He who
hates the Son hates the Father. The two are in the closest possible
connection. For the opposite truth see 13 : 20.

24 The truth of the two preceding verses is further brought out
and emphasized. First Jesus points out the significance of the
"works". This term certainly includes the miracles, but also more.
It covers the whole life of Jesus (which makes inadequate
"miracles", the translation of Rieu and Weymouth). He had
done among the Jews works such as nobody else had ever done
(*cf.* the similar truth concerning His words, 7 : 46). There was an
obligation resting on them accordingly to take note of these works.
The appeal to the works is noteworthy and classically Johannine
(see further Additional Note G, pp. 684ff.). The works are distinctive.[55] Had such works not been done among them they would
not have been held to be sinners. For "having" sin see on v. 22.
But now things are different. They have both seen and hated
both Christ and the Father.[56] Both verbs are in the perfect tense

---

[53] The verb ἔχω is used with ἁμαρτίαν as its object in 9 : 41; 15 : 22, 24;
19 : 11 and in I John 1 : 8 only in the New Testament. The expression implies
that the sin in question remains like a personal possession with the person
who commits it. It is not something that can be over and done with. The form
εἴχοσαν is found only here and in v. 24 in the New Testament. BDF notes
it as a Doricism still found in one village in Rhodes. The –σαν ending "enlarged
its domain still further in the Hellenistic period" (84). It is possibly used here
to avoid any confusion since εἶχον could be misunderstood as first person
singular.

[54] πρόφασις can denote the real reason for an action (see AG). It is what
is put forth to justify it, whether this is the real reason or a mere excuse. Jesus
is saying that they have nothing to bring forward which can justify the position
they have taken up.

[55] This is the significance of οὐδεὶς ἄλλος ἐποίησεν.

[56] Murray comments: "This is a tremendous sentence. And when we stand
face to face with the Cross, we admit its justice. There was no flaw in the
presentation of the appeal of His love. Our rejection of that appeal was absolute
and inexcusable. Granted that, in the fullest sense, none of those who slew
Him were fully aware of what they were doing, yet they were themselves to
blame for their ignorance."

which must here indicate a permanent attitude (*cf.* v. 18). It is interesting that it is said that the Father as well as the Son has been "seen". This will be in the sense of 14 : 9 for right at the beginning of the Gospel John has assured us that nobody has seen God (1 : 18). Once again the closeness of the unity between the Father and the Son is stressed. The guilt of the Jews consisted in this, that they rejected the revelation of the Father which was made known in the Son. Jesus does not speak of "the Father", but of "my Father". His special relationship to God is very much in the forefront.

25 "But" is somewhat unexpected.[57] The meaning evidently is that the Jews' conduct is the opposite of what might reasonably have been expected. The construction is elliptical and we must supply "they did this" or "this cometh to pass" (as ARV).[58] What stands written in the law must be fulfilled. The law is spoken of as "their" law. It is the law that they of all people might have been expected to heed.[59] "Law" strictly applies to the Pentateuch, but sometimes it is used of Scripture in general. It must be the latter use here for the passage quoted is from Psalm 35 : 19 or Psalm 69 : 4, or possibly Psalm 109 : 3. All these passages speak of hatred which lacks any reasonable foundation.[60] It is this kind of hatred that the Jews had exercised toward Jesus.

5. The Work of the Holy Spirit, 15 : 26–16 : 15

Jesus has a good deal to say about the Holy Spirit in this discourse. Without ceasing to think of persecution He unfolds further teaching on the work of the Spirit. As He is thinking of the attitude of the world to Christian men it is perhaps not surprising that He deals here with the one activity of the Spirit with regard to the world, namely that the Spirit convicts the world of sin, righteousness and judgment.

---

[57] All the more so since it is the strong adversative ἀλλά (see on 1 : 8).

[58] For this use of ἵνα with the omission of the preceding verb see on 1 : 8.

[59] *Cf.* Hoskyns: "The writer, moreover, names the Law *your* Law (viii. 17, x. 34), not so much that he may dissociate himself from it, as so many modern commentators maintain . . . but rather in order to rivet upon the Jews those scriptures in which they boast themselves so proudly, and then to prove those same scriptures prophetic of their apostasy."

[60] δωρεάν is found here only in John. It means "gift-wise", "without payment", and so comes to mean without adequate cause, "gratuitously".

(a) The Witness of the Spirit, 15 : 26, 27

26 But when the ¹Comforter is come, whom I will send unto
you from the Father, even the Spirit of truth, which ²pro-
ceedeth from the Father, he shall bear witness of me: 27 ³and
ye also bear witness, because ye have been with me from the
beginning.

¹Or, *Advocate* Or, *Helper* Gr. *Paraclete.* ²Or, *goeth forth from* ³Or, *and bear
ye also witness*

26 For "the Comforter" see Additional Note F, pp. 662ff. Notice
that whereas in 14 : 16 Jesus said that the Father would give the
Spirit in response to His prayer, and in 14 : 26 that the Father
would send Him in Christ's name, now Jesus says that He
Himself[61] will send Him from the Father. It is plain that the Spirit
is regarded as being connected in the most intimate fashion with
both the Father and the Son. The sending of the Spirit is an
activity which concerns them both. For "the Spirit of truth" see
on 14 : 17. The Spirit's relationship to the Father is brought out
by saying that He "proceedeth from[62] the Father". Probably not
too much emphasis should be placed on the meaning of this verb.
The passage is not concerned with the eternal mutual relationships
of the Persons of the Trinity, but with the work the Spirit would
do in this world as a continuation of the ministry of Jesus. The
particular function of the Spirit[63] which occupies us here is that
of witness, and specifically of witness to Christ. For the concept

---

[61] Notice the use of the emphatic $\dot{\epsilon}\gamma\dot{\omega}$ (see on 1 : 20). We should also observe
that the $\H{o}\tau\alpha\nu$ which introduces the verse leaves the time indefinite, "whenever".

[62] After $\dot{\epsilon}\varkappa\pi\sigma\varrho\epsilon\acute{\nu}\epsilon\tau\alpha\iota$ we would expect the preposition $\dot{\epsilon}\varkappa$ rather than $\pi\alpha\varrho\acute{\alpha}$.
John is fond of this preposition to express what comes from God and he uses
it 17 times in this way. Especially does he use it of the Son (1 : 14; 6 : 46; 7 : 29;
9 : 16, 33; 16 : 27; 17 : 8). Westcott thinks that "The use of $\pi\alpha\varrho\acute{\alpha}$ in this place
seems . . . to show decisively that the reference here is to the temporal mission
of the Holy Spirit, and not to the eternal Procession." He points out that the
Creeds which refer to the latter doctrine uniformly use $\dot{\epsilon}\varkappa$, and that the Greek
Fathers who use the present passage to support the doctrine of the Procession
change the $\pi\alpha\varrho\acute{\alpha}$ to $\dot{\epsilon}\varkappa$.

[63] The masculine $\dot{\epsilon}\varkappa\epsilon\tilde{\iota}\nu\sigma\varsigma$ should be noted, for $\tau\grave{o}$ $\Pi\nu\epsilon\tilde{\nu}\mu\alpha$ . . . $\H{o}$ is nearer
than is $\Pi\alpha\varrho\acute{\alpha}\varkappa\lambda\eta\tau\sigma\varsigma$. It does not prove that the Spirit is personal, but it is
an indication that John tended to think of the Spirit in personal terms. This,
of course, accords also with the function ascribed to Him here, that of bearing
witness, for this is normally a personal activity. Bernard comments: "However

of witness in this Gospel see on 1 : 7. When Christ is taken from the earth, the Spirit will continually bear witness concerning Him. The passage strengthens the conviction that the word translated "Comforter" has legal significance. The Spirit, so to speak, conducts Christ's case for Him before the world.

27 The apostles are linked closely with the Spirit in this activity of witness (cf. Acts 4 : 33). Their witness[64] is linked with that of the Holy Spirit. It is the same Christ to whom they bear witness, and it is the same salvation of which they bear witness. At the same time it is *their*[65] witness. They cannot simply relax and leave it all to the Spirit. They have a particular function in bearing witness in that they were with Jesus from the very beginning.[66] There is a responsibility resting on all Christians to bear their witness to the facts of saving grace. They cannot evade this. But the really significant witness is that of the Holy Spirit, for He alone can bring home to the hearts of men the truth and the significance of all this.[67]

ADDITIONAL NOTE G: MIRACLES

John has his own particular way of referring to the miracles of Christ. He never uses $\delta \dot{\nu} \nu \alpha \mu \iota \varsigma$, the favored word in the synoptic Gospels. This word is to all intents and purposes the only word for miracles in the first three Gospels (Matthew uses it 12 times, Mark 10 times, Luke 15 times). This makes John's total omission of the word all the more striking. Instead he uses two words,

---

little modern conceptions of *personality* and of what it implies were present to the mind of the first century, the repeated application of $\dot{\varepsilon} \varkappa \varepsilon \tilde{\iota} \nu o \varsigma$ to the Spirit in these chapters ($16^{8 \cdot 13 \cdot 14}$ 14^{26}) shows that for Jn. $\tau \dot{o}$ $\pi \nu \varepsilon \tilde{\nu} \mu \alpha$ $\tau \tilde{\eta} \varsigma$ $\dot{\alpha} \lambda \eta \vartheta \varepsilon \dot{\iota} \alpha \varsigma$ meant more than a mere tendency or influence."

[64] $\mu \alpha \varrho \tau \nu \varrho \varepsilon \tilde{\iota} \tau \varepsilon$ is usually taken as indicative, but it might well be imperative, "And you also, bear your witness . . ." (so Goodspeed, "you must bear testimony"). *Berkeley* renders with a future, "you too will testify" (Knox, *Amplified*, and others are similar), but this does not appear to be justified.

[65] The pronoun $\dot{\nu} \mu \varepsilon \tilde{\iota} \varsigma$ puts some emphasis on this.

[66] $\dot{\alpha} \pi' \dot{\alpha} \varrho \chi \tilde{\eta} \varsigma$ points to the beginning of Jesus' public ministry. This was the decisive thing. The present tense $\dot{\varepsilon} \sigma \tau \varepsilon$ is a continuous tense which "gathers up past and present time into one phrase" (M, I, p. 119).

[67] The Spirit, of course, does much of His work through human agency. But His witness is not to be confused with that of men. *Cf.* Godet: "The Spirit does not teach the facts of history; He reveals their meaning."

σημεῖον, "a sign", and ἔργον, "a work".[68] Neither of these words is absent from the synoptic Gospels, but neither is used in the synoptics in the same way as in John. σημεῖον is found in Matthew 13 times, Mark 7 times, Luke 11 times, but in none of them is it applied to the miracles of Jesus. It is used of "the signs" that the Jews asked of Him and which He refused to supply. And it is used of "the sign of the Son of man", which will appear in the last days. But it is not applied to the actual miracles that Jesus did. It is almost the same with ἔργον. This word is used by Matthew 6 times, Mark twice, Luke twice. Twice indeed it may refer to Christ's miracles, namely, when Matthew reports that John the Baptist heard in prison "the works of the Christ" (Matt. 11 : 2), and when Luke reports that Jesus was "mighty in deed and word" (Luke 24 : 19). But this is exceptional in these Gospels. John, by contrast, uses both words very freely in a way which reveals his characteristic view of miracles.

He uses σημεῖον 17 times. On one occasion this refers to John the Baptist who "did no sign" (10 : 41). Jesus' opponents used the word on two occasions when they asked Him what sign He showed (2 : 18; 6 : 30); and on another occasion when they asked themselves whether the Christ when He came would do more signs than Jesus (7 : 31). Jesus used the word on two occasions. Once He complained that His hearers would not believe unless they saw "signs and wonders" (4 : 48), and again He referred to those who sought Him out because they ate of the loaves, and not because of the signs (6 : 26).

On the other 11 occasions σημεῖον always refers to the miracles of Christ.[69] Here we must regard the intrinsic meaning of the

---

[68] He uses τέρας, "a wonder", "a portent", only in 4 : 48, "Except ye see signs and wonders, ye will in no wise believe". This word is however used in Acts of Christ's miracles. Barclay sees significance in the fact that τέρας, δύναμις, and σημεῖον are all used in the New Testament of Jesus' miracles: "In any miracle, then, there are three things. There is the wonder which leaves men dazzled, astonished, aghast. There is the power which is effective, which can deal with and mend a broken body, an unhinged mind, a bruised heart, a power which can do things. There is the sign which tells us of the love in the heart of the God who does such things for men" (I, pp. 107f.). It is the last point which is significant for John.

[69] P. Riga, in an important article, "Signs of Glory" in *Interpretation*, XVII, 1963, pp. 402–424, says that σημεῖον "does not necessarily mean an extra-ordinary miracle (2 : 1–12, 14–21), but it can" (*op. cit.*, p. 407). Elsewhere

word as significant. It is connected with σημαίνω, "to signify, indicate, make known". In other words a σημεῖον is something full of meaning.[70] It is not an end in itself, but it points men beyond itself. The word has no necessary connection with the miraculous. Indeed, in LXX it is usually used of "signs" which are not miraculous. But John uses it exclusively of miracles. The miracle, as John sees it, is a means of teaching men spiritual truth, and specifically of pointing them to God. Thus he quotes the words of Nicodemus, "no one can do these signs that thou doest, except God be with him" (3 : 2). And negatively he records the words of the man born blind: "How can a man that is a sinner do such signs?" (9 : 16). The signs then take their origin from God and they point men to God.[71] It is not surprising that they therefore result in faith. On the occasion of the first of them, the changing of water into wine at Cana it is said that "his disciples believed on him" (2 : 11). Many in Jerusalem came to believe on account of the signs (2 : 23), and indeed John can speak of his whole Gospel as an account of "signs" recorded that men might believe (20 : 30f.). In accordance with this people who saw the signs but refused to believe are blamed for that very reason (12 : 37). The chief priests and the Pharisees on one occasion expressed their deep concern. Jesus, they said, "doeth many signs", and the consequence they thought, might well be that "all men will believe on him" (11 : 47f.). On more than one occasion John records that people came to Jesus on account of the signs (6 : 2; 12 : 18), while on the occasion of the feeding of the multitude the people who saw the sign concluded: "This is of a truth the prophet that cometh into the world" (6 : 14). It is of interest that Jesus

---

he distinguishes between "a miraculous happening" and "a supernatural but significant event" (*op. cit.*, p. 402). I cannot understand this distinction, and I see no evidence that John uses σημεῖον with reference to Christ of any non-miraculous event.

[70] In LXX it most commonly translates אוֹת and Barrett can say, "The אוֹת-σημεῖον . . . becomes a special part of the prophetic activity; no mere illustration, but a symbolical anticipation or showing forth of a greater reality of which the σημεῖον is nevertheless itself a part" (p. 63).

[71] R. H. Lightfoot sees the term, as used in the Old Testament and among the Jews, as denoting a present event pointing forward to the future: "In St. John's gospel the contrast in the end is not so much between present and future, as between seen and and unseen, external event and internal truth" (p. 22).

did not reject the faith that rested on the signs. It is, of course, not the highest kind of faith, but it is better than none at all. So on one occasion He blamed people who had a wrong attitude to the signs: "Ye seek me, not because ye saw signs, but because ye ate of the loaves, and were filled" (6 : 26). These people went on to ask Jesus for a sign (6 : 30), but their desire was not granted. No more than the Synoptists does John depict a Jesus who works the kind of miracle that will compel faith. The signs stimulate faith indeed. But they are not of such a type that men must believe when they see them as John 6 shows. Jesus' words about those who demand "signs and wonders" before they believe leave us in no doubt but that He repudiates their attitude (4 : 48).

It is plain that John uses "sign" in a distinctive fashion. For him the miracles were significant events. They set forth spiritual truths. We see this, not only in the meaning of this one word, but in the way John arranges his narratives. In them he exposes facet after facet of human need, showing at one and the same time man's inadequacy and Jesus' all-sufficiency. At Cana with the turning of water into wine this concerns man's inability to cope with the demands of those festivities which are normal to human life. In the case of the nobleman's son and of the man lame for thirty-eight years it is man's helplessness in the face of disease and of the tragedy of crippling physical disability. The feeding of the multitude shows up the barrenness of human resources even to supply necessary food (a lesson very much in place in the modern world), while Jesus' walking on the water contrasts with man's helplessness in the face of the awesome forces of nature unleashed in a storm. The opening of the eyes of the blind man shows man's failure to cope with innate handicaps while it also shows Jesus to be the light of the world. The raising of the dead Lazarus underlines human defeat by death while it reveals Jesus as the resurrection and the life. Each miracle is significant, meaningful.[72] Rightly considered it points men to

---

[72] Hoskyns points out that the "signs" in the Bible, and supremely in John, "are usually of such a kind as to anticipate and show forth the nature both of what will take place and of the work of Him whom they authenticate . . . They are not narrated as prodigies, or wonders, nor do they merely authenticate Jesus. They are quite properly signs or parables of the nature of His work" (p. 190).

God,[73] and to God's provision in Jesus. If men will only view the miracles as they should they will be led into an ever deeper faith. From this point of view the σημεῖα represent a challenge, a call to faith.[74]

It is also worth pointing out that for John the "sign" was something akin to the "signs" employed by the prophets and which are now widely recognized as an integral part of their message. The "sign" did things. Thus the sign at Cana set forth the life-giving power of Christ over against the ritualism of Judaism and His disciples believed (2 : 11). The healing of the nobleman's son points to Jesus as the Life, and the life came to the nobleman and his house (4 : 53). The healing of the man born blind shows Jesus as "the Light of the world" and leaves the man with light for his body and light for his soul (9 : 38). So is it with other signs. For John the "sign" is effectual.

We should also notice that on all three occasions when John uses the cognate verb σημαίνω it refers to death (twice the death of Jesus, 12 : 33; 18 : 32, and once that of Peter, 21 : 19). The "signs" are significant for they are wrought as part of the work of Him whose supreme work was to die for men.

But this is not all John has to say about the miracles, and his use of ἔργον is also interesting. The word can be used of the deeds of men, whether these deeds are good or evil. For the evil see 3 : 19, 20; 7 : 7; 8 : 41, and for good deeds 3 : 21; 6 : 28, 29; 8 : 39; 14 : 12. It is not without its interest that these good deeds may sometimes be spoken of as "the works of God" (6 : 28, 29). It may be that this hints at the derivative nature of good works. They do not originate in man himself. The one passage in which Jesus looks forward to the works that His followers would do after He is taken from them is very striking, for He assures them that "He that believeth on me, the works that I do shall he do also; and greater works than these shall he do" (14 : 12).

---

[73] Barrett insists on the Christological significance of the signs: "The miracles of Jesus, then, are not merely, as in the synoptic gospels, signs that the kingdom of God is at hand, but also clear indications that he by whom the signs are wrought is the Son of God and equal to God himself" (p. 65).

[74] Riga sees in the signs of the Fourth Gospel an equivalent to the parables of the Synoptics. Both at one and the same time conceal and reveal truth. And both are a challenge to believe in Jesus.

But John's characteristic use of ἔργον is for the works of Jesus.[75] Of the 27 times he uses the word 18 times he applies it to what Jesus has done. He uses the term in a variety of ways. Clearly it applies to the miracles on some occasions, *e.g.*, "I did one work, and ye all marvel because thereof" (7 : 21). On other occasions it refers to the whole of Jesus' earthly work, as when He refers in prayer to "having accomplished the work which thou hast given me to do" (17 : 4). The word may be used in the singular, of an individual act or of the sum total of His earthly life, or the plural may be used of many individual deeds.

Jesus' works are characterized as "the works which none other did" (15 : 24). They are distinctive works. They are not to be compared to those of other men. Indeed, in a sense they are not the works of Christ at all but of His Father. The Father, He says, "loveth the Son, and showeth him all things that himself doeth: and greater works than these will he show him, that ye may marvel" (5 : 20). There is no doubt but that it is the works done by Christ that are meant. But Jesus recognizes these to be the Father's works. He Himself does not originate them. "The Father abiding in me doeth his works" (14 : 10). Thus He can say that it is His very meat to accomplish the Father's work (4 : 34; the word is singular), and He can speak of the works that the Father has given Him to do (5 : 36). Again, at the end of His life He could say, "I glorified thee on the earth, having accomplished the work which thou hast given me to do" (17 : 4). ἔργον here

---

[75] A. Richardson does not notice this when he says that John "does not call (the miracles) δυνάμεις but σημεῖα; occasionally he uses the relatively colourless word 'works' (ἔργα) . . ." (*The Miracle Stories of the Gospels*, London, 1959, p. 30). It is perhaps this failure to perceive the importance of John's use of ἔργον which leads him to deny any distinctiveness in the Johannine view of miracles. It is true that for John, as for the Synoptists, the miracles "are evidence (not to the general public, but only to those who have eyes to see) as to Who Jesus is" (*op. cit.*, p. 31). But there is more to it in John. "Works", for him, is not a colorless term, but a way of linking the miracles with the non-miraculous. It shows that the whole of Jesus' life glowed with the divine glory, and that the miracles and the rest of Jesus' life alike represent the outworking of a single consistent divine purpose.

stands for His complete life work. On one occasion He says that a man was born blind "that the works of God should be made manifest in him", and He adds: "We must work the works of him that sent me" (9 : 3f.). Again, Jesus can say to the Jews: "Many good works have I showed you from the Father" (10 : 32). It is plain enough that Jesus regards His characteristic works as originating with the Father.

Now these works have a function in teaching men. They have value as revelation. More than once Jesus spoke of the works that He did as "testifying" of Him (5 : 36; 10 : 25). And if His works testified, it is important that men should heed their testimony. So He could tell His hearers not to believe Him if He does not do the works of the Father. He adds: "But if I do them, though ye believe not me, believe the works: that ye may know and understand that the Father is in me, and I in the Father" (10 : 37f.). So again He can say, "believe me for the very works' sake" (14 : 11). His word and works are closely connected, for He can say, "the words that I say unto you I speak not from myself: but the Father abiding in me doeth his works" (14 : 10). Clearly the works, like the signs, have a revelatory function.

From all this we see that ἔργον is an important word in John's understanding of the miracles. It is not without its interest that this is the term Jesus usually employs for the miracles in this Gospel. He uses σημεῖον on two occasions, but apart from these He always refers to ἔργα. This is surely a very important fact, but it is missed by many who see no farther than John's preference for σημεῖον over the Synoptic δύναμις. There must be significance in Jesus' own preference for ἔργον. We may discern part of this at any rate from the intrinsic meaning of the word, and the fact that it can be applied to the ordinary deeds of men. What to men are miracles, to God and to Christ are no more than "works". This is their normal way of working.

And besides being used more often than σημεῖον, ἔργον is used in a greater variety of ways. Perhaps it would be true to say that where John sees miracles from one point of view as σημεῖα, activities pointing men to God, from another point of view he sees them as ἔργα, activities which take their origin in God. But because they originate with God they have a revelatory function and they also point men to God. Therefore John can look for faith on the basis of the "works" just as much as on the basis of

690

"signs". ἔργον for him is the fuller word.[76] It includes what we would call the "natural" activities of Jesus as well as the "supernatural". It reminds us that these are all of a piece, that Jesus' whole life was consistently spent in doing the will of God and in accomplishing His purpose. Not only in the miracles, but in all His life He was showing forth God's glory.[77]

There is probably another thought behind John's use of the term ἔργον. The same word is used consistently in the Old Testament of the works of God. Perhaps especially important are the passages in which it is used of His works in creation (Gen. 2 : 2f.; Ps. 8 : 3; 104 : 24, etc.), and in delivering His people from Egypt (Ps. 44 : 1; 95 : 9, etc.). But in view of the way in which Jesus is seen in this Gospel to be fulfilling what is foreshadowed in other works of God in the Old Testament (giving the true manna, the living water, the true light, etc.) we should not limit the use of the word too narrowly. What John is doing then is indicating the continuity of the work of God in the Old Testament with that which He does in the ministry of Jesus. This is seen in all manner of activities but especially in those of creation and salvation. The "wondrous works" of God are brought to their climax and fulfilment in the "works" of Christ. There is a unity here. And it is probably no coincidence that the great saying "I and the Father are one" (10 : 30) is made in a context which deals with the "works". Unity of action means unity of being.[78]

---

[76] R. H. Lightfoot misses this in his preference for σημεῖον. He says that Jesus' "whole life is a sign, in action, of the love of God" (p. 23). But to get this into the word he has had to say "it would be a mistake to confine the word to those of His actions which are expressly so described." The point about ἔργον is that it is not necessary to make such an assertion. It is used expressly of the whole range of Jesus' activities. E. M. Sidebottom can say that the works "include the signs but are also more than these . . . In the Fourth Gospel the works are closely associated with the manifestation of the character of God. John in fact stresses that like produces like and that only the good produces the good, so that good works reveal God" (*The Christ of the Fourth Gospel*, London, 1961, p. 157).

[77] Westcott says that τὰ ἔργα in John describes "the whole outward manifestation of Christ's activity, both those acts which we call supernatural and those which we call natural. All alike are wrought in fulfilment of one plan and by one power" (on 5 : 36).

[78] Riga says with reference to John 10 : 30 as set in a context of works: "The operation or activity of these works is, in reality, that of the Father; the works of salvation and life-giving are given to the Son while remaining the Father's. Christ has the full power of judgment and vivification because he does not work of himself or alone, but works in unity with the power of the Father" (*op. cit.*, p. 419).

CHAPTER XVI

(b) A Warning of Coming Persecutions, 16 : 1–4

1 These things have I spoken unto you, that ye should not be caused to stumble. 2 They shall put you out of the synagogues: yea, the hour cometh, that whosoever killeth you shall think that he offereth service unto God. 3 And these things will they do, because they have not known the Father, nor me. 4 But these things have I spoken unto you, that when their hour is come, ye may remember them, how that I told you. And these things I said not unto you from the beginning, because I was with you.

The work of the Holy Spirit in the church is done in the context of persecution. The Spirit is not a guide and a helper for those on a straight way perfectly able to manage on their own. He comes to assist men caught up in the thick of battle, and tried beyond their strength. Jesus makes it quite plain that the way before His followers is a hard and a difficult way.

1 For "these things have I spoken unto you" see on 14 : 25. Jesus' discourse is purposive. He has spoken *in order that* His followers may not "be caused to stumble".[1] This last expression looks forward to excommunication and the like. The disciples will undergo sore trials and Jesus is preparing them for them. As Temple reminds us, "it is hard to believe that a cause is truly God's when it seems to meet with no success, and all power is on the other side." But Jesus prepares them so that they will not be taken by surprise and overcome in the collapse of a starry-eyed optimism.

2 Their enemies will excommunicate them.[2] The term indicates the loss of all fellowship. Jesus has often spoken of His "hour".

---

[1] For $\sigma\kappa\alpha\nu\delta\alpha\lambda\acute{\iota}\zeta\omega$ see on 6 : 61. Knox's rendering, "so that your faith may not be taken unawares", brings out the element of surprise involved in the release of the bait-stick of a trap, while *Berkeley's*, "so you may not be trapped" stresses the metaphor. *Cf.* Lenski: "The disciples are fully informed as to what discipleship really means; all of its hard and painful features are fully disclosed – no trap is laid for them."

[2] For $\dot{\alpha}\pi\sigma\sigma\upsilon\nu\acute{\alpha}\gamma\omega\gamma\sigma\varsigma$ see on 9 : 22.

In this passage[3] "the hour"[4] and again "their hour" (v. 4) may possibly be meant to awake memories of the other expression. Be that as it may, Jesus looks forward to a time when men's values will be so perverted that a man who kills[5] His followers will think[6] that he is serving[7] God.[8] It is not persecution by a secular state that is in mind, but that set in train by religious authorities. Pilcher aptly reminds us that "A sermon was preached at the burning of Archbishop Cranmer, and the horrors of the Inquisition were carried out with a perfectly good conscience." It is the tragedy of religious man that he so often regards persecution as in line with the will of God.

3 "These things will they do" indicates certainty. Jesus is not speaking about one possible outcome of present circumstances. He is warning His followers of what will certainly follow. They will suffer for their faith. The reason for the action of the persecutors is their complete ignorance[9] both of the Father and of

---

3 The strong adversative ἀλλ' (ARV, "yea") is used once again to introduce a proposition contrary, not to the preceding statement, but to everything that might have been expected. The adversative force might perhaps be retained with such a rendering as "Nay, more". BDF sees it as an example of ἀλλά in the sense, " 'not only this, but also', used to introduce an additional point in an emphatic way" (448(6)). Turner sees it as "Introducing a strong addition" with the sense, "yes, indeed" (M, III, p. 330). For John's use of the term see on 1 : 8.

4 ἔρχεται ὥρα is rather a stately expression, and not at all what one might have anticipated. Indeed the point could well have been made without it. Thus one is reminded of other references in this Gospel to a coming "hour" (see on 2 : 4). On the other hand there is no article with ὥρα and this may be significant. We should probably not connect it too closely with these other passages.

5 Notice the characteristic πᾶς ὁ with participle for "he who". The aorist (which is not common in John in this connection) regards the act as a completed whole.

6 Is δόξῃ connected with John's frequent use of δόξα? The error of the man in question is that he has a wrong idea of δόξα.

7 λατρεία, here only in John (elsewhere in the New Testament, Rom. 9 : 4; 12 : 1; Heb. 9 : 1,6), denotes worship as well as the more general idea of the service of God. This gives a piquant flavor to the use of the term here. *Twentieth Century* translates, "will think that he is making an offering to God".

8 In the Mishnah homicide was encouraged against those who committed certain offences (*Sanh.* 9 : 6). SBk cites a Midrash on Num. 25 : 13, "whoever sheds the blood of the godless is as one who offers a sacrifice" (II, p. 565).

9 The aorist οὐκ ἔγνωσαν may signify "failed to recognize" (Weymouth); *cf.* Rieu: "did not learn to know".

693

the Son. Characteristically this passage links the two together. The Father is known as He really is only through the revelation made in the Son. To be ignorant of the one is therefore necessarily to be ignorant of the other. There is, of course, an ignorance which is natural and which is not blameworthy. But in this Gospel the ignorance of the Jews is always regarded as culpable, because they ought to have known the truth. God had revealed Himself, but they had not considered the revelation. In this verse He is called "the Father", not "my Father", nor "him that sent me". Jesus speaks of Him in the relationship in which the Jews ought to have recognized Him.

4 Jesus gives the reason for His warning at this particular time. It had not been necessary for Him to say these things earlier because He had been with them. His presence in the flesh had meant that He could give guidance day by day, and it also meant that the venom of the enemy would be directed against Him rather than them. While the Master was with them the disciples were a negligible quantity in the eyes of their opponents. The removal of the Master would transform the situation. Now the hostility will be directed at them. Therefore on the threshold of His departure from them Jesus tells them plainly what is going to happen so that they will not be overtaken by surprise. When the trials come they will know that they are no more than Jesus[10] had predicted. Thus, instead of being a difficulty to faith, the trials would actually strengthen faith. When the trials came they would remember that this is just what Jesus said would happen. There is dramatic fitness in the use of "their hour", when we recall the way in which Christ's own "hour" is spoken of (see on 2 : 4). Just as His "hour" would certainly come, so would His enemies' "hour" certainly come. But in how different a sense! This section of discourse ends with an indication that things were changing. At the beginning[11] Jesus had not said these things for He was with them. The implication is that persecution then would fall on Him, not them. But not at the time of which He speaks. Things will be different.

---

[10] Note the emphatic ἐγώ, "that *I* told you" (see on 1 : 20).
[11] For the unusual ἐξ ἀρχῆς see on 6 : 64.

(c) The Work of the Spirit, 16 : 5–15

5 But now I go unto him that sent me; and none of you asketh me, Whither goest thou? 6 But because I have spoken these things unto you, sorrow hath filled your heart. 7 Nevertheless I tell you the truth: It is expedient for you that I go away; for if I go not away, the ¹Comforter will not come unto you; but if I go, I will send him unto you. 8 And he, when he is come, will convict the world in respect of sin, and of righteousness, and of judgment: 9 of sin, because they believe not on me; 10 of righteousness, because I go to the Father, and ye behold me no more; 11 of judgment, because the prince of this world hath been judged. 12 I have yet many things to say unto you, but ye cannot bear them now. 13 Howbeit when he, the Spirit of truth, is come, he shall guide you into all the truth: for he shall not speak from himself; but what things soever he shall hear, these shall he speak: and he shall declare unto you the things that are to come. 14 He shall glorify me: for he shall take of mine, and shall declare it unto you. 15 All things whatsoever the Father hath are mine: therefore said I, that he taketh of mine, and shall declare it unto you.

¹Or, *Advocate* Or, *Helper* Gr. *Paraclete.*

From the thought of the persecutions His followers will have to face Jesus turns to the resources available to them. He will send them the Spirit who will supply their need abundantly. We have already had the thought of the Spirit as a Helper and Advocate (14 : 16f., 26; 15 : 26f.). Now we have the additional thought that He is a Prosecutor, convicting sinful men of being in the wrong.

5 "But now" points to altered circumstances. A change is imminent. Jesus is about to go to the Father, typically spoken of as "him that sent me" (*cf.* 7 : 33; and see on 3 : 17); Jesus' sense of mission remains. A difficulty is posed by His statement that nobody[12] asks "Whither goest thou?" in the light of Simon Peter's earlier question, "Lord, whither goest thou?" (13 : 36). But that question had not really indicated a serious inquiry as to Jesus' destination. Peter was diverted immediately and he made no real

---

12   καί is used in the sense of καίτοι, "and yet", as often in this Gospel, especially in the expression καὶ οὐδείς (see on 1 : 5).

attempt to find out where Jesus was going. He had been concerned with the thought of parting from Jesus, not with that of the Master's destination. He had in mind only the consequences for himself and his fellows. Neither he nor they had as yet made serious inquiry as to what was to become of Jesus.[13] So does self-interest blind men.

6 For "I have spoken these things unto you" see on 14 : 25. Because[14] of Jesus' words, sorrow,[15] He says, "hath filled your heart" (for the singular, "heart", see on 14 : 1). The perfect is somewhat strange since sorrow was to give way to joy (v. 20). The thought may be that when Jesus was taken from them a sorrow would enter their hearts that would not cease until the Easter joy replaced it. The pain of parting would be very real.

7 Jesus now assures the disciples that it is expedient for them that He should leave them. The word "It is expedient" is the same as that used by Caiaphas (11 : 50), and we may profitably reflect that this is the supreme illustration of the way God takes the acts of wicked men and uses them to effect His purpose. Caiaphas thought the crucifixion expedient. So it was, but in a way and for a reason that he could not guess. The statement here is important and Jesus prefixes it with "Nevertheless I tell you the truth" (*cf.* 8 : 45f.). These words are not necessary for the sense but they add weight and emphasis to what follows. The expression "It is expedient for you"[16] should be noted. To the disciples the departure of Jesus seemed disastrous: actually it was for their profit.[17] There are two things involved. The one is that it is better

---

[13] Strachan reminds us that this is often the case still: "Exclusive interest to-day in the historic Jesus, as distinct from the risen and ascended Lord, still exemplifies this refusal to ask the question He desired His disciples to ask, *Whither goest thou?* We cannot understand Jesus, and the mind of Jesus, unless we take into account that He Himself did not regard His earthly life as a sufficient revelation."

[14] For causal ὅτι see on 1 : 50.

[15] λύπη receives some stress in this chapter (vv. 20, 21, 22), but it does not occur elsewhere in John.

[16] συμφέρει ὑμῖν. AG give the verb's meaning as "1. *bring together* . . . 2. *help, confer a benefit, be advantageous* or *profitable* or *useful*. . . ."

[17] Bernard comments, "there is a better education in discipleship than that which can be supplied by a visible master, whose will for his disciples can never be misunderstood. The braver and more perfect disciple is he who can walk by faith, and not by sight only. . . ." He goes on to quote Gore, "the Coming of the Holy Ghost was not merely to supply the absence of the Son, but to complete His presence."

for them not to be dependent on the visible, bodily presence of Christ. But the other, and more important, reason is that the Spirit (for "the Comforter" see Additional Note F, pp. 662ff.) will not come until Jesus goes away.[18] Why is not said, but in 7 : 39 (where see note) John has explained that the Spirit was not then given "because Jesus was not yet glorified". So now the implication is that the cross is critical. Before that Jesus could not send the Spirit. Afterwards He will send Him (*cf.* 15 : 26). It is the divine concern to bring about a full salvation for men. That salvation can be based on nothing but Christ's atoning work. Only when that is accomplished can men receive the Spirit in all His fullness. The truth behind Jesus' words may be discerned by reflecting that at the end of His visible sojourn with them "they all left him, and fled" (Mark 14 : 50). But at the beginning of the new era inaugurated by the coming of the Spirit "they spake the word of God with boldness" (Acts 4 : 31); they were found "rejoicing that they were counted worthy to suffer dishonor for the Name" (Acts 5 : 41).

8 When the Spirit is come He will "convict the world". This is the one place in Scripture where the Spirit is spoken of as performing a work in "the world". The many other references refer to what He will do with believers. We have seen that the word translated "Comforter" is a word with legal implications (see Additional Note F, pp. 662ff.). Normally it denotes a person whose activities are in favor of the defendant. Here, however, the meaning is that the Spirit will act as prosecutor and bring about the world's conviction.[19] This is given a threefold qualification which is further developed in the succeeding verses. Apart from

---

[18] For "go away" ἀπέλθω replaces ὑπάγω of v. 5, while a third verb, πορευθῶ, appears in "but if I go". It seems useless to try to distinguish between these. The change from one to another is sufficiently accounted for by John's habit of introducing minor changes in repetitions. There is no significant difference in meaning. For John's use of ὑπάγω see on 7 : 33.

[19] *Cf.* Bernard, "ἐλέγχειν is to cross-examine for the purpose of convincing or refuting an opponent (the word being specially used of legal proceedings)". He sees an example of what is meant in Acts 2 : 36f. where those who heard the preaching were "pricked to the heart". *Cf.* also I Cor. 14 : 24. Some measure of the difficulty of finding an exact English equivalent may be gauged from the fact that both Rieu and Phillips use four different translations in verses 8–11, and they do not agree in any one of the four places.

the Holy Spirit men do not really know the truth about sin or righteousness or judgment. [20]

9 The Greek underlying these verses can be taken in any one of three principal ways. It may mean "He will convict the world (of wrong ideas) of sin, in that they do not believe", [21] "He will convict the world of its sin because they do not believe" (*i.e.* their unbelief is a classic illustration of their sin), [22] or "He will convict the world of its sin (which consists in the fact) that they do not believe" (*i.e.* their unbelief is their sin). None of these is impossible, and in the Johannine manner more than one may be intended. If we have to choose, then (with Barrett) it seems as though the second is most likely to be correct. The basic sin is the sin which puts self at the centre of things and consequently refuses to believe. This is the world's characteristic sin and it received classic expression when God sent His Son into the world and the world refused to believe in Him. The world is guilty, but it requires the Spirit to sheet this home. The Spirit convicts the world in two senses. In the first place He "shows the world to be guilty", *i.e.* He secures a verdict of "Guilty" against the world. But in the second place we should take the words to mean also that the Spirit brings the world's guilt home to itself. The Spirit convicts the individual sinner's conscience. Otherwise men would never be convicted of their sin.

10 The righteousness [23] which is shown by Christ's going to the Father is surely that righteousness which is established by the Christ. It is precisely this righteousness which requires the work

---

[20] *Cf.* Westcott: "He will not simply convict the world as sinful, as without righteousness, as under judgement, but He will show beyond contradiction that it is wanting in the knowledge of what sin, righteousness, and judgement really are". He further points out that the world regarded Jesus as a sinner (9 : 24), and itself as righteous (Luke 18 : 9), and that it was on the point of giving judgement against Him. On all three points it was in disastrous error, and needed correction.

[21] Taking περί to mean "with regard to".

[22] In the second and third cases ἐλέγχειν means "to convict of", but in the second case ὅτι means "because" and in the third, "that".

[23] δικαιοσύνη is found in John only here and in v. 8. Barrett sees the death and resurrection of Jesus as showing the righteousness both of Christ and of God: "Jesus' death proved his complete obedience to the will of God, and his exaltation proved that his righteousness was approved by more than human acclamation."

of the Holy Spirit for men to be convinced about it. [24] The Spirit shows men (and no-one else can do this) that their righteousness before God depends not on their own efforts but on Christ's atoning work for them. "Ye behold me no more" might refer to the cross, when Jesus was removed from them. Or it might look through the cross to the ascension when His bodily form was finally taken aware from them.

11 The work of judgment is referred to the defeat of Satan on the cross. For "the prince of this world" see on 12 : 31. The defeat of Satan is not an arbitrary feat of power, but a judgment. Justice is done in the overthrow of the evil one.

It should not be overlooked that all three aspects of the work of the Holy Spirit dealt with in these verses are interpreted Christologically. Sin, righteousness and judgment are all to be understood because of the way they relate to the Christ.

12, 13 From the work of the Spirit in the world Jesus turns to His work in believers. First He speaks of having many things yet to say to the disciples. He does not explain "but ye cannot bear them now". "Bear" is an unusual verb in this connection.[25] It may mean that their experience thus far sets a limit to their ability to perceive. There are vistas of truth set before them which they cannot as yet enter, but they will enter when the Spirit[26] comes. More probably it refers to their inability, until the Spirit should come, to live out the implications of the revelation.[27] This

---

[24] Barclay comments: "When you think of it, it is an amazing thing that men should put their trust for all eternity in a crucified Jewish criminal. What *convinces* men that this crucified Jew is the Son of God? *That is the work of the Holy Spirit.* It is the Holy Spirit who convinces men of the sheer righteousness of Christ. . . ."

[25] βαστάζω is used of raising stones (10 : 31), of carrying a burden (19 : 17 and often), and figuratively of enduring anything burdensome (Gal. 6 : 2). It may be used of bearing Christ's name (Acts 9 : 15), but the present passage is the only one where the thought is that of bearing words. Pallis suggests that it may be a Latinism, reproducing *tenere*.

[26] The conjunction, ἐκεῖνος, τὸ Πνεῦμα τῆς ἀληθείας, is noteworthy, with the masculine pronoun in immediate juxtaposition to the neuter noun. It emphasizes the fact that John thought of the Spirit as personal.

[27] *Cf.* MiM: "the most glorious and encouraging truths may become a burden to one too immature to bear them. Not, therefore, because the disciples could not in a certain sense even now understand further revelation, but because they had not yet the Christian experience to give that revelation power, does Jesus say that they cannot bear the many things that He has yet to say unto them."

latter is more in keeping with the meaning of the verb "bear". The Spirit is called "the Spirit of truth" (see on 14 : 17), for His work here is to guide[28] the followers of Jesus into "all the truth".[29] As the days go by the Spirit will lead them deeper and deeper into a knowledge of truth.[30] In passing we should notice that the attempt of some scholars to "go back to the original Jesus" and by-pass the teaching of the apostles is shown by our Lord Himself to be misguided. The same source lies behind both. The Spirit's teaching is not from Himself, but He teaches "what things soever he shall hear". It is not said whether He hears them from the Father or the Son, but the point is probably not material. The emphasis in these verses is on the Spirit rather than on either of the other Persons. This expression will indicate His harmony with Them. He is not originating something radically new, but leading men in accordance with the teaching already given from the Father and the Son. The declaring of "the things that are to come" is somewhat puzzling. While the Spirit has on occasion revealed the future, that is not His characteristic work. Usually even spiritually-minded Christians are ignorant of what lies ahead. Perhaps the expression means that He will supply what is needed as it is

---

[28] This is the only place where John uses the verb ὁδηγέω (cf. Rev. 7 : 17). It may connect with the fact that Christ is the ὁδός, as He is also the Truth to which the Spirit leads (14 : 6).

[29] There are textual problems in this verse, notably whether we should read εἰς τὴν ἀλήθειαν πᾶσαν with AB (πᾶσαν τὴν ἀλήθειαν, f13 28 700) or ἐν τῇ ἀληθείᾳ πάσῃ with ℵ D W (Θ). Some think the variants significant, the former signifying "lead you into all the truth", i.e. bring you to further knowledge, and the latter "lead you in all the truth", i.e. lead you in the path of the truth already revealed. In view of the difficulty of making a firm distinction between εἰς and ἐν not too much, however, should be made of this. It seems that εἰς should be accepted as the right reading, but even if ἐν be accepted the meaning will not differ greatly. Barrett, however, who accepts ἐν, thinks this reading "suggests guidance in the whole sphere of truth". FF renders: "He will instruct you in all the truth". I. de la Potterie argues that εἰς in John always has a dynamic sense as in the classics (Biblica, XLIII, 1962, pp. 366–387). In this verse he discerns a "formula which describes very well the penetration into (εἰς) the whole truth of Christ under the action of the Spirit" (op. cit., p. 373).

[30] The significance of the article in τὴν ἀλήθειαν is stressed by Tasker. The words do not mean that the church will be led to a full knowledge of the truth on all manner of subjects. What is meant is "the specific truth about the Person of Jesus and the significance of what He said and did." Perhaps we could say that the words must be interpreted in the light of 14 : 6.

needed. More likely "the things to come" is a way of referring to the whole Christian system, yet future when Jesus spoke, and to be revealed to the disciples by the Spirit, not by natural insight.[31] Not a few scholars discern an eschatological reference. They remind us of the fact that Jesus foretold calamities, and specifically dire persecution of His followers, in the last days. They remind us also that He promised the help of the Spirit when they stood before hostile tribunals (Mark 13 : 11). This passage they see accordingly as the Johannine counterpart of this strand of Synoptic teaching. This is not impossible, but it does seem to be reading something into the words. It is better to take the sense as, "He will show you the whole Christian way". Hoskyns sees vv. 16–24 as supporting if not actually rendering necessary the view that these "things to come" refer to what is imminent rather than to the End.

14 The work of the Spirit is Christocentric. He will draw attention not to Himself but to Christ.[32] He will glorify Christ. It is the things of Christ[33] that He takes and declares,[34] i.e. His ministry is built upon and is the necessary sequel to that of Christ.

15 There is no division in the Godhead. What the Father has the Son has (cf. 17 : 10). The previous verse does not mean that the Spirit will concentrate attention on Christ to the exclusion of the Father. It is because of the community between the Father and Himself that Jesus can speak in the way He has just done. Just as the Spirit is concerned to set forward the things of Christ so is He concerned to set forward the things of the Father.

6. SOME DIFFICULTIES SOLVED, 16 : 16–33

Jesus proceeds to deal with certain difficulties felt by the

---

[31] Calvin takes the words in this sense: "in my opinion it signifies the future state of His spiritual kingdom, which the apostles saw soon after His resurrection but were then quite unable to comprehend."

[32] $\dot{\epsilon}\mu\dot{\epsilon}$ is emphatic both from its form and its position. There is some emphasis also on $\dot{\epsilon}\varkappa\epsilon\tilde{\iota}\nu o\varsigma$.

[33] Notice the typical Johannine variation, $\dot{\epsilon}\varkappa\ \tau o\tilde{v}\ \dot{\epsilon}\mu o\tilde{v} \ldots \dot{\epsilon}\mu\acute{a} \ldots \dot{\epsilon}\varkappa\ \tau o\tilde{v}\ \dot{\epsilon}\mu o\tilde{v}$. There does not seem to be a real difference between singular and plural.

[34] There is a typical Johannine variation in the threefold "he shall declare unto you" (vv. 13, 14, 15). First the object is $\tau\grave{a}\ \dot{\epsilon}\varrho\chi\acute{o}\mu\epsilon\nu a$ while both the others concern $\dot{\epsilon}\varkappa\ \tau o\tilde{v}\ \dot{\epsilon}\mu o\tilde{v}$. But in v. 14 the verb "take" is in the future and in v. 15 it is in the present. Notice another Johannine characteristic in the repetition of the words $\dot{a}\nu a\gamma\gamma\epsilon\lambda\epsilon\tilde{\iota}\ \dot{v}\mu\tilde{\iota}\nu$, which puts emphasis on this aspect of the Spirit's work.

disciples. This does not mean that His words were immediately understood in all the fulness of their meaning or that the disciples consciously felt that their problems had been solved. In some ways they were just as puzzled as before. But important truths were spoken. The answer was given. In due course the full implications of Jesus' words would be unfolded.

(a) The Disciples' Perplexity, 16: 16–18

16 A little while, and ye behold me no more; and again a little while, and ye shall see me. 17 Some of his disciples therefore said one to another, What is this that he saith unto us, A little while, and ye behold me not; and again a little while, and ye shall see me: and, Because I go to the Father? 18 They said therefore, What is this that he saith, A little while? We know not what he saith.

It is not surprising that these words of Jesus proved a difficulty to the men in the upper room. They have puzzled Christians ever since. The main problem concerns the meaning of the coming again of which Jesus speaks. Does He mean that He will come again in the person and work of the Holy Spirit? Or is He referring to the post-resurrection appearances? Or even to the ascension and the parousia? Great names can be urged in support of each of these views. Barrett is of opinion that the ambiguity is deliberate: "By this ambiguity John means to convey that the death and resurrection were themselves eschatological events which both prefigured and anticipated the final events." In these verses we are concerned not with the resolution of the difficulty, but with its statement. But it seems to me that the language accords better with a reference to Jesus' death and then to the post-resurrection appearances than to anything else (though this is not to deny that, as often, there may also be a secondary meaning as well). 16 Jesus declares that there is but "a little while"[35] before He will be taken from them.[36] There can scarcely be any doubt but

---

[35] For μικρόν see on 13 : 33.

[36] οὐκέτι, rendered "no more" ("ye behold me no more"), means "no longer". It carries no necessary implication of "never again" (for John's use of οὐκέτι see on 4 : 42).

702

that this refers to His approaching death. He uses the same expression for the time interval, "a little while", before they will see Him again. The words seem to favor a literal seeing of Jesus Himself rather than a metaphorical reference to the work of the Spirit.[37] As far as they go then, the words point to the post-resurrection appearances.

17 The words certainly were mysterious to men who stood on the other side of the cross. It is not surprising that the disciples were puzzled. Some of them express their bewilderment (characteristically there is a small change from the way Jesus puts it in the previous verse[38]). It is noteworthy that they couple "Because I go to the Father" with the words about the "little while"[39] when they shall not see Him and then shall see Him. Either they perceive that there is some link between the two, or else they are carrying on a difficulty that they felt earlier (the words about going to the Father were spoken in v. 10). Notice that they do not ask Jesus to explain Himself. Their words are spoken "one to another".

18 The heart of the difficulty for them was the reference to "a little while".[40] They concentrate on that.[41] And they see no solution. Godet sagely remarks: "Where for us all is clear, for

---

[37] ὄψεσθε is sometimes used of spiritual vision (1 : 51) and it is argued accordingly that here it must refer to the coming of the Holy Spirit (so also in v. 19). This, however, scarcely seems to be justified. The verb can be used of ordinary, earthly sight (1 : 39). That it is suitable for referring to the post-resurrection appearances seems clear from the use of the perfect ἑώρακα for seeing the risen Lord in 20 : 18, 25, 29. It is not easy to find in the verb itself evidence that the coming of the Spirit is meant (though cf. ὤφθησαν of the tongues of fire in Acts 2 : 3). A small point telling against the distinction from θεωρέω is the double use of the latter verb in 14 : 19 where we might legitimately have expected variation if John really did distinguish between the two verbs. For ὁράω see on 1 : 18, and for θεωρέω on 2 : 23.

[38] Jesus says οὐκέτι θεωρεῖτε με, but their negative is οὐ: "not" is substituted for "no more". In taking up their words (v. 19) Jesus uses their version and not His own original form of the saying.

[39] "The way in which the changes are rung on the expression a little while, suggests that the Evangelist has before him the actual expression used by Jesus" (Strachan).

[40] The article before μικρόν has the effect of marking out this word as the difficult one.

[41] ἔλεγον may well be continuous "they were saying" or "they kept saying"; cf. Weymouth: "they asked one another repeatedly".

them all was mysterious. If Jesus wishes to found the Messianic kingdom, why go away? If He does not wish it, why return?"

(b) The Disciples' Joy, 16: 19–24

19 Jesus perceived that they were desirous to ask him, and he said unto them, Do ye inquire among yourselves concerning this, that I said, A little while, and ye behold me not, and again a little while, and ye shall see me? 20 Verily, verily, I say unto you, that ye shall weep and lament, but the world shall rejoice: ye shall be sorrowful, but your sorrow shall be turned into joy. 21 A woman when she is in travail hath sorrow, because her hour is come: but when she is delivered of the child, she remembereth no more the anguish, for the joy that a man is born into the world. 22 And ye therefore now have sorrow: but I will see you again, and your heart shall rejoice, and your joy no one taketh away from you. 23 And in that day ye shall ¹ask me no question. Verily, verily, I say unto you, If ye shall ask anything of the Father, he will give it you in my name. 24 Hitherto have ye asked nothing in my name: ask, and ye shall receive, that your joy may be made full.

¹Or, *ask me nothing* Comp. ver. 26; ch. 14. 13, 20.

Jesus replies to the need, rather than to the question, of the disciples. He points out that there may be anguish, like that of a travailing woman, that is purposeful. It must be gone through, but when that is done the person forgets it for the joy at the result. So they must go through a time of deep sorrow. But out of it will emerge an abounding joy.

19 It is not likely that John wants us to think of Jesus' understanding that the disciples were perplexed[42] as due to supernatural knowledge. After all, they were speaking openly to one another.[43]

---

[42] Abbott notes a difference between $\vartheta\acute{\epsilon}\lambda\omega$ with the aorist (*e.g.* 6 : 21; 7 : 44) and with the present, even when, as here, the reference is to particular actions. He suggests that, perhaps, $\grave{\epsilon}\varrho\omega\tau\tilde{\alpha}\nu$, " 'to be asking,' means 'to ask all about' the mysterious saying, and not merely to put a definite question. Or possibly... the present may denote an action *almost begun but stopped because Jesus anticipated the question*, 'they wished *(and were almost beginning)* to ask' " (2498).

[43] There is no thought of dispute. In John $\mu\epsilon\tau\acute{\alpha}$ after a verb of speaking *etc.* always seems to imply that the speakers are in agreement (6 : 43; 11 : 56; *cf.* Abbott, 2349). Moreover the verb is $\zeta\eta\tau\epsilon\tilde{\imath}\tau\epsilon$ not $\sigma\nu\nu\zeta\eta\tau\epsilon\tilde{\imath}\tau\epsilon$.

Jesus repeats their words. Interestingly He does not use exactly
the same words as in His original statement (v. 16), though the
difference is slight.[44] There was apparently some constraint on
the part of the disciples. They wanted to ask Him, yet they did
not.
20 For "Verily, verily" see on 1 : 51. The following words are
marked out as important. Jesus makes it clear that His followers
will have a difficult time while their enemies triumph, but He does
not explain this in detail. The saying is enigmatic. "Weep and
lament" combines the thoughts of deep grief and of the outward
expression given to that grief, while there is an emphatic contrast
between "ye" and "the world"[45] (for this latter term see Additional
Note B, pp. 126ff.). But Jesus does not end on the note of sorrow.[46]
The disciples' sorrow will become joy[47] (*cf.* 20 : 20). Again He
does not define this closely. They would still not understand
exactly what He had in mind. It may be significant that He does
not speak of their sorrow being replaced by joy, but of turning
into it. The very same thing, the cross, that would be to them
first a cause of sorrow would later become a source of joy. This
corresponds exactly to the illustration that follows. In childbirth
it is one and the same thing which is first a source of pain, then of
joy. Jesus is not speaking of an anguish which would be replaced
by a quite different joy.[48] Calvin sees the further thought that
"Christ means that the sorrow which they will endure for the sake
of the Gospel will be fruitful."

---

[44] The negative is changed from οὐκέτι to οὐ. In both places He uses
θεωρεῖτε in the first clause and ὄψεσθε in the second. For the suggestion that
ὄψεσθε denotes spiritual vision and thus points to the coming of the Spirit see
on v. 16.
[45] The emphatic pronoun ὑμεῖς is used, and it is placed at the very end
of its clause, immediately before ὁ δὲ κόσμος.
[46] Again the emphatic ὑμεῖς puts stress on the fact that it is they who
will suffer sorrow.
[47] "But" in this clause is ἀλλά, and not δέ as in the preceding. It indicates
that there is something unexpected in the joy which follows sorrow (*cf.* Abbott,
2058).
[48] Loyd sees another point: the woman "finds herself again in her child.
The disciples found themselves again in the risen Lord. Here is another purpose
of this darkness and anguish that we have to endure; namely, that we may
die to ourselves, in order that we may live in Christ, and through Him in
others."

705

21 Elsewhere in Scripture the thought of the travailing woman[49] is generally used to bring out such thoughts as the suddenness and the inevitability of the birth when the time has come. Here the thought is rather the contrast between the state of mind of the mother before and after the birth. During travail, she is in great distress.[50] But when the child is born[51] the distress is forgotten. What matters then is that "a man[52] is born into the world." Specially important as a background to these words are Old Testament passages like Isa. 26 : 17ff. (which combines the thoughts of childbirth and resurrection), Hos. 13 : 13–15 and perhaps Isa. 66 : 7–14.[53] Such passages point to an anguish like that of childbirth from which the new Israel would emerge. This leads to the well known thought of the birth pangs that would precede the coming of the Messiah. Such thoughts are important for an understanding of the present passage.[54]

22 The point of the "therefore" is difficult to see. What is clear is that Jesus sees the "sorrow" of the disciples[55] as already present. He is not looking to the distant future, but speaking of something that is imminent. It is even now upon them. But that is not the end. He will see them again.[56] This is not explained, but it seems to be another reference to the post-resurrection appearances. When this takes place a new state of affairs will have emerged. The disciples

---

[49] ἡ γυνή is general, the article denoting the class. Bernard points out that Abbott's view that it means *the* woman of a household, *i.e.* the wife, "is to miss the point." The words are "universally true".

[50] Both λύπη and θλῖψις are strong words. There is to be no doubt about the reality of the anguish that is to be turned into joy.

[51] ARV perhaps obscures the change of tense. τίκτῃ depicts the woman as in the act of childbirth, but the aorist γεννήσῃ sees the process as complete, "when she has given birth".

[52] "ἄνθρωπος is used in its proper sense, a *human being* (contrast ἀνήρ, an *adult male*)" (Barrett).

[53] See n. 56 below.

[54] Chrysostom says with reference to "a man" being born, "to my mind He here alludeth to His own Resurrection, and that He should be born not unto that death which bare the birth-pang, but unto the Kingdom" (LXXIX. 1; p. 292).

[55] For the third time in this passage the emphatic ὑμεῖς is used when the subject is the sorrow of the disciples. There can be no missing the point.

[56] The language resembles that of Isa. 66 : 14, καὶ ὄψεσθε, καὶ χαρήσεται ὑμῶν ἡ καρδία. We might have expected ὄψεσθε here also, but *cf.* I Cor. 13 : 12; Gal. 4 : 9. It is the divine knowledge and sight that matter, not the human.

will then rejoice[57] in a way which is permanent. No one will take away the joy they will then have. The thought is not, of course, that believers never know sorrow. It is rather that after they have come to understand the significance of the cross they are possessed by a deep-seated joy. This joy is independent of the world. The world did not give it and the world cannot take it away.

23 "In that day" perhaps points us to the rather frequent use of "that day" (or the plural, "those days") for the last great day (Mark 13 : 17, 19, 24, 32, *etc.*; *cf.* also Mark 13 : 11). But the primary reference will surely be to the time after the resurrection. It is not certain what meaning we should give to the word for "ask" in the first part of the verse.[58] ARV takes it to mean "ask a question". This is the proper meaning of the verb, though in late Greek it may be used also of asking for a boon. In view of the second part of the verse some suggest that this is the way it should be taken here. If ARV is right Jesus is saying that after the resurrection the disciples will not need further information from Him.[59] This probably points to an activity of the Holy Spirit who would be with them to teach them "all things", to remind them of all that Jesus had said (14 : 26) and to guide them into all the truth (16 : 13). They will have all the knowledge that is really necessary. This is probably the way the words should be taken. The disciples had hitherto asked Jesus many questions. Not least was this the case in the upper room (*cf.* 13 : 6, 25, 36f.; 14 : 5, 22), and this makes a reference to questions very appropriate. But they had not prayed to Him. There is no reason for thinking that the words would have made them think at this time of prayer to Jesus. Moreover "verily, verily" commonly introduces a new thought. It does not simply repeat the old. The asking in prayer at the end of the verse thus appears to be something different from the asking at the beginning. The alternative view is that the whole verse has to do with prayer. In that case Jesus is saying that prayer will be directed not to Him, but to the Father. In either case the events now to take place will alter everything. The disciples will not again return to the kind of situation in which

---

[57] For the singular καρδία see on 14 : 1.

[58] ἐρωτήσετε. In the second part of this verse and in the next the verb is αἰτέω. See on 11 : 22 for these two verbs in John.

[59] ἐμέ is emphatic both from its form and its position.

they have hitherto been. They will in future direct their prayers to the Father who will give them "anything"[60] they ask in the name of the Son. The expression "in my name" is usually attached to asking, rather than giving, and some scholars suggest that here it should be understood as AV, "Whatsoever ye shall ask the Father in my name". But the word order favors ARV. The meaning is that the atoning death of Jesus will revolutionize the whole situation. On the basis of the Son's atoning work men will approach God and know the answers to their prayers. The saying does not, of course, exclude altogether the possibility of prayer to the Son. But it reminds us that, for Christians, prayer is normally addressed to the Father in the name of the Son, and that such prayer is all-prevailing. It is on the grounds of all that the Son is and does that men receive gifts from the Father.[61] Notice that part of the thought of this verse is a repetition of that in 15 : 16, characteristically, with small variations.

24 A new state of affairs is about to be inaugurated. Up till now the disciples have asked Jesus for things directly or they have asked the Father directly. They have not asked the Father for anything[62] in the name of the Son. Jesus exhorts them to ask (the present tense may have its full significance: "keep on asking"). Then they will receive. And the purpose of all this is their joy. God is interested in the wellbeing and the happiness of His people. They will go through trials (*cf.* v. 33), but when their trust is in Him He puts a joy into their hearts that can never be removed. Notice that this is connected with prayer. They are to pray in order that their joy may be made complete. It cannot be made complete in any other way.

(c) The Disciples' Faith, 16 : 25-30

25 These things have I spoken unto you in ¹dark sayings: the hour cometh, when I shall no more speak unto you in ¹dark sayings, but shall tell you plainly of the Father. 26 In that

---

[60] τι is very general. It sets no limits to what the Father will give.

[61] Dods comments: "Prayer must have been rather hindered by the visible presence of a sufficient helper, but henceforth it was to be the medium of communication between the disciples and the source of spiritual power."

[62] There is an emphatic double negative οὐκ ἠτήσατε οὐδέν.

day ye shall ask in my name: and I say not unto you, that
I will ²pray the Father for you; 27 for the Father himself
loveth you, because ye have loved me, and have believed
that I came forth from the Father. 28 I came out from the
Father, and am come into the world: again, I leave the
world, and go unto the Father. 29 His disciples say, Lo, now
speakest thou plainly, and speakest no ³dark saying. 30 Now
know we that thou knowest all things, and needest not that
any man should ask thee: by this we believe that thou camest
forth from God.

¹Or, *parables* ²Gr. *make request of.* ³Or, *parable*

Jesus further explains His going away. He is to leave the
world and go to the Father. The disciples find this plain speaking,
and it elicits from them a statement of faith – they believe now
that Jesus came forth from God.
25 For "These things have I spoken unto you" see on 14 : 25.
A good deal here hinges on the meaning of the word rendered
"dark sayings".⁶³ It can mean parables, but it is also used of a
variety of clever sayings of one kind or another. There is often
the implication that the meaning does not lie on the surface, but
must be searched for and thought about. "Dark sayings" does
therefore bring out an important part of what the word conveys.
Schonfield translates: "I have spoken to you enigmatically thus
far." Up till now Jesus has spoken figuratively, with the implication
that the figure is not easy to penetrate. The reference will be to
the discourse as a whole rather than to the immediately preceding
figure of the woman in childbirth (which is fairly obvious; it is
not a "dark saying", even though there are depths of meaning
in it which the disciples are as yet unable to plumb). Jesus goes
on to refer to "the hour" when He will speak plainly. One would
have expected that this would be now, and, indeed, the disciples
apparently take it this way (v. 29). Yet Jesus does seem to be
looking forward to the time after the resurrection (v. 26), and this
was the time when things which had been obscure began to be
clear for them. This is probably the best way to take the words.
There is a marked difference in the apostles when we come to

---

⁶³ παροιμία (παρά+ οἶμος, a way, a path) is "a wayside saying . . . a
byword, maxim, proverb" (AS). AG speaks of it as denoting "in Johannine
usage *dark saying, figure* of speech, in which esp. lofty ideas are concealed". See
further on 10 : 6.

Acts. There there is a sureness of touch, a certainty, a conviction, which could not take place until after the events narrated in the Gospels.

26 In the light of their fuller knowledge the disciples will then pray as they should, in Christ's name (*cf.* vv. 23f.). Notice that Jesus does not undertake to intercede for them then (contrast 14 : 16; 17 : 9, but these refer to prayers of Jesus during His earthly ministry; after the resurrection there will be a new state of affairs). Asking in His name is not a way of enlisting His support. It is rather a pleading of His person and of His work for men. It is praying on the basis of all that He is and has done for our salvation. There is no contradiction with passages speaking of Christ's perpetual intercession for His people (Rom. 8 : 34; Heb. 7 : 25), nor with that in which John calls Him "an Advocate with the Father" (I John 2 : 1). In all four passages there is one basic underlying thought, namely, that our approach to the Father rests firmly on Christ's priestly work for us.[64] That work is itself a perpetual intercession. It does not require to be supplemented by further intervention on our behalf. There is also a firm exclusion of the thought that the disciples should enlist Christ's prayers for them as though He were more merciful and more ready to hear than is the Father. Rather the passage insists on the unity of the Son with the Father.[65] The Son does not persuade the Father to be gracious. The whole of the work of the Son rests on the loving care of the Father who sent Him.

27 The reason that Christ will not intercede for them is now given. There will be no need. The Father *Himself*[66] loves them.

---

[64] *Cf.* Calvin: "when Christ is said to intercede with the Father for us, let us not imagine anything fleshly about Him, as if He were on His knees before the Father offering humble supplications. But the power of His sacrifice, by which He once pacified God towards us, is always powerful and efficacious. The blood by which He atoned for our sins, the obedience which He rendered, is a continual intercession for us. This is a remarkable passage, by which we are taught that we have the heart of God as soon as we place before Him the name of His Son."

[65] Perhaps also with the believer. *Cf.* MacGregor: "John so closely identifies Christ with the Father, and the believer with Christ, that he regards no such separate intercession on the part of the Risen Christ as necessary."

[66] αὐτός puts some emphasis on the fact that it is the Father, and none less than He, that loves them. Barrett notes and rejects the suggestion that αὐτός is unemphatic, being simply the representation of "an Aramaic proleptic pronoun".

He does not need to be persuaded to be gracious. In this case the ground of acceptance is the relationship in which they stand to Jesus. They have loved Him (the perfect tense in this verb and the next probably implies continuance). This does not, of course, mean that their love merits the Father's love, or that He loves only because of their prior love. Rather they owe their love to Christ to a prior divine work in them, and this proceeds from God's love. As Augustine says, "He would not have wrought in us something He could love, were it not that He loved ourselves before He wrought it."[67] They have also had faith in Him, faith that He "came forth from[68] the Father".[69] Notice that a right faith is informed. It has regard to Christ's heavenly origin. It is true that from one point of view the Father loves all men. But it is also true that He has a special regard for those who believe, and it is this that is in mind here.

28 Here we have the great movement of salvation. It is a twofold movement, from heaven to earth[70] and back again.[71] Christ's heavenly origin is important, else He could not be the Saviour of men. But His heavenly destination is also important, for it witnesses to the Father's seal on the Son's saving work.

29 These words of Jesus cause the disciples to say that He is no longer using dark sayings (for this expression see on v. 25 and 10 : 6). They appear to think that their difficulty has been cleared up, but it is not easy to hold that this is really the case. It is true that Jesus is not now speaking figuratively, and their words are

---

[67] CIII. 5; p. 391.

[68] In the expression "from the Father" the preposition here is παρά, in verse 28 it is ἐκ (though some MSS read παρά), and when the disciples take up the words they use ἀπό (v. 30). It is difficult to think that John wants us to see different meanings. The prepositions are not used with narrowly defined meanings.

[69] ARV follows the reading τοῦ Πατρός with BC*D co etc. Most recent commentators prefer τοῦ θεοῦ, C³W f1 f13 28 565 700, or θεοῦ, P5 ℵ* AΘ 33 etc. They are probably right for, as Godet puts it, "It is the *divine* origin and mission of Jesus, and not his *filial* relation with God, which must be emphasized at this moment".

[70] John uses the aorist ἐξῆλθον for the act of leaving the Father (*cf.* 8 : 42, etc.), but the perfect ἐλήλυθα of arriving (and staying) in the world (so also in 12 : 46; 18 : 37).

[71] Abbott takes πάλιν here in the sense "*reversely, or returning back*, I leave the world" (2649(ii)). But this seems unnecessary. The sense "again" is sufficient.

justified to that extent. He is indeed speaking plainly. The difficulty is not so much with the words as with the situation in which the disciples find themselves. On the farther side of Calvary no man could know what was involved in Christ's leaving the Father and then returning to Him.

30 It is probably significant that they do not say that they understand fully all that Jesus is saying. Instead they say that they know that He knows all things. They have full confidence in Him. Christ has answered the question in their heart (it had not been spoken, v. 19), and they ascribe to Him the power to do this always (*cf.* 2 : 25). There is no need for any man to ask Him. This[72] in turn gives them assurance of His divine origin. Their confession is certainly an inadequate one,[73] but we should not overlook the fact that they bring their words to a close with an expression of trust.

(d) The Disciples' Peace, 16 : 31–33

31 Jesus answered them, Do ye now believe? 32 Behold, the hour cometh, yea, is come, that ye shall be scattered, every man to his own, and shall leave me alone: and yet I am not alone, because the Father is with me. 33 These things have I spoken unto you, that in me ye may have peace. In the world ye have tribulation: but be of good cheer; I have overcome the world.

Jesus shows that He is not deceived by the disciples' confidence. He knows that there are limitations to their faith, and that these limitations will speedily be shown up. But His final word to them is one of peace. The opposition of the world is real. But Jesus has overcome it.

31 Jesus' words might be taken as a statement rather than as a question as ARV. McClymont comments that in any case "it

---

[72] BDF sees in ἐν τούτῳ an example of the extension of instrumental ἐν in imitation of the Hebrew בְ with the meaning, "for that reason" (219(2)).

[73] *Cf.* Westcott: "This common confession of faith shows how little even yet the disciples had apprehended the nature of Christ. As a body they had not advanced as far as the Baptist." So also R. H. Lightfoot: "a belief resting on the ground of His knowledge was found at the outset in Nathanael (1[47-50]) and in the Samaritan woman (4[29]); and a faith which has now seen greater things than these (1[50]) should have a deeper basis."

is more an exclamation than a question". Jesus is not calling in question the reality of their faith, but directing attention to its inadequacy. They do believe. But they do not, as yet, know the quality of faith that stands firm in the face of difficulty and danger. There is possibly some emphasis on "now"; in this hour they have professed to believe (v. 30). But, as Jesus' next words show, in reality they have not yet come to know some of the important consequences of faith in Him. It is not without its interest that Jesus uses "believe" absolutely, whereas the disciples had said that they believed that ——. The two are not so very different. (See further Additional Note E, pp. 335ff.)

32 The limitations of the disciples' faith are shown in that they will shortly abandon their Lord. Their failure at the moment of crisis is faithfully recorded and it has its importance. The church depends ultimately on what God has done in Christ, not on the courage and wit of its first members.[74] "The hour cometh, yea, is come" (*cf.* 12 : 23) stresses the imminence of this. They have just professed faith. But in the immediate future they will be unable to stand the test. They will be scattered, perhaps to their homes;[75] at any rate they will be separated from one another and from Him (*cf.* Mark 14 : 50). The little band will have lost all cohesion. The disaster will destroy it as an entity (though only temporarily). Christ they will abandon. But the thought that Jesus will be left "alone" leads on the to other thought[76] that in view of His relationship to the Father He will not really be alone.[77]

---

[74] *Cf.* Dodd: "It is part of the character and genius of the Church that its foundation members were discredited men; it owed its existence not to their faith, courage, or virtue, but to what Christ had done with them; and this they could never forget" (*IFG*, p. 416 n. 1).

[75] This is the meaning of εἰς τὰ ἴδια in 19 : 27 and elsewhere, and it may be what is meant here. There is a contrast in κἀμέ. They will go to their homes. Jesus they will abandon (ἀφῆτε) and leave lonely.

[76] καί is used in the sense of καίτοι as often in John.

[77] Some suggest that John is writing in conscious contradiction of the saying in Mark 15 : 34: "My God, my God, why hast thou forsaken me?" This seems to be reading a great deal into the present passage. It is better to see Mark as presenting starkly one aspect of the truth, that at the crisis of the process in which God made Christ sin for us (II Cor. 5 : 21) the presence of the Father was withdrawn. John is giving us another part of the picture, namely, that when the disciples forsook Jesus He was not alone. Human abandonment could not make Him alone. His communion with the Father was too real for that. The two Evangelists are speaking about different things. See further the note in Tasker.

The present tenses, which Jesus uses of the Father's presence with Him, are natural for an abiding reality. Always the Father is with Him. *Cf.* 8 : 16, 29.

33 For "These things have I spoken unto you" see on 14 : 25, and for "peace" on 14 : 27. Christ's words to the disciples conclude on the note of peace and victory. There are three contrasts here: "in me" is set over against "in the world", "ye may have" over against "ye have", and "peace" over against "tribulation". The second of these does not, of course, mean that there is any doubt that the man who is "in" Christ has peace.[78] Rather it points to the contrast between the life that all must lead, a life in this world, and a life which all do not lead, a life in Christ. All must live in the world and thus have tribulation. But they may also live in Christ and thus have peace. The speaking of these words just at this time has a significance rather like the reference to the trials that would befall them in v. 4. When they had all forsaken Jesus they might well feel so ashamed that they would remain uneasy whenever they thought of Him. But He predicted their desertion in the very saying in which He assured them of the peace He would give them. He loved them for what they were and despite their shortcomings. When in the future they looked back on their desertion they could reflect that Jesus had predicted it. And, in the full knowledge that they would act in this way, He had promised them peace. The world will infallibly bring them "tribulation".[79] That is its characteristic. But He can bid them "be of good cheer".[80] He[81] had overcome[82] the world, the perfect tense denoting an abiding victory. This statement, spoken as it is in the shadow of the cross, is audacious. The cross would

---

[78] In the expression ἵνα ἐν ἐμοὶ εἰρήνην ἔχητε the conjunction ἵνα is fully telic. It is Jesus' purpose that they have peace.

[79] The word is θλῖψις (used in this Gospel elsewhere only at v. 21). It denotes great and pressing affliction, not some mild malady.

[80] For the strong adversative ἀλλά which introduces the clause *cf.* v. 20 and the note there (see also on 1 : 8). It indicates that this is something for which the circumstances have not prepared us.

[81] Note the ἐγώ: "I, none else, have overcome" (see on 1 : 20).

[82] The verb νικάω is used here only in this Gospel. It is found 6 times in I John, including the expression νικάω τὸν κόσμον (I John 5 : 4f.) as here. It is especially frequent in Revelation (17 times), being used there as here of Christ's victory.

714

seem to the outsider to be Christ's total defeat. He sees it as His complete victory over all that the world is and can do to Him. He goes to the cross not in fear or in gloom, but as a conqueror.

CHAPTER XVII

7. THE HIGH PRIESTLY PRAYER, 17 : 1–26

The farewell discourse is followed by the great high priestly prayer. Barrett objects to describing the prayer in this way, or as the "prayer of consecration", since this "does not do justice to the full range of the material contained in it." Everything I suppose depends on what range one would expect to find in a "high priestly prayer". This common name does draw attention to the solemn consecration which is so much a feature of the prayer and to the way it looks forward to the cross as the consummation of Christ's priestly work. This is the longest of our Lord's recorded prayers, and, spoken as it is in the shadow of the cross, it is invested with a peculiar solemnity. "No attempt to describe the prayer can give a just idea of its sublimity, its pathos, its touching yet exalted character, its tone at once of tenderness and triumphant expectation" (MiM). The last words are important. We so often understand this prayer as though it were rather gloomy. It is not. It is uttered by One who has just affirmed that He has overcome the world (16 : 33), and it starts from this conviction. Jesus is looking forward to the cross, but in a mood of hope and joy, not one of despondency. The prayer marks the end of Jesus' earthly ministry, but it looks forward to the ongoing work which would now be the responsibility first of the immediate disciples and then of those who would later believe through them. Jesus prays for them all.

The prayer is difficult to subdivide for it is essentially a unity. However it is possible to discern a movement. At the beginning Jesus prays about His own glorification (1–5), then He goes on to the main part of the prayer which concerns the circle of the disciples (6–19), and He concludes by praying for those who will believe through their ministry (20–26). Common to all these sections is the desire that the Father's purpose be set forward.[1]

---

[1] Bernard draws attention to an interesting group of coincidences with the Lord's Prayer, and says, "None of these coincidences or parallels is likely to have been invented by one setting himself to compose a prayer for the lips of Christ on the eve of His Passion; but, when taken together, they show that

(a) Prayer for the Glorification of the Son, 17 : 1-5

1 These things spake Jesus; and lifting up his eyes to heaven, he said, Father, the hour is come; glorify thy Son, that the Son may glorify thee: 2 even as thou gavest him authority over all flesh, that [1] to all whom thou hast given him, he should give eternal life. 3 And this is life eternal, that they should know thee the only true God, and him whom thou didst send, even Jesus Christ. 4 I glorified thee on the earth, having accomplished the work which thou hast given me to do. 5 And now, Father, glorify thou me with thine own self with the glory which I had with thee before the world was.

[1] Gr. *whatsoever thou hast given him, to them he &c.*

This part of the prayer is often said to be Jesus' prayer for Himself. As He prays that He may be glorified (vv. 1, 5) there is perhaps something in this. But this is not prayer "for" Himself in the way we usually understand this. Since His glorification is to be seen in the cross it is a prayer rather that the Father's will may be done in Him. If we do talk about this as Jesus' prayer for Himself we should at least be clear that there is no self-seeking in it.

1 The farewell discourse is ended. There follows our Lord's prayer. Lifting up the eyes to heaven was the accepted posture for prayer (*cf.* 11 : 41; Mark 7 : 34; Ps. 123 : 1; the publican in the parable however would not lift up his eyes to heaven, Luke 18 : 13).[2] The form of address is the simple "Father", the address of a child to its parent.[3] It marks the close familiarity between

the spirit which breathes throughout c. 17 is similar to that with which we have been made familiar when reading Jesus' words as recorded by the Synoptists and elsewhere in Jn." Wright also sees a connection with the Lord's Prayer. He speaks of this prayer as "a kind of expanded paraphrase" of it.

[2] The worshipper might sometimes prostrate himself in prayer presumably when he wished to adopt an especially lowly place in earnest petition. Our Lord did this in Gethsemane (Matt. 26 : 39).

[3] G. Dalman points out that the Greek πάτερ (used here) like ὁ πατήρ or πάτερ μου presupposes an Aramaic אַבָּא (as in Mark 14 : 36). The significance of this is that, "The usage of family life is transferred to God: it is the language of the child to its father" (*The Words of Jesus*, Edinburgh, 1902, pp. 191f.). The Jews preferred a less intimate form when addressing God, *e.g.* "Our Father in heaven".

Jesus and the Father. For "the hour" in this Gospel see on 2 : 4. Now with the cross in immediate prospect Jesus can speak of the hour as having come.[4] This is that to which the whole ministry of Jesus has led up. For the idea of "glory" see on 1 : 14; *cf.* also 12 : 28. It is significant that with the cross in view Jesus prays that God will glorify Him. To men the cross appeared an instrument of shame. To Christ it was the means of true glory. The prayer makes it clear moreover that the glory of the Son and the glory of the Father are closely connected. To glorify the Son is to glorify the Father.[5] The two are one.

2 The thought of the glory continues ("even as"). The giving[6] of eternal life to men is the outworking of the glory of which Christ speaks. The authority of Christ is God-given and it is an authority over the whole human race (*cf.* 5 : 27; Matt. 11 : 27; 28 : 18). This does not mean that He exercises a sovereignty over mankind like the sovereignty of earthly kings. It is an authority[7] given for the express purpose[8] of conferring eternal life (*cf.* 3 : 35f.; 10 : 28; see on 1 : 4; 3 : 15). The thought that the authority is

---

[4] There is an air of finality about the perfect ἐλήλυθεν. *Cf.* 12 : 23.

[5] ἵνα will be fully telic. Jesus prays for His own glorification not as an end in itself, but as a means to the greater glory of the Father. For ἵνα in John see on 1 : 8.

[6] The repeated use of δίδωμι in this chapter should not be overlooked (see vv. 4, 6, 7, 8, 9, 11, 12, 14, 22, 24). The verb is a favorite one of this Evangelist, being found 76 times in the Gospel (Matthew 56 times, Mark 39 times, Luke 60 times). In this prayer of our Lord it occurs 17 times. Often the perfect tense is used (11 – 13 times depending on the resolution of textual points) denoting the permanence of the gift. Thirteen times the Father is the subject of the verb and on every occasion the gift is made to the Son. The other four occasions all refer to the Son's giving to the disciples. Abbott comments on the frequency of the verb in this Gospel, "What '*grace*' is in the Pauline Epistles, '*giving*' is in the Fourth Gospel" (2742). For the Father's gifts to the Son see on 3 : 35.

[7] ἐξουσία is also connected with the giving of life in the Prologue, though there it is translated "the right", and it refers to an authority given to believers (1 : 12).

[8] Again we have the telic ἵνα. It appears to be followed by the future indicative δώσει, though this is corrected in various ways, some of which have strong attestation. It is, of course, possible also that δώσει is no more than an orthographical variant of δώσῃ. This latter form presents problems. Some posit a rare future subjunctive which Moulton and Howard dismiss as an "imaginary mood", speaking of all the few examples cited (including the present example) as "only new aorists made from the future stem by the usual analogy" (M, II, p. 218).

given to Christ to convey life, used as it is in a context dealing with the passion, reminds us of that other thought which meant so much to some of the Fathers, that Christ reigned from the tree. The cross was not to be defeat but victory. He exercised authority in bringing men life even as He hung, apparently helpless, on the cross. But, though life is His gift, He does not confer it on all indiscriminately. Once again we have the thought of the divine predestination. Life is given "to all[9] whom thou hast given him". For eternal life see on 3 : 15.[10]

3 Here we have something of a definition of eternal life.[11] Really to know[12] God means more than knowing the way to life. It *is* life.[13] In this world we are familiar with the truth that it is a blessing and an inspiration to know certain people. Much more

---

[9] The neuter $\pi\tilde{\alpha}\nu$ $\ddot{o}$ where we might have expected the masculine, puts an emphasis on the quality as God-given, rather than on the persons as such. There is also a hint at unity, which would not be conveyed in $\pi\acute{\alpha}\nu\tau\epsilon\varsigma$ (*i.e.* "the whole" rather than "all"). In strict grammar, of course, the meaning ought to be: "so that he should give them all that thou hast given him, namely eternal life". But there can be no doubt but that $\pi\tilde{\alpha}\nu$ refers to all believers, not to all God's gift. There is a similar neuter in v. 24. It is a further example of John's love of variety that he refers to men in the present passage first with the use of "flesh", $\pi\acute{\alpha}\sigma\eta\varsigma$ $\sigma\alpha\varrho\varkappa\acute{o}\varsigma$, then with the neuter $\pi\tilde{\alpha}\nu$, and finally with the masculine pronoun $\alpha\dot{\upsilon}\tau o\tilde{\iota}\varsigma$. "All flesh" is, of course, a Hebrew expression to denote all mankind, especially mankind as weak and temporary over against the strength and eternity of God.

[10] When "eternal life" is repeated in the next verse there is a characteristic slight alteration. Here we have $\zeta\omega\grave{\eta}\nu$ $\alpha\dot{\iota}\acute{\omega}\nu\iota o\nu$, there $\acute{\eta}$ $\alpha\dot{\iota}\acute{\omega}\nu\iota o\varsigma$ $\zeta\omega\acute{\eta}$. The article, of course, will point back to the previous use of $\zeta\omega\acute{\eta}$.

[11] This verse is often said to be a parenthesis in which John gives us his view of eternal life. In favour of this is the difficulty of seeing why Jesus should give such an explanation in prayer, and the use of "Jesus Christ" rather than "me" (but He uses the third person in vv. 1f.). Against it is the use of the second person ($\sigma\acute{\epsilon}$ and $\dot{\alpha}\pi\acute{\epsilon}\sigma\tau\epsilon\iota\lambda\alpha\varsigma$), and the difficulty of seeing why John should put his explanation so late in the Gospel after having used the concept so often. A similar passage where the explanation is that of the writer (and is in the third person) may be seen in I John 5 : 20.

[12] MiM maintain that "know" here "does not mean to know fully or to recognise, but to learn to know: it expresses not perfect, but inceptive and ever-growing knowledge." This may be reading a bit much into the use of the present tense, but the point is surely valid that Jesus has in mind an ever-increasing knowledge, not something given in its completeness once and for all.

[13] This point is overlooked by Barrett in his otherwise excellent note. He gathers many parallels to show the stress placed on the knowledge of God in both Hebrew and Hellenistic thought. But when he says "Knowledge of God

is it the case when we know God. To know Him transforms a man and introduces him to a different quality of living. Eternal life is simply the knowledge of God.[14] Jesus stresses that there is but one God (cf. 5 : 44) and He the true[15] God. It is not knowledge of "a god" that is meant but knowledge of the supreme Ruler of the universe. This is linked with the knowledge of Christ.[16] The only way to know God is through the revelation He has made, and He has revealed Himself in His Son. It is not possible to know God in any way that we choose. We must know Him in Him whom He has sent,[17] namely Jesus Christ (for "Christ" see on 1 : 20, 41). **4** Now comes a statement that Jesus has completed the task for which He came. "I glorified thee"[18] indicates a completed task. This is further defined as "having accomplished the work which

and Christ gives life" he is introducing a different thought. To say that the knowledge of God and Christ *brings* life is one thing; to say that it *is* life is quite another. Temple writes: "At one time I was much troubled that the climax of the *Veni Creator* should be

Teach us to know the Father, Son,
And Thee, of Both, to be but One.

It seemed to suggest that the ultimate purpose of the coming of the Holy Spirit was to persuade us of the truth of an orthodox formula. But that is mere thoughtlessness. If a man once knows the Spirit within him, the source of all his aspiration after holiness, as indeed the Spirit of Jesus Christ, and if he knows this Spirit of Jesus Christ within himself as none other than the Spirit of the Eternal and Almighty God, what more can he want? *This is the eternal life.*" Tenney stresses the importance of the passage: "the definition of eternal life is important because Jesus differentiated it from the current concept of endless existence."

14 Philo comes close to this thought without actually reaching it when he speaks of "holding that the knowledge of him is the consummation of happiness and long life" (*De Spec. Leg.* I, 345: τὴν ἐπιστήμην αὐτοῦ τέλος εὐδαιμονίας εἶναι νομίζοντες καὶ ζωὴν μακραίωνα).

15 For ἀληθινός see on 1 : 9. Only here and at 4 : 23 does John have this adjective used attributively precede its noun. This makes it emphatic.

16 The compound noun "Jesus Christ" is found elsewhere in this Gospel only at 1 : 17 (where see note). Here a few take it to mean, "that they know... Jesus as Christ" (Lenski, for example, favors this). It seems better, however, to take it in the normal fashion as the compound name. The alternative does seem to be straining the Greek.

17 The aorist ἀπέστειλας with its indication of a definite act will refer to the incarnation. See further on 3 : 17.

18 The juxtaposition of the pronouns ἐγώ and σέ is to be noted (though the latter is not emphatic). It points to the fact that the work of *Christ* was nothing other than to glorify the Father.

thou hast given me to do". Jesus says that He has brought to its due end[19] the task that was assigned Him (see on 4 : 34). There is nothing flamboyant about this utterance. But there is a quiet recognition that Jesus has completed His task adequately, and brought glory to the Father in the process. The supreme place of the Father is guarded with the expression "given". Even the work that Jesus did was work which the Father gave Him. The initiative is seen as resting with the Father.

5 Now Jesus prays God to glorify Him. He looks for glory in the last place that men would seek it, namely in the cross. And He sees this glory for which He prays as linked with His pre-incarnate[20] glory with the Father.[21] There is a clear assertion of Christ's pre-existence here (we have already seen such a claim, 1 : 1; 8 : 58; 16 : 28). There is also the claim that He had enjoyed a unique glory with the Father in that pre-existent state.[22] And now, as men are about to do their worst to Him, He looks for the Father to glorify Him again in the same way.[23] It is the Father who will glorify Him with true glory in the cross, and in what follows. Paul tells us that Jesus "was raised from the dead through the glory of the Father" (Rom. 6 : 4). In the passion and all associated with it Jesus would be glorified with the true glory, a glory continuous, and indeed identical, with the glory He had

---

[19] This will be the significance of τελειώσας. Jesus has glorified the Father in that He has finished His assigned task (cf. Rieu: "by finishing the task"). The expression, of course, looks forward to the cross (cf. the use of τετέλεσται in 19 : 30).

[20] For the articular infinitive πρὸ τοῦ ... εἶναι see on 1 : 48. BDF notes the present passage as the only one in the New Testament where πρὸ τοῦ is followed by the present infinitive, the aorist being invariable elsewhere (403).

[21] παρὰ σεαυτῷ looks for a glory beyond this world with the Father. It is reinforced with παρὰ σοί. The preposition παρά when used with the dative often has the meaning "in the house of" (see LS, s.v.), and there may be a hint at such a meaning here. Cf. also 1 : 1, πρὸς τὸν θεόν.

[22] Murray comments: "His words imply that for His human consciousness, presence in human flesh in this world involved the surrender, for the time, of the joy of full uninterrupted communion, an absence from the Father, even the possibility of that hiding of His face which makes the darkest of all human utterances a true expression of His experience as man: 'My God, my God, why didst Thou forsake me?'"

[23] The statement of v. 4 and the prayer of this verse are illuminated by the principle laid down in I Sam. 2 : 30, which reads in LXX, τοὺς δοξάζοντάς με δοξάσω.

"before the world was". For "the world" see Additional Note B, pp. 126ff. The noun occurs eighteen times in this prayer, which is considerably more than in any section of comparable length anywhere else in this Gospel. Clearly the right relationship of the disciples to the world was of great moment to our Lord as He contemplated leaving them.

(b) Prayer for the Disciples, 17 : 6–19

6 I manifested thy name unto the men whom thou gavest me out of the world: thine they were, and thou gavest them to me; and they have kept thy word. 7 Now they know that all things whatsoever thou hast given me are from thee: 8 for the words which thou gavest me I have given unto them; and they received them, and knew of a truth that I came forth from thee, and they believed that thou didst send me. 9 I [1]pray for them: I [1]pray not for the world, but for those whom thou hast given me; for they are thine: 10 and all things that are mine are thine, and thine are mine: and I am glorified in them. 11 And I am no more in the world, and these are in the world, and I come to thee. Holy Father, keep them in thy name which thou hast given me, that they may be one, even as we are. 12 While I was with them, I kept them in thy name which thou hast given me: and I guarded them, and not one of them perished, but the son of perdition; [2]that the scripture might be fulfilled. 13 But now I come to thee; and these things I speak in the world, that they may have my joy made full in themselves. 14 I have given them thy word; and the world hated them, because they are not of the world, even as I am not of the world. 15 I [1]pray not that thou shouldest take them [3]from the world, but that thou shouldest keep them [3]from [4]the evil one. 16 They are not of the world, even as I am not of the world. 17 [5]Sanctify them in the truth: thy word is truth. 18 As thou didst send me into the world, even so sent I them into the world. 19 And for their sakes I [5]sanctify myself, that they themselves also may be sanctified in truth.

[1]Gr. *make request.* [2]Ps. xli. 9? [3]Gr. *out of.* [4]Or, *evil* [5]Or, *consecrate*

The main part of the prayer is concerned with the disciples. They had depended very heavily on the visible presence of their Master. This presence was soon to be taken from them. Though

Jesus has already promised them that the Holy Spirit will come, and has even assured them that this will be better for them than His continuing bodily presence, yet He knows that the coming hours will be a great trial to them. Despite everything they are not ready for the shock of Calvary. Tenderly now He commits them to the care of the heavenly Father.

6 Jesus recalls that He has revealed God to the disciples. The "name" stands for the whole person (see on 1 : 12). To manifest the name of God then is to reveal the essential nature of God to men. Later He says that He has made the Father's "name" known (v. 26), and in between He twice refers to the disciples as "kept" in the Father's "name" (v. 11, where He prays that God will keep them in this name, and v. 12, where He says that He Himself has kept them in that name). Clearly "the name" is an important concept for the understanding of this prayer. Here the point is that the revelation was not made indiscriminately. It was made to those[24] whom God gave Jesus (*cf.* 6 : 37) out of[25] the world[26] (for "world" see Additional Note B, pp. 126ff.). The priority of the Father is implied in "thine". These men belonged first to Him, then He gave them to the Son (for the things the Father gives the Son see on 3 : 35). The disciples' continuance in the right way is described as a keeping of the Father's word. They have persevered and they have persevered in keeping the "word" of God. Elsewhere we are told that Jesus keeps God's word (8 : 55), but this is the one place where men are said to have kept it (as distinct from commands to keep it).[27] "Word" is an important concept in this Gospel (see Additional Note A, pp. 115ff.).

7 "Now" may be either logical or temporal, probably the latter. It seems that Jesus is saying that only now, now at long last, have

---

[24] Abbott draws attention to the fact that, whereas the accusative αὐτούς is found often in the Synoptists in connection with what Jesus did to "them", it occurs four times only in this way in John until we come to this prayer. Here it is used of the disciples nine times (2376). *Cf.* also the use of the nominative αὐτοί in vv. 8, 11, 19, 21.

[25] ἐκ here will have something of the thought of separation from.

[26] *Cf.* Westcott: "It is only by the influence of the Father that men can come to Christ, vi. 44,65. Yet the critical act admits of being described from many sides. The Father is said to 'draw' men (vi. 44), and Christ also draws them (xii. 32). Christ 'chooses' men (vi. 70, xv. 16); and men freely obey His call."

[27] For τηρέω see on 8 : 51.

they come into the knowledge of which He speaks. This knowledge
is not described so plainly as to be beyond any possible misunderstanding. But it appears to mean the knowledge that Jesus'
mission is divine, that He has nothing except what the Father
has given Him. All is of God. This is an important truth. So long
as we stay with the figure of the Galilean Jesus (perhaps roman-
ticizing over the beauty of His holiness and lowliness) so long we
miss what really matters. What is central is that all that we see
in Him is of God. It is not so much the Man of Galilee as the
eternal God on whom our attention should rest.

8 "The words which thou gavest me" points to a God-given
message. It is this that Jesus passed on to the disciples (*cf.* 7 : 16;
12 : 48f.). It is important to note the stress placed on the divine
revelation in this passage. The essential thing is not the example
of Jesus or the like, but "the words which thou gavest me". The
rest of the verse is taken up with the attitude of the disciples,
which is described in three ways. First, they "received" the words
in question. This sets them in contrast with other men of their
day. Some, like the chief priests or the Pharisees, might have
been expected to welcome a genuine divine revelation. They did
not. But the disciples did.[28] Secondly, they came to know, and
to know of a certainty, that Jesus was of divine origin, that He
came forth from God. This is, of course, an essential part of the
revelation. So central is it that it is given a special mention. The
disciples still had misconceptions and their faith was still weak.
But Jesus recognizes that basically their attitude to Him is right.
They know that He has come from God (*cf.* 16 : 30). Thirdly,
they can be described as men of faith (for the connection between
receiving and believing *cf.* 1 : 12; the parallel is all the more
impressive in that there is no personal object expressed for
"received" here). They have come to believe that the Father[29]
sent Christ. This point is very much like the previous one (the
connection between knowledge and faith is close), but it is not
identical. The second point concerns the Son's divine origin, the

---

[28] Godet comments: "The harvest seems scanty, no doubt: eleven Galilean
artisans after three years of labor! But this is enough for Jesus: for in these
eleven He beholds the pledge of the continuance of the divine work on the
earth."

[29] There is some emphasis imparted by the use of σύ: "They believed that
it was none less than thou. . . ."

third His mission. He was sent to do a divine task. It was this that the disciples had come to believe. There is a similar combination of believing and knowing in 6 : 69.

9 Very simply Jesus prays[30] for them. He makes a distinction between the little band of disciples and the world. His prayer is not for "the world". This does not mean that "the world" is beyond God's love. Elsewhere we are specifically told that He loves it (3 : 16). And throughout this chapter it is plain that Jesus came with a mission to the world, and that the disciples were now to carry it on. A little later Jesus prays that the disciples may do certain things "that the world may believe . . ." (v. 21), and "that the world may know . . ." (v. 23). The world is to be reached through the disciples and it is for His agents that Jesus prays.[31] But He could scarcely pray for "the world" as such. As "the world" it was ranged in opposition to God. Its salvation lay precisely in its ceasing to be "the world". Prayer for the world could only be that it be converted and no longer be the world. But that would be a different prayer. We see it for example in His prayer for those who crucified Him (Luke 23 : 34).[32] Now He prays rather for the little group of His friends. Notice that they are again described in terms of their relationship to the Father. They have been "given" to Christ. They belong to the Father.

10 It is characteristic of this Gospel to describe them with reference to the divine act and not their own. It is also a frequently made point that there is community between the Father and the Son. What[33] belongs to the One belongs to the Other. It is worth noting that "thine are mine" goes beyond "mine are thine". This latter expression might perhaps be said by any creature, but

---

[30] For the use of ἐρωτάω (used here) and αἰτέω in this Gospel see on 11 : 22. For περί see on v. 20.

[31] *Cf.* Morgan: "He was praying for the instrument He was creating, through which He would reach the world."

[32] Ryle ranges himself with those who think that Jesus did not pray for the world on the grounds "that it is derogatory to our Lord's honour to suppose that He can ever ask anything in vain; and that His intercession specially belongs to 'those who come unto God by Him' (Heb. vii. 25)."

[33] As persons are in view we might have anticipated the masculine instead of the neuter possessives τὰ ἐμά and σά. But the neuter is more general and inclusive. Grammatically αὐτοῖς could be neuter and refer to ἐμά and σά. But it is more likely to be masculine, perhaps looking back to ὧν (v. 9).

"thine are mine" points to a very special relationship. As Luther is reported to have said, "This no creature can say with reference to God." It is worth noting that Jesus now returns to the thought of glory which we saw in the earlier part of the chapter. But now He says that He has been glorified[34] in the disciples. This really is very like Jesus' attitude to the glory seen in the cross. Outwardly the little group was not distinguished. The men of the day saw nothing about its members to mark them off as eminent in any respect. But, just as the world's values were all wrong concerning the cross, so were the world's values all wrong concerning the apostolic band. In them the Son of God, none less, was actually glorified.

11 Jesus' departure from the world is so near that he can use the present tense of it. His work in the world is done. He is no longer in it. But[35] the disciples[36] are in it. Just as it is His task to go out of the world, so it is their task to remain in the world. The address, "Holy Father", is unique (though *cf.* I Pet. 1 : 15f.; Rev. 4 : 8; 6 : 10). Holiness is ascribed to God the Father in surprisingly few New Testament passages, especially considering the importance of the idea of holiness in the Old Testament. We are probably right in deducing that the reason for this is that the work of the men of the Old Testament had been well done. In their day men tended to presume on the love and tender care of God. They thought that because God was the God of their nation they could rely on Him to help them no matter what the circumstances. The dishonoring of Israel they thought meant the dishonoring of Israel's God. It was necessary that they should be taught that God is a holy God. No man may presume. If Israel did not respect the holiness of God, Israel could not expect the blessing of God. So the sovereignty of God and the awe-fulness of God and the holiness of God received great emphasis. But by

---

[34] The perfect tense δεδόξασμαι may point to the very real measure of glorification that has already taken place. Perhaps more likely it is proleptic, pointing forward to the glory that was yet to come, but which was certain. For this verb in John see on 7 : 39.

[35] καί here in a contrasted statement has much the force of "but". Burney regards this as a literal translation of ן adversative, which is found in both Hebrew and Aramaic (M, II, p. 469; Howard, however, points out that this use of καί can be found in classical Greek).

[36] The use of the pronoun αὐτοί marks a certain emphasis on "they".

New Testament days this lesson had been learned all too well. Now God was often thought of as remote and lofty, as a Being great and dignified indeed, but distant and aloof. The need now was for a stress on His love and His care. So Jesus speaks mostly of God in terms like "Father". But the holiness is still there. It is not to be overlooked or forgotten. The expression "Holy Father" is a reminder of both aspects of God's nature. Jesus goes on to pray that the Father will "keep" the disciples. This probably means keep them from evil, but the object is not expressed, and the end of the verse makes it possible that what is meant is keeping them from disunity. But the wider meaning is more likely. "In thy name which[37] thou hast given me" points to the whole revealed character of God. Jesus prays that God, the God He has revealed, may in that revealed character keep those who have such need of Him. The purpose[38] of His keeping of them is "that they may be one",[39] a thought which recurs (vv. 21, 22, 23). The latter half of our Lord's prayer for His followers shows an impressive concern for unity and is a rebuke to our "unhappy divisions". The nature of the unity is to be noted. It is a unity already given. Jesus does not pray that they may "become" one, but that they may "continually be" one.[40] It is a unity "in" the Father and the Son (v. 21). Christ is to be "in" them (v. 23). We should be clear that the unity for which Christ prays is a unity which rests on a common basic attitude, that of abiding in Him and having Him abide in them. "It is the Divine unity of love that is referred to, all wills bowing in the same direction, all affections burning with the same flame, all aims directed to the same end – one blessed harmony of love" (MiM). Enthusiasts for the ecumenical movement sometimes speak as though the reunion of Christendom would

---

[37] The reading ᾧ, which must be accepted on the evidence, can refer back only to ὄνομα. We might have expected οὕς (which in fact is read by A C³ Dᶜ Θ fl fl3 28 69 lat etc.; it seems clearly to be a scribal "correction"). But Jesus here speaks of the "name" as being given Him, i.e. He has been entrusted with the revelation of God as He is.

[38] Seven times in this prayer Jesus prays for His followers with the expression ἵνα ὦσιν (vv. 11, 19, 21bis, 22, 23, 24). Four of these are connected with unity.

[39] "One" is neuter, ἕν: "The disciples are to be kept by God not as units but as a unity" (Barrett).

[40] This appears to be the force of the present subjunctive ἵνα ὦσιν. Lenski stresses this, and points out that γένωνται would be required for the sense, "get to be one".

mean the answer to Christ's prayer. While it is true that unity of organization can be an impressive witness to unity of spirit, yet as such it is merely outward. It is not this that is in mind here. It is something much more difficult. It is unity of heart and mind and will. It is well that we work to bring the sundered denominations together. But it is better to look for a grander unity than that, and it is this grander unity for which Christ prays.

12 Now comes a brief retrospect. During His earthly ministry Jesus used to keep them. He did it "in thy name which thou hast given me". Again there is the thought of revelation. It was in the power of the God who revealed Himself that Jesus kept the disciples. He guarded[41] them safely so that none perished but Judas. "The son of perdition"[42] points to character rather than destiny. The expression means that he was characterized by "lostness", not that he was predestined to be "lost". Both parts of this statement are important. The disciples need not fear, for Christ had kept them, so that none was lost. And if attention be drawn to Judas, then the retort must be that the Father's will was done both in the eleven and in the one, for Scripture was fulfilled. The reference to the fulfilling of Scripture brings out the thought of divine purpose. This does not mean that Judas was an automaton.[43] He was a responsible person and acted freely. But God used his evil act to bring about His purpose. There is a combination of the human and the divine, but in this passage it is the divine side rather than the human which receives stress. God's will in the end was done in the handing over of Christ to be crucified. The particular passage of Scripture which is meant is not

---

[41] There is probably little significance in the change of verb from ἐτήρουν, "kept", to ἐφύλαξα, "guarded". The imperfect tense, however, may indicate an activity continued through the years and the aorist regard the action as complete.

[42] The exact expression, ὁ υἱὸς τῆς ἀπωλείας, is used of the man of sin in II Thess. 2 : 3. It perhaps is impossible to reproduce in English the word play of the original, where ἀπωλείας refers back to ἀπώλετο. Phillips tries with "not one of them was destroyed, except the son of destruction", while NEB reads: "Not one of them is lost except the man who must be lost".

[43] Cf. Calvin: "It would be wrong for anyone to infer from this that Judas' fall should be imputed to God rather than to himself, in that necessity was laid on him by the prophecy."

said, but probably Ps. 41 : 9 is in mind (though some prefer to think of Ps. 109 : 4–13).

13 Once more we have the thought that Christ is going to the Father. But He is still "in the world". And as He is in the world He speaks these things with a view to[44] the benefit of His disciples. He prays for them in order that they may have His joy (see on 15 : 11) in all its fulness in themselves. On an earlier occasion He had said that He came "that they may have life, and may have it abundantly" (10 : 10). It is something like this that He has in mind here.

14 Jesus' gift to them was God's "word" (*cf.* v. 6). The supremely significant thing is the revelation. The Word of the Father is not a natural possession. It is given only by Christ. "Word" here will mean the entire message that has been revealed. It is a natural transition to the thought that the world hated the disciples. During the time they had been with Jesus they had been given over to learning of God. This meant that inevitably the world opposed them. The disciples and the world were ranged on opposite sides. Now it can be said "they are not of the world". That Jesus is not of the world is easy enough to understand. This Gospel reiterates the truth that His essential being is heavenly. He came forth from God. But now He says that His followers are not "of the world" even as He is not "of the world". In a sense of course they were. They were born originally into the world, and as part of the world. But in His conversation with Nicodemus (ch. 3) Jesus has made it clear that men must be born all over again if they are to see the Kingdom of God. It is in this re-born state that the disciples are thought of as not "of the world". And the re-born state is the significant state. *Berkeley* translates: "they are not worldly, just as I am not worldly." This is a valiant attempt, but perhaps it is not quite right; "they do not belong to the world" (Knox, Goodspeed, *etc.*) is better. It is origin and character rather than outlook that is meant.[45]

15 Since they are not "of the world" it might be thought that

---

[44] Once again we have ἵνα to express purpose.

[45] Some have seen a parallel with Qumran with its sharp division between the community and outsiders. But there is an important difference. As Raymond E. Brown puts it, "St. John's theology still presents a great clarification: our hatred is for evil as represented in the world, and not for the people who do evil" (*SNT*, p. 288, n. 74).

the prayer would be made that they should be removed "from the world". Jesus now makes it plain that He has nothing of the sort in mind. Their place is still in the world. It would be bad for them and disastrous for the world to have them taken out of the world. Prayers were offered by Moses and Elijah and Jonah that they be taken out of the world (Num. 11 : 15; I Kings 19 : 4; Jon. 4 : 3, 8), but in no case was the request granted. The place of God's people is in the world, though, of course, not of it. The church has often sought to contract out, to become a kind of holy club. But this is not the prayer of the Master. His prayer is rather that they should be kept from evil, or perhaps better, from "the evil one". With our background we should expect here a general reference to evil (Lagrange takes this view), but the thought is probably akin to that in I John 5 : 19, "We know that we are of God, and the whole world lieth in the evil one." Jesus recognizes the power of the evil one and prays for His own to be kept from him (*cf.* I John 5 : 18, and for other references to the devil, 12 : 31; 14 : 30; 16 : 11; I John 2 : 13f.; 3 : 12). They are to be "in" Christ (16 : 33; I John 5 : 20) and therefore "out of" the evil one. They have a task to do in the world so it is important that they should be in the world. But it is equally important that they should be kept from evil, for evil is fatal to the discharge of their task.

16 The statement of verse 14 is repeated.[46] As they belong to a Master they share His detachment from the world. The world is no more the source of their distinctives than it is of His.

17 "Sanctify" means "make holy, separate". They are not to be worldly men. They are to be holy men, separated from the world to be of service to the world. This sanctification is to be "in the truth" (for "truth" see Additional Note D, pp. 293ff.).[47] Elsewhere we read that the disciples are to "do" the truth (3 : 21), and there may be some such idea here. The sanctification that Jesus looks for the Father to accomplish will be worked out in their doing of the truth. This is now connected with "thy word".[48]

---

[46] Characteristically with a small change, one of word order. In v. 14 we have, οὐκ εἰσὶν ἐκ τοῦ κόσμου and in this verse, ἐκ τοῦ κόσμου οὐκ εἰσίν.

[47] With this we might compare the Qumran passage "cleansing him with a holy spirit from all wicked deeds. And he will sprinkle upon him a spirit of truth" (IQS, iv. 20f.; *DSS*, p. 376).

[48] This is possibly a quotation from LXX of Ps. 119 : 142. The MS evidence for that passage is divided between νόμος and λόγος, but Swete, for example, reads ὁ λόγος σου ἀλήθεια (*cf.* II Sam. 7 : 28).

That is to say the divine revelation is in mind once again. Sanctification is not effected apart from the divine revelation.[49] And the divine revelation is eminently trustworthy. It is not only true, but truth. It is not without its interest that Jesus earlier connected His own "word" with truth, that truth that makes men free (8 : 31f.). The Father's Word, all that He has revealed, is of the same kind. It is truth and may therefore be unhesitatingly accepted and acted upon. It is in this way that sanctification takes place.

18 The mission of Christ forms the pattern for the mission of the apostles.[50] Earlier we have read that the Father sanctified Him and sent Him into the world (10 : 36). He has just prayed that the Father will sanctify them and now He sends[51] them into the world. The parallel is impressive. Their lives are not to be aimless. They are given a definite commission by their Lord. Their task is to discharge it, even as He discharged His mission.

19 Again we have the thought of sanctification, but now Jesus says that He "sanctifies" Himself.[52] He sets Himself apart for the

---

[49] There is no article with ἀλήθεια in the final clause. This may well be to indicate that "thy word" and "truth" are not interchangeable terms (as the use of the article might be held to imply; see A. T. Robertson, *A Grammar of the Greek New Testament in the light of Historical Research*, London, n.d., p. 768). Or it may be an example of Colwell's rule that definite predicate nouns which precede the verb have no article (see on 1 : 1).

[50] The emphatic ἐμέ and κἀγώ stress this. For "send" see on 3 : 17.

[51] The aorist ἀπέστειλας (referring to Christ) is plain enough. It will refer to the single past action involved in the incarnation. But when we come to the apostles we should have expected a present or a future in place of ἀπέστειλα. Jesus may be referring to His commissioning of His followers earlier, and to His sending of them out on missions. It is perhaps more probable that the word is used proleptically. It adds a touch of certainty to the future sending out of the disciples.

[52] The verb, ἁγιάζω, is used in LXX of the setting apart of both people and things for the service of God (more often of people than things). Two uses in particular are important for the present passage, namely, those when the verb is used for the sanctifying of priests (Exod. 28 : 41; 29 : 1, 21 *etc.*), and of sacrifices (Exod. 28 : 38; Num. 18 : 9 *etc.*). Both are appropriate in the present passage. The verb does not signify in itself a setting apart for death, but in this context the meaning can scarcely be anything else. Some think this excluded by the subsequent statement with respect to the disciples, but this does not follow. Jesus sets Himself apart to do the will of God and He looks for them to be set apart to do God's will. But the implications are not the same in the two cases. For Him the consecration issued in an atoning death: for them in lives of service (sometimes crowned with the death of the martyr). There does not appear to be a parallel to Jesus' statement, "I sanctify myself". See further the lengthy note in Hoskyns.

doing of the Father's will, and in this context this must surely mean death. It points us to Calvary and all that Calvary means.[53] This is connected with the disciples in two ways. It is "for their sakes".[54] He dies for them, to do for them that which they could not do for themselves. And further it is "that they themselves also may be sanctified in truth."[55] It is purposeful. He dies with a view to the disciples being sanctified, being set apart for God. It is only on the basis of what He has done for them that His prayer for their being sanctified may be answered.

(c) Prayer for those who will in future believe, 17: 20–26

20 Neither for these only do I [1]pray, but for them also that believe on me through their word; 21 that they may all be one; even as thou, Father, art in me, and I in thee, that they also may be in us: that the world may believe that thou didst send me. 22 And the glory which thou hast given me I have given unto them; that they may be one, even as we are one; 23 I in them, and thou in me, that they may be perfected into one; that the world may know that thou didst send me, and lovedst them, even as thou lovedst me. 24 Father, [2]I desire that they also whom thou hast given me be with me where I am, that they may behold my glory, which thou hast given me: for thou lovedst me before the foundation of the world. 25 O righteous Father, the world knew thee not, but I knew thee; and these knew that thou didst send me; 26 and I made known unto them thy name, and will make it known; that the love wherewith thou lovedst me may be in them, and I in them.

[1]Gr. *make request.* [2]Gr. *that which thou hast given me, I desire that where I am, they also may be with me, that &c.*

The concluding section of the prayer is of the greatest of interest for in it Jesus prays for all believers. It is thus a prayer

---

[53] *Cf.* Lüthi: "He serves as Mediator between Heaven and earth. He sanctifies Himself by placing Himself completely at His Father's service and saying, 'Not my will, but thine, be done.' His path of duty leads through the Cross and the grave to Resurrection, and up to the right hand of the Father, from whence He shall come again. This absolute, voluntary filial obedience is the secret of Christ's self-sanctification. That is what He means when He stands alone before the Father here and vows to Him, 'I sanctify myself.'"

[54] For ὑπέρ see on 6 : 51.

[55] For ἵνα ὦσιν in this prayer see on v. 11.

for us as for those of previous generations. The dominant concern in the section is for unity and for the divine glory.

20 Jesus names those for whom He is about to pray. His intercession is not confined to the apostles. It looks out to the result of their mission and prays for[56] all who will believe[57] in Jesus[58] through their message. We have three times in this prayer had references to "thy word" referring to the Father (vv. 6, 14, 17). Now Jesus refers to "their word". This will stand for the whole of their message. Their message is one which will lead to faith in Christ.

21 The content of the prayer follows. The first petition is "that they may all be one" (*cf.* 10 : 30).[59] This is followed by a statement of the mutual indwelling of the Father and the Son and a prayer that believers may be "in" them both. The structure is markedly similar to that in v. 23, where there is also a concern for unity. In both places we have four parts. Here they are as follows: (1) "thou, Father, art in me," (2) "and I in thee," (3) "that they may be in us" (4) "that the world may believe that thou didst send me." In v. 23 these are the four parts: (1) "I in them," (2) "and thou in me," (3) "that they may be perfected into one;" (4) "that the world may know that thou didst send me". In each case the effect of this structure is to add solemnity and emphasis. Jesus prays first that the disciples may be one and then that they may be "in" the Father and the Son, just as the Father[60] and

---

56 The preposition is περί, which is usual with this verb to convey the meaning "ask about". But John uses it of praying for people in 16 : 26; 17 : 9, as well as here. The meaning is much the same as ὑπέρ, to which περί sometimes approximates (see BDF, 229(1)).

57 The present participle, τῶν πιστευόντων, might perhaps be held to signify those who at that moment believed on account of the disciples' word. But this is unlikely. The future almost certainly gives the sense of it. Turner regards this as a present participle for future, perhaps under Hebrew or Aramaic influence (M, III, p. 87). *Cf.* RSV: "who are to believe".

58 Taking εἰς ἐμέ with πιστευόντων rather than with λόγου (*i.e.* "their word with respect to me"). The former is more in accordance with Johannine style, but the latter is not impossible and it is favored by the word order.

59 For ἵνα ὦσιν in this prayer see on v. 11. Note further that John sets πάντες and ἕν side by side to emphasize that the great number of believers is to be one.

60 The address is Πατήρ as in vv. 24, 25 whereas in vv. 1, 5, 11 the vocative Πάτερ was used (there is some textual variation, but this appears to be the true text). Clearly there is not much difference between the two.

the Son are "in" one another (cf. 15 : 4ff.; I John 1 : 3). This does not mean that the unity between the Father and the Son is the same as that between believers and God. But it does mean that there is an analogy. The Father is in the Son and does His works (14 : 10). The Son is in the Father. The two are one (10 : 30) and yet are distinct. So in measure is it with believers. Without losing their identity they are to be in the Father and the Son. Apart from the Son they can do nothing (15 : 5).[61] In other words the unity for which He prays is to lead to a fuller experience of the Father and the Son. And this in turn will have the further consequences "that the world may believe".[62] Typically the faith that is to be produced in the world is expressed in terms of Christ's mission ("that thou didst send me"). The fact that the Father sent the Son is for this Gospel of the very first importance.

22 Jesus now says that He has given His followers the glory which the Father gave Him. That is to say, just as His true glory was to follow the path of lowly service culminating in the cross, so for them the true glory lay in the path of lowly service wherever it might lead them. The little band and its Master were both insignificant as the world counts importance. But the apostles are

---

[61] *Cf.* Barrett: "The unity of the Church is strictly analogous to the unity of the Father and the Son; the Father is active *in* the Son – it is the Father who does his works (14. 10) – and apart from the Father the deeds of the Son are meaningless, and indeed would be impossible; the Son again is in the Father, eternally with him in the unity of the Godhead, active alike in creation and redemption. The Father and the Son are one and yet remain distinct. The believers are to be, and are to be one, in the Father and the Son, distinct from God, yet abiding in God, and themselves the sphere of God's activity (14. 12)."

[62] Strachan has a helpful note: "The basis of this unity is religious. Even what is called 'oecumenical' union, the world-wide Church remains imperfect without a unity in our doctrine of God and of salvation, and a unity of purpose in our mission. The size and extent of the Church alone will not impress the world. This inward unity expressing itself in a common mission and message will alone impress the world." J. C. Earwaker is of opinion that the *ἵνα* which precedes this clause should not be taken as final but as introducing a third petition. Christ is praying, he thinks, "(1) that all may be one; (2) that they may be in us; (3) that the world may believe" (*ExT*, LXXV, 1963-64, p. 317). This is attractive, but it does not face the fact that the prayer is "for them also that believe on me through their word" (v. 20). It is not easy to see how a prayer for such people, who before believing were part of "the world", could include a petition "that the world may believe". Moreover Earwaker's view seems almost to require a *καί* before the third *ἵνα*.

right with God and therefore they are supremely significant. They have the true glory. They are walking in the way of God. We have seen often in this Gospel that for Jesus the cross is the true glory. Elsewhere it is recorded that He called on His followers to take up their cross in following Him (*e.g.* Luke 9 : 23). For them, too, the way of the cross is the way of true glory.[63] The purpose[64] of this giving of glory to the disciples is unity. This time Jesus prays that they may be one just as the Father and the Son are one. The bond which unites believers is to be of the very closest.

23 For the structure of this verse and its significance see on v. 21. Indwelling is the secret of it all. Christ indwells believers and the Father indwells Him. It is through Christ that they have their unity with the Father (*cf.* 14 : 6).[65] This indwelling is purposive.[66] It looks for the disciples to be "perfected into one".[67] They already had a unity of a sort. But this unity is not regarded as being sufficient. There is to be a closer unity, a "perfected" unity. As in v. 21 the unity of believers is to impress the world. In the former place the purpose was that the world might believe that the Father sent the Son. Here it is that the world may know that the Father sent the Son. Actually there is little difference, since for John believing gives further knowledge, and knowledge to all intents and purposes means faith (*cf.* v. 8). The world is to

---

[63] *Cf.* Barclay: "We must never think of our cross as our penalty; we must think of it as our glory ... The harder the task we give a student, or a craftsman, or a surgeon, the more we honour him. We, in effect, say that we believe that nobody but him could attempt that task at all. So when it is hard to be a Christian, we must regard it as our glory, as our honour given to us by God."

[64] ἵνα here is fully telic. For ἵνα see on 1 : 8, and for κἀγώ on 1 : 31.

[65] *Cf.* Lagrange: "The manner of this union is explained here: the Son is in the faithful, He is in the Father: it is thus by Him that the faithful are united with the Father: not that they pass from the one to the other, but because they find the Father in the Son".

[66] Again we have telic ἵνα.

[67] The perfect tense τετελειωμένοι may denote a state they should attain and remain in. On the meaning of the verb Temple remarks: "The word translated *perfected* does not primarily suggest ethical perfection but complete realisation of ideal or type; a fair rendering of the original would be: *that they may become full grown into one*." εἰς is somewhat surprising in a context where we would expect ἐν. According to BDF εἰς here "denotes rather the purpose, the result" (205).

know not only that the Father sent the Son, but also that He loves believers[68] as He loves the Son[69] (*cf.* Rev. 3 : 9). The unity of believers will be explicable to the world only on the basis of the divine love. It will transcend all human unity. The unity in question, while it is a spiritual unity rather than one of organization, as we have seen, yet has an outward expression, for it is a unity which the world can observe, and which will influence the world.
24 Jesus' final petition is for them to be with Him. "I desire"[70] (ARV) is a verb which expresses the action of the will. It is more than a mere wish. Here when Jesus is thinking of the disciples He uses the expression "I will", but when He is thinking of Himself He prays, "not what I will, but what thou wilt" (Mark 14 : 36). The petition looks for the disciples[71] to be with Jesus in the next world rather than this (*cf.* 14 : 3). He wants them to be "where I am"[72] and He has already said, "I am no more in the world" (v. 11). He looks for them to be with Him so that they may see the glory that the Father has given Him. It is possible that "glory" here is used in the more common sense, rather than denoting lowliness as earlier in this prayer. Jesus may be referring to the majesty and splendour that will be His in the life to come. It is also possible that He is praying that they will have the insight to know what the true glory really is, that they may see lowly service as truly glorious. Paul gives us a thought somewhat similar to this when he speaks of "beholding as in a mirror the glory of

---

[68] Taking αὐτούς to refer to the same group as the preceding αὐτοῖς. It is possible to take it as an *ad sensum* construction, referring to "the world" (so Bernard).

[69] Notice that there is one ὅτι for σύ με ἀπέστειλας and ἠγάπησας αὐτούς κτλ. The two are a unity. The love of God and the sending of the Son are inseparable.

[70] θέλω. We should bear in mind the point made by Bailey, that "the consciousness of the union of His will with the Father's destroys any distinction between 'I pray' and 'I will' ".

[71] As in v. 2 there is an alternation of genders. The neuter ὅ of that which the Father has given is quite general. Then we have the masculine κἀκεῖνοι as the personal note becomes more prominent. The clause with the neuter, ὅ δέδωκάς μοι, is in a specially prominent position which may indicate that John wants to give it emphasis. Turner thinks that "the gift is depicted first in its unity = ὅ, then individually = κἀκεῖνος" (M, III, p. 21).

[72] The word order εἰμί ἐγώ distinguishes this from the formula ἐγὼ εἰμί used to such effect elsewhere in this Gospel (see on 8 : 58 *etc.*). But the personal pronoun enables emphasis to be given to "I" (see on 1 : 20).

the Lord" and being "transformed into the same image from glory to glory" (II Cor. 3 : 18). The glory that the Father gave the Son arose out of the love with which He loved Him before this universe came into existence.[73] Again we have the thought of pre-existence, and again the greatness of the love of the Father for the Son.

25 The last two verses are something of a retrospect. They might, perhaps, be separated off as a separate division of the prayer. There is no petition in them. Jesus is no longer praying for those who should believe through the apostolic witness. He is making certain statements about what He has done and the purpose of it. The address "righteous Father" is unique (though cf. "Holy Father", v. 11). It reminds us of the character of the Father. Jesus is not looking for an attitude of favoritism from the Father. He is bearing in mind, as He prays for His followers, that it is God's nature to be righteous. It is probably significant that immediately after addressing God as righteous He proceeds to distinguish between "the world" and His followers. It is because God is righteous that He treats both groups as He does.[74] Jesus proceeds to contrast "the world"[75] with Himself. The world, in its very nature, was ignorant of God (cf. 8 : 55). But Jesus is different. He has a complete knowledge of God (see on 4 : 18). The knowledge of the disciples is related to the incarnation. It is not said that they knew God, but that they knew that God sent Jesus.

---

[73] Godet comments: "This saying of Jesus is that which leads us farthest into the divine depths. It shows Christian speculation on what path it must seek the solution of the relations of the Trinity; love is the key of this mystery."

[74] Cf. Dods: "The Father's justice is appealed to, that the believing may not share the fate of the unbelieving world." Cf. also Lenski: "Jesus closes with a word of complete confidence in the righteousness of the Father, yet he leaves unsaid what action he expects from this righteousness. He does not need to say this, for the Father will most assuredly act in righteous accord with what Jesus here lays before him."

[75] καί before ὁ κόσμος is a little surprising. It can scarcely mean "even", but "also" is not much easier. Perhaps we should take ἐγὼ δέ σε ἔγνων as a parenthesis and understand the two καί as "both ... and", "both the world did not know thee ... and these knew...." The ignorance of the world and the knowledge of the disciples are a pair. Moule notes that Abbott favors this view, and proceeds, "but the first καί does not seem so easily explicable" (IBNTG, p. 167). However he gives no alternative explanation, preferring apparently to regard the καί as displaced. Turner favors the view adopted here (M, III, p. 335). NEB renders "although" (so also Goodspeed, Schonfield etc.). FF has "indeed".

26 Throughout the ministry Jesus has made[76] the Father known (*cf.* v. 6). For the use of "thy name" in this prayer see on v. 6, and for "the name" see on 1 : 12. Jesus has revealed the Father to His followers and He says now that He will do this again. This may refer to the revelation in the cross, or it may refer to the work of the Holy Spirit whom He has promised to send (15 : 26). The following reference to love[77] may perhaps make it a little more likely that it is the cross that is primarily in mind. The purpose of this future revelation is that the love with which the Father loved His Son might be "in" the disciples. In Johannine fashion this probably has a double meaning: the love in question will be "within" them ("in their hearts", *Twentieth Century*), and also "among" them (the relation uniting them to one another). With this purpose is linked another, that Christ Himself may be "in" them (within them and among them). The love of God is thus associated with the indwelling of Christ. We know the love of God because the Son dwells in our hearts.[78]

---

[76] The aorist ἐγνώρισα points to a completed activity.

[77] For ἀγάπη see on 5 : 42. The cognate accusative coupled with a personal object, ἡ ἀγάπη ἣν ἠγάπησάς με, is most unusual. Abbott finds no parallel except Eph. 2 : 4, and there the accusative may be due to the attraction of the relative into the case of the antecedent. He thinks that the Evangelist "shrank from representing the love of God as instrumental ('wherewith')" and he proceeds to connect it with the statement that God *is* love (2014).

[78] *Cf.* Westcott: "The last word of the Lord's prayer corresponds with the last word of His discourses; ἐγὼ νενίκηκα τὸν κόσμον (xvi. 33). He is Himself the source of victory and life."

CHAPTER XVIII

V.   THE CRUCIFIXION, 18 : 1 – 19 : 42

As in the other Gospels it is the events surrounding the crucifixion and the resurrection that form the climax of the whole book. John has his own way of handling these events, a way which stresses the divine overruling. Thus his account of the arrest stresses Jesus' complete mastery of the situation, and there are touches like the "It is finished" of the dying Saviour which indicate plainly that the outcome was completely in God's control. Here supremely we see the purpose of God worked out, and here supremely is the glory of Jesus displayed.

1.   THE ARREST, 18 : 1–12

1 When Jesus had spoken these words, he went forth with his disciples over the ¹brook ²Kidron, where was a garden, into which he entered, himself and his disciples. 2 Now Judas also, who ³betrayed him, knew the place: for Jesus ofttimes resorted thither with his disciples. 3 Judas then, having received the ⁴band of soldiers, and officers from the chief priests and the Pharisees, cometh thither with lanterns and torches and weapons. 4 Jesus therefore, knowing all the things that were coming upon him, went forth, and saith unto them, Whom seek ye? 5 They answered him, Jesus of Nazareth. Jesus saith unto them, I am he. And Judas also, who ³betrayed him, was standing with them. 6 When therefore he said unto them, I am he, they went backward, and fell to the ground. 7 Again therefore he asked them, Whom seek ye? And they said, Jesus of Nazareth. 8 Jesus answered, I told you that I am he; if therefore ye seek me, let these go their way: 9 that the word might be fulfilled which he spake, Of those whom thou hast given me I lost not one. 10 Simon Peter therefore having a sword drew it, and struck the high priest's ⁵servant, and cut off his right ear. Now the ⁵servant's name was Malchus. 11 Jesus therefore said unto Peter, Put up the sword into the sheath: the cup which the Father hath given me, shall I not drink it? 12 So the ⁴band and the ⁶chief captain, and the officers of the Jews, seized Jesus and bound him,

¹Or, *ravine* Gr. *winter-torrent.* ²Or, *of the Cedars* ³Or, *delivered him up* ⁴Or, *cohort* ⁵Gr. *bondservant.* ⁶Or, *military tribune* Gr. *chiliarch.*

739

As in the Synoptists, Jesus is arrested in the Garden. But there are important differences. A striking omission is the agony in Gethsemane. Many conjectures have been put forward as to why John does not mention this, but none is universally accepted. Perhaps the most convincing is that which refers us to John's purpose. He was not giving a complete account of all that happened, but painting a picture. This incident did not suit his purpose so he omitted it (though such words as those of 12 : 27; 18 : 11 show that he has the essential teaching of the incident).[1] John makes it clear, as the others do not, that the garden was a frequent resort of Jesus and His followers (though *cf.* Luke 22 : 39). He also uses a technical term for the band of soldiers (Matthew and Mark use this term, but not in connection with the arrest, Matt. 27 : 27; Mark 15 : 16). Above all, he stresses the majesty of Jesus by telling us that He spoke and acted in such a way as to strike awe into the soldiers who came to arrest him so that they "went backward, and fell to the ground" (v. 6).

1 The opening words perhaps militate against the view that some of the preceding discourse was spoken on the road. They seem to indicate that it was after it was concluded that Jesus "went forth" (*i.e.* from the house) with[2] the apostles. It is not impossible that the meaning is "went out of the city"; but "went out of the house" seems more probable. It is John alone who tells us that they went to a garden,[3] though he does not name the place (as do Matthew and Mark). He does however give its

---

[1] *Cf.* Murray: John "has no wish to conceal or deny the reality of the deep waters through which the soul of Jesus had to pass. He has already recorded (12 : 27) an agony in the Temple Courts. But he seems to have felt, as he looked back over the whole story, that there was another side even to the human experience than that which met the eye. We have already seen that to him the Cross, so far from connoting humiliation and defeat, was the symbol of uplifting, of glory, and of victory. So here, he is content to recall the spiritual struggle by a single phrase (verse 11). He records exclusively words and deeds which shewed that Jesus remained throughout absolute master of the situation. He is so, of course, even in the Synoptic account: but there is so much else in the picture that the fact may easily be overlooked."

[2] This is one of only three places in which John uses the preposition σύν (elsewhere, 12 : 2; 21 : 3). Some put a distinction of meaning between σὺν τοῖς μαθηταῖς here and μετὰ τῶν μαθητῶν in the next verse, but it is better seen as another example of Johannine variation.

[3] His word is κῆπος (which some render "orchard"). Matthew and Mark call it a χωρίον (Matt. 26 : 36; Mark 14 : 32), while Luke simply says that they went to the Mount of Olives (Luke 22 : 39). Clearly the place was situated

location, namely on the further side of the Kidron.[4]

2 Judas is characterized, as elsewhere, by the betrayal. John uses the present participle which conveys the meaning "who was betraying Him (*i.e.* at that moment)". The information that Jesus and the disciples often went to the Garden is found here only, though Luke tells us that Jesus lodged "in" the mount of Olives every night during passion week (Luke 21 : 37). This probably means that He and the disciples used to bivouac, sleeping in the open air, and probably in this very garden. Ryle reminds us that "Excepting at the institution of the Lord's Supper, we have no mention of our Lord ever being in any *house* in Jerusalem." "Ofttimes" would be a curious way of referring to Jesus' custom on the present visit only. It probably indicates that He had been in the habit of using the garden through the years.

3 "Band" is a technical term for the "cohort".[5] Judas apparently

---

on the lower slopes of Olivet, though we cannot be sure of exactly where. A very old garden with olive trees is the traditional site, and it may be correct. But it is impossible to be certain. Indeed there may be significance in the use of ἦν, "there *was* (not *is*) a garden". It may perhaps indicate that the garden had been destroyed by the time the Gospel was written.

[4] The reading τοῦ Κεδρών though supported only by A *pc* lat has much to commend it, the other two variants, τοῦ Κέδρου and τῶν Κεδρών having the appearance of corrections. This will indicate that the name of the brook was Κεδρών, the word being indeclinable. Some think that the plural article should be read to give the meaning "the brook of the cedars" (τῶν Κέδρων), but this seems less probable. As far as is known no cedars grew there, and this looks like an attempt at providing an etymology for a previously existent name. Κεδρών is the transliteration of the Hebrew קדרון which appears to have the meaning "dark". The connection with "cedar" is purely fortuitous. The Kedron is described as a χείμαρρος, *i.e.* a wadi for the most part dry in the summer, but with a flowing stream in the winter. John is the only New Testament writer to speak of it.

[5] The term is σπεῖρα, "the Gk. word used to transl. the Lat. 'cohors' ... In our lit. prob. always *cohort*" (AG). A cohort was the tenth part of a legion and thus normally comprised 600 men (though in practice the number varied a good deal). It was commanded by a χιλίαρχος (*cf.* v. 12). John will not of course, mean that 600 or so soldiers took part in the arrest but that the "cohort" performed the task, *i.e.* a detachment was sent. Some point out that σπεῖρα was used on occasion of a maniple, which was one third of a cohort, *i.e.* 200 men. But even this is rather large. John is surely not saying that the whole σπεῖρα was present, but rather using a form of speech like our "the police came to arrest the man". Yet we must bear in mind that the Romans could use surprisingly large numbers of soldiers where one prisoner was in question (Acts 23 : 23), and that here they may well have feared a riot.

was guiding a knot of Roman soldiers and if the article is significant
it will have been a known, definite cohort (*cf.* Abbott, "A.V. ('a
band') has missed the reference to '*the* band' that regularly kept
guard in the fortress called Antonia"⁶). It is likely that the
Jewish authorities would have brought in the Romans as soon as
possible in view of their ultimate aim (and, we might add, in view
of the fact that on a previous occasion the temple guards had failed
to arrest Jesus, 7:44ff.). With passions running high at the festival
period, the Romans would be unlikely to refuse a request for help
from the high priest. They would always have to reckon with
the possibility that Jesus and the eleven would resist arrest and
that a host of excited Galileans might join them. With the soldiers
was a group sent from the Sanhedrin (this will be the force of
the linking of "chief priests" with "Pharisees"). Moffatt distinguishes the two components of this force as "troops" and "atten-
dants". The band was armed⁷ and they carried lights.⁸ They were
thus prepared for trouble and equipped to meet it. The lights
indicate that they thought Jesus might hide away in the dark
recesses of the garden. As it was full moon, they would not be
needed otherwise (unless the night was cloudy; since, however,
we are told that it was cold, v. 18, it would seem to have been
clear).

4, 5 Jesus' complete knowledge of the situation dictates His action

---

⁶   1994 *b.*

⁷   The temple guard was on occasion unarmed (*cf.* Josephus, *Bell.* iv, 293),
but now they, as well as the soldiers, carried weapons.

⁸   John mentions φανοί as well as λαμπάδες. Commentators cite a statement
from Phrynichus which shows that in earlier days the two terms were synonymous. By New Testament times, however, φανός had come to mean a lantern.
λαμπάς will be a torch, made of resinous strips of wood fastened together. It
is sometimes rendered "lamp" in the New Testament, but Plummer suggests
that this translation is best left for λύχνος. There is a good discussion of "The
Household Lamps of Palestine in New Testament Times" by Robert Houston
Smith in *BA*, XXIX, Feb. 1966, pp. 2–27. He agrees that λαμπάς here denotes
a torch, though it will be a lamp in the story of the Ten Virgins (on this,
however, see J. Jeremias, "Lampades in Mt 25.1–13" in *Soli Deo Gloria*, ed.
J. McD. Richards, Richmond, Va., 1968, pp. 83ff.). He thinks of φανοί as
"roughly cylindrical terracotta vessels with an opening on one side large enough
for a household lamp to be inserted, its wick facing outward; a ceramic ring –
or strap – handle on the top permitted easy carrying. Occasionally lanterns
may have had built-in lamps" (*op. cit.*, p. 7; no lanterns of precisely this period
are known, but Smith describes what are found both before and after).

(see on 2 : 24; 4 : 18). John omits any reference to the kiss of Judas (Matt. 26 : 49; Mark 14 : 45; Luke 22 : 47), which would have taken place at this juncture. He is not concerned to tell us everything that happened, but rather to show Jesus' complete control of the situation. The Lord knows all the things that are coming upon Him, and in the light of this knowledge goes out[9] to meet the soldiers. He is not "arrested" at all. He has the initiative and He gives Himself up. First He asks whom they are seeking. When they say, "Jesus of Nazareth",[10] He replies, "I am", which may well mean "I am Jesus of Nazareth". But the answer is in the style of deity (see on 8 : 58).[11] This must have been a most unexpected move on His part. The soldiers had come out secretly to arrest a fleeing peasant. In the gloom they find themselves confronted by a commanding figure, who so far from running away comes out to meet them and speaks to them in the very language of deity. At this point John reiterates that Judas was there. As in v. 2, he speaks of him in terms of the betrayal. It had obviously made a deep impression on the minds of the early Christians. In the Synoptic Gospels Judas identifies Jesus with a kiss. Here he is simply mentioned as standing there, though John's "with them" is probably significant. It indicates on whose side he was.

6 The effect of Jesus' bearing is now brought out. His fearlessness, the gloom with its atmosphere of mysteriousness, His numinous words, all combined to produce a moment of terror, or perhaps awe. The soldiers retreated and fell to the ground. It is possible

---

[9] ἐξῆλθεν corresponding to εἰσῆλθεν (v. 1) probably means that He went out from the garden. Others suggest that it means out of the gloom into the light of the torches, or out of the recesses of the garden into the open places where the soldiers were.

[10] 'Ιησοῦν τὸν Ναζωραῖον. Jesus is characteristically described with this term (Ναζωραῖος is found 13 times and Ναζαρηνός 6 times). Its meaning is not certain, and many have pointed out that linguistically the transition from Ναζαρέτ to Ναζωραῖος is not easy. However, it appears to have been made, for there can be no doubt but that in the New Testament Ναζωραῖος = ὁ ἀπὸ Ναζαρέτ. See the note by G. F. Moore in *The Beginnings of Christianity*, I (London, 1920), pp. 426–432, and the literature cited in AG.

[11] Dodd reminds us that the repetition of the saying in the two following verses is not unlike that of ὁ υἱός σου ζῇ in 4 : 50, 51, 53. He adds, "In each place an expression entirely natural in the circumstances is given a special importance by a repetition which is sufficiently unnatural to draw the reader's attention" (*HTFG*, p. 75 n. 2).

that those in front recoiled from Jesus' unexpected advance, so
that they bumped those behind them, causing them to stumble
and fall. C. B. Williams translates: "took a lurch backward and
fell to the ground". But clearly what concerns John is the majesty
of Jesus thus underlined. Some find it too difficult to think of the
soldiers as recoiling, and emend the text to read "he" (*i.e.* Judas)
instead of "they" (so, for example, Schonfield and Torrey). This
certainly makes for an easier text, but it raises the insuperable
difficulty of how, if this were original, it has left no mark on the
manuscript tradition.

7 Jesus repeats His question and the soldiers their answer
(characteristically John has a small variant; he replaces "they
answered him" with "they said").

8, 9 Jesus repeats His declaration of identity (retaining the same
mystical words). He adds a request that the soldiers permit His
followers to go away.[12] Their business is with Him, not them.
The Good Shepherd takes thought for His sheep at the very hour
in which He goes forth to arrest, trial and death. It may be that
this is behind His request for them to repeat that it is "Jesus of
Nazareth" for whom they are looking. Out of their own mouth, in a
twice-repeated statement, He leads them to declare in effect that
their business is not with the disciples. John adds an interesting
expression. It is common to find it said that such and such a thing
happened "in order that the scripture might be fulfilled". Here
it is "that[13] the word might be fulfilled which he spake". To John
it was inconceivable that a word of Jesus would fail of fulfilment.
It is put into the same category as Scripture. The "word" referred
to is found in 17 : 12, but the repetition, as usually in John, has
its variations. Here Jesus speaks of the disciples as given to Him,
there it was the "name" of God (the disciples were earlier said
to be "given" to Him, 17 : 6; see also on 3 : 35). Here there is
no reference to His "guarding" them, while "I lost not one"[14]
replaces "not one of them perished". These changes do not affect
the sense, and there is exactness in John's saying that this saying
of Jesus was fulfilled. Some object that the object of the saying

---

[12] The construction εἰ . . . ζητεῖτε conveys the sense "If (as is the case)
you seek Me". Jesus accepts the concentration of their attention on Himself
in order to ensure the freedom of His followers.

[13] For ἵνα without a preceding principal verb see on 1 : 8.

[14] For the redundant pronoun see on 1 : 27.

as originally given was spiritual, but here it is physical. But an arrest of the disciples at this moment would have been a very severe test of faith and it might well have caused them great spiritual harm. It is unnecessary to see an opposition. To preserve them physically at this moment was to preserve them spiritually.

10 John names Peter as the man who wielded the sword,[15] whereas the Synoptists leave him nameless. The reason is not apparent. It is sometimes said that Mark wishes to spare Peter, but this is difficult to maintain in view of his inclusion of the denial. It may be a further example of John's love of being exact with names and places. He also tells us that the man whose right ear (this detail is shared with Luke) was cut off[16] was Malchus. Nothing more is known of him. The use of the definite article (*the* servant of the high priest, not *a* servant) marks Malchus out, but our ignorance of the man and his position prevents us from knowing just what the significance of this is.[17]

11 Jesus immediately intervenes. "Put up the sword" is a

---

[15] μάχαιρα denotes a long knife or a short sword (ῥομφαία being the large sword). It is frequently said that it was illegal to carry such a weapon at Passover. J. Jeremias disposes of this contention by drawing attention to Mishnah *Shab.* 6 : 4, wherein R. Eliezer declares that a man's weapons, including his sword, are his "adornments" and therefore legal. Jeremias contends that R. Eliezer is "the constant champion of the earlier tradition" (*The Eucharistic Words of Jesus*, Oxford, 1955, p. 50). This may be so, but in the passage in question Eliezer is cited for a dissenting opinion, the one put forward being that these weapons are not legal. Jeremias's argument can scarcely be called impressive. This does not, however, mean that it cannot have been the feast. Desperate men do not normally respect ecclesiastical niceties.

[16] D. Daube draws attention to Jewish passages referring to the slitting of men's ears as a means of disqualifying them for priestly office and he thinks that the high priest was being insulted through his servant: "he would be seriously and suggestively disgraced by having his servant mutilated in this particular manner" (*JThS*, n.s., XI, 1960, p. 61). There may be something in this, but I am inclined to think that the striking of the ear was probably not deliberate. After all it is a small target, and Peter was not an expert swordsman. It is more likely that he struck out wildly in the general direction of the head and in the uncertain light hit only the ear.

[17] Calvin comments: "it was exceedingly thoughtless in Peter to try to prove his faith by the sword, while he could not do so by his tongue. When he is called to make confession, he denies; but now unbidden by his Master he raises a riot. Warned by such a striking example, let us learn to moderate our zeal. And as the wantonness of our flesh ever itches to dare more than God commands, let us learn that our zeal will turn out badly whenever we dare to undertake anything beyond God's Word."

somewhat vigorous expression,[18] and leaves no doubt but that swordplay is forbidden. Then Jesus speaks of the cup which the Father has given Him and His question indicates the necessity for drinking it.[19] There are references to the cup in the other Gospels (Matt. 26 : 39; Mark 14 : 36; Luke 22 : 42). But in them it occurs in the prayer in the Garden. This is the only passage which assigns the origin of the "cup" to the Father. In the Old Testament the "cup" often has associations of suffering and of the wrath of God (Ps. 75 : 8; Isa. 51 : 17, 22; Jer. 25 : 15; Ezek. 23 : 31-33, *etc.*; *cf.* Rev. 14 : 10; 16 : 19). We cannot doubt but that in this solemn moment these are the thoughts that the term arouses. Weymouth renders "cup of sorrow".

12 Jesus' summary rejection of resistance leads immediately to His arrest. The conjunction of the word rendered "chief captain" with that rendered "band"[20] seems to make it clear that a cohort of Roman soldiers and their officer is meant. Either term is used on occasion of something else, but the conjunction seems conclusive. The Jews are linked with them in the arrest. The reason for the binding of Jesus is not apparent. Since, however, there is no suggestion of escape, it must be simply the standard practice in arresting prisoners. There may also be something of a rebound from their earlier fear. The Synoptists do not mention this detail. Contrariwise John does not tell us, as they do, that the disciples all deserted Jesus and ran away (Mark 14 : 50).

2. The Jewish Trial and the Denials, 18 : 13–27

The narratives of the trial and of Peter's denials in the four Gospels are not easy to fit in to one another.[21] The trial seems to have had several clearly defined stages. Thus all our Gospels

---

[18] Βάλε τὴν μάχαιραν εἰς τὴν θήκην.

[19] The emphatic οὐ μή leaves no room for doubt.

[20] ὁ χιλίαρχος and ἡ σπεῖρα. The former term may, of course, be used of officers other than the tribune, the commander of a cohort, *e.g.* Mark 6 : 21; Rev. 6 : 15; 19 : 18. But it is generally used in the technical sense, and the conjunction here with σπεῖρα seems to put the matter beyond doubt.

[21] See J. Blinzler, *The Trial of Jesus* (Westminster, Maryland, 1959); P. Winter, *On the Trial of Jesus* (Basel, 1961). There is a very valuable chapter in William Barclay's, *Crucified and Crowned* (London, 1961), pp. 56–78, and see also J. Moffatt's article in *HDCG*; J. Juster, *Les Juifs dans l'Empire Romain*, II (Paris, 1914), pp. 127–152. A. N. Sherwin-White has a very useful discussion and he makes some cogent criticisms of the positions taken up by Winter and Juster (*Roman Society and Roman Law in the New Testament*, Oxford, 1963, pp. 24–47). He shows that all four Gospels have impressive agreements with Roman

speak of a trial before the Jewish authorities (which had two or three stages) and another before Pilate. John is the only one of the four to tell us that Jesus appeared before Annas, though all four speak of two stages. There seems little doubt but that Jesus was first given an informal examination, and that He was later brought before the Sanhedrin for the formal sentence. As the visit to Annas is mentioned only by John some have thought that it is to be rejected. But if nothing of the sort took place it is hard to see why John says it did.[22] It could not have been in order to secure Jesus' condemnation by Annas, for no such condemnation is recorded. Moreover, John is not ignorant of the fact that Jesus was brought before Caiaphas (v. 24), nor of the other fact that it was from Caiaphas that He was taken to Pilate (v. 28). Acceptance of John's story leads to fewer difficulties than its rejection.[23]

Godet reminds us that according to Jewish law a prisoner could not be sentenced on the same day as his trial, and he connects the two examinations with this. The appearance before Annas did not fully meet the legal requirements, but "they must at least try to save appearances as far as possible, and to offer the semblance of a first preliminary meeting, before that at which the sentence should be pronounced." It has been suggested that the house of Annas was not far from Gethsemane,[24] and if this was the case it is unlikely that Annas would let the opportunity pass of having a preliminary examination of Jesus before sending Him on to Caiaphas. It is also to be borne in mind, that, though we naturally think of Jesus as being brought before Annas in that priest's house his house is not mentioned in the narrative.

---

law and custom. His discussion is more valuable than most of the others because of his intimate acquaintance with Roman legal procedure.

[22] *Cf.* Moffatt: "the insuperable difficulty about eliminating the Annas trial is the impossibility of detecting any adequate motive for its invention and introduction" (*HDCG*, II, p. 751).

[23] Lord Charnwood comments that in this scene "there is no doctrinal purpose served, but it is a scene full of character and life, which really enriches the history which we obtain as a whole when we take the Gospels together" (*According to St. John*, London, n.d., p. 99).

[24] MacGregor thinks that Annas may have resided at the "bazaars of the sons of Hanan" and that these were on the Mount of Olives. If this were so Annas would have lived close to the place of arrest and it would be very natural to take Jesus there. But there does not appear to be a great deal of evidence to support the conjecture. Calvin also suggests that Annas's house may have been convenient to the place of arrest.

It is possible that Annas saw Jesus in the temple (so Barrett on v. 15). The references to the doorkeeper (vv. 16f.), however, make it more probable that a private house is meant, though not necessarily the house of Annas.

There are other difficulties which some try to solve by changes of order. Thus an examination took place before "the high priest" (v. 19), though Jesus was not sent to Caiaphas until v. 24.[25] Again, John's scheme of things might be held to give us one denial by Peter in the courtyard of Annas and the other two in that of Caiaphas, whereas in the Synoptic accounts they all appear to be at the same place. The first denial is separated from the second and third in this Gospel by the examination before the high priest, whereas in the Synoptists the three denials follow on. But this does not necessarily mean a dislocation in John's original order. It is likely that John preserves the order of events, and in any case part of his aim appears to have been to contrast our Lord's steadfastness under stress with Peter's fickleness. This is well brought out by interposing the examination between two of the denials. Some more or less plausible alterations to the order of verses have been suggested,[26] but these solutions break down on

---

[25] But it is to be borne in mind that all who had held the office of high priest were designated by the term. Josephus affords a number of examples (*e.g. Bell.* iv, 151, 160). See Schürer, *A History of the Jewish People*, II, i (Edinburgh, 1885), pp. 202f. Thus Annas may well be meant (though the reference to Caiaphas in v. 13 makes this less likely). Annas is specifically referred to as high priest (Luke 3 : 2; Acts 4 : 6). It is also to be borne in mind that John uses the plural "high priests" in v. 35. It is difficult to envisage what this means unless Annas be included. It is best to retain the order and take the term here to refer to Annas.

[26] Some lay stress on the fact that the Sinaitic Syriac has the order 13, 24, 14–15, 19–23, 16–18, 25. Such an order makes sense, but it is more likely that some scribe altered the accepted order to this one because of the difficulties he saw in the text than that this MS alone preserves the correct order. The simplest alternative is to read v. 24 immediately after v. 13. Torrey suggests that this was the original order. He thinks that a scribe when writing v. 13 had in his mind 11 : 51, so that his eye naturally alighted on v. 14. Having written it he realized that the had omitted a verse and, to repair the damage, inserted the omitted words at the first possible opportunity, in this case after v. 23. But it is too much to say, with Torrey, "the explanation is both simple and certain". It gives no account of the fact that the MSS almost unanimously have the present order, and this is the big stumbling block. Why should the overwhelming majority of the scribes transform their intelligible order of verses to conform to this one scribe's error (which Torrey thinks "presents a most astonishing contradiction")? Had scribes no capacity for astonishment?

the difficulty of explaining how the present order got into the vast majority of the MSS. No really convincing explanation has been given as to why an original tidy order with no or very little difficulty about Annas and Caiaphas and the denials should have been all but universally corrupted into the present scheme. There is also the suspicion that harmonizing motives have been at work. The Synoptists speak of an examination before Caiaphas, but John does not. If however we move v. 24 so that it precedes v. 14 an "agreement" is brought about. This however, introduces another difficulty for the subject matter of the examination here is different from that in the Synoptists. It is better to accept the order of the bulk of the MSS as John's original order, and to attempt to understand the text as it stands.

(a) Jesus brought before Annas, 18 : 13, 14

13 and led him to Annas first; for he was father in law to Caiaphas, who was high priest that year. 14 Now Caiaphas was he that gave counsel to the Jews, that it was expedient that one man should die for the people.

13 It might have been thought that Jesus would have been brought before Caiaphas, since he was the ruling high priest. But Annas had been high priest, and may well have been thought by many to be still the only legitimate high priest. The high priesthood in the Old Testament was for life, and such depositions as the Romans carried out were not lawful. But we do not know how far men were prepared to accept the authority of the Romans in this matter. In any case Annas appears to have been a very wily person and one well able to assert himself. Not only was he high priest, but in time five of his sons occupied that office, as did Caiaphas, his son-in-law. There is little doubt but that through these changes the astute old man at the head of the family exercised a good deal of authority. He was in all probability the real power in the land, whatever the legal technicalities. There is nothing surprising in Jesus' being brought before him, especially if his house were near the scene of the arrest.[27] We owe to John

---

[27] *Cf.* Barclay: "If the stalls in the Temple which Jesus had overturned really were the property of Annas and his family, no doubt Annas used his position to arrange that Jesus should be brought to him first, that he might gloat over the downfall of the presumptuous Galilaean" (*op. cit.*, p. 61).

the information that Caiaphas had married Annas's daughter and John proceeds to tell us that this man held the office of high priest. "That year" (as in 11 : 49, 51) should not be taken to signify that John thought of the office as an annual one. It surely means "at that time", "that fateful year", "that year of all years". John tells us that Jesus was brought "first" to Annas. This requires a "second", which is evidently the appearance before Caiaphas (v. 24).

14 In John's mind the thing that marked out Caiaphas was his unconscious prophecy that Jesus would die for the people (11 : 49f.). So here he distinguishes him by referring back to this prophecy. His recall of those words may also be meant to indicate that Jesus might expect little from such a judge. Here was no idealist ready to see that justice was done, but a cynical politician who had already spoken in favor of Jesus' death.[28]

(b) Peter's First Denial, 18 : 15–18

15 And Simon Peter followed Jesus, and so did another disciple. Now that disciple was known unto the high priest, and entered in with Jesus into the court of the high priest; 16 but Peter was standing at the door without. So the other disciple, who was known unto the high priest, went out and spake unto her that kept the door, and brought in Peter. 17 The maid therefore that kept the door saith unto Peter, Art thou also one of this man's disciples? He saith, I am not. 18 Now the [1]servants and the officers were standing there, having made [2]a fire of coals; for it was cold; and they were warming themselves: and Peter also was with them, standing and warming himself.

[1]Gr. *bondservants*. [2]Gr. *a fire of charcoal*.

There are difficulties about the story of the denial. One of them arises from the fact that John separates the first denial (v. 17) from the second and third (vv. 25–27) by interposing the story of the examination of Jesus before the high priest. To some this appears to place one denial in the courtyard of Annas and the others in that of Caiaphas (unless there has been dislocation of the text). This, however, does not follow. It is quite possible that Caiaphas and Annas shared the same palace (Godet thinks that John's narrative leads us to this conclusion; Hendriksen and Dods also think of one residence). But even this is not necessary. Wherever

[28] For John's use of ἄνθρωπος of Jesus see on 4 : 29.

they lived it would have been quite possible for them both to have
been in the same place on this particular night. In any case it
is not necessary to postulate a change of courtyard. It is true that
v. 24 speaks of Annas sending Jesus to Caiaphas, but this may
be John's way of rounding off this part of his narrative. Then,
having finished with Annas he returns to complete the story of
the denials. He does not speak of Peter as moving from one
courtyard to another, and it is not necessary to read this into his
narrative. Even if Jesus was taken from one building to another,
or even from one part of Jerusalem to another, it does not follow
that Peter moved in between his denials. John does not always
narrate events in strict sequence, and we have no reason for
demanding this of him here. This still leaves us with the problem
that, whereas the Synoptists tell of the three denials in order John
interposes an examination of Jesus by the high priest between the
first and second. The Synoptists finish off their denial stories once
they start. This means neither that there was nor that there was
not an interval between the denials. The Synoptists ought not to
be pressed as though they meant that the denials followed in
quick sequence and that nothing happened in between. They
simply do not address themselves to the problem (except for Luke's
brief notices; see below). There is nothing inherently unlikely
about John's statement. On the contrary, it seems probable that
an interval of time elapsed between Peter's withstanding of the
challenge of the doorkeeper and the raising of the issue by the
others (Luke tells us that there was an interval which he calls "a
little while" between the first and second denials, and another
interval, this time of "about one hour" between the second and
third, Luke 22 : 58f.).

15 The reason that Peter followed Jesus is not given. It is clear,
though, that neither the incident with Malchus nor the subsequent
flight of the disciples had completely shaken him. It is probable
that he simply wished to see what the outcome of the arrest would
be, and in any case it is natural in such a man to wish to be near
his Lord.[29] Another disciple is now introduced, but not named.

---

[29] *Cf.* Chrysostom: "no one should wonder that he followed, or cry him
up for his manliness. But the wonder was that matter of Peter, that being in
such fear, he came even as far as the hall, when the others had retreated. His
coming thither was caused by love, his not entering within by distress and
fear" (LXXXIII. 2; p. 308).

He is simply described as "known unto the high priest."[30] It has often been suggested that he was John, the beloved disciple.[31] In favor of this is the fact that if so it would explain some of the peculiar knowledge of this Evangelist. It would mean that he had a close connection with Jerusalem, and access to sources not normally open to the Christians. But against it is urged the improbability that a son of Zebedee would occupy a position of such eminence.[32] Other names have been suggested, such as Joseph of Arimathea or Nicodemus. Such men would have the entree to

---

[30] On this point *cf.* Dodd: "It is now generally recognized that γνωστός implies something more than mere acquaintance. It means that the person so described was a member of the High Priest's circle, possibly a kinsman and himself of priestly birth, or at any rate one who stood in intimate relations with the governing high priestly family" (*HTFG*, pp. 86f.).

[31] Murray takes this for granted. Westcott thinks that "The reader cannot fail to identify the disciple with St. John" (the expression used here, ἄλλος μαθητής, is used of the beloved disciple in 20 : 2, 3, 4, 8). Calvin, however, calls this "a weak conjecture".

[32] It is possible to account for it, however. One line of argument is that John seems to have come of a priestly family. The woman Salome, who stood by the cross of Jesus, appears to have been his mother, as a comparison of Mark 15 : 40 and Matt. 27 : 56 shows. John does not mention Salome, nor his own mother specifically, but he does speak of the Virgin Mary's sister (John 19 : 25) in such a way as to lead to the conclusion that she is Salome. Now Mary was related to Elizabeth (Luke 1 : 36) who is called one "of the daughters of Aaron" (Luke 1 : 5). Salome thus had priestly connections. The conclusion is that John was of a priestly family and could well have come in contact with the high priest in connection with his priestly duties. This is supported by the passage in the letter of Polycrates (*c.* 190 A.D.) which says that John "was a priest wearing τὸ πέταλον" (Eusebius *HE*, III. xxxi, 3). The passage is obscure. It is not known for certain what the πέταλον was, nor whether others than the high priest might wear it. But Polycrates certainly supports the view that John was a priest. There is nothing improbable about all this, but the reasoning comes short of proof. Others point out that there was a large trade in salt fish between Galilee and Jerusalem and that Zebedee was a sufficiently well established citizen to employ workmen (Mark 1 : 20). They suggest that there is nothing unlikely in holding that merchants in a big way may have had contacts with the high priest, possibly even to the extent of supplying his household with salt fish. This, again, is possible. But it cannot be demonstrated. The most that we can say is that quite reasonable ways in which the son of Zebedee might have become known to the high priest have been suggested.

the high priest's house and one of them may well have known Peter. But all this is conjecture. There is really no way of identifying him. But his acquaintance with the high priest was such that he was readily admitted to the courtyard, whereas Peter was not.
16 Peter stood outside at the door.[33] But the unknown had sufficient influence to secure his admission. He spoke to the doorkeeper (for a female doorkeeper cf. Acts 12 : 13 and the references in MM), and this was enough to ensure that Peter came in.[34]
17 But the doorkeeper clearly had some reservations. She proceeded to resolve her doubts by asking whether Peter were not one of Jesus' disciples. All four Gospels agree that this challenge came from a slave girl. It may be that this is part of the reason for Peter's fall. He may well have been nerving himself to face some stiff challenge. But instead he was asked a simple question from a little slave girl. Her question incidentally implies the answer "No". "*You* aren't one of the disciples of this man too, are you?" is the force of it.[35] And Peter went along with this. "I am not", he said. The question suggested a line of escape. Peter gratefully took it up. Almost certainly he did not reflect where it would lead him.[36] Once committed, he must have found it hard to go back on his denial.

---

[33] The expression πρὸς τῇ θύρᾳ is to be noted, for πρός with the dative is found in this Gospel four times only, here and at 20 : 11, 12 *bis* (by contrast John uses the accusative after this preposition 97 times). In each case close proximity is signified.
[34] The subject of εἰσήγαγεν is uncertain. The meaning might be "he brought Peter in" or "she admitted Peter".
[35] The question is introduced with μή as is that in v. 25. But in v. 26 there is a change to οὐ. Moffatt and RSV miss this by rendering all three questions as though the answer expected was "Yes". Rieu translates here: "Surely you are not another of that man's disciples?" He has a similar rendering in v. 25, but in v. 26: "Didn't I see you with him in the garden?" This is surely the way the Greek should be understood.
[36] Temple (on vv. 25–27) remarks that "To accept the suggestion" of this first question "is scarcely more than a refusal to look for trouble. The suggestion is that he is not likely to be a disciple, and no one will suppose he is unless he says so; he had little more to do than to let well alone. But that little more is fatal."

18 Now we have a little detail about the circumstances. It was evidently a cold night, and the slaves and officers[37] of the high priest had made[38] a charcoal[39] fire in the courtyard. They were standing round it warming themselves and Peter joined them. There was possibly danger in this, but then there would probably have been danger in not doing it. It would have been conspicuous to stay in the courtyard, but away from the group. And in any case Peter was cold. He warmed himself with the others.

(c) The Examination before Annas, 18 : 19-24

19 The high priest therefore asked Jesus of his disciples, and of his teaching. 20 Jesus answered him, I have spoken openly to the world; I ever taught in [1]synagogues, and in the temple, where all the Jews come together; and in secret spake I nothing. 21 Why askest thou me? ask them that have heard me, what I spake unto them: behold, these know the things which I said. 22 And when he had said this, one of the officers standing by struck Jesus [2]with his hand, saying, Answerest thou the high priest so? 23 Jesus answered him, If I have spoken evil, bear witness of the evil: but if well, why smitest thou me? 24 Annas therefore sent him bound unto Caiaphas the high priest.

[1]Gr. synagogue. [2]Or, with a rod

As we have already seen, none of the other Evangelists mentions that Jesus was brought before Annas. Moreover, John has already told us that Caiaphas was high priest at that time (v. 13). Some accordingly feel that this examination was in fact conducted by Caiaphas and not Annas. Sometimes this view is furthered by transferring v. 24 to a place between verses 13 and 14, which would remove any doubt. But unless we resort to this tactic it is difficult to see how the case can be made out. The

---

[37] οἱ δοῦλοι will be the high priest's slaves and οἱ ὑπηρέται members of the temple guard (cf. v. 3).

[38] The perfect πεποιηκότες seems a little strange. But John is fond of the perfect, and there may be no more significance to it than that.

[39] John alone speaks of a charcoal fire. He uses ἀνθρακία again in 21 : 9, the only places in the New Testament where the word is found. In both it is a mark of his fondness for exact detail.

natural force of the present arrangement of the text is that Jesus was brought before Annas first (v. 13), and that he remained there until that worthy sent Him on to Caiaphas (v. 24). As already noted, there is evidence that men such as Annas who had once held the office of high priest were still called by that title. This would be all the more likely in the case of Annas in that he was in strictness still the legitimate high priest according to Jewish law.

19 The high priest interrogated Jesus. In a trial this was not legal, for Jewish law provided strict safeguards for the accused.[40] He was not to be called upon to incriminate himself. The case had to be established by witnesses. It was the responsibility of Jesus' accusers to bring forth their witnesses. It was not His responsibility to demonstrate His innocence. Perhaps Annas regarded this as an informal inquiry, when the rules of court procedure would not apply. His question about the disciples is puzzling.[41] One would have thought that they would have been known (though we must bear in mind that apparently those of the household did not know Peter by sight). But possibly the high priest inquired as to what they did, what was expected of them, rather than as to who they were. This is rendered all the more likely in that the other topic of his questioning was Jesus' teaching.

20, 21 Jesus' reply does not mention the disciples. He is clearly determined to protect them to the end. This may be the significance of the fact that three times he uses the emphatic "I": "*I* have spoken openly . . . *I* ever taught . . . behold, these know the things which *I* said." He takes attention from them and fixes it on Himself. From our standpoint we might

---

[40] According to Barrett this is not attested explicitly before Maimonides. But he agrees with Abrahams that the earlier texts that we have imply the principle. Barclay says: "One curious feature of legal procedure in the Sanhedrin was that the man involved was held to be absolutely innocent, and, indeed, not even on trial, until the evidence of the witnesses had been stated and confirmed. The argument about the case could only begin when the testimony of the witnesses was given and confirmed. That is the point of the conversation between Jesus and Annas in John 18. 19–21. Jesus in that incident was reminding Annas that he had no right to ask him anything until the evidence of witnesses had been taken and found to agree" (*op. cit.*, p. 58).

[41] Hendriksen thinks the order of the questions, first the disciples and then the teaching, is significant: "That is exactly what one can expect from Annas! He was far more interested in the 'success' of Jesus – how large was his following? – than in the truthfulness or untruthfulness of that which he had been teaching. That is ever the way of the world."

perhaps incline to regard His answer as very uncooperative. It is not that. He is not simply refraining from any attempt to help the high priest or to let him know what He stood for. His point is that the high priest is not proceeding in the correct legal form. It was his duty to bring forth his witnesses (and in Jewish law witnesses for the defence should be called first). Jesus is saying that that should not be at all difficult. He has always spoken openly[42] in places like the synagogues and the temple.[43] The Jews had heard[44] Him often. He had not taught in secret. There was no reason accordingly for addressing questions to Him. The right way to go about things, now that an arrest has taken place and the law set in motion, was to bring out the witnesses and let them tell their story.[45] We should not misunderstand what Jesus says about teaching in secret. He does not mean that He had nothing to say to His followers when they were apart from the crowds. All four Gospels disprove this. What He means is that He did not have two kinds of teaching, a harmless one for the general public and a very different one for the secret revolutionaries. What He said to the disciples did but unfold the implications of His words to men at large. The essence of His teaching was public property.[46]

22 One of the high priest's retainers did not like this independent tone, so struck Jesus with his hand.[47] He does not appear to have

[42] παρρησία, "openly", is a word which is often rendered "boldly" so that here there will be the thought of outspokenness as well as of publicity.

[43] There is no article with ἐν συναγωγῇ, "in synagogue", i.e. in the synagogues generally. But there is only one temple so the next phrase is ἐν τῷ ἱερῷ.

[44] The perfect ἀκηκοότας may mean "heard and retained".

[45] οὗτοι and ἐγώ are set in balance at opposite ends of the clause. This puts a certain emphasis on both words and sets them in contrast with one another.

[46] Lagrange makes the interesting point that the interrogation was necessarily self-defeating, for the high priest was looking for something Jesus had not disclosed in his public teaching. That is to say the high priest thought Jesus had dissembled. But "What would be the use of his own testimony if one suspected him of having concealed his teaching?"

[47] ῥάπισμα originally meant a blow with a rod or the like, but it came to mean a blow struck with the open hand, a slap, and especially a slap in the face. This seems to be its New Testament meaning. In the New Testament it is found only in the passion narratives (Mark 14 : 65; John 19 : 3), and Dodd thinks it may have been suggested from its use in Isa. 50 : 6 (*HTFG*, p. 39, n. 3).

been a person of any importance, being simply described as "one of the officers standing by". His action, was, of course, a further illegality.[48]

23 Jesus brings out the wrongness of this action by inviting the man to bear witness of any evil that He has spoken. That is surely the proper course of action. Incidentally it is worth noting that throughout this Gospel there is a stress on witness. It accords with this that now at the climax Jesus demands that His enemies bear witness. NEB brings out the legal flavour of the term by rendering, "If I spoke amiss, state it in evidence". And if they cannot bear witness to any evil He has spoken the question remains: "why smitest thou me?"[49]

24 This concludes the examination.[50] Annas apparently decided that he would get nothing from such a prisoner, and sent[51] Him on. Caiaphas would have to be the one to take action before

---

[48] Commentators sometimes adduce this incident as evidence that the examination must have been informal. They reason that before the Sanhedrin an officer would not behave in this fashion. It is, however, recorded in the Talmud that in a case before R. Papa an attendant "nudged" (or kicked; the verb is בעט) one of the parties to make him stand (*Sheb.* 30b). The inquiry before Annas may well have been informal but this incident from the Talmud shows that the blow in the face does not prove it.

[49] Those who complain that Jesus is not obeying His own injunction to turn the other cheek (Matt. 5 : 39) were answered long ago by Augustine: "those great precepts of His are to be fulfilled not by bodily ostentation, but by the preparation of the heart. For it is possible that even an angry man may visibly hold out his other cheek. How much better, then, is it for one who is inwardly pacified to make a truthful answer, and with tranquil mind hold himself ready for the endurance of heavier sufferings to come" (LXI. 4; p. 420).

[50] *Cf.* Hamilton: "the examination is inadequate, illegal, and, in verse 22, brutal."

[51] AV translates the aorist ἀπέστειλεν "had sent". This is a way of getting round the difficulty of the examination before Annas and not Caiaphas. It indicates that, though it is only now mentioned that Jesus has been sent to Caiaphas, this in fact took place earlier. The examination then will have taken place before Caiaphas. But it is more than doubtful whether the translation is legitimate (though it is adopted by Knox). The aorist can, of course, on occasion be rendered by the English pluperfect. But there is nothing in the present context to indicate it and the οὖν makes it very unlikely. Burton, indeed, sees the "valid objection" to the pluperfect "in the presence of οὖν, which is, in John especially, so constantly continuative, and in the absence of any intimation in the context that the events are related out of their chronological order" (*Moods*, 48).

Pilate, so to him Jesus must go. John notes that Jesus was "bound" as He was sent. Precisely opposite conclusions have been drawn from this. Some understand it to mean "still bound" (Goodspeed), "bound as He was", and infer that He had been bound throughout the interrogation. Others maintain that it was standard practice to free a prisoner's hands while he was examined, but that Jesus was now bound once more. There is no evidence, and we must decide the point on our estimate of the probabilities. John does not say that Jesus was sent to Caiaphas's house and as far as the language of this verse is concerned He might have been sent to another room within the same building. Or He might have been sent to a session of the Sanhedrin in the Temple buildings, with Caiaphas presiding. In view of what the other Gospels tell us this is the way we should take it. The appearance before Annas was a preliminary inquiry after which more formal (though still not strictly legal) proceedings were taken before the Sanhedrin.

(d) Peter's Second and Third Denials, 18 : 25–27

25 Now Simon Peter was standing and warming himself. They said therefore unto him, Art thou also one of his disciples? He denied, and said, I am not. 26 One of the [1]servants of the high priest, being a kinsman of him whose ear Peter cut off, said, Did not I see thee in the garden with him? 27 Peter therefore denied again: and straightway the cock crew.

[1] Gr. *bondservants.*

The sequence of the denials is now resumed. As noted earlier, the scene may still be the courtyard of Annas's house, or Annas and Caiaphas may have shared the same residence in which case there would have been one courtyard. It is not impossible, as some commentators have thought, that Jesus was taken through the courtyard on the way to the wing where Caiaphas lived, and that this was the occasion for Jesus to turn and look at Peter just after the third denial (Luke 22 : 61). But we have no certain knowledge on these points.

25 As Peter was warming himself (the tense is continuous) another approach was made. There is a difficulty arising from the fact that the Gospels do not agree as to the way in which the question was put. John does not particularize, but simply says "they" spoke to him. Matthew and Mark mention a maid in this

connection (Matt. 26 : 71; Mark 14 : 69; Mark appears to have in mind the same maid as on the first occasion, Matthew another one), while Luke speaks of a man (Luke 22 : 58). Our difficulty probably arises because we unconsciously think that in each case one person asked the question and that was that. A moment's reflection, however, shows that this would almost certainly not have been the case. With a group of servants talking informally round a fire in the courtyard when one asked whether Peter were a disciple it is almost certain that others would take the question up, especially if there were any hesitation about the answer. Matthew and Mark do not say that their maids addressed Peter. They said "This man was. . . ." Clearly the servants, more especially the maidservants, are talking among themselves. Luke's "man" and John's "they" specifically address Peter. It is perhaps significant that Luke says Peter replied to the questioner ("Man, I am not"), whereas in all the other three the denial is quite general and is not said to be addressed to the maids or to the crowd.[52] What certainly happened was that somebody started the question and it was taken up by others. This is perfectly natural and it seems implied by Mark. It is not to be understood that John's "they" means a chorus. It points rather to several people taking up the question from one to another.[53] Mark says that the second denial took place in the porch (Mark 14 : 68; cf. Matt. 26 : 71), whereas John appears to mean that it took place in the courtyard. Hendriksen solves the difficulty by suggesting that John omits Mark's second denial, and breaks up Mark's third into two. It might be better to split up the second, with Peter retreating to the porch after being challenged and there repeating his denial. In this case Mark would be speaking of the end so to speak of the second denial and John of its beginning. Again the form of question expects the answer, "No". This was the last place where one might expect to find one of Jesus' followers. This may explain

---

[52] Mark uses the imperfect ἠρνεῖτο of the second denial (Mark 14 : 70) whereas he prefers the aorist in the other two cases. This may point to a continuing action. The question kept getting put and Peter kept denying.

[53] Milligan and Moulton see in this sort of thing the explanation of all the apparent discrepancies in the stories of the denials. "Not one only but many of the eager and excited spectators would ask the question, and of that number Luke and John might easily single out the person peculiarly prominent" (the last words apply to the third denial).

why no attempt was made to hold Peter for questioning, though he was asked a number of times whether he followed Jesus. The question was indeed put but the questioners did not treat the possibility seriously. And now, as before, they received a prompt emphatic denial.

26 The last questioner was different, and his question looks for an affirmative answer. He was related to Malchus (only John tells us this), and therefore would have had a peculiar interest in the man who had struck out with a sword. But it had been done in an uncertain light, and the relative could not be absolutely sure that it was Peter that he had seen. All the more would this have been the case in that he was now seeing Peter in a very dim light indeed. A charcoal fire glows red, but does not emit bright flames. But he was more confident than the earlier questioners, as his words show. He refers to the incident, and asks whether he did not see Peter in the garden.

27 For the third time Peter denies any connection with Jesus.[54] John does not give his exact words this time, but simply says that he "denied again". He records the fact that a (not "the") cock crew at that moment (*cf.* 13 : 38),[55] but he says nothing of its effect on Peter (Mark 14 : 72f.; Luke 22 : 62f.). Lightfoot points out that, except for Pilate's fear (19 : 8), no mention is made of

---

[54] Barclay has a helpful comment: "it was the real Peter who protested his loyalty in the upper room; it was the real Peter who drew his lonely sword in the moonlight of the garden; it was the real Peter who followed Jesus, because he could not leave his Lord alone; it was *not* the real Peter who cracked beneath the tension and who denied his Lord. *And that is just what Jesus could see* . . . The forgiving love of Jesus is so great that He sees our real personality, not in our faithlessness, but in our loyalty, not in our defeat by sin, but in our reaching after goodness, even when we are defeated."

[55] A number of scholars think that not an actual cock's crow is meant, but the bugle call which ended the third watch of the night, the *gallicinium*, or in Greek, ἀλεκτοροφωνία. This would give a precise time by which Jesus prophesied the denials. Bernard points out that the four watches of the night were called ὀψέ, μεσονύκτιον, ἀλεκτοροφωνία and πρωΐ, so that if the trumpet sound were meant there would be singular appropriateness in the use of πρωΐ in verse 28. The events of that verse would than take place during the period technically known as πρωΐ. As noted there, however, this is not likely. It is better to take πρωΐ in the non-technical sense. In any case it is not certain that the Jews (as opposed to the Romans) divided the night into four watches. The Talmud describes a dispute as to whether there were three or four watches, and seems to favor the view that there were three (*Ber.* 3a).

people's emotions throughout chapters 18, 19. John concentrates on the facts.

3. THE ROMAN TRIAL, 18 : 28–19 : 16

In contrast to his handling of the Jewish trial John gives considerable attention to the Roman trial. He scarcely notices the former, merely contenting himself with a sketchy account of Jesus' interview with Annas, and with the information that it was Caiaphas who sent Jesus on to Pilate. But when he comes to deal with what happened before Pilate his account is much more full. This would probably have been of great interest to his readers who must themselves have come in continual contact with the Romans. And it was part of John's plan to show that Pilate both bore his testimony to the innocence of Jesus (18 : 38; 19 : 4, 6), and also tried very hard to deliver Him. It was only at the insistence of the high priestly party that he finally consented to the crucifixion. John has several pieces of information which he alone supplies. Indeed, it is to John's account that we owe most of our knowledge of the Roman trial. The Synoptists allude but sketchily to Pilate's examination of Jesus. One example of our debt to John is the wonderful scene in which Jesus confronts Pilate (18 : 33–38). Westcott conjectures that John may well have entered the Praetorium and thus have been in a position to observe what was going on. He points out that apparently the only thing that kept the Jews outside was their fear of defilement, which would scarcely have deterred a follower of Jesus at that moment. Moreover the man who entered the high priest's house would not have hesitated at the Praetorium. This is very possible, but we must bear in mind that it is all speculation. We do not know how John obtained his information.

(a) Jesus delivered up to Pilate, 18 : 28–32

28 They lead Jesus therefore from Caiaphas into the [1]Praetorium: and it was early; and they themselves entered not into the [1]Praetorium, that they might not be defiled, but might eat the passover. 29 Pilate therefore went out unto them, and saith, What accusation bring ye against this man? 30 They answered and said unto him, If this man were not an evil-doer, we should not have delivered him up unto thee. 31 Pilate therefore said unto them, Take him yourselves, and judge him according to your law. The Jews said unto him, It is not lawful for us to put any man to death: 32 that the

word of Jesus might be fulfilled, which he spake, signifying by what manner of death he should die.

¹ Or, *palace*

John tells us nothing of what happened in the house of Caiaphas. He has already told us that Jesus was brought there (v. 24), but he adds nothing to that. Evidently his source of information was connected with the house of Annas. So he says nothing of the trial narrated in the Synoptics. He simply tells us that Caiaphas sent Jesus on. This opening paragraph of the Roman trial shows us Jesus in the hands of the Romans, and the Jews unwilling either to see Him freed or to enter the Roman's residence lest they be defiled. There is irony in John's concise story.

28 The Praetorium was the official residence of the Roman governor.[56] They brought Jesus there from Caiaphas. John inserts a characteristic time note: "it was early" (for this last term see on v. 27; for John's habit of noting the time of day see on 1 : 39). If this word is used in a technical sense to denote the fourth watch of the night the time will have been before 6 a.m. It seems more likely that it was later than this. The day began at this hour, and there was a Jewish law that cases involving the death sentence could not be held during the night. The chief priests may well have held a session of the Sanhedrin after daybreak in order to give a semblance of legality to the proceedings (this would be the "second trial" of Mark 15 : 1). "Early" will then mean "in the early part of the day", perhaps between 6 a.m. and 7 a.m.[57] We

---

[56] The traditional view is that Pilate's residence was in the tower of Antonia. This may be right, but it is difficult to find evidence to support it. Philo tells us that on one occasion Pilate hung up certain shields in Herod's palace (*Leg. ad Gai.*, 299). Some years later Florus when governor lodged in the same palace (Josephus, *Bell.* ii, 301, 328). This evidence is not enough to prove that Pilate must have lodged there and the whole matter must be regarded as uncertain. In any case it would have been a temporary residence, for the Roman governor lived in the Praetorium at Caesarea (Acts 23 : 35).

[57] It is perhaps worth mentioning that Roman courts evidently began the day quite early, so that there would be no great impropriety in seeking Pilate around dawn. Seneca speaks of "thousands hurrying to the forum at break of day – how base their cases, and how much baser are their advocates!" (*De Ira*, II, vii. 3; Loeb translation). Martial, it is true, mentions the third hour: "The first and the second hour wearies clients at the levee, the third hour sets hoarse advocates to work" (*Epigrams* IV, viii. 1–2; Loeb translation). But this can scarcely be taken to mean that the courts did not begin until the third hour.

owe to this Evangelist the information that the Jewish leaders would not enter the Praetorium lest they contract defilement and render themselves unable to keep the feast. It was the rule that "The dwelling-places of gentiles are unclean."[58] Any Jew who entered such a dwelling would immediately contract defilement, a defilement which lasted seven days. This would effectively prevent him from observing the feast.[59] It is a curious commentary on human nature that they were scrupulous about contracting a defilement that would prevent them from keeping the feast, but they were not at all concerned about taking part in an act of judicial murder. And it is a characteristic example of John's irony that he simply mentions the fact without stopping to draw out its implications. For the bearing of this verse on the date of the crucifixion see Additional Note H, pp. 774ff.

29 Pilate is introduced into the narrative somewhat abruptly.

---

[58]   Mishnah, *Ohol.* 18 : 7. This does not apply to colonnades (*Ohol.* 18 : 9), to the open space in a courtyard and certain other appurtenances to the dwelling (*Ohol.* 18 : 10). Thus the Jews would be able to appear before the Praetorium, but not to enter it.

[59]   Barrett accuses John of error here. He says: "The uncleanness the Jews would have incurred by entering the Praetorium would last only till the end of the day when it could be removed by a bath; in the immediately ensuing evening (the beginning of the next day) the Passover could be eaten." But Barrett appears to be guilty of a failure to look into the type of uncleanness that was contracted. It is true that in some cases uncleanness lasted only until evening, but in other cases, for example that due to contact with a dead body, it lasted for seven days (Num. 19 : 11). This was so even without physical contact. Anyone who entered a tent in which a man had died was expressly said to be unclean for seven days (Num. 19 : 14). Now the reason that the houses of the Gentiles were regarded as conveying uncleanness was that the Gentiles were thought to throw abortions down the drains (SBk, II, p. 839; Danby, p. 675, n. 10). It was thus the defilement connected with the dead, and hence a seven-day defilement, that the houses of the Gentiles conveyed. It is Barrett, and not John who is in error. Barrett further cites *Pes.* 7 : 6, "if the congregation or the greater part thereof contracted uncleanness, or if the priests were unclean but the congregation clean, the Passover may be kept in uncleanness". It is difficult to see why he cites this. There is no question of the greater part of the congregation contracting uncleanness, nor yet of the priests as a whole (Barrett himself notices that "only a small number of priests" were involved). The passage has no relevance to the situation in John. Had Jesus' accusers gone into the Praetorium there could have been no more than a handful admitted. The result would have been that the Passover would have gone on and those admitted would have been excluded from its observance. Moreover, even if

John evidently regards him as quite well known. The governor[60] reveals himself as very accommodating in the matter of Jewish scruples. Because the Jews would not go in he came out[61] and inquired what the accusation was that they were making.[62] This does not mean necessarily that he did not know what was in their mind. He is simply observing due form and asking for a formal charge.

30 Jesus' enemies were in a somewhat difficult position. They had no charge that would stand up in a Roman court of law and they knew it. So they did not answer Pilate's question directly, but took refuge in a generality. They speak of Jesus as an "evil-doer"[63] and let it go at that. But this is an allegation about His character, not an accusation that He has committed a specific crime. They imply that Pilate should trust them. They would not hand over to him anyone other than a criminal. It is possible

---

by some miracle all the priests or most of the congregation could have crowded into the Praetorium we have no reason for thinking that either priests or people would have regarded with equanimity the prospect of holding the Passover "in uncleanness". That was a desperate remedy for use only in desperate situations. It was on every count much more desirable to bring Pilate out and keep the feast in the normal way.

Barrett concludes his note with, "This is an important example of the way in which some of John's detailed historical notes, which add verisimilitude to his narrative and have led to the view that he was an eyewitness, break down when they are subjected to criticism." But it is Barrett's statement, not John's, that will not stand up to criticism. The significance of this, in what Barrett himself calls "an important example", should not be overlooked. Richardson thinks that the Jews simply "wished to avoid having to undergo the necessary rites of purification". But this is assumption. It is not what John says. MiM holds that the priests had had their Passover slain, but that the events of the night had prevented them from eating it. They must eat it almost immediately in order to do so before daybreak. Hence they could not afford a defilement that would last until evening. There is a good deal that is conjectural here. But in any case the hypothesis is scarcely necessary once we have seen that the uncleanness in question lasted seven days. See further *SFG*, pp. 192ff.

[60] Pilate is usually called a "procurator", but it now seems that the correct designation in pre-Claudian times was *praefectus* or "prefect". Pilate is given this title in an inscription recently found in Caesarea (Sherwin-White, *op. cit.*, p. 12).

[61] The οὖν must be held to have its full meaning here. Strictly ἔξω is redundant, but its insertion makes it quite plain that Pilate went outside.

[62] For John's use of ἄνθρωπος with reference to Jesus see on 4 : 29.

[63] They choose a description which emphasizes continuity: ἦν ... κακὸν ποιῶν, "habitually doing wrong".

that they were taken by surprise at Pilate's indication that he would try the case himself. They had had his cooperation in making the arrest. Now they apparently expected that he would take their word for it that the man the Romans had helped to arrest was dangerous and should be executed.

31 Not unnaturally Pilate wants none of this. If there is no offence against Roman law than let the Jews look to it themselves.[64] They have their own procedures. They can judge Him according to their own law. The Romans respected the laws and customs of conquered peoples and allowed them a considerable latitude in their administration of justice. Their governor possessed the supreme power, the *imperium*, which meant that he did pretty well what he liked. But normally he would allow subject peoples to preserve their legal habits. All the more was this the case since the Romans did not normally set up a bureaucracy in conquered countries. The governor had enough assistants to enable him to deal with such matters as came within his purview. But of necessity he left much to local courts.

Pilate's attitude brings out into the open the Jews' intention and their difficulty. They are out for an execution and nothing less will suffice them. But they have a difficulty in bringing this about and they look to Pilate to resolve their dilemma. The question of whether the Jews could or could not inflict the death penalty is a perplexing one,[65] but the evidence as we have it appears to support John. In any case the Jews are determined to have Pilate pass sentence which will lead to crucifixion. Without ever explaining why, this Evangelist puts some emphasis on the fact that the death of Jesus was by crucifixion and not in some other way, as by stoning. Indeed twice he records that Jesus escaped stoning (8 : 59; 10 : 31), and on another occasion he mentions that the disciples spoke strongly to prevent Jesus dying that way (11 : 8). By contrast he speaks of Jesus as being "lifted up" (3 : 14; 8 : 28) and says both that this signifies the manner of death that He would die (12 : 32f.), and that He "must" die in this way (12 : 34).

---

[64] His ὑμεῖς is emphatic: "*You* take him".
[65] The difficulty arises from the fact that on occasion the Jews did put men to death, *e.g.* Stephen. See the discussion in Additional Note I, pp. 786ff.

32 This is the fulfilment of another of Jesus' prophecies (*cf.* v. 9).[66] Just as is the case with Scripture, a word of Jesus cannot lack fulfilment. The particular saying John has in mind is evidently 12 : 32, "I, if I be lifted up from the earth, will draw all men unto myself", for he uses exactly the same expression to describe that saying as he uses here.[67] In view of the extreme rarity of exact repetitions in this Gospel this must be held to be significant. Jesus' prophecy was that He would be crucified, and John now records its fulfilment. Caiaphas's determination to secure a crucifixion fulfils the divine purpose.[68] This perhaps supports the view that the question at issue was not whether the Jews could execute a man, but the way in which he should die. John sees it as necessarily (and the Jews as demanding) a death by crucifixion. I do not see how this is to be explained other than by reference to the curse: "he that is hanged is accursed of God" (Deut. 21 : 23). Caiaphas would see this as a way of discrediting Jesus, John as the way Jesus took away the sin of the world.[69]

(b) Jesus examined before Pilate, 18 : 33–40

33 Pilate therefore entered again into the ¹Praetorium, and called Jesus, and said unto him, Art thou the King of the Jews? **34** Jesus answered, Sayest thou this of thyself, or did others tell it thee concerning me? **35** Pilate answered, Am I a Jew? Thine own nation and the chief priests delivered thee unto me: what hast thou done? **36** Jesus answered, My kingdom is not of this world: if my kingdom were of this world, then would my ²servants fight, that I should not be delivered to the Jews: but now is my kingdom not from hence.

---

[66] The ἵνα that introduces the clause is seen by some as imperatival ("let the word be fulfilled"). But this seems unlikely. See on 1 : 8.

[67] The words are σημαίνων ποίῳ θανάτῳ ἤμελλεν ἀποθνήσκειν.

[68] Strachan thinks that "the Evangelist sees divine significance in the shrewd and far-seeing determination of Caiaphas and his confederates to have Jesus crucified, not stoned."

[69] *Cf.* A. G. Hebert and N. H. Snaith: "When Caiaphas decided that Jesus must be crucified, there can be no doubt that his intention was to attach to him the curse of Deut. 21 : 22-23: 'he that is hanged (on a tree) is accursed of God', so that every Jew would regard it as demonstrated that this was not God's Blessed One but a blasphemous imposter on whom God had broken out, and would say 'Jesus is anathema' (cf. 1 Cor. 12 : 3)" (*BT*, 3, 1952, p. 112).

37 Pilate therefore said unto him, Art thou a king then? Jesus answered, [3]Thou sayest that I am a king. To this end have I been born, and to this end am I come into the world, that I should bear witness unto the truth. Every one that is of the truth heareth my voice. 38 Pilate saith unto him, What is truth?

And when he had said this, he went out again unto the Jews, and saith unto them, I find no crime in him. 39 But ye have a custom, that I should release unto you one at the passover: will ye therefore that I release unto you the King of the Jews? 40 They cried out therefore again, saying, Not this man, but Barabbas. Now Barabbas was a robber.

[1]Or, *palace* [2]Or, *officers:* as in ver. 3, 12, 18, 22. [3]Or, *Thou sayest* it, *because I am a king*

In a scene full of dramatic power John pictures for us the lowly majesty of Jesus confronting the proud majesty of Rome's representative. At this moment all the other actors in the passion recede from the attention – Annas, Caiaphas, even the disciples with impetuous Peter at their head. Perhaps we should understand the Jews in the background to indicate that the power of the State is swayed by unseen forces. But the basic thing is the confrontation of Caesar by Christ, with kingship as the topic for discussion.[70] Subtly, but very definitely, John brings out the supreme royalty of Jesus. He will be slain, but this does not detract from His majesty. He has committed no crime. As Caesar's representative inquires into what Jesus has done he soon comes to the conclusion that He is innocent. But to come to this conclusion and to act on it are two different things. Pilate does try, even if not very resolutely. He begins by attempting simply to release Jesus in accordance with the custom that a prisoner was set free at that feast. But he is met by the demand that a robber be released instead.

33 Having talked with the Jews Pilate went back[71] into the Praetorium to interrogate the prisoner. It is uncertain whether Jesus was brought into the Praetorium only at this point, or whether

---

[70] *Cf.* Barrett: "it must be repeated that John has with keen insight picked out the key of the passion narrative in the kingship of Jesus, and has made its meaning clearer, perhaps, than any other New Testament writer."

[71] πάλιν here can scarcely be used in the sense of "again", as there is no previous mention of Pilate's entering the Praetorium. The meaning must be "back" as in 6 : 15; 10 : 40 (where see notes).

v. 28 means that Jesus was then brought right inside the Praetorium. It would be interesting to know whether Pilate spoke
Aramaic or whether he used Greek, the *lingua franca* of the Roman
world. If the latter, the conversation will be reported in the language
in which it was originally spoken.[72] Pilate's opening question
shows that more had been said by the Jews than is recorded. His
"Thou" is emphatic. "Art *thou* the King of the Jews?" In all
four Gospels this is Pilate's first question to Jesus (Matt. 27 : 11;
Mark 15 : 2; Luke 23 : 3), and in all four his "thou" is emphatic.[73]
Pilate was incredulous. *This* man a king? From what he had
been told he had evidently been expecting a revolutionary, one
who had set himself up as monarch and who had styled himself
"King of the Jews". One glance at his prisoner was enough to
enable the governor to see that it was fantastic to see Jesus in this
role. Hence his incredulous question.

34, 35 Jesus is interested to know whether this is Pilate's own
line of questioning,[74] or whether he has been coached by others.
Pilcher brings out the significance of this. "If Pilate asked it of
himself, the question would have meant, 'Art thou a political

---

[72] There is no mention of Pilate as calling for an interpreter. As it seems
unlikely that the governor would have taken the trouble to learn Aramaic
the inference is that Jesus spoke Greek, and conversed with Pilate in that
language.

[73] "The trial of Christ was peculiar in that the accused made no attempt
to defend himself. This was rare in Roman courts, but to prevent any mis-
carriage of justice there was a usage by which the direct question was put three
times to the defendant before his case was allowed to go by default. Hence
it was a correct technicality in Mark and Matthew, and also in John, when
Pilate repeated his question to the silent Christ (Mark 15. 2-4; Matt. 27. 11-14;
John 18. 33-7)" (A.N. Sherwin-White, in *Historicity and Chronology in the New
Testament*, S. P. C. K. Theological Collections no. 6, London, 1965, p. 105).

[74] Recent editors tend to read ἀφ' ἑαυτοῦ with W Θ 33 etc. against ἀπὸ
σεαυτοῦ with אBC etc. Moulton points out that in the plural the reflexive
pronouns all tend to take the same form in Hellenistic Greek, namely ἑαυτούς.
In the singular, however, the variant forms remain except with uncultured
scribes. He says: "The presence or absence of this confusion in the singular
is a nice test of the degree of culture in a writer of Common Greek. In the
papyri there are a few examples of it in very illiterate documents . . ." (M, I,
p. 87). He thinks that "late scribes, reflecting the developments of their own
time, have introduced it" into the text here, at Rom. 13 : 9 and perhaps Gal.
5 : 14 *(ibid.)*. BDF see only "doubtful authority" for the form anywhere in
the New Testament [64(1)].

King, conspiring against Caesar'! If he had asked it of Caiaphas' prompting, it would have meant, 'Art Thou the Messianic King of Israel?' The answer to the first question would have been, 'No'. The answer to the second question, 'Yes.' " The question evokes a contemptuous response. "I am not a Jew, am I?" (C. B. Williams) is the force of it.[75] Pilate cannot be expected to know about things of this kind from his own knowledge. The initiative came from "Thine own nation", and from this nation the chief priests are especially singled out for notice. So Pilate inquires what Jesus has done. That, for Pilate, is the important thing. He is not prepared to accept the accusation of the chief priests at its face value. But something lies behind all this. What is it? Jesus has done something to arouse the hostility of the chief priests. Pilate wishes to drag this out into the open in order to see whether it is something that offends against Roman law or not.

36 Jesus' reply admits that there is a sense in which He has a "kingdom".[76] But He stresses that it is not a kingdom as this world understands kingdoms. It does not take its origin from this world,[77] and it is not basically concerned with this world. To demonstrate His point Jesus refers to the absence of all military activity on the part of His followers.[78] Had He been interested in what this world calls a "kingdom" a necessary first step would have been to recruit soldiers. His servants would be fighting men. But now, as things are, it is plain to all that He looks for no kingdom from this world. The words "that I should not be delivered to the Jews" are rather strange since He is being accused of being "the King of the Jews". But the setting of "the Jews" in opposition to "the King of the Jews" brings out the absurdity of the charge.

37 Pilate's words can be taken in more ways than one.[79] They

---

[75] Μήτι ἐγὼ 'Ιουδαῖός εἰμι; In the New Testament μήτι seems always to imply a strong negative. There is force also in the use of ἐγώ (see on 1 : 20).

[76] βασιλεία here probably has the sense "reign", "rule", "kingship" (RSV) rather than "realm" (Moffatt).

[77] This will be the force of the preposition ἐκ, as also ἐντεῦθεν later in the verse.

[78] The continuous tense ἠγωνίζοντο may be significant: "they would be fighting" i.e. fighting now, not simply "they would have fought" at the time of the arrest. The same word ὑπηρέται is used of the disciples in this character, as was used of the high priest's retainers (18 : 3, 18 etc.).

[79] The problem concerns the significance of οὐκουν. This might be accented οὔκουν, "not therefore", or οὐκοῦν, "with the negative element lost" (AS),

might be a statement, "Then (since you speak of a kingdom) you are a king". Or they might be spoken in irony, "So then, it is a king that *you* are!" Or they might be a question, but if so the question will not be a simple request for information. "So you are a king?" will be the meaning with a note of irony, an irony underlined by the use of the emphatic pronoun "thou". Irony or not, the words affirm Jesus' kingship, one of John's great themes. Jesus' reply is not easy to translate. His "Thou sayest"[80] does not negate Pilate's words but it is not enthusiastic. "I didn't say that, but if you put it that way I can scarcely say 'No' " is about the force of it. "It is your word, not mine".[81] The kingship which the Jews completely rejected and Pilate affirmed ironically is a fact. John will not let us miss it. Then Jesus proceeds to the kind of statement that He prefers. His "I" stands in sharp contrast with "Thou". There is a purpose in His life, and this purpose is to be seen in connection with the truth (for this term see Additional Note D, pp. 293ff.). He came to bear witness to the truth, to point men to the real truth. This is not the abstract concept of truth over against falsehood, but the religious truth that we have seen elsewhere throughout this Gospel. It is closely related to Christ's person (14 : 6) as well as to His mission. And the witness that

---

"therefore", "so then". The latter would introduce a question expecting an affirmative answer "So you are a king?" or for that matter a statement, "Well then, you are a king" (Weymouth, "So then *you* are a king!"). The former, according to LS, is used in impassioned questions and is almost equivalent to οὐ. This would mean that Pilate looked for an affirmative answer, but this is most unlikely. The word should be taken as οὐκοῦν and probably most modern versions are right in taking the words as a question (so RSV, *Berkeley*, NEB *etc.*).

[80] Σὺ λέγεις ὅτι βασιλεύς εἰμι. Turner points out that the personal pronouns do not always convey emphasis in the New Testament, but he singles out this passage as one when the pronoun is significant, "you have said it, not me" (M, III, p. 37; for personal pronouns in John see on 1 : 20). Moffatt, C. B. Williams and others are too strong with their "Certainly I am a king". Jesus is not receiving the suggestion warmly, but refraining from denying it outright.

[81] NEB renders: " 'King' is your word". It is, of course, possible to take the words as a question, "Do *you* say that I am a King?" though this is hardly likely. A further ambiguity arises from the use of ὅτι: "You say that I am a King" or "You say (this) because I am a King". With the question this would be, "Do you say so? For I am a King." BDF is definite on the point, saying, "not 'that', 'because, for' " is the translation of ὅτι [441(3)]. Westcott, however, regards this as "both unnatural as a rendering of the original phrase, and alien from the context." In my opinion the word should be translated "that".

Christ bears to this truth elicits a response from "every one that is of the truth".[82] Such will indeed hear Jesus and accept what He says.

This verse also has an unusual statement about Jesus' birth. He speaks of Himself as having been born and as having come into the world.[83] Both statements can be paralleled elsewhere, but the combination is unusual, and in such a situation, unexpected. The governor might not have understood all the meaning that Jesus could put into the expression. But at least it would impress him with the fact that Jesus was an unusual person, and that He was speaking of an unusual coming to this world. It is difficult to see how the implication is to be avoided that Jesus is claiming pre-existence. He says that He had a purpose in coming to this world in the first place.

38 Pilate dismisses the subject. It is difficult to know whether he is "jesting Pilate"[84] or whether he is wistful – his words could be taken in either sense. Either way his question ends the interview. He does not wait for an answer, which indicates that he did not look to his prisoner for information on the subject. This does not mean that John feels there is no answer. He records no answer in words, but the whole of the following narrative of the death and resurrection of Jesus is John's answer in action (see further Additional Note D, pp. 293ff.). On the cross and at the empty tomb we may learn what God's truth is. But Pilate's question was not an attempt to add to his store of knowledge. It was a way of dismissing the subject. Pilate has learned what he wants to know. Jesus is no revolutionary.[85] He represents no danger to

---

[82] For the force of the construction $\dot{\alpha}\varkappa o \dot{\nu}\omega$ with the genitive see on 5 : 25. There is a parallel to $\dot{o}$ $\mathring{\omega}\nu$ $\dot{\varepsilon}\varkappa$ $\tau\tilde{\eta}\varsigma$ $\dot{\alpha}\lambda\eta\vartheta\varepsilon\dot{\iota}\alpha\varsigma$ in 8 : 47, where we read, $\dot{o}$ $\mathring{\omega}\nu$ $\dot{\varepsilon}\varkappa$ $\tau o\tilde{\nu}$ $\vartheta\varepsilon o\tilde{\nu}$. For $\varepsilon\tilde{\iota}\nu\alpha\iota$ $\dot{\varepsilon}\varkappa$ see on 3 : 31. The men of Qumran linked themselves with the truth. See on 5 : 33.

[83] $\gamma\varepsilon\gamma\acute{\varepsilon}\nu\nu\eta\mu\alpha\iota$ strictly refers to the action of the male parent, but in the present context is used (as often) loosely of the whole process of birth. To "come into the world" is a typically Johannine expression (6 : 14; 9 : 39; 11 : 27; 16 : 28) though not confined to John (I Tim. 1 : 15). *Cf.* also references to Jesus as being "sent" into the world (3 : 17; 10 : 36 *etc.*).

[84] *Cf.* Francis Bacon's well known words from his essay *Of Truth:* "What is truth? said jesting Pilate; and would not stay for an answer."

[85] The emphatic position of $o\dot{\upsilon}\delta\varepsilon\mu\dot{\iota}\alpha\nu$ should not be overlooked. Pilate sees nothing at all amiss in Jesus. The pronoun $\dot{\varepsilon}\gamma\acute{\omega}$ may be meant to convey the sense "Whatever be the case with you, *I*...." Turner, however, sees no stress in it and takes it to be an example of "superfluous $\dot{\varepsilon}\gamma\acute{\omega}$" (M, III, p. 37). See further on 1 : 20.

the state.[86] He may safely be released, and indeed He ought in common justice to be released. Pilate accordingly sets himself to do this. He goes outside and speaks to the Jews. John does not refer to "the high priests" or the like. His words seem to mean that Pilate addresses himself to the crowd. He tells them that he has found no crime in Jesus. This statement is found three times altogether (here, 19 : 4, 6), characteristically with slight variations which do not affect the main sense. On this occasion Pilate evidently had in mind an appeal to the sympathies of the crowd. If they could be induced to give some support to Jesus it would be easy to release Him. It is possible, as Westcott thinks, that there was some division of opinion among the crowds, but that eventually the high priests prevailed (cf. Mark 15 : 11).

39 He proposes to release Jesus. He draws attention to a custom which he speaks of as theirs ("ye have a custom"), not as his own or that of the Romans. The custom of releasing a prisoner at Passover[87] is not attested elsewhere. There is nothing inherently unlikely about it. Prisoners were on occasion released elsewhere on special occasions. But this custom is shrouded in mystery. The Synoptists do not add much to what John tells us; they simply refer to the custom as known and accepted. We learn from Mark 15 : 6 that the choice of the prisoner to be released lay with the people. We should have gathered this from John's account, but he does not say so in so many words. Pilate was evidently trying to get the best of both worlds. If his plan succeeded he would be able to release Jesus, as he plainly wished to do. But he would also technically be convicting Jesus, and by refraining from an acquittal he doubtless hoped to please the high priestly party. Notice that in framing his question Pilate refers to Jesus as "the King of the Jews". The use of this full title might be expected to sway the people in Jesus' favor.

---

[86] Indeed it is possible that his question is to be taken as meaning much this. Cf. McClymont: "It was the question of a practical politician, who attached no importance to the speculations of philosophers or the dreams of enthusiasts. If truth was all that Jesus was concerned about, there was no need (Pilate thought) to take him seriously."

[87] Mark does not mention the Passover but speaks of the release of a prisoner κατὰ ἑορτήν, "at festival time" (Mark 15 : 6). Some have felt that Mark wishes this to be taken to mean "at a feast". This, however, is unjustified (see Vincent Taylor, in loc.). There is no reason for doubting John's more definite statement.

40 If that was the reason for it it failed. John tells us that the people cried out again (this last word in puzzling, as they have not been recorded as crying out up till this point[88]), emphatically refusing Jesus, and asking for Barabbas.[89] It may be that some, at any rate, from among the crowd had been hoping for the release of Barabbas, even before Jesus was arrested. It is very likely that his supporters had planned to take advantage of the custom. Even if this were not so it is likely that the crowd would have thought Pilate should give them someone other than Jesus. There cannot have been many among them who thought of Jesus as a guilty man. To release Him would not be to release a real criminal, and it was this for which they looked. The name Barabbas is thrust into the narrative without warning, and John proceeds to explain that its bearer was a brigand.[90] Incidentally this is all he does tell us, and it is a mark of his capacity for concentrating on what matters to him that he does not even tell us that Barabbas was released. Mark tells us that Barabbas was imprisoned with men who had taken part in an insurrection and who had committed murder during it (Mark 15 : 7), while Luke adds the point that Barabbas himself had done this (Luke 23 : 18f.). Matthew says that Barabbas was "a notable prisoner" (Matt. 27 : 16).[91] Putting all this together it would seem that Barabbas

---

[88] R. H. Lightfoot notes that a similar problem arises concerning the same word and the same incident in Mark 15 : 13. His solution is that πάλιν "not only is often used as a very light and unemphatic particle, but can also have a negative sense, 'on the other hand', e.g. Lk. 6⁴³ 2 Cor. 10⁷ 1 Jn. 2⁸." Probably a better solution is that of Black, who sees a translation of the Aramaic inferential conjunction *tubh* "thereupon" (*AA*, p. 82; he is referring to the Marcan passage).

[89] Βαραββᾶς = בַּר־אַבָּא "son of Abba" (or "son of father"), or less probably בַּר רַבָּן "son of the master". The "son of Abba" is likely to have had a personal name of his own, and it is this which gives point to the reading "Jesus Barabbas" in Matt. 27 : 16f. If his name were really Jesus there is obvious reason why the Christians should not have used it, preferring to call him simply "Barabbas". But the evidence is slight and falls a long way short of carrying conviction. Many have drawn attention to the fact that Barabbas, "Son of the father" was released, while Another, who may well be called "the Son of the Father", was condemned.

[90] The word is λῃστής, used in 10 : 1, 8 of those set in opposition to the Good Shepherd. The Jews at this critical moment chose a robber in preference to the Shepherd.

[91] The use of the article by John may point to the same thing, "the well-known Barabbas".

was a member of the local resistance movement. Because of his opposition to the Romans he would be a hero to many of the Jews, and they had no hesitation in preferring him to the Galilean. There is irony in the fact that the chief priests persuaded the people to ask for and secure the release of a man who was guilty of the very crime of which, though He was innocent, they accused Jesus.[92]

ADDITIONAL NOTE H: THE LAST SUPPER AND THE PASSOVER

A problem is posed by the fact that the Synoptic Gospels appear to record the Last Supper as a Passover meal (*e.g.* Mark 14 : 12ff.), while the fourth Gospel seems to indicate that Jesus was actually crucified when the Passover victims were being slain,[93] so that the Last Supper preceded the Passover (John 13 : 1, 29; 18 : 28; 19 : 36). The principal points urged in favor of the idea that the Last Supper was a Passover meal are as follows:

1. There are explicit statements in Matt. 26 : 2, 17, 18, 19; Mark 14 : 1, 12, 14, 16; Luke 22 : 1, 7, 8, 11, 13, 15. These seem to make it plain that the meal held by Jesus and His disciples was in fact a Passover.

2. The meal took place at night as commanded for the Passover, whereas other meals were normally held earlier in the day.

3. The participants reclined instead of sitting (which was the usual posture at ordinary meals). This point is not decisive, but as far as it goes it indicates the Passover.

4. A dish preceded the breaking of bread, whereas at meals other than the Passover the breaking of bread seems usually to have been the first part of the meal.

5. Red wine was drunk, as is prescribed for the Passover.

6. The meal ended with the singing of a hymn, which points to the Hallel at the end of the Passover meal.

---

[92] Plummer quotes from *Ecce Homo:* "Pilate executed Him on the ground that His kingdom was of this world; the Jews procured His execution precisely because it was not."

[93] This is approximate only. The only time note in John is that it was "about the sixth hour" shortly before Pilate delivered Him up for crucifixion (19 : 14). The evening burnt offering was offered at half after the eighth hour unless the eve of the Passover coincided with the eve of a Sabbath when it was half after the seventh hour. The Passover was slaughtered after this (Mishnah *Pes.* 5 : 1).

7. After the meal Jesus went to Gethsemane, not to Bethany. Bethany was outside the area to which one might go on Passover night.[94]

8. The words of institution remind us of the custom that the president at the Passover feast explained its significance.

9. John 13 : 29, "that he should give something to the poor", may point to a giving of alms in connection with the feast.

10. The arguments urged against it may all be fairly disputed.

However many scholars are not at all convinced and the following reasons are urged against the identification:

1. The bread is spoken of as ἄρτος, not as ἄζυμα. At the Passover unleavened bread should have been used. (The Eastern church uses leavened bread at Holy Communion; so apparently did the Western church until about the eleventh century.[95])

2. There is no mention of the characteristic articles eaten in the Passover feast, namely, the paschal victim and the bitter herbs.

3. A common cup was used whereas individual cups were prescribed for the Passover.

4. The Synoptists tell us that Jesus was not to be arrested during the feast (Matt. 26 : 5; Mark 14 : 2). If the Last Supper was the Passover, then He was arrested during the feast.

5. A number of events took place which it is urged were forbidden on the feast day:

(a) Jesus' going to Gethsemane (which was outside the limits of Jerusalem).[96]

(b) The carrying of arms.

(c) The session of the Sanhedrin and the condemnation of our Lord on the very night of the Passover.

(d) The coming of Simon from the fields (Mark 15 : 21) which seems to indicate that he had been working.

(e) The purchase by Joseph of Arimathea of linen on the eve of the feast.

(f) The burial of the body on the feast day.

---

[94] It seems that the outer limit of Jerusalem was regarded as reaching to Bethphage (*Men.* 11 : 2 and several passages in the Talmud, as *Pes.* 63b, 91a; *Men.* 78b etc.).

[95] See A. J. B. Higgins in *NTS*, I (1954–55), p. 202, and n. 3.

[96] This point will not stand since Jerusalem was regarded as extending to Bethphage (see n. 94). I mention it because it is urged by some. But their point seems quite invalid.

6. The Passover was essentially a family meal, but this does not accord with the Last Supper. There are no women present, as there would be in a family. And it is Jesus, not the *paterfamilias*, who presides.

7. There is a Jewish tradition that Jesus was executed "on the eve of the Passover" (*Sanh.* 43a).

8. The main weight of the case against rests on the Johannine chronology. At the beginning of the farewell discourses John says, "Now before the feast of the passover, Jesus knowing . . ." (John 13 : 1). It is not impossible to understand this as meaning that Jesus knew certain things long before the feast. But it can also be understood to mean that the events now to be described took place before the feast began. A little later John says, with respect to a remark of Jesus to Judas, "For some thought, because Judas had the bag, that Jesus said unto him, Buy what things we have need of for the feast" (John 13 : 29). The next reference is usually held to be more important. It tells us that "They lead Jesus therefore from Caiaphas into the Praetorium: and it was early; and they themselves entered not into the Praetorium, that they might not be defiled, but might eat the passover" (John 18 : 28). This seems to most to mean that the passover at this time had not yet begun. This is perhaps reinforced by a later statement, "Now it was the Preparation of the passover" (John 19 : 14). The doubt arises because "the Preparation" had become almost equivalent to "Friday" (from its use for "the Preparation of the sabbath"). Thus the term probably means no more than "Friday in Passover week", "Passover Friday".[97] Finally John tells us that

---

[97] There is a discussion of the term παρασκευή by A. J. B. Higgins, *op. cit.*, pp. 206ff. He shows that the term had come to mean "Friday", so that in John 19 it will refer to the day of the week rather than "Passover-eve". The critical point appears to be the absence of evidence that the term was used for the "eve" of any festal day other than the sabbath. Barrett says categorically that the term does not mean Friday in Passover week (on 19 : 14), but he cites no example of its use for the eve of any day other than the Sabbath. C. D. Buck says equally categorically: "The day before the Sabbath was called παρασκευή" (*A Dictionary of Selected Synonyms in the Principal Indo-European Languages*, Chicago, 1949, p. 1008). Bernard points out that had the meaning been "the Preparation day of the Passover" we would expect the definite article (on 19 : 14). Mark almost gives us a definition when he speaks of Παρασκευή, ὅ ἐστιν προσάββατον (Mark 15 : 42). This does not, of course, contain the expression, τοῦ πάσχα, but it does give a strong presumption that παρασκευή by itself, as in John 19 : 31, 42 means Friday. And in any case Mark is speaking of the same day

a soldier plunged a spear into the side of Jesus rather than breaking his legs, "For these things came to pass, that the scripture might be fulfilled, A bone of him shall not be broken" (John 19 : 36). This appears to be a reference to the requirement for the Passover victim that its bones should not be broken (Exod. 12 : 46; Num. 9 : 12). It would seem that John means us to think that Jesus' death was the real Passover sacrifice (*cf.* the similar view of Paul, I Cor. 5 : 7).[98]

Such then is the evidence. It is possible to take up any one of a number of positions with respect to it. Both accounts may be regarded as untrustworthy and rejected, which leaves us with very little knowledge of what went on. Confining ourselves to views which allow for substantial historicity in one or more accounts the following views are possible:

1. The two accounts cannot be harmonized and John is to be preferred.
2. The two accounts cannot be harmonized and the Synoptists are to be preferred.
3. The Passover took place as in the Synoptists (*i.e.* the Last Supper was a Passover meal) and John is not really in contradiction.
4. The Passover took place as in John and the Synoptists are not really in contradiction.
5. There are calendrical differences so that the Synoptists follow one reckoning and John another.

---

as John. MiM draws attention to a weakness in the "day before the Passover" idea: "It has never been shown that the day before the Passover was called 'The preparation of the Passover.' It has been *conjectured* that it was, because it is believed that the day before the Sabbath was called 'The preparation of the Sabbath.' *No such name as this last has been pointed out*" (on 19 : 14). The fact must be faced that no example of the use of παρασκευή is cited for any day other than Friday. The use for Friday is cited, both by linking the term with the sabbath (Josephus, *Ant.* xvi, 163), and, from the second century, absolutely (*Didache*, viii. 1; *Martyrdom of Polycarp*, vii. 1). The evidence that the term was used for Friday must be accepted.

[98] The Johannine date is supported by an argument from astronomy. The Synoptic date requires that 14th Nisan in the year of the crucifixion fall on a Thursday. George Ogg cites evidence, mainly from K. Schoch and J. K. Fotheringham, to show that the only year from A. D. 26 to 36 when this happened (unless we assume abnormal circumstances) was A. D. 27, a year most scholars regard as impossible. But 14th Nisan was on a Friday, as required by John, in A. D. 30 and 33, both of which are real possibilities (*Historicity and Chronology in the New Testament*, S. P. C. K. Theological Collections no. 6, London, 1965, pp. 92–96).

We need say little about the first two suggestions. The evidence has been summarized. If it be held that no harmonization is possible then it is a matter of making up one's mind which is to be preferred. Most modern authorities prefer the first view.[99]

The third suggestion is one which has been adopted by very many. On this view John 13 : 1 is interpreted to mean, "Before the paschal feast began, Jesus already knew that the time had come . . ." (Knox's translation; so also Moffatt, Goodspeed, *Amplified, Twentieth Century, etc.*; Bultmann in his commentary supports this view). Grammatically εἰδώς could be taken with the preceding as required by this translation, though it must be borne in mind that ARV is also possible, "Now before the feast of the passover, Jesus knowing that his hour was come. . . ."[100] But the principal difficulty is with the expression "that they . . . might eat the passover" (John 18 : 28). This has to be taken to mean "keep the feast of unleavened bread" or perhaps to refer to one or other of the sacrificial meals therein. In support of this are great names like Zahn and others, and recently Geldenhuys has embraced this view. The great difficulty is that there does not appear to be an example of this expression from antiquity which does not mean "eat the passover supper". Geldenhuys cites examples of the use of τὸ πάσχα to denote the whole feast of unleavened bread (Luke 22 : 1; Acts 12 : 1), and says that "John himself frequently uses τὸ πάσχα in this sense, e.g., in John ii. 13, vi. 4, xi. 55, xviii. 39 etc."[101] But in none of these passages does τὸ πάσχα clearly point to the feast of unleavened bread in distinction from the Passover supper itself and this is the crucial point. Geldenhuys does not notice that his position requires τὸ πάσχα to mean not the Passover plus the feast of unleavened bread, but, because, on his view, the

---

[99] N. Geldenhuys has a very important Excursus on "The Day and Date of the Crucifixion" in his *Commentary on the Gospel of Luke* in this series (pp. 649–670). In it he lists the principal authorities who hold these views (those who hold to the Synoptists, pp. 649f.; those who prefer the Johannine chronology, p. 650).

[100] George Ogg finds this the most natural understanding of the Greek: "Standing at the head of the sentence, this time-note is most naturally referred to its direct affirmation, 'he was to show them the full extent of his love'. Since according to what follows he did so on the occasion of the Last Supper, John here indicates clearly that that supper with all that Jesus did and said during and immediately after it took place *before* Passover" (*op. cit.*, p. 76).

[101] *Op. cit.*, p. 662.

Passover proper had already been eaten when the words of John 18 : 28 were spoken, the feast of unleavened bread *without the Passover*. G. Ogg points out that some deny even the former possibility. "Passover, they maintain, never meant anything other than the Paschal Supper; and, had not the need been felt of harmonising the Synoptic and the Johannine Passion narratives, the idea of understanding it in any other way would never have occurred to anyone".[102]

I do not think that the extreme position can be maintained. The evidence of the New Testament itself, and the other evidence cited by Geldenhuys and others, is clear proof that the word could mean more than the Paschal supper. But the words of Zahn are important: "the usage of the expression 'to eat the Passover' loosely and popularly for the entire seven days' or, properly, seven and a half days' feast, *beginning with the slaughter of the Passover lamb*, is adequately attested."[103] That the expression could apply to the Passover plus the feast of unleavened bread is, in my opinion, clear. That it could be used of the feast of unleavened bread without the Passover, which is what is required if John 18 : 28 is to be squared with the theory, is not.

This way of understanding the evidence, perhaps, cannot be ruled out as impossible. It has commended itself to many scholars of great eminence. Yet it certainly comes a long way short of final demonstration. To my mind the absence of any example of the use of "the Passover" in the sense required is decisive. Until evidence is produced that "the Passover" can on occasion mean "the feast of unleavened bread without the Passover", John 18 : 28 remains a stumbling block.[104]

If we adopt view number four, that the Passover took place at the time indicated in John, then the meal described in the Synoptics was not the Passover. Some suggest that it was a *kiddush*. [105] This was a little ceremony observed by religious groups who met

---

[102] *The Chronology of the Public Ministry of Jesus* (Cambridge, 1940), p. 209.

[103] *Introduction to the New Testament*, III (Edinburgh, 1909), pp. 282f. (my italics).

[104] Another view is expressed in NEB mg. at John 18 : 28 which reads, "*Or* could share in the offerings of the Passover season". But it is difficult to see how this can be got out of the Greek.

[105] See, for example, J. Stephen Hart, *A Companion to St. John's Gospel* (Melbourne, 1952), pp. 152ff.

on the eve of a Sabbath or festival "to say a prayer of sanctification *(kiddush)* of the day over a cup of wine".[106] A difficulty which seems to most people to make the idea impossible is that if the Last Supper were a *kiddush* it must have been put back twenty-four hours. Jesus died on Friday afternoon, so the meal must have been held on Thursday evening. But the Sabbath *kiddush* could not take place on Thursday evening which would be twenty-four hours before the commencement of the day in question. It had to take place as the day was beginning, *i.e.* on the Friday evening. Again the Passover *kiddush* "is the opening of the Passover meal and is said over the first cup."[107] It could not take place twenty-four hours earlier. It seems that the *kiddush* simply will not do.

Others feel that the situation is best met by thinking of the meal as a *ḥaburah* meal, *i.e.* a meal held by a small company of likeminded people. Dom Gregory Dix argues for this and he makes the point that had the Eucharist been instituted at a Passover we should have expected it to be an annual observance. The weekly celebration corresponds rather to the proceedings of the *ḥaburah*. He also argues that Mark's account bears traces of adaptation to liturgical interest.[108] The difficulty is that none of the *ḥaburoth* known to us quite fills the bill. A. J. B. Higgins cites E. Gaugler for the view that "the *ḥaburah* was an association of a particular kind, concerned with the observance of the Torah and with the performance of religious duties including attendance at special ritual meals held in connection with circumcisions, engagements, weddings, and funerals. There is no evidence of any other meals being held by these *ḥaburoth*".[109] Clearly Jesus and His followers do not form a group of this kind. N. Clark thinks that Higgins is too cavalier, but he likewise finds the *ḥaburah* hypothesis untenable.[110]

Somewhat akin to this is G. D. Kilpatrick's idea. He agrees that Jeremias has disposed of the idea that the Last Supper was a *kiddush*, but on the basis of an examination of a Jewish romance, *Joseph and Asenath*, he argues that there were other possibilities.

---

[106] A. J. B. Higgins, *The Lord's Supper in the New Testament* (London, 1952), p. 14.
[107] Higgins, *op. cit.*, p. 15. This is indicated by Mishnah *Pes.* 10 : 2.
[108] *Jew and Greek* (London, 1955), pp. 100f.
[109] *Op. cit.*, pp. 15f.
[110] *An Approach to the Theology of the Sacraments* (London, 1956), pp. 45–48.

There is evidence for the existence of a Jewish religious meal quite distinct from the Passover and sufficiently similar to the Last Supper for these two to have a common origin independent of the Passover.[111]

K. G. Kuhn gives this a somewhat greater precision by arguing from *Joseph and Asenath* to the meals of the Qumran covenanters. He argues that the Qumran cult meal gives us the clue to the Last Supper. There are four important points at which the Supper differs from the Passover, and in each it agrees with Qumran, namely: (i) It was confined to men, whereas the Passover was essentially a family observance with women and children present. (ii) It was confined to the Twelve, the chosen members of Christ's circle. (iii) Jesus, not the *pater familias*, presides. (iv) Jesus pronounces the benedictions over both bread and cup, whereas at the Passover the guest of honor was normally called on to give the benediction over "the cup of blessing".[112] Such arguments provide food for thought though they have not convinced all. Matthew Black, in fact, rejects any argument based on *Joseph and Asenath*, which he holds "is not only late . . . but obviously, in its only available form, a christianized document, and cannot be admitted as evidence."[113]

Another view is that the Supper was a special meal preceding the Passover.[114] This seems more readily demonstrable than that the Synoptists regarded it as such. Any view which denies that the Synoptists regarded the Last Supper as a Passover meal seems unsatisfactory.

The idea that the Last Supper was not the Passover, but a meal of some such sort as those we have noticed cannot be ruled out absolutely. But it appears to be in conflict with the statements in the Synoptic Gospels and few find the solution satisfactory. The Synoptists do seem to be talking about a Passover meal, and not about a meal of a quite different kind. As G. Ogg says, "According to all three Synoptists it was for a Paschal Supper that Jesus ordered

---

[111] *ExT*, LXIV, 1952–55, pp. 4–8; see the reply of Jeremias, *ibid.*, pp. 91f.

[112] See *SNT*, ch. V, especially pp. 83f.

[113] *The Scrolls and Christian Origins* (London, 1961), pp. 105f.

[114] Vincent Taylor cites Chr. N. Ghiaouroff for such a way of reconciling the Synoptists and John (*Theology*, LVII, 1954, pp. 60f.).

preparation to be made, and that the meal to which he subsequently sat down with his disciples was such a supper is what all three of them plainly intend their readers to understand".[115]

Some suggest that Jesus anticipated the proper Passover date, knowing that He was about to be killed, and held His own Passover a day early.[116] Against this Ogg quotes Luthardt: "A roasted lamb and a few cups of wine do not make a supper a passover supper. There would be needed in addition a series of ritual presuppositions or preliminaries (slaying in temple, etc.), which the individual could not supply for himself, and without which the passover meal was not conceivable for the Jewish consciousness."[117]

Views such as these have not commended themselves as widely as those under heading three. But they cannot be ruled out altogether. While the *kiddush* view would seem to be untenable it is not at all impossible to hold that the Last Supper was a fellowship meal of some sort, but not the Passover. As it was held very close to Passover time, and it was the only Passover the disciples held that year, for them it became the Passover.

The fifth view is that put forward originally by D. Chwolson and modified by Strack-Billerbeck.[118] There is some evidence that the Pharisees and the Sadducees used slightly different calendars. For the calculation of the date of the Feast of Weeks Lev. 23 : 15 provides: "ye shall count unto you from the morrow after the sabbath".[119] The Pharisees took "sabbath" to mean "festival", *i.e.* the Passover, and they counted from the day following Passover whatever day of the week it was. The Sadducees took "sabbath" in its normal sense of the seventh day of the week so they counted from the Sunday after Passover (*Men.* 10 : 3; *Hag.* 2 : 4). The Samaritans (or some of them) incidentally seem to have agreed with the Sadducees on this point[120] as did the Karaites and possibly others.[121] J. van Goudoever says, "In the beginning of our era there

---

[115] *Op. cit.*, p. 215.
[116] R. H. Fuller, for example, argues for an anticipated Passover, *The Mission and Achievement of Jesus* (London, 1954), pp. 70f.
[117] *Op. cit.*, p. 217.
[118] SBk, II, pp. 812–853.
[119] For a discussion of the interpretations of this verse with reference to the calendar see R. H. Charles's note on Jubilees 15 : 1 (*The Apocrypha and Pseudepigrapha of the Old Testament*, II, Oxford, 1963, pp. 34f.).
[120] J. van Goudoever, *Biblical Calendars* (Leiden, 1961), pp. 20ff.
[121] *Op. cit.*, pp. 22ff.

were two rival countings in Israel: a priestly and a more popular counting."[122] He sees John's calendar as different from that in the Synoptics, and he regards it as a compromise between the Pharisaic and the Sadducean.[123] The Talmud gives further evidence of calendrical confusion, as in the dispute recorded between R. Jose and the Rabbis (*Shabb.* 86b–87a), with the former holding that the New Moon was fixed on a Sunday and the latter that it came on Monday. It is perhaps worth pointing out that Matthew seems to presuppose a different method of counting the beginning of the day when he says, "Now late on the sabbath day, as it began to dawn toward the first day of the week" (Matt. 28 : 1).[124] It is difficult to reconcile this with the view that the day began at sunset, unless we translate "after the sabbath day".[125]

J. Morgenstern in a series of articles in the *Hebrew Union College Annual* has argued that there were three different calendars in use in biblical times.[126] This does not help us in our particular difficulty, but it reinforces the evidence for the use of differing calendars during the period under discussion.[127]

A. Jaubert argues strongly that there were two calendars, the older, priestly calendar that we see in the Book of Jubilees, and the more usual one.[128] She thinks that Jesus was arrested on the Wednesday, not Friday of Holy Week, an arrangement which

---

[122]   *Op. cit.*, p. 29.

[123]   *Op. cit.*, p. 226.

[124]   *Cf.* the discussion by G. R. Driver, *JThS*, n.s. XVI, 1965, pp. 327–331. He thinks that certain groups "probably Galilaean in origin, long clung to the ancient custom of reckoning it from sunrise to sunrise" (*op. cit.*, p. 327), and he thinks that the men of Qumran did likewise.

[125]   The significant Greek word is ὀψέ which usually means "late". LS, however, give "after" as a possible meaning, when followed by the genitive. MM cite both meanings for the papyri, and see the discussion in M, I, pp. 72f.

[126]   I (1924) pp. 13–78; III (1926), pp. 77–108; X (1935), pp. 1–148. See also H. H. Rowley, *The Relevance of Apocalyptic* (London, 1963), pp. 101ff.

[127]   E. Stauffer says forthrightly, "in Palestinian Judaism in the time of Jesus it is usual for the calendar of feasts to be calculated differently in different groups and regions – particularly in the calculation of the Passover" (*Jesus and His Story*, London, 1960, p. 95). A. Finkel makes it clear that different calendars were in use in New Testament times (*The Pharisees and the Teacher of Nazareth*, Leiden, 1964, pp. 70ff.).

[128]   *La Date de la Cène* (Paris, 1957). N. Walker summarizes her argument, *ExT*, LXXII, 1959–60, pp. 93f.

would give more time for the events between the arrest and the crucifixion, but which seems to be in conflict with the statements of all four Gospels (Matt. 27 : 62; Mark 15 : 42; Luke 23 : 54; John 19 : 31, 42). This conflict plus the speculative nature of some of her key material[129] makes it difficult to accept her theory in its entirety.[130] But the evidence she brings forward strengthens the case for calendrical confusion at the time.

It is sometimes said that there is no evidence of divergent practice over against divergent theory. Men might argue about the correct calendar, but they followed the official one. However, this appears to be refuted by the practice of the men of Qumran. They had strong views on the calendar and refused to abide by the rules of the temple authorities. Matthew Black says forthrightly, "we can be certain that the Qumran sectarians or Essenes, an important and numerous minority in the Palestinian scene of the first century, did celebrate the Passover in the year of the Crucifixion at a different time from the official time promulgated by the Jerusalem Temple authorities".[131] W. M. Christie cites a further example, which is even more relevant. He refers to an occasion when the Sadducees bribed witnesses to give false evidence as to the date of the New Moon. However the Pharisaic rabbis came to know what had happened and kept the feast on the correct day. The result was that "these were sitting down (reclining) to-day, and those were sitting down on the morrow".[132] Here we have divergent practice as well as different ways of understanding the correct date. A point in favor of the calendar divergence view is that the accounts of the Last Supper make no mention of the lamb nor of such characteristic Passover dishes as the bitter herbs.

---

[129] See the review by Jeremias, *JThS*, n.s., X, 1959, pp. 131ff. J. T. Milik also draws attention to some weighty objections (*Ten Years of Discovery in the Wilderness of Judaea*, London, 1959, pp. 112f.).

[130] She is, however, supported by J. Daniélou, *The Dead Sea Scrolls and Primitive Christianity* (New York, 1962), pp. 27f., and, more cautiously, by A. Gilmore, *SJT*, 14, 1961, pp. 256–269.

[131] *Op. cit.*, pp. 200f. Black argues for the view that there was calendrical confusion behind the Last Supper. Similarly F. F. Bruce thinks that "a study of the calendar used by the Qumran community has strengthened the reasons for thinking that the discrepancies between the Synoptists and John regarding the chronology of Holy Week are due to the following of two distinct calendars" (*Faith and Thought*, 90, 1958, p. 99).

[132] *ExT*, XLIII, 1931–32, p. 518; the citation is from Jer. *Rosh.* 10b.

If the temple authorities held one day to be the correct day and Jesus and His followers agreed with those who had the alternative view, then they would not be able to obtain a lamb and their celebration would necessarily differ from what might have been expected.[133] This is not final, but it may be a pointer.

* * * * * * *

The evidence is thus confusing, and it is not in the least surprising that different conclusions have been drawn by different scholars. I do not see how with our present knowledge we can be dogmatic. But on the whole it seems to me most probable that the explanation is to be found in calendrical confusion. The most natural reading of the Synoptists shows the meal there to be the Passover. The most natural reading of John shows Jesus as crucified at the very time the Passover victims were slain in the temple. While it is undoubtedly possible so to interpret the evidence as to make both tell the same story it seems preferable to see them as following different calendars. According to the calendar Jesus was following the meal was the Passover. But the temple authorities followed another, according to which the sacrificial victims were slain the next day. John appears to make use of this to bring out the truth that Christ was slain as our Passover.

There are many discussions of the problem, but the following may be cited: N. Geldenhuys, *Commentary on the Gospel of Luke* (London and Grand Rapids, 1950), pp. 649–670; T. Zahn, *Introduction to the New Testament*, III (Edinburgh, 1909), pp. 273–283, 296–8; A. J. B. Higgins, *The Lord's Supper in the New Testament* (London, 1952), ch. II, also *NTS*, I, 1954–55, pp. 200–209; A. Jaubert, *La Date de la Cène* (Paris, 1957); J. Jeremias, *The Eucharistic Words of Jesus* (Oxford, 1955), ch. I; N. Clark, *An Approach to the Theology of the Sacraments* (London, 1956), ch. IV; W. M. Christie in *ExT*, XLIII, 1931–32, pp. 515ff.; K. G. Kuhn in *The Scrolls and the New Testament*, ed. K. Stendahl (London, 1958), ch. V; G. Ogg, "The Chronology of the Last Supper", in *Historicity and Chronology in the New Testament*, S. P. C. K. Theological Collec-

---

[133] Bertil Gärtner argues that Jesus observed a "lambless Passover" such as might have been held anywhere outside Jerusalem (*John 6 and the Jewish Passover*, Lund, 1959, pp. 44ff.). This could be a further way of reconciling the evidence, with the lambless Passover celebrated in this case a night before the orthodox Passover.

tions no. 6 (London, 1965), pp. 75–96; A. R. C. Leaney, "What was the Lord's Supper?" in *Theology*, LXX, 1967, pp. 51-62.

ADDITIONAL NOTE I: THE RIGHT OF THE JEWS TO INFLICT THE DEATH PENALTY

The statement in John 18 : 31 is categorical: the Jews had no legal right to inflict the death penalty. But the situation is complicated by the fact that the Romans clearly had no hand in the execution of Stephen. It is, of course, possible to regard Stephen's death as a lynching rather than as an official legal execution. Against this, Stephen was brought before the Sanhedrin (Acts 6 : 12), presided over by the high priest (Acts 7 : 1). There were wild scenes at the end of his speech (Acts 7 : 54, 57), but on the other hand the stoning may have taken place in proper legal form for the witnesses laid down their clothes, apparently in an orderly manner, at the feet of a young man called Saul (Acts 7 : 58).

Josephus mentions another stoning at a slightly later time, namely that of James the Lord's brother.[134] But this was carried out at a time when there was no governor in the country and Josephus makes it clear that it was considered highly irregular. Indeed, the high priest was deposed on account of it. The Mishnah, in addition to giving many and detailed regulations about the methods of execution, tells us that R. Eliezer spoke of the execution of a priest's daughter for adultery.[135]

It is also argued that the inscription prescribing the death penalty for any Gentile who entered the inner courts of the Temple presupposes the right to carry out the sentence. Even Romans were subject to this penalty.[136] Actually this proves the opposite. It was a special concession granted by the Romans on account of the delicate situation in Jerusalem. Had the Sanhedrin possessed this power there would have been no necessity for the special arrangement. In any case this provision applied expressly to Gentiles. It gave the Sanhedrin no rights whatever against Jews. Further, certain statements in Josephus appear to mean that only

---

[134] *Ant.* xx, 200.
[135] *Sanh.* 7 : 2.
[136] Josephus, *Bell.* vi, 126.

the Romans could inflict the death sentence.[137] There is also a Jewish tradition that the right of executing the death penalty was taken from the Jews forty years before the destruction of the Temple. Schürer maintains that from the time procurators were appointed over Judea the Jews had no right to impose the death sentence.[138] This is inherently likely, for the Romans could not allow their supporters among a conquered people to be put to death by their enemies. The number of executions cited by those who hold that the Jews did have authority to carry out the death sentence is very low indeed, a fact which seems to indicate that the procedure was irregular.

The facts are best explained if we hold that the Romans retained for themselves the right to impose the death penalty, but that, in exceptional circumstances, when there was considerable popular support, the Jews might take the law into their own hands without much fear of Roman reprisals. Another view which amounts to much the same thing, is that they could pass the death sentence, but carry it out only when the Roman authorities had confirmed it. On this occasion, however, the amount of popular support on which the priests could rely was very uncertain. They themselves feared to arrest Jesus during the feast lest there be a riot (Mark 14 : 2). Clearly this was a time for sticking to the letter of the regulations, and getting the Romans to take action (and bear responsibility!).

An interesting view is that of Hoskyns. He thinks that the use of the verb ἀποκτείνω is important, and that it means death by crucifixion and not death by stoning (the Jews would not have regarded the latter as "killing" any more than did the officers of the Inquisition the burning of a heretic). The Jews, he thinks, could stone a man but not crucify him. On this occasion they wanted the penalty to be that for sedition, not blasphemy. Hoskyns takes the words, "judge him according to your law", as permission to carry out a stoning.[139] This is a possible reading of the evidence but it falls short of demonstration. Incidentally, Chrysostom long ago maintained that the Jews could stone Jesus, but that they wanted a crucifixion.[140] Strachan should also be mentioned. He

---

[137]   *Bell.* ii, 117; *Ant.* xx, 202f.
[138]   *Op. cit.*, II. i, p. 188, n. 515.
[139]   P. 518.
[140]   LXXXIII. 4; p. 310.

thinks that the Jews retained the right to stone for religious offences, but that they had no such authority in cases of sedition. For reasons of their own they wanted Jesus convicted of the latter offence, which meant crucifixion by the Romans.

The best discussion appears to be that of A. N. Sherwin-White.[141] He makes it clear that "the capital power was the most jealously guarded of all the attributes of government, not even entrusted to the principal assistants of the governors",[142] and that the available evidence strongly supports John's statement.

[141] *Op. cit.*, pp. 36–43.
[142] *Op. cit.*, p. 36.

CHAPTER XIX

(c) Behold, the Man, 19 : 1–6a

1 Then Pilate therefore took Jesus, and scourged him. 2 And the soldiers platted a crown of thorns, and put it on his head, and arrayed him in a purple garment; 3 and they came unto him, and said, Hail, King of the Jews! and they struck him ¹with their hands. 4 And Pilate went out again, and saith unto them, Behold, I bring him out to you, that ye may know that I find no crime in him. 5 Jesus therefore came out, wearing the crown of thorns and the purple garment. And Pilate saith unto them, Behold, the man! 6 When therefore the chief priests and the officers saw him, they cried out, saying, Crucify him, crucify him!

¹ Or, *with rods.*

Pilate's attempt to free Jesus by way of complying with the custom of release of a prisoner at the feast having failed, he tried another tack. He had Jesus flogged, maltreated and mocked and then paraded before the mob. This may have been a way of appealing to the pity of the Jews. Pilate may have reasoned that they might respond when they saw one of their own people treated in this fashion. Perhaps more probably he meant it as a visual demonstration of the impossibility of taking the charge seriously. The helpless object of this violence and derision was clearly not a king! If Pilate was making an appeal to the people in either form he was guilty of a serious miscalculation. The only effect of it was to provoke the cry, "Crucify him!"

There is a difficulty in that Matthew and Mark appear to place the scourging after the sentence of crucifixion (though they do not actually say so), whereas here the sentence appears not to have been given. But then neither Matthew nor Mark nor John appears to record a formal sentence so this is not decisive. John's narrative is supported by Luke 23 : 16, 22 (though Luke does not actually mention that the scourging took place). It is unlikely that such a fearsome punishment was inflicted twice. The probability accordingly is that the first two Evangelists are not following chronology too closely at this point. They knew that

Jesus had been scourged before being crucified and said so, but they did not bother to insert it in its exact place in the sequence of events. Alternatively they do insert it in its right place and the trouble arises only because John does not say exactly when sentence was passed. It is perhaps more likely that John puts the scourging in its right place. Scourging was standard practice before a crucifixion and the Synoptists mention it accordingly. But it is only John who lets us see "that Jesus was not scourged in order to be crucified but in order to escape crucifixion" (Lenski).

1 John does apparently intend us to understand that this followed next.[1] He gives no reason for the scourging. Luke however tells us that Pilate said, "I will therefore chastise him, and release him" (Luke 23 : 16, 22), which makes it appear that it was an attempt to induce the Jews to think that Jesus had been punished enough. But neither Luke nor John actually says this and we are left to infer the motive from the fact. Scourging was a brutal affair. It was inflicted by a whip of several thongs, each of which was loaded with pieces of bone or metal. It could make pulp of a man's back.[2] It is a further example of the reserve of the Gospels that they use but one word to describe this piece of frightfulness. There is no attempt to play on our emotions.

2 Now the soldiers engage in some crude horse-play. The prisoner had been accused of being "King of the Jews", so a "King" they will make Him. They plait a chaplet of some thorny material[3]

---

[1] This appears to be the force of τότε οὖν; cf. BDF, "Jn uses τότε οὖν ... with a fuller sense = 'now' (in contrast to the preceding time)" [459(2)].

[2] The severity of this form of punishment is seen in certain incidental references. Thus Josephus tells us that a certain Jesus, son of Ananias, was brought before Albinus and "flayed to the bone with scourges" (*Bell.* vi, 304). Eusebius narrates that certain martyrs at the time of Polycarp "were torn by scourges down to deep-seated veins and arteries, so that the hidden contents of the recesses of their bodies, their entrails and organs, were exposed to sight" (*HE*, iv, 15, 4). Small wonder that men not infrequently died as a result of this torture (*cf.* the passages from Cicero cited by Godet). Incidentally if Jesus' scourging was a severe one (we do not know how many blows He received) this would explain why He died after such a comparatively short time on the cross.

[3] στέφανος strictly denotes a wreath of victory rather than a royal crown (διάδημα). It was awarded, for example, to the winners at the Games. The στέφανος might also be used at feasts. For the crown of thorns *cf.* H. St. J. Hart in *JThS*, n.s., III, 1952, pp. 66–75. Hart argues that it was a caricature

and use this to "crown" Him. The purple[4] garment will be the chlamys (Matt. 27 : 28), a cloak worn by military officers and men in high position. Since it was used by officers they would have had no great difficulty in obtaining one for their fun. In Matthew, and probably Mark, the mockery took place after Jesus' condemnation, and it is more thoroughgoing than here. Westcott suggests that it took place in two stages. He thinks that Pilate arranged the incident recorded here, with a view to presenting Jesus before the crowd and securing His release. Then, immediately before the crucifixion, the soldiers took up the idea on their own initiative and carried it further. There is nothing improbable about this. The mockery will have been aimed at the Jews generally rather than at Jesus specifically. He simply formed a convenient means whereby the soldiers showed their contempt for the nation at large.

3 "They came unto him" seems to mean that they kept on coming up,[5] probably in some formal manner, as though doing homage to royalty. "Hail" was a normal method of greeting (used, for example, in Matt. 28 : 9), but it was also used in acclaiming royalty (*cf.* "Hail, Caesar"). "King of the Jews" shows what had caught the soldiers' attention about their prisoner and what it was that gave point to their mockery. At the same time their

---

of the "radiate" crown, a crown in which spikes radiate outwards. He suggests that such a crown might well be made from the palm tree. It was a form of crown which pointed to the ruler as divine. If it was this form of crown that was used, then Jesus "was presented as at once θεός and βασιλεύς – he was as it were *divus Iesus radiatus*. Accordingly he was the object in mockery of *proskynesis*" (*op. cit.*, p. 74). This is, of course, not proven, and the traditional idea that the crown was an instrument of torture may be correct. But we do not know for sure, and Mr. Hart's suggestion is an interesting one. Tasker is inclined to accept it.

[4] John's word is πορφυροῦν (*cf.* Mark 15 : 17, πορφύραν). Matthew speaks of a χλαμύδα κοκκίνην (Matt. 27 : 28). In strictness scarlet was the color formed from the dried bodies of a scale insect that lived on the oak, while purple, a very costly color, came from the shellfish *murex*. But the ancients do not seem to have distinguished very sharply between colors, at least in their nomenclature. Purple was the color for royalty, but the soldiers would not have had access to a genuine purple cloak. A scarlet cloak, however, would be easy to obtain, and it would give the general idea well enough. See further R. C. Trench, *Synonyms of the New Testament* (London, 1880), pp. 185f.

[5] There are three imperfects here, ἤρχοντο, ἔλεγον, and ἐδίδοσαν. They indicate that the soldiers kept on doing these things.

choice of words makes it plain that they *are* mocking.[6] The soldiers doubtless conceived of themselves as witty fellows, able to devise an ironical situation. But the real irony is that the One whom they so mock is "King of kings, and Lord of lords". They struck Him, apparently with their hands.[7] This seems to be meant to take the place of some expression of homage, such as the dutiful kiss or the bringing of a present. John's account of the mockery is briefer than those in Matthew and Mark. There we read that the soldiers hit Him on the head with a reed, which they had previously put in His hand, apparently as a sceptre. If John is referring to the same thing the blows will be not with the hand, but with this reed. Matthew and Mark also tell us that the soldiers knelt before Him and spat on Him.

4 Once again Pilate went outside (as in 18 : 38). The language appears to mean that Pilate came out first and announced that he was going to have Jesus brought out. Only after he had told the crowd what he intended did he cause the prisoner to come outside. He told the people that he found nothing blameworthy in Jesus (*cf.* v. 6; 18 : 38). He would now bring Him out so that they could see for themselves. It is not clear how Pilate's bringing of Jesus out will enable the people to know that the governor finds no fault in Him. Perhaps His general demeanour is held to show there is no substance in the charges levelled against Him.

5 Jesus therefore came out, dressed as He was in His "royal" robes and the "crown". It was plainly ludicrous to take seriously any suggestion that this figure of scorn had pretensions to kingship. The very sight of Him ought to be enough to demonstrate this, and allow Pilate to release Him. As Jesus came out the governor

---

[6] This appears to be the force of ὁ Βασιλεύς. *Cf.* Moulton: "we may represent the *nuance* by . . . . 'Hail, you "King"!' In the latter passage we can easily feel the inappropriateness of the βασιλεῦ found in ℵ, which would admit the royal right, as in Ac 26[7]. Its appearance in Mk 15[18] is merely a note of the writer's imperfect sensibility to the more delicate shades of Greek idiom" (M, I, pp. 70f.). Similarly BDF points out that "Attic used the nominative (with article) with simple substantives only in addressing inferiors, who were, so to speak, thereby addressed in the 3rd person" [147(3)]. This must not be applied rigorously in the New Testament, as God may be addressed with ὁ θεός or ὁ Πατήρ. But in the present passage it is likely that there is an element of contempt.

[7] For ῥάπισμα see the note on 18 : 22.

introduced Him with the words, "Behold, the man!"[8] Abbott points out that in the classics this on occasion means "the poor man", "the poor creature".[9] Pilate may be using the words in a somewhat contemptuous manner. The expression need mean no more than "Here is the accused", but it is likely that John saw more in it than that. Jesus is THE man, and in this dramatic scene the supreme governing authority gives expression to this truth. Some suggest that John may intend an allusion to "the Son of man". It is impossible to imagine Pilate using exactly this form of words. It is not at all unlikely, however, that John intends "the man" to evoke memories of Jesus' favorite self-designation.[10]

6a If Pilate had meant by all this to appeal to the pity of the Jews or their natural aspirations or anything else that might prove favorable to Jesus he was disappointed. The only effect of bringing Jesus out was to cause the chief priests and their retainers[11] to call[12] for crucifixion. This is the first use of the term "crucify" in the narrative. It is perhaps significant that it is not "the Jews" or "the crowd" who raise the cry, but the chief priests and their retainers. Pilate brought forth Jesus in an attempt to win men over to his way of thinking. The chief priests waste no time. They do not attempt to persuade the crowd. They and their henchmen immediately cry, "Crucify". The use of the verb as a one word slogan (there is nothing in the Greek corresponding to "him") is the kind of cry that a crowd might well take up.

---

8   For John's use of ἄνθρωπος of Jesus see on 4 : 29.

9   1960.

10   *Cf.* Richardson: "Adam (a Hebrew word meaning 'man') was created by God to be a king over the whole created world; all creation was to be ruled by a son of man (Hebrew, *ben adam*) (Ps. 8 . . .). In Christ, the Son of Man, God's original intention in the creation is fulfilled. He is the new Adam, the Messianic King. Thus, we have in Pilate's words a striking example of Johannine *double entendre*; whereas Pilate might merely have meant, 'Look, here is the fellow,' his words contain the deepest truth about the person of Christ." *Cf.* also Pilcher: "Jesus summed up in His own Person the ideal Humanity – and this was how humanity treated Him."

11   The repetition of the article before ὑπηρέται should not be overlooked. It separates the two groups and prevents us from taking them as a unified whole. Contrast Matt. 16 : 21; 26 : 47; 27 : 3, 12; Luke 9 : 22, all of which regard the high priests and elders as forming a kind of unity. John once links the Pharisees and the high priests in this way (7 : 45), but otherwise he always has the high priests as a separate group. *Cf.* M, III, p. 182.

12   ἐκραύγασαν denotes a loud shout, "roared" (Dods); "yelled" (Moffatt).

(d) Pilate's Final Decision, 19 : 6b–16

Pilate saith unto them, Take him yourselves, and crucify him: for I find no crime in him. 7 The Jews answered him, We have a law, and by that law he ought to die, because he made himself the Son of God. 8 When Pilate therefore heard this saying, he was the more afraid; 9 and he entered into the ¹Praetorium again, and saith unto Jesus, Whence art thou? But Jesus gave him no answer. 10 Pilate therefore saith unto him, Speakest thou not unto me? knowest thou not that I have ²power to release thee, and have ²power to crucify thee? 11 Jesus answered him, Thou wouldest have no ²power against me, except it were given thee from above: therefore he that delivered me unto thee hath greater sin. 12 Upon this Pilate sought to release him: but the Jews cried out, saying, If thou release this man, thou art not Caesar's friend: every one that maketh himself a king ³speaketh against Caesar. 13 When Pilate therefore heard these words, he brought Jesus out, and sat down on the judgment-seat at a place called The Pavement, but in Hebrew, Gabbatha. 14 Now it was the Preparation of the passover: it was about the sixth hour. And he saith unto the Jews, Behold, your King! 15 They therefore cried out, Away with him, away with him, crucify him! Pilate saith unto them, Shall I crucify your King? The chief priests answered, We have no king but Caesar. 16 Then therefore he delivered him unto them to be crucified.

¹Or, *palace* ²Or, *authority* ³Or, *opposeth Caesar*

This section marks Pilate's final abortive attempt to release Jesus. It was sparked off by the Jews' remark that Jesus had claimed to be the Son of God. This apparently struck a chord in Pilate's superstitious nature and induced him to speak further with Jesus. Confirmed in his conviction that there was no case against Jesus he tried again to set Him free. But when the Jews raised the ominous issue of "Caesar's friend", *i.e.* a veiled threat to let it be known in Rome if he did not sentence the Galilean as they desired, Pilate capitulated. Jesus was delivered over to crucifixion.

6b Possibly Pilate's reply is somewhat petulant. Otherwise it is difficult to see why he should have told the Jews to crucify Jesus. They had no power to carry out this particular form of execution, whatever may be thought of their power to inflict some other

794

form of death penalty (see on 18 : 31). Moreover Pilate's "your-selves" and his "I" are set in emphatic contrast. It is as though he is saying, "I want nothing to do with this. Do it yourselves." But the trouble is that the Jews could not do this themselves. Their method of execution was by stoning. He might mean, "He will be crucified, but the responsibility will be yours, not mine". But the emphatic pronouns are against this. It looks more like the sudden wild statement of a man who is goaded into speaking unreasonably. He may mean: "If you are not going to take any notice of me, then crucify Him yourselves – if you can."

7 Now the Jews come to the real issue. Pilate had used emphatic pronouns in telling them what to do and they respond with one of their own. "*We* have a law" (whatever be the case with you Romans). The term "law" is used here, not of the whole Pentateuch, but of one particular ordinance, in this case clearly the law of blasphemy (Lev. 24 : 16). By this law, they say, Jesus ought to die because He has made Himself Son of God (*cf.* 5 : 18; 8 : 53; 10 : 33 for this accusation). It was His religious claims that antag-onized them. "Son of God" is in an emphatic position. It was nothing less than this that He had made Himself.[13] Pilate, from his own point of view, sees no crime in Jesus. Very well. Let him look at it from theirs.

8, 9 Pilate was evidently superstitious. He can scarcely be called a religious man, but the news that his prisoner had made divine claims scared the governor. He had possibly been affected by a message from his wife about a dream she had had (Matt. 27 : 19). And every Roman of that day knew of stories of the gods or their offspring appearing in human guise. He had plainly been impressed by Jesus as he talked with Him. Now that he hears of the possibility of the supernatural he is profoundly affected.[14] In view of the habit of referring to the Roman Emperor as *divi filius* it may be that Pilate feared that, after all, Jesus was claiming to be King in a political sense. But a superstitious fear seems more likely. He left

---

[13] The anarthrous $Yιὸν \ Θεοῦ$ may be meant to put some stress on the quality.

[14] $μᾶλλον \ ἐφοβήθη$ is somewhat curious. There has been no previous mention of Pilate as being afraid which makes it seem as though the meaning is "was afraid rather than –". Perhaps the Jews expected him to be angry or the like, but rather than that, he was afraid. Or the term may be elative, "he was very much afraid".

the Jews and questioned Jesus in the Praetorium. It is not certain
when Jesus went back inside. He was brought out (v. 5), but
there is no mention of His return. Probably He was still outside
during the conversation of vv. 6f., and Pilate then had Him brought
back inside, preferring to talk with Him in the absence of the Jews.
He proceeded to ask Him where He had come from. It is a curious
question,[15] but the answer might be determinative for any claim
to divinity. But Jesus does not answer. The reason is not clear.
He had answered Pilate readily enough before. Possibly He felt
that then Pilate had been discharging his function as judge, whereas
now he was exceeding it. The question to be decided was Jesus'
guilt or innocence, and His origin was irrelevant. But, in view of
Jesus' free conversation both before and after, His silence on this
one question stands out. It may be that the answer must be such
that Pilate would never have believed it, or possibly, have understood it.[16] It was not a simple question. Or again, it may be that
the answer had in effect already been given (18 : 37). It still stood.
Jesus' silence at one point or another of His trial is mentioned
elsewhere (Matt. 26 : 63; 27 : 14; Mark 14 : 60f.; 15 : 5; Luke
23 : 9). Both Augustine and Chrysostom see in this the fulfilment
of the prophecy of Isaiah 53 : 7.

10 Pilate does not like this. He is very conscious of his dignity
and position of power. It is incredible that Jesus will not speak
to *him*[17] of all people. So he reminds his prisoner that he has
power[18] both to release Him and to crucify Him. The question

---

[15] It is also somewhat strange that Pilate should use the emphatic pronoun
σύ. Abbott points out that σύ in questions and imperatives "sometimes implies
contempt" (2403), but he prefers the explanation that, as in Epictetus, there
is a suggestion of incredulity: "he comes back into the Praetorium repeating
to himself 'This man son of God!' and then utters his thought aloud to the
prisoner, '*How could you possibly be* (Son of God)?'" (2404). Another suggestion
is that the question was a natural one at the beginning of an inquiry, and that
Pilate is beginning his inquiry all over (Luke records that at an early stage
Pilate asked whether Jesus were a Galilean, Luke 23 : 6).

[16] *Cf.* Temple: "With his mind full of stories about gods who married
women, and of the offspring of such unions, how can he begin to understand
the relation of Jesus, Son of God, to the Father?"

[17] He uses the emphatic pronoun ἐμοί and begins his sentence with it:
"To *me* you do not speak?" In view of the almost unlimited power possessed
by the Roman prefect in the exercise of his *imperium* the question is not unnatural.

[18] The word is ἐξουσία, "authority". Pilate repeats the word, thus giving
it a certain emphasis, and the same word is then taken up by Jesus in the
next verse as the true nature of authority is brought out.

is illuminating. In the last resort it was Pilate alone who could say "Crucify" or "Release", and this frank recognition of it makes nonsense of all the shifts to which he resorted in the attempt to avoid making a decision. Ultimately he could not avoid responsibility and these words show that deep down he must have realized this.

11 These are Jesus' final words to Pilate, and, indeed, the only words He is recorded to have said after the scourging. First He corrects a misapprehension. Pilate has[19] no inherent authority over[20] Jesus, but only that granted him "from above" (*cf.* 3 : 27). This will mean "from heaven", not "delegated from your superiors in Rome". Jesus is asserting that God is over all and that an earthly governor can act only as God permits him (*cf.* Rom. 13 : 1). Since then Pilate is limited in what he can do the greater sin rests with him that handed Jesus over. This must mean Caiaphas. It cannot mean Judas, for he did not deliver[21] Jesus to Pilate, but to the Jews. In any case in this context it must be the man who is ultimately responsible who is meant, and that means Caiaphas. Judas was but a tool. This does not mean that Pilate is excused. After all "greater sin" implies "lesser sin", and that was the governor's. He did not bear all the responsibility he thought he did. But he was a responsible man, and therefore guilty for his actions in this case.[22]

---

[19] We would have anticipated ἄν with οὐκ εἶχες. Its omission does not, however, appear to affect the sense.

[20] κατ' ἐμοῦ should probably be translated "over me" (as RSV, Moffatt, Rieu *etc.*) rather than "against me" (ARV). It is the sense, "in respect of", "concerning" (LS, A, II, 7). κατά often does have the meaning "against", but it is difficult to think that Jesus is thinking here exclusively of Pilate's power to crucify. There is also the power to release, and this is not a power "against" Jesus.

[21] The verb παραδίδωμι is used characteristically of Judas who is described as ὁ παραδιδοὺς αὐτόν (18 : 2, 5). But it is also used of the Jews in their giving up of Jesus to Pilate (18 : 30, 35). For that matter it can be used of Pilate himself (19 : 16).

[22] Some hold that the comparison is not with Pilate, but with what would otherwise be the case. Thus Bernard cites Wetstein: "Your power and authority are delegated to you from God, therefore Caiaphas is more guilty than he would be if you were only an irresponsible executioner, for he has used this God-given authority of yours to further his own wicked projects." But this is scarcely a natural interpretation, and the more usual view is to be preferred.

12 Something in Jesus' answer won Pilate, though it is not easy to see just what. He did not excuse Pilate for what he was doing, but simply affirmed that another had a greater guilt and that Pilate's own part was less than he thought. Perhaps Pilate saw in the answer something which strengthened the case that Jesus was the Son of God. At the very least the answer presupposes a familiarity with God's ways. Therefore (or "from this time")[23] Pilate was trying[24] to release Jesus. John does not tell us in what this attempt consisted. He moves immediately to the opposition it aroused. But the governor probably said something to the Jews. He certainly went outside the Praetorium where he was in v. 11, for here the Jews are addressing him. They give a shout, setting Jesus in opposition to Caesar. Some hold that "Caesar's friend" is used in a technical sense,[25] but this seems unlikely. It is a general term for a loyal supporter of Rome. The Jews are maintaining that there is an antagonism between Jesus[26] and Caesar. Again we have John's irony, for there is a sense in which this is true, though not the sense in which the Jews meant it. Jesus was no revolutionary. A just judge could well release an innocent man and still be Caesar's friend. But the claims of Christ are such that Caesar cannot have the principal place. In that sense it is really "Christ or Caesar?" John will not want us to miss this. The Jews go on to point out that the charge they are preferring is one of high treason. To make oneself a king is to oppose Caesar. The Jews do not spell out their threat. But there cannot be any doubt but that the mention of Caesar in this way is meant to remind the governor that, if he released Jesus, they could bring a damaging accusation against him at Rome. They could report that he had failed to deal firmly with a man guilty of treason. A man with a good record need not, of course, take notice of such a palpably false accusation. But Pilate's record was not one to be subjected

---

[23] ἐκ τούτου. See also 6 : 66 for the same expression and the same ambiguity.

[24] Note the imperfect ἐζήτει.

[25] See AG sub Καῖσαρ for examples of the phrase as an official title; also Deissmann, *LAE*, pp. 377f., Sherwin-White, *op. cit.*, p. 47.

[26] τοῦτον is probably used with a touch of contempt, "this fellow".

to a close scrutiny,[27] and Tiberius's suspicious nature was very
well known. Plummer comments on the tactics of the Jewish
leaders: "They know their man: it is not a love of justice, but
personal feeling which moves him to seek to release Jesus; and
they will overcome one personal feeling by another still stronger."
13 Pilate got the message.[28] Humanly speaking, the mention of
Caesar sealed Jesus' fate. The prefect made no answer to the Jews,
but brought Jesus out and sat down[29] on the judgment seat.[30]
This looks like the solemn preparation for the end of the case.
Pilate will now give the official sentence which will conclude
matters. John gives us both the Greek and the Aramaic names[31]

---

[27] Philo tells us that on another occasion when certain Jewish leaders
spoke of referring a certain matter to the Emperor Tiberius, Pilate "feared
that if they actually sent an embassy they would also expose the rest of his
conduct as governor by stating in full the briberies, the insults, the outrages
and wanton injuries, the executions without trial constantly repeated, the
ceaseless and supremely grievous cruelty" (*Leg. ad Gai.*, 302). We need not
doubt that Philo was overplaying his hand. But it is plain enough that Pilate
would not relish an imperial scrutiny of his governorship.

[28] For $\dot{\alpha}\varkappa o\acute{v}\omega$ with the genitive see on 5 : 25.

[29] The verb $\varkappa\alpha\vartheta\acute{\iota}\zeta\omega$ is often transitive, and some take it in this sense here.
This gives the meaning, Pilate sat Jesus on the judgment seat (so, for example,
Weymouth, Moffatt, Goodspeed, Schonfield). This, however, is most unlikely.
In the first place it is impossible to imagine the governor doing such a thing
(whether with his approval or not, it was the soldiers who carried out the
mockery). Pilate wanted to set Jesus free, not mock Him. In the second place,
the transitive use is not very common in the New Testament. John uses the
verb elsewhere only in 12 : 14 where it is intransitive (it also occurs in 8 : 2,
again intransitively). And in the third place $\varkappa\alpha\vartheta\acute{\iota}\zeta\omega\ \dot{\epsilon}\pi\grave{\iota}\ \beta\acute{\eta}\mu\alpha\tau o\varsigma$ is quite a
natural expression for taking one's place on the judgment seat (it is used of
Pilate himself by Josephus, *Bell.* ii, 172). Barrett sees a typical Johannine
double meaning: "We may suppose then that John meant that Pilate did in
fact sit upon the $\beta\tilde{\eta}\mu\alpha$, but that for those with eyes to see behind this human
scene appeared the Son of man, to whom all judgement has been committed
(5. 22), seated upon his throne."

[30] This is the only place in the New Testament where $\beta\tilde{\eta}\mu\alpha$ is used of the
judgment seat without having the article prefixed, *i.e.*, it is "a" judgment seat
not "the" judgment seat. It may well signify that a temporary judgement seat
was set up on the Pavement. One would have expected that the normal $\beta\tilde{\eta}\mu\alpha$
would have been inside the Praetorium.

[31] $\Lambda\iota\vartheta\acute{o}\sigma\tau\varrho\omega\tau o\nu$ may mean "a stone pavement" or "a mosaic pavement".
$\Gamma\alpha\beta\beta\alpha\vartheta\tilde{\alpha}$, a word which occurs here only, is of uncertain meaning. It has been
suggested that it is from גב ביתא, *gab baitha'*, "the hill of the House", *i.e.* the
mound on which the Temple was built. The appropriateness of this is difficult
to see. It is the same with other explanations. In our present state of knowledge

of the place[32] where the judgment-seat was set. This is not required by the sense, and it looks like a personal reminiscence.

14 John puts in a characteristic time note (see on 1 : 39), but this one arouses some problems. "The Preparation of the passover" almost certainly means "Friday in passover week", rather than "the day before passover" (see Additional Note H, pp. 774ff.). The other problem concerns the time of day. Mark tells us that Jesus was crucified at "the third hour" (Mark 15 : 25).[33] Here John speaks of the trial as still not completed at "about the sixth hour". Westcott thought that John used the "Roman" method of computing time, whereby the day began at midnight as with us. The sixth hour would thus be about 6 a.m. whereas Mark, using the Palestinian method of beginning the day at sunrise, would mean about 9 a.m. by his "third hour". This is attractive, but there appears to be no evidence that the so-called Roman method of computing time was used other than in legal matters like leases. At Rome, as elsewhere, the day was reckoned to begin at sunrise.[34]

---

neither the meaning of the name, nor the situation of the place so named, can be known with certainty. Λιθόστρωτον is not, of course, meant as a translation of the Aramaic term. The two appear to have quite different meanings. They are alternative names for the same spot. Some think the "Pavement" was a portable site for the judgment seat and cite Suetonius, *Vit. Div. Jul.* XLVI in support. Suetonius, however, speaks of the portable "tesselated and mosaic floors" as evidence of unusual luxury, not as the normal state of affairs, and he does not connect them with judgment. W. F. Albright thinks that L. H. Vincent has demonstrated that the place referred to is the courtyard of the Tower of Antonia, where there was a Roman pavement covering at least 2,500 square metres. As it stood on a rocky height the name *gabbetâ*, "ridge", was applicable (*BNT*, pp. 158f.).

[32] The preposition εἰς before τόπον is curious. It may be due to the influence of the earlier verb ἤγαγεν, or it may simply be equivalent to ἐν.

[33] *I.e.* taking the usual sentence division. A. Mahoney, however, argues that the words "at the third hour" should be taken with the preceding words about the casting of lots and not with the following words about the crucifixion (*CBQ*, XXVIII, 1966, pp. 292–99). He thinks that this casting of lots took place at the time of the scourging, well before the crucifixion. If this be accepted is no contradiction with the present passage.

[34] Westcott, however, draws attention to Polycarp's martyrdom "at the eighth hour" (*Mart. Pol.* 21), which he thinks must mean 8 a.m. and not 2 p.m. He also cites the martyrdom of Pionius "at the tenth hour" and maintains that this cannot be 4 p.m. since this kind of thing usually took place in the morning. From these two references he reasons that in Asia Minor people counted from midnight. It is a slender basis on which to erect a theory which involves John

Where a definite hour is given ("the first hour", "the fourth hour", *etc.*) the reference always appears to be to the hour of the day, and not to the interval since midnight. It is more likely that in neither Mark nor John is the hour to be regarded as more than an approximation. People in antiquity did not have clocks or watches, and the reckoning of time was always very approximate. The "third hour" may denote nothing more firm than a time about the middle of the morning, while "about the sixth hour" can well signify getting on towards noon. Late morning would suit both expressions unless there were some reason for thinking that either was being given with more than usual accuracy. No such reason exists here.[35]

Pilate had Jesus brought out, and sat on the judgment-seat. However, he did not deliver sentence as might have been expected,

---

in a method of counting the hours at variance with what is established in every other place. W. M. Ramsay further points out that the games were over when Polycarp was tried, and that this is unlikely to have occurred much before midday (*Expositor*, 4, vii, 1893, pp. 221ff.; he also regards Pionius as having died in the afternoon, *op. cit.* p. 223). Pliny, commenting on the fact that different people reckon time in different ways, says: "The actual period of a day has been differently kept by different people: the Babylonians count the period between two sunrises, the Athenians that between two sunsets . . . the common people everywhere from dawn to dark, the Roman priests and the authorities who fixed the official day, and also the Egyptians and Hipparchus, the period from midnight to midnight" (*Natural History*, II,188;Loeb translation). There is a good discussion in *HDB*, V, pp. 475–79. The critical point is the absence of evidence for dividing this "official day" into hours reckoned from midnight. No passage is cited for this. See also on 1 : 39.

[35] Barrett thinks the difficulty may be a purely transcriptional one. The Greek numerals Γ (3) and F (6) could easily be confused and he notes a similar possibility in Hebrew characters. He prefers to think, however, that John has altered the time so as to bring the death of Jesus to the time the passover victims were being killed. Ryle has a good account of the various attempts to solve the problem. C. C. Cowling thinks that in Mark ὥρα can have the meaning "watch", and, as the third watch was from noon onwards, that Mark means essentially what John does (*ABR*, V, nos. 3–4, pp. 155–160). The argument is ingenious, but comes short of demonstration. W. M. Ramsay's article "About the Sixth Hour" (*Expositor*, 4, vii, 1893, pp. 216–23) takes the line I have adopted. He says, "The Apostles had no means of avoiding the difficulty as to whether it was the third or the sixth hour when the sun was near mid-heaven, and they cared very little about the point" (*op. cit.*, p. 218). He illustrates the normal vagueness about time by pointing out that "in Latin idiom, 'in the lapse of an hour' *(horae momento)* is used where we should now say 'in a second' " *(ibid.)*.

but said, "Behold, your King!" As in the case of "Behold, the man!" (v. 5) John's irony lurks behind the words. For Pilate there was no question of kingship. It was plain to him that Jesus was not a king in any sense in which he understood the term. He was simply using the terms of the accusation in a last-ditch effort to get the Jews to drop proceedings. But for John the kingship was real. He wants us to see Jesus as King in the very act in which He went to death for the salvation of men.

15 Inevitably this feeble effort resulted in failure, just as all Pilate's previous efforts had done. His words provoked a mighty yell, as the crowd called[36] for Jesus to be taken away[37] and crucified. Pilate made yet one more ineffectual protest. When he says, "Shall I crucify your King?" he puts the word "King" in an emphatic position. He gives the title all it will stand. But this is not enough. The mob is past reasoning and wants only blood. Pilate is answered, however, not by the mob but by the chief priests. And they of all people assure him, "We have no king but Caesar"! Nothing could be more ludicrous than this protestation of loyalty on the lips of such men. It is another fine example of Johannine irony. They certainly claimed, in accordance with the Old Testament, to be God's people. They held that God was their King (Judg. 8 : 23; I Sam. 8 : 7). On this occasion they spoke in terms of cynical expediency. But they expressed the real truth. They showed in their lives that they gave no homage to God. They had no king but Caesar. And it is the chief priests, the religious leaders, who utter the words.

16 There was nothing more Pilate could do. He recognized defeat and handed Jesus over to execution.[38] He could now release Him only at the cost of facing an accusation of having failed in his duty to Caesar. He had troubles enough without inviting this for taking action in favor of a powerless Galilean peasant. Pilate

---

[36] The aorist ἐκραύγασαν perhaps points to a great shout (rather than a continuing noise, which, however, almost certainly followed). ἐκεῖνοι will set the Jews in emphatic contrast to Pilate.

[37] Ἆρον is usually taken to mean "Away with him", but Lightfoot points out that the verb also means "raise". He thinks there may be a subtle Johannine reference to the exaltation of Jesus. Curiously C. K. Williams translates: "Down with him". But the word has the meaning "up" rather than "down".

[38] *Cf.* Sherwin-White: "the implication that Pilate adopted, or was willing to adopt, the sentence of the Sanhedrin – is entirely within the scope of the procurator's imperium" (*op. cit.*, p. 47).

handed Him over. Grammatically "them" ought to refer to the chief priests. But the execution was carried out by the Romans. It was not a Jewish form of death, and in any case the Jews would not have been permitted to carry it out. But John's turn of phrase reveals that, whoever carried out the actual execution, Jesus was being delivered over to the will of those who sought His death (*cf.* Luke 23 : 25). NEB renders: "Then at last, to satisfy them, he handed Jesus over to be crucified."

4. Jesus Put to Death, 19 : 17–42

John proceeds to deal with the crucifixion proper. His narrative brings before us certain items not in the Synoptics: the information that the title over Jesus' head was in three languages, the Jews' challenge of the wording, and three of Jesus' "words" from the cross: "Woman, behold thy son" with the corresponding "Behold thy mother", "I thirst", and "It is finished". It is to John also that we owe our information about Jesus carrying His cross during the first part of the journey to Golgotha, about the piercing of Jesus' side, and about the part of Nicodemus in the burial.

(a) Jesus Crucified, 19 : 17–22

17 They took Jesus therefore: and he went out, bearing the cross for himself, unto the place called The place of a skull, which is called in Hebrew Golgotha: 18 where they crucified him, and with him two others, on either side one, and Jesus in the midst. 19 And Pilate wrote a title also, and put it on the cross. And there was written, JESUS OF NAZARETH, THE KING OF THE JEWS. 20 This title therefore read many of the Jews, [1]for the place where Jesus was crucified was nigh to the city; and it was written in Hebrew, and in Latin, and in Greek. 21 The chief priests of the Jews therefore said to Pilate, Write not, The King of the Jews; but, that he said, I am King of the Jews. 22 Pilate answered, What I have written I have written.

[1]Or, *for the place of the city where Jesus was crucified was nigh at hand*

17 "They" is not defined, but we should probably understand it to refer to the soldiers[39] (*cf.* NEB: "Jesus was now taken in charge"). It was usual for a condemned prisoner to carry to the place of execution all or part of the cross to which he was to be fastened. John's "for himself" puts a certain stress on the fact that Jesus did this particular piece of work.[40] John's emphasis may be on the fact that Jesus accomplished the world's salvation alone. Many have discerned a reference to Gen. 22 : 6, Isaac being seen as a type of Christ. The Synoptists tell us that on the way Simon of Cyrene was pressed into service to relieve Jesus of this burden (Matt. 27 : 32; Mark 15 : 21; Luke 23 : 26; Mark and Luke add that he was coming "from the country"). Jesus will thus have carried the cross at first, but along the way, probably because He was weak through the flogging He had endured, He was relieved of the burden. This is the more likely in that the cross piece usually carried was not an unduly heavy burden for a normal man.[41] John tells us the name of the place where the crucifixion took place in both Greek and Aramaic.[42] The name means "a skull",

---

[39] Grammatically, of course, it refers very naturally to the chief priests. If that was what John meant the expression will recall 1 : 11, and Westcott's comment will be in point: "The Jews received Christ from the hands of the Roman governor for death: they did not receive Him from the teaching of their own prophets for life." Some scholars take "they" to refer to the Jews who then proceeded to crucify Jesus by the hands of the Romans. But it seems better to take it of the soldiers, or as NEB.

[40] It may, however, reflect the Aramaic *dativus ethicus*, "carried him the cross", as Black thinks (*AA*, p. 76).

[41] Some find further evidence for Jesus' weakened state in the use of the verb φέρουσιν to describe His progress after Simon took the cross (Mark 15 : 22). The most natural meaning of this is "they carried" (Him), though too much should not be placed on this since the verb is often used in the sense "lead", "conduct".

[42] Γολγοθᾶ = גֻּלְגָּלְתָּא. AG thinks this may point to an Aramaic גֻּלְגָּלְתָּא = Heb. גֻּלְגֹּלֶת (II Kings 9 : 35). Our word Calvary is from the Latin *calvaria* which also means "skull". The neuter relative ὅ is rather strange since τόπος is masculine. Perhaps it refers to Κρανίον, a neuter noun. Or the expression Κρανίον τόπον may be regarded as a unity and treated as a neuter place name. There are somewhat similar neuters in Matt. 27 : 33 and Mark 15 : 22, referring to this same name and its interpretation. The expressions ὅ ἐστιν and τοῦτ' ἐστιν are often used as explanatory formulas (like the Latin *id est*) quite irrespective of gender [see BDF, 132(2)]. It may be that a similar force is at work here.

but why a place was given this name is not known.[43] It is another example of John's knowledge of the topography of Jerusalem before its destruction, but we do not share his knowledge. The traditional site or "Gordon's Calvary" may be right. But we have no means of knowing.

18 John describes the horror that was crucifixion[44] in a single word. As in the case of the scourging, he simply mentions the fact and passes on. Popular piety, both Protestant and Catholic, has often tended to make a great deal of the sufferings of Jesus, to reflect on what was done and to dwell on the anguish He suffered. None of the Gospels does this. The Evangelists record the fact and let it go at that. The death of Jesus for men was their con-

---

[43] The usual explanation is that Jesus was crucified on a hill which was in the shape of a skull. This may be right. But there is no ancient tradition to that effect and we should also bear in mind that, despite frequent references in hymns, sermons and the like to the hill on which Jesus was crucified, nothing in the Gospels indicates that Jesus was crucified on a hill. Another explanation is that skulls from executed victims lay there. But this would require the plural "skulls", not "skull". Moreover Jews would certainly not have permitted unburied bodies, or even skulls, to lie about. Nor would Joseph's tomb have been near to a place so unclean. Moreover there was a garden "in" this place (v. 41) which makes it highly improbable that bodies or parts of them were allowed to lie about. Another suggestion, dating from the time of Origen, is that Adam was buried there. But there is no reason for thinking that this tradition is pre-Christian. The plain fact is that we have no evidence at all to determine the point. We do not know why such a curious name was used.

[44] There was some variety in crucifixion. Sometimes a single stake was used, or a tree perhaps shaped like a Y. Sometimes there was a cross beam either at the top of a vertical stake (the *crux commissa* or *patibulata*) or lower down (the *crux immissa* or *captitata*) or a diagonal cross might be used. The victim was fastened to the cross either with cords or nails. The cross beam was fixed so that the victim's feet were off the ground, but not necessarily very high off the ground. There was a horn-like projection (the *sedile*), which the crucified man straddled. This took some of the weight of the body and prevented the flesh tearing from the nails. It was a frightful death. Goguel quotes A. Réville's description: "it represented the acme of the torturer's art: atrocious physical sufferings, length of torment, ignominy, the effect on the crowd gathered to witness the long agony of the crucified. Nothing could be more horrible than the sight of this living body, breathing, seeing, hearing, still able to feel, and yet reduced to the state of a corpse by forced immobility and absolute helplessness. We cannot even say that the crucified person writhed in agony, for it was impossible for him to move. Stripped of his clothing, unable even to brush away the flies which fell upon his wounded flesh, already lacerated

cern.[45] They make no attempt to play on the heartstrings of their readers.

John, like the other Evangelists, tells us that there were two others crucified with Jesus, and that Jesus was in the middle. From the point of view of the enemies of Jesus this may have been meant as a final indignity. He was among criminals in His death, and in no sense separate. But John probably records the fact in order to bring out the truth that Jesus was one with sinners in His death.

19 Pilate wrote out a "title". "Also" may mean "in addition to the other indignities he had shown the Jews". The "title" was a placard listing the crimes of the condemned,[46] and attached to

---

by the preliminary scourging, exposed to the insults and curses of people who can always find some sickening pleasure in the sight of the tortures of others, a feeling which is increased and not diminished by the sight of pain – the cross represented miserable humanity reduced to the last degree of impotence, suffering, and degradation. The penalty of crucifixion combined all that the most ardent tormentor could desire: torture, the pillory, degradation, and certain death, distilled slowly drop by drop. It was an ideal form of torture" (*The Life of Jesus*, London, 1958, pp. 535f.). It is not certain what actually caused the death of the crucified. Both the circulation and the respiration would have been affected and this in a body already weakened by the vicious flogging that was the normal preliminary, and now subject to prolonged exposure. Some suggest that the combination might bring on heart failure. A further possibility is brain damage caused by a reduced supply of blood reaching it.

The shape of our Lord's cross has traditionally been held to be the *crux immissa*, and this may well be correct. Support for the argument is found in the fact that Pilate's τίτλος was set over His head. This, however, is not conclusive because with the *crux commissa* the body would sink down low enough for a τίτλος to be affixed.

[45] *Cf.* Morgan: "It may be a challengeable opinion, but I think the Church of God has suffered more than it knows by pictures of the crucifying of Jesus; and sometimes by very honest and well-intentioned sermons, trying to describe the matter on the physical side. I am not denying the tragedy and the pain of it physically, but the physical suffering of Jesus was nothing compared to the deeper fact of that Cross."

[46] Dods describes it thus: "The 'title,' αἰτία, was a board whitened with gypsum (σανίς, λεύκωμα) such as were commonly used for public notices." Suetonius speaks of a slave whom Caligula ordered to be punished by having his hands cut off and hung from his neck, "and that he then be led about among the guests, preceded by a placard *(titulo)* giving the reason for his punishment" *(Calig.* xxxii).

the cross. Over Jesus he wrote, "Jesus of Nazareth,[47] the King of the Jews", thus maintaining the position he took up in vv. 14f. and securing a certain grim revenge against those who had hounded him into consenting to Jesus' execution. It is worth noticing that John stresses the kingship motif right to the end. For him the royalty of Jesus is the significant thing. He does not let us forget it.

20 John adds some information not contained in the other Gospels. He tells us that the title was read by many people. Probably not a great number had heard Pilate when he spoke of Jesus as King outside the Praetorium. But executions were popular functions in the first century and people would tend to watch a crucifixion, especially in a case like this where it was close to the city.[48] The reading was aided also by the fact that the inscription was tri-lingual. Anyone in the crowd who could read could almost certainly read Aramaic or Latin or Greek. Thus Pilate's description of Jesus would become widely known through the city and beyond. Moreover each of the languages has a significance of its own. Aramaic was the language of the country, Latin the official language, and Greek the common language of communication throughout the Roman world. This will surely symbolize the universality of Jesus' kingship. Incidentally the fact that the inscription was in three languages will sufficiently account for the fact that divergent accounts are given of its content in the four Gospels.

21, 22 Not unnaturally the chief priests (here called "the chief priests of the Jews"[49]) did not like this. They had refused to have Jesus as their King, though they had made His claim to being a King a chief point in their accusation before the governor. They lodged an objection,[50] though with the title already written and

---

47 For Ναζωραῖος see on 18 : 5.

48 The words John uses mean something like "the place of the city where Jesus was crucified was near" (*cf.* ARV mg.). This manner of phrasing it is, according to MiM, "because a closer connection is thus established between the crime committed there and the guilty city of Jerusalem."

49 οἱ ἀρχιερεῖς τῶν Ἰουδαίων. This appears to be the only place where this expression is found (though *cf.* Acts 25 : 15). A contrast with "the King of the Jews" may be intended.

50 Turner sees in the present imperative μὴ γράφε the significance "*stop writing*, i.e. *alter what you have written*" (M, III, p. 76). Moule, however, includes this in a list of passages where "the reason for the use of the tense is difficult to detect" (*IBNTG*, p. 21). See further on 2 : 16.

affixed it was a little late in the day. They wanted to have substituted for "The King of the Jews" something which said that He
claimed that He was King.[51] Instead of the fact, they wanted the
claim. But Pilate would not hear of it. With an air of finality
he refused to alter what he had written.[52] John will want us to
see that there is a kingship that Jesus exercises, and that nothing
can change this. Whether Pilate sensed anything of this or whether
his title is a further touch of mockery of Jesus, or whether it is
meant as a mockery of Jesus' accusers John does not say. Perhaps
the last-mentioned is most probable.

(b) The Division of Jesus' Clothing, 19 : 23–25a

23 The soldiers therefore, when they had crucified Jesus, took
his garments and made four parts, to every soldier a part;
and also the [1]coat: now the [1]coat was without seam, woven
from the top throughout. 24 They said therefore one to
another, Let us not rend it, but cast lots for it, whose it shall
be: that the scripture might be fulfilled, which saith,
[2]They parted my garments among them,
And upon my vesture did they cast lots.
25 These things therefore the soldiers did.

[1]Or, *tunic* [2]Ps. xxii. 18.

23 It was customary for the soldiers who performed a crucifixion
to take the clothing of the executed man. It was a recognized
perquisite of their office. In accordance with this custom the
soldiers who crucified Jesus divided His clothing[53] into four, one

---

[51] After "Write not" there is an article, ὁ Βασιλεύς, but this is lacking
when the expression is repeated after "he said". Abbott draws attention to
the distinction in the classics between βασιλεύς, " 'King' uniquely, the name
given to the sovereign of the East, and ὁ βασιλεύς *'the* king' of this or that
barbarous tribe." He sees accordingly "perhaps an inner evangelistic meaning"
in John's usage here (1966a). This, however, is to overlook the New Testament
usage whereby a definite predicate noun which precedes the verb regularly
lacks the article (see on 1 : 1). Here Βασιλεύς precedes εἰμι and is therefore
anarthrous. The meaning is "The King".
[52] This is reflected in the double use of the perfect tense, Ὃ γέγραφα,
γέγραφα. The aorist might well have been used in place of the first γέγραφα,
so that the substitution of the perfect increases the air of finality.
[53] The plural ἱμάτια is used, but this may be a general item for "clothing"
(like our "clothes") and not mean a plurality of garments. See Mark 5 : 27, 30

part for each soldier. It is this which enables us to see that there were four soldiers concerned in this execution. The "coat", however, was in a different class. This was the undergarment, and, instead of being made out of separate pieces of cloth, sewn together, it was woven in one piece, without a seam.[54] It was thus of some value.

24, 25a Accordingly the soldiers decided not to divide it up among them but to give it to one of their number as it was. They cast lots[55] to determine who should be the fortunate fellow. John sees in this the literal fulfilment of a certain passage of Scripture (Ps. 22 : 18).[56] He stresses that this is the reason for the soldiers'

---

for the interchangeability of the singular and plural of this word. In strictness it denoted the outer garment in distinction from the $\chi\iota\tau\dot\omega\nu$, the undergarment. The normal clothing of the time comprised a loin cloth, a $\chi\iota\tau\dot\omega\nu$, a $\iota\mu\dot\alpha\tau\iota o\nu$, a belt, a head covering and sandals (see Daniel-Rops, *Daily Life in Palestine at the Time of Christ*, London, 1962, pp. 211–18). It is possible that in the case of Jesus the $\iota\mu\dot\alpha\tau\iota o\nu$ was divided at the seams. Or the four parts may have been made up by including such items as the belt and the head-cloth. If so the one who got the $\iota\mu\dot\alpha\tau\iota o\nu$ got a good deal more than did his fellows. It is probable that the casting of lots mentioned in Mark 15 : 24 has to do with this (notice "what *each* should take"). The soldiers cast lots to determine which article belonged to which soldier. The seamless $\chi\iota\tau\dot\omega\nu$ remained over when each had something. So, rather than divide it, they cast lots again.

[54] Josephus tells us that the high priest's $\chi\iota\tau\dot\omega\nu$ was of this type, woven in one piece (*Ant.* iii, 161). John may wish us to discern a reference to Christ's priestly activity as He offered Himself in death. Christian commentators, both ancient and modern, have sometimes seen in the seamless robe a reference to the unity of Christ's followers, gathered together through His death. There is truth here, but it is a trifle fanciful to see it in the seamless robe. M. F. Wiles's citation of Theodore of Mopsuestia has point: "Christ's seamless robe woven from the top, which suggested to Origen the wholeness of Christ's teaching, to Cyprian the unity of the church, and to Cyril the virgin birth of Christ, receives from Theodore no other comment than that such methods of weaving were common in the time of Christ, although in his day they had died out except for soldiers' uniforms" (*The Spiritual Gospel*, Cambridge, 1960, p. 25). The term $\check\alpha\rho\alpha\varphi o\varsigma$ incidentally is found nowhere else in the New Testament, and the same is true of $\dot\upsilon\varphi\alpha\nu\tau\dot o\varsigma$.

[55] The verb $\lambda\alpha\gamma\chi\dot\alpha\nu\omega$ means "to obtain by lot", as in Acts 1 : 17. However it seems clear that in the present passage the meaning must be "cast lots".

[56] SBk has a long note on the use of Ps. 22 in ancient Jewish writings (II, pp. 574–80). This is valuable in view of the frequent citation of this Psalm in the passion narratives.

action.[57] Once again we see his master-thought that God was over all that was done, so directing things that His will was accomplished, and not that of puny man. It was because of this[58] that the soldiers acted as they did.

(c) Jesus Provides for Mary, 19 : 25b–27

But there were standing by the cross of Jesus his mother, and his mother's sister, Mary the wife of Clopas, and Mary Magdalene. 26 When Jesus therefore saw his mother, and the disciple standing by whom he loved, he saith unto his mother, Woman, behold, thy son! 27 Then saith he to the disciple, Behold, thy mother! And from that hour the disciple took her unto his own home.

25b Jesus was not entirely forsaken in the hour of His death. Some women stood by His cross. His mother is mentioned first, unnamed as always in this Gospel. It is not clear whether "his mother's sister" is also unnamed, or whether she is to be equated with "Mary the wife of Clopas".[59] It seems better to think of these as two different persons. In the first place, it is unlikely that sisters should both bear the name "Mary". And in the second place, if the two are distinct there are four believing women who

---

[57] He introduces the quotation from Ps. 22 with the purposive conjunction ἵνα (for ἵνα without a preceding principal verb see on 1 : 8), and after citing the passage from the Psalm he adds "These things therefore (οὖν) the soldiers did." Some scholars think that the whole gambling motif has been introduced in order to find a fulfilment of prophecy. One feels that their zeal for finding an Evangelist manipulating the facts to square with a theory outruns their knowledge of the ways of fighting men. Nothing is more natural than a little gambling in such circumstances.

[58] μὲν οὖν is found in John only here and in 20 : 30. In the New Testament it is usually resumptive and many hold that that is its significance here.

[59] The Greek does not use the term "wife". It reads Μαρία ἡ τοῦ Κλωπᾶ. This could mean "the wife of" or for that matter "the mother of" or "the sister of" or "the daughter of" Klopas. The expression would perhaps most naturally be taken to mean "the daughter of" were it not that the woman in question seems to have had grown up sons. A lady of this age would be known by reference to her husband rather than her father. Godet thinks that this lady is identical with "his mother's sister" and that there were three woman at the cross. He meets the objection that two sisters are not likely to have borne the same name by suggesting that ἀδελφή here may be used in the sense of the rare term γαλόως. This is possible, but scarcely convincing.

stood by the cross. They will stand over against the four unbelieving soldiers who crucified Jesus,[60] quite in the Johannine
manner. It is probable that "his mother's sister" here is to be
equated with Salome (Mark 15 : 40), and that she was "the
mother of the sons of Zebedee" (Matt. 27 : 56), who was standing
at a distance with the other women when Jesus died. If so, and
if the beloved disciple is John the son of Zebedee a reason for the
omission of her name appears. He never names himself nor his
brother nor any of his family. It would be quite in keeping that
he should not name his mother. Clopas is mentioned here only in
the New Testament.[61] Mary Magdalene[62] is mentioned here for
the first time in this Gospel, but in the next chapter John tells
us of Jesus' appearance to her after the resurrection.

26   Even in His bitter anguish Jesus took thought for His mother.[63]

---

[60]   In the light of Matt. 27 : 55 and Luke 8 : 2f. it is not impossible that
these women had provided the very clothes over which the soldiers gambled.

[61]   It is unlikely that this man is to be identified with Cleopas (Luke 24 : 18).
As *NBD* points out, the names appear to be distinct, for εο does not contract
to ω but to ου. Moreover, there is agreement that Κλεοπᾶς is a contraction
of Κλεόπατρος whereas Κλῶπας is Semitic. Some identify Clopas with Alphaeus
(Matt. 10 : 3 *etc.*), maintaining that these are variant Greek forms of the same
Aramaic name, חלפי. This, however, is disputed (see Deissmann, *BS*, p. 315,
n. 2), and some roundly deny the possibility. Those who maintain the identity
point out that Alphaeus is the father of James the less (Matt. 10 : 3), and that
the Mary mentioned here as Clopas's wife is apparently the mother of James
(Mark 15 : 40). The identification cannot be ruled out as impossible, but in
our present state of knowledge it is best not to be dogmatic. Hegesippus,
according to Eusebius, says that Clopas was the brother of Joseph (*HE*, III,
xi, 1).

[62]   Her name is given here as Μαρία (as also in 20 : 1, 11; א, however,
reads Μαριάμ in all three places). In 20 : 16, 18 it is Μαριάμ, which corresponds
more nearly to the Aramaic form (which would have used by Jesus in addressing
her). ἡ Μαγδαληνή probably means "the woman from Magdala", a town
not far from Tiberias on the West side of the Sea of Galilee. We read of this
woman in the passion narratives of all four Gospels, both as being present
at the crucifixion, and also as coming to the tomb early on the morning of the
resurrection. Apart from this we read of her only that seven demons went out
of her (this is not further explained) and that she was one of the women who
ministered to Jesus (Luke 8 : 2f.).

[63]   *Cf.* Barclay: "There is something infinitely moving in the fact that Jesus
in the agony of the Cross, in the moment when the salvation of the world hung
in the balance, thought of the loneliness of His mother in the days when He
was taken away. Jesus never forgot the duties that lay to His hand."

He saw her and the disciple "whom he loved" (see on 13 : 23). This man has not been mentioned, though the others by the cross are listed. Is this perhaps the touch of one who remembers who were there, but records them as he saw them and thus does not mention himself? Jesus then said to Mary, "Woman,[64] behold, thy son!" This is surely a way of saying that the beloved disciple would take His place in being her protector and provider, now that His earthly course was finished. It is perhaps a little strange that Jesus commends Mary to the beloved disciple rather than to His brothers. But they did not believe in Him (7 : 5) and Mary did. However, the crucifixion and resurrection seem to have worked a change in them for shortly after the ascension we find them associated with the apostles and with Mary (Acts 1 : 14).

27 His words to Mary are complemented by similar words to the disciple. These he would remember as a sacred charge. There is a typical Johannine note of time, "from that hour".[65] That he took her into his own home[66] implies, of course, more than that he provided her with a roof. From that time he took the responsibility for her.

(d) The Death of Jesus, 19 : 28–30

28 After this Jesus, knowing that all things are now finished, [1]that the scripture might be accomplished, saith, I thirst. 29 There was set there a vessel full of vinegar: so they put a sponge full of the vinegar upon hyssop, and brought it to

---

[64] For γύναι as a form of address see on 2 : 4.

[65] This may mean that the beloved disciple took Mary away immediately so that she did not witness the death of her Son. This is supported by the fact that she is not mentioned in the group of women who were there when Jesus died (Matt. 27 : 56; Mark 15 : 40). Against it is the difficulty of seeing how the beloved disciple could have taken her home and returned in time for the events of vv. 31–37 (most agree that he witnessed them whether or no he is directly mentioned in v. 35). "From that hour" need not mean "from that moment". When we consider the way in which "the hour" is used in this Gospel it is clear that it need mean no more than "from the time of the crucifixion". It is also urged that if Jesus' mother came to the place of execution it is most unlikely that she would have left before the end, all the more so in that the other women remained.

[66] The expression εἰς τὰ ἴδια does not, of course, necessarily denote one's permanent home. It is used of all the disciples in 16 : 32 and they would certainly not all have had homes in Jerusalem.

his mouth. 30 When Jesus therefore had received the vinegar, he said, It is finished: and he bowed his head, and gave up his spirit.

¹Ps. lxix. 21.

28 "After this" signifies a short interval.[67] John is narrating how things happened, and there was little time between the last incident and this. Jesus knew that the end was at hand. Once again John sees Him as in complete command. It is not certain whether we should take "that the scripture might be accomplished"[68] with the preceding ("knowing that all was finished that the scripture might be accomplished") or with the following, in which case the "I thirst" will perhaps refer to Ps. 69 : 21. Either is possible, or, in the Johannine manner, there may be a reference to both.[69]

29 "Vinegar" is a term which signifies a cheap wine,[70] the kind of drink that was used by the masses. There was some of it there in a container of some sort. "There was set there" makes it seem as though it was provided for use at the crucifixion. It was not some wine that somebody just happened to have with them. The fact that there were also a sponge and some hyssop appears to indicate that it had been provided for the crucified, and not simply for the soldiers. They now soaked a sponge in the wine, put it on "hyssop",[71] and thus raised it to Jesus' mouth. The

---

[67] The expression is μετὰ τοῦτο, for which see on 2 : 12.

[68] The verb τελειόω is used only here in the New Testament in the sense of the fulfilment of Scripture. It has about it the air of bringing to its end or aim (τέλος). It will point to the complete fulfilment of Scripture in Christ.

[69] J. M. Spurrell argues that the thirst is to be interpreted in terms of being "cut off from the knowledge and the Spirit of God" (it being a thirst to be understood in terms of the "living water"). He thinks of it accordingly as being akin in meaning to the cry: "My God, my God, why hast thou forsaken me?" of Mark 15 : 34 (CQR, CLXVII, 1966, pp. 12–18).

[70] ὄξος was the Roman posca, a vinegar well diluted with water.

[71] There has been a good deal of argument about this term. Many point out that the plant in question is one which is well adapted for sprinkling, but that it does not grow stems long enough for the purpose here mentioned. The implication is that John was not concerned with accuracy, but only with some symbolical meaning. Some see this in connection with purification, but a better suggestion is that, since hyssop was used in connection with Passover ceremonies (Exod. 12 : 22), John may be calling attention to Jesus as the

sponge was a useful way of conveying liquid to the lips of a crucified man, a cup of any sort being manifestly unsuitable.

30 Jesus drank the vinegar. Matthew and Mark tell us that He refused drugged wine before the crucifixion (Matt. 27 : 34; Mark 15 : 23).[72] We should probably conclude that He wished to undergo His sufferings with a clear mind. But now He is at the point of death. He wishes to say something that will be heard, so calls for a drink to moisten His parched throat. He drinks, then says, "It

---

perfect Passover sacrifice. Some have been so impressed by the difficulty of using hyssop in this way that in place of ὑσσώπῳ they conjecture an original ὑσσῷ, "javelin", a reading actually found in the 11th century cursive 476. No good reason has been adduced, however, why this reading, if original, should have been so universally corrupted. G. D. Kilpatrick remarks that the conjecture has been welcomed rather by the translators than the commentators. He rejects it on two main grounds – it does not agree with the nature of John's vocabulary and the meaning of the term is the *pilum*, a weapon of legionaries, but not of the auxiliaries who were stationed in Palestine (*Transactions of the Victoria Institute*, LXXXIX, 1957, p. 99). Tasker accepts the conjecture, regarding it as due to dittography of the two letters ωπ (*GNT*, p. 429). But the conjecture should be rejected. The difficulty appears to be due to the fact that too many critics are too sure that they know what ὕσσωπος was. AG, for example, describes it as "a small bush w. blue flowers and highly aromatic leaves", from which one would never gather that the experts are not too sure what plant the term denotes. Thus W. E. Shewell-Cooper says, "I find it difficult to discover what hyssop really is" (*Plants and Fruits of the Bible*, London, 1962, p. 75). He mentions a number of possibilities and concludes that the term does not denote one plant, but two or three different plants of which one "may have been like the rosemary with long branches well furnished with leaves" (*op. cit.*, p. 76). *NBD* thinks that the plant meant in the present passage "was probably the *Sorghum vulgare*, var. *durra* . . . a maize-like grass attaining at least 6 feet in height." In view of all this there seems no real reason for doubting that by ὑσσώπῳ John meant a plant with a stem sufficiently long for the purpose indicated. It should be borne in mind, moreover, that a very long rod was not needed as the crucified were not normally raised very high. All that was necessary was that the feet be clear of the ground, so that Jesus' mouth would probably be within reach of a man of average height. Quite a short cane would suffice.

[72] It is good to know that it was customary for a drug to be offered to the crucified so that some of the pain was mitigated. We read of the custom in *Sanh.* 43a, "When one is led out to execution, he is given a goblet of wine containing a grain of frankincense, in order to benumb his senses, for it is written, *Give strong drink unto him that is ready to perish, and wine unto the bitter in soul.* And it has also been taught: The noble women in Jerusalem used to donate and bring it" (Soncino edn., pp. 279f.).

is finished".[73] Immediately He dies. John does not speak of the tone in which He uttered the word, but elsewhere we read that Jesus uttered a loud cry just before His death (Matt. 27 : 50; Mark 15 : 37; Luke 23 : 46; the first two mention that Jesus was given a drink just before this). It would appear then that the loud cry was, "It is finished". Jesus died with the cry of the Victor on His lips. This is not the moan of the defeated, nor the sigh of patient resignation. It is the triumphant recognition that He has now fully accomplished the work that He came to do.[74] Then He bowed His head, a detail mentioned only by John, and possibly the touch of an eyewitness. It is perhaps worth noting that the same expression is used of going to bed: "the Son of man hath not where to lay his head" (Matt. 8 : 20; Luke 9 : 58).[75] There is the thought of a peaceful death, the death of One who trusts His Father.[76] John goes on, "and gave up his spirit". This is not the usual way of referring to death.[77] Indeed in none of the four Gospels is there any usual expression to describe the

---

[73] In the Greek this is one word, τετέλεσται. It is another of John's ambiguous terms. It could mean that Jesus' life was finished (*i.e.* He was about to die). This will be part of the meaning, but it is highly improbable that it is the whole. More important is the truth that Jesus' work was finished. He came to work God's work, and this meant dying on the cross for the world's salvation. This mighty work of redemption has now reached its consummation. It is finished.

[74] Anton Baumstark sees in this the central point for John: "In the mind of the great Apostle of Asia Minor, St. John, the Beloved Disciple, who stood under the dying Master's Cross until the final *Consummatum est*, even the Resurrection could add nothing to the remembrance of that triumphant cry" (*Comparative Liturgy*, London, 1958, p. 174). A. Corell can say, "Surely it is not an exaggeration to think that τετέλεσται is the key word of the Fourth Gospel, the key to the solution of its theological problem." He proceeds: "The whole of the Fourth Gospel is really the story of the death of Jesus regarded as an eschatological fact" (*Consummatum Est*, London, 1958, p. 106).

[75] Matthew and Luke have ποῦ τὴν κεφαλὴν κλίνῃ. John's expression is κλίνας τὴν κεφαλήν. That resting place for His head which He did not have on earth He found on the cross.

[76] Murray cites a comment of Origen: Jesus "bent the head and took His departure in the act of resting it, as it were, on the lap of the Father, who could cherish it and strengthen it in His bosom."

[77] παρέδωκεν τὸ πνεῦμα. Bernard points out that the Hebrew of Isa. 53 : 12, "he poured out his soul unto death", might well be translated παρέδωκεν εἰς θάνατον τὴν ψυχὴν αὐτοῦ. He thinks that John may well be alluding to this passage. He goes on to maintain that the verb παραδιδόναι "expresses a voluntary act".

manner of Jesus' end. His relation to death is not the same as that of other people. It may be going too far to say that He "dismissed His spirit", but there does seem to be an element of voluntariness that is not found in the case of others.[78]

(e) The Piercing of Jesus' Side, 19 : 31–37

31 The Jews therefore, because it was the Preparation, that the bodies should not remain on the cross upon the sabbath (for the day of that sabbath was a high day), asked of Pilate that their legs might be broken, and that they might be taken away. 32 The soldiers therefore came, and brake the legs of the first, and of the other that was crucified with him: 33 but when they came to Jesus, and saw that he was dead already, they brake not his legs: 34 howbeit one of the soldiers with a spear pierced his side, and straightway there came out blood and water. 35 And he that hath seen hath borne witness, and his witness is true: and he knoweth that he saith true, that ye also may believe. 36 For these things came to pass, [1]that the scripture might be fulfilled, A bone of him shall not be [2]broken. 37 And again another scripture saith, [3]They shall look on him whom they pierced.

[1]Ex. xii. 46; Num. ix. 12; Ps. xxxiv. 20. [2]Or, *crushed* [3]Zech. xii. 10.

This incident is peculiar to this Gospel. It indicates that the death of Jesus took place fairly quickly, more quickly than in the case of either of the others crucified with Him. John sees scriptural significance in the facts that His bones were not broken, and that His side was pierced. Despite the attempts to find an edifying meaning in the latter incident it seems best understood as the touch of an eyewitness who recorded it because it impressed him.

31 "The Preparation" had become a technical term for "the Preparation for the sabbath", *i.e.* Friday (see Additional Note H).

---

[78] Another interpretation of this last phrase is that Jesus handed over the Spirit to the believers gathered near the cross (*cf.* 7 : 37–9). This seems to me very difficult to get from the text, but Hoskyns, in the light of I John 5 : 8 finds it "not only possible, but necessary". M. F. Wiles tells us that among the patristic commentators πνεῦμα here "is never interpreted of the Holy Spirit" (*The Spiritual Gospel*, Cambridge, 1960, p. 67). Elsewhere he tells us that the expression used "is almost universally interpreted of the essentially voluntary nature of his death" (*op. cit.*, p. 62).

According to Jewish Law the dead body of an executed criminal was not to remain all night "upon the tree", but was to be buried, "that thou defile not thy land which Jehovah thy God giveth thee for an inheritance" (Deut. 21 : 23). Thus a body should be removed from a cross[79] on any day before evening.[80] But especially was this the case when a sabbath was approaching, and even more so when the sabbath[81] was "a high day"[82] *i.e.* one of the important feasts (*Berkeley,* "a specially important day"). The Jews were thus insistent that in this case the bodies should be removed before the feast began. Therefore they asked Pilate that the legs of the crucified be broken.[83] The Roman custom was to leave the bodies of crucified criminals on their crosses as a warning to others. It was therefore necessary to obtain permission before removing a body. The victims of this cruel form of execution could ease slightly the strain on their arms and chests

---

[79] $\grave{\epsilon}\pi\grave{\iota}$ $\tauο\tilde{υ}$ $\sigmaτανρο\tilde{υ}$ is singular, though "the bodies", $\tau\grave{α}$ $\sigma\acute{ω}ματα$, is plural. But the construction is perfectly intelligible.

[80] Josephus attests this as the Jewish custom: "the Jews are so careful about funeral rites that even malefactors who have been sentenced to crucifixion are taken down and buried before sunset" (*Bell.* iv, 317).

[81] The expression $\acute{η}$ $\acute{η}μέρα$ $το\tilde{υ}$ $\sigmaαββάτου$, evidently a translation of the Hebrew הַשַּׁבָּת יוֹם, is found in a number of places (Luke 13 : 14, 16; 14 : 5). Sometimes the plural $τ\tilde{ω}ν$ $\sigmaαββάτων$ replaces $το\tilde{υ}$ $\sigmaαββάτου$ with the same meaning (Luke 4 : 16; Acts 13 : 14; 16 : 13). This is the only example of the construction in John and the only place in the New Testament where $\grave{\epsilon}κε\tilde{ι}νο$ accompanies $τ\grave{ο}$ $\sigma\acute{α}ββατον$.

[82] SBk point out that this Sabbath could be called "great" whether it were Nisan 15, since that was the first day of the Passover festival, or whether it were Nisan 16, for on that day the Omer sheaf was offered according to the Pharisaic tradition (II, pp. 581f.). The reference thus does not help in deciding the question of whether the Last Supper was a Passover meal or not. It accords with either of the two important theories. I. Abrahams finds no instance before John 19 : 31 of the use of the term the "great Sabbath" and he mentions an opinion that the later Rabbinic use was borrowed from the church (*Studies in Pharisaism and the Gospels,* II, Cambridge, 1924, p. 68). This, however, is unlikely, and John's use of the expression seems inexplicable unless the term was already in use among the Jews.

[83] It is unusual to find in John the plural verb with a neuter plural subject, and it is difficult to see a reason for it here. All the more is this the case in that we have just had the singular $μείνη$ with the subject $τ\grave{α}$ $\sigma\acute{ω}ματα$. It is, of course, possible that $τ\grave{α}$ $\sigmaκέλη$ is accusative, "that they might have their legs broken". This has the further advantage that it avoids an awkward change of subject when we come to the following verb $\grave{α}ρθ\tilde{ω}\sigma\iotaν$. The subject of this verb can scarcely be $τ\grave{α}$ $\sigmaκέλη$.

by taking some of their weight on the feet. This helped to prolong their lives somewhat. When the legs were broken this was no longer possible. There was then a greater constriction of the chest, and death came on more quickly. This was aided also, of course, by the shock attendant on the brutal blows as the legs were broken with a heavy mallet. So the Jews wanted the process of death speeded up and the bodies removed.[84] It is perhaps significant that this is the last action of "the Jews" recorded in this Gospel. The Jews did not want their land defiled by their dead, but they were not concerned that they were themselves defiled by their deed.

32, 33 It is not said that Pilate gave his approval, but evidently he did for the soldiers came to break the legs of the sufferers. They did actually break the legs of both the men who were crucified with Jesus. This indicates that they were at this time still alive. But when they came to[85] Jesus they saw that He was already dead. Therefore they did not break His legs. There was no point in it.

34 But one of the soldiers was not content simply to pass by. Either out of brutality or to make sure that Jesus was really dead he thrust[86] his spear[87] into His side. Immediately blood and water came out (*cf.* I John 5 : 6). The significance of this is not clear. In view of the following verse it is plain that John wants us to take this as a record of what actually happened. He is not manufacturing an edifying piece of symbolism, but describing an event. The author was struck by it, so included it in his Gospel. But this does not exclude the possibility that John saw spiritual significance in what he records. Some appear to deny this, holding that it points to

---

[84] Plummer cites from Lactantius: "His executioners did not think it necessary to break His bones, as was their prevailing custom." If this is accurate the horror of broken legs was habitually added to that of crucifixion.

[85] This use of ἐπί with the accusative to denote motion right up to a person is found here only in John. It occurs more often in the Synoptic Gospels.

[86] νύσσω occurs only here in the true text of the New Testament (though it is found in some MSS of Matt. 27 : 49, and in a different sense in one or two of Acts 12 : 7). It is perhaps another example of John's love for slight variation that the verb differs from that used in the citation of Scripture which he sees fulfilled in the incident, namely ἐκκεντέω (v. 37).

[87] The λόγχη was originally the iron point or spearhead. Then it came to denote a lance, a shaft tipped with an iron point (see GT, LS).

the manner of Jesus' death, namely by a ruptured heart.[88] Or it may be held that there is in mind a Jewish belief that the body consists of half water and half blood.[89] The thrust of the spear shows Jesus' body to be a genuine human corpse (in opposition to Docetic teaching that the body was a phantom). Others, however, see a mystical significance,[90] or a reference to the sacraments.[91] It is more likely that the explanation should be in terms of John's

---

[88] This was argued by William Stroud, M. D., in his book, *Treatise on the Physical Cause of the Death of Christ* (London, 1847). He maintained that rupture of the heart may be caused by great mental agony and that it "is usually attended with immediate death, and with an effusion into the pericardium (the capsule containing the heart) of the blood previously circulating through that organ; which when thus extravasated, although scarcely in any other case, separates into its constituent parts, so as to present the appearance commonly termed blood and water" (*op. cit.*, 2nd edn., 1871, pp. 74f.). This view was accepted by Sir Alexander Simpson (*Expositor* 8, xi, 1916, pp. 334ff.) who said that he had examined several cases "in which the pericardial bag was greatly distended and the blood had separated into clot and watery serum" (*op. cit.*, p. 336). It has been urged against it that John does not tell us whether it was the left or right side that was pierced. We cannot be certain that the spear was thrust into the region of the heart. Tasker cites a paper by a medical man, J. L. Cameron, arguing that the passage indicates a flow of blood from the heart and great blood vessels adjacent, and water from the acutely dilated stomach. Dodd refers us to a study by Raymond Schmittlein which sees traumatic shock as the fundamental cause of death (*HTFG*, p. 136).

[89] SBk gives the evidence (II, pp. 582f.). *Cf.* F. C. Burkitt: "According to 1 Joh v 6–8 the living personality has in it three elements, viz. spirit, water, blood. From the 'water' we are begotten, by the 'blood' we are sustained, and the 'spirit' or breath is the immaterial element that enters at birth and leaves at death. The spirit quitted Jesus when He died (Joh xix 30), leaving behind the water and blood of a human body, the existence of which was demonstrated to the onlookers by the spear-thrust of the soldier" (*The Gospel History and its Transmission*, Edinburgh, 1907, p. 233, n. 1).

[90] Thus Westcott says, "The issuing of the blood and water from His side must therefore be regarded as a sign of life in death . . . Though dead, dead in regard to our mortal life, the Lord yet lived; and as He hung upon the cross He was shown openly to be the source of a double cleansing and vivifying power, which followed from His death and life." But this is based on a view of the connection between blood and life which appears to be untenable. See my *The Apostolic Preaching of the Cross* (London and Grand Rapids, 3rd edn., 1965), ch. III. Hoskyns has an interesting list of patristic interpretations.

[91] *E.g.* Richardson: "The symbolism is profound: from Christ's self-oblation there flow the healing waters of baptism and the life-giving blood of the Eucharist." One would feel happier about this type of interpretation if it could be demonstrated that the early church did use "water" to mean "baptism" and "blood" to signify "Holy Communion."

use of the terms "blood" and "water" elsewhere. Apart from the statement that men are born "not of bloods" (1 : 13) John uses the former term only in ch. 6 from which we learn that life comes through appropriating the blood of Christ (6 : 53–56). Water is used more often, but perhaps the significant references are those to being born "of water and the Spirit" (3 : 5), to the "living water" which is the gift of Christ (4 : 10, 11, 14), and to the "living water" which would flow from the inner being of the believer, which is explained as referring to the Spirit (7 : 38f.). There is a consistent reference in the use of both terms to the life that Christ gives. We conclude, then, that John is reminding us that life, real life, comes through Christ's death.[92]

35 This incident evidently made a profound impression on the mind of the Evangelist. He brings out emphatically the point that he has good evidence for what he is saying. This evidence in the opinion of many is the testimony of the Beloved Disciple. He is mentioned in vv. 26f., the last reference to the followers of Jesus before this verse. Moreover John mentions no other disciple as being present at the scene. The identification is not certain, but it is probable.[93] Be that as it may, there was someone there who saw it and who has borne his testimony,[94] a testimony that is reliable.[95] This may be understood in more ways than one. The

---

[92] *Cf.* Barrett: "He was not concerned to support this or that detail of sacramental practice or terminology, but to emphasize, perhaps against those who controverted it, that the real death of Jesus was the real life of men." Some see a reference to purification in the water, and this is quite possible. Purification is connected with the life in the Spirit as a necessary preliminary. Ryle is reminded of the opening of "a fountain . . . for sin and for uncleanness" (Zech. 13 : 1).

[93] *Cf.* W. G. Kümmel: "Since only the Beloved Disciple was mentioned as present at the cross (in addition to the women), it is natural to find him mentioned in the ἑωρακώς and witness of 19 : 35, though, to be sure, that is not clearly said" (*Introduction to the New Testament*, London, 1966, p. 166).

[94] The perfect, μεμαρτύρηκεν, will signify "he has set it on permanent record."

[95] Plummer brings out the force of it: "S. John first says that his evidence is adequate; then he adds that the contents of it are true. Testimony may be sufficient (e.g. of a competent eyewitness) but false: or it may be insufficient (e.g. of a half-witted child) but true. S. John declares that his testimony is both sufficient and true." For the importance of witness in this Gospel see on 1 : 7, and for ἀληθινός on 1 : 9. This is one of the places where Kilpatrick reads ἀληθής (with ℵ 124 Chrys).

writer may be referring to himself as a witness, which seems to be the implication of Weymouth's translation: "This statement is the testimony of an eye-witness, and it is true. He knows that he is telling the truth – in order that you also may believe."[96] Or the writer may be distinguishing between himself as the author and another man who is the witness. Thus Rieu translates: "This is vouched for by the man who saw it, and his evidence may be relied on. Also, to assure you, the writer knows that he is telling the truth."[97] It is also possible that the writer is calling God to witness, as Moffatt renders: "He who saw it has borne witness (his witness is true; God knows he is telling the truth), that you may believe."[98] When experts can differ so widely it is unwise to

---

[96] Lagrange notes an objection to understanding the writer to be referring to himself on the grounds that he has twice recorded the truth that a man's witness to himself is not valid (5 : 31; 8 : 13; he himself thinks that the writer is the witness). This would have more weight if he were in fact bearing witness to himself here. But he is not. It is witness to an observed fact that is meant. Barclay sees a reference to the writer: "he goes out of his way to say that this is an eye-witness account of what actually happened, and that he personally guarantees that it is true." That ἐκεῖνος is not impossible in Greek with reference to the writer is shown by Josephus's use of the pronoun in just this way (*Bell.* iii, 202; *cf.* also John 9 : 37). Support for the view that the writer is referring to himself may perhaps be found in the strong emphasis on personal witness in I John 1 : 1–3.

[97] The principal advantage of this view (and it is a considerable one) is that this is a very natural way of understanding ἐκεῖνος. Torrey maintains that ἐκεῖνος here reflects the Aramaic *hāhū gabrā*, "a common Jewish substitute for the pronoun of the first person singular." An objection is the difficulty of seeing how the writer, if not an eyewitness himself, could know that the witness was speaking the truth as he solemnly assures us is the case. Those who understand the words to refer to a witness other than the author often think of that witness as the Beloved Disciple. However this is not said.

[98] This is sometimes supported by the contention that in this Gospel, apart from dialogue, ἐκεῖνος is generally emphatic and is often used of God or of Christ. Lagrange sees a reference to Jesus Christ, as does Hoskyns, who regards it as "almost necessary" to refer the words to our Lord. This, however, is not borne out by the facts. Dodd has shown that the usage of ἐκεῖνος in this Gospel supports the view that the reference is to the witness (*HTFG*, p. 134, n. 1). Bernard reminds us that John uses ἐκεῖνος not only of the Deity but quite often also of men, as John the Baptist (5 : 35), Moses (5 : 46), the blind man (9 : 10), *etc.* It requires more than this pronoun to demonstrate a reference to God or to Christ. Strachan sees a threefold witness, the Evangelist in v. 34, the Beloved Disciple in v. 35 and Christ Himself, also in v. 35. This is attractive but hard to discern in the text. Incidentally John rarely uses καὶ ἐκεῖνος as here, preferring κἀκεῖνος.

be dogmatic. I incline to the view that the first suggestion is the correct one, but one cannot be sure. What is plain is that John is placing some emphasis on the fact that this incident may be relied on.[99] He is maintaining that it is recorded "that ye also may believe".[100] The production of faith in the readers is the main purpose of the writing of this Gospel (20 : 31).[101] John does not explain how faith will result from the narration of the issuing of water and blood from the side of the crucified Saviour, but clearly he expected it to do so.[102]

36 Characteristically John sees a fulfilment of Scripture in these happenings. The purpose of God had to be fulfilled.[103] He refers to two separate things, the fact that Jesus' bones were not broken, and the fact that His side was pierced. It is really extraordinary that this should be the case. Jesus escaped the breaking of the legs though this happened to those crucified with him, and He ex-

---

[99] *I.e.*, assuming that we have the text of what he wrote at this point. Blass was most uncertain of this, saying, "In this passage, however, *everything* is doubtful, so far as criticism is concerned. There is doubt about the whole verse, which is wanting in e and Cod. Fuldensis of the Vulgate, about this particular clause, about the text of this clause, as Nonnus read ἐκεῖνον οἴδαμεν, etc. . . . . The fact that so many theologians have based their theories as to the origin of the 4th Gospel on this verse and the meaning ordinarily attached to it is only explicable on the ground of a complete neglect of textual criticism" (*Grammar of New Testament Greek*, London, 1905, p. 172, n. 2). It may, however, be doubted whether Blass is being fair to the evidence. While the textual variants he notes should be weighed we should not attach to them more than their due weight. After all, there is a limit to the value we attach to the combination e, Cod. Fuldensis, and Nonnus. These can scarcely outweigh the mass of the authorities especially as they do not all say the same thing. Turner is another who is hesitant about this verse. He draws attention to variation in John's use of ἐκεῖνος and concludes, "it is inadvisable to build any theories of authorship on the notorious ἐκεῖνος (= *he*, the eye-witness) in Jn 19³⁵" (M, III, p. 46).

[100] If, as seems likely, the present subjunctive should be read, ἵνα πιστεύητε may be meant to indicate a continuing faith rather than merely an entry into faith. But many MSS read the aorist so the point should not be pressed.

[101] J. Ramsay Michaels connects this verse with the confession of faith of the centurion recorded in Mark 15 : 39. He suggests a tentative identification of the centurion with the "witness" of this verse (*CBQ*, XXIX, 1967, pp. 102–109). There is much that is speculative here, but Michaels certainly draws attention to the fact that John understands what he records to be for the purpose of establishing faith.

[102] Westcott has a very useful Additional Note on the interpretation of this passage among the Fathers. He cites many, both Greek and Latin.

[103] Note the significance of ἵνα.

perienced a hard spear thrust, which appears to have been unusual, but which yet did no bone damage. Most think that the particular passage John has in mind for the first is Exod. 12 : 46 or Num. 9 : 12, both referring to the Passover. When that sacrifice was instituted the command was given that not one bone was to be broken. If this is the allusion then John is viewing Jesus as the perfect Passover offering. This is a motif that we have seen elsewhere and it seems to me that it is the most likely explanation of the reference here. Some, however, who do not stress the Passover, think the reference is to Ps. 34 : 20. This is a general reference to the way God watches over His own, with the specific assertion that "He keepeth all his bones: not one of them is broken." This is possible but it does not seem as probable as the Passover allusion.[104]

37 The other Scripture in mind does not seem so difficult. There is agreement that John is referring to Zech. 12 : 10[105] (*cf.* also Rev. 1 : 7). It is not the kind of allusion that a modern student would readily discern, but it fits in with the habit of mind of the first century.[106] And this passage from the prophet certainly

---

[104] The correspondence with the Greek text is not as close as in the case of the other two passages. For example the words ὀστοῦν and αὐτοῦ are absent from Ps. 34 : 20, though present in the other two passages. There is poetic parallelism in the expression in the Psalm, but not in John or in the Pentateuchal passages. Moreover the Psalm is concerned with the preservation of the righteous from death. It is concerned with saving his life, not with the condition of the bones in his corpse. The other two passages do refer to the treatment of a dead body. In favor of the reference to the Psalm are the facts that the Pentateuchal passages both give a command and are in the active, whereas the Psalm and John represent a prediction and are passive. But I do not think that these considerations outweigh the others.

[105] The quotation follows the Hebrew text, not the LXX which reads κατωρχήσαντο ("mocked", reflecting the misreading רקדו for דקרו) instead of John's ἐξεκέντησαν. But Theodotion and Aquila agree with John, so we cannot regard it as proved that John is translating direct from the Hebrew. He may have used a translation which on this point is like Theodotion and Aquila, but which has now perished. The most natural understanding of it, however, is that John knew and used the Hebrew. The LXX translators may well have been deterred by the bold anthromorphism of the original (the piercing of God).

[106] Calvin denies that the passage refers to Christ in the literal sense: "Rather he shows that Christ is the God who had complained through Zechariah, that the Jews had pierced His heart (Zech. 12 : 10). Now God here speaks in a human way, meaning that He is wounded by the sins of His people".

strengthens the Evangelist in his conviction that in the events associated with the crucifixion the will of God was done. John was evidently impressed with the fact that, though Jesus' body was pierced not one bone was broken, and that this corresponded exactly with Scripture.

(f) The Burial, 19 : 38–42

38 And after these things Joseph of Arimathaea, being a disciple of Jesus, but secretly for fear of the Jews, asked of Pilate that he might take away the body of Jesus: and Pilate gave him leave. He came therefore, and took away his body. 39 And there came also Nicodemus, he who at the first came to him by night, bringing a [1]mixture of myrrh and aloes, about a hundred pounds. 40 So they took the body of Jesus, and bound it in linen cloths with the spices, as the custom of the Jews is to bury. 41 Now in the place where he was crucified there was a garden; and in the garden a new tomb wherein was never man yet laid. 42 There then because of the Jews' Preparation (for the tomb was nigh at hand) they laid Jesus.

[1]Some ancient authorities read *roll.*

38 Some time later[107] Joseph of Arimathea[108] began to make arrangements for Jesus' burial. John introduces Joseph rather abruptly. We hear of him neither before nor after this incident. The burial of Jesus is the one thing by which he is known. There is not much description of him. We are told only that he was from Arimathea, and that he was a secret disciple. Neither Mark nor Luke tells us in so many terms that he was a disciple, though this may perhaps be implied when they say that he "was looking for the kingdom of God" (Mark 15 : 43; Luke 23 : 51). Matthew

---

[107] μετὰ ταῦτα (see on 2 : 12). The expression does not appear to denote strict chronological sequence. Thus it does not necessarily place Joseph's approach to Pilate immediately after the incident with the spear. It may mean that Joseph went to Pilate as soon as Jesus' death appeared imminent, or perhaps had taken place.

[108] The location of Arimathea is not known. It may be identical with Ramathaim-Zophim (I Sam. 1 : 1), but this does not help for the site of this place is uncertain. Since Joseph had a tomb near Jerusalem it seems that Arimathea was his birthplace, but that he had now moved to the capital.

does say that he was a disciple (Matt. 27 : 57), and also that he was rich. Mark and Luke do not say this, but they tell us that he was a councillor, and Luke adds that he was "a good and righteous man" and that he had not consented to "their counsel and deed" (Luke 23 : 51). It would not have been easy for a member of the Sanhedrin to profess himself a follower of Jesus, so that John's information has nothing inherently improbable about it. But the death of Jesus apparently affected him in a way different from that of the closer disciples. They all fled. Joseph now went to Pilate (Mark tells us that he went in "boldly") and asked permission to take Jesus' body away for burial. It may be that he felt that in Jesus' lifetime he had paid him little honor, and that he was now presented with his last opportunity. The Jews of that day regarded proper burial of their dead as most important. Many went out of their way to see that fellow-countrymen received proper burial, and this may have had something to do with Joseph's action. He came now to ask Pilate's permission to remove Jesus' body. Pilate gave the necessary permission and Joseph took the body away.

39 The other Evangelists speak of Joseph's part in the burial, but they do not mention Nicodemus. Indeed they mention him nowhere. It is to John that we owe all our information about him. He is characterized here by his first coming to Jesus by night (see on 3 : 2). Clearly this fact meant a good deal to John. Nicodemus brought spices for the burial, about seventy pounds weight in our measures, of myrrh and aloes (for this conjunction *cf.* Ps. 45 : 8; aloes is mentioned only here in the New Testament). It was the custom to put spices of this kind in with the sheets round the body, so Nicodemus was performing a normal courtesy. What is unusual is the amount, though if Nicodemus wished to cover the body completely the quantity is not excessive. But there is evidence that large quantities were used in royal burials (*cf.* II Chron. 16 : 14), and the probability is that John is reminding us again of Jesus' kingship.[109] The thought may well be in mind that when He spoke with Nicodemus Jesus talked of the kingdom (3 : 3).

---

[109] SBk cites an incident in which the proselyte Onkelos burned more than 80 minas of spices at the funeral of R. Gamaliel the elder. Asked why he did this he drew attention to Jer. 34 : 5 and went on: "Is not R. Gamaliel better than a hundred kings?"

The lavish provision may also be meant to show that Nicodemus, like Joseph, was trying in the hour of Jesus' death to make some reparation for his failure to do more in Jesus' life. The amount shows that Nicodemus must have been a man of some wealth. It is possible that in this incident we are to see the consequence of Jesus' prediction of the passion in His first interview with Nicodemus. If on that night Jesus had told the Pharisee that He would one day die for men this may explain why Nicodemus was ready to do what he could at the burial at a time when the disciples had all run away. It is not without its interest that, whereas the disciples who had openly followed Jesus ran away at the end, the effect of the death of Jesus on these two secret disciples was exactly the opposite. Now, when they had nothing at all to gain by affirming their connection with Jesus, they came right out into the open.

40 These men gave Jesus decent burial according to the Jewish custom. This provided for an embalming, but unlike, for example, the Egyptian practice, there was no mutilation of the body. They first prepared the body by wrapping it in linen cloths.[110] This will mean long bandage-like strips rather than a shroud or the like. Between the folds they put the spices.

41 There was a tomb in a garden (only John mentions the garden) very near to the place of execution. John actually says it was "in" the place, so it must have been very close indeed. The tomb is described as "new", as one "wherein was never man yet laid." Tombs were commonly hewn out of the solid rock, and closed with heavy stones. The stone at the mouth would run in a groove and finish right over the opening. Such tombs were expensive, and there would be a tendency to use them again and again. Sometimes this would arise because from the beginning the tomb was designed to take more than one body. But on this occasion John tells us that the tomb had never[111] before been used, a detail which Luke also mentions (Luke 23 : 53). Matthew tells us that it was Joseph's own tomb (Matt. 27 : 60).

---

[110] ὀθόνιον according to MM in Egypt at any rate denoted fine linen. They cite as parallels to the present passage papyri where it is used of "fine linen-wrappings for a mummy". It is generally agreed that the term denotes thin strips or bandages whereas σινδών (Matt. 27 : 59; Mark 15 : 46; Luke 23 : 53) refers to a sheet or shroud.

[111] The double negative οὐδέπω οὐδείς puts emphasis on this fact.

42 There was need for haste, for clearly it would be getting near to sundown when the sabbath would start. It was necessary therefore to get the burial completed before then. So, because it was Friday (for the term "the Preparation" see on v. 31 and Additional Note H, pp. 774ff.), and because[112] this tomb was near, they buried Jesus there.

---

[112] For causal ὅτι see on 1 : 50.

CHAPTER XX

VI. THE RESURRECTION, 20 : 1–29

All four Gospels come to their climax in the resurrection narratives, but each does it in its own way. The accounts are very different. John, for example, has none of the stories that the others have.[1] His account is peculiar to himself throughout. He agrees on the fact of the resurrection, and he speaks of the empty tomb as do the others. But he lacks the stories the others tell, and he tells stories that they do not. It is not easy to arrange the details given by the four Evangelists into a connected narrative. But it is not impossible, and Westcott, for example, has drawn up an approximate time table of the events on that first Easter Day with everything arranged in sequence. We cannot be certain that his account is correct, but it is certainly possible. The differences between the Gospels amount to no more than a demonstration that here we have the spontaneous evidence of witnesses, not the stereotyped repetition of an official story.

1. THE EMPTY TOMB, 20 : 1–10

1 Now on the first day of the week cometh Mary Magdalene early, while it was yet dark, unto the tomb, and seeth the stone taken away from the tomb. 2 She runneth therefore, and cometh to Simon Peter, and to the other disciple whom Jesus loved, and saith unto them, They have taken away the Lord out of the tomb, and we know not where they have laid him. 3 Peter therefore went forth, and the other disciple, and they went toward the tomb. 4 And they ran both together: and the other disciple outran Peter, and came first to the tomb; 5 and stooping and looking in, he seeth the linen cloths lying; yet entered he not in. 6 Simon Peter therefore also

---

[1] Luke 24 : 12 mentions Peter's visit to the tomb (though the Beloved Disciple is not included). Some regard that verse as inauthentic on the grounds of its omission by certain Western authorities (notably D) and the possibility of its being derived from the present passage. If the latter were the case, however, it is difficult to see why John should not be mentioned, nor the appearance to Mary.

cometh, following him, and entered into the tomb; and he beholdeth the linen cloths lying, 7 and the napkin, that was upon his head, not lying with the linen cloths, but rolled up in a place by itself. 8 Then entered in therefore the other disciple also, who came first to the tomb, and he saw, and believed. 9 For as yet they knew not the scripture, that he must rise again from the dead. 10 So the disciples went away again unto their own home.

The Synoptists inform us that on the first Easter morning a number of women came to the tomb with spices. Matthew speaks of Mary Magdalene and "the other Mary" (Matt. 28 : 1), Mark mentions these two and Salome (Mark 16 : 1), Luke the two Marys and Joanna (Luke 24 : 10). Presumably this means that the burial on the Friday had had to be hurried, and when the Sabbath was over the ladies wished to complete the burial in a seemly manner. John does not speak of any woman as being there other than Mary Magdalene. She is mentioned by the Synoptists (Matt. 28 : 1; Mark 16 : 1; Luke 24 : 10). But they do not actually tell us that she saw the risen Lord. It is possible that after the vision of angels mentioned in the Synoptists she became separated from the others and that the vision of the Lord took place then. It is perhaps surprising that our Lord's first appearance after the resurrection was to Mary who, as far as we know, held no official position. Her only claim was that she was one of those who had served Jesus (Luke 8 : 2f.).[2] We should not miss the implication that God's priorities are not ours. We should have expected one or more of the apostles, or, if a woman, then Jesus' mother.

It is worthy of note that all the Evangelists put some emphasis on the empty tomb. Nowadays some scholars suggest that we should not be too confident in our exposition of the resurrection, for we do not really know what took place. We may agree that there is room for some reverent agnosticism. There is much here of which we must say "We cannot explain this." But this does not mean that we must surrender the great biblical emphases. Specifically the empty tomb witnesses to the fact that the resurrec-

---

[2] It is possible that it was her need that determined our Lord's appearance. *Cf.* Tasker: "She who owed so much to her Master during His earthly life (see Mk. xvi. 9) needed most of all to be reassured at the earliest possible moment that death had not put an end to the benefits she could receive from Him."

tion of Christ had physical aspects. Alan Richardson says, "If we truly believe that God performed the stupendous act of raising Jesus from the dead, we will not quibble about how he could or could not have done it. The bodily resurrection of the Lord is theologically very important in shewing that the whole of creation is to be redeemed, the physical no less than the spiritual" (on v. 19).

1 Mary Magdalene came to[3] the tomb very early[4] on the first[5] day of the week,[6] for John tells us that it was "yet dark".[7] That it was still dark will perhaps explain why Mary did not see the things Peter and John saw later. However, she does not appear to have paused for long enough to see much, whatever the state of the light. Her early arrival is evidence of a determination to get on with the task at the soonest possible moment. It is not clear why John does not mention any woman other than Mary when all the other Gospels tell us that she was not alone. It may be that he knew that she was the first to see the Lord Jesus (*cf.* Mark 16 : 9) and that he was not concerned accordingly with the others who did not see Jesus at the same time as did Mary.[8] This is not entirely convincing but it is difficult to see a better

---

[3] εἰς is used here in much the sense of πρός. It can scarcely be taken to mean "into". Yet later in this chapter the same expression is used where the meaning must be "into" (vv. 6, 8).

[4] For πρωΐ see on 18 : 27f.

[5] The cardinal number μιᾷ is used and not the ordinal. This is not conclusive proof of Semitic influence (see M, I, pp. 95f.), but it certainly agrees with a Semitic background, for such a use is found in both Hebrew and Aramaic.

[6] σάββατα, though plural in form, is used with the singular meaning. It can signify either "sabbath" or "week". The plural form appears to be due to the fact that the Aramaic שבתא, when transliterated, has the appearance of a Greek neuter plural. This would be helped by the analogy of plurals for festivals such as τὰ ἐγκαίνια. The meaning "week" would derive from the interval between sabbath and sabbath.

[7] A problem is posed by the fact that according to Mark 16 : 2 the sun had risen when the women reached the tomb. Several commentators suggest that the women came in groups, all arriving about sunrise. Those who were a little earlier would have arrived in darkness, and those a little later when the sun was up. Another view is that John's statement refers to the time of Mary's departure from her home, Mark's to the time of arrival at the tomb.

[8] Matthew of course tells us that the other women saw Jesus (Matt. 28 : 9). But this may mean that they saw Him after becoming separated from Mary Magdalene.

explanation. The synoptists tell us that the women came with spices to anoint the body. Why this should be done when Nicodemus had brought such a large quantity is not clear. It may be that they were not aware of what Nicodemus had done, but this seems unlikely in the light of the fact that two of them "beheld where he was laid" (Mark 15 : 47). More probably, in view of the lateness of the hour and the nearness of the sabbath, Nicodemus was not able to use all the spices he had brought in the way intended. Something remained to complete the process of burial, and the women came to do this. John proceeds to tell us that Mary saw that the stone had been taken away from the tomb.[9] The women had been anxious about this, since they knew they could not roll it away themselves (Mark 16 : 3).

2 Mary's immediate reaction was to tell the menfolk. She ran off to Simon Peter (who thus appears still to have been recognized as the leading apostle, despite the denials), and to the Beloved Disciple[10] (for this expression see on 13 : 23). She had seen that the tomb was empty and concluded that the body had been stolen[11] (what else?). It is interesting to notice that apparently the thought of a resurrection did not enter her head. So she told the two men that the body had been taken away. Her "they" is not defined, but it can scarcely mean "people in general". It will refer to the enemies of Jesus, perhaps especially the chief priests, or it may be an impersonal plural equivalent to our passive.[12]

---

[9] "Taken away" is the translation of ἠρμένον. The verb has the meaning "lift up", "take up", and it is not the word we might have anticipated. When the stone was put in place it was "rolled" (the verb is προσκυλίω, Matt. 27 : 60; Mark 15 : 46). John may imply violence, all the more so since the preposition following is ἐκ. This seems to imply that the stone was lifted out of the groove in which it ran (*Amplified* renders, "lifted out of (the groove across the entrance of) the tomb"). The perfect of this verb is unusual and may be intended to give an air of finality.

[10] It is difficult to see why the preposition πρός is repeated. Perhaps the two disciples were not together at first. The easiest supposition is that the two were lodging in different places and that Mary went to Peter first, then with Peter to the lodgings of the other. But it is difficult to get all this out of one preposition.

[11] We might have expected the perfect instead of the aorist ἦραν. But the perfect of this verb is very rare, the only example in John being the participle in v. 1. It appears that the aorist was sometimes used in the sense which we associate with the perfect.

[12] This view is favored by Black, who sees in it an Aramaism (*AA*, p. 91).

She adds, "we know not where they have laid him." The plural "we" indicates that other women were associated with her in the discovery, though she is the only one John mentions (*cf.* the singular in v. 13). It is in any case inherently likely, considering that the visit to the tomb was made "while it was yet dark", that others were with her. A woman would scarcely have ventured outside the city alone at such an hour with Jerusalem crowded with visitors for the feast, visitors who might be of uncertain character and who might be bivouacking anywhere! For "the Lord" see on 4 : 1.

3 The disciples apparently wasted no time talking. They set off to see for themselves. Peter is mentioned first as though he took the initiative and set off. The other then decided to come, too. They were going to the tomb.[13]

4 The result was that they were both running.[14] But he who started second was faster than Peter and he reached the tomb first. It is often said that he was a younger man than Peter, and he may well have been. But the text does not say so and we must bear in mind that speed and youth are not synonymous. It is not impossible moreover that the Beloved Disciple was more familiar with the way than Peter and took a short cut to the tomb. We do not know.

5 Apparently the Beloved Disciple was a somewhat diffident or hesitant man. He had not begun this race to the tomb, but had waited till Peter took the initiative. Now, arrived at his destination, he hesitated to go inside the tomb. He contented himself with standing outside and looking in.[15] From this position he could see the linen clothes lying. No mention is made of the headcloth. Presumably this was not visible from where he stood, but when Peter (in the next verse) went into the tomb he would see it straight away.

---

[13] The imperfect, ἤρχοντο, pictures the action as in progress, "they were coming", or perhaps, "they began to come".

[14] ARV says, "they ran both together". ὁμοῦ here must be taken in the sense "at the same time" rather than "in company with each other", for Peter started out without the other, and the other passed Peter and arrived first.

[15] "Stooping and looking in" is the translation of one word, παρακύψας. The verb conveys the idea of bending over (*i.e.* to see something better). In the New Testament period this seems often to have passed over to the meaning "peer into", "peep into".

6, 7 Some time later (how much later is not specified) Peter arrived. Typically, he did not hesitate. He went straight into the tomb. He saw the cloths that had been round the body, and John mentions that the cloth that had been on Jesus' head was not with the others, but was wrapped up in a place of its own (*Berkeley* renders, "in its particular place", but this seems to go beyond the meaning of the Greek). In recent years this has often been taken to mean that the grave clothes were just as they had been when placed round the body. That is to say, Jesus' body rose through the grave-clothes without disturbing them. This is not inconsistent with the language, but it should be borne in mind that John does not say this. That the headcloth was not with the others scarcely supports this, for had this been the case it would have been right alongside them, with no more than the length of the neck (if that) between them. Moreover "rolled up" does not look like a description of the way it would have appeared had the head simply passed through it. However, whatever be the truth of this, John is plainly describing an orderly scene, not one of wild confusion. This means that the body had not been taken by grave-robbers. They would never have left the cloths wrapped neatly. They would have taken the body, cloths and all, or would have torn the cloths off and scattered them.[16]

8 Emboldened by Peter the other disciple also entered the tomb. John repeats that he came first. He tells us that "he saw[17] and believed". Neither verb has an object. We may fairly conjecture that the object of the first is the grave clothes. These are at the

---

[16] Long ago Chrysostom remarked: "For neither, if any persons had removed the body, would they before doing so have stripped it; nor if any had stolen it, would they have taken the trouble to remove the napkin, and roll it up, and lay it in a place by itself; but how? they would have taken the body as it was. On this account John tells us by anticipation that it was buried with much myrrh, which glues linen to the body not less firmly than lead . . ." (LXXXV. 4; pp. 320f.).

[17] This is the third different verb used for "see" in this chapter. βλέπει is used of Mary in v. 1 and of the Beloved Disciple in v. 5, θεωρεῖ is used of Peter in v. 6 and now we have εἶδεν. Some make a good deal of the changes, but these may simply be due to John's love of variety (see on 1 : 32 for words for "see" and on 3 : 5 for John's variations). It is, however, probable that θεωρεῖ in v. 6 denotes a more prolonged scrutiny than does βλέπει in vv. 1, 5. Moffatt tries to bring out the force of some of these changes by rendering "glanced" in v. 5, "noticed" in v. 6, and "saw" in v. 8.

moment the centre of attention. There is no real uncertainty here.[18] But what did he believe? That Jesus rose is the natural answer, but immediately John goes on to tell us that they did not yet know the scripture that Jesus must rise. He may mean that, on the basis of the evidence before his eyes, the Beloved Disciple believed that a resurrection had taken place, even despite his ignorance at this time of the significance of the scripture bearing on this point. This will be supported by the meaning attaching to "believe" in vv. 25, 27, 29. Hoskyns is in no doubt about this and goes as far as to say, "The pre-eminence of the faith of the Beloved Disciple is the climax of the narrative. His faith was not derived from ancient prophetic texts; the fact of the empty tomb illuminated the sense of scripture". Some have felt that the recording of the fact that he was the first to believe shows a certain pride. In view of v. 29 it is more likely to be humility. "He saw, and believed" – and therefore did not attain to the blessing promised to those who believed without seeing. The possibility should also be mentioned that John's meaning is that, though he did not attain to a knowledge of the resurrection, he did attain some sort of faith. Whatever had happened in the tomb had been wonderful. Or he may simply mean that he believed Mary's story. It had sounded incredible enough, but now that John saw the tomb he recognized the truth of what she had said. He believed her.[19] It is worth noting that John puts some emphasis on the fact of the empty tomb. Not only was it seen to be empty by Mary, but also by Peter and the Beloved Disciple.

9 "As yet they knew not" appears to mean that eventually they did know.[20] But at this time they did not know the scripture which spoke of the resurrection. John's habit is to use "the scripture" as a way of referring to a specific passage rather than to the general tenor of scriptural teaching. Which raises the question, Which passage is meant? Paul also tells us that Jesus

---

[18] Despite Phillips: "saw what had happened". This is an addition to the text and not a translation.

[19] G. W. Broomfield strongly urges this explanation: "This interpretation removes all difficulties with regard to the story, and it has the great advantage of being the most obvious and natural interpretation of the text as it stands" (*John, Peter, and the Fourth Gospel*, London, 1934, p. 49).

[20] But I do not think it implies that they came to know this right away as NEB appears to mean: "until then they had not understood the scriptures".

was raised "on the third day according to the scriptures" (I Cor. 15 : 4), but he does not say what passage he has in mind either. It is usual to point to Hos. 6 : 2 or Jon. 1 : 17 for "the third day". Neither of these is convincing to modern ears, but they may well have sounded differently to men of the first century. For the idea of resurrection though without specification of the day, Isa. 53 : 10-12 (which speaks of the Servant as alive and active subsequent to speaking of His death) and Ps. 16 : 10 may be cited. It is clear from the New Testament that the early Christians saw the resurrection as foretold in the Old Testament. But this verse shows plainly that it was belief in the resurrection that came first. The believers did not manufacture a resurrection to agree with their interpretation of prophecy. They were first convinced that Christ was risen. Then they came to see a fuller meaning in certain Old Testament passages. "Must" is important (see on 4 : 4).[21] Since they came to see the resurrection in inspired prophecy it was no chance happening. The hand of God was in it. It must happen.

10 John rounds off this section of the narrative by telling us that the disciples went off home[22] again. They did not figure in the appearance of the Lord to Mary. When they had seen the tomb they went away.

2. THE APPEARANCES, 20 : 11-29

Each of the four Gospels recounts appearances of Jesus after the resurrection (with the exception of Mark if it really ended originally at 16 : 8; but resurrection appearances are prophesied in 16 : 7, and there is good reason for holding that from the be-

---

[21] There is a touch of inevitability about δεῖ. It is not only that He *did* rise, but He *must* rise. *Cf.* Rieu: "the Scripture where it is ordained that he should die and then come back to life."

[22] Some allege that πρὸς αὐτούς does not mean "went home", for which εἰς τὰ ἴδια would be required as in 1 : 11; 19 : 27. The expression used here is found however, in just this sense in Josephus, *Ant.* viii, 124 (where, incidentally, the meaning is not that they went to the same place, but each to his own home). Black sees evidence of an Aramaic construction, the use of the *dativus ethicus*. He thinks the present expression "corresponds to Aramaic '*azal leh*, as in the example from the Elephantine Papyrus above, 'took him off', 'went him away' " (*AA*, p. 77). This must be treated with respect, and the Aramaic may not be altogether out of mind. But in view of the passage in Josephus it is difficult to deny the correctness of ARV.

ginning that Gospel, like the others, included accounts of appearances of the risen Lord). But the four differ in the appearances they relate. Characteristically John makes his own selection. There is no question of his having derived these stories from any of the other Gospels.[23]

(a) The Appearance to Mary, 20 : 11–18

11 But Mary was standing without at the tomb weeping: so, as she wept, she stooped and looked into the tomb; 12 and she beholdeth two angels in white sitting, one at the head, and one at the feet, where the body of Jesus had lain. 13 And they say unto her, Woman, why weepest thou? She saith unto them, Because they have taken away my Lord, and I know not where they have laid him. 14 When she had thus said, she turned herself back, and beholdeth Jesus standing, and knew not that it was Jesus. 15 Jesus saith unto her, Woman why weepest thou? whom seekest thou? She, supposing him to be the gardener, saith unto him, Sir, if thou hast borne him hence, tell me where thou hast laid him, and I will take him away. 16 Jesus saith unto her, Mary. She turneth herself, and saith unto him in Hebrew, Rabboni; which is to say, Teacher. 17 Jesus saith to her, [1]Touch me not; for I am not yet ascended unto the Father: but go unto my brethren, and say to them, I ascend unto my Father and your Father, and my God and your God. 18 Mary Magdalene cometh and telleth the disciples, I have seen the Lord; and that he had said these things unto her.

[1]Or, *Take not hold on me*

There is something very moving about this first meeting of the risen Lord with any of His followers. There is moreover a wonderful condescension involved, for we have no reason for thinking of Mary as being a particularly important person. Yet it was to her and not to any of the outstanding leaders in the apostolic band that the Lord appeared first. The story is told simply, and with conviction.[24]

---

[23] For Luke 24 : 12 see p. 828, n. 1. It is manifestly impossible to hold that John derived his story from that verse.

[24] *Cf.* Dodd: "I cannot for long rid myself of the feeling (it can be no more than a feeling) that this *pericopé* has something indefinably first-hand about it" (*HTFG*, p. 148).

11 "But", *i.e.* in contrast to the two who went home, Mary was standing just outside the tomb and weeping.[25] John says nothing about her return to the tomb, nor about whether she got there before the two men left. He simply pictures her as standing at the tomb[26] and weeping. While she continued weeping she stooped down and peeped[27] in. Though she had been at the tomb before, this is the first mention of her looking inside it.

12, 13 She sees (the tense is present for greater vividness) two angels[28] in white sitting, where the body of Jesus had lain, one at the head and the other at the feet. The angels do not play a major part in the incident that John is describing. Their one function is to ask Mary why she is crying,[29] after which we hear no more of them. For "Woman" as a form of address see on 2 : 4. It is obvious that in this context there can be nothing harsh about the term. Mary's reply[30] is much like her words to the disciples in v. 2, though now she uses the singular "I know not". There are no other women to be associated with her at this moment. The question concerns her personal grief and her answer relates to this only. The depth of her grief is perhaps due to the emphasis the Jews of the day placed on correct and seemly burial. They regarded with abhorrence any disrespect paid to a corpse. Un-

---

[25] The verb κλαίω denotes not a quiet, restrained shedding of tears, but the noisy lamentation typical of Easterners. *Cf.* its use of wailing at the tomb of Lazarus (11 : 31).

[26] πρὸς τῷ μνημείῳ. For πρός with the dative see on 18 : 16. The expression denotes close proximity. Indeed *Twentieth Century* renders it here by "close".

[27] The verb used, παρακύπτω, is that used of the Beloved Disciple in v. 5 (where see note).

[28] We read of one angel in Matt. 28 : 2ff., of "a young man" in Mark 16 : 5 and of "two men . . . in dazzling apparel" in Luke 24 : 4ff., these latter being apparently angels (Luke 24 : 23). On the question of whether there was one angel or two Temple comments: "It is not to be presumed that angels are physical objects reflecting rays of light upon the retina of the eye. When men 'see' or 'hear' angels, it is rather to be supposed that an intense interior awareness of a divine message leads to the projection of an image which is then experienced as an occasion of something seen and heard. That divine messengers were sent and divine messages received we need not doubt; that they took physical form so that all who 'saw' anything must 'see' the same thing we need not suppose."

[29] On this question Lenski comments: "Indeed, why does she weep? – when we should all have had cause to weep to all eternity if what she wept for had been given her, the dead body of her Lord!"

[30] There is an ambiguity caused by the use of ὅτι. If it is recitative the meaning will be simply, "They have taken away my Lord . . . .." But it may mean "Because" as in ARV.

certainty as to what had happened to Jesus' body was worrying Mary and distressing her deeply.

14 No answer of the angels is recorded. Perhaps Mary withdrew abruptly. She may have heard a movement behind her. Or, as many commentators from Chrysostom down have held, the angels may have made some motion at the sight of the Lord behind Mary. We do not know. At any rate she turned right round[31] and saw Jesus standing there. Why she did not recognize Him is not said. It is possible that tears were blurring her vision, but then tears are not usually a reason for failure to recognize someone well known. There seems to have been something different about the risen Jesus so that He was not always recognized. The walk to Emmaus is the outstanding example of this, but we see the same thing at the miraculous draught of fishes (21 : 4), and Matthew tells us that when the disciples saw Jesus on a mountain in Galilee they worshipped, "but some doubted" (Matt. 28 : 17). *Cf.* also Luke 24 : 37.

15 Jesus repeats the question of the angels, "Woman, why weepest thou?" and adds, "whom seekest thou?"[32] Notice that He says "whom" and not "what". This might have started Mary along the right track. She was looking for a corpse whereas she should have been seeking a person. Why Mary took Him for the gardener is not clear. Perhaps it was the only logical thing. Who else would be in the garden so early, and who else would question her as to what she was doing? What is certain is that she did take Him for the gardener and she leapt to the conclusion that he may well have carried off[33] the body of her Lord. So she asks whether this were the case, and lets Him know that she wants to take the body away. She does not say "in order to give it decent burial"

---

[31] ἐστράφη εἰς τὰ ὀπίσω.

[32] Ryle sees an implied rebuke in this question, "Whom seekest thou? Who is this person that thou art seeking among the dead? Hast thou not forgotten that He whom thou seekest is one who has power to take life again, and who predicted that He would rise?"

[33] Of the supposed gardener Mary uses the verb βαστάζω. Of the supposed grave robbers (vv. 2, 13) and of herself she uses αἴρω. This is probably not meant to denote difference of meaning, but is another example of the slight variation so typical of this Gospel.

but that is implied. Interestingly, she says nothing of whose body
she meant, nor even that she did mean a body. Her answer
presupposes quite a bit of knowledge of the circumstances. But
that is quite understandable, given the depths of her grief. A
thoroughly grief-stricken person does not make allowances and go
into full explanations. Notice the repetition of "him". This was
what filled her thoughts to the exclusion of all else. It has often been
pointed out that it would have been difficult for Mary unaided
to "take him away". So it would. But grief such as Mary's does
not perform exact calculations as to the weight which can be lifted.

16 With a masterly economy of language John tells how Mary
came to know that it was the Lord. Jesus utters but one word,
her name. Mary turns. Evidently, after turning towards Jesus
(v. 14) she had turned back to the tomb. This further act of
turning indicates that something in the way the name was spoken
caught her attention. When the Good Shepherd calls His sheep
they know His voice (10 : 3f.). Immediately she calls out in
Aramaic the word "Rabboni",[34] which John translates for the
benefit of his Greek readers. It indicates plainly enough that
Mary had come to recognize Jesus. This seems, however, to have
been an unusual form of address. In the older Jewish literature
it appears to be used but seldom with reference to men and never
as a mode of address. As a mode of address it is confined to
addressing God in prayer.[35] John may mean us to understand

---

[34] The Greek is ʽΡαββουνι as in Mark 10 : 51. Black points out that this
is the form in the Palestinian Pentateuch Targum, whereas the later Targum
of Onkelos has the form רְבּוֹנִי (*AA*, p. 21). Thus the form is "Rabbouni" rather
than "Rabboni".

[35] So SBk, II, p. 25; G. Dalman, *The Words of Jesus* (Edinburgh, 1902),
pp. 324ff. It is often said that the word means much the same as "Rabbi".
Etymologically this may be so, though we should not overlook the point made
by W. F. Albright that the term is a caritative with a meaning like "my (dear
(or) little) master" (*BNT*, p. 158). But the usage is decisive. "Rabbi" is frequently used as a form of address, but "Rabboni" is not cited in this way (other
than in prayer, of address to God). Black, however, points to its use in the old
Palestinian Pentateuch Targum (see p. 119, n. 163; he regards it as a much
more reliable guide to first-century Aramaic than the Onkelos Targum which
is the basis of much of Dalman's argument), which "shows that it cannot
have been uncommon in earlier Palestinian Aramaic for a human lord" (*AA*,
p. 21). He does not, however, cite any example of the term as a form of address
to a human lord.

Mary's reaction to the presence of the risen Lord as similar to that of Thomas who said, "My Lord and my God" (v. 28). Against this are the facts that "Rabboni" is used by the blind man in Mark 10 : 51 (where there is no reason to hold that he thought he was addressing God), that the Palestinian Targum may point to a different use,[36] and that John here interprets the word as meaning "Teacher". This last point is probably decisive. We should hold that Mary's understanding of Jesus' person is not complete.

17 This verse presents us with some problems. The first is in the words "Touch me not". There seems no reason why Mary should not touch Him, and indeed Matthew tells us that when the women first saw the risen Lord "they came and took hold of his feet, and worshipped him" (Matt. 28 : 9).[37] Probably we should understand the Greek tense here in the strict sense. The present imperative with a negative means "Stop doing something" rather than "Do not start something".[38] Here it will mean "Stop clinging to Me" (RSV, "Do not hold me"; NEB, "Do not cling to me"), and not, "Do not begin to touch Me". Evidently Mary in her joy at seeing the Lord had laid hold on Him, possibly in the same way and for the same purpose as the ladies of whom Matthew writes.[39]

The references to ascending are not completely clear. It is not easy to see what difference the ascension could make to Mary's clinging to Jesus. Some point out that, whereas we use "the Ascension" as a technical term, this was not so in New Testament days. The point may be conceded, but it does not get us far. Whether "ascend" is used in the technical sense in this verse or

---

[36]   See n. 34 and n. 35 above.

[37]   That there is no great significance in the use of ἐκράτησαν in Matt. 28 : 9 and ἅπτου here is shown by the use of both verbs to describe the same action (Matt. 8 : 15; Mark 1 : 31).

[38]   For this use of the present tense in prohibitions see on 2 : 16. Of the present passage BDF says, "μή μου ἅπτου (which therefore has already happened or has been attempted)" (336(3)).

[39]   Bernard favors emending μή μου ἅπτου to μή πτόου, largely on the grounds that in the other Gospels people who first saw the angels or the risen Lord usually were afraid and had to be reassured (Matt. 28 : 5, 10; Mark 16 : 8; Luke 24 : 5). Rieu renders "Do not be alarmed", accepting the emendation. The grounds for this, however, seem inadequate. It is much better to take the text given in the MSS and to understand the present tense in the normal fashion.

not it clearly refers to a decisive parting as Jesus returns to His Father. Part of the thought appears to be that Jesus was not simply returning to the old life. Mary was reacting as though He were. As He had not yet ascended He could appear to her, but she must not read into this a simple return to the former state of affairs (such as no doubt happened in the case of Lazarus).[40] But part of the thought also will be concerned with the fact that the ascension was as yet future. Some exegetes maintain that John thought that the ascension took place on the same day as the resurrection and cite the passage as proof. But this is to ignore the subsequent happenings narrated in this very chapter. Vv. 26ff., to name no other, show clearly that John thought of Jesus as active here on earth after the day of the resurrection. The words we are discussing must be understood in the light of a future ascension. It is as though Jesus were saying, "Stop clinging to Me. There is no need for this, as I am not yet at the point of permanent ascension.[41] You will have opportunity of seeing Me." In the message to the "brethren" the verb "I ascend" is in the present tense. This tense may denote future action, but if so it is with the thought either of imminence or certainty. It is the latter which is required here. We should probably accept Lagrange's suggestion that the adversative conjunction appended to "go" applies also to "ascend". The words will then mean, "Stop clinging to Me. I have not yet ascended to My Father, it is true. But I shall certainly do so. Tell this to My brothers."[42]

A further problem is the meaning to be attached to "my brethren" to whom Mary was to deliver a message. In this context we naturally expect a message to be sent to the disciples, and in

---

[40] *Cf.* Chrysostom: "To have said, 'Approach Me not as ye did before, for matters are not in the same state, nor shall I henceforth be with you in the same way,' would have been harsh and high-sounding; but the saying, 'I am not yet ascended to the Father,' though not painful to hear, was the saying of One declaring the same thing" (LXXXVI. 2; p. 324).

[41] This may be the significance of the perfect tense, ἀναβέβηκα. The only other place where John uses the perfect of this verb is in 3 : 13, where the reference is also to ascending to heaven.

[42] Barrett gives the meaning in these terms: "The resurrection has made possible a new and more intimate spiritual union between Jesus and his disciples; the old physical contacts are no longer appropriate, though touch may yet (v. 27) be appealed to in proof that the glorified Lord is none other than he who was crucified."

fact Mary does go to them (v. 18). But they are not normally called Christ's "brethren" (though *cf.* Matt. 12 : 50). His brothers are, of course, referred to with this term (2 : 12; 7 : 3, 5, 10). But we are expressly told that they did not believe on Him (7 : 5) so it is not easy to see why He should be sending a message to them. Yet Luke tells us that from the earliest times after the resurrection the "brethren" of Jesus were found with the disciples (Acts 1 : 14). Obviously there was a change in them by that time, so it is possible to hold that they are in mind in this verse. But on the whole this does seem too soon after the resurrection for a special message to them. After all they were unbelieving. A little time seems required for their change of heart. The same problem arises in connection with Matt. 28 : 10, where the risen Lord gives a message to "my brethren" through the women. All in all it seems as though we should understand the term as denoting the disciples.

Finally we should notice that Jesus refers to God as "my Father and your Father" and as "my God and your God". It seems as though He is of set purpose placing Himself in a different relationship to the Father from that which His followers occupy.[43] This has important implications for an understanding of Christ's Person.

18 If Mary was intended to speak to the brothers of Jesus it does not appear that she carried out the instruction. She told the disciples that she had seen the Lord and that He had said certain things to her. There is a change from direct speech, "I

---

[43] *Cf.* R. H. Lightfoot: "the disciples must never forget that, whereas His Sonship to the Father is by nature and right, theirs is only by adoption and grace, in and through Him; and therefore He speaks of 'my Father and your Father', not of 'our Father'." Long ago Augustine drew attention to the significance of this point: "He saith not, Our Father: in one sense, therefore, is He mine, in another sense, yours; by nature mine, by grace yours . . . my God, under whom I also am as man; your God, between whom and you I am mediator" (CXXI. 3; p. 438). C. F. D. Moule disputes this. He says that the expression must not be taken as proof of a different relationship, "for this need only mean 'Your Father *who is also mine* . . .'" (*Worship in the New Testament*, London, 1964, p. 77). Again he says, "it can equally well, or more plausibly, be construed in precisely the opposite sense, to stress the identity of approach between Christ and the disciples: 'my Father *who is also* your Father, my God *who is also* yours'" (*The Phenomenon of the New Testament*, London, 1967, p. 51). This caution must be borne in mind. The words are not proof of a different relationship. But, with all respect, it seems that the most natural way of taking the words is to see a difference between Jesus' relationship to God and that of the disciples.

have seen the Lord", to indirect speech, "that he had said these things". This has the effect of highlighting the significant words and putting emphasis on Mary's experience.

(b) The Appearance to the Ten, 20 : 19–23

19 When therefore it was evening, on that day, the first day of the week, and when the doors were shut where the disciples were, for fear of the Jews, Jesus came and stood in the midst, and saith unto them, Peace be unto you. 20 And when he had said this, he showed unto them his hands and his side. The disciples therefore were glad, when they saw the Lord. 21 Jesus therefore said to them again, Peace be unto you: as the Father hath sent me, even so send I you. 22 And when he had said this, he breathed on them, and saith unto them, Receive ye the Holy Spirit: 23 whose soever sins ye forgive, they are forgiven unto them; whose soever sins ye retain, they are retained.

Luke mentions an appearance of the Lord to the disciples on the evening of the first Easter Day (Luke 24 : 36ff.). This comes after those who had walked the Emmaus road with Jesus had returned to Jerusalem and had been told by the assembled disciples that Peter had seen Jesus. John's story resembles Luke's in the greeting and in the fact that Jesus showed His friends His hands and His side (in Luke, His hands and His feet). But Luke says nothing about Jesus breathing on the disciples, or about the Holy Spirit, or about forgiving and retaining sins. John, by contrast, does not speak of the disciples' fear at seeing what they thought was a spirit or of Jesus as eating some broiled fish. Though both Evangelists seem to be referring to the same occasion there is no question of John's setting before us a variant of Luke's story. Here, as elsewhere, he is quite independent.

19 This incident is introduced with a typical Johannine note of time (see on 1 : 39). It was evening. It was on that same day, the first[44] day of the week. When he tells us that the doors[45] were

---

[44] For μιᾷ see on v. 1.

[45] In view of the fact that John uses the plural of θύρα only here and in v. 26 it seems that more than one door was involved. There may have been double doors or, perhaps more probably, a door into the room and a door into the house entrance.

"shut" we should understand this to mean "locked" as the following explanation, that this was due to fear of the Jews, shows.[46] The group met together is called simply "the disciples". Some think this means the apostles only (or rather ten of them, for Thomas was not present). But the term is wide enough to include others and there is no real reason for thinking that apostles only are in mind. Certainly if the occasion is that referred to in Luke 24 : 33 there were others present, for Luke expressly mentions them. It should also be borne in mind that in this very chapter John speaks of "the twelve" (v. 24), so that presumably he means something different when he says "the disciples". The disciples were afraid (understandably), and they took their precautions. Now Jesus came and stood among them.[47] This appears to mean that He had not come through the door in the normal fashion (else what is the point of mentioning the shut door?). Some suggest that Jesus came right through the closed door, or that the door opened of its own accord or the like. But Scripture says nothing of the mode of Jesus' entry into the room and we do well not to attempt too exact a definition. We can scarcely say more than that John wants us to see that the risen Jesus was not limited by closed doors. Miraculously He stood in their midst. But the precise manner of the miracle is not indicated. "Peace be unto you" is the usual Hebrew greeting (e.g. I Sam. 25 : 6). However it is likely that on this occasion we should see more in the words than a conventional greeting. After their conduct on Good Friday the disciples might have expected rebuke or blame. Instead Jesus pronounces peace upon them. For the term "peace" see on 14 : 27.

20 No reason is given for His showing His hands and side.[48] But these were places where He bore the prints of the wounds (John does not mention wounds in the feet), so that this was a

---

[46]   This will be supported also by the fact that the verb is perfect, κεκλεισμένων. This is the case also in v. 26.

[47]   The expression is εἰς τὸ μέσον. There will be something of the idea of motion towards, He came "into their midst". But εἰς here will not differ greatly from ἐν. Moule sees this as an example of what he calls the "pregnant" use of εἰς, "apparently *combining* the ideas of motion and rest". He renders the present passage "he came and stood among them" (*IBNTG*, p. 68).

[48]   καὶ . . . καί (if this is the true reading; many MSS omit the first καί), "both his hands and his side", puts a certain emphasis on the completeness of the process. John alone of the Evangelists tells us that Jesus showed the disciples His side.

means of convincing them that it was He, the same Jesus they
had known, however much He might now be transformed. We
should probably understand this in the light of what Luke tells
us, that when Jesus appeared among the disciples on the evening
of the first Easter Day, "they were terrified and affrighted, and
supposed that they beheld a spirit" (Luke 24 : 37). It must have
been unnerving for them to have Jesus suddenly appear in their
midst, though the doors remained fast closed. What could this be
other than a spirit? Seeing is not always believing and it must
have been very hard for them to credit a resurrection. So the Lord
immediately took steps to convince them of His identity and to
take away their fear. He dealt gently with their difficulty. The
following "therefore" shows that the sight of the hands and side
was effective. On account of this they rejoiced,[49] convinced now
that it was the Lord that they saw. We should certainly see in
this the fulfilment of our Lord's prophecy that the disciples would
have sorrow while the world rejoiced, but that they would see
Him again and their sorrow be turned to joy (16 : 20–22).

21 Now comes Jesus' commissioning of His disciples.[50] He repeats
the greeting, "Peace be unto you", the repetition giving it emphasis.
It may not be fanciful to think of this peace thus emphasized as
the peace that comes as the result of His death and resurrection
(*cf.* 14 : 27). After all He has just shown them His hands and side
with their marks of the passion. The thought that the Father has
sent the Son is one of the master thoughts of this Gospel. It is
repeated over and over. Thus it is not surprising that it comes
out once more in this solemn moment. Now, as Jesus has brought
to its consummation the task that He came to accomplish, the task
that the Father laid upon Him, He sends His followers into the

---

[49] The aorist may point to the sudden joy which came over them as they
realized that it was Jesus.

[50] Bernard maintains that the words apply to the apostles alone and not
to any others who may have been present. But he presents no real evidence
that this is the case. He argues that in passages like 13 : 20 the apostles are in
mind and that "Language of this kind is addressed in the Fourth Gospel
to the apostles *alone*". But this is begging the question. The indications are that
in this chapter these words are addressed to others than apostles. To most it
seems self-evident that the words of 13 : 20 are quite general and apply to
others than the apostles.

world.[51] The charge is given added solemnity from being linked
thus to the mission of the Son. Their mission proceeds from His.
It is only because He has accomplished His mission, and indeed
precisely because He has accomplished it, that they are sent into
the world. There is emphasis on the link between His mission
and theirs. The thought is very similar to that in the prayer of
17 : 18, though characteristically there are slight changes in the
wording.[52]

22 Having commissioned them Jesus bestows on them the
equipment they will need for the discharge of their commission.
He breathed[53] and said "Receive Holy Spirit".[54] It is perhaps
significant that there is no "on them" in most MSS[55] (*cf.* Schonfield: "he expelled a deep breath"). John is not writing as though
there were a series of gifts made to individuals. Rather he speaks

---

[51] There is a change of verb from ἀπέσταλκεν of the Father's sending of
the Son, to πέμπω of the Son's sending of the apostles. There is unlikely to
be any significance in this as John appears to use the verbs without distinction
of meaning (see on 3 : 17). In this passage the improbability of any change
of meaning is heightened by the use of καθώς. It is the resemblance which
occupies attention. κἀγώ (see on 1 : 31) puts a certain stress on the activity
of Christ. It is *His* commission that they bear. The perfect tense in ἀπέσταλκεν
may have reference to the fact that His mission on earth is now completed.

[52] In 17 : 18 the same verb ἀποστέλλω, and the same tense, the aorist, is
used of both sendings. Here we have the perfect of ἀποστέλλω for the Father's
sending of the Son and the present of πέμπω for the Son's sending of His
followers. In ch. 17 both sendings are explicitly "into the world" whereas here
the verbs are left quite general.

[53] The verb is ἐνεφύσησεν here only in the New Testament. It is the same
verb as is used in Gen. 2 : 7 where God "breathed into his nostrils the breath
of life; and man became a living soul." There will be the thought that there
is now a new creation. This verb is used also in Ezek. 37 : 9 of the word of
the Lord, "Come from the four winds, O breath, and breathe upon these slain,
that they may live." It is not unlikely that both these passages are in mind,
the coming of the Spirit bringing both a new creation and life from the dead.
Augustine sees in the fact that Christ gave the Spirit by breathing on the
apostles evidence that the Spirit is His as well as the Father's.

[54] Πνεῦμα Ἅγιον is anarthrous from which some have drawn the conclusion that not the Holy Spirit, but a gift of the Spirit is in mind. This, however,
seems very unlikely. The absence of the article may do no more than fasten
our attention on the quality of the gift as Holy Spirit rather than on the
individuality of the Spirit. But there is no solid reason to doubt that what is
meant here is "the Holy Spirit".

[55] von Soden cites only Tatian's Diatessaron, D, syr^c for these words. They
should not be read.

of a collective gift made to the church as a whole. "The gift was once for all, not to individuals but to the abiding body" (Westcott). There is possibly a recollection here that the primary meaning of the word we render "spirit" is "breath" or "wind". But the important thing is not this, but the presence of the Holy Spirit within them. The relation of this gift to that made on the day of Pentecost is obscure. Some scholars hold that the two are incompatible. They maintain that Luke thought that the Spirit was not bestowed until ten days after the ascension, whereas John thought of this gift as taking place on the evening of the day of resurrection. But this may be going too fast. The circumstances of the two gifts are completely different. And, whereas that in Acts 2 is followed immediately by some very effective preaching, no sequel to this gift is narrated. It is the teaching of the New Testament that "there are diversities of gifts, but the same Spirit" (I Cor. 12 : 4), and the problem is probably to be solved along these lines.[56] It is false alike to the New Testament and to Christian experience to maintain that there is but one gift of the Spirit. Rather the Spirit is continually manifesting Himself in new ways. So John tells us of one gift and Luke of another.

23 On the basis of the gift of the Spirit whom the Lord Jesus has given to His church, that church is now given authority to declare that certain sins are forgiven[57] and certain sins are retained.[58] This is not to be understood in any mechanical way.

---

[56] Hoskyns sees in the predictions of 14 : 16, 26; 16 : 7, 13 evidence that John thought of a gift of the Spirit which would be given after Jesus' return to the Father. "There is therefore a distinction between the two gifts of the Spirit. The Resurrection scenes in the Fourth Gospel are all preparatory scenes, preparatory for the mission. What the Lord will do invisibly from heaven He here does visibly on earth. The mission is inaugurated, but not actually begun. The disciples still remain in secret, behind closed doors. The actual beginning of the mission lies outside the scope of the Fourth Gospel. There remains, therefore, room for the Pentecostal outpouring. . . ."

[57] The word order is interesting: ἄν τινων ἀφῆτε τὰς ἁμαρτίας. By using ἀφῆτε to separate τινων from τὰς ἁμαρτίας (which must in any case be taken together), a certain emphasis is imparted to the verb, "of whomsoever you *forgive* the sins. . . ."

[58] The verb κρατέω is an unusual one in such a connection. It signifies "take hold of", "hold", "retain", but in this verse the significance appears to be that of holding something on to someone else. There does not appear to be a parallel to this. In Matt. 16 : 19; 18 : 18 the verb is δέομαι (with λύω in the antithesis). Dodd points out that neither this expression nor ἀφιέναι

It is the result of the indwelling Spirit and takes place only as that Spirit directs.[59] The verse is sometimes understood as though it gave the apostles, and through them the individual Christian minister, the power to forgive or not to forgive the sins of individual men.[60] There are, however, objections to this In the first place it overlooks the fact that there were almost certainly others than the apostles present. There seems no reason for thinking that this group of Christians was anything other than that mentioned in Luke 24 : 33ff., and that certainly included Cleopas and the friend who walked with him to Emmaus. The gift Christ made was made to the church as a whole. We have no reason at all for thinking that those present formed a "ministry". They were rather the representatives of the whole church. Strachan indeed thinks that the words give the authority in question "to any disciple of Christ". This does not seem to me correct. The words apply to the church as a whole and not to individuals.[61] But at least the fact that Strachan can take up this position shows how difficult it is to insist that the words apply to the ordained ministry

---

ἁμαρτίας is found elsewhere in the Fourth Gospel, which makes it unlikely that the saying is either a free creation of the Evangelist, or the result of his editing of Matt. 16 : 19. It is much more likely that the passage is independent, and that John is faithfully transmitting the words as he heard them (*HTFG*, pp. 348f.).

[59] *Cf.* Filson: "This is no promise of official power which leaders may exercise regardless of whether they are personally true and loyal to Christ; only as Spirit-filled and Spirit-guided men may they thus speak for him with authority, but as Spirit-guided men they need not hesitate to speak and act with assurance".

[60] Thus R. E. Brown can say: "The power to absolve and to hold men's sins is explicitly given to (ten of) the Twelve in 20 : 23" (*Interpretation*, XXI, 1967, p. 391). Despite Brown's "explicitly" it is very difficult to see this. The passage does not mention the Twelve and I see no evidence that the gift was given to the Ten. John speaks of "the disciples" as being present (20 : 19, 20). Brown admits that John's use of the term "disciples" sometimes at least is a way of indicating that Jesus "is really speaking to all believers" (*loc. cit.*). He gives no reason for a different usage here.

[61] *Cf.* Barclay: "This sentence does not mean that the power to forgive sins was ever entrusted to any man or to any men; it means that the power to proclaim that forgiveness was so entrusted; and it means that the power to warn that that forgiveness is not open to the impenitent was also entrusted to them. This sentence lays down the duty of the Church to convey forgiveness to the penitent in heart, and to warn the impenitent that they are forfeiting the mercy of God".

only. Those who refer the words to the ministry usually concentrate on the power of absolution. They think of the Christian priest as a man with a God-given authority to declare to men that their sins are forgiven. It ought not to be overlooked that the power to declare sins forgiven is on all fours with the power to declare them retained. I do not think that this verse teaches that any individual Christian minister has the God-given authority to say to a sinner, "I refuse to forgive your sins. They are retained." But unless this can be said the words about forgiveness cannot be said. The one goes with the other.[62]

It should also be borne in mind that, according to the best text, the verbs "are forgiven" and "are retained" are in the perfect tense.[63] The meaning of this is that the Spirit-filled church can pronounce with authority that the sins of such-and-such men have been forgiven or have been retained. If the church is really acting under the leadership of the Spirit it will be found that her pronouncements on this matter do but reveal what has already been determined in heaven.

Further, it ought not to be overlooked that the words for "whose" are plural. It is not the sins of whatever[64] *man*, but the sins of whatever *men*, of which this verse speaks. Jesus is not speaking of individuals, but of classes. He is saying that the Spirit-filled church has the authority to declare which are the sins that are forgiven and which are the sins that are retained.[65] This

---

[62] *Cf.* Westcott: "It is impossible to contemplate an absolute individual exercise of the power of 'retaining'; so far it is contrary to the scope of the passage to seek in it a direct authority for the absolute individual exercise of the 'remitting.' At the same time the exercise of the power must be placed in the closest connexion with the faculty of spiritual discernment consequent upon the gift of the Holy Spirit."

[63] In the case of κεκράτηνται this can be taken as beyond doubt. No variants are cited, but the perfect is universal. ἀφέωνται is read by ℵ^c AD f1 f13 565 *al*. The late MSS led by W Θ read the present ἀφίενται, while B has ἀφίονται. ℵ* reads the future ἀφεθήσεται. It seems tolerably clear that the perfect is right here also.

[64] There is a certain ambiguity posed by the use of ἄν. This could mean "if" as in RSV, "If you forgive . . ." but equally it may be held to be the "– ever" suffix as in ARV, "whosoever sins. . . ."

[65] *Cf.* MiM: "Nor does there seem to be ground for thinking that we have here a special application by one individual, whether minister or not, to another of the remission (or retention) of sin spoken of. The use of 'any' in

accords with Rabbinical teaching which spoke of certain sins as "bound" and others as "loosed".[66] This referred to classes, not to individuals, and this is surely what Jesus is saying also. Of course, what applies to classes has its application to individual cases. That cannot be denied and it should not be overlooked. But it is not the subject of this gift of Christ.

(c) The Appearance to Thomas, 20 : 24–29

24 But Thomas, one of the twelve, called [1]Didymus, was not with them when Jesus came. 25 The other disciples therefore said unto him, We have seen the Lord. But he said unto them, Except I shall see in his hands the print of the nails, and put my finger into the print of the nails, and put my hand into his side, I will not believe.

26 And after eight days again his disciples were within, and Thomas with them. Jesus cometh, the doors being shut, and stood in the midst, and said, Peace be unto you. 27 Then saith he to Thomas, Reach hither thy finger, and see my hands; and reach hither thy hand, and put it into my side: and be not faithless, but believing. 28 Thomas answered and said unto him, My Lord and my God. 29 Jesus saith unto him, Because thou hast seen me, [2]thou hast believed: blessed are they that have not seen, and yet have believed.

[1]That is *Twin.* [2]Or, *hast thou believed?*

This incident, peculiar to this Gospel, is of the utmost importance for an understanding of the way the first Christians came to know that the resurrection had indeed taken place. Some writers almost give the impression that at first there was no thought of a resurrection, but that bit by bit the apostles became familiar with the thought. Eventually they built up more and

---

the plural number appears to be inconsistent with such a view. It is not a direct address by one person to another that is thought of, – 'I declare that *thy* sins are thus authoritatively remitted or retained.' It is a proclamation from one collective body to another, – from the Church to the world."

[66] Among the Rabbis the "binding" and the "loosing" referred primarily to forbidding and permitting. But the terms were also used with respect to excommunication, when they meant "excommunicate" and "receive into communion". It is possible that this latter is what is meant in the present passage. But the terms used here are not the natural ones, which would be rather δέομαι and λύω (as in Matt. 16 : 19; 18 : 18).

more circumstantial tales until eventually the whole church was convinced.[67] The church at first had no idea of a resurrection. That is plain enough. But there was no gradual acceptance of the idea with more and more "appearances" being manufactured. The plain fact is that all told we read of five appearances on the one day (to Mary Magdalene, to the women, to the two on the way to Emmaus, to Peter, and to the ten). Then there are five more spread out over forty days, and after that no more with the exception of the appearance to Saul of Tarsus.[68] This is no gradual building up of "appearances" but rather the reverse. They were progressively restricted, not built up. Moreover, as Thomas makes abundantly clear, the appearances were not at first welcomed. They were resisted as idle talk, and those who had not actually seen Christ for themselves refused point blank to accept the stories. Only the plainest of evidence could have convinced a sceptic like Thomas. But convinced he was, which shows us that the evidence was incontrovertible.

24 First the scene is set. Thomas is described with some precision as one of the Twelve, and as the one called "Didymus", or "twin" (see on 11 : 16). He was not with the others when Jesus came. No reason is given, and there is neither praise nor blame for his absence.

25 The others told[69] Thomas that they had seen Jesus, a statement which met with blank incredulity. Thomas demands visual and tactual proof before he will believe. Unless he can both see the

---

[67] *Cf.* the classical statement of A. Harnack: "The Easter *message* tells us of that wonderful event in Joseph of Arimathea's garden, which, however, no eye saw; it tells us of the empty grave into which a few women and disciples looked; of the appearance of the Lord in a transfigured form – so glorified that his own could not immediately recognise him; it soon begins to tell us, too, of what the risen one said and did. The reports become more and more complete, and more and more confident" (*What is Christianity?* 5th edn., London, 1958, pp. 119f.). But this is not what the Gospels tell us.

[68] R. H. Kennett put a good deal of emphasis on Paul. He regards his conversion as having taken place within five years of the crucifixion and points out that "within a very few years of the time of the crucifixion of Jesus, the evidence for the resurrection of Jesus was in the mind of at least one man of education absolutely irrefutable" (*The Interpreter*, V, 1908–09, p. 267).

[69] The imperfect ἔλεγον may imply that they "kept saying to him" (C. B. Williams, so also Phillips).

nailprints[70] and put his finger into them,[71] and put his hand into Jesus' side he will certainly not[72] believe. No scepticism could be more thoroughgoing than this. Normally this is taken to indicate that Thomas was of a more sceptical turn of mind than the others, and, of course, he may have been. But another possibility should not be overlooked, namely that he was so shocked by the tragedy of the crucifixion that he did not find it easy to think of its consequences as being annulled. In support of this is urged his preoccupation with the wounds of Jesus, as his words quoted in this verse show.

26 "Eight days" according to the inclusive method of counting signifies a week. This incident then is dated on the Sunday evening after the first Easter Day. The disciples were again gathered indoors, this time with Thomas in the number. As before, the doors were closed (the same expression as in v. 19 where see note). As before, Jesus came among them and gave them the usual greeting. John seems to be at pains to make clear that all was just as it had been on the first occasion.

27 After the greeting Jesus addressed Himself to His hard-headed disciple. With some rather unexpected vocabulary[73] He invites Thomas to carry out the tests he himself had nominated, to put his finger into the nail prints and his hand into the side. Our Lord

---

[70] Some have suggested that the detail is unhistorical, urging that nails would not support the weight of a body and that ropes must have been used. J. A. Bailey, however, cites O. Zöckler as showing that the hardness of the nails used in crucifixion was proverbial, and that Xenophon of Ephesus mentions the use of ropes in crucifixions in Egypt as though this was unusual (*The Traditions Common to the Gospels of Luke and John*, Leiden, 1963, p. 101, n. 3). It seems clear that the detail is historical.

[71] There is a textual problem, namely whether Thomas speaks of putting his finger into the print, $\tau \acute{v} \pi o v$, or into the place, $\tau \acute{o} \pi o v$, of the nails. The former has the stronger attestation, but it would be easy to corrupt an original $\tau \acute{o} \pi o v$ into $\tau \acute{v} \pi o v$, which might reasonably be expected. Not much hinges on the point. NEB, accepting $\tau \acute{o} \pi o v$, renders, "unless I put my finger into the place where the nails were".

[72] He uses the emphatic double negative $o \grave{v} \ \mu \acute{\eta}$.

[73] "Reach hither" is $\varphi \acute{e} \varrho \varepsilon$, which is an unusual verb for this kind of action. Nor do we expect $\emph{i} \delta \varepsilon$ of the action of the hands. $\beta \acute{a} \lambda \varepsilon$ was used in v. 25 of putting the finger into the nail prints, and now of putting the hand into the wound in the side.

concludes by urging Thomas to cease being an unbeliever[74] and[75] become a believer.

28 But Thomas was not quite such a sceptic as he had thought he was. At the sight of Jesus all his doubts vanished and he did not need to apply any of his tests. It is possible that it was the words of Jesus more than anything which brought conviction, for they showed that Jesus was perfectly aware of what Thomas had laid down as his demands. How did He come by this knowledge unless He was there, unseen? Perhaps we should mention here that some think that Thomas did actually put his finger into the nailprints and his hand into the spearwound. They think that if Jesus commanded him he had no choice. But John says nothing of the sort and it seems very improbable. It is much more likely that Jesus' words give us the truth of the matter: "Because thou hast *seen* me, thou hast believed" (v. 29). Thomas gave utterance to his new-found faith in the memorable words "My Lord and my God".[76] If, as many scholars think, ch. 21 is an appendix and the original Gospel ended at 20 : 31 this will be the last statement made by anyone in the Gospel. It is significant that it is an ascription to Jesus of deity, corresponding to "the Word was God" in 1 : 1. For the term "Lord" see on 4 : 1. It is an expression which is used by others of the Master, sometimes with more and sometimes with less content. Here we must evidently give the term all that it will hold. "My God" is a quite new form

---

[74] The present imperative is used, $\mu\dot\eta$ $\gamma\acute\iota\nu o\upsilon$. For the force of this construction see on 2 : 16.

[75] "But" is the strong adversative, $\dot\alpha\lambda\lambda\acute\alpha$, "but, on the contrary . . ." (see on 1 : 8).

[76] It is common to take 'Ο Κύριός μου καὶ ὁ Θεός μου as a form of address, the nominative being used for vocative. Abbott, however, objects that ὁ Κύριος is not so used, though ὁ Θεός is. He cites occurrences of κύριε ὁ θεός which seem to show that a difficulty was felt in taking ὁ κύριος as vocative. If we accept it as a true nominative here the meaning will probably be "It is my Lord and my God". Alternatively we could take the expression as a subject with the rest of the clause omitted, such as "My Lord and my God (has indeed risen)". Abbott favors the latter (feeling that ἐστιν could scarcely have been omitted from the former) (2049–51). However it is not to be overlooked that Thomas's words are introduced by εἶπεν αὐτῷ, so that in fact he is addressing Jesus. Nor that the very words used here are used (in the reverse order) in an address to God in Ps. 34 (35) : 23. We should take the words as a vocative, albeit an unusual one.

of address. Nobody has previously addressed Jesus in this way. It marks a leap of faith. In the moment that he came to see that Jesus was indeed risen from the dead Thomas came to see something of what that implied. Mere men do not rise from the dead in this fashion. The One who was now so obviously alive, though He had died, could be addressed in the language of adoring worship.

29 Jesus addresses to Thomas a word of approval, but one which goes far beyond Thomas to those who had not required so much before believing. Thomas believed on the basis of sight.[77] He saw Jesus and believed.[78] Some think that Jesus is administering a rebuke to His hard-headed follower. This may be, but if so it is a very gentle rebuke. We must bear in mind that if it is true that Thomas believed only on the basis of what he himself saw, this is so also with all the others John has so far mentioned. While doubtless some believed on the basis of the testimony of Mary Magdalene and the others John has not said so. There is possibly significance also in the fact that when Jesus goes on to speak of those who believed without seeing He says "blessed", not "more blessed", are they. This does not look like a comparison, with Thomas worse off than the others. However, the Master does pronounce a blessing on those who have believed without seeing. At the time the words were spoken this would not be a large number, but perhaps not all the first Christians were as sceptical as Thomas. Some had believed Peter and the others (*cf.* Luke 24 : 34). These are now said to be blessed. And, of course, the words will refer also to all those who in the future would follow in the same way. There is a special blessing for those possessed of a faith which can trust absolutely, and which does not need to "see" at every turn.

VII.   THE PURPOSE OF THE GOSPEL, 20 : 30, 31

30 Many other signs therefore did Jesus in the presence of the disciples, which are not written in this book: 31 but these are written, that ye may believe that Jesus is the Christ, the Son of God; and that believing ye may have life in his name.

---

[77]   For causal ὅτι see on 1 : 50.
[78]   The words to Thomas could, of course, be a question: "Because thou hast seen me, hast thou believed?" (ARV mg.).

30 In this statement of intention John first makes it clear that in his Gospel he has made a selection. He has not by any means written all that he knows about Jesus.[79] There were many other "signs" (for this term see on 2 : 11 and Additional Note G, pp. 684ff.) that Jesus did. He has written what served his purpose and has omitted much.[80] Notice that he speaks of the signs as having been done "in the presence of the disciples". That is to say the disciples were witnesses of them. This way of putting it reminds us of a characteristic emphasis throughout this Gospel. Though John does not choose to use the term "witness" in this verse his choice of words is one which reminds us that there is adequate "witness" borne to the things of which he writes.

31 Now John gives us the purpose of his book, that purpose which he has had steadily in mind from the beginning.[81] He uses the perfect tense in the verb "are written", a tense which perhaps indicates that what he has written stands. There is an air of permanence about it as in Pilate's "What I have written I have written" (19 : 22). He tells us that the purpose of his writing is that men may believe. This appears to mean that John has an evangelistic aim, and if the aorist subjunctive of the verb be read

---

[79] This is overlooked by some scholars who appear to think that John was, for example, incapable of supplementing the Synoptists in matter he shares with them. It must never be assumed that John has written all he knows on a given topic. In the light of this plain statement our presumption must always be that John has made a selection, including what he deemed relevant to his purpose and excluding what he deemed of less importance.

[80] Karl Heim regards this silence about other signs as significant. One collects everything possible about a dead prophet. It is all one has of him. But one tells only enough of a living person to introduce one's hearers to him. For the disciples, and John in particular, Jesus was alive (*Jesus the Lord*, London, 1959, p. 182).

[81] It is important that this be not overlooked. Dodd's brilliant work, *The Interpretation of the Fourth Gospel*, suffers from its declared purpose. Dodd tells us that "I shall try to show how the whole shape of the gospel is determined by the idea expressed in the words, ὁ λόγος σάρξ ἐγένετο, with the context of the term λόγος supplied by the Prologue as a whole" (*op. cit.*, p. 285). But, with all respect, that is not what this Gospel is about. We should not overlook its author's express words. Elsewhere Dodd in fact recognizes the evangelistic purpose (*op. cit.*, p. 9).

[82] The present is read by P66 (vid) ℵ* B Θ – a strong combination. Since the aorist might well be expected in a sentence like this the present has transcriptional probability and it is likely to be correct.

855

this is beyond reasonable doubt. Some, however, accept the present (which seems not improbable)[82] and argue from it that the meaning is "that you may continue to believe". They reason that the Gospel is addressed to believers. It seems that this is reading a great deal into the tense and it is more probable that we should see an evangelistic aim whatever the tense.[83] Faith is fundamental, and John longs to see men believe. He has not tried to write an impartial history. He is avowedly out to secure converts. He is bearing his witness to those great events in which God has acted for man's salvation. For he is sure that God has acted, and that His action is seen supremely in Jesus Christ. John does not think of faith as a vague trust, but as something with content (see further Additional Note E, pp. 335ff.). Faith means believing that –. Here he singles out two things in faith's content. The one is that Jesus is the Christ, *i.e.* the Messiah, the long expected One. The other is that He is the Son of God. We take these two as more or less identical, but Jews of the day did not. The Messiah was not expected to stand in that very close relationship to the Father of which John speaks. John's conception of messiahship is fuller and richer than is that of contemporary Judaism[84] (see on 1 : 20, 41). The combination of terms indicates the very highest view of the Person of Jesus, and it must be taken in conjunction with the

---

[83]   *Cf.* Dodd: "the continuous present could be justified, even as addressed to those who were not yet Christians, if the writer were thinking not so much of the moment of conversion, as of the continuing union with Christ, the condition of which is faith, and which means the perpetual possession of eternal life" (*IFG*, p. 9). Bultmann denies that the tense has any real significance in this case: "In the sense of the Evangelist it is a matter of indifference whether his potential readers are already 'Christians' or not; for the faith of the 'Christians' is certainly for him not a conviction present once and for all, but something which must continually be finding its certainty anew and which must therefore constantly hear the Word anew." We may certainly agree that faith is an adventure which must be renewed each day, and even that John's words may be used with profit by those who are already Christians. But this does not mean that the words are without meaning for unbelievers. As applied to unbelievers they will mean that there is a continuing attitude of faith, a constant union with Christ, and that nothing less is John's aim for them. That is why he wrote.

[84]   The Qumran scrolls show a great interest in messianism, this being often urged as a point of contact with this Gospel. But there is this decisive difference, that the covenanters looked for a future Messiah or Messiahs, whereas for John the Messiah has already come. That is the point of his whole Gospel.

fact that John has just recorded the confession of Thomas which hails Jesus as "My Lord and my God". There cannot be any doubt but that John conceived of Jesus as the very incarnation of God.

It is only because He has this high dignity that He can be the kind of Saviour that John conceives Him to be. So John thinks of the faith of which he writes not as an end in itself, but as the means of bringing men life, life in Christ's name. Life is another of John's great themes (see on 1 : 4; 3 : 15). He writes of it constantly, and invariably he thinks of real life as something to be had only through Christ. So here life is to be had by believers, and they have it in the "name" of Christ (for "the name" see on 1 : 12; 14 : 13). That is to say, the abundant life of which he writes is connected with the very person of Christ. It is His gift.

CHAPTER XXI

VIII. The Epilogue, 21 : 1-25

There are two opinions about John 21, one which sees it as an integral part of the Gospel from the very first, and the other which regards it as an addition to an already completed work. We can subdivide the second group into those who think that, apart from verses 24f., it was written by the author of chs. 1–20 and those who think of a different author. If it was no part of the original Gospel it must nevertheless be very early as the manuscript tradition knows nothing of a twenty-chapter Gospel.[1]

The principal reasons for thinking of it as a later supplement are first, that 20 : 30f. looks suspiciously like the end of a Gospel, and secondly, that chapter 21 is held to contain within it a sufficient indication of how it came to be added. When the Beloved Disciple was growing old and some thought that Jesus had said He would return before His beloved follower's death, it was necessary to correct the error. Harm could occur to the church if he died and still the Lord had not come. This chapter is held to be the result. Those who see this section as integral to the Gospel point to the fact that there is no break in style. As far as we can see this last chapter came from the same pen as did the first twenty.[2] To maintain that the closing words of chapter 20 form the end of the

---

[1] R. H. Lightfoot does speak of a Syriac MS which lacks this chapter, but he does not say which it is, and other authorities do not appear to mention it. On the other hand there are many strong statements like those of Strachan, "There is no trace of any manuscript of the Gospel without this chapter", or Lenski, "No copies of the Fourth Gospel have ever been found from which chapter 21 is omitted, and no trace of such copies has ever been discovered".

[2] Thus Plummer lists twenty-five points of vocabulary, grammar, etc., which tell in favor of identity of authorship. See also Howard, *FGRCI*, pp. 279f. On the other hand, Moffatt finds several indications of divergence, *An Introduction to the Literature of the New Testament* (Edinburgh, 1927), p. 572. G. W. Bloomfield counters this by pointing out that in every chapter of this Gospel there are divergences from all other chapters and that chapter 21 contains rather less than the average (*John, Peter, and the Fourth Gospel*, London, 1934, pp. 147f.; he also discounts some of the evidence adduced by Moffatt). Bultmann in his commentary gives perhaps as good a case against identity of authorship as the linguistics will allow. It is all the more significant accordingly that Barrett,

Gospel is to impose a standard of consistency on this writer which he does not always display elsewhere. Our ideas of what is proper are not necessarily his. And it may be relevant to note that I John 5 : 13 is not dissimilar to this verse, but it does not end the Epistle. It is further contended that, while chapter 21 does indeed deal with the expected return of the Lord before the death of the Beloved Disciple, yet this is not the main thrust of the chapter. It is more concerned with Peter's reinstatement. Hoskyns makes the important point that "a Christian gospel ends properly, not with the appearance of the risen Lord to His disciples, and their belief in Him, but with a confident statement that this mission to the world, undertaken at His command and under His authority, will be the means by which many are saved". He points out that the first three Gospels all end this way. John 21 agrees with this, but John 20 does not.[3] Lagrange is of opinion that 20 : 30f. originally stood after 21 : 23, and that this formed the original conclusion of the Gospel. Subsequently 21 : 24 was added and this caused the removal of the words to their present place. This is ingenious but it has not convinced very many.

There does not seem to be any way of reaching a final solution. I must confess to being a little mystified by the certainty of those who regard it as self-evident that this last chapter is a late addition. While I think I see the strength of their arguments I incline the other way. If it is original to the Gospel then, of course, there is no question as to authorship. If it is not original it is more probable that it was a later addition by the same author than that it was written by someone else altogether.

1. THE MIRACULOUS DRAUGHT OF FISHES, 21 : 1–14

1 After these things Jesus manifested himself again to the disciples at the sea of Tiberias; and he manifested himself

---

who favors a different author for ch. 21, does not find this convincing. He thinks the differences "not in themselves sufficient to establish the belief that ch. 21 was written by a different author." He is convinced by evidence other than the linguistic.

   [3] Similarly Temple notes that to end the Gospel at 20 : 31 "would be in a very real sense misleading. For the work of the Lord, which is at once the ground of faith in Him and the vindication of that faith, was in one sense incomplete. The victory was won; but its fruits had still to be gathered".

on this wise. 2 There were together Simon Peter, and Thomas called [1]Didymus, and Nathanael of Cana in Galilee, and the sons of Zebedee, and two other of his disciples. 3 Simon Peter saith unto them, I go a fishing. They say unto him, We also come with thee. They went forth, and entered into the boat; and that night they took nothing. 4 But when day was now breaking, Jesus stood on the beach: yet the disciples knew not that it was Jesus. 5 Jesus therefore saith unto them, Children, have ye aught to eat? They answered him, No. 6 And he said unto them, Cast the net on the right side of the boat, and ye shall find. They cast therefore, and now they were not able to draw it for the multitude of fishes. 7 That disciple therefore whom Jesus loved saith unto Peter, It is the Lord. So when Simon Peter heard that it was the Lord, he girt his coat about him (for he [2]was naked), and cast himself into the sea. 8 But the other disciples came in the little boat (for they were not far from the land, but about two hundred cubits off), dragging the net full of fishes. 9 So when they got out upon the land, they see [3]a fire of coals there, and [4]fish laid thereon, and [5]bread. 10 Jesus saith unto them, Bring of the fish which ye have now taken. 11 Simon Peter therefore went [6]up, and drew the net to land, full of great fishes, a hundred and fifty and three: and for all there were so many, the net was not rent. 12 Jesus saith unto them, Come and break your fast. And none of the disciples durst inquire of him, Who art thou? knowing that it was the Lord. 13 Jesus cometh, and taketh the [7]bread, and giveth them, and the fish likewise. 14 This is now the third time that Jesus was manifested to the disciples, after that he was risen from the dead.

[1]That is, *Twin.* [2]Or, *had on his undergarment only* Comp. ch. 13. 4; Is. 20. 2; Mic. 1. 8, 11. [3]Gr. *a fire of charcoal.* [4]Or, *a fish* [5]Or, *a loaf* [6]Or, *aboard* [7]Or, *loaf*

This passage is the longest account we have of any appearance of the risen Lord in Galilee.[4] The fishing expedition plainly reveals the uncertainty of the disciples, an uncertainty which contrasts

---

[4]   I am not impressed by the efforts made by some scholars to derive the miraculous catch in Luke 5 from this story or vice versa. Bultmann performs the interesting feat of doing both. In his commentary he maintains that the Johannine story is original (pp. 545f.), but in his *The History of the Synoptic Tradition* (Oxford, 1963), he affirms that "The variant in Jn. 21[1-14] seems to me a later version, which in some way derives from Luke" (*op. cit.*, pp. 217f.).

sharply with their assured sense of purpose from the day of Pentecost on. It is of interest that Peter has a place of leadership, even despite his fall. And, as happened when He appeared to Mary Magdalene, Jesus was not immediately recognized.

1 This verse forms a descriptive heading to the section. "After these things" is a general time note and does not locate the following events with any exactness (see on 2 : 12). "Manifested", twice repeated in this verse, is very much a Johannine word.[5] It points us to the very real existence of Jesus in a sphere beyond this world of time and sense. He and His glory were from time to time "manifested" to men here and now. He showed Himself as He is. John locates this incident "at the sea of Tiberias" (for this term see on 6 : 1).

2 John proceeds to list those present. For the full name "Simon Peter" see on 1 : 40, for Thomas on 11 : 16, for Nathanael on 1 : 45 and for Cana on 2 : 1. John does not name "the sons[6] of Zebedee", in keeping with his omission of their names throughout the Gospel. But the expression is precise. For reasons of his own he does not tell us who the other two were, but his love of precision comes out in the information that there were just two of them.

3 Peter proposed a fishing trip[7] and evoked apparently a unanimous response. The impression left is that the proposal was completely spontaneous. There is no plan, no settled aim. There may have been economic reasons behind the suggestion. It is possible that the thoughts of the fishermen were beginning to turn to their former occupation, now that they had lost the presence of Jesus. We do not know, and this incident is not enough to tell us. All

---

[5] φανερόω is found 9 times in this Gospel (3 times in Mark including twice in the ending to ch. 16, and not at all in Matthew or Luke) and 9 times in I John. It is not by any means exclusively Johannine, being also found 22 times in the Pauline Epistles. John does not use it outside this chapter of the resurrection appearances, though it is used this way in Mark 16 : 12, 14.

[6] Actually his expression is οἱ τοῦ Ζεβεδαίου. Elsewhere, where the expression is plural, υἱοί is always inserted but Ζεβεδαίου lacks the article, thus: οἱ υἱοὶ Ζεβεδαίου. In the singular, however, υἱός is not used, and Ζεβεδαίου regularly has the article, as Ἰάκωβος ὁ τοῦ Ζεβεδαίου. The present passage must be taken as resembling the usual construction in the singular, rather than as one where we should supply some other word than υἱοί.

[7] This seems to be the meaning of Ὑπάγω ἁλιεύειν. Whatever Peter's ultimate intentions it is pressing the meaning of the present tense too hard to see in it a proposal to resume his former life as a fisherman. The verb ἁλιεύειν is used here only in the New Testament.

that we can say is that this is a possibility and that the general impression left is that of men without a purpose.[8] They went out, though John does not say from where. In v. 2 he has told us only that they were "together" and in v. 1 that the location of the incident was "at the sea of Tiberias". They embarked in "the" (not "a") boat, but there is no way of knowing what this means. John evidently had the details clear in his mind, but we cannot enter into his knowledge. He proceeds to tell us that that night[9] they caught nothing.

4 Just at dawn[10] Jesus stood on the beach. It is not said that He came there or the like, and the choice of language may be a hint at the kind of thing we see in earlier passages, where Jesus suddenly appears behind closed doors. John adds the note that the disciples did not recognize the Lord (being apparently much like Mary Magdalene is this respect).

5 Jesus hails them. The diminutive, "children", is not common as a form of address, though parallels can be found.[11] Jesus asks whether they have any food. This is apparently directed to discovering whether they had caught any fish, but the word used does not denote fish specifically.[12] However in this context it is

---

[8] Loyd, however, draws the lesson that "when the pause comes and the vision begins to be less vivid, we are not to be idle or despondent. We are to go on with the obvious tasks of every day ... How wise were these disciples who calmly went back to their fishing!"

[9] Turner and Mantey cite Aristotle: "Fishermen, especially, do their fishing before sunrise and after sunset." They add: "This is still the custom of commercial fishermen who fish in the Sea of Galilee." *Cf.* Luke 5 : 5.

[10] πρωΐας indicates first light. The present γινομένης (with A B *al* bo) is to be preferred to γενομένης (ℵ W Θ *etc.*). It shows that day was in process of arriving rather than that it had already come. Dawn was just breaking.

[11] παιδία occurs, for example, in I John 2 : 14, 18. More usual as a form of address is τεκνία, found in John 13 : 33; I John 2 : 1, 12, 28 *etc.*, MM find a parallel to παιδία only in modern Greek (the Klepht ballad where it is used of soldiers). They draw attention also to the English use of "Lads" and the Irish of "Boys". Parallels are cited from Aristophanes (*Clouds* 137, *Frogs* 33), but clearly it is far from common as a form of address. NEB renders "Friends", which is to forsake the original.

[12] The word is προσφάγιον, defined by AS as "Hellenistic for ὄψον ... a *relish* or *dainty* (esp. *cooked fish*), to be eaten with bread". MM cite a papyrus giving a stonecutter's wages as ἄρτον ἕνα καὶ προσφάγιον, and others to show that the term refers to one of the items in an ordinary meal. But, addressed to a party of fishermen in their boat, there can be no doubt as to what is in mind.

quite clear that "fish" is meant. The question appears to expect a negative reply ("you haven't caught any fish, have you?"),[13] and the answer is a laconic negative.[14] The brevity of the reply is natural in a conversation shouted by disappointed men over a hundred yards of water.

6 The miracle is described with the greatest reserve. First we have Jesus' instruction to cast the net on the right side of the boat.[15] I have been unable to find any evidence which indicates which side of the boat was normally used by fishermen on the sea of Galilee so that it is difficult to know whether this was unusual or not. Some commentators draw attention to passages in classical authors showing that the right side is the fortunate side but it is difficult to see what relevance this has to the the New Testament. Obedience to Christ, not luck, is the important thing.[16] Jesus' instruction is clear, and there appears to have been no discussion. The fishermen simply did as He told them. Possibly they thought that a man standing on the shore might detect some indication of fish that was not apparent to them.[17] In any case, after a fruitless

---

13 Abbott points out that μή is used thus interrogatively in this Gospel more often than in all the others put together, but whereas they confine it to the words of Jesus John uses it in this way twice only, here and in 6 : 67 (2235).

14 For οὔ see on 1 : 21.

15 The expression is εἰς τὰ δεξιὰ μέρη τοῦ πλοίου. It is found here only in the New Testament. Robertson classes it among the idiomatic plurals of the New Testament (A Grammar of the Greek New Testament in the Light of Historical Research, London, n.d., p. 408), which makes it equivalent to our "on the right side". I have not discovered any other example of this phrase applied to a boat. Bernard likewise finds no linguistic parallel. Hendriksen says it "is simply an idiom" but he cites no other example of its use. μέρη is used a number of times in Hermas of directions. Thus εἰς τὰ δεξιὰ μέρη and εἰς τὰ ἀριστερὰ μέρη are used of sitting on the right hand or the left (Vis. III. i. 9; III. ii. 1). He also refers to "the four parts" (or directions, Sim. IX. ii. 3) and "the outer parts" (the outside of a building, Sim. IX. ix. 3). J. Schneider speaks of these passages as the only ones in which μέρος is used in this way (TDNT, IV, pp. 595f.). We must regard John's expression as an unusual one. But the meaning is clear enough.

16 "There is no need to seek symbolical meanings for the right and left side. The difference is not between right and left, but between working with and without Divine guidance" (Plummer).

17 H. V. Morton tells of seeing a fisherman casting a hand net in the Sea of Galilee when a friend on shore cried out that he should fling the net to the left. When he did this he caught fish. Morton says, "It happens very often that the man with the hand-net must rely on the advice of someone on shore,

night anything would be worth trying. When they cast the net as directed they found themselves unable to draw it (Phillips: "they were now not strong enough to pull it in") for the multitude of fish. "Draw" here probably means "draw into the ship",[18] for a little later we read of Peter's drawing it to land.

7 The miracle gave the Beloved Disciple all the clue that he needed. In what had happened he recognized the touch of the Master, so could say to Peter, "It is the Lord" (for "the Lord" see on 4 : 1). Impulsively Peter threw his coat[19] around him and cast himself into the sea. Presumably he made his way to the shore, though this is not said in so many words. Peter is not said in fact to do anything between throwing himself into the water here and drawing the net to land in v. 11. It is not said that he reached the shore first or what he did when he got there, and Hoskyns, for example, can state that the disciples in the ship reached land before Peter did. From the point where Peter leapt into the sea the story is told from the viewpoint of someone in the boat. The actions of both disciples are in character, the one being first to discern the Lord and the other first to take action. The statement that Peter was naked may indicate something of the custom of the time when fishing, though the singling of Peter out might alternatively be held to mean that the others were not in the same state of undress. It is, however, not at all certain that Peter wore no clothing whatever, as the English would lead us to expect. Both LS and AG cite passages where the word means "without an outer garment", "dressed in one's underwear". The probability

---

who tells him to cast either to the left or right, because in the clear water he can often see a shoal of fish invisible to the man in the water" (*In the Steps of the Master*, London, 1935, p. 199). Whether this would be valid for people one hundred yards apart is another matter. But Morton's incident is interesting and may be relevant.

[18] Trench maintains that the verb ἑλκύω used here and at v. 11 means to draw to a certain point (here into the ship, in v. 11 to Peter on the shore), whereas σύρω in v. 8 simply means dragging the net after the boat (*Synonyms of the New Testament*, London, 1880, pp. 73f.).

[19] The word is ἐπενδύτης, here only in the New Testament. It denotes an outer garment, without being specific. Barrett draws attention to a Jewish idea that since offering a greeting was a religious act it could not be performed unless one was clothed. Thus greetings were not given in the baths, since all were naked. If the point is relevant, as seems likely, Peter wanted to be sufficiently clad when he reached the shore to give the usual religious greeting.

here is that the word means that parts of the body normally covered were exposed so that Peter was not naked but rather "stripped for work" (RSV, Barclay). This may mean that he wore a loincloth, or perhaps a sleeveless tunic which would not impede his movements.

8 Peter's example of diving into the water was not followed. The rest of the party came ashore more decorously in the little boat.[20] We have another example of John's love of precision in the statement that they were about two hundred cubits (*i.e.* a hundred yards) from[21] the shore. They dragged the net full of fishes to shore.[22]

9 When they reached the land and disembarked they saw a charcoal fire (see on 18 : 18) with fish set on it, evidently cooking, and bread. The picture is one of a breakfast made ready.

10 Evidently there was not an abundant supply, for Jesus now tells them to supplement it from their recent haul.[23] "Fish" in the previous verse could mean "a fish" as ARV mg.[24] This probably means that there was not enough cooked for a meal for all, and that Jesus is requesting a further supply. Some, however, think that He wanted the disciples to do no more than simply exhibit some of their catch. They prefer to hold that Jesus was supplying the whole meal, perhaps in a miraculous feeding analogous to

---

[20] The word used here is πλοιάριον. Strictly this is the diminutive of πλοῖον. But as the latter term seems to be used of the same vessel in vv. 3, 6, there appears to be no difference in the meaning. We should probably put it down to John's love of variation. There is a somewhat similar situation in ch. 6, where some see a difference in meaning (see on 6 : 22), as do a few commentators here. They think that the πλοῖον was a large fishing vessel, which drew too much water to come near the shore. So the disciples left it and came ashore in the dinghy. This is possible, but it does seem to be getting a lot out of a change of word. In both passages it is better to see the two words as referring to the one boat.

[21] For ἀπό in measuring distance *cf.* 11 : 18; Rev. 14 : 20.

[22] τὸ δίκτυον τῶν ἰχθύων, literally "the net of the fishes". The expression is unusual, but there can be no doubt but that the meaning is "the net full of fish".

[23] "Bring" translates ἐνέγκατε, noteworthy as the solitary example of the aorist imperative of this verb in the New Testament (elsewhere the present is invariable, even in contexts where we might expect an aorist). It may be that this is meant to give special urgency to the command.

[24] Though, as Bultmann notes, in that case we should have expected that there would have been a ἕν with ὀψάριον.

that in ch. 6. It is true that nothing is said of the disciples actually eating the fish they caught, but it is also true that there is no mention of a miraculous feeding. It is best to hold that the fish were directed to be brought for use in the meal.

11 When the Master spoke it was Peter who hastened to answer, or rather to act. He went up[25] and dragged the net to land. Since the net has already been described as too heavy for the combined strength of the others to haul into the boat this may mean that Peter organized the hauling of the net to shore rather than that he did it all himself.[26] John goes on to tell us that the fishes were big ones and that there were 153 of them. It seems probable that he says this for no more profound reason than that this was the actual number that was caught. After all, a love for exactness and a readiness to supply numerical detail can be documented elsewhere in this Gospel. Temple says forthrightly, "It is perverse to seek a hidden meaning in the number; it is recorded because it was found to be the number when the count was made." A number of commentators remind us that, since the catch was presumably to be shared among the fishermen, it was necessary to count the fish preparatory to assigning shares. Fishermen, moreover, have always loved to preserve the details of unusual catches. Yet we must bear in mind that there was no absolute necessity for including the number (in the unusual haul described in Luke 5 no number is given). The fact that John does record it may mean that he saw significance in it. This leaves us free to consider the suggestions that are offered, yet bearing in mind that John sometimes records numbers when there is probably no inner significance (such as the number of waterpots in ch. 2).

It is sometimes said that the significance of the number lies in the fact that the ancients held that the total number of kinds of fish in existence was 153. The number is accordingly held to symbolize the universal appeal of the Gospel. It is meant for all men, not some restricted circle. The trouble with this is that the evidence so far adduced to show that this belief was held fails to carry conviction. We have no good reason for thinking that this was,

---

[25] "Went up" translates $\dot{\alpha}\nu\acute{\epsilon}\beta\eta$, and provokes the question "went up where?" The verb is, however, used of embarking on a ship and that is probably the meaning here.

[26] There is no $\alpha\dot{\upsilon}\tau\acute{o}\varsigma$ or $\mu\acute{o}\nu o\varsigma$ or the like, such as would indicate a solo performance.

in fact, the case.[27] Another suggestion arises from the fact that 153 is the sum of numbers from 1 to 17. That is to say it is the sum of 10, the number of the commandments and hence of the Law, and 7, representing the sevenfold gifts of the Spirit. Some point out that 153 dots can be arranged in an equilateral triangle with 17 dots along each side. This is an interesting geometrical fact but, as R. H. Lightfoot says, "it remains to be explained, in a form which will carry conviction, what bearing this has upon the number of fish here taken." Such explanations of the number may carry conviction to some, but I must confess to remaining completely unimpressed. So with other suggestions that have been made.[28] If John meant us to see such meanings he has given us no guidance. It is much simpler to see a fisherman's record of a fact.

John goes on to record the detail that the net did not break,

---

[27] The belief would have to be a widespread one, else the point would be missed. But very little evidence for it can be cited, and none of real weight. Attention is usually called to Jerome's comment on Ezek. 47 : 9–12: "Those who write on the nature and properties of animals, who have learned ἁλιευτικά as well in Latin as in Greek, among whom is Oppianus Cilix, a very learned poet, say that there are one hundred and fifty-three different kinds of fish all of which were caught by the Apostles. . . ." This has all the appearance of a comment called forth in the attempt to find an edifying meaning in the number actually found in the text of John rather than an objective statement of a widespread ancient belief. Jerome cites no writer other than Oppian, and no one else appears to have found the statement in this author. W. F. Howard accordingly thinks that "until some more reliable evidence than Jerome's vague statement is forthcoming, we can hardly make use of this interpretation, and it would be well to leave Oppian's name out of the question" (*FGRCI*, p. 184). Moreover Pliny says that the total number of fish in existence is 74 (*Natural History*, IX, 43), and he is much nearer to the date of the New Testament than is Jerome.

[28] For example there is a view which sees a reference to the numerical values of the letters in the names Σίμων = 76 and ἰχθύς = 77, total 153. Those who espouse this view see Peter in the capacity of a divinely empowered fisherman or the like. Others see a reference to the Trinity, the number being 3 times 50 plus 3. Some, missionary minded, think of 100 as representing the Gentiles, 50 as standing for Israel, and three for the Trinity. See the article by J. A. Emerton in *JThS*, n.s., IX, 1958, pp. 86–89 (with the further comment by P. R. Ackroyd, *JThS*, n.s., X, 1959, p. 94) for references to lists of interpretations, a refutation of some previous suggestions and the author's own view that there is a reference to the places in Ezek. 47 where the fishermen spread their nets. There seems no end to the "meanings" that can be extracted from the number. But that John intended any of them is another matter.

as it did in the corresponding stage of the catch in Luke 5. This
may point to something added after the resurrection. It was in
the power of the risen Lord that the net did not break. "This
would signify that the Church's resources, with Christ in its midst,
are never overstrained" (Strachan).

12 Jesus now invited the disciples to have breakfast.[29] John
mentions no response to this invitation. Instead he informs us
that none of them dared to ask who Jesus was. This seems curious.
If they knew[30] who Jesus was why should they ask such a question?
One usually does not ask those one knows well who they are.
Yet it must be borne in mind that there was something unusual
about Jesus' appearance. Earlier Mary Magdalene had not recognized Him, and that very morning, just a short time before,
none of them knew Him and even Peter had needed to be told
who it was. But with this unasked question in their minds it must
have been a strange meal.

13 Evidently the disciples found it hard to begin eating. There
is no record of their responding to Jesus' invitation in v. 12.
Perhaps because they did not respond, Jesus now comes (comes
where? He had already called them to come to Him, v. 12) and
gives them bread, and fish too.[31] This would have the effect of
starting the meal, though John does not mention it. Indeed from
this point he mentions nothing until the meal is concluded. And
he tells us no more about the disciples, all the rest of the incident
being concerned with Peter.

14 He rounds off this opening section of the story by reminding his

---

[29] He says, ἀριστήσατε. There were normally two meals a day for first-
century Jews, and the ἄριστον was the first of them. It would be eaten as a
rule before starting the day's work, though on occasion it could be an early
luncheon. The other meal was the δεῖπνον (see on 12 : 2).

[30] The construction is curious since εἰδότες does not agree with anything.
But the anacoluthon is quite effective. The meaning of the participle might
be "because they knew" or "although they knew".

[31] In 6 : 11 He also gave bread and fish to eat, but it is not easy to draw a
satisfactory conclusion from the fact. Some think there is a eucharistic reference
here on account of the connection with ch. 6. But as the link with the eucharist
is far from certain there it will need more than a mention of bread and fish
to see it here. Others draw attention to the use of bread and fish in some early
eucharistic representations. But this forms too hazardous a link for us to
connect up the kind of food that would naturally be used for a lakeside meal
with the sacrament. Strachan says bluntly, "The meal described in *vv.* 12, 13,
is not a Eucharist" (similarly, Bailey).

readers that this was the third occasion on which Jesus was manifested to His disciples after the resurrection.[32] This must refer to meetings with the Twelve, or most of them, for he has already recorded three meetings, one with Mary Magdalene, one to the disciples without Thomas and one to the disciples with Thomas. But this is the third occasion on which He appeared to any considerable group of disciples.

2. PETER RESTORED, 21 : 15-19

15 So when they had broken their fast, Jesus saith to Simon Peter, Simon, son of [1]John, [2]lovest thou me more than these? He saith unto him, Yea, Lord: thou knowest that I [3]love thee. He saith unto him, Feed my lambs. 16 He saith to him again a second time, Simon, son of [1]John, [2]lovest thou me? He saith unto him, Yea, Lord; thou knowest that I [3]love thee. He saith unto him, Tend my sheep. 17 He saith unto him the third time, Simon, son of [1]John, [3]lovest thou me? Peter was grieved because he said unto him the third time, [3]Lovest thou me? And he said unto him, Lord, thou knowest all things; thou [4]knowest that I [3]love thee. Jesus saith unto him, Feed my sheep. 18 Verily, verily, I say unto thee, When thou wast young, thou girdedst thyself, and walkedst whither thou wouldest: but when thou shalt be old, thou shalt stretch forth thy hands, and another shall gird thee, and carry thee whither thou wouldest not. 19 Now this he spake, signifying by what manner of death he should glorify God. And when he had spoken this, he saith unto him, Follow me.

[1]Gr. *Joanes*. See ch. 1. 42, margin. [2][3]*Love* in these places represents two different Greek words. [4]Or, *perceivest*

This passage must be taken in conjunction with Peter's threefold denial of his Lord. Just as he had a short time ago in the presence of the enemy denied all connection with the Lord, so now in the presence of his friends he affirms three times over that he loves his Lord. There can be no doubt but that Peter was under a cloud with his fellow-disciples after the denial. This triple affirmation, accompanied as it was by a triple commission from Jesus, must have had the effect of giving an almost "official"

---

[32]   The use of ἤδη is rather curious. Perhaps as Godet thinks, it "allows us to suppose other *subsequent* appearances".

sanction to his restoration to his rightful place of leadership. Yet this should not be pressed too hard in the manner of some exegetes. Peter is accorded no absolute primacy, and in particular there is nothing in this passage to indicate that he was in any way superior to John. Throughout this chapter John is regarded as specially close to his Lord.

15 The meal concluded,[33] Jesus addressed a question to Peter. There is an air of solemnity about John's use of the full name, Simon Peter, and then of his reporting Jesus as using the expanded form, Simon son of John (cf. 1 : 42).[34] The question is a significant one, and it is accordingly prefaced by a serious form of address. Jesus asks, "lovest thou me more than these?" The latter term is not defined, which leaves the question ambiguous. It might mean "Do you love me more than these men love me?" or "Do you love me more than you love these men?" or "Do you love me more than you love these things?" Against the first way of taking the words is the difficulty of thinking that Jesus would invite one of His followers to compare the strength of his love with that of other disciples. Yet it must be remembered that Peter had explicitly professed a devotion to Christ which exceeded that of the others in the apostolic band (Matt. 26 : 33; Mark 14 : 29; cf. also John 13 : 37; 15 : 12f.). It may be that Christ is asking Peter whether, in the light of what has since happened, he still thinks that his love for Christ exceeds that of all the others.[35] Not many have taken the words to mean "Do you love me more than you love these men?" But this is possible.[36] Peter had three times denied Jesus, so that his devotion must be held to be suspect. But he had remained with his fellows and gone fishing with them. Where did

---

[33] οὖν here appears to be no more than resumptive (see on 1 : 21).

[34] It is interesting that though Jesus gave to Simon the name Peter there is only one subsequent occasion recorded when He addressed him by it (Luke 22 : 34). His habit is to call him Simon. The Synoptists usually refer to him as Peter, but John often uses Simon Peter (he uses the name Peter 34 times and it is combined with Simon 17 times). The Received Text reads here Σίμων Ἰωνᾶ (with A Θ f1 f13), but Σίμων Ἰωάννου is to be preferred with (ℵ) BDW lat co.

[35] This is accepted by Westcott, Bultmann, Lenski, Barclay and others. It is seen also in the translations of Goodspeed, Weymouth, Moffatt, Amplified, and others.

[36] See, for example, BDF, 185(1).

870

his supreme affection lie? With his companions with whom he resorted, or with Jesus whom he denied? In the third case we should take the term to refer to the fishing equipment and all that it stood for.[37] This symbolized an entire way of life. Taken this way the question challenges Peter as to his whole future. Was this to be spent in the pursuit of fishing and the like? Or did he love Christ more than that? It is perhaps against this interpretation that in his reply Peter drops the comparison. There would be no point in this if it were his fishing which was in mind, but very much if people were involved. Perhaps there is most to be said for the first way of looking at the question. We are sometimes inclined to think that a question about Peter's love was superfluous. But this is not the case. His actions showed that Peter had not wanted a crucified Lord. But Jesus was crucified. How did Peter's devotion stand in the light of this? Was he ready to love Christ as He was, and not as Peter wished Him to be? That was the question and it was an important one. Peter must face it and answer it.

His reply is an ungrudging affirmative. "Yea, Lord" is his own assent, and he goes on: "thou knowest that I love thee". "Thou" is emphatic, as the disciple appeals to the sure knowledge possessed by the Master. His own actions have not been such as to reveal his love and he is not in a position to point to them. But he can and does appeal to Christ's full understanding of the situation. A problem is posed by the use of different words for "love". Peter uses the same verb throughout, but Jesus uses a different word in His first two questions. In the third, however, Jesus uses Peter's word.[38] Not a few commentators hold that the change of word is significant.[39] Some maintain that the word Jesus uses in the first

---

[37] This is accepted by C. B. Williams, Rieu, and others.

[38] Peter's verb throughout is φιλέω. Jesus asks ἀγαπᾷς με; on each of the first two occasions but uses φιλέω in His third question.

[39] Perhaps the best case for seeing a distinction of meaning is that made out by Hendriksen in his special note (II, pp. 494–500). But he fails to notice that it is John's habit to introduce slight variations in repetitions and this makes his argument less cogent. We may well agree that, while the two verbs are of very similar meaning, there is yet a distinction on occasion. But it does not follow that a writer who elsewhere shows himself prone to slight variations, including the use of synonyms, without appreciable difference of meaning (see on 3 : 5), does intend a difference of meaning here. It is this which does not appear to have been made out. A. Marshall says he has never met an explanation

two questions denotes a higher type of love, while Peter's word points to a lower form of love, perhaps no more than a liking.[40] Seen in this way Jesus questions Peter as to whether he has a profound love for Him, and Peter, not daring to claim so much, replies that he is fond of Jesus. Then in his third question Jesus descends to Peter's level. Other commentators, however, reverse the meanings of the two words. They see Jesus as inquiring whether Peter has a rather cool type of affection for Him and Peter as replying that he has more than that, he has a warm love. Then in the last question our Lord rises to Peter's word.[41]

---

of the difference between the two terms which satisfies all the requirements. He adds to his note the interesting point that in the formation of compounds $\varphi\iota\lambda-$ is always used to express love, never $\dot{\alpha}\gamma\alpha\pi-$ (BT, 6, 1955, p. 48). If there were a real difference it would seem necessary for $\dot{\alpha}\gamma\alpha\pi-$ to be used on occasion.

[40] Among those who see $\dot{\alpha}\gamma\alpha\pi\dot{\alpha}\omega$ as denoting a higher form of love are Westcott, Lenski, Plummer, and Temple. The last-mentioned affirms that no two words are ever exactly synonymous. He points out that in the list given by Bernard which is intended to show that the words have much the same meaning we always have $\varphi\iota\lambda\dot{\epsilon}\omega$ or $\dot{\alpha}\gamma\alpha\pi\dot{\alpha}\omega$ alone. When the two occur together a difference must, he thinks, be intended; but he does not refer to John's habit of introducing minor verbal changes. This view is seen also in some translations, e.g. *Twentieth Century*. Goodspeed renders $\dot{\alpha}\gamma\alpha\pi\tilde{\alpha}\varsigma$ $\mu\epsilon$; by "are you devoted to me?" and $\varphi\iota\lambda\tilde{\omega}$ $\sigma\epsilon$ by "I love you", while Schonfield reverses the translations. We may take Hendriksen's summary as giving a typical view from the standpoint of those who see $\dot{\alpha}\gamma\alpha\pi\dot{\alpha}\omega$ as denoting a superior type of love, "we believe that $\dot{\alpha}\gamma\alpha\pi\dot{\alpha}\omega$ *in this story* (and generally throughout the Gospels, though *with varying degree of distinctness in meaning*) indicates love, deep-seated, thorough-going, intelligent and purposeful, a love in which the entire personality (not only the emotions, but also the mind and the will) plays a prominent part, which is based on esteem for the object loved or else on reasons which lie wholly outside of this object; while $\varphi\iota\lambda\dot{\epsilon}\omega$ indicates (or at least tends in the direction of) spontaneous natural affection, in which the emotions play a more prominent role than either the intellect or the will."

[41] Perhaps the typical representative of this point of view is Trench, who comments on $\dot{\alpha}\gamma\alpha\pi\tilde{\alpha}\varsigma$ $\mu\epsilon$; "At this moment, when all the pulses in the heart of the now penitent Apostle are beating with a passionate affection towards his Lord, this word on that Lord's lips sounds far too cold; to very imperfectly express the warmth of his affection toward Him. The question in any form would have been grievous enough (ver. 17); the language in which it is clothed makes it more grievous still. He therefore in his answer substitutes for the $\dot{\alpha}\gamma\alpha\pi\tilde{\alpha}\varsigma$ of Christ the word of a more personal love, $\varphi\iota\lambda\tilde{\omega}$ $\sigma\epsilon$ (ver. 15). And this he does not on the first occasion only, but again upon a second. And now at length he has triumphed; for when his Lord puts the question to him a third time, it is not $\dot{\alpha}\gamma\alpha\pi\tilde{\alpha}\varsigma$ any more, but $\varphi\iota\lambda\epsilon\tilde{\iota}\varsigma$" (*op. cit.*, pp. 42f.). C. B. Williams translates $\dot{\alpha}\gamma\alpha\pi\tilde{\alpha}\varsigma$ $\mu\epsilon$; by, "are you really devoted to me?" and $\varphi\iota\lambda\tilde{\omega}$

The unfortunate thing about these two interpretations, of course, is that they cancel one another out. A priori, one would have thought that a variation in vocabulary like this would be significant. But against it are certain difficulties. First there is the difficulty just noted, that the precise difference is not easy to discern and that competent commentators take opposite sides. Secondly, there is John's habit of introducing slight variations in all sorts of places without real difference of meaning (see on 3 : 5). There is no reason, on the grounds of Johannine usage, for seeing a difference in meaning between the two verbs. This point is rendered all the more significant in that the original conversation would have been in Aramaic, so that the choice of word in Greek would be John's rather than that of the original participants in the conversation. Thirdly, Peter's "Yea, Lord" does not look like a correction. As Bernard asks, "why should he say 'Yes,' if he means 'No'?" Peter seems concerned that his love is called in question, not as to the precise quality of love that he displays. He is accepting Jesus' word, not declining it. It is simplest to see here a further example of John's love of variation in triple repetitions. Peter and Jesus will be referring to essentially the same thing.[42]

σε by, "I tenderly love you." MacGregor takes this kind of distinction as that most likely to be drawn. He understands ἀγαπάω to mean "the esteem existing between benefactor and recipient" and φιλέω "the personal affection existing between members of the same family". He cites Strachan as one who takes this view (but Strachan in his commentary denies a distinction in this passage while admitting that one may be drawn in classical Greek). It is possible that the Vulgate should be included here with its use of *diligo* to render ἀγαπάω and *amo* for φιλέω. MiM refuses to grade the verbs as higher and lower, but nevertheless regards ἀγαπάω as "less expressive of emotions of tenderness, of personal feeling and affection, than that verb used by Peter in his reply."

[42] This is the position taken up by most modern commentators, *e.g.* Barrett, Bernard. Many recent translations do not distinguish between the two verbs, as RSV, Rieu, Moffatt, NEB text (the margin renders φιλέω by "be a friend"), *etc.* Moffatt examines the Johannine use of the two terms and decides that there is no significant difference (*Love in the New Testament*, London, 1932, pp. 46f.). He concludes, "The use of φιλέω and ἀγαπάω in this dialogue is therefore no more than a literary variation, and to read anything recondite into it is to be subtle where simplicity is the mark of the writer's thought and expression." Barrett reminds us that the Beloved Disciple is several times called ὃν ἠγάπα and once ὃν ἐφίλει (20 : 2) and proceeds, "it is highly improbable that there were two 'beloved disciples', one loved in a rather better way than the other". Bernard has a thorough analysis of the use of the two verbs and finds no difference. He points out also that the patristic commentators, Syriac, Greek and Latin

There is a slightly more complicated variation in the triple commission given to Peter.[43] ARV reflects the variation in the Greek where both noun and verb are changed in the second charge, while on the third occasion the verb is that from the first and the noun from the second version. Some have drawn from this an indication that Peter is charged to do more things than one and to do them both to the lambs and to the sheep.[44] But most people see the variation as no more than stylistic.[45] Peter is being commissioned to tend the flock of Christ. The absence of any good reason for seeing differences of meaning here strengthens the case for seeing none in connection with the words for love.

16 Jesus' question is repeated without the "more than these". Attention is concentrated on the question of love and the comparison drops out. Peter's reply is exactly as before. Again there is the agreement with Jesus' word, again the emphatic "Thou", and again the appeal to Jesus' own knowledge that Peter does indeed love his Lord. As noted in the previous verse, the commission varies. The verb used here has a somewhat broader meaning. It is "Exercise the office of shepherd" over against simply "Feed". The word rendered "sheep" in ARV is actually a diminutive and strictly speaking means "lambs" (unless a different reading is followed; see n. 44 for the evidence). But it is so often used without diminutive force that it is impossible to quarrel with the translation "sheep". However, it is equally impossible to maintain that there is a change of meaning.

17 As before noted, the third time Jesus changes to Peter's word for love, though no particular attention is drawn to this. Peter was very sad,[46] but it was because he was asked the question three

---

alike (except possibly for Ambrose), do not treat the variation of words here as significant. He also reminds us that the Syriac and Old Latin translations make no distinction (though the Vulgate does).

[43] Here Jesus says Βόσκε τὰ ἀρνία μου. There are intricate textual problems about the next two verses but we should probably read in v. 16 Ποίμαινε τὰ προβάτιά μου, and in v. 17 Βόσκε τὰ προβάτιά μου.

[44] There are textual variants. Thus for ἀρνία here C*D it read πρόβατα. In v. 16 προβάτια is read by BC pc and should probably be accepted, and πρόβατα by ℵ ADW Θ f13.

[45] The Vulgate renders both verbs by Pasce.

[46] ἐλυπήθη. This word refers to grief; it is not "was vexed" (Barclay, Schonfield).

times,[47] not because of a change of meaning. This seems further evidence that there is no real difference in meaning between the words for love. Had there been Peter would have been asked two different questions, not the one question three times over. His sorrow at the threefold question impelled him to a rather fuller reply. But, though his reply is fuller, it lacks the "Yea, Lord" of the two previous replies. Peter does not venture on his own affirmative this time, but relies on the Lord's intimate knowledge of all things, and specifically of His servant. "Lord, thou knowest all things", he said, a statement which has important implications for Christology (*cf.* 2 : 25; 16 : 30). In the context it means at least that Jesus fully understood what went on in the hearts of men, and specifically in Peter's heart. Incidentally we have another example of variation in vocabulary here. In his final "thou knowest that I love thee" Peter uses a word for "knowest" different from that used in the previous replies.[48] But again, I see no real difference in meaning. Jesus' final commission, as we saw, combines the verb from the first form with the noun from the second form.[49]

There can be little doubt but that the whole scene is meant to show us Peter as completely restored to his position of leadership. He has three times denied his Lord. Now he has three times affirmed his love for Him, and three times he has been commissioned to care for the flock. This must have had the effect on the others of a demonstration that, whatever had been the mistakes of the past, Jesus was restoring Peter to a place of trust. It is further worth noting that the one thing about which Jesus questions Peter prior to commissioning him to tend the flock is love. This is the basic qualification for Christian service. Other qualities may be desirable but love is completely indispensable (*cf.* I Cor. 13 : 1–3).

---

[47] The text runs, ὅτι εἶπεν αὐτῷ τὸ τρίτον, Φιλεῖς με; This should surely be taken to mean that the same question had been asked three times, rather than that the verb on the third occasion was Φιλεῖς. This is supported by the use of δεύτερον in v. 16.

[48] Peter has twice said σὺ οἶδας. Now he retains this verb in his πάντα σὺ οἶδας, but then he says, σὺ γινώσκεις ὅτι φιλῶ σε. For οἶδα and γινώσκω see on 2 : 24.

[49] This latter point is not certain. προβάτια is read by ABCW^c *pc*, but there is also strong support for πρόβατα, namely ℵ D W* Θ f1 f13 *pl*. Some hold that a threefold variation is intended, but it seems to me that on this occasion twofold is more probable. The substitution of προβάτια by scribes is intelligible, but that of προβάτια is not so easily explained.

18, 19 The commission is followed by a prophecy. It is introduced by the solemn "Verily, verily" (see on 1 : 51). Jesus refers to Peter's past state,[50] rather than his present position, perhaps to contrast his first state with his last. Two things are singled out, the fastening of the belt and the going where he willed. In youth Peter had done both of these things. In old age he will do neither. He will be restrained, and no longer master of his movements.[51] John proceeds to an explanation of these rather enigmatic words They refer to the death by which Peter will glorify God (for death as a glorifying of God *cf.* 12 : 23, *etc.*; 15 : 8 may also be relevant). The words are very general, but there is evidence that the stretching forth of the hands was held in the early church to refer to crucifixion.[52] If this understanding of the expression goes back to the time of Christ then we have a prophecy of the exact mode of Peter's death. But unless we can be sure of this we cannot hold that the verse points to more than martyrdom in some form. Against it is the word order, for the "carrying" would necessarily precede the crucifixion (though the order may be determined here not by the sense, but by the parallelism with the first part of the verse).[53] This prophecy is followed by a call to Peter to follow

---

[50] The comparative form $νεώτερος$ is used, strictly signifying "younger".

[51] The singular $ἄλλος$ invites comment. For any form of martyrdom one would expect a plural, for several people would be involved. It may be that Christ Himself or God is intended, the point then being that Peter would fulfil the divine will in his martyrdom. But this may be over-subtle. Perhaps nothing more is meant than a personification of the persecuting authorities.

[52] Barrett draws attention to the interpretation of $ἐξεπέτασα$ $τὰς$ $χεῖράς$ $μου$ (Isa. 65 : 2) as foreshadowing the crucifixion by Barnabas (12 : 4), Justin (I Apol. 35), Irenaeus (*Demonstration of the Apostolic Preaching*, 79), and Cyprian (*Test.* II, 20). There are similar interpretations of Moses' outstretched hands (Exod. 17 : 12), and Barrett finds one use of $ἐκτείνω$ with reference to crucifixion in Epictetus (AG also cite Josephus, *Ant.* xix, 94, but this is dubious to say the least). Trench cites some passages in Christian writers, the Epictetus passage and also one from Seneca (*Notes on the Miracles of our Lord*, London, 1895, p. 503). If these references be accepted as demonstrating the point, confirmation will perhaps be seen in the use of $ζώννυμι$, for the crucified were sometimes fastened to their crosses with ropes. Tertullian tells us that Peter was crucified in Rome under Nero and he sees in crucifixion the fulfilment of the words about being girt by another (*Scorp.* 15). Eusebius reports that at his own request Peter was crucified head downwards (*HE*, III, i. 2).

[53] Cullmann, however, cites W. Bauer that the order is correct for "the criminal had to carry the cross to the place of execution with arms spread out and chained to it" (*Peter, Disciple, Apostle, Martyr*, London, 1962, p. 88, n. 87).

Christ. There is possibly significance in the use of the present tense here. "Keep on following" will be the force of it. Peter had followed Christ, but not continuously in the past. For the future he was to follow steadfastly in the ways of the Lord.

3. THE ROLE OF THE BELOVED DISCIPLE, 21 : 20-23

20 Peter, turning about, seeth the disciple whom Jesus loved following; who also leaned back on his breast at the supper, and said, Lord, who is he that ¹betrayeth thee? 21 Peter therefore seeing him saith to Jesus, Lord, ²and what shall this man do? 22 Jesus saith unto him, If I will that he tarry till I come, what is that to thee? follow thou me. 23 This saying therefore went forth among the brethren, that that disciple should not die: yet Jesus said not unto him, that he should not die; but, If I will that he tarry till I come, what is that to thee?

¹Or, *deliniereth thee up* ²Gr. *and this man, what?*

20 Happy in his own position, Peter now gave thought to his friend. He turned and saw the Beloved Disciple (see on 13 : 23) following. Quite in the Johannine manner, he is characterized by his question at the Last Supper (13 : 23ff.; *cf.* similar ways of describing Nicodemus, 19 : 39; Judas, 6 : 71, *etc.*; Caiaphas, 18 : 14).[54] In view of the preceding, the term "following" is probably significant. What Peter had been twice urged to do John was already doing. "His obedience is assured; it was Peter's love that had been shown to be uncertain" (Hoskyns). The term may be used here partly in the literal sense, if, as many commentators think, Jesus was withdrawing a little with Peter, and John behind them. But the more important sense of the term throughout the passage is surely "follow as a disciple".
21 Peter, then, saw this man. Doubtless he was emboldened by his restoration to leadership, and the prophecy about his martyrdom. All this put him in a very different light. So now he inquired

---

54 There is a characteristic Johannine variation. In 13 : 25 the question was Κύριε, τίς ἐστιν; there was no reference to betrayal, as here. But as the question refers back to Jesus' statement of 13 : 21, εἷς ἐξ ὑμῶν παραδώσει με, its present form is quite intelligible.

as to John's future. His question is a very general one: "But this man, what?"

22 Jesus, however, declines to satisfy Peter's curiosity. It is no business of Peter's what is to happen to the other. Even if Jesus wills that he remains alive until[55] He returns what is that to Peter? The question is an emphatic way of reminding the impulsive leader of the apostolic band that there are some things which are quite outside his province. It is followed up by a repetition of the command of v. 19, "follow thou me".[56]

23 John proceeds to deal with an error that had arisen. A report went out among the brethren (this way of designating Christians is common in Acts, but here only in the Gospels, though *cf.* Matt. 23 : 8 and see note on John 20 : 17). This report was that the disciple would never die.[57] He would live right through until the day when Jesus would return again. One can see how such an interpretation would arise. But John wants his readers to be clear that it was an interpretation. It was not what Jesus had said. He did not say, "He will not die".[58] He only asked what it mattered to Peter if in fact this man were to remain alive until the return of Christ. John wants us to be clear on what Jesus said and what He did not say. His "but" is a strong adversative.[59] The two are in sharp contrast. In view of the fact that in this Gospel slight variations when statements are repeated are almost universal, it

---

[55] Both here and in the repetition of the statement in the next verse ἕως is followed by the indicative, a construction found fairly rarely in the New Testament. It puts some stress on the factuality of the coming. The present tense is curious, but it is reading too much into it to assert that it shows that John thought of the coming as a continuous process. Indeed, to take the coming in this way is to render the saying practically meaningless.

[56] There is a slight difference in the wording, for this time the pronoun σύ puts emphasis on "thou". The present imperative is used both times, which is consonant with a stress on the continuous process involved. In the former place the verb precedes μοι, here it follows. Schonfield brings out some of the difference by translating "Follow me ... You follow me". Similarly Rieu has "For yourself, follow me" in the second place.

[57] We would have anticipated the future tense for the verb "die", but John uses the present, ὁ μαθητὴς ἐκεῖνος οὐκ ἀποθνήσκει, "that disciple dies not".

[58] There is actually an ambiguity here. ὅτι is usually taken to mean "that", giving the sense as ARV. But it could possibly mean "because", "Jesus did not say (this) to him because he would not die". ARV, however, is much to be preferred.

[59] He uses ἀλλ' (see on 1 : 8).

878

is noteworthy that here the statement is reported exactly from v. 22.[60] The precise words used are significant and the writer is at pains to be accurate. Some have concluded from this section that John was already dead when it was written. But it is hard to see how such a conclusion can stand. After John died Christians would not keep saying "He will not die"! The fact that an explanation was called for surely shows that the Beloved Disciple was still alive, though possibly quite old.

4. AUTHENTICATION, 21 : 24, 25

The last two verses look like a conclusion written by someone other than the author of the preceding.[61] The conclusion brings in a number of people to authenticate what has been written. They can say, "we know that his witness is true". Who these people were it is idle to speculate. They have left no indication as to their identity, and we can only conjecture that they were people who were respected in the church and who knew the facts of the case. So they tell us now that this disciple "wrote these things" and they certify that his witness is to be relied on. The strongest objection to this is that v. 23 is a curious if not impossible way to end a Gospel. This leads to the suggestion that the author is here supported by others who can vouch for his testimony and that he then goes on to write v. 25 in his own name (but see I Thess. 2 : 18 for a transition from plural to singular when there is no question as to authorship).

> 24 This is the disciple that beareth witness of these things, and wrote these things: and we know that his witness is true.
> 25 And there are also many other things which Jesus did, the

---

[60] This is not the case if we omit the words τί πρὸς σέ with ℵ* 565 *a e* syr^s. But the words should be read. Their attestation is strong.

[61] This is not completely certain. In the first place the word οἴδαμεν might conceivably be read as οἶδα μέν, corresponding to ἔστιν δέ. This, however, gives an unnatural sequence and should probably be rejected. In the second place the plural is sometimes used of one person plus his associates as in 3 : 11; 6 : 5; I John 1 : 1 *etc.* In favor of this is the fact that, if added by others, we would expect the attestation to stand right at the end, but it does not do so. V. 25 with its singular οἶμαι follows. However this does not appear to be decisive and the sense strongly favors a genuine plural, giving the attestation of others than the author of the preceding (though perhaps including him).

which if they should be written every one, I suppose that even the world itself would not contain the books that should be written.

24 The concluding words form a testimony to the reliability of the Gospel's author. The first words of this verse make it clear that the witness behind the Gospel is the man just spoken of, *i.e.* the Beloved Disciple. The use of the present tense may be another indication that he was still living. It is not easy to fit in to the hypothesis that he had died. "And wrote these things" seems to indicate also that he was the actual author.[62] Some hold that the Beloved Disciple was the witness in the sense that he vouched for the facts included in the Gospel, but that he was not the man responsible for the actual wording of the Gospel. This conclusion does not come from such words as those written here. They ascribe authorship to the Beloved Disciple.[63] They do not however indicate the extent of the authorship and some hold that "these things" refer to no more than this final chapter. This seems unlikely. The words seem like a reference to the witness of 19 : 35. Again, there seems no reason for a solemn attestation that the Beloved Disciple had written a few paragraphs to be tacked on to the end of someone else's Gospel. It is much more probable

---

[62] This is especially the case if the ὁ before γράψας be omitted with אֲ* AW fl *pl*, or if we read ὁ καὶ γράψας with Θ f13 33. καὶ ὁ γράψας is read by BD it syr.

[63] "The most natural meaning of these words, and therefore the meaning to be adopted unless very strong reasons are brought against it, is that the disciple himself not only bore witness to but also wrote down ταῦτα" (Barrett; he regards as "conceivable but perhaps not probable the view that γράψας means "caused to be written"). Sometimes curious inferences are drawn from this word. Thus Bernard cites Pilate's writing of the Titulus on the cross and Paul's use of the verb of his own "writing" of Romans (Rom. 15 : 15) though we know that the actual penman was Tertius (Rom. 16 : 22). He reasons that the verb may mean "dictated", and that here "the Beloved Disciple *caused these things to be written*. They were put into shape by the writer who took them down". On this H. P. V. Nunn comments: "No one supposes that Pilate actually wrote on the board any more than that he nailed it to the cross, but we are told in the immediate context that he identified the words which he caused to be written with his intention in a most emphatic manner. Any scribe who ventured 'to put them into shape' would have got into serious trouble. We do not know that it has ever before been suggested that Tertius did anything more than write down the exact words which St. Paul dictated to him" (*The Authorship of the Fourth Gospel*, Eton, 1952, p. 8).

that "these things" refers to the whole book. It is a pity that there is no clue as to the identity of the "we". It would be a help to know who these people were who speak so confidently about the authorship of the Gospel. All that we can say is that the words (and hence their authors) must be very early, for there is no textual doubt about these concluding verses.[64] Barrett regards the plural as very important. "The 'we' is to be taken with full seriousness; there exists an apostolic Church capable of verifying and affirming the apostolic witness".

25 The Gospel closes with a reminder that the author has done no more than make a selection from the mass of material available. He has not written all he knows about Jesus. If all were to be written he thinks the world itself could not[65] contain[66] the books to be written.[67] With this delightful hyperbole he lets us see that there is much more about Jesus than we know. It is fitting for us to bring our study of the Gospel to a close with the reminder of the limitations of our knowledge. It is well for us to be appreciative of the knowledge we have and to show a due gratitude to God for what He has revealed. But we should not exaggerate. Our knowledge of the truth is at best partial. The reader who appreciates the significance of these final words is kept humble.

---

[64] Tasker cites evidence that the verse was originally lacking in Sinaiticus but that the original scribe erased an ornamental colophon and inserted the verse. This is not without its interest, but it cannot be allowed to outweigh the consensus of the manuscripts.

[65] The negative $o\dot{v}\delta$' is noteworthy since it is to be taken with the infinitive $\chi\omega\varrho\acute{\eta}\sigma\epsilon\iota\nu$. It is perhaps more emphatic than $\mu\eta\delta$' would have been. BDF take the negative with $o\check{\iota}\mu\alpha\iota$ (429), but Turner dissents, in my judgment rightly (M, III, p. 285).

[66] It is not certain whether $\chi\omega\varrho\acute{\eta}\sigma\epsilon\iota\nu$ is a true future infinitive, as its form indicates (M, I, p. 204, n. 2), or whether it is an example of the use of a present ending on the aorist stem to form an aorist infinitive (M, II, p. 216). The future infinitive is rare but then so is the use of the present ending to form an aorist infinitive. Not much hinges on our verdict, for the meaning is much the same in either case. It should be added that some MSS here read $\chi\omega\varrho\ddot{\eta}\sigma\alpha\iota$.

[67] There is an interesting parallel in Philo, *De Post. Cain*, 144: "Were (God) to choose to display His own riches, even the entire earth with the sea turned into dry land would not contain *($\chi\omega\varrho\ddot{\eta}\sigma\alpha\iota$)* them." SBk cites a saying of Jochanan b. Zakkai (who died *c.* A.D. 80): "If all the sky were parchment, and all the trees were writing pens, and all the seas were ink there would not be enough to write down my wisdom which I have learned from my teachers; and yet I have had the pleasure of only as much of the wisdom of the wise as a fly, who plunges into the ocean, takes away" (II, p. 587).

APPENDIX

53 [1](And they went every man unto his own house: 1 but Jesus went unto the mount of Olives. 2 And early in the morning he came again into the temple, and all the people came unto him; and he sat down, and taught them. 3 And the scribes and the Pharisees bring a woman taken in adultery; and having set her in the midst, 4 they say unto him, Teacher, this woman hath been taken in adultery, in the very act. 5 [2]Now in the law Moses commanded us to stone such: what then sayest thou of her? 6 And this they said, trying him, that they might have whereof to accuse him. But Jesus stooped down, and with his finger wrote on the ground. 7 But when they continued asking him, he lifted up himself, and said unto them, He that is without sin among you, let him first cast a stone at her. 8 And again he stooped down, and with his finger wrote on the ground. 9 And they, when they heard it, went out one by one, beginning from the eldest, even unto the last: and Jesus was left alone, and the woman, where she was, in the midst. 10 And Jesus lifted up himself, and said unto her, Woman, where are they? did no man condemn thee? 11 And she said, No man, Lord. And Jesus said, Neither do I condemn thee: go thy way; from henceforth sin no more.)

[1]Most of the ancient authorities omit John 7. 53–8. 11. Those which contain it vary much from each other. [2]Lev. xx. 10; Dt. xxii. 22f.

The textual evidence makes it impossible to hold that this section is an authentic part of the Gospel.[1] It is not attested in the oldest manuscripts, and when it does make its appearance it is sometimes found in other positions, either after v. 36, or after

---

[1] There is a convenient summary of the evidence in Hoskyns, pp. 563f. The most considerable support for it is D, but the evidence against it is overwhelming. It is not found in any of the oldest MSS apart from D, nor is it referred to by the Fathers other than Western ones. Its only attestation is Western or late, and it is omitted even by some of the Western witnesses.

v. 44, or at the end of this Gospel,[2] or after Luke 21:38. It seems clear enough that those scribes who felt it too important to be lost were not at all sure where to attach it. And if they could not agree on the right place for it, they could not agree either on the true text for it. The manuscripts which have it do not agree closely. The very large number of variants indicates that the textual history of this pericope is different from that of the fourth Gospel. In addition to the textual difficulty many find stylistic criteria against the story.[3] While the spirit of the narrative is in accordance with that of this Gospel the language is not quite that of John. The passage is too short for this argument to be completely decisive, but for what it is worth it does tell against Johannine authorship. There is also the point that the section does not fit well into the context, whereas 8 : 12 follows naturally after 7 : 52.

But if we cannot feel that this is part of John's Gospel we can feel that the story is true to the character of Jesus. Throughout the history of the church it has been held that, whoever wrote it, this little story is authentic.[4] It rings true. It speaks to our condition. It is thus worth our while to study it, though not as an authentic part of John's writing. The story is undoubtedly very ancient. Most authorities agree that it is referred to by Papias.[5] It is mentioned also in the *Apostolic Constitutions*.[6] But it is not mentioned very often in early days. The reason probably is that in a day when the punishment for sexual sin was very severe

---

[2]   In this position it may be intended as an appendix to the four Gospels rather than specifically to this Gospel.

[3]   Note such things as the frequent use of δέ instead of John's οὖν; πορεύομαι εἰς (v. 53) where John prefers πρός (14 : 12, 28; 16 : 28, *etc.* though εἰς is used in 7 : 35); ὄρθρου (v. 2) as in Luke 24 : 1, whereas John uses πρωΐ (18 : 28; 20 : 1); λαός (v. 2) is used often in Matthew and Luke, but only occasionally in John, who prefers ὄχλος; ἀπὸ τοῦ νῦν (v. 11) is not found in John, though frequent in Luke (Luke 1 : 48; 5 : 10 *etc.*).

[4]   Tenney speaks of "its ancient character and undoubtedly historic truthfulness". Most would accept this as a fair statement.

[5]   Eusebius reports Papias as having "expounded another story about a woman who was accused before the Lord of many sins, which the Gospel according to the Hebrews contains" (*HE*, III, xxxix, 17; cited from Loeb edn.). Though Papias speaks of "many sins" and our narrative of but one it is not unlikely that Papias is referring to another version of this story. No other is known of a woman accused before our Lord of sinning.

[6]   *Apostolic Constitutions* ii. 24.

among the Christians this story was thought to be too easily misinterpreted as countenancing unchastity. When ecclesiastical discipline was somewhat relaxed the story was circulated more widely and with a greater measure of official sanction.

53 This verse shows that the story originally was attached to some other narrative, but what that was we can only guess.

1 The Synoptic Gospels tell us that the pattern followed by Jesus during the closing days of His life was to teach in Jerusalem during the day, and to retire outside the city to spend the night. Luke specifically speaks of Him as lodging on the Mount of Olives (Luke 21 : 37; *cf.* Luke 22 : 39).[7] It would seem to have been one of our Lord's favorite places. On the occasion mentioned here He evidently passed the night there. The Mount of Olives is not mentioned in the fourth Gospel, though it is in each of the other three.

2 "Again" indicates that the narrative from which this story was taken included a previous visit or visits to the temple. Evidently it also included a reference to teaching. So on this occasion Jesus went to the temple early in the morning. "Came" ("all the people came") and "taught" are continuous tenses. When He reached the temple courts people kept coming to Him, so He sat and engaged in teaching them.

3 The group is joined by some religious leaders bringing a woman they had taken in the act of sin. "Scribes and Pharisees" is a conjunction found quite often in the Synoptic Gospels, but the scribes are never mentioned in John.[8] The two terms do not mean the same people, for scribes need not necessarily be Pharisees (though of course many of them were). In days when writing was far from universal the scribes were members of a skilled profession. Among the Jews their principal study was the law, and as this was the chief interest of the Pharisees, the two groups had much in common. Accordingly it is never strange to find the two acting in conjunction.[9] Yet we should not overlook the other

---

[7] Mark mentions Bethany as the place to which Jesus withdrew (Mark 11 : 11f.). But, as C. E. B. Cranfield says, Luke "does not contradict this, since Bethany could be regarded as on the Mount of Olives" (on Mark 11 : 11).

[8] γραμματεύς is found in Matthew 22 times, in Mark 21 times, and in Luke 14 times so that John's total omission of the term is striking.

[9] For a useful account of the scribes and the Pharisees see W. Barclay, *The Mind of Jesus* (London, 1960), pp. 158ff. He neatly sums up the differences between the two by saying, "It was the scribes who worked out all these rules and regulations; it was the Pharisees who devoted their whole lives to the keeping of them" (*op. cit.*, p. 161).

fact that the Synoptic Gospels also link the scribes very often with the high priests, who were Sadducees. In other words the scribes had their links with the Pharisees, but also with others, notably the official hierarchy.

The woman these people bring had been taken[10] in adultery. This is interesting, for apparently it implies that witnesses had seen the very act.[11] Compromising circumstances were not enough. If the conditions required by Jewish law were as stringent as J. Duncan M. Derrett maintains[12] this can scarcely indicate anything other than a trap deliberately set.[13] All the more is this likely to be the case in that the man was not present. Why not? Since the woman was taken in the very act there should have been two sinners, not one, before Jesus. But if the whole thing was engineered provision would have been made for the man to escape. Moreover the witnesses ought to have warned the woman in accordance with the maxim, "No penalty without a warning". There is no hint that they did anything of the sort. All the indications are that her accusers had some special vindictiveness against her. This is shown also in the fact that they brought the woman along publicly (*cf.* Knox: "made her stand there in full view"). There was no need for this. She might have been kept in custody while the case was referred to Jesus.

---

10 The perfect, κατειλημμένην, indicates a meaning like "taken with her shame upon her". It points to her continuing character as an adulteress.

11 *Cf.* the dictum of R. Samuel: "In the case of adulterers, they (sc. the witnesses) must have seen them in the posture of adulterers" (*BM*, 91a; Soncino edn., p. 524).

12 In his very valuable article on this incident in *NTS*, X, 1963–64, pp. 1–26. He stresses that the witnesses must have seen the couple *in coitu.* "There is absolutely no question of their having seen the couple in a 'compromising situation', for example, coming from a room in which they were alone, or even lying together on the same bed. The actual physical movements of the couple must have been capable of no other explanation, and the witnesses must have seen exactly the same acts at exactly the same time, in the presence of each other, so that their depositions would be identical in every respect" (*op. cit.*, pp. 4f.). He points out that conditions were so stringent that they could have been met only on rare occasions. Thus provision was made for the ordeal *(soṭāh)* when the husband was suspicious, but had not the proof required.

13 There is more than one possible motive. A good one is the material one. If a husband divorced his wife she would take her property with her. But if she died he would succeed to it.

4 They address Jesus with the polite "Teacher", and explain the circumstances. "Teacher" is appropriate in a context where Jesus is to be asked to decide a point of the law. "Hath been taken" is again in the perfect tense. The woman's guilt is plain.[14] She was taken "in the very act".[15] The word puts some stress on her part in the affair.

5 They put to Jesus the question of what should be done with the woman, first pointing out that the law of Moses specifically provides for the death penalty in such cases. It is perhaps worth noticing that they slightly manipulate the text of the law. They speak of "such" as being stoned, the word being feminine, "such women", whereas Lev. 20 : 10 and Deut. 22 : 22 both lay it down that the man as well as the woman is to be put to death. They are also a little more specific than the Old Testament, for they speak definitely of stoning, whereas the passages we have cited do not indicate the manner of execution. Stoning is prescribed for the guilty pair when the woman is "a virgin betrothed unto a husband" (Deut. 22 : 23f.).[16] It seems fairly clear that what they were envisaging was a lynching. There is no mention of a trial,[17] and it would seem that this group proposed to take the law into their own hands. Their "thou" is emphatic. The law, they infer,

---

[14] BDF take μοιχευομένη as middle in accordance with Attic use (101; the active would be used of the man). AG however remind us of the use of the accusative of the object τινά (γυναῖκα) after the active, which "explains the use of the passive in the case of the woman". They cite a number of examples including this passage. *Cf.* also Matt. 5 : 32. LS cite the passive as classical.

[15] The word is αὐτόφωρος. From φώρ, "a thief", it properly denotes "caught in the act of stealing", but comes to be used of other offences. It leaves no room for doubt.

[16] Strangulation is the penalty for adultery according to the Mishnah (*Sanh.* 11 : 1), though stoning is, of course, the method of execution when the woman is betrothed (*Sanh.* 7 : 4). But there does not appear to be evidence of the use of strangling in Jewish penal procedure before the fall of Jerusalem. See P. Winter, *On the Trial of Jesus* (Berlin, 1961), pp. 67–74; he notes that Herod had certain people strangled (*op. cit.*, p. 188, n. 21), but denies that Jewish penal procedure knew this form of execution until the second century. Derrett says, "We know now that the traditional punishment for adultery by a married woman was stoning" (*op. cit.*, p. 11).

[17] It is possible that there was no properly constituted Jewish court to conduct such a trial. See the evidence in Derrett, *op. cit.*, p. 9, n. 4. Lynching would then be the only way of securing execution, for the Romans would not order death for such an offence.

is plain. What now do *you* say? The next verse makes it clear
that they were not sincere, but the exact nature of the trap is not
certain. Most accept the view that Jesus faced a charge under
either Roman law or the law of Moses. If He said "Stone her"
He would lay himself open to the charge of counselling action
contrary to Roman law, which did not provide for a death
penalty in such cases.[18] If He said "Do not stone her" He could
be charged with offending against the law of God. The question
was a loaded one. Either answer would involve Jesus in difficulties.
This may indeed be the dilemma His opponents had in mind,
though evidence does not seem to be adduced that the Romans
would, in fact, have taken strong action in such a case. Another
possibility is that a verdict for stoning would have set those who
favored leniency against Him, while one against would leave Him
opposed by the legalists. There is some evidence that a good
number of people did view the death penalty as too severe,[19]
but the objection to this is that v. 6 looks for a definite charge,
not a shift in popularity. In any case Jesus' views were clearly
well known and the accusers almost certainly felt that they could
count on Jesus not to endorse the provision of the law. They felt
they could rely on Him to be lenient, so that we need not concern
ourselves unduly with looking for the consequences of an alternative answer. He could, of course, have refused to give a decision.
There was no compulsion, and He would have been safe. But in

---

[18] *Cf.* Bernard: "although the Roman authorities were lax on occasion
about such acts of violence (as in the case of Stephen, Acts 7[58]), there would
have been a good pretext for handing Him over to them to deal with." J.
Jeremias similarly argues that the Jews had no right to put anyone to death,
so that an answer affirming the death penalty could be construed as usurping
the functions of the Roman authorities (*ZNTW*, 43, 1950–51, pp. 145–50).

[19] The main reasons for thinking this are that the death penalty seems
rarely to have been carried out, and that the offence was common. According
to I. Abrahams the death penalty for adultery "can never have been frequently
enforced" (*Studies in Pharisaism and the Gospels*, I, Cambridge, 1917, p. 73). It
was apparently much more usual for the husband to divorce his erring wife
and receive compensation from the man. Abrahams speaks also of "the great
prevalence of adultery" (*op. cit.*, p. 74), so that demanding the death penalty
would imply a readiness for many executions. The Mishnah tractate *Sotah*
seems to take it for granted that the punishment for adultery would be divorce,
and it does not look for the death penalty. For example, it provides that an
adulteress is forbidden both to her husband and to her paramour (*Sot.* 5 : 1),
which indicates that neither party was executed.

that case the woman would certainly have been lynched.
6 Their motives are made clear. They are not really seeking
guidance, but "trying" Him. The word is often translated "tempt",
and it signifies to put to the test with a view to failing. They
wanted a legal basis on which to accuse Him. Jesus' reaction was
to ignore them.[20] He simply stooped and made marks in the dust.
There is no hint of why He wrote or what He wrote. It is not
even certain that He wrote, for the verb used can mean "to draw".[21]
But the word more naturally in this context points to writing. A
not unlikely suggestion is that He wrote the words He later spoke.
In other words His sentence was written as well as pronounced.[22]
Derrett is of opinion that He will have written some words from
the law (thus showing on what He would rely if He were to
give a decision), and that He will have used unpointed Hebrew.
This would have enabled Him to suggest all the meanings
associated with the various possible pointings. This gives a motive
for writing. If the words were spoken the speaker was committed
to one interpretation. Derrett thinks the writing was the opening
part of Exodus 23 : 1b: "put not thy hand with the wicked to

---

[20] Some think that He did not wish to look at the hideous sight of pro-
fessedly godly men hounding the woman. *Cf.* Temple: "But the Lord is tortured
with the horror of it all. He will not look at them or at her. He stoops down
to hide the burning confusion of His face and relieves His agitation by tracing
patterns in the dust." Calvin is of opinion that the gesture is to show that Jesus
despises them.

[21] The verb is $\varkappa\alpha\tau\dot{\varepsilon}\gamma\varrho\alpha\varphi\varepsilon\nu$. It is not found elsewhere in the New Testament.
The imperfect denotes a continuing activity. The uncompounded $\dot{\varepsilon}\gamma\varrho\alpha\varphi\varepsilon\nu$,
however, is found in v. 8 which points to a meaning here of "was writing"
rather than "was drawing". Godet sees in the action "a meaning analogous to
that of the saying of Jeremiah (xvii. 13); 'Those who turn aside from Me shall
be written in the earth.' "

[22] T. W. Manson is of this opinion. He says, "the action of Jesus might
be explained from the well-known practice in Roman criminal law, whereby
the presiding judge first wrote down the sentence and then read it aloud from
the written record . . . Jesus by this motion says in effect: 'You are inviting
me to usurp the functions of the Roman Governor. Very well, I will do so;
and I will do it in the approved Roman manner.' He then stoops down and
pretends to write down the sentence, after which he reads it out: 'whoever
among you is without sin, let him be the first to cast a stone at her.' . . . Jesus
defeats the plotters by going through the form of pronouncing sentence in the
best Roman style, but wording it so that it cannot be executed" (*ZNTW*, 44,
1952–3, pp. 255f.). An ancient opinion is that Jesus wrote the sins of the accusers
(*cf.* Job 13 : 26).

be an unrighteous witness." This was a reminder that the whole affair was unsavoury,[23] and it carried a warning lest innocent men contract guilt by association with evil witnesses.

7 Evidently the accusers felt that Jesus' silence arose from an inability to evade giving them the opening for which they were looking. So they pressed their question ("they persisted in questioning him", AG). But Jesus stood up and invited any one one among them who was sinless[24] to throw the first stone. This answer completely disarmed them. It could not possibly be construed as a rejection of the law. Jesus specifically enjoined that a stone be thrown. But His limitation on who might throw it effectively prevented any harm coming to the guilty woman. The saying "does not deny that she may be stoned, but insists upon the innocency and therefore the competence of whoever stands forth against her as accuser and witness."[25] If, for example, the witnesses were guilty of not giving a warning (as the facts of the case make almost certain) then the woman could not be convicted on their evidence. For anyone to take part in a stoning on the basis of such evidence would be to incur the guilt of "joining with the wicked". The words of Jesus are both an appeal to conscience and a warning to the hearers that their own lives might very well be at stake. If they stoned the woman they must be very sure of the witnesses.

8, 9 Jesus stooped again and resumed His writing.[26] But as the

---

[23] "Now if one reads רֵשַׁע instead of רָשָׁע ... the result is impressive. Jesus is then considering joining with Evil in the abstract, associating in an evil matter" (Derrett, *op. cit.*, p. 20). If Jesus did in fact write this those who read it might be uncertain whether He was warning others about associating with evil witnesses, or with an unsavoury deed, or whether He Himself was refusing to have any contact with a case which involved immorality. This would give a reason for them to press Him to speak.

[24] Some have thought that the word means "innocent of that particular sin". ἀναμάρτητος is not found elsewhere in the New Testament, but its use in LXX shows that it is not specific. It can denote innocence of various kinds of sin. In this present context it is important that this wide meaning be understood. It was not their indulgence in one particular sin, but their general sinfulness that disqualified them from arrogating to themselves the position of God's agents in punishing the sin of others.

[25] Derrett, *op. cit.*, p. 22. The well known case of Susanna stood as a reminder of the fate of false witnesses.

[26] Derrett thinks that this time Jesus wrote, "Keep thee far from a false matter", which the readers would complete with the rest of the verse: "and

significance of His words sunk in the men went out. The continuous tense in this last verb gives the thought of something like a procession. They kept on going out. They began with the elders (the word is plural), who would naturally be expected to give a lead, and whose greater experience would enable them more quickly to grasp the implications of Jesus' words. They, moreover, would have a certain responsibility to see that justice was done. If the witness was false, or not legally valid, and the woman was killed, the oldest men present would have a major share of the responsibility. So they went out. But the action was not confined to them. The consciences of all were touched, and all went.[27] The woman was left alone. "Left" is a strong word, and might be translated "abandoned".[28] When the force of Jesus' words struck home they were no longer interested in her sin, but in their own. They made no attempt to interfere with her for she was left "where she was".[29]

10 The Lord addresses the woman. "Woman" is not a harsh form of address. It is used by Jesus on the cross as He addresses His mother (19 : 26). Now He asks the adulteress where her accusers are, and goes on to inquire whether no one has condemned her. She assures Him that this is indeed the case.

11 Jesus' answer brings the incident to a fitting conclusion. He, too, will not condemn her. But that does not mean that He condones her sin. He tells her to sin no more. The form of the command implies a ceasing to commit an action already started: "Stop your

---

the innocent and righteous slay thou not: for I will not justify the wicked (= acquit the guilty)" (Exod. 23 : 7). In the apocryphal book of Susanna Daniel used this very text to condemn the false elders (verse 53). It had thus been the means of bringing wicked men to their death, and the text might well arouse memories of the incident.

[27] "One by one" is εἷς καθ' εἷς. BDF explains the curious nominative after κατά as a development from the distributive use of this preposition, "since καθ'ἕνα ἕκαστον became fixed as καθένα ἔκ. and a corresponding nom. was created". They add, "not many examples of this vulgarism are found in the NT" (305). GT thinks that "either κατά is used adverbially, or εἷς as indeclinable" (sub εἷς).

[28] The word is κατελείφθη. It is used of Levi's abandoning his position as tax collector to follow Jesus (Luke 5 : 28), and of a man's dying and leaving his wife (Mark 12 : 19).

[29] Augustine in a telling phrase says, Relicti sunt duo, misera et misericordia (XXXIII. 5).

sinful habit".[30] And the "no more" points to the thought of no return. She is to make a clean break with sin. Jesus does not refer specifically to adultery, though there cannot be any doubt that that is primarily in mind. His words are perfectly general. He is calling the woman to amendment of life, the whole of life. It should not be overlooked that He says nothing about forgiveness. The guilty woman has given no sign of repentance or of faith. What He does is to show mercy and to call to righteousness.[31]

---

[30] μηκέτι ἁμάρτανε.
[31] *Cf.* Hoskyns: "Here then the mercy of God and His truth meet. For only in the mouth of the sinless Jesus can the full condemnation of sin, and the full demand for the righteousness of God, march with the authoritative pronouncement of His mercy and charity."

INDEXES

GENERAL INDEX

895

INDEX OF AUTHORS

INDEX OF SCRIPTURE REFERENCES

OLD TESTAMENT

NEW TESTAMENT

4 : 8	726	7 : 17	700	16 : 19	746
4 : 11	620	12 : 12	103	19 : 11	170
6 : 10	726	14 : 10	746	19 : 13	71, 124
6 : 15	746	14 : 14	320	19 : 18	746
7 : 9	584	14 : 20	865		

INDEX OF GREEK WORDS